The
World Book
Encyclopedia

F Volume 7

World Book–Childcraft International, Inc.

A subsidiary of The Scott & Fetzer Company

Chicago London Paris Sydney Tokyo Toronto

The World Book Encyclopedia

Copyright © 1979, U.S.A.
by
World Book–Childcraft International, Inc.

Ff

F is the sixth letter of our alphabet. Historians believe that the letter came from a symbol used by the Semites, who once lived in Syria and Palestine. They named it *waw*, meaning *hook*. The ancient Greeks later took the symbol into their own alphabet and called it *digamma*. They used it to represent the sound of *w* in English. The Romans were the first to use the letter to represent our sound for *f*. See ALPHABET.

Uses. *F* or *f* is about the 15th most frequently used letter in books, newspapers, and other material printed in English. When used on a report card, *F* usually means failure in a school subject. In music, it names one note of the scale. As an abbreviation, *F* shows that a temperature reading is in Fahrenheit degrees. *F* means *fluorine* in chemistry, *function* in mathematics, *fluid* in pharmacy,

free energy in physics, and *frequency* in statistics. In photography, *f* refers to the focal length of the lens divided by its actual opening. The *f* also stands for *franc* (in France).

Pronunciation. In English, a person pronounces the *f* by placing his lower lip against the edges of his upper front teeth and forcing his breath out. He pronounces *ff* as a single *f*, except when the letter appears in combinations of two words, such as *self-fed*. In some English nouns, such as *knife*, the *f* becomes a *v* in the plural form of the word. The *f* in French, Italian, Spanish and German words resembles the English *f* sound. The Latin pronunciation of *f* was also similar to the English *f* sound.   I. J. GELB and JAMES M. WELLS

See PRONUNCIATION.

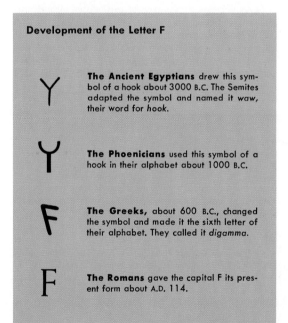

Development of the Letter F

The Ancient Egyptians drew this symbol of a hook about 3000 B.C. The Semites adapted the symbol and named it *waw*, their word for *hook*.

The Phoenicians used this symbol of a hook in their alphabet about 1000 B.C.

The Greeks, about 600 B.C., changed the symbol and made it the sixth letter of their alphabet. They called it *digamma*.

The Romans gave the capital F its present form about A.D. 114.

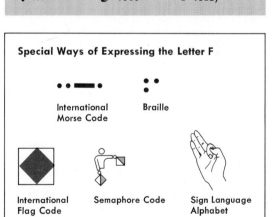

The Small Letter f developed about A.D. 500 from Roman writing. Monks who copied manuscripts modified the letter during the 800's. By about 1500, the f had its present shape.

A.D. 500   1500   Today

Special Ways of Expressing the Letter F

International Morse Code

Braille

International Flag Code

Semaphore Code

Sign Language Alphabet

Common Forms of the Letter F

Ff *Ff*

Handwritten Letters vary from person to person. *Manuscript* (printed) letters, *left*, have simple curves and straight lines. Cursive letters, *right*, have flowing lines.

Ff *Ff*

Roman Letters have small finishing strokes called *serifs* that extend from the main strokes. The type face shown above is Baskerville. The italic form appears at the right.

Ff *Ff*

Sans-Serif Letters are also called *gothic letters*. They have no serifs. The type face shown above is called Futura. The italic form of Futura appears at the right.

F

Computer Letters have special shapes. Computers can "read" these letters either optically or by means of the magnetic ink with which the letters may be printed.

FABER, EBERHARD

FABER, EBERHARD (1822-1879), an American businessman born in Bavaria, built the first mass-production pencil factory in the United States. His great-grandfather had started making pencils in Bavaria in 1761. Faber moved to New York City in 1848 and opened a branch of the family firm there the next year. He sold pencils shipped from Bavaria and also exported cedar boards from Florida to European pencil manufacturers.

Faber had to pay a tariff on the pencils he imported, and so he decided it would be cheaper to make them himself. He developed labor-saving machinery to avoid high production costs and, in 1861, built a pencil factory in New York City. Faber later expanded the business to include pens, erasers, and other stationery products. Faber was born in Stein, near Nuremberg in what is now West Germany.   BARRY W. POULSON

FABIAN SOCIETY is a group of British socialists. The society was founded in 1884. It was named for Quintus Fabius Maximus, a Roman general who avoided defeat by refusing to fight any decisive battles against Hannibal. The Fabians teach that socialism can be achieved gradually, through a series of reforms (see SOCIALISM). They differ from the Communists, who believe that the people can gain ownership of the means of production only through revolution. Noted Fabians have included George Bernard Shaw and H. G. Wells. Fabian ideas became the basis of the British Labour Party (see LABOUR PARTY). See also WEBB (family).   BASIL D. HENNING

FABIUS, *FAY bee uhs*, was the name of one of ancient Rome's greatest families. The Fabius family alone fought against Veii, an Etruscan city that often fought against Rome. According to the Roman historian Livy, 306 members of the Fabius family were killed in an ambush at Cremera in 447 B.C. Only one male survived to carry the Fabius name.

Quintus Fabius Maximus Rullianus (? -290 B.C.) was *consul* (chief government official) five times. He defeated the Samnites and Gauls at Sentinum in 295 B.C., and Rome gained control of most of Italy. He is said to have limited the power of the poor people of Rome by placing them all in four of Rome's 31 tribes.

Quintus Fabius Maximus Cunctator (? -203 B.C.) was also consul five times. He was known as "the Delayer" because of his war strategy of annoying and tiring the enemy while avoiding an actual battle. This method, known as *Fabian tactics*, has been used by many later generals, including George Washington. Fabius was also called the "Shield of Rome" for his defense of Rome against Hannibal of Carthage.

Quintus Fabius Pictor (250?-190? B.C.) was the first Roman to write the history of Rome from its beginning to his own time. He wrote the story in Greek rather than in Latin.   HERBERT M. HOWE

FABLE is a brief fictitious story that teaches a moral. In most fables, one or more of the main characters is an animal, plant, or thing that talks and acts like a human being. A fable may be told in prose or in verse. In many fables, the moral is summed up at the end in the form of a proverb.

Famous fables include "The Fox and the Grapes," "The City Mouse and the Country Mouse," and "The Wolf in Sheep's Clothing." These tales have been told and retold for more than 2,000 years. They remain

Detail of *The Fox and the Crow* (1839), a woodcut by J. J. Grandville from *Fables of La Fontaine;* the Newberry Library, Chicago

In the Fable of the Fox and the Crow, a fox robs a crow of some cheese by telling him what a fine singer he must be. As the crow opens his mouth to caw, the cheese drops from his beak.

popular because they illustrate truths that almost anyone can recognize. In "The Fox and the Grapes," for example, a fox decides that some grapes growing too high for him to reach are probably sour anyway. A person who hears the tale recognizes the fox's attitude as a common human failing. The moral of the fable—that people often express a dislike for what they cannot have—is summed up in the expression "sour grapes."

Nearly all ancient peoples invented folk tales in which animals had human traits. The fox was often pictured as sly, and the owl as wise. In time, people began to tell the stories to teach various morals. The tales thus became fables.

Most of the fables that are popular in Western countries can be traced back to ancient Greece and India. The majority of the Greek fables are credited to Aesop, a Greek slave who lived about 600 B.C. Aesop had a reputation for telling wise, witty tales about animals, but scholars know little else about him. The fables known as "Aesop's fables" probably came from several ancient sources. Some of the stories originated in India.

The fables of the people of India were influenced by their belief that after death, human beings might be reborn as animals. Indian storytellers made up many tales of such rebirths and used them to teach a variety of morals. Some of these fables had reached the West by the start of the Christian era and were included in early collections of Aesop's fables. During the 200's B.C. or after, the Indians collected their best-known fables in a work called the *Panchatantra*.

Through the centuries, many writers have retold the ancient fables. The most famous such writer was Jean de La Fontaine, a French poet of the 1600's. La Fontaine retold Aesop's fables in elegant verse and expanded their meanings. Fables had always made fun of human follies, but La Fontaine turned such satire into biting social criticism. In "The Fox and the Crow," for example, a fox robs a crow of some cheese by telling him what a fine singing voice he must have. As the flattered crow opens his mouth to caw, the cheese drops from his beak. Earlier versions of the fable poked fun at the crow for being fooled by the fox's flattery. La Fontaine's version includes the trickery of the fox and ends with a thoughtful moral: "Every flatterer lives at the expense of his listeners." La Fontaine wrote his fables mainly for adults, but they have long been favorites of French children.

La Fontaine has had many imitators. One of the most successful was Ivan Krylov, a Russian poet of the early 1800's. Krylov translated La Fontaine's fables into Russian and also wrote many of his own. Like La Fontaine, he intended his stories mainly for adults. But through the years, Krylov's fables have become the most popular children's stories in Russia.

During the 1900's, writers have continued to develop the fable as a literary form. The Irish novelist James Joyce wove "The Fox and the Grapes" and "The Ant and the Grasshopper" into his *Finnegans Wake*. The fables help create the mood of fantasy that characterizes this novel. The American humorist James Thurber revived the fable as a form of social criticism. His fables are noted for their stinging portrayal of the anxieties of modern life.   DARCY O'BRIEN

See also AESOP'S FABLES; ALLEGORY; FOLKLORE; LA FONTAINE, JEAN DE; LITERATURE FOR CHILDREN (Folk Literature).

FABRE, *FAH br'*, **JEAN HENRI CASIMIR** (1823-1915), a French naturalist, spent his life observing insects and spiders. He wrote simply of what he saw in the gardens and fields near his home. He received the ribbon of The Legion of Honor, but was fired from his teaching position because he allowed girls to attend his science classes. Fabre was almost unknown outside of France until he was nearly 80. Then the great scientific societies recognized his accomplishments. He wrote a 10-volume *Souvenirs Entomologiques*. Fabre was born in St. Léon, France, to a poor family.   LORUS J. MILNE and MARGERY MILNE

Bettmann Archive
Jean Henri Fabre

FABRIC. See TEXTILE.

FACE is the front part of a person's head. It consists of the forehead, eyes, nose, mouth, cheeks, and chin. The face is covered with muscles and skin. The eyes are protected from glare and dust by the eyelids, lashes, and eyebrows. The tip of the nose is made up of cartilage and skin, which act as a flexible cushion. The channels of the nose are covered with tiny hairs which strain out dust and dirt in the air going through the nose. The mouth includes the lips, teeth, tongue, and roof, and is lined with mucous membrane. The lower jaw is the only bony part of the face that moves.

The skeleton of the face is made up of 14 bones and 32 teeth. The upper bones of the face are the *nasals*, which unite to make the bridge of the nose, and the *lachrymals*, which lie between the eyes. The lower bones

of the face are the *malars*, or cheekbones, the *maxillae*, or upper jawbones, and the *mandibles*, or lower jawbones. The lower jawbone is also called the *inferior maxillary*. The *vomer*, *ethmoid*, and *palatines* lie deeper in the face. There are also a number of muscles in the face. There is a circular muscle around the mouth and one around each eye. Other muscles spread out over the face from the edges of the circular muscles.

The face is the most distinctive part of a human being. It differs in each person because of variations in the nose, eyes, and other parts of the face. It is because of these variations that we recognize each other and tell one another apart. Much of what goes on in our mind finds expression in our face. Our facial muscles often show the kind of emotions we feel. We cannot always control our expression.   W. B. YOUMANS

See also BLUSHING; HEAD (picture); MANDIBLE.

FACE FLY is an annoying pest for livestock. Groups of adult face flies feed on the fluid around the eyes, noses, and mouths of livestock, especially cattle. They also feed on blood from the wounds that other flies make on cattle. Face flies do not bite, and are not known to carry human diseases. The face fly is very similar to the common housefly. The two look almost exactly alike. They differ mainly in their habits.

The female face fly lays eggs in fresh cow manure. Face fly *larvae* (maggots) develop faster than housefly larvae. Mature face fly larvae are yellowish instead of white, but otherwise resemble housefly maggots. Face flies hibernate in large numbers in barns, houses, and other shelters.

Illinois Natural History Survey
The Face Fly

The first known face flies in North America were discovered in Nova Scotia in 1952. They probably came from Europe. The flies soon spread throughout most of the United States.

Scientific Classification. The face fly is in the order *Diptera*. It belongs to the housefly family, *Muscidae*, genus *Musca*, species *M. autumnalis*.   DALE W. JENKINS

FACET. See DIAMOND (How Diamonds Are Cut to Make Jewels); ANT (Head).

FACING. See SEWING (Facings).

FACSIMILE, *fak SIM uh lee*, or FAX, is a way of sending pictures and handwritten or printed material by wire or radio. News services often use facsimile to transmit news to newspapers and television stations. Banks, railroads, and other organizations have adopted facsimile for business purposes. Small newspapers have been published experimentally by facsimile.

Facsimile is made possible because radio currents can be modified by light as well as by sound. Any change in the waves caused by light at the sending station will be reproduced at the receiving station.

A picture to be sent by facsimile is placed on a revolving cylinder at the sending station. A tiny beam of light about $\frac{1}{100}$ inch (0.25 millimeter) wide is passed over the picture. The beam is reflected on a photoelectric

FACTOR

Facsimile carries news and pictures from press services to newspapers and television stations. Other businesses also use this electronic device to speed communications between offices.
Wide World

cell that changes light waves into electric current. When the light ray strikes the lighter parts of the picture, more of the ray is reflected, and the photoelectric cell sends out a stronger current. When the light ray strikes a dark part of the picture, less light is reflected, and the photoelectric cell sends out a weaker current. In this way, the light and dark places of the picture are reproduced in terms of electric current. When the electric signal reaches the receiving set, it passes from a printer blade through damp, chemically treated paper to a wire that is wound around a revolving cylinder. The chemicals in the paper react as the current passes from the blade through the paper to the wire. A strong current makes a dark spot, and a weaker current produces a lighter spot. The different degrees of black and white in the picture are reproduced on the paper.

Many inventors in Europe and the United States worked on facsimile in the late 1800's and early 1900's. Facsimile first attracted attention in 1924, when a picture was sent from Cleveland to *The New York Times*. It came into widespread use in the mid-1930's. In 1954, the International News Service began simultaneous transmission of pictures and voice recordings by facsimile. EARL F. ENGLISH

See also LIBRARY (Information Boom); TELEPHOTO.

FACTOR. The factors of a number are the numbers which when multiplied together give the original number. For example, the numbers 3 and 4 are factors of 12 because $3 \times 4 = 12$. The other whole number factors of 12 are 2 and 6, and 1 and 12. *Factoring* (determining factors) provides insight into one of the many relationships among numbers.

Every whole number, except 1, can be expressed as the product of at least two factors. A number that has only two possible factors, itself and 1, is called a *prime number*. The number 7 is prime because 1 and 7 are its only factors. The eight smallest primes are 2, 3, 5, 7, 11, 13, 17, and 19. A number that has more than two factors is called a *composite number*. The number 4 is composite because it has three factors, 1, 2, and 4. The eight smallest composite numbers

are 4, 6, 8, 9, 10, 12, 14, and 15. The number 1 is neither composite nor prime.

Prime Factors of a number are those prime numbers which when multiplied together equal the number. Each number is a product of only one set of prime numbers. For example, 24 can only be expressed as a product of prime numbers as $2 \times 2 \times 2 \times 3$ (in any order). The *prime factorization* of 24 is $2 \times 2 \times 2 \times 3$ and the *prime factors* of 24 are 2 and 3.

To find the prime factors of a number, divide the number by the smallest *prime number* that goes into it evenly. For example, to find the prime factors of 220, begin by dividing by 2 ($220 \div 2 = 110$). Continue dividing the *quotient* (the number obtained) by 2 until it is no longer divisible by 2 ($110 \div 2 = 55$). But 55 cannot be divided by 2 without leaving a remainder. The next prime, 3, does not divide 55 without a remainder either. But the next greater prime, 5, does divide 55 equally ($55 \div 5 = 11$). The number 11, like 2 and 5, is a prime number. Therefore the prime factorization of 220 is $2 \times 2 \times 5 \times 11$ and the prime factors are 2, 5, and 11. The product $2 \times 2 \times 5 \times 11$ (in any order) is the only way 220 can be expressed as the product of prime numbers. The process may be written like this:

$$2 \underline{|220}$$
$$2 \underline{|110}$$
$$2 \underline{|55} \quad \text{(leaves a remainder)}$$
$$3 \underline{|55} \quad \text{(leaves a remainder)}$$
$$5 \underline{|55}$$
$$11 \quad \text{(prime)}$$

The only factors of a prime number are the number itself and 1.

Common Factors. If a number is a factor of two or more numbers, it is called a *common factor* of those numbers. For example, 1, 3, 5, and 15 are the factors of 15; and 1, 2, 4, 5, 10, and 20 are the factors of 20. One and 5 are common to both these sets of factors. Since 1 is a factor of every number, it is ignored. Therefore, 5 is the only common factor of 15 and 20.

If two numbers have more than one common factor, the greatest one is called the *greatest common factor*. It is also the *greatest common divisor* since a factor of a number is also a divisor of that number. For example, the numbers 30 and 45 have three common factors: 3, 5, and 15. The greatest common factor is 15. To find the greatest common factor of two or more numbers, first find the set of all the factors for each number. Then select the largest factor which is in all the sets. The greatest common factor of 18, 30, and 42 is found in this example:

Number	Set of Factors
18	1, 2, 3, 6, 9, 18
30	1, 2, 3, 5, 6, 10, 15, 30
42	1, 2, 3, 6, 7, 14, 21, 42

The number 6 is the greatest factor common to all the sets, so 6 is the greatest common factor of 18, 30, and 42.

Relative Primes. Two numbers that have no common prime factors are *relatively prime* or *prime in relation to each other*. For example, the prime factors of 12 are 2 and 3. The prime factors of 35 are 5 and 7. Twelve and 35 have no common factors. They are relatively prime.

Algebraic Factors. *Algebraic expressions* ($2x + 4$ is an algebraic expression) also have factors. For example, *1, 3, a, b,* and *ab* are factors of *3ab*. The expressions *1, a, a^2, b* and *a^2b* are factors of *a^2b*. The factors of algebraic expressions are found in the same way as the factors of whole numbers. Multiplying *2ab* by *(a + 2b)* gives *$2a^2b + 4ab^2$*. Therefore, *2ab* and *a + 2b* are factors of *$2a^2b + 4ab^2$*. The other factors of *$2a^2b + 4ab^2$* are *1, 2, a, b,* and *ab*. The expression *$a^2 + b^2$* cannot be factored using real numbers only. Its factors are *complex numbers* (the square roots of negative numbers). See SQUARE ROOT (Square Roots of Negative Numbers). HENRY VAN ENGEN

See also ALGEBRA (Factoring).

FACTORY is a building or group of buildings in which products are manufactured. It may be as small as a house, and have only a few simple machines and two or three workers. Or it may have several buildings and cover one or more city blocks. Factories make almost all the products we use except food. And many food products are processed in factories. About a fourth of the workers in the United States and about a fifth of the workers in Canada are employed in factories. See INDUSTRY; MANUFACTURING.

Before the development of factories, workers in homes or small shops produced most of the products needed by the average family. But the development of automatic machines in the 1700's and 1800's made the modern factory system possible (see INDUSTRIAL REVOLUTION). Until the 1900's, factories were often dirty, poorly lighted, dangerous places to work. Most of them were cramped in industrial sections of large cities. Today, more and more factories are being built in country or suburban areas. Most modern factories have good lighting and air conditioning. Many provide music, cafeterias, and nurses or complete medical staffs.

Kinds of Factories. The factory system of production uses a *division of labor*. That is, it divides the work into a series of different operations. Most factories use one of two methods of manufacturing, or a mixture of the two.

One is the *serialized* or *assembly-line* method. In an automobile plant, for example, the auto frame is placed on a conveyer which moves through the plant. As the frame moves along, parts arrive on other conveyers that join the main conveyer, as branches flow into a river. Finally, a completed automobile comes off the assembly line, ready for the road. See AUTOMOBILE (illustration: Assembling an Automobile).

Some factories use a *job-lot*, or *intermittent*, type of manufacturing. Each department performs a particular set of operations on the product. Workers in one section of a television factory may make the cases, those in another section may install the tubes, and so on.

Location and Design. Most new factories are being built in suburban areas where land costs less than it does in cities, and where the factories benefit by the transportation, labor, and materials available in the cities. These new factories have plenty of space for parking as well as for expansion. Manufacturers generally plan a layout for their machines, and then design a factory to fit around them. Most new factories are one-story buildings that permit materials to move easily from one part of the plant to another, without having to go up or down stairs. This also allows machinery to be installed and rearranged easier than could be done in a multistory building. Industries that make such materials as flour, paints, or chemicals still use factories with two or more stories. In these, raw materials may be started on an upper floor and moved downward through the various operations needed to make the finished product. FRANK F. GROSECLOSE

Related Articles in WORLD BOOK include:

Automation	Industry	Mass Production
Electricity (In Business and Industry)	Invention	Sweatshop
	Labor Force	Technology
Industrial Relations	Management	Workers'
Industrial Revolution	Manufacturing	Compensation

FACTORY ACT. See GREAT BRITAIN (The Era of Reform).

FAERIE QUEENE, THE. See SPENSER, EDMUND.

FAEROE ISLANDS, *FAIR oh,* also spelled FAROE and FØROYAR, are a group of 18 islands and some reefs in the North Atlantic Ocean. They lie between Iceland and the Shetland Islands. The group has an area of 540 square miles (1,399 square kilometers), and a population of about 42,000. Major islands are Streymoy, Eysturoy, Vágar, Sudhuroy, and Sandoy.

The 140-mile (225-kilometer) coastline is steep and deeply indented. Treacherous currents along the shores make navigation difficult. The islanders are hardy people of Norse origin who fish and raise sheep. They also sell the eggs and feathers of the many sea birds that nest on the cliffs. The islanders do little farming.

Norway ruled the islands from the 800's until 1380, when they came under the

Boeing Co.
Aircraft Factory Workers assemble a Boeing 747 superjet passenger plane in the company's huge plant near Everett, Wash.

WORLD BOOK map
Location of Faeroe Islands

control of Denmark. British forces occupied the islands during World War II, but the civil government remained the same. In 1948, Denmark granted the Faeroes self-government. The islanders have their own parliament, or *Lagting*, and send representatives to the Danish parliament in Copenhagen. The seat of government is Tórshavn on Streymoy.   JENS NYHOLM

FAFNIR, *FAHV nihr*, was the brother of Regin and Otter in Norse mythology. He changed himself into a dragon to guard the great pile of gold that had been made by the ring of the dwarf Andvari. Sigurd killed Fafnir while Fafnir was in the form of a dragon. Sigurd ate Fafnir's heart and was able to understand the language of the birds. See also SIGURD; SIEGFRIED.

FAGIN was a receiver of stolen goods and a trainer of young thieves. He was a character in the novel *Oliver Twist*, by Charles Dickens.

FAHRENHEIT, *FAR un hite*, **GABRIEL DANIEL** (1686-1736), a German physicist, developed the Fahrenheit temperature scale. He also made the thermometer more accurate by using mercury instead of alcohol in the thermometer tube (see THERMOMETER). He determined three fixed temperatures: 0° for the freezing point of ice, salt, and water; 32°, the freezing point of pure water; and 96° F. for the normal temperature of the human body. These three temperatures, from lowest to highest, are equal to −18°, 0°, and 36° on the Celsius temperature scale. Later experiments proved the body temperature to be 98.6° F., or 37° C. Fahrenheit was born in Danzig (now Gdańsk, Poland).   CARL T. CHASE

FAÏENCE, *fah YAHNS*, or *fy AHNS*, is a soft earthenware made in England, France, Germany, Italy, and other countries. It has an opaque white glaze made of tin enamel, and may be decorated with iron, copper, and manganese oxides. The iron oxide produces a brown, tan, or yellow color; the copper oxide, a green color; and the manganese oxide, a brown, tan, or purple color. Faïence resembles majolica because of its white glaze, but differs from it in design and technique (see MAJOLICA). The name *faïence* comes from Faenza, Italy, the center for the production of tin enamel earthenware during the 1500's.   PAUL BOGATAY

Metropolitan Museum of Art, New York City,
Museé de Cluny, Paris (Art Institute of Chicago)

Faïence Dish and Plate show the elaborate decoration which made this kind of pottery famous. The pottery bird, made in France during the 1700's, rests on a gilded bronze mount. The plate shows a tiger attacking a gazelle.

FAILLE, *file*, is a ribbed fabric of silk or soft rayon. Faille is used for dresses, neckties, hats, robes, coats, curtains, and slipcovers.

FAINTING is a temporary loss of consciousness. The fainting person becomes pale, begins to perspire, and then loses consciousness and collapses. The person also has a weak pulse and breathes irregularly. Fainting usually lasts only a few minutes. As the fainting passes, the muscles become firm, the pulse is stronger, and breathing becomes regular. Fainting is caused by a rapid and great fall in blood pressure which results in a too small supply of blood to the brain. Usually the fall in blood pressure is caused by a mental or physical shock.

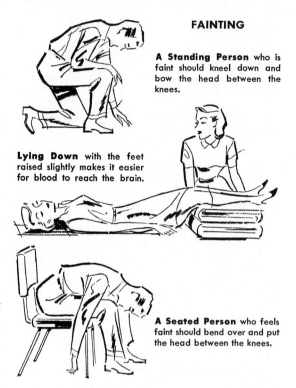

FAINTING

A Standing Person who is faint should kneel down and bow the head between the knees.

Lying Down with the feet raised slightly makes it easier for blood to reach the brain.

A Seated Person who feels faint should bend over and put the head between the knees.

Fainting should be treated by letting the person lie stretched out with the head slightly lower than the body. The person's clothing should be loosened, and the individual should be given plenty of room and air. In a few cases, hot applications to the back and legs can be used. In some cases, a person can be revived by bathing the face with cool water or by passing a whiff of ammonia under the nostrils.   JOHN B. MIALE

See also FIRST AID (Fainting).

FAIR. See FAIRS AND EXPOSITIONS.

FAIR DEAL is the name President Harry S. Truman gave to his domestic legislative program. He said it offered to the American people "the promise of equal rights and equal opportunities." See also TRUMAN, HARRY S. (The Fair Deal).

FAIR EMPLOYMENT PRACTICES try to give everyone the right to any job, regardless of race, color, or national origin. Fair employment regulations aim particularly at anti-black and anti-Jewish discrimination. In the United States, President Franklin D. Roosevelt established the Committee on Fair Employment Practice, called FEPC, in 1941. This organization, which continued until 1946, tried to prevent job discrimination in factories that worked on government contracts. In 1953,

Fairbanks, Alaska, the chief financial and trade center of the interior of Alaska, lies on the banks of the Chena River, center. Fairbanks is in the heart of a great gold-mining region.

Fairbanks Chamber of Commerce

President Dwight D. Eisenhower set up a Committee on Government Contracts to serve the same purpose. The federal Civil Rights Act of 1964 banned discrimination in employment on the basis of race, religion, or sex. The first such U.S. federal law, it set up the Equal Employment Opportunity Commission to review discrimination cases. Most fair employment (FEPC) laws were made by states. New York passed the first FEPC law in the U.S., in 1945. Over 30 states and 50 cities now have FEPC laws. Many such laws also ban discrimination in public housing, hotels, and restaurants. Five states prohibit discrimination against older workers.

Ontario passed the first Canadian antidiscrimination law in 1951. Five other provinces followed, and a federal act took effect in 1953.   H. G. HENEMAN, JR.

See also EQUAL EMPLOYMENT OPPORTUNITY COMMISSION.

FAIR HOUSING LAWS. See OPEN HOUSING.

FAIR LABOR STANDARDS ACT. See CHILD LABOR (U.S. Federal Laws); MINIMUM WAGE.

FAIR TRADE is a term that refers to the prevention of unfair cutting of prices. Such cutting can be prevented by (1) a court order or (2) the establishment of minimum retail prices. Suppose that a large chain store cuts its prices below cost to force smaller merchants out of business. The large store can afford a dip in profits. If the small merchants drop out, shoppers must go to the chain store. As a result, the chain might boost its prices far above the original levels. Since the early 1900's, courts in the United States have ordered such price cutting stopped in many cases and have awarded damages to dealers hurt by it.

In 1931, California passed the first state fair-trade law. Other states soon followed with their own laws. The laws permitted manufacturers and retailers to agree on a minimum retail price for a manufacturer's products. Ordinarily, price fixing of this kind would violate federal antitrust laws (see TRUST). But the Miller-Tydings Act of 1937 suspended the laws in such cases. It permitted fair-trade agreements, provided that they dealt with trademarked products and were legal in the state involved. The McGuire Act of 1952 allowed states to make any fair-trade agreement binding on all sellers.

Opponents of fair-trade laws argued that the laws cost consumers millions of dollars a year in higher prices. Through the years, many states repealed their fair-trade laws. Congress abolished the remaining ones in 1975.   JOHN ALAN APPLEMAN and JEAN APPLEMAN

FAIRBANKS, Alaska (pop. 36,874), the state's second largest city, is the center of a great gold-mining region. It is the closest city in North America to the Arctic Circle, which lies 130 miles (209 kilometers) north. Fairbanks lies on the banks of the Chena River (see ALASKA [political map]). Major occupations include mining and construction. In 1967, a flood in Fairbanks caused about $75 million in damage and six deaths.

Fairbanks is often called *The Heart of the Golden North.* It lies at the northern end of the Alaska Railroad and near the northern end of the Alaska Highway. The architecture of Fairbanks is an interesting mixture of log cabins and modern office buildings. The University of Alaska, a U.S. Air Force base, and an army post are in the area. The city has a council-manager government.

Felix Pedro, a prospector, found gold 12 miles (19 kilometers) north of Fairbanks in 1902. Its name honors Charles W. Fairbanks, Vice-President of the United States (1905-1909). The temperature in Fairbanks averages 60° F. (16° C) in June and about −11° F. (−24° C) in January.   LYMAN E. ALLEN

FAIRBANKS is the family name of a father and son who became noted for playing dashing, gallant heroes in adventurous motion pictures.

Douglas Fairbanks, Sr.
Wide World

Douglas Fairbanks, Jr.
Wide World

FAIRBANKS, CHARLES WARREN

Douglas Fairbanks, Sr. (1883-1939), ranked as one of the most popular stars of his day. His great charm and energy made him an international favorite. He and his second wife, Mary Pickford, were called the "King and Queen of Movieland." He acted on the stage in New York City before he entered motion pictures in 1915. A skilled athlete, Fairbanks performed daring feats in such motion pictures as *Robin Hood*, *The Iron Mask*, and *The Thief of Bagdad*. He died of heart failure caused by overexertion. He was born in Denver, Colo.

Douglas [Elton] Fairbanks, Jr. (1909-   ), acted in many motion pictures, and became a television producer in the 1950's. He appeared in such motion pictures as *Dawn Patrol*, *The Prisoner of Zenda*, and *Gunga Din*. President Franklin D. Roosevelt sent him to South America on a political mission in 1941. He served in the U.S. Navy in World War II, and received the Silver Star for bravery in action. Fairbanks was born in New York City, the son of Ann Beth Sully Fairbanks. He made his home in London, England, in the 1950's. He has published stories and poems.   NARDI REEDER CAMPION

Culver
Charles W. Fairbanks

FAIRBANKS, CHARLES WARREN (1852-1918), served as Vice-President of the United States from 1905 to 1909 under President Theodore Roosevelt. He hoped to be the Republican presidential candidate in 1908. But he did not get along well with Roosevelt, and the President helped William Howard Taft win the nomination. Fairbanks again was Republican vice-presidential candidate in 1916. But he and presidential candidate Charles Evans Hughes lost the election to Woodrow Wilson and Thomas R. Marshall.

He was born on a farm near Unionville Center, Ohio, and was graduated from Ohio Wesleyan University. He became a successful railroad lawyer in Indianapolis, Ind. Fairbanks served as a U.S. senator from Indiana from 1897 to 1905. He headed the American delegation to the Joint High Commission that tried to settle all outstanding difficulties with Canada in 1898. He rejected an offer from Mark Hanna, Republican political leader, to be William McKinley's running mate in the 1900 presidential campaign.   IRVING G. WILLIAMS

FAIRBANKS, THADDEUS (1796-1886), invented the platform scale in 1831. It replaced the large hooks and lifting apparatus necessary for weighing heavy loads.

Fairbanks was born in Brimfield, Mass. He suffered from poor health as a boy, and had little formal education. He established a small iron foundry in St. Johnsbury, Vt., in 1823, and, over a period of 60 years, made many improvements in such products as plows and stoves.   ROBERT P. MULTHAUF

FAIRBURN, WILLIAM ARMSTRONG (1876-1947), an American businessman and inventor, found methods to remove the poisonous effect of phosphorus used in match heads and the hazard of afterglow in the wood of matches (see MATCH). He discovered the processes in 1911 for the Diamond Match Company, but released his findings for use by competitors. He was president of the company from 1915 until his death. Fairburn was born in Huddersfield, England.   RICHARD D. HUMPHREY

FAIRCHILD, DAVID GRANDISON (1869-1954), an American botanist and explorer, brought more than 200,000 species of plants to the United States. He helped found the Section of Foreign Seed and Plant Introduction in the U.S. Department of Agriculture, and directed that section from 1906 to 1928. He established the Fairchild Tropical Garden, 12 miles (19 kilometers) south of Miami, Fla., in 1938. It became the largest botanical garden in the United States. Fairchild wrote such books as *Garden Islands of the Great East* and *The World Grows Round My Door*. He was born in Lansing, Mich., and studied at Kansas State and Iowa State colleges, and at Rutgers University.   C. B. BAKER

FAIRCHILD, SHERMAN MILLS (1896-1971), an American inventor and businessman, was called the "father of aerial mapping photography." He invented many cameras and an automatic photoengraver. Fairchild invented the Fairchild Flight Analyzer Camera in 1953. It was the first camera to take pictures without distortion in a continuous sequence of action. It has been used to track guided missiles and to study the take-offs and landings of missiles and planes.

Fairchild developed the FC-1 and FC-2 planes, the first to have enclosed cockpits. He built the C-119 transport plane so that equipment could be rolled in or out of its rear cargo doors. He also developed a radio compass and hydraulic landing gear. Fairchild was born in Oneonta, N.Y.   R. E. WESTMEYER

FAIRFIELD, CICILY ISABEL. See WEST, DAME REBECCA.

FAIRFIELD UNIVERSITY. See UNIVERSITIES AND COLLEGES (table).

FAIRLEIGH DICKINSON UNIVERSITY is a private, coeducational school with campuses in Rutherford, Teaneck, and Madison, N.J. It also operates a two-year college and a dental school in Hackensack, N.J.; an extension center in Wayne, N.J.; Wroxton College in Wroxton, England; and a marine biology laboratory on St. Croix, U.S. Virgin Islands.

The university grants bachelor's and master's degrees in allied health, business administration, education, engineering, liberal arts, and science. Doctor's degrees are awarded in dentistry and educational leadership. Wroxton College offers a graduate program in English literature and various undergraduate courses. Fairleigh Dickinson was founded in 1941. For enrollment, see UNIVERSITIES AND COLLEGES (table).

Critically reviewed by FAIRLEIGH DICKINSON UNIVERSITY

FAIRLESS, BENJAMIN FRANKLIN (1890-1962), was an American industrialist. He was president of U.S. Steel Corporation from 1938 to 1953 and chairman of the board from 1952 to 1955. He held several positions with the American Iron and Steel Institute and served as its president from 1955 until his death. Fairless received the Bessemer Medal in 1951 for distinguished service to the iron and steel industry. He was born Benjamin F. Williams in Pigeon Run, Ohio, the son of a coal miner. He took the name Fairless from an uncle who adopted him. He graduated from Ohio Northern University.   W. H. BAUGHN

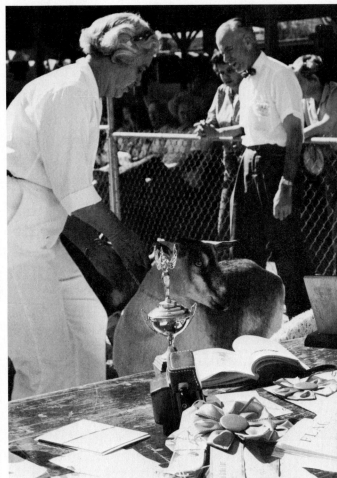

Herb and Dorothy McLaughlin

Herb and Dorothy McLaughlin

State Fairs are held every summer and fall throughout the United States. Exhibits, games, and exciting rides attract large crowds to a state fair midway, *left*. These fairs also hold competitions, *right*, to select outstanding livestock raised in the state.

FAIRS AND EXPOSITIONS are events where people gather to present or see exhibitions that show how other people work, live, or play. The terms are often used interchangeably. But many persons classify *fairs* as events that attract an audience from one locality or a limited region and *expositions* as events that draw people from greater distances.

Fairs

A fair is a special kind of gathering of people for buying and selling, for holding contests, and for having a good time. Fairs first came about as a means of carrying on peaceful trade between different tribes. Thousands of years ago, tribesmen gathered at certain places to exchange goods. They regarded these places as holy and believed that the gods would punish anyone who fought or cheated there.

Ancient Fairs were connected with religion. Beginning about 1000 B.C., the Arabic city of Mecca was the scene of great festivals held by pilgrims who journeyed

there. On the day of a festival, huge Phoenician caravans would arrive, and a fair would be held. The fairs of ancient Egypt and Ireland were held at tombs and burying grounds. They were part of ceremonies and games honoring the dead.

Ancient Greek fairs were held along with festivals honoring the gods. The finest glassware, cloth, spices, carpets, and armor were sold at these fairs. One such fair featured the Olympic Games.

The ancient Romans held a yearly festival honoring Jupiter. The festival was followed by a fair. Other fairs took place in connection with festivals honoring other gods or goddesses. Rome also had fairs that were not part of ceremonies honoring the gods. These fairs were held on holidays, and trading was carried on.

Fairs of the Middle Ages. In the 1200's, the Chinese trade center Kinsai (now Hangchow) held large fairs. These fairs took place in 10 huge squares 4 miles (6 kilometers) apart on the city's main street. Half a million people visited the fairs and bought tremendous

9

County Fairs feature exhibits ranging from home canning and farm products to flower arrangements. Judges award prizes to the best entries.

The Atomium was the symbol of the World's Fair which was held in Brussels, Belgium, in 1958. The giant structure represented the atomic make-up of a metal molecule, enlarged about 200 billion times. The highest sphere housed a skyline restaurant, and the other spheres held exhibits from Belgium and other countries.

amounts of meat, vegetables, fruits, wine, and jewelry.

During the same period, important fairs were held in four towns in the French province of Champagne. These towns—Bar, Lagny, Provins, and Troyes—had held fairs before. But in the 1200's, the counts of Champagne built them up to new greatness, and the fairs of Champagne became major centers of European trade.

The most famous Russian fair was that of Nizhni Novgorod (now Gorki). It was first held in the early 1300's and was not discontinued until 1930, when the Communists banned all Russian fairs. It was held mainly to exchange goods, and huge piles of cotton, furs, metals, and tea surrounded the fairground. Caravans brought Chinese products by one of the longest and most dangerous routes in the history of trade.

Later Fairs. During the 1600's, the chief English fair was Stourbridge Fair. It opened on St. Bartholomew's Day, August 24. A message from the king was read, urging the people "to keep the king's peace." Rules about honest weights and measures were also read. The fair had a long row of shops where people could buy clothing, jewelry, toys, and other items. But the biggest business was the trade among the merchants.

Bartholomew Fair in London was the first great fair to put amusement above everything else. Circus and vaudeville acts and other entertainments were developed or improved. But at the fair, the old, strict rules about honesty were broken. Pickpockets and cheats appeared, and the crowds were loud and disorderly.

In the United States, the Berkshire Agricultural Society held a fair called the Berkshire Cattle Show in 1810 in Pittsfield, Mass. Prizes were given for the best livestock and for other products, such as jellies, pickles, and mincemeat made by housewives. This type of fair became popular throughout the country. Later, athletic contests, corn huskings, horse races, and quilting bees were added. These fairs developed into agricultural and industrial fairs sponsored by counties and states. Today,

The Milan Fair in Italy is Europe's largest sample fair. It exhibits more than a million samples of goods from all parts of the world every year.

livestock breeders and 4-H Clubs and other organizations exhibit and sell products at county and state fairs throughout the United States.

Expositions

An exposition features industrial, commercial, and scientific developments. Some expositions are open to the public. Others are held for groups of people with similar special interests.

The Crystal Palace Exposition. In 1851, the London Society of Arts organized the "Exposition of the Industry of All Nations." It was housed in a Crystal Palace that covered almost 19 acres (8 hectares). The event drew more than 6 million visitors. The chief exhibits included such inventions as the McCormick reaper and the Colt repeating pistol.

Later Expositions. In 1853 and 1854, the New York Crystal Palace Exhibition featured the first passenger elevator and demonstrations of the sewing machine. The Centennial Exposition in Philadelphia in 1876 honored Alexander Graham Bell for inventing the telephone. In 1893, the World's Columbian Exposition in Chicago featured electricity and structural steel. The Brussels World's Fair in 1958 displayed developments in nuclear physics. The theme of the 1962 Seattle World's Fair was the 21st century. The New York World's Fair of 1964 and 1965 offered the latest views of science and the arts. The theme of Expo 67, held in Montreal in 1967, was "Man and His World." In 1970, Expo '70 was held in Osaka, Japan. It was the first world's fair held in Asia. "Celebrating Tomorrow's Fresh, New Environment" was the theme of Expo 74, held in Spokane, Wash.   EDWARD J. LEE

Related Articles. For the dates and locations of fairs in the United States and Canada, see the Annual Events section of the state and province articles. See also:

Bazaar
Centennial Exposition
Century of Progress Exposition
Expo 67
Louisiana Purchase Exposition
New York World's Fair
Pan American Exposition
Sesquicentennial Exposition
Texas (Places to Visit)
Toronto (Other Interesting Places to Visit)
World's Columbian Exposition

The Unisphere ® became the symbol of the New York World's Fair of 1964-1965. This stainless steel structure, 140 feet (43 meters) high, symbolized the fair's theme, "Peace Through Understanding." The three orbit rings shown encircling the globe called attention to man's accomplishments in investigating space.

Engraving (1800's) by W. J. Linton; Bettmann Archive

The King and Queen of the Fairies were named Oberon and Titania in many tales. William Shakespeare featured them and the mischievous fairy Puck in his comedy *A Midsummer Night's Dream*.

Engraving (1917) from *Grimm's Fairy Tales* by Louis Rhead; Copyright 1917 by Harper & Row Publishers, Inc. By permission of the publisher

Rumpelstiltskin was a wicked fairy in German folklore. He wove gold from straw for a girl in exchange for her promise to give him her first child after she married a king. In this picture, Rumpelstiltskin demands the child from the unhappy girl.

FAIRY is an imaginary creature that appears in the folklore of Western Europe. Fairies have magic powers, which they use to perform both good and bad deeds. Fairies are usually helpful, but they often behave mischievously and occasionally act cruelly.

There are several kinds of fairies, and each lives in a certain area. For example, *brownies, buccas,* and *pixies* live in England; *goblins* in France; *kobolds* and *nixes* in Germany; and *trolls* in the Scandinavian countries. Although the word *fairy* generally refers to various characters in Western European folklore, fairylike creatures exist in the folklore of many other parts of the world. Hawaiian folklore includes stories about dwarfs called *Menehune,* who work at night. Japanese folk stories tell of a water demon known as the *kappa.*

Fairies make themselves invisible to human beings. However, some people have the power to see fairies and the places where they live. Sometimes fairies become visible to a person who steps into a *fairy ring.* Fairy rings are dark green circles found in a field or meadow. Fairies enjoy dancing and use fairy rings as dancing places.

Fairies appear in two kinds of folk stories—*legends* and *fairy tales.* Legends take place in the real world, and fairy tales occur in some imaginary land. Legends are told as true stories, but fairy tales are told as fiction. Actually, fairies appear in few fairy tales. Most stories about fairies are really legends.

A number of beliefs and stories about fairies have been popular for hundreds of years. For example, many children believe that the *sandman* comes each night and puts "sleepy dust" in their eyes to help them sleep. American children especially like the *tooth fairy.* After losing a baby tooth, a child puts it under a pillow or in a glass of water. During the night, while the youngster is asleep, the tooth fairy takes the tooth and leaves money. The *bogeyman,* an evil fairy, kidnaps boys and girls who leave home without permission. The *bogey beast,* also called the *bug-a-boo,* carries off naughty children.

No one knows how the belief in fairies began. In some stories, fairies were angels who were forced to leave heaven because of some wrongdoing. In other stories, fairies were spirits of the dead. Some scholars believe that fairies began as ancient nature spirits, such as the spirits of mountains, streams, and trees. Many stories about fairies represent attempts to explain various happenings. For example, if a cow goes dry for no apparent reason, a farmer may blame fairies for stealing her milk.

What Fairies Look Like. Fairies vary in size, but the majority are smaller than adult human beings. Most fairies have various human features. Some fairies, including pixies, have great beauty. Others have misshapen faces or deformed bodies. For example, trolls are short, ugly men with crooked noses and humped backs. Leprechauns are wrinkled little men. The *banshees* of Ireland and Scotland have long, streaming hair, and their eyes are fiery red from continual crying. Many fairies wear green or white clothing with red caps. Brownies wear brown cloaks and hoods.

Where Fairies Live. Fairies may live alone or in a large group. The banshee is an example of a fairy that lives alone. In Scotland, she can be heard wailing by a river as she washes the clothes of a person who soon will die. In Ireland, banshees often live near a particular family. The sound of a wailing banshee means that someone in the family will soon die.

Large groups of fairies live in fairyland, a fairy society with its own government and territory. In most stories, a king and queen rule fairyland, with the queen having the most power. Queen Mab is a famous fairy queen in Irish folklore. Oberon is king of the fairies in many legends. Fairyland may be under the earth, inside a hollow hill, or beneath a lake. The entrance may be a door in a hill or under the roots of trees.

Life in fairyland closely resembles life in the human world. Fairies work, marry, and have children. But time passes extremely slowly in fairyland, and so there is no old age or death. Many legends describe the difference between time in fairyland and in the human world. In one legend, a man spends what he believes is one night in fairyland. But after he returns to his home, he discovers that hundreds of years have passed —and no one remembers him.

In fairyland, fairies often have trouble giving birth. A common type of fairy legend tells how fairies kidnap a human woman and take her to fairyland to help deliver a baby. The fairies blindfold the woman before she enters and leaves fairyland so the entrance will remain secret. Fairies nearly always pay the woman well for her help.

Fairies and Human Beings. People and fairies sometimes marry. A man might go to fairyland to live with his bride, or he might bring his fairy wife back to his home. In many stories, the human being must follow strict rules to remain married to a fairy. For example, a human husband must never scold or strike his fairy wife or refer to her being a fairy. If he does, the fairy immediately returns to fairyland.

Fairies often aid people in various ways. They might help with the housework or with such farmwork as reaping and threshing. In some cases, a person is not allowed to thank the fairy, to offer it gifts, or even to watch it work. If the person breaks one of these rules, the fairy runs away and never returns.

Sometimes fairies reward people for doing them a favor. According to one story, a farmer who mends a fairy oven or chair will receive delicious food in return. Grateful fairies also may leave money for people who have treated them well.

However, fairies are not always helpful and kind. They may steal grain or lead travelers astray. Occasionally, fairies commit cruel acts. In one legend, a woman helps deliver a fairy baby. As she puts some magic ointment on the baby's eye, she accidentally rubs some on one of her own eyes. The ointment enables her to see fairies who are normally invisible to human beings. Later, the woman sees a fairy in a market place and speaks to him. The fairy asks which eye the woman sees him with. After she tells him, he blinds her in that eye.

Fairies sometimes try to trick women into caring for fairy babies. The fairies may exchange their babies, called *changelings*, for healthy newborn human infants. Usually a human mother can see that a changeling has been substituted for her child because the fairy baby has some ugly physical feature or habit. If the mother threatens to burn the changeling, it may leave and give back the woman's own child.

Many people believe in fairies and have developed ways to win their favor or to protect themselves from evil ones. Fairies love milk, and so people may pour milk into the ground for them. Parents may hang an open pair of scissors over a child's crib as a charm to prevent fairies from stealing the infant. Parents also may place a cross or a container of holy water beside the baby for protection. If travelers lose their way because of what they believe is a fairy's spell, they try to break the spell by turning a piece of their clothing inside out and burning it.

Fairies in Literature. For hundreds of years, authors have written about fairies in novels, plays, and stories. The English playwright William Shakespeare used fairies as major characters in his comedy *A Midsummer Night's Dream*. This play includes Oberon and Titania, the king and queen of the fairies, and the mischievous fairy Puck. Shakespeare may have based Puck on any of several fairies from British folklore, including *Pooka* of Ireland, *Pwca* of Wales, and *Robin Goodfellow* of England. A fairy named Ariel is an important character in Shakespeare's *The Tempest*. The playwright also wrote a famous description of Queen Mab in *Romeo and Juliet*.

In 1697, the French author Charles Perrault published a collection of folk stories called *Tales of Mother Goose*. This book included some stories that are still popular. In one tale, Cinderella's fairy godmother changes a pumpkin into a carriage and mice into horses —and changes them back again. In another story, an evil fairy condemns Sleeping Beauty to death. But a good fairy changes the curse from death to sleep, so that a handsome prince can awaken the girl with a kiss.

In the early 1800's, two German scholars, the brothers Jakob and Wilhelm Grimm, published a collection of folk stories called *Grimm's Fairy Tales*. Only a few of the stories include fairies. One tale, "Rumpelstiltskin," tells of a fairy who spins gold from straw.

Some authors have made up their own stories about fairies. The Danish writer Hans Christian Andersen wrote several volumes of stories from 1835 until his death in 1875. In one tale, "Little Tiny," the main character springs from a magic flower. The Italian author Carlo Collodi wrote *Pinocchio* (1883), a famous children's novel that has a fairy character. *Peter Pan* (1904), a popular children's play by the English writer Sir James M. Barrie, has a number of fairies, including one of the main characters.

The English author J. R. R. Tolkien included fairies and other imaginary creatures in his works. In *The Hobbit* (1937) and the three-volume *The Lord of the Rings* (1954-1956), Tolkien described a race of wise and gifted elves. They live in the Undying Lands, where nothing ever ages or dies.   ALAN DUNDES

Related Articles in WORLD BOOK include:

For a list of collections of fairy tales, see LITERATURE FOR CHILDREN (Books to Read [Folk Literature—Fairy Tales]).

FAIRY FALLS

FAIRY FALLS is a waterfall in Mount Rainier National Park in western Washington. It stands 5,500 feet (1,676 meters) above sea level at the head of Stevens Canyon. Fairy Falls is 700 feet (213 meters) high, fifth in size among U.S. waterfalls. WALLACE E. AKIN

FAIRY TALE. See FAIRY.

FAISAL, *FIE sal*, or FEISAL, is the name of two kings of Iraq, grandfather and grandson. They were members of the Hashemite family, which traced its descent from the prophet Muhammad (see MUHAMMAD).

Faisal I (1885-1933) became the first king of Iraq after the British took Iraq from the Ottoman Empire during World War I. He was elected king in 1921, while the country was a British mandate under the League of Nations. Faisal and the British cooperated in overthrowing the ruling Ottoman Turks in 1915. The famed Lawrence of Arabia was his close friend. Under Faisal's rule, Iraq became an independent country in 1932.

Faisal II (1935-1958) became king in 1939 at the age of three when his father, Ghazi I, was killed in an automobile accident. His uncle, Prince Abdul Ilah, ruled Iraq as regent during Faisal's youth. Faisal II began his reign on May 2, 1953. He and his uncle were killed by revolutionaries on July 14, 1958. SYDNEY N. FISHER

See also IRAQ (History).

FAISAL, *FY suhl* (1906?-1975), was king of Saudi Arabia from 1964 to 1975. He became an important world leader because of his control over Saudi Arabia's vast oil resources. In 1975, Faisal was assassinated by one of his nephews.

Faisal used government profits from oil for such things as industrialization projects and the expansion of public education in Saudi Arabia. During the early 1970's, he supported an oil embargo against nations friendly to Israel. He also favored sharp price increases for petroleum exports.

Faisal ibn Abdul Aziz al Faisal al Saud was born in Riyadh. He was crown prince from 1953 to 1964, and served as prime minister from 1953 to 1960 and from 1962 to 1964 when his brother Saud was king. See also SAUD; SAUDI ARABIA (History). JOHN R. RANDALL

FAITH. See PHILOSOPHY (Faith); RELIGION.

FAKIR, *fuh KEER*, is a Muslim or Hindu who practices extreme self-denial as part of his religion. *Fakir* is an Arabic word meaning *poor*, especially *poor in the sight of God*. Fakirs usually live on charity and spend most of their lives in religious contemplation. Some fakirs can actually perform such feats of will power as walking on hot coals. But they also frequently practice deception. Some fakirs live in religious communities. Others wander about alone. Men whose way of life resembles that of fakirs include Muslim *dervishes* and Hindu *yogis*. ALI HASSAN ABDEL-KADER

See also ASCETIC; DERVISH; YOGA.

FALANGE ESPAÑOLA, or SPANISH PHALANX, was the only legal political party in Spain under dictator Francisco Franco. The Falange Española was founded in 1933 as a fascist group that tried to overthrow the republic with terrorism and violence. José Antonio Primo de Rivera, son of former dictator Miguel Primo de Rivera, founded the party. Falangists supported Franco during the Spanish Civil War. In 1937, Franco took control of the party. In 1976, after Franco's death, the Spanish government legalized other political parties. STANLEY G. PAYNE

FALCON AND FALCONRY. The falcon is a hawk-like bird that is trained to hunt other birds in the sport called *falconry*. Falcons are often called hawks, but they differ from true hawks in having long pointed wings, fairly long tails, and a different kind of flight. Their wing strokes are rapid, and they do not soar. There are about 60 species of falcons found throughout the world.

The largest of these birds are the *gyrfalcons*, which are 2 feet (61 centimeters) or more long. They live in the Arctic regions of North America, Europe, and Asia. The smallest are the *pygmy falcons* of southern Asia, with a length under 6 inches (15 centimeters). Females are somewhat larger than males, but both usually have the same colors. Both sexes have hooked beaks and powerful feet with sharp *talons* (claws). Falcons attack prey as large as themselves and larger. They kill many birds.

The larger falcons have become rare in North America, largely because of overuse of the insecticide DDT. The nesting habits of falcons are similar to those of hawks, but the nests are usually smaller and barer.

The Peregrine Falcon once lived throughout the world, but it has become extremely rare in some places. Few can be found in North America east of the Rocky Mountains. Probably few birds can fly faster than this powerful falcon. Its speed when it swoops on its prey is estimated at 180 miles (290 kilometers) per hour. It can easily overtake the swiftest ducks, pigeons, grouse, and pheasants. The falcon measures about 18 inches (46 centimeters) in length, and has a wingspread of about 43 inches (109 centimeters). It is blue-gray above, and white below with blackish-brown bars. This falcon prefers to nest on a shelf of a steep cliff. It lays two to six cream-and-brown eggs on the bare rock.

The American Kestrel, or sparrow hawk, is the smallest American falcon, and one of the most handsome birds of prey. It ranges from Canada southward into South America, and is one of the commonest birds of prey. Its average length is only about 10 inches (25

The Peregrine Falcon is one of the fastest flying birds. It dives at speeds up to 180 miles (290 kilometers) per hour. The falconer keeps the bird from escaping by holding the straps hanging from its legs.

Ron Austing

FALCON

Aplomado Falcon
Falco femoralis
Found in Central and South America
and the extreme southwestern United
States
Body length: 16 inches
(41 centimeters)

Philippine Falcon
Microhierax erythrogonys
Found in the Philippines
Body length: 6½ inches
(16.5 centimeters)

American Kestrel
Falco sparverius
Found throughout the Western
Hemisphere
Body length: 12 inches
(30 centimeters)

Gyrfalcon
Falco rusticolus
Found near the Arctic Circle
Body length: 24 inches
(61 centimeters)

WORLD BOOK illustrations
by Walter Linsenmaier

Russ Kinne, Photo Researchers

The Prairie Falcon is sometimes used for falconry. The falconer wears a heavy leather glove to protect his hand from the bird's sharp claws.

centimeters), and its wingspread about 22 inches (56 centimeters). The colors are mostly reddish-brown, ashy-blue, black, and white. They are duller in the female than in the male. Of all birds of prey, the American kestrel is one of the most helpful to farmers, because it eats insects such as grasshoppers and beetles which injure the crops. At times it catches field mice and other small rodents. It rarely harms birds. This bird nests in tree holes, rock crevices, small openings in buildings, and occasionally in a large birdhouse. It usually lays 4 or 5 buff or reddish-white eggs with spots of brown, and both sexes sit on the eggs.

The Merlin, or *pigeon hawk,* is much like the peregrine falcon in color, but almost as small as the American kestrel. It nests mainly in the woods of eastern Canada, northern Maine, Michigan, and Minnesota. Merlins are seen in other parts of the country chiefly when they migrate to and from their wintering grounds in Mexico and South America.

Other Falcons. The *prairie falcon* lives in dry, treeless parts of the western United States. It resembles the peregrine falcon in general appearance, but it has much paler markings. The large white and black *gyrfalcons* sometimes migrate southward from the far north in the winter when their food becomes scarce. The medium-sized *Aplomado falcon* lives in the extreme Southwest.

Falconry, or Hawking, is a method of hunting game with trained falcons or hawks. The Persians began it

about 4,000 years ago. In the Middle Ages it was a popular sport among the noblemen of Europe. The sport became much less widespread after guns were invented and feudalism ended. Groups in Europe, the Middle East, and North America keep up the sport. In the United States, falconry is regulated by the federal government and most state governments. Conservationists oppose the sport because it decreases the already dwindling number of large wild falcons.

Training falcons is an art that takes skill, months of time, and endless patience. First they must become used to having men around them. This is called being "manned." They must also be "broken" to the hood which is placed over their heads while they are carried in the field. The hood is removed only when the game is seen and the falcon is turned loose to pursue it. Finally, the birds must be trained to "lure," so that they will not fly off with the game after they have struck it down or pounced on it.

Scientific Classification. Falcons belong to the family *Falconidae.* The peregrine falcon is classified as genus *Falco,* species *F. peregrinus.* Other members of the falcon family include the American kestrel, *F. sparverius;* the merlin, *F. columbarius;* the prairie falcon, *F. mexicanus;* the gyrfalcon, *F. rusticolus;* and the Aplomado falcon, *F. femoralis.*   OLIN SEWALL PETTINGILL, JR.

See also BIRD (color picture: Hunters of the Sky); HAWK; KESTREL.

FALCON DAM is owned jointly by the United States and Mexico. This dam spans the Rio Grande 75 miles (121 kilometers) southeast of Laredo, Tex. Its maximum height is 150 feet (46 meters). Its length totals 26,294 feet (8,014 meters), about two-thirds of which lies in the United States. Falcon Dam forms a lake about 60 miles (97 kilometers) long. Two power plants serve both countries. The dam was completed in 1954.   T. W. MERMEL

FALK FOUNDATION, MAURICE AND LAURA. See FOUNDATIONS (Citizenship).

FALKLAND ISLANDS, *FAWK lund,* make up a British dependency in the South Atlantic Ocean. The islands lie 300 miles (483 kilometers) east of the Strait of Magellan (see SOUTH AMERICA [political map]). They form the southernmost part of the British Empire outside the British Antarctic Territory. Argentina also claims ownership of the Falkland Islands. The islands' name in Spanish is *Islas Malvinas.*

The dependency includes two large islands, East and West Falkland, and about 200 smaller ones. East Falkland covers 2,580 square miles (6,682 square kilometers) and West Falkland covers 2,038 square miles (5,278 square kilometers). All the islands together have a coastline of 610 miles (982 kilometers). The climate is damp and cool. Strong winds limit tree growth.

Most of the 2,045 inhabitants of the Falkland Islands are of British origin. The islanders raise many sheep and export the wool. Fishermen get oil from whales killed near the Falklands, then ship it to the island of South Georgia where it is re-exported. The islands' exports usually have a much greater value than the imports. About half the people live in Stanley, the chief town. Located on East Falkland Island, Stanley receives mail by ship about once a month from Montevideo, Uruguay. A steamship then carries the mail from island to island.

History and Government. A governor rules the dependency, aided by an executive and a legislative council. The government provides schools which children must attend. Traveling teachers give instruction to children in isolated settlements.

The English explorer John Davis sighted the Falklands in 1592. British Captain John Strong first landed on the islands in 1690. He named them for Viscount Falkland, the British treasurer of the navy. France, Spain, and Argentina later laid claim to the islands. British rule was established in the islands in 1833, and the Falklands are now an important British base. The British won a great naval victory over Germany near the Falklands in 1914.

Dependencies. A vast area of islands and ocean became dependencies of the Falkland Islands Colony in 1908. The principal islands in the dependencies included South Georgia, South Orkney, South Shetland, and South Sandwich. About 500 persons live in a whaling and sealing settlement in South Georgia.

The South Orkney and South Shetland island groups became part of the British Antarctic Territory in 1962. The newly created territory includes all of the area south of 60° south latitude, between 20° and 80° west longitude. H. F. RAUP

FALL. See AUTUMN.

FALL, ALBERT B. See HARDING, WARREN G. (Government Scandals); TEAPOT DOME.

FALL LINE is a line where rocky or hilly country meets softer soil or plains. A stream running down from the rocky highlands cuts deeply into the soft soil. The water carries away the softer soil and in time wears a deep channel at the point where it passes from the rocky bed to the soft soil. Waterfalls are created where a stream passes from the rocky soil to the soft plain.

The eastern coast of the United States is a lowland with mountains rising inland. Rivers flowing from the mountains to the Atlantic Ocean have left a series of waterfalls stretching all the way from southern Georgia to New Jersey.

The fall line is a great source of electric power. The falling water can be used to turn turbines and generate electricity. Also, the waterfall is usually as far inland as a ship can go. For both these reasons, important cities are often found along the fall line. ELDRED D. WILSON

See also PIEDMONT REGION; PLAIN; WATERFALL.

FALL RIVER, Mass. (pop. 96,898; met. area 169,549), was once the cotton manufacturing center of the country. It lies in southeastern Massachusetts, about 50 miles (80 kilometers) southwest of Boston, where the Taunton River flows into Mount Hope Bay (see MASSACHUSETTS [political map]). Fall River's moist climate, good harbor, and available water power form ideal conditions for textile manufacturing. During the peak production years, Fall River had over a hundred cotton mills. The number of mills declined after 1929, but the manufacture of textile products is still the chief industry. Three out of every four industrial workers in Fall River work in the textile trades. The garment industry has become important in Fall River. Emphasis is on high-grade cottons, often blended with synthetic (man-made) fibers. Rubber and latex products are also manufactured in Fall River.

Fall River was settled about 1656 as part of a land grant from Plymouth called Freeman's Purchase. Additional land, known as the Pocasset Purchase, was added and the area became known as Freetown (1683). Fall

The Fall Line in the Eastern United States extends from New Jersey to Alabama. A series of waterfalls lies along the fall line and provides electric power to many cities on the line.

River became a separate town and changed its name to Troy in 1804. The city's present name, in use since 1834, is the translation of the Indian name for the Quequechan (*falling water*) River, which flows through the city. The Battle of Fall River occurred in 1778 during the Revolutionary War, when the townspeople put up a stout defense against a British landing force. The site of the battle is marked by a tablet on the city hall. Fall River received its city charter in 1854 and has a mayor-council form of government. It is an important port for the importation of bulk cargoes, especially petroleum products. WILLIAM J. REID

FALLA, *FAH yah,* **MANUEL DE** (1876-1946), a Spanish composer, did much to develop interest in the music of his homeland. He gained world fame with the first performance of his ballet *The Three-Cornered Hat* in 1919. It ranks as one of the finest works of contemporary Spanish music. He also wrote the ballet *El Amor Brujo* (Love, the Sorcerer); the puppet opera, *Master Peter's Puppet Show;* three pieces for piano and orchestra, "Nights in the Gardens of Spain"; and "Seven Popular Spanish Songs."

His opera *La Vida Breve* (Life Is Short), written in 1905, won first prize in a contest for the best national opera. This work contains his well-known "Spanish Dance No. 1." Falla was born in Cadiz, and studied at the Madrid Conservatory. He settled in Argentina in 1939, and died there. HOMER ULRICH

FALLACY may refer either to an unsound argument or to the method used to arrive at an unsound conclusion. Philosophers speak of two kinds of fallacies: formal fallacies and nonformal fallacies.

Formal fallacies are arguments in which the *premises*

17

(statements used as evidence) fail to justify or support the conclusion. For example, if some students in a class are good at geometry and some students are handsome, it does not necessarily follow that some students good at geometry are handsome.

Nonformal fallacies may take various forms. An argument in which the conclusion depends on evidence not to the point is called a *fallacy of relevance*. For example, we cannot prove that an accused man is innocent by showing he attends church regularly. An argument in which a person presents as evidence his own assurance that he is telling the truth is a fallacy of *begging the question*. Other nonformal fallacies rest on false comparisons, wrong observations, and *ambiguous* (unclear) terms.

LOUIS O. KATTSOFF

See also LOGIC.

FALLEN TIMBERS, BATTLE OF. See INDIAN WARS (Other Midwestern Conflicts); INDIANA (Territorial Days); WAYNE, ANTHONY.

FALLING BODIES, LAW OF. Several laws, or rules, tell what an object does when it is allowed to fall to the ground without anything stopping it. These are called the laws of falling bodies. From the time of Aristotle to the end of the 1500's, people believed that if two bodies of different mass were dropped from the same height at the same time, the heavier one would hit the ground first. The great Italian scientist, Galileo, did not believe this was true. He reasoned that if two bricks of the same mass fall at the same speed, side by side, they ought to fall at the same speed even when cemented together. Therefore, a single brick would fall just as fast as the heavier two bricks that were cemented together.

Other scientists disagreed with Galileo. According to a story that probably is not true, he proved his theory about 1590 in an experiment at the famous Leaning Tower of Pisa. Galileo is supposed to have gone to the top of the tower with two cannon balls, one large and the other small. He dropped them both at the same instant, and they reached the ground at nearly the same time. There was a small difference, but not nearly so great as the difference between their weights. Galileo

Falling Bodies are not influenced by horizontal motion when their descent is caused by gravity. Although the ball on the left must travel farther, it will strike the bottom at the same time as the other ball. Horizontal motion caused by the slide does not influence the speed of the fall.

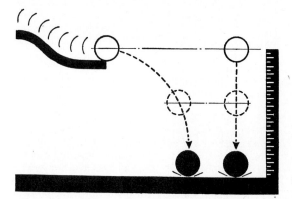

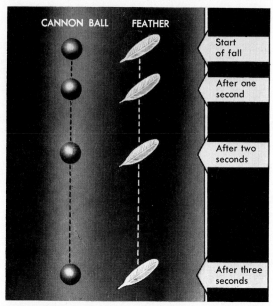

Bodies Falling Freely in a Vacuum have the same rate of speed regardless of size and weight. But objects falling through the air may have different speeds. This is because the resistance of the air acts most strongly on those objects which are lightest in proportion to their size.

concluded that it was the resistance of the air which caused the difference in time of fall between the two cannon balls. Whether or not Galileo actually conducted this experiment, his reasoning was correct.

The dispute was not finally settled until the air pump was invented about 1650 (see PUMP). Then it was shown that if the air were pumped from a long tube, and a feather and a coin were dropped down the tube at the same instant, they would fall side by side and reach the bottom together. The force which draws bodies toward the earth is called *gravity* (see GRAVITATION).

It has been found that this force of gravity acts on all bodies alike, regardless of shape, size, or density. The earth attracts bodies toward its center, so all bodies fall in a direct line toward that point. This is the direction called *down*, and it is exactly perpendicular to the surface of still water.

There are three things to consider in studying the laws of falling bodies. One is the *distance* the body travels when it falls. The second is its *velocity*, or speed (see VELOCITY). The third is its *acceleration*, the rate at which its speed increases as it falls (see ACCELERATION). The abbreviations of these three terms are d, v, and a.

The longer a freely falling body falls, the *faster* it travels. The first law of falling bodies says that, under the influence of gravity alone, all bodies fall with equal acceleration. If they start from rest, and their velocity increases at the same rate, they fall at the same velocity.

Actually, when various kinds of bodies fall through the air, they fall at different velocities. The air *resists* the falling bodies, so they are not falling under the influence of gravity alone. You can test this resistance by dropping two sheets of newspaper, one unfolded and the other crushed into a ball. Both pieces have the same weight, so they give a perfect illustration that the difference of *shape* and not of *mass* causes the difference in the speed at which various kinds of bodies fall.

The acceleration of a falling body is the same for each second. There are no spurts in its "pickup," and its fall is described as *uniformly accelerated* motion. This is true if gravity is the only force acting on the body. Gravity acting on a body that falls from rest *increases* its velocity during *each* second of fall by the same amount of velocity that the body had at the end of its *first* second of fall. The velocity at the end of the first second is 32.16 feet (9.802 meters) per second (in the latitude of New York City). The speed of the body increases at a rate of 32.16 feet per second for each second it falls. The body's acceleration is expressed as *32.16 feet per second per second*. This figure is used in most calculations.

At the end of the 1st second $v = (0[\text{rest}] + 32.16) = $ 32.16 feet a second.
At the end of the 2nd second $v = (32.16 + 32.16) = $ 64.32 feet a second.
At the end of the 3rd second $v = (64.32 + 32.16) = $ 96.48 feet a second.
At the end of the 4th second $v = (96.48 + 32.16) = $ 128.64 feet a second.

A simple formula to get the velocity of a falling body at the end of any second is to multiply 32.16 feet per second per second by the number of seconds.

There is also a simple formula to find the distance a body falls in a given second. Multiply the distance it falls the first second by twice the total number of seconds, minus 1. Since the distance fallen during the first second is always 16.08 feet (4.901 meters), the distance fallen during the third second is $(2 \times 3 - 1) \times 16.08 = 80.40$. The distance fallen during the fourth second is $(2 \times 4 - 1) \times 16.08 = 112.56$. You can compare these results with the table given above.

By adding the distance during any given second to the distances for all the preceding seconds, you can find the total distance traveled at the end of that given second. For instance, at the end of the third second, a body has fallen $16.08 + 48.24 + 80.40$ feet, which adds up to 144.72 feet. Now 144.72 can also be divided up this way: $3 \times 3 \times 16.08$. The total distance fallen in 4 seconds, 257.28 feet, can be divided this way: $4 \times 4 \times 16.08$. So a shorter formula has been worked out which says that the distance a falling body travels in a given time is 16.08 times the square of the number of seconds.

The laws just stated can be written in the form of equations. For velocity at the end of any second:

$$v = 32.16 \times t$$

For distance traveled during any second:

$$d = \left(\frac{32.16}{2}\right) \times (2t - 1) = 16.08 \times (2t - 1)$$

For total distance traveled at the end of any second:

$$d = \left(\frac{32.16}{2}\right) \times t^2 = 16.08 \times t^2$$

These equations are true not only for falling bodies, but for any bodies with uniformly accelerated motion. Any other acceleration, *a*, can be substituted in place of 32.16 feet per second per second. Then we are able to use the more general equations: $v = at$, and $d = \frac{1}{2}at^2$.

ROBERT F. PATON

FALLING SICKNESS is another name for epilepsy. See EPILEPSY.

FALLING STAR. See METEOR.

FALLOUT is radioactive material that settles over the earth after an atomic bomb or hydrogen bomb explosion. Radiation from intense fallout can cause sickness and death. Fallout radiation can also affect inheritance in living things. In this way, it may affect future generations. The effects of fallout depend on the kind of radioactivity involved and the length of exposure to it.

How Fallout Is Produced. All nuclear explosions produce a giant fireball of intensely hot gases. When a nuclear device explodes close to the earth's surface, this fireball may touch the ground. If it does, everything within the area that the fireball touches, including natural and man-made objects, is *vaporized* (turned into a gas). The fireball then begins to rise, carrying this vaporized material with it. As the fireball rises, a low-pressure area forms beneath it. Air rushes in to fill this partial vacuum carrying along with it dust, dirt, and other small particles. Much of this debris may be lifted up through the atmosphere along with the fireball.

As the vaporized materials rise and cool, some of them condense into solid particles. Atoms of the various radioactive elements that are produced by the blast cling to these particles. These radioactive materials eventually return to the earth in the form of fallout. Fallout particles range in size from fine invisible dust to ash of snowflake size.

The Fallout Pattern. Fallout is described as either *local* or *distant*, depending on how far from the blast site it settles to the earth.

Local Fallout consists of the larger and heavier particles that fall to earth within a few hundred miles or kilometers of the blast site. The time it takes for these particles to reach the earth, and the distance they travel from the blast site depend on a number of factors. These include (1) their size and composition, (2) the altitude they reach before they begin to fall, (3) the pattern of the winds that carry them, (4) the latitude at which the explosion takes place, and (5) the time of year. When a nuclear device explodes on the surface of the earth, more than half of the total fallout produced is local fallout.

Local fallout may settle over an irregularly shaped area, depending upon the winds that carry it. In general, the intensity of radiation within this area decreases as the distance from the blast site increases. But there may be *hot spots* (areas of intense radioactivity) scattered within the zone of fallout.

Distant Fallout consists of fine radioactive material that may be scattered by winds to any part of the world. Some of this fallout remains in the atmosphere for years before it settles. Winds traveling through the *troposphere* (the lowest layer of the atmosphere) carry some distant fallout. But fallout particles produced by the most powerful nuclear explosions may rise as high as the *stratosphere* (the layer of atmosphere above the troposphere), where they are blown about by the winds.

Winds traveling at an altitude of about 50,000 feet (15,000 meters) carry most of the fallout in the troposphere. These winds move in a generally eastward direction. They make a complete circle around the earth in

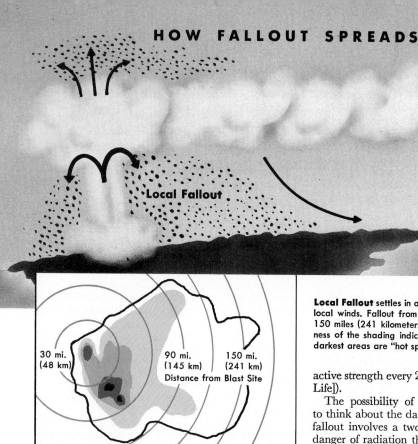

Local Fallout

30 mi.
(48 km)

90 mi.
(145 km)

150 mi.
(241 km)

Distance from Blast Site

Local Fallout settles in an irregularly shaped pattern caused by local winds. Fallout from a 5-megaton blast may extend over 150 miles (241 kilometers) from the bomb burst, *left*. The darkness of the shading indicates the strength of the radiation. The darkest areas are "hot spots" of deadly radiation.

from one to two months. As a result, the fallout material from the troposphere may settle anywhere on a fairly narrow band around the earth near the latitude of blast site. Fallout debris is carried down to earth from the troposphere by fog, rain, or snow.

The fine fallout particles that penetrate into the stratosphere spread over the globe and settle back to earth slowly. The length of time they remain in the stratosphere varies from many months to many years. Eventually, the fallout particles descend from the stratosphere to the troposphere and are carried to earth by rain or other precipitation. Hydrogen bombs produce much less of the distant type of fallout than atomic bombs do because they create a kind of radioactivity that loses strength in the stratosphere.

The Fallout Hazard. Fallout can be dangerous to plants, animals, and people because of the radioactive elements it contains (see RADIATION SICKNESS). These elements include about 200 isotopes of more than 30 chemical elements produced by a nuclear explosion (see ISOTOPE).

The radioactive elements in fallout give off radiation for varying periods of time. Most fallout radioactivity dies off in a matter of hours or days. As a result, the radioactivity at the end of two weeks is only one-thousandth as strong as the radioactivity one hour after the explosion. But even at the end of two weeks, local fallout can be so intense that it remains a serious hazard. A few of the fallout elements continue to give off radiation over a long period of time. Strontium-90, for example, loses only one half its radio-

active strength every 28 years (see RADIOACTIVITY [Half Life]).

The possibility of nuclear war has caused people to think about the danger of local fallout. This type of fallout involves a twofold problem. First, there is the danger of radiation that is emitted by the radioactive debris on the ground. Persons can best protect themselves from this danger by taking refuge in underground fallout shelters. For example, 3 feet (91 centimeters) of earth overhead will reduce the intensity of the radiation to one-thousandth of its original intensity. See FALLOUT SHELTER.

Second, there is the danger that certain fallout elements may be taken into the body. These elements may get into the human body as part of the air a person breathes and the food a person eats. Strontium-90, for example, may enter the body as part of milk or other dairy products. Cows may feed on grass or other plants that have been contaminated by strontium-90. Milk produced by these cows may contain atoms of radioactive strontium, which could be transferred to the body of anyone drinking this milk. In the human body, some atoms of strontium-90 could be absorbed by bones and teeth. The body absorbs strontium-90 because of the similarity between several chemical properties of strontium and calcium.

History. From the mid-1940's to the early 1960's, the United States, Russia, and a few other nations exploded many experimental nuclear weapons. As a result, distant fallout increased to alarming levels. In 1963, more than 100 nations, including the United States and Russia, signed a treaty that banned the testing of nuclear weapons everywhere but underground. Fallout then decreased greatly. However, China and France did not sign the treaty. China continued to test nuclear weapons aboveground throughout the 1970's.   RALPH E. LAPP

See also ATOMIC BOMB (Fallout); CIVIL DEFENSE (Surviving Radiation Danger); HYDROGEN BOMB (Fallout; Steps); RADIATION (Effects of Exposure to Radiation).

Stratosphere

Distant Fallout

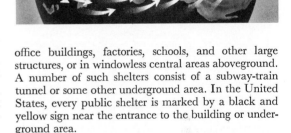

High Altitude Fallout may remain in the stratosphere for years before it settles. The arrows, *inset right*, represent winds in the stratosphere that carry this fallout. For example, some fallout from a bomb test in Russia will be carried over North America. This fallout settles as part of rain, snow, or fog.

FALLOUT SHELTER is a building or an underground area that protects people from fallout. A nuclear explosion scatters bits of radioactive material into the air. Within a few hours, the fallout particles settle on an area of hundreds of square miles or kilometers. Fallout gives off radiation that can cause burns, illness, or even death. The particles could endanger almost everyone in the United States if a nuclear attack hit the nation's major cities.

People can protect themselves from fallout by taking shelter in a building made of thick layers of a heavy material, such as brick, concrete, or stone. Any such building blocks radiation and can serve as a fallout shelter. Underground areas, including mines and tunnels, also provide protection from fallout.

The U.S. government has designated many buildings and underground areas as public fallout shelters. Some families have their own fallout shelter. An emergency shelter, which can be built quickly of heavy materials at hand, provides some protection from radiation.

The United States public fallout shelter program began in 1961. Civil defense agencies urge people without a public shelter nearby to build a home fallout shelter or to locate and improve protective areas already in their home. These agencies also provide instructions for building emergency shelters. By the mid-1970's, the nation had thousands of public shelters and an unknown number of private ones.

Various agencies of the federal government have administered national programs concerned with the designation and construction of fallout shelters. These programs are the responsibility of the Defense Civil Preparedness Agency (DCPA), a part of the Department of Defense. Public fallout shelters have been established by the government of many other nations, including Canada, Denmark, Finland, Russia, Sweden, Switzerland, and West Germany.

Public Shelters. Most public fallout shelters have been established in the basement of apartment and office buildings, factories, schools, and other large structures, or in windowless central areas aboveground. A number of such shelters consist of a subway-train tunnel or some other underground area. In the United States, every public shelter is marked by a black and yellow sign near the entrance to the building or underground area.

Many U.S. public fallout shelters have radiation detection instruments and emergency medical and sanitation kits. Local civil defense agencies plan to make food, water, and other necessities available to

CAPACITY 3075

FALLOUT SHELTER

A Black and Yellow Sign like the one shown above marks the entrance to public fallout shelters in the United States.

Kinds of Home Fallout Shelters

These drawings show four types of fallout shelters that can be built in or near the home. The emergency shelter shown below probably would not provide complete protection from fallout, but it might block enough radiation to save lives. A permanent shelter, which provides better protection, can be built in a basement or outdoors—either above or below the ground.

An Emergency Shelter may be prepared by piling heavy materials on and around a sturdy table. Books, bricks, and boxes or dresser drawers filled with earth provide some fallout protection.

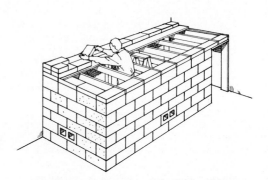

A Basement Shelter may consist of several layers of bricks or of concrete blocks that have been filled with sand. The shelter ceiling should lie below the level of the earth around the basement.

An Underground Shelter may be built with a roof that serves as a patio. The shelter shown above has a trap door entrance at the right of the patio. Some shelters connect with a basement.

An Aboveground Shelter must have thick, windowless walls. The shelter shown above has a shingled roof that covers a thick concrete ceiling. The building also serves as a storage space.

WORLD BOOK illustrations by David Cunningham

people in shelters if nuclear war becomes likely. In some cases, people going to an unstocked shelter might be asked to bring food and other essential items. Civil defense agencies would supplement those supplies.

Most of the public fallout shelters in the United States are in cities. Suburban and rural areas have few public shelters. The DCPA sponsors various programs to increase the number of shelters. These programs have helped architects and engineers design buildings that include public fallout shelter areas. In many cases, a building can be designed to provide such protection at little or no increase in the cost of construction.

Home Shelters. A family may build its own home fallout shelter, or several families may share in constructing a shelter. A basement makes a good place for a home fallout shelter because the earth around the building helps block radiation. Two walls of a shelter could be provided by a windowless basement corner. Two more walls and a ceiling would complete the structure. A fallout shelter may also be built outside the home. Such a shelter may be aboveground or partly or completely underground. In most cases, an underground shelter provides the most protection.

A shelter can be built with any heavy construction material. For example, a basement shelter may consist of walls and ceiling made of solid concrete 8 inches (20 centimeters) thick, brick 10 inches (25 centimeters) thick, or wood 32 inches (81 centimeters) thick. An aboveground outdoor shelter would require walls of solid concrete about 20 inches (50 centimeters) thick and a ceiling of the same material about 8 inches (20 centimeters) thick. An underground outdoor shelter should have at least 8 inches (20 centimeters) of concrete or 14 inches (35 centimeters) of earth above it. Any additional thickness improves the protection.

Any fallout shelter should have at least 10 square feet (0.9 square meters) of floor space for each person who uses it. It also should have a drain, an electrical outlet, and adequate ventilation. An underground shelter should have a mechanical blower to provide fresh air. An aboveground shelter or a basement shelter can be ventilated by leaving an open doorway. But a wall must be built just outside the doorway and parallel to it. This wall would help keep fallout and radiation from entering the doorway.

A home shelter should be stocked with a two-week supply of food and water. Equipment and supplies for medical, sanitation, and personal hygiene needs must also be provided. A battery-powered radio is necessary to receive information and instructions from civil defense officials. An outside antenna may have to be installed to provide good radio reception in the shelter.

Other important supplies for a shelter include batteries, bedding, clothing, fire-fighting equipment, flashlights, tools, and eating utensils. If space permits, various items may be provided to make shelter life more pleasant. They include reading and writing materials, toys and games, and nonessential foods.

Plans for various kinds of home shelters may be obtained from a local or state civil defense agency or from the Defense Civil Preparedness Agency. The DCPA's headquarters are at the Pentagon, Washington, D.C. 20301. Instructions are available for building an emergency shelter in a few hours.

Emergency Shelters. Most emergency shelters provide less protection from fallout than do permanent shelters. But an emergency shelter may block enough radiation to save lives. Such a shelter may be built if better protection is not available, and if fallout will not reach a community for at least several hours.

An emergency shelter should be in a basement or storm cellar if possible. Otherwise, it can be built in an inner room of a building. First, one or more large, sturdy tables are moved to the area where the shelter is to be constructed. Next, various heavy materials are piled on and around the tables as a shield against radiation. An opening is left among the piles of shielding materials to serve as a doorway. Such materials might include books and magazines, bricks, firewood and lumber, metal appliances, paving stones from a patio, and containers filled with earth or gravel. The containers could be boxes, strong sacks, or even dresser drawers. After the shelter has been stocked with water and other supplies, the doorway should be blocked from the inside with some of the shielding materials.

Living in a Shelter need not be difficult if the proper preparations have been made and if reasonable rules of conduct are followed. The daily routine in the shelter must be supervised, and everyone should share in such tasks as preparing food and keeping the shelter clean. Food and water should be rationed carefully, and cleanliness maintained at all times. Someone in the shelter should know how to administer first aid. Fire must be guarded against, and gasoline or other explosive fuels should not be used for cooking or heating. If a mechanical blower ventilates the shelter, it should be operated on a regular schedule.

Every person should stay in the shelter until radio broadcasts announce that radiation in the area has decreased to a safe level. Fallout loses much of its radioactivity fairly quickly. In most areas, people would have to remain in the shelter for only two or three days. They then could go outside safely, at least for short periods. Even in areas of heavy fallout, people could probably leave their shelter after a week or two to perform emergency tasks. Such tasks would include obtaining food or medical care.

Critically reviewed by the DEFENSE CIVIL PREPAREDNESS AGENCY

See also CIVIL DEFENSE; FALLOUT; RADIATION SICKNESS.

FALLS. See WATERFALL.

FALLS OF SAINT ANTHONY are waterfalls in the upper Mississippi River. They were sighted by Father Louis Hennepin in 1680 on the site of present Minneapolis. They are 49 feet (15 meters) high. See also HENNEPIN, LOUIS; MINNEAPOLIS.

FALSE FACE. See MASK; INDIAN, AMERICAN (color pictures).

FALSE IMPRISONMENT is any unlawful restraint of a person, whether by confinement in a jail or elsewhere, by threats, or by force. An unlawful arrest, called a *false arrest*, is a form of false imprisonment. But false imprisonment also may follow a legal arrest. False imprisonment is an offense against both the victim and the state. The victim may sue for damages, charge the offender with a crime, or both.   FRED E. INBAU

FALSE RIB. See RIB.

FALSE TEETH. See DENTISTRY (Prosthodontics).

FALSTAFF, SIR JOHN is one of William Shakespeare's most famous comic characters. Falstaff is a bragging, self-indulgent knight who first appeared in the two parts of Shakespeare's *Henry IV*. He was so popular with audiences that Shakespeare wrote *The Merry Wives of Windsor* to feature him. Falstaff's death is mentioned in *Henry V*, but he does not appear in that play. Giuseppe Verdi's opera *Falstaff* (1893) is based on Shakespeare's plays. See also SHAKESPEARE, WILLIAM (Shakespeare's Plays [Henry IV]).

FAME, HALL OF. See HALL OF FAME; BASEBALL (table: National Baseball Hall of Fame); MERCHANDISE MART.

FAMILY, in biology, is a unit of scientific classification. Animals and plants are classified in seven major groups called kingdoms, phyla, classes, orders, families, genera, and species. Members of a family are more closely related than members of an order, but not so closely related as members of a genus. See also CLASSIFICATION (table).   WILLIAM V. MAYER

A Nuclear Russian Family

Jonathan T. Wright, Bruce Coleman Inc.

Doug Wilson, Black Star

A Single-Parent American Family

U.S. Department of Agriculture

A Childless Chinese Couple

An Extended South West African Family

Edward S. Ross

An Extended South West African Family

People of All Known Cultures Live in Family Groups. Such groups range from two persons to *extended families,* in which grandparents, parents, and children share a home. The most common family unit is the *nuclear family,* consisting of a mother, a father, and their children.

FAMILY

FAMILY is one of the oldest and most common human institutions. Since prehistoric times, the family has been an important organization in society. Most people grow up in a family and, as adults, establish a family of their own.

In the United States and Canada, the term *family* commonly means a group of related persons who share a home. There are over 56 million such families in the United States and about 6 million in Canada. The word *family* also refers to all a person's ancestors and other relatives. Most families are based on *kinship*—that is, the members belong to the family through birth, marriage, or adoption. However, some groups that are not based on kinship think of themselves as a family because they share a home or feel ties of affection. For example, foster children and their foster parents are not

Nona Glazer, the contributor of this article, is Professor of Sociology and Women's Studies at Portland State University. She is the author of Old Family/New Family *and coeditor of* Woman in a Man-Made World.

related by adoption, birth, or marriage. But they live together and consider themselves a family.

American and Canadian families consist, on the average, of a mother, a father, and one or two children. However, there are many other types of family structures. The smallest family unit consists of two persons, such as a parent and child or a couple who share a home and companionship. When a couple have children, the parents and their children make up a *nuclear family.* If married children and their offspring live with the parents, the family is called an *extended family.* An extended family's household might also include aunts, uncles, and cousins. Such relatives, along with grandparents, grandchildren, and others, form part of an extended family group even if they live in separate homes. Some cultures recognize a large kinship unit called the *clan.* A clan consists of all people who are descended from a common ancestor through their mother's or father's side of the family.

The family fulfills many important functions in society, but the kinds of functions vary from one culture to another. In most societies, the family is the social unit into which children are born. The family also provides protection and training for the children. Human beings are born helpless and need care for several years after birth. Family life also helps children learn the culture of their society.

The family provides economic support for its members. Commonly, the adults receive income from jobs, investments, public welfare, or other sources. This money is then shared with the other members of the family. In some cases, the family functions as a group to make a living. All family members work together at farming or some other economic activity. The family may also be a means of preserving property. The children become heirs to their parents' land and other wealth. Increasingly, the most important function of the family in industrialized societies is to meet certain emotional and social needs of family members. Each member is expected to provide the others with affection, emotional support, and a sense of belonging.

This article deals mainly with families that share a household. It concentrates on families in the United States, but much of the information also applies to families in Canada and other industrialized nations.

Family Relationships

People are related to one another by *blood* (through birth), by *affinity* (through marriage), or through adoption. Most nuclear families consist of a mother, a father, and their *biological children* (the children born to them). Many other nuclear families have members who are included through adoption or remarriage. When a couple adopt a child, the child becomes a member of their family. The adopted child gains all the legal rights of a member of that family. When a divorced or widowed parent remarries, the parent's new *spouse* (husband or wife) becomes the children's *stepfather* or *stepmother*. The children become the new parent's *stepchildren*. Children from the couple's previous marriages become *stepbrothers* and *stepsisters* to one another. *Half brothers* and *half sisters* share either the same biological mother or the same biological father.

The parents of a person's mother or father are that person's *grandparents*. *Great-grandparents* are the parents

Edward S. Ross

Touring Places of Interest is a popular family activity throughout the world. In Thailand, many families enjoy visiting their country's beautiful temples, such as this one in Bangkok.

of a person's grandparents. An *aunt* is the sister of a person's mother or father. An *uncle* is a parent's brother. An uncle's wife is also called aunt, and an aunt's husband is also called uncle, but they are not a person's blood relatives. A *first cousin* is the child of a person's aunt or uncle. The child of a first cousin is a person's *first cousin once removed*. Children of first cousins are *second cousins* to each other, and children of second cousins are *third cousins* to each other. The child of a second cousin is a person's *second cousin once removed*.

When people marry, they gain a new set of relatives, called *in-laws*. The mother of a person's spouse is called a *mother-in-law*, the brother is called a *brother-in-law*, and so on throughout the rest of the family.

Some families consider certain friends as family members because they feel special affection for them. Such friends are *fictive kin*, and family members might call them by family names. For example, children might call their parents' best friends "aunt" and "uncle."

Almost all societies prohibit *incest*—that is, marriage or sexual relations between certain relatives. They especially forbid sexual relations between all members of a nuclear family except the husband and wife. Most societies also prohibit marriage between such relatives as grandparent and grandchild or uncle and niece, and some extend the ban to first cousins.

Family Living

In the United States, as in other industrialized countries, many people are turning away from traditional family patterns. They are adopting new roles for family members and various kinds of family structures. Many of these changes reflect scientific, economic, and social developments and changing attitudes. For example, modern birth control methods enable couples to limit the size of their family and to space their children. Many young people are postponing marriage and childbearing, and many couples want to have fewer children than people had in the past.

The number of employed married women has been growing dramatically. In the United States, the percentage of married women who work outside the home has risen from about 15 per cent in 1940 to about 45 per cent today. This increased number of working wives and mothers has led to many changes in family life. It has contributed to the ideal of the *equalitarian family*, in which each member is respected and neither parent tries to be the head of the family.

Divorce has become more and more common. In the United States, about half of all marriages end in divorce. But Americans also have a high remarriage rate. This fact suggests that many people have not given up on family life. Instead, they believe they can find happiness in marriage with a new partner.

Home Life. The home is the center of family activities. These activities include caring for the children, playing games, watching television, keeping house, and entertaining friends. In the home, children learn basic social skills, such as how to talk and how to get along with others. They also learn health and safety habits there. In addition, family meals can be a major source of nutrition for family members.

A family's home life is influenced by which members

live in the home and by the roles each member plays. Home life can also be affected by relatives who live outside the family's home. Traditions, laws, and social conditions help determine who lives in a home and the place each family member holds.

Traditions, which are based on a family's cultural background, strongly influence family life. American families vary because they represent many cultural heritages. For example, some Americans have little contact with relatives outside the nuclear family. But many others—especially those who belong to such cultural groups as Chinese Americans and Mexican Americans—feel strong ties to such relatives and see them often. Aunts, uncles, and cousins traditionally are important in the lives of these people.

Laws regulate family behavior in various ways. In the United States, each state has its own family laws. Generally, these laws set forth the legal rights and responsibilities people have as husbands, wives, parents, and children. Family laws also deal with such matters as marriage, divorce, and adoption.

Social conditions can affect family life in many ways. For example, many black American men have been discriminated against in getting well-paying jobs. Thus, black wives have been more likely than white wives to work outside the home to help support the family. As a result, many black wives have tended to have more authority in family affairs than have white wives.

The Nuclear Family, consisting of a husband, a wife, and their children, is considered the traditional American family. As husband and wife, the couple hope to share companionship, love, and a sexual relationship. As parents, they are required by law to feed, clothe, shelter, and educate their children.

Children depend on their parents for love and the basic necessities of life. The children, in turn, give emotional support to their parents and to their brothers and sisters. As the children grow older, they may be given various household chores. Most grown children eventually leave their parents' home.

Under the laws of most states, the father in particular is required to support his wife and children. The mother, in turn, is expected to run the home and care for the children. In many such families, the father alone makes the major family decisions and is considered the head of the family.

Today, however, many Americans are turning away from these traditional family roles and toward an equalitarian relationship. The parents make family decisions together. They hold the authority in the family but try to consider the children's opinions. The children may express their desires and opinions, and they have much freedom within the family. In most such families, both parents probably work outside the home. The father and children may share in chores, such as washing clothes and cooking, that traditionally were performed by the mother alone.

Other Family Patterns. Not all people choose to marry and live in a nuclear family. For example, some married couples decide not to have children. Also, some couples *cohabit* (live together without marrying). They want the companionship of a person of the other sex but, for various reasons, prefer not to marry. Some

such couples have children and live as a nuclear family, and some cohabiting couples eventually do marry. Although an increasing number of couples are deciding to cohabit, some people object to cohabitation because it conflicts with their moral standards.

In some cases, divorced or widowed parents choose not to remarry. Instead, they and their children live together as a *single-parent family*. In most cases of divorce, the children stay with their mother, but they may visit their father regularly. A judge might require the father to help support his minor children. However, more and more divorced fathers are being given custody of their children. In many such cases, working mothers must contribute to their children's support. Increasingly, never-married fathers and mothers are deciding to raise their biological or adopted children in a single-parent family. In some families, children of unwed mothers are raised by their grandparents.

Some groups of people live together as *communal families*. The members of a communal family might include married and unmarried couples, single adults, and children. They might share child care, housework, and living expenses.

Family Problems. Almost every family has problems as a normal part of living together. Many problems can be solved by working them out in the home. But some problems are difficult to solve. Unsolved problems may result in unhappiness and lead to a breakdown of the family.

The question of divorce can be one of the most serious problems a family may face. Divorce can affect every member of the family deeply. The husband and wife must make a new life for themselves, and the children may grow up in a fatherless or motherless home. But many experts believe that living with one parent may be better for children than living with both parents in an unhappy home.

Couples get divorced for numerous reasons. One of the main reasons is that they expect a great deal from family life. For example, many Americans expect the family to be a constant source of love and personal satisfaction. However, family members spend much of their time at work, in school, and at other places outside the home. Thus, they have limited time together to give one another emotional support. In addition, their experiences outside the home affect their behavior as family members. They might not always feel as loving as they are expected to be.

Many families can receive help with some of their problems by consulting a trained family counselor, a member of the clergy, a social worker, or a psychologist. Many such specialists use a technique called *family therapy*. They meet with the entire family as a group to help them work out their problems together. Various public welfare agencies offer guidance and economic aid. Many other organizations counsel family members who have a specific problem. For example, an organization called Alateen helps teen-agers who have an alcoholic parent. Other groups aid runaway children or battered children and wives. Numerous high schools, colleges, and universities offer courses in family living, which can help students prepare for family life.

Many Americans tend to view the family as separate from society. They think all family problems can be solved by dealing only with the family itself. They fail to realize that the family is part of society and that society greatly influences family life. Such social problems as drug traffic, poor housing, and unemployment directly affect family life.

Increasingly, sociologists are finding that alcoholism, child abuse, runaway children, unhappy marriages, and certain other family problems are related to problems in society. They believe that such family problems can be reduced by dealing with the social conditions that help promote them. For example, programs that improve housing or restrict drug traffic help support family life. With such programs, the family is no longer solely responsible for overcoming all the social problems that affect it.

History of the Family

Early Families. Scientists believe that family life began among prehistoric people more than 300,000 years ago. It may have developed because of the infant's need of care and the mother's ability to nurse the child.

The earliest prehistoric people probably lived in groups made up of several families. They moved from place to place, hunting animals and gathering wild plants for food. Everyone worked for the survival of the group by searching for food. At first, the early people hunted small animals. In time, they developed the means to kill or capture large animals. Some researchers think that the hunting of large game eventually led to a division of labor between men and women. Such hunting required the hunters to be away from the camp for hours or days. The women probably found such hunting difficult during pregnancy and, after giving birth, stayed near home to nurse their young. But the men could go off to hunt large game. The women probably gathered plants and hunted near the camp.

The division of labor between men and women may have helped the men gain power within the family. Prehistoric people eventually learned how to raise plants and animals for food. In many cultures, the women raised crops, and the men turned from hunting to the herding of goats, sheep, and other animals. A family's wealth depended on its herd because the animals provided a steady source of food and could also be traded for other goods. The father controlled the family's herd and thus its wealth. This control gave the father economic power within his family, and eventually he came to be considered the head of the family. A family in which the father has the most power is called a *patriarchal family*.

Patriarchal families were common in early civilizations. Among the ancient Hebrews, who lived in the Middle East about 2000 B.C., the father had the power of life and death over his wife and children. He also controlled the family's property. Strong patriarchal societies also existed in ancient China, Egypt, Greece, and Rome and among the Hindu people of India.

The Family in Western Culture developed from the traditions of the ancient Hebrews and other patriarchal societies. The father remained the most powerful figure in the family. The nuclear family was common throughout history. But some households included other relatives, servants, or an apprentice, who lived with the family and learned the father's trade.

Until the Industrial Revolution began in the 1700's, most of the people of Europe lived in rural villages or small towns. Families produced their own food and made most of their clothing, furniture, and tools. Most manufactured goods were produced under the *domestic system*. Under this system, an entire family worked together in the home to make clothing, textiles, or other products for market.

Among the pioneers in America, the whole family worked together to clear the land and to plant, cultivate, and harvest crops. At about 6 years of age, children had to begin doing various chores. Many settlers wanted, and needed, a large family to help with the family's work. In addition, older children could hunt and help protect the family against Indian attacks, fire, and other dangers.

In rural areas of Europe and America, the family also served as a center of education, religious instruction, health care, and recreation. Girls learned how to cook,

Photograph (1908) by Lewis Wickes Hine; International Museum of Photography, Rochester, N.Y.

A Family of the Early 1900's made artificial flowers in their home to sell, *left*. Working as a group to earn a living was an important function of the family everywhere before the Industrial Revolution began in the 1700's. But by the time this photograph was taken, few families in industrial societies still worked together at home to support themselves.

sew, spin, and weave from their mother. Boys learned farming or a trade from their father or were apprenticed to a skilled worker. In many families, the children also received religious training from their parents. Old, orphaned, and sick relatives were cared for in the home. In addition, much of a family's social life took place there. For example, family members might gather in the evening for games or conversation or to entertain neighboring families.

In Western societies, the family served as a means for passing land and other wealth from one generation to the next. Commonly, property was inherited through the male line. Families hoped for sons, who would carry on the father's name and inherit his property.

As Western nations became increasingly industrialized, many rural people moved to the cities to seek factory work. Family life in the city differed from that in rural areas because people had to leave home each day to work. Commonly, the mother and children also held a job to help support the family. Family members had little time together, and the home became less central to family life. Hospitals, schools, and other social institutions took over many family functions. In addition, families could look to police and fire departments to help protect their lives and property.

Traditional Families in Other Cultures. Most early non-Western civilizations probably also had a patriarchal family system. Some may have had an *equalitarian system*, which gave women and men equal power in the family. Researchers have found no evidence of a truly *matriarchal system*, in which the mother headed the family and held the most power in society. But in some cultures, the mother was especially honored.

Throughout history, most Western and non-Western societies have practiced a form of marriage called *monogamy*. Monogamy means a person has only one spouse at a time. But many other cultures, especially non-Western ones, have permitted *polygamy*. Polygamy allows a person to have more than one spouse at a time. There are two kinds of polygamy, *polyandry* and *polygyny*. Polyandry permits a woman to have more than one husband at a time, and polygyny allows a man more than one wife.

Today, many people in non-Western cultures follow family patterns that are probably similar to those their ancestors practiced centuries ago. Most such traditional families live in remote rural areas. The following discussion describes some non-Western family patterns of the past and the present.

Hunter and Gatherer Societies still exist among the Pygmies and Bushmen of Africa; among various groups of Eskimos, Australian Aborigines, and South American Indians; and among certain other peoples. The people live in bands of about 20 to 200 members. The nuclear family is the main family structure in many groups, but some groups live in extended families. The men hunt, and the women gather wild plants. The women also practice, and probably invented, such crafts as weaving, basketry, and pottery making.

The Chinese. From ancient times to the mid-1900's, the Chinese worshiped their ancestors and felt great loyalty to their father's clan. The family was a strong patriarchal unit, and women had little freedom. The

Edward S. Ross

Bushmen Families in southwestern Africa live much as their ancestors did centuries ago. The women and young children gather wild plants for food, *above*, and the men hunt.

father decided whom his children should marry. Commonly, a bride went to live in her in-laws' home. She was considered an outsider because she came from another clan. The only way she could gain respect was to bear many sons and so increase her husband's clan.

In 1949, the Communists gained control of China's government. They began a program to make China a strong, industrialized nation. As part of the program, they tried to abolish many ancient family customs. Today, many Chinese people live in nuclear families much as do people in other industrialized countries.

The Muslim Arabs have had an extended, patriarchal family system for centuries. Family ties are extremely strong, and many related families commonly live near one another. The culture allows polygyny, but few men practice it. Women have little freedom and live in separate women's quarters in the house. If a husband divorces his wife, their children remain in his home.

Increasingly, the family patterns of some Muslim Arab communities are changing and coming to resemble those of Western cultures. This change is most common in the large, industrialized cities, where the people are exposed to Western ideas.

North American Indians practiced a wide variety of family customs before white settlers arrived. After the Indians were forced onto reservations, most tribes tried to keep their family customs. However, more and more individuals turned away from their traditional way of life and adopted family patterns of the white American culture.

Some tribes, such as the Hopi of the Southwestern United States, still follow their traditional way of life. To the Hopi, women are the center of family life. The oldest woman is honored as the head of the family, but her brother or maternal uncle commonly holds the most authority in the family.

In many cases, a woman shares her home with her unmarried children and her married daughters and their families. A husband lives in his wife's household. But he considers his mother's or his sister's house as his home and often returns there for family ceremonies.

Children are considered part of their mother's *line*, or ancestral family. The mother's brother, as a member of her line, has the most authority over her children. Her husband gives his children love but has little authority over them. Instead, he disciplines and has authority over his sisters' children. NONA GLAZER

Related Articles. See the *Way of Life* or *Family Life* section of various country articles, such as MEXICO (Way of Life). See also the articles on groups of people, such as ESKIMO and INDIAN, AMERICAN. Other related articles in WORLD BOOK include:

CHILDREN

Adolescent	Child	Children's Bureau
Adoption	Child Welfare	Growth
Baby		

FAMILY LIFE THROUGH HISTORY

Colonial Life in America	Greece, Ancient (Family Life)	Prehistoric People
Egypt, Ancient (Family Life)	Pioneer Life in America	Roman Empire

FAMILY NEEDS

Clothing	Food	Housing	School
Cooking	Home Economics	Nutrition	Shelter

PARENTS

Divorce	Guardian	Parent
Foster Parent	Marriage	Parent Education

OTHER RELATED ARTICLES

Birth Control	Court of Domestic Relations	Genealogy Health
Budget	Cousin	Planned
Clan	Family Service Association of America	Parenthood
Community		Polygamy
		Tribe

Outline

I. Family Relationships
II. Family Living
   A. Home Life   C. Other Family Patterns
   B. The Nuclear Family   D. Family Problems
III. History of the Family
   A. Early Families
   B. The Family in Western Culture
   C. Traditional Families in Other Cultures

Questions

What is a *patriarchal family?*
How was family life affected as Western nations became increasingly industrialized?
What responsibilities do parents have toward their children?
How are *second cousins* related to each other?
What is a *nuclear family?* An *extended family?*
Who are *in-laws?*
What are some functions the family fulfills in society?
What are some reasons for the changes in traditional family patterns?
What is an *equalitarian family?*
How do some researchers think the division of labor between men and women developed in prehistoric times?

Reading and Study Guide

See *Family* in the RESEARCH GUIDE/INDEX, Volume 22, for a *Reading and Study Guide.*

FAMILY NAME. See NAME, PERSONAL.
FAMILY PLANNING. See BIRTH CONTROL.
FAMILY SERVICE ASSOCIATION OF AMERICA is a national federation of about 300 social work-counseling agencies. These agencies provide professional help for a wide range of personal and family problems. They serve about a million people each year in about 300 communities throughout North America. The association is dedicated to preventing family breakdowns.

It was founded in 1911 and has headquarters at 44 E. 23rd St., New York, N.Y. 10010. It publishes two monthly magazines, *Social Casework* and *Family Service Highlights.*

Critically reviewed by the FAMILY SERVICE ASSOCIATION OF AMERICA
FAMILY TREE. See GENEALOGY.

David Austen, Stock, Boston

Famine Victims receive food and other emergency aid from their government and such international agencies as the Red Cross and United Nations (UN). The people shown above are waiting for food at a famine relief center in Dacca, Bangladesh.

FAMINE is a prolonged food shortage that causes widespread hunger and death. Throughout history, famine has struck at least one area of the world every few years. Most of the developing nations of Africa, Asia, and Latin America have barely enough food for their people. Millions in these countries go hungry. When food production or imports drop for any reason, famine may strike and thousands or millions of people may die.

Causes of Famine

Many famines have more than one cause. For example, the great Bengal famine of 1943 in eastern India was caused by both natural and historical events. World War II (1939-1945) created a general food shortage and led to the cutoff of rice imports from Burma, which had been occupied by the Japanese. Then a cyclone destroyed much farmland. Famine struck, and more than $1\frac{1}{2}$ million persons died.

Nearly all famines result from crop failures. The chief causes of crop failure include (1) *drought* (prolonged lack of rain), (2) too much rainfall and flooding, and (3) plant diseases and pests. Many other factors may also help create a famine.

Drought ranks as the chief cause of famine. Certain regions of China, India, and Russia have always been those hardest hit by famine. All three have large areas, near deserts, where the rainfall is light and variable. In

FAMINE

a dry year, crops in those areas fail and famine may strike. In the 1870's, for example, dry weather in the Deccan plateau of southern India caused a famine that took about 5 million lives. During the same period, a famine in China killed more than 9 million persons.

In the late 1960's and early 1970's, lack of rain produced widespread famine in a region of Africa called the Sahel. The estimated number of deaths was about a million. The Sahel lies just south of the Sahara. It includes parts of Chad, Mali, Mauritania, Niger, Senegal, the Sudan, Upper Volta, and other nations.

Too Much Rainfall may also bring famine. Rivers swollen by heavy rains overflow their banks and destroy farmland. Other crops rot in the field because of the excess water. In the 1300's, several years of heavy rains created widespread famine in western Europe. The Hwang Ho River in northern China is called *China's Sorrow* because it often floods, ruining crops and bringing famine. In 1929 and 1930, flooding along this river caused a famine that killed about 2 million persons.

Plant Diseases and Pests sometimes produce famine. During the 1840's, a plant disease destroyed most of Ireland's potato crop. Between 1841 and 1851, Ireland's population dropped by about $2\frac{1}{2}$ million persons through starvation, disease, and emigration.

Other Causes of famine include both natural and human ones. Such natural disasters as cyclones, earthquakes, early frosts, and tidal waves may affect a large area, destroying enough crops to create a famine. War may result in a famine if many farmers leave their fields and join the armed forces. In some cases, an army has deliberately created a famine to starve an enemy into surrender. The army destroys stored food and growing crops and sets up a blockade to cut off the enemy's food supply. Blockades prevented shipments of food from reaching the region of Biafra during the Nigerian Civil War (1967-1970). A famine resulted, and more than a million Biafrans probably starved.

Poor transportation may also contribute to a famine because of the difficulty of shipping food where it is needed. Many of the famines in China, India, and Russia resulted largely from primitive transportation. For example, a famine in what is now the state of Uttar Pradesh in northern India killed about 800,000 persons in 1837 and 1838. Lack of transportation prevented the shipment of grain from other areas of India.

Effects of Famine

The chief effects of famine include (1) death and disease, (2) destruction of livestock and seed, (3) crime and other social disorders, and (4) migration.

Death and Disease are the main and most immediate effects of famine. People who lack sufficient food lose weight and grow extremely weak. Many famine victims become so feeble that they die from diarrhea or some other simple ailment. The weakened condition of a starvation victim is called *marasmus*. Old people and young children are the first to die.

Children who have some food but do not receive enough protein develop a condition called *kwashiorkor*. One of its symptoms is *edema* (puffy swelling of the face, forearms, and ankles). Changes in the color and texture of the hair and skin also may occur. Young famine vic-

tims who do not die from kwashiorkor or starvation may grow up with severe mental and physical handicaps.

Famines also increase the possibility of epidemics. Cholera, typhus, and other diseases take many lives because people weakened by hunger do not recover easily from disease. Large numbers of the victims have fled from their homes and live in crowded refugee camps where disease spreads quickly. People frequently must drink impure water, which can carry disease.

Destruction of Livestock and Seed during a famine prolongs the disaster. Many farm animals die or are killed for food. Farmers, to avoid starvation, may have to eat all their seed before the planting season begins. Such damaging losses hinder them from returning to a normal life and may lower production levels.

Crime and Other Social Disorders increase during a famine. Such crimes as looting, prostitution, and theft multiply. Desperate people steal food and other items they could not obtain otherwise. They may sell stolen goods to buy something to eat. There may be scattered outbreaks of violence, particularly near food distribution centers. However, large riots rarely occur.

Migration. Large numbers of famine victims leave their homes and flock to cities or other areas where food may be available. In the confusion, parents and children may be separated, leading to panic. Youths may band together to obtain food by looting or theft.

Prolonged famine may result in emigration. The potato famine in Ireland caused about a million persons to settle in other countries, chiefly the United States.

Fighting Famine

The United Nations (UN) and several other international organizations provide emergency help for famine victims. Various agencies also work to increase the world's food supply and thus prevent future famines. Many nations hope to prevent famine by increasing their food production. If a nation can build up a large enough reserve of food, regional crop failures will not cause disastrous shortages. For additional information about world food programs and methods of producing more food, see the WORLD BOOK articles on UNITED NATIONS (Fighting Hunger) and FOOD SUPPLY (Methods to Increase the Food Supply; Food Supply Programs).

If a nation's population grows as fast as its food production, little food will be left over to build up a reserve. For this reason, many nations have promoted birth control programs to limit their population growth (see BIRTH CONTROL [In Other Countries]). However, such programs have had little effect in areas where large numbers of people remain poor. Many poor people want large families so the children can help with the work and, later, care for the parents.   JEAN MAYER

FAN. Long ago, men learned they could make themselves feel cooler on hot days by waving a leaf through the air and creating an artificial breeze. The early Assyrians and Egyptians used hand fans made of palm leaves. Wealthy persons had servants fan them with these huge leaves. Artists decorated many early Greek vases with pictures of pretty fans. Fans were used to brush flies from sacred vessels in the Christian church from about A.D. 300 until about 1300.

Historians believe that the folding fan was invented in Japan about A.D. 700. The inventor may have made his fan after noticing the way in which a bat folds

A Chinese Fan of the Late 1700's shows one of the first American vessels to enter a Chinese port.

its wings. Japanese artists often painted fans with bright colors and used them in ceremonial dances.

The Chinese soon began using the folding fan, and in the 1500's the Portuguese brought it to Europe. European women adopted and used painted fans. For a short time, during the reign of Louis XV of France, men also carried dainty folding fans.

In the 1800's, noted artists painted fans which sold for high prices. They made the more expensive ones from asses' skin, parchment, or silk. They also made fine fans from lace, gauze, ostrich feathers, and peacock feathers. They mounted the fans on beautifully carved handles of ivory, tortoise shell, horn, bone, or sandalwood. Americans used many palm-leaf and cardboard fans in the 1800's and early 1900's, especially in public meeting places. The Japanese have made beautiful painted fans of silk and paper.

As a device for keeping cool, the electric fan has largely replaced the hand fan. EFFA BROWN

See also ELECTRIC FAN.

FAN, ALLUVIAL. See ALLUVIAL FAN.

FANEUIL, *FAN uhl* or *FAN yuhl,* **PETER** (1700-1743), a Boston merchant, built Faneuil Hall for the city of Boston as a public market and meeting place. It was completed in 1742. It now has historical paintings, a library, and a military museum. It became known as the *Cradle of Liberty* because of the historic meetings there during the Revolutionary and Civil wars. Faneuil was born in New Rochelle, N.Y., and moved to Boston at the age of 12 to live with his uncle Andrew. He inherited his uncle's fortune in 1738. JOHN B. MCFERRIN

See also BOSTON (Downtown Boston; picture: Historic Faneuil Hall).

FANFANI, *fahn FAHN ee,* **AMINTORE** (1908-   ), was elected president of the Italian Senate in 1968. He previously had served as premier and had held several Cabinet posts.

Fanfani, a member of the Christian Democratic Party, was elected to the Constituent Assembly in 1946 and to Parliament two years later. He became minister of labor in 1947, and was named minister of agriculture in 1951. In 1953, he was chosen minister of the interior. Fanfani became premier in January, 1954, but resigned when the opposition parties failed to support his government. He again was named premier in 1958, and served until 1959 and also from 1960 to 1963. He was minister of foreign affairs from 1965 to 1968, except for one brief period. Fanfani was born in Tuscany.

FANG. See DOG (Mouth); SNAKE (Fangs and Venom Glands; diagram); SPIDER (Chelicerae).

FANJET. See JET PROPULSION (Turbofan).

FANNIE MAE. See FEDERAL NATIONAL MORTGAGE ASSOCIATION.

FANNING ISLAND. See LINE ISLANDS.

FANTASIA, *fan TAY zhuh,* or *FAN tuh ZEE uh,* is a free musical form written according to the composer's impulse. Unlike the rondo or sonata forms, it does not follow a prescribed pattern. Bach wrote many fantasias for the organ. Musicians also give the name of fantasia to an improvisation or enlargement on the theme of a known piece of music. Modern *swing* music is a kind of fantasia.

Fantasia was the name of a motion picture produced in 1940 by Walt Disney (see DISNEY, WALT). It was an animated, feature-length cartoon with classical music themes. CHARLES B. RIGHTER

FAO. See FOOD AND AGRICULTURE ORGANIZATION.

FAR EAST is a term used for the easternmost region of Asia (see ASIA). The same region is now often referred to as EAST ASIA. According to the United States Department of State, the Far East includes China, Japan, Korea, and eastern Siberia. But it is also common practice to extend the term Far East to include Burma, Cambodia, Indonesia, Laos, Malaysia, Mongolia, the Philippines, Singapore, Thailand, and Vietnam, and smaller political units such as Hong Kong and Timor. WORLD BOOK has separate articles on each of the places named above.

The countries of the Far East vary greatly in geography. Japan, Korea, and China have temperate climates. Large parts of China and Mongolia have barren deserts. As one nears the equator south of China, the climate becomes increasingly tropical. Much of the Far East is mountainous, and most of the people live on short coastal plains, or on the great plains of the Hwang, Yangtze, and Si Kiang rivers. Most of the people in these areas are farmers. More and more people in the Far East have moved to cities to work in factories or enter business. Today, Tokyo and Shanghai are among the world's largest cities. Other cities, such as Singapore and Hong Kong, are also great trade centers.

Most of the world's natural rubber comes from the Far East. Other important resources include iron ore, coal, tin, and tungsten. Rice is the chief crop in the Far East. Many farmers grow tea bushes, which take little space and yield a large crop. A large part of the world's spices comes from islands in the Far East.

The Far East has changed greatly since 1900. It had little industry and little importance in world affairs then. Today, some nations are as highly industrialized as European countries, and are highly active in world affairs. China has become an important Communist country and since October 1971, has been a member of the United Nations (UN). Until then, the Nationalist Chinese government on Taiwan had represented China in the UN. Since the 1940's, Burma, Cambodia, Indonesia, Korea, Laos, Malaya (now part of Malaysia), the Philippines, Singapore, and Vietnam have won independence. JOHN WHITNEY HALL

FARAD, *FAR uhd,* is a unit of electrical capacity. The farad is named for the English physicist Michael

Faraday. The charge in any condenser is directly proportional to the applied voltage. If one coulomb of electricity gives a condenser an electrical pressure (potential difference) of one volt, the capacity of the condenser is one farad. For practical purposes, one millionth of a farad, called a *microfarad* (mF), is used. In radio and electronic work, one millionth of a microfarad is often used. Physicists call this unit a *picofarad* (pF). D. D. EWING

See also CAPACITANCE; COULOMB; VOLT.

FARADAY, *FAIR uh day,* **MICHAEL** (1791-1867), one of the greatest English chemists and physicists, discovered the principle of electromagnetic induction in 1831 (see ELECTROMAGNETISM). He found that moving a magnet through a coil of copper wire caused an electric current to flow in the wire. The electric generator and the electric motor are based on this principle. Joseph Henry, an American physicist, discovered induction shortly before Faraday, but failed to publish his findings (see HENRY, JOSEPH).

Faraday's work in electrochemistry led him to discover a mathematical relationship between electricity and the *valence* (combining power) of a chemical element. Faraday's law states this relationship. It gave the first

Chicago Historical Society
Michael Faraday

clue to the existence of electrons (see ELECTRON). Many industrial processes are based on this law. Faraday was the first to liquefy many gases and to distill benzene from fish oil. Liquid gases are now used as rocket fuels. Benzene is a base for dyes, perfumes, and explosives.

Faraday was born near London. He was first apprenticed to a bookbinder. He became Sir Humphry Davy's assistant at the Royal Institution in London in 1813, and remained there for 54 years. Faraday was a popular lecturer. He gave scientific lectures for children every Christmas. The most famous of these lectures is "The Chemical History of a Candle." SIDNEY ROSEN

See also ELECTRICITY (Flowing Electricity); MAGNESIUM (History).

FARALLON ISLANDS, *FAIR uh lahn,* are seven small islands in the Pacific Ocean. They lie about 30 miles (48 kilometers) west of San Francisco. Seven miles (11 kilometers) of open water divides them into two groups. Southeast Farallon, 1 square mile (2.6 square kilometers) in area, is the largest island. The islands are uninhabited. But the U.S. Coast Guard maintains a lighthouse on Southeast Farallon, and the U.S. Navy has radar equipment there. JOHN W. REITH

FARCE. See COMEDY (picture); DRAMA (Comedy).

FAREWELL ADDRESS. See WASHINGTON, GEORGE (Farewell Address).

FAREWELL-TO-SPRING. See GODETIA.

FARGO, N.Dak. (pop. 55,815), is the largest city in North Dakota. It lies in the valley of the Red River of the North, one of the nation's great farming regions (see NORTH DAKOTA [political map]). Fargo and Moorhead,

Minn., together form a metropolitan area with 120,261 persons. For Fargo's rainfall and monthly temperatures, see NORTH DAKOTA (Climate).

The city's industries manufacture canvas, grain silos, bridges, concrete products, and metal products. The meat-packing plants and stockyards in suburban West Fargo are among the largest in the country. Fargo is known as the *Transportation Hub of the Northwest.* Railroad passenger trains and two rail freight lines serve the city. Five bus lines and two major airlines also link Fargo to other cities. North Dakota State University is located in Fargo.

The city was founded in 1871, and was named for William G. Fargo of the famed Wells, Fargo & Company express. Fargo has a commission form of government. RUSSELL REID

FARGO, WILLIAM GEORGE (1818-1881), was a partner in the gold rush express company of Wells, Fargo & Company (see WELLS, FARGO & COMPANY). His company's stagecoaches provided the best and fastest transportation between the East and the West in the mid-1800's. The city of Fargo, N.Dak., is named for him.

In Buffalo, N.Y., as a young man, Fargo served as a messenger with Wells and Company. Later, he became part owner. This was the first express company to go west of Buffalo. Wells and Company joined with two other companies to form the American Express Company in 1850. Fargo became its secretary. But the new firm was not equipped to handle the difficult gold rush business. So a new company, under the name of Wells, Fargo & Company, was formed to carry freight and express across the continent to San Francisco.

Wells, Fargo operated in most parts of the country. When the Union Pacific Railroad finished its tracks to the Pacific Coast in 1869, it took most of the express business. Mergers and reorganizations led to the creation of a new American Express Company in 1873.

Fargo was born in Pompey, N.Y. He served as mayor of Buffalo from 1862 to 1866. THOMAS D. CLARK

FARIGOULE, LOUIS. See ROMAINS, JULES.

FARJEON, ELEANOR. See REGINA MEDAL.

FARLEY, *FAHR lee,* **JAMES ALOYSIUS** (1888-1976), a politician and businessman, served as postmaster general of the United States from 1933 to 1940. During his term he greatly improved airmail service. He was also chairman of the Democratic National Committee from 1932 to 1940. Farley managed the national presidential campaigns of Franklin D. Roosevelt during the elections of 1932 and 1936. He resigned before the 1940 election campaign. Farley also served as chairman of the New York State Democratic Committee from 1930 until he resigned in 1944.

United Press Int.
James A. Farley

Farley was born in Grassy Point, N.Y., and entered the building supply business. He became chairman of the Coca-Cola Export Corporation in 1940. He wrote two books about his career, *Behind the Ballots* (1940) and *Jim Farley's Story* (1948). HARVEY WISH

The Vast Farmlands of the United States are among the most productive in the world. Efficient management and the use of much labor-saving machinery help to account for the high productivity.

FARM AND FARMING

FARM AND FARMING. Farming is the most important occupation in the world. People cannot live without food, and nearly all the food they eat comes from crops and livestock raised on farms. Various industrial materials, such as cotton and wool, also come from plants and animals raised on farms.

Farming was once the chief way of life in nearly every country. For example, the typical American family of the 1700's and early 1800's lived on a small farm. The family raised cattle, chickens, and hogs and grew corn, fruits, garden vegetables, hay, and wheat. Everyone in the family worked long and hard, but the results were often disappointing. Most families produced barely enough food for themselves. This situation began to change during the last half of the 1800's—and it has changed remarkably during the 1900's.

Scientific advances since the 1800's have made farming increasingly productive. The development of better plant varieties and fertilizers has helped double and even triple the yields of some major crops. Scientific livestock care and breeding have helped increase the amount of meat that animals produce. At the same time, the use of tractors and other modern farm machines has sharply reduced the need for farm labor.

Lester V. Boone, the contributor of this article, is an agronomist at the University of Illinois.

Farming is no longer the chief way of life in countries where farmers use scientific methods and labor-saving machinery. In these countries, farmers produce more food than ever before, and most of the people live and work in urban areas. These changes have occurred in all industrialized nations and have been dramatic in the United States. In 1850, each farmer in the United States produced, on the average, enough food for 5 persons. Most Americans lived on farms. Today, each farmer produces enough food for nearly 50 persons, and only 4 per cent of all Americans live on farms. But even with the great decrease in the number of farmers, the nation's farms produce more food than the American people use. The surplus has enabled the United States to become the world's chief food exporter. About a sixth of all food exports come from American farms.

As farming has become less important as a way of life in the United States, it has become more and more important as a business. The successful farmers of today are expert not only in agriculture but also in accounting, marketing, and financing. Farms that are not run in a businesslike way have great difficulty surviving.

This article deals mainly with farms and farming in the United States. It discusses the various kinds of U.S. farms and the methods that American farmers use to raise crops and livestock scientifically. The article also discusses farming as a business. Much of the information about American farming also applies to such countries as Canada, Australia, and New Zealand. For information about farming in other countries and about the history of farming, see AGRICULTURE.

Farms in the United States can be divided into two main groups: (1) specialized farms and (2) mixed farms. A specialized farm concentrates on a particular type of crop or livestock. A mixed farm raises a variety of crops and livestock.

Specialized farming is profitable only if there are large commercial markets for farm products. The United States had few such markets before the late 1800's because the majority of the people lived on farms and raised their own food. Most U.S. farms, therefore, were mixed farms. Specialized farming was important mainly in the South. Unlike the North, the South has a long enough *growing season* (frost-free period) to raise such warm-weather crops as cotton, rice, and sugar cane. The North provided a large commercial market for these products, and many Southern farmers specialized in raising them.

The surpluses from mixed farms could feed the relatively few people who lived in U.S. cities and towns before the mid-1800's. But the urban areas began to grow rapidly during the last half of the 1800's, creating a demand for larger and larger food supplies. Farmers started to meet the demand by specializing. During the 1900's, specialized farms have increased at nearly the same rapid rate as the population of U.S. cities and towns. Today, about 95 per cent of the nation's farms are specialized farms.

Specialized Farms

Farmers who practice specialized farming raise the kind of crop or livestock that is best suited to their region. For example, corn is often the most profitable crop to grow in regions that have level land, fertile soil, and a warm, moist growing season. Wheat grows best in a drier and somewhat cooler climate. Dairy farming is often the most profitable kind of farming in regions with rolling land, rich pastures, and a short growing season. Much of the western half of the United States is too dry for any crops to grow without irrigation. But the West has vast grasslands, which farmers use to graze beef cattle and sheep. Irrigated farms in the West specialize in such crops as citrus fruits, cotton, rice, or vegetables. For more information on how soils and climate influence the kinds of crops and livestock that a farmer can raise, see AGRICULTURE (Agriculture Around the World).

In the United States, a farm is classed as a specialized farm if it earns more than half its income from the sale of one kind of crop or livestock. Many specialized farms raise other products in addition to their main one. Numerous crop farms, for example, also raise livestock, and many livestock farms also raise crops.

Specialized Crop Farms make up about 50 per cent of all the farms in the United States. Most of them raise *field crops*. Field crops are crops that must be grown on a relatively large amount of land to be profitable. They include nearly all crops except nuts and most vegetables and fruits. Nuts and most vegetables and fruits have a higher market value than do field crops. They may therefore be raised profitably on as little as 1 to 2 acres (0.4 to 0.8 hectare) of land. However, such vegetables and fruits as potatoes and pineapples must be grown in large fields to produce a crop big enough to be profitable. They are thus classed as field crops.

The most important field crops are *cereal grains*. Foods made from grain make up a large part of the American diet. In addition, grain is a major ingredient in livestock feed, and so it is essential to large-scale egg, meat, and milk production. The chief cereal grains grown in the United States are, in order of value, corn, wheat, sorghum, rice, barley, oats, and rye. Farmers raise these crops either to sell or to feed to their livestock. A farm that concentrates on raising grain for sale is called a *cash grain* farm.

Cash Grain Farms mainly raise cereal grains. However, farms that specialize in dry field beans, dry peas, or soybeans are also considered to be cash grain farms. These crops are *legumes* (members of the pea family), not grains. But they are grown much like cereal grains and, in many cases, on the same farms.

Mississippi Agricultural and Industrial Board

A Mechanical Cotton Picker, *above, can harvest as much cotton as 80 workers picking the crop by hand. Farms throughout the southern half of the United States grow this important crop.*

Grant Heilman

Vegetable Farming uses both machines and hand labor. This machine on a California tomato farm cuts and gathers tomato plants. Workers then remove the tomatoes from the stems by hand.

Some cash grain farmers raise dry field beans, dry peas, rice, sorghum, or soybeans as their principal crop. However, most cash grain farmers specialize in corn or wheat. The majority of the nation's wheat farms are in the Great Plains region and the Pacific Northwest. Most farms that specialize in corn are in the Midwest and the South. Wheat is the only cash crop that most farmers in the Great Plains region grow. But in sections of the plains that have enough rainfall, many wheat farmers raise a secondary cash crop of corn or sorghum. Many corn farmers grow another grain or soybeans as a secondary cash crop.

Other Field Crop Farms specialize in such crops as cotton, peanuts, pineapples, potatoes, sugar cane, sugar beets, or tobacco. All the cotton and peanut farms in the United States are in the southern half of the nation. Farms in Hawaii produce all the nation's commercial pineapple crop. California and the states that border Canada, especially Idaho and Maine, have most of the potato farms. Sugar cane is grown in Florida, Hawaii, and Louisiana. Farms in various parts of the country specialize in sugar beets. Most of the tobacco farms are in the South.

Vegetable Farms raise such produce as cucumbers, green beans, lettuce, sweet corn, and tomatoes. Many of these farms grow only one kind of vegetable. Most vegetable farms are relatively small, but some cover 2,000 acres (810 hectares) or more. About half the nation's vegetable farms are in seven states—California, Florida, Michigan, New Jersey, New York, Texas, and Wisconsin.

Fruit and Nut Farms concentrate on raising tree fruits, berries, grapes, and nuts. Tree fruits are the most common fruit crops by far. These fruits include apples, cherries, citrus fruits, peaches, pears, and plums. Most fruit and nut farms raise only fruits or nuts. Many of them specialize in one crop, such as grapes, oranges, or pecans. About three-fourths of the farms are in five states—California, Florida, Michigan, New York, and Washington.

Other Specialized Crop Farms raise flowers, nursery products, or forest products. Flower farms and nurseries are found throughout the United States. About half the farms that specialize in forest products are in the South.

Specialized Livestock Farms account for about 45 per cent of all U.S. farms. They can be divided into three main groups: (1) beef cattle, hog, and sheep farms, (2) dairy farms, and (3) poultry farms.

Beef Cattle, Hog, and Sheep Farms produce most of the nation's meat animals. The majority of the farms specialize in one kind of animal. In the eastern half of the United States, many livestock farmers raise crops to feed their animals. However, most livestock farmers in the western half of the nation engage in ranching—that is, they graze beef cattle and sheep on rangeland.

Milt and Joan Mann

An Orange Picker in Florida is one of thousands of workers hired by U.S. fruit farms each year at harvesttime. Fruits bruise easily, and so they are harvested mainly by hand.

Nicholas deVore III, Bruce Coleman Inc.

Cattle Ranching is the main type of farming on the Western grasslands of the United States. This Montana ranch has fairly rich grazing land. Many other ranches are located in dry regions of the West. They must cover a huge area to provide enough grass for large numbers of cattle.

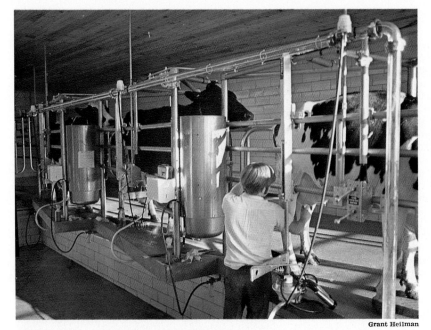

Grant Heilman

Machines Milk Cows in a milking parlor, *left*. The majority of U.S. dairy farms use milking machines. Because it is expensive to ship milk great distances, most large dairy farms are located near big-city markets.

Most of the rangeland is dry. In many areas, a rancher needs as many as 125 acres (51 hectares) of land to provide enough grass for one animal. A ranch must therefore cover a huge area to make a profit. Ranches are by far the largest kind of farm. They average nearly 3,350 acres (1,356 hectares) in size, and some cover 40,000 acres (16,000 hectares) or more.

Dairy Farms specialize in raising milk cows. Most of the farms are concentrated near big-city markets. Many dairy farmers buy all or some of the feed they require from commercial suppliers. However, farmers in the Northeast and the Great Lakes region have large areas of pastureland that are ideal for the grazing of dairy cattle. The two regions have long been the nation's chief centers of dairy farming.

Poultry Farms raise chickens, turkeys, and other poultry for meat. They also raise laying hens for eggs. Most of the farms specialize in broiler chickens or eggs. The broiler industry is centered in the South. Egg farms are scattered throughout the country. Nearly half the poultry farms grow no crops. The great majority of poultry farms buy most or all of their feed.

Other Specialized Livestock Farms raise horses, mules, goats, rabbits, minks, chinchillas, bees, or fish. Usually, only *domesticated* (tame) animals are regarded as livestock. Minks, chinchillas, bees, and fish are not domesticated. But farms that raise them are often classed as livestock farms.

Farmers raise horses mainly for riding and racing. They raise mules to be work animals. Goats are raised for milk and wool, and rabbits for meat and fur. Farmers raise minks and chinchillas for their valuable fur. They keep bees for honey. Fish farms produce food fish, especially catfish, pompano, and trout. Farmers raise the fish in ponds and use special feeding methods to make the fish grow bigger and faster than they grow in the wild.

Mixed Farms

About 5 per cent of the farms in the United States produce a variety of crops and livestock. These mixed, or *diversified*, farms differ greatly from the mixed farms of the 1700's and 1800's. Like specialized farms, today's mixed farms are operated for profit and raise the kinds of crops and livestock that are best suited to their region. In the Midwest, for example, the typical mixed farm raises beef cattle, hogs, and cash grains. The typical mixed farm in the South produces beef cattle, peanuts, and tobacco.

Ray Atkeson, DPI

Poultry Farming requires relatively little land—about 70 acres (28 hectares) for a typical farm. Most poultry farmers buy the grain to feed their birds. This farm in Oregon raises turkeys.

This section discusses how farmers grow field crops scientifically. Field crops are grown on more than 95 per cent of the harvested cropland in the United States, and most of them are raised in a similar manner. The science of field crop production is called *agronomy*. In many cases, farmers must use special methods to grow fruits, vegetables, and nuts. The science of growing these crops is called *horticulture*. The articles FRUIT and GARDENING discuss horticultural methods. But fruits and vegetables grown in large fields are raised in much the same way as any field crop.

Basic Principles of Crop Production

All crops require *nutrients* (nourishing substances) and water to grow. Soil supplies most of the nutrients. It also stores the water that the crops need. Crops take root in the soil and absorb the nutrients and water through their roots.

Crops differ, however, in the amount of nutrients and water they require. A farmer must therefore make sure that the soil and water resources meet the needs of each crop. A farmer must also plan measures to control pests, which could damage or ruin a crop. Most farmers plan their methods of soil and water management and of pest control well in advance of the growing season.

Soil Management. Soil consists chiefly of mineral particles mixed with decaying *organic* (plant and animal) matter. Chemical reactions involving these substances produce most of the nutrients that crops need. But some of the most important chemical reactions, such as the decay of organic matter, require the help of certain microbes. To be fertile, therefore, soil must consist of the right mixture of minerals, organic matter, and helpful microbes. It must also have the proper amounts of air and water. A plant's roots need air to function properly, and microbes need air to survive. Too much water in the soil reduces the supply of air and so drowns the plant roots and destroys helpful microbes. Too little water deprives crops of moisture.

Plants need 17 nutrients for healthy growth. The major nutrients are the elements calcium, carbon, hydrogen, magnesium, nitrogen, oxygen, phosphorus, potassium, and sulfur. Most crops require relatively large amounts of these elements. Elements needed in lesser amounts are called *trace* elements. They are boron, chlorine, cobalt, copper, iron, manganese, molybdenum, and zinc. Water and air supply all the necessary carbon, hydrogen, and oxygen. The 14 other nutrients must come from the soil. But plants differ somewhat in their food requirements, and so the need for particular nutrients varies from one kind of crop to another.

After deciding which crops to grow, farmers analyze their soil to learn if any nutrients are insufficient or lacking. To get an accurate analysis, most farmers send samples of the soil to a soil-testing laboratory. The test results help farmers plan a scientific fertilizer program. Chemical companies provide fertilizers for almost any crop requirement. Most crops absorb large amounts of nitrogen, phosphorus, and potassium, and so most commercial fertilizers consist chiefly of these elements.

The richest soil lies at and just below the surface. If this topsoil is not protected, it may be blown away by strong winds or washed away by heavy rains—a process called *erosion*. Effective soil management therefore also includes methods of soil conservation. These methods are discussed later in this section.

Water Management. Crops cannot grow without water. In most cases, farmers rely entirely on rainfall for the necessary moisture. In extremely dry areas, however, farmers must irrigate their crops. For a detailed discussion of irrigation techniques, see IRRIGATION.

Where rainfall is light or uncertain, many farmers practice *dry farming*. In dry farming, part of the cropland is left *fallow* (unplanted) each year. The fallow soil can store moisture for a crop the following year. Wheat is the main crop grown by dry farming.

Many farms often have too much water rather than too little. In most instances, the problem is greatest on low-lying land and on land crossed by streams or rivers. Fields that tend to collect water must have a drainage system. Most drainage systems consist of lengths of tile pipe buried 3 to 4 feet (0.9 to 1.2 meters) below the surface of the field. Excess moisture filters through cracks in the pipe and then flows to open drainage ditches at the edge of the field.

Grant Heilman

Irrigation Systems enable farmers to grow crops in dry regions. These Nebraska cornfields are watered by a *center-pivot* system. In each circular field, a central well supplies water to a series of sprinklers on a long arm. The arm rotates around the well and distributes water evenly throughout the field.

Pest Control. Agronomists use the word *pests* in referring to weeds, plant diseases, and insects that threaten crops. Most farmers control pests with chemicals called *pesticides.* Scientists have developed hundreds of pesticides for use on farms. Each one is designed to fight certain types of weeds, plant diseases, or harmful insects. All pesticides must be used with extreme care. If they are used improperly, they may pollute the environment or the food supply and so endanger people's health. To help prevent this problem, the U.S. government sets and enforces standards for the manufacture, sale, and use of pesticides.

Farmers also use other methods of pest control in addition to pesticides. For example, turning the soil with a plow or mechanical cultivator kills most weeds. Pesticides, however, control weeds more thoroughly. A pesticide remains active in the soil for some time and so kills weed seedlings as they develop. Plant scientists have developed varieties of corn, wheat, and other crops that are more resistant to diseases and insects than were earlier varieties.

Basic Methods of Crop Production

Crop farming involves at least five separate operations: (1) preparing the soil, (2) planting, (3) cultivating, (4) harvesting, and (5) processing and storage. Modern farm equipment can perform each of these operations easily and quickly. The most important item of equip-

Tillage and Planting Equipment

These drawings show some of the equipment that farmers use to *till* (work) the soil and to plant crops. Plows are used for *primary tillage*—the original turning over of the soil each year. Harrows are tillage devices that further break up plowed soil to prepare it for planting. Harrows may also be used for light primary tillage. Planting machines, called *seed drills,* plant seeds in rows. Cultivators till the soil between the rows and so control weeds that appear while a crop is growing.

WORLD BOOK illustrations by Robert Keys

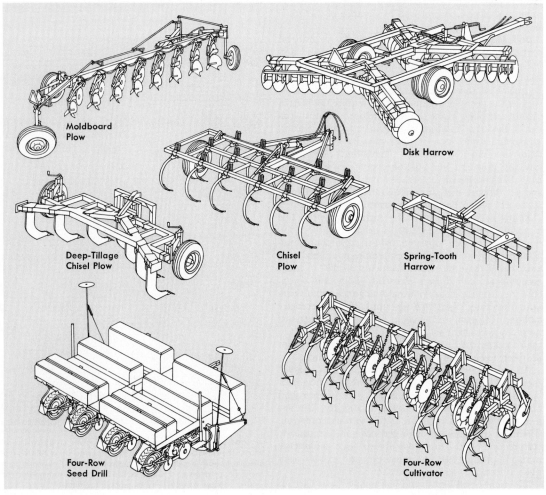

Moldboard Plow

Disk Harrow

Deep-Tillage Chisel Plow

Chisel Plow

Spring-Tooth Harrow

Four-Row Seed Drill

Four-Row Cultivator

ment is the tractor, which is used to pull or push other field machinery. The use of modern equipment—and of improved plant varieties and fertilizers—has enabled American farmers to produce bigger and bigger harvests with less and less labor. In the early 1900's, a farmer had to work about 135 hours, on the average, to produce 100 bushels of corn. Today, a farmer can produce 200 bushels of corn with 12 hours work.

Preparing the Soil. The main purpose of soil preparation is to make a *seedbed*—that is, an area of soil in which seeds can be planted and in which they will sprout, take root, and grow. Most farmers make the seedbed by an age-old process called *tillage*. Tillage involves digging into the soil and mixing it. Some farmers prepare a seedbed with no or little tilling. Such methods are called *no-tillage* or *reduced tillage*.

Tillage loosens the soil, kills weeds, and improves the circulation of the water and air in the soil. Plows are the chief tillage devices. The most widely used plows are *moldboard* plows. The bottom of a moldboard plow is built to turn over the top 6 to 10 inches (15 to 25 centimeters) of soil. This *clean* plowing buries most weeds and other plant matter that were on the surface. See PLOW (The Moldboard Plow Bottom).

At plowing time, most farm fields are scattered with dead stalks, leaves, and other plant wastes from the preceding crop. Other fields may have a *cover crop*, such as alfalfa or grass. Plant wastes and cover crops help protect soil from erosion. They also enrich the soil with nutrients if they are plowed under. Microbes cause the buried plant matter to decay. The decayed matter provides nutrients.

In many areas, the topsoil is too thin or too fragile for clean plowing. Farmers then use special plows that break up the soil without turning it over completely. This method kills fewer weeds than clean plowing does. But it leaves more plant matter on the surface and so helps reduce erosion. This kind of plowing is called *conservation tillage*.

Other plowing methods also help conserve soil. On sloping land, for example, farmers plow across, rather than up and down, the slope. The plowed soil forms ridges across the slope, which helps prevent erosion by rainwater. Such plowing is called *contour* plowing.

Soil that has been completely turned over in plowing often remains stuck together in large chunks. Most farmers therefore go over the plowed field with a device called a *harrow*. Harrows have sharp metal teeth or disks that break the chunks into smaller pieces and so smooth the surface for planting. Many farmers add fertilizers and pesticides to the soil during harrowing. The chemicals may be distributed by equipment attached to the harrow. Farmers may also attach this equipment to the plow and add the fertilizers and pesticides during plowing. In some cases, fertilizers and pesticides are applied before the soil is plowed.

No-Tillage and Reduced Tillage. In the no-tillage system, wastes from the preceding crop are left on the field as a covering called a *mulch*. Farmers spray the mulch with a *herbicide* (weedkiller) and then apply fertilizer. Rainwater eventually washes the chemicals down through the mulch and into the soil. In most cases, no

Grant Heilman

A Special Method of Plowing called *conservation tillage* leaves some of the wastes from the previous crop on the surface of the soil. The wastes help prevent soil erosion. This tractor is pulling a chisel plow, a chief tool of conservation tillage.

further soil preparation is necessary. The seedbed is ready for planting.

The no-tillage method improves on traditional tillage systems in several ways. For example, the mulch helps prevent erosion and helps keep moisture in the soil. By eliminating plowing and harrowing, the method saves both time and tractor fuel. However, no-tillage may have certain disadvantages. Some weeds are not killed by herbicides, and so weed control may become a problem. Planting may be delayed because the mulch tends to keep fields cooler and moister than is desirable at the start of the growing season. In addition, the heavy use of herbicides may cause environmental problems.

Few U.S. farmers used no-tillage until herbicides became readily available in the 1960's. Today, a growing number of farmers use the method. Many other farmers have adopted a reduced tillage system. Under such a system, a farmer may eliminate all tillage except clean plowing. This technique helps control weeds but makes soil conservation difficult because little plant matter is left on the surface. To avoid this problem, a farmer may substitute conservation tillage for clean plowing. In this method, the plowing is done with a chisel plow, a harrow, or a cultivator. These devices leave more plant wastes on the surface, and so their use helps control erosion. Experts believe that more and more farmers will adopt no-tillage or reduced tillage systems, especially to conserve tractor fuel.

Planting. American farmers plant certain varieties of barley, oats, and wheat early in the fall. The plants begin to develop before the growing season ends and then rest during the winter. The young plants start to grow again in the spring and are ready to be harvested

Grant Heilman

A Seed Drill plants seeds. It cuts furrows, drops seeds into them, and then covers them. The drill shown above plants eight rows at a time. As part of the operation, it also applies a *herbicide* that kills weeds and thus promotes the growth of the new crop.

by midsummer. Except in the warmest regions of the country, however, farmers plant most crops in the spring after the danger of frost has passed.

Nearly all the field crops grown in the United States are planted by machines called *drills*. Drills cut furrows in the soil, drop seeds into each furrow, and cover the seeds with soil—all in one operation. Most drills plant several rows of seeds at a time. The largest drills can plant 12 or more rows. Drills plant some crops in closely spaced rows. These crops include the *small* grains, such as barley, oats, and wheat. Other crops are planted in widely spaced rows. These *row crops* include corn, cotton, sorghum, and soybeans. Drills designed for no-tillage operations are similar to conventional drills. However, they also have sharp blades that slice through the mulch so that the furrows can be dug.

Farmers use special planting methods to help conserve soil. On sloping land, for example, small-grain crops are often planted in long strips between bands of thick clover or grass. The clover or grass helps slow the flow of rainwater down the slope. This method of planting is called *strip cropping*.

Some fertilizers and pesticides are applied to the soil during planting. Equipment to distribute the chemicals may be attached to the seed drill just as it is to a harrow or a plow.

Cultivating. Herbicides applied before or during planting kill many kinds of weeds but not all. Some weeds may therefore develop with the crops. In most cases, weeds are not a problem in small-grain fields because the plants grow close together. In fields where

J. C. Allen and Son

A Cultivator turns over the soil between rows of corn, *above*. This process, used on crops planted in broadly spaced rows, uproots any weeds that herbicides have not controlled.

Grant Heilman

A Combine cuts and threshes grain in one operation. Combines have replaced most of the machines that only cut or only thresh a grain crop. This combine is harvesting sorghum.

row crops are grown, however, weeds can multiply rapidly between rows. Farmers control such weeds with harrows or special cultivators. These devices stir up the soil between rows and so uproot and bury any weeds.

Harvesting. Nearly all farmers in the United States harvest their field crops with machines, especially *combines*. Farmers use combines to harvest most grain and seed crops, including barley, corn, rice, soybeans, and wheat. A combine performs several tasks. First, it cuts the plant stalks. Then, it *threshes* the cuttings—that is, separates the grain or seeds from the straw and other wastes. The combine leaves the wastes on the ground and collects the grain or seeds in a tank or bin. Some farmers harvest corn with special machines. The machines pick the ears from the stalks but do not remove the grain from the ears. The grain is removed later. The grain is then processed to produce corn oil or to make livestock feed. In the case of sweet corn, the ears are left whole and sold for human consumption.

Special machines are also used to harvest other field crops, including peanuts, potatoes, and sugar beets. Some machines mow such crops as alfalfa and clover. The mowed crops are left on the ground, where they dry and become hay. Machines called *hay balers* gather the hay and bind it into bales.

Some farmers harvest green grain or grass to make a kind of livestock feed called *silage*. To make silage, the entire plant is harvested and then chopped up. Some silage machines harvest the crop and chop up the plants in one operation.

Processing and Storage. Crops raised to supply food for human beings are called *food crops*. Many food crops tend to spoil quickly, and so farmers ship these crops to market as soon as possible after harvesting. Food grains, however, can be stored for months on farms that have the proper facilities. Before grain is stored, it must be dried. Most farms that store large amounts of grain have grain-drying equipment and large storage bins.

Crops raised to supply feed for livestock are called *feed crops*. Hay, silage, soybeans, and such grains as corn and sorghum are the principal feed crops. Hay must be kept dry until it is used, and so it is usually stored in barns. Unlike hay, silage must be kept moist. Most farmers store it in airtight structures called *silos*. Soybeans must be specially processed to produce meal for livestock feed. Most farmers buy soybean meal ready-made from commercial suppliers (see SOYBEAN [How Soybeans Are Used]). Many farmers have equipment for milling feed grains other than soybeans. Corn is often fed to hogs without any processing.

Special Crop-Growing Methods include (1) organic farming and (2) hydroponics. Organic farming is the raising of crops without the use of synthetic chemicals. Hydroponics is the science of growing crops in water.

Organic Farming. American farmers depend heavily on chemical fertilizers and pesticides. However, these

An Automated Grain Storage System

Grain can be stored for months after harvesting if it has been dried to prevent spoilage. Many farms that store large quantities of grain have an automated system for drying the grain and for transferring it to and from storage bins. The drawings below show how such a system works.

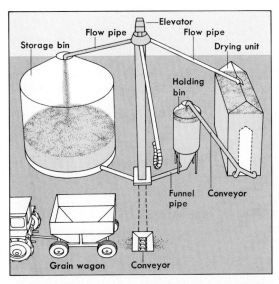

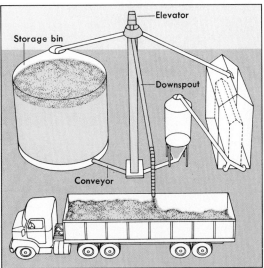

WORLD BOOK diagrams by Robert Keys

Drying and Storage. Grain is brought from the fields by grain wagon and dumped on a conveyor, which carries it to an elevator. The elevator lifts the grain and releases it through a flow pipe into the drying unit. Here, hot forced air dries the grain. The dried grain, represented by the gold-colored areas, is moved by a conveyor to a holding bin. The grain funnels from the bin onto the elevator, which lifts it to a flow pipe at the top of the elevator. The grain flows through the pipe and into the storage bin.

Unloading from Storage. Farmers often store grain in hopes that the market price will rise. An automated storage system enables a farmer to ship stored grain to market quickly in case of a sudden increase in prices. To ship the stored grain, the farmer activates a conveyor at the foot of the storage bin. The conveyor removes grain from the bin and carries it to the elevator. The elevator lifts the grain and releases it into a downspout. The grain flows through the spout and into a waiting truck.

chemicals can cause soil and water pollution if they are overused or used improperly (see ENVIRONMENTAL POLLUTION [Water Pollution; Soil Pollution]). In extreme cases, the chemicals may also enter the food or water supply and so directly endanger people's health. For these reasons, some experts believe that farmers should use organic farming methods whenever possible.

Organic farming relies on natural substances rather than on synthetic chemicals to fertilize the soil and control pests. *Manure* (wastes from animals) is the most widely used organic fertilizer. It is readily available on farms that raise livestock. However, most specialized crop farms raise too few livestock to provide enough manure for fertilizer.

Many farmers rotate their crops from year to year to reduce the need for chemical fertilizers. The rotation crop is usually a legume, such as alfalfa or soybeans. Unlike corn, wheat, and most other crops, legumes restore nitrogen to the soil. If corn or wheat is grown in a field one year, a legume may be grown in the field the next year to replace the nitrogen used by the corn or wheat. See NITROGEN CYCLE.

Crop rotation also helps control insect pests and plant diseases. Most insects and disease-causing microbes are attracted only to particular crops. If the same kind of crop is grown in the same field year after year, the insects and microbes attracted to that crop can multiply out of control. But they gradually die out if a crop they are not attracted to is grown in the field for several years.

Hydroponics involves growing crops in large tanks filled either with water or with sand or gravel covered with water. Chemicals added to the water provide the nutrients that crops normally get from soil. Hydroponics has certain advantages over the growing of crops in soil. For example, the tanks can be kept in a greenhouse, and so crop losses due to pests or bad weather can largely be prevented. But hydroponics is unsuited to large-scale crop production. Its commercial importance is therefore limited. See HYDROPONICS.

An Automated Livestock Farm

The farm in this drawing uses a variety of automatic machinery to mass-produce beef cattle. The farm also grows corn, hay, and silage to feed the animals. After the feed crops are harvested, they are loaded into the tall storage structures at the left through blower pipes. Conveyors remove them from storage as they are needed and carry them to a feed preparation room in the livestock building. Here, machinery mixes the feed and sends it by conveyor to the feeding trough in the main livestock room. The cattle remain in this room most of the time. Machinery scrapes their manure from the floor and pumps it into the outdoor storage tank at the right. The manure is used as fertilizer. As the cattle grow fat enough for slaughter, they are herded aboard trucks and shipped to market.

WORLD BOOK diagram by Robert Addison; with technical assistance of A. O. Smith Harvestore Products, Inc.

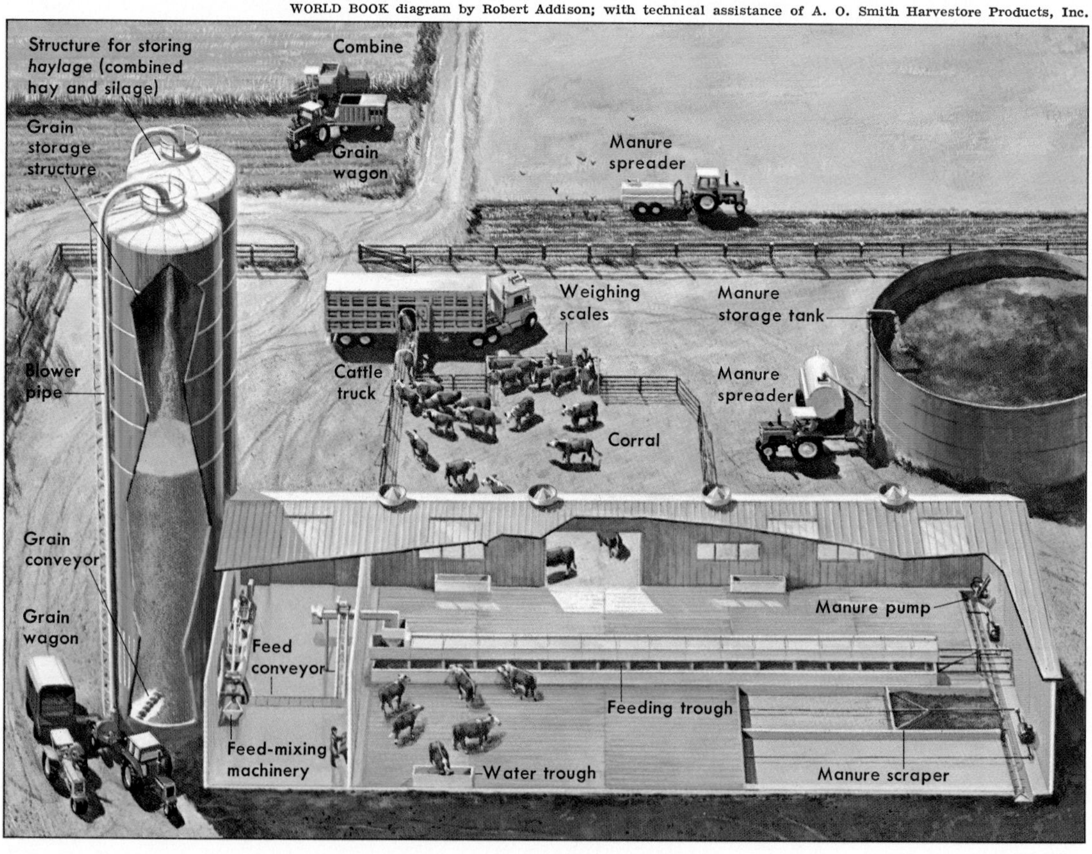

Structure for storing haylage (combined hay and silage)

Combine

Grain storage structure

Grain wagon

Manure spreader

Blower pipe

Weighing scales

Manure storage tank

Cattle truck

Manure spreader

Corral

Grain conveyor

Grain wagon

Manure pump

Feed conveyor

Feeding trough

Feed-mixing machinery

Water trough

Manure scraper

In the past, almost all the chores on livestock farms were done by hand. These chores included milking the cows, gathering eggs, feeding all the animals, and cleaning the livestock buildings of animal wastes. Farmers had to do many of these tasks once or twice a day every day of the year.

The chores oh a livestock farm must still be done regularly. However, farmers now have machines to do most of the work. On most large farms, cows are milked by machines, and eggs roll into collection troughs automatically as soon as they are laid. Feed is distributed to the livestock buildings by conveyor belts or other machinery. Similar machinery keeps the buildings cleared of wastes.

The use of machines has enabled livestock farmers to raise many more animals than they could in the past. In addition, improvements in livestock breeds and in livestock care have greatly increased the amount of eggs, meat, or milk that an animal can produce. The output of livestock and livestock products in the United States has more than doubled since the early 1900's—and with less than one-fourth the labor.

Basic Principles of Livestock Production

To raise livestock successfully, farmers must provide the animals with the proper care. They must also select certain animals for *breeding* (reproductive) purposes to replace the animals that are marketed or that outgrow their usefulness.

Livestock Care consists of providing feed and shelter for the animals and safeguarding their health. The success of a livestock farm largely depends on how skillfully the farmer does each of these jobs.

Feed. Livestock feeds can be divided into two main groups: (1) forage and (2) feed concentrates. Forage consists of plants that livestock graze on or that have been cut to make hay or silage. Forage supplies livestock mainly with *roughage* (coarse food). Feed concentrates consist chiefly of feed grains, such as corn and sorghum, and soybean meal. They supply much food energy and little roughage. In most cases, the grain is milled and mixed with vitamins and minerals. Many farmers also add synthetic *hormones* (growth-regulating chemicals) to feed concentrates to stimulate their animals' growth. Some farmers produce their own concentrates. Others buy them from commercial suppliers.

The digestive system of cattle and sheep enables them to convert forage into the protein and other nutrients they require. These animals can therefore live mainly on forage. Sheep get most of their forage by grazing. Cattle can also get forage by grazing. If cattle are kept indoors, however, they are fed hay or silage. Although cattle and sheep can live on forage, farmers also feed them concentrates to ensure a balanced diet. Cattle and sheep that are being prepared for slaughter are usually fed large amounts of concentrates. The high-energy content of such a diet helps fatten the animals quickly. Unlike cattle and sheep, hogs and poultry cannot digest forage efficiently. They are therefore raised chiefly on concentrates.

Most livestock farms require great quantities of prepared feed. A herd of about 40 dairy cows, for example,

may eat as much as 2 short tons (1.8 metric tons) of hay and other feed each day. An egg farm with about 20,-000 laying hens uses about $2\frac{1}{2}$ short tons (2.3 metric tons) of feed concentrates daily.

Shelter. Most kinds of livestock need protection against extremely cold weather. Mature beef cattle and sheep, however, are less affected by the cold than are the majority of livestock. Ranchers may keep these animals on open rangeland throughout the year. Most other farmers provide shelter for their animals at least part of the time. Some livestock, including most poultry, are raised entirely indoors.

Health Care for livestock has been made much easier by the development of vaccines and other modern drugs. Before these drugs were available, such diseases as anthrax and hog cholera killed large numbers of livestock. Farmers now prevent many kinds of diseases by having their animals vaccinated. Animals that have infectious diseases can be treated with penicillin and other germ-killing *antibiotics*. Many farmers add antibiotics to livestock feed as a preventive measure.

Livestock Breeding. Most farm animals are raised to provide livestock products. However, farmers also raise *breeding stock*—that is, animals of superior quality which are used mainly to produce offspring. In many cases, the offspring will inherit their parents' qualities, such as superior size and weight or exceptional milk- or egg-producing ability. Farmers select animals to be breeding stock on the basis of their qualities and those of their offspring. For example, a cow that gives much

Grant Heilman

Baby Hogs depend on their mother's milk for nourishment. Many hog farmers keep the babies partially separated from the mother while they are nursing, *above*, to prevent them from being crushed.

Rugged Grazing Land, such as this ranch land in Colorado, is well suited to raising sheep. Sheep are among the hardiest of livestock. They need little food other than grass.

A Modern Egg Farm raises hundreds or thousands of laying hens in a *confinement building,* above. The birds are kept in small cages to conserve their energy and to make egg-gathering easier.

milk and whose daughter does the same may be removed from the milk herd and placed in the breeding herd. Over a period of years, such *selective breeding* can greatly improve the quality of all the animals on a farm. For detailed information about livestock breeding, see LIVESTOCK (Breeding Livestock).

Basic Methods of Livestock Production

Livestock production involves three main types of operations. They are (1) livestock grazing, (2) livestock fattening, and (3) confinement operations.

Livestock Grazing. About 55 per cent of all U.S. farmland is used for the grazing of livestock, especially beef cattle and sheep. Most of this land is native grassland. The rest is pasture. Pastures are fields of cultivated grasses or other forage crops. They are used mainly to graze dairy cattle. In regions with enough rainfall, many farmers who raise beef cattle or sheep also have pastures for their animals.

Most of the grassland used to graze beef cattle and sheep is on ranches in the western half of the United States. However, ranches do not produce enough grain or other high-energy feed to fatten the animals for slaughter. Most ranchers therefore ship their meat animals to other farms for fattening after the animals are 5 to 12 months old. Sheep raised for wool live mainly on grass, and so these animals remain on the ranch.

Dairy cows do not have to be fattened. In most cases, they are allowed to graze in pastures when the weather permits. Dairy farmers supply the cows with any additional feed they need for efficient milk production.

Livestock Fattening, or *finishing,* depends on the large-scale use of feed concentrates. Most livestock

finishing therefore takes place in major grain-producing areas. Hog farms, for example, are highly specialized finishing operations. The great majority of them are in the chief corn-producing states, especially Iowa and Illinois.

Some farmers fatten beef cattle, hogs, or sheep that they have raised from birth. Many others sell their young animals for finishing, either to farmers who have excess feed grain or to *feed lots.* Feed lots specialize in fattening young beef cattle or sheep. The animals are kept in pens and fed large amounts of feed concentrates. The largest feed lots fatten hundreds of animals at a time.

Confinement Operations mass-produce certain kinds of livestock and livestock products. The largest operations produce poultry and eggs. Feed lots are a form of confinement operation. However, most feed lots are simply areas of open land that have been fenced in and divided into large pens. The animals can roam about freely inside the pens. In a full confinement operation, the animals are kept inside a building in small pens or cages that limit their movements. The animals therefore use less energy by not moving about and so produce more meat or other products.

Many confinement buildings have enclosures for hundreds or even thousands of animals. Most of these buildings are equipped with automatic machinery that brings feed to the animals and clears away their wastes. In the United States, nearly all broiler chickens and a large share of laying hens are raised in confinement. A growing number of American farmers also use confinement techniques to raise hogs and beef and dairy cattle.

The United States today has about 2,300,000 farms, compared with about 6,500,000 in the 1930's. Yet the nation's total farm output is far greater today than ever before. Much of this increase in production is due to efficient management. Businesslike farming therefore not only earns profits for farmers, but it also helps meet the ever-increasing demand for food.

Farm Owners and Farm Operators

Since 1945, the average size of U.S. farms has more than doubled—from 195 acres (79 hectares) to 440 acres (178 hectares). At the same time, the average cost of a farm has increased nearly 20 times. Today, the typical farm requires an investment of $100,000 to $500,000 or more, depending on the type and location of the farm. Most of the investment is in real estate. The rest is chiefly in supplies and equipment.

Most of the nation's farms are owned by individuals. In many cases, the owners also operate their farms. Other owners rent all or part of their land. More than half of all U.S. farmland is rented. Some farmers, called *tenant* farmers, rent all their land. Many other farmers rent part of their land and own the rest.

Some farms are owned by business partnerships or by corporations rather than by individuals. In a partnership, two or more persons combine their resources to buy and operate a business. The partners then share the profits or the losses. The majority of farm partnerships consist of two or more members of a farm family.

Farms owned by corporations are called *corporate farms*. Most corporate farms, like most farm partnerships, are formed by farm families. A family corporate farm provides certain tax benefits that individual ownership and partnerships do not offer. The benefits are usually small, however, unless a farm has an exceptionally high income. The majority of family corporate farms have an income well above the average.

Some corporate farms are owned by stock corporations, such as food-processing firms and feed manufacturers. The food processors and feed manufacturers own such farms to supply the products that the companies process. The farms are operated by hired managers or by tenants and have a high average income.

Farm Management

Farm management includes everything that farmers do to make farming profitable. To make a profit, farmers must sell their goods for more money than it costs to produce them. Farmers try to keep production costs as low as possible. They also try to find the highest-paying markets for their products. However, farm production costs have been increasing much faster than market prices. Farmers regularly borrow money to finance their operations. As farm production costs increase, the average debt per farm also increases.

Expert management helps lessen some of the financial

Changes in U.S. Farming Since 1900

	1900	1925	1950	1975
Farm population	29,875,000	31,190,000	23,048,000	8,253,000
Total land in farms (in acres*)	839,000,000	924,000,000	1,202,000,000	905,600,000
Number of farms	5,737,000	6,471,000	5,648,000	2,314,000
Average size of farms (in acres*)	146	143	213	440
Average assets per farm†	unknown	unknown	$23,436	$185,396
Average crop production per acre* (index numbers**)	50	62	77	122
Average annual gross income per farm	$1,306	$2,120	$5,718	$34,956

*One acre equals 0.4047 hectare.
†Includes value of land, buildings, livestock, motor vehicles, machinery, stored crops, and household furnishings.
**The index numbers show changes in relation to the base year of 1967, which equals 100.
Sources: U.S. Department of Agriculture, U.S. Department of Commerce.

risks of farming. But farmers have little or no control over risks caused by the weather. Crops can be damaged or ruined by heavy rains at planting time or during the harvest season. A drought, flood, severe hail, or frost can destroy a crop at any time. A sudden cold spell or violent storm can endanger livestock on ranges or in pastures. Hazards like these can wipe out an entire year's profit. They thus make efficient farm management all the more important. An efficiently run farm should earn enough profit in most years to survive an occasional loss because of bad weather.

Managing Production Costs. The average cost of running a farm in the United States increased almost 300 per cent from 1950 to 1975—and the cost continues to climb rapidly. The steep rise in farm expenses is caused partly by inflation. Higher prices for farm *inputs* (production materials and equipment) add to the cost of farming. But the rising costs are mainly due to the fact that farmers have greatly increased their use of such inputs as chemical fertilizers and pesticides, fuel, and farm machinery. Farmers depend on these inputs to expand production, and so their expenses cannot be sharply reduced without also lowering productivity. Farmers must thus manage their production costs carefully to ensure a profit.

Production costs are usually figured in terms of the *cost per unit* of the product. To arrive at this figure, farmers add up the estimated cost of all the inputs they will need to produce a certain amount of their product —for example, 1,000 bushels of corn. They then divide the total cost by 1,000 to find the cost per bushel. Farmers compare the estimated cost per unit with the estimated selling price per unit to learn if the product can earn a profit. Sometimes, the unit cost may have to be reduced to show a profit. Farmers reduce unit costs by cutting expenses if possible and by making their farms more productive.

Many farmers lower expenses by joining a *purchasing cooperative*. Purchasing cooperatives provide their members with farm materials and equipment at reduced prices. Nevertheless, most modern farm equipment is still increasingly expensive. Many farmers therefore rent equipment that they use only once or twice a year. Such equipment includes seed drills and combines.

In many cases, farmers have to increase their inputs to increase productivity. They can often make up for the added expense of the inputs if they make better use of their resources. For example, efficient methods of soil and water management can help expand a farm's total output at little or no added cost. The higher output lowers the cost per unit and thus raises the profit.

Marketing Farm Products. Some farmers sell directly to food processors, stores, or consumers. This marketing method is not particularly desirable, however, because a farmer may have difficulty finding the highest-paying buyers. For this reason, many farmers belong to *marketing cooperatives*. A marketing cooperative finds the best markets for its members' products.

Cooperatives assure farmers of a market, but they do not usually guarantee a specific selling price. If the supply of a product exceeds the demand, the price normally falls. American farms often produce a surplus,

Milt and Joan Mann

Bookkeeping is an essential part of farm management. Like any other business manager, a farmer must carefully keep track of a wide variety of expenses as well as the farm's income.

and so farmers risk having their profit reduced or wiped out by falling prices.

Farmers can nearly eliminate marketing risks by an arrangement called *contract farming*. In contract farming, a farmer signs a contract with a food-processing or food-distributing firm. In most cases, the firm agrees to pay a certain price for a specified amount of the farmer's product. Much of the nation's broiler chickens, eggs, fruits, milk, and vegetables are produced under such agreements. However, contract farming has not won enthusiastic approval of all farmers. Many contracts specify which farming methods the farmer must use. Most farmers prefer to make such decisions themselves. In addition, farmers who sell on contract cannot benefit if market prices rise.

Many farmers sell beef cattle, hogs, and sheep at *auction markets*. The buyers at a livestock auction bid on the animals to determine the selling price. The animals are sold to the highest bidder. For more information about livestock marketing methods, see LIVESTOCK (Marketing Livestock).

Financing Farm Operations. Production costs are so high that most American farmers cannot afford to pay them all out of annual earnings. Instead, they must regularly borrow money to finance their operations. The average debt per farm, including mortgages, amounts to more than $30,000. Farmers pay back part of their debt each year plus interest. The interest becomes an added production expense.

Farmers often borrow small sums from commercial banks. For large loans, most farmers deal with cooperatives. A farmer who belongs to a lending cooperative

Nicholas deVore III, Bruce Coleman Inc.

A Grain Dealer buys truckloads of wheat from local farmers. The wheat is stored in elevators, *background.* It is later resold, either through a grain exchange or directly to a milling company.

Grant Heilman

Bidding at a Cattle Auction determines the price of animals offered for sale. The cattle are sold to the highest bidder. Farmers often sell hogs and sheep, as well as cattle, at auctions.

can borrow funds at reduced interest. The largest such cooperatives are part of a nationwide system supervised by the Farm Credit Administration, an agency of the federal government. For a detailed discussion of these cooperatives, see FARM CREDIT ADMINISTRATION. Another federal agency, the Farmers Home Administration, provides small, low-interest loans for farmers who cannot get funds from other sources (see FARMERS HOME ADMINISTRATION).

Many farmers buy insurance policies for protection against severe financial losses. Most of the policies insure farmers against crop losses due to bad weather or other natural hazards. The federal government provides such insurance through the Federal Crop Insurance Corporation. However, most crop insurance policies give farmers only partial protection. A serious crop loss is costly even to insured farmers.

Obtaining Management Assistance. To manage a farm successfully, a person needs a variety of skills. A crop farmer must have thorough knowledge of agronomy, including soil science and plant biology. Livestock farmers must know the principles of animal nutrition, animal breeding, and veterinary medicine. Every farmer has to be familiar with bookkeeping and other accounting techniques and with agricultural economics, including marketing and financing. Farmers need engineering skills to operate and service modern farm machinery. Farming requires so much specialized knowledge that most young people who plan to become farmers attend an agricultural college.

Even the best-trained farmers occasionally need help in solving management problems. Farmers can get such

J. C. Allen and Son

Keeping Farm Equipment in Working Condition is a major task on today's highly mechanized farms. This farmer is servicing his combine, *right,* and its special corn-picking attachment, *left.*

47

Management Assistance for Farmers is provided by a variety of organizations. This course in the use of pesticides is sponsored by the U.S. Environmental Protection Agency.

assistance from various public and private agencies. Every state and nearly every county in the United States has an agricultural *extension service*, which provides management help for farmers. The services are part of a nationwide system sponsored by the U.S. Department of Agriculture. Each county extension service is headed by a *county agent*. Many farmers go to the county agent for up-to-date information about farming methods. County agents get much of their information from research centers sponsored by state agricultural colleges and the United States Department of Agriculture.

A growing number of private firms provide management assistance for farmers. Unlike government agencies, a private consulting firm charges a fee for its services. Several hundred agricultural periodicals are published in the United States. Some of them print articles of general interest to farmers. However, most deal with specialized subjects, from poultry breeding to soil conservation.

Farm Income

Farm income consists chiefly of earnings from the sale of agricultural products plus payments from government farm programs. In the mid-1970's, the annual income per farm in the United States averaged about $10,000 after the payment of all expenses. Many farms have an income well above the average, but the majority have a below-average income or no income after expenses.

Most farm families cannot live on the money they make from farming. As a result, the great majority of farmers have other sources of income in addition to their farm earnings. Many farmers hold jobs as factory workers, truckdrivers, salespeople, teachers, or business executives. Farmers also earn outside income from

the rental of property and from other investments. About two-thirds of all farmers earn at least half their personal income from nonfarm sources.

Federal Farm Programs

During the 1900's, U.S. farmers have often produced surpluses of corn, wheat, and other major crops. Such surpluses can help lower consumer food prices somewhat. However, the lower prices can reduce farm income so severely that many farmers cannot remain in business. The nation might then face a food shortage. To help prevent such a crisis, the United States government sets minimum prices that farmers receive for certain products. The government keeps prices from falling below the minimum levels through *price support programs*.

Most price support programs establish minimum prices for selected key farm products, such as corn, milk, and wheat. The government buys the products at these prices from farmers if the market prices fall much below the minimum, or support, levels. The government uses most of its food purchases for public aid and disaster relief programs.

Price support programs have often been tied to *acreage allotments*. To take part in the programs, farmers have had to restrict the acreage they use to grow certain crops, such as corn and wheat. In addition to qualifying for price supports, these farmers have received payments for the crops they might have grown but did not.

The chief purpose of acreage allotments is to eliminate farm surpluses. When the worldwide demand for grain and other crops is high, however, American farmers can sell their surpluses in other countries. At such times, the federal government may remove acreage allotments from most of its farm programs and adjust the price supports for various crops. Acreage allotments may be restored and price support payments may increase if the supply once again greatly exceeds the demand.

Farm Organizations

A number of private organizations work to promote the interests of American farmers. Some of the organizations represent the interests of farmers in general. These general farm organizations include the American Farm Bureau Federation, the National Farmers Organization, the National Farmers Union, and the National Grange. Farmers who specialize in a particular product have formed *commodity organizations* to promote their interests. Each commodity organization represents a certain group of farmers, such as cattle producers or wheat growers. The general farm organizations and the commodity organizations both work to promote farm programs and legislation that they consider favorable.

Several labor unions represent the interests of hired farm workers. Many such workers are *migrants*. Migrant laborers move from one farming region to another to help harvest crops, especially vegetables and fruits. The United Farm Workers of America is the chief labor union concerned with improving the wages and working conditions of migrant workers. LESTER V. BOONE

Related Articles. See AGRICULTURE with its list of *Related Articles.* See also the *Agriculture* section of the state, province, country, and continent articles. Additional related articles include:

KINDS OF FARMING

Aquaculture	Gardening	Plantation
Dairying	Horticulture	Ranching
Floriculture	Hydroponics	Tree Farming
Fur (Fur Ranching)	Nursery	Truck Farming

MAJOR CROPS

Alfalfa	Corn	Oats	Rice	Soybean	Vegetable
Barley	Cotton	Peanut	Rye	Sugar	Wheat
Bean	Fruit	Potato	Sorghum	Tobacco	

CHIEF KINDS OF LIVESTOCK

Cattle	Duck	Hog	Poultry	Sheep
Chicken	Goat	Horse	Rabbit	Turkey

FARM BUILDINGS AND EQUIPMENT

Barn	Milking Machine	Separator
Combine	Plow	Silo
Drill	Pump	Threshing Machine
Greenhouse	Rake	Tractor
Harness	Reaper	Truck and Trucking
Harrow	Scythe	Windmill

METHODS AND PROBLEMS

Breeding	Erosion	Irrigation
Conservation	Fertilizer	Migrant Labor
Cropping System	Fungicide	Rainmaking
Drainage	Hybrid	Shelter Belt
Dry Farming	Insecticide	Weed

GOVERNMENT AGENCIES AND PROGRAMS

Agricultural Marketing Service	Federal Crop Insurance Corporation
Agricultural Research Service	Land Management, Bureau of
Agricultural Stabilization and Conservation Service	Reclamation, Bureau of
Agriculture, Department of	Rural Electrification Administration
Commodity Credit Corporation	Soil Bank
Farm Credit Administration	Soil Conservation Service
Farmers Home Administration	

FARM ORGANIZATIONS

American Farm Bureau Federation	Future Farmers of America
	Grange, National
Cooperative	National Farmers Organization
Flying Farmers	National Farmers Union
4-H	United Farm Workers of America

OTHER RELATED ARTICLES

Agribusiness	Electricity (On Farms)
Agricultural Education	Food
Agricultural Experiment Station	Food Supply
Agronomy	Grain
Airplane (Special-Purpose Planes)	Helicopter (On the Farm)
Chemurgy	Land-Grant College or University
County Agricultural Extension Agent	Livestock
	Soil
	Tenant Farming

Outline

I. Kinds of Farms
  A. Specialized Farms
  B. Mixed Farms
II. Modern Crop Production
  A. Basic Principles of Crop Production
  B. Basic Methods of Crop Production
III. Modern Livestock Production
  A. Basic Principles of Livestock Production
  B. Basic Methods of Livestock Production
IV. Farming as a Business
  A. Farm Owners and Farm Operators
  B. Farm Management
  C. Farm Income
  D. Federal Farm Programs
  E. Farm Organizations

Questions

What is the largest kind of farm? What do farms of this type raise?

Why do farmers use special crop-growing methods on sloping land? What are two such methods?

What are the two main kinds of farms? Which is more important in the United States today?

Why can farmers today produce more food with less labor than in the past?

What kinds of skills are required to manage a farm successfully?

Why must soil contain certain microbes to remain fertile?

What are *field crops?* Which ones are the most important?

How do livestock farmers improve the quality of their animals?

How does crop rotation help enrich the soil and control plant diseases and harmful insects?

Why has the cost of running a farm risen rapidly since the mid-1900's?

Reading and Study Guide

See *Farm and Farming* in the RESEARCH GUIDE/INDEX, Volume 22, for a *Reading and Study Guide.*

Books for Young Readers

BENSON, CHRISTOPHER. *Careers in Agriculture.* Lerner, 1974.

BUEHR, WALTER. *Food from Farm to Home.* Morrow, 1970.

FLOETHE, LOUISE L. *Farming Around the World.* Scribner, 1970.

KEEN, MARTIN L. *The World Beneath Our Feet: The Story of Soil.* Simon & Schuster, 1974.

LARSSON, CARL. *A Farm.* Putnam, 1976. Text by Lennart Rudström.

Books for Older Readers

BOONE, LESTER V., and others. *Producing Farm Crops.* 2nd ed. Interstate, 1975.

CONRAT, MAISIE and RICHARD. *The American Farm: A Photographic History.* Houghton, 1977.

EVANS, EVERETT F., and DONAHUE, R. L. *Exploring Agriculture.* 4th ed. Prentice-Hall, 1974.

GUITHER, HAROLD D. *Heritage of Plenty: A Guide to the Economic History and Development of U.S. Agriculture.* Interstate, 1972.

HARLAN, JACK R. *Crops & Man.* American Society of Agronomy, 1975.

McCOY, JOSEPH J. *To Feed a Nation: The Story of Farming in America.* Nelson, 1971.

"The New Rural America," ed. by Frank Clemente, in *The Annals of the American Academy of Political and Social Science,* January 1977.

SEIM, RICHARD K. *The American Farmer: A Glimpse into the World and Heart of the American Food Grower and His Family, Shaped by All Seasons, Sustained by a Belief in Spring.* Rand McNally, 1974.

U.S. DEPARTMENT OF AGRICULTURE. *Yearbook of Agriculture.* U.S. Govt. Printing Office, Washington, D.C. These handbooks cover various topics in agriculture and are published annually.

FARM BUREAU FEDERATION, AMERICAN. See AMERICAN FARM BUREAU FEDERATION.

FARM CREDIT ADMINISTRATION (FCA) is an independent government agency that supervises the *Farm Credit System*. This system provides loans to farmers and their marketing, purchasing, and business service cooperatives in the United States and Puerto Rico. The FCA was established in 1933. The federal government provided the original capital for the system. But farmers gradually replaced the government's capital, and now they own all the stock in the system's cooperatives.

Organization. There are 12 farm credit districts in the United States. Each district has a Federal Land Bank, a Federal Intermediate Credit Bank, and a Bank for Cooperatives. A Federal Farm Credit Board sets FCA policies. The President of the United States appoints one board member from each district. The secretary of agriculture appoints the 13th member as his or her representative. This board selects the FCA's governor, the organization's full-time administrator.

During the mid-1970's, banks and associations in the system loaned about $30 billion a year to farmers and their cooperatives. The system obtains most of its loan funds from the sale of securities to the public. All FCA expenses are paid from assessments against member banks and associations it supervises.

Federal Land Banks provide long-term loans to farmers. These loans run from 5 to 40 years. Farmers may receive loans for general agricultural purposes such as buying land and constructing or remodeling farm buildings. To be eligible for a loan, farmers must be members of a Federal Land Bank Association. The borrower buys stock in the association usually equal to 5 per cent of the loan. The association then buys the same amount of stock in its district bank. When the loan is repaid, the stock in the bank is retired. There are 550 land bank associations operating today, with a membership of about 400,000 farmers. The land banks and associations were authorized by Congress in 1916. Government capital invested in the banks was repaid by 1947.

Production Credit Associations offer loans for general agricultural purposes for periods up to seven years. Farmers must belong to an association to obtain a loan. About 550,000 farmers belong to the 430 associations. The associations are supervised by their district Federal Intermediate Credit Bank. They were authorized by Congress in 1933.

Federal Intermediate Credit Banks do not lend money directly to farmers and ranchers. Most of the banks' business is done with production credit associations. They provide funds to the associations in connection with their loans. The banks also discount negotiable instruments from livestock loan companies and other lending groups that make loans directly to farmers. Loans accepted for discount range from less than one year to seven years. Congress authorized Federal Intermediate Credit Banks in 1923.

Banks for Cooperatives make loans to farmer cooperatives. Over 3,000 farmer cooperatives use the loan facilities of the banks. To be eligible to borrow, a cooperative must be an association in which farmers act together in marketing farm products, purchasing farm supplies, or furnishing farm business services. A Central Bank for Cooperatives in Denver makes loans to the 12 district banks and participates in loans that exceed the limits of the district banks. Banks for cooperatives were authorized by Congress in 1933.

Critically reviewed by the FARM CREDIT ADMINISTRATION

FARM MACHINERY. See FARM AND FARMING with its list of Related Articles.

FARMER. See FARM AND FARMING; AGRICULTURE (Careers in U.S. Agriculture).

FARMER, JAMES LEONARD (1920-   ), an American civil rights leader, was assistant secretary of the Department of Health, Education, and Welfare in 1969 and 1970. He helped establish the Congress of Racial Equality (CORE) in 1942, and was its national director until 1966. He guided CORE through the freedom marches and sit-ins of the 1960's (see CONGRESS OF RACIAL EQUALITY).

Farmer served as program director of the National Association for the Advancement of Colored People (NAACP) from 1959 to 1961. He was a professor of social welfare at Lincoln (Pa.) University in 1966 and 1967. In 1968, he ran unsuccessfully for a seat in the United States House of Representatives from Brooklyn. In 1976, Farmer became associate director of the Coalition of American Public Employees, a group of labor and professional organizations.

Wide World

James L. Farmer

Farmer was born in Marshall, Tex. He graduated from Wiley College in 1938, and from the Howard University School of Religion in 1941.   C. ERIC LINCOLN

See also BLACK AMERICANS (picture).

FARMER-LABOR PARTY was a leading Minnesota political party. It was founded in 1920 and later took over the work of the Nonpartisan League (see NONPARTISAN LEAGUE). Its platform included government ownership of some industries, social security laws, and protection for farmers and labor union members. The party's outstanding leader was Floyd B. Olson, Minnesota governor from 1931 to 1936. The party elected candidates to state and national offices. In 1944, the party merged with the Minnesota Democratic Party to form the Democratic-Farmer-Labor Party.

Farmer-Labor Party was also the name of an organization formed in Chicago in 1919. It lasted until 1924, but elected no candidates.   DONALD R. MCCOY

FARMERS' ALLIANCE. See POPULISM; LEASE, MARY ELIZABETH.

FARMERS HOME ADMINISTRATION is an agency of the U.S. Department of Agriculture. The agency coordinates a nationwide rural development program and promotes cooperation between the federal government and state and local rural-development projects. It offers credit designed to improve the income of the small farm owner. It also provides financing for business and industrial development, community facilities, and housing in rural areas. Farmers may receive loans for farm supplies, land purchases, living needs, and special disaster relief. Community loans are made for such improvements as fire protection, medical facilities, and waste disposal systems. In most cases, financing becomes available when it is shown that the applicant has no other source of credit. Repayment terms range from short periods to up to 40 years. Congress established the agency in 1946.

Critically reviewed by the FARMERS HOME ADMINISTRATION

FARMERS' MUSEUM. See NEW YORK (Places to Visit); COLONIAL LIFE IN AMERICA (A Visitor's Guide to Colonial America [picture: Blacksmith Shop]).

FARMERS OF AMERICA, FUTURE. See FUTURE FARMERS OF AMERICA.

FARMERS ORGANIZATION, NATIONAL. See NATIONAL FARMERS ORGANIZATION.

FARMERS UNION, NATIONAL. See NATIONAL FARMERS UNION.

FARMING. See AGRICULTURE; FARM AND FARMING.

FARNESE BULL is a famous group sculpture. It is now in the National Museum in Naples. Its name comes from the Farnese Palace in Rome, where the sculpture was first kept. The sculpture is based on a story in Greek mythology. The story tells of Dirce's death on the horns of a bull. Dirce was the second wife of Lycus, king of Thebes. She was jealous of Antiope, his divorced first wife and mother of his two sons. Dirce ordered the sons to bind their mother to a bull's horns. But the sons loved their mother, and they tied Dirce to the bull instead. PAUL BOGATAY

Museo Nazionale, Naples (Anderson from Art Reference Bureau)
The *Farnese Bull* is a marble copy made in the A.D. 200's of the original Greek sculpture—now lost—carved in the 100's B.C.

FARNSWORTH, PHILO TAYLOR (1906-1971), was an American inventor of electronic devices. At the age of 16, he developed the idea of the *image dissector*, one of the pioneering inventions that led to television. Six years later, he patented it. Many years passed before his inventions were put to commercial use. He established an independent research laboratory and licensed his

inventions to Radio Corporation of America (now RCA Corporation), and American Telephone and Telegraph Company. He began the Farnsworth Television and Radio Corporation in Fort Wayne, Ind., in 1938. Later, Farnsworth became technical director for the Farnsworth Electronics Company. He was born in Beaver, Utah. W. RUPERT MACLAURIN

FAROE ISLANDS. See FAEROE ISLANDS.

FAROUK I. See FARUK I.

FARQUHAR, *FAR kwar,* **GEORGE** (1678-1707), is a transitional figure in the history of English drama. His plays contain the wit found in Restoration comedy of the late 1600's and the emphasis on character and plot found in English plays of the 1700's.

Farquhar wrote eight comedies during his brief life, and is best known for two of them. In *The Beaux' Stratagem* (1707), two young Londoners visit a country town seeking rich wives in order to regain their wasted fortunes. Both have comic adventures, and one wins an heiress. *The Recruiting Officer* (1706) describes the adventures of army recruiters in an English country town.

Farquhar was born in Londonderry, Ireland, and moved to London to find a career. A careless young man, he lived in constant need. THOMAS H. FUJIMURA

FARQUHAR ISLANDS. See BRITISH INDIAN OCEAN TERRITORY.

FARRAGUT, *FAR uh gut,* **DAVID GLASGOW** (1801-1870), an American naval officer, won fame at the Civil War battle of Mobile Bay with his slogan: "Damn the torpedoes. Full steam ahead!" Congress created the rank of full admiral for him in 1866.

Farragut showed his loyalty to the Union when he gave up his home in Norfolk, Va., at the start of the Civil War to fight on the Northern side. He took command of the important Western Gulf Blockading Squadron, and cooperated brilliantly with General B. F. Butler and General E. R. S. Canby in operations against New Orleans and the forts at Mobile Bay. He won the nickname of *Old Salamander* when he ran his boats under heavy gunfire between

The Smithsonian Institution
David G. Farragut

the New Orleans forts on April 24, 1862, and the Mobile Bay forts on Aug. 5, 1864.

Farragut sailed up the Mississippi River with his heavy seagoing ships to bombard Vicksburg in 1862, a year before Grant captured the city by land. Farragut led a fleet that attacked Mobile in 1864. He forced his way into the bay, captured or destroyed enemy ships, and occupied the forts.

Farragut was born near Knoxville, Tenn., on July 5, 1801. He took the name David after his adoption in 1810 by Captain David Porter. He served under Porter as a midshipman on board the U.S.S. *Essex* in that vessel's famed battle with the British *Phoebe* and *Cherub*. Later, he fought pirates in the West Indies, took part in the war with Mexico, and helped establish the

Mare Island Navy Yard in San Pablo Bay. He became a captain in 1855. RICHARD S. WEST, JR.

See also CIVIL WAR (Mobile Bay); PORTER (David).

FARRAR, *fuh RAHR*, **GERALDINE** (1882-1967), an American soprano, enjoyed a brilliant career in opera and on the concert stage. Her striking dramatic and musical ability, coupled with her charm and personality, placed her among the outstanding American singers. She excelled in the role of Madama Butterfly.

She was born in Melrose, Mass., and studied in Boston, Paris, and Berlin. She made her debut in Berlin in 1901 as Marguerite in *Faust*. She sang with the Metropolitan Opera Company from 1906 until she retired in 1922. Her autobiography, *Such Sweet Compulsion*, was published in 1938. DANIEL A. HARRIS

FARRELL, EDELMIRO J. See ARGENTINA (Years of Dictatorship).

FARRELL, JAMES T. (1904-   ), is an American writer best known for his novels about lower middle-class life in a decaying neighborhood of a large city. Farrell followed the theory of naturalism in his early works, believing that people are influenced overwhelmingly by their environment (see NATURALISM). Farrell's best-known work is the *Studs Lonigan* trilogy— *Young Lonigan* (1932), *The Young Manhood of Studs Lonigan* (1934), and *Judgment Day* (1935). These novels are written largely in the language of Lonigan, a young tough. They explore the impact of urban industrial life on a boy growing up in a poor Chicago neighborhood.

James Thomas Farrell was born and raised in Chicago. After attending the University of Chicago, he became a writer. Following the Lonigan series, he wrote five novels featuring Danny O'Neill, a stronger and more sensitive hero than Lonigan. The O'Neill stories show Farrell's newly found faith in the ability of people to deal with their circumstances. The first O'Neill novel was *A World I Never Made* (1936). JOSEPH N. RIDDEL

FARRIER. See BLACKSMITH.

FARSIGHTEDNESS, or HYPEROPIA, is an eye defect in which the diameter of the eyeball from front to back is too short for proper vision. Consequently, light rays from an object strike the retina of the eye before they can be brought to a focus, and the image formed is blurred. To get a clear image of a distant object, a farsighted person must *accommodate* (focus with the lens of the eye) more than a person with normal vision. This limits the amount of accommodating power left for near objects and they seem fuzzier than distant objects. Constant accommodation causes eyestrain and headaches. Doctors treat farsightedness by prescribing convex or magnifying glasses that cause the light rays to focus on the retina. WILLIAM F. HUGHES

See also EYE (illustration: Some Defects of the Eye).

FARTHING was a bronze coin of the lowest value in British currency. It was worth one-fourth of a penny, or the 960th part of a pound sterling (see POUND STERLING). The farthing was first issued in 1279, during the reign of King Edward I (1272-1307). The farthing remained a silver coin until 1613. The British government withdrew the farthing from circulation on Jan. 1, 1961. The word *farthing* is sometimes used to mean a measure of land. FRED REINFELD

FARTHINGALE. See CLOTHING (The Renaissance).

FARUK I, *fuh ROOK* (1920-1965), also spelled *Farouk*, was the last king of Egypt. He became king in 1936, succeeding his father, Fuad I. Faruk enjoyed great popularity at first. But he shirked his duties and followed a life of luxury and dissipation. A rebel group, directed by General Muhammad Naguib, forced Faruk to abdicate in July, 1952. They charged there was corruption in the government. Faruk went into exile in Europe. He was born in Cairo. T. WALTER WALLBANK

See also EGYPT (History); NASSER, GAMAL ABDEL.

FASCES, *FAS eez*, were a symbol of power in the days of the Roman Republic, of the Roman Empire, and, later, of Benito Mussolini's Fascist government in Italy. Fasces consisted of a bundle of birch or elm rods bound together by a red strap. The blade of an ax projected from the bundle. Servants called *lictors* carried these bundles ahead of such officials as magistrates, governors, and emperors (see LICTOR). The fasces stood for the official's power to punish or put to death, and also symbolized unity. In modern times, fasces appear on the back of some American dimes.

ROMAN FASCES

The Fascists, or Fascisti, took their name from the fasces, and used them as a symbol of unity.

FASCISM, *FASH ihz uhm*, is a form of government headed, in most cases, by a dictator. It involves total government control of political, economic, cultural, religious, and social activities.

Fascism resembles Communism. But unlike Communism, which calls for the government to own all industry, fascism allows industry to remain in private ownership, though under government control. Other important features of fascism include extreme patriotism, warlike policies, and persecution of minorities.

The word *fascism* also describes any governmental system or political belief that resembles those of Benito Mussolini and Adolf Hitler. Fascist governments ruled Italy under Mussolini from 1922 to 1943, and Germany under Hitler from 1933 to 1945.

Fascism has varied from country to country. This

Chase Manhattan Bank Money Museum

The Farthing Was a British Coin. One side showed the British monarch. The other side pictured a perching wren. The photograph has been greatly enlarged to show the details.

article discusses fascism mainly as it existed in Italy under Mussolini and in Germany under Hitler.

Life Under Fascism

Political Life. In most cases, fascists have come to power after a nation has suffered an economic collapse, a military defeat, or some other disaster. The fascist party wins mass support by promising to revive the economy and to restore national pride. The fascists may also appeal to a fear of Communism or a hatred of Jews and other minorities. Eventually, the fascists may gain control of the government—through peaceful elections or by force.

After the fascist party takes power, its members replace the men and women in the executive, judicial, and legislative branches of the government. In most cases, one individual—usually a dictator with great popular appeal—becomes the leader of the government. Sometimes, a committee of party members holds the government leadership. Fascists permit no other political party and no opposition to their policies.

The fascist desire for national glory leads to an increase in military spirit and a build-up of the armed forces. After the military forces become strong enough, they may invade and occupy other countries.

Economic Life. A fascist government permits and even encourages private enterprise—as long as such activity serves the government's goals. However, the government maintains strict control of industry to make sure it produces what the nation needs. The government discourages imports by putting high tariffs on certain essential products or by banning imports of those products. It does not want to depend on other countries for such vital products as oil and steel.

The government also forbids strikes so that production will not be interrupted. Fascism outlaws labor unions and replaces them with a network of organizations in the major industries. These organizations, which consist of both workers and employers, are called *corporations*, but they differ from those in other countries. Fascist corporations supposedly represent both labor and management but actually are controlled by the government. Through the corporations, the government determines wages, hours, and production goals. As a result, a fascist country is sometimes called a *corporative state*.

Personal Liberty is severely limited under a fascist government. For example, the government limits travel to other countries and restricts any contact with their people. The government also controls the newspapers, radio, and other means of communication in its country. It issues propaganda to promote its policies, and it practices strict censorship to silence opposing views. All children are required to join youth organizations, where they exercise, march, and learn fascist beliefs. A secret police force crushes any resistance. Opposition may lead to imprisonment, torture, and death.

Fascists consider all other peoples inferior to those of their own nationality group. As a result, a fascist government may persecute or even kill Gypsies, Jews, or members of other minority groups.

History

The word *fascism* comes from ancient Roman symbols of authority called *fasces* (see FASCES). Benito Mussolini

originated the term in 1919, but fascism itself is much older than its name.

Many historians trace the beginning of modern fascism to Napoleon I, who ruled France as a dictator during the early 1800's. Napoleon carried out many liberal reforms and was not a true fascist. But fascists later adopted many of his methods. Napoleon promised his people that he would restore the glory of France through military conquest. To prevent opposition, he established one of the first secret police systems. Napoleon also controlled the French press and used propaganda and strict censorship to win support of his programs.

Fascism in Italy. Italy was on the winning side when World War I ended in 1918, but the war left the nation in poor economic condition. In addition, the peace treaties gave Italy far less territory than it had expected to receive. The Fascist Party promised to give Italians prosperity and to restore the prestige Italy had held during the days of the Roman Empire. The party gained the support of many landowners, business and military leaders, and members of the middle class. By 1922, the Fascists had become powerful enough to force the king of Italy to make Mussolini prime minister. Mussolini, who became known as *Il Duce* (the leader), soon began to create a dictatorship. He abolished all political parties except the Fascist Party and seized control of the nation's industries, newspapers, police, and schools.

In 1940, under Mussolini's leadership, Italy entered World War II on the side of Nazi Germany. The Fascist government was overthrown in 1943, when Italy surrendered to the Allies.

Fascism in Germany. Germany was defeated in World War I and lost much of its territory under the peace treaties. The treaties also forced Germany to disarm and to pay heavy penalties for war damages. Severe inflation during the 1920's, followed by a worldwide depression in the early 1930's, left the German economy in ruins.

A fascist party called the National Socialist German Workers' Party, or Nazi Party, gained strength rapidly during the postwar period of crisis. By 1933, the Nazis were the strongest party in the nation. Their leader, Adolf Hitler, became the head of the government that year. Hitler soon overthrew the constitution and began to make Germany a fascist state. His secret police wiped out any opposition.

Hitler, who was called *der Führer* (the leader), preached that Germans were superior people and that Jews, Slavs, Gypsies, and other minorities were inferior. His followers used these beliefs to justify the brutal Nazi persecution of Jews and other groups. The Nazis eventually killed about 6 million Jews.

Hitler vowed to extend Germany's borders and to avenge the nation's humiliation in World War I. He began to build up the armed forces and prepare for war. In 1939, World War II began when German armies invaded Poland. The Allies defeated Germany in 1945, and the Nazi government crumbled.

Fascism in Other Countries. In Hungary, a fascist party called the Arrow Cross gained much support in the early 1930's. During the same period, a fascist organization called the Iron Guard became the strongest political party in Romania. Fascist groups also achieved considerable strength in Japan during the 1930's. All these fascist movements disappeared after the Nazi defeat in 1945.

In Argentina, Juan D. Perón established a fascist dictatorship in 1943 and ruled until 1955, when a revolt forced him to resign. His supporters remained active, however, and Perón returned to power in 1973 during a period of economic difficulty in Argentina. He ruled until his death the next year.

During the Spanish Civil War (1936-1939), a fascist group called the Falange Española supported the revolutionary forces led by Francisco Franco. Franco's forces won the war, and he ruled Spain as a dictator from 1939 until his death in 1975. Many people consider the Franco government to have been fascist, but most historians and political scholars think it lacked essential features of fascism.

Today, the rulers of many developing nations are following fascist policies in an effort to promote industrial growth and national unity. But because of the association of fascism with racism—and with Mussolini and Hitler—these leaders deny any similarity to fascist dictators. MICHAEL HURST

Related Articles in WORLD BOOK include:

Black Shirt	Nazism
Fasces (with picture)	Police State
Germany (Nazi Germany)	Romania (Depression and
Hitler, Adolf	Fascism)
Italy (Italy Under	Totalitarianism
Mussolini)	World War II (The Rise
Mussolini, Benito	of Dictatorships)
Nationalism	

See also *Fascism* in the RESEARCH GUIDE/INDEX, Volume 22, for a *Reading and Study Guide*.

FASHION is a term commonly used to describe a style of clothing worn by most of the people of a country. However, popular styles of automobiles, furniture, homes, and many other products are also fashions. The kinds of art, music, literature, and sports that many people prefer can likewise be fashions. Thus, a fashion is —or reflects—a form of behavior accepted by most people in a society.

A fashion remains popular for a few months or years before being replaced by another. A product or activity is *in fashion* or is *fashionable* during the time that a large segment of society accepts it. It becomes *old-fashioned* when the majority of people no longer accept it.

Most people do not easily accept extreme changes in fashion. Therefore, most new fashions closely resemble those they replace.

A clothing style may be introduced as a fashion, but its use becomes a *custom* if it is handed down from generation to generation. For example, in the early 1800's, long trousers replaced knee-length pants and stockings as the fashion in men's clothing in the United States and Europe. Today, wearing long trousers is a custom for men in most countries. But fashionable variations in the color and shape of trousers have occurred through the years.

A fashion that quickly comes and goes is frequently called a *fad*. The majority of people do not accept fads. Some people may become involved in faddish behavior because fads can be widely publicized. Fads of the mid-1900's included playing with such toys as hula hoops and skateboards.

Why People Follow Fashion

Before the 1800's, some nations had laws that regulated the clothing fashions of people in certain social classes. Many of these *sumptuary laws* were designed to preserve the class system. Sometimes, they forced people to buy products manufactured in their own country. An English law of the 1600's required men of the lower classes to wear woolen caps made in England. However, this same law permitted men of high position to wear velvet hats from France and Italy.

Today, people follow fashion for various reasons. For example, they may want to identify with a select group. New fashions may be adopted immediately by well-known people, including athletes, motion-picture stars, and political figures. Then, other people may follow these fashions so they can identify with this privileged group. Some people think that having fashionable clothes and surroundings raises their status in life.

Following fashion provides a way for people to gain acceptance from others. This adoption of fashion applies more to clothes and social behavior than to cars, houses, and other items that most people cannot afford to replace frequently. During the 1960's, many young people identified with one another's political and social beliefs by wearing blue jeans. After a while, blue jeans became a fashion that was accepted by a wide variety of people.

People also follow fashion to make themselves more attractive. Standards of beauty change through the years, and people decorate themselves to fit their society's changing standards. Ideas of beauty also vary from culture to culture. For example, people in many countries use cosmetics to increase their attractiveness. In some countries, people use tinted cream on their cheeks. In other countries, people decorate themselves with tattoos and with scars filled with colored clay.

Men and women have always enjoyed changing their appearance. Following new fashions in clothes, hair styles, and makeup allows people to alter their appearance in a generally accepted way.

What Causes Fashion to Change

Major changes in fashion occurred infrequently before the 1300's. Since then, the political and social conditions of a nation, plus technological developments, have influenced fashion in various ways.

Political and Social Conditions. During the 1300's, the rulers of many European nations began to set fashions that were followed by the members of their courts. In the mid-1600's, King Louis XIII of France began wearing a wig to hide his baldness. Fashionable Frenchmen soon began to shave their heads and wear wigs. In the mid-1800's, English women are said to have copied Queen Victoria's stout figure by wearing puffy dresses with padding underneath.

Some fashion changes have accompanied a breakdown in the system of social classes. The members of the nobility lost much of their power during the 1300's, when rigid class systems were weakened in Europe. The nobility began to dress more elaborately to distinguish themselves from the middle classes.

Fashions in clothing, furniture, and interior decoration change through the years. The decorative styles of the 1890's, *left,* gradually gave way to the simpler fashions of the 1940's, *right.*

During the mid-1800's, mass production of clothing made fashionable clothes available to more people at lower prices. People of all social classes began to wear similar styles of clothing. Today, it is easier to identify an expensive garment by the quality of its fabric and manufacture than by its style.

Through the years, fashions in games and sports have influenced the way people dress. During the 1700's, people in England adopted simpler clothing styles after they became interested in fox hunting and other outdoor sports. Today, many people wear special outfits for such activities as golf, horseback riding, hunting, and tennis.

Wars have also affected the style of dress in a country. European soldiers returning from the crusades during the 1100's and 1200's brought back various Eastern ideas of dress styles. The crusaders also returned with rich silk and other textiles that were not available in Europe.

During the French Revolution (1789-1795), the elegant dress styles associated with the French nobility were replaced by plainer fashions. After Napoleon became emperor in 1804, he brought back elaborate fashions in clothing for the court.

During World War II (1939-1945), the shortage of fabrics limited new fashions. The governments of many countries restricted the amount of fabric that could be used in various garments. Nylon stockings were also scarce during World War II, and many women began wearing leg paint.

Technological Developments. The development of new dyes, machinery, and textiles has greatly affected most areas of fashion, especially clothing. The style of dress has changed frequently in countries that have highly mechanized production systems.

During the early 1700's, new dyes made new color combinations possible in clothes. In the late 1700's the invention of the cotton gin, the power loom, and other machines sped up the production of fabric and yarn.

Industrial mass production of clothing began after the development of improved sewing machines during the mid-1800's. The production of many identical garments resulted in a more uniform clothing style for many people. Since that time, the garment industry has influenced the design of new clothing fashions.

In the early 1900's, manufacturers began to make clothing and other products from synthetic fabrics. These materials have become popular because they are easier to care for and less expensive than some natural fibers. People began to wear lighter weight clothing in the 1900's, following the development of more efficient heating systems.

At one time, changes in fashion spread slowly from one country to another. Today, various communication systems keep people informed on current fashion developments in all parts of the world.   Mary Ellen Roach

Related Articles in World Book include:

Brummell, George B.	Hairdressing	Modeling
Clothing	Hat	Shoe
Dior, Christian		

FAST is abstinence from food, or certain kinds of food, for a period of time. The origin of *fasting* is unknown. But the custom of fasting has played a part in the practices of every major religious group at some time.

There are many purposes for fasting. In many early religions, fasting may have been related to man's desire to keep the gods friendly, or to improve the food supply. It has often been a way in which persons have sought pardon for their misdeeds. In some religions, people fast during times of mourning. In others, the people believe that fasting will take their minds away from physical things, and produce a state of spiritual joy and happiness.

There are important fast days in Judaism, Christianity, and Islam. Jewish law orders a yearly fast on *Yom Kippur*, the Day of Atonement. Many orthodox Jews follow the custom of having the bride and groom fast on the day before their wedding. Many Christians fast

FAT

during Lent, the period of 40 days from Ash Wednesday until Easter, commemorating the 40 days that Jesus spent fasting in the wilderness. In general, for Christians, fasting seldom means doing without all food for an entire day at a time. In addition, persons who are not well can usually receive permission from their religious leaders allowing them not to fast.

Muslims fast from dawn to sunset every day during Ramadan, the ninth month of their year. During these fasting hours, Muslims abstain from both food and beverage, even though this month often comes in the hottest season of the year. Buddhists and Hindus also make use of fasts.

Most people have fasted at some time during their lives, either for religious reasons, for initiation ceremonies, or for help in developing magical powers or control over the body. In some religions, such as Zoroastrianism, religious leaders have protested against fasting from food. They claim that the food fast actually has no moral value, when compared with "fasting from evil" with eyes, hands, tongue, or feet.

Sometimes, personal or political goals are sought through fasting. Mohandas Gandhi of India used fasting both as a penance and as a means of political protest (see GANDHI, MOHANDAS KARAMCHAND).

Scientists have studied the effects of fasting on the body. They know that the intake of food affects the body by increasing its metabolism (see METABOLISM). After fasting, metabolism can become as much as 22 per cent lower than the normal rate. But research has also shown that, after long periods of fasting, the body tends to adjust itself by lowering the rate of metabolism itself. After fasting, a person should gradually resume eating. Religious groups do not intend fasting to be harmful. They believe that it promotes self-control and strengthens the will.   FLOYD H. ROSS

FAT is one of the most important foods of animals and plants. Without it they would die. Fats are found in the tissues of animals and in plants, particularly in the seeds. They are made up of carbon, hydrogen, and oxygen, in combinations of glycerol and certain acids. Therefore fats are sometimes called *glycerides of fatty acids*. Some fats are called *hard*, some *soft*, and some *liquid*,

Sources of Fats and Oils

Vegetable oils account for about 70 per cent of the world's production of fats and oils. Animal fats make up the remainder.

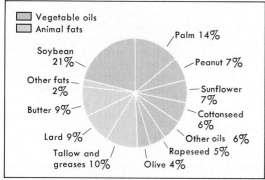

- Vegetable oils
- Animal fats

Soybean 21%
Other fats 2%
Butter 9%
Lard 9%
Tallow and greases 10%
Olive 4%
Rapeseed 5%
Other oils 6%
Cottonseed 6%
Sunflower 7%
Peanut 7%
Palm 14%

Source: *Foreign Agricultural Circular: Oilseeds and Products*, U.S. Department of Agriculture, September 1976.

according to their degree of firmness at ordinary temperatures. Hard fats include human fat and fat of beef and mutton. Lard and butter are soft fats. Liquid fats include all animal and plant oils that stay in a fluid state at ordinary temperatures. Hard and soft fats may be liquefied by heat, and liquid fats may be hardened by a chemical process called *hydrogenation* (see HYDROGENATION). This process keeps the liquid fat in a solid form so that it does not spoil. The most important of the fatty acids are *palmitic*, *stearic*, and *oleic* acids. Hard fats have comparatively large amounts of palmitic and stearic acids. Liquid fats, such as olive and cottonseed oils, contain more oleic acids. Mineral oils, such as petroleum, are not considered fats because they do not contain combinations of glycerol and fatty acids. The body does not absorb mineral oils. Most fats dissolve in chloroform, ether, gasoline, and benzine. For this reason, many cleaning fluids contain these substances.

Fats in the Diet. Fats furnish more than twice as much fuel and energy for the body as the same amount of proteins or carbohydrates. This is because fats contain more carbon and hydrogen. When carbon and hydrogen burn, they give off huge amounts of heat. A pure fat has a fuel value of 4,040 calories per pound (8,907 per kilogram), while sugar, a typical carbohydrate, has a fuel value of 1,820 calories per pound (4,012 per kilogram). People in cold countries need more fat in their diet than do people in warm countries. Less fat should be eaten in summer, as the body demands less heat then. In winter, more fat should be eaten so that the body can resist cold. Eskimos eat a great amount of fat or tallow in order to store up fat in their bodies. This serves as a source of heat and also as an insulation against cold. All fat not used for fuel energy, or growth, is stored in the tissues as body fat.

The bodies of some people do not burn up all the fat that they take in, but store up the excess fat in the body tissues. Such persons generally gain too much weight. In general, a person can lose weight either by eating less, or by doing more physical exercise, or both. People who wish to lose weight try to regulate the diet so that the body must draw on its reserve stores of fat. Each person must follow the diet best suited to his or her own physical condition. A person who is greatly overweight or underweight should consult a physician (see DIET; WEIGHT CONTROL).

Nearly all the fat found in food is digestible. But it takes a long time for digestive juices to work on fat. Thus, fried foods that are covered with fat will be digested more slowly than boiled foods. Fatty foods therefore keep a person from feeling hungry for a longer period of time than do nonfatty foods. Cooking other foods in fat makes the food tasty, but care must be taken not to overheat the fat-covered foods, as this makes them less digestible. Fat is digested in the small intestine.

Vitamins A and D are found in most fats. Vitamin A is necessary for growth, and vitamin D prevents the disease called rickets. Butter and cream, and the liver oils of cod, halibut, and shark contain these vitamins.

Industrial Uses. Besides its importance as a food, fat serves as a base for all soap. Coconut oil and palm oil are two of the chief fats used in making soaps. Fat is also a chief ingredient in the making of candles. Manufacturers use fats to make paints, varnishes, leather, artificial rubber, polishes, waxes, carbon paper, salves, insecticides, lubricants, cosmetics, drugs, dyes, petroleum, and synthetic resin. Another important use for fat is as a cooking oil. Some fats, such as castor oil and cod-liver oil, can be used as medicines. The glycerol in fat is an important ingredient of explosives. During World War II, homemakers saved used cooking fats to be used in making soap; and its by-product, glycerol, was used in making explosives. Thus, soapmaking was vital to the war effort.   LEONE RUTLEDGE CARROLL

Related Articles in WORLD BOOK include:

Blubber	Margarine	Stearic Acid
Butter	Nutrition (Carbo-	Stearin
Detergent	hydrates; Fats)	Suet
and Soap	Oil	Tallow
Lanolin	Perfume	Vegetable Oil
Lard	Shortening	Wax

FATA MORGANA. See MIRAGE.

FATALISM, *FAY tuh lihz uhm,* is the belief that all events are determined by fate. Fatalists believe that one cannot choose how to act by free will. They accept every event which occurs in human life or in nature as something which must happen as it does because it has been predetermined. Such a belief implies that some force, divine or physical, determines all events.

See also PREDESTINATION.

FATES were three goddesses who ruled people's lives. According to Greek and Roman mythology they spun and cut the thread of life. They were called *Parcae* among the Romans and *Moirai* among the Greeks. Clotho was the spinner of the thread and Lachesis decided how long it was to be. Atropos cut the thread.

The Fates were stern and gloomy goddesses. Nothing could make them change their minds. People offered them gifts to escape death, but never to thank them for any kind of blessings.

Ancient artists represented Clotho as holding the spindle of thread. Lachesis carries rods which she shakes to decide a person's fate. Atropos has a tablet in her hand on which she writes the decision.   PADRAIC COLUM

See also NORNS.

FATHER is a title of honor given to men who establish anything important in human affairs. A man who occupies an unusual place in history is sometimes also called a *Father*. The title has no official standing. It is given only by custom. The following list represents some of the best-known holders of this title:

Father of America. Samuel Adams, one of the most active patriots in the cause of American independence.

Father of American Methodism. Francis Asbury.

Father of Angling. Izaak Walton, who wrote about the delights of fishing in *The Compleat Angler* (1653).

Father of Comedy. Aristophanes, who was the greatest of the Greek writers of comedy.

Father of English History. The Venerable Bede, who wrote an *Ecclesiastical History of the English Nation.*

Father of English Poetry. Geoffrey Chaucer, who wrote the famous *Canterbury Tales.*

Father of English Pottery. Josiah Wedgwood, who made the manufacture of pottery in England an art.

Father of English Printing. William Caxton, who introduced printing into England in 1476.

Father of English Prose. Alfred the Great, who inspired and partly wrote the first English history to appear in his native language.

Father of Epic Poetry. Homer, who, tradition says, wrote the famous Greek epic poems, the *Iliad* and the *Odyssey.*

Father of Greek Tragedy. Aeschylus, the first great writer of Greek tragedy.

Father of His Country. George Washington is the Father of His Country to the people of the United States. The title has also been given to other men in history. The Romans called Cicero the Father of His Country because he saved the state from the plots of Catiline. Julius Caesar and the Emperor Augustus also received the title.

Father of History. Herodotus, who wrote the first great history of Greece and other ancient countries.

Father of Medicine. Hippocrates, who was a Greek physician and the most famous one of ancient times.

Father of New France. Samuel de Champlain.

Father of the Constitution. James Madison.

Father of the Faithful. Abraham, who was the ancestor of the Hebrew race.

Father is sometimes applied to anything of chief importance. For example, the Mississippi is often called the "Father of Waters" because of its many branches.

Father is also the title given to priests of the Roman Catholic and Anglican churches.   JOHN F. CUBER

There is a biography in THE WORLD BOOK ENCYCLOPEDIA for each man named.

FATHER ABRAHAM was a popular name for Abraham Lincoln. See LINCOLN, ABRAHAM.

FATHER OF THE CONSTITUTION. See MADISON, JAMES.

FATHER'S DAY is a day on which the people of many countries express gratitude and appreciation by giving their fathers presents or greeting cards. In the United States and Canada, Father's Day comes on the third Sunday in June. Some groups hold special programs to celebrate the day. Mrs. John Bruce Dodd of Spo-

Oil painting attributed to Francesco Salviati and Michelangelo; Pitti Palace, Florence, Italy (Alinari from Art Reference Bureau)

The Three Fates ruled people's lives. Clotho spun the thread of life, Lachesis set its length, and Atropos cut it.

FATHERS OF CONFEDERATION

kane, Wash., started the U.S. observance of Father's Day in 1910. In 1936, a national Father's Day Committee was formed.   ELIZABETH HOUGH SECHRIST

FATHERS OF CONFEDERATION. See CANADA, HISTORY OF (Confederation; table; color picture).

FATHOM, *FATH uhm,* is a unit of length used to measure ropes or cables and the depths of water. One fathom equals 6 feet (1.8 meters). Navigators mark a rope in fathoms and drop it into the water to measure the depth. Sailors of average height often measured fathoms roughly by extending both arms and measuring the rope from finger tip to finger tip.   E. G. STRAUS

FATHOMETER, *fa THAHM uh tuhr,* is an instrument used on ships to measure the depth of the water. It works by sending a sound down through the water to be echoed back from the bottom. Navigators can measure the depth below the ship by measuring the time it takes the sound to return. The speed of sound in water is known. Continuous soundings of this kind can be taken all during a voyage. The fathometer contains two parts, a *submarine oscillator,* which produces the sound, and a hydrophone *echo receiver.* They are kept in tanks of water at the bottom of the ship. The echo is amplified and sent to a *depth indicator* and a *recorder* near the bridge. The fathometer is less reliable in shallow water than in deep water. See also SONAR.   RAWSON BENNETT

Sound waves travel down through water

Depth known from the time taken by sound to leave vessel and return to the receiver

The Fathometer is used to determine the depth of water. This information makes it possible to chart the ocean floor.

FATIGUE, *fuh TEEG,* is another name for tiredness. People often say they are "fatigued" when they feel tired. If we work hard, play hard, or go without rest or sleep, we expect to feel fatigued. In such cases, fatigue is normal. We know from experience that this feeling will disappear after we rest. But sometimes fatigue is a symptom of illness. A physically ill person often feels weak and becomes fatigued after even a

slight amount of work or exertion. Such persons need a great deal of rest, often much more than they would need if they were well. Doctors have found that fatigue occurs frequently in many different kinds of illnesses. Rest in bed has become a part of the treatment for almost every kind of physical illness.

Fatigue may be one of the symptoms of a mental or a physical illness. In either case, rest helps a person feel less tired. But no amount of rest will cure the tendency to become tired easily. This tendency will disappear or improve only if the physical or mental illness that causes the fatigue is improved or cured.

Cause. Doctors do not know exactly what causes fatigue. They do not know why a person feels tired after muscular exertion or mental effort. However, they do know that psychological as well as physical factors contribute to fatigue. The effect of fatigue has been closely studied. Research workers have shown that persons who spend long hours at things that bore them or at tasks they do not want to do soon develop fatigue. If the person's *morale* (general attitude) and *incentive* (promise of reward) are good, it takes longer for fatigue to develop. But, no matter how good morale or incentive might be, a person who works or plays long enough or hard enough will develop a feeling of fatigue.

Fatigue in Physiology. *Physiologists* (persons who study the action of living tissue) use the word fatigue in a somewhat different sense. These people sometimes study the reaction of muscles to stimuli. They make a muscle contract again and again by stimulating it with an electric current. They do not let the muscle rest, but make it contract and relax continually for a long time. As the stimulation continues, the contractions become weaker and weaker. When the muscle becomes very weak, the researchers allow it to rest for a while. When they stimulate it again after the rest period, it contracts as strongly as ever. The progressive weakening of the muscle is called fatigue. It differs from the *feeling* of fatigue people have after muscular exertion. But the two conditions are so much alike that they are called by the same name.   CHARLES BRENNER

See also HEALTH.

FATIGUE, METAL. Engineers use the term fatigue to describe certain changes that occur in substances like metals. After extensive use, the substance gradually weakens. Repeated stress, such as continued weight, tension, or pressure, causes this weakening. Such stress often alters the molecular structure of the materials so· that they bend or crack. Metal fatigue usually begins at the surface of a metal piece where small defects, or even minute tool marks, serve as a concentration point for stress. The crack spreads through the piece, making it too weak to carry its normal load. Engineers allow for fatigue when planning airplanes, bridges, and machinery. See also STRENGTH OF MATERIALS.

FATIMA. See MUHAMMAD (Early Life).

FÁTIMA, *FA tih muh* (pop. 6,433), is a town in west-central Portugal and the site of a famous religious shrine. For location, see PORTUGAL (political map). The Virgin Mary, also called Our Lady of Fátima, reportedly appeared near Fátima in 1917. On May 13 of that year, three Portuguese children told of seeing a vision of a lady near Fátima while they were tending their sheep. The children said that the lady, dressed in a white gown and veil, told them to come there on the 13th day of each month until the following October when she would tell them who she was. On October 13, she said that she was Our Lady of the Rosary, and told the children to recite the rosary every day. She called for people to reform their lives and asked that a chapel be built in her honor.

In 1930, the Roman Catholic Church authorized devotion to Our Lady of Fátima. Since then, millions of persons have made pilgrimages to Fátima. FRANCIS L. FILAS

FATIMITE DYNASTY, *FAT ih myt*, was a line of Muslim *caliphs* (rulers) who claimed that they were descended from Fatima, the daughter of Muhammad. They rose to power in northwest Africa in A.D. 909, and won control of Egypt in 969. Their empire at one time included Sicily, part of Arabia, and Syria. For a long time, their capital was Kairwan (now Al Qayrawan), Tunisia. Later the Fatimites established their capital in Cairo. They gathered a great library there, and had another one at Tripoli, in Lebanon.

The Fatimite caliphs were good leaders. But, as time went on, they became lazy, and lost their authority. The Cairo caliph realized that his dynasty was growing weaker, and sent to Nur al-Din, a Muslim leader, for help. Nur al-Din responded by sending a strong force which included Saladin, a soldier who overthrew the Fatimite Dynasty in 1171. ALI HASSAN ABDEL-KADER

See also MUHAMMAD; SALADIN; CAIRO (History).

FATTY ACID. See FAT; ACID.

FAUCET. See PLUMBING.

FAULKNER, WILLIAM (1897-1962), ranks among the leading American authors of the 1900's. He gained fame for his novels about the mythical "Yoknapatawpha County" and its county seat of Jefferson. Faulkner patterned the county after the area around his hometown, Oxford, Miss. He explored the county's geography, history, economy, and social and moral life. He also described the decay of its aristocratic families and their inability to adjust to modern life.

Faulkner received the 1949 Nobel prize for literature. He won Pulitzer prizes in 1955 for *A Fable* and in 1963 for *The Reivers.*

Faulkner's work is characterized by a remarkable range of technique, theme, and tone. In *The Sound and the Fury* (1929) and *As I Lay Dying* (1930), he used stream-of-consciousness, in which the story is told through the thoughts of a character. In *Requiem for a Nun* (1951), Faulkner alternated sections of prose fiction with sections of a stage play. In *A Fable* (1954), he created a World War I soldier whose experiences symbolize the passion of Christ. Faulkner was especially skillful in creating characters with differing reactions to the same person or situation. He used this technique to make his readers recognize the difficulty of arriving at true judgments.

The traditions and history of the South were a favorite Faulkner theme. *Sartoris* (1929) and *The Unvanquished* (1938) tell the story of several generations of the Sartoris family. *The Reivers* (1962) is a humorous

Wide World

William Faulkner

story of a young boy's adventures during a trip from Mississippi to Memphis. Faulkner examined the relationship between blacks and whites in several works, including *Light in August* (1932); *Absalom, Absalom!* (1936); and *Go Down, Moses* (1942). Here, he was especially concerned with persons of mixed racial background and their problems in establishing their identity.

Most of Faulkner's novels have a serious tone, but some are flavored with comedy. *The Hamlet* (1940), *The Town* (1957), and *The Mansion* (1959) make up an often humorous trilogy that shows the evil impact of the unscrupulous Snopes family on their neighbors. Faulkner's short stories have the same range of technique, theme, and tone as his novels.

Faulkner was born on Sept. 25, 1897, in New Albany, Miss. He grew up in Oxford. He traveled occasionally, but he preferred to stay in Oxford writing, or hunting with old friends.

Many early critics of Faulkner denounced his books for their emphasis on violence and abnormality. *Sanctuary* (1931), a story involving rape and murder, was most severely criticized. Later, many critics recognized that Faulkner had been criticizing the faults in society by showing them in contrast to what he called the "eternal verities." These verities are universal values such as love, honor, pity, pride, compassion, and sacrifice. Faulkner often said it is the writer's duty to remind readers of these values. OLGA W. VICKERY

FAULT, in geology, is a movement of the two masses of rocks on each side of a break in the earth's crust. The masses move on surfaces called *fault planes.*

See also EARTHQUAKE (Why Earthquakes Occur; illustration: An Earthquake Focus).

FAUN, *fawn*, was a half-human god of the woods and herds in Roman mythology. The fauns corresponded to the *satyrs* of Greek mythology. They had pointed ears, short horns, and a tail. Their legs are sometimes represented as human, sometimes as covered with shaggy hair and with feet like a goat. The fauns were followers of Pan, god of the fields and woods, and Bacchus, god

The Satyr among the Peasants (early 1600's), an oil painting by Jacob Jordaens; Mrs. Richard Ederheimer collection

A Faun, *left,* was a half-human god in Roman mythology. Fauns were often represented with hairy legs and the feet of a goat.

of wine. They were generally represented as playful creatures.   PHILIP W. HARSH

See also SATYR.

FAUNA, *FAW nuh,* is the name given to the animal life of a certain period of time or of a certain part of the world. It corresponds to the word *flora,* which means the plant life of a certain place or time. Thus we may speak of the fauna and flora (animals and plants) of North America or of a past geological period. The term *fauna* comes from the name of a Roman goddess of fields and flocks.   L. B. AREY

FAURÉ, *foh RAY,* **GABRIEL URBAIN** (1845-1924), a French composer, organist, and teacher, helped to free French music from German influences. The most outstanding characteristic of his music is its elegance and reserve. Fauré was born in Pamiers in southern France. He played the organ in Parisian churches for many years, and directed the Paris Conservatory of Music from 1905 to 1920. His works include a Requiem Mass, the musical dramas *Pénélope* and *Prométhée,* incidental music for plays such as Maeterlinck's *Pelléas et Mélisande,* many works for piano, several chamber music compositions, and a number of songs.   HOMER ULRICH

FAUST (1480?-1538?) was a magician who amazed German audiences in the early 1500's with weird exhibitions and far-fetched boasts. He claimed to be in league with Satan. After his death, marvelous tales circulated about him, and the mythical deeds of famous sorcerers were often credited to him.

An anonymous author published a book about Faust in 1587 to show the dangers of making agreements with evil spirits. Many others followed, and Faust became a frequent character in plays. In all the early books and plays, Faust sold his soul to the devil in return for magic powers. This was usually for a period of 24 years, after which the devil dragged Faust to hell.

A slightly changed version of the German book of 1587 was translated into English by P. F. Gent and published in England in 1592. Gent's translation inspired the British dramatist Christopher Marlowe to write a play, *The Tragical History of Dr. Faustus.* Marlowe added little to the story, but his talent lifted it to the level of fine literature. In the play *Faust,* the German author Johann Wolfgang von Goethe produced a famous portrayal of Faust. Goethe made the tragedy into a dramatic story in which God permitted the devil to mislead Faust on earth but redeemed him in the end. The novelist Thomas Mann published a novel called *Doctor Faustus* in 1947 about a musical composer of the early 1900's who led a life similar to Faust's.   FRANK GOODWYN

See also MEPHISTOPHELES; OPERA (The Opera Repertoire); GOETHE, JOHANN WOLFGANG VON.

FAUVES, *fohvz,* were a group of French artists who painted in a style that emphasized intense color and rapid, vigorous brushstrokes. Fauvism flourished from about 1903 to 1907. Henri Matisse led the movement, and members included André Derain, Raoul Dufy, Maurice de Vlaminck, and Georges Rouault. The Fauves tried to express as directly as possible the vividness and excitement of nature. They were influenced by

Fauve Paintings show the emphasis of this group of painters on intense color and bold brushstrokes. André Derain, a leader of the Fauves, painted *London Bridge* in 1906.

the bright colors, bold patterns, and brushwork of such artists of the 1880's and 1890's as Paul Cézanne, Paul Gauguin, Georges Seurat, and Vincent van Gogh.

The word *fauves* means *wild beasts* in French. An art critic gave the painters this name because of the unusual boldness of their style. Most of the Fauves changed their style of painting by about 1907. But the movement had great influence throughout Europe, especially on German expressionism.   MARCEL FRANCISCONO

Each artist mentioned in this article has a separate biography in WORLD BOOK. See also PAINTING (Fauvism).

FAVELA. See RIO DE JANEIRO (The City; History).

FAWCETT, JOHN. See HYMN (Blest Be the Tie).

FAWKES, *fawks,* **GUY** (1570-1606), led a group who tried to blow up King James I and the Parliament on Nov. 5, 1605, to avenge the persecution of Roman Catholics in England (see GUNPOWDER PLOT). Fawkes was born in York, England, and served in the Spanish army from 1593 to 1604. He was hanged in 1606, after the plot against the king failed. England observes Guy Fawkes Day each November 5.   WILLARD M. WALLACE

FAWN is the name for a young deer during the first year of its life. See ANIMAL (color picture: Animal Camouflage); DEER.

FAX. See FACSIMILE.

FAYETTEVILLE, N.C. (pop. 53,510; met. area pop. 212,042), is a tobacco, cotton, and livestock trade center in the south-central part of the state (see NORTH CAROLINA [political map]). Settled by Highland Scots in 1739, it became a Tory center during the Revolutionary War. Campbelltown and Cross Creek combined during the war, and the name was changed to Fayetteville in 1783. North Carolina ratified the Constitution there in 1789. Fayetteville has a council-manager government.   HUGH T. LEFLER

FAZENDA. See LATIN AMERICA (Country Life).

FBI. See FEDERAL BUREAU OF INVESTIGATION.

FCA. See FARM CREDIT ADMINISTRATION.

FCC. See FEDERAL COMMUNICATIONS COMMISSION.

FCIC. See FEDERAL CROP INSURANCE CORPORATION.

FDA. See FOOD AND DRUG ADMINISTRATION.

FDIC. See FEDERAL DEPOSIT INSURANCE CORPORATION.

FEAR. See EMOTION; PHOBIA.

FEAR, CAPE. See CAPE FEAR.

FEAST OF FOOLS was a festival celebrated in many European countries from early medieval times down to the 1600's. The Feast of Fools came in December and was a Christian form of the Roman Saturnalia (see SATURNALIA). People celebrated the feast with merriment and foolish, boisterous pranks. The ceremonies usually included dramatic performances in the principal church of the town. The people often elected a mock pope, cardinal, archbishop, bishop, or abbot. They gave these "officials" such names as Pope of Fools, Abbot of Unreason, or Boy Bishop. The mob took over the churches on election day and sometimes imitated church rites.

The feast was most popular in the time of Queen Elizabeth I. It survived in the south of France until 1644. The festival finally became so lawless that the church forbade it.   ELIZABETH HOUGH SECHRIST

FEAST OF LIGHTS. See HANUKKAH.

FEAST OF WEEKS. See SHABUOT.

Omar Marcus

A Highlight of the Christmas Festival in Mexico is the breaking of the *piñata,* a decorated earthen jar filled with sweets. Blindfolded guests try to hit the piñata with a long stick to spill its contents on the floor.

FEASTS AND FESTIVALS are religious celebrations that express people's joys, fears, and feelings of gratitude. Most people think of feasts as happy family celebrations. Many churches refer to joyous religious services as feasts. People hold festivals for the same reasons as feasts, but all the people of a community celebrate together at festivals.

Pagan Sources. Scholars think that feasts and festivals originated in the fears and superstitions of primitive people. Many things in nature puzzled or frightened them, and they came to worship objects and events they could not understand. Primitive people bowed to the sun because it brought light and warmth. They offered the first fruit and grain of the harvest to the gods of the earth. Many early civilizations continued these customs. Semitic tribe members offered animal sacrifices to their gods during festivals held in the springtime and at harvest time. The Babylonians celebrated their New Year's festival with sacrifices and gifts of gold, silver, and precious stones.

As civilizations developed, festivals became more elaborate, and included many nonreligious elements. The ancient Greeks honored their gods with festivals that often included athletic games. The most important were the Olympian, Isthmian, Nemean, and Pythian festivals and games. The Romans often held huge fairs to celebrate their festivals. Beginning on December 17, they honored the god Saturn with a festival called Saturnalia. During the festivities, the Romans chose a king by lot, and masters served their slaves.

In Russia, dancers dressed in colorful national costumes bid goodbye to the *Shrovetide*, a festival that precedes the Lenten season.

Lars Hedman

In Spain, *left*, penitent Christians wear white pointed hoods in the *Semana Santa* procession, held during Holy Week.

New Year's Day in China features folk dances by men wearing huge lion and dragon masks.

▼

Church Festivals took over many pagan customs, giving them new meanings. The Hebrews of ancient Palestine celebrated their festival of Pentecost by bringing the first fruits of their harvest to the Temple in Jerusalem. Many features of the Roman Saturnalia appeared in Christian festivals. Bishops washed the feet of priests on Maundy Thursday, much as Roman masters served their slaves. During the medieval Feast of Fools, a boy bishop presided over church festivities. He resembled the king chosen by lot during Saturnalia. Many religious festivals stressed recreation. They allowed people to forget the hardships of their daily life.

Christian Feasts today fall into two groups, *movable* and *immovable* feasts. Immovable feasts fall on the same day each year. They include Epiphany, or Little Christmas, on January 6; All Saints' Day, on November 1; and Christmas Day, on December 25. Movable feasts occur on different dates each year. Easter is the principal movable feast, and its date determines the date of most other movable feasts. Church feasts dated from Easter include Ash Wednesday; Palm Sunday; Good Friday; Ascension Day, or Holy Thursday; Pentecost, or Whitsunday; and Trinity Sunday.

Many unusual celebrations accompany Christian feasts and festivals. On June 23, many Christians observe St. John's Eve with bonfires, dancing, and rites that are supposed to insure health and success in love. In France, Italy, Portugal, Spain, and many Latin-American countries, the people hold a joyous carnival just before Lent. This carnival survives in the United States in the Mardi Gras of New Orleans. Siena, Italy, draws thousands of people to the horse races held on July 2 and again on August 16 at the Festival of the Palio. This festival honors the Virgin Mary.

Jewish Festivals honor both religious and national events. Among the most important are Yom Kippur (Day of Atonement), Rosh Hashanah (New Year), Hanukkah, and Pesah (Passover). Israelis observe the festival of Purim with costume parties and dramatic presentations of the story of Queen Esther.

Other Festivals. The Muslims observe two important feast days in the year. One ends the month-long fast, called *Ramadan*, during which Muslims fast from sunrise to sunset every day. The other feast day concludes the pilgrimage to Mecca made by devout Muslims. The Chinese celebrate their New Year in midwinter with religious ceremonies, parades, firecrackers, and great merrymaking. The Japanese celebrate a colorful festival on April 8 to honor the birthday of Buddha. Some Japanese call this festival Flower Day. They decorate temples with flowers and pour sweet tea over small statues of the infant Buddha.   ELIZABETH HOUGH SECHRIST

Related Articles in WORLD BOOK include:

All Saints' Day	Halloween	New Year's Day
All Souls' Day	Hanukkah	Olympic Games
Ascension Day	Holiday	Palm Sunday
Ash Wednesday	Holy Innocents' Day	Passover
Assumption	Holy Year	Pentecost
Candlemas Day	Islam (Customs	Purim
Christmas	and Ceremonies)	Pythian Games
Doll (Doll	Isthmian Games	Rogation Days
Festivals and	Judaism (table:	Rosh Hashanah
Customs)	Jewish Feasts	Sabbath
Easter	and Fasts)	Saturnalia
Epiphany	Lag Ba'Omer	Shabuot
Fairs and	Mardi Gras	Simhat Torah
Expositions	Martinmas	Sukkot
Feast of Fools	Maundy Thursday	Tishah B'Ab
Fiesta	May Day	Trinity Sunday
Good Friday	Michaelmas	Tu B'Shebat
Guadalupe Day	Nemean Games	Yom Kippur

FEATHER. The feathers of birds help them fly and also keep them warm. People use feathers to stuff pillows, to guide the flight of arrows, and to decorate hats and other garments. Until the steel pen was invented in the early 1800's, pens were made from feathers.

Parts of a Feather. Birds have two chief kinds of feathers—contour and down.

Contour feathers are the large feathers that cover the wings, body, and tail. They are shaped somewhat like fern leaves. A contour feather has a strong, flexible center shaft. The lower part of the shaft is called the *quill*. The *rhachis*, or upper part of the shaft, supports the *web* or *vane*, the flat part of the feather. The web is made up and held together by parts called barbs, barbules, and hooklets. *Barbs* branch out from the shaft like the branches of a tree. Several hundred *barbules* branch out from each barb. The *hooklets* interlock with those on nearby barbules and hold the web together.

Down is a small, soft feather found beneath the outer feathers of ducks, geese, and other waterfowl. Down has no central shaft. The silky fibers of down grow outward from a common center.

Feathers for Stuffing pillows, quilts, and upholstery are judged on the basis of springiness, shape, texture, odor, density, and their ability to hold up under weight. Size is another important factor. If a feather is too large, the bony quills make the stuffing uncomfortable. If the feathers are too small, the stuffing will have no body.

The finest feather-stuffed pillows contain a mixture of three-fourths down and one-fourth goose feathers. Down alone does not have the needed ability to hold up under weight. Goose feathers alone, or a mixture of goose and duck feathers, also make satisfactory fillings. Chicken and turkey feathers make poor stuffing. They are stiff, hard, heavy, and have little bounce. They tend to mat.

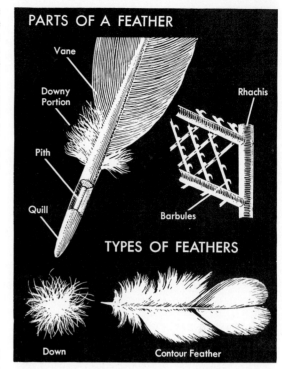

PARTS OF A FEATHER

Vane

Downy Portion

Rhachis

Pith

Quill

Barbules

TYPES OF FEATHERS

Down

Contour Feather

Other Uses. Designers often decorate hats and clothes with dyed or natural feathers.

Manufacturers often use feathers to make toothpicks and artists' brushes. The demand for feathers to make arrows has also grown. Manufacturers still make some quill pens.

Members of the National Audubon Society and other bird lovers have long fought against killing wild birds for their feathers. The *aigrette*, the long plume of the egret, was a popular ornamental feather in the 1800's. Hunters killed so many egrets for their feathers that the birds faced extinction. State and federal laws now protect wild birds, and it is illegal to import bird feathers into the United States.   EFFA BROWN

Related Articles in WORLD BOOK include:

Bird (Feathers; picture:	Egret	Peacock
Parts of a Bird)	Molting	Pen
Bird of Paradise	Ostrich	Pheasant

FEATHER STAR. See SEA LILY.

FEATHERWEIGHT. See BOXING (Weight Classes).

FEBOLD FEBOLDSON, *FEE bold FEE bold son*, is a mythical, tall-tale hero of Nebraska. His humorous exaggerations reflect the ingenuity of the pioneers in solving their problems and "laughing off" their hardships. The "Big Swede" was developed and publicized by two Nebraska newspapermen, Don Holmes and Wayne T. Carroll. Beginning in 1927 or 1928, they patterned Feboldson after legendary men like Paul Bunyan and Pecos Bill. For example, Febold started tree-planting on the plains by tossing handfuls of cottonwood seeds into prairie-dog holes. He also devised a way of digging postholes by using the happy auger, a creature that spun around on its augerlike tail when it sat down, and drilled a perfect posthole. Paul R. Beath collected the Feboldson yarns into a book in 1948.   B. A. BOTKIN

FEBRUARY

FEBRUARY is the second month of the year, and the shortest. According to legends, Romulus did not include it when he made the first Roman calendar, which had only 10 months. Numa Pompilius, who followed Romulus, added two months, making February the last month of the year. Its name, *Februarius*, came from a Latin word meaning *to purify*. The Romans purified themselves in February to prepare for festivals at the start of the new year. But Julius Caesar moved the beginning of the year from March to January, making February the second month.

February usually has 28 days. But it has one extra day in every leap year. February had 30 days until the time of Julius Caesar. Caesar took one day off to add to the month named after him, July. The emperor Augustus took another day off to add to August, the month named after him.

February is usually cold and stormy in the northern half of the world. But sunny days now and then show that spring is not far off. February is not nearly so dark and gloomy as the other winter months. The air is often crisp and clear, and ice and snow cover the ground. People in the Southern Hemisphere enjoy mid-summer weather during February.

Special Days. People in Christian countries celebrate Valentine's Day on February 14. Many schools hold Valentine's Day parties when the children make special decorations for their classrooms. Old and young alike exchange Valentine cards with their friends. The custom of exchanging greetings on Valentine's Day goes back hundreds of years. Scholars have found records of Valentine notes that date from as early as the Middle Ages.

Two of America's greatest men, George Washington and Abraham Lincoln, were born during February. Many states honor these men with official holidays in February. Other states informally celebrate the birthdays. Charles Dickens, Henry Wadsworth Longfellow, and many other famous men were born in February.

The Roman Catholic Church celebrates February 2

IMPORTANT FEBRUARY EVENTS

1 U.S. Supreme Court met for the first time, 1790.
—American composer Victor Herbert born 1859.

Wide World

—Louis S. St. Laurent, second French-Canadian prime minister of Canada, born 1882.
—American writer Langston Hughes born 1902.
2 Ground-Hog Day.
—By the Treaty of Guadalupe Hidalgo, Mexico gave New Mexico and California to the United States, 1848.
—Fritz Kreisler, Austrian-born violinist, born 1875.
—James Joyce, Irish novelist and poet, born 1882.
—Violinist Jascha Heifetz born 1901.
—The last German troops surrendered in the Stalingrad pocket, completing the Russian victory at Stalingrad, 1943.
3 Joseph E. Johnston, Confederate general, born 1807.
—German composer Felix Mendelssohn born 1809.
—Horace Greeley, American publisher, born 1811.
—Sidney Lanier, American poet, born 1842.
4 Confederate States of America formed by a temporary committee meeting at Montgomery, Ala., 1861.
—Philippine Rebellion against the United States began, 1899.
—Charles A. Lindbergh, American aviator, born 1902.
—Yalta Conference began, 1945.
—Amendment 24 to the U.S. Constitution, banning poll tax, proclaimed, 1964.
5 Evangelist Dwight L. Moody born 1837.
6 Queen Anne of England born 1665.
—Aaron Burr, American political leader, born 1756.
—Massachusetts ratified the Constitution, 1788.
—Home run king "Babe" Ruth born 1895.

United Press Int.

—The United States Senate ratified the peace treaty ending the Spanish-American War, 1899.
—Amendment 20 to the United States Constitution,

moving Inauguration Day to January 20, proclaimed, 1933.
7 Novelist Charles Dickens born 1812.
—Dmitri Mendeleev, Russian chemist, born 1834.
—Nobel prize novelist Sinclair Lewis born 1885.
8 Mary, Queen of Scots, executed, 1587.
—College of William and Mary, second oldest college in the United States, chartered, 1693.
—John Ruskin, English essayist and critic, born 1819.
—William T. Sherman, Union general, born 1820.
—Jules Verne, French novelist, born 1828.
—Russo-Japanese War began, 1904.
—Boy Scouts of America incorporated, 1910.
—Elizabeth II proclaimed queen of England, 1952.
9 William Henry Harrison, ninth President of the United States, born in Charles City County, Virginia, 1773.
—George Ade, American humorist, born 1866.
—United States Weather Service established, 1870.
—Amy Lowell, American poet, born 1874.
10 France surrendered Canada to Great Britain by the Treaty of Paris, 1763.
—English essayist and critic Charles Lamb born 1775.
11 Thomas A. Edison, American inventor, born 1847.
12 Thaddeus Kosciusko, Polish patriot, born 1746.
—Peter Cooper, American philanthropist, born 1791.
—Abraham Lincoln, 16th President of the United States, born near present-day Hodgenville, Ky., 1809.
—Charles Darwin, British naturalist, born 1809.
—Chile gained its independence from Spain, 1818.
—John L. Lewis, American labor leader, born 1880.
—Chinese Republic formed, 1912.
13 Talleyrand, French statesman, born 1754.
—Grant Wood, American painter, born 1892.
14 Valentine's Day.
—Oregon became the 33rd state to join the Union, 1859.
—John Barrymore, American actor, born 1882.
—Arizona became the 48th state, 1912.
15 Galileo, Italian astronomer and physicist, born 1564.
—Inventor Cyrus McCormick born 1809.
—Susan B. Anthony, American woman suffrage leader, born 1820.

as Candlemas Day. The candles used in the church during the rest of the year are blessed on this day.

Popular Beliefs. People often refer to the second day of February as Ground-Hog Day. According to many old stories, the ground hog, or woodchuck, comes out of his burrow on February 2 to look for his shadow. If the sun is shining and the ground hog can see his shadow, he goes back to sleep for a while, and winter is not over. If the ground hog cannot see his shadow, he begins his springtime activities. Only superstitious people believe this story.

February Symbols. Many people consider the primrose the special flower for February. The amethyst is the birthstone for February.　　　　　GRACE HUMPHREY

Quotations

The February sunshine steeps your boughs,
And tints the buds and swells the leaves within.
　　　　　William Cullen Bryant

I crown thee king of intimate delights,
Fireside enjoyments, home-born happiness,

And all the comforts that the lowly roof
Of undisturb'd retirement, and the hours
Of long uninterrupted evening know.
　　　　　William Cowper

Hail to thy returning festival, old Bishop Valentine! Like unto thee, assuredly, there is no other mitred father in the calendar.
　　　　　Charles Lamb

Thirty days hath September,
April, June, and November;
All the rest have thirty-one,
Excepting February alone
Which hath but twenty-eight, in fine,
Till leap year gives it twenty-nine.
　　　　　Old saying

Related Articles in WORLD BOOK include:

Amethyst	Leap Year
Calendar	Primrose
Candlemas Day	Valentine's Day
Ground-Hog Day	

IMPORTANT FEBRUARY EVENTS

15 Elihu Root, U.S. statesman and lawyer, born 1845.
　—U.S.S. *Maine* blew up in Havana Harbor, 1898.
16 Henry Adams, American historian, born 1838.
　—Van Wyck Brooks, American historian, born 1886.
　—Katharine Cornell, American actress, born 1893.
17 Thomas Malthus, British economist, born 1766.
　—Montgomery Ward, mail-order merchant, born 1844.
　—Marian Anderson, American singer, born 1902.

HARRISON　　　LINCOLN　　　WASHINGTON

18 Mary I, first reigning queen of England, born 1516.
　—John Bunyan's *Pilgrim's Progress* was licensed for publication, 1678.
　—Jefferson Davis took the oath as provisional President of the Confederate States of America, 1861.
　—Wendell Willkie, American political leader, born 1892.
　—San Francisco's Golden Gate International Exposition opened, 1939.
19 Astronomer Nicolaus Copernicus born 1473.
　—David Garrick, English actor, born 1717.
　—Edison patented the phonograph, 1878.
　—U.S. forces landed on Iwo Jima, 1945.
20 U.S. astronaut John H. Glenn, Jr., orbited the earth three times, 1962.
21 John Henry Cardinal Newman, British religious leader, born 1801.
　—Battle of Verdun began, 1916.
　—Richard M. Nixon became first U.S. President to visit China, 1972.
22 George Washington, first U.S. President, born in Westmoreland County, Va., 1732.
　—Philosopher Arthur Schopenhauer born 1788.

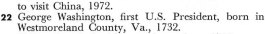

United Press Int.

22 James Russell Lowell, American poet, born 1819.
　—The United States bought the Florida territory from Spain, 1819.
　—Heinrich Rudolph Hertz, discoverer of radio waves, born 1857.
　—Boy Scout founder Robert Baden-Powell born 1857.
　—Edna St. Vincent Millay, American poet, born 1892.
23 Samuel Pepys, English diarist, born 1633.
　—Composer George Frideric Handel born 1685.
　—W. E. B. Du Bois, American civil rights leader, historian, and sociologist, born 1868.
　—Smith-Hughes Act passed, setting up the Federal Board of Vocational Education, 1917.
　—Amendment 25 to the U.S. Constitution, on presidential succession, proclaimed, 1967.
24 John Adams appointed first United States Minister to Great Britain, 1785.
　—Winslow Homer, American painter, born 1836.
　—Chester W. Nimitz, American admiral, born 1885.
25 José de San Martín, liberator of Argentina, Chile, and Peru, born 1778.
　—Painter Pierre Auguste Renoir born 1841.
　—Enrico Caruso, Italian singer, born 1873.
　—Amendment 16 to the Constitution, setting up the income tax, proclaimed, 1913.
26 Victor Hugo, French poet and novelist, born 1802.
　—Napoleon escaped from island of Elba, 1815.
　—American frontiersman William Frederick Cody, better known as "Buffalo Bill," born 1846.

Brown Bros.

27 Henry Wadsworth Longfellow, American poet, born 1807.
　—David Sarnoff, American radio executive, born 1891.
28 Ben Hecht, American author and newspaperman, born 1894.
　—Vincent Massey took the oath as the first Canadian-born governor general of Canada, 1952.
29 Marquis de Montcalm, French commander in Quebec, born 1712.
　—Gioacchino Antonio Rossini, Italian operatic composer, born 1792.

FECES. See ALIMENTARY CANAL; DIGESTION.

FEDERAL AVIATION ADMINISTRATION (FAA) is an agency in the U.S. Department of Transportation. It controls air traffic; certifies aircraft, airports, and pilots and other personnel; and operates navigation aids. The FAA writes and enforces air safety regulations and air traffic procedures. It requires airlines and airport operators to provide anti-hijacking security. The agency also conducts aviation research and promotes the safety and development of civil aviation. Its research and development services deal with air traffic, airway facilities, flight standards, logistics, security, and systems. Founded in 1958, the agency absorbed the Civil Aeronautics Administration, Airways Modernization Board, and safety rule-making functions of the Civil Aeronautics Board. An administrator appointed by the President directs the FAA.

Critically reviewed by FEDERAL AVIATION ADMINISTRATION

FEDERAL BUREAU OF INVESTIGATION (FBI) is the chief investigating branch of the United States Department of Justice. The FBI investigates more than 180 kinds of federal crimes, including bank robbery and kidnapping. It also collects evidence in lawsuits that involve the federal government. In addition, the bureau gathers *intelligence* (information) about individuals or groups that it believes are dangerous to national security. FBI investigators are called *special agents*.

A director, appointed by the President with the approval of the Senate, supervises the FBI from headquarters in Washington, D.C. The FBI has about 60 offices in the United States and Puerto Rico and 15 offices in other countries. It employs more than 19,000 men and women, of whom about 8,600 are special agents. It has an annual budget of about $450 million.

FBI Operations

Criminal Investigation. The FBI investigates such federal crimes as assault on the President, bank robbery, bombing, hijacking, and kidnapping. It handles cases involving stolen money, property, or vehicles that have been taken from one state to another. The bureau fights organized crime and, at the request of state or local authorities, it helps capture fleeing criminals. The FBI also examines reported violations of civil rights laws. In all criminal investigations, the FBI gives its findings to the Justice Department, which determines whether to take further action.

Intelligence Operations of the FBI consist of gathering information about individuals or organizations engaged in activities that may endanger national security. These operations include the investigation of rebellions, riots, spy activities, treason, and threats to overthrow the government. The FBI gives its reports to the President, Congress, or the Justice Department for action.

Other Services. The FBI provides various services to law enforcement agencies throughout the United States and in other countries. Such agencies may request help from the FBI Identification Division, the FBI Laboratory, and the National Crime Information Center (NCIC). The bureau also trains selected police officials in advanced methods of fighting crime.

The FBI Identification Division has the world's largest collection of fingerprints. Its files contain about 169 million prints. Police officials use these prints to identify over 40,000 suspects annually.

Federal Bureau of Investigation

The FBI National Academy in Quantico, Va., trains future agents in the use of firearms and other crime-fighting methods.

The FBI Laboratory is the finest crime laboratory in the world. FBI scientists examine over 600,000 pieces of evidence yearly, including bullets, handwriting samples, and tire prints. These experts testify in court if state or local authorities ask them to do so.

The NCIC is a computerized information system that stores almost 5 million records concerning criminal suspects and stolen property. A network of about 90 computer terminals links the NCIC with law agencies in the United States, Puerto Rico, and Canada. The NCIC daily handles more than 170,000 requests for information, or replies to questions.

The FBI issues an annual publication called *Uniform Crime Reports for the United States*, which includes a record of rates and trends in major crimes. The bureau also distributes a list with descriptions of its *Ten Most Wanted Fugitives*. The FBI National Academy at Quantico, Va., provides training in advanced methods of fighting crime for more than 5,000 police officials annually.

FBI Agents

Men and women who wish to be special agents must be U.S. citizens between 23 and 34 years old and in excellent physical condition. They must have a law degree or a degree in accounting. The FBI sometimes hires college graduates with special skills in such fields as investigation, language, or science.

Future agents go through a 15-week training program at the FBI National Academy. They study crime detection, evidence, constitutional and criminal law, and methods of investigation. They also learn self-defense and how to use firearms. Agents later receive periodic refresher training to keep them up to date.

History

In 1908, Attorney General Charles J. Bonaparte organized a group of special investigators in the Justice Department. This group, called the Bureau of Investigation, investigated such offenses as illegal business practices and land sales. Its first director was Stanley W. Finch, an attorney. J. Edgar Hoover, a Justice Department lawyer, became director of the bureau in 1924 and headed it until his death in 1972. Congress gave the bureau its present name in 1935.

A wave of bank robberies, kidnappings, and other violent crimes broke out in the United States during the 1930's. Congress passed laws giving the FBI increased authority to combat this lawlessness. FBI agents, who were nicknamed *G-Men*, or *Government Men*, became admired for tracking down such gangsters as John Dillinger and George "Machine Gun" Kelly.

During World War II (1939-1945), the FBI broke up enemy spy rings in the United States. In the 1950's and 1960's, special agents arrested Communist spies who had stolen secret atomic and military information. The bureau also investigated protest organizations in the 1960's and early 1970's. Clarence M. Kelley, a former special agent, became director of the FBI in 1973.

In 1975, a Senate committee reported that the FBI had acted illegally or improperly in a number of cases. The committee revealed that FBI agents had committed burglaries during some investigations and had spied illegally on U.S. citizens. The Senate investigators also charged that Hoover had given certain Presidents damaging personal information about some of their political opponents. In 1976, Kelley apologized for the FBI's past abuses of power. He said some of the bureau's activities under Hoover had been "clearly wrong and quite indefensible." The Justice Department set up guidelines to prevent further abuses by the FBI. William H. Webster, a federal judge, became director of the bureau in 1978.   GEORGE T. FELKENES

See also HOOVER, J. EDGAR; CRIME.

FEDERAL COMMUNICATIONS COMMISSION (FCC) is an independent agency of the United States government. The FCC was created in 1934 to centralize the regulation of U.S. interstate and foreign communication by radio, wire, and cable. It also regulates radio and television stations, without censorship authority.

The FCC (1) allocates bands of frequencies for different types of radio and television operations; (2) assigns specific frequencies, power, and call letters; and (3) issues licenses to stations and their transmitter operators. It also regulates the Communications Satellite Corporation, a private corporation that owns and operates the U.S. portion of the global satellite system. The FCC monitors radio broadcasts to detect unlicensed operations and technical violations, and to assist ships and planes in distress.

The FCC has about 2 million license- and permit-holders. They operate about 9 million transmitters in 70 categories of services. The transmitters are used for communication by aircraft, ships, land transportation services, police and fire departments, individuals, business and industry, AM, FM, and television broadcast services, and telephone and telegraph systems.

The FCC has seven members. The President of the United States appoints them for seven-year terms. The Senate approves the appointments. The President also names one commissioner as chairman.

Critically reviewed by FEDERAL COMMUNICATIONS COMMISSION

See also RADIO (Government Regulation); TELEVISION (Government Regulations); MONITORING STATION.

FEDERAL COURT. See COURT; UNITED STATES, GOVERNMENT OF THE (The Judicial Branch).

FEDERAL CROP INSURANCE CORPORATION (FCIC) is an agency of the U.S. Department of Agriculture. It offers farmers insurance against loss of crops because of such natural hazards as drought, flood, or freeze. Federal Crop Insurance does not guarantee a profit, nor does it cover losses that result from bad farming practices. The FCIC was created in 1938.

Critically reviewed by FEDERAL CROP INSURANCE CORPORATION

FEDERAL DEPOSIT INSURANCE CORPORATION (FDIC) insures the deposits of about 97 per cent of the banks in the United States. If an insured bank closes and is unable to pay its depositors, the FDIC pays the depositors up to $40,000 each. It also makes loans to reopen closed insured banks or to keep insured banks from closing. The FDIC has authority to examine all insured banks to make sure they are using safe banking practices. It also passes on bank mergers and acts on applications of nonmembers of the Federal Reserve System to change location or establish branches.

A board of three directors manages the FDIC. The President appoints two directors for six-year terms. The comptroller of the currency, who is appointed by the President, is an ex-officio member. The FDIC was created in 1933 to help end the banking crisis of the 1930's. Its funds come from assessments paid by insured banks and from earnings on United States government securities.   Critically reviewed by the

FEDERAL DEPOSIT INSURANCE CORPORATION

FEDERAL DISTRICT is a tract of land which a country sets apart as the seat of its national capital. The U.S. District of Columbia is a federal district. Other countries that have a federal district include Australia, Brazil, Malaysia, Mexico, and Venezuela. See also CANBERRA; MEXICO CITY; WASHINGTON, D.C.

FEDERAL ELECTION CAMPAIGN ACT OF 1971. See CORRUPT PRACTICES; ELECTION CAMPAIGN (Changes).

FEDERAL ELECTION COMMISSION is an agency of the United States government. The commission establishes and enforces the rules that govern campaign financing for election to federal offices. These rules include requirements to disclose campaign contributions and expenses, restrictions on the amounts any individual or group may contribute to a candidate, and prohibitions on the use of corporation or labor union funds for contributions. The commission also administers the public financing of presidential campaigns and national party nominating conventions.

The agency has the power to conduct investigations and audits of campaign funds. It serves as a national clearing house for information and research about the administration of elections.

The commission was established by Congress in 1974. It has six members who are appointed by the President, subject to the approval of the Senate. No more than three members may belong to the same political party.

Critically reviewed by the FEDERAL ELECTION COMMISSION

FEDERAL EMERGENCY RELIEF ADMINISTRATION. See NEW DEAL (Helping the Needy; table).

FEDERAL ENERGY ADMINISTRATION. See ENERGY, DEPARTMENT OF.

FEDERAL GOVERNMENT. See FEDERALISM.

FEDERAL HALL

FEDERAL HALL, in New York City, was the first Capitol of the United States under the Constitution. City Hall, the original building on the site, was erected in 1699. It also housed the Stamp Act Congress (1765), and the Congress of the Confederation from 1785 to 1789. On April 30, 1789, George Washington took the oath as President there. The present structure was built in 1842. Federal Hall became a national memorial in 1955. See also L'ENFANT, PIERRE C.   MARSHALL SMELSER

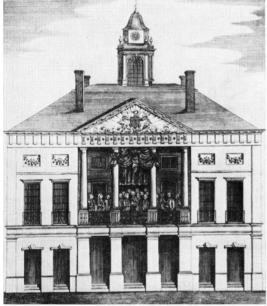

Engraving (1790) by Amos Doolittle; National Park Service
Federal Hall, New York. George Washington was inaugurated President on the balcony of this building in 1789.

FEDERAL HIGHWAY ADMINISTRATION (FHWA) is an agency of the United States Department of Transportation. It supervises federal aid for highway construction and improvement. This program involves about 900,000 miles (1,400,000 kilometers) of highways out of a total of 3,700,000,000 miles (5,950,000,000 kilometers) of roads and streets in the United States. The program costs billions of dollars annually.

The federal government pays 90 per cent of the cost of construction or improvement in the interstate highway system, and the states pay 10 per cent. For work involving state or local highways, the government pays 70 per cent and the states pay 30 per cent.

The FHWA, which is directed by an administrator appointed by the President, has offices in every state. Congress established the FHWA in 1966. The agency replaced the Bureau of Public Roads.

Critically reviewed by the FEDERAL HIGHWAY ADMINISTRATION

FEDERAL HOME LOAN BANK BOARD is an independent federal agency that supervises most savings and loan associations in the United States. It directs the Federal Home Loan Bank System, which provides credit to member institutions that issue mortgages. It also directs the Federal Savings and Loan Insurance

Corporation, which insures the savings of depositors in member associations for up to $40,000.

The board has three members, whom the President appoints to four-year terms. Nominees are subject to confirmation by the Senate. The board was created in 1932.   Critically reviewed by the FEDERAL HOME LOAN BANK BOARD

FEDERAL HOUSING ADMINISTRATION (FHA) is a U.S. government agency that works with private industry to provide good housing. The FHA insures mortgages on private homes, multifamily rental housing projects, cooperative and condominium housing, housing in urban renewal areas, housing for the elderly, and nursing homes. It also insures loans to improve property and to buy mobile homes, but does not normally lend money itself. The loans are made by banks, building associations, mortgage firms, and other approved lending institutions. The borrower applies to the lender for the loans. Most FHA operations are paid for by the agency's income from fees, insurance premiums on loans, and interest on investment of insurance reserves.

The FHA also determines minimum property standards for housing, analyzes local housing markets, and makes appraisals, land-planning surveys, and technical studies. Created in 1934, the FHA forms part of the Department of Housing and Urban Development. A commissioner heads the FHA and also serves as assistant secretary for housing.

Critically reviewed by FEDERAL HOUSING ADMINISTRATION

FEDERAL INTERMEDIATE CREDIT BANK. See FARM CREDIT ADMINISTRATION.

FEDERAL LAND BANK. See FARM CREDIT ADMINISTRATION.

FEDERAL MARITIME COMMISSION is an independent agency of the United States government that administers the nation's shipping laws. It regulates the rates, services, and agreements of U.S. shipping firms. It also regulates ocean freight forwarders and terminal operators.

The commission requires evidence of financial responsibility from owners and charterers of vessels that carry 50 or more passengers and that sail from U.S. ports. This policy ensures that the owners and charterers can pay any claims involving accidental injuries and deaths. It also ensures that they can refund fares if a voyage is canceled.

Owners, charterers, and operators of vessels that transport substances which can cause pollution also must prove financial responsibility. If one of their vessels spills such a substance onto U.S. waters or shores, they may have to pay to remove the pollutant.

The Federal Maritime Commission was established in 1961. The President appoints the commission's five members.   Critically reviewed by the FEDERAL MARITIME COMMISSION

FEDERAL MEDIATION AND CONCILIATION SERVICE (FMCS) is an independent agency of the United States government. It helps prevent or settle disputes between labor unions and management that affect interstate commerce. (Another government agency, the National Mediation Board, handles such disputes in the airline and railroad industries.) Mediation involves giving both sides in a dispute various solutions to consider in working for a compromise.

The law requires either management or a union to give 60-day notice of any intention to end or change a labor contract. If the employer and the union do not

The Federal Reserve System is the national banking system of the United States. The nation is divided into 12 districts, each with a Federal Reserve Bank. These banks issue Federal Reserve notes, which make up nearly all the paper money in circulation. A number on each note identifies the bank that issued it. The system also includes 25 Federal Reserve branch banks throughout the country.

★ Federal Reserve Bank

• Federal Reserve Branch Bank

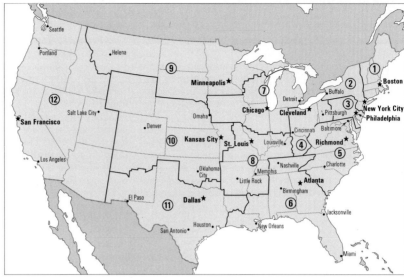

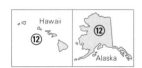

WORLD BOOK map

reach an agreement within 30 days after such a notice, they must notify the FMCS. The service then investigates the case and decides whether to intervene. In most disputes, the FMCS intervenes at the request of one or more of the opposing parties. But it may intervene in any dispute without such a request. The FMCS does not serve as a law enforcement or regulatory agency. It depends on persuasion.

The FMCS has about 250 mediators in 78 offices in principal industrial areas. The agency also maintains a roster of qualified private citizens who *arbitrate* (judge) labor-contract disputes (see ARBITRATION [Industrial, or Labor, Arbitration]). The FMCS was established under the Taft-Hartley Act of 1947.   Critically reviewed by the
FEDERAL MEDIATION AND CONCILIATION SERVICE

FEDERAL NATIONAL MORTGAGE ASSOCIATION (FNMA) is a private corporation chartered by the United States government. It helps assure that enough money is available to home buyers. The FNMA buys home mortgages from banks, savings and loan associations, mortgage companies, and insurance companies. It also sells mortgages to private institutions. These mortgages are insured or guaranteed by government agencies, such as the Federal Housing Administration (FHA) and the Veterans Administration (VA).

The FNMA was established in 1938 as a government-owned corporation and was placed under the Housing and Home Finance Agency in 1950. In 1954, the FNMA was reorganized as a corporation owned jointly by the government and private stockholders. It became a totally private corporation in 1970. The agency has the nickname "Fannie Mae."

Critically reviewed by the FEDERAL NATIONAL MORTGAGE ASSOCIATION

FEDERAL OPEN MARKET COMMITTEE. See FEDERAL RESERVE SYSTEM.

FEDERAL POWER COMMISSION. See ENERGY, DEPARTMENT OF.

FEDERAL RESERVE SYSTEM (FRS) is the central banking organization of the United States. Its most important job is to influence the flow of credit and money. Generally, if credit is plentiful, businesses can borrow money easily to expand, and consumers can obtain

money to buy such items as appliances and automobiles at lower interest rates. But too much credit, as well as too little credit, can hurt a nation's economy.

Organization. About 5,700 banks belong to the FRS. All national banks are required by law to belong. State banks may join if they meet certain requirements. Each member bank operates in one of 12 Federal Reserve districts covering the United States. Each district has a Federal Reserve Bank. There are also 25 Federal Reserve Bank branches within the districts (see map).

Member banks hold the stock of the Federal Reserve Banks, but they do not operate them. A nine-member board of directors supervises each Federal Reserve Bank. Each member buys a certain amount of the capital stock of the reserve bank in its district. The specific amount depends on the member's capital and surplus.

The FRS *Board of Governors* has general supervision over the system. The board consists of seven members. Each member is appointed by the President to a 14-year term, with the advice and consent of the U.S. Senate.

The *Federal Advisory Council* advises the board on general business conditions and makes recommendations to the board. The council consists of 12 members, one from each reserve district.

The *Federal Open Market Committee* consists of the seven members of the Board of Governors and five Federal Reserve Bank representatives. The committee establishes the FRS's open-market policy.

What the System Does. The Board of Governors has authority to set *reserve* requirements for member banks. These banks must set aside an established percentage of their deposits. A bank can use the rest of its money to make loans. By increasing or decreasing the reserve percentage, the FRS controls how much money banks can loan. This, in turn, influences such business activities as building homes or buying machinery for factories.

Through *open-market* operations, the FRS can reduce bank reserves by selling government securities. Checks issued to pay for these securities are usually drawn on member banks. When the checks are paid, the reserve that member banks must maintain is reduced. They

69

must replace this reserve with money they might otherwise loan. The system can increase bank reserves by buying government securities.

The FRS also influences credit conditions through the *discount rate*. This is the rate that banks must pay when they borrow money from Federal Reserve Banks. If the FRS increases the rate of discount, banks tend to charge customers higher interest rates.

In addition, the FRS sets *margin* requirements for the purchase of certain securities. The margin is the percentage of the price that must be put up in cash. Before margin requirements were established, purchasers sometimes bought large amounts of stock almost entirely on credit. This method of buying often led to dangerous speculation.

As the national clearing house for U.S. banks, the FRS handles trillions of dollars in checks yearly. The U.S. government uses the FRS as its bank.

The Board of Governors supervises the reserve banks, which examine state member banks to make certain they follow sound operating procedures. The board also regulates the maximum rate of interest the member banks may pay on deposits. The board acts on applications for membership submitted by state banks and trust companies. It regulates the activities of bank holding companies and sets regulations under the Truth in Lending Act, the Equal Credit Opportunity Act, and other consumer protection laws. The board also passes on the establishment of state member bank branches, and bank mergers that create state member banks. The board supervises the activities of member banks in other countries and also charters and regulates certain corporations engaging in international finance.

History. The FRS was established in 1913 when Congress passed the Federal Reserve Act. Previously, many banks had failed in each financial panic or business depression. The FRS enabled banks to borrow money temporarily to meet seasonal and sudden demands from depositors. A major FRS function was to improve bank supervision and credit conditions. The power to issue bank notes was also transferred from privately owned banks to Federal Reserve Banks.

Later legislation made many changes in the FRS, including changes in the organization of the Board of Governors. These laws also gave the FRS authority to set maximum interest rates and reserve requirements for member banks, and to set margin requirements. Critically reviewed by the FEDERAL RESERVE SYSTEM

See also BANKS AND BANKING; MONEY.

FEDERAL SAVINGS AND LOAN INSURANCE CORPORATION. See INVESTMENT (Savings Accounts); FEDERAL HOME LOAN BANK BOARD.

FEDERAL SECURITY AGENCY (FSA). See HEALTH, EDUCATION, AND WELFARE, DEPARTMENT OF (History).

FEDERAL SYSTEM. See FEDERALISM.

FEDERAL TRADE COMMISSION (FTC) is an independent U.S. government agency that works to (1) maintain free and fair competition in the economy and (2) protect consumers from unfair or misleading practices.

The FTC issues *cease and desist orders* against companies or individuals that it believes engage in unlawful practices. The firms or persons must then stop such practices unless a court decision sets aside the orders.

The FTC also issues trade regulation guides for business and industry and conducts a wide variety of consumer-protection activities. Congress created the FTC in 1914. The President appoints the five FTC commissioners, subject to Senate approval, to seven-year terms.

Critically reviewed by the FEDERAL TRADE COMMISSION

See also MONOPOLY AND COMPETITION (History).

FEDERALISM is a system in which political power is divided between a *central* (national) government and smaller governmental units. The central government is often called the *federal government*, and the smaller units, *states* or *provinces*. The division of powers is usually defined in a constitution. The United States, Canada, Australia, and Switzerland have federal systems. To a degree, so do Mexico and India.

Federal systems of government differ from *unitary* systems. In a unitary system, the central government holds the principal powers. States or provinces have only those powers that the central government gives them. Some nations that appear to use the federal system really use the unitary system. Their provinces are administrative units rather than political units with separate powers. Russia outwardly has a federal system, but all countries that allow only one political party or are under military rule really use the unitary system.

In a true federal system, citizens owe their loyalty directly to the central government, even though they live in states or provinces. The central government has direct authority over the people concerning powers granted to it in the constitution. This feature distinguishes a federal system from a loose grouping of states, commonly called a *confederation*. ROBERT G. DIXON, JR.

See also GOVERNMENT; STATE GOVERNMENT; CANADA, GOVERNMENT OF; UNITED STATES, GOVERNMENT OF THE; and the Government sections of the countries mentioned. For a *Reading and Study Guide*, see *Federalism* in the RESEARCH GUIDE/INDEX, Volume 22.

FEDERALIST, THE, is a series of 85 letters written to newspapers by Alexander Hamilton, James Madison, and John Jay. The letters urge ratification of the Constitution. The letters sought to influence the New York ratifying convention. All except eight of the essays appeared during 1787 and 1788 under the signature "Publius." They appeared in the *Independent Journal*, a semiweekly New York newspaper. Hamilton wrote 51 of the essays, Madison 29, and Jay 5. The collected essays appeared in book form as *The Federalist*.

The Federalist authors used both logical argument and appeal to prejudice. They emphasized the weaknesses in the Articles of Confederation, the dangers in British sea power and Spanish intrigue, the desirability and need of a stronger central government, and the safeguards of the new Constitution.

The authors did not defend every point in the proposed Constitution. But they argued that it was the best document on which agreement could be reached. They asserted that the check and balance system of the Constitution would create a strong government and still protect the states' rights. The Federalist papers greatly influenced acceptance of the Constitution. They are still important in interpreting it. MARSHALL SMELSER

FEDERALIST PARTY was one of the first political organizations in the United States. The Federalists favored a strong central government.

After George Washington became President, a political division soon appeared between those who favored a strong federal government and those who opposed it. The Federalist Party developed under the leadership of Alexander Hamilton, Washington's secretary of the treasury. Hamilton believed that the Constitution should be loosely interpreted to build up federal power. He had aristocratic views and favored the interests of business. He wanted the new federal government on a sound financial basis, and sponsored a national bank.

Thomas Jefferson opposed Hamilton. Jefferson's followers called themselves Republicans. Historians often use the name Democratic-Republicans for Jefferson's party. The Democratic-Republicans believed that the Constitution should be strictly interpreted, and that the states and the citizens should retain as many of their powers and rights as possible. The Federalists controlled the national government until 1801, when Jefferson became President. They continued to oppose Democratic-Republican policies until their party broke up soon after the election of 1816.

The term *Federalists* also is used to indicate those persons who fought for the adoption of the Constitution in 1787 and 1788.   JOHN R. ALDEN

See also POLITICAL PARTY (Development of Parties in the United States); ADAMS, JOHN (Vice-President; Adams' Administration); ANTI-FEDERALISTS; DEMOCRATIC-REPUBLICAN PARTY; HAMILTON, ALEXANDER.

FEDERATION is a union of states in a government, or a union of organizations. Many federations of workers are listed in THE WORLD BOOK ENCYCLOPEDIA under the key word in the name of the federation, such as MUSICIANS, AMERICAN FEDERATION OF.

FEE, in modern law, describes the kind of ownership that may pass to an owner's heirs on his or her death. A *fee simple absolute* is complete ownership of land. A *fee simple determinable* is ownership that is automatically lost if the property is used in a way prohibited by the previous owner. A *fee simple conditional* gives the previous owner a choice of whether to retake land used in a certain way. A *fee tail* is ownership that must pass in a certain way, as from father to eldest son. The term *fee,* or *fief,* also referred to the method of owning land under the English feudal system. A fief was also the piece of land that a lord granted to a servant in return for certain services (see FEUDALISM).   ROBERT E. SULLIVAN

FEE SIMPLE. See ESTATE; FEE.

FEED, LIVESTOCK. Livestock feed is a general term for food given to farm animals. *Roughage feeds* (coarse foods) include soybeans, cowpeas, and pasture plants such as grass and alfalfa. Some of these plants are dried and fed to livestock as hay. Farmers often preserve whole corn plants and other crops, and use them as a feed called *silage*. Grains of corn, grain sorghum, or barley can be ground and mixed with other ingredients to make another kind of feed. Farmers give livestock extra and unused products from milling, brewing, meat packing, and other industries. Farmers give animals a combination of feeds to make sure the livestock get the nutrients necessary for good health.   ALLEN D. TILLMAN

Related Articles in WORLD BOOK include:

Alfalfa	Cotton (Uses)	Hay
Cattle (Feeding)	Dairying (Feeding)	Hog (Raising Hogs)
Chicken (Food)	Grain	Silo
Corn (Uses)	Grass	Soybean

FEEDBACK. See AUTOMATION; CYBERNETICS.

FEEDING STATION. See BIRD (How to Attract Birds).
FEELER. See ANTENNAE (picture).

FEELING is a part of consciousness that some psychologists consider separate from will or knowledge. Early philosophers believed that the mind was divided into three *faculties* (powers) known as *feeling, intellect,* and *will.* They defined feeling as the emotional effect that any mental or physical activity produced upon a person. A person might feel good or bad about any given thing, and the feeling might be pleasant or unpleasant. But a person always *feels*.

Modern psychologists have discarded the general term *feeling*, because they cannot define feelings and cannot study them objectively. This is chiefly because feelings cannot clearly be distinguished from emotions. Some psychologists describe emotions as strong feelings (see EMOTION).

Generally we experience feelings of pleasure and displeasure in connection with sensations. For example, it is the sensing that the candy tastes pleasant that is the feeling. We may call this reaction to the sensation of taste a feeling.

The word feeling is sometimes used to describe the total consciousness of a number of separate physical sensations, such as a feeling of good health or a feeling of drowsiness.   FRANK J. KOBLER

See also AMBIVALENCE.

FEET. See FOOT.

FEININGER, *FY nihng uhr,* **LYONEL** (1871-1956), was an American painter whose works combine qualities found in cubism and expressionism. The subject matter of his mature work is based on nature, and is charac-

Oil painting; Neue Staatsgalerie, Munich, Germany

Feininger's *The Market Church in Halle* shows how the artist used straight lines to divide forms and space into flat planes.

terized by flat crystalline planes of color and thin straight lines.

Feininger was born in New York City. His parents were musicians. In 1887, he went to Germany to join his parents, who were on tour. Feininger stayed in Europe and was a political and satirical cartoonist in Berlin and Paris from 1894 to 1908. He then turned to painting and soon earned an international reputation for his work while living in Germany. In 1919 Feininger became the first professor chosen by Walter Gropius for the Bauhaus school of art and design in Germany. He returned to the United States in 1937, after the Nazis labeled him a "degenerate artist."   GEORGE EHRLICH

See also BAUHAUS.

FEISAL. See FAISAL.

FEKE, *feek,* **ROBERT** (1705?-1750?), was the earliest noteworthy American-born painter. He was one of the first of many persons born in America who, in spite of little encouragement or training, painted memorable works that captured the faith, dignity, and spirit of early Americans. His *Portrait of Isaac Royall and His Family* is reproduced in the article COLONIAL LIFE IN AMERICA.

Feke was born in Oyster Bay, Long Island, N.Y. Little is known about his life. By 1741 he was established as a portrait painter in Boston. He was married in 1742 in Newport, R.I., where he lived until 1750. In 1744, a visiting Scot wrote in his journal that he had met Feke. The Scot described Feke as "the most extraordinary genius ever I knew for he does pictures tolerably well by force of genius, never having had any teaching."   EDWARD H. DWIGHT

FELDSPAR is the most abundant mineral in the rocks at and near the earth's surface. This group of minerals usually occur as glassy white, reddish, bluish, or greenish crystals. All feldspars contain aluminum and silica, but the varieties differ in the amounts and kinds of other elements that are present. *Microcline, orthoclase,* and *sanidine* are called *alkali feldspars.* They contain sodium and potassium in various amounts. Green microcline, also known as *Amazone stone* is a feldspar that can be cut and polished to make ornaments. *Moonstone* is a milky translucent alkali feldspar that people treasure as a gem.

Minerals in the *plagioclase* group contain sodium and calcium. *Labradorite* is a kind of plagioclase that sometimes shows a beautiful display of colors when light strikes it. Architects use plates of rock containing such crystals to ornament buildings. The rock can also be made into decorative objects such as paperweights.

Rocks containing feldspar *weather* (decompose) when they are exposed to the atmosphere. They break down into other minerals, especially the clay minerals. Much of the potassium is held in the weathered rocks and in the soil. These rocks are the chief source for the potassium which all plants need for growth.

Pottery manufacturers use much feldspar. They use the clay materials formed by weathered feldspar to make porcelain and glass. *Kaolin,* the most important of these clays, is the chief material used in making high-grade chinaware (see KAOLIN).

Feldspar is mined almost entirely from bodies of *pegmatite,* a special kind of rock containing large crystals of quartz and feldspar. In the United States, feldspar is mined in California, Connecticut, North Carolina, and South Carolina.   ERNEST E. WAHLSTROM

See also GRANITE; HARDNESS; IGNEOUS ROCK; MOONSTONE.

FELIBRIGE. See MISTRAL, FRÉDÉRIC.

FELICIANA COUNTRY. See LOUISIANA (Places to Visit).

FELLAHIN. See EGYPT (Village Life).

FELLER, BOB (1918-   ), became the strike-out king of baseball during 18 seasons with the Cleveland Indians. His blazing fast ball won him the nickname *Rapid Robert.* He pitched three no-hit games, and set a season strike-out record of 348 in 1946. Sandy Koufax broke the record in 1965. Robert William Andrew Feller was born in Van Meter, Iowa. He joined the Indians after finishing high school. In 1962, he was elected to baseball's Hall of Fame.   ED FITZGERALD

FELLINI, FEDERICO (1920-   ), is one of the world's most famous motion picture directors. He originates his own ideas for his movies, usually developing the story as the film is being made. His films often blend realism and social satire with fantasy. His use of symbolism and dreamlike scenes makes his movies difficult for many people to understand. Fellini's artistic effects and imaginative use of images have won him praise.

Fellini was born in Rimini, Italy, and first gained recognition in the 1940's as a screenwriter. He directed his first motion picture, *Variety Lights,* in 1950. His first international success was *La Strada (The Road,* 1954). This grimly realistic, yet poetic, film describes the relationship between a brutal circus strongman and a half-witted young girl. *La Dolce Vita (The Sweet Life,* 1959) is a complex study of moral corruption in present-day society. In $8\frac{1}{2}$ (1963) and *Juliet of the Spirits* (1965), Fellini used deeply symbolic dream sequences to explore inner emotions. Fellini's *Amarcord* won the 1974 Academy Award as best foreign film. Fellini's other major motion pictures include *I Vitelloni* (1953) and *Nights of Cabiria* (1957).   ARTHUR KNIGHT

FELLOWSHIP is a sum of money given to scholars so they can continue their studies. Some fellowships are for specified periods of time, but others are for life. Fellowships have been made since the Middle Ages.

Today, fellowships are usually given by universities, foundations, corporations, and governments. Universities give fellowships for graduate work. Sometimes fellows teach classes. Foundations give fellowships for graduate study and individual research in such areas as adult education, medicine, and international relations. Large foundation fellowship programs in the United States include those of the American Council of Learned Societies, the General Electric Foundation, the John Simon Guggenheim Memorial Foundation, the Social Science Research Council, and the Woodrow Wilson National Fellowship Foundation. Corporation fellowships often encourage study and research in fields of interest to the sponsoring corporation. The federal government's Department of Health, Education and Welfare awards fellowships to educate teachers. The government conducts other fellowship programs through the National Foundation on the Arts and the Humanities, and the National Science Foundation.

In the United States, fellowships are usually granted for one or two years. The amount of money given may vary from a few hundred to several thousand dollars. In Great Britain, the grants are often given for three to five years. JOSEPH C. KIGER

See also FOUNDATIONS; SCHOLARSHIP.

FELONY, *FEHL uh nee,* is a crime for which punishment is death or imprisonment for a year or more. Felonies include murder, robbery, burglary, kidnaping, treason, and certain other serious crimes. A violation of law less serious is called a *misdemeanor* and is punishable by a fine or jail sentence (see MISDEMEANOR).

The person directly injured by a felony may sometimes agree not to prosecute in return for some payment or other valuable consideration. For example, a person may promise not to prosecute a thief who gives back the stolen goods. This is called *compounding a felony* and is a crime punishable by fine or imprisonment. FRED E. INBAU

See also BURGLARY; ROBBERY.

FELS, SAMUEL SIMEON (1860-1950), was an American civic leader, industrialist, and philanthropist. He helped establish such Philadelphia civic agencies as the Philadelphia Bureau of Municipal Research and the Crime Prevention Association of Philadelphia. He also established the Samuel S. Fels Fund (see FELS FUND, SAMUEL S.). With his father and brother, Fels founded Fels and Company, the maker of Fels-Naphtha soaps, in 1881. In 1933, Fels published *This Changing World.* He was born in Yanceyville, N.C. SYLVESTER K. STEVENS

FELS FUND, SAMUEL S., was established in 1936 by Samuel S. Fels, an American industrialist. The purpose is "the furtherance of scientific, educational or charitable projects to improve human life."

Fels, who died in 1950, desired that the fund be used within 40 years of his death. But there is no legal obligation to do this. Most grants are made to support major projects of the fund, such as the Fels Research Institute for the study of Human Development, the Fels Research Institute at Temple University, and the Fels Center of Government at the University of Pennsylvania. Some grants are also made to social and civic projects. The offices are at 2 Penn Center Plaza, Philadelphia, Pa. 19102. Critically reviewed by the SAMUEL S. FELS FUND

FELSITE. See ROCK (Extrusive Rocks).

FELT is a fabric made of wool fibers or animal hair matted together by steam and pressure. Felt varies greatly in weight, thickness, and value. Manufacturers use felt to make hats, chalkboard erasers, rug pads, slippers, and billiard-table covers. Felt is usually made 72 inches (183 centimeters) wide. See also BAIZE; HAT (Hat Production and Distribution).

FEMININE GENDER. See GENDER.

FENCE. Many types of fences are used to enclose land, mark boundaries, keep in animals, insure privacy, or add a decorative touch to homes. In farm areas, fences protect valuable crops from destruction by roaming animals. Temporary snow fences stand along highways to prevent drifting snow from blocking traffic.

Stone Fences. Persons living in rocky areas often mark boundaries with low stone fences that are made by simply piling stones one on top of another. Some persons use stone fences to add a rustic note to their gardens.

Wire Fences. Wire is used in many ways to make fences. *Barbed wire* ranks as an extremely effective and economical means of fencing off large areas (see BARBED WIRE). *Wire mesh* serves well for small enclosures for animals. A strong *chain link* fence withstands winds of great strength. These are made of heavy woven steel wire supported by steel posts. *Electrified* fences are sometimes used in prisons, on farms, and in other places where protection is needed. See WIRE (Uses of Wire).

Wood Fences. *Brush* or *deadwood* formed the earliest type of fences. These were simply brush and tree limbs cleared from the land and piled up to make an obstacle. The more carefully built *zigzag* or *Virginia rail* fences developed from this. These consist of *rails,* or split logs, placed one above the other at an angle. The *post and rail* fence resembles short, wide ladders placed side by side. Poles placed at intervals support horizontal rails. *Solid board* fences can be made easily by adding boards to the post and rail type.

Picket fences, made of narrow slats in a variety of patterns, can be purchased already cut. The *woven* picket fence consists of thin pieces of wood wired together. Interesting *basket weave* fences are made by weaving wooden strips through a framework of posts and spacers. The *lattice* fence has x-shaped wooden strips set within panels. Modern *louver* fences have vertical or horizontal boards set at an angle with spaces between them. The *English hurdle* fence resembles racing hurdles.

Wooden fence posts should be treated with a preservative, such as creosote, to prevent rotting (see CREOSOTE). Some lumber firms sell fence posts already treated.

FENCING is skillful swordplay. When quarrels were settled by dueling with swords, fencing was a necessary part of every gentleman's training (see DUEL). It first

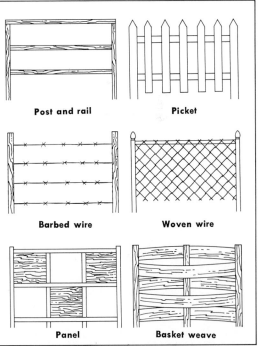

Post and rail   Picket

Barbed wire   Woven wire

Panel   Basket weave

WORLD BOOK illustration

Different Types of Fences can be used for practical or decorative purposes. The post and rail and picket fences form attractive backgrounds for shrubs and flowers. Barbed wire has been used to fence western cattle ranges since the 1870's. Woven wire makes sturdy animal pens. A panel fence serves as a windbreaker, and the basket weave type screens unsightly views.

French
Foil Grip

Belgian
Foil Grip

Italian
Foil Grip

French
Épée Grip

Hungarian
Saber Grip

Area of
Outside
Highline

Area of
Inside
Highline

Area of
Outside
Lowline

Area of
Inside
Lowline

**DEFENSIVE
AREAS OF
VALID TARGET**

WORLD BOOK photos
by E. F. Hoppe

became a sport in the mid-1700's. Today, it is a well-developed sport that requires muscular coordination and a thorough knowledge of technique and tactics.

It is a sport in the Olympic Games. More than 65 countries belong to the International Fencing Federation. In the United States, the Amateur Fencers League of America, founded in 1891, conducts sectional and national championships. Fencing is taught at most colleges, and intercollegiate championships are held each year.

Fencing Rules. The object in fencing is to touch the opponent on a certain part of the body and to avoid being touched. Three weapons, each with its own rules, may be used by men. These are the foil, the épée, and the saber. Women's fencing is limited to the foil.

The *foil* is the original fencing weapon. It has a four-sided, flexible blade and a circular guard for the hand. It weighs about 17 ounces (482 grams), and is about 43 inches (109 centimeters) long. Foil touches can be scored only by touching the target with the blunted point. The target in foil fencing is limited to the trunk of the opponent's body. The rules provide a regular sequence of play. The fencer who attacks has the "right of way" until the defender *parries*, or defends against a thrust. Then the defender has the right of way. If each fencer touches the other, only the first touch counts. If both are hit at about the same time, only the touch that has the right of way counts.

The *épée* is the fencing counterpart of the dueling sword. It is the same length as the foil, but may weigh up to 27 ounces (765 grams). Its rigid, three-sided blade ends in a pronged or burred tip (*pointe d'arrêt*). A large, circular guard protects the hand. There is no right of way in épée. If both fencers are touched at the same time, both touches count. The target includes any point

Guard

Lunge

on the body. Touches can only be made with the blade tip.

The *saber* has a flat, thin blade, and is about the same length and weight as the foil. The hand guard curves around the hand to protect the knuckles against cuts. Touches are scored either with the blade's point or the cutting edges. The target includes any part of the body except the legs. The rules of play are similar to foil rules.

Fencers must wear a strong wire-mesh mask with a cloth bib, a jacket and trousers of closely-woven material, and a glove for the weapon hand. Five touches are necessary to win a men's bout, and four for women. The bouts take place on a playing area that is 40 to 60 feet (12 to 18 meters) long and 3 to 6 feet (0.9 to 1.8 meters) wide. Courtesy in combat is part of the rules. Matches are judged by a director and touches are scored by four judges. An electrical device indicates touches in most foil and épée matches. It includes cables that connect each fencer to a buzzer, a bell, and one or two lights.

Method of Fencing. The technique of swordsmanship is based on precision, speed, timing, and distance. The fencing attack must coordinate hand- and footwork, with a minimum of wasted motion. To *parry*, the defender blocks or beats off the incoming thrust with the strong part of the blade. The defender's immediate

Touché

ÉPÉE

SABER

Parry   Head Cut

daytime. At night, they seek such food as birds and birds' eggs, insects, lizards, rodents, and various bulbs and fruits. Fennecs have pale reddish-orange, sandy, or white fur. The tail has a black tip. A fennec weighs about 3½ pounds (1.6 kilograms). Its exceptionally large ears may grow as long as 6 inches (15 centimeters). Fennecs live in family groups.

Scientific Classification. The fennec belongs to the dog family, *Canidae*. It is a member of the genus *Fennecus*, species *F. zerda*.   E. LENDELL COCKRUM

See also Fox (Fennecs).

Arthur H. Fisher

The Fennec Is a North African Fox Noted for Huge Ears.

counterattack, the *riposte*, follows the parry. Every attack can be avoided or parried if the defender has time enough to react. Thus, success depends on split-second speed, fractions of an inch in distance, and sound tactical judgment.   MIGUEL A. DE CAPRILES

FÉNELON, *fain LAWN*, **FRANÇOIS DE SALIGNAC DE LA MOTHE-** (1651-1715), was a French author and a Roman Catholic archbishop, known for his advanced political, social, and educational ideas. Fénelon's *Treatise on the Education of Girls* (1687) shows his keen understanding of child psychology. His best-known work is *Telemachus* (1699), a novel written to instruct the Duke of Burgundy, grandson of King Louis XIV. The book is about a young man who observes the governments of many countries. It was intended to teach the duke the duties of high office. Fénelon's criticism of absolute monarchy was implied in *Telemachus* and clearly stated in a *Letter to Louis XIV*, published after Fénelon's death. In *Maxims of the Saints* (1697), Fénelon favored *quietism*, a religious movement that denied the value of conventional religious practices. The church condemned the *Maxims*, and Fénelon lost his influence in religious and court life. Fénelon was born at Périgord. He was ordained about 1675 and was appointed Archbishop of Cambrai in 1695.   JULES BRODY

FENIAN MOVEMENT was a struggle by Irish nationalists to free Ireland from English rule. In the late 1850's, a group of Irish patriots called *Fenians* began to plan a revolution to achieve independence. The Fenians took their name from the *Fianna*, a band of mythical Irish warriors.

Most Fenians belonged to a secret society called the Irish Republican Brotherhood (IRB), which was founded in the United States in 1858. In 1866 and 1867, the Fenians attacked police stations in Ireland and set off bombs in England. But the English authorities put down the rebellion and imprisoned hundreds of suspected rebels.

Many people who had emigrated from Ireland to the United States supported the Fenians. In the late 1860's, Irish-American Fenians staged three unsuccessful raids on Canada, a member of the British Empire. They hoped to take over Canada and hold it as a "hostage" to force England to grant Ireland independence.

The Fenian goal of independence through revolution was adopted by later Irish republican movements. Ireland became independent in 1921, after several years of guerrilla warfare.   L. PERRY CURTIS, JR.

FENNEC is a small fox that lives in the deserts of North Africa and Arabia. Fennecs rest in burrows in the

FENNEL is a perennial plant related to parsley. It grows wild in southern Europe. Botanists cultivate fennel throughout the United States and in various parts of Europe. Finely divided fragrant leaves grow on the plant. The fennel plant also has fragrant seeds which have a licorice taste. People use both leaves and seeds to flavor medicines, liqueurs, candy, and foods. Oil of fennel, which is made from the seeds, is used in soaps and perfumes. The United States imports about 300,000 pounds (140,000 kilograms) of fennel seeds every year. Writers often referred to the fennel plant as a symbol of strength and valor.

Fennelflower is the name of a group of plants related to the buttercup. These plants grow in the Mediterranean region and in western Asia. The wrinkled black or brown seeds of one variety of fennelflower serve as seasoning for breads and pastries.

Scientific Classification. Fennel belongs to the parsley family, *Umbelliferae*. It is genus *Foeniculum*, species *F. vulgare*. Fennelflower is in the crowfoot family, *Ranunculaceae*. It is *Nigella hispanica*.   HAROLD NORMAN MOLDENKE

J. Horace McFarland

Fennel

FEPC. See Fair Employment Practices.

FERBER, EDNA (1885-1968), an American novelist and playwright, wrote many books about the colorful American life of the 1800's. She won the 1925 Pulitzer prize for fiction for her first best-selling novel, *So Big* (1924). She also wrote *Show Boat* (1926), *Cimarron* (1930), *Saratoga Trunk* (1941), *Giant* (1952), and *Ice Palace*

Doubleday
Edna Ferber

(1958). *Show Boat* was made into a popular musical comedy, and all of these books became successful motion pictures. She said that she intended her books to be social criticism as well as good stories. Her other novels include *Dawn O'Hara* (1911), her first book; *The Girls* (1921); and *Come and Get It* (1935). *Roast Beef, Medium* (1913) is a collection of stories. She had considerable success with the plays she

wrote with George S. Kaufman. The best known of these are *The Royal Family* (1927), *Dinner at Eight* (1932), and *Stage Door* (1936).

Ferber was born in Kalamazoo, Mich., but grew up in Appleton, Wis. Her first ambition was to be an actress. But at 17, when her father went blind, she took a newspaper job with the *Appleton Daily Crescent*. She told her life story in two books, *A Peculiar Treasure* (1939) and *A Kind of Magic* (1963). Arthur Mizener

FER-DE-LANCE, *fair duh LAHNSS*, is one of the largest and deadliest of the poisonous snakes. It lives in tropical North and South America. It has velvety scales, marks of rich brown and gray, and a yellowish throat. The fer-de-lance lives in both wet and dry places, in forests as well as open country. It eats birds and small animals. There may be over 60 young snakes in one brood. The baby snakes are about 1 foot (30 centimeters) long. They have fully formed fangs at birth, and can give a poisonous bite. A fer-de-lance strikes swiftly. The snake may grow to be 8 feet (2.4 meters) long. Its

Nature Magazine
The Deadly Fer-de-Lance lives in the Americas, from tropical Mexico to the northern edge of the Amazon Basin.

name is French and means *lance head*. See also Viper.

Scientific Classification. The fer-de-lance belongs to the pit viper family, *Crotalidae*. It is a member of genus *Bothrops*, and is species *B. atrox*. Clifford H. Pope

FERDINAND was the name of three Holy Roman emperors. Ferdinand I (1503-1564) was the brother of Charles V and became emperor in 1556. Ferdinand II (1578-1637), the grandson of Ferdinand I, ruled during the Thirty Years' War. He failed in his attempt to stamp out Protestantism in north Germany. His son, Ferdinand III (1608-1657), was the emperor at the close of the war. He delayed, but finally signed the Peace of Westphalia in 1648. See also Holy Roman Empire; Hapsburg; Thirty Years' War. Robert G. L. Waite

FERDINAND I, king of Bulgaria. See Boris III.

FERDINAND I, king of Romania. See Romania.

FERDINAND I, king of the Two Sicilies. See Bourbon (In Naples); Sicilies, Kingdom of the Two.

FERDINAND V (1452-1516), king of Castile and Aragon, married his cousin, Isabella I, in 1469. This marriage led to the unification of Castile and Aragon, Spain's two largest kingdoms (see Isabella I). The two rulers increased Spain's power by conquering the Moors in 10 years of war and by sending Christopher Columbus to America. After Isabella's death in 1504, Ferdinand added Naples and the province of Navarre to his kingdom. He was also known as Ferdinand II of Aragon and Sicily, and as Ferdinand III of Naples. He was born in Sos, Aragon. Franklin D. Scott

See also Castile and Aragon; Spain (History).

FERDINAND, ARCHDUKE. See World War I (Death of an Archduke; picture).

FERLINGHETTI, *fir lin GET tee,* **LAWRENCE** (1919-), is an American poet who was a major figure in the *beat* literary movement of the 1950's. Beat writers rebelled against what they felt was the use of outmoded forms in literature. Ferlinghetti's *A Coney Island of the Mind* (1958) registers less violent contempt for technique and order than did books by other beat writers. But he stresses the value of "risking absurdity" in life and art. By this, he means that people should try to free themselves from old-fashioned and conventional traditions in life and art. Ferlinghetti has also composed *oral messages* —poems to be spoken to jazz.

Ferlinghetti was born in Yonkers, N.Y. He publishes and sells the works of beat and *avant garde* (experimental) authors in his San Francisco book store and publishing company, City Lights. Mona Van Duyn

See also Ginsberg, Allen.

FERMAT, *fer MAH,* **PIERRE DE** (1601-1665), a French mathematician, won fame for his work in the theory of numbers or integers. He also shared in the invention of analytic geometry and calculus. He formulated the least-time law to explain the *diffraction* (bending) of light, and also developed an equation for the graph of a straight line. His "last theorem" has never been proved or disproved. Fermat knew integral solutions of the equation $x^2 + y^2 = z^2$ (for example, $3^2 + 4^2 = 5^2$). His theorem held that there was no whole number solution of $x^n + y^n = z^n$ if the exponent, n, is larger than 2. Fermat, along with Blaise Pascal, is credited with originating the theory of probability, now widely used in insurance and statistics (see Probability). Fermat practiced law in Toulouse and studied mathematics only as a hobby. He was born in Beaumont-de-Lomagne. Phillip S. Jones

FERMENTATION, *FUR mehn TAY shuhn,* is a change that takes place in animal or vegetable matter when certain chemicals called *ferments*, or *enzymes*, act upon it. Fermentation changes the chemicals which make up animal and vegetable matter, and also changes the taste, smell, and form.

Some examples of fermentation include the souring of milk, the ripening of cheese, the curing of silage, the change of apple juice to hard cider, and of the alcohol in hard cider to vinegar. The ferments which cause these changes are built up by the cells of plants and animals. Many come from bacteria and various other low forms of plants, such as molds and yeasts. Fermented foods include buttermilk, chocolate, and sauerkraut.

The action of yeast on bread dough is a useful kind of fermentation. The ferment from the yeast changes the starch in the flour to sugar. It then breaks down the sugar into carbon dioxide gas and alcohol. The gas forms bubbles which honeycomb the mass of dough and puff it out until it *rises*.

Fermentation also aids in the digestion of food. The gastric juice of the stomach contains two ferments, *rennin* and *pepsin*. Rennin curdles milk, and pepsin softens the albumen of food so it will dissolve in water and pass into the blood. When certain harmful bacteria enter into the stomach, the acid in the gastric juice can usually destroy them. But if for some reason the acid is too weak, these bacteria ferment the food and turn it sour. An attack of indigestion will result.

Fermentation helps growing plants. Plants get all their food from the ground and air. When a plant or animal dies, bacteria act on it and cause it to decay. In decay, the chemical compounds of its body are broken down into elements that return to the soil and air. Then living plants can use them over again. The breakdown of dead matter sometimes gives off bad odors, and the products may be poisonous. Scientists call this kind of fermentation *putrefaction*. Cold storage, freezing, smoking, and canning can prevent the action of putrefying bacteria on food.　　　GEORGE L. BUSH

Related Articles in WORLD BOOK include:

Alcoholic Drink	Digestion	Pasteurization
Bacteria	Enzyme	Refrigeration
Chemurgy	Food Preservation	Yeast
Decay	Mold	Yogurt

FERMENTED LIQUOR. See ALCOHOLIC DRINK; BREWING; WINE (How Wine Is Made).

FERMI, *FUR mee,* **ENRICO** (1901-1954), a physicist, designed the first atomic piles and produced the first nuclear chain reaction in 1942. He later worked on the atomic bomb project at Los Alamos, N.M. He won the 1938 Nobel prize in physics for his nuclear research, especially his theoretical work on nuclear processes. In 1943, he won the Hughes Medal of the Royal Society, the oldest scientific society in Great Britain.

Fermi began bombarding many elements with neutrons in 1934. He proved that slow neutrons are very effective in producing radioactive atoms. This discovery was particularly important, because slow neutrons can split U-235. As a result of these experiments, Fermi announced in 1934 what he thought were elements lying beyond uranium, not realizing that he had actually split the atom. Otto Hahn and Fritz Strassmann of Germany performed the same experiment in 1938. Lise Meitner and Otto Frisch proved that the uranium

atom had been split, and named the process *nuclear fission* (see MEITNER, LISE).

Fermi was born in Rome. He studied at the University of Rome, and received a doctor's degree from the University of Pisa in 1922. He became a professor of theoretical physics at the University of Rome in 1926. Fermi left Italy in 1938 to escape the Fascist regime, and settled in the United States. He became

University of Chicago Press
Enrico Fermi

a professor of physics at Columbia University in 1939. He moved to the University of Chicago as a professor of physics in 1942. Fermi led the work on the first nuclear chain reaction. After World War II, he pioneered in research on high energy particles. RALPH E. LAPP

See also NUCLEAR ENERGY (Development).

FERMI NATIONAL ACCELERATOR LABORATORY is a physics research laboratory near Batavia, Ill. Its name honors Enrico Fermi, the Italian-American physicist who produced the first nuclear chain reaction. Scientists from all over the world come to the laboratory to do research on mesons, neutrinos, protons, and other atomic particles.

The laboratory's main instrument is a particle accelerator, or atom smasher, called a *synchrotron*. The world's largest particle accelerator, it lies in an underground tunnel that forms a circle $1\frac{1}{3}$ miles (2 kilometers) in diameter. It accelerates protons almost to the speed of light. The accelerated protons reach an energy of up to 500 *giga* (billion) electron volts. Scientists direct a beam of protons at a target and study the result of the collision.

The United States Department of Energy pays for the operation of the Fermi National Accelerator Laboratory. Universities Research Association, Incorporated, a group of 53 universities in the United States and Canada, manages it.　　　FRANCIS T. COLE

See also PARTICLE ACCELERATOR; SYNCHROTRON; MESON; PROTON; ATOM (Neutrinos).

FERMIUM, *FUR mee uhm* (chemical symbol, Fm) is a man-made radioactive element. Its atomic number is 100. Its most stable isotope has a mass number of 257 (see ATOM [Atomic Weight]). Other isotopes have mass numbers ranging from 244 to 257. A team of American scientists led by Albert Ghiorso discovered fermium in 1953. They found the element in radioactive debris produced by the first hydrogen bomb explosion in 1952. Fermium was named for Enrico Fermi, the Italian-American nuclear physicist who produced the first controlled nuclear chain reaction (see FERMI, ENRICO).

Scientists produce fermium in the laboratory by bombarding lighter transuranium elements with charged nuclear particles, or by the capture of neutrons by these elements. No weighable amounts have been isolated and the chemical properties are not completely known to scientists.　　　GLENN T. SEABORG

See also ELEMENT, CHEMICAL; RADIOACTIVITY; TRANSURANIUM ELEMENTS.

Licorice fern

Five-finger fern

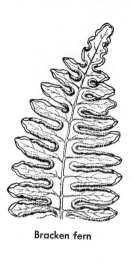

Bracken fern

California wood fern

FERN is a flowerless plant. Ferns are most commonly found in moist, shady woods among rocks and cliffs. They grow almost anywhere in the world. Some kinds grow in cold climates, even north of the Arctic Circle and on high mountains at altitudes over 15,000 feet (4,570 meters). Ferns are more common, however, in warm regions such as the tropics. There are about 10,-000 kinds of ferns. Approximately 300 varieties of ferns grow in the United States.

Ferns have many sizes and shapes. Some are so small that they look like moss, and others grow to be as large as trees. The large ferns of South America and the Pacific Islands may become 40 feet (12 meters) tall. They have thick, woody trunks with feathery crowns of large leaves. Many other tropical ferns have long stems which creep upward on tree trunks and grow high above the

ground. Botanists call these ferns air plants, or *epiphytes*. Air ferns get nourishment from the moist air and from decayed matter which collects on the bark of the trees. Still other ferns grow in ponds and lakes.

In most ferns, the leaves are the parts of the plant which people usually notice. The stem and roots usually grow underground. The leaves, called *fronds*, are large compared to the stem and have different forms. Some are shaped like hearts, or like long straps with smooth edges. Usually, the developing leaves are coiled at the top and are covered with brown scales.

The fern reproduces by means of spores and sex cells. Small, brownish cases contain the spores. They grow grouped in dots or lines on the backs or sides of the leaves. When the spores ripen, the cases burst open, and the spores fall to the ground. Each spore then de-

Fronds of a Cinnamon Fern unfold as they grow. Young fern fronds are covered with a thick coating of pale fuzz. They are tightly coiled, but gradually unwind during growth.

Spore Cases on a Fern Frond. Ferns have neither flowers nor seeds. Instead, they multiply by means of tiny spores, which the parent plant scatters from groups of spore cases like these.

California maidenhair

Chain fern

Gold fern

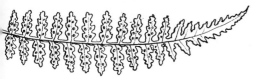

Silvery Spleenwort Grows in Rich, Moist Woods.

Lady fern

velops into a tiny green plant shaped like a heart. This plant is different from the original fern plant, and belongs to a different generation. This tiny plant develops special tissues which produce male and female sex cells. The male cell comes from an organ called the *antheridium*, which is comparable to the anther in flowers. Botanists call the female organ of the fern an *archegonium*. When the sex cells become mature, the male cell, or *antherozoid*, swims through the moisture on the plant to the female cell, and fertilizes the *egg*. Then the egg grows into the mature fern plant. Botanists call this process of reproduction in the fern the *alternation of generations*. The two generations are the large fern plant which produces spores, and the tiny fern plant which produces sex cells.

Ferns are hardy and will grow from year to year with little care. Many gardeners cultivate the Boston fern, maidenhair, and holly fern. Doctors use the oil from another kind called the *male fern*. The oil is helpful for treating diseases caused by worms in the digestive tract. Some people eat the stems of ferns.

Ferns flourished on earth thousands of years ago during the geological age known as the *Carboniferous Period*. Ferns supplied some of the vegetable matter which later formed the great coal deposits.

Scientific Classification. The ferns are divided into 12 families. The most common and widely distributed family is *Polypodiaceae*. It includes many genera such as *Pteridium* (the bracken), *Adiantum* (maidenhair), *Dryopteris* (woodferns), *Asplenium* (spleenworts), *Polypodium* (polypody), *Camptosorus* (walking-leaf), *Onoclea* (sensitive fern), and *Polystichum* (holly ferns). Some genera that belong to other families are *Trichomanes* (filmy fern), *Lygodium* (climbing fern), *Ophioglossum* (adder's-tongue), and *Botrychium* (rattlesnake fern).   ROLLA M. TRYON

See also AIR PLANT; FOSSIL (picture: A Split Rock); PLANT (pictures); SPORE.

Bureau of Insular Affairs

A Tree Fern of the Philippine Islands. Its rosette of leaves grows at the top of a strong, woody stalk like the trunk of a tree. Tree ferns are most common in damp mountainous regions in the tropics, where they may grow 40 feet (12 meters) high.

79

FERN-TREE JACARANDA. See JACARANDA.
FERNÁNDEZ, JUAN. See JUAN FERNÁNDEZ.
FERNÁNDEZ DE LIZARDI, JOSÉ JOAQUÍN. See MEXICO (Literature).
FERNANDINA. See GALAPAGOS ISLANDS.
FERNANDO PO. See EQUATORIAL GUINEA.
FERRARI. See AUTOMOBILE (picture: Sports Cars).
FERRET is a small, bold animal that is closely related to the weasel. The *common ferret* lives in Europe. Hunters there use it to drive rabbits and other animals from their holes. Ratcatchers sometimes use

N.Y. Zoological Society

The Black-Footed Ferret has a long neck and a slender body. It preys on prairie dogs, and may use one of their burrows as a nest.

trained ferrets. This ferret may be one of several colors but its eyes are usually pink. It grows about 12 inches (30 centimeters) long. Ferrets can be tamed, but they are not affectionate animals.

The *black-footed ferret* lives in the Great Plains of the United States and Canada. The number of black-footed ferrets has declined because people have turned grasslands into farms and killed off many prairie dogs, the chief food of the ferret. Many wildlife experts believe this ferret will soon become extinct. This ferret has a tan body, and its feet and the tip of its tail are black. Some black-footed ferrets live in prairie dog burrows.

Scientific Classification. Ferrets belong to the weasel family, *Mustelidae*. The common ferret is classified as genus *Mustela*, species *M. furo*. The black-footed ferret is *M. nigripes*.   ROBERT K. ENDERS.

FERRIS STATE COLLEGE. See UNIVERSITIES AND COLLEGES (table).

FERRIS WHEEL is an entertainment device used at fairs, carnivals, and amusement parks. Present-day Ferris wheels stand about 40 to 45 feet (12 to 14 meters) high and usually carry 12 to 16 two-person seats. A gasoline-powered engine turns the giant wheel.

The largest of all Ferris wheels was built by G. W. Gale Ferris, a mechanical engineer in Galesburg, Ill. Ferris built it for the World's Columbian Exposition

Chicago Historical Society

The Ferris Wheel at the World's Columbian Exposition in Chicago in 1893 was the largest ever built. Its 36 cars could carry 2,160 persons.

in Chicago in 1893. The wheel was 250 feet (76 meters) in diameter. Each of the 36 cars could hold 60 persons. This Ferris wheel was used at the St. Louis exhibition in 1904 and then was sold for scrap metal.

In 1900, William E. Sullivan began making Ferris wheels in Jacksonville, Ill. The company he founded, the Eli Bridge Company, is the largest maker of Ferris wheels. Accidents to Ferris wheels have been rare. The wheels can withstand winds of 60 miles per hour (97 kilometers per hour).   LEE A. SULLIVAN

FERROMANGANESE. See MANGANESE.

FERROUS ALLOY. See ALLOY (Alloys of Iron).

FERROUS SULFATE, *FEHR us SUL fayt* (chemical formula, $FeSO_4 \cdot 7H_2O$), is a substance which occurs in light-green crystals. It has a puckery taste and an unpleasant odor. It is also known as *green vitriol* and *copperas*. The crystals turn rusty brown if they absorb water from the air. Ferrous sulfate is an iron salt of sulfuric acid. It can be made by combining iron with sulfuric acid or by oxidizing *iron pyrites*, a compound of iron and sulfur. Ferrous sulfate is used to dye fabrics black, to make ink, and to purify water. It is also used as a disinfectant.

FERRY is a boat used to carry persons, vehicles, and freight across narrow bodies of water. Most ferries have

DPI

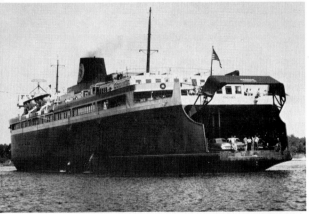

Chesapeake and Ohio R.R. Co.

Ferries carry persons, vehicles, and freight across rivers, lakes, bays, and other bodies of water.

a large opening at each end so they can be loaded and unloaded without being turned around.

People have used ferries for hundreds of years. Early ferries included rafts and small boats that were rowed, sailed, or moved by poles across water. Many ferries were guided by cables stretched between shores, and were pulled by ferry workers on the shore of destination. Some cable-guided ferries are pushed by motor boats. Most large ferries in use today are powered by their own engines.

Bridges over water and tunnels under water have replaced many ferries. Ferries still operating include those between Manhattan and Staten islands in New York, and between New Jersey and New York. ROBERT H. BURGESS

See also SHIP (Other Passenger Vessels).

FERRY, ELISHA PEYRE. See WASHINGTON (History [Statehood]).

FERTILE CRESCENT was a crescent-shaped region in Asia. It began at the Mediterranean Sea, stretched between the Tigris and Euphrates rivers, and ended at the Persian Gulf. In this area, the Sumerians developed one of the first great civilizations about 5,000 years ago. Archaeologist James H. Breasted named it the *fertile crescent* because these people and their successors created rich, irrigated farmlands. The Assyrian, Babylonian, Eblaite, Hebrew, Mitannian, and Phoenician civilizations also began there.   JOHN WILLIAM SNYDER

See also ASIA (History); SYRIA (introduction).

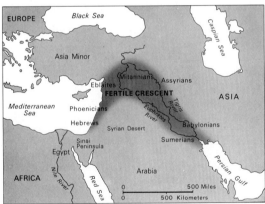

WORLD BOOK map

The Fertile Crescent was a historic region that curved around the Syrian Desert in Asia. The Sumerians built one of the world's first important civilizations there about 5,000 years ago. Other advanced ancient cultures also developed in the region.

FERTILITY DRUG. See MULTIPLE BIRTH.

FERTILIZATION, *FUR tuh luh ZAY shuhn*, is the process in which the male and female sex cells unite to form a new individual. The male sex cells, known as *spermatozoa*, in animals are produced in the male organs, or *testes*. The female sex cells, or *eggs*, are formed in the female gland, or *ovary*. In lower plants and animals, both male and female organs may be found on one individual. In higher animals and in some higher plants, however, the sexes are separate. Many animals which live in water discharge their eggs and sperm into the water. The sperm cells then swim about until they fertilize an egg. The *zygote* (fertilized egg) becomes a new animal.   George W. Beadle

Related Articles in World Book include:

Breeding
Embryo (Fertilization)
Flower (How Flowers Reproduce)
Germ Cell

Plant (How Plants Reproduce)
Pollen and Pollination
Reproduction
Sex

FERTILIZER is a substance that is added to soil to help plants grow. Farmers use various kinds of fertilizers to produce abundant crops. Home gardeners use fertilizers to raise large, healthy flowers and vegetables. Landscapers spread fertilizers on lawns and golf courses to help grow thick, green grass.

Fertilizers contain *nutrients* (nourishing substances) that are essential for plant growth. Some fertilizers are made from organic waste, such as manure or sewage. Others are manufactured from certain minerals or from synthetic compounds produced in factories.

Man has used fertilizer for thousands of years—even though he once did not know why it was good for plants. Long before he understood plant nutrition, he noticed that animal droppings, wood ashes, and certain minerals helped plants thrive. During the 1800's and early 1900's, scientists discovered that certain chemical elements were essential for plant nutrition.

Today, farmers throughout the world use billions of dollars worth of fertilizer yearly. Fertilized crops probably make up about a fourth of the world's total crop production. Crop yields would be much lower without fertilizer, and greater amounts of land and manpower would be needed to produce the same quantity of food and fiber.

The Importance of Fertilizer

Green plants produce the food they use for growth. They produce it by means of the process of photosynthesis (see Photosynthesis). To make this food, plants require large amounts of nine chemical elements—carbon, hydrogen, oxygen, phosphorus, potassium, nitrogen, sulfur, calcium, and magnesium. They also must have smaller amounts of several other elements. These elements, called *micronutrients* because so little of each is needed, include boron, copper, iron, manganese, molybdenum, and zinc.

Air and water provide most of the carbon, hydrogen, and oxygen that green plants need for growth. The other elements must come chiefly from the soil.

The elements plants receive from soil are normally provided by decaying plant and animal matter and dissolved minerals. But sometimes soil does not have enough of these substances, resulting in a need for fertilizer. The harvest of crops, for example, involves removing plants from the soil before they die and decay. The soil does not receive the mineral elements contained in the crops, and so fertilizer must be added to supply them. Nitrogen, phosphorus, and potassium are the elements in which soil is most frequently deficient. They are the main fertilizer elements.

Kinds of Fertilizers

There are two chief kinds of fertilizers, *mineral* and *organic*. Manufacturers produce mineral fertilizers from

certain minerals or synthetic substances. Organic fertilizers come from decayed plant or animal matter.

Mineral Fertilizers are the most widely used fertilizers. They supply three main elements: (1) nitrogen, (2) phosphorus, and (3) potassium.

Nitrogen Fertilizers, the most widely used mineral fertilizers, are produced mainly from ammonia gas. Manufacturers use ammonia in making such liquid fertilizers as anhydrous ammonia and aqua ammonia. They also use it in producing solid fertilizers, such as ammonium sulfate, ammonium nitrate, ammonium phosphate, and an organic compound called *urea*. Each of these fertilizers provides the soil with large amounts of nitrogen. Some of them, including ammonium sulfate and ammonium phosphate, furnish other elements as well.

Phosphorus Fertilizers, also called *phosphates*, are made from the mineral apatite. Finely ground apatite may be applied to soil as a solid fertilizer called *rock phosphate*. Apatite also may be treated with sulfuric acid or phosphoric acid to make liquid fertilizers called *superphosphates*.

Potassium Fertilizers come largely from deposits of potassium chloride. Manufacturers mine the deposits or extract them with water to produce such fertilizers as potassium chloride, potassium nitrate, and potassium sulfate.

Other Mineral Fertilizers provide soil with various elements. Those made from gypsum, for example, supply sulfur. Manufacturers also produce fertilizers that provide specific micronutrients.

Organic Fertilizers are made from a variety of substances, including manure, plant matter, sewage water, and packing house wastes. These fertilizers contain a smaller percentage of nutrients than do mineral fertilizers. Therefore, they must be used in larger quantities to obtain the same results. Some organic fertilizers may also cost more. But they solve a disposal problem because organic waste has few other uses than as fertilizer. Plant matter is used as fertilizer in two main ways, (1) as a compost pile or (2) as green manure.

A compost pile consists of alternate layers of plant matter and soil. Fertilizer mixed with lime is also usually added. The pile is allowed to decay for several months before being used as fertilizer. See Compost.

Green manure consists of certain crops that farmers use as fertilizer. For example, some plants have bacteria in *nodules* (knotlike growths) on their roots. These bacteria take nitrogen out of the air. Such plants, called *legumes*, include alfalfa, beans, and clover. Farmers may plant a crop of legumes and then plow the young plants into the soil. As the plants decay, nitrogen returns to the soil and enriches it for other crops.

The Fertilizer Industry

The United States manufactures more fertilizer than any other country. It produces about $5½ billion worth of fertilizer annually and exports about $680 million of it. About 95 per cent of the fertilizer produced in the world is used on farm crops.

Raw Materials for fertilizer come from several sources. Ammonia, the basic source of nitrogen fertilizer, is formed by combining nitrogen from the air with hydrogen from natural gas. Several U.S. oil firms produce ammonia because they have supplies of natural gas.

The United States has about 40 per cent of the

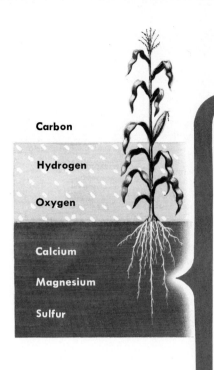

Carbon

Hydrogen

Oxygen

Calcium

Magnesium

Sulfur

Some Essential Elements for Plant Growth

Green plants need various chemical elements to grow and reproduce. Air and water supply carbon, hydrogen, and oxygen. The soil usually contains sufficient calcium, magnesium, sulfur, and micronutrients for plant growth. Additional nitrogen, phosphorus, and potassium are the most common needs that must be provided by fertilizers. The chief sources of these elements are listed below.

Nitrogen

Most nitrogen fertilizer is either liquefied ammonia or a product made from ammonia, such as ammonium sulfate or ammonium nitrate. Manure and other organic fertilizers also contain nitrogen.

Phosphorus

The mineral apatite is the chief source of phosphorus fertilizers. Apatite is sometimes finely ground and applied to the soil, but more often it is treated with acids to produce liquid fertilizers called superphosphates.

Potassium

Potassium chloride mined from mineral deposits is the chief potassium fertilizer. Other potassium fertilizers include potassium nitrate and potassium sulfate.

world's supply of phosphate rock. The main sources are in Florida, Idaho, Missouri, Montana, North Carolina, Tennessee, Utah, and Wyoming. Morocco and Russia rank as the chief suppliers after the United States.

The largest deposits of potassium chloride, the major source of potassium fertilizer, occur in Canada and Russia. Canada furnishes about 75 per cent of the potassium chloride used in the United States. Potassium chloride is mined in several states, including California, New Mexico, and Utah.

Production and Sale. Fertilizer is produced and sold in four basic forms. *Straight goods fertilizer* is any chemical compound that contains one or two fertilizer elements. *Bulk blend fertilizer* is a mixture of straight goods in certain proportions. *Manufactured fertilizer* consists of two or more chemicals that are mixed and then formed into small grains. Each grain contains nitrogen, phosphorus, and potassium and perhaps certain micronutrients. *Liquid fertilizer* consists of one or more fertilizer materials dissolved in water. It may be sprayed on plants or soil, injected into soil, or added to irrigation water.

Most fertilizers release their plant nutrients into the soil almost immediately. Manufacturers also produce a special type of fertilizer, called *slow-release fertilizer*, that gives up its nutrients gradually. This type has been found useful when plants need a constant supply of nutrients over a long period of time.

Problems of the Fertilizer Industry. Every year, large amounts of fertilizer must be produced to meet the world's growing need for food. The fertilizer industry tries to match its production with this need. If it does not do so, severe food shortages might result.

A shortage of raw materials could cause a low supply of fertilizer. Some materials, such as natural gas and phosphorus, have uses other than in making fertilizer. Their use by other industries could cause a shortage for fertilizer manufacturers.

The mining and processing of the raw materials needed to make fertilizer may damage the environment. Many minerals used in making fertilizer come from open-pit mines, which cause large unproductive areas unless properly landscaped. In addition, the excessive use of fertilizer can contribute to water pollution. For example, erosion may carry fertilized soil into lakes and streams. The nutrient elements in the soil then increase the growth of simple plants called *algae* in the water. When the algae die, they produce large amounts of waste. As the waste decays, it uses up the oxygen supply of the water.   FREDERICK R. TROEH

Related Articles in WORLD BOOK include:

FERTILIZER MATERIALS

Ammonia	Guano	Nitrogen
Anhydrous	Lime	Phosphate
Ammonia	Limestone	Phosphoric Acid
Ash	Manure	Phosphorus
Calcium	Marl	Potassium
Compost	Mulch	Sulfur
Dolomite	Nitrate	Urea

OTHER RELATED ARTICLES

Agricultural Education
Agriculture (New Agricultural Chemicals)
Agronomy
Eutrophication
Soil (Characteristics of Soil)
Water Pollution

O. M. Scott & Sons Co.

Alta Fescue Grass

FÈS. See FEZ (city).

FESCUE is the name of a group of grasses that grow in the United States and other temperate regions. Most fescue grasses tend to grow in tufts, or bunches. Fescue may grow to a height of 6 to 48 inches (15 to 122 centimeters) or more. Many perennial fescues serve as important foods for livestock in the grazing regions of the West. These include *Arizona fescue, Idaho fescue, greenleaf fescue,* and *Thurber fescue. Alpine fescue* is a variety of *sheep fescue* that grows above the timber line from the Rocky Mountains westward.

Farmers in humid areas of Tennessee, Missouri, and Kansas use *Kentucky 31* and *alta fescue* for hay and pasture. Sheep fescue and *red fescue* may be grown in lawns and pastures in the eastern United States. Creeping red fescue and *chewings,* a variety of red fescue, grow in a thick mat of fine leaves ideal for lawns.

Scientific Classification. The fescue grasses belong to the grass family, *Gramineae.* Arizona fescue is genus *Festuca,* species *F. arizonica.* Idaho fescue is *F. idahoensis;* greenleaf fescue, *F. viridula;* Thurber fescue, *F. thurberi.* Kentucky 31 and alta fescue are *F. arundinacea;* sheep fescue is *F. ovina;* and red fescue is *F. rubra.* WAYNE W. HUFFINE

See also GRASS.

FESSENDEN, REGINALD AUBREY. See RADIO (Early Development).

FESSENDEN, WILLIAM PITT (1806-1869), a United States senator from Maine, helped found the Republican Party in the 1850's. He served in the Senate from 1854 to 1864, and from 1865 to 1869. He was secretary of the treasury under Abraham Lincoln in 1864. Fessenden opposed slavery and favored harsh measures against the South after the Civil War. However, he voted "not guilty" at the impeachment trial of President Andrew Johnson in 1868. Johnson had opposed Congress' harsh treatment of the South. Fessenden was born in Boscawen, N.H. ROBERT M. YORK

FESTIVAL. See FEASTS AND FESTIVALS.

FESTIVAL OF LIGHT. See SWEDEN (Holidays).

FESTUS, PORCIUS. See PAUL, SAINT (Later Years).

FETID BUCKEYE. See HORSE CHESTNUT.

FETISH, *FEE tihsh,* or *FEHT ihsh,* is an object that supposedly has magic powers. Many peoples worship bones, carved statues, unusual stones, and other objects as fetishes. In some societies, people carry such fetishes as a rabbit's foot or a "lucky" penny to bring them good luck.

Europeans first learned about *fetishism* (the worship of fetishes) when Portuguese explorers colonized Africa during the late 1400's. Many African tribes had fetishes and treated them with great devotion and respect. Fetishism is a type of *animism,* the belief that lifeless things have a spirit (see ANIMISM). Fetish worshipers believe that the spirit protects them from evil and

Marc & Evelyne Bernheim, Woodfin Camp, Inc.

Fetishes, such as these two statues of the Mina tribe of Togo, supposedly have magic power because spirits live in them. A woman of the tribe gives these fetishes food. She believes they are inhabited by the souls of her twins who died in infancy.

brings good luck. A fetish may become an *idol,* the image of a god, if word of its power spreads beyond the tribe (see IDOL).

Psychiatrists use the term *fetishist* for a person who has an abnormal sexual attachment for a lifeless object. Such objects may include a lock of hair, a shoe, or a piece of clothing. ALAN DUNDES

See also MYTHOLOGY (African); SCULPTURE (African); SUPERSTITION.

FETUS. See EMBRYO; GENETIC COUNSELING.

FEUD, *fyood,* is a bitter and sometimes murderous quarrel between families or groups. Feuds are especially common in regions far from any central authority. The people in such regions may take the law into their own hands and seek revenge for a real or a fancied wrong. Often no living person can remember how a feud started, but new acts of violence keep the hatreds alive. Sometimes a feud wipes out whole families.

Feuds breed in mountain regions because law officers cannot police them well. Feuds occurred often in the mountains and highlands of Afghanistan; in Corsica, Sicily, Montenegro, and in the Balkans; as well as in the southern Appalachian Mountains of the United States. An occasional feud still flares in eastern Kentucky. The bloody private war between the Hatfield and McCoy families became the most famous of the Kentucky feuds. It began in the 1860's and went on for nearly 50 years. Many stories and songs are based on this feud.

Feuds resemble a custom of primitive society called *blood vengeance.* This custom grew up in the days when there was no strong public authority to punish acts of violence. When a man killed or seriously hurt another, the dead or injured person's nearest relative considered it his sacred duty to take vengeance on the murderer or injurer. But the killing of the murderer usually imposed a duty on *his* nearest relative to seek revenge in turn. Thus a whole series of killings often resulted from one act of violence. JOHN F. CUBER

See also VENDETTA.

FEUDALISM was the political and military system of western Europe during the Middle Ages. In a period when there was little security, feudalism fulfilled the basic need for government, justice, and protection against attack.

Feudalism is often confused with manorialism. Manorialism was primarily a system for making a living from land. It was an economic relationship between a lord and his peasants. Feudalism, on the other hand, was mainly a political and military system. It was an arrangement between feudal aristocrats—a lord and his vassals. The lord gave vassals land in exchange for military and other services. The lord and the vassals were honor bound to be faithful and to fulfill their obligations to each other. The peasants had no part in such arrangements. See MANORIALISM.

Feudalism was a useful system for its time. It helped to create order out of the disorder that existed in Europe in the early Middle Ages. Under feudalism, a capable ruler could bring efficient government and peace to his people.

Feudalism began to appear in the A.D. 700's. During the 1000's and 1100's, it spread from northern Europe into England and southern Europe. The crusaders also introduced feudalism into Syria. Feudalism developed most fully in England and in the region between the Pyrenees and the Rhine River. It reached its height in the period from the 800's to the 1200's. During the 1400's, it rapidly disappeared from Europe.

The word *feudal* came from *feodum*, the Latin term for *fief*. In the Middle Ages, a *fief* was an estate granted by a lord in return for military or political service.

The Beginnings of Feudalism. Feudalism had two main roots. One was a relationship of honor that existed among the German war bands that roamed over much of Europe in the early Middle Ages. These bands consisted of a leader and a group of warriors of proven skill and bravery. The warriors pledged on their honor to fight for their leader, to the death if necessary. The leader, in turn, treated the warriors honorably. The bands fought for glory, adventure, and whatever valuables they could seize in war.

When the Germans settled in lands that had been part of the Roman Empire, they found the second main root of feudalism already established. This was a system of land *tenure* (holding). Sometimes a lord would give a small plot of land to a man in exchange for his labor in the lord's fields. At other times, men who owned land would turn it over to a lord in exchange for his protection. The lord let them stay on the land as long as they worked for him. These former landowners became the peasants of the manorial system, which spread in the Middle Ages throughout western Europe.

The land tenure relationship between lord and peasant in time became a relationship between noblemen. The change came about in the 700's, when Muslims from Africa were spreading into Europe by way of Spain. The European rulers, needing men to fight off the invaders, began granting fiefs to noble warriors for their service. These fiefs included land, the buildings on it, and the peasants who worked it. The warriors receiving the fiefs were called *vassals* (from the Latin *vassallus*, meaning *military retainer*). By the 800's, the relationship of honor that existed between leader and warrior in the German war bands was combined with a

Archives Générales du Royaume, Brussels

A Knight Armed for Battle in the 1200's carried a cross-hilted sword and a kite-shaped shield. His helmet completely covered his head. Other knights could identify him only by his heraldic symbol. The symbol of the Flemish lion that appears on the shield and horse's coverlet in this seal identifies the knight as Guy de Dampierre, the Count of Flanders.

system for the holding of land. Vassalage was joined to fief holding. This was feudalism.

The Principles of Feudalism. Only noblemen or aristocratic warriors could take part in feudal practices. These practices centered on the fief. No man could receive a fief until he became a vassal of the lord. The ceremony by which he became a vassal was called *homage*. The future vassal promised to fight for the lord and became his *man* (*homo* in Latin). The lord promised to treat the vassal with honor. If either broke his promise, he was considered guilty of feudal *perfidy*, a serious crime. See HOMAGE.

After doing homage, the new vassal was *invested* with (given the rights to) his fief. This was done in an *investiture* ceremony.

The vassal received only possession of a fief, not ownership of it. He could keep possession as long as he fulfilled his feudal duties. The vassal had many powers over his fief. He received what the land produced, collected taxes, held court, executed sentences, and obtained labor as needed on the castle, other buildings, and roads of the fief.

When the vassal died, his son could take over the fief. But the son had to be able to provide the military and other services required by the lord. And he had to become a vassal through homage. The eldest surviving son was granted the fief. This custom was called *primogeniture*. It insured that the fief would not be broken up among many sons and that one person would remain

Bryce Lyon, the contributor of this article, is Professor of Medieval History at Brown University and the author of several books on medieval history, including From Fief to Indenture.

responsible for the services to the lord. See PRIMO-GENITURE.

If the vassal died without heirs, the fief *escheated* (went back) to the lord. The lord then granted it to another man. If the dead vassal left a very young son, the lord had the right of *wardship*. This meant that the lord became responsible for the boy and managed the fief until the young heir was old enough to become a vassal and receive the fief. If the vassal left only a daughter, the lord had the right to have her married to a man of his choice. This man then would become the vassal and receive the fief. Such rights of the lord were called feudal *incidents*.

The lord had other rights called feudal *aids*. All the vassals were required to contribute money when the lord's eldest son was knighted and when his eldest daughter married. If the lord was captured in battle and held for ransom, the vassals had to pay it.

Feudal rights were limited. The lord, for example, could not burden his vassals with extra taxes without their consent. This tradition later led to the rule that a king could levy no taxes without the consent of his subjects.

Knighthood Under Feudalism. The main service the vassal owed his lord was military. From the 700's on,

vassals had to contribute the services of a certain number of knights for a certain number of days each year. *Knights* were heavily armed men mounted on war horses. At first, the vassals kept the knights in their own households. They fed, clothed, and armed them. But knights sometimes behaved too rudely to live so closely with vassals, who were lords of the knights. Knights also began to want their own fiefs. It became the custom for a vassal-lord to grant his knights parts of his own fief. They then became his vassals. This practice was called *subinfeudation*. By the 1200's, it had gone so far that several layers of feudal relations separated the humblest knight from a great count or king. Between them were various levels of lords. Each was a vassal of the lord of the next higher rank.

Justice Under Feudalism. Differences among vassals were settled at the lord's *court*, consisting of all the vassals. Many of the customs that developed there continue today in American and British courts of law. The lord presided over the feudal court. In courts today, judges preside. A vassal received judgment from other vassals. These were his feudal *peers* (social equals). Modern citizens receive judgment from their peers, who form a jury. But other judicial customs of feudal days have died. One of them was *trial by combat*, which the

Feudal Courts settled differences among noblemen. This miniature shows England's King Richard II presiding over his royal court. The king gave the final verdict on the advice of his vassals, who were lords and churchmen. This court settled a dispute in 1398 between Thomas Mowbray and Henry of Bolingbroke (later King Henry IV) by banishing both noblemen from England.

From the Harley Manuscript of *Froissart's Chronicles*, British Museum

Bibliothèque Nationale, courtesy *Life Magazine*

The Battle of Crécy in 1346 introduced new methods of warfare that helped cause the decline of feudalism. Infantry armed with new weapons made knights almost powerless. In this battle, English foot soldiers, *right*, used the longbow to defeat French knights. The knights, slowed by bulky armor, could not escape the storm of arrows shot at close range by the archers.

peers often ordered as a way of deciding disputes between vassals. The vassals fought, and the one who won the fight won his case. See TRIAL BY COMBAT.

A vassal had to answer the *summons* (order to appear) of a feudal court and obey the court's decisions. If he failed, the lord could take back his fief. The vassal then would be declared a feudal *felon*. Such disputes often led to wars. In the early 1200's, King John of England failed to heed the summons to the court of his lord, King Philip Augustus of France. War broke out, some of John's fiefs were taken away, and the English kings thus lost most of their possessions in France.

At the feudal court, the lord also was required to get the advice and consent of his vassals before making laws. In time, this practice led to the basic rule of democracy that no ruler can make laws without the consent of the people he governs.

The Decline of Feudalism. Two things happened in the 1200's that led to the decline of feudalism. The economic revival of Europe put money back into use, and new methods of warfare were developed. Since the services of soldiers could now be paid for with money, fiefs became unnecessary. Feudal relationships among nobles weakened. The coming of gunpowder, of new weapons, and of effective infantry ended the usefulness of knights. Foot soldiers from Flemish cities defeated the best French knights in the battle of Courtrai in 1302. Longbowmen from England also beat the French knights in battles at Crécy in 1346, Poitiers in 1356, and Agincourt in 1415. Stone castles no longer could stand against cannons. Today their remains serve only as reminders of the age of feudalism.   BRYCE LYON

Related Articles in WORLD BOOK include:

For a *Reading and Study Guide on Feudalism*, see the RESEARCH GUIDE/INDEX, Volume 22.

FEUERBACH, LUDWIG

FEUERBACH, *FOY uhr BAHK,* **LUDWIG** (1804-1872), was a German philosopher. He studied in Berlin under G. W. F. Hegel, but later turned against philosophical idealism and stressed instead the importance of the scientific study of man. He declared that *Der Mensch ist, was er isst* (Man is what he eats). His ideas deeply influenced those of Karl Marx. Feuerbach published his major work, *The Essence of Christianity,* in 1841. He was born in Landshut, Bavaria.   WALTER KAUFMANN

FEVER is the rise in the temperature of the body. It accompanies many different diseases and infections. When fever is an outstanding symptom, it may be the name of the disease as in *scarlet fever* or *yellow fever.*

When fever is present, the body produces more heat than it gives off. The temperature of the body may reach 105° F. (41° C). A temperature of 98.6° F. (37° C) is normal. In a few diseases and in sunstroke, the temperature may reach 112° or 115° F. (44° or 46° C).

A fever which lasts for a long time usually starts as the period of *invasion.* In this first stage, the patient shows weakness, languor, loss of appetite, rapid pulse, and a chill. In the next stage, or period of *height,* the pulse remains rapid, the body becomes hot, dry, and flushed, and the temperature rises. The patient also manifests thirst, headache, restlessness, and rapid breathing. During the last stage, or period of *decline,* the temperature falls, the breathing slows down, the skin becomes moist, and the patient begins to feel better. At the height of the fever, the patient sometimes suffers from delirium, but during the decline, he usually falls into a natural sleep.

There are several types of fever. A *continued* fever is one in which the temperature remains above normal for several days. An *intermittent* fever is one in which the temperature drops to normal and then rises again after certain periods of time. In a *remittent* fever, the temperature alternately falls to a point above normal and then rises. In a *relapsing* fever, the temperature falls to normal and suddenly rises again after a few days. A slight fever in a healthy person is usually a sign of infection.

The disease or condition causing the fever should determine the treatment. Bathing the patient in either warm or cold water, or applying cold applications to the head, may reduce the temperature. Drugs such as *salicylic acid, aspirin,* and *phenacetin* may relieve the aches and pains which accompany a fever. Ice-water baths can relieve the high fever of sunstroke. In all cases, the person should consult a doctor.

In the 1920's, Julius Wagner von Jauregg (1857-1940), a Viennese scientist, discovered that high fever can kill bacteria which cause some diseases. Doctors at one time gave *artificial fever* cures to persons suffering from gonorrhea and syphilis.   PAUL R. CANNON

Related Articles in WORLD BOOK include:

Antipyretic	Rocky Mountain	Typhoid Fever
Dengue	Spotted Fever	Typhus
Relapsing Fever	Scarlet Fever	Undulant Fever
	Tick Fever	Yellow Fever

FEVER BLISTER. See COLD SORE.

FEVERFEW is a low, hardy plant that requires little attention. Its cluster of small, white, daisy-like flowers appears in late summer. Its leaves have a strong scent when crushed. People once believed that feverfew could drive away fever. Its name means *to put fever to flight.*

Scientific Classification. Feverfew is a member of the composite family, *Compositae.* It is genus *Chrysanthemum,* species *C. parthenium.*   ROBERT W. SCHERY

FEW, WILLIAM (1748-1828), was a signer of the United States Constitution. He was born near Baltimore, Md., but later lived in North Carolina, Georgia, and New York. Few fought in the Revolutionary War. He served several terms in the Georgia general assembly and as a delegate to the Continental Congress and the Constitutional Convention. Later, he served as a U.S. senator and as a federal judge.   ROBERT J. TAYLOR

FEYNMAN, RICHARD PHILLIPS (1918-   ), of the United States, shared the 1965 Nobel prize in physics with Julian S. Schwinger and Sin-itiro Tomonaga. Working independently, the three men developed an improved theory of quantum electrodynamics in the late 1940's. *Quantum electrodynamics* is the study of the interaction of electrons and electromagnetic radiation. The theory enables scientists to predict accurately the effects of electrically charged particles on each other in a radiation field.

Feynman was born in New York City. He earned a B.S. degree from Massachusetts Institute of Technology in 1939 and a Ph.D. degree from Princeton University in 1942. From 1942 to 1945, he was a theoretical physicist at the Los Alamos Scientific Laboratory, Los Alamos, N.Mex. He joined the faculty of California Institute of Technology in 1951.   R. T. ELLICKSON

FEZ, or FÈS (pop. 325,327), is the religious center of Morocco and one of its traditional capitals. It boasts the Mosque of Mulai Idris, a noted Muslim shrine, and Karaouiyine University, one of the world's oldest universities, which was founded in 859.

Fez lies in the deep valley of the Fez River in northern Morocco (see MOROCCO [map]). Railroads connect it with other North African cities. It is noted for its silk, woolen, and leather goods.

J. Horace McFarland

Leaves and Blossoms of Feverfew. This plant is a native of Europe, but is now common in American fields and gardens.

The Moorish ruler Idris II founded Fez as his capital in 808. The city declined in the 1600's, when Sultan Ismail built his palace in Meknès. But it again became the capital from 1728 until the French occupation of Morocco in 1912.   KEITH G. MATHER

FEZ is a tall, red, brimless cap with a colored tassel of silk or wool. It is worn in Egypt and in North Africa where it is sometimes called a *tarboosh*. All fezzes were once colored with a dye made from the juice of red berries found only in Morocco. This same color can now be produced by chemical dyes. The fez was first made in Fez, Morocco.   WARREN S. SMITH

FHA. See FEDERAL HOUSING ADMINISTRATION.

FIANNA FÁIL. See IRELAND (Politics; The Irish Free State).

FIAT, *FY at*, in government is an order or decree that has the force of a law. It is usually an executive order from a ruler who may be acting arbitrarily, rather than a statute from a legislative body. The term *fiat* also means approval or endorsement of an act. A legislature may require a ruler's fiat to pass laws. For example, in Great Britain, Parliament could not pass laws without the fiat of George II. A ruler gives this approval by including the term *fiat* in the order. It is the Latin word for *let it be done*.   ARTHUR E. SUTHERLAND

FIAT MONEY. See MONEY (Money Terms).

FIBER is a threadlike strand of a substance. Some fibers occur in nature, and others are manufactured. Many can be spun into yarns that are made into fabrics by knitting, weaving, and other methods. Manufacturers use fibers in clothing and such home furnishings as carpets and upholstery. They also use fibers in industrial fabrics, including filter cloths and insulation, and in many other products for industrial use.

The chemical composition and arrangement of molecules in a fiber determine its properties, such as absorbency, durability, and elasticity. Manufacturers use fibers that have properties best suited to their products. For example, glass fibers, commonly called *fiberglass*, have the highest resistance to stretching. Manufacturers use fiberglass to reinforce plastics for automobile bodies and boat hulls. Some fibers are blended to make yarns that have specific properties.

There are two major forms of fibers, *staples* and *continuous filaments*. These forms are based on length. Most staples measure from $\frac{1}{2}$ inch to 8 inches (1.3 to 20 centimeters) long, though some are longer than 40 inches (100 centimeters). Manufacturers spin staples into yarns or use them for stuffing mattresses, pillows, and similar products. Most natural fibers are staples. Continuous filaments range from more than 300 yards (270 meters) long for silk fibers to indefinite lengths for manufactured fibers. They can be used singly as yarns, or they can be combined into yarns or cut into staple lengths.

Natural Fibers

Natural fibers are obtained from plants, animals, and minerals. They account for more than half the fibers produced in the world yearly.

Plant Fibers. *Cotton* is the most widely used natural fiber. Staples from cotton *bolls* (seed pods) are spun into yarns for clothing and home and industrial fabrics. Cotton cloth is absorbent, crisp, and soft. *Flax*, a strong, silky fiber from the stems of flax plants, is used in making clothing and napkins and other linen products. *Hemp*, *jute*, and *sisal* are coarse fibers used in cords, ropes, and rough fabrics.

Animal Fibers include fur and hair. *Wool*, the hair sheared from sheep and certain other animals, is popular in clothing and home furnishings. Rough surfaces on wool fibers give bulk and warmth to wool clothing and blankets. *Silk* is the strongest natural fiber. Manufacturers unwind silk filaments from silkworm cocoons and make silk yarn for clothing and household fabrics.

Mineral Fibers. Various minerals—chiefly serpentine and amphibole—that occur in fibrous form are called *asbestos*. They resist high temperatures and are used in insulation, shingles, and fireproof products.

Manufactured Fibers

Most manufactured fibers are plastics. The study of plastics has helped chemists learn how to combine chemicals to create fibers that have specific properties. Machines melt the chemicals or mix them in various

HOW VARIOUS KINDS OF FIBERS DIFFER

Wool Fibers have scales that make them stick together during spinning. This fiber is magnified about 6,200 times.

International Wool Secretariat

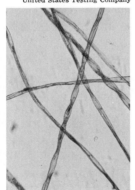

Cotton Fibers are easy to spin because of the natural twist of the fiber. This fiber is magnified 84 times.

United States Testing Company

Asbestos Fibers resist high temperatures and are used in fireproof products. This fiber is magnified 66 times.

Johns-Manville Sales Corp.

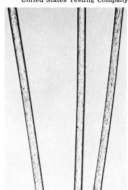

Nylon Fibers resist wearing because they are round and smooth. This fiber is magnified about 200 times.

United States Testing Company

liquids. The machines then force streams of the chemical through tiny holes. The streams harden into continuous filaments that are wound onto spools or cut into staple lengths.

Manufactured fibers account for more than two-thirds of the fibers processed by textile mills in the United States. The variety and qualities of these fibers make them popular with consumers and manufacturers. See TEXTILE (table: Manufactured Fibers).

There are two main groups of manufactured fibers, *cellulosics* and *noncellulosics*, commonly called *synthetics*.

Cellulosics are fibers derived from cellulose. Manufacturers process cotton and wood pulp to make cellulosic fibers. *Rayon*, a cellulosic fiber, was the first successful manufactured fiber. It has many properties that resemble those of cotton. Cellulose treated with acetic acid produces *acetate*, a fiber that is silkier than rayon. Rayon and acetate are used in clothing, and rayon is used in tires as well.

Synthetics, or noncellulosics, are fibers manufactured from simple chemicals. Most synthetics are stronger than natural or cellulosic fibers. The most widely used kinds of synthetics are (1) nylon fibers, (2) polyester fibers, (3) acrylic fibers, and (4) olefin fibers.

Nylon Fibers were the first synthetic fibers. They are lightweight and strong and are widely used in carpets, ropes, and tires. Such nylon fibers as Cantrece and Qiana are popular in clothing.

Polyester Fibers, such as Dacron and Kodel, are durable and quickly regain their shape after being stretched or wrinkled. They are used in clothing, sheets, and pillows. Manufacturers also use polyester fibers in filters, sails, and other industrial fabrics.

Acrylic Fibers, including Acrilan and Orlon, are soft and durable. A number of acrylic yarns resemble wool and are used in clothing and carpeting. Many artificial furs are also made from acrylic fibers.

Olefin Fibers are strong and resist stains. These properties make Herculon, Marvess, and other olefin fibers useful in carpets, upholstery, and ropes.

Other Synthetics. Yarns called *Lastex* are made from manufactured rubber fibers wrapped in cotton, nylon, or other fibers. Lastex and *spandex*, a group of elastic fibers including Lycra and Glospan, add stretch to garments. Special metal treatments produce *metallic fibers*, such as gold and silver filaments, that can be used to decorate fabrics.   ELIJA M. HICKS, JR.

Related Articles in WORLD BOOK include:

NATURAL FIBERS

Abacá	Flax	Jute	Silk
Asbestos	Hemp	Kapok	Sisal
Bast	Henequen	Ramie	Wool
Cotton			

MANUFACTURED FIBERS

Acrylic	Fiberglass	Orlon	Rayon
Dacron	Nylon	Polyester	Saran

OTHER RELATED ARTICLES

Agriculture (Natural Fibers)	Mohair
Cellulose	Palm
Clothing (Clothing Materials;	Plastics
Protecting the Public)	Textile
Linen	Thread
Lisle	Wallboard

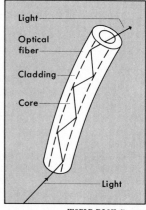

Bell Laboratories   WORLD BOOK diagram

Optical Fibers, shown at the left above, are thin, transparent fibers of glass or plastic used to transfer light. Some have a covering called *cladding* that reflects the light carried through the core, as shown in the cross-section drawing at the right.

FIBER OPTICS is a field of physics. It deals with the transfer of light from one place to another through long, thin, flexible fibers of glass or plastic called *optical fibers*. Although light travels in a straight line, optical fibers can transfer light around corners or along a twisting path. The sides of the fiber reflect the light and keep it inside as the fiber bends and turns. Improved fibers have a thin core and a special outer covering, called *cladding*. The core carries the light. The cladding helps "bend" the light back to the core.

Optical fibers have many important uses. One type of fiber optic device can transfer an image formed by a lens at one end of a group of fibers to the other end. Physicians use instruments utilizing these devices to examine body cavities and the inside of hollow organs, such as the bladder and stomach. Other fiber optic devices can transmit television programs, telephone conversations, and other forms of communication. Sounds or pictures can be sent by varying the amount of light sent. At the receiving end of the fibers, a receiver changes the varying amounts of light into copies of the original sounds or pictures.   BRIAN J. THOMPSON

FIBERBOARD is a building material made of wood or other plant fibers pressed into sheets. Builders use it as insulation, as wall covering, and as a base for plastering and floor covering. It is also used for the bottoms of drawers and the backs of furniture. Manufacturers make fiberboard chiefly from wood, but also use waste paper, straw, sugar cane, and cornstalks. Other materials, such as asphalt and rosin, may be added to increase strength or resistance to fire, decay, or moisture. See also WALLBOARD.   GEORGE W. WASHA

FIBERGLASS, or FIBROUS GLASS, is glass in the form of fine *fibers* (threads). The fibers may be many times finer than human hair, and may look and feel like silk. The flexible glass fibers are stronger than steel, and will not burn, stretch, rot, or fade.

Uses. Manufacturers use fiberglass to make a variety of products. Fiberglass is woven into cloth to make such products as curtains and tablecloths. The cloth does not change its properties when dyed. It will not wrinkle or soil easily, and needs no ironing after washing. Fiberglass textiles are also used for electrical insula-

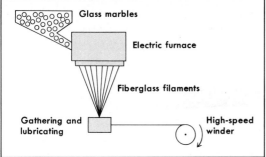

Glass marbles

Electric furnace

Fiberglass filaments

Gathering and lubricating

High-speed winder

WORLD BOOK diagram

Fiberglass is often made by melting glass marbles in a furnace. The melted glass flows through tiny holes at the bottom of the furnace and comes out in the form of fine filaments. The filaments are then gathered together, lubricated, and wound around a reel.

tion. In bulk form, fiberglass is used for air filters and for heat and sound insulation. Air trapped between the fibers makes it a good insulator.

Fiberglass reinforced plastics are extremely strong and light in weight. They can be molded, shaped, twisted, and poured for many different uses. Manufacturers use fiberglass reinforced plastics to make automobile bodies, boat hulls, building panels, fishing rods, and aircraft parts. The fibers used to strengthen plastic may be woven or matted together, or they may be individual strands. The form used depends on the nature and price of the final product.

How Fiberglass Is Made. Fiberglass is made from sand and other raw materials used to make ordinary glass (see GLASS [Recipes for Making Glass]). Strands of fiberglass may be made in different ways. In one method, the raw materials are heated and formed into small glass marbles so workers can examine them for impurities. The marbles are then melted in special electric furnaces. The melted glass runs down through tiny holes at the bottom of the furnace. A spinning drum catches the fibers of hot glass and winds them on bobbins, like threads on spools. Because the drum revolves much faster than the glass flows, tension pulls the fibers and draws them out into still finer strands. The drum can pull out 2 miles (3.2 kilometers) of fibers in a minute. Up to 95 miles (153 kilometers) of fiber can be drawn from one marble $\frac{5}{8}$ inch (16 millimeters) in diameter. The fiber can be twisted together into yarns and cords. The yarns may be woven into cloth, tape, and other kinds of fabrics. In another method, called the *direct melt process*, the marble-making steps are omitted.

Bulk fiberglass, or *fiberglass wool*, is made somewhat differently. Sand and other raw materials are melted in a furnace. The melted glass flows from tiny holes in the furnace. Then high-pressure jets of steam catch it and draw it into fine fibers from 8 to 15 inches (20 to 38 centimeters) long. The fibers are gathered on a conveyor belt in the form of a white wool-like mass.

History. The Egyptians used coarse glass fibers for decorative purposes before the time of Christ. Edward Drummond Libbey, an American glass manufacturer, exhibited a dress made of fiberglass and silk at the Columbian Exposition in Chicago in 1893. During World War I, fiberglass was made in Germany as a substitute for asbestos. Finally, in experiments conducted from 1931 to 1939, the Owens Illinois Glass Company

(now called Owens-Illinois, Inc.) and the Corning Glass Works developed practical methods of making fiberglass commercially. C. J. PHILLIPS

FIBIGER, *FEE bee gur,* **JOHANNES ANDREAS GRIB** (1867-1928), was a Danish bacteriologist. He won the 1926 Nobel prize for physiology or medicine. He produced stomach cancer in rats by feeding them cockroaches infested with *nematodes* (small worms). The nematode, called *Spiroptera carcinoma,* provided a means of producing cancer experimentally. Fibiger was born in Silkeborg, Denmark. HENRY H. FERTIG

FIBONACCI, LEONARDO. See MATHEMATICS (The Middle Ages).

FIBRILLATION. See HEART (Fibrillation).

FIBRIN, *FIE brihn,* is a white, fibrous protein substance that makes up the most important part of a blood clot. The formation of a clot is called *coagulation.* Fibrin is formed from *fibrinogen,* a protein that is present in blood serum. When blood flows out of a cut area, molecules of fibrinogen unite to become long fibers of fibrin. These fibers make a meshlike plug over the entire cut area. Red blood cells become caught in the mesh, and help to form the blood clot. Blood clots may also form inside blood vessels. BENJAMIN F. MILLER

FIBROVASCULAR BUNDLE. See BOTANY (table: Terms Used in Botany).

FICHTE, *FICK tuh,* **JOHANN GOTTLIEB** (1762-1814), was a German philosopher. He strongly influenced German nationalism, as well as the philosophies of Friedrich Schelling, G. W. F. Hegel, and Arthur Schopenhauer.

Fichte decided to devote his own life to philosophy, after reading Immanuel Kant's three *Critiques,* published in 1781, 1788, and 1790. His *Attempt at a Critique of Revelation* won the favor of Kant, who asked his own publisher to accept the manuscript. It appeared in 1792, without Fichte's name and preface, and was widely hailed as a new work by Kant. When Kant corrected this misunderstanding, Fichte became famous overnight. The University of Jena made him a professor.

Fichte was a popular lecturer, but his technical works are difficult. Accused of atheism, he lost his position and moved to Berlin. His *Addresses to the German Nation* was his most popular work. He was born in Rammenau, near Bautzen. WALTER KAUFMANN

FICTION, in literature, is any narrative work that is not pure fact. A novel or a short story is fiction, even when it is based on fact. Real persons or events may form the background or take minor or major parts in the narrative, but they are interwoven with people who never were and things that never happened. The word comes from the Latin *fictio,* which means *something invented.* In its narrowest sense, it is applied only to the novel, but it also applies to other kinds of literature.

Importance of Fiction. Good fiction serves many purposes:

(1) Fiction is entertainment and affords pleasure.

(2) Fiction is escape. It takes people's minds out of their own familiar existences to a different world.

(3) Fiction is education. Often it gives a true picture of places, people, or times. It often gives a realistic picture of one segment or period of life. It helps us to understand ourselves and each other better.

(4) Fiction is personal. Readers identify themselves,

their families, or their friends and enemies, with a character or characters. The readers live the events and make the choices.

Types of Fiction. There are several types of fiction, and most early types exist today.

Folk Tales are fictionized stories of characters who figured in the life of a people. The stories of Robin Hood in England and Paul Bunyan in the United States are examples. Myths and legends are, in a measure, folk tales, because they are pure fiction on a spiritual, or supernatural, scale. See FOLKLORE.

Fables are brief fiction about animals. They are almost anecdotal, and all point a moral. See FABLE.

Tales are stories with little or no plot. Many of Washington Irving's writings are tales.

Short Stories are compact, crisp pieces of fiction, with definite setting, good characterization, and a plot.

Novels are longer than short stories. They employ more characters and their plots usually are more involved. There are many kinds of novels, with a wide range of subject matter and treatment. See NOVEL.

Essays and Sketches may also be fiction, such as an imaginary journey to the moon. See ESSAY.

Plays and Poetry. Most dramatic works are fiction, although some have historical backgrounds. Such poems as Longfellow's *Evangeline* and Scott's *Lady of the Lake* are fictionized history. See DRAMA; POETRY.

The Development of Fiction was slow. Folk tales and hero stories were first handed down by word of mouth and in cave pictures. Long, rambling tales, usually about heroes and often in verse, were written from the time of the early Greeks to the Middle Ages. A fine example of these early tales is Homer's *Iliad*.

The *Decameron*, a collection of tales by the Italian, Boccaccio, was written about 1350. Malory's *Le Morte Darthur*, romantic tales of an English court, came about the middle of the 1400's. John Bunyan's *Pilgrim's Progress* (1678) was a different kind of fiction, pointing a moral. Daniel Defoe's *Robinson Crusoe* (1719) was an important development in the English novel. By 1800, many novels were being written.   MARTHA F. SIMMONDS

Related Articles. See the articles on various national literatures, such as FRENCH LITERATURE. See also the following articles:

Detective Story	Pulitzer Prizes
Literature for Children	(table: Fiction)
(Fiction)	Romance
National Book Awards	Science Fiction
(table: Fiction)	Short Story

FIDDLER CRAB is a burrowing animal which lives along sandy or muddy beaches and salt marshes in tropical and temperate regions. It belongs to the class *Crustacea*. The male has a huge front *pincer* (claw) that he moves back and forth much as a fiddler moves his arm when playing a violin. This claw is used for courting females and for fighting with other males. The fiddler crab feeds on water plants, called *algae*, mixed with mud. In the fall, the crabs in cold regions close their burrows and hibernate.

Scientific Classification. The fiddler crab belongs to the order *Decapoda*. It makes up the genus *Uca*. There are various species.   J. LAURENS BARNARD

See also BIOLOGICAL CLOCK (Other Rhythms); CRAB.

FIDELIO. See BEETHOVEN, LUDWIG VAN.

FIEDLER, *FEE dlur,* **ARTHUR** (1894-   ), has conducted the Boston Pops Orchestra since 1930. He organized and conducted the Boston Sinfonietta, later known as the Arthur Fiedler Sinfonietta, and the Boston Esplanade Concerts. Fiedler was born in Boston, and studied at the Royal Academy of Music in Berlin. He taught at Boston University.   DAVID EWEN

FIEF. See FEUDALISM; FEE.

FIELD was the family name of three distinguished sons of David Dudley Field (1781-1867), a well-known Congregational clergyman and the author of several histories of Massachusetts.

David Dudley Field, Jr. (1805-1894), a brilliant lawyer, won recognition for his work as a reformer of legal procedure. He started work on a code of legal procedure in 1847. His code formed the basis for legal procedure reforms in many states and in England.

David became the first president of the International Law Association, founded in Brussels in 1873 to reform and codify international law. He was born in Haddam, Conn., and studied at Williams College.

Stephen Johnson Field (1816-1899) was an associate justice of the Supreme Court of the United States from 1863 to 1897. He handed down many opinions that helped develop United States constitutional law. He also served on the Electoral Commission in 1877 (see ELECTORAL COMMISSION). Stephen was born in Haddam, Conn., and graduated from Williams College.

Cyrus West Field (1819-1892) promoted the first telegraph cable across the Atlantic (see CABLE). The first fully successful cable was laid in 1866, after four previous attempts.

The first cable, laid in 1857, broke 360 miles (579 kilometers) from shore. An attempt in June 1858, also failed. Field promoted a successful effort to lay a cable between Ireland and Newfoundland in August 1858. Technical carelessness ruined the cable's insulation, and it failed four

Chicago Historical Society
Cyrus W. Field

weeks later. In 1865, Field chartered the steamship *Great Eastern* to lay a new cable. The cable broke when the project was almost done. The project succeeded in

American Museum of Natural History
A Fiddler Crab uses its large claw to fight other males. If it is caught, it can break it off to escape. A new small claw grows in its place, and the other front claw grows to be a big claw.

Detail of oil painting (1870) by M. J. Deming; Lighthouse Gallery, Shelburne Museum, Shelburne, Vt.

1866, with the laying of a new cable and the repair of the old. Field later promoted the New York elevated railroad. He also wanted to lay a cable to the Hawaiian Islands, Asia, and Australia. He was born in Stockbridge, Mass.   DANIEL J. DYKSTRA and RICHARD D. HUMPHREY

FIELD is the name of an American family prominent in merchandising, publishing, and philanthropy. Marshall Field I built the family fortune as a wholesaler to thousands of Midwestern retail stores, as a Chicago department store owner, and through real estate investments. His grandson, Marshall Field III, entered the publishing field, and his great, great grandson, Marshall Field V, carries on that tradition.

Marshall Field I (1834-1906) was a New England farm boy who became a great Chicago merchant by developing the world-famous Marshall Field & Company department store in Chicago.

His Early Life. Field was born on Aug. 18, 1834, on a farm in Conway township, Massachusetts. His schooling was limited. He worked on the farm of his brother Chandler until he was 17. Then he went to Pittsfield with his brother Joseph to work in a dry goods store.

Field decided in 1856 to go west. Arriving in Chicago, Field found a boom town of about 80,000 with muddy streets and creaking boardwalks. He got a job with Cooley, Wadsworth and Company, a wholesale dry goods firm in the city.

Soon he was sent out as a traveling salesman for the store. In 1860, he borrowed money to buy a junior partnership in the firm. The Civil War brought a business boom, and the store prospered. About 1865, Field and an associate, Levi Z. Leiter, bought an interest in a rival business owned by Potter Palmer. In nine years, Field had risen from a $400-a-year

Chicago Historical Society
Marshall Field I

clerk's job to head of a successful business in which he had an interest of $260,000. By 1881, the 47-year-old Field had bought out his two partners, and the firm became known as Marshall Field & Company.

His Policies introduced a new era in merchandising. Prices were plainly marked on merchandise, and goods were not misrepresented. Customers could exchange goods if they were dissatisfied. Field undersold competitors because he bought goods for cash at wholesale in anticipation of consumer demand. His competitors bought later on the open market.

Field's slogan was "Give the Lady What She Wants," and he made a special effort to attract women to his store. His was the first store to use its basement to sell goods. It was a leader in developing advertising techniques and window displays.

Philanthropist. Field gave 10 acres (4 hectares) of ground as a site for the new University of Chicago, and later he gave the university $100,000. He gave $1 million in 1893 to establish a museum in Chicago. A later bequest by him of $8 million built the Field Museum of Natural History.

Marshall Field II (1868-1905) was the son of Marshall Field I. Poor health prevented him from taking part in the family enterprises, and he spent much time traveling in Europe with his family.

Marshall Field III (1893-1956), son of Marshall Field II, was a noted publisher, philanthropist, and civic leader. He launched several successful business undertakings, and believed that the great wealth he inherited from his grandfather, Marshall Field I, carried with it certain obligations. He used it to establish a wide variety of charitable, educational, and scientific programs and to promote social justice.

His Early Life. Field was born in Chicago on Sept. 28, 1893. He was educated at Eton and Trinity College, Cambridge, in England. At 21 he returned to the United States.

Following World War I, in which he rose from a private to a captain, Field became associate director of a Chicago bureau that found jobs for ex-servicemen and

Field Enterprises, Inc.
Marshall Field II

Philippe Halsman
Marshall Field III

Arthur Siegel, *Chicago Sun-Times*
Marshall Field IV

Henry Gill, *Chicago Daily News*
Marshall Field V

helped organize community centers for young people. In 1920, he joined an investment banking firm and a year later formed his own investment firm, Marshall Field, Glore, Ward & Company. Field retired from the investment business in 1935.

The Publisher. During the Great Depression of the 1930's, Field developed a deep interest in the communications field. He became convinced that a fully informed public was essential to the orderly functioning of a democracy.

In 1940, Field was a founder of the New York City daily newspaper, *PM*, and later served as publisher. *PM* carried no advertising and was dedicated to complete freedom from influence by Field or any outside source. In 1948, he disposed of his interest in *PM*.

Field founded *The Chicago Sun*, a morning newspaper, in 1941. The *Sun* was handicapped at first because it was denied the services of the Associated Press. But in 1945, the Supreme Court of the United States ruled that denial of Associated Press services to the *Sun* was a violation of the Sherman Anti-Trust Act.

In 1947, Field purchased control of another Chicago paper, the *Daily Times*. The next year he merged them into a daily and Sunday tabloid-sized newspaper called the *Chicago Sun-Times*.

Field consolidated his communications activities under Field Enterprises, Inc. These activities included: the *Sun-Times; The World Book Encyclopedia* and *Childcraft* (which became Field Enterprises Educational Corporation); the Sunday newspaper supplement, *Parade;* the book publishing houses of Simon & Schuster and Pocket Books; the background music company, Functional Music; and a number of radio stations.

Philanthropist and Civic Leader. Field's charitable and social welfare contributions were substantial and widespread. He gave the 38-story Pittsfield Building in Chicago to the Field Museum of Natural History. As a champion of low-rent housing, Field directed construction of one of the first privately financed, low-rent, large-scale housing projects in the United States. Called the Marshall Field Garden Apartments, it was built on Chicago's Near North Side in 1929.

Field became one of the best informed laymen in the United States on child welfare activities. He started the Field Foundation in 1940 to deal with problems relating to child welfare, social and racial relations, and education (see FIELD FOUNDATION). He gave it his equity in the 45-story Field Building in Chicago. He served as president of the Child Welfare League of America in 1950.

Marshall Field IV (1916-1965) expanded and increased the scope of the publishing enterprises developed by his father. He built the Sun-Times Building and purchased the *Chicago Daily News*, moving it into the Sun-Times Building. He renamed the structure the Sun-Times and Daily News Building.

His Early Life. Marshall Field IV was born on June 15, 1916, in New York City, and was graduated *magna cum laude* from Harvard University in 1938. He graduated third in his class from the University of Virginia Law School in 1941, and was on the *Law Review* there. He then served as secretary to a United States Circuit Court judge until he entered the U.S. Navy during World War II. He saw action in most of the major naval battles in the South Pacific and received the Silver Star for bravery.

Field started work on *The Chicago Sun* in 1946 as an apprentice. In 1947, he went to New York City to work on the *New York Herald Tribune.* When his father merged the *Daily Times* and *The Chicago Sun* to form the *Chicago Sun-Times* in 1948, Field became the assistant publisher and associate editor. He was named editor and publisher in 1950.

Editor and Publisher. When his father died in 1956, Field became president of Field Enterprises, Inc., and later was named chairman of the board. He bought the *Chicago Daily News* in 1959 and made it part of Field Enterprises, Inc. He became president, editor, and publisher of two of Chicago's leading newspapers, the morning *Sun-Times* and the afternoon *Daily News.*

His policies strengthened the papers. He enlarged their staffs and increased the space devoted to news. Under his leadership, the *Daily News* won its 12th Pulitzer prize in 1963, and the *Sun-Times* became the newspaper with the largest circulation in Chicago proper in 1965.

Field purchased the Manistique (Mich.) Pulp and Paper Company in 1960. In 1962, he acquired Publishers Syndicate and combined this service with the Sun-Times-Daily News Syndicate. He formed the Publishers Newspaper Syndicate in 1963. Now known as Field Newspaper Syndicate, it serves more than 2,000 daily and weekly newspapers with columns, comic strips, and other news features.

In 1965, Field formed Field Communications Corporation and became its president. Field Communications built an ultra-high frequency (UHF) television station, WFLD, channel 32, in Chicago. The station went on the air on Jan. 4, 1966.

Field was publisher of Field Enterprises Educational

Corporation (now World Book—Childcraft International, Inc.). Translation of *The World Book Encyclopedia* into braille, the largest braille printing project in history, was completed in 1961, and a large-type edition of *World Book* was produced in 1964. The *Cyclo-teacher®* Learning Aid was developed in 1961. *The World Book Year Book* began publication in 1962, *The World Book Dictionary* in 1963, and *Science Year* in 1965.

Marshall Field V (1941-   ) became publisher of the *Sun-Times* and *Daily News* in October 1969. This post had not been filled since the death of his father in 1965. At the age of 28, he became the youngest publisher of any major newspaper in the United States. Since then, the *Sun-Times* has won five Pulitzer prizes. The *Daily News* won three before it ceased publication in March 1978.

His Early Life. Field was born in Charlottesville, Va., on May 13, 1941. He attended St. Albans School in Washington, D.C., and graduated from Deerfield (Mass.) Academy. He earned a bachelor's degree in fine arts from Harvard University in 1963. While attending Harvard, Field worked as a summer intern in the editorial departments of *The Boston Globe* and *Mademoiselle* magazine.

After graduating, Field joined Random House, Inc., a publishing firm, and later worked on the circulation staff of the *New York Herald Tribune.* He took graduate courses at the University of Chicago Business School. After his father's death, he moved to Chicago and began an intensive four-year training program at Field Enterprises, Inc.

Field has been a member of the board of directors of Field Enterprises, Inc., since 1965, and chairman of the board since 1972. He and his brother Frederick Woodruff Field are co-owners of the company.

Marshall Field served as president and chief executive officer of the corporation from January 1973 to February 1974. He is publisher of World Book—Childcraft International, Inc., and a board member of all national and international divisions and subsidiaries of Field Enterprises, Inc.

Corporate Activities. In 1972, Field Communications Corporation joined as a minority partner with Kaiser Broadcasting Corporation in forming Kaiser Broadcasting Company. In 1973, the firm was licensed to operate the Kaiser television stations, which include stations in Chicago, Boston, Detroit, Philadelphia, and San Francisco. In July 1977, Field Communications acquired full ownership of the five UHF stations.

Under Field, Field Enterprises formed two new wholly owned subsidiaries to undertake real estate projects and also entered the energy field. It purchased Rapoca Energy Corporation of Cincinnati in 1975 and merged it with Field Resources, Inc., in 1976. The company's activities include the mining, processing, and brokerage of coal.

Field's numerous business, civic, and educational activities include cultural and educational institutions, a hospital, and conservation organizations. He has one son, Marshall, Jr., from his marriage to Joan Best Connelly in 1964. He is now married to Jamee Beckwith Jacobs and they have two daughters, Jamee and Stephanie Caroline.   VIRGINIA BUTTS

FIELD, EUGENE (1850-1895), a popular American author and journalist, has often been called the *Poet of*

Chicago Historical Society
Eugene Field

Childhood. Many of his verses are whimsical and fanciful, picturing the make-believe world of childhood. They show his desire to help explore the child's world in a spirit of adventure.

Such poems as "Wynken, Blynken, and Nod," "Seein' Things at Night," "The Ride to Bumpville," "The Delectable Ballad of the Waller Lot," and "The Duel" are favorites of boys and girls. Sometimes he wrote in a serious, even sorrowful vein. "Little Boy Blue," perhaps his most famous poem, is very sad, and appeals to adults rather than to children. The American composers Reginald De Koven and Ethelbert Nevin both set to music "Little Boy Blue" and "Wynken, Blynken, and Nod."

The simplicity and genuineness of children's thoughts appealed to Field. He believed children should be encouraged to cultivate imagination. He thought that they grow best in an atmosphere of fancy, rather than in one of cold facts. He wrote his poems to give this atmosphere. He wrote *A Little Book of Western Verse* (1890), *With Trumpet and Drum* (1892), *Love Songs of Childhood* (1894), and *Lullaby-land* published in 1897.

Early Life. Field was born on Sept. 2 or 3, 1850, in St. Louis, Mo. His parents were of New England stock. His father, Roswell Field, was the lawyer who defended Dred Scott, a slave, in the first trial of Scott's historic case (see DRED SCOTT DECISION). When Field was six years old, his mother died, and he and his younger brother were sent to Amherst, Mass., where they were cared for by a cousin, Mary French Field.

United Press Int.
A Eugene Field Memorial, by the sculptor Edward McCartan, stands in Lincoln Park in Chicago. Most of the memorial's cost was paid for by donations from American children.

FIELD, MARSHALL

Field received his early schooling in Amherst and Monson, Mass. He was keenly intelligent, but very mischievous and never a good student. He was sweet-tempered and warmhearted, but more interested in the things of nature—birds and animals, flowers and trees—than in lessons or books. As one biographer wrote, "Schools in the way of 'book larnin'' did not count for much in his young life." He entered Williams College in 1868, and the next year became a sophomore at Knox College in Galesburg, Ill. Later, he attended the University of Missouri, but left without graduating.

Field made many admiring friends during his college career, and gained a reputation as a "genial, song-singing, fun-loving companion." He was fond of the theater, and wrote and acted in several amateur plays, but was remembered best for the practical jokes he played on his professors and on his fellow students.

When Field was 19, his father died. With the $8,000 he inherited, he visited Europe in 1872. When he returned to the United States from Europe in 1873, he told his friends, "I spent six months and my patrimony in France, Italy, Ireland, and England."

The First Columnist. During the next 10 years Field worked as a newspaperman in St. Joseph and Kansas City, Mo., and in Denver, Colo. He was very successful in this work. In 1883, he moved from Denver to Chicago, where he wrote a humorous column in the Chicago *Daily News*. This column, called "Sharps and Flats," showed his ability to write quaint, satirical, and pathetic stories. He was considered the first columnist, and one of the most talented.

One of Field's hobbies was collecting books. His taste for classical works is shown in his *Echoes from the Sabine Farm* (1893), which he and his brother, Roswell M. Field, translated from the works of the Latin poet Horace. He also wrote a book of essays, *The Love Affairs of a Bibliomaniac*, published in 1896, after his death.

His Personality. Field was a kind man, extravagant in his tastes, and generous to a fault. He loved pleasure, gaiety, and children. He had eight children of his own, and was an adoring and indulgent father. His marriage to Julia Comstock of St. Joseph, Mo., and his home life were both exceptionally happy.

A beautiful bronze statue was erected to Field's memory in 1922 in Chicago, where he had done most of his writing. The monument shows an angel sprinkling the sand of dreams into the eyes of two sleeping children. Carved on the base are lines from two of his best-known poems, "Wynken, Blynken, and Nod" and "The Sugar Plum Tree." JEANNETTE C. NOLAN

FIELD, MARSHALL. See FIELD (family).

FIELD, RACHEL (1894-1942), an American author, is best known for her books for children. She won a Newbery medal in 1930 for *Hitty, Her First Hundred Years* (1929), a story of a doll's adventures. Some critics consider *Calico Bush* (1931) to be her best book. This story describes the experiences of a French servant girl in pioneer Maine.

Field's other works include *Taxis and Toadstools* (1926) and other books of poetry; several children's plays; and books for adults, including the novels *All This and Heaven Too* (1938) and *And Now Tomorrow* (1942). Field was born in New York City. ELOISE RUE

FIELD, STEPHEN JOHNSON. See FIELD (family).

FIELD-EMISSION MICROSCOPE. See ION MICROSCOPE.

FIELD ENTERPRISES, INC. See FIELD (Marshall).

FIELD EVENT. See TRACK AND FIELD.

FIELD FOUNDATION, INC., is an organization that administers a fund set aside for charitable, educational, and scientific purposes. The Field Foundation was established in 1940 by publisher and philanthropist Marshall Field III.

The foundation's grants total about $2 million a year. Grants are made to organizations with programs to fight discrimination, poverty, and the wrongful uses of governmental power. The foundation is particularly interested in child welfare.

The Field Foundation was chartered in New York as a nonprofit membership corporation. It has its office at 100 E. 85th Street, New York, N.Y. 10028.

Critically reviewed by the FIELD FOUNDATION, INC.

See also FIELD (Marshall Field III); FOUNDATIONS (Social Welfare).

FIELD GEOLOGIST. See GEOLOGY (Careers; picture).

FIELD GLASSES. See BINOCULARS.

FIELD HOCKEY is a fast team sport. In the United States, field hockey is primarily played by girls and women, but it is a popular male sport in many other countries. Men's field hockey has been part of the Summer Olympic Games since 1908. World championship tournaments for national men's and women's teams are held every two years.

The teams compete on a smooth grass field 90 to 100 yards (82 to 91 meters) long and 50 to 60 yards (46 to 55 meters) wide. Each team has 11 players. The basic formation has five forwards, three halfbacks, two fullbacks, and a goalkeeper. However, teams may use other combinations of players.

The goal cages are placed in the center of the end lines. The goal posts are 7 feet (2.13 meters) high and 12 feet (3.66 meters) apart. The posts are connected by a crossbar. A net is attached to the posts and the crossbar.

Each player carries a stick with a curved end that is always flat on its left side and rounded on its right. Only the flat side of the stick may be used to hit the ball. Most players use sticks that are about 35 inches (89 centimeters) long. The ball, about 9 inches (23 centimeters) in circumference, has a cork and twine center and a leather covering.

The Game is divided into two halves and varies in length from 30 to 70 minutes. The players try to move the ball with their sticks until they are in a position to shoot it through the other team's goal. A goal counts 1 point. It occurs each time a player hits the ball from within an area called the shooting circle and drives it over the goal line between the goal posts.

The game starts with a *bully*. Two opposing players stand in the center of the field, facing the side lines. First, they hit the ground on their side of the ball and then their opponent's stick, repeating this three times. Then each tries to hit the ball to a teammate. Play resumes with a bully after each goal. The rules allow no body contact or dangerous hitting, and the players cannot raise any part of the stick above their shoulders. The goalkeepers may kick the ball, but they may not advance it with their hands. The rules

Field Hockey is a fast-moving team sport played on a smooth grass field. The players try to hit a ball toward their opponents' goal, using sticks that are curved at one end. The sport requires skill, speed, and endurance and is popular in many countries throughout the world.

are made by the Women's International Hockey Rules Board. These rules have been modified for girls by the United States Field Hockey Association.

History. The exact origin of the sport is not known. Friezes carved by the ancient Greeks show players using crooked sticks to hit a small object. The French played field hockey at an early date and later introduced it to Great Britain. The word *hockey* evidently came from the Old French word *hoquet*, meaning shepherd's crook. In its early days, field hockey was known in Ireland as *hurling*, in Scotland as *shinty* or *shinny*, and in Wales as *banty*.

Only men played field hockey at first. But women tried the sport in 1887, and the All England Women's Hockey Association was formed in 1889.

Constance M. K. Applebee of the British College of Physical Education arranged a match in 1901 at Harvard College in Cambridge, Mass. She promoted the game in the United States. The United States Field Hockey Association (USFHA) was organized in 1922, and the first U.S. touring team went to Great Britain in 1924. Each year the USFHA sponsors a national field hockey tournament.

The International Federation of Women's Hockey Associations (IFWHA) was formed in 1927. Members of the IFWHA send touring teams on visits to other countries in the federation. About 35 countries throughout the world belong to the federation. BETTY SHELLENBERGER

See also HOCKEY.

FIELD-ION MICROSCOPE. See ION MICROSCOPE.

FIELD MAGNET. See ELECTRIC MOTOR (Parts of the Electric Motor).

FIELD MARSHAL. See MARSHAL.

FIELD MUSEUM OF NATURAL HISTORY, in Chicago, is one of the largest and best-known natural history museums in the world. It contains more than 13 million objects in four major fields—anthropology, botany, geology, and zoology.

Each year, more than a million people view the museum's collections. Its department of education provides lectures, short courses, and workshops. The museum also conducts natural history tours and sends traveling exhibits to schools. Its library has more than 185,000 volumes for the use of scientists and the general public. The museum is privately supported. But it receives some funds from the city, state, and federal governments.

Exhibits. In the Hall of the Stone Age, types of prehistoric human beings are exhibited in life-size dioramas that depict scenes and activities typical of their period. Other outstanding anthropology exhibits include collections from the civilizations of the ancient Egyptians and of North American Indians. There are also collections of gems and jewels, primitive art, and Chinese jade.

The museum's botany department includes a world-famous collection of plant models. The geology exhibits are classified in two groups, one illustrating the scientific, and the other showing the economic and industrial relations of mineral products of the earth. The geology department is noted for its great hall of paleontology, which has many fossil displays, including a number of dinosaurs. The department also has the most extensive collection of meteorites in the world. Another large exhibit in the museum represents in life-size a section of a forest of the coal age. The zoology exhibits

FIELD OF FORCE

Field Museum of Natural History, Chicago

The Field Museum of Natural History, in Chicago, is one of the world's largest and most famous museums of its kind.

include displays of the mammals of the world in habitat groups. Other exhibits illustrate facts and theories about animals in their relation to each other and to human beings.

History. The Chicago merchant and philanthropist Marshall Field I founded the museum in 1893 and gave it more than $9 million during his lifetime. The museum was first called the Columbian Museum of Chicago. Within a year of its founding, its name was changed to the Field Columbian Museum. In 1905, the museum received its present name. But from 1943 to 1966, it was called the Chicago Natural History Museum.

Critically reviewed by the FIELD MUSEUM OF NATURAL HISTORY

FIELD OF FORCE. See FORCE (Fields of Force).

FIELD SPANIEL is a hunting dog. For many years, owners separated field spaniels from cockers and other kinds of spaniels on the basis of size alone. The dog they called the field spaniel stands about 18 inches (46 centimeters) high and weighs 35 to 50 pounds (16 to 23 kilograms). It has a flat, glossy coat, usually black or some other solid color. The breed originated in England in the 1700's, but it has never been popular in the United States. This spaniel is intelligent and has great perseverance.   MAXWELL RIDDLE

FIELDING, HENRY (1707-1754), an English author, wrote *The History of Tom Jones, a Foundling* (1749), one of the world's great novels. The book is an exciting, humorous story of an orphan and his adventures. Although it begins when Tom is a baby, most of the story concerns the hero as a young man. Tom's many adventures include a variety of love affairs, ranging from passing encounters to his true love for Sophia Western.

In *Tom Jones,* Fielding did more than create a humorous adventure story. He skillfully incorporated the plot's many twists into a unified structure, beginning each of the novel's 18 *books* (chapters) with a brilliant and related essay. He filled his story with unforgettable characters whom he described in a sophisticated and lively style. These qualities greatly influenced later novelists, as did Fielding's realistic, basically unsentimental attitude toward life. Fielding ridiculed hypocrites and selfish persons but avoided

Detail of an engraving by William Hogarth; The British Museum, London

Henry Fielding

a preaching tone. His tongue-in-cheek irony makes *Tom Jones* an outstanding satire on society.

Fielding's novel *Joseph Andrews* (1742) is a *parody* (mock imitation) of *Pamela,* Samuel Richardson's serious novel about the rewards of a virtuous life. *The Life of Jonathan Wild the Great* (1743) is fictional, but its criminal hero was a real person whom Fielding treated ironically to contrast "greatness" with "goodness." Fielding's last novel, *Amelia* (1751), is a relatively sober work. It attacks social evils more directly than *Tom Jones,* but is less successful as a novel.

Early in his career, Fielding supported himself by writing plays. The most enjoyable is *The Tragedy of Tragedies; or, The Life and Death of Tom Thumb the Great* (1730-1731), a burlesque of English heroic drama. *Pasquin* (1736) and *The Historical Register for The Year 1736* (1737) attack Prime Minister Robert Walpole. These satires helped bring about the Licensing Act of 1737, which resulted in strict control and censorship of the London theater.

Fielding was also an excellent journalist and essayist. In 1752, he published the *Covent Garden Journal,* a satirical review of society and literature of his time that appeared twice a week. His *Journal of a Voyage to Lisbon,* published in 1755 after his death, describes a trip he made to Portugal.

Fielding was born near Glastonbury in Somerset. He attended Eton College and then studied law. He be-

Walter Chandoha

The Field Spaniel Has a Glossy Coat.

came a justice of the peace in 1748. Throughout his life, Fielding fought for social and legal reforms, both as a writer and as a magistrate.   FRANK W. WADSWORTH

FIELDS, W. C. (1879-1946), was an American motion-picture comedian. He played swindling characters who seemed dedicated to the philosophy that there is a "sucker born every minute." In his movies, Fields was always at war with the world, battling both people and objects. He hated children, and they hated him. Fields' trademarks included a top hat, a monstrous nose, and a distinctive side-of-the-mouth manner of speaking. His major films include *The Old-Fashioned Way* (1934), *It's a Gift* (1934), *The Man on the Flying Trapeze* (1935), *You Can't Cheat an Honest Man* (1939), *My Little Chickadee* (1940), *The Bank Dick* (1940), and *Never Give a Sucker an Even Break* (1941).

Fields was born in Philadelphia. His real name was William Claude Dukenfield. He began a vaudeville

Penguin Photo

W. C. Fields was a popular stage and motion-picture comedian. He and Mae West starred in the film *My Little Chickadee, above.*

and musical comedy career at the age of 14. He featured monologues, juggling, and tricks with a corkscrew billiard cue on stage and in his movies. RICHARD GRIFFITH

FIESOLE, FRA GIOVANNI DA. See FRA ANGELICO.

FIESTA, *fee EHS tuh,* is the Spanish word for *feast day* or *holiday.* Most fiestas are either religious or political. They may celebrate saints' days and holydays or such events as a nation's independence. All Latin-American nations and Spain hold fiestas. ELIZABETH HOUGH SECHRIST

See also FEASTS AND FESTIVALS; MEXICO (Holidays); SPAIN (Religious Holidays; pictures).

FIFE is a simple type of woodwind instrument similar to the flute (see FLUTE). The player blows across an opening in the head of the instrument to produce the tone. The pitch is controlled by closing and opening the 6 finger holes. The fife has no keys and cannot produce chromatic scale tones. The English probably brought fifes from Switzerland to Britain in the 1500's.

In the United States, some patriotic groups have fife and drum corps. A corps in Chester, Conn., is one of the most famous. But few people now play the fife. Usually

a piccolo replaces it. Archibald M. Willard's painting *The Spirit of '76* pictures a man playing a fife while his two companions beat snare drums (see REVOLUTIONARY WAR IN AMERICA [picture]). CHARLES B. RIGHTER

FIFTEENTH AMENDMENT to the United States Constitution guarantees that an American citizen shall not be discriminated against in exercising the right to vote. It states that the federal and state governments cannot bar a citizen from voting because the person had been a slave or because of race. Amendment 15 was ratified on Feb. 3, 1870. Seven Southern states tried to bypass it by adding *grandfather clauses* to their constitutions. One such clause gave the right to vote to persons who could vote on Jan. 1, 1867, and to their family descendants. In 1915, the Supreme Court of the United States declared grandfather clauses unconstitutional. For information on more recent legislation protecting the right to vote, see VOTING (Restrictions on Voting). See also GRANDFATHER CLAUSE; CONSTITUTION OF THE UNITED STATES.

FIFTH AMENDMENT to the United States Constitution guarantees that people cannot be forced to testify against themselves in a criminal case. It also provides that a person cannot be placed in jeopardy twice for the same offense. Amendment 5 also guarantees that (1) a person cannot be deprived of life, liberty, or property without due process of law; (2) a person cannot be held to answer for a "capital, or otherwise infamous crime" unless he or she has been indicted by a grand jury, except that military personnel are subject to court-martial; (3) property cannot be taken from a person without just compensation. Amendment 5 is a part of the Bill of Rights ratified on Dec. 15, 1791. See also BILL OF RIGHTS; DUE PROCESS OF LAW; CONSTITUTION OF THE UNITED STATES.

FIFTH COLUMN refers to undercover agents operating within the ranks of an enemy to undermine its cause. The agents pave the way for military or political invasion. They may work in an army, political party, or industry. Their activities include spying, sabotage, propaganda, agitation, infiltration, and even, terror and revolt. The term *fifth column* was first used during the Spanish Civil War (1936-1939) to describe the work of Francisco Franco's followers in Loyalist Madrid. Emilio Mola, a leader under Franco, said, "I have four columns moving against Madrid, and a fifth will rise up inside the city itself." STEFAN T. POSSONY

FIFTH REPUBLIC. See FRANCE (Government; History).

FIFTY-FOUR FORTY OR FIGHT was a slogan used during a boundary dispute between the United States and Great Britain. An 1818 treaty allowed both nations to occupy the Oregon Country, lying between 42° and 54°40' north latitude. In the 1830's and 1840's, American expansionists wanted to take the whole area, by force if necessary. When James K. Polk became president, the U.S. made a new treaty that set 49° as a boundary, except for Vancouver Island. The U.S. secured the land south of the line, and Great Britain obtained the land to the north. OSCAR O. WINTHER

See also BRITISH COLUMBIA (The Border Dispute); POLK, JAMES KNOX ("Oregon Fever").

FIG is the name of a popular fruit and the plant on which it grows. The fig plant may grow as a low, spreading bush or as a tree, depending on how it is pruned. The fig is native to the Mediterranean region. People have eaten figs since earliest times and the fruit is mentioned in the Bible and other ancient records. In the United States, fig trees grow chiefly in the southern half of the country and in central California. However, figs may be grown as far north as Michigan, if the trees are protected against frost in winter.

Growing Figs. New trees may be grown by cutting two- or three-year-old branches and planting them in early spring. The plant may produce a few fruits within the second or third year after planting.

The fig is sometimes called a fruit without a flower. However, the inside of each fruit has several hundred tiny flowers. An opening at the top of the fruit permits a small wasp to enter and pollinate the flowers. The common fig produces two crops of fruit each year. The first crop, called *breba*, is produced on branches made the previous season. The first crop matures in late June or early July. The second crop is produced on new branches and matures in late August or early September.

Types of Figs include caprifigs, Smyrna figs, and common figs. *Caprifigs*, which usually cannot be eaten, are commonly known as *male* figs. They contain both male and female flowers. Fig wasps, which live in caprifigs, carry pollen from the male flowers to the female flowers of the *Smyrna* figs. Smyrna figs have only female flowers which must be pollinated by the pollen from caprifigs before the fruit will grow. The Calimyrna fig, a variety of Smyrna fig, is grown in California. *Common* figs also contain only female flowers, but they do not have to be pollinated by the caprifig.

People may eat figs fresh, canned, preserved, or pickled. But most figs are eaten dried. Dried figs contain large amounts of sugar, calcium, and iron. Bakers use figs to make fig bars and fig newtons.

Scientific Classification. Fig trees belong to the mulberry family, *Moraceae*. The common fig is classified as genus *Ficus*, species *F. carica*.   JULIAN C. CRANE

See also Bo Tree.

J. Horace McFarland

Clusters of Figs grow close to the stem of the fig tree. They are surrounded by deeply lobed leaves.

FIGARO, *FIG uh roh,* is the rascally hero of Pierre de Beaumarchais' comedies, *The Barber of Seville* (1775) and *The Marriage of Figaro* (1784). As a barber, Figaro blocks Dr. Bartolo's attempts to marry his ward, Rosina, and promotes her marriage to Count Almaviva. In the latter play, Figaro succeeds in marrying Countess Almaviva's ward, Susanna. Rossini and Mozart based operas on these witty comedies.   GEORGE ROBERT CARLSEN

See also BEAUMARCHAIS, PIERRE; OPERA.

FIGHTER. See AIR FORCE, U.S. (Fighters); BOXING.

FIGHTING FISH is a small, quarrelsome fish that lives in the waters around the Malay Archipelago. It is often

G. J. M. Timmerman, *Tropical Fish Hobbyist*

Fighting Fish grow about 2½ inches (6.4 centimeters) long. The beautiful veil-tailed variety is a favorite in the aquarium.

called the *Betta* or *Siamese fighting fish*. It has a long waving tail and fins. When the male is excited, it becomes colored with reds, greens, purples, and blues. Only the male is a fighter. Fighting fish dash at one another, biting the opponent's fins until one of the fish is exhausted. One will even attack its own image in a mirror. Watching fights between male fighting fish is a popular sport among the people of Thailand.

Scientific Classification. The fighting fish is a member of the family *Anabantidae*. It is genus *Betta*, species *B. splendens*.   LEONARD P. SCHULTZ

See also FISH (pictures: Fish of Tropical Fresh Waters; A Male Siamese Fighting Fish).

FIGUERES, JOSÉ. See COSTA RICA (Revolutions and Reforms; Recent Developments).

FIGURE OF SPEECH is the use of words in certain conventional patterns of thought and expression. For example, we might read that "The spy was cornered *like a rat* . . . The crowd *surged* forward . . . The *redcoats* withdrew . . . Justice *hung her head* . . . Here was *mercy* indeed! . . . The *entire nation* screamed vengeance."

Each of these figures of speech has its own name. The first is *simile*, when the spy is directly compared with a rat. The second is simple *metaphor*, when the author implies that the movement of the crowd is like that of an oncoming wave. The third is *metonymy*, when the word "redcoats" stands for the soldiers who wear them. The fourth, *personification*, speaks of justice as though it were a person. The fifth is *irony*, because the author means the opposite of mercy. The sixth is *hyperbole*, or exaggeration for special effect.

Figures of speech are the flowers of rhetoric. They give to poetry much of its beauty and fragrance, its sweetness and germinal power. John Milton wrote, in "On His Being Arrived at the Age of Twenty-Three,"

How soon hath Time, the subtle thief of youth,
Stolen on his wing my three and twentieth year!
My hasting days fly on with full career,
But my late spring no bud or blossom shew'th.

Without consciously analyzing the personification, metonymy, and metaphor used, the reader still senses the richness of imagery and poetic thought. Everyday speech also uses many such figures.   CHARLES W. COOPER

See also HYPERBOLE; IRONY; METAPHOR; METONYMY; SIMILE.

FIGURE SKATING. See ICE SKATING.

FIGWORT FAMILY, *FIG wurt,* or SCROPHULARIACEAE, *SKRAHF yoo LAY ree AY see ee,* is a group of about 3,000 species of herbs, shrubs, and small trees. Some of these plants are used in medicines. They have bell-shaped flowers which are divided into two lips. The flowers grow at the top of a slender stem, while the leaves often grow in pairs on the stem. The family flourishes especially in temperate regions. It includes wild flowers and weeds such as mullein, butter-and-eggs, speedwell, and lousewort. The cultivated varieties include foxglove, snapdragon, and calceolaria.

Certain figworts live partially as parasites on other plants. The drug *digitalis,* used for heart ailments, comes from a kind of foxglove. Scrophularia, from which the family is named, is a medicinal figwort. People at one time believed that it would cure scrofula (see SCROFULA).   HAROLD NORMAN MOLDENKE

Related Articles in WORLD BOOK include:

Beardtongue	Indian Paintbrush	Slipperwort
Digitalis	Monkey Flower	Snapdragon
Foxglove	Mullein	Toadflax

FIJI, *FEE jee,* is a country in the South Pacific Ocean made up of more than 800 scattered islands. Fiji has a total land area of 7,055 square miles (18,272 square kilometers). The island of Viti Levu (Big Fiji) covers about half this area, and Vanua Levu (Big Land) occupies about a third. Many of the other islands are merely piles of sand on coral reefs. Suva, Fiji's capital and largest city, lies on Viti Levu's southern coast (see SUVA).

Fiji has about 627,000 people, of whom 40 per cent are native Fijians of chiefly Melanesian descent. About 50 per cent of the people are descendants of laborers imported from India. The remaining 10 per cent—Fiji's so-called "general" population group—have Chinese, European, Micronesian, or Polynesian ancestry. Fiji became independent in 1970 after being a British crown colony since 1874. It remained a member of the Commonwealth of Nations.

Government. Fiji has two houses of parliament. The Senate consists of 22 members appointed to six-year terms. The people elect the 52 members of Fiji's House of Representatives to five-year terms. Fiji's political leader, the prime minister, is the leader of the majority party in the House of Representatives.

Under Fiji's Constitution, adopted in 1970, the voters are divided into three groups—Fijian, Indian, and general. In every election, a fixed number of candidates from each group must be chosen. For example, the House of Representatives must have 22 Fijians, 22 Indians, and 8 others.

People. Most native Fijians live in rural areas. They follow such traditional customs as the ceremonial drinking of *kava,* a beverage made from pepper plants. The men wear skirts called *sulus,* and the women wear

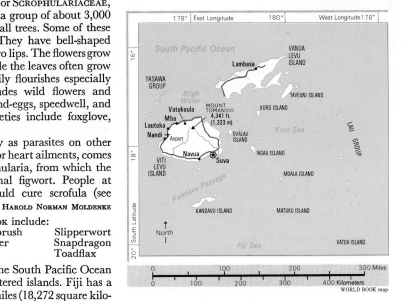

Fiji

⊛ National capital
• Other city or town
━━ Road
〜 River
▲ Mountain

WORLD BOOK map

bright cotton dresses or occasionally grass skirts. Most native Fijians are Christians.

The Indians are descendants of about 60,000 laborers brought from India between 1879 and 1916 to work on Fiji's sugar plantations. Many Indians still work in the cane fields, but others have become prosperous shopkeepers or business people. Indians control much of Fiji's business and industry. The Indian women wear the *sari,* the traditional dress of India. Most of the Indians are Muslims or Hindus.

English, the official language of Fiji, is used in the schools. But the country also has two other main languages, Fijian and Hindustani. The law does not require children to go to school, but over 85 per cent of those from 6 to 13 years old do so. Most Fijian and Indian youngsters attend separate schools. The University of the South Pacific in Suva, Fiji's only university, serves students from hundreds of the Pacific Islands.

Land. Most of the Fiji islands were formed by volcanoes. Coral reefs surround nearly all the islands. The larger islands have high volcanic peaks, rolling hills, rivers, and grasslands. Tropical rain forests cover more than half the total area of Fiji. The islands also have fertile coastal plains and river valleys.

Stuart Inder, the contributor of this article, is Publisher of Pacific Islands Monthly, *a magazine published in Sydney, Australia.*

Nitin Lal, Fiji Visitors Bureau

Suva, the Capital and Largest City of Fiji, is also the nation's chief port and commercial center. Many modern buildings stand along the shoreline of the city.

Milt and Joan Mann, Van Cleve Photography

Sugar Cane is one of Fiji's chief products. The photograph above shows a team of oxen pulling a farmer's cartload of sugar cane stalks to market. The cart runs on tracks.

Cool winds make Fiji's tropical climate relatively comfortable. Temperatures range from about 60° F. (16° C) to 90° F. (32° C). Heavy rains and tropical

---

FACTS IN BRIEF

Capital: Suva.

Official Language: English.

Form of Government: Constitutional monarchy.

Head of State: British monarch.

Head of Government: Prime minister.

Parliament: *Senate*—22 members appointed to 6-year terms; *House of Representatives*—52 members elected to 5-year terms.

Total Land Area: 7,055 sq. mi. (18,272 km²). *Greatest Distances*—north-south, 364 mi. (586 km); east-west, 334 mi. (538 km). *Coastline*—925 mi. (1,489 km).

Elevation: *Highest*—Mount Tomaniivi, on Viti Levu, 4,341 ft. (1,323 m) above sea level. *Lowest*—sea level.

Population: *Estimated 1979 Population*—627,000; distribution, 72 per cent rural, 28 per cent urban; density, 88 persons per sq. mi. (34 persons per km²). *1966 Census*—476,727. *Estimated 1984 Population*—696,000.

Chief Products: *Agriculture*—bananas, coconuts, forest products, sugar. *Manufacturing*—beer, cement, cigarettes. *Mining*—gold, silver.

National Anthem: *God Save the Queen.*

Flag: The British Union Jack appears in the upper left on a light blue field. On the right is the shield from Fiji's coat of arms with a British lion, a dove, coconut palms, and such agricultural products as bananas and sugar cane. Adopted on Oct. 10, 1970. See FLAG (color picture: Flags of Asia and the Pacific).

Money: *Basic Unit*—Fijian dollar. See MONEY (table).

storms occur frequently between November and April.

Economy of Fiji is based primarily on agriculture. Most Fijians grow such crops as sugar cane and coconuts. Many also work in the country's tourist industry.

Sugar and coconut products account for about three-fourths of Fiji's exports. Other exports include bananas, gold, and timber. Manufactured products include beer, building materials, cement, and cigarettes.

Fiji has been called the "crossroads of the South Pacific." The airport at Nandi, on Viti Levu, is the busiest terminal south of the equator for planes flying the Pacific. Fiji also lies on major shipping routes and has several excellent harbors.

History. Melanesians migrated to Fiji thousands of years ago, probably from Indonesia. A small group of Polynesians settled there during the A.D. 100's. In 1643, Abel Tasman, a Dutch navigator, became the first European to see Fiji. Captain James Cook, a British explorer, visited Vatoa, one of the southern islands in 1774. During the 1800's, traders, Methodist missionaries, and escaped Australian convicts visited or settled in Fiji.

The Fijians were cannibals, and various tribes fought one another until 1871, when a chief named Cakobau extended his influence over much of Fiji. With the help of King George Tupou I, of nearby Tonga, Cakobau brought peace to Fiji. To protect the country from outside interference, Cakobau asked Britain to make Fiji a crown colony. Britain did so on Oct. 10, 1874. Fiji remained a colony until, at its own request, it gained independence on Oct. 10, 1970.   STUART INDER

See also CLOTHING (picture: Policeman in Fiji).

FILAMENT. See ELECTRIC LIGHT.

FILAMENT. See FLOWER (The Stamens).

FILARIA, *fih LAIR ee uh,* is a long threadlike round-worm that lives as a parasite in the bodies of human beings and animals. Filariae are commonly found in tropical and subtropical countries. The male worm is shorter than the female and it has a curved tail.

The *larvae* (young worms) are born alive. They can be seen in the blood near the body surface of the *host* (the animal in which the larvae live). When a blood-sucking fly or mosquito bites an infected person, it takes up the larvae with the blood. The larvae develop in the mosquito's or fly's head near the mouth. Then when the insect bites another animal, the larvae enter the wound and infect a new host.

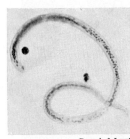

Bausch & Lomb

Filaria Under a Microscope clearly shows its transparent, threadlike body.

Wuchereria (Filaria) ban-crofti is harmful to human beings. It is found in Africa, South America, and the Far East. The adult worms live in the *lymph,* a body fluid (see LYM-PHATIC SYSTEM). When the worms block the flow of lymph, a severe swelling of body organs called *ele-phantiasis* results (see ELEPHANTIASIS). *Wuchereria ban-crofti* can be eliminated by controlling the mosquitoes that carry the larvae. Other kinds of filariae infect such animals as cattle and dogs.

Scientific Classification. Filariae are members of the phylum *Aschelminthes* and the roundworm class *Nema-toda.* JAMES A. MCLEOD

See also MANSON, SIR PATRICK.

FILBERT is the name for both the nut and the plant of a group of trees and shrubs closely related to the birches. The nuts from these plants are also called *hazelnuts* and *cobnuts* (see HAZEL). Some filberts grow into large trees 60 feet (18 meters) tall. Others are shrubs that normally grow from 2 to 30 feet (0.6 to 9 meters) high, depending upon what kind they are and their environment. Filberts are native to North America, Europe, and Asia. They thrive in orchards in the Pacific Northwest in the United States and in southern Europe. The cultivated seeds taste better than the wild ones, and are better roasted than raw.

The nuts form in compact clusters, with each nut

Arthur H. Fisher

Filberts, or Hazelnuts, grow inside a smooth shell, *left,* shaped somewhat like an acorn. When the shell is cracked, *center,* the tasty meat can easily be taken out, *right.*

encased within its own husk. The nuts have smooth, hard, but brittle shells. The kernels are single.

Scientific Classification. Filberts belong to the birch family, *Betulaceae.* They are genus *Corylus.* Most cultivated varieties are species *C. avellana.* REID M. BROOKS

FILENE, *fih LEEN,* **EDWARD ALBERT** (1860-1937), an American merchant, pioneered in improving retail distribution. He helped organize the Boston, the United States, and the International chambers of commerce. He promoted the credit union movement in the United States. He also founded the Twentieth Century Fund to study major economic problems. He supported the League of Nations and other movements for international understanding. Filene was born in Salem, Mass. W. H. BAUGHN

FILIBUSTER, *FIHL uh buhs tuhr,* originally meant a pirate of the 1600's. The word comes from the Dutch *Vrijbuiter,* which means *freebooter.* Beginning about 1850, *filibuster* came to mean an adventurer who organized an armed expedition against a nation with which his own country was at peace. In the mid-1800's, many adventurers led filibustering expeditions from the United States to attack various Latin-American countries. In 1850 and 1851, Narciso López, a former officer of the Spanish army, led two unsuccessful attempts to end Spanish rule in Cuba. The most notorious American filibuster, a Californian named William Walker, organized invasions of Lower California, Nicaragua, and Honduras (see WALKER, WILLIAM). JOHN DONALD HICKS

FILIBUSTERING is the practice by which a minority in a legislature uses extended debate to block or delay action on a proposed bill. Members of the minority make endless speeches, demand roll calls, propose useless motions, and use other delaying tactics. If they can keep the bill from coming to a vote, they can defeat it even though the majority favors it.

The U.S. Senate has the tradition of unlimited debate. A senator who holds the floor may speak without interruption. Senators may filibuster alone or with a group. The Senate can end a filibuster only by invoking the cloture rule, adopted in 1917 and amended in 1959 and 1975. Under the rule, a vote of 60 senators, three-fifths of the Senate membership, can limit each senator to one hour of debate on most bills. However, filibusters on proposed changes in the Senate rules can be stopped only by a two-thirds majority of the members present and voting. See CLOTURE.

A filibuster against the civil rights bill of 1964 lasted 75 days, the longest since the rule was adopted. When cloture was invoked, it was the first time in 12 attempts that the filibuster on a civil rights bill was limited.

Several senators have filibustered for half a day or more. Robert M. La Follette, Sr., filibustered 18 hours and 23 minutes in 1908. Huey Long held the floor for 15 hours and 30 minutes in 1935. In 1957, Strom Thurmond filibustered 24 hours and 18 minutes in a debate over a civil rights bill. ROBERT A. DAHL

FILIOQUE. See EASTERN ORTHODOX CHURCHES.

FILIPINOS. See PHILIPPINES (The People); RACES, HUMAN (table: Geographical Races [Asian]).

FILIPPO LIPPI. See LIPPI (Fra Filippo).

FILLING STATION. See PETROLEUM (Moving the Oil; Service Stations).

MILLARD
FILLMORE

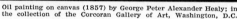

POLK
11th President
1845 — 1849

TAYLOR
12th President
1849 — 1850

PIERCE
14th President
1853 — 1857

BUCHANAN
15th President
1857 — 1861

Oil painting on canvas (1857) by George Peter Alexander Healy; in the collection of the Corcoran Gallery of Art, Washington, D.C.

13TH PRESIDENT OF THE UNITED STATES 1850-1853

FILLMORE, MILLARD (1800-1874), the second Vice-President to inherit the nation's highest office, became President when Zachary Taylor died. During his 32 months in office, Fillmore's most important action was his approval of the Compromise of 1850. This series of laws helped delay the Civil War for more than 10 years.

A self-made man, Fillmore had been a poor boy who was once a clothmaker's apprentice. He studied law, then won election to the New York state legislature and to Congress. He became known nationally only after the Whig political party chose him to be Taylor's vice-presidential running mate in 1848.

As Vice-President, Fillmore presided coolly over the heated Senate debates between slavery and antislavery forces. The Compromise of 1850, which he helped achieve, had been opposed by President Taylor because of its concessions to the South. But when Taylor died, Fillmore urged passage of the compromise, and quickly signed it into law. Fillmore personally did not approve of slavery. But he loved the Union, and preferred compromise to the risk of war.

Fillmore faithfully enforced the compromise, including its provision for the return of runaway slaves. This policy lost him the support of most Northerners, and he was not nominated for President in 1852.

A conservative dresser, Fillmore always wore a dark frock coat and a high-collared shirt with a black silk neckcloth tied in a bow in front. He had kindly blue eyes and a gracious, courteous manner. People admired his modesty. When Oxford University offered him an honorary degree, Fillmore replied that he had done nothing to deserve the honor, and would not accept it.

Early Life

Millard Fillmore was born in Locke, N.Y., on Jan. 7, 1800. He was the second child in a family of three girls and six boys. His parents, Nathaniel and Phoebe Millard Fillmore, had moved to the frontier from Bennington, Vt. The elder Fillmore had hoped to improve his fortune, but he lost his farm through a faulty title. He then moved to another part of Cayuga County where he rented a heavily wooded piece of land. Millard helped his father clear timber and work the farm.

Education. Millard attended school for only short periods, but he learned reading, spelling, arithmetic, and geography. His father owned two books, the Bible and a hymnbook.

At the age of 14, Millard was apprenticed to a clothmaker. His master treated Millard so badly that the boy once threatened him with an ax. He found a new

---

IMPORTANT DATES IN FILLMORE'S LIFE

1800 (Jan. 7) Born in Locke, N.Y.
1826 (Feb. 5) Married Abigail Powers.
1832 Elected to U.S. House of Representatives.
1848 Elected Vice-President of the United States.
1850 (July 10) Succeeded to the presidency.
1852 Defeated in bid for presidential nomination.
1853 Mrs. Abigail Fillmore died.
1856 Defeated in presidential election.
1858 (Feb. 10) Married Mrs. Caroline McIntosh.
1874 (March 8) Died in Buffalo, N.Y.

master, but he bought his freedom from the apprenticeship in 1819 for $30. In the same year, he also purchased the first book he had ever owned, a dictionary. Fillmore decided to become a lawyer. He taught school while he studied with a local judge. In 1823, he opened a law office in East Aurora, N.Y.

Fillmore's Family. During one of his periods of schooling, Fillmore's teacher was Abigail Powers (March 13, 1798-March 30, 1853), the daughter of a Baptist minister. He was 19 and she was 21, and they fell in love. After he became a lawyer, they were married in 1826. But she continued to teach until 1828. The couple had two children, Millard Powers Fillmore (1828-1889) and Mary Abigail Fillmore (1832-1854). In 1830, the family moved to Buffalo, N.Y.

Political and Public Career

Fillmore won election to the New York House of Representatives in 1828 with the help of Thurlow Weed, an Albany publisher who helped form the Whig party. Fillmore was twice re-elected.

Congressman. In 1832, Fillmore was elected to the U.S. House of Representatives. He served from 1833 to 1835 and from 1837 to 1843. He generally favored the nationalistic policies of Henry Clay. As chairman of the Ways and Means Committee, Fillmore was the chief author of the tariff of 1842, which raised duties on manufactured goods. He ran for governor of New York in 1844, but was defeated and returned to his law practice. In 1846, he became the first chancellor of the University of Buffalo. The next year, he was elected comptroller of New York.

Vice-President. The Whigs nominated Fillmore for Vice-President in 1848 on a ticket headed by General Zachary Taylor, the hero of the Mexican War. The Democrats nominated Senator Lewis Cass of Michigan for President and former Congressman William O. Butler of Kentucky for Vice-President. During the campaign, the Democrats split over the slavery issue, and many voted for the Free Soil ticket (see FREE SOIL

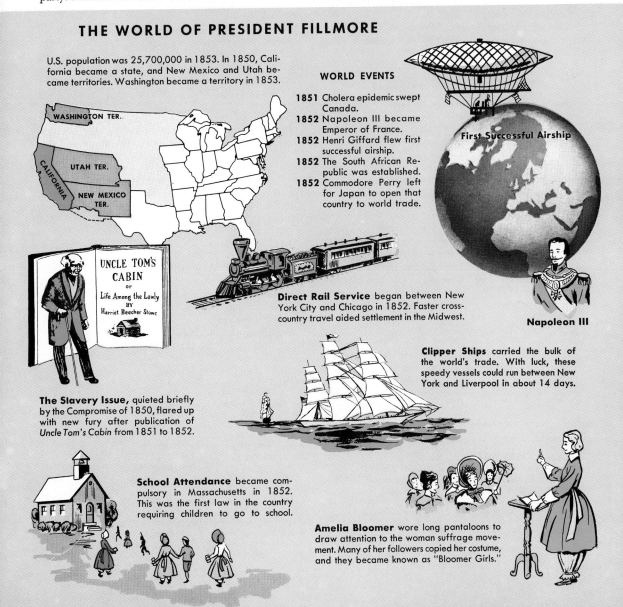

THE WORLD OF PRESIDENT FILLMORE

U.S. population was 25,700,000 in 1853. In 1850, California became a state, and New Mexico and Utah became territories. Washington became a territory in 1853.

WASHINGTON TER.

CALIFORNIA

UTAH TER.

NEW MEXICO TER.

WORLD EVENTS

1851 Cholera epidemic swept Canada.
1852 Napoleon III became Emperor of France.
1852 Henri Giffard flew first successful airship.
1852 The South African Republic was established.
1852 Commodore Perry left for Japan to open that country to world trade.

First Successful Airship

Napoleon III

Direct Rail Service began between New York City and Chicago in 1852. Faster cross-country travel aided settlement in the Midwest.

UNCLE TOM'S CABIN or Life Among the Lowly BY Harriet Beecher Stowe

Clipper Ships carried the bulk of the world's trade. With luck, these speedy vessels could run between New York and Liverpool in about 14 days.

The Slavery Issue, quieted briefly by the Compromise of 1850, flared up with new fury after publication of *Uncle Tom's Cabin* from 1851 to 1852.

School Attendance became compulsory in Massachusetts in 1852. This was the first law in the country requiring children to go to school.

Amelia Bloomer wore long pantaloons to draw attention to the woman suffrage movement. Many of her followers copied her costume, and they became known as "Bloomer Girls."

Courtesy of Cayuga Museum of History and Art, Auburn, New York

Fillmore's Birthplace was a log cabin in Locke, N.Y. The cabin, now restored, appears here as it looked during Fillmore's youth.

The Buffalo Historical Society

Abigail Powers Fillmore, the President's wife, found her official duties a heavy burden.

Mary Abigail Fillmore, their only daughter, often served as White House hostess.

PARTY). Taylor and Fillmore won the election by a margin of 36 electoral votes.

Fillmore presided impartially over the Senate debate on the Compromise of 1850 (see COMPROMISE OF 1850). Before the issue was settled, President Taylor died on July 9, 1850. Fillmore took office the next day.

Fillmore's Administration (1850-1853)

Accomplishments. After becoming President, Fillmore came forth strongly in favor of compromise on slavery. As his first act, he replaced Taylor's Cabinet with men who had led the fight for compromise.

In September, Congress passed the series of laws that made up the Compromise of 1850. Fillmore promptly signed them. The compromise abolished the slave trade in the District of Columbia, admitted California as a free state, and organized the territories of Utah and New Mexico with no reference to slavery. It also settled the Texas boundary dispute and established a stricter fugitive slave law (see FUGITIVE SLAVE LAW).

Also during Fillmore's administration, Congress reduced the basic postal rate from five to three cents. Late in 1852, the President sent Commodore Matthew C. Perry on an expedition to the Far East. Two years later, after Fillmore had left the presidency, this voyage resulted in the first trade treaty with Japan.

Life in the White House. Abigail Fillmore found her responsibilities as First Lady a heavy burden on her health. Her 18-year-old daughter Mary took over many official tasks. Mrs. Fillmore arranged for the purchase of the first cooking stove in the White House. She also set up the first White House library. When the Library

---

FILLMORE'S CABINET

Secretary of State . . . . *Daniel Webster
 *Edward Everett (1852)
Secretary of the Treasury . . . Thomas Corwin
Secretary of War . . . . Charles M. Conrad
Attorney General . . . . John J. Crittenden
Postmaster General . . . . Nathan K. Hall
 Samuel D. Hubbard (1852)
Secretary of the Navy . . . . . . William A. Graham
 John P. Kennedy (1852)
Secretary of the Interior . . . . Thomas M. T. McKennan
 Alexander H. H. Stuart (1850)
 *Has a separate biography in WORLD BOOK.

of Congress burned in 1851, Fillmore and his Cabinet helped fight the blaze.

Election of 1852. When the Whigs met to nominate a presidential candidate in 1852, the Southerners supported Fillmore. But the President's zeal in enforcing the Fugitive Slave Law made many Northerners reject him. The delegates nominated an antislavery candidate, General Winfield Scott.

Later Years

Mrs. Fillmore died less than a month after her husband left office. She was buried in Washington, D.C.

Fillmore returned to Buffalo and resumed his law practice. The Know-Nothing and the Whig parties both nominated him for President in 1856. But the Republican party, which nominated General John C. Frémont, cut into his support. Democrat James Buchanan won. Fillmore ran third, carrying only one state, Maryland.

In 1858, Fillmore married Mrs. Caroline Carmichael McIntosh (Oct. 21, 1813-Aug. 11, 1881), a widow. During the Civil War, he opposed many of Abraham Lincoln's policies. After the war, he favored the Reconstruction program of President Andrew Johnson. Fillmore died on March 8, 1874, and was buried in Forest Lawn Cemetery in Buffalo.   BRAINERD DYER

Outline

I. Early Life
 A. Education   B. Fillmore's Family
II. Political and Public Career
 A. Congressman   B. Vice-President
III. Fillmore's Administration (1850-1853)
 A. Accomplishments   C. Election of 1852
 B. Life in the White House
IV. Later Years

Questions

What did Fillmore do that is credited with delaying the Civil War for 10 years?

How did Fillmore meet his first wife?

Why did Fillmore support some proslavery measures even though he opposed slavery?

Why did he refuse a degree from Oxford University?

How did the argument over slavery help Zachary Taylor and Fillmore win office in 1848?

FILM. See MOTION PICTURE (Film); PHOTOGRAPHY.

FILM CITY. See ROCHESTER (N.Y.).

FILM FESTIVAL. See MOTION PICTURE (Festivals and Awards).

FILMSTRIP is a related series of still pictures on 35 mm. film. A projector flashes one after another of these pictures on a screen. Teachers use filmstrips for instruction. They are easier to use, can be stored in less space, and cost less than slides.

Filmstrips are black and white or in color. A record player or tape recorder attached to the projector may provide sound for the filmstrips. The recording explains the film and sometimes has music and sound effects. Some recordings can change pictures automatically by transmitting a silent signal to a special type of projector. Other types give a beep when the operator should change pictures. But teachers often prefer to explain the picture themselves or to have a pupil do it. In this way, the picture can be changed whenever desired. Students can ask questions immediately instead of waiting until the end of the picture.   BEAUMONT NEWHALL

FILTER is a device that removes unwanted quantities from the flow of liquids or gases, or from the transmission of electric currents, beams of light, and sound waves. Filters that remove solid particles or other impurities from liquids or gases are made from paper, cloth, charcoal, porcelain, fiber glass, asbestos, or some other porous material. Glass or gelatin filters are used on cameras to filter out certain light rays (see PHOTOGRAPHY [Accessories]).

Gasoline engines use various types of filters to remove impurities from air, lubricating oils, or fuel. Dry-paper filters on automobile carburetors remove impurities from air before it enters the engine. Most oil filters also are made of fibrous paper. Many fuel filters have a stack of ceramic or metal disks separated by narrow spaces, but a few consist of wire screen. Some high-temperature engines also use magnetic filters. The filters attract metallic particles smaller than 1 micron (0.001 millimeter, or 0.000039 inch).

Cigarette filters, usually made of cellulose acetate, remove some of the tar and nicotine particles from cigarette smoke. Air conditioners use filters made of fiber glass or metal, coated with an adhesive, to remove dust and pollen from the air. Almost all large cities have filtration plants to filter water.   JAMES B. JONES

See also AIR CONDITIONING (Cleaning the Air); AQUARIUM (picture).

FILTRATION. See WATER (City Water Systems).

FIN. See AIRPLANE (The Tail Assembly); FISH (The Bodies of Fish).

FINALE. See MUSIC (table: Terms Used in Music).

FINANCE. See ECONOMICS; BANKS AND BANKING; BUDGET; MONEY.

FINANCE BILL. See BILL OF EXCHANGE.

FINANCE COMPANY is a firm that loans money to people who promise to repay the loan with interest in a specified period of time. A borrower must offer some guarantee that he will repay the loan, such as a lien on his salary or personal possessions (see LIEN). Some finance companies also offer credit card services that enable the holder to buy merchandise. Finance companies also make loans to merchants and manufacturers. A merchant may offer the finance company a purchaser's contract to buy goods on installment pay-

ments as security for cash loans (see INSTALLMENT PLAN). Some finance companies purchase these contracts. A businessman who needs a loan can offer his property, merchandise, or unpaid bills due to him as security.   L. T. FLATLEY

See also LOAN COMPANY.

FINBACK. See WHALE (Kinds of Whales).

FINCH is the name given to birds that belong to the family of seedeaters. About 1 of every 7 birds is a member of this family, the largest of all the families of birds. Finches live in all parts of the world. Several species live in Australia, though finches are not native to that continent. Also in Australia, some birds of a different family are commonly referred to as finches. The black-ringed finch, for example, is not really a finch. It belongs to the family *Ploceidae*.

Many finches sing beautifully. Most species have dull colors, but a few are brilliantly colored. All have sharp, pointed, cone-shaped bills, strong enough to crush seeds. Great numbers of finches live in the United States and Canada. They include the chewink, goldfinch, bunting, and grosbeak.

Scientific Classification. The family of seedeaters is named *Fringillidae*.   ARTHUR A. ALLEN

Related Articles in WORLD BOOK include:

Bird (pictures)	Cardinal	Grosbeak	Pine Siskin
Bullfinch	Crossbill	Junco	Sparrow
Bunting	Goldfinch	Linnet	Towhee
Canary			

FINCH, ROBERT HUTCHISON (1925-   ), was United States secretary of health, education, and welfare (HEW) under President Richard M. Nixon in 1969 and 1970. From 1970 to 1972, Finch served as counsellor to the President—a post with Cabinet rank—and a member of the Domestic Council.

Finch was one of Nixon's closest friends and most trusted political advisers. He served as Nixon's administrative assistant from 1958 to 1960, while Nixon was Vice-President. He directed Nixon's unsuccessful campaign for President in 1960. He became lieutenant governor of California in 1967. When Nixon was elected President in 1968, he offered Finch his choice of Cabinet posts.

Finch was born in Tempe, Ariz., and grew up in southern California. He graduated from Occidental College and the University of Southern California Law School. Finch served as a Marine, both in World War II and the Korean War.   DAVID S. BRODER

FINE is a payment of money ordered by a court from a person who has been found guilty of violating a law. The word comes from the Latin *finem facere*, meaning *to put an end to*. The term originated in England in 1275, when the courts began to permit convicts to be released from prison when they paid a required amount of money. A fine is often the punishment for a *misdemeanor* (minor crime). But a fine and a prison sentence can be the penalty for a major crime. If a person cannot pay a fine assessed against him, he is usually ordered to serve a prison sentence.   FRED E. INBAU

FINE ARTS are concerned with making or performing beautiful products or products that appeal in some way to man's aesthetic tastes. People expect to enjoy a poem, a painting, or a symphony for its own sake, not merely as a means to something else. People also expect a great work of art to develop their minds by expressing and clarifying the best thoughts of great men and women.

Grouping the Arts. In a broad sense, the fine arts include music, literature, opera, and ballet, as well as painting, sculpture, architecture, and the decorative arts. Here the word *fine* is often taken to mean *beautiful* or *aesthetically pleasing*. But an artist does not always try to make things beautiful or pleasing. Sometimes he tries instead to shock or arouse the public to indignation or pity. He may do this by showing the tragic, evil, or ugly sides of life.

In a narrower sense, the fine arts include only the arts that appeal to aesthetic taste through the sense of sight. These arts include painting, sculpture, architecture, landscape design, furniture, ceramics, jewelry, and textile design. Many colleges have departments of "fine arts" that cover only these arts. But most authorities now prefer to call these the *visual arts*. They classify music and spoken literature, as in a dramatic performance, as *auditory arts*. Some authorities group music, dance, and the theater arts together as *performance arts*, because they must be performed, either by living artists or by mechanical means such as films and phonograph records. Many art authorities group painting, sculpture, and architecture together as *plastic arts*, because they consist of solid objects. Works of art that do not move, including most paintings, sculptures, and architecture, are called *static*. Those works that do move are called *mobile*, as in mobile sculptures and animated films. Perfume and cooking are sometimes called *lower-sense arts*, but they are rarely classed as fine arts.

Older Groupings. Many persons believe that there are seven fine arts. This idea developed in the Middle Ages. Scholars at that time grouped together seven kinds of learning, most of which we call sciences today. This group included grammar, dialectic (a kind of logic), rhetoric, arithmetic, geometry, music, and astronomy.

Another ancient idea is that fine arts can be separated from useful arts, because fine arts are only supposed to be beautiful, not to be useful. This idea developed in ancient times, when men believed that gentlemen and ladies could not use their hands for any useful work. But few people in democratic societies today believe that this is true. We regard architecture, furniture design, and ceramics as fine arts, even though their products are useful, when artists use good design and make their objects satisfying to our eyes, ears, and minds. The Greeks and Romans called all useful skills arts, including agriculture, mining, and medicine. But we regard the hundreds of arts as those which are concerned with beauty and aesthetic appeal, regardless of their practical use. THOMAS MUNRO

Related Articles in WORLD BOOK include:

Aesthetics	Ballet	Drawing	Music
Architecture	Beauty	Furniture	Painting
Art and	Dancing	Literature	Poetry
the Arts	Drama	Muse	Sculpture

FINE ARTS, COMMISSION OF, is an independent U.S. government agency. It advises the federal government and District of Columbia agencies on questions of architecture, art, and design. It reviews proposals for public buildings, monuments, parks, and other landmarks that affect the appearance of the nation's capital. It also reviews building permit applications for private property in such historic areas of Washington as Georgetown. The commission also advises on designs for coins, medals, and insignia. The commission has seven members, each appointed by the President for a four-year term. *Critically reviewed by the* COMMISSION OF FINE ARTS

FINGER. See HAND.

FINGER, CHARLES JOSEPH (1871-1941), an American adventure writer, won the 1925 Newbery medal for his children's book, *Tales from Silver Lands*. The book is a collection of South American Indian legends.

Finger's colorful adventures as a young man furnished him with rich background material for the 35 books he wrote during his life. His works include *Courageous Companions* (1929), *Heroes from Hakluyt* (1927), *Tales Worth Telling* (1927), *A Dog at His Heel* (1935), and *Golden Tales from Far and Near* (1935).

Finger left home when he was 16. He roamed Africa, Alaska, and the Antarctic, and explored much of the United States. He spent 10 exciting years in South America, hunting gold, herding sheep, and living with Indians, sailors, miners, and *gauchos* (cowboys). When he was past 50, he bought a farm in the Ozark hills of Arkansas and began to write stories.

Finger was born in Willesden, England. He studied in England and Germany. EVELYN RAY SICKELS

FINGER LAKES are a group of long, narrow lakes in west-central New York. They received their name because they are shaped somewhat like the fingers of a hand. For the location of the lakes, see NEW YORK (physical map).

Geographers differ on how many lakes should be included in the group. Most experts include 11 lakes, however. The lakes are, from east to west, Otisco, Skaneateles, Owasco, Cayuga, Seneca, Keuka, Canandaigua, Honeoye, Canadice, Hemlock, and Conesus.

Geographers also differ on how the lakes were formed. Some believe they were created when river water filled valleys dammed by glacial deposits. Others believe ice from glaciers carved out valleys as much as 175 feet (53 meters) below sea level, allowing the lakes to form.

Seneca is the largest of the Finger Lakes. It is 37 miles (60 kilometers) long and 4 miles (6.4 kilometers) wide at its broadest point. This lake lies 444 feet (135 meters) above sea level and is 600 feet (180 meters) deep at some points. Watkins Glen, a famous summer resort, is located on Seneca Lake.

Cayuga Lake is 40 miles (64 kilometers) long, 2 miles (3 kilometers) wide, 435 feet (133 meters) deep, and lies 381 feet (116 meters) above sea level. Taughannock Falls (215 feet, or 66 meters), near the head of Cayuga Lake, is one of the highest falls east of the Rocky Mountains. Seneca and Cayuga lakes are connected at their northern ends by the Cayuga and Seneca Canal, part of the New York State Barge Canal System. Frontenac Island, in Cayuga, is one of the few islands in the Finger Lakes.

Most of the Finger Lake Valley lies in rolling country, with rounded hills from 60 to 800 feet (18 to 240 meters) above the level of the lakes. Thick woods cover most of the lake shores. GEORGE MACINKO

See also CANANDAIGUA LAKE; NEW YORK (color picture: Vineyards).

WORLD BOOK photo

A Young Artist swirls finger paint on a piece of paper. The pasty paint can be spread into countless designs.

Finger Painting Equipment includes paints, glossy paper, water to dampen the paper, and sticks to scoop out the paint.

FINGER PAINTING is one of the simplest forms of art. A finger painter smears a thick, pasty paint on damp paper with his fingers. He may shake powdered paint onto the paper. He needs no other materials, and develops his own technique. Finger paints limit the artist in the kinds of pictures he can paint. The lines are too broad to allow detail. But he can express his imagination freely. A finger painter also develops rhythmic, free movements. Leonardo da Vinci told students to make finger paintings to develop rhythm and imagination.

Elementary schools often teach finger painting. Children enjoy it because even a beginner can make attractive designs. Adults finger-paint as a hobby. Doctors who treat mental illnesses often ask their patients to make finger paintings. Mental patients tend to express their thoughts and feelings freely in such work. Doctors sometimes find their patients' hidden troubles from these paintings.

A finger painter should choose his paper and working surface carefully. The paper must have a shiny glaze. Some companies make special paper for finger painting, but any shiny-surfaced paper is satisfactory. The paper should be large, so that the painter can move his hands and arms freely when painting. The working sur-

Mysterious Designs, *right,* result when an imaginative artist uses his fingers, the palms and sides of his hands, his lower arm, and even his elbows.

Lifelike Portraits done in finger paints, *left,* may reveal the artist's personality and his ideas about his subject.

face under the paper should be smooth and hard. Linoleum and masonite make excellent working surfaces, because they can be washed easily.

In preparing to paint, the artist soaks the paper thoroughly. Next, he spreads it on the working surface, shiny side up, and smooths out all wrinkles and air bubbles. Then he puts about a teaspoonful of the paint in the center of the paper. A beginner should work with a single color until he becomes familiar with the techniques of finger painting. Standing in a relaxed position, the artist smears the paint evenly across the surface of the paper with the palm of his hand. If the paint is too thick and starts to dry, he sprinkles a few drops of water over the work.

The artist is now ready to start painting. He can use free movements across the paper with his hand, fingers, and forearm to make all kinds of patterns. To make fine lines, he can draw the backs of his fingernails across the paper. With experience, the painter develops techniques of his own. He can create abstract designs, or try to paint flowers, birds, and other subjects from nature. Experienced finger painters sometimes blend their colors, creating many different color effects. They also add contrasting pure colors by wiping part of the background clean with a sponge and spreading on the fresh color. Thomas Munro

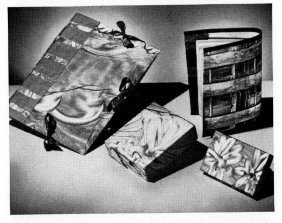

The Finished Design, on its paper base, carries with it the personal and original touch of the artist. It may be used to wrap gifts or cover books, or for other decorative purposes.

FINGERNAIL. See NAIL (finger).

FINGERPRINTING is the chief method of identifying a person with absolute certainty. Fingerprints are the impressions made by ridges on the *bulbs* (end joints) of the fingers and thumbs. These ridges form the fingerprint pattern, which remains unchanged throughout a person's life. No two fingerprints have as yet been found to be exactly alike. Therefore, fingerprints are a foolproof means of identification.

Classification. Fingerprints can be classified according to the types of patterns and the number of ridges appearing between designated points within the patterns. They fall into three main groups: the *arch*, the *loop*, and the *whorl*. In *arch* patterns, the ridges extend all the way across the bulb, and rise slightly in the center or make a more definite tented rise. In *loop* patterns, one or more ridges curve into a hairpin turn. Both ends of a *loop* ridge stop on the same side of the bulb. In the *whorl* pattern, the ridges follow a spiral or circular direction. There are eight subclassifications of the main pattern types.

Recording. To make a permanent fingerprint record, a person first coats a small piece of glass or metal with a thin film of printer's ink. Next, he presses the finger and thumb ridges against the inked surface. Finally, he presses the inky bulbs against a white card, where the prints are reproduced in exact detail.

Uses. Fingerprinting has proved to be an infallible method of identification. Its superiority over older methods has been demonstrated many times. The older methods include branding, tattooing, distinctive clothing, photography, and body measurements or the Bertillon system (see BERTILLON SYSTEM). The use of these methods has resulted in many cases of mistaken identification. But to date the fingerprints of no two persons have been found to be exactly the same.

A person may leave *latent* (hidden) fingerprints when he touches an object. The value of the latent print for identification depends on the clearness of the print and where the print is found. Latent prints are often impossible to see and require the use of chemicals and powders to make them visible. Latent fingerprints are used in solving crimes, such as murder, kidnaping, and bank robberies, and in the investigation of forgery and similar cases.

Fingerprinting is often associated with criminal investigation only, because of its wide use by law enforcement officers. But fingerprint identification services cover a broad field that includes amnesia victims, missing persons, unknown dead, establishment of military status, applicants for service in the armed forces, employment applicants, government workers, alien registrations, and applications for citizenship.

History. Historians believe that the Chinese used thumbprints to sign documents long before the birth of Christ. Many persons in the past sought to set up on a

Arch

Loop

Whorl

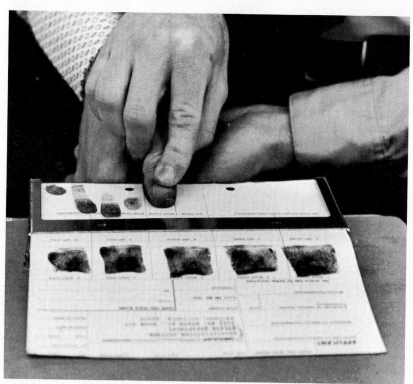

WORLD BOOK photo, courtesy Chicago Police Department

Fingerprinting is a positive means of identification because no two persons have the same fingerprints. Fingerprints are classified into three main pattern groups—the *arch*, the *loop*, and the *whorl*. In an arch pattern, *upper right*, the ridges arch across the bulb of the finger. The loop pattern, *center right*, consists of one or more curved ridges that form a loop on the bulb. Ridges in the whorl pattern, *lower right*, follow a spiral or circular formation on the finger.

FBI

Mike Fink shoots a tin cup full of whiskey from the head of a friend named Carpenter. Fink and Carpenter took turns shooting the cup from each other's head at a distance of 70 yards (64 meters). But tradition says that this game led to the deaths of both Fink and Carpenter.

Wood engraving (1847) by John R. Telfer (Bettmann Archive)

scientific basis the permanent character of fingerprints as a means of identification. Sir William J. Herschel (1833-1917) is credited with being the first to devise a workable method of fingerprint identification. He was a British government official in Bengal, India. By 1858, he was making use of a simple form of such identification to prevent impersonations then common among the people. Historians credit Sir Francis Galton with founding the present system of fingerprint identification. In the 1880's, he established a bureau for the registration of civilians by means of fingerprints and measurements. In 1891, Juan Vucetich of Argentina developed a method of classification that could be applied to criminal investigations. Sir E. R. Henry, who later became chief commissioner of the London Metropolitan Police, developed a simplified system for classifying and filing fingerprints in 1901. Most bureaus of identification in the United States use this system.

The use of fingerprint identification forms an inseparable part of law enforcement today. In this connection, the Federal Bureau of Investigation (FBI) of the United States Department of Justice has developed the largest collection of fingerprints in the world. The FBI has about 169 million fingerprints on file in the offices of its Identification Division in Washington, D.C.   J. Edgar Hoover

See also Footprinting.

FINISTERRE, CAPE. See Cape Finisterre.

FINITE SET. See Set Theory.

FINK, MIKE (1770-1823), an American frontiersman and boatman, is the subject of many folk tales. He first won fame as an expert shot while serving as an Indian scout near his boyhood home of Fort Pitt (now Pittsburgh), Pa. Legend has it that he never lost a shooting contest with his rifle, "Bang-all."

He was big, strong, and boastful. Fink described himself as "half horse, half alligator and half snapping turtle." Davy Crockett is said to have challenged him to a shooting match once, but the two men proved evenly matched at driving nails, snuffing out candles, and shooting flies from a cow's horn. Finally, Fink shot half a comb from Mrs. Fink's head. Crockett refused the shot and admitted he was beaten.

Fink worked on keelboats on the Ohio and Mississippi rivers in the early 1800's. He was a good boatman and he loved to fight. Many stories circulated about his rough deeds and great strength. When the steamboat began to replace the keelboat, Fink joined the Rocky Mountain Fur Company as a boatman and trapper. One of his companions killed him on his first expedition.

Many stories have been told about how he met death. One is that Fink shot a lifelong friend named Carpenter in a rifle contest. Carpenter, in shooting a can from Fink's head, grazed his scalp. Fink became so enraged that when his turn came, he shot his friend through the forehead. Later, one of the dead man's friends murdered Fink.   Howard R. Lamar

FINLAND

Embassy of Finland

Thick Forests and Island-Dotted Lakes cover most of Finland. This small farm lies in the scenic Lake District, a land region that occupies the central part of the country.

FINLAND is a country in northern Europe famous for its scenic beauty. Thousands of lovely lakes dot Finland's landscape, and thick forests cover more than two-thirds of the land. The country has a long, deeply indented coast, marked by colorful red and gray granite rocks. Thousands of scenic islands lie offshore.

Finland is a little larger than New Mexico. Sweden lies to the west, northern Norway to the north, and Russia to the east. The Gulf of Finland and the Gulf of Bothnia, two arms of the Baltic Sea, border Finland on the south and southwest. The northernmost part of the country lies inside the Arctic Circle in a region called the *Land of the Midnight Sun.* In this region, the sun shines 24 hours a day for long periods each summer. Helsinki—the country's capital, largest city, and chief port—lies in the south on the Gulf of Finland.

Most of Finland's people live in the southern part of the country, where the climate is mildest. The Finns love both the outdoors and the arts. They have a high standard of living and receive many welfare benefits from the government. Most of Finland's wealth comes from its huge forests. The forests form the basis of the country's thriving forest-products industry, which includes woodworking and the manufacture of paper and pulp.

Finland's location between Russia on the east and Sweden on the west has played an important role in the country's history. In the 1000's, Sweden and Russia began to battle for possession of Finland. Sweden gradually gained control in the 1100's and 1200's, but conflict between Sweden and Russia over Finland continued for centuries. Today, Swedish remains equal with Finnish as an official language of Finland. Russia controlled the country from 1809 until 1917, when Finland declared its independence. The nation became a republic with a president and parliament. During World War II (1939-1945), Finland fought two disastrous wars with Russia. Today, Finland tries to maintain friendly relations with both Russia and Western nations by remaining strictly neutral in foreign affairs.

Pekka Kalevi Hamalainen, the contributor of this article, is Professor of History and Chairman of the Western European Area Studies Program at the University of Wisconsin at Madison, and the author of several books and articles on Finland.

FACTS IN BRIEF

Capital: Helsinki (in Swedish, Helsingfors).

Official Languages: Finnish and Swedish.

Official Name: Republic of Finland. Finland's name in Finnish is *Suomi.*

Form of Government: Republic.

Area: 130,120 sq. mi. (337,009 km²), including 12,206 sq. mi. (31,613 km²) of inland water. *Greatest Distances*—east-west, 320 mi. (515 km); north-south, 640 mi. (1,030 km). *Coastline*—1,462 mi. (2,353 km).

Elevation: *Highest*—Mount Haltia, 4,344 ft. (1,324 m) above sea level. *Lowest*—sea level.

Population: *Estimated 1979 Population*—4,783,000; distribution, 67 per cent urban, 33 per cent rural; density, 36 persons per sq. mi. (14 persons per km²). *1970 Census*—4,598,336. *Estimated 1984 Population*—4,879,000.

Chief Products: *Agriculture*—barley, cattle, dairy products, eggs, oats, potatoes, rye, sugar beets, wheat. *Forestry*—birch, pine, spruce. *Manufacturing*—chemicals, machinery, metals, paper and pulp, processed foods, textiles and clothing, transportation equipment, wood and wood products. *Mining*—copper, granite, iron, limestone.

National Anthem: "Maamme" (in Finnish) or "Vårt Land" (in Swedish), meaning "Our Land."

Money: *Basic Unit*—markka. For its value in U.S. dollars, see MONEY (table: Values). See also MARKKA.

Finland is a democratic republic. Its Constitution, adopted in 1919, guarantees the people such rights as freedom of speech, freedom of worship, and equality before the law. All Finns 18 years and older may vote.

The President is Finland's head of state and chief executive. He is elected to a six-year term by the Electoral College, whose 300 members are chosen by the people. A president may be re-elected any number of times. The president has far-reaching powers. He may issue orders that do not violate existing laws, *veto* (reject) bills passed by the parliament, and dissolve the parliament and call for new elections. The president handles foreign relations and acts as commander in chief of the armed forces. But the parliament must approve all decisions concerning war and peace.

The Prime Minister and Cabinet. The president appoints the prime minister, who is head of government. The prime minister, with the president's approval, selects the members of the Cabinet to head the government departments. The prime minister presides over the Cabinet and works with it in setting government programs, which must be acceptable to the parliament.

The Parliament of Finland is a one-house legislature called the *Eduskunta* (in Swedish, the *Riksdag*). The people elect its 200 members to four-year terms. But the president may dissolve the Eduskunta and call for new elections at any time. The parliament, in turn, may force the Cabinet to resign by not supporting its programs. The Eduskunta can also repass a bill by a simple majority vote after the president has vetoed it.

Local Government. For purposes of local government, Finland is divided into 12 provinces. The president appoints a governor to administer each province. The provinces are subdivided into more than 500 *communes*. They range in size from thinly populated rural areas to large cities. A council elected by the people governs each commune. Communes collect their own taxes to support hospitals, schools, police and fire departments, and other local institutions.

Political Parties. Election to the Eduskunta is based on a system called *proportional representation*. This system gives a political party a share of seats in the parliament according to its share of the total votes cast in an election. The system encourages small parties to put up candidates and makes it hard for any one party to win a majority. As a result of proportional representation, a number of parties usually have seats in the Eduskunta. See PROPORTIONAL REPRESENTATION.

The Social Democratic Party, supported mostly by working-class and lower-middle-class voters, generally receives the most votes. Other parties include the Center Party, Christian League, Conservative Party, Finnish Rural Party, Liberal Party, People's Democratic League, and Swedish People's Party.

Courts. Finland's highest court of appeal is the Supreme Court. Four regional courts hear appeals of decisions made by lower courts. Special courts handle such matters as impeachment of government officials and labor disputes.

Armed Forces. Finland has about 42,000 men in its army, navy, and air force. Healthy men between 17 and 60 must serve 9 to 11 months in the armed forces.

Kay Honkanen from Carl Östman

Parliament Building in Helsinki is the meeting place of Finland's one-house legislature, the *Eduskunta*. The Eduskunta has 200 members, elected by the people to four-year terms.

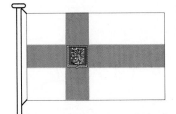

Finland's State Flag, used by the government, was adopted in 1918. The national flag has no coat of arms.

The Finnish Coat of Arms was adopted in its present form in 1918. But its basic design dates back to the 1500's.

WORLD BOOK map

Finland is a northern European country that borders Norway, Russia, and Sweden. Its coastline stretches along the Baltic Sea.

**FINLAND
Political Map**

International boundary	Canal
Road	⊛ National capital
Railroad	• Other city or town
Ferry	

WORLD BOOK map

Cities and Towns

Äänekoski ....10,724..F 3
Borgå
  (Porvoo) ...16,963..H 3
Ekenäs
  (Tammisaari) ..6,836..H 3
Esbo (Espoo) ..98,920..H 3
Forssa ....16,102..G 3
Grankulla
  (Kauniainen)* ..6,313..H 3
Haapajärvi ......8,371..E 3
Hämeen-
  linna ....38,171..G 3
Hamina ....11,087..G 4
Hangö
  (Hanko) ......9,998..H 3
Harja-
  valta* ....8,311..G 3
Heinola ....14,197..G 4
Helsinki
  (Helsing-
  fors) 513,254
            *817,370..H 3
Hyvinkää ....34,753..G 3
Iisalmi ....20,984..E 4
Ikaalinen* ....785..G 2
Imatra ....34,932..G 4
Jakobstad
  (Pietar-
  saari) ....19,311..E 2
Jämsä ....12,815..G 3
Järvenpää .....16,593..H 3
Joensuu ....37,105..F 5
Jyväskylä ......59,295..F 3
Kajaani ....20,140..E 4
Kan-
  kaanpää .....12,751..G 2
Karhula ....22,026..H 4
Karis
  (Karjaa) ......7,993..H 3
Karkkila* ....8,731..G 3
Kaskö
  (Kaskinen) ...1,335..F 2
Kemi ....29,131..D 3
Kemijärvi ....6,302..C 4
Kerava* ....14,600..H 3
Kokkola (Gam-
  lakarleby) ...21,375..E 3
Kotka ....34,011..H 4
Kouvola ....26,642..G 4
Kristinestad
  (Kristiinan-
  kaupunki) ....2,710..F 2
Kuopio ....65,602..F 4
Kurikka ....11,400..F 2
Kuusankoski ...22,764..G 4
Lahti 90,699
            *114,967..G 3
Lappeenranta ..51,877..G 4
Lapua ....15,514..F 3
Lieksa ....4,929..F 5
Lohja (Lojo) ...12,487..H 3
Loimaa ....6,403..G 3
Lovisa
  (Lovisa)* ....7,261..H 4
Mänttä* ....7,445..F 3
Mariehamn
  (Maarian-
  hamina) ....8,770..H 1
Mikkeli ....25,713..G 4
Naantali ....6,847..H 2
Nokia ....19,712..G 3
Nurmes ....2,637..E 4
Nykarleby
  (Uusikaar-
  lepyy) ....1,462..E 2
Oulainen ....7,446..E 3
Oulu 87,343
            *106,075..D 3
Outokumpu ....11,027..F 4
Pargas
  (Parainen) ...10,974..H 2
Pieksämäki ....12,880..F 4
Pori ....74,362..G 2
Raahe ....7,561..E 3
Raisio ....14,562..H 2
Rauma ....25,918..G 2
Riihimäki ......23,097..G 3
Rovaniemi .....28,499..C 3
Salo ....17,574..H 3
Savonlinna .....18,256..G 4
Seinäjoki ....20,616..F 3
Suolahti* ....5,735..F 3
Suonenjoki ......9,702..F 4
Tampere 158,731
            *225,040..G 3
Toijala* ....7,761..G 3
Tornio ....7,824..D 3
Turku
  (Åbo) 155,834
            *221,655..H 2
Uusikau-
  punki ....8,169..G 2
Vaasa
  (Vasa) ....49,288..F 2
Valkeakoski ...16,756..G 3
Vammala ....6,457..G 3
Varkaus ....24,328..F 4
Ylivieska ....10,636..E 3

*Does not appear on map; key
shows general location.
*Population of metropolitan
area, including suburbs.
Source: Official estimates (1971).

Volker von Bonin

The Gleaming Lights of Downtown Helsinki, heart of Finland's capital and largest city, brighten the 18-hour nights of midwinter. The rest of Finland, like Helsinki, is also dark most of the time in winter. About a sixth of the nation's people live in Helsinki and its suburbs.

Ancestry and Population. Over 90 per cent of Finland's people are Finnish by descent, and nearly 7 per cent are Swedish. Most people in both groups are tall, with fair skin, blue or gray eyes, and blond or light brown hair. About 2,300 Lapps live in northern Finland. The ancestors of these short, stocky people lived in Finland long before the first Finns arrived in the A.D. 100's (see LAPLAND). Finland also has about 6,000 Gypsies and small groups of Jews and Turks.

Finland has a total population of about 4¾ million. Most of the people live in the south, and about two-thirds live in cities and towns. Helsinki, Finland's capital and largest city, has over 500,000 persons. About a sixth of the nation's people live in Helsinki and its suburbs. Finland has two other cities—Tampere and Turku—with more than 150,000 persons each. See HELSINKI; TAMPERE; TURKU.

Languages. Finland has two official languages—Finnish and Swedish. About 93 per cent of the people speak Finnish, and almost 7 per cent speak Swedish. Most of the Swedish-speaking people live on the south and west coasts and on the offshore Aland Islands. Finnish and Swedish belong to different language families. The Lapps speak a language related to Finnish. See LANGUAGE (Language Families).

Way of Life. In Finland's cities, most people own or rent apartments. Most countrypeople live in one-family homes on farms or in villages.

The Finns enjoy fish, especially herring, perch, pike, and salmon. Popular meats include beef, veal, pork, and sausage. Smoked reindeer is a special treat. Boiled potatoes covered with butter and dill sprigs make up a favorite side dish. Butter and milk are important parts of the Finnish diet.

The most famous feature of Finnish life is a special kind of bath called a *sauna*. Most Finns take a sauna at least once a week for cleansing and relaxation. In a sauna room or bathhouse, stones are heated over a stove or furnace. The temperature in the sauna rises to between 176° and 230° F. (80° and 110° C). Bathers sit or lie on wooden benches until they begin to perspire freely. After a while, they may throw water on the stones to produce steam and make the sauna feel even hotter. The bathers may beat themselves gently with leafy birch twigs to stimulate circulation. Finally, they take a cold shower or plunge into a lake. After repeating the entire cycle, they lie down to rest until their body returns to normal temperature.

Social Welfare. The government of Finland provides the people with many welfare services. Since the 1920's, maternity and child welfare centers have given free health care to pregnant women, mothers, and children. Since 1948, families have received an allowance every time they have had a new baby as well as a yearly allowance for each child under the age of 16.

In 1939, Finland began an old-age and disability insurance program. This program guarantees monthly pensions to people 65 years and older and to permanently disabled citizens. In 1963, Finland set up a health insurance program for all citizens.

Bob and Ira Spring, FPG

Lapp Schoolchildren in northernmost Finland place their skis against a rack after skiing to school. The Lapp people lived in Finland long before the first Finns arrived in the A.D. 100's.

Embassy of Finland

A Finnish Farmwife uses a wood-burning stove for baking. Such stoves are common in rural Finland, where forests provide plentiful wood. More than a third of the people live in rural areas.

Keystone

Family Camping Vacations are popular among the Finns, who love the outdoors. Other favorite summer activities include boating; hiking; and playing *pesäpallo*, a Finnish form of baseball.

Bud Guyon, Keystone

Finnish Glassware is internationally prized for its high quality and simplicity of design. These women are admiring beautiful glass objects on display in a Helsinki store.

Since 1917, Finnish law has limited the workday to 8 hours. In 1965, the workweek was limited to 40 hours. The government began to guarantee workers annual holidays in the 1920's. Today, workers who remain in the same job for one year receive a 24-day annual vacation. After 10 years, they receive 26 days.

Recreation. The Finns love outdoor sports. In winter, they enjoy ice hockey, ice skating, ski jumping, and cross-country skiing. Popular summer sports include *pesäpallo* (a Finnish form of baseball); swimming; boating; and hiking. In summer, thousands of city families flock to their cottages and saunas on lakes, the seacoast, or the offshore islands. Favorite spectator sports include track-and-field events and ice hockey matches. The Finns also enjoy ballets, concerts, motion pictures, plays, and operas.

Education. All adult Finns can read and write. Children between the ages of 7 and 15 must attend school. All elementary school students and most other students go to public schools. The rest attend private schools, which may charge a small tuition fee. Elementary school students receive free one meal a day, books, and medical and dental care.

All Finnish communities had a *parallel system* of education until 1972. In 1972, some communities began to adopt a *basic system*. This system is expected to replace the parallel system completely by 1978. Under the parallel system, students may attend either (1) six years of elementary school and two years of *continuation* school or (2) four years of elementary school and five years of junior high school. Students who complete the first program may enter a trade school. Those who complete the second program may enter either a vocational school or a three-year high school, which prepares them for university study.

Under the basic system, students attend elementary school for six years and junior high for three years. They may then enter a vocational school, trade school, or high school. The system aims at providing a similar basic education for all students.

Finland has 6 universities and 11 other institutions

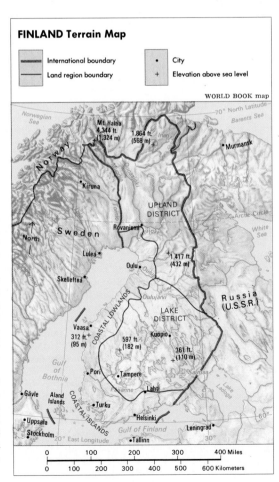

Finland covers 130,120 square miles (337,009 square kilometers). This area includes 12,206 square miles (31,613 square kilometers) of inland water. Finland is largely a plateau broken by small hills and valleys and low ridges and hollows. The land rises gradually from south-southwest to north-northeast, but the average altitude is only 400 to 600 feet (120 to 180 meters) above sea level. Mount Haltia, the country's highest point, stands 4,344 feet (1,324 meters) above sea level in far northwestern Finland. About 60,000 lakes dot the country, and forests cover more than two-thirds of the land.

Land Regions

Finland has four main land regions: (1) the Coastal Lowlands, (2) the Lake District, (3) the Upland District, and (4) the Coastal Islands.

The Coastal Lowlands lie along the Gulf of Bothnia and Gulf of Finland. Finland's coastline is 1,462 miles (2,353 kilometers) long. Many small lakes lie in the Coastal Lowlands. The region has less forestland and a milder climate than the Lake and Upland districts have. The lowlands also have some of the country's most fertile soil. As a result, the region offers the best

Francis O. Spalding, Tom Stack & Associates

The Town of Tapiola, near Helsinki, has become world famous as a model for city planning. A private organization developed Tapiola as an entirely new community in the 1950's.

of higher learning. The University of Helsinki is the country's largest university.

Religion. The Evangelical Lutheran Church is the state church of Finland, and the national government has supreme authority over it. But the people have complete freedom of worship. Almost 95 per cent of all Finns are Evangelical Lutherans. The Finnish Orthodox Church makes up the next largest religious group, with about 1 per cent of the population. Finland also has other, smaller Protestant groups as well as small groups of Jews, Muslims, and Roman Catholics.

The Arts. Finland has a rich folk culture, which is reflected in the country's crafts, literature, music, and painting. The person most responsible for preserving Finland's oral folklore was Elias Lönnrot, a country doctor. He collected the centuries-old song-poems and chants of the Finnish peasants and published them in 1835. This huge collection, called the *Kalevala*, became Finland's national epic.

During the 1800's and 1900's, the *Kalevala* inspired many artists. Akseli Gallen-Kallela used its themes in many paintings. The composer Jean Sibelius based most of his symphonic poems on the work. The American poet Henry Wadsworth Longfellow patterned the rhythm of his poem *Hiawatha* on the *Kalevala*.

In the early 1800's, Johan Ludvig Runeberg became known as Finland's national poet. His poem "Vårt Land" is the country's national anthem. Other writers of the 1800's include the novelist Aleksis Kivi and the playwright Minna Canth, an early champion of women's rights. In the 1900's, the novelists Frans Eemil Sillanpää and Mika Waltari gained international fame. Sillanpää won the Nobel prize for literature in 1939.

Finnish glassware, ceramics, furniture, and textiles are world famous for the simple beauty of their design. This same simplicity of line and shape can be seen in the works of Finland's best-known architects—Eliel Saarinen and Alvar Aalto. Saarinen's famous designs include the railroad station and the National Museum in Helsinki. Aalto gained fame not only as an architect, but also as a town planner and furniture designer.

FINLAND Terrain Map

International boundary
Land region boundary
City
Elevation above sea level

WORLD BOOK map

Norwegian Sea
70° North Latitude
Barents Sea
Mt. Haltia 4,344 ft. (1,324 m)
1,864 ft. (568 m)
Murmansk
Norway
Kiruna
UPLAND DISTRICT
Arctic Circle
White Sea
Rovaniemi
Sweden
North
Luleå
1,417 ft. (432 m)
Oulu
Skellefteå
COASTAL LOWLANDS
Oulujärvi
Russia (U.S.S.R.)
LAKE DISTRICT
Vaasa 312 ft. (95 m)
597 ft. (182 m)
Kuopio
361 ft. (110 m)
Gulf of Bothnia
Pori
Tampere
Lahti
Gävle
Åland Islands
COASTAL ISLANDS
Turku
Helsinki
Uppsala
Stockholm
20° East Longitude
Gulf of Finland
Tallinn
Leningrad
30°
60°

| 0 | 100 | 200 | 300 | 400 Miles |
| 0 | 100 200 | 300 | 400 500 | 600 Kilometers |

The Coastal Lowlands along the Gulf of Finland are the home of most of the Finnish people. The picturesque town of Borgå, above, with its centuries-old wooden buildings, lies in this region.

The Upland District is Finland's northernmost, hilliest, and least densely populated region. Several rivers in the region provide energy for hydroelectric power stations.

conditions for farming. The Coastal Lowlands of the south have the mildest climate and the most productive farms. Most of Finland's people live in this area.

The Lake District occupies central Finland north and east of the Coastal Lowlands. The region has thousands of island-dotted lakes. The lakes cover about half the total area of the district. Narrow channels or short rivers connect many of the lakes. Saimaa, the largest lake in Finland, covers about 680 square miles (1,760 square kilometers) in the southeastern part of the region. The Saimaa Lake System, which is about 185 miles (298 kilometers) long, links several lakes in the area. A fleet of steamers travels the system, stopping at towns on the shores of the lakes. Forests of birch, pine, and spruce cover most of the land in the Lake District. Most farmlands lie in the southwestern part of the region.

The Upland District is Finland's northernmost and least densely populated region. It covers about 40 per cent of the country. The Upland District has a harsher climate and less fertile soil than the other regions have. As one travels north through the Upland District, plant life becomes increasingly scarce. Stunted pines and arctic birches grow in parts of the district. However, the northernmost part makes up a *tundra*—a frozen, treeless plain.

Most of Finland's hills rise in the Upland District. Swamps and marshlands separate the hills. Several rivers in the region provide energy for hydroelectric power stations.

The Coastal Islands consist of thousands of islands in the Gulf of Bothnia and Gulf of Finland. The great majority of islands are small and uninhabited. The thin, rocky soil on many islands cannot support much plant life, but many kinds of plants thrive on a few of the larger islands. Although fishermen maintain summer bases on some islands, Finland's islands serve chiefly as recreation areas. Many Finns have summer cottages or saunas on them.

The most important islands are the Aland group, which consists of about 6,500 islands off Finland's southwest coast. People, almost all of whom speak Swedish, live on about 80 of these islands. The land area of the Aland Islands totals 572 square miles (1,481 square kilometers). The main island, also called Aland, is Finland's largest island. It covers 285 square miles (738 square kilometers) and is a major tourist and shipping center.

Rivers

Finland's longest river is the Kemijoki. It rises in the Upland District near the Russian border and winds southwestward 340 miles (547 kilometers) to the Gulf of Bothnia. The Kemijoki and its chief branch, the Ounasjoki, provide important logging routes and rich salmon catches. Several hydroelectric stations have been built along both rivers.

The Muonio River begins about 60 miles (97 kilometers) southeast of the point where the Norwegian, Swedish, and Finnish borders meet. The river flows south about 110 miles (177 kilometers), forming part of the border between Sweden and Finland. The Muonio provides a logging route. The Oulujoki rises in the northern part of the Lake District and empties into the Gulf of Bothnia. The river is only about 80 miles (130 kilometers) long. But it serves as an important logging route. Its 105-foot (32-meter) Pyhä Falls provides power for a major hydroelectric plant.

Finland has a much milder climate than most other regions of the world that lie as far north. In January, for example, Helsinki's temperatures often average 25° to 35° F. (14° to 18° C) higher than the temperatures in parts of Canada at the same latitude. Finland's climate is influenced chiefly by the Gulf Stream, a warm ocean current that flows off Norway's west coast. Finland's many lakes and the gulfs of Bothnia and Finland help give the country a relatively mild climate.

July temperatures in Finland average 55° to 63° F. (13° to 17° C). The temperature reaches 50° F. (10° C) or higher on 110 to 122 days a year in the south and on 50 to 85 days a year in the north. February is usually Finland's coldest month, with temperatures averaging from −7° F. (−22° C) to 26° F. (−3° C). In northern Finland, winter temperatures sometimes drop as low as −22° F. (−30° C).

The amount of *precipitation* (rain, melted snow, and other forms of moisture) varies between southern and northern Finland. The south receives about 27 inches (69 centimeters) a year, and the north only about 16 inches (41 centimeters). August usually has the heaviest rainfall.

Snow covers the ground in southern Finland from December to April, and northern Finland is snowbound from October to April. Most of the country is icebound in winter, but icebreakers keep the major ports open for passenger traffic and shipping.

Northern Finland lies in the Land of the Midnight Sun and so has continuous daylight each summer. The number of days of constant daylight increases as one goes farther north. Constant daylight lasts a few days near the Arctic Circle. In northernmost Finland, the sun stays above the horizon for about $2\frac{1}{2}$ months. Southern Finland never has continuous daylight, but it averages 19 hours of daylight a day in midsummer. See MIDNIGHT SUN.

In winter, Finland is dark most of the time. The sun never rises above the horizon for about 2 months in the northernmost areas of the country. Southern Finland has some daylight each day, but it receives only about 6 hours of daylight a day in midwinter. The winter night sky—especially in the northern areas—often becomes glorious with brilliant displays of the *aurora borealis*, or northern lights (see AURORA BOREALIS).

Finland's economy is based mostly on private ownership. However, the national government has a monopoly in certain businesses, such as the telephone, telegraph, and postal systems. In forestry and certain other industries, government-owned businesses compete with private companies.

Natural Resources. Finland's greatest natural resource is its widespread forests. They cover more than 70 per cent of the land—a higher percentage than in any other European country. But Finland's other resources are limited. Its soil is poor, and the crop-growing season short. The country has no deposits of oil, natural gas, or coal. Water power produces much of the country's electricity. Finland's most important mineral is copper, which comes from large deposits near Outokumpu.

Forestry forms the basis of Finland's economy. Forestry and forest-products industries provide about half of Finland's exports. The government owns about a third of Finland's forests, chiefly in the north. But these northern forests make up only about 15 per cent of the country's annual forest growth because of the short growing season in the north. Most private forests are owned by individual farmers. They work their farmland in summer and cut trees in their forests throughout the year.

Finland produces more than 1.1 billion cubic feet (30 million cubic meters) of timber a year. Pine accounts for almost half the production, followed by spruce and birch.

Manufacturing. Woodworking, pulp and paper production, and other forest-based industries are Finland's chief manufacturing industries. Finland ranks as the world's top producer of plywood. It is also a leading producer of paper. Other major forest products include cardboard; wood paneling; and *prefabricated houses*, which are erected in factory-made sections.

Finland's metalworking industry has expanded rapidly since the 1940's. The chief metal products include farm machinery and equipment; electric motors and generators; and industrial machinery. Finland also produces buses, ships, and other transportation equipment. The shipbuilding industry is especially known for its sturdy, powerful icebreakers. Other manufactured products include chemicals, metals, processed foods, and textiles and clothing.

Agriculture. Most of Finland's farmland lies in the south and west. The farms are small, averaging about 22 acres (9 hectares). The Finnish government owns less than 2 per cent of the farmland.

Dairy farming and livestock production account for about 80 per cent of Finland's farm income. Finland's farmers produce all the dairy products, eggs, and meat needed by the people. They also produce almost all the bread grains needed in Finland. Wheat and rye are the main grain crops. Other crops include barley, oats, potatoes, and sugar beets.

Foreign Trade. Finland depends heavily on foreign trade. It imports large quantities of fuels, fruits, vegetables, industrial raw materials, and manufactured goods not produced in Finland. Paper, pulp, and wood products make up about 50 per cent of the country's exports. Other major exports include products of the metalworking industry, such as machinery and ships.

Finland does more than 90 per cent of its trade with European nations, especially Great Britain, Sweden, West Germany, and Russia. Russia is the chief importer of Finnish machinery and other metal products.

FINLAND

Herbert Fristedt from Carl Östman

Stacks of Lumber await loading onto ships at Kotka, a city on Finland's south coast. Lumber and other forest products make up about half the value of the country's exports.

Herbert Fristedt from Carl Östman

Finland's Shipbuilding Industry has expanded rapidly since the 1940's. The industry produces cargo and passenger ships but is best known for its icebreakers. This shipyard is in Helsinki.

FINLAND'S GROSS NATIONAL PRODUCT

Total gross national product in 1972—$12,000,000,000

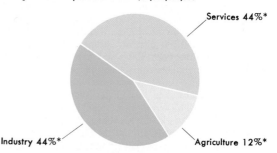

Services 44%*

Industry 44%*

Agriculture 12%*

The gross national product (GNP) is the total value of goods and services produced by a country in a year. The GNP measures a nation's total annual economic performance. It can also be used to compare the economic output and growth of countries.

PRODUCTION AND WORKERS BY ECONOMIC ACTIVITIES

Economic Activities	Per Cent of GDP* Produced	Employed Persons	
		Number of Persons	Per Cent of Total
Manufacturing	30	570,000	27
Community, Business, & Personal Services	14	419,000	20
Banking, Insurance, Real Estate, & Trade	13	399,000	19
Construction	10	180,000	8
Transportation & Communication	7	150,000	7
Agriculture	7	339,000	16
Forestry	5	60,000	3
Housing	5	—	—
Government	5	†	†
Utilities	3	**	**
Mining	1	**	**
Total	100	2,117,000	100

*GDP is gross domestic product (gross national product adjusted for net income sent or received from abroad).
†Included in Community, Business, & Personal Services.
**Included in Manufacturing.
Sources: Economic Department of Ministry of Finance, Helsinki; U.S. Department of State.

Western European countries are the main customers for forest products. Finland is an associate member of the eight-nation European Free Trade Association (EFTA). EFTA members have eliminated most tariffs on imports of manufactured goods from one another. Finland extends EFTA policies to its trade with Russia. In 1973, EFTA members, including Finland, entered into free trade agreements with another economic group, the European Community. See EUROPEAN FREE TRADE ASSOCIATION; EUROPEAN COMMUNITY.

Transportation. The government owns more than 90 per cent of Finland's 3,600 miles (5,794 kilometers) of railroad. Finland has over 45,000 miles (72,000 kilometers) of roads and highways, of which about 30 per cent are paved. About 900,000 Finns own an automobile. The Finnish airline, Finnair, is owned mostly by the government. The airline operates international and domestic flights. As a result of the great distances between many major Finnish communities and the watery nature of the land, Finland has one of the busiest and most extensive domestic air networks in Europe.

Finland's merchant fleet includes more than 500 ships. Over 3,000 miles (4,800 kilometers) of inland waterways connect various lakes and seaports.

Communication. Finland publishes about 60 daily newspapers, with a total circulation of about 1,783,000 copies. The largest dailies include *Helsingin Sanomat* of Helsinki, *Aamulehti* of Tampere, and *Turun Sanomat* of Turku. Finland has almost 70 television stations and more than 100 radio stations. The government owns about 90 per cent of the stock in the main radio and television network. Government-owned telegraph and telephone lines connect all areas of Finland. Most families have a radio, TV set, and telephone.

FINLAND /History

Early Years. The earliest-known inhabitants of Finland were the Lapps. These people lived as *nomadic* (wandering) hunters. About A.D. 100, the ancestors of present-day Finns began to move into the country from the south shores of the Gulf of Finland. Their original homeland may have been between the Volga River and the Ural Mountains in Russia. The Finns gradually pushed the Lapps farther and farther north. The early Finns were divided into three loosely organized tribes that often fought one another. They lived by farming, hunting, and fishing.

In the 1000's, Sweden and Russia began a struggle for control of Finland. Both nations wanted to extend their boundaries. In addition, Sweden wanted to convert the Finns to Roman Catholicism, and Russia wanted to convert them to Eastern Orthodoxy.

Swedish Rule. During the 1100's and 1200's, Sweden gradually conquered all Finland and established Roman Catholicism as the official religion. Many Swedes settled in Finland, and Swedish became the official language. However, Finns shared equal rights with Swedes. About 1540, the Swedish king made Lutheranism the official religion.

From the 1500's through the 1700's, Sweden and Russia fought several wars over Finland. Russia won the Finnish province of Vyborg after the Great Northern War (1700-1721), which was known in Finland as the *Great Wrath.* For several years during that war and from 1741 to 1743, Russia occupied all Finland. Sweden and Russia fought over Finland again from 1788 to 1790.

After the 1788-1790 war, some Finns began to think Sweden could not protect their land. But a plot to create an independent Finland under Russian protection failed to win wide support.

Annexation by Russia. In 1808, Russia again invaded Finland. It conquered the country in 1809 and made it a grand duchy of the Russian Empire with the czar as grand duke. The duchy had local self-rule based on government systems developed during Swedish control. Russia returned Vyborg to the duchy.

During the 1800's, Finns began to develop feelings of nationalism as they took increasing pride in their country and its culture. In 1835, Elias Lönnrot published the *Kalevala,* whose heroic themes strengthened the growing sense of nationalism. Many Finnish leaders began to urge that Finnish be made an official language equal with Swedish. But Finnish did not become a fully equal official language until 1902.

In 1899, Czar Nicholas II began a program to force the Finns to accept Russian government and culture. He took away most of Finland's powers of self-rule and appointed a Russian governor as dictator. Russian was made the official language. Finnish resistance reached a peak in 1905 with a six-day nationwide strike. The czar then restored much of Finland's self-government.

In 1906, the Finns created their first parliament elected by all adult citizens, women as well as men. During the next several years, Russia again tried to Russianize Finland.

Finland stayed out of World War I (1914-1918). But its merchant ships were blockaded in the Gulf of

IMPORTANT DATES IN FINLAND

About A.D. 100 The ancestors of present-day Finns began to move into Finland.

1100's-1200's Sweden gradually conquered all Finland.

1500's-1700's Sweden and Russia fought several wars for possession of Finland.

1809 Finland became a grand duchy of the Russian Empire.

1917 Finland declared its independence from Russia.

1918 Finnish socialists and nonsocialists fought a civil war.

1919 Finland adopted a republican constitution and elected Kaarlo Juho Ståhlberg president.

1939-1940 Russia defeated Finland in the Winter War.

1941-1944 Russia defeated Finland in the Continuation War.

1946 President Juho K. Paasikivi established a policy of Finnish neutrality in international politics.

1955 Finland joined the United Nations (UN) and the Nordic Council.

1956 Urho Kekkonen became president. He was re-elected in 1962 and 1968.

1973 The Finnish parliament extended Kekkonen's term to 1978. Finland and other EFTA members entered into free trade agreements with the European Community.

Bothnia, and the country suffered food shortages and unemployment. In 1917, a revolution in Russia overthrew the czar. Finland then decided to declare its freedom.

The New Republic. Finland declared its independence from Russia on Dec. 6, 1917. Russia's new Bolshevik (Communist) government recognized the new nation, but some Russian troops remained in Finland. In preparing for independence, the Finns had become divided into two groups—socialists, who formed armed units called the Red Guard, and nonsocialists, who formed armed units called the White Guard. Both groups had demanded Finnish independence, but the socialists also wanted revolutionary social changes.

In January, 1918, the White Guard, led by Carl Gustav Mannerheim, began operations in western Finland to expel the Russian troops. Meanwhile, the Red Guard attempted to take over the Finnish government in Helsinki. A bloody civil war broke out between the two groups. The Whites received aid from Germany, and the Reds from Russia. The war ended in a White victory in May, 1918.

In 1919, Finland adopted a republican constitution, and Kaarlo Juho Ståhlberg became the first president. But Finland's relations with Sweden and Russia remained unsettled. Finland and Sweden quarreled over possession of the Aland Islands. In 1921, the League of Nations awarded the islands to Finland. Disputes with Russia centered on Karelia, a large region east of present-day Finland. Finland demanded that the eastern part of Karelia be made part of Finland, like the rest of Karelia, or that it be made independent of Russia. Russia accepted neither demand, and relations between the two countries remained tense for years.

World War II (1939-1945). Although Finland never officially allied itself with any nation in World War II, Russia invaded the country twice. The *Winter War* began on Nov. 30, 1939, when Russian troops marched into Finland. Mannerheim led the strong Finnish resistance, which included troops on skis. But Finland had to surrender in March 1940. Under the peace treaty, Finland was forced to give up the southern part of Karelia, where 12 per cent of the Finnish people lived. The area made up a tenth of Finland's territory and included Lake Ladoga and Finland's second largest city, Viipuri (now Vyborg). Russia also received a naval base at Hangö in southwestern Finland.

In 1941, Finland allowed Germany to station troops in northern Finland and to move them through the region to attack Russia. Russia then bombed Finland, beginning the *Continuation War*. Finnish troops recaptured southern Karelia. But in 1944, the Russians pushed farther and farther into Finland, and the country had to give up. On Sept. 19, 1944, Finland and Russia signed an armistice. As the German troops retreated from northern Finland, they burned towns, villages, and forests behind them.

The destruction by the Germans was only part of Finland's heavy war losses. About 100,000 Finns died, and about 50,000 were permanently disabled. Russia regained southern Karelia and won other Finnish territories as well. Russia also leased a military base at Porkkala, near Helsinki, but gave up its base at Hangö. About 420,000 Karelians fled to Finland, where the government gave them new land. Finland also had to pay Russia about $225 million in *reparations* (payment for damages). See RUSSO-FINNISH WARS.

Postwar Developments. Mannerheim became Finland's president in 1944, but he retired in 1946 because of poor health. Juho K. Paasikivi finished Mannerheim's term and was elected to a full term in 1950. Paasikivi set a policy of Finnish neutrality in international politics. Under him, Finland also developed close economic and cultural ties with Russia and the Scandinavian countries—Denmark, Norway, and Sweden. In 1955, Russia returned Porkkala to Finland, and the two nations renewed a 1948 treaty of friendship and assistance.

Also in 1955, Finland joined both the United Nations (UN) and the Nordic Council, which includes Denmark, Iceland, Norway, and Sweden. Citizens of Nordic Council countries may work and receive social benefits in any member nation and travel among member nations without a passport or visa. As a result, many Finns have moved to Sweden, which has a more developed economy and more social welfare benefits than Finland has.

In 1956, Urho Kekkonen was elected president. He continued to emphasize neutrality in international affairs and was re-elected in 1962 and 1968.

Finland Today stresses friendship with all nations, especially Russia, and cooperation with Scandinavia. In late 1973, Finland and the other members of EFTA entered into agreements with another economic group, the European Community. The agreements reduced tariffs among all the nations of both groups. Earlier, in January 1973, Finland's parliament passed a special bill to extend Kekkonen's term from 1974 to 1978. Parliament hoped the bill would assure Russia that Kekkonen's policies of neutrality would not change because of the economic agreement with the European Community. Kekkonen was re-elected in 1978.

By 1990, Finland plans to have completed construction of 10 nuclear power plants, which are expected to supply half the nation's future energy needs. Meanwhile, Finland hopes to improve the economy in the underdeveloped north and so relieve overcrowding in the booming south.

PEKKA KALEVI HAMALAINEN

FINLAND / Study Aids

Questions

What are Finland's two official languages?

In which region of Finland do most of the people live?

How has Finland's location between Russia and Sweden influenced its history?

What are the chief manufacturing industries in Finland?

What is the *Kalevala?* How has it affected Finnish arts?

Why does Finland have a much milder climate than most other regions of the world that lie as far north?

What area did Russia receive from Finland after the Winter War?

What is a *sauna?*

What are some of Finland's social welfare policies?

About how many lakes does Finland have?

FINLAND, GULF OF. See BALTIC SEA.

FINLAY, CARLOS JUAN (1833-1915), was the first man to report evidence that yellow fever might be transmitted by the bite of the *Stegomyia* mosquito (*Aedes aegypti*). The American Yellow Fever Commission went to Havana, Cuba, in 1900, and Finlay convinced its members that his theory was correct. Finlay was born in Puerto Principe (now Camagüey), Cuba. He was chief sanitary officer of Cuba from 1902 to 1908. He studied at Jefferson Medical College in Philadelphia. See also YELLOW FEVER.   NOAH D. FABRICANT

FINN MACCOOL was the leader of the Fenians, or Fianna, Irish warriors of the A.D. 100's or 200's. Stories about Finn are deeply colored by fancy. Finn studied poetry with a master named Finegas who had been trying to catch the "salmon of knowledge." Finegas caught the fish. He asked Finn to cook it, but not to taste it. In turning the fish, Finn burned his thumb and instinctively put it in his mouth. From that day on, Finn had only to put his thumb against a certain tooth to obtain supernatural knowledge.

A charm was laid on Finn to marry a deer, though he recognized the deer as a woman under a spell. Their child was named Oisin, or Little Fawn. Finn, as an old widower, wooed a beautiful lady, Grainne, but she eloped with Finn's friend, Diarmuid. In James Macpherson's Ossianic poems, Finn was called Fingal and Oisin was called Ossian.   KNOX WILSON

See also MYTHOLOGY (Celtic); IRISH LITERATURE (Heroic Tales, Romances, and Sagas); GIANT'S CAUSEWAY).

FINNAN HADDIE. See HADDOCK.

FINNEY, CHARLES GRANDISON (1792-1875), was a Presbyterian and Congregationalist revival preacher. He served as president of Oberlin (Ohio) College from 1851 to 1866. Finney was a lawyer before he became a revivalist, and his preaching was logical and direct, free from pulpit mannerisms. He invited converts to come forward to an "anxious bench." Finney emphasized human free will, and taught that it is possible for people, with God's help, to live perfect lives free from sin.

His preaching helped reforming crusades, including the antislavery and temperance movements. The Broadway Tabernacle in New York City was built for him. He made two preaching tours of Great Britain. He wrote *Lectures on Revivals* and *Lectures on Systematic Theology*. He also founded and edited the *Oberlin Evangelist*. Finney was born in Connecticut.   LEFFERTS A. LOETSCHER

FINNS. See FINLAND (People).

FINSEN, NIELS RYBERG. See NOBEL PRIZES (table: Nobel Prizes for Physiology or Medicine—1903).

FIORD, *fyawrd,* or FJORD, is a long, narrow inlet of the sea. *Fiord* is a Norwegian word, applied to the deep bays and inlets along the ragged coastline of Norway. Geologists believe that rivers cut these fiords, and glaciers deepened them millions of years ago. Most fiords have steep, rocky walls with thick woods and foaming, roaring waterfalls. Small stretches of fertile farmland lie below some of these cliffs.

The coasts of Maine, British Columbia, Alaska, and New Zealand contain inlets like Norway's fiords. *Sea loch* or *firth* is the name for such an inlet in Britain. The southwest coast of the South Island of New Zealand has many interesting fiords.   JOHN D. ISAACS

See also FIRTH; NORWAY (The Land; picture).

U.S. Forest Service; William M. Harlow

The Balsam Fir has needles that give off a fragrant aroma as they dry. Fir cones grow upright on the branches, above.

FIR is a common name for a number of handsome evergreen trees that belong to the pine family. The Douglas fir is not a true fir. It belongs to a separate *genus* (group) in the pine family (see DOUGLAS FIR).

The fir tree is shaped somewhat like a pyramid. It has dense foliage. Its needles are its leaves. They do not grow in clusters like pine needles, but are distributed evenly all around the branch. They are usually soft, blunt, and fragrant. In many species the needles are dark green above, with two light colored lines on the bottom surface. Firs have distinctive cylinder-shaped cones that grow upright on the branches. When the cones mature, they shed their scales, leaving a bare, spinelike axis. The bark of the young trees contains blisters that are filled with a resin called *balsam*.

Nine types of true firs grow in the United States. Two of these grow in the East and seven in the mountains of the West. In northeastern North America and in the states bordering the Great Lakes, the *balsam fir* is a favorite Christmas tree. From its bark comes *Canada balsam*, a substance used in medicine and varnish. The *Fraser fir,* sometimes called the *she-balsam,* grows in the mountains of North Carolina, Virginia, and Tennessee, and is often used as a Christmas tree. Western firs grow quite large and are valuable for their timber. One *California red fir* grew 230 feet (70 meters) high and 10 feet (3 meters) in diameter.

Scientific Classification. Firs belong to the pine family, *Pinaceae,* and make up genus *Abies.* The balsam fir is genus *Abies,* species *A. balsamea.* Fraser fir is *A. fraseri.* The California red fir is *A. magnifica.*   RICHARD J. PRESTON, JR.

See also BALSAM; CONE-BEARING PLANT.

FIRDAUSI, *fur DOU see,* or FIRDUSI, *fur DOO see* (940?-1020?), means the *Heavenly One.* It was the name taken by Abul Qasim Mansur, one of the great epic poets of Persia. His *Shah Namah* (Book of Kings) traces the history of Persia from its mythical period, perhaps before 3600 B.C., to the Moslem conquest in A.D. 641. It is a poem of 60,000 lines, and is about seven times as long as the *Iliad.* Iranian folklore now includes parts of the poem.   WALTER J. FISCHEL

Fire is essential in various industrial processes, particularly the manufacture of steel. Intense flames melt scrap iron, iron ore, and other raw materials in an open-hearth furnace to produce molten steel, *left.*

Jones & Laughlin Steel Corp.

FIRE. The earliest use people made of fire was to keep warm. As civilizations advanced, people learned to use fire in many other ways. Even in earliest times, people had learned to use fire to cook food, to shape weapons and tools, to change clay into pottery, and to furnish light. But primitive peoples had very slow and unsatisfactory ways of kindling fires. Today, people have not only improved the methods of kindling fires, but they also use fire in many more ways. Fire furnishes the energy to drive machines, and keeps vast industries running. It supplies the power to drive trains, ships, and planes; and it generates electricity. Fire is used to remove and destroy waste materials and to kill harmful bacteria.

Fire is also used in separating most metals from their ores, as well as in forging and shaping metals into useful things. Many chemical changes of materials are either made possible or speeded up by the use of fire. A few of these chemical changes are made in such places as sugar refineries and petroleum plants.

Controlled fire is useful. Uncontrolled fire kills thousands of people and destroys millions of dollars' worth of property each year.

What Is Fire?

Fire is the heat and light that comes from burning substances. In 1777, Antoine Lavoisier, a French chemist, proved that burning is the result of the rapid union of oxygen with other substances (see LAVOISIER, ANTOINE L.). As a substance burns, heat and light are produced. Burning is also called *combustion*. Often oxygen unites with other substances at such a slow rate that little heat and no light are given off. When this happens, we call the process *oxidation*, rather than *burning* or *combustion*. Oxidation takes place whenever oxygen unites with other substances either rapidly or slowly. For example, when oxygen unites with gasoline, the action takes place rapidly and heat and light are given off. This process may be described by any of the three words, burning, combustion, or oxidation. When oxygen unites with iron and causes it to rust, burning, or combustion, does not take place, but oxidation does.

Kinds of Fire. All substances do not burn in the same manner. Charcoal, for example, gives off heat with a faint glow. But other substances, such as coal, gas, magnesium, oil, and wood, give off heat with a flame. The color of the flame depends chiefly on the kind of material being burned and on the temperature.

Substances may burn in different ways, but they all require oxygen to burn. Sometimes old rags soaked with oil or paint are thrown aside and forgotten. Oxygen from the air may slowly unite with the oil in the rags. At first, there will not be a fire. But as oxidation gradually takes place, enough heat accumulates to set the rags on fire. This type of burning, called *spontaneous combustion*, causes many fires.

Very rapid burning may cause explosions like those produced by gunpowder and dynamite. Here, oxidation takes place so rapidly that great volumes of gases are produced. These require many hundreds of times the space that was formerly occupied by the gunpowder or dynamite before it was oxidized. These gases expand so rapidly and violently that they produce an explosion. An explosion is really a sudden increase in volume, caused by rapid burning.

How Fire Is Produced. Three conditions must exist before a fire can be made. There must be a fuel or a substance that will burn. The fuel must be heated to its *kindling temperature*. This is the temperature at which oxygen will rapidly unite with the fuel. Finally, there must be plenty of oxygen, which usually comes from the surrounding air.

Fuels are of three classes, solids, liquids, and gases. Coal and wood are examples of solids. Oil and gasoline are liquid fuels. Natural gas and hydrogen are gaseous fuels.

The burning of a solid fuel often depends upon its form. For example, you may not be able to light a large log with a match, but a small twig from the same tree may catch fire easily with the same match. This is because the twig has more air (oxygen) available in proportion to the wood that is to be burned. This explains why it is easy to start a fire with splinters or shavings. Also, the kindling temperatures of fuels differ. Some,

Methods of Making Fire. In ancient times, people twisted sticks in holes in wood until friction caused flames. They also struck rocks together to create sparks. Today, matches ignite when their heads, made of chemicals, are struck on rough surfaces.

such as dry wood or gasoline, have a low kindling temperature, and we can easily set a fire to them. Others, such as hard coal and coke, have a high kindling temperature and are difficult to ignite. A substance known as phosphorus has such a low kindling point that it will start burning in the air at normal temperatures. It must be placed under water in order to keep it from burning. Sodium is another substance that has a low kindling point. It will even burn in water, by taking the oxygen from the water. In order to keep sodium from burning, it has to be placed in kerosene.

If the kindling temperature of a fuel is high, we may place the fuel in a fire already going, as we often do in firing a furnace or stove. We may apply the fire to the fuel as we do with matches when we start a fire. We may produce the kindling temperature of a substance by rubbing it over another substance by *friction*. The early Indians rubbed sticks together to start a fire.

The supply of oxygen for a fire is usually taken from the air, since air is about one-fifth oxygen. If enough oxygen is not available, we often fan the fire to move more air to it. The oxygen supply to furnaces is regulated by openings which can be closed with check drafts. In locomotives and large boilers, air is often forced to the fuel by blowers.

Fireproof Materials. Substances that will not burn easily are called fireproof materials and are used in fireproofing.

There are two reasons why they will not burn easily.

Some fireproofing materials have already combined with as much oxygen as possible. Others will not unite with oxygen at ordinary temperatures. Examples of fireproof materials are asbestos, sand, brick, and stone. Metals like steel and copper are considered fireproof because they combine with oxygen very slowly except at higher temperatures than those which ordinary flames produce.

Methods of Starting Fires. There are several methods of starting a fire, but in each of them the three necessary conditions for a fire must be present. Before matches were invented, the flint and steel method was used. This method required a piece of steel, a flint (hard rock), and a tinder. The tinder was generally made from cotton or linen cloth, or from dried, powdered bark from certain trees. It was heated in an oven until it was nearly ready to burn. It was then placed in a tinderbox to keep it perfectly dry. When the fire was to be started, tinder was placed on the ground and the flint struck against the steel. Some of the sparks made by the flint and steel would fly into the tinder and light it.

Another early method of starting fires was by friction. This method consisted of whirling a stick in a notch in a board until the wood powder that was produced began to glow. Enough oxygen to turn the glow into a blaze was supplied by blowing carefully on the glowing powder.

The first match was invented in 1827 by the English pharmacist John Walker. The tip of this match was

KINDLING TEMPERATURES OF COMMON MATERIALS Kindling temperature, or kindling point, is the temperature to which a substance must be heated to burst into flame. Every burnable substance has its own kindling temperature. The lower the kindling temperature, the more easily a substance will catch fire.

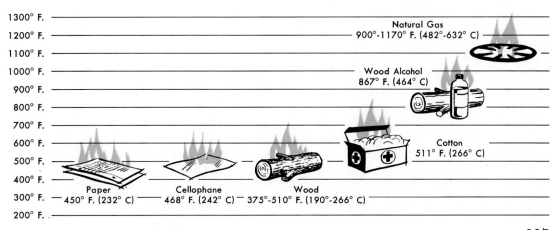

1300° F.
1200° F. — Natural Gas 900°-1170° F. (482°-632° C)
1100° F.
1000° F. — Wood Alcohol 867° F. (464° C)
900° F.
800° F.
700° F.
600° F. — Cotton 511° F. (266° C)
500° F.
400° F.
300° F. — Paper 450° F. (232° C) — Cellophane 468° F. (242° C) — Wood 375°-510° F. (190°-266° C)
200° F.

coated with a mixture of antimony sulfide and potassium chlorate that was held on the wooden matchstick by gum arabic and starch. When this tip was rubbed on a rough surface, friction produced enough heat to ignite the chemicals. The burning chemicals then produced enough heat to ignite the matchstick. More efficient matches were developed later. See MATCH (History).

What Fire Produces

An entire piece of wood or coal will not burn, even if there is sufficient oxygen present. Most of us have taken the ashes from a charcoal grill or fireplace. The ash, generally a mixture of minerals, is present in the fuel, but will not unite with the oxygen. Some fuels have a lower ash content than others. This is important to remember when buying charcoal or wood because you want the fuel with the lowest ash content, provided that it is good in other respects.

Often the bottom of a pan or a skillet becomes black when it is placed over a fire. This is because of the un-burned carbon, and soot. Soot forms when there is not enough oxygen present to burn all the carbon of the fuel. If a furnace produces great quantities of soot, some of the carbon of the fuel is not being burned, and is wasted. This can be remedied by seeing that sufficient air is supplied to burn all the carbon in the fuel.

Gases. Substances that burn in air are nearly always composed of two elements, carbon and hydrogen, or their compounds. For example, coal, coke, and charcoal are mostly carbon. Natural gas, gasoline, and fuel oils consist of many compounds of hydrogen and carbon. When these fuels burn, the oxygen of the air unites with the carbon and hydrogen to form carbon dioxide gas and water vapor. These usually mix with the air and disappear. The uniting of the oxygen with the hydrogen and the carbon is what produces the heat and flame of the fire.

Often, a deadly gas called carbon monoxide forms when there is not enough oxygen to burn the fuel completely. For example, when gasoline burns in an automobile engine, some of this gas forms and comes out the exhaust pipe. If you are in a closed garage when this happens, you are in danger of breathing this gas. Death may result. A person should never run the engine of an automobile in a closed garage.

Smoke, like soot, is produced when too much fuel is added for the amount of oxygen present. It is unburned carbon going out the chimney. Smoking furnaces are wasteful because all the fuel is not burned and the heat energy is lost. The smoke is also a nuisance, because it makes a neighborhood dirty.

Light. Most of the energy caused by a fire goes into heat, but some of it goes into light. The light results either because the carbon particles in the flame become so hot that they give off light energy, or because the gas that is burning is a type that gives off light.

Ever since fire was discovered, people have been trying to make more energy from heat go into light energy. People first used flaming pieces of wood as torches. They later discovered that if the wood was dipped into pitch before lighting it, the light lasted longer and was much brighter. Years afterward, people poured oil in a dish, placed a wick in it, and lighted the wick. This gave a

better light. Later, the tallow candle, which was convenient to carry around, was invented. The kerosene lamp, with its chimney to help control the air currents, was a big improvement over the candle. After electricity was made usable, Thomas A. Edison sent an electric current through a carbon *filament* (wire) until the filament became so hot that it gave off light.

Fire in Legend and Religion

We can only guess that prehistoric people may have gained a knowledge of fire from observing things in nature, such as lightning, the fire of volcanoes, and the heat of the sun. They also must have noticed that sparks fly when stones are struck upon one another, or when the hoofs or claws of an animal strike some hard substance. In Persian literature, there is a story of the discovery of fire in a fight with a dragon. One of the stones which the hero used as weapons missed the monster and struck a rock. Light shone forth and human beings saw fire for the first time. The mythology of nearly all primitive races contains some account of accidental or supernatural happenings which first revealed fire to human beings. Fire was regarded as a true gift of the gods.

Fire was considered sacred because it was so essential to the welfare of people. Fire worship and sun worship have existed since very early times. Because fire was so hard to produce, the custom soon became common of keeping a public fire, which was never allowed to die out. These fires were kept in every village among the Egyptians, Persians, Greeks, and Romans. They were often in the civic center of the community.

The Temple of Vesta in Rome was an outstanding example of the importance of fire to the Romans. Vesta was originally the goddess of the hearth, and her shrine was in every home. But when religion became an affair of state, a temple was erected in which the sacred fire was kept constantly burning. This temple consisted merely of a round hearth. For its service, there were selected the Vestal Virgins, who devoted their lives to the duty of attending the fire. They were selected by the high priest, or pontifex maximus, and the safety of the state was thought to depend upon the faithfulness of the Vestal Virgins.   ERNEST O. BOWER

FIRE ALARM. See FIRE DEPARTMENT.

FIRE ANT. See ANT (picture: Fire Ants).

FIRE BLIGHT. See PEAR (Diseases); BLIGHT.

FIRE CLAY. See CLAY.

FIRE CONTROL is the aiming and firing of guns, rockets, torpedoes, and other weapons at targets. Fire-control equipment includes all devices used in calculating and adjusting fire. Aiming a gun tube or rocket launcher is the simplest form of fire control. More complicated systems guide rockets or missiles after launching. This guidance may be in the form of a device built into the missile. Guidance may also be provided from the launching site through the use of radar beams or attached wires.   HUGH M. COLE

See also GUIDED MISSILE; GYROSCOPE; RADAR (In the Military); RANGE FINDER.

Fighting Fires is one of the most important tasks of a fire department. Many fire fighters and a variety of equipment are needed to put out a large building fire, such as the one shown above.

FIRE DEPARTMENT

FIRE DEPARTMENT is one of the most important organizations in a community. Fire departments battle fires that break out in homes, factories, office buildings, stores, and other places. Fire fighters risk their lives to save people and protect property from fires. They have one of the most dangerous of all occupations. In the United States, a higher percentage of fire fighters are killed or injured on the job than are workers in any other occupation.

The men and women who work for fire departments also help people in many kinds of emergencies besides fires. For example, they rescue persons who may be trapped in cars or trains after an accident. They aid victims of such disasters as tornadoes and floods.

Fire departments work to prevent fires by enforcing fire safety laws. They also teach people about possible fire dangers in their homes and places of work. People cause most fires through carelessness. They could prevent these fires if they knew about fire hazards and followed certain safety measures. Every year in the United States, fires kill about 8,000 persons, injure more than 300,000 others, and destroy over $4 billion worth of property. To reduce the damage caused by fires, local fire departments need the support of the people in the community.

James W. Smith, the contributor of this article, teaches fire protection at Tidewater Community College in Virginia Beach, Va. The article was critically reviewed by the National Fire Prevention and Control Administration.

In colonial America, fires often destroyed whole settlements. When a fire broke out, all the people in the community rushed to the scene. They passed buckets of water from one person to another to put out the fire. As cities and towns grew larger, volunteer and paid fire departments were organized. Today, U.S. fire departments have well-trained men and women and a variety of modern fire-fighting equipment.

The Work of a Fire Department

Fire Fighting. The two basic fire-fighting units in most fire departments are *engine companies* and *ladder companies*. Engine companies operate trucks called *pumpers*, which carry a pump and hoses for spraying water on a fire. Ladder companies use *ladder trucks*, which carry an extension ladder or elevating platform to rescue people through the windows of buildings. Ladder trucks also have other rescue equipment and fire-fighting tools. In most large cities, each neighborhood fire station has at least one engine company and one ladder company. At a fire, the members of the engine and ladder companies work together as a team under the direction of an officer.

Fire departments must handle many types of fires. Each type requires a different plan of action to put it out. For example, the methods used to fight a building fire differ greatly from those used to fight a forest or grassland fire. The following discussion describes how fire fighters battle the two types.

Fighting a Building Fire. After an alarm is received, the engine and ladder companies speed to the fire. They often arrive within a few minutes after receiving the alarm. The officer in command quickly sizes up the situation and directs the fire fighters into action.

FIRE DEPARTMENT

The members of the engine company first connect a hose from the pump to a nearby fire hydrant. They then stretch hose lines from the pump to the building on fire and try to locate the fire within the building. Their first concern is to keep the fire from spreading. The fire fighters spray water on any nearby buildings that are in danger of catching fire. They then direct water on the fire itself until it is out.

Meanwhile, the members of the ladder company search for people who may be trapped in the building. In some buildings, they use ladders to rescue people through windows. However, the ladders on most trucks extend up to only about eight stories. Fire fighters must use elevators or stairs to get to persons trapped on floors above the reach of the ladders.

Ladder company members must also ventilate the building to let out the smoke, heat, and gases that build up during a fire. They open or break windows and sometimes cut holes in the roof or walls. If the building were not ventilated, the heat and the pressure of the gases could cause an explosion.

The ladder company tries to save any furniture or other property not damaged by the fire. The members spread canvas or rubber covers over such property to prevent water damage. Finally, the ladder company searches the building for hidden sparks that might cause another blaze.

After the fire is out, the fire fighters try to find out exactly where and how the fire started. The officer in charge makes out a report that gives all the important facts about the fire. The report includes information on the number of persons killed, if any; the cause of the fire; and the estimated cost of damage.

Fighting a Grassland or Forest Fire. Many grassland and forest fires occur in areas that are hard to reach and far from a source of water. Local fire departments have trucks that carry water and can travel over rough land.

Observers in helicopters or airplanes may fly over the fire and report on its size and behavior. Sometimes, helicopters or airplanes are also used to carry fire fighters to the fire or to drop chemicals that slow the spread of the fire.

Grassland and forest fires often spread rapidly and are difficult to put out. Fire fighters try to keep the fire within the smallest area possible, and so they may first create a *firebreak*, or *fireline*. The fire fighters clear a strip of land some distance in front of the racing flames. They cut down the grass or trees and scrape away some of the soil with shovels or a bulldozer. The fire fighters may then set a *backfire* to burn the area between the firebreak and the onrushing fire. The firebreak and the backfire prevent the flames from spreading. After the fire has been contained, the fire fighters spray water or throw dirt on the flames until the fire is out.

Emergency Rescue Operations. Large fire departments have rescue companies to handle nonfire emergencies. For example, rescue workers may be called to free persons trapped under the wreckage of a fallen building or in a car after an accident. Rescue workers sometimes have to break through walls or cut through metal doors to reach an injured person.

Rescue companies also go to major fires. At a building fire, for example, the rescue workers help the ladder company get people out of the building. They give first aid to people overcome by smoke or suffering from burns and then rush them to a hospital.

Some fire departments have *paramedic units*, which give on-the-scene medical care in an emergency. Fire fighters trained as paramedics treat heart attack victims and other persons needing emergency attention. The paramedics operate ambulances that carry medical equipment, drugs, and a two-way radio for contact with a nearby hospital. See PARAMEDIC.

Fire Prevention and Fire Safety. To help prevent fires and reduce fire losses, local fire departments inspect public buildings and private homes. They also

Fire Fighters Ventilate a Building by chopping holes in the roof, if necessary. Ventilation lets out smoke and gases that build up during a fire and that could cause an explosion.

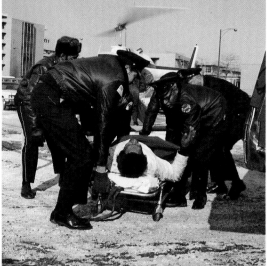

Fire Department Paramedics treat persons needing emergency medical care and rush them to a hospital. The paramedics operate ambulances that carry medical equipment and drugs.

teach people about fire safety and conduct *arson* investigations. Arson is the crime of purposely setting fire to a building or other property. Many fire departments have a separate division that carries out fire prevention and fire safety programs.

Public Building Inspections. Most cities have a fire safety code that applies to such buildings as theaters, department stores, schools, and hospitals. Under these codes, the buildings may not be constructed of materials that burn easily. The codes also require portable fire extinguishers, a certain number of exits, and other fire safety features in public buildings.

Fire department officials inspect public buildings from time to time to enforce the local code. The officials check the condition of the electrical equipment and the heating system. They note the number and location of exits and fire extinguishers. The inspection also covers housekeeping conditions and many other matters that affect fire safety. Fire department inspectors may also review plans for a new building to make sure it meets the safety code.

Home Inspections. Most of the deaths caused by fires occur in private homes. For this reason, many fire departments have home safety programs. They will send a fire fighter to inspect a private home if asked by the owner. After the inspection, the fire fighter recommends ways to make the home safer from fire.

During home inspections, fire fighters check the heating and air-conditioning systems and the cooking equipment. They look for unsafe practices, such as overloading electrical outlets or running electrical cords under a rug. The fire fighters also instruct families on what to do if a fire breaks out. To leave the home safely and quickly in case of fire, families are advised to make escape plans and to practice fire drills. For other recommended instructions, see the table *What to Do in Case of Fire* on this page.

Most fire departments advise people to install *smoke detectors* in their homes. Smoke detectors are devices that sound an alarm if smoke builds up in a room. The devices are attached to the ceiling or wall in several areas of the home. Most home fires that result in deaths occur at night when the family is asleep. Smoke detectors will awaken the family before the fire and the smoke build up to the point where escape is impossible. *Heat detectors*, which sound an alarm if the temperature rises to a certain point, are also available. However, smoke detectors generally give an earlier warning than do most heat detectors.

Fire departments also recommend that people have portable fire extinguishers in their homes. A person must be sure, however, to use the right kind of extinguisher for the type of fire involved. For example, a water extinguisher cannot put out a grease fire. Such a fire can be fought with a special gas extinguisher. For more information on the kinds of fires and extinguishers, see the article FIRE EXTINGUISHER.

Public Education Programs. Many fire departments work with other local agencies to teach people how to prevent fires and what procedures to follow during a fire. In some communities, fire department officials serve as instructors or advisers in fire safety courses in the schools. They also supervise school fire drills.

Arson Investigations. Many fire departments have a squad of specially trained investigators who gather

What to Do in Case of Fire

1. **Leave the Building Immediately.** Do not try to fight the fire unless it is confined to a small area.

2. **Never Open a Door That Feels Hot.** Before opening any door, place your hand on it. If the door feels hot, the fire on the other side may be blazing fiercely. You could be killed by the heat and smoke if you opened the door. Try another escape route or wait for help.

3. **Crawl on the Floor When Going Through a Smoky Area.** Smoke and heated gases tend to rise, and so they will be thinnest near the floor.

4. **Do Not Run if Your Clothes Catch Fire.** Running fans and spreads flames. Roll on the floor to smother the flames.

5. **Do Not Return to the Building for Any Reason.** After you have escaped, call the fire department. If people are still trapped in the building, wait for the fire department to rescue them.

evidence in cases where arson is suspected. Fire department officials in some cities estimate that nearly half the fires in their cities are purposely set.

Fire Department Equipment

The most important equipment of a fire department includes (1) communication systems, (2) fire trucks, and (3) special fire vehicles. In addition, the fire fighters themselves require protective clothing.

Communication Systems are necessary to alert fire departments to the outbreak of a fire. Most fire alarms are telephoned to the fire department. Other alarms are sent from (1) fire alarm boxes or (2) automatic signaling devices. All alarms go to the department's *alarm headquarters*, which then quickly alerts the neighborhood station closest to the fire.

Milt and Joan Mann

The Alarm Headquarters of a fire department receives all alarms reporting the outbreak of a fire. An operator alerts the nearest fire station, which sends fire fighters to the scene.

FIRE DEPARTMENT

Fire Alarm Boxes stand on street corners in most large cities. Some of these boxes operate by telegraph. Others contain a telephone or two-way radio. The telegraph boxes send a coded signal to alarm headquarters when a person pulls the lever. The signal indicates the location of the box. The boxes that have a telephone or two-way radio are used to talk directly to operators at the alarm center.

Automatic Signaling Devices are installed in many public buildings. These devices include smoke and heat detectors that are wired to send an alarm automatically to alarm headquarters. A *sprinkler system* can also be wired to alert the fire department automatically. Such a system consists of a network of pipes installed throughout a building. The pipes carry water to nozzles in the ceiling. The heat from a fire causes the nozzles directly above the fire to open and spray water. When the water starts to flow through the pipes, an alarm is automatically sent to the fire department.

Alarm Headquarters in a small fire department may consist of one switchboard operator. Some large fire departments have a computerized system of receiving alarms and notifying fire stations.

After fire fighters arrive at a fire, they advise alarm headquarters how serious the situation is and, if necessary, ask for more help. With each call for additional help, more equipment and companies are sent to the fire. Each fire truck has a two-way radio for communication with headquarters.

Fire Trucks. Fire departments have several types of fire trucks. The main kinds are (1) pumpers, (2) ladder trucks, and (3) rescue trucks.

Pumpers have a large pump that takes water from a fire hydrant or other source. The pump boosts the pressure of the water and forces it through hose lines. The size of a pump is determined by the amount of water it can discharge per minute. The most common sizes deliver 750 to 1,500 gallons (2,840 to 5,680 liters) per minute.

Pumpers carry several sizes of hoses and nozzles. Many pumpers also have a small-diameter hose called a *booster line*, which is wound on a reel. The booster line

Three Kinds of Fire Trucks   The illustrations below show an elevating platform truck, a pumper, and an aerial ladder truck. All three trucks are used to spray water on a fire. Elevating platform and aerial ladder trucks can also be used to rescue people through the windows of a burning building.

WORLD BOOK illustrations by George Suyeoka

Elevating Platform Truck — Articulating boom — Platform — Water nozzle — Portable ladders — Turntable — Storage compartment — Supporting jacks

Pumper — Booster line — Hard suction hose — Water hose — Pump — Hose connection — Storage compartment — Extension ladder

Aerial Ladder Truck — Booster line — Portable ladders — Turntable — Pump — Storage compartment

is used chiefly to put out small outdoor fires. Pumpers used for fighting grass or brush fires carry a tank of water and such tools as shovels and rakes.

Ladder Trucks. There are two kinds of ladder trucks— *aerial ladder* and *elevating platform.* An aerial ladder truck has a metal extension ladder mounted on a turntable. The ladder can be raised as high as 100 feet (30 meters), or about eight stories. An elevating-platform truck, commonly called a *snorkel,* has a cagelike platform that can hold several persons. The platform is attached to a lifting device, either an *articulating boom* or a *telescoping boom,* which is mounted on a turntable. The boom on the largest trucks can extend 150 feet (46 meters). A built-in hose runs the length of the boom and is used to direct water on a fire.

Ladder trucks are equipped with portable ladders, stretchers, and first-aid kits. They also carry *forcible entry tools* to break into a building or a room. These tools include axes, power saws, and sledge hammers.

Rescue Trucks are enclosed vehicles equipped with many of the same kinds of forcible entry tools that ladder trucks carry. But rescue trucks also carry additional equipment for unusual rescues. They have such tools as oxyacetylene torches, for cutting through metal, and hydraulic jacks, for lifting heavy objects. They also carry scuba gear, fire-resistant suits, and emergency medical supplies and equipment.

Special Fire Vehicles include *airport crash trucks* and *fireboats.* Airport crash trucks are pumpers that spray foam or dry chemicals on burning aircraft. Water is ineffective against many aircraft fires, such as those that involve jet fuel, gasoline, or certain aircraft metals. Fireboats fight fires on ships and piers and in waterfront buildings. These boats have pumps that draw water from a river, lake, or ocean. Large seagoing fireboats can pump about 10,000 gallons (38,000 liters) of water per minute.

Protective Clothing. Fire fighters require special clothing for protection against flames, falling objects, and other hazards. They wear knee-length coats made of fire-resistant material and protective pants and shirts. Other clothing includes specially made boots, gloves, and helmets. Fire fighters also use masks to avoid inhaling smoke and toxic gases. The masks are connected to small air cylinders strapped on the back.

On certain rare occasions, fire fighters must walk through flames. For instance, they may do so when rescuing passengers from a burning airplane. They then wear *heat-reflective suits.* These suits are fire resistant and coated with aluminum to reflect heat. They cover the whole body, leaving no part unprotected.

Kinds of Fire Departments

The main kinds of fire departments are (1) volunteer, (2) paid, and (3) special purpose. About 27,000 volunteer and paid fire departments protect communities in the United States. Most of these departments are volunteer organizations. Special-purpose departments are maintained by certain government agencies and some private industries.

Volunteer Departments provide protection mainly in small towns and rural communities. They are staffed by men and women who serve part time. Some departments have a few paid fire fighters but rely chiefly on volunteers. When a fire breaks out in the community,

Some Equipment Carried on Fire Trucks

Fire trucks carry a variety of *forcible entry tools,* such as axes and crowbars, which are used to break into a building or room. Other equipment on fire trucks includes first-aid kits, oxygen tanks and masks, and smoke ejectors.

WORLD BOOK illustrations by David Cunningham

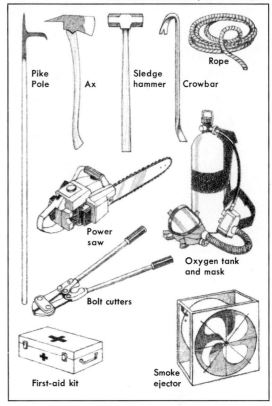

Pike Pole Ax Sledge hammer Crowbar Rope

Power saw

Bolt cutters

Oxygen tank and mask

First-aid kit Smoke ejector

Chicago Fire Department

Protective Clothing worn by fire fighters includes helmets, knee-length coats, gloves, and boots. The clothing protects fire fighters from flames, water, and other job hazards.

FIRE DEPARTMENT

Owens-Corning Fiberglas Corporation

Heat-Reflective Suits are worn by fire fighters in special cases when they have to walk through flames. The suits are fire resistant and coated with aluminum to reflect heat.

the volunteers leave their jobs or homes and rush to the fire station. In some departments, the volunteers are paid for their work, but in others they receive no pay.

Many volunteer departments have only enough equipment and volunteers for routine fires. In case of a major fire, departments from neighboring communities help one another. Most volunteer departments are headed by a fire chief, who is either appointed by the mayor or elected by members of the department.

Paid Departments serve chiefly in larger cities. Some departments are organized on a county, district, or regional level. Paid departments are staffed by full-time fire fighters.

Paid fire departments in large cities have many fire-fighting companies, which operate from neighborhood fire stations. Each company is commanded by a captain or a lieutenant. Several companies make up a *battalion* or a *district*. Battalions may be further grouped into *divisions*. Large departments also have separate staffs that work in such areas as fire prevention, training, communications, and arson investigations. A fire chief, who is appointed by the mayor or some other city official, directs the entire fire department.

Special-Purpose Departments. The U.S. government maintains fire departments at all military bases and other large federal installations. These departments are trained to handle fires and other emergencies unique to a particular installation, as well as routine fires. For example, Air Force bases train fire fighters to battle aircraft fires, and nuclear power installations train fire fighters to deal with radiation emergencies. Certain federal and state agencies maintain fire-fighting units to watch for and put out forest fires.

Some industrial plants, such as those that manufacture fuels or explosives, organize their own fire departments. In addition, all major airports have a fire department to fight aircraft fires.

History

One of the first fire-fighting organizations was established in ancient Rome. Augustus, who became emperor in 27 B.C., formed a group called the *vigiles*. The vigiles patrolled the streets to watch for fires. They also served as the police force in Rome.

Scholars know little else about the development of fire-fighting organizations in Europe until after the Great Fire of London in 1666. This fire destroyed much of the city and left thousands of people homeless. Before the fire, London had no organized fire protection system. After the fire, insurance companies in the city formed private *fire brigades* to protect the property of their clients.

The Development of U.S. Fire Protection. The early American colonists fought building fires by forming *bucket brigades*. One row of volunteers passed buckets from a source of water to the fire. Another row passed back the empty buckets. The fire fighters also pulled down buildings next to the burning structure with iron hooks attached to ropes. In this way, they created a separation between the buildings to help prevent the fire from spreading.

Peter Stuyvesant, the governor of a colony that included what is now New York, made one of the first efforts to establish a fire prevention system. In 1648, he appointed four fire wardens to inspect homes in New Amsterdam, which later became New York City. The wardens' chief duty was to inspect chimneys for fire hazards. In 1658, Stuyvesant began one of the first community alarm systems. He appointed a number of men to patrol the streets at night and watch for fires. The men were called the *rattle watch* because they shook wooden rattles to alert the townspeople whenever a fire was discovered.

In 1679, Boston established the first paid fire department in the American Colonies. It consisted of a crew of men who operated a hand pump. In 1736, Benjamin Franklin founded the colonies' first volunteer fire department in Philadelphia.

By the early 1800's, many U.S. cities had volunteer fire departments. The departments required numerous volunteers to pull and operate the hand pumps and hose wagons. In many cities, the most prominent citizens belonged to the volunteer departments, which became powerful social and political organizations.

In the mid-1800's, steam pumpers pulled by horses began to replace hand pumps. The steam pumpers required fewer persons to operate them. About this time, many of the larger cities changed from volunteer to paid fire departments. During the early 1900's, steam pumpers were replaced by gasoline fire engines. Since then, many improvements have been made in the equipment and methods used in fire fighting.

Recent Developments. During the 1970's, the U.S. government encouraged fire departments to devote more time and money to fire prevention activities. In 1974, the government established the National Fire Prevention and Control Administration (NFPCA). The NFPCA serves as an information center for the nation's

Steam Pumpers Pulled by Horses were used by fire departments from the mid-1800's to the early 1900's. At the time, they were a major improvement over the hand pumps formerly used.

fire departments and develops new fire prevention and control techniques for use by local departments. It also operates the National Academy for Fire Prevention and Control in Washington, D.C. The academy develops training programs for fire fighters and others who work in the field of fire prevention and control.

Since the 1960's, U.S. fire departments have been faced with drastic increases in arson. Between the mid-1960's and 1977, the arson rate increased about 300 per cent. In efforts to reduce the problem, some fire departments have hired more arson investigators and pushed for stronger laws against arson.

False alarms have also become a serious problem. In some U.S. cities, a third or more of all alarms received by the fire department are false. Some departments have removed alarm boxes from areas with a long record of false alarms. Others send fewer companies to answer alarms during peak false alarm periods.

A number of paid fire departments began to hire women as fire fighters during the 1970's. Women had served in volunteer fire departments since the 1800's but were not admitted into any paid departments until the 1970's.

Careers

The requirements for becoming a paid fire fighter vary among fire departments. In general, an applicant must be at least 19 years old and in excellent physical condition. An applicant must also have a high school education and pass a written test.

After being accepted by a fire department, a probationary fire fighter takes a training program that lasts one to three months. The program covers such subjects as fire behavior, fire-fighting tactics and strategy, and forcible entry techniques. After the probationary period, a fire fighter may receive specialized training in such areas as rescue work, fire prevention, arson investigation, or emergency medical care.

Many fire departments provide continuing education programs for fire fighters. In addition, nearly 400 community colleges in the United States offer courses in subjects related to fire protection.   JAMES W. SMITH

Critically reviewed by the
NATIONAL FIRE PREVENTION AND CONTROL ADMINISTRATION

Related Articles in WORLD BOOK include:

Outline

I. **The Work of a Fire Department**
   A. Fire Fighting
   B. Emergency Rescue Operations
   C. Fire Prevention and Fire Safety
II. **Fire Department Equipment**
   A. Communication Systems
   B. Fire Trucks
   C. Special Fire Vehicles
   D. Protective Clothing
III. **Kinds of Fire Departments**
   A. Volunteer Departments   C. Special-Purpose
   B. Paid Departments   Departments
IV. **History**
V. **Careers**

FIRE DRILL

Questions

What rules should a person follow in case of fire?

What services does the National Fire Prevention and Control Administration provide?

How did the early American colonists fight fires?

What is the purpose of firebreaks and backfires?

What duties does an engine company perform at a building fire? A ladder company?

Why do fire departments inspect buildings and homes?

What are *paramedic units?*

What kinds of equipment do pumpers, ladder trucks, and rescue trucks carry?

How do smoke and heat detectors work?

Why must fire fighters ventilate a burning building?

Who founded the first volunteer fire department in the American Colonies?

FIRE DRILL in schools is an exercise to teach children to leave a school safely and speedily if fire breaks out. Many states have laws that require regular school fire drills. In many schools, each classroom has signs that tell the class its route out of the building. There are signs and red lights in the halls. These show the nearest exit for children who are not in their classroom when the fire bell rings. When the alarm is given, the teacher sees that the class leaves the school in a quiet and orderly manner. The children march out in single file. Without the practice that a fire drill provides, people may become frightened and crush each other in leaving a burning building. Fire drills are also practiced on ships and at such places as airports and oil refineries.

FIRE ENGINE. See FIRE DEPARTMENT (Fire Department Equipment).

FIRE EXTINGUISHER is a metal container filled with water or chemicals used to put out fires. Fire extinguishers are portable and easy to operate and can be used to put out small fires before the flames spread.

In the United States, state and local fire laws require that extinguishers be installed in easily seen places in public buildings. Such buildings include factories, schools, stores, and theaters. School buses and most public vehicles also must be equipped with fire extinguishers.

There are many kinds of fire extinguishers. The kind used depends on the type of fire involved. Fire prevention experts divide fires into four classes—A, B, C, and D—depending on the burning material. *Class A* fires involve such ordinary combustible materials as cloth, paper, rubber, or wood. *Class B* fires involve combustible gases or such combustible liquids as cooking grease, gasoline, or oil. *Class C* fires involve motors, switches, or other electrical equipment. *Class D* fires involve combustible metals, such as magnesium chips or shavings. Most extinguishers have information printed on them that tells the class, or classes, of fire for which they can be used.

Class D fires require special extinguishers designed for specific metals. But most other fire extinguishers can be classified, by their contents, as one of three main types: (1) water extinguishers, (2) liquefied gas extinguishers, and (3) dry chemical extinguishers.

Water Extinguishers are used to fight only class A fires. Water conducts electricity, and so it must never be used on a fire involving electrical equipment. A water extinguisher is operated by a valve or a hand pump, depending on the model. Either action shoots the water through a hose that is attached to the container.

Liquefied Gas Extinguishers may be used on class B and class C fires. There are two main kinds—*carbon dioxide extinguishers*, which contain a gas called carbon dioxide; and *Halon extinguishers*, which contain another gas. Each of these types has the gas in liquid form under pressure in the container. The operator, by squeezing a handle, converts the liquid to gas, which flows out and covers the fire. Liquefied gas extinguishers leave no water or powder as do other extinguishers. For this reason, the gas types are the most suitable for class C fires involving computers or other delicate electrical equipment that could be damaged.

Dry Chemical Extinguishers are used on class B and class C fires. One type, the *multipurpose dry chemical extinguisher*, also can be used against class A fires. Dry chemical extinguishers contain a chemical powder and a gas under pressure. The gas expels the chemical after the operator opens a valve or punctures a gas cartridge attached to the extinguisher. A heat reaction between the expelled chemical and the fire creates carbon dioxide, which puts out the fire. C. R. FREDRIKSEN

FIRE FIGHTING. See FIRE DEPARTMENT.

FIRE INSURANCE. See INSURANCE (Fire Insurance).

KINDS OF FIRE EXTINGUISHERS

The chief kinds of fire extinguishers are *water, liquefied gas,* and *dry chemical.* To operate most extinguishers, a person pulls the locking pin and squeezes the operating lever while aiming the nozzle at the base of the fire.

Water Extinguishers are filled with water. They are used to fight Class A fires, which involve wood, paper, cloth, or other combustible solids. Water extinguishers must never be used for fires that involve electrical equipment.

Liquefied Gas Extinguishers contain either carbon dioxide gas or a gas called *Halon.* They are used for Class B fires, which involve a combustible liquid, such as gasoline or cooking grease. People also use these extinguishers to fight Class C fires, which involve motors, switches, or other electrical equipment.

Dry Chemical Extinguishers contain a chemical powder. They are used on Class B or C fires. A type called multipurpose dry chemical can also be used on Class A fires.

PARTS OF A FIRE EXTINGUISHER

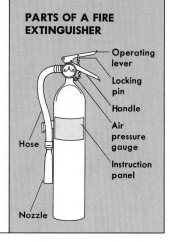

Operating lever
Locking pin
Handle
Air pressure gauge
Instruction panel
Hose
Nozzle

FIRE PREVENTION is a term for the many safety measures used to keep harmful fires from starting. Each year, about $2\frac{1}{2}$ million fires are reported to fire departments in the United States. The fires cause about 8,000 deaths and billions of dollars worth of damage. In Canada, about 65,000 fires cause more than 600 deaths annually. More than a fourth of all the people killed or injured by fire are children.

Individuals, groups, and communities work to prevent fires. They use three main methods: (1) laws and regulations, (2) inspection of buildings and other property, and (3) education about fire safety.

Most cities and states have laws that require certain types of fireproof materials and electric wiring to be used in buildings. Fire departments and other public agencies inspect public buildings for fire hazards and recommend corrective action. In some communities, homeowners may agree to have their homes inspected. Education is a vital part of fire prevention programs because people cause—and could prevent—almost all fires. Fire departments, community groups, and schools teach children and adults about fire hazards and work to reduce fires throughout the community.

In Homes and Schools, trash and old clothing, drapes, and furniture should be discarded, not stored in attics, basements, or closets. They could quickly catch fire in any of those places. Such liquids as gasoline and paint burn easily and should be stored in tightly closed cans, away from heat. Gasoline should not be stored in a house, and it must never be used to start a barbecue fire or bonfire.

In old homes and schools, an electrician should regularly check electric wiring and replace any that appears weak or worn. An electrician should also replace cords on electric appliances as soon as the outside coverings become worn. Cords should never be run under carpeting, where they might become damaged and set the carpeting on fire. A fire can also result from overloading one outlet with several appliances. See ELECTRICITY (How to Use Electricity Safely); SAFETY (Home).

FIRE HAZARDS IN THE HOME

Every day, fires strike more than 1,500 homes in the United States. Most of these fires are caused by carelessness. These pictures show some of the careless habits that can result in fire.

Smoking in Bed can cause linen or clothing to catch fire if the smoker falls asleep.

An Electrical Outlet overloaded with appliances can cause overheated wires to burn.

Playing with Matches can result in rugs, clothing, and other items being set aflame.

Storing Flammable Liquids near a furnace can cause escaping fumes to catch fire.

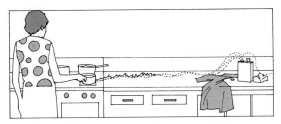
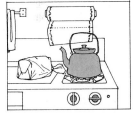

Gasoline should not be used to start fires because it is too flammable and uncontrollable.

A Flashback Fire can begin when fumes escape from cleaning fluid or some other flammable liquid and come in contact with a flame. A flashback fire travels along the path of the fumes.

Dish Towels and other burnable items can be set ablaze if placed too near a stove.

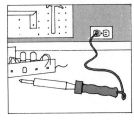
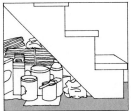

WORLD BOOK illustrations by David Cunningham

Throwing Away Cigarettes that are still burning can start a wastebasket fire.

A Soldering Iron can set a workbench on fire if not disconnected after being used.

Stored Rags soaked with grease, oil, or paint can quickly burst into flame.

Space Heaters located too close to blowing curtains can cause the fabric to catch fire.

FIRE PREVENTION

Dow Chemical Co.

A Fire Retardancy Test shows how easily a fabric can burn. Many fabrics are treated chemically to make them less flammable.

Many types of fabrics burn easily. Wise parents teach children to avoid clothing fires by not playing near lighted stoves, not standing near bonfires, and not playing with matches. Children playing with matches cause almost 75,000 fires yearly in the United States.

Many school programs train children to be alert to fire hazards. Young children may learn these dangers by coloring sheets of pictures, rhymes, and slogans about fire prevention. Many older children visit fire departments. Fire fighters also give talks and demonstrations for classes and assemblies. School and community groups sponsor children's clubs, called junior fire departments, to promote fire safety in the home.

In the Community, fire departments and other public agencies work to improve fire prevention through laws, inspections, and educational programs. Such groups as chambers of commerce and youth clubs promote fire prevention through newspapers, pamphlets, posters, and radio and television appeals.

Some groups sponsor programs to alert the community to fire hazards that occur during various seasons. For example, the number of fires in homes increases every winter, when heating equipment comes into use. Some of this equipment has not been kept in good condition or has been misused. In many communities, groups put safety tags on Christmas trees. Halloween programs stress the dangers of bonfires, candles, and costumes made of materials that burn easily.

Local clean-up weeks encourage homeowners, stores, and factories to discard rubbish and eliminate other fire hazards. Each year, the United States and Canada observe National Fire Prevention Week during the week including October 9, the anniversary of the Chicago Fire of 1871. Most communities have laws that require regular inspections of commercial, public, and some residential buildings. Fire department officials conduct these inspections for fire dangers.

In Industry, fire prevention presents special problems because fire must be used for so many jobs. Fire per-

forms such tasks as melting metals, heating chemicals, and generating electricity. Machines and furnaces used for these jobs must be carefully designed to keep the flames under control. Inspectors check for fire hazards near machines and in other areas of a factory. Employers teach workers to operate machines safely and to report any problems that could cause fire.

Workers must take special care when using dry or liquid chemicals and oils. Some liquids give off easily ignited vapors and have to be stored in metal safety cans. Spilled chemicals, and dust and chips from wood and other materials, must be cleaned up immediately.

Many industries sponsor special classes and demonstrations to teach workers how to prevent fire at their jobs. Factory bulletin boards, pamphlets, and articles in company magazines also promote fire safety.

Fire Prevention Laws began with building regulations in ancient times. About 18 B.C., the Roman Emperor Augustus set maximum heights for houses and minimum thicknesses for their walls. Later laws required minimum separations between buildings to prevent fires from spreading from one structure to the next. In the A.D. 300's, Emperor Julian issued controls on the work of blacksmiths and other tradespeople who used fire. For example, he banned smoking chimneys that could cause roof fires. Princes in parts of Italy and Germany used some of these laws as late as the 1600's.

In the American Colonies, the earliest fire laws dealt with fighting, rather than preventing, fires. But colonial newspapers sometimes advised their readers about fire hazards. Late in the 1800's, insurance companies worked for the passage of many fire prevention laws and required businesses to follow fire prevention programs. In 1922, the United States and Canada observed National Fire Protection Week, the first campaign to educate the public in fire safety. Since then, public education programs have become important supplements to well-developed fire prevention laws and inspection programs. Many of these programs go on the year around, with emphasis on seasonal hazards.

Australia, Great Britain, The Netherlands, and Sweden also stress public education in fire prevention. But most other industrialized nations rely more on laws, inspections, and worker training. In many other countries, insurance requirements form the basis of fire prevention programs.

Critically reviewed by the

NATIONAL FIRE PROTECTION ASSOCIATION

See also COMBUSTION; FIRE DEPARTMENT; FIRE DRILL; FIRE EXTINGUISHER; FIREPROOFING; SHIP (picture: Safety at Sea).

FIRE TEST. See BUILDING CONSTRUCTION.

FIRE TOWER. See FORESTRY.

FIRE-TUBE BOILER. See BOILER.

FIRE UNDERWRITERS, NATIONAL BOARD OF. See INSURANCE (Fire Insurance).

FIRE WORSHIP is an ancient religious practice followed by peoples who believe a god or spirit inhabits fire and gives it its power. It is somewhat like fetish worship, since those who practice it believe a god or spirit lives in the fire. The ancient religion of Persia and India, called Zoroastrianism, used fire as a symbol or emblem of its god. Many peoples have held hearth fires sacred. The Aztec Indians of Mexico lighted new fires in their hearths when the year began. See also FETISH; ZOROASTER; VESTA.　　WILSON D. WALLIS

FIREARM is any weapon that uses gunpowder to fire a bullet or shell. Generally, the term is used for light firearms, such as rifles, shotguns, and pistols. They are often called *small arms*. Heavier firearms are generally referred to as *artillery*.

Mechanism. Any firearm, large or small, has four essential parts: (1) barrel, (2) chamber, (3) breech mechanism, and (4) firing mechanism. The *barrel* is a long tube. It may be smooth, as in a shotgun, or with spiral grooves on the inner surface, as in a rifle. The *chamber* is a widened hole at the *breech* (rear) end of the barrel. It holds the *cartridge* (explosive charge). The *breech mechanism* closes the rear end of the barrel, holding the cartridge in the chamber. Every up-to-date firearm has some way by which the breech can be opened for loading and locked for safety in firing. Artillery uses screw plugs or breechblocks. Machine guns, rifles, and other small arms usually have a metal cylinder, or *bolt*, that is locked when the gun is fired, and drawn back to eject the empty cartridge case and to reload. The *firing mechanism* may be electric, as in some large artillery pieces. In small arms, a spring drives a pointed firing pin through the breech bolt against a sensitive *primer* in the cartridge. The firing pin is *cocked* (drawn back) against a hook called the *sear*. When the trigger is pulled, the sear releases the firing pin, which in turn leaps forward to strike the primer. A jet of flame from the primer ignites the rest of the powder, forming a gas. This explosive gas propels the bullet from the barrel.

In World War II, American soldiers carried semiautomatic Garand rifles that fired and ejected cases automatically with each pull of the trigger. The M1 carbine used a less powerful cartridge, but was quite similar. Both the Garand rifle and M1 carbine fired .30-caliber bullets. Soldiers and officers also used .45-caliber semiautomatic pistols.

History. The Chinese may have used firearms thousands of years ago. But firearms as we know them were not developed in the Western world until Europeans learned to use gunpowder during the 1200's. The first firearms were cannons, but men soon developed firearms that they could carry.

The invention of firearms led to great changes in warfare. Bullets could penetrate armor. Castles had easily withstood the attacks of men armed with battle-axes, swords, spears, and bows and arrows. But they crumbled before the assault of new weapons such as cannon balls. Soldiers used pistols, blunderbusses, and muskets. They had to load their hand-held firearms from the muzzle, and found these weapons heavy and clumsy. But, clumsy as they were, they revolutionized warfare.

The rifle was invented about 1500. It had spiral grooves inside the barrel that made it more accurate than any previous firearm. Smokeless powder was developed in the 1800's. Breechloading systems replaced dangerous muzzle loading. Many improvements since have resulted in high-powered firearms. JACK O'CONNOR

Related Articles in WORLD BOOK include:

Ammunition	Carbine	Machine Gun
Armor	Explosive	Musket
Artillery	Flintlock	Pistol
Bazooka	Garand Rifle	Revolver
Blunderbuss	Gun	Rifle
Cannon	Harquebus	Shotgun

TYPES OF FIREARMS

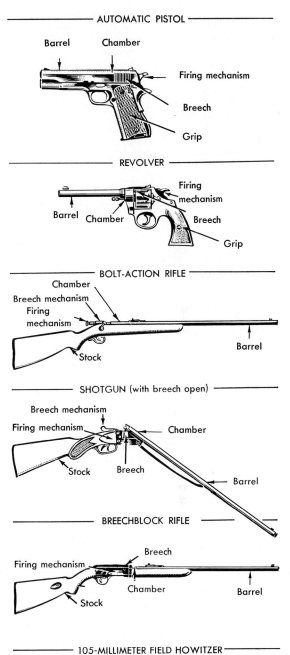

— AUTOMATIC PISTOL —

Barrel   Chamber

Firing mechanism

Breech

Grip

— REVOLVER —

Firing mechanism

Barrel   Chamber   Breech

Grip

— BOLT-ACTION RIFLE —

Chamber

Breech mechanism
Firing mechanism

Barrel

Stock

— SHOTGUN (with breech open) —

Breech mechanism

Firing mechanism   Chamber

Stock   Breech

Barrel

— BREECHBLOCK RIFLE —

Breech

Firing mechanism

Chamber   Barrel

Stock

— 105-MILLIMETER FIELD HOWITZER —

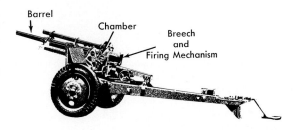

Barrel

Chamber

Breech
and
Firing Mechanism

FIREBALL

FIREBALL is a meteor that burns brightly as it plunges through the earth's atmosphere. If the fireball explodes at the end of its path, it is generally called a *bolide*. Some pieces may survive the explosion, and fall to the earth. Only brightness makes a fireball different from an ordinary meteor. A fireball is as bright as Jupiter or Venus. In rare cases, a fireball may be as bright as the full moon. A sound like thunder occasionally accompanies the passage of a fireball.   I. M. LEVITT

See also METEOR.

FIREBIRD. See BALTIMORE ORIOLE.

FIREBOAT. See FIRE DEPARTMENT (Special Vehicles).

FIREBRICK. See BRICK (Kinds of Brick).

FIRECRACKER FLOWER is a perennial plant of the amaryllis family. It grows in California. Its low, narrow leaves look like blades of grass. The slender stalk may grow to be 3 feet (91 centimeters) high. The tube-shaped flowers are scarlet, tipped with green. They grow in a cluster at the top of the stalk. The plant grows best in partial shade in deep, loose, well-drained soil with some leaf mold.

Scientific Classification. The firecracker flower belongs to the amaryllis family, *Amaryllidaceae*. It is genus *Dichelostemma*, species *D. idamaia.*   DONALD WYMAN

The Firecracker Flower

FIREDAMP. See DAMP.

FIREFLY is the name commonly given to several kinds of beetles that glow like sparks of fire in the dark. Fireflies are often called *lightning bugs* or *lightning beetles*. Fireflies live in warm and tropical countries. Most of the fireflies in the United States live east of the Rocky Mountains. One of the most common fireflies is about $\frac{1}{2}$ inch (13 millimeters) long, and black in color with red and yellow spots. It is most abundant during midsummer. It eats pollen and other foods during the day, and spends the warmer part of the night flying about and flashing its light. The flashing usually occurs just as the beetle starts on its up-and-down course.

Five chemicals—adenosine triphosphate, luciferin, oxygen, magnesium, and luciferase—are bound up in the firefly's abdomen by a chemical controller. When nerve stimulations release another chemical, inorganic pyrophosphate, the bond breaks and the reaction produces the light. This light area usually appears on the sides of the firefly's abdomen. Seconds later the light goes out, because another chemical destroys the pyrophosphate. The firefly is one of the few insects that use vision to find a mate. Male fireflies find the females by following their flashing lights.

Sometimes the *larvae* (young fireflies), and even the eggs, give light. Most fireflies have wings. But some, such as the common *glowworm* of Europe, have no wings. The wingless female glowworm gives off light. The males have wings, but they give off little or no light. The *railway beetle* of Paraguay also has no wings but

can give light. It is about 3 inches (8 centimeters) long and sends forth a red light from both ends of its body. It sends out a green light from other points on its body. It is called the railway beetle because its red and green lights look like railway signals.

Fireflies are sometimes used for decoration and for light. Cuban women sometimes pin a firefly called a *click beetle* on their gowns,

Black Star

Glowing Brazilian Firefly

or attach one to a golden chain. The click beetles give off a strong green light that is ornamental. People in tropical countries sometimes put many in a bottle and use them for lanterns. They give their light in flashes. But when many are in a bottle at the same time, some are lighting constantly. Together they give continuous, though wavering, light. People who travel through dense tropical forests at night sometimes attach fireflies to their boots to light the path in front of them. Biochemists use fireflies to study *bioluminescence*, the heatless light given off by certain plants and animals.

Scientific Classification. Fireflies are members of the class *Insecta*, order *Coleoptera*. They make up the firefly family, *Lampyridae.*   H. H. ROSS

See also BEETLE (pictures: The Firefly's Glow, De Geer's Firefly); BIOLUMINESCENCE; CLICK BEETLE.

FIREMAN. See FIRE DEPARTMENT (Careers).

FIREMAN, LOCOMOTIVE. See RAILROAD (Railroad Workers).

FIREPLACE. See HEATING (Local Heating Systems); PIONEER LIFE IN AMERICA (picture: A Frontier Home).

FIREPROOFING is the name given to the covering or chemical treatment which protects materials against fire. The term *fireproof* is generally applied to buildings which are either constructed of fire-resistant materials or materials protected with a fire-resistant covering. The fire-resistant materials include masonry of such various kinds as stone, brick, hollow tile, gypsum blocks, and concrete. These materials cannot be set afire and will resist intense heat for several hours. Therefore, if fire starts in the building, the parts of the building which are fireproofed will probably not be damaged so much that they cannot be repaired.

In judging the fireproofing qualities of a particular material, the builder must also take into account its resistance when streams of water are directed against it to extinguish a fire. Some materials, such as glass products, may split, chip, or lose strength if squirted suddenly with cold water while they are hot.

The fact that a material will not burn does not mean that it is fireproof. Steel is an example of this. Steel beams and columns in buildings must be insulated with some material which will protect them against excessive heat. If the temperature of steel rises above 500° F. (260° C), as often happens in burning buildings, its strength is reduced. In "fireproofing" buildings, steel is covered with a layer of brick, hollow tile, concrete, or gypsum from 2 to 4 inches (5 to 10 centimeters) thick. Laws generally require that a *fireproof* building must be able to resist fire for 3 or 4 hours without collapsing.

Wood can catch fire, but soaking or painting it with fire-retarding chemicals reduces its tendency to burn. Ammonium phosphate, ammonium sulfate, borax, boric acid, and zinc chloride are effective. Such treatments are sometimes called *fireproofing*, but the term is wrong. No treatment will make wood fireproof. Papers and fabrics may also be treated with such chemicals.

Asbestos is another fireproofing material. It is made by weaving fire-resistant fibrous minerals into fabrics or by cementing them together into heat-resisting paper board. Fireproof theater curtains of asbestos fabric protect audiences from fires which may start on the stage, or backstage. See ASBESTOS. GEORGE W. WASHA

FIRESTONE, HARVEY SAMUEL (1868-1938), was an American industrial leader who pioneered in the field of automobile tires. He founded the Firestone Tire & Rubber Company in Akron, Ohio, in 1900. He served as president of this company from 1903 to 1926, and was chairman of the board of directors until his death.

The company produced its first tires, made of solid rubber, in 1903. Firestone's keen interest in technical progress caused his company to lead in numerous improvements. It developed and, in 1931, became the first to market a practical air-filled tire for farm machinery.

Firestone Tire & Rubber Co.
Harvey S. Firestone

In 1924, Firestone took over a small plantation in Liberia to produce rubber. Two years later he signed an agreement with the Liberian government to lease 1 million acres (400,000 hectares) of land for the development of rubber plantations. He made large loans to Liberia, and built for it a new and improved harbor. Firestone was also a leader in investigating the rubber resources of the Philippines and South America, and he encouraged American investment in rubber-growing countries. He also helped organize rubber production for World War I.

Firestone was born and grew up on an Ohio farm. His first jobs were as a clerk and a bookkeeper. He became interested in rubber tires while he was working for a carriage factory. This lifetime interest caused him to carry on extensive rubber research and publish two books on the subject. In 1927, he joined Henry Ford and Thomas A. Edison in projects searching for substitutes for natural rubber. W. H. BAUGHN

FIRESTONE TIRE & RUBBER COMPANY. See RUBBER (Leading Manufacturers); FIRESTONE, HARVEY.

FIREWEED, or WILLOW HERB, is an erect plant which thrives in the North Temperate Zone. It gets its name because it springs up so quickly after a forest fire. It grows about 3 to 6 feet (0.9 to 1.8 meters) high and looks like a long wand. The narrow leaves are 2 to 6 inches (5 to 15 centimeters) long. In the summer, clusters of rose-purple flowers bloom along the upper stalk. The slender fruits are four-sided pods. Fireweed is the official flower of the Yukon Territory.

Scientific Classification. Fireweeds belong to the evening primrose family, *Onagraceae*. They are genus *Epilobium*, species *E. angustifolium*. EARL L. CORE

FIREWOOD. See CAMPING (Campfires).

FIREWORKS are combinations of gunpowder and other ingredients that explode with loud noises and colorful sparks and flames when they burn. Fireworks are also called *pyrotechnics*. Fireworks that only make a loud noise are called *firecrackers*. Fireworks are dangerous because they contain gunpowder. They should be handled only by experts. Fireworks handled improperly can explode and cause serious injury to the untrained user. Most states prohibit the use of fireworks by individuals. The federal government limits the explosive power of fireworks that can be used by individuals.

Most fireworks are made by packing gunpowder in hollow paper tubes. A coarse gunpowder tightly packed is used to *propel* (drive) rockets into the air. Another type of gunpowder that is finer and more loosely packed explodes to break up the rocket once it is in the air. See GUNPOWDER.

Manufacturers add small amounts of special chemicals to the gunpowder to create colors. They add sodium compounds to produce yellow, strontium compounds for red, and copper and barium compounds for blue and green. Charcoal is another substance that can be added. It gives the rocket a sparkling, flaming tail.

How Fireworks Work. Fireworks rockets, also called *skyrockets*, operate on a principle close to that used in large military rockets. A *fuse* ignites the coarse gunpowder charge, which forms gases that stream out of the end of the paper tube. This propels the rocket into the air. When the rocket is near its highest point of flight, the coarse gunpowder ignites the finer charge, and the finer charge explodes. The explosion breaks up the rocket and ignites many small firecrackers in the *nose* (forward section) of the rocket.

Roman candles have gunpowder charges separated by inactive material so they shoot out separate groups of sparks and colored flames with series of booming noises. *Pinwheels* have a gunpowder charge packed in a long, flexible tube. The tube is attached to the outside edge of a cardboard disk that has a hole in its center. A stick is placed in the hole. As the charge ignites and burns, it makes the disk whirl around the stick, throwing off sparks and flames. *Lances* are thin paper tubes filled with color-producing fireworks. They are arranged in a pattern on a wooden frame so that when they are set afire, they outline a scene, a portrait, or a flag.

Other Uses of Fireworks. Fireworks are also used for serious purposes. A device called a *fusee* burns with a bright red flame and is used as a danger signal on highways and railroads. Railroads use giant firecrackers called *torpedoes*. The torpedoes explode while the train is passing over them to warn the engineer of danger ahead.

People can signal for help by using a *Very* pistol. The pistol shoots a flare into the air that can be seen far away. *Parachute flares* are used to light up landing areas. A kind of fireworks rocket can be used to shoot lifelines to shipwrecks. *Star shells* are used in wartime to light up battlefields. JULIUS ROTH

See also EXPLOSIVE; INDEPENDENCE DAY.

FIRING GLASSES. See GLASSWARE.

FIRMAMENT. See SKY.

First-Aid Courses teach the proper emergency treatments for a variety of injuries and illnesses. The students in this class are learning how to bandage an injured shoulder. The American National Red Cross offers free first-aid instruction in many communities.

American National Red Cross (WORLD BOOK photo)

FIRST AID

FIRST AID is the immediate care given to a victim of an accident, sudden illness, or other medical emergency. Proper first aid can save a victim's life, especially if the victim is bleeding heavily, has stopped breathing, or has been poisoned. First aid also can prevent the development of additional medical problems that might result from an injury or illness.

Emergency treatment should be administered by the person on the scene who has the best knowledge of first aid. The treatment should be continued until professional medical help is available. First aid also involves reassuring a victim, relieving his pain, and moving him, if necessary, to a hospital or clinic.

This article describes some basic first-aid techniques for common medical emergencies. Persons interested in taking a complete first-aid training course should contact their local chapter of the American National Red Cross.

General Rules for First Aid

Analyze the situation quickly and decide whether you can help the victim. If you decide to treat the victim, begin at once. But if you are confused or unsure of yourself, do *not* attempt to give treatment. In many cases, the wrong treatment causes more damage than no treatment at all. For professional help in giving first aid, call a hospital, the fire department, or the police.

The general steps to take in any situation requiring first aid include the following: (1) provide urgent care

Morris Green, contributor of this article, is Professor and Chairman, Department of Pediatrics, Indiana University School of Medicine.

for life-threatening emergencies, (2) examine the victim for injuries, (3) treat the victim for shock, and (4) call a physician for assistance.

Provide Urgent Care. Certain medical emergencies require immediate care to save the victim's life. If the victim is bleeding severely, has been poisoned, or has stopped breathing, treatment must begin at once. A delay of even a few minutes can be fatal in these cases. The treatments for these emergencies are discussed in this article in the sections on *First Aid for Bleeding, Treatment for Poisoning,* and *Restoring Breathing.*

Do not move a victim who may have a broken bone, internal injuries, or damage to the neck or spine, unless absolutely necessary to prevent further injury. If he is lying down, keep him in that position. Do not allow him to get up and walk about. Never give food or liquid to a person who may require surgery.

If the victim is unconscious, turn his head to one side to help prevent him from choking on blood, saliva, or vomit. But do *not* move the head of a person who may have a broken neck or a spinal injury. Never pour a liquid into the mouth of an unconscious person.

Make certain that the victim has an open airway. The *airway* consists of the nose, mouth, and upper throat. These passages must remain open in order for the victim to breathe. For information on keeping the airway open, see the section of this article on *Giving Artificial Respiration.*

Examine the Victim for injuries only after treating him for any life-threatening emergencies. Then treat the individual injuries. The victim may suffer from diabetes, heart trouble, or some other disease that can cause sudden illness. Many persons with such medical problems carry a medical tag or card. The tag or card lists special instructions for medical care that should be followed exactly. If you must examine the victim's identification papers to look for a medical card, you should do so in the presence of a witness, if possible.

Make the victim comfortable, but handle him as little as possible. If necessary, shade the victim from the sun or cover him to prevent chilling. Loosen the person's clothing. But do not pull on the victim's belt, because this pressure could damage an injured spine.

Remain calm and reassure the victim. Explain what has happened and what is being done. Ask any spectators to stand back.

Treat for Shock. Shock results from the body's failure to circulate blood properly. Any serious injury or illness can cause a victim to suffer from shock. When a person is in shock, his blood fails to supply enough oxygen and food to his brain and other organs. The most serious form of shock may result in death.

A victim in shock may appear fearful, light-headed, weak, and extremely thirsty. In some cases, he may feel nauseous. His skin appears pale and feels cold and damp. His pulse is rapid and his breathing is quick and shallow or deep and irregular. It is best to treat a seriously injured person for shock even if these signs are not present. The treatment will help prevent shock.

To treat shock, place the victim flat on his back, with his legs raised slightly. If he has trouble breathing in this position, place him in a half-sitting, half-lying position. Warm him by placing blankets over and under his body.

Call for Assistance. Send someone else to call for a doctor, an ambulance, or other help while you care for the victim. If you are alone with the victim, you must decide when you can safely leave him to call for assistance. Always treat the victim for any life-threatening conditions before leaving him to summon aid.

When telephoning for help, be ready to describe the nature of the victim's illness or injury, the first-aid measures you have taken, and the exact location of the victim. Also be prepared to write down any instructions a physician may give you. Repeat the instructions and ask questions to clarify orders you do not understand.

If you decide to take the victim to a hospital emergency room, first telephone the hospital to say you are coming. The hospital staff will then be better prepared to treat the victim's particular problems.

Every home should have a list of emergency phone numbers posted on or near the telephone. However, if such numbers are not available, the telephone operator can assist the caller in contacting the proper person or emergency unit.

First Aid for Bleeding

Severe *hemorrhage* (bleeding) can cause death within minutes. Bleeding from most small wounds stops by itself in a short time, after the blood begins to *clot* (thicken). But clotting alone cannot stop the flow of blood from large wounds. Emergency treatments for severe bleeding include such techniques as (1) direct pressure, (2) pressure on arteries carrying blood to the wound, and (3) the use of a tourniquet.

Direct Pressure. The most effective way of controlling heavy bleeding is to press directly on the wound itself. If possible, have the victim lie down and elevate the bleeding part above the rest of his body. Then place a sterile dressing over the wound and press firmly on it with your hand. If you do not have a sterile dressing, use a clean handkerchief, towel, or other cloth folded to make a pad. If no cloth is available, press your hand directly on the wound while someone else obtains the necessary material.

If the victim bleeds through the first dressing, add another on top of it and apply firmer pressure. Do not

How to Control Bleeding These photographs show how to stop bleeding from an arm or leg. The person giving the treatment applies pressure directly to the wound and raises it above the rest of the body. With his other hand, he helps control the bleeding by pressing on the arteries that supply blood to the affected limb. The diagram indicates the pressure points for the arteries of the arms and legs.

American National Red Cross (WORLD BOOK photos); WORLD BOOK illustration by Mary Ann Olson

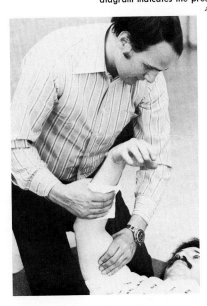
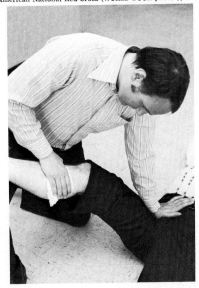
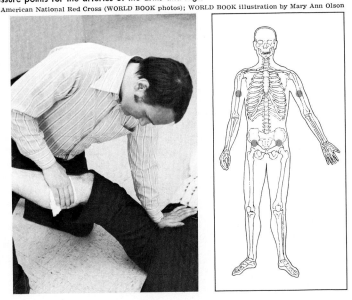

remove the first dressing. After the hemorrhage has stopped, secure the dressing with a bandage.

Pressure on Arteries. Sometimes, direct pressure and elevation fail to stop severe bleeding. If such bleeding is from an arm or leg, you may be able to stop it by applying pressure to the artery that supplies blood to the injured limb. The illustrations in this article on *How to Control Bleeding* show the points at which pressure should be applied to these arteries. Pressure on arteries should be used in addition to—not instead of —direct pressure and elevation.

Applying a Tourniquet. A tourniquet should be used only to control bleeding from serious injuries, such as the accidental amputation of a hand or foot. In other cases, the use of a tourniquet should be avoided because it can cause *gangrene* (tissue death). It may also damage uninjured nerves and blood vessels. Never apply a tourniquet unless all other means of hemorrhage control have failed, and it is apparent that the victim will die unless the bleeding is stopped.

If a tourniquet must be applied, use strips of cloth at least 2 inches (5 centimeters) wide. Wrap the material two to six times around the injured limb, just above the wound, between it and the heart. Knot the ends of the material together. Then tie a stick or similar object on top of this knot with a square knot. Twist the stick to tighten the tourniquet until the bleeding stops. Do not loosen the tourniquet until a physician advises you to do so. See TOURNIQUET.

Treatment for Poisoning

A person who has swallowed a poisonous substance may die within minutes if not treated. First aid for poisoning consists of two kinds of treatment: (1) neutralizing the poison or (2) removing it from the body. The most effective way to neutralize a poison is to administer the proper antidote. An *antidote* is a substance that counteracts a particular poison. The best first-aid procedure for removing a poison is to make the victim vomit, if he is conscious. In all cases, take the victim to a hospital or clinic as quickly as possible. Take with you the poisonous substance, in its container. A physician may need the container to identify the kind or amount of poison taken.

Giving an Antidote. If the victim has swallowed a commercial product, check the label of the container. It should indicate the procedures to follow in administering the proper antidote. Give the antidote immediately. But do *not* attempt to make an unconscious person swallow a liquid antidote. The table with this article lists the antidotes for various common household products.

Making the Victim Vomit. You may not know what poison has been swallowed or what the correct antidote is. The victim also may have swallowed a substance for which there is no antidote, or for which the antidote is not readily available. In such cases, have the victim drink plenty of water or milk to dilute the poison. Then make the victim vomit. Do not *induce* (cause) vomiting if the victim is unconscious or convulsing. Also, do not induce vomiting if he may have swallowed a petroleum product or a chemical that causes burns. Smell his breath for the odor of petroleum products, such as

EMERGENCY TREATMENT FOR SOME COMMON POISONS

For emergency treatment of poisoning, immediately telephone a physician, a poison information center, or a hospital. If possible, tell the physician the name of the poison. If no other advice has been given, emergency steps may be taken for the following poisons:

Acids (toilet bowl cleaners, phenol). Do not induce vomiting. Give a mixture of 1 ounce (30 milliliters) milk of magnesia, baking soda solution, or other antacid in a large glass of water. Then give 2 ounces (59 milliliters) of olive oil or vegetable oil, or the whites of two raw eggs.

Alcohol. Induce vomiting.

Alkalis (lye, drain cleaners). Do not induce vomiting. Give a mixture of 2 tablespoons (30 milliliters) vinegar in 2 glasses of water; or give orange juice, lemon juice, or milk. Then give 2 ounces (59 milliliters) of olive oil or vegetable oil, or the whites of 2 raw eggs.

Ammonia. See Alkalis.

Amphetamines ("pep" pills). Give one glass of milk, then induce vomiting.

Antihistamines (nasal sprays, cold capsules). Induce vomiting.

Arsenic (ant poisons). Induce vomiting, then give the whites of two raw eggs and several glasses of milk.

Aspirin. Induce vomiting.

Barbiturates (sedatives). Induce vomiting if victim is conscious. Then have the victim drink large quantities of hot coffee or tea. Give artificial respiration if the victim stops breathing.

Gas (inhaled cooking gas, carbon monoxide). Move victim to fresh air. Give artificial respiration if necessary.

Petroleum Products (gasoline, kerosene, furniture polish). Do not induce vomiting. Give one or two glasses of water or milk.

Oil of Wintergreen. Induce vomiting.

Tranquilizers. Induce vomiting.

---

gasoline or kerosene. Examine his lips and mouth for burns caused by harsh chemicals.

One of the most reliable ways of making a person vomit is to use a drug called *syrup of ipecac*. To induce vomiting, give 1 tablespoon (15 milliliters) of syrup of ipecac mixed in half a glass of water. Afterwards, have the victim drink as much water as he can. Keep him moving about, because activity promotes vomiting. If vomiting does not occur within 15 to 20 minutes, administer another dose of syrup of ipecac. Do not repeat a third time.

If syrup of ipecac is not available, you can make the victim vomit by pressing your finger or the blunt end of a spoon at the back of his throat. Or you can give him a mixture of 2 tablespoons (30 milliliters) of salt in a glass of warm water.

When the victim vomits, lay him on his stomach with his head hanging down over the edge of a bed or over your knees. This position will prevent him from inhaling the poisoned vomit into his lungs. Catch the vomit in a pan so that it can be examined by a physician.

If a victim is unconscious, make sure that his airway remains open. Administer artificial respiration if necessary. Take him to a hospital immediately.

Restoring Breathing

Begin artificial respiration as soon as possible for any victim whose breathing has stopped. Two or three minutes without breathing can cause permanent brain damage, and six minutes can be fatal. Signs of breath stoppage include the lack of regular chest movements and a blue color in lips, tongue, or fingernails.

Removing the Cause of Breathing Failure. The steps you take before administering artificial respiration depend on why the victim's breathing has stopped. For example, if the victim's airway is blocked, you must remove the obstruction before beginning artificial respiration.

Electric shock also can cause respiratory failure. In cases of electric shock, free the victim from contact with the current before attempting artificial respiration. Turn off the current if possible. Do not touch the victim with your bare hands or with a wet or metal object until the contact has been broken. If you cannot turn off the current, free the victim from contact by using a dry stick, rope, or cloth. Be sure to stand on a dry surface that will not conduct electricity.

Respiratory failure can also result from breathing air that lacks sufficient oxygen. Such air may be present in storage bins, poorly ventilated mines, and closed vaults. Breathing also may stop because the victim has inhaled large quantities of carbon-monoxide, a substance that interferes with the blood's ability to carry oxygen. In any of these cases, move the victim into fresh air before beginning artificial respiration.

Giving Artificial Respiration. The most efficient method of artificial respiration is *mouth-to-mouth resuscitation*. To administer mouth-to-mouth resuscitation, place the victim on his back, on a firm surface if possible. Kneel down near his head and, using your fingers or a handkerchief, quickly remove such objects as food or vomit from his mouth. Place one of your hands under the victim's neck and the other on his forehead. Tilt the victim's head back by lifting with the hand under his neck and pressing down with the one on his forehead. This position—with the chin pointing upward and the neck arched—opens the airway. If necessary, remove your hands momentarily from the victim's neck and forehead to pull his jaw forward. This action prevents his tongue from blocking the airway.

To treat an infant or small child, take a deep breath and place your mouth over both his mouth and nose. Blow gently into the child's mouth and nose. Then remove your mouth and listen for air to flow back out of the child's lungs. Take a deep breath and blow again. Repeat this procedure every three seconds.

If the victim is an older child or an adult, pinch his nostrils shut with the hand you have placed on his forehead. Take a deep breath, cover his open mouth tightly with your own, and blow hard enough to make his chest rise. Then remove your mouth and listen for the return air flow. Repeat this procedure every five seconds.

If the victim's mouth is too large for you to make a tight seal over it with your own, or if he has suffered a severe mouth injury, use mouth-to-nose resuscitation. Remove your hand from the victim's neck and place it under his chin. Then blow into the victim's nose while holding his mouth tightly shut.

If the victim's chest does not rise when you blow in, check his mouth again to be sure that there is nothing

How to Give Artificial Respiration

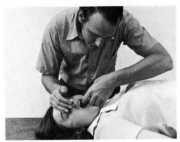
Clear the Victim's Mouth with your fingers. Remove food, vomit, or other objects that could block the flow of air.

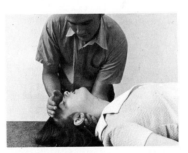
Place One Hand under the victim's neck and the other on the forehead. Then tilt the victim's head backward.

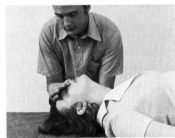
For the Mouth-to-Mouth Method, pinch the victim's nostrils shut between your thumb and index finger.

Take a Deep Breath and place your mouth tightly over the victim's mouth. Blow until the victim's chest rises.

For the Mouth-to-Nose Method, hold the victim's mouth closed and blow air into the person's nose.

American National Red Cross (WORLD BOOK photos)
Listen for Air Being Exhaled. Repeat every five seconds for an adult, and every three seconds for a child.

in it. Also make certain that his head is tilted back far enough and that his lower jaw is pulled forward. If you still cannot make the victim's chest expand, it may mean that an object is blocking his airway. Turn the victim on his side and strike him sharply several times between the shoulder blades. This should free any object blocking the upper throat. Continue artificial respiration until the victim starts to breathe or until professional help arrives.

Other First-Aid Procedures

Animal Bites can result in serious infections and diseases if left untreated. Wash the area of the bite thoroughly with soap and water. Rinse the wound and cover it with a gauze dressing. Call a physician. If possible, the animal should be kept under observation by a veterinarian to determine if it has rabies.

Bites made by poisonous snakes require immediate medical treatment. For information regarding such treatment, see the *Snakebite* section of this article.

Burns. The first-aid treatment of burns depends on the severity of the injury. Burns are classified, in order of increasing severity, as first-, second-, or third-degree. *First-degree burns* produce a reddening of the top layer of skin. *Second-degree burns* damage deeper skin layers. These burns give the injured skin a red or spotted appearance and cause blisters. *Third-degree burns* destroy tissues in the deepest layer of skin. The injury has a white or charred appearance.

To treat first- and second-degree burns, place the injured area in cool water to relieve the pain. Then blot the area dry and apply a dry, sterile dressing.

Third-degree burns should be covered immediately with a thick, dry, sterile dressing. Do not use water on these injuries. Large burns may be wrapped in a clean sheet or towel, or in plastic bags or kitchen wrap. Plastic bags or wrap should never be placed over the face. Clothing stuck to the wound should not be pulled away.

In treating any kind of burn, do not open blisters, and do not smear the injury with petroleum ointment, butter, or any greasy substance. If the victim has suffered burns around the face or has been exposed to smoke, watch for respiratory difficulties. If the victim has trouble breathing, give artificial respiration. Severe burns cause much pain and a loss of body fluids and may send the victim into shock. In such cases, take the first-aid measures to prevent or treat shock.

Victims of third-degree burns should be examined by a physician as soon as possible. Those suffering first- or second-degree burns on the face or over an area larger than the size of one's hand should also receive professional medical attention.

Chemical burns should be flushed with large amounts of water. Use a hose, shower, or bucket. Wash the injury for at least 10 minutes. Remove any clothing that has been covered by the chemical and cover the burn with a sterile dressing. Take the victim to a physician immediately.

Sunburn, in most cases, is a first-degree burn. Extremely deep sunburn may cause second-degree burns, with blistering. Do not open any blisters. Apply cool compresses to relieve pain. Consult a physician in cases of severe sunburn.

Choking occurs when food or some other object blocks the windpipe. A person who is choking cannot breathe or speak. After a short time, the victim's skin turns blue and he collapses. If the object is not removed in 4 to 6 minutes, death occurs.

An effective way to remove an object blocking the windpipe is a technique called the *Heimlich maneuver.* To perform this maneuver, stand behind the victim and place your arms around his waist. Make a fist and place it so that the thumb is against the victim's abdomen, slightly above the navel and below the ribcage. Grasp your fist with your other hand and then press your fist into the victim's abdomen with a quick upward thrust. This action forces air out of the victim's lungs and blows the object from the windpipe.

If the victim has collapsed or is too large for you to support or place your arms around, lay him on his back. Then face the victim and kneel straddling his hips. Place one of your hands over the other, with the heel of the bottom hand on the victim's abdomen, slightly above the navel and below the ribcage. Then press your hands into the victim's abdomen with a quick upward thrust.

When applying the Heimlich maneuver, be careful not to apply pressure on the victim's ribs. Such pressure may break the ribs of a child or an adult.

WORLD BOOK photos courtesy of Henry J. Heimlich, M.D.

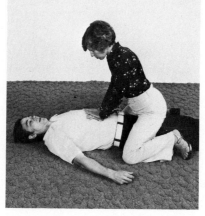

A Treatment for Choking on an object stuck in the windpipe can be applied to a standing victim, *left,* or one who is lying down, *right.* In this technique, called the *Heimlich maneuver,* the person giving the treatment presses sharply on the victim's abdomen. The pressure forces air out of the victim's lungs and blows the blockage from the windpipe.

Concussion is a head injury that results from a violent blow or shock. If the injury has knocked the victim unconscious, place him on his side and keep his airway open. Give artificial respiration if his breathing stops. Get medical assistance as soon as possible.

Victims of a violent head blow might not lose consciousness at the time of the injury. However, they should be watched closely for the next 12 to 24 hours. They may develop delayed symptoms that should be treated by a physician. Such delayed symptoms include loss of consciousness, repeated vomiting, severe headache, pale appearance, weakness in the arms or legs, unsteady walking, convulsions, unusual behavior, difficulty in talking, pupils of unequal size, double vision, watery discharge from the ears or nose, and excessive drowsiness. Check the victim for alertness every 15 minutes immediately following the injury and awaken him every 3 hours during that night. If signs of a concussion appear, consult a physician.

Convulsion and Epileptic Seizure. A person suffering a convulsion experiences violent, completely involuntary contractions of the muscles. Major convulsions, particularly those associated with epileptic seizures, also involve loss of consciousness. The victim falls to the ground. His muscles twitch and jerk or become rigid. Most attacks last a few minutes.

Try to prevent the victim from injuring himself during the attack. Leave him in the position in which he falls, but move aside objects that he might strike during the seizure. Do not attempt to restrain him. You may, however, place a blanket or some other soft material behind his head and loosen his clothing. Put a folded handkerchief between his teeth to prevent him from biting his tongue. But be careful not to place your fingers in his mouth, because he could bite down on them. After the attack, turn the victim's head to one side to prevent him from choking in case he vomits.

Eye Injury. If acids or alkalis have been splashed into the eye, immediately flush the eye with water. Flush at least 10 minutes for acids and 20 minutes for alkalis. Use a stream of water from a tap or a hose, or pour the water from a cup or other container. Flush the eye from the inside corner outward, to avoid washing the chemical into the other eye. Cover the eye with sterile gauze or a clean pad and take the victim to an eye doctor.

Dust particles or other foreign objects can be removed from the eye by gently flushing with water. Or they can be removed with the corner of a clean handkerchief. However, do not wipe across the *cornea* (clear, central part of the eye) with a handkerchief or any other material.

Fainting is a brief, sudden period of unconsciousness. It occurs when blood pressure falls to the point where the brain does not receive enough oxygen. In most cases, fainting occurs when a person is standing. The victim falls to the ground as he loses consciousness. Leave the victim lying down. Loosen his clothing and raise his feet slightly. Blood will flow back into his head, and he should regain consciousness promptly. Should he fail to do so, lay him on his side and make certain his airway remains open. Call a physician.

Just before fainting, a person may feel weak or numb.

Other symptoms include nausea, light-headedness, blurred vision, pale appearance, sweating, or excessive yawning. A person experiencing these symptoms should lie down or sit with his head between his knees.

Fractures and Dislocations. A *fracture* is a break in a bone. A *dislocation* occurs when the end of a bone is forced out of its normal position in a joint. Fractures and dislocations frequently result from automobile and sports accidents.

Signs of fractures and dislocations include pain, an unusual position of a joint or bone, and tenderness and swelling around the injury. The victim may also experience a grating sensation, caused by fragments of broken bone rubbing together. He may find himself unable to use a hand or a foot.

Keep the victim quiet and treat for shock. Whenever possible, do not move him until expert help arrives. Improper handling of an injured bone or joint may seriously damage arteries, muscles, or nerves. It may also increase the severity of the fracture or dislocation.

If you must move the victim before help arrives, apply a splint to the injured area. The splint prevents broken or dislocated bones from moving. You can make a splint from any material that will support the injured part without bending. For fractures of the arm or leg, the splint should be long enough to prevent movement of joints above and below the injury. Pad the splint surfaces that touch the body. Do not try to correct any deformities before splinting. Do not push bone fragments back into an open wound.

Use strips of cloth to tie the splint above and below the point of injury. Do not tie the splint so tightly that it interferes with circulation. Blueness or swelling in fingers, for example, indicates that a splint has been tied too tightly to an arm.

Do not move a person who may have suffered a broken neck or other spinal injury. A person may receive such an injury by diving into shallow water, falling from a considerable height, or striking his head in an auto accident. Moving such an accident victim may cause permanent paralysis or death.

Frostbite may occur when the skin is exposed to extreme cold. It most frequently affects the skin of the cheeks, chin, ears, fingers, nose, or toes.

Frostbitten skin appears whitish and feels numb. It should be handled gently. Never massage frostbitten skin, and do not rub it with snow or bathe it in cold water. Warm the affected area with the heat of your hand or cover it with a heavy cloth until you can get the victim indoors. Thaw the affected skin by soaking it in lukewarm water. The temperature of this water should be between 100° and 105° F. (38° and 41° C). Keep the temperature in this range by adding more warm water as needed. Never use water hotter than 105° F. (41° C). If warm water is not available, wrap the frostbitten area with blankets. Obtain medical assistance as quickly as possible. If the victim must be moved, protect him from additional exposure.

Never treat frostbite with heat from a stove or with a heating pad, hot water bottle, or heat lamp. Such treatment may produce temperatures that can damage frostbitten tissue. If frostbite blisters occur, do not break them. Bandage them to prevent infection.

Heart Attack. Most heart attacks begin with a crushing tightness or intense pressure behind the breast bone. This pain may spread across the chest, affecting the arms, the neck, the jaw, or the pit of the stomach. In most cases, it lasts more than five minutes. The victim appears worried and has difficulty breathing. He may also perspire heavily and experience feelings of weakness and nausea. He may vomit.

Call a physician or summon an ambulance that has oxygen equipment. Stay calm and reassure the victim that help is on its way. Do not pick him up or carry him and do not allow him to move himself. Place him in the most comfortable sitting or half-sitting, half-lying position. If his breathing stops, give artificial respiration until help arrives. Do not give the victim liquids without a doctor's orders.

Heatstroke and Heat Exhaustion can occur when the body becomes overheated. Heatstroke is the more serious of the two conditions. A person suffering heatstroke feels hot but cannot sweat. His skin becomes hot, dry, and red. His body temperature rises so high that it can cause brain damage if not lowered quickly. Undress the victim. Either place the victim in a tub of cool water or apply cold, wet towels to his entire body. Get medical attention as quickly as possible.

A person suffering heat exhaustion, or *heat prostration*, displays many of the symptoms of shock. Such symptoms include faintness, headache, and nausea. His skin is cold, gray, and wet with perspiration. In most cases, his body temperature remains about normal. Treat the victim as if he were in shock. Take him to a hospital, in an air-conditioned vehicle if possible.

Nosebleed. To control a nosebleed, sit the victim up and have him lean forward. Then press his nostrils firmly together for 5 to 10 minutes. In some cases, a cold cloth placed on the victim's face helps stop the bleeding. Consult a physician if the bleeding does not stop within 10 to 15 minutes.

Snakebite. The treatment of a snakebite depends on whether or not the snake is poisonous. If the snake is nonpoisonous, the bite should be washed thoroughly with soap and water.

A person bitten by a poisonous snake requires medical attention. Most poisonous snakebites cause deep, burning pain along with swelling and discoloration. Within minutes the victim may begin to feel numb and have difficulty breathing. Call a physician or take the victim to a hospital. If possible, kill the snake and bring it along for identification.

Keep the victim motionless and quiet, because activity increases the spread of the poison. Place the bitten portion of the body at a level below that of the heart. If the bite is on an arm or a leg, tie a band above the wound, between it and the heart. The band should be loose enough for you to slip your finger under it. Release the band for 90 seconds every 10 minutes to prevent damage from lack of circulation.

If the victim shows symptoms of poisoning but cannot receive medical attention within 30 minutes, begin first-aid treatment. Sterilize a knife or razor blade in a flame. Make a single shallow cut, parallel to the limb, at each fang mark and over the area where the venom appears most concentrated. Cut only deep

enough to break the skin. A deeper cut can damage nerves and muscles. Apply suction to the cuts to remove the poison. Many first-aid kits include a *suction syringe*, a bulblike device for sucking up liquids. If you do not have a suction syringe, suck the wound by mouth and spit out the venom. Be sure that you have no cuts or open sores in your mouth. Continue suction for 30 to 60 minutes or until the swelling stops. Take the victim to a physician as soon as possible.

Transporting the Victim

Moving a seriously injured person to a medical facility requires great care. Rough or careless handling can make the victim's injuries even more serious. If a victim must be moved, call for an ambulance.

If you must transport the victim yourself, be sure that you have thoroughly examined him to determine the full extent of his injuries. All bleeding should be under control, and breathing should be satisfactory and comfortable. Treat the victim for shock and splint any fractures and dislocations. If the victim must be lifted, get someone to help you, in order to avoid rough handling. Whenever possible, use a stretcher to carry a seriously injured person.

If a person may have suffered a back or neck injury, wait for professional help. Move such a victim only if it is necessary to save his life. Take great care not to bend or twist his body or neck. Carry him on a wide, hard surface, such as a lightweight door.

During transport, drive safely. If possible, two persons should transport the victim. One can ensure that the victim's airway remains open and comfort him while the other drives. Morris Green

Related Articles in World Book include:

Conditions Requiring First Aid

Apoplexy	Drowning	Poison Ivy
Asphyxiation	Fainting	Rabies
Bee (Sting)	Fracture	Shock
Bleeding	Frostbite	Snakebite
Blister	Hemorrhage	Sunburn
Bruise	Nosebleed	Sunstroke
Burns and Scalds	Poison	Wound
Dislocation		

Other Related Articles

Ambulance	Bandage	Resuscitator
Antidote	Emetic	Safety
Antiseptic	Red Cross	Tourniquet
Artificial Respiration		

Outline

I. General Rules for First Aid
  A. Provide Urgent Care   C. Treat for Shock
  B. Examine the Victim   D. Call for Assistance
II. First Aid for Bleeding
  A. Direct Pressure
  B. Pressure on Arteries
  C. Applying a Tourniquet
III. Treatment for Poisoning
  A. Giving an Antidote
  B. Making the Victim Vomit
IV. Restoring Breathing
  A. Removing the Cause of Breathing Failure
  B. Giving Artificial Respiration
V. Other First-Aid Procedures
  A. Animal Bites   C. Choking
  B. Burns   D. Concussion

E. Convulsion and Epileptic Seizure
F. Eye Injury
G. Fainting
H. Fractures and Dislocations
I. Frostbite
J. Heart Attack
K. Heatstroke and Heat Exhaustion
L. Nosebleed
M. Snakebite
VI. **Transporting the Victim**

Questions

Under what conditions should a poisoning victim not be made to vomit?

Why should an animal that has bitten a person be kept under observation by a veterinarian?

What is the purpose of a splint?

What information should a person administering first aid tell the doctor when calling him in an emergency?

Why is it especially important to keep a snakebite victim motionless? What precautions should be taken before sucking the poison from a snakebite by mouth?

Why should a victim be examined for a medical tag or medical identification card?

What are the three types of burns? Which types should be treated with cool water?

When should a tourniquet be used? What are the dangers involved in its use?

What are some of the signs of a concussion?

What kinds of injuries may cause the condition called *shock?*

FIRST CONTINENTAL CONGRESS. See CONTINENTAL CONGRESS.

FIRST LADIES. See pictures of the First Ladies in the separate biographies of each President of the United States. See also the separate articles ADAMS, ABIGAIL SMITH; LINCOLN, MARY TODD; MADISON, DOLLEY PAYNE; ROOSEVELT, ELEANOR; WASHINGTON, MARTHA CUSTIS.

FIRST NATIONAL CITY BANK. See CITIBANK.

FIRST RIEL REBELLION. See RED RIVER REBELLION.

FIRTH is a deep, narrow arm of the sea. The term is used mostly in Scotland, but the word *firth* comes from the language of Iceland. In Scandinavia, the word *fiord* has a similar meaning, but fiords always have high walls, and the walls of firths may be low.

See also FIORD.

FIRTH OF CLYDE is the broad, irregularly shaped mouth of the River Clyde in southwestern Scotland. The firth is a large bay 50 miles (80 kilometers) long and more than 30 miles (48 kilometers) wide in places. The North Channel connects it with the Atlantic Ocean and with the Irish Sea. Shipping from Glasgow, which lies inland on the River Clyde, has an outlet through the firth.   JOHN W. WEBB

FIRTH OF FORTH is the large mouth of the River Forth on the east coast of Scotland. The baylike firth connects with the North Sea. The Firth of Forth is 50 miles (80 kilometers) long and 30 miles (48 kilometers) wide at its widest point.

One of the world's longest suspension bridges spans the firth at Queensferry. The bridge was completed in 1964. It is 8,244 feet (2,513 meters) long and has a 3,300-foot (1,006-meter) center span. A cantilever railroad bridge 1 mile (1.6 kilometers) long also crosses the firth at Queensferry.   JOHN W. WEBB

See also GREAT BRITAIN (physical map).

FISCAL SERVICE. See TREASURY, DEPARTMENT OF.

FISCHER, BOBBY (1943-), became the first American to win the official world chess championship. Fischer won the title in 1972 by defeating defending champion Boris Spassky of Russia in the most publicized chess match in history. In 1975, the International Chess Federation took away

Wide World Photos
Bobby Fischer

Fischer's title after he refused to play Russian challenger Anatoly Karpov under rules set by the federation.

Robert James Fischer was born in Chicago and raised in New York City. He dropped out of high school in 1958, when he was 14 years old. That year, he won his first U.S. chess championship. He held the title until 1968, except in 1962, when he passed up the tournament. At 15, he became the youngest international grandmaster in chess history.   HERMAN WEISKOPF

See also CHESS (picture).

FISCHER, EMIL (1852-1919), a German chemist, won the 1902 Nobel prize in chemistry for his wide research. He discovered a method of identifying sugars, and did basic research on proteins, enzyme actions, and purine derivatives such as uric acid and caffeine. He also won fame for his work on dyes. During World War I, he conducted research on carbon, rubber, oils, fats, and other materials. Fischer was born in northern Germany. He taught at the University of Berlin from 1892 until his death.   K. L. KAUFMAN

FISCHER, ERNST. See NOBEL PRIZES (table: Nobel Prizes for Chemistry—1973).

FISCHER, HANS (1881-1945), a German biochemist, received the 1930 Nobel prize in chemistry for his work on the composition of the coloring matter in leaves and blood. He isolated hemin from bile pigments. Hemin is a chemical compound contained in hemoglobin. Fischer synthesized hemin from substances of known composition in 1928.

Fischer was born at Höchst, now a part of Frankfurt, West Germany. He studied at Marburg and Munich universities, and then taught chemistry.   PAUL R. FREY

FISCHER-DIESKAU, DIETRICH (1925-), a German baritone, is considered the finest singer of *lieder* (German art songs) of his time. Fischer-Dieskau's lieder recitals set new standards of taste and musicianship, especially those accompanied by pianist Gerald Moore. See LIEDER.

Fischer-Dieskau won international fame for his concerts and his many phonograph recordings. But he also achieved great success in opera. His voice is relatively light and not well suited to heavier heroic operatic roles. His success came from his attractive voice and his intelligence in interpreting and performing roles.

Fischer-Dieskau was born in Berlin, and studied music there. He made his debut at the Berlin State Opera when he was only 23.   MAX DE SCHAUENSEE

FISCHER QUINTUPLETS. See QUINTUPLETS.

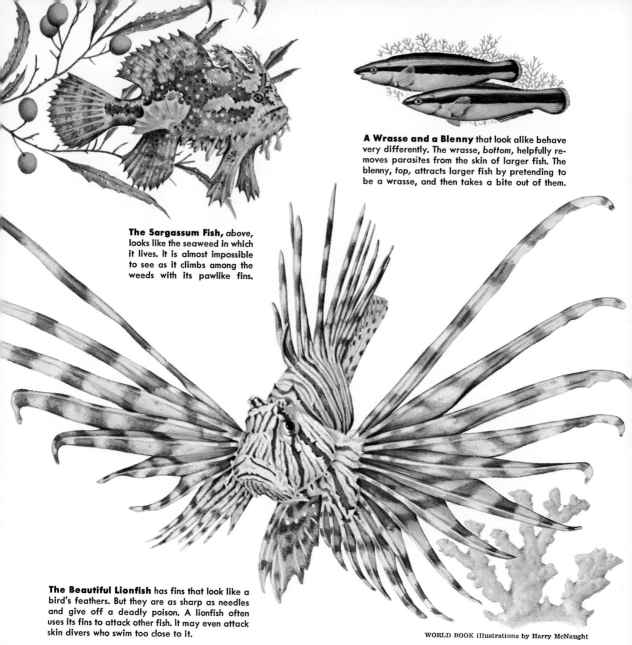

A Wrasse and a Blenny that look alike behave very differently. The wrasse, *bottom*, helpfully removes parasites from the skin of larger fish. The blenny, *top*, attracts larger fish by pretending to be a wrasse, and then takes a bite out of them.

The Sargassum Fish, *above,* looks like the seaweed in which it lives. It is almost impossible to see as it climbs among the weeds with its pawlike fins.

The Beautiful Lionfish has fins that look like a bird's feathers. But they are as sharp as needles and give off a deadly poison. A lionfish often uses its fins to attack other fish. It may even attack skin divers who swim too close to it.

WORLD BOOK illustrations by Harry McNaught

FISH

FISH are *vertebrates* (backboned animals) that live in water. There are more kinds of fish than all other kinds of water and land vertebrates put together. The various kinds of fish differ so greatly in shape, color, and size that it is hard to believe they all belong to the same group of animals. For example, some fish look like lumpy rocks, and others like wriggly worms. Some fish are nearly as flat as pancakes, and others can blow themselves up like balloons. Fish have all the colors of the rainbow. Many have colors as bright as the most

C. Lavett Smith, the contributor of this article, is Curator in the Department of Ichthyology at the American Museum of Natural History and coauthor of The Hidden Sea.

brightly colored birds. Their rich reds, yellows, blues, and purples form hundreds of beautiful patterns, from stripes and lacelike designs to polka dots.

The smallest fish is the pygmy goby of the Philippines, which grows less than ½ inch (13 millimeters) long. The largest fish is the whale shark, which grows up to 60 feet (18 meters) long and weighs up to 15 short tons (14 metric tons). It feeds on small sea animals and plants and is completely harmless to most other fish and to man. The most dangerous fish weigh only a few pounds or kilograms. They include the deadly stonefish, whose poisonous spines can kill a human being in a matter of minutes.

Fish live almost anywhere there is water. They are found in the near-freezing waters of the Arctic and in the steaming waters of tropical jungles. They live in roaring mountain streams and in quiet underground

The Porcupine Fish is covered with protective spines. For added protection, the fish fills itself with water to change from its normal appearance, *bottom*, to that of a prickly balloon, *top*.

Roy Pinney, Globe

An Archerfish catches an insect resting above the surface by spitting drops of water at it. The drops strike with enough force to knock the insect into the water, where the fish can eat it.

The Smallest Fish is the pygmy goby of the Philippines. It measures less than ½ inch (13 millimeters) when fully grown.

The Largest Fish is the whale shark. It weighs up to 15 short tons (14 metric tons)—more than twice as much as an African elephant. This fish is harmless to man. It eats small water plants and animals.

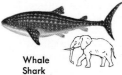

Whale Shark

A Four-Eyed Fish, the anableps, has eyes divided in two. When the fish swims just below the surface, the top half of each eye sees objects above the surface and the bottom half sees underwater objects.

Four-Eyed Fish

The Black Swallower can swallow fish twice its own size. Its jaws have "hinges" that enable them to open wide, and its stomach can stretch to several times its normal size. A fish swallowed whole is gradually digested in the stomach.

Black Swallower

The Flying Hatchet Fish is one of the few fish that can really fly. A hatchet fish can take off from the water's surface and fly as far as 10 feet (3 meters). The fish uses its side fins as wings.

Flying Hatchet Fish

The Walking Catfish lives for days out of water and even "walks" on land from one lake to another. The fish has special air-breathing organs and uses its side fins and tail to help it crawl along the ground.

Walking Catfish

The Largest Group of Fish are bristlemouths, a kind of tiny salt-water fish. Scientists believe that bristlemouths number in the billions of billions.

rivers. Some fish make long journeys across the ocean. Others spend most of their life buried in sand on the ocean bottom. Most fish never leave water. Yet some survive for months in dried-up riverbeds.

Fish have enormous importance to man. They provide food for millions of people. Fishermen catch them for sport, and many people keep them as pets. Fish are also important in the *balance of nature*. They eat plants and animals and, in turn, become food for plants and animals. Fish thus help keep in balance the total number of plants and animals on the earth.

All fish have three main features in common. (1) They have a backbone, and so they are vertebrates. (2) They breathe mainly by means of gills. (3) They are *cold-blooded* animals—that is, they cannot regulate their body temperature, which changes with the temperature of their surroundings. In addition, almost all fish have

fins, which they use for swimming. All other water animals differ from fish in at least one of these ways. For example, dolphins, porpoises, and whales look like fish and have a backbone and fins. But they are *mammals* (animals that feed their young with the mother's milk). Mammals breathe with lungs rather than gills. They are also *warm-blooded*—their body temperature remains about the same when the air or water temperature changes. Some water animals are called *fish*, but they do not have a backbone and so are not fish. These animals include jellyfish and starfish. Clams, crabs, lobsters, oysters, scallops, and shrimps are called *shellfish*. But they also lack a backbone.

The first fish appeared on the earth about 500 million years ago. They were the first animals to have a backbone. Most scientists believe that these early fish became the ancestors of all other vertebrates.

139

Fish benefit human beings in many ways. Fish make up a major part of the people's diet in such nations as Japan and Norway. In other countries, the people eat fish to add variety to their meals. For thousands of years, people have also enjoyed fishing for sport. Fish are also important in the balance of nature.

Food and Game Fish. Fish rank among the most nourishing of all foods. Fish flesh contains about as much protein as meat does. Each year, millions of tons of cod, herring, tuna, and other ocean food fish are caught commercially. Commercial fishing also takes place in inland waters, where such fresh-water food fish as perch and trout are caught. The WORLD BOOK article on FISHING INDUSTRY discusses commercial fishing throughout the world.

Businesses called *fish farms* raise certain types of fish for food. Fish farms in the United States raise catfish, salmon, and trout. In other countries, they raise carp and milkfish. Fish farmers raise the fish in ponds and use special feeding methods to make the fish grow larger and faster than they grow in the wild.

Some persons enjoy fishing simply for fun. Many of these people like to go after *game fish*. Game fish are noted for their fighting spirit or some other quality that adds to the excitement of fishing. They include such giant ocean fish as marlin and swordfish and such fresh-water fish as black bass and rainbow trout. Most game fish are also food fish. See the article on FISHING for detailed information on sport fishing.

Other Useful Fish. Certain fish, such as anchovettas and menhaden, are caught commercially but are not good to eat. Industries process these fish to make glue, livestock feed, and other products. Scientists often

FISH IN THE BALANCE OF NATURE

Fish help keep the number of plants and animals on the earth in balance. They feed on some plants and animals and themselves become food for others. This process is called a *food chain*. Fish are part of many food chains, as shown in the diagram below. The blue symbols represent plants and animals that fish eat. The red symbols represent living things that eat fish or are nourished by the matter that remains after fish die and decay.

WORLD BOOK diagram

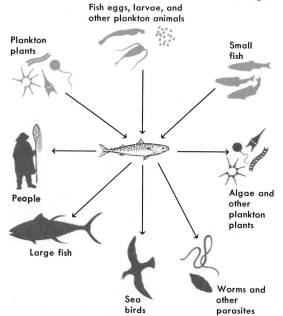

Fish eggs, larvae, and other plankton animals

Plankton plants

Small fish

People

Algae and other plankton plants

Large fish

Sea birds

Worms and other parasites

Jen & Des Bartlett, Bruce Coleman Inc.

Fish Hatcheries raise fish that are used to stock rivers. The workers at the left are removing the eggs from a female salmon. The eggs are then fertilized with *milt* from a male salmon, *center*. The fertilized eggs are kept in an *incubator, right*, until they hatch into baby salmon.

use goldfish and other small fish as experimental animals in medical research. They do not require so much space or so much care as do other experimental animals. Some fish produce substances used as medicines. For example, a chemical produced by puffers is used to treat asthma. Many people enjoy keeping fish as pets in home aquariums (see AQUARIUM). Popular aquarium fish include goldfish, guppies, and tetras.

Harmful Fish. Few species of fish will attack a human being. They include certain sharks, especially hammerhead and white sharks, which occasionally attack swimmers. Barracudas and moray eels may also attack a swimmer if provoked. Certain types of piranhas are bloodthirsty fish with razor-sharp teeth. A group of them can strip the flesh from a human being or an alligator or other large animal in minutes or even seconds. Some other fish, including sting rays and stonefish, have poisonous spines that can injure or kill anything that comes in contact with them. The flesh of filefish, puffers, and some other fish is poisonous and can cause sickness or death if eaten. A few species of fish have become pests after being introduced into certain waters. For example, sea lampreys that entered the Great Lakes and Asian catfish introduced into inland waters of Florida have become a threat to native fish.

Fish in the Balance of Nature. All the fish in a particular environment, such as a lake or a certain area of the ocean, make up a *fish community*. The fish in a community are parts of a system in which energy is transferred from one living thing to another in the form of food. Such a system is called a *food chain*. Every food chain begins with the energy from sunlight. Plants use this energy to make their food. In the ocean and in fresh water, the most important kinds of plant life are part of the *plankton*—the great mass of tiny plants and animals that drifts near the surface. Certain fish eat plankton and are in turn eaten by other fish. These fish may then be eaten by still other fish, by people, or by birds or other animals. Many fish die naturally. Their bodies sink and decay. The decayed matter provides nourishment for water plants and animals.

Every fish community forms part of a larger natural community made up of all the plants and animals in an area. A natural community includes numerous food chains, which together are called a *food web*. The complicated feeding patterns involved in a food web keep any one form of life from becoming too numerous and so preserve the balance of nature.

The balance of a community may be upset if large numbers of one species in the community are destroyed. People may upset the balance in this way by catching too many fish of a particular kind. Or they may pollute the water so badly that certain kinds of plants and animals, including certain fish, can no longer live in it. To learn how people conserve fish, see FISHING INDUSTRY (Conservation).

FISH/Kinds of Fish

Scientists have named and described about 21,000 kinds of fish. Each year, they discover new species, and so the total increases continually. Fish make up more than half of all known species of vertebrates.

Scientists who study fish are called *ichthyologists* (pronounced IHK thee AHL uh jihsts). They divide fish into two main groups: (1) *jawed* and (2) *jawless*. Almost all fish have jaws. The only jawless species are lampreys and hagfish. Jawed fish are further divided into two groups according to the composition of their skeletons. One group has a skeleton composed of a tough, elastic substance called *cartilage*. Sharks, rays, and chimaeras make up this group. The other group has a skeleton composed largely or partly of bone. Members of this group, called *bony fish*, make up by far the largest group of fish in the world. The section of this article called *A Classification of Fish* lists the major subgroups into which bony fish are divided. This section discusses the chief characteristics of (1) bony fish; (2) sharks, rays, and chimaeras; and (3) lampreys and hagfish.

Bony Fish

Bony fish can be divided into two main groups according to the composition of their skeletons. One group consists of *modern bony fish*, whose skeletons are composed largely of bone. The second group consists of *primitive bony fish*, whose skeletons are partly bone and partly cartilage.

Modern Bony Fish include about 20,000 species. They make up about 95 per cent of all known kinds of fish. Because of their bony skeletons, these fish are called *teleosts*, which comes from two Greek words meaning *complete* and *bone*. Nearly all food, game, and aquarium fish are teleosts. They include such well-known groups of fish as bass, catfish, cod, herring, minnows, perch, trout, and tuna. Each group consists of a number of species. For example, Johnny darters, walleyes, and yellow perch are all kinds of perch.

Thousands of species of teleosts are not so well known. Many live in jungle rivers or coral reefs. Some are deep-sea species seldom seen by human beings. They include more than 150 kinds of deep-sea anglers. These small, fierce-looking fish have fanglike teeth and flashing light organs. They live in the ocean depths and seldom if ever come to the surface. Many teleosts have unusual names and are as strange and colorful as their names. For example, the elephant-nose mormyrid has a snout shaped much like an elephant's trunk. The fish uses its snout to hunt for food along river bottoms. Another strange fish, the upside-down catfish, is the only fish that regularly swims on its back.

Many millions of years ago, there were only a few species of teleosts. They were greatly outnumbered by sharks and the ancestors of certain present-day bony fish. The early teleosts looked much alike and lived in only a few parts of the world. Yet they became the most

Bill Noel Kleeman, Tom Stack & Associates

A Leaping Trout, *above, is a sight familiar to many people. But some species of fish are seldom seen by man. Many kinds of fish live in such places as jungle rivers or deep parts of the ocean.*

numerous, varied, and widespread of all fish mainly because they were better able than other fish to *adapt* (adjust) to changes in their environment. In adapting to these changes, their bodies and body organs changed in various ways. Such changes are called *adaptations*.

Today, the various species of teleosts differ from one another in so many ways that they seem to have little in common. For example, many teleosts have flexible, highly efficient fins, which have helped them become excellent swimmers. Sailfish and tuna can swim long distances at high speed. Many teleosts that live among coral reefs are expert at darting in and out of the coral. But a number of other teleosts swim hardly at all. Some anglerfish spend most of their adult life lying on the ocean floor. Certain eellike teleosts are finless and so are poor swimmers. They burrow into mud on the bottom and remain there much of the time. Many teleosts have fins that are adapted to uses other than swimming. For example, flying fish have winglike fins that help them glide above the surface of the water. The mudskipper has muscular fins that it uses to hop about on land.

Primitive Bony Fish include about 50 species of bichirs, bowfins, coelacanths, gars, lungfish, paddlefish, and sturgeon. They make up less than 1 per cent of all fish species. These odd-looking fish are related to fish that lived many millions of years ago.

All the primitive bony fish except the coelacanths and some sturgeon live in fresh water. Coelacanths live off the south and southeast coast of Africa. They are not closely related to any other living fish, and there is only

one known species of coelacanth. Some sturgeon live in salt water but return to fresh water to lay their eggs.

Bichirs live in tropical Africa. They are slow-moving fish with a long, thin body and thick scales. Bowfins and gars are extremely fierce fish of eastern North America. They have unusually strong jaws and sharp teeth. Lungfish live in Africa, Australia, and South America. They breathe with lunglike organs as well as gills. The African and South American species can go without food and water longer than any other vertebrates. They live buried in dry mud for months at a time, during which they neither eat nor drink. The paddlefish, a strange-looking fish found only in China and the Mississippi Valley of the United States, has a huge snout shaped somewhat like a canoe paddle. Sturgeon rank as the largest of all fresh-water fish. A sturgeon may weigh more than 3,000 pounds (1,400 kilograms). Instead of scales, sturgeon have an armorlike covering consisting of five rows of thick, bony plates.

Sharks, Rays, and Chimaeras

Sharks, rays, and chimaeras total about 600 species, or about 3 per cent of all known fish. All have jaws and a skeleton of cartilage rather than bone. Almost all live in salt water. Sharks and rays are by far the most important members of the group and make up about 570 species.

Most sharks have a torpedo-shaped body. The bodies of most rays are shaped somewhat like pancakes. A large, winglike fin extends outward from each side of a ray's flattened head and body. But the angel shark and a few other sharks have a flattened body, and the sawfish and a few other rays are torpedo shaped. As a result, the best way to tell a shark from a ray is by the position of the *gill slits*. In sharks and rays, gill slits are slotlike openings on the outside of the body, leading from the gills. A shark's gill slits are on the sides of its head just back of the eyes. A ray's are underneath its side fins.

Chimaeras, or ratfish, include about 30 species. They are medium-sized fish with large eyes and a long, slender, pointed tail. They live near the ocean bottom. Several species called elephant fish have a long snout.

Lampreys and Hagfish

Lampreys and hagfish are the most primitive of all fish. There are about 30 species of lampreys and about 15 kinds of hagfish. They make up less than 1 per cent of all fish species. Lampreys live in both salt water and fresh water. Hagfish live only in the ocean.

Lampreys and hagfish have slimy, scaleless bodies shaped somewhat like the bodies of eels. But they are not closely related to eels, which are teleosts. Like sharks, rays, and chimaeras, lampreys and hagfish have a skeleton made of cartilage. But unlike all other fish, lampreys and hagfish lack jaws. A lamprey's mouth consists mainly of a round sucking organ and a toothed tongue. Certain types of lampreys use their sucking organ to attach themselves to other fish. They use their toothed tongue to cut into their victim and feed on its blood (see LAMPREY [picture: The Lamprey's Mouth]). Hagfish have a slitlike mouth with sharp teeth but no sucking organ. They eat the insides of dead fish.

THE CHIEF KINDS OF FISH

WORLD BOOK illustration by Marion Pahl

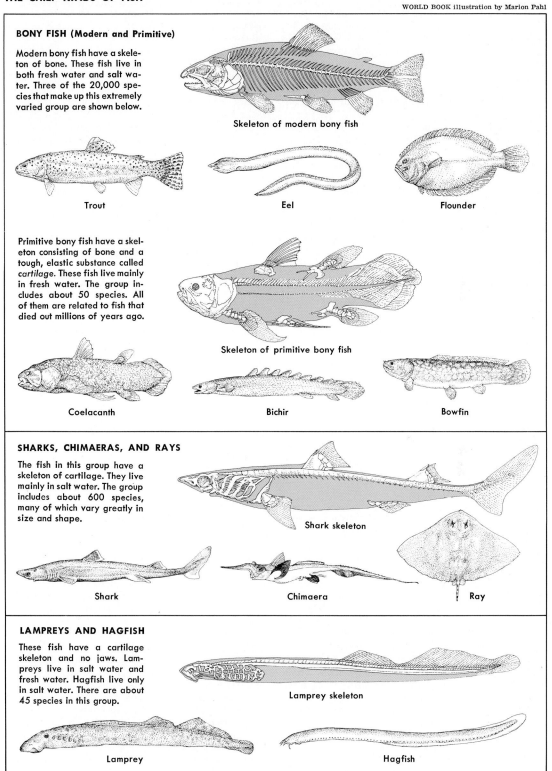

BONY FISH (Modern and Primitive)

Modern bony fish have a skeleton of bone. These fish live in both fresh water and salt water. Three of the 20,000 species that make up this extremely varied group are shown below.

Skeleton of modern bony fish

Trout

Eel

Flounder

Primitive bony fish have a skeleton consisting of bone and a tough, elastic substance called *cartilage*. These fish live mainly in fresh water. The group includes about 50 species. All of them are related to fish that died out millions of years ago.

Skeleton of primitive bony fish

Coelacanth

Bichir

Bowfin

SHARKS, CHIMAERAS, AND RAYS

The fish in this group have a skeleton of cartilage. They live mainly in salt water. The group includes about 600 species, many of which vary greatly in size and shape.

Shark skeleton

Shark

Chimaera

Ray

LAMPREYS AND HAGFISH

These fish have a cartilage skeleton and no jaws. Lampreys live in salt water and fresh water. Hagfish live only in salt water. There are about 45 species in this group.

Lamprey skeleton

Lamprey

Hagfish

Fish live almost anywhere there is water. They thrive in the warm waters of the South Pacific and in the icy waters of the Arctic and Antarctic oceans. Some live high above sea level in mountain streams. Others live far below sea level in the deepest parts of the ocean. Many fish have adapted themselves to living in such unusual places as caves, desert water holes, marshes, and swamps. A few fish, including the African and South American lungfish, can even live for months out of water.

Fish thus live in many environments. But all these environments can be classified into two major groups according to the saltiness of the water: (1) salt-water environments and (2) fresh-water environments. Some fish can live only in the salty waters of the ocean. Others can live only in fresh water. Still others can live in either salt water or fresh water. The sections on *The Bodies of Fish* and *How Fish Live* discuss how fish adjust to their environment. This section describes some of the main salt-water and fresh-water environments. It also discusses fish migrations from one environment to another. A series of color illustrations shows the kinds of fish that live in the various environments. The illustration for each fish gives the fish's common and scientific names and the average or maximum length of an adult fish.

Salt-Water Environments. About 14,000 species—or about two-thirds of all known fish—live in the ocean. These salt-water, or *marine*, fish live in an almost endless variety of ocean environments. Most of them are suited to a particular type of environment and cannot survive in one much different from that type. Water temperature is a chief factor in determining where a fish can live. Water temperatures at the surface range from freezing in polar regions to about 86° F. (30° C) in the tropics.

Many salt-water species live where the water is always warm. The warmest parts of the ocean are the shallow tropical waters around coral reefs. More than a third of all known salt-water species live around coral reefs in the Indian and Pacific oceans. Many other species live around reefs in the West Indies. Coral reefs swarm with angelfish, butterfly fish, parrot fish, and thousands of other species with fantastic shapes and brilliant colors. Barracudas, groupers, moray eels, and sharks prowl the clear coral waters in search of prey.

Many kinds of fish also live in ocean waters that are neither very warm nor very cold. Such *temperate* waters occur north and south of the tropics. They make excellent fishing grounds. The richest fishing grounds lie off the northeast coast of North America and the northwest coast of Europe. There, fishermen bring in huge catches of cod, flatfish, herring, and other food fish.

The cold waters of the Arctic and Antarctic oceans have fewer kinds of fish than do tropical and temperate waters. Arctic fish include bullheads, eelpouts, sculpins, skates, and a jellylike, scaleless fish called a sea snail. Fish of the Antarctic Ocean include the small, perchlike Antarctic cod, eelpouts, and the icefish, whose blood is nearly transparent rather than red.

Different kinds of fish also live at different depths in the ocean. The largest and fastest-swimming fish live near the surface of the *open ocean* and are often found great distances from shore. Fish that live near the surface of the open ocean include bonito, mackerel, marlin, swordfish, tuna, and a variety of sharks. Some of these fish make long annual migrations that range from tropical to near-polar waters.

Many more kinds of ocean fish live in midwater and in the depths than near the surface. Their environment differs greatly from that of species which live near the surface. Sunlight cannot reach far beneath the ocean's surface. Below about 600 feet (180 meters), the waters range from dimly lit to completely dark. Most fish that live in midwater far out at sea measure less than 6 inches (15 centimeters) long and are black, black-violet, or reddish-brown. Most of them have light organs that flash on and off in the darkness. Many also have large eyes and mouths. A number of midwater species are related to the herring. One such group includes the tiny bristlemouths. Scientists believe that bristlemouths outnumber all other kinds of fish. They estimate that bristlemouths number in the billions of billions.

Some fish species live on the ocean bottom. Many of these fish, such as eels, flounders, puffers, sea horses, and soles, live in shallow coastal waters. But many others live at the bottom far from shore. They include rattails and many other fish with large heads and eyes and long, slender, pointed tails. The tails help the fish navigate over the slimy ocean floor. Many species of rattails grow 1 foot (30 centimeters) or more long. One of the strangest bottom dwellers of the deep ocean is the tripod, or spider, fish. It has three long fins like the legs of a tripod or a three-legged stool. The fish uses its fins to sit on the ocean bottom.

Some kinds of fish live in *brackish* (slightly salty) water. Such water occurs where rivers empty into the ocean, where salt water collects in coastal swamps, and where pools are left by the outgoing tide. Brackish-water fish include certain species of barracudas, flatfish, gobies, herring, killifish, silversides, and sticklebacks. Some salt-water fish, including various kinds of herring, lampreys, salmon, smelt, and sticklebacks, can also live in fresh water.

Fresh-Water Environments. Fish live on every continent except Antarctica. They are found in most lakes, rivers, and streams and in brooks, creeks, marshes, ponds, springs, and swamps. Some live in streams that pass through caves or flow deep underground.

Scientists have classified about 7,000 kinds of freshwater fish. They make up about a third of all fish species. Almost all fresh-water fish are bony fish. Most of these bony fish belong to a large group that includes carp, catfish, characins, electric eels, loaches, minnows, and suckers. In this group, catfish alone total more than 2,000 species.

Like ocean fish, fresh-water fish live in a variety of climates. Tropical regions of Africa, Asia, and South America have the most species, including hundreds of kinds of catfish. Africa also has many cichlids and mormyrids. A variety of colorful loaches and minnows live in Asia. South American species include electric eels, piranhas, and tetras. Temperate regions, especially in North America, also have many fresh-water species, including bass, carp, minnows, perch, and trout. Blackfish and pike live in the Arctic.

In every climate, certain kinds of fresh-water fish require a particular kind of environment. Some species, including many kinds of graylings, minnows, and trout, live mainly in cool, clear, fast-moving streams. Many species of carp, catfish, and fresh-water drumfish thrive in warm, muddy, slow-moving rivers. Some fish, such as bluegills, lake trout, white perch, and whitefish, live chiefly in lakes. Black bullheads, largemouth bass, muskellunge, northern pike, rainbow trout, yellow perch, and many other species are found both in lakes and in streams and rivers.

Like marine fish, fresh-water fish live at different levels in the water. For example, many cave, spring, and swamp fish live near the surface. Gars, muskellunge, and whitefish ordinarily live in midwater. Bottom dwellers include darters, sturgeon, and many kinds of catfish and suckers.

Some fresh-water species live in unusual environments. For example, some live in mountain streams so swift and violent that few other forms of life can survive in them. These fish cling to rocks with their mouth or some special suction organ. A number of species live in caves and underground streams. These fish never see daylight. Most have pale or white skin, and many are blind. A few kinds of fresh-water fish live in hot springs where the temperature rises as high as 104° F. (40° C).

Fish Migrations. Relatively few kinds of fish can travel freely between fresh water and salt water. They make such migrations to *spawn* (lay eggs). Salt-water fish that swim to fresh water for spawning are called *anadromous* fish. They include alewives, blueback herring, sea lampreys, smelt, and most species of salmon and shad. Fresh-water fish that spawn in salt water are called *catadromous* fish. They include North American and European eels and certain kinds of gobies. Some normally anadromous fish, including large numbers of certain species of alewives, lampreys, salmon, and smelt, have become *landlocked*—that is, they have become fresh-water natives. After hatching, the young do not migrate to the ocean. The section *How Fish Adjust to Change* explains why most fish cannot travel freely between salt water and fresh water.

Many salt-water species migrate from one part of the ocean to another at certain times of the year. For example, many kinds of mackerel and certain other fish of the open ocean move toward shore to spawn. Each summer, many species of haddock and other cold-water fish migrate from coastal waters to cooler waters farther out at sea. Some fresh-water fish make similar migrations. For example, some trout swim from lakes into rivers to spawn. Some other fish of temperate lakes and streams, such as bass, bluegills, and perch, live near the warm surface during summer. When winter comes, the waters freeze at the surface but remain slightly warmer beneath the ice. The fish then migrate toward the bottom and remain there until warm weather returns.

WHERE OCEAN FISH LIVE

Many kinds of salt-water fish live far from shore. There, the sea can be divided into three main levels according to the amount of sunlight that reaches various depths, *below left*. Different kinds of fish live at each level.

WORLD BOOK illustration by Marion Pahl

600 feet
(180 meters)

Upper waters
(brightest sunlight)

3,000 feet
(910 meters)

Midwaters
(dim sunlight)

Depths
(little or
no sunlight)

Fish of the Upper Waters include such fast swimmers as the marlin and tuna. The largest kinds of fish, including the giant manta ray, also live in this region. Many upper-water fish travel great distances and range from tropical to arctic waters. Some often swim close to shore.

Bluefin Tuna

Blue Marlin

Manta Ray

Fish of the Midwaters include the oarfish, which grows as long as 50 feet (15 meters). But most midwater fish grow less than 6 inches (15 centimeters) long. The lantern fish and hatchet fish have light-producing organs, as do most midwater fish. Some kinds of midwater fish swim into upper waters to feed or lay eggs.

Oarfish

Lantern Fish

Hatchet Fish

Fish of the Depths live in waters that are always cold and almost totally dark. Such waters extend from lower midwaters to the bottom. Lower-midwater fish include anglerfish and many other species with a large mouth and sharp teeth. The rattail and the tripod fish live near the ocean bottom.

Deep-Sea Angler

Tripod Fish

Rattail

FISH

FISH OF COASTAL WATERS
AND THE OPEN OCEAN

Some salt-water fish live along the coasts of continents. Others live far from shore in the open ocean, though many of these fish also swim close to shore from time to time. Both coastal and open-ocean species are pictured in these drawings. Fish of the open ocean shown here include dolphin fish, flying fish, herring, mackerel, manta rays, marlin, ocean sunfish, sailfish, swordfish, and tuna. Most of the other fish pictured live mainly in coastal waters. Some coastal fish, such as bull sharks and sawfish, always stay close to land. Others, such as bluefish and great barracuda, sometimes swim far out to sea.

Exciting Game Fish, such as this striped marlin, live throughout upper ocean waters. Many salt-water game fish are also important food fish. Commercial fishermen catch many far out at sea.

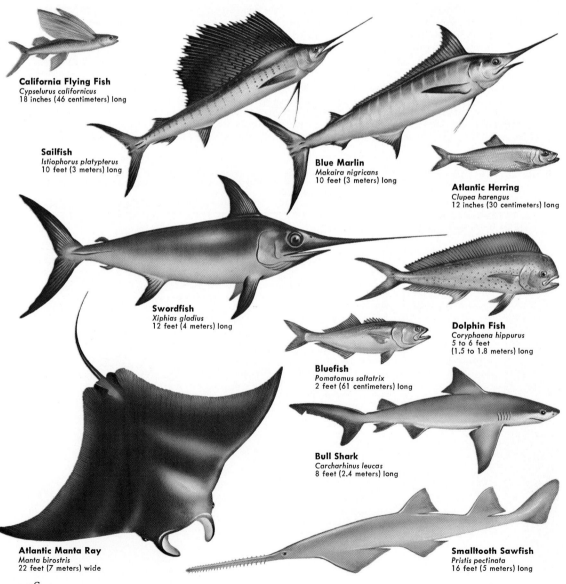

California Flying Fish
Cypselurus californicus
18 inches (46 centimeters) long

Sailfish
Istiophorus platypterus
10 feet (3 meters) long

Blue Marlin
Makaira nigricans
10 feet (3 meters) long

Atlantic Herring
Clupea harengus
12 inches (30 centimeters) long

Swordfish
Xiphias gladius
12 feet (4 meters) long

Dolphin Fish
Coryphaena hippurus
5 to 6 feet
(1.5 to 1.8 meters) long

Bluefish
Pomatomus saltatrix
2 feet (61 centimeters) long

Bull Shark
Carcharhinus leucas
8 feet (2.4 meters) long

Atlantic Manta Ray
Manta birostris
22 feet (7 meters) wide

Smalltooth Sawfish
Pristis pectinata
16 feet (5 meters) long

A Slow Swimmer, the enormous jewfish keeps close to the bottom in coastal waters. Many fish move slowly unless stirred to fast action by an approaching prey or a fisherman's bait.

A Spotted Eagle Ray glides swiftly through coastal waters in search of prey. This dangerous fish has poisonous spines in its tail that can injure or even kill a human swimmer.

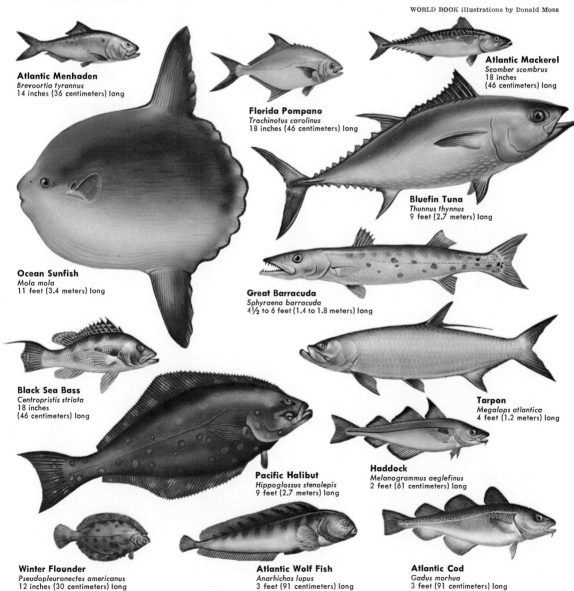

Atlantic Menhaden
Brevoortia tyrannus
14 inches (36 centimeters) long

Florida Pompano
Trachinotus carolinus
18 inches (46 centimeters) long

Atlantic Mackerel
Scomber scombrus
18 inches
(46 centimeters) long

Bluefin Tuna
Thunnus thynnus
9 feet (2.7 meters) long

Ocean Sunfish
Mola mola
11 feet (3.4 meters) long

Great Barracuda
Sphyraena barracuda
4½ to 6 feet (1.4 to 1.8 meters) long

Black Sea Bass
Centropristis striata
18 inches
(46 centimeters) long

Tarpon
Megalops atlantica
4 feet (1.2 meters) long

Pacific Halibut
Hippoglossus stenolepis
9 feet (2.7 meters) long

Haddock
Melanogrammus aeglefinus
2 feet (61 centimeters) long

Winter Flounder
Pseudopleuronectes americanus
12 inches (30 centimeters) long

Atlantic Wolf Fish
Anarhichas lupus
3 feet (91 centimeters) long

Atlantic Cod
Gadus morhua
3 feet (91 centimeters) long

147

FISH

FISH OF CORAL REEFS

Hundreds of kinds of salt-water fish live in the warm, shallow waters around coral reefs. Most of these reefs are in the Indian and Pacific oceans and around the West Indies. A reef's clear, sunlit waters swarm with fish that dart in and out of the coral. Many of them are among the most beautiful in the world. Reef fish differ greatly in appearance and in many other ways. For example, some are mainly plant eaters, such as parrotfish and surgeonfish. Others, including triggerfish and trunkfish, eat small water animals as well as plants. Still others are *predators* that hunt smaller fish. Such fish include groupers and moray eels.

A Fierce Hunter, this speckled moray eel lives in and around coral reefs and catches smaller fish as prey. The moray, a snake-like fish with sharp teeth, can attack with lightning speed.

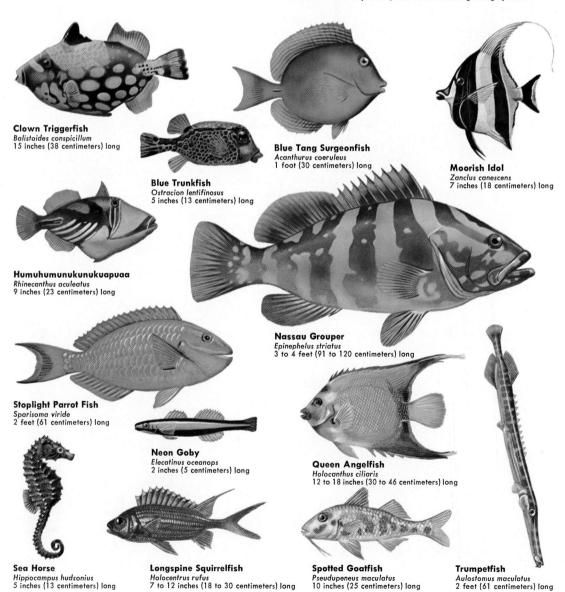

Clown Triggerfish
Balistoides conspicillum
15 inches (38 centimeters) long

Blue Trunkfish
Ostracion lentifinosus
5 inches (13 centimeters) long

Blue Tang Surgeonfish
Acanthurus coeruleus
1 foot (30 centimeters) long

Moorish Idol
Zanclus canescens
7 inches (18 centimeters) long

Humuhumunukunukuapuaa
Rhinecanthus aculeatus
9 inches (23 centimeters) long

Nassau Grouper
Epinephelus striatus
3 to 4 feet (91 to 120 centimeters) long

Stoplight Parrot Fish
Sparisoma viride
2 feet (61 centimeters) long

Neon Goby
Elecatinus oceanops
2 inches (5 centimeters) long

Queen Angelfish
Holocanthus ciliaris
12 to 18 inches (30 to 46 centimeters) long

Sea Horse
Hippocampus hudsonius
5 inches (13 centimeters) long

Longspine Squirrelfish
Holocentrus rufus
7 to 12 inches (18 to 30 centimeters) long

Spotted Goatfish
Pseudupeneus maculatus
10 inches (25 centimeters) long

Trumpetfish
Aulostomus maculatus
2 feet (61 centimeters) long

David Doubilet, Animals, Animals

Allan Power, Bruce Coleman Ltd.

Small, Lively Swimmers, such as this school of French grunts, create almost constant movement around a reef. Some swim about hunting for food during the day, and others do so at night.

The Harlequin Tuskfish is one of the many brilliantly colored species that live among the coral. Dazzling colors or color patterns may help protect these fish by confusing their enemies.

WORLD BOOK illustrations by Donald Moss

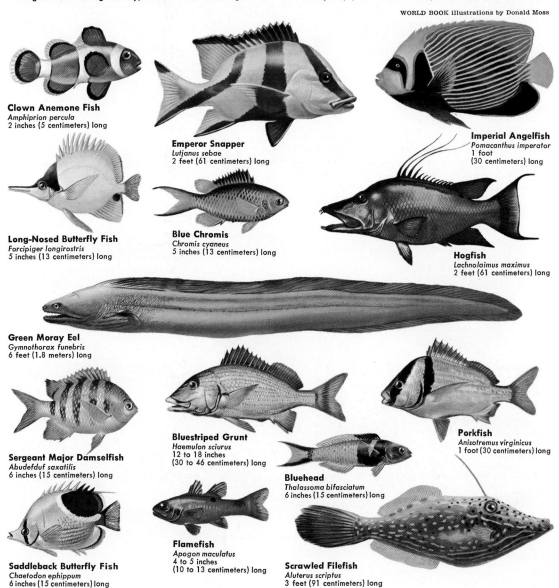

Clown Anemone Fish
Amphiprion percula
2 inches (5 centimeters) long

Emperor Snapper
Lutjanus sebae
2 feet (61 centimeters) long

Imperial Angelfish
Pomacanthus imperator
1 foot
(30 centimeters) long

Long-Nosed Butterfly Fish
Forcipiger longirostris
5 inches (13 centimeters) long

Blue Chromis
Chromis cyaneus
5 inches (13 centimeters) long

Hogfish
Lachnolaimus maximus
2 feet (61 centimeters) long

Green Moray Eel
Gymnothorax funebris
6 feet (1.8 meters) long

Sergeant Major Damselfish
Abudefduf saxatilis
6 inches (15 centimeters) long

Bluestriped Grunt
Haemulon sciurus
12 to 18 inches
(30 to 46 centimeters) long

Porkfish
Anisotremus virginicus
1 foot (30 centimeters) long

Bluehead
Thalassoma bifasciatum
6 inches (15 centimeters) long

Saddleback Butterfly Fish
Chaetodon ephippum
6 inches (15 centimeters) long

Flamefish
Apogon maculatus
4 to 5 inches
(10 to 13 centimeters) long

Scrawled Filefish
Aluterus scriptus
3 feet (91 centimeters) long

148a

FISH

FISH OF THE DEEP OCEAN

Fish of the deep ocean include some of the most unusual and least-known fish in the world. Many of them have large eyes, huge mouths, fanglike teeth, and light organs that flash on and off in the dark waters of the depths. Most deep-ocean fish seldom, if ever, come to the surface. Oarfish, however, sometimes swim up from the lower midwaters and create the strange appearance of a "sea serpent" as they break the surface. A number of species of deepwater fish are familiar only to scientists and have been given only scientific names. These fish include various brotulids and stomiatoids and certain species of anglers.

Ron Church, Tom Stack & Associates

A Channel Rockfish rests on the ocean bottom, 4,000 feet (1,200 meters) down. There, the ocean is almost totally dark. This photograph was taken from a submarine with the aid of lights.

Blue Lantern Fish
Tarletonbeania crenularis
5 inches (13 centimeters) long

Oarfish
Regalecus glesne
20 to 30 feet
(6 to 9 meters) long

Hatchet Fish
Argyropelecus gigas
3½ inches (9 centimeters) long

Stomiatoid Fish
Bathophilus longipinnis
2 inches (5 centimeters) long

Spiny Eel
Notacanthus bonaparti
8 inches (20 centimeters) long

Umbrella Mouth Gulper Eel
Eurypharynx pelecanoides
2 feet (61 centimeters) long

Common Blackdevil Deep-Sea Angler
Melanocetus johnsoni
3½ inches (9 centimeters) long

Deep-Sea Angler
Lasiognathus saccostoma
3 inches (8 centimeters) long

Bristlemouth
Gonostoma elongatum
3 inches (8 centimeters) long

Brotulid Fish
Dicrolene nigra
12 inches (30 centimeters) long

California Rattail
Nezumia stelgidolepis
12 to 15 inches
(30 to 38 centimeters) long

Tripod Fish
Bathypterois quadrisilis
10 inches (25 centimeters) long

FISH OF TROPICAL FRESH WATERS

Tropical regions of Africa, Asia, and South America have a tremendous variety of fresh-water fish. Many of the smaller species are popular aquarium fish. These fish include the guppies, mollies, and swordtails of North and South America and the Siamese fighting fish of Asia. Large tropical fresh-water fish include the giant arapaima, which lives in jungle rivers of South America. The arapaima is one of the largest fresh-water fish in the world. Some arapaimas weigh more than 200 pounds (91 kilograms). The elephant-nose mormyrid of tropical Africa uses its long snout to hunt for food under stones and in mud on river bottoms.

Giuseppe Mazza

The South American Leaf Fish is one of many unusual species that live in tropical fresh waters. By imitating a floating leaf, this fish escapes its enemies and surprises its prey.

WORLD BOOK illustrations by Donald Moss

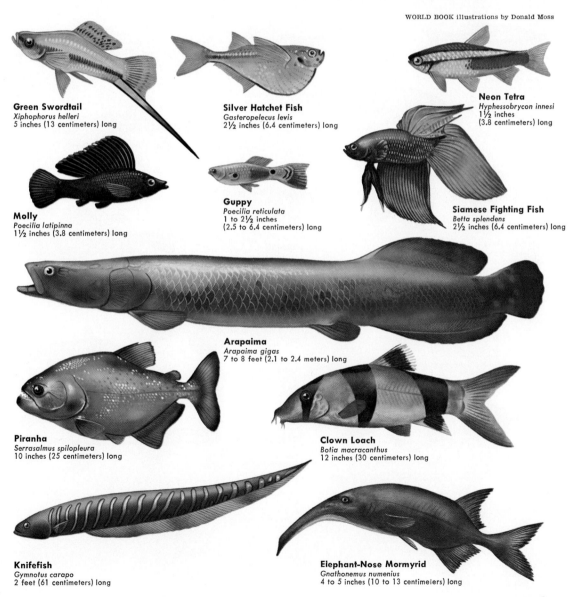

Green Swordtail
Xiphophorus helleri
5 inches (13 centimeters) long

Silver Hatchet Fish
Gasteropelecus levis
2½ inches (6.4 centimeters) long

Neon Tetra
Hyphessobrycon innesi
1½ inches
(3.8 centimeters) long

Molly
Poecilia latipinna
1½ inches (3.8 centimeters) long

Guppy
Poecilia reticulata
1 to 2½ inches
(2.5 to 6.4 centimeters) long

Siamese Fighting Fish
Betta splendens
2½ inches (6.4 centimeters) long

Arapaima
Arapaima gigas
7 to 8 feet (2.1 to 2.4 meters) long

Piranha
Serrasalmus spilopleura
10 inches (25 centimeters) long

Clown Loach
Botia macracanthus
12 inches (30 centimeters) long

Knifefish
Gymnotus carapo
2 feet (61 centimeters) long

Elephant-Nose Mormyrid
Gnathonemus numenius
4 to 5 inches (10 to 13 centimeters) long

FISH

FISH OF TEMPERATE FRESH WATERS

Unlike tropical waters, temperate waters become cold during part of the year. Fish that live in such waters must adjust their living habits to changes in water temperature. For example, in lakes that freeze over during winter, most fish move down to warmer water near the bottom and remain there until spring. The fish pictured here live in temperate lakes, rivers, and streams of North America. Many alewives, coho salmon, rainbow trout, and white sturgeon live in salt water but swim into fresh water to lay their eggs. American eels live in fresh water but swim to the ocean to lay their eggs.

Ron Church, Tom Stack & Associates

Cave Fish live without seeing in the dark waters of caves and underground rivers. These Ozark cave fish have small, sightless eyes, but some other cave fish have no eyes at all.

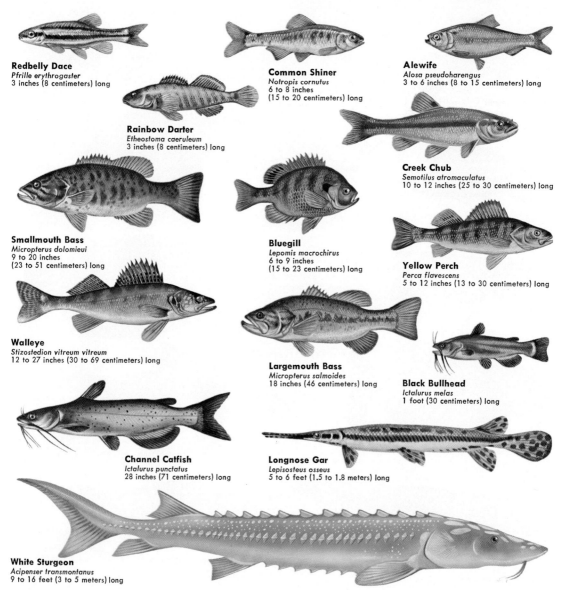

Redbelly Dace
Pfrille erythrogaster
3 inches (8 centimeters) long

Common Shiner
Notropis cornutus
6 to 8 inches
(15 to 20 centimeters) long

Alewife
Alosa pseudoharengus
3 to 6 inches (8 to 15 centimeters) long

Rainbow Darter
Etheostoma caeruleum
3 inches (8 centimeters) long

Creek Chub
Semotilus atromaculatus
10 to 12 inches (25 to 30 centimeters) long

Smallmouth Bass
Micropterus dolomieui
9 to 20 inches
(23 to 51 centimeters) long

Bluegill
Lepomis macrochirus
6 to 9 inches
(15 to 23 centimeters) long

Yellow Perch
Perca flavescens
5 to 12 inches (13 to 30 centimeters) long

Walleye
Stizostedion vitreum vitreum
12 to 27 inches (30 to 69 centimeters) long

Largemouth Bass
Micropterus salmoides
18 inches (46 centimeters) long

Black Bullhead
Ictalurus melas
1 foot (30 centimeters) long

Channel Catfish
Ictalurus punctatus
28 inches (71 centimeters) long

Longnose Gar
Lepisosteus osseus
5 to 6 feet (1.5 to 1.8 meters) long

White Sturgeon
Acipenser transmontanus
9 to 16 feet (3 to 5 meters) long

Jay Schmidt, FPG

Fighting Foaming Rapids, a rainbow, or steelhead, trout swims from the ocean to fresh water, where it will lay its eggs. This yearly trip makes the rainbow a popular fresh-water game fish.

Tom Myers, FPG

Kokanee Salmon are a *landlocked* form of sockeye salmon. They live entirely in fresh water, unlike most other sockeye salmon, which live in the ocean but enter fresh water to lay their eggs.

WORLD BOOK illustrations by Donald Moss

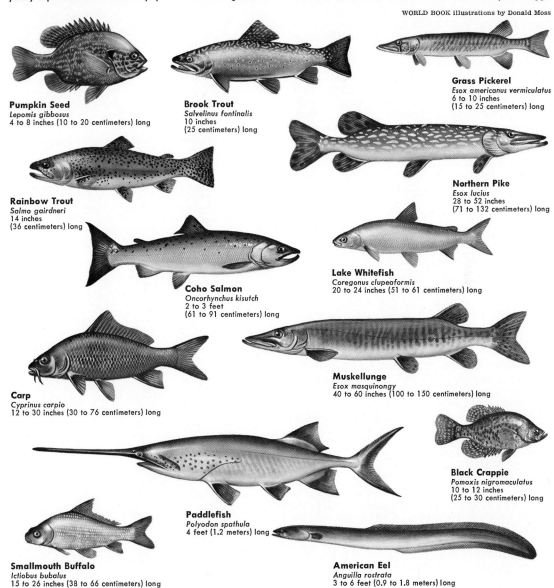

Pumpkin Seed
Lepomis gibbosus
4 to 8 inches (10 to 20 centimeters) long

Brook Trout
Salvelinus fontinalis
10 inches
(25 centimeters) long

Grass Pickerel
Esox americanus vermiculatus
6 to 10 inches
(15 to 25 centimeters) long

Rainbow Trout
Salmo gairdneri
14 inches
(36 centimeters) long

Northern Pike
Esox lucius
28 to 52 inches
(71 to 132 centimeters) long

Coho Salmon
Oncorhynchus kisutch
2 to 3 feet
(61 to 91 centimeters) long

Lake Whitefish
Coregonus clupeaformis
20 to 24 inches (51 to 61 centimeters) long

Carp
Cyprinus carpio
12 to 30 inches (30 to 76 centimeters) long

Muskellunge
Esox masquinongy
40 to 60 inches (100 to 150 centimeters) long

Black Crappie
Pomoxis nigromaculatus
10 to 12 inches
(25 to 30 centimeters) long

Paddlefish
Polyodon spathula
4 feet (1.2 meters) long

Smallmouth Buffalo
Ictiobus bubalus
15 to 26 inches (38 to 66 centimeters) long

American Eel
Anguilla rostrata
3 to 6 feet (0.9 to 1.8 meters) long

148e

In some ways, a fish's body resembles that of other vertebrates. For example, fish, like other vertebrates, have an internal skeleton, an outer skin, and such internal organs as a heart, intestines, and a brain. But in a number of ways, a fish's body differs from that of other vertebrates. For example, fish have fins instead of legs, and gills instead of lungs. Lampreys and hagfish differ from all other vertebrates—and from all other fish—in many ways. Their body characteristics are discussed in an earlier section on *Lampreys and Hagfish*. This section deals with the physical features that most other fish have in common.

External Anatomy

Shape. Most fish have a streamlined body. The head is somewhat rounded at the front. Fish have no neck, and so the head blends smoothly into the trunk. The trunk, in turn, narrows into the tail. Aside from this basic similarity, fish have a variety of shapes. Tuna and many other fast swimmers have a torpedolike shape. Herring, fresh-water sunfish, and some other species are flattened from side to side. Many bottom-dwelling fish, including most rays, are flattened from top to bottom. A number of species are shaped like things in their surroundings. For example, anglerfish and stonefish resemble rocks, and pipefish look like long, slender weeds. This type of camouflage, called *protective resemblance*, helps a fish escape the notice of its enemies and its prey.

Skin and Color. Most fish have a fairly tough skin. It contains blood vessels, nerves, and connective tissue. It also contains certain special cells. Some of these cells produce a slimy *mucus*. This mucus makes fish slippery and gives them their "fishy" smell. Other special cells, called *chromatophores* or *pigment cells*, give fish many of their colors. A chromatophore contains red, yellow, or brownish-black pigments. These colors may combine and produce other colors, such as orange and green. Some species have more chromatophores of a particular color than other species have or have their chromatophores grouped differently. Such differences cause many variations in coloring among species. Besides chromatophores, many fish also have whitish or silvery pigments in their skin and scales. In sunlight, these pigments produce a variety of bright rainbow colors.

The color of most fish matches that of their surroundings. For example, most fish that live near the surface of the open ocean have a blue back, which matches the color of the ocean surface. This type of camouflage is called *protective coloration*. But certain brightly colored fish, including some that have poisonous spines, do not blend with their surroundings. Bright colors may protect a fish by confusing its enemies or by warning them that it has poisonous spines.

Most fish can change their color to match color changes in their surroundings. Flatfish and some other fish that have two or more colors can also change the pattern formed by their colors. A fish receives the impulse to make such changes through its eyes. Signals from a fish's nerves then rearrange the pigments in the chromatophores to make them darker or lighter. The darkening or lightening of the chromatophores produces the different color patterns.

Scales. Most jawed fish have a protective covering of scales. Teleost fish have thin, bony scales that are rounded at the edge. There are two main types of teleost scales—*ctenoid* and *cycloid*. Ctenoid scales have tiny points on their surface. Fish that feel rough to the touch, such as bass and perch, have ctenoid scales. Cycloid scales have a smooth surface. They are found on such fish as carp and salmon. Some primitive bony fish, including bichirs and gars, have thick, heavy *ganoid* scales. Sharks and most rays are covered with *placoid* scales, which resemble tiny, closely spaced teeth. Some fish, including certain kinds of eels and fresh-water catfish, are scaleless.

Fins are movable structures that help a fish swim and keep its balance. A fish moves its fins by means of muscles. Except for a few finless species, all modern bony fish have *rayed fins*. Some primitive bony fish also have rayed fins. These fins consist of a web of skin supported by a fan-shaped skeleton of rods called *rays*. Some ray-finned fish have *soft rays*. Others have both soft rays and *spiny rays*, which are stiff and sharp to the touch. Some primitive bony fish have *lobed fins*, which consist of a fleshy base fringed with rays. Lobed fins are less flexible than rayed fins. Sharks, rays, and chimaeras have fleshy, skin-covered fins supported by rods of cartilage.

Fish fins are classified according to their position on

KINDS OF FISH SCALES

These drawings show examples of the four main types of fish scales and the pattern each type forms on the fish's body. Most modern bony fish have ctenoid or cycloid scales. Some catfish and a few other species have no scales at all.

WORLD BOOK illustration by Marion Pahl

Ctenoid scale (Perch)

Cycloid scale (Salmon)

Ganoid scale (Gar)

Placoid scale (Shark)

EXTERNAL ANATOMY OF A FISH

This drawing of a yellow perch shows the external features most fish have in common. Many kinds of fish do not have all the fins shown here, or they lack such features as gill covers or scales. For example, lampreys and hagfish have no scales and no pelvic or pectoral fins.

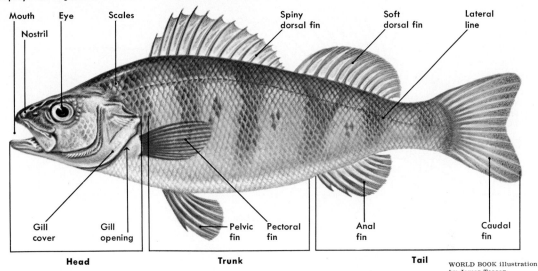

Mouth   Eye   Scales   Spiny dorsal fin   Soft dorsal fin   Lateral line

Nostril

Gill cover   Gill opening   Pelvic fin   Pectoral fin   Anal fin   Caudal fin

Head   **Trunk**   **Tail**   WORLD BOOK illustration by James Teason

the body as well as according to their structure. Classified in this way, a fin is either *median* or *paired*.

Median fins are vertical fins on a fish's back, underside, or tail. They include *dorsal, anal,* and *caudal* fins. The dorsal fin grows along the back and helps a fish keep upright. Almost all fish have at least one dorsal fin, and many have two or three. The anal fin grows on the underside near the tail. Like a dorsal fin, it helps a fish remain upright. Some fish have two anal fins. The caudal fin is at the end of the tail. A fish swings its caudal fin from side to side to propel itself through the water and to help in steering.

Paired fins are two identical fins, one on each side of the body. Most fish have both *pectoral* and *pelvic* paired fins. The pectoral, or shoulder, fins of most fish grow on the sides, just back of the head. Most fish have their pelvic, or leg, fins just below and behind their pectoral fins. But some have their pelvic fins as far forward as the throat or nearly as far back as the anal fin. Pelvic fins are also called *ventral* fins. Most fish use their paired fins mainly to turn, stop, and make other maneuvers.

Skeleton and Muscles

A fish's skeleton provides a framework for the head, trunk, tail, and fins. The central framework for the trunk and tail is the backbone. It consists of many separate segments of bone or cartilage called *vertebrae*. In bony fish, each vertebra has a spine at the top, and each tail vertebra also has a spine at the bottom. Ribs are attached to the vertebrae. The skull consists chiefly of the brain case and supports for the mouth and gills. The pectoral fins of most fish are attached to the back of the skull by a structure called a *pectoral girdle*. The pelvic fins are supported by a structure called a *pelvic girdle* back of the skull, or they are supported by muscular tis-

sue in the abdomen. The dorsal fins are supported by structures of bone or cartilage, which are rooted in muscular tissue above the backbone. The caudal fin is supported by the tail, and the anal fin by structures of bone or cartilage below the backbone.

Like all vertebrates, fish have three kinds of muscles: (1) *skeletal muscles,* (2) *smooth muscles,* and (3) *heart muscles.* Fish use their skeletal muscles to move their bones and fins. A fish's flesh consists almost entirely of skeletal muscles. They are arranged one behind the other in broad vertical bands called *myomeres.* The myomeres can easily be seen in a skinned fish. Each myomere is controlled by a separate nerve. As a result, a fish can bend the front part of its body in one direction while bending its tail in the opposite direction. Most fish make such movements with their bodies to swim. A fish's smooth muscles and heart muscles work automatically. The smooth muscles are responsible for operating such internal organs as the stomach and intestines. Heart muscles form and operate the heart.

Systems of the Body

The internal organs of fish, like those of other vertebrates, are grouped into various systems according to the function they serve. The major systems include the respiratory, digestive, circulatory, nervous, and reproductive systems. Some of these systems resemble those of other vertebrates, but others differ in many ways.

Respiratory System. Unlike land animals, almost all fish get their oxygen from water. Water contains a certain amount of dissolved oxygen. To get oxygen, fish gulp water through the mouth and pump it over the gills. Most fish have four gills enclosed in a *gill chamber* on each side of the head. Each gill consists of two rows of fleshy *filaments* attached to a *gill arch.* Water passes

148g

THE SKELETON OF A FISH

The skeletons of most fish consist mainly of (1) a skull, (2) a backbone, (3) ribs, (4) fin rays, and (5) supports for fin rays or fins. The skeleton of a yellow perch is shown below.

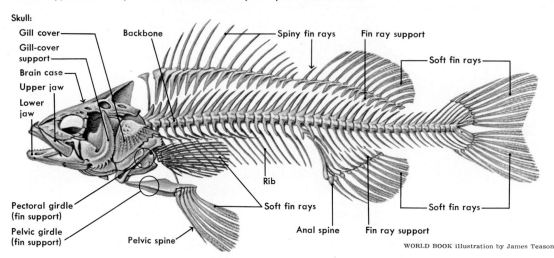

Skull:
Gill cover
Gill-cover support
Brain case
Upper jaw
Lower jaw
Backbone
Spiny fin rays
Fin ray support
Soft fin rays
Pectoral girdle (fin support)
Pelvic girdle (fin support)
Pelvic spine
Rib
Soft fin rays
Anal spine
Fin ray support
Soft fin rays

WORLD BOOK illustration by James Teason

into the gill chambers through *gill slits*. A flap of bone called a *gill cover* protects the gills of bony fish. Sharks and rays do not have gill covers. Their gill slits form visible openings on the outside of the body.

In a bony fish, the breathing process begins when the gill covers close and the mouth opens. At the same time, the walls of the mouth expand outward, drawing water into the mouth. The walls of the mouth then move inward, the mouth closes, and the gill covers open. This action forces the water from the mouth into the gill chambers. In each chamber, the water passes over the gill filaments. They absorb oxygen from the water and replace it with carbon dioxide formed during the breathing process. The water then passes out through the gill openings, and the process is repeated.

Digestive System, or *digestive tract*, changes food into materials that nourish the body cells. It eliminates materials that are not used. In fish, this system leads from the mouth to the *anus*, an opening in front of the anal

fin. Most fish have a jawed mouth with a tongue and teeth. A fish cannot move its tongue, which is used only for tasting. Most fish have their teeth rooted in the jaws. They use their teeth to seize prey or to tear off pieces of their victim's flesh. Some of these fish also have teeth on the roof of the mouth or on the tongue. Most fish also have teeth in the *pharynx*, a short tube behind the mouth. They use these teeth to crush or grind food.

In all fish, food passes through the pharynx on the way to the *esophagus*, another tubelike organ. A fish's esophagus expands easily, which allows the fish to swallow its food whole. From the esophagus, food passes into the *stomach*, where it is partly digested. Some fish have their esophagus or stomach enlarged into a *gizzard*. The gizzard grinds food into small pieces before it passes into the intestines. The digestive process is completed in the intestines. The digested food enters the blood stream. Waste products and undigested food pass out through the anus.

HOW A FISH'S GILLS WORK

Like all animals, fish need oxygen to change food into body energy. These drawings show how a fish's gills enable it to get oxygen from the water and to get rid of carbon dioxide, a body waste.

WORLD BOOK illustration by Margaret Ann Moran

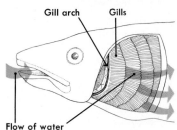

Gill arch   Gills

Flow of water

Most fish have four gills on each side of the head. Water enters the mouth and flows out through the gills. Each gill is made up of fleshy, threadlike *filaments*.

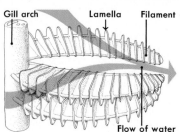

Gill arch   Lamella   Filament

Flow of water

Water from the mouth passes over the filaments, which are closely spaced along a gill arch in two rows. Three of the many filaments of a gill are shown above.

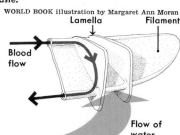

Lamella   Filament

Blood flow

Flow of water

Each filament has many tiny extensions called *lamellae*. Blood flowing through a lamella takes oxygen from the water and releases carbon dioxide into the water.

INTERNAL ORGANS OF A FISH

This view of a yellow perch shows the chief internal organs found in most fish. These organs are parts of the systems that perform such body processes as breathing and digestion.

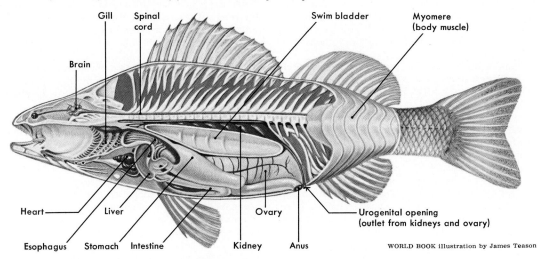

Gill — Spinal cord — Swim bladder — Myomere (body muscle) — Brain — Heart — Liver — Ovary — Urogenital opening (outlet from kidneys and ovary) — Esophagus — Stomach — Intestine — Kidney — Anus

WORLD BOOK illustration by James Teason

Circulatory System distributes blood to all parts of the body. It includes the heart and blood vessels. A fish's heart consists of two main chambers—the *atrium* and the *ventricle*. The blood flows through *veins* to the atrium. It then passes to the ventricle. Muscles in the ventricle pump the blood through *arteries* to the gills, where the blood receives oxygen and gives off carbon dioxide. Arteries then carry the blood throughout the body. The blood carries food from the intestines and oxygen from the gills to the body cells. It also carries away waste products from the cells. A fish's kidneys remove the waste products from the blood, which returns to the heart through the veins.

Nervous System of fish, like that of other vertebrates, consists of a *spinal cord*, *brain*, and *nerves*. However, a fish's nervous system is not so complex as that of mammals and other higher vertebrates. The spinal cord, which consists of soft nerve tissue, runs from the brain through the backbone. The brain is an enlargement of the spinal cord and is enclosed in the skull. The nerves extend from the brain and spinal cord to every part of the body. Some nerves, called *sensory* nerves, carry messages from the sense organs to the spinal cord and brain. Other nerves, called *motor* nerves, carry messages from the brain and spinal cord to the muscles. A fish can consciously control its skeletal muscles. But it has no conscious control over the smooth muscles and heart muscles. These muscles work automatically.

Reproductive System. As in all vertebrates, the reproductive organs of fish are *testes* in males and *ovaries* in females. The testes produce male sex cells, or *sperm*. The sperm is contained in a fluid called *milt*. The ovaries produce female sex cells, or *eggs*. Fish eggs are also called *roe* or *spawn*. Most fish release their sex cells into the water through an opening near the anus. The males of some species have special structures for transferring sperm directly into the females. Male sharks, for example, have such a structure, called a *clasper*,

on each pelvic fin. The claspers are used to hold the female and insert sperm into her body.

Special Organs

Most bony fish have a swim bladder below the backbone. This baglike organ is also called an air bladder. In most fish, the swim bladder provides *buoyancy*, which enables the fish to remain at a particular depth in the water. In lungfish and a few other fish, the swim bladder serves as an air-breathing lung. Still other fish, including many catfish, use their swim bladders to produce sounds as well as to provide buoyancy. Some species communicate by means of such sounds.

A fish would sink to the bottom if it did not have a way of keeping buoyant. Most fish gain buoyancy by inflating their swim bladder with gases produced by their blood. But water pressure increases with depth. As a fish swims deeper, the increased water pressure makes its swim bladder smaller and so reduces the fish's buoyancy. The amount of gas in the bladder must be increased so that the bladder remains large enough to maintain buoyancy. A fish's nervous system automatically regulates the amount of gas in the bladder so that it is kept properly filled. Sharks and rays do not have a swim bladder. To keep buoyant, these fish must swim constantly. When they rest, they stop swimming and so sink toward the bottom. Many bottom-dwelling bony fish also lack a swim bladder.

Many fish have organs that produce light or electricity. But these organs are simply adaptations of structures found in all or most fish. For example, many deep-sea fish have light-producing organs developed from parts of their skin or digestive tract. Some species use these organs to attract prey or possibly to communicate with others of their species. Various other fish have electricity-producing organs developed from muscles in their eyes, gills, or trunk. Some species use these organs to stun or kill enemies or prey.

Like all vertebrates, fish have sense organs that tell them what is happening in their environment. The organs enable them to see, hear, smell, taste, and touch. In addition, almost all fish have a special sense organ called the *lateral line system*, which enables them to "touch" objects at a distance. Fish also have various other senses that help them meet the conditions of life underwater.

Sight. A fish's eyes differ from those of land vertebrates in several ways. For example, most fish can see to the right and to the left at the same time. This ability makes up in part for the fact that a fish has no neck and so cannot turn its head. Fish also lack eyelids. In land vertebrates, eyelids help moisten the eyes and shield them from sunlight. A fish's eyes are kept moist by the flow of water over them. They do not need to be shielded from sunlight because sunlight is seldom extremely bright underwater. Some fish have unusual adaptations of the eye. For example, adult flatfish have both eyes on the same side of the head. A flatfish spends most of the time lying on its side on the ocean floor and so needs eyes only on the side that faces upward. The eyes of certain deep-sea fish are on the ends of short structures that stick out from the head. These structures can be raised upward, allowing the fish to see overhead as well as to the sides and front.

A few kinds of fish are born blind. They include certain species of catfish that live in total darkness in the waters of caves and the whalefish, which lives in the ocean depths. Some of these fish have eyes but no vision. Others lack eyes completely.

Hearing. All fish can probably hear sounds produced in the water. Fish can also hear sounds made on shore or above the water if they are loud enough. Catfish and certain other fish have a keen sense of hearing.

Fish have an inner ear enclosed in a chamber on each side of the head. Each ear consists of a group of pouches and tubelike canals. Fish have no outer ears or eardrums to receive sound vibrations. Sound vibrations are carried to the inner ears by the body tissues.

Smell and Taste. All fish have a sense of smell. It is highly developed in many species, including catfish, salmon, and sharks. In most fish, the *olfactory organs* (organs of smell) consist of two pouches, one on each side of the snout. The pouches are lined with nerve tissue that is highly sensitive to odors from substances in the water. A nostril at the front of each pouch allows water to enter the pouch and pass over the tissue. The water leaves the pouch through a nostril at the back.

Most fish have taste buds in various parts of the mouth. Some species also have them on other parts of the body. Catfish, sturgeon, and a number of other fish have whiskerlike feelers called *barbels* near the mouth. They use the barbels both to taste and to touch.

Touch and the Lateral Line System are closely related. Most fish have a well-developed sense of touch. Nerve endings throughout the skin react to the slightest pressure and change of temperature. The lateral line system senses changes in the movement of water. It consists mainly of a series of tiny canals under the skin. A main canal runs along each side of the trunk. Branches of these two canals extend onto the head. A fish senses the flow of water around it as a series of vibrations. The vibrations enter the lateral line through pores and activate certain sensitive areas in the line. If the flow of water around a fish changes, the pattern of vibrations sensed through the lateral line also changes. Nerves relay this information to the brain. Changes in the pattern of vibrations may warn a fish of approaching danger or indicate the location of objects outside its range of vision.

Other Senses include those that help a fish keep its balance and avoid unfavorable waters. The inner ears help a fish keep its balance. They contain a fluid and several hard, free-moving *otoliths* (ear stones). Whenever a fish begins to swim in other than an upright, level position, the fluid and otoliths move over sensitive nerve endings in the ears. The nerves signal the brain about the changes in the position of the body. The brain then sends messages to the fin muscles, which move to restore the fish's balance. Fish can also sense any changes in the pressure, salt content, or temperature of the water and so avoid swimming very far into unfavorable waters.

THE LATERAL LINE SYSTEM

The lateral line system makes a fish sensitive to vibrations in the water. It consists of a series of tubelike *canals* in a fish's skin. Vibrations enter the canals through *pores* (openings in the skin) and travel to sensory organs in the canals. Nerves connect these organs to the brain.

WORLD BOOK illustration by Marion Pahl

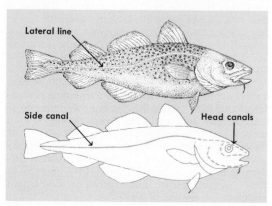

Lateral line

Side canal

Head canals

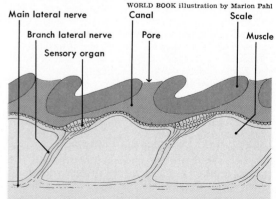

Main lateral nerve

Branch lateral nerve

Sensory organ

Canal

Pore

Scale

Muscle

Every fish begins life in an egg. In the egg, the undeveloped fish, called an *embryo*, feeds on the yolk until ready to hatch. The section *How Fish Reproduce* discusses where and how fish lay their eggs. After a fish hatches, it is called a *larva* or *fry*. The fish reaches adulthood when it begins to produce sperm or eggs. Most small fish, such as guppies and many minnows, become adults within a few months after hatching. But some small fish become adults only a few minutes after hatching. Large fish require several years. Many of these fish pass through one or more *juvenile* stages before becoming adults. Almost all fish continue to grow as long as they live. During its lifetime, a fish may increase several thousand times in size. The longest-lived fish are probably certain sturgeon, some of which have lived in aquariums more than 50 years. For the life spans of various other fish in captivity, see ANIMAL (table: Length of Life of Animals).

How Fish Get Food. Most fish are *carnivores* (meat-eaters). They eat shellfish, worms, and other kinds of water animals. Above all, they eat other fish. They sometimes eat their own young. Some fish are mainly *herbivores* (plant-eaters). They chiefly eat algae and other water plants. But most plant-eating fish probably also eat animals. Some fish live mainly on plankton. They include many kinds of flying fish and herring and the three largest fish of all—the whale shark, giant manta ray, and basking shark. Some fish are *scavengers*. They feed mainly on waste products and on the dead bodies of animals that sink to the bottom.

Many fish have body organs specially adapted for capturing their prey. Certain fish of the ocean depths attract their prey with flashing lures. The dorsal fin of some anglerfish dangles above their mouth and serves as a bait for other fish. Such species as gars and swordfish have long, beaklike jaws, which they use for spearing or slashing their prey. Barracudas and certain piranhas and sharks are well known for their razor-sharp teeth, with which they tear the flesh from their victims. Electric eels and some other fish with electricity-producing organs stun their prey with an electric shock. Many fish have comblike *gill rakers*. These structures strain plankton from the water pumped through the gills.

How Fish Swim. Most fish gain *thrust* (power for forward movement) by swinging the tail fin from side to side while curving the rest of the body alternately to the left and to the right. Some fish, such as marlin and tuna, depend mainly on tail motion for thrust. Other fish, including many kinds of eels, rely chiefly on the curving motion of the body. Fish maneuver by moving their fins. To make a left turn, for example, a fish extends its left pectoral fin. To stop, it extends both pectorals.

A fish's swimming ability is affected by the shape and location of its fins. Most fast, powerful swimmers, such as swordfish and tuna, have a deeply forked or crescent-shaped tail fin and sickle-shaped pectorals. All their fins are relatively large. At the other extreme, most slow swimmers, such as bowfins and bullheads, have a squared or rounded tail fin and rounded pectorals.

How Fish Protect Themselves. All fish, except the largest ones, live in constant danger of being attacked

HOW A FISH DEVELOPS

Most fish develop from egg to adult in stages. The photographs below show three stages in the development of brook trout.

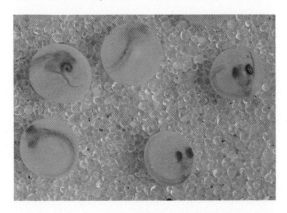

These tiny trout eggs lie among grains of sand. Curled inside each egg is an undeveloped fish called an *embryo*. The large dots are the embryo's eyes. The yolk of the egg nourishes the embryo.

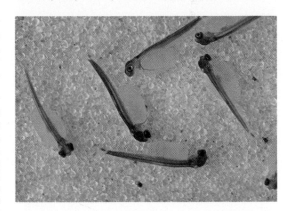

A newly hatched fish, called a *larva* or *fry*, continues to draw nourishment from the egg yolk by means of blood vessels that extend through the yolk. The yolk is contained in a *yolk sac*.

Treat Davidson, NAS

This 3-month-old trout has used its supply of yolk and now hunts for food. As it grows, it will take on the appearance of an adult trout. Most trout become adults in 2 to 5 years.

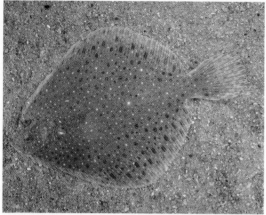

Runk/Schoenberger from Grant Heilman

A Flounder, which has both eyes on one side of its body, lies on the ocean bottom with both eyes facing up. Flounders change their color pattern to match the background.

Stan Keiser from Ron Church

The Electric Eel stuns its enemies and prey with a powerful electric shock. The electricity-producing organs take up most of the body. The other inner organs lie just back of the head.

and eaten by other fish or other animals. To survive, fish must be able to defend themselves against predators. If a species loses more individuals each generation than it gains, it will in time die out.

Protective coloration and protective resemblance are the most common methods of self-defense. A fish that blends with its surroundings is more likely to escape from its enemies than one whose color or shape is extremely noticeable. Many fish that do not blend with their surroundings depend on swimming speed or maneuvering ability to escape from their enemies.

Fish also have other kinds of defense. Some fish, such as gars, pipefish, and sea horses, are protected by a covering of thick, heavy scales or bony plates. Other species have sharp spines that are difficult for predators to swallow. In many of these species, including scorpionfish, sting rays, and stonefish, one or more of the spines are poisonous. When threatened, the porcupine fish inflates its spine-covered body with air or water until it is shaped like a balloon. The fish's larger size and erect spines may discourage an enemy. Many eels that live on the bottom dig holes in which they hide from their enemies. Razor fish dive into sand on the bottom. A few fish do the opposite. For example, flying fish and needlefish escape danger by propelling themselves out of the water.

How Fish Rest. Like all animals, fish need rest. Many species have periods of what might be called sleep. Others simply remain inactive for short periods. But even at rest, many fish continue to move their fins to keep their position in the water.

Fish have no eyelids, and so they cannot close their eyes when sleeping. But while asleep, a fish is probably unaware of the impressions received by its eyes. Some fish sleep on the bottom, resting on their belly or side. Other species sleep in midwater, in a horizontal position. The slippery dick, a coral-reef fish, sleeps on the bottom under a covering of sand. The striped parrot

HOW FISH SWIM

The dogfish and most other fish swim by swinging their tail from side to side, while curving the rest of their body in the opposite direction. Some fish, such as tuna, move the front of their body little in swimming. Eels and some other fish bend their body in snakelike curves.

WORLD BOOK illustration by Marion Pahl

Dogfish

Tuna

Eel

Boyd Wells, Pictorial Parade

Giuseppe Mazza

A Fleshy Bait grows from the head of an anglerfish, *above left,* and out of the mouth of a star-gazer, *above right.* The wormlike bait attracts smaller fish. Anglerfish and stargazers snap up small fish with astonishing speed, but they move slowly at most other times.

fish, another coral-reef fish, encloses itself in an "envelope" of mucus before going to sleep. The fish secretes the mucus from special glands in its gill chambers.

Certain air-breathing fish, such as the African and South American lungfish, sleep out of water for months at a time. These fish live in rivers or ponds that are dry during the summer. The fish lie buried in hardened mud until the return of the rainy season. This kind of long sleep during summer is called *estivation.* During estivation, a fish breathes little and lives off the fat stored in its body.

How Fish Live Together. Among many species, the individual fish that make up the species live mainly by themselves. Such fish include most predatory fish. Many sharks, for example, hunt and feed by themselves and join other sharks only for mating.

Among many other species, the fish live together in closely knit groups called *schools.* About a fifth of all fish species are schooling species. A school may have few or many fish. A school of tuna, for example, may consist of fewer than 25 individuals. Many schools of herring number in the hundreds of millions. All the fish in a school are about the same size. Baby fish and adult fish are never in the same school. In some schooling species, the fish become part of a school when they are young and remain with it throughout their lives. Other species form schools for only a few weeks after they hatch. The fish in a school usually travel in close formation as a defense against predators. But a school often breaks up at night to feed and then regroups the next morning. The approach of a predator brings the fish quickly back together.

Allan Power, Bruce Coleman Ltd.

Fish Protected by Spines include the demon stinger, *above left,* and the stonefish *above right.* Both fish give off poison through their spines. The stonefish's poison is the deadliest of all fish poisons. It can kill a human being in minutes.

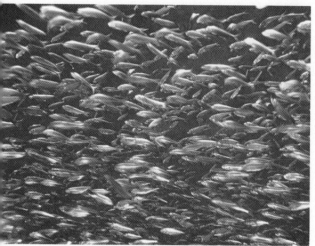

Thousands of Sardines make up this school. They live together most of the time but may separate at night to feed. They swim quickly back together when threatened by an enemy.

A Sweetlips and a Wrasse help each other. The small wrasse is removing parasites from the gills of the sweetlips. The large sweetlips, in turn, protects the wrasse from predators.

Three Remoras Ride on a Lemon Shark. The remoras use a sucking disk on their head to hold on to the shark. They also eat scraps of the shark's food.

Fish also form other types of relationships. Among cod, perch, and many other species, a number of individuals may gather in the same area for feeding, resting, or spawning. Such a group is only temporary and is not so closely knit as a school. Some fish, including certain angelfish and wrasses, form unusual relationships with larger fish of other species. In many such relationships, the smaller fish removes parasites or dead tissue from the larger fish. The smaller fish thus obtains food, and the other is cleaned. The larger fish also protects the smaller one from predators.

How Fish Adjust to Change. Fish sometimes need to adjust to changes in their environment. The two most common changes are (1) changes in water temperature and (2) changes in the salt content of water.

In general, the body temperature of each species of fish equals that of the water in which the species lives. If the water temperature rises or falls, a fish can adjust to the change because its body temperature changes accordingly. But the change in the water temperature must not be too great and must occur gradually. Most fish can adjust to a change in the water temperature of up to 15° F. (8° C)—if the change is not sudden. Water temperatures usually change slowly, and so there is time for a fish's body to make the necessary adjustment. But occasionally, the temperature drops suddenly and severely, killing many fish. In addition, fresh-water fish are sometimes endangered by *thermal pollution*, which occurs when factories and electric power plants release hot water into rivers or lakes. The resulting increase in water temperature may be greater than most fish can adjust to.

Both fresh water and ocean water contain various salts, many of which fish need in their diet. But ocean water is far saltier than fresh water. Fish that migrate between the two must adjust to changes in the salt content of the water. Relatively few fish can make such an adjustment.

Both fresh-water and ocean fish have about the same amount of dissolved salts in their body fluids. But the body fluids of ocean fish are not so salty as the water in which the fish live. According to a law of nature, if two solutions containing different amounts of salt are separated by a porous *membrane* (thin layer of tissue), water from the weaker solution will flow into the stronger solution. This process is called *osmosis*. As a result of osmosis, ocean fish constantly lose water through their skin and the membranes of their gills. To make up for this loss, they must drink much water. But ocean water contains more salt than marine fish need. The fish pass the extra salt out through their gills and digestive tract. Salt-water fish need the water they drink. As a result, these fish produce only small amounts of urine.

Fresh-water fish have the opposite problem with osmosis. Their body fluids are saltier than fresh water. As a result, the fish constantly absorb water through their membranes. In fact, they absorb so much water that they do not need to drink any. Instead, the fish must get rid of the extra water that their bodies absorb. As a result, fresh-water fish produce great quantities of urine.

All fish reproduce sexually. In sexual reproduction, a sperm unites with an egg in a process called *fertilization*. The fertilized egg develops into a new individual. In almost all fish species, males produce sperm and females produce eggs. In a few species, the same individual produces both sperm and eggs.

The eggs of most fish are fertilized outside the female's body. A female releases her eggs into the water at the same time that a male releases his sperm. Some sperm come in contact with some eggs, and fertilization takes place. This process is called *external fertilization*. The entire process during which eggs and sperm are released into the water and the eggs are fertilized is called *spawning*. Almost all bony fish reproduce in this way.

Sharks, rays, chimaeras, and a few bony fish, such as guppies and mosquito fish, reproduce in a different manner. The eggs of these fish are fertilized inside the female, a process called *internal fertilization*. For internal fertilization to occur, males and females must mate. The males have special organs for transferring sperm into the females. After fertilization, the females of some species release their eggs into the water before they hatch. Other females hatch the eggs inside their bodies and so give birth to living young. Fish that bear living young include many sharks and rays, guppies, and some halfbeaks and scorpionfish.

This section discusses spawning, the method by which most fish reproduce.

Preparation for Spawning. Most fish have a *spawning season* each year, during which they may spawn several times. But some tropical species breed throughout the year. The majority of fish spawn in spring or early summer, when the water is warm and the days are long. But certain cold-water fish, such as brook trout and Atlantic cod, spawn in fall or winter.

Most fish return to particular *spawning grounds* year after year. Many fresh-water fish have to travel only a short distance to their spawning grounds. They may simply move from the deeper parts of a river or lake to shallow waters near shore. But other fish may migrate tremendous distances to spawn. For example, European fresh-water eels cross 3,000 miles (4,800 kilometers) of ocean to reach their spawning grounds in the western Atlantic.

At their spawning grounds, the males and females of some species swim off in pairs to spawn. Among other species, the males and females spawn in groups. Many males and females tell each other apart by differences in appearance. The females of some species are larger than the males. Among other species, the males develop unusually bright colors during the spawning season. During the rest of the year, they look much like females. In some species, the males and females look so different that for many years scientists thought they belonged to different species. Among other fish, the sexes look so much alike that they can be told apart only by differences in behavior. For example, many males adopt a special type of *courting* behavior to attract females. A courting male may swim round and round a female or perform a lively "dance" to attract her attention.

HOW FISH REPRODUCE

Fish reproduce *sexually*—by uniting a *sperm* (male sex cell) with an *egg* (female sex cell). In most species, the union of sex cells takes place in the water. Trout reproduction is shown below.

The female trout, *above center*, makes a nest for her eggs. She uses her tail to scoop the nest out on the gravelly bottom. The male trout, *left*, does not help make the nest.

After the nest has been made, the male moves alongside the female. As the female releases her eggs, the male releases his sperm. The sperm cells unite with the eggs in the nest.

WORLD BOOK illustration by Harry McNaught

The female then covers the nest to protect the eggs. She heads into the current and swishes her tail in the gravel to stir it up. The current carries the loosened gravel back over the eggs.

Among some species, including cod, Siamese fighting fish, and certain gobies and sticklebacks, a male claims a territory for spawning and fights off any male intruders. Many fish, especially those that live in fresh water, build nests for their eggs. A male fresh-water bass, for example, uses its tail fin to scoop out a nest on the bottom of a lake or stream.

Spawning and Care of the Eggs. After the preparations have been made, the males and females touch in a certain way or make certain signals with their fins or body. Depending on the species, a female may lay a few eggs or many eggs—even millions—during the spawning season. Most fish eggs measure $\frac{1}{8}$ inch (3 millimeters) in diameter or less.

Some fish, such as cod and herring, abandon their eggs after spawning. A female cod may lay as many as 9 million eggs during a spawning season. Cod eggs, like those of many other ocean fish, float near the surface and scatter as soon as they are laid. Predators eat many of the eggs. Others drift into waters too cold for hatching. Only a few cod eggs out of millions develop into adult fish. A female herring lays about 50,000 eggs in a season. But herring eggs, like those

1480

of certain other marine fish, sink to the bottom and have an adhesive covering that helps them stick there. As a result, herring eggs are less likely to be eaten by predators or to drift into waters unfavorable for hatching.

A number of fish protect their eggs. They include many fresh-water nest builders, such as bass, salmon, certain sticklebacks, and trout. The females of these species lay far fewer eggs than do the females of the cod and herring groups. Like herring eggs, the eggs of many of the fresh-water nest builders sink to the bottom and have an adhesive covering. But they have an even better chance of surviving than herring eggs because they receive some protection. The amount and kind of protection vary greatly. Salmon and trout cover their fertilized eggs with gravel but abandon them soon after. Male fresh-water bass guard the eggs fiercely until they hatch. Among ocean fish, female sea horses and pipefish lay their eggs in a pouch on the underside of the male. The eggs hatch inside the male's pouch. Some fish, including certain ocean catfish and cardinal fish, carry their eggs in their mouth during the hatching period. In some species, the male carries the eggs. In other species, the female carries them.

Hatching and Care of the Young. The eggs of most fish species hatch in less than a month. Eggs laid in warm water hatch faster than those laid in cold water. The eggs of some tropical fish hatch in less than 24 hours. On the other hand, the eggs of certain cold-water fish require four or five months to hatch. The males of a few species guard their young for a short time after they hatch. These fish include fresh-water bass, bowfins, brown bullheads, Siamese fighting fish, and some sticklebacks. But most other fish provide no protection for their offspring.

Runk/Schoenberger from Grant Heilman

A Male Siamese Fighting Fish blows bubbles that stick together to make a nest for eggs laid by the female. He then collects the eggs in his mouth and blows them into the nest.

Ray Duke, Pictorial Parade

Most Female Sharks hatch their eggs inside their bodies. The swimmer, above, is observing the birth of a baby grey nurse shark. The females of some shark species lay their eggs in the water.

William M. Stevens, Tom Stack & Associates

Mouthbreeding Fish hold their eggs in their mouth during much of the time before hatching. This male jawfish has a mouthful of eggs. Females of some species and males of others hold the eggs.

A Fish That Lived 58 Million Years Ago left its "picture" in this fossil. Such fossils reveal many details about fish that are now extinct. Scientists study fossils to discover how fish developed through the ages.

Scientists learn how fish developed by studying fish fossils. The fossils show the changes that occurred in the anatomy of fish down through the ages.

The First Fish appeared on the earth about 500 million years ago. These fish are called *ostracoderms*. They were slow, bottom-dwelling animals covered from head to tail with a heavy armor of thick bony plates and scales. Like today's lampreys and hagfish, ostracoderms had no jaws and poorly formed fins. For this reason, scientists group lampreys, hagfish, and ostracoderms together. Ostracoderms were not only the first fish, but they were also the first animals to have a backbone. Most scientists believe that the history of all other vertebrates can be traced back to the ostracoderms. They gave rise to jawed fish with backbones, and these fish in turn gave rise to *amphibians* (vertebrates that have legs and live both on land and in water). The amphibians became the ancestors of all land vertebrates.

Ostracoderms probably reached the peak of their development about 400 million years ago. About the same time, two other groups of fish were developing—*acanthodians* and *placoderms*. The acanthodians became the first known jawed fish. The placoderms were the largest fish up to that time. Some members of the placoderm group called *Dinichthys* grew up to 30 feet (9 meters) long and had powerful jaws and sharp bony plates that served as teeth.

The Age of Fish was a period in the earth's history when fish developed remarkably. Scientists call this age the Devonian Period. It began about 405 million years ago and lasted about 60 million years. During much of this time, dinichthys and other large placoderms ruled the seas.

The first bony fish appeared early in the Devonian Period. They were mostly small or medium-sized and, like all fish of that time, were heavily armored. These primitive bony fish belonged to two main groups—*chondrosteans* and *sarcopterygians*.

The chondrosteans had rayed fins. They were the

ancestors of today's ray-finned fish, which make up about 95 per cent of all fish species. But the chondrosteans differed in many ways from modern ray-finned fish. The paddlefish and sturgeons are the only surviving chondrosteans, though some scientists also include the African bichir. The sarcopterygians had fleshy or lobed fins. Few fish today are even distantly related to this group. The coelacanth and the lungfish are the only surviving sarcopterygians. However, some scientists include the bichir in this group rather than with the chondrosteans. Bichirs share some of the characteristics of both groups. The most important members of the sarcopterygian group were the *rhipidistians*, which died out more than 200 million years ago. Most scientists believe that the rhipidistians were the direct ancestors of the first amphibians.

The first sharks appeared during the Devonian Period. They looked much like certain sharks of today. The first rays appeared about 200 million years after the first sharks. By the end of the Devonian Period, all jawless fish had died out, except for the ancestors of today's lampreys and hagfish. Some acanthodians and placoderms remained, but they also died out in time.

The First Modern Fish, or teleosts, appeared during the Triassic Period, which began about 225 million years ago. The chondrosteans of the Devonian Period had given rise to another group of primitive bony fish, the *holosteans*. The holosteans, in turn, became the ancestors of the teleosts. The only surviving holosteans are the bowfin and fresh-water gars.

The teleosts lost the heavy armor that covered the bodies of most earlier fish. At first, all teleosts had soft-rayed fins. These fish gave rise to present-day catfish, minnows, and other soft-finned fish. The first spiny-finned fish appeared during the Cretaceous Period, which began about 130 million years ago. These fish were the ancestors of such highly developed present-day fish as perch and tuna. Since the Cretaceous Period, teleosts have been by far the most important group of fish.   C. LAVETT SMITH

Ichthyologists classify fish into various groups according to the body characteristics they have in common. They divide all fish into two superclasses: (1) *Agnatha*, meaning *jawless*, and (2) *Gnathostomata*, meaning *jawed*. The superclass *Agnatha* consists of a single class, also called Agnatha, which is divided into two orders. The much larger superclass *Gnathostomata* is divided into classes, subclasses, superorders, and orders. The orders are further divided into families, the families into genera, and the genera into species.

SUPERCLASS AGNATHA. Mouth jawless; skeleton of cartilage; no paired fins, air bladder, or scales; about 45 species in 2 orders:

Order Petromyzoniformes—lampreys. Large sucking mouth; 7 pairs of external gill openings; some species parasitic; live in salt and fresh water.

Order Myxiniformes—hagfish. Small nonsucking mouth; 1 to 16 pairs of external gill openings; nonparasitic; salt water.

Lamprey
(Petromyzoniformes)

SUPERCLASS GNATHOSTOMATA. Mouth jawed; most species have paired fins and scales; about 21,000 species in 2 classes:

Class Chondrichthyes. Skeleton of cartilage; no air bladder; about 600 species in 3 orders:

Order Squaliformes—sharks. Most have torpedo shape; upturned tail; 5 to 7 pairs of gill slits; no gill covers; placoid scales; mostly salt water.

Order Rajiformes—rays. Most have body flattened from top to bottom; whiplike tail; 5 pairs of gill slits under pectorals rather than on sides; no gill covers; placoid scales; mostly salt water.

Order Chimaeriformes—chimaeras. Short-, long-, and elephant-nosed species; pointed tail; 4 pairs of gill slits; gill covers; scaleless; salt water.

Class Osteichthyes. Skeleton largely or partly bone; most species have 5 pairs of gill slits, gill covers, air bladder, and cycloid or ctenoid scales; over 20,000 species in 2 subclasses:

Subclass Sarcopterygii. Lobed fins; skeleton partly cartilage and partly bone (primitive bony); 7 species in 2 orders:

Order Dipteriformes—lungfish. Air bladder an air-breathing lung; fresh water.

Order Coelacanthiformes—coelacanth. Single ancient species; salt water.

Subclass Actinopterygii. Rayed fins; skeleton largely or partly bone; single dorsal and anal fins in most orders; divided into 3 superorders:

Superorder Chondrostei. Skeleton largely cartilage with little bone (primitive bony); sharklike tail; about 40 species in 2 orders:

Order Polypteriformes—bichirs. Slender body; thick ganoid scales; long dorsal fin composed of separate finlets; lunglike air bladder; fresh water.

Order Acipenseriformes—paddlefish, sturgeon. Heavy body; paddlefish nearly scaleless; sturgeon have bony plates instead of scales; fresh water; some sturgeon anadromous.

Superorder Holostei. Skeleton mostly bone with little cartilage (primitive bony); nearly symmetrical tail; fresh water; 8 species in 2 orders:

Order Semionotiformes—gars. Long, slender body and jaws; short, far-back dorsal fin; diamond-shaped ganoid scales; lunglike air bladder.

Order Amiiformes—bowfin. Stout body, rounded tail fin; long, wavy dorsal fin; cycloid scales; bony plate under chin; single species.

Superorder Teleostei. Skeleton largely bone (modern bony); soft or spiny fin rays; symmetrical tail fin; about 20,000 species in 30 orders:

Order Elopiformes—bonefish, tarpon, ten-pounders. Soft fin rays; low pectorals; abdominal pelvics; deeply forked tail; silvery body; mostly salt water.

Order Anguilliformes—eels. Soft fin rays; many species lack pectorals; no pelvics; some species scaleless; snakelike; mostly salt water; some catadromous.

Order Notacanthiformes—spiny eels. Soft and spiny fin rays; low pectorals; abdominal pelvics; no tail fin; long, tapering body; salt water, on bottom.

Order Clupeiformes—anchovies, herring, sardines, shad. Soft fin rays; low pectorals; abdominal pelvics; deeply forked tail; silvery body flattened from side to side; travel in large schools; mostly salt water.

Order Mormyriformes—Mormyrids. Soft fin rays; low pectorals; abdominal pelvics; many have long snout; electricity-producing organs; fresh water.

Order Osteoglossiformes—bony tongues, fresh-water butterfly fish, mooneyes. Soft fin rays; low pectorals; abdominal pelvics; many have large scales and rounded tail fins; extremely varied body forms; fresh water.

Order Salmoniformes—dragonfish, mudminnows, pike, salmon, viperfish. Soft fin rays; salmon have a second, *adipose* (fatty and rayless) dorsal fin; most have low pectorals; abdominal pelvics; salt and fresh water.

Order Myctophiformes—lantern fish, lizard fish. Soft fin rays; many species have a second, adipose dorsal; fairly low pectorals; abdominal pelvics; many have light-producing organs; mostly deep salt water.

Order Cypriniformes—characins, gymnotid eels, loaches, minnows, suckers. Soft fin rays; most characins have a second, adipose dorsal; most species have low pectorals, abdominal pelvics; air bladder connected to inner ear by series of bones called *Weberian apparatus*; extremely varied body forms; fresh water.

Blue Shark
(Squaliformes)

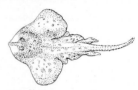

Little Skate
(Rajiformes)

Australian Lungfish
(Dipteriformes)

Sturgeon
(Acipenseriformes)

Longnose Gar
(Semionotiformes)

Bonefish
(Elopiformes)

American Eel
(Anguilliformes)

American Shad
(Clupeiformes)

Mormyrid
(Mormyriformes)

This table lists the major groups down through orders into which fish are classified. The groups are arranged according to their probable evolutionary development. One or more representative families are listed after the name of each order, along with important characteristics of the fish in the order. The table lists 41 orders. But some ichthyologists list fewer than 41, and others list more. Ichthyologists also disagree on the names of some orders, the way the orders should be arranged, and the species included in each.

SUPERCLASS GNATHOSTOMATA (continued)

Order Siluriformes—catfish. Soft fin rays, but some species have dorsal and pectoral spines; some have a second, adipose dorsal; low pectorals; abdominal pelvics; most scaleless; all have Weberian apparatus and barbels; mostly fresh water.

Blue Catfish
(Siluriformes)

Order Gonorhynchiformes—sandfish. Soft fin rays; low pectorals; pelvics behind abdomen; slender body; beaked snout; primitive Weberian apparatus; salt water.

Order Percopsiformes—cave fish, pirate perch, trout perch. Soft fin rays except for a few spiny rays in pirate perch and trout perch; trout perch have a second, adipose dorsal; low pectorals; pelvics far forward but lacking in most cave fish; large lateral line canals in head; fresh water.

Trout Perch
(Percopsiformes)

Order Batrachoidiformes—toadfish. Spiny and soft fin rays; two dorsal fins—one spiny, one soft; pectorals midway up sides; pelvics under throat; some have light-producing organs; many have poisonous spines; mostly salt water.

Order Gobiesociformes—clingfish. Soft fin rays except for single spines in pelvics; pectorals midway up sides; pelvics, under throat, form sucking disk that enables fish to cling to rocks; scaleless; small body; mostly salt water.

Order Lophiiformes—anglers, batfish, frogfish, goosefish. Spiny and soft fin rays; dorsal fin has spiny ray at front, forming dangling lure; pectorals midway up sides, forming fleshy flaps; pelvics under throat or lacking; broad, flat body; many species have light-producing organs; salt water.

Goosefish
(Lophiiformes)

Order Gadiformes—cod, eelpouts, pearlfish. Most have soft fin rays; some cod have three dorsals, two anals; high pectorals; pelvics far forward; mostly salt water.

Order Atheriniformes—flying fish, halfbeaks, killifish, needlefish, live-bearing top-minnows. Most have soft fin rays; pectorals high or midway up sides; abdominal pelvics; near surface of salt, fresh, and brackish water.

Flying Fish
(Atheriniformes)

Order Polymixiiformes—beardfish. Spiny and soft fin rays; pectorals midway up sides; pelvics under chest; forked tail; two chin whiskers; salt water.

Order Beryciformes—pinecone fish, squirrelfish. Spiny and soft fin rays; pectorals midway up sides; pelvics under chest; brilliantly colored; salt water.

Order Zeiformes—boarfish, dories. Spiny and soft fin rays; pectorals midway up sides; pelvics under chest; body extremely flattened from side to side; upturned mouth; salt water.

Order Lampridiformes—crestfish, oarfish, opahs, ribbonfish. Soft fin rays; many species have unusually long dorsal and anal fins; pectorals midway up sides; pelvics under chest or lacking; varied body forms; salt water.

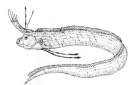

Oarfish
(Lampridiformes)

Order Gasterosteiformes—pipefish, sea horses, sticklebacks, trumpetfish. Spiny and soft fin rays; pectorals midway up sides; pelvics under chest; slender body; tubular snout; many encased in bony plates or rings; salt and fresh water.

Order Channiformes—snakeheads. Soft fin rays; low pectorals; pelvics under chest or lacking; special air-breathing organs; fresh water.

Order Scorpaeniformes—scorpionfish, sculpins. Spiny and soft fin rays; usually two dorsals—one spiny, one soft; pectorals midway up sides; pelvics under chest; cheek covered by bony plate; many have extremely sharp, poisonous spines; varied body forms; salt and fresh water.

Snakehead
(Channiformes)

Order Pegasiformes—sea moths. Spiny and soft fin rays; large, spiny, winglike pectorals high on sides; small pelvics between chest and abdomen; small body encased in bony plates and rings; extended snout; salt water.

Order Dactylopteriformes—flying gurnards. Spiny and soft fin rays; two dorsal fins—one spiny, one soft; huge, winglike pectorals midway up sides; pelvics under chest; head encased in heavy bone; salt water.

Order Synbranchiformes—swamp eels. Soft fin rays; dorsal and anal fins rayless; no pectorals; pelvics under throat or lacking; gill openings under head; special air-breathing organs; eel-shaped body; fresh and brackish water.

Order Perciformes—bass, blennies, gobies, jacks, mackerel, perch. Spiny and soft fin rays; many have two dorsal fins—one spiny, one soft; pectorals midway up sides; pelvics under chest and composed of one spine and five soft rays in most species; extremely varied body forms; largest fish order, with 8,000 to 10,000 species; salt and fresh water.

Common Jack
(Perciformes)

Order Pleuronectiformes—flounders, soles, tonguefish. Most have soft fin rays; long dorsal and anal fins; pectorals and pelvics small or lacking; flattened body; adults have both eyes on same side of head; mostly salt water.

Order Tetraodontiformes—boxfish, ocean sunfish, puffers, triggerfish. Spiny and soft fin rays; pectorals midway up sides; pelvics under chest or lacking; scaleless or covered with spines, bony plates, or hard scales; many are poisonous to eat; varied body forms; mostly salt water.

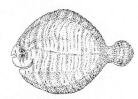

Naked Sole
(Pleuronectiformes)

FISH / *Study Aids*

Related Articles in WORLD BOOK include:

FRESH-WATER FISH

Alewife	Eel	Pickerel
Anableps	Electric Eel	Pike
Archerfish	Electric Fish	Piranha
Bass	Fighting Fish	Pupfish
Blindfish	Flame Tetra	Roach
Bowfin	Gar	Salmon
Buffalo Fish	Goldfish	Sculpin
Bullhead	Grayling	Smelt
Carp	Lamprey	Stickleback
Catfish	Lungfish	Sturgeon
Chub	Minnow	Sucker
Crappie	Muskellunge	Sunfish
Darter	Paddlefish	Trout
Drum	Perch	Whitefish

SALT-WATER FISH

Alewife	Haddock	Sardine
Amber Jack	Hagfish	Sawfish
Anchovy	Hake	Sculpin
Angelfish	Halibut	Scup
Barracuda	Herring	Sea Bat
Bass	Jewfish	Sea Horse
Blackfish	John Dory	Shad
Bluefish	Kingfish	Shark
Bonefish	Lamprey	Skate
Bonito	Lantern Fish	Smelt
Butterfish	Lumpfish	Snapper
Candlefish	Mackerel	Sole
Catfish	Marlin	Spot
Cod	Menhaden	Sprat
Coelacanth	Mullet	Stickleback
Cutlass Fish	Oarfish	Sting Ray
Doctorfish	Pilot Fish	Sturgeon
Dogfish	Pipefish	Swordfish
Dolphin	Pollack	Tarpon
Drum	Pompano	Tilefish
Eel	Porcupine Fish	Toadfish
Electric Fish	Porgy	Torpedo
Flatfish	Puffer	Trout
Flounder	Ray	Tuna
Flying Fish	Redfish	Turbot
Grouper	Remora	Wahoo
Grunion	Rosefish	Weakfish
Grunt	Sailfish	Wolf Fish
Gurnard	Salmon	

OTHER RELATED ARTICLES

Animal (pictures)	Ichthyology
Aquaculture	Instinct
Aquarium	Ocean (pictures: Life in
Conservation (picture:	the Ocean)
"Planting" Fish)	Plankton
Evolution (chart)	Prehistoric Animal
Fish and Wildlife Service	Reproduction (Sexual Re-
Fishery	production in Animals)
Fishing	Sea Serpent
Fishing Industry	Spawn
Fossil (picture: Fish	Tropical Fish
Skeleton)	

Outline

I. The Importance of Fish
  A. Food and Game Fish
  B. Other Useful Fish
  C. Harmful Fish
  D. Fish in the Balance of Nature
II. Kinds of Fish
  A. Bony Fish
  B. Sharks, Rays, and Chimaeras
  C. Lampreys and Hagfish

III. Where Fish Live
  A. Salt-Water Environments
  B. Fresh-Water Environments
  C. Fish Migrations
IV. The Bodies of Fish
  A. External Anatomy
  B. Skeleton and Muscles
  C. Systems of the Body
  D. Special Organs
V. The Senses of Fish
  A. Sight
  B. Hearing
  C. Smell and Taste
  D. Touch and the Lateral Line System
  E. Other Senses
VI. How Fish Live
  A. How Fish Get Food
  B. How Fish Swim
  C. How Fish Protect Themselves
  D. How Fish Rest
  E. How Fish Live Together
  F. How Fish Adjust to Change
VII. How Fish Reproduce
  A. Preparation for Spawning
  B. Spawning and Care of the Eggs
  C. Hatching and Care of the Young
VIII. The Development of Fish
  A. The First Fish   C. The First Modern Fish
  B. The Age of Fish
IX. A Classification of Fish

Questions

What kind of food do most fish eat?

How are lampreys and hagfish different from other fish?

What are *median fins? Paired fins? Chromatophores?*

How great a change in water temperature can most fish survive?

What are *fish farms?*

What is the name of the process by which most fish eggs are fertilized?

Which parts of the world have the most species of fresh-water fish?

What were *ostracoderms?*

How do fish turn and make other swimming maneuvers?

What are the two main groups of jawed fish? How do they differ?

Books for Young Readers

COOPER, ALLAN. *Fishes of the World.* Grosset, 1971.

FLETCHER, ALAN M. *Fishes Dangerous to Man.* Addison-Wesley, 1969. *Fishes That Travel.* 1971. *Fishes That Hide.* 1973. *Fishes and Their Young.* 1974.

NATIONAL GEOGRAPHIC SOCIETY. *Wondrous World of Fishes.* Rev. ed. The Society, 1969.

WOODS, LOREN P. *Fishes.* Follett, 1969.

ZIM, HERBERT S., and SHOEMAKER, H. H. *Fishes.* Golden Press, 1956.

Books for Older Readers

BUDKER, PAUL. *The Life of Sharks.* Rev. ed. Columbia, 1971.

GRZIMEK, BERNHARD, ed. *Grzimek's Animal Life Encyclopedia: Vol. 4, Fishes I.* Van Nostrand, 1973. *Vol. 5, Fishes II/Amphibians.* 1974.

HERALD, EARL S. *Living Fishes of the World.* Doubleday, 1961. *Fishes of North America.* 1972.

LAGLER, KARL F., and others. *Ichthyology.* Wiley, 1962.

MARSHALL, NORMAN B. *The Life of Fishes.* World Publishing Co., 1966.

NORMAN, JOHN R. *A History of Fishes.* 3rd ed. by P. H. Greenwood. Wiley, 1975.

OMMANNEY, FRANCIS D. *The Fishes.* Time Inc., 1970.

FISH is the name of a family which became prominent in American public life.

Hamilton Fish (1808-1893) was a distinguished lawyer and statesman. He was a member of the Whig Party and served as a New York representative in Congress from 1843 to 1845. He was governor of New York from 1849 to 1850, and one of New York's U.S. senators from 1851 to 1857. When the Whig Party broke up, he became a Republican. Fish served as secretary of state under President Ulysses S. Grant from 1869 to 1877. He negotiated the Treaty of Washington, which submitted the *Alabama* claims to arbitration and settled other problems with England (see ALABAMA [ship]; WASHINGTON, TREATY OF). He was born in New York City and was graduated from Columbia College.

Hamilton Fish (1849-1926), son of Hamilton Fish, was a politician and lawyer. He served as U.S. assistant treasurer from 1903 to 1908, and as a Republican representative from New York in the United States Congress from 1909 to 1911. Fish was born in Albany, N.Y.

Stuyvesant Fish (1851-1923), another son of the first Hamilton Fish, became a banker and railroad official. He started as a clerk for the Illinois Central (now Illinois Central Gulf) Railroad in 1871 and served as its president from 1887 to 1906. While Fish was president, the Illinois Central increased its mileage by 175 per cent and became one of the most prosperous American railroads. Fish was born in New York City and was graduated from Columbia College.

Hamilton Fish (1888-   ), son of the second Hamilton Fish, served as a Republican United States representative from New York from 1920 to 1945. He was born in Garrison, N.Y., and was graduated from Harvard University.

Hamilton Fish, Jr. (1926-   ), grandson of the second Hamilton Fish, has represented New York in the U.S. House of Representatives as a Republican since 1969. He was born in Washington, D.C. He graduated from Harvard University and earned a law degree at New York University School of Law.   NELSON M. BLAKE

FISH AND CHIPS. See ENGLAND (Food and Drink).

FISH AND WILDLIFE SERVICE is an agency of the United States government that helps protect the nation's birds, mammals, fish, and other wildlife. It operates more than 350 wildlife refuges and several research centers.

The service surveys waterfowl breeding grounds to help the states establish hunting regulations. It controls the breeding of various kinds of fish and manages about 100 hatcheries that maintain the supply of fish in inland waters. The agency works to enforce the Endangered Species Conservation Act of 1969 and regulates the importation of foreign species of animals. It also cooperates with other groups devoted to protecting wildlife.

The Fish and Wildlife Service provides funds to the states and territories for wildlife conservation. It also publishes booklets on wildlife. The agency was established in 1940 as part of the Department of the Interior.

Critically reviewed by the FISH AND WILDLIFE SERVICE

See also BIRD (Birdbanding).

FISH COMMUNITY. See FISH (Fish in the Balance of Nature).

FISH FARM. See FISH (Food and Game Fish).

FISH HAWK. See OSPREY.

FISH LADDER. See SALMON (The Life of a Salmon); NEW BRUNSWICK (picture: Fish Ladder); OREGON (Places to Visit [Bonneville Dam]; picture).

FISH NET. See NET.

FISHER. See MARTEN.

FISHER, BUD. See COMICS (History).

FISHER, CARL. See LINCOLN HIGHWAY.

FISHER, DOROTHY CANFIELD (1879-1958), an American novelist, became noted for her stories about the problems of normal married couples and of children. *The Deepening Stream* is perhaps her best novel, and she also published such short stories as "Portrait of a Philosopher," essays on education and literature, plays, and books for children. She also translated Giovanni Papini's *Life of Christ*.

She was born in Lawrence, Kans., and was graduated from Ohio State University. She received her Ph.D. degree from Columbia University.   HARRY H. CLARK

FISHER, IRVING (1867-1947), was an American mathematical economist and monetary reformer. He believed that booms and depressions were caused by unstable prices.

Fisher advocated monetary reforms in order to stabilize the value of the dollar. His remedies included changing the gold content of the dollar and limiting the expansion of bank credit. He pioneered in making index numbers for measuring changes in production and the cost of living. He believed economics should be a mathematical science.

Fisher was born in Saugerties, N.Y. He was graduated from Yale University, and was a professor there from 1898 to 1935.   DUDLEY DILLARD

FISHER, SAINT JOHN (1469?-1535), was the Roman Catholic bishop of Rochester, England, who was beheaded for saying that King Henry VIII was not the supreme head of the Catholic Church in England. He was born in Beverley, Yorkshire, and received his education at Cambridge University. Later, he founded St. John's College there. While he was awaiting death in prison, Pope Paul III made him a cardinal. His feast day is July 9.   JAMES A. CORBETT

FISHER, VARDIS (1895-1968), an American author, became best known for his fictional history of the Mormons, *The Children of God* (1939). His 12-volume novel series, *The Testament of Man*, traced human thought from its beginnings to the present. The first novel in this series, *Darkness and the Deep*, was published in 1943. Fisher was born in Annis, Ida. He was graduated from the University of Utah and received a Ph.D. degree from the University of Chicago.   BERNARD DUFFEY

FISHERY is an area which supplies abundant fish for commercial purposes. Species of cod, flatfish, herring, sardines, and tuna make up the world's most important fishery resources. Many governments practice *fishery management* to conserve fish. Rules limit the size and amount of fish that may be caught, and the fishing season. The United States federal and state governments operate fish-culture stations, sometimes called *fisheries*. Here fishes are grown to be placed in various bodies of water. See also FISHING INDUSTRY.

FISHES, AGE OF. See DEVONIAN PERIOD.

FISHHOOK. See FISHING (Hooks).

FISHING

FISHING is one of the most popular forms of recreation. People of all ages enjoy fishing in streams, rivers, lakes, bays, and oceans for many kinds of fish.

Some people fish with simple cane poles, but others use rods, reels, and additional equipment that requires more skill to operate. People who fish for sport are called *anglers*. They enjoy the challenge of hooking and landing fish. Many anglers try to catch certain species of fish. Some fish are especially prized for their beauty. Others are unusually strong or fast and fight hard to escape. Some species are considered crafty game that must be outwitted in order to catch them.

Some common methods of fishing include *casting*, *still fishing*, *drift fishing*, *trolling*, and *ice fishing*. Casting is one of the most popular methods. The angler casts the *lure* (artificial bait) into the water and carefully *retrieves* (gathers in) the line in an attempt to lure the fish to bite. In still fishing, the angler throws the bait into the water from a bank or anchored boat and waits for a fish to bite. When drift fishing, the angler trails the bait behind a boat, which is allowed to drift freely with the current. In trolling, the bait is trailed behind a moving boat. Ice fishing is a popular winter sport in which the angler fishes through a hole chopped in the ice.

This article discusses recreational fishing. For information on commercial fishing, see FISHING INDUSTRY.

Fishing Equipment

Manufacturers produce a wide variety of *tackle* (equipment) designed for every type of fishing. Fishing tackle includes rods, reels, lines, leaders, sinkers, floats, hooks, and bait. The choice of equipment depends chiefly on the kind of fish sought.

The two most basic fishing tools are the rod and reel. Both are available in a wide range of sizes, from those designed for freshwater *pan fish* to those made for large saltwater fish. Pan fish are small fish, such as bluegill, crappie, and yellow perch, that can fit into a frying pan. Large saltwater species include marlin, sailfish, and tuna.

Rods are tapered poles made of fiberglass, bamboo, graphite, steel, or other materials. Fiberglass and graphite rods are the most popular because they are lightweight yet strong and flexible.

All fishing rods have a handle, shaft, *reel seat*, and *guides*. The reel seat is the area on the rod where the reel is attached. On some rods, the reel is fastened below the handle, and on others it is above the handle. Guides are attachments along the shaft of the rod through which the line is strung. Some rods consist of two or more sections joined by *ferrules* (sockets and plugs) that enable them to be taken apart and carried easily.

Rods are made in many lengths, weights, and designs. Each rod is designed for use with a particular type of reel. For example, a fly rod is used with a fly reel. Rods also vary in *action* (flexibility), ranging from limber to stiff. Rods with greater flexibility are needed to catch larger fish.

Reels are used to store, release, and retrieve fishing line. Many reels have an adjustable *drag-setting device* that controls the tension of the line on the spool. There are four basic kinds of reels: (1) spinning, (2) spin-

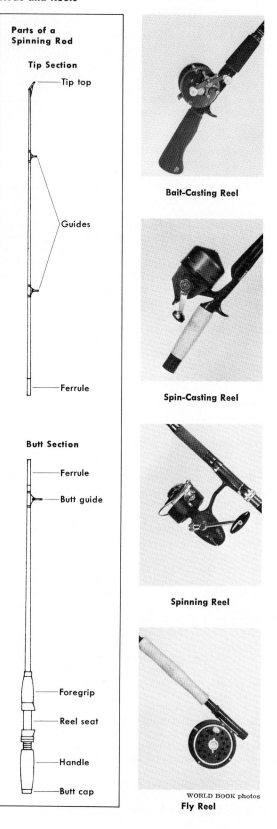

Parts of a
Spinning Rod

Tip Section

— Tip top

— Guides

— Ferrule

Butt Section

— Ferrule

— Butt guide

— Foregrip

— Reel seat

— Handle

— Butt cap

Bait-Casting Reel

Spin-Casting Reel

Spinning Reel

WORLD BOOK photos
Fly Reel

Some Basic Types of Lures

A Popping Plug floats on top of the water. When the rod is jerked, the plug's hollowed mouth goes underwater and makes popping sounds that attract fish.

A Spinner has a metal blade that spins as it is drawn through the water. Spinners attract fish by their motion, vibration, and bright flashing colors.

Flies are made of feathers, hair, or other materials. They may be wet or dry. A wet fly, *left*, sinks below the surface of the water. A dry fly, *right*, floats on the surface.

A Floating and Diving Plug floats on the surface of the water until the line is *retrieved* (gathered in). The plug then dives below the surface.

A Plastic Worm can be made to slide or hop along the bottom of the water by slowly retrieving the line. It does not catch on weeds as easily as other lures.

A Streamer Fly has a long wing made of feathers or hair. It is designed to imitate a small bait fish. Most streamer flies sink below the surface.

A Deep Diver Plug dives quickly while the line is being retrieved. It may dive to a depth of 10 to 20 feet (3 to 6 meters) or more.

A Jig sinks quickly after hitting the water. As the rod is jerked, a jig attracts fish by making short, rapid hops along the bottom of the water.

WORLD BOOK illustrations by James Teason

A Spoon flutters or wobbles when pulled through the water. The action of this type of lure is designed to imitate that of a wounded bait fish.

casting, (3) bait-casting, and (4) fly. Each is manufactured in various sizes and designs. Spinning and spin-casting reels are the easiest to use and the most popular.

Spinning Reels have an open-faced spool mounted on the reel seat in a vertical position parallel to the rod. The spool does not turn when the line is cast or retrieved. When cast, the line simply slips off the open end of the spool. Spinning reels have a handle for gathering in line. A device called a *bail* winds the line around the spool. The spool moves in and out of its frame so that the line is wound evenly. The spool itself turns only when a fish pulls on the line against the drag setting.

Spin-Casting Reels resemble spinning reels, but the spool is enclosed within a hood or cap. The line passes through a hole in the center of the cap. Most spin-casting reels are operated by a push button that releases the line for casting. They have a handle for gathering in the line. A device built into the hood winds the line on the spool and keeps it from tangling.

Bait-Casting Reels have a wide spool that lies horizontally across the reel seat. The reel has a handle that turns to release and retrieve line. For each turn of the reel handle, the spool revolves several turns. Some bait-casting reels have a device called a *level wind* that guides the line evenly on the spool.

Fly Reels serve chiefly to store line and to feed line to a hooked fish. A fly reel is not designed to cast line. In fly casting, the line is pulled off the reel by hand and cast into the water with the rod.

There are two basic types of fly reels, *single-action* and *automatic*. A single-action fly reel has a handle that turns to gather in the line. An automatic fly reel has a spring mechanism that draws in the line at the push of a lever or trigger. Fly reels and rods are especially popular for trout fishing.

Lines may consist of natural fibers, such as linen or silk; or synthetic fibers, such as nylon or Dacron. Some lines are made of many fibers braided or twisted together. Others consist of *monofilaments*, which are single strands of fiber.

Monofilament lines are widely used on spinning, spin-casting, and bait-casting reels. These lines are sturdy and lightweight. Braided lines are often used with fly reels. These lines are heavier than monofilament lines. Their extra weight plays an important part in fly casting because it helps carry the line smoothly through the air.

All lines are made in a variety of thicknesses and lengths. Lines are also rated in *pounds test*, which is the weight they can lift without breaking. They range from $\frac{1}{4}$ pound (0.1 kilogram) test to 100 pounds (45 kilograms) test. The weight and strength of the line used depends on the size of the rod and reel and the kind of fish sought.

Leaders are lengths of line made of a synthetic or metal material. A leader is connected to the end of a line and attached to a hook. Synthetic monofilament leaders are used with braided lines because they provide a less visible link between the line and the hook. Fish cannot see these leaders as well as they can see a braided line. Metal leaders are used when casting for sharp-toothed or rough-scaled fish that may break a line. Leaders range in length from 12 inches (30 centimeters) to 12 feet (3.7 meters) or longer. A leader may be attached to a line with a device called a *swivel*. A swivel allows the leader to rotate freely and thus prevents twisting of the line and leader.

FISHING

Sinkers are lead weights that are attached to lines or leaders. They lower the bait and hold it in the water. An angler selects a sinker that is just heavy enough to hold the bait at the desired depth. Sinkers also provide extra weight on the line, enabling it to be cast farther. Sinkers are made in various styles designed for waters with rocky, muddy, or sandy bottoms. They range in weight from $\frac{1}{16}$ ounce (1.8 grams) to 3 pounds (1.4 kilograms).

Floats hold the bait suspended in the water. They are made of cork, plastic, or some other material that floats. The amount of line between the float and the bait determines the depth at which the bait is suspended.

Floats, which are also called *bobbers*, bob when a fish bites the hook, and so they may indicate a strike. Some floats attract fish by making a popping noise when the rod is jerked. Other floats can be partially filled with water to provide additional weight for casting.

Hooks are made in many sizes and hundreds of styles. The choice depends on several factors, such as the kind of tackle used and the size of fish sought. A hook made of fine wire should be used with a light rod. A heavier wire hook can be used with heavy tackle.

Bait used to catch fish may be either natural or artificial.

Natural Bait. Most freshwater and saltwater game fish feed chiefly on smaller fish. Therefore, a small live fish on a hook is one of the best kinds of natural bait. Fishes used as bait include freshwater minnows and saltwater herring, mullet, and smelt.

Fish also feed on such animals as worms, crayfish, grasshoppers, and frogs, all of which are used as live bait in freshwater fishing. Eels, clam worms, and shrimp may be used in saltwater fishing.

Many species of fish feed on dead animals as well as live ones. Such fish can be caught with *cut bait*, which consists of pieces of dead fish or other animals. Anglers also use cheese, marshmallows, fish eggs, and bread dough as bait for some freshwater fish.

Artificial Bait consists of a variety of items called *lures*. Some lures look like natural bait, and others attract fish by means of their unusual color, design, motion, or sound. Lures, unlike natural bait, can be reused and can be cast farther and harder. Basic types of lures include *flies, plugs, spinners,* and *spoons.*

Flies are lightweight lures made of feathers, hair, yarn, or other materials tied onto a hook. Flies are used mainly with fly rods in fishing for trout, salmon, bass, and a variety of pan fish. Some flies look like insects, small fish, or other natural food of fish. Others attract fish by their unusual color or appearance. There are two basic types of flies, *wet flies* and *dry flies*. Wet flies sink beneath the surface of the water. Dry flies float.

Plugs are wooden or plastic lures designed to resemble small fish, frogs, and other natural bait. There are two chief kinds of plugs, *surface plugs* and *sinking plugs*. Surface plugs float on top of the water. Some sinking plugs sink when they hit the water, and others dive to various depths while the line is being retrieved. Many plugs twirl, wobble, or make popping or gurgling sounds to attract fish.

Spinners have metal or plastic blades that whirl as

Some Popular Bait Hooks

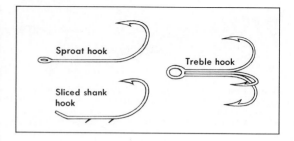

Parts of a Fishhook

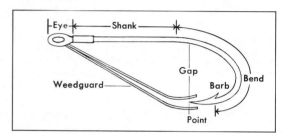

Some Fishing Tackle

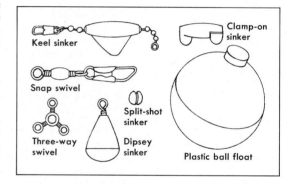

Two Basic Fishing Knots

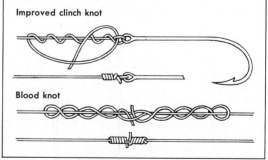

WORLD BOOK illustrations by David Cunningham

Fishing Knots are used for a variety of purposes. Two important fishing knots are the *improved clinch knot* and the *blood knot*. An improved clinch knot is used to tie lines or leaders to hooks, lures, or *swivels*. Swivels are attachments that allow a line or leader to rotate freely and thus prevent twisting of the line or leader. A blood knot is used to join two lines or two leaders together.

Five Ways to Rig a Fishing Line

The illustration below shows five of the many ways of rigging a fishing line. For fly fishing, the line may be rigged with a long leader. For bottom fishing, drift fishing, and *trolling* (fishing from a moving boat), sinkers are used to hold the bait or lure at the proper depth. In *still fishing* (fishing from a shore or anchored boat), a float may be used to suspend the bait in the water.

WORLD BOOK illustration by David Cunningham

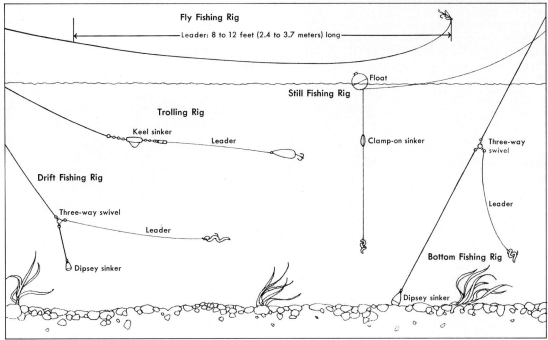

the spinner is retrieved through the water. They attract fish by their color, motion, and the sound they make. Spinners also work well in cloudy water, where fish might not notice silent lures. They may be used alone or with other lures or natural bait.

Spoons are rounded or dished-out metal lures that flutter when pulled through the water. Their action imitates that of wounded bait fish. Spoons are made in various sizes, shapes, and colors to catch different fish. A spoon that weighs only $\frac{1}{16}$ of an ounce (1.8 grams) may be used for pan fish. A spoon weighing 2 ounces (57 grams) or more may be used to catch muskie, lake trout, and a variety of saltwater fish.

Other Equipment includes nets, tackle boxes, *stringers*, *creels*, and various electronic devices. Tackle boxes hold lures, hooks, and other fishing equipment. *Stringers* are cords or chains that anglers use to hold the fish they catch. A stringer is run through the mouth of the fish, which are placed in the water to keep them fresh. Creels are canvas, rattan, or willow containers used to carry fish. Some anglers use various electronic devices that measure the depth and temperature of the water or even locate fish.

Fishing Tips

Successful fishing requires much practice and study. A person can learn only from experience how to hook and *play* (tire out) a fish properly. To catch a particular species of fish, an angler must study its habits—what it eats, the kinds of waters it lives in, and the water depth and temperature it prefers.

The habits of a fish influence the choice of bait, the

fishing technique used, and the place chosen for fishing. For example, rainbow trout thrive in cool, clear streams with swift currents. They often feed near the surface of the water, where the current brings them insects to eat. A favorite method of catching these fish is fly fishing with a dry fly, casting upstream. On the other hand, many kinds of catfish live in muddy lakes and streams near the bottom of the water. They find their food chiefly by smell or touch. Such fish may be caught by fishing near the bottom, using an odorous bait made of cheese, meat, or bread dough.

The temperature of the water influences the hunger and activity of fish. Each species prefers a certain temperature range and seeks the level of water within that range. Fish become less active when the water temperature is above or below their preferred range. Certain species may even wait until night or early dawn to feed if the water temperature near the surface is too warm. Anglers often measure the water temperature at various depths to find the level suitable for the fish they seek.

In the United States and Canada, state and provincial fishing laws regulate the times of year when certain fish can be caught and kept. These regulations, which are published by state and provincial conservation departments, also limit the number of fish that a person may catch. In addition, the departments provide information about places to fish and the best methods of catching fish in various areas.   LARRY GREEN

See the articles on the game fish mentioned in this article. See also ANGLING; FISH; SPEARFISHING.

FISHING BANKS. See GRAND BANKS.

FISHING
INDUSTRY

FISHING INDUSTRY is one of the oldest and most important activities of man. Man began to harvest the wealth of lake, sea, and stream thousands of years ago. An Egyptian tomb more than 4,000 years old contains a picture of fishermen. Today, about 5 million fishermen make their living by bringing in fish and shellfish. In the United States there are about 140,000 commercial fishermen. These men who catch fish create jobs for thousands of others in canning, packing, inspecting, and selling fish.

Fish and shellfish contain proteins, unsaturated fats, and other important food elements. As the world's population has grown, the demand for this rich source of nourishment has grown, too. In some countries, such as Japan, fish may make up a major portion of the food. The fishing industry catches over 145 billion pounds (65.8 billion kilograms) a year. This is about 38 pounds (17 kilograms) for each person in the world.

The fishing industry has grown and changed greatly since 1900. In some places men still fish by hand, as the ancient Egyptians did. But in others, great fleets range the oceans in search of fish. They use helicopters, radar, and other electronic gear to locate fish and fishing grounds. They use machines to haul in the nets. These methods have located great quantities of fish in areas where few men fished before. Fish processors are changing, too. They seek new ways of preparing food fish and new uses for parts of fish that cannot be used for food.

FISHING INDUSTRY/Where Fish Are Caught

Off the North Atlantic Coast of North America, there is a wide continental shelf which in some places extends as far as 500 miles (800 kilometers) from the shore. Large areas of this shelf rise to form underwater plateaus called *banks*. The Grand Banks off Newfoundland are part of this system of banks (see GRAND BANKS). Fishermen from Canada's eastern provinces, the U.S. Atlantic Coast, and Europe take about 10 billion pounds (4.5 billion kilograms) of fish from this area each year. They catch haddock, hake, ocean perch, cod, and herring. Canadians and New Englanders also harvest the clams, lobsters, oysters, and scallops that grow along the coast. These are not true fish, but are sea products of the fishing industry.

The fastest-growing U.S. fisheries lie off the South Atlantic and Gulf states. In 1950 they produced 17 per cent of the United States catch. By the mid-1970's, they accounted for about a third of the U.S. production. The main reason was the rapid growth in the menhaden catch. Menhaden, used to make fish oil and meal, make up about two-fifths of U.S. fish tonnage. This area also has the world's largest shrimp fisheries. Other food fish are included in the tonnage of fish caught in the area each year.

The Mississippi River, Great Lakes, and several large Canadian lakes are the major inland fisheries of North America. Inland fisheries produce about 266 million pounds (120.7 million kilograms) a year for the commercial market. Most of these freshwater fish are caught with nets or traps. The freshwater catch is about 3 per cent of the U.S. total.

Since 1940, the fishing industry of the western U.S. has dropped sharply in tonnage. In that year, fishermen from California, Oregon, Washington, and Alaska accounted for half the U.S. catch. By the mid-1970's, the same four states accounted for about three-tenths of the catch. Much of the drop was caused by the disappearance of huge numbers of sardines off the coast of California. The fall sardine run once produced 1 billion pounds (0.5 billion kilograms) a year. In the mid-1970's, the yearly sardine catch totaled about 150,000 pounds (68,000 kilograms). The herring catch off Alaska has also declined greatly since the late 1930's.

But West Coast fisheries get good returns from crab, tuna, salmon, and other products. Fishermen catch about 1¾ billion pounds (0.8 billion kilograms) of fish in Pacific waters off the United States and Canada. Further expansion and development of Pacific continental shelf and deepwater fishing is likely.

Many American fishermen now work in a growing fishery area in the Pacific off Central and South America. Some of this catch is taken through the Panama Canal to tuna canners in Puerto Rico.

Alaska and California lead all the other states in the value of sea products caught. San Pedro, Calif., is the leading U.S. port in value of fish landed. Other leading states in tonnage or value of fish landed are Florida, Louisiana, Massachusetts, and Texas.

In the mid-1970's, the total catch in the United States and off its shores was worth more than $907 million a year to the fishing industry.

The world's most heavily fished areas are the Northwest and Southeast Pacific, the Northeast Atlantic, the inland waters of Asia, and the Northwest Atlantic. Among the major world fisheries are those for anchovy and anchovetta, cod, mackerel, pollack, and sardine and pilchard. Tuna is a leading product of fisheries in Japan, California, and Taiwan. Japan accounts for about 47 per cent of the total, the United States for about 13 per cent, and Taiwan for about 8 per cent.

The newest of the major fishing grounds is in the southeastern Pacific, off South America. Vast catches of anchovetta there have made Peru a leading fishing nation. The world catch tripled between 1948 and 1973, but the catch in the southeastern Pacific increased 29 times during the same period. New fishing grounds have also been found off Angola and South Africa.

Fishermen from Canada, Great Britain, France, Portugal, Spain, and several other countries seek *ground fish* in the North Atlantic. Ground fish live on or near the bottom of the sea. Cod, hake, pollack, and flounder are included among this group.

In many parts of the world, fish are raised commercially on fish farms. Such fish provide about six per cent of the world's total fish catch. Fish farms use special breeding methods that make fish grow larger and faster than they would naturally. In some Asian and European countries, carp and other fish raised commercially are a major source of protein. In the United States, fish farmers raise catfish and trout. U.S. scientists raise various fish on an experimental basis.

Millions of Tons of Fish are taken from the seas every year. The fish serve as food and are also used in manufacturing industrial products. Canadian fishermen, *left*, haul huge nets of haddock from the North Atlantic Ocean near Newfoundland.

FISHING INDUSTRY/How Fish Are Caught

In commerical fishing, there are three basic ways of catching fish and other water creatures. These are snaring, luring, and attacking. Snaring includes the use of nets or traps. Luring employs bait to get the fish to enter a trap or bite on a hook. Attacking consists of direct attack with dredges, harpoons, or other devices.

Snaring is the most important fishing method used commercially. Snares include traps made in many shapes, from small circular hoop nets to the large Alaska *set traps* and the *pound*, or *trap*, *nets* of the Great Lakes. Traps are made of fine wire, nylon, and cotton webbing.

Nets for catching fishes are made in numerous shapes. *Drag*, or *trawl*, *nets* are huge bag-shaped nets. The trawl net called a *beam trawl* is weighted along the bottom lip and has its mouth held open by a wooden beam or metal frame across the top. The *otter trawl* is kept open by two huge doors at either side of the mouth, and by floats strung along the top edge and weights on the bottom edge. The pressure of the water against the doors of the otter trawl holds the net open. In *bottom trawling*, the trawl nets are dragged along the bottom of the sea and used to catch flounder, king crab, shrimp, sole, and other ground fishes. In *midwater trawling*, the nets are dragged along at various depths between the surface and the bottom of the water. Fishermen use this method to catch herring and other fishes that live at levels above the bottom of the water. Trawl nets are dragged by one or two boats.

Gill and *trammel nets* are designed so they entangle the fish in their meshes. The gill net floats like a curtain in the water. Its meshes allow the fish to thrust only its head into the net. When the fish tries to back out, its gills catch in the net. The trammel net is made of two or three layers of webbing, one or two of big-mesh and the other of smaller webbing. The fish strike the fine mesh and carry it through the large, forming pockets in which they are caught.

Of all the snaring techniques, the ones that provide the largest catches are the various forms of *seining*. Basically,

Dept. of Fisheries of Canada

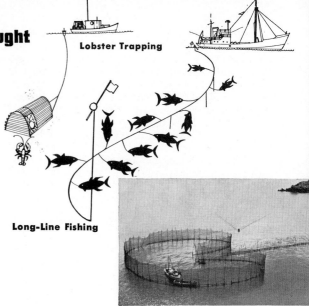

Lobster Trapping

Long-Line Fishing

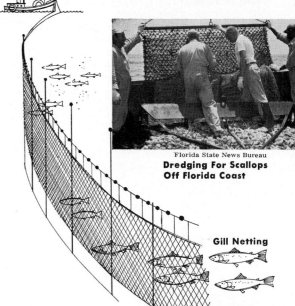

National Film Board

Trapping Sardines Off New Brunswick Coast

Florida State News Bureau

Dredging For Scallops Off Florida Coast

Gill Netting

Oyster Fishermen, *left,* gather tasty oysters in Malpeque Bay, off Prince Edward Island, Canada. They work with long wooden tongs that reach down into the shallow waters.

A Clam Jet Hose blasts clams out of the mud of Long Island Sound and sucks them up into metal baskets, *right.*

Goodyear

beach, or *drag*, *seining* makes use of a long net which is drawn in a circle around the school of fish being pursued. The net is then hauled onto the beach or a platform, pocketing the fishes in a small section or dragging them onto land inside the net. The most complex seine is the *purse seine*. It uses a line running through rings along the bottom edge to close the net and pocket the fish. Salmon, mackerel, sardines, menhaden, and tuna may be caught in this way.

The Pacific Coast purse seiners encircle a school of fish, with one boat carrying the seine. The East Coast menhaden seiners use two boats from a mother ship. Each boat carries part of the seine and together they encircle the dense schools of fish.

Luring. In *trolling*, the fishermen trail hooked, active lures attached to lines set from long poles on the boat. Lines and poles are arranged so the different lines do not tangle. Various species of tuna, salmon, and many other varieties of fish are caught in this manner. Fishermen use sails, oars, gasoline engines, or diesel engines to power their craft. *Long-line fishing* is another method of luring. It employs branch lines off a long main line, each bearing a baited hook. These are set along the ocean floor in a long, continuous string, and used to catch the hundreds of species of ground fishes. Japanese tuna long-lines may be 50 miles (80 kilometers) long.

Attacking. In commercial fishing, the attacking method is employed by swordfish fishermen and by killer ships pursuing whales. Harpoons attached to main lines or cords are shot by gun or thrown by hand. New harpoon guns use electric shocks to kill whales. When the harpoon strikes its prey, a killing charge of electricity is shot through a wire encased in a waterproofed rope attached to the harpoon.

American Can Co.

A Modern Tuna Clipper uses a diesel engine to reel in its huge net, called a *purse seine*. Many clippers carry freezers and can start to preserve tuna soon after they are caught. Tuna clippers sail the Pacific Ocean from Washington to Chile.

J. D. Williamson

Purse Seines are used to catch Alaska salmon. Fishermen also trap mackerel, menhaden, tuna, and sardines with these nets.

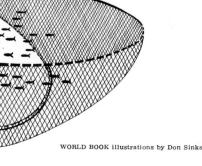

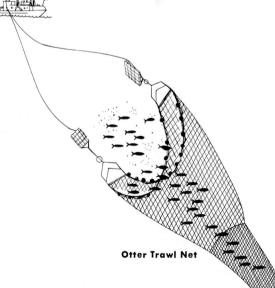

Otter Trawl Net

WORLD BOOK illustrations by Don Sinks

North American Waters attract many fishermen to the northwest Atlantic, a historic fishing ground. Europeans fished in these waters before Christopher Columbus discovered America. Today, fishermen of Asia, Europe, and North America come to the area.

Chesapeake Bay Oyster Boats

F.P.G.

ARCTIC OCEAN

CANADA
BLUE PICKEREL
CISCO
PIKE

COD
HALIBUT
SHARK

COD
COALFISH
HADDOCK
HERRING

ANCHOVY
CLAM
COD
CRAB
HALIBUT
HERRING
LOBSTER
MACKEREL
OYSTER
SABLEFISH
SALMON
SEAL
STRIPED BASS
TUNA

UNITED STATES
CARP
CATFISH
CHUB
HERRING

ANCHOVY
COD
HADDOCK
HAKE
HERRING
PERCH
SARDINE
SCALLOP
OYSTER

OYSTER
SARDINE

MEXICO
CATFISH
CARP

ANCHOVY
COD
CRAB
HADDOCK
HAKE
HALIBUT
HERRING
LOBSTER
MACKEREL
MENHADEN
OYSTER
SARDINE
TUNA
WHITING

ATLANTIC OCEAN

GROUPER
MENHADEN
RED SNAPPER
SHRIMP

ANCHOVY
FLOUNDER
HERRING
RED SNAPPER
SARDINE

BONITO
MULLET
RED SNAPPER
SEA TROUT
SHRIMP

Northwestern European Waters include primarily the North Sea. This sea, an arm of the Atlantic Ocean, lies between Great Britain and the European mainland. The North Sea is one of the richest fishing grounds in the world.

East Indian Waters include parts of both the Indian Ocean and the Pacific Ocean. They form a major world fishing area. These waters are especially important to the growing fishing industry of India, and also to Indonesia and the Philippines.

South American Waters along the west coast of South America are the world's newest fishing grounds. South America's fishing industry has grown since the early 1960's.

SOUTH AMERICA
CHARACIN
DORADO
SABALO
SILVERSIDE

BONITO
COD
HADDOCK
HAKE
MACKEREL
PILCHARD
TUNA

ANCHOVETTA
COD
HADDOCK
HAKE
HERRING
LOBSTER
MUSSEL
TUNA
WHALE

Florida Sponge Boat

Authenticated News

HEAVILY FISHED

LIGHTLY FISHED

FISHING AROUND THE WORLD

This map shows the world's most important commercial fishing areas. The different kinds of ocean fish are listed outside the continents. Freshwater fish are listed in the land areas. The tables show the leading fishing industry countries and the ocean fish and shellfish they catch.

LEADING FISHING INDUSTRY COUNTRIES

	Fish Caught in 1973	
	In short tons	In metric tons
JAPAN	11,797,000	10,701,900
RUSSIA	9,501,000	8,618,700
CHINA	8,349,000	7,574,000
NORWAY	3,279,000	2,974,500
UNITED STATES	2,943,000	2,669,900
PERU	2,535,000	2,299,300
INDIA	2,158,000	1,958,000
THAILAND	1,865,000	1,692,300
SOUTH KOREA	1,824,000	1,654,600
SPAIN	1,731,000	1,570,400

Source: *Yearbook of Fishery Statistics, 1973,* FAO.

East Asian Waters provide more fish than any other fishing ground in the world. Fishermen of China, Japan and Russia catch a large part of the world's supply of fish there. Their catch includes tuna, sardines, herring, mackerel and many kinds of shellfish.

Japanese Refrigerator Ship

HADDOCK
HAKE
HERRING
MACKEREL
OYSTER
PERCH
SARDINE
SOLE

RUSSIA
CARP
PERCH
PIKE
ROACH
STURGEON

COD
HADDOCK
HERRING
PLAICE
REDFISH

EUROPE
BREAM
EEL
PERCH
WHITEBAIT

JAPAN
CARP
EEL
UGUI MINNOW

ANCHOVY
COD
FLOUNDER
HAKE
HADDOCK
HALIBUT
HERRING
MACKEREL
SARDINE
SALMON
SAURY
SEA BREAM
SEA TROUT
SMELT
TUNA

ANCHOVY
BONITO
HERRING
MACKEREL
SHRIMP
TUNA

CHINA
CARP
MOUTHBREEDER

ANCHOVY
HERRING
JACK
MULLET
SALMON
SARDINE
SAURY
SEA BASS
SEA BREAM

SOUTH AFRICA
BASS
BLUEGILL SUNFISH
CARP
MOUTHBREEDER
PERCH
SILVERFISH
TROUT

INDIAN OCEAN

PACIFIC OCEAN

JACK
MULLET
OYSTER
SALMON
SARDINE
SEA BASS

Portuguese Sardine Boat

Island Fishing, Martinique

ANTARCTIC OCEAN

CHIEF KINDS OF OCEAN FISH AND SHELLFISH CAUGHT

	Fish Caught in 1973			Fish Caught in 1973	
	In short tons	In metric tons		In short tons	In metric tons
POLLACK	5,821,410	5,281,100	SHRIMP AND PRAWN	1,124,910	1,020,500
ANCHOVY AND ANCHOVETTA	3,771,000	3,421,000	MENHADEN	996,500	904,000
SARDINE AND PILCHARD	3,539,850	3,211,300	OYSTER	840,000	762,000
MACKEREL	3,368,330	3,055,700	SQUID	792,670	719,100
COD	3,006,330	2,727,300	SHAD	695,890	631,300
HERRING	2,750,370	2,495,100	CLAM	688,900	625,000
SMELT	2,305,700	2,091,700	HADDOCK	682,440	619,100
HAKE	2,229,530	2,022,600	REDFISH	672,960	610,500
JACK MACKEREL	1,803,050	1,635,700	SANDEEL	552,040	500,800
TUNA	1,422,530	1,290,500	SAURY	543,770	493,300

Source: *Yearbook of Fishery Statistics, 1973*, FAO.

FISHING INDUSTRY/Processing

Details vary in the canning of different species of fish but the fundamental process is the same. The fishes are prepared by grading, cleaning, and cutting for the filling machines or for hand packing. After the fishes are packed and seasoned, the air is exhausted from the cans, which are then sealed and cooked. Some oily fishes, such as sardines and tuna, are precooked before packing. Specialty products such as fish soups require more preparation. In the United States, about one-fifth of the total fish catch is canned each year.

A much smaller portion of the U.S. catch is cured. Curing includes drying, smoking, salting, and pickling fish. Methods of drying fish by blowing warm, dry air on them have replaced sun-drying in some areas.

Herring, salmon, smelt, and mackerel are fishes commonly smoked. The cleaned fish is salted, washed, and drained in preparation for smoking. It is then partially dried and hung in the smokehouse for curing.

Salting, or pickling, fish is done entirely by hand, and each producer develops his own characteristic flavor. The process consists of salting, draining, and drying.

Freezing keeps fish longer and in better condition. Quick-freezing at extremely low temperatures ensures fresh flavor and texture. In the early 1970's, about 360 million pounds (163 million kilograms) of fish a year were frozen.

Processors also make breaded fish sticks and meal-sized portions of breaded fish that are sold cooked or ready to cook. In the early 1970's, the industry produced about 325 million pounds (147 million kilograms) of such fish.

Scraps and waste from fish contain much protein. Much of this waste is processed into dried meal and concentrates that are used for animal feeds. During the early 1970's, many nations sought ways to convert fish waste into food for human beings. They worked to develop an odorless, tasteless fish protein concentrate that

Authenticated News

Smoking preserves fish and adds color and flavor. At the port of Boulogne, France, herring are salted and water-soaked, then hung on frames to dry. Smoking completes the process.

could be added to foods. Scientists believe that in time this substance can be used to enrich food in parts of the world where people lack sufficient protein in their diets.

The commercial value of fish is not limited to its use as food. Various industrial products contain fish parts or fish by-products. For example, manufacturers make shoes from the skins of sharks. Abalone shells are made into buttons. Menhaden, sardines, herrings, and sharks produce valuable oils. These oils are used in making paints and varnishes, in tanning leather, and in the manufacture of linoleum and synthetic materials.

Manufacturers use by-products of fish to make glue. In addition, a kind of gelatin called *isinglass* is made from the air bladders of certain fish. See ISINGLASS.

National Film Board

Drying fish in the sun to preserve them started in primitive times. In Newfoundland, cod are spread outdoors to dry and harden on wire frames called *flakes*.

Fin and Tail Foods, Inc.

Quick-Freezing cooked fish keeps it fresh tasting for a long time. These ocean perch fillets are entering a freezing tunnel, where they will be sprayed with liquid nitrogen.

National Film Board

Biologists Help the Fishing Industry in many ways. To study the habits of fish, scientists sometimes tag salmon before releasing them to spawn in rivers.

National Film Board

Laboratory Tests conducted by government agencies and food companies make certain that the millions of tons of fish caught each year meet all standards for marketing.

Most countries have fish conservation programs to prevent certain kinds of fish from becoming scarce. In addition, various international agencies control many of the world's major fishing areas to prevent overfishing. For example, Canada and the United States regulate halibut fishing in the Pacific Northwest through the International Pacific Halibut Commission. The area was once threatened by overfishing, and drastic restrictions were used to rebuild the stocks. Today, these grounds produce most of the world's halibut supply. Although some problems remain, scientists believe the fish catch is as large as it can be while still permitting a steady, continuing supply of fish.

The International Pacific Salmon Fisheries Commission controls the fishing of salmon in order to build up and maintain salmon runs. The International Commission for the Northwest Atlantic Fisheries, established by a 10-nation treaty, provides a similar function for the Grand Banks-New England area. The 22-nation International Whaling Commission tries to regulate the catch of whales and to protect the rarest species. The Inter-American Tropical Tuna Commission protects eastern Pacific tunas. It consists of Canada, the United States, and several Central and South American nations.

Scientific research promotes fish conservation in many ways. For example, scientists study how water pollution affects certain fish. Many fish have been killed by oil being spilled or industrial wastes being discharged into waters where fish live. Concern for fish and other marine life ranks as a major consideration in setting water pollution control standards.

Oceanographers investigate the fish populations in various parts of the oceans and determine what areas are being overfished. Marine biologists follow the movements of migratory fish in coastal areas. They also study the effects on fish of variation in ocean waters

near and away from the shore. Laws based on these studies regulate the type of boats and gear and the size of nets that can be used. Fishing seasons and other fish conservation regulations are also based on information collected by scientists.

Marine biologists conduct experiments to change the size, the rate of growth, and other qualities of fish. Such research is helpful to fish farmers, who raise commercial and sport fish. Commercially-raised fish have greatly increased the fish population in certain parts of the world, chiefly in some Asian and European countries.

Many nations have laws to protect waters off their coasts from fishing crews of other countries. For example, the United States, Canada, Russia, and many countries of Latin America bar foreigners from fishing within 200 nautical miles (370 kilometers) of their shores without a permit.

Disputes over fishing rights have sometimes led to violence. In the mid-1970's, for example, Icelandic gunboats clashed with British trawlers fishing within 200 nautical miles of Iceland's coasts. Iceland set the 200-mile limit in 1975, claiming its coastal waters were being overfished. At first, the British held that the limit was illegal. But in 1976, Britain agreed to reduce the catch its trawlers take within the 200-mile limit. In 1977, Britain and several other European countries claimed their own 200-mile limits.

The United Nations has held talks aimed at establishing uniform fishing limits for all nations. In 1976, delegates from about 150 countries generally agreed on a 200-nautical-mile *economic zone*, within which coastal countries would have control over fishing, mining, and other commercial activity. Most developing nations favored the 200-mile limit. But some countries that are landlocked or have short coastlines demanded guaranteed fishing rights within the zone.

Fishermen in Ancient Egypt fished with hand nets from reed boats called *bindings*. Scientists discovered this fishing scene in an Egyptian tomb built more than 4,000 years ago.

FISHING INDUSTRY/History

Prehistoric man fished for food. Stone Age men made hooks, lines, nets, and traps. Later, fishing grew as an industry in widely scattered places. Hundreds of years before Christ, the Chinese spun silk fishing lines. Egyptians used twine made from flax to weave strong nets. The ancient Greeks built large traps to catch tuna which traveled past the Greek shores in the Mediterranean Sea.

Bigger fish in deeper waters tempted the early fishermen to build larger boats and learn the art of seaman-

ship. As a result of this, many early nations became sea powers. Fishing has changed the course of history. Holland and Great Britain went to war in the 1600's over the herring fisheries of the North Sea. Fishermen who came to the Grand Banks helped develop the United States and Canada.

New England seamen killed so many whales during the early 1800's that the United States led the world in whaling then. The wealth that was created by whaling helped the country establish its foreign trade. The fishing industry was also important in the development of Canada. The waters off the Atlantic Coast have been fished since colonial times. Fishing towns founded in Nova Scotia and Newfoundland were among Canada's first settlements. Fishing is Canada's oldest industry.

Fishermen from Europe settled along the coasts of the United States and continued their occupation. Today, people of many nationalities contribute greatly to the U.S. fishing industry. Cubans and Greeks work as sponge fishermen in Florida. Yugoslavs and Norwegians work in the Northwest salmon and halibut fisheries. Portuguese and Italians are Atlantic Coast fishermen, and also fish for tuna off California.

After 1900, many nations turned to the fishing industry. Governments provided money for ships and equipment. Better transportation and new methods of processing widened the market for the industry's products. Probably most important, the world's increasing population needed more food. Fishermen caught more fish by using better equipment, including airplane spotters, radar, radio-telephones, and sonar. Mechanical pulleys for reeling in purse seines enabled fishermen to greatly increase catches of tuna and herringlike fishes. They searched places where few had fished before, and found new fishing grounds.

The world catch increased about 29 times from 1900 to the early 1970's. But by the mid-1970's, it had begun to decrease by about 3 billion pounds (1.4 billion kilograms) a year. China, Japan, and Russia caught more fish during this period, but Peru's catch dropped. The U.S. catch remained about the same.   RICHARD A. WADE

FISHING INDUSTRY/Study Aids

Related Articles. Many WORLD BOOK articles on countries, states, and provinces have a section on fishing industry. See, for example, JAPAN (Fishing Industry); ALABAMA (Fishing Industry). See also:

IMPORTANT FOOD FISHES

Outline

I. **Where Fish Are Caught**
II. **How Fish Are Caught**
   A. Snaring
   B. Luring
   C. Attacking
III. **Processing**
IV. **Conservation**
V. **History**

Questions

Why are fish highly valued as food?
Where are the world's most heavily fished areas?
What is a purse seine? How does it work?
What is luring?
Describe three ways of processing fish.
What are the leading nations of the world in the fishing industry?
Who protects the fishing grounds from overfishing?
How has the fishing industry changed since 1900?
What modern equipment helps fishermen find fish?

FISHING LAWS. See FISHING INDUSTRY (Conservation).

FISHWORM. See EARTHWORM.

FISK, JAMES, JR. See BLACK FRIDAY.

FISK UNIVERSITY. See UNIVERSITIES AND COLLEGES (table).

FISKE, JOHN (1842-1901), an American philosopher and historian, helped spread the theory of evolution developed by Charles Darwin and Herbert Spencer. Fiske also lectured and wrote on early American history. He wrote *Excursions of an Evolutionist, The Destiny of Man, The Beginnings of New England, The American Revolution, A History of the United States for Schools*, and more than 30 other books. He was born in Hartford, Conn., and graduated from Harvard University.   MERLE CURTI

FISKE, MINNIE MADDERN (1865-1932), was one of America's leading actresses for more than 60 years. She starred in both serious and comic parts. Among her greatest hits were the title roles in *Becky Sharp, Tess of the D'Urbervilles, Salvation Nell*, and as Nora in *A Doll's House*. She was born Mary Augusta Davey in New Orleans, and made her stage debut when she was three years old.   WILLIAM VAN LENNEP

FISSION. *Cellular fission* is a method of reproduction used by certain simple plants and animals. *Nuclear fission* is the splitting of an atom into smaller atoms.

Cellular Fission is a form of reproduction. It occurs in certain single-celled plants and animals, such as protozoa and bacteria, and in a few many-celled animals, such as those that produce coral. In *binary*, or *simple*, fission, the organism divides into two equal parts. In *multiple* fission, it divides into more than two parts.

Nuclear Fission is the splitting of the nucleus of an atom into two parts. Fission can occur when an atomic particle, such as a neutron, strikes the nucleus of an atom. The atom may split into two smaller atoms. When this occurs, atomic particles and energy are released. The fission of certain heavy atoms, such as uranium and plutonium, produces the energy for an atomic bomb. See NUCLEAR ENERGY (Nuclear Fission); FUSION; PLUTONIUM; URANIUM.

FISTULA, *FISS tyoo luh*, is a deep, sometimes twisting, passage in the body. It may lead from the deep tissues to the outside through an abnormal opening in the skin. Or it may form an abnormal connection between two deep organs. It may connect a deep organ, such as the stomach, with the surface. Sometimes a fistula drains pus from a deep abscess. Or it may connect two hollow organs such as the bladder and rectum. Fistulas may be caused by wounds or disease. They can be corrected by surgery.   JOHN B. MIALE

FITCH. See POLECAT.

FITCH, CLYDE (1865-1909), was an extremely productive and successful American playwright. His works cover a broad range and include farces, problem plays, historical plays, and plays about high society. Several of Fitch's plays are notable for their realistic presentation of familiar scenes from life in his day. Fitch served as stage manager for his plays, controlling every detail of their production. From *Beau Brummell* (1890) to *The City* (1909), Fitch wrote 60 plays. *Beau Brummell*, written for Richard Mansfield, was one of the many plays Fitch wrote for a specific star. In 1901, Fitch had four plays running in New York City at the same time: *Lovers' Lane, Captain Jinks of the Horse Marines, The Climbers*, and *Barbara Frietchie*. His other plays include *The Girl with the Green Eyes* (1902), *Her Great Match* (1905), and *The Truth* (1907). William Clyde Fitch was born in Elmira, N.Y.   RICHARD MOODY

FITCH, JOHN (1743-1798), was an American inventor and metal craftsman. He built and operated a mechanically successful steamboat 20 years before Robert Fulton's *Clermont* made its first trip on the Hudson River. Fitch had constant trouble with his financial affairs, and did not succeed in attracting enough public support to make his boats profitable. Although he was energetic and had many ideas, the steamboat age did not arrive until after his death.

In 1787, he demonstrated the first workable steamboat in the United States. The boat sailed on the Delaware River. It was propelled by six paddles on a side like an Indian canoe, but was driven by a steam engine.

Lithograph by Henry Reigart (Brown Brothers)
One of John Fitch's Earliest Steamboats sailed on the Delaware River. Philadelphia can be seen on the opposite shore.

Fitch launched a 60-foot (18-meter) boat in 1788. He launched another boat in 1790. It operated in regular passenger service from Philadelphia to Burlington, N.J., but there was not enough demand for passage to make it pay. After other disastrous attempts in this field, Fitch moved west and died in Bardstown, Ky.

Fitch was born on a farm in Windsor Township, Connecticut. After six years of schooling and trying out a number of trades, he became a successful brassworker and silversmith in Trenton, N.J. The business was wiped out by the Revolutionary War, in which Fitch served as a lieutenant. He turned his attention to the construction of a steamboat in 1785.   JOHN H. KEMBLE

See also FULTON, ROBERT; STEAMBOAT.

FITCHBURG, Mass. (pop. 43,343), lies in a valley along a branch of the Nashua River. The city is in the north-central section of the state, about 46 miles (74 kilometers) northwest of Boston (see MASSACHUSETTS [map]). Fitchburg and Leominster form a metropolitan area with 97,164 persons. Fitchburg is an industrial city and a trading center for a dairy farming and fruit orchard area. The city is the home of Fitchburg State College. It was settled in the 1740's and incorporated as a town in 1764. Fitchburg became a city in 1872. It has a mayor-council government.   WILLIAM J. REID

FITZGERALD, EDWARD (1809-1883), is known chiefly as the translator of the *Rubaiyat* of Omar Khayyam. His aim as translator was to capture the sense of the author's poetry rather than its exact meaning. Instead of a literal translation, FitzGerald created a poem of remarkable beauty in which countless readers have found strong appeal. FitzGerald was born in Suffolk, England. See also OMAR KHAYYAM; RUBAIYAT.   C. L. CLINE

FITZGERALD, ELLA (1918-   ), ranks among the best and most popular jazz singers of all time. She is known for her pure and personal tone, remarkable vocal control, ability to improvise, and flawless intonation and phrasing as an interpreter of ballads.

Ella Fitzgerald was born in Newport News, Va. She won several amateur contests as a singer before joining Chick Webb's band in 1935. She recorded her first hit, "A Tisket A Tasket," with Webb's band in 1938. Webb died in 1939, and she took over leadership of the band for two years. In 1941, Miss Fitzgerald began to work as a solo performer and with vocal groups. She gained world fame while working with the "Jazz at the Philharmonic" touring group of musicians and singers beginning in 1946.   LEONARD FEATHER

FITZGERALD, F. SCOTT (1896-1940), was the leading writer of America's *Jazz Age*, the *Roaring Twenties*, and one of its glittering heroes. The chief quality of Fitzgerald's talent was his ability to be both a leading participant in the high life he described, and a detached observer of it. Few readers saw the serious side of Fitzgerald, and he was not generally recognized as a gifted writer during his lifetime. But later readers realized that Fitzgerald's books have a theme of morality that goes beyond the "fun" the stories seem merely to record and celebrate.

Francis Scott Key Fitzgerald was born in St. Paul, Minn., on Sept. 24, 1896. He attended Princeton University, where he wrote amateur musical comedies. He left Princeton in 1917 without a degree. Years later he remarked that perhaps he should have continued writing musicals, but said, "I am too much a moralist at heart, and really want to preach at people in some acceptable form, rather than entertain them."

Fitzgerald won fame for his first novel, *This Side of Paradise* (1920). The book is an immature work, but it was the first novel to portray the pleasure-seeking generation of the Roaring Twenties. A similar novel, *The Beautiful and Damned* (1921), and two collections of short stories, *Flappers and Philosophers* (1920) and *Tales of the Jazz Age* (1922), increased Fitzgerald's popularity.

The Great Gatsby (1925) was less popular than Fitzgerald's early works, but this book was the first of three successive novels that give him lasting importance. The lively yet deeply moral novel centers around a wealthy bootlegger named Jay Gatsby, and presents a penetrating portrait of the moral empti-

Carl Van Vechten

F. Scott Fitzgerald

ness of wealthy American society during the 1920's.

Fitzgerald's next novel, *Tender Is the Night* (1934, revised edition by Malcolm Cowley, 1951), is a beautifully written account of the general decline of a few glamorous Americans in Europe. The book failed because readers during the Great Depression of the 1930's were not interested in Jazz Age "parties." Fitzgerald died before he completed *The Last Tycoon* (1941), a novel about Hollywood life.

Critics generally agree that Fitzgerald's early success damaged his personal life and marred his literary production. This success led to extravagant living and a need for large income. It probably contributed to Fitzgerald's alcoholism and the mental breakdown of his wife Zelda. The success also probably led to his physical and spiritual collapse, which he described frankly in the long essay *The Crack-Up* (1936). Fitzgerald spent his last years as a scriptwriter in Hollywood. A few years after his death, his books won him the recognition he had desired while alive.   PHILIP YOUNG

See also AMERICAN LITERATURE (The "Lost Generation"); ROARING TWENTIES (Cultural Trends).

FITZPATRICK, SIR CHARLES (1853-1942), served as chief justice of the Supreme Court of Canada from 1906 to 1918. He was the first Canadian chief justice appointed directly to that office, without serving first as a judge of the court.

Fitzpatrick was born and educated in Quebec. He gained recognition as a fine criminal lawyer and as a professor of criminal law at Laval University in Quebec. Fitzpatrick became a national figure in 1885, when he acted as chief defense counsel for Louis Riel, leader of the Northwest Rebellion of 1885 (see RIEL, LOUIS). He also served as dominion minister of justice and lieutenant governor of Quebec.   J. E. HODGETTS

FITZSIMMONS, BOB (1862-1917), held the world's heavyweight boxing championship from 1897 to 1899. Fitzsimmons also held the world's middleweight title from 1891 until he gave it up in 1897. He was the light-heavyweight champion of the world from 1903 until 1905. He gained the heavyweight title by knocking out James J. Corbett in 14 rounds. He is credited with originating the solar plexus punch in this fight (see SOLAR PLEXUS). Fitzsimmons lost the title to James J. Jeffries on a knockout in the 11th round.

Born Robert Prometheus Fitzsimmons in England, Fitzsimmons grew up in New Zealand and did his early fighting there. He moved to the United States in 1890.   LYALL SMITH

See also BOXING (picture).

FITZSIMMONS, FRANK EDWARD (1908-   ), became president of the Teamsters union, the largest labor union in the United States, in 1971. Most of the Teamsters are truckdrivers.

Fitzsimmons was born in Jeannette, Pa. He began his union career in 1937 as business agent of the Teamsters local in Detroit. In 1940, he became vice-president of the local. The international union appointed him to a vice-presidency in 1961. Fitzsimmons became acting head of the Teamsters after union president James R. Hoffa was imprisoned in 1967. Fitzsimmons succeeded as president after Hoffa resigned in June 1971. The union elected Fitzsimmons to a full term the next month. Fitzsimmons was re-elected to another five-year term in 1976.   JAMES G. SCOVILLE

FITZSIMONS, THOMAS (1741-1811), or FITZSIM-MONS, a Philadelphia businessman, was a signer of the United States Constitution. He served in the Congress of the Confederation in 1782 and 1783. As a Pennsylvania delegate to the U.S. Constitutional Convention of 1787, FitzSimons favored a strong central government. As a Federalist Party member of the House of Representatives from 1789 to 1795, he supported Alexander Hamilton's fiscal policies and favored a protective tariff. FitzSimons helped found and became a director of the Bank of North America and the Insurance Company of North America. FitzSimons was born in Ireland.   ROBERT J. TAYLOR

FIUME. See RIJEKA.

FIVE BOOKS OF MOSES. See PENTATEUCH.

FIVE CIVILIZED TRIBES is the name given to five Indian tribes by the United States Bureau of Indian Affairs after these tribes had settled in Indian Territory (now Oklahoma). The Cherokee, Chickasaw, Choctaw, Creek, and Seminole Indians received this name because they quickly adopted civilized life and customs, especially in government and education. The settlement of the Five Civilized Tribes is regarded as a necessary first step in making peace between the white man and the Southern Plains tribes.

The Seminole were once a hunting group in the Florida swamps. The other tribes formed confederations of farming villages. They occupied most of the inland country in the Southern States from the Carolinas to Mississippi. They began intermarrying with the whites at an early date, and soon adopted English ways. Many became Christians. One of the Cherokee composed an Indian alphabet (see SEQUOYA).

But the Southern States did not like these separate nations within their boundaries. By a series of treaties in the 1830's, the tribes sold their lands and moved to Indian Territory. A part of the Seminole tribe and some Cherokee, Creek, and Choctaw refused, and still live near their old homes.

The Five Civilized Tribes suffered from bad management on the move. The Cherokee speak of the trip as "the trail of tears." But, after the tribes settled in Oklahoma, each organized its own government, schools, and churches. The Civil War disorganized the tribes, but they soon developed new governments and progressed steadily. The Five Civilized Tribes' reservations in Oklahoma have been broken up. The Indians own parts of them. Most of the Indians live in communities like those of their non-Indian neighbors. A museum of the Five Civilized Tribes is in Oklahoma. WILLIAM H. GILBERT

Related Articles in WORLD BOOK include:

Alabama (History)	Choctaw Indians	Oklahoma
Cherokee Indians	Creek Indians	(History)
Chickasaw Indians	Indian Territory	Seminole Indians

FIVE-FINGER. See CINQUEFOIL.

FIVE NATIONS. See IROQUOIS INDIANS.

FIVE-YEAR PLAN is a program to increase a country's standard of living. Russia began its first Five-Year Plan in 1928. It set up economic goals to be reached in five years. The country began other plans in 1934, 1938, 1946, 1951, and 1956. In 1958, it replaced the five-year plan with a seven-year plan (1959-1965) aimed at surpassing the industrial progress of the United States. Russia stressed production in heavy industries, such as steel and coal. India and other countries have also

adopted five-year plans. See also RUSSIA (History); INDIA (Economy; History).   WILLIAM B. BALLIS

FIVEPINS. See BOWLING (Canadian Fivepins).

FIXED STAR is an expression often used in referring to the stars, because their places in the sky relative to one another do not seem to change. Actually, however, the stars are moving in many directions, and the pattern of the heavens is slowly changing.

But the changes are scarcely noticeable within a person's lifetime, because the stars are so far away and the distances between them are so great. Even Barnard's star, the one believed to move the fastest, changes position by a distance equal only to the moon's diameter in 200 years. Compared to the planets, which can be seen constantly shifting their positions in the sky, the starry background seems "fixed."

Astronomers use photography to study the motions of all the bright stars and many faint ones. In photographs taken at different times many years apart, they compare the positions of the stars and note how they have changed. Then they can tell how the *constellations* (groups of stars) will change in the future. For example, you can see in the diagram of the Big Dipper, that the opening of the cup at the present time appears to be quite a bit wider than it was 50,000 years ago. And 50,000 years from now, the opening will be so much wider that this constellation will no longer look like a dipper.   CHARLES A. FEDERER, JR.

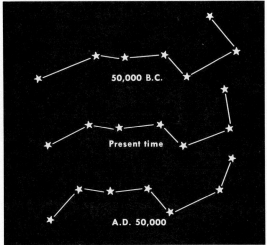

Adapted from Baker's *Introduction to Astronomy*, D. Van Nostrand Co.
Movements of the Fixed Stars in the Big Dipper

FIXTURE, in law, refers to personal property which has been affixed to houses or land. Fixtures are generally considered to become part of the property to which they are attached. Thus, when a tenant installs electric wiring, this fixture may become the property of the landlord. The courts usually try to determine the intention of the parties concerned in deciding who is the owner. But to be safe, the tenant should secure a written statement from the landlord that he agrees to the installation of the fixtures and to their removal when the lease ends.   WILLIAM TUCKER DEAN

Flag

The Flags in Front of the United Nations Building. WORLD BOOK photo

Whitney Smith, the contributor of this article, is Director of the Flag Research Center (Winchester, Mass.), editor of The Flag Bulletin, and author of The Flag Book of the United States and The Bibliography of Flags of Foreign Nations. Colors, sizes, proportions, and designs are all based on information supplied by official sources and checked by the Flag Research Center. Text information on the flags of countries, states, and provinces can be found in the separate articles in WORLD BOOK.

FLAG. A nation's flag is a stirring sight as it flies in the wind. Its bright colors and striking design stand for the country's land, its people, its government, and its ideals. A country's flag can stir people to joy, to courage, and to sacrifice. Many persons have died to protect their national flags from dishonor and disgrace. People should know how to honor their nation's flag.

There are many kinds of flags besides national ones. Some countries fly a special state flag over embassies and other government buildings at home and abroad. Presidents, kings, queens, or other government leaders have their own flags. Some flags stand for international organizations, such as the United Nations and the Red Cross. Some regional groups, such as the North Atlantic Treaty Organization (NATO) and the Council of Europe, have flags. States, provinces, and cities also have flags. Other flags represent youth groups, such as the Boy Scouts and the Girl Scouts. Still others stand for ideas, such as Christianity and peace. Some flags are even used to send messages.

The Egyptians flew the first flaglike symbols many thousands of years ago. They tied streamers to the tops of long poles. Soldiers carried these poles into battle, hoping that their gods would help them win. The people of Assyria and, later, the Greeks and Romans used symbols in the same way. Their symbols usually stood for their gods or their rulers.

Flags became important in battles. Generals watched the flags to see where their soldiers were. The flags showed which way the wind blew, and helped soldiers see the direction to aim their arrows. The flags stood for each side in a battle, and the fighting often centered around them. If the soldier carrying the flag was killed or wounded, others would "rally around the flag" to prevent the enemy from capturing it. If the flag was captured, many soldiers would give up the fight.

The symbols used in flags may go back thousands of years. The Shield of David, an ancient symbol of the Jews popularly known as the "Star of David," appears on the flag of Israel. The cross, a symbol of Christianity, is on the flags of many Christian nations. The crescent and star in the flags of many Muslim countries are symbols of peace and life. Generally, stars on flags stand for unity. The number of stars may show how many states are united in the country.

Most national flags use one or more of only seven basic colors. These colors are red, white, blue, green, yellow, black, and orange. The colors were all used in *heraldry*, a system of designs that grew up during the Middle Ages (see HERALDRY). Designs on many flags follow rules of heraldry, such as a strip of white or yellow separating two colors. The Mexican flag, with white between red and green bands, follows this rule.

Years of history lie behind the colors of many flags. Denmark is said to have used the same national flag for more than 750 years. King Valdemar the Victorious of Denmark saw a white cross in the red sky just before he won a battle. Denmark has used the white cross on red since about 1219.

Popular stories often explain why flags have certain colors. The Austrian flag supposedly dates from an event in 1191, during the Third Crusade. Duke Leopold V took off his blood-stained cloak after a battle and found that his belt had kept a band of the cloth white. From then on, he used a red flag with a white stripe across it. Austria adopted this design in 1919.

Several nations may use the same colors in their flags. Blue and white appear in the flags of five Central American countries. These nations were once joined together in the United Provinces of Central America, which had a blue and white flag (see CENTRAL AMERICA, UNITED PROVINCES OF). Four colors—black, green, red, and white—stand for Arab unity. They appear in the flags of Iraq, Jordan, Kuwait, the Sudan, the United Arab Emirates, and Yemen (Sana).

The study of the history and symbolism of flags is called *vexillology*. The name comes from the Latin word *vexillum*, meaning a square flag or banner. Soldiers of ancient Rome carried a square military flag that hung from a crossbar fastened to a staff.

The First Flags were probably carried by ancient Egyptian soldiers, *far left*. They carried long poles with streamers attached. Roman battle flags, *center, below*, identified army units. The white cross of Denmark, *right, below*, is one of the oldest national flags. It has been used for over 750 years.

flags
of the
Americas

Argentina

Bahamas

Barbados

Bolivia

Brazil

Canada

Chile

Colombia

Costa Rica

Cuba

Dominican Republic

Ecuador

El Salvador

Grenada

Guatemala

Guyana

Haiti

Honduras

Jamaica

Mexico

Nicaragua

Panama

Paraguay

Peru

Surinam

Trinidad and Tobago

United States

Uruguay

Venezuela

Albania

Andorra

Austria

Belgium

Bulgaria

Czechoslovakia

Denmark

Finland

France

Germany (East)

Germany (West)

Great Britain

Greece

Hungary

Iceland

Ireland

Italy

Liechtenstein

Luxembourg

Malta

Monaco

The Netherlands

Norway

Poland

Portugal

Romania

Russia

San Marino

Spain

Sweden

Switzerland

Vatican City

Yugoslavia

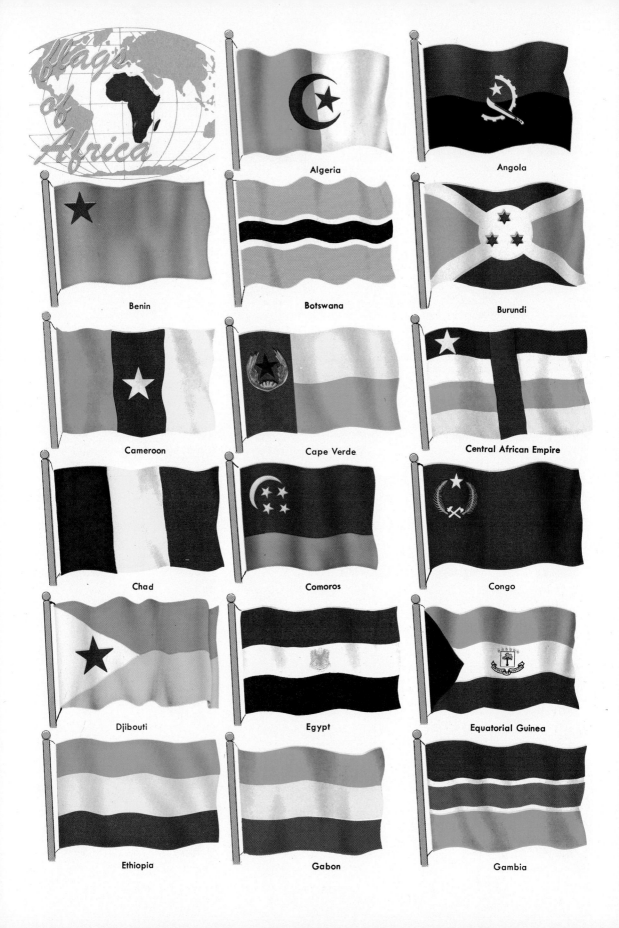

Flags of Africa

Algeria

Angola

Benin

Botswana

Burundi

Cameroon

Cape Verde

Central African Empire

Chad

Comoros

Congo

Djibouti

Egypt

Equatorial Guinea

Ethiopia

Gabon

Gambia

Ghana

Guinea

Guinea-Bissau

Ivory Coast

Kenya

Lesotho

Liberia

Libya

Madagascar

Malawi

Mali

Mauritania

Mauritius

Morocco

Mozambique

Niger

Nigeria

Rhodesia

Flags of Africa are continued on the next page.

I 77

flags
of
Africa
—continued

Rwanda

Saint Helena

São Tomé and Príncipe

Senegal

Seychelles

Sierra Leone

Somalia

South Africa

Sudan

Swaziland

Tanzania

Togo

Tunisia

Uganda

Upper Volta

Zaire

Zambia

Afghanistan

Australia

Bahrain

Bangladesh

Bhutan

Brunei

Burma

Cambodia

China

Cyprus

Fiji

Hong Kong

India

Indonesia

Iran

Flags of Asia and the Pacific are continued on the next page.

flags of Asia and the Pacific
—continued

Iraq

Israel

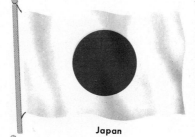

Japan

Jordan

Korea (North)

Korea (South)

Kuwait

Laos

Lebanon

Malaysia

Maldives

Mongolia

Nauru

Nepal

New Zealand

Oman

Pakistan

Papua New Guinea

Philippines

Qatar

Saudi Arabia

Singapore

Sri Lanka

Syria

Taiwan

Thailand

Tonga

Turkey

United Arab Emirates

Vietnam

Western Samoa

Yemen (Aden)

Yemen (Sana)

flags of World Organizations

The United Nations

North Atlantic Treaty Organization (NATO)

Organization of African Unity (OAU)

Council of Europe

Arab League

Olympic Games

Organization of American States

Red Cross   Red Crescent   Red Lion and Sun

Flags of the Geneva Convention are recognized symbols of mercy. The Red Cross flies in Christian countries, the Red Crescent in most Muslim ones, and the Red Lion and Sun in Iran.

historical

Roman Flags. For years, soldiers carried the *vexillum*, *left*. The emperor Constantine became a Christian in the A.D. 300's, and added *XP*, meaning Christ, to the staff of the *labarum*, *right*.

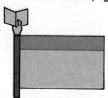

Later Roman Flags bore letters standing for the Latin *senate and people of Rome*.

Muhammad's Flag. The ornament on this later staff is a hand holding the Koran.

Early French Flags. The French Royal Banner with three fleurs-de-lis, *left*, was used from the 1300's to the 1600's. French soldiers carried the oriflamme, *right*, between 1124 and 1415.

Early English Flags. William the Conqueror's flag, *left*, first flew in England in 1066. King Richard I adopted the three lions, *right*, in 1195. They still appear on the royal standard.

Crusaders' Flags usually had plain white crosses on red, but the Knights of St. John or Knights of Malta used a Maltese cross, *left*. The Knights Templars used a black-and-white flag.

Traders' Flags. Ships from Venice flew the symbol of St. Mark, patron of the city, *left.* Merchants in northern Europe flew the flag of the Hanseatic League, *right.*

Holy Roman Empire Flag flew in what is now Germany from the 900's until 1806.

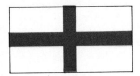

Crosses in the British Flag. The British Union Flag, *left,* combines symbols of England, Scotland, and Ireland. The cross of St. George, *above,* was a national symbol of England as early as the 1200's. The cross of St. Andrew, *above,* had long been a symbol for Scotland, and the cross of St. Patrick, *right,* for Ireland. This Union Flag first flew in Great Britain in 1801.

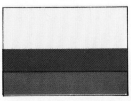

Latin-American Flags. Simón Bolívar's flag, *left,* first flew in Venezuela and Colombia in 1810. The Army of the Andes raised José de San Martín's flag, *center,* in Argentina in 1817. The flag of the United Provinces of Central America, *right,* flew from 1823 to 1840.

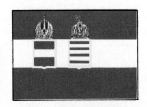

Flags of Four Empires disappeared in the early 1900's. The Chinese Empire flag, *left,* came down when the empire collapsed in 1912. The flag of the Russian Empire, *above,* was torn down during the Russian Revolution of 1917. The flags of the Austro-Hungarian Empire, *above,* and German Empire, *right,* were replaced by flags of republics at the end of World War I in 1918.

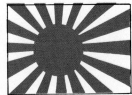

Spain's Republican Flag flew from 1931 to the end of the Spanish Civil War in 1939.

Flags Under Two Dictatorships. The Germans used the Nazi swastika from 1933 to 1945. The Japanese navy flew the rising sun with rays during World War II and readopted it in 1952.

The Viking Flag of Leif Ericson was the first flag in North America, in the 1000's.

The Spanish Flag carried by Columbus in 1492, *left*, combined the arms of Castile and Leon. Columbus' own flag, *right*, bore the initials F and Y for Ferdinand and Isabella (Ysabel).

This French Flag was one of many flown in North America between 1604 and 1763.

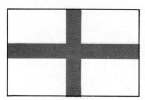

The English Flag of John Cabot, *left*, flew in Canada in 1497. The British flag, *right*, adopted in 1606, flew over the British colonies in North America, beginning with Jamestown, 1607.

Dutch East India Company flag of Henry Hudson flew in the New York area in 1609.

Russian-American Company flag was raised at Russian settlements in Alaska in 1806.

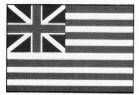

The Continental Colors served as America's first national flag from 1775 to 1777.

The Flag of 1777 had no official arrangement for the stars. The most popular design had alternating rows of 3, 2, 3, 2, and 3 stars. Another flag with 13 stars in a circle was rarely used.

The Flag of 1795 had 15 stripes, as well as 15 stars, to stand for the 15 states.

New England Flags. The Taunton Flag, *left*, was raised at Taunton, Mass., in 1774. The Bedford Flag, *above*, flown in 1775, bears the words *vince aut morire*, meaning *conquer or die*. The

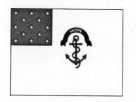

Rhode Island Flag, *above*, was carried in battle until 1781. The Bennington Flag, *right*, a variation of the original Stars and Stripes, may have flown during the Battle of Bennington in 1777.

Navy Flags. American ships in New England waters flew a liberty tree flag, *left*, in 1775. Later that year, the Continental Navy began using a striped flag with a rattlesnake design.

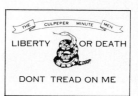

Southern Flags often had rattlesnake designs, as in the flag of Virginia's Culpeper Minutemen, 1775. William Moultrie's flag was flown by defenders of Charleston, S.C., in 1776.

flags of the United States

The *Stars and Stripes* is the most popular name for the red, white, and blue national flag of the United States. No one knows where this name came from, but we do know the origin of several other names. Francis Scott Key first called the U.S. flag the *Star-Spangled Banner* in 1814 when he wrote the poem that became the national anthem (see STAR-SPANGLED BANNER). William Driver, a sea captain from Salem, Mass., gave the name *Old Glory* to the United States flag in 1824 (see DRIVER, WILLIAM).

The Stars and Stripes stands for the land, the people, the government, and the ideals of the United States, no matter when or where it is displayed. Some other flags also stand for the United States, or its government, in certain situations. The *Navy Jack*, a blue flag with white stars, stands for the United States whenever it flies from a U.S. Navy ship. The stars, stripes, and colors of the U.S. flag appear in many federal and state flags.

First United States Flags

At the start of the Revolutionary War, Americans fought under many different flags. The first flag to represent all the colonies was the *Continental Colors*, also called the *Cambridge*, or *Grand Union*, *Flag*. This flag, on which the British flag appeared at the upper left, was the unofficial American flag from 1775 to 1777. It was also the first American flag to receive a salute from another country. On Nov. 16, 1776, the Dutch governor

Today's 50-Star United States Flag has the following dimensions: hoist (width) of flag, 1.0 unit; fly (length) of flag, 1.9; hoist of union, .5385 (7/13); fly of union, .76; width of each stripe, .0769 (1/13); and diameter of each star, .0616.

of St. Eustatius in the West Indies saluted Isaiah Robinson's ship, *Andrea Doria*.

But after the Declaration of Independence, the British flag was no longer appropriate as part of the U.S. flag. On June 14, 1777, the Continental Congress resolved that "the Flag of the united states be 13 stripes alternate red and white, and the Union be 13 stars white in a blue field representing a new constellation."

This flag received its first salute from another country on Feb. 14, 1778, when French vessels in Quiberon Bay, France, saluted John Paul Jones and his ship *Ranger*.

No one knows who designed this flag, or who made

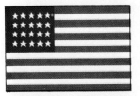 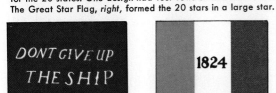  

The Flag of 1818 went back to 13 stripes, and had 20 stars for the 20 states. One design had four rows of five stars each. The Great Star Flag, *right*, formed the 20 stars in a large star.

The Flag of 1861, used in the Civil War, had stars for 34 states, including the South.

The 48-Star Flag served as the national flag the longest of any flag, from 1912 to 1959.

Perry's Flag in 1813 bore the last words of James Lawrence, a hero of the War of 1812.

Texas Flags. The Alamo Flag of 1836, *left*, bore the date of Mexico's constitution, showing loyalty to the idea of constitutional government. The Texas Navy Flag, *right*, had a lone star.

The Bear Flag flew over an independent California republic for a few months in 1846.

Confederate Flags. The Stars and Bars, *left*, adopted in 1861, had stars for 7 seceding states. It looked too much like the U.S. flag, so troops carried a battle flag, *above*. It had

stars for 11 states and for secession governments in Kentucky and Missouri, as did the flag of 1863, *above*. This looked too much like a flag of truce, so a red bar was added in 1865, *right*.

Alabama

Alaska

American Samoa

Arizona

Arkansas

California

Colorado

Connecticut

Delaware

District of Columbia

Florida

Georgia

Guam

Hawaii

Idaho

Illinois

Indiana

Iowa

Kansas

Kentucky

Louisiana

Maine

Maryland

Massachusetts

Michigan

Minnesota

Mississippi

Missouri

Montana

Nebraska

Nevada

New Hampshire

New Jersey

New Mexico

New York

North Carolina

North Dakota

Ohio

Oklahoma

Oregon

Pennsylvania

Puerto Rico

Rhode Island

South Carolina

South Dakota

Tennessee

Texas

Utah

Vermont

Virgin Islands

Virginia

Washington

West Virginia

Wisconsin

Wyoming

flags of the
United States
government

President

Vice-President

Secretary of State

Secretary of the Treasury

Secretary of Defense

Attorney General

Secretary of the Interior

Secretary of Agriculture

Secretary of Commerce

Secretary of Labor*

Secretary of Health,
Education, and Welfare

Secretary of Housing
and Urban Development

Secretary of
Transportation

Secretary of
Energy*

U.S. Air Force

flags of the armed forces

U.S. Army

U.S. Coast Guard

U.S. Marine Corps

U.S. Navy

*Secretary does not have a personal flag; flies the flag of the department.

184

flags of Cities of the United States

Baltimore

Boston

Chicago

Cleveland

Dallas

Detroit

Houston

Los Angeles

Milwaukee

New Orleans

New York

Philadelphia

Pittsburgh

Saint Louis

San Antonio

San Diego

San Francisco

Canada

Royal Union

Queen

Governor General

Armed Forces

flags of the Provinces and Territories of Canada

Alberta

British Columbia

Manitoba

New Brunswick

Newfoundland

Northwest Territories

Nova Scotia

Ontario

Prince Edward Island

Quebec

Saskatchewan

Yukon Territory

the first one. Soon after the flag was adopted, Congressman Francis Hopkinson claimed that he had designed it (see HOPKINSON, FRANCIS). In 1870, William J. Canby claimed that his grandmother, Betsy Ross, had made the first U.S. flag. Betsy Ross was a Philadelphia seamstress who made flags during the Revolutionary War. But most historians do not support the claim that she made the first U.S. flag. See ROSS, BETSY.

The Colors. The Continental Congress left no record to show why it chose red, white, and blue as the colors for the flag. But, in 1782, the Congress of the Confederation chose these same colors for the newly designed Great Seal of the United States. The resolution on the seal listed meanings for the colors. *Red* is for hardiness and courage, *white* for purity and innocence, and *blue* for vigilance, perseverance, and justice.

The Stripes in the flag stand for the thirteen original colonies. The stripes were probably adopted from the flag of the Sons of Liberty, which had five red and four

────── **THE STARS AND STRIPES FIRST FLEW...** ──────

. . . **in a Land Battle** on Aug. 16, 1777, when troops under John Stark fought in the Battle of Bennington on the New York-Vermont border.

. . . **on a U.S. Navy Ship** on Nov. 1, 1777, when John Paul Jones left Portsmouth, N.H., in the *Ranger.*

. . . **in a Foreign Port** on Dec. 1, 1777, when Jones sailed into Nantes, France, on the *Ranger.*

. . . **over Foreign Land** on Jan. 28, 1778, when John Rathbone of the sloop *Providence* captured Fort Nassau in the Bahamas.

. . . **in the Pacific Ocean** in 1784 when John Green and the *Empress of China* sailed to Macao, near Hong Kong.

. . . **around the World** from Sept. 30, 1787, to Aug. 10, 1790, on the ship *Columbia* of Boston.

. . . **over a Fort in the Eastern Hemisphere** on April 27, 1805, when U.S. Marines captured Derna, Tripoli.

. . . **over a Schoolhouse** in May, 1812, at a log school at Catamount Hill, Colrain, Mass.

. . . **in a Naval Battle in the Pacific** on March 25, 1813, when the frigate *Essex*, commanded by David Porter, captured the Peruvian cruiser *Nereyda.*

. . . **in Antarctica** in 1840 on the pilot boat *Flying Fish* of the Charles Wilkes expedition.

. . . **in a Flag Day Celebration** in 1861 throughout Connecticut. An editorial in the *Hartford Courant* suggested the state-wide observance.

. . . **at the North Pole** on April 6, 1909, when Robert E. Peary of the U.S. Navy planted it there.

. . . **on the Moon** on July 20, 1969, after U.S. astronauts Neil A. Armstrong and Edwin E. Aldrin, Jr., landed there in their Apollo 11 spacecraft.

white stripes (see SONS OF LIBERTY). The British Union Jack was added to show that the colonists did not at first seek full independence.

The Stars. The resolution passed by Congress in 1777 stated that the flag should have 13 stars. But Congress did not indicate how the stars should be arranged. The most popular arrangement showed the stars in alternating rows of three, two, three, two, and three stars. Another version had 12 stars in a circle with the 13th star in the center. A flag with 13 stars in a circle is often associated with the period. But there is little evidence that such a design was used. There is also no historical basis for assigning each star to a particular state.

Changes in the United States Flag

By 1794, two new states had joined the Union. Congress decided to add two stars and two stripes to the flag. It ordered a 15-stripe flag used after May 1, 1795. The stars appeared in five rows, three in a row. Americans carried this flag in the War of 1812.

Five more states had come into the Union by 1817. Congress did not want the flag to have 20 stars and 20 stripes, because it would be too cluttered. Samuel Chester Reid (1783-1861), a navy captain, proposed a flag of 13 stripes, with a star for each state. Congress accepted the idea, because it could then change the stars easily. On April 4, 1818, it set the number of stripes at 13 again. It ordered a new star to be added to the flag on the July 4th after a state joined the Union.

Congress still did not say how the stars should be arranged, so flagmakers used various designs. For example, the *Great Star Flag* of 1818 had its 20 stars arranged in the form of a five-pointed star. In the years that followed, various Presidents sometimes proclaimed new arrangements for the stars when a new state entered the Union. In some cases, the army and navy worked out the new designs. And, in some cases, no official action was ever taken. During the Civil War, President Abraham Lincoln refused to have the stars for southern states taken from the flag. Union troops fought under a 33-star flag for the first three months of the war, a 34-star flag until 1863, and a 35-star flag until the end of the war. No one ever decided on the design of the 46-star flag, used from 1908 to 1912. Presidential orders fixed the positions of the stars in 1912 (for 48 stars), in 1959 (for 49), and in 1960 (for 50).

★★★ *honoring a national flag* ★★★

Every person should know how to display his country's flag and how to salute it. Owning a flag and displaying it properly are marks of patriotism and respect.

Most countries agree that one national flag may not be flown above another. Some countries have additional rules. For example, when the U.S. flag is flown with other flags, all staff heights should be equal and the U.S. flag should be on its own right. There are two exceptions to this rule. (1) The United Nations flag flies above all flags at UN headquarters in New York City. (2) The church pennant flies above the U.S. flag while naval chaplains conduct services at sea.

Many countries have *flag codes*, or sets of rules for displaying and honoring national flags. The UN also has a

flag code. Some countries, such as Canada and Great Britain, do not have such codes. They simply expect their citizens to treat their flags with respect. Congress passed the first U.S. flag code in 1942. The President may proclaim changes in it. The following sections give the basic rules for honoring *any* national flag.

Displaying the Flag

A national flag is usually displayed outdoors only in good weather, between sunrise and sunset. It may be flown at night on special occasions such as parades.

Flag customs vary from one country to another. For example, the U.S. flag flies over the White House whether or not the President is in Washington, D.C.

DISPLAYING THE FLAG

The flag should be honored as a symbol of the nation it represents. These pictures illustrate points to remember in displaying the flag.

Salute the Flag at the moment it passes in a parade. Put your hand over your heart or give the military salute. **Use Bunting** for patriotic decorations, never the flag.

Marching Right. Carry the flag to the right of any other flag in a procession.

Marching in Front. If there are many other flags, carry the flag alone in front of the center of the line.

With Grouped Staffs, place the flag at the center and highest point. **With Crossed Staffs,** put the flag on its own right, its staff on top.

On a Casket, drape the flag with its canton at the head and over the left shoulder of the body. Do not lower the flag into the grave.

On an Automobile, tie the flag to the antenna or clamp the flag-staff to the right fender. Do not drape the flag over the vehicle.

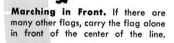
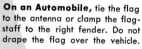

As a Color Bearer, hold the staff at a slight angle from your body. Or carry it with one hand, resting the staff on your right shoulder.

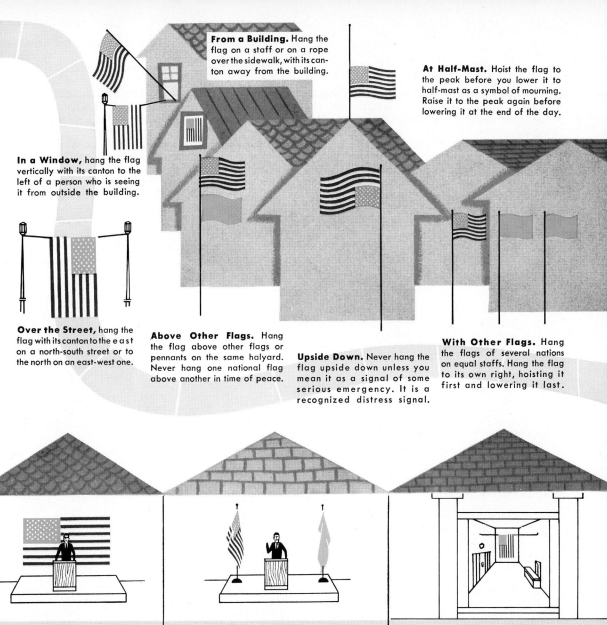

From a Building. Hang the flag on a staff or on a rope over the sidewalk, with its canton away from the building.

At Half-Mast. Hoist the flag to the peak before you lower it to half-mast as a symbol of mourning. Raise it to the peak again before lowering it at the end of the day.

In a Window, hang the flag vertically with its canton to the left of a person who is seeing it from outside the building.

Over the Street, hang the flag with its canton to the e a s t on a north-south street or to the north on an east-west one.

Above Other Flags. Hang the flag above other flags or pennants on the same halyard. Never hang one national flag above another in time of peace.

Upside Down. Never hang the flag upside down unless you mean it as a signal of some serious emergency. It is a recognized distress signal.

With Other Flags. Hang the flags of several nations on equal staffs. Hang the flag to its own right, hoisting it first and lowering it last.

Behind a Speaker, hang the flag flat against the wall. Do not gather or drape it on the rostrum. Use bunting for such decorations.

Beside a Speaker, put the flag in the position of honor on the person's right. At a religious service, the flag should go to the right of the minister, priest, or rabbi.

In a Corridor or Lobby, hang the flag vertically opposite the main entrance with its canton to the left of a person coming in the door.

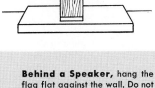

As a Color Guard, keep in a straight line, with your escorts on the outside and the flag always to the right of your organizational banner.

189

But the personal flag of the Queen of England flies only from the building she is in at the time. The U.S. flag flies over the Capitol every day. The British flag flies over the Houses of Parliament in London only when Parliament is meeting, or on holidays and special days. The same rule applies to the Canadian flag.

In the United States, the national flag should be displayed every day except when weather conditions are severe enough to damage the flag. The flag is customarily displayed from sunrise to sunset, but it is not illegal to fly the flag 24 hours a day. When flown at night, it should be spotlighted. Congress has authorized the U.S. flag to be flown day and night at Flag House Square in Baltimore, Md., and the Battle Green in Lexington, Mass. Presidential proclamation has made the same authorization for Fort McHenry in Baltimore, the Marine Corps War Memorial in Arlington, Va., U.S. Customs ports of entry, and the Washington Monument and the White House in Washington, D.C.

The U.S. flag should be flown at polling places on election days. Legal public holidays and other special days for flying it include the following:

New Year's Day, January 1
Presidential Inauguration Day, January 20 (every 4th year)
Lincoln's Birthday, February 12
Washington's Birthday, the third Monday in February
Easter Sunday, no fixed date
Mother's Day, the second Sunday in May
Armed Forces Day, the third Saturday in May
Memorial Day, the last Monday in May
Flag Day, June 14
Independence Day, July 4
Labor Day, the first Monday in September
Citizenship Day, September 17
Columbus Day, the second Monday in October
Veterans Day, November 11
Thanksgiving Day, the fourth Thursday in November
Christmas Day, December 25

In Canada, the national flag may fly from government buildings from sunrise to sunset. It also flies on holidays and special days, including the following:

New Year's Day, January 1
Good Friday, no fixed date
Easter Monday, no fixed date
Victoria Day and *the Queen's Birthday,* the Monday before May 25
Dominion Day, July 1
Labour Day, the first Monday in September
Thanksgiving Day, the second Monday in October
Remembrance Day, November 11
Christmas Day, December 25

Hanging the Flag Outdoors

When the flags of several countries are displayed, they should be flown from separate staffs of about equal size. The flags should also be about the same size. Almost every country requires that its own flag be given the position of honor among the flags. This position is to the left of observers as they face the main entrance to a building. The national flag may also be placed in the center of the group of flags, or at each end of a line of flags. At headquarters of international organizations, such as the UN, flags are flown in the alphabetical order of their country names in English.

From a Building, a national flag should be hoisted, top first, either on a staff or on a rope over the sidewalk.

Over a Street, a national flag should be suspended vertically with its top to the north on an east-west street, or to the east on a north-south street.

Hanging the Flag Indoors

A national flag should have a prominent place on a speaker's platform, but it should not be used to decorate the platform. Instead, bunting in the national colors should be used for decoration. In the United States, the red, white, and blue bunting should be arranged with the blue at the top. In the United States, the national flag must hang free, either flat against a wall or from a staff. In Canada, the national flag may be gathered up like bunting in a display.

If a national flag is displayed with another flag from crossed staffs against a wall, it should be on the observer's left. When a number of flags are grouped on staffs, the national flag should be in the center and at the highest point of the group.

When a national flag is displayed flat on a wall on a speaker's platform, it should be above and behind the speaker. When hung from a staff in a church or auditorium, the flag should be at the speaker's right. Any other flag that is displayed should be on the speaker's left.

Raising and Lowering the Flag

A national flag should be *hoisted* (run up) briskly. It is lowered slowly, and should be gathered and folded before it touches the ground. When displayed with other flags from several staffs, the national flag should be raised first and lowered last.

Breaking the Flag means unfurling it dramatically at the top of the staff. The flag is folded or rolled loosely. Before it is hoisted, the halyard is tied loosely around it. When the halyard is pulled sharply, the flag unfolds.

Striking the Flag means lowering it at sea, or taking it down in battle as a sign of surrender.

Dipping the Flag means lowering it slightly, then immediately raising it again as a salute. In Canada and Great Britain, certain flags may be *trailed* (lowered until the peaks of their staffs touch the ground), as a salute to the queen. The U.S. flag should not be dipped to any person or thing, and should never be trailed. But when a ship from a country recognized by the United States dips its flag to a U.S. Navy ship, the naval vessel returns the salute. Most other navies follow this rule.

Flying Upside Down, a national flag is traditionally a signal of distress. However, it is often displayed upside down as a political protest.

Flying at Half-Mast, halfway up the staff, a national flag is a signal of mourning. The flag should be hoisted to the top of the staff for an instant before being lowered to half-mast. It should be hoisted to the peak again before being lowered for the day or night. On Memorial Day, the flag should be displayed at half-mast until noon only, then raised to the top of the staff. By tradition, the national flag flies at half-mast only when the entire country mourns. It is not lowered to half-mast for occasions of local mourning. If local flags are flown at half-mast, the national flag may be flown at full mast with them. Citizens may salute and pledge allegiance to the flag when it flies at half-mast.

In the United States, the U.S. flag flies at half-mast (1) for 30 days after the death of the President or a former President; (2) for 10 days after the death of the Vice-President, the Chief Justice or a retired Chief Justice, or the Speaker of the House of Representatives; and (3) from the day of death until burial of an Associate Justice, a secretary of an executive department or a military department, or the governor of a state, territory, or possession. The flag also flies at half-mast in Washington, D.C., on the day of death and the following day for a U.S. senator or representative, a territorial delegate, or the resident commissioner of Puerto Rico. The U.S. flag flies at half-mast in a state from the day the governor or one of the state's U.S. senators dies until burial. The same practice is followed in (1) a congressional district for a representative, (2) a territory for a territorial governor or delegate, and (3) Puerto Rico for the governor or resident commissioner.

In Canada, the national flag flies at half-mast only on occasions of national mourning, such as the death of the sovereign. The flag on the Parliament Buildings in Ottawa is lowered to half-mast on certain occasions. They include the day of the funeral of a member of the Senate, the House of Commons, or the Privy Council.

Carrying the Flag

A national flag should always be held aloft and free, never flat or horizontal. The person who carries the flag is called the *colorbearer.*

A Color Guard, in military and patriotic organizations, usually includes the colorbearer, two escorts, and a bearer of an organizational flag or some other flag. The colorbearer with the national flag must be on the marching right of the other colorbearer. For this reason, a color guard cannot perform an "about face." The escorts march on each side of the two bearers. Nonmilitary color guards may include only one colorbearer and two escorts. Armed escorts may accompany the U.S. flag, but usually not the Canadian flag.

When a national flag is carried into a meeting hall, everyone in the hall should stand facing the platform. The colorbearer marches to the front and faces the audience, followed by the escorts. They stand on each side as the colorbearer puts the flag into its stand.

In a Parade, when a national flag is carried with other flags, it should always be on the marching right. If there is a line of other flags, the colorbearer with the national flag marches alone in front of the center of the line.

On a Float, a national flag should be hung from a staff with its folds falling free, or it should be hung flat.

On a Car, a national flag should hang free and not drape over the car. It may be tied to the antenna or to a staff that is fixed firmly to the chassis or clamped to the right fender.

Saluting the Flag

When a national flag is raised or lowered as part of a ceremony, or when it passes by in a parade or in review, all persons present should face it and stand at attention. A man or woman in a military uniform should give a hand salute. A man not in uniform salutes by removing his hat with his right hand and holding it at his left shoulder, with his right palm inward over his heart. A man without a hat salutes by placing his right hand over his heart. A woman also salutes by placing her right hand over her heart. Women do not remove their hats to salute the flag. The flag should be saluted at the moment it passes by in a parade or in review. Citizens of other countries stand at attention, but need not salute.

U.S. citizens give the *Pledge of Allegiance* to the flag by holding the right hand over the heart. But civilians also show respect for the flag when the pledge is given by standing at attention and by men removing their hats. Persons in uniform should salute.

If the national anthem is played while the U.S. flag is displayed, everyone present should face it and salute in the same manner as when the flag is raised or lowered or passes by in a parade. If the flag is not displayed, all persons should stand and face toward the music. Persons in uniform should salute throughout the anthem. All others should stand at attention, and men should remove their hats.

Permitted and Prohibited Uses

At any funeral, a national flag may be used to cover the casket. An armed color guard may accompany the flag-draped casket of a person who served in the armed forces, but not into the church or chapel. The flag should be removed before the color guard fires a salute. It should not be lowered into the grave or allowed to touch the ground. It may be used again after the funeral.

At an unveiling of a statue or monument, a national flag should have a prominent place. But the U.S. flag should never be used as part of the covering for the monument. The Canadian flag may be used in the covering, but must be lifted off the statue.

Countries usually forbid some uses of their national flags. The United Nations flag code also lists some prohibited uses of the UN flag. A national flag should never be used for receiving, carrying, holding, or delivering anything. It should never be used as bedding, drapery, or wearing apparel, such as a costume or athletic uniform. But a flag patch may be attached to the uniform of military personnel, fire fighters, police officers, and members of patriotic organizations. A lapel flag pin should be worn on the left lapel near the heart. The national flag should not be printed on paper napkins, boxes, or other items that will be discarded. The U.S. flag should never be used for advertising purposes. It should never be marked or have anything attached to it. Advertising signs should not be fastened to the staff or halyards. Federal and state laws provide penalties for persons who use it improperly.

Caring for the Flag

A national flag should be folded carefully and put away when not in use. The U.S. flag may be given a special *military fold.* It should first be folded twice lengthwise to form a long strip. Then, starting at the stripe end, it should be given a series of triangular folds. The resulting compact triangle looks like a cocked hat. If the flag is permanently attached to its staff, it should be *furled* (wrapped around the staff). It should then be *cased* (wrapped with a cover).

A national flag may be mended, dry-cleaned, or washed. An old flag, or one with an out-of-date design, may be displayed as long as it is in a respectable condition. When it is no longer fit for display, it should be destroyed in some dignified way, preferably by burning.

National flags are in many ways the most important flags in the world. They stand for all the people in a country, just as state and city flags stand for the people in smaller areas. But there are many other kinds of flags. Some flags stand for only one person, and others for one part of the government. Some flags are used only by the armed forces, and others only at sea. Some flags are used only to send messages.

Flags of Individuals

Many rulers and important government leaders have personal flags. For example, the President and Vice-President of the United States and members of the Cabinet have special flags. The Queen of England and members of the royal family have special flags. The queen's flag, called the *Royal Standard*, is raised over a building as she enters it and lowered when she leaves. The queen also has a *personal standard* for use in the Commonwealth countries that have become republics. The governor general of Canada, as her personal representative, also has a special flag.

Many personal flags are older than national ones. They developed during the Middle Ages, and became especially important in battle. Noblemen flew banners of various sizes, depending on their rank. With the development of national unity in Europe, flags symbolizing the personal authority of a ruler became less important. National flags representing all the people developed.

Military Flags

Flags have always been important in the armed forces. Most countries have special flags for individual units. Some also have separate flags for each branch of their armed forces and for top-ranking officers.

Army Flags. Armies once went into combat carrying *battle flags*. Some of them were quite different from the national flags of the times. But soldiers now carry flags mostly for parades and ceremonies. Large units, such as regiments, have special *colors*. These flags often bear the names of the battles or campaigns where the unit served with distinction. U.S. Army units attach *battle streamers* to their flags to show where they have fought. Smaller units carry *guidons* in parades so the marching men can have something to guide on.

Navy Flags. Navy ships usually fly several flags. An ensign, displayed when a ship is at sea, is usually flown from a flagstaff at the stern or from a *gaff* (crossbar) on the mast. In peacetime, the ensign may not be displayed if the ship is out of sight of land and no other ships are nearby. In wartime, the ensign is always displayed to show the nationality of the ship.

PARTS OF A FLAG

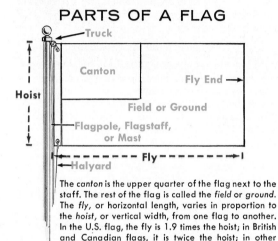

The *canton* is the upper quarter of the flag next to the staff. The rest of the flag is called the *field* or *ground*. The *fly*, or horizontal length, varies in proportion to the *hoist*, or vertical width, from one flag to another. In the U.S. flag, the fly is 1.9 times the hoist; in British and Canadian flags, it is twice the hoist; in other flags, it may be 1.5 times the hoist.

STAFF ORNAMENTS

The ornaments on flagstaffs include, *left to right*, the spread eagle, halberd, ball, flat truck, star, and colors or guidon.

THE SHAPES OF FLAGS

Flags may have many shapes, including rectangular, square, and tapering. The tapering flags include triangular ones called *pennants* and ones that end in two points called *swallowtails*. Swallowtail flags may be broad or long and narrow.

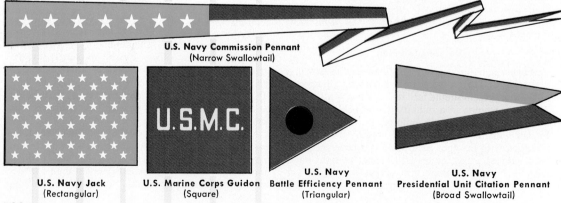

U.S. Navy Commission Pennant
(Narrow Swallowtail)

U.S. Navy Jack
(Rectangular)

U.S. Marine Corps Guidon
(Square)

U.S. Navy
Battle Efficiency Pennant
(Triangular)

U.S. Navy
Presidential Unit Citation Pennant
(Broad Swallowtail)

Badge is an emblem or design, usually on the fly.

Battle Flag is carried by armed forces on land.

Battle Streamer, attached to the flag of a military unit, names battles or campaigns where the unit served with distinction.

Bend On means to attach signal flags to a halyard.

Breadth, a measurement for flags, is 9 inches (23 centimeters) wide. A four-breadth flag is 36 inches (91 centimeters) wide. The term originated when flag cloth was made in 9-inch (23-centimeter) strips.

Bunting is cloth decorated with stripes of the national colors. The term is also used for the woolen cloth used in making flags.

Burgee is a flag or pennant that ends in a swallow-tail of two points.

Canton is the upper corner of a flag next to the staff where a special design, such as a union, appears.

Color is a special flag carried by a military unit or officer. In the armed forces of many countries, regiments and larger units often carry two colors—the national flag and a unit flag.

Courtesy Flag is the national flag of the country a merchant ship visits, hoisted as the ship enters port.

Device is an emblem or design, usually on the fly.

Ensign is a national flag flown by a naval ship. Some countries also have ensigns for other armed services.

Ensign Staff is the staff at the stern of a ship.

Field is the background color of a flag.

Fimbriation is a narrow line separating two other colors in a flag.

Flag Hoist is a group of signal flags attached to the same halyard and hoisted as a unit.

Fly is the free end of a flag, farthest from the staff. The term is also used for the horizontal length of the flag.

Garrison Flag, in the U.S. Army, flies over military posts on holidays and special days. It is 20 feet (6 meters) wide by 38 feet (12 meters) long, twice as wide and long as a post flag.

Ground is the background color of a flag.

Guidon is a small flag carried at the front or right of a military unit to guide the marchers.

Halyard is a rope used to hoist and lower a flag.

Hoist is the part of the flag closest to the staff. The term is also used for the vertical width of a flag.

House Flag is flown by a merchant ship to identify the company that owns it.

Jack is a small flag flown at the bow of a ship.

Jackstaff is the staff at the bow of a ship.

Merchant Flag is a flag flown by a merchant ship.

National Flag is the flag of a country.

Pennant is a triangular or tapering flag.

Pilot Flag is flown from a ship that wants the aid of a pilot when entering port.

Post Flag, in the U.S. Army, flies regularly over every army base. It is 10 feet (3 meters) wide by 19 feet (5.8 meters) long.

Reeve means to pull the halyard through the truck, raising or lowering a flag.

Staff is the pole a flag hangs on.

Standard is a flag around which people rally. Today, the term usually refers to the personal flag of a ruler, such as Great Britain's *Royal Standard*.

State Flag is the flag flown by the government of a country. Many state flags are the same as national flags but with the country's coat of arms added.

Storm Flag, in the U.S. Army, flies over an army base in stormy weather. It is 5 feet (1.5 meters) wide by 9 feet 6 inches (2.9 meters) long, half as wide and half as long as a post flag.

Truck is the wooden or metal block at the top of a flagpole below the *finial* (staff ornament). It includes a pulley or holes for the halyards.

Union is a design that symbolizes unity. It may appear in the canton, as the stars do in the U.S. flag. Or it may be the entire flag, as in the *Union Flag* of Great Britain.

Vexillology is the study of flag history and symbolism. The name comes from the Latin word *vexillum*, which means flag.

A FAMILY OF FLAGS

Many governments have official flags for various purposes. For example, the British have a family of flags. The Queen has two flags she can use: the Royal Standard, as queen, and her own standard, as head of the Commonwealth.

The Royal Standard
The Queen's Flag

The Queen's Standard
The Queen's Personal Flag

The Union Flag
The National Flag

The Red Ensign
Flown by Merchant Ships

The Blue Ensign
Flown by Public Servants

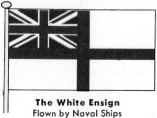

The White Ensign
Flown by Naval Ships

The Army Flag
Flown at Army Bases

The Royal Air Force Ensign
Flown at RAF Bases

When a navy ship is in port or at anchor, a small flag called the jack flies from the *jackstaff* (short flagpole at the bow), and the ensign is flown from the flagstaff at the stern. Ships of most navies fly *command flags* to show the title or command of any flag officer on board. If no officer higher than the commanding officer is on board, a flag called a *commission pennant* is flown to show that the ship is in active service.

Air Force Flags often are flown over air bases. For example, the British air force flies a pale-blue ensign with the aircraft recognition emblem used on planes in the ensign's fly. Air force units also have their own flags and guidons.

Other Government Flags

Some countries have a special *state flag* that only the government uses. It flies over government buildings, embassies, and UN headquarters. Usually, a state flag is a national flag with a coat of arms added to it. Most flags in this article are national flags. State flags are shown for Andorra, Argentina, Austria, Bolivia, Costa Rica, Ecuador, El Salvador, Equatorial Guinea, Finland, Guatemala, Haiti, Iran, Peru, Poland, San Marino, Spain, and Venezuela.

Many government agencies have their own flags. Such United States units as the Foreign Service have special flags. Many British agencies fly the Blue Ensign, usually with a badge in the fly.

Flags of the Sea

A merchant ship flies a *house flag* of the company that owns it. At the stern, it also flies the national flag of the country in which it is registered. The ships of some countries fly a *merchant flag* that differs from the national flag used on land. Canadian and U.S. ships fly their national flags, but British ships fly the Red Ensign. When a ship's captain wants a pilot to help the ship enter port, the captain may hoist a *pilot flag*. As a courtesy, ships also fly the flag of the country they visit.

Flags That Talk

Flags are often used for signaling. Sailors may use special flags to relay orders to other ships. The United States National Weather Service uses two *storm warning flags* to provide weather warnings.

Hand Signal Flags. In signaling, a person uses one *wigwag flag* to indicate the dots and dashes of the Morse Code (see MORSE CODE). A signaler uses two *semaphore flags* to spell out a message, holding them in various positions to indicate letters and numerals (see SEMAPHORE).

The International Flag Code, the most complete flag signaling system, has more than 40 flags. Each flag stands for a letter of the alphabet and pennants stand for zero and the numerals 1 through 9. To send messages, sailors fly *hoists* of one to five flags that have code meanings or spell out words.

Each ship carries a code book that explains the flags in nine languages—English, French, German, Greek, Italian, Japanese, Norwegian, Russian, and Spanish. With the code book, any captain can understand messages sent to the ship. Warships fly the *code and answering*

A U.S. Navy Signalman uses a system of signaling called *semaphore*. He holds a flag in each hand and moves his arms to spell out messages. Each arm position stands for a letter or a number.

Semaphore Flags are used to send messages between ships or between a ship and shore. Red-and-yellow flags, *left*, are used at sea, and red-and-white ones, *right*, on land.

pennant when they use the international code, so other ships will know that they are not using some type of secret code.

Sailors use certain flags from the international code for warnings or announcements. A ship that is about to sail hoists the flag for the letter *P*. Sailors once called this symbol the *blue peter*. A ship flies the *D* if it is having difficulty steering, and the *O* if it has lost someone overboard. The flags for the letters *R* and *X* together warn of a mutiny, and *P*, *Y*, and *U* wish another ship a good voyage.

THAT TALK

International Flag Code has 36 flags and pennants for letters and numerals, a code and answering pennant, *right*, and three substitutes. A signal-receiving ship raises its answering pennant to show that the hoist has been understood. The substitutes repeat letters or numerals that precede them and make it unnecessary to carry extra sets of flags and pennants. The North Atlantic Treaty Organization and other western navies use a fourth substitute.

INTERNATIONAL ALPHABET FLAGS

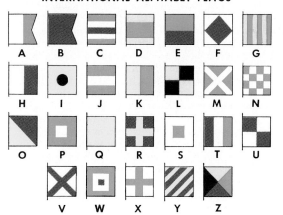

A B C D E F G

H I J K L M N

O P Q R S T U

V W X Y Z

U.S. Navy

Four Flag Hoists, or groups of flags, fly from the signal bridge of a U.S. Navy cruiser. Sailors clip the flags together to form messages. The right-hand hoist spells the word *drill*.

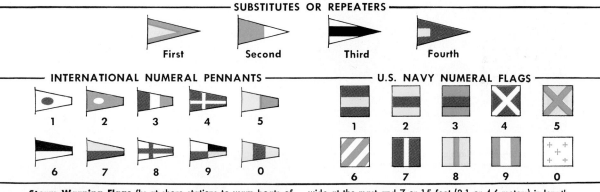

━━ SUBSTITUTES OR REPEATERS ━━

First   Second   Third   Fourth

━ INTERNATIONAL NUMERAL PENNANTS ━

1 2 3 4 5

6 7 8 9 0

━ U.S. NAVY NUMERAL FLAGS ━

1 2 3 4 5

6 7 8 9 0

Storm Warning Flags fly at shore stations to warn boats of hazardous wind and sea conditions. The red pennants for small craft and gale warnings measure 4 or 7½ feet (1.2 or 2.3 meters)

wide at the mast and 7 or 15 feet (2.1 or 4.6 meters) in length. The flags for storm and hurricane warnings are 4 or 8 feet (1.2 or 2.4 meters) square. They have a black square on a red field.

Small Craft Warning
Winds up to 38 mph (61 kph)

Gale Warning
Winds from 39 to 54 mph (63 to 87 kph)

Storm Warning
Winds from 55 to 73 mph (89 to 117 kph)

Hurricane Warning
Winds at least 74 mph (119 kph)

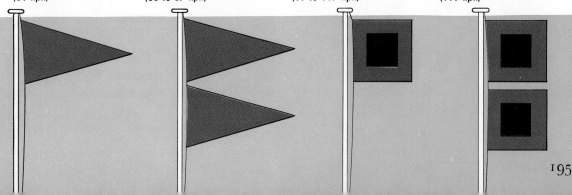

Cutting Out the Stars, a worker uses a star-shaped die. His machine cuts through many layers of cloth at a time.

Sewing the Stars in Place after they have been put on with a spot of glue, a worker attaches them to both sides at once.

Sewing the Stripes Together into long panels, workers add individual strips of the proper widths of red and white cloth.

Some governments issue specifications for the design, proportions, and colors of official flags. Many color specifications refer to the *Standard Color Card of America*, the *British Colour Council Dictionary of Colour Standards*, and other color systems. But flags are subject to variations as manufacturers standardize common colors and proportions to reduce costs.

Almost all flags are made of cloth. Most flags that fly outdoors are made with synthetic fabrics. The most commonly used fabric is a blend of nylon and wool fibers. These fabrics are light, strong, and colorfast. For many years, flagmakers used *bunting* in flags. This woolen cloth came in long strips called *breadths*, which were 9 inches (23 centimeters) wide. Most inexpensive flags are made of cotton, and the cotton fabric is sometimes also called bunting. Special ceremonial flags are made of rayon or silk. Such flags are richer looking than those made with cotton, nylon, or wool.

Sewing is the most common method of making flags. Strips of flag material are sewn together in the proper positions and sizes to create the flag. Elaborate designs, such as the complicated seals within some flags, may be painted on cloth and then *appliquéd*, or sewn, onto the background cloth of the flag. They may also be embroidered on the flag by hand. Especially complicated flags, such as Great Britain's Royal Standard, may be painted or embroidered entirely by hand.

Many flags are printed, usually on paper or plastic materials, but sometimes on cloth. Flags and pennants are often printed on cloth by the silk-screen process. A separate silk-screen stencil is used for each color in the flag (see SILK-SCREEN PRINTING).

In making a U.S. flag, workers cut stars from white cloth in the appropriate size, then attach them to the blue field of the canton with a spot of glue, just for position. The stars are then sewn permanently in place on the blue cloth. At the same time, other workers sew

Checking the Sewn Flags, other workers trim off any extra threads. At the same time, they watch for any defective flags.

Dettra Flag Company

together long strips of red and white fabric to form the stripes. Many flagmakers sew panels of six stripes for the area below the blue field and seven stripes for the area beside it, then cut the panels into the proper lengths. The blue field and panels of stripes are then sewn together. A strip of strong *heading* material is sewn along the hoist for strength. A machine punches holes at the top and bottom of the heading and inserts metal rings in them for tying the flag to the halyard.

In making small Canadian flags, workers use silk-screen printing. With the maple leaf and red stripes as a stencil, they paint the red areas on rolls of white cloth. Then they cut up the cloth into individual flags. For large flags, three pieces of cloth, two red and one white, are sewn together and the maple leaf is appliquéd on each side of the white material.

In most countries, private firms make all the flags, although some governments make their own. Annin and Company is the world's largest flagmaker. It makes millions of flags a year, including U.S. flags and flags for other countries. The company has offices in Verona, N.J., and New York City, and plants in Bloomfield and Verona, N.J. Annin produced one of the world's largest flags, a 60-by-90-foot (18-by-27-meter) Stars and Stripes for the Port Authority of New York and New Jersey. This flag hangs from the George Washington Bridge on holidays. The J. L. Hudson Company, a department store in Detroit, Mich., owns the world's largest U.S. flag. The flag is 104 feet (32 meters) wide by 235 feet (72 meters) long. WHITNEY SMITH

Related Articles in WORLD BOOK include:

Christian Flag	Hopkinson,	Ross, Betsy
Color (table: Mean-	Francis	Semaphore
ing of Color in	Jones, John Paul	Star-Spangled
Heraldry)	Key, Francis Scott	Banner
Flag Day	Navy Jack	Tricolor
Flag of Truce	Pennant	Union Jack
Flag Officer	Pledge to the Flag	Wigwagging
Heraldry		

Outline

I. Flags of the World

II. Flags of the United States

A. First United States Flags
  1. The Colors   3. The Stars
  2. The Stripes
B. Changes in the United States Flag

III. Honoring a National Flag

A. Displaying the Flag
  1. In the United States
  2. In Canada
B. Hanging the Flag Outdoors
  1. From a Building
  2. Over a Street
C. Hanging the Flag Indoors
D. Raising and Lowering the Flag
  1. Breaking the Flag   4. Flying Upside Down
  2. Striking the Flag   5. Flying at Half-Mast
  3. Dipping the Flag
E. Carrying the Flag
  1. A Color Guard   3. On a Float
  2. In a Parade   4. On a Car
F. Saluting the Flag
G. Permitted and Prohibited Uses
H. Caring for the Flag

IV. Kinds of Flags

A. Flags of Individuals
B. Military Flags
  1. Army Flags   3. Air Force Flags
  2. Navy Flags
C. Other Government Flags
D. Flags of the Sea
E. Flags That Talk
  1. Hand Signal Flags
  2. The International Flag Code

V. Manufacturing Flags

Questions

What country has used the same national flag for more than 750 years?

How does the *union* of a flag differ from the *canton?*

What do the stars stand for in the United States flag? What do the stripes stand for?

When is a national flag flown at half-mast?

Who flew the first flaglike emblems?

When are new stars added to the United States flag?

What is the *hoist* of a flag? The *fly?*

How are most flags made?

What is the meaning of *dipping* a flag? Of *striking?*

How can ship captains understand signals at sea?

Adding the Heading Strip and metal rings, workers complete a flag strong enough to fly in a high wind without tearing.

Packing the Finished Flags for shipping, workers add booklets that give the rules for displaying and honoring the flag.

Dettra Flag Company

FLAG DAY is celebrated on June 14 in memory of the day in 1777 when the Continental Congress adopted the Stars and Stripes as the official flag of the United States. Flag Day is not an official national holiday, but the President proclaims a public Flag Day observance every year. Pennsylvania celebrates Flag Day as a legal holiday.

On Flag Day, people in the United States display the flag on their homes, businesses, and public buildings. Some schools honor the flag with special programs that may feature discussions of the flag's origin and meaning. Many patriotic organizations hold parades and other Flag Day demonstrations.

Flag Day was first officially observed in 1877 to celebrate the 100th anniversary of the selection of the flag. Congress requested all public buildings to fly the flag on June 14 of that year. Some people suggested that Flag Day be observed each year. In 1885, Bernard J. Cigrand (1866-1932), a schoolteacher in Waubeka, Wis., began a lifetime fight to establish Flag Day as an annual national celebration. In 1897, the governor of New York proclaimed a Flag Day celebration for the first time as an annual event in that state. President Woodrow Wilson established Flag Day as an annual national celebration in his proclamation issued on May 30, 1916.   Elizabeth Hough Sechrist

See also Flag (First United States Flags).

FLAG OF TRUCE is a plain white flag used by opposing sides on a battlefield when they want to discuss peace terms. It is also used to arrange for a prisoner exchange or for wounded to be rescued. Both sides stop fighting while their leaders discuss terms of the truce, or temporary peace. All armies recognize the white flag of truce.   Whitney Smith, Jr.

FLAG OFFICER is the rank of the five highest officer grades in the United States Navy. These are fleet admiral, admiral, vice-admiral, rear admiral, and commodore. A flag officer usually commands a fleet or squadron. His ship flies a flag which indicates his rank. See also Rank in Armed Services.   Whitney Smith, Jr.

FLAGELLATE. See Protozoan (Kinds).

FLAGELLUM is the singular form of flagella. See Protozoan (Kinds); Bacteria (Movement).

FLAGEOLET, *FLAJ oh LET*, is a small wood-wind instrument. It is made of a wooden or metal tube with a whistle block at one end. It has four finger holes on top and two underneath. A Frenchman named Juvigny invented it in 1581. The *English flageolet* has all six holes on top. It was popular in the early 1800's. The flageolet's tone is high like a piccolo's, but softer.

FLAGG, JOSIAH. See Dentistry (History).

FLAGLER, HENRY MORRISON (1830-1913), helped organize Standard Oil Company in 1870. He was vice-president of the company until 1908. But after the early 1880's, his main business interest was in Florida. In 1886, he helped organize the railroad that became the Florida East Coast Railroad. By 1896, his railroad reached from Jacksonville to Miami. It was later extended across more than 100 miles (160 kilometers) of water and islands to Key West. Flagler built luxurious resort hotels in St. Augustine, Palm Beach, Miami, and other cities. He was born in Hopewell, N.Y. See also Miami (History).   Rembert W. Patrick

FLAGSTAD, *FLAHG staht,* **KIRSTEN** (1895-1962), a Norwegian operatic soprano, became famous as an interpreter of the heroines in the operas of Richard Wagner. Previously unknown to American audiences, her 1935 debut as Sieglinde in *Die Walküre* at the Metropolitan Opera House in New York City was a storybook triumph. Miss Flagstad also became a renowned recitalist. She helped revive interest in the songs of her countryman, Edvard Grieg. Although she retired from the operatic stage in 1952, she continued to sing in concerts and to record opera and German songs. She became director of the new Norwegian State Opera in 1958. Born in Oslo, she made her operatic debut there when she was 18.   Martial Singher

FLAGSTAFF, Ariz. (pop. 26,117), is the center of a lumbering region near the colorful San Francisco Mountains in northern Arizona. Flagstaff is the home of Northern Arizona University and the Museum of Northern Arizona. Lowell Observatory, from which astronomers discovered the planet Pluto, is in Flagstaff. Sunset Crater National Monument is nearby.

In 1876, settlers who had camped in the area made a flagstaff from a pine tree and flew the American flag from it. People believe the city's name came from this incident. A city council and mayor govern Flagstaff. It is the seat of Coconino County. For location, see Arizona (political map).   Alice B. Good

FLAHERTY, ROBERT JOSEPH (1884-1951), was an American explorer and pioneer in producing documentary motion pictures. He became noted for his treatment of the lives of primitive peoples in the silent films *Nanook of the North* (1922) and *Moana* (1926) and the sound film *Man of Aran* (1934). His short film *The Land* (1942) showed the effects of erosion, and *Louisiana Story* (1948) showed the effects of the discovery of oil in Louisiana. Flaherty was born in Iron Mountain, Mich., and grew up in Canada.   Barnard Hewitt

FLAHIFF, GEORGE BERNARD CARDINAL (1905-   ), archbishop of Winnipeg, Man., was appointed a cardinal of the Roman Catholic Church in 1969 by Pope Paul VI. He became the first Canadian cardinal named in a province west of Ontario.

Cardinal Flahiff was born in Paris, Ont. He attended the University of Toronto and universities in Strasbourg and Paris, France. He was ordained a priest in 1930. From 1954 to 1961, Flahiff served as Superior-General of the Basilian Fathers, a Canadian order. He became archbishop of Winnipeg in 1961.   Thomas P. Neill

FLAIL, *flayl,* is a hand implement used to thresh small grain crops such as wheat, barley, and oats. The flail was made up of a short stick or club fastened by a leather strip to a long wooden handle. Farmers beat the grain from the straw with this crude implement. Then they tossed the mixture of grain and straw into the air to be separated by the wind or by fanning it with a large sheet. The threshing machine and motor-operated combine took the place of the flail on most farms. But the flail is still used in some underdeveloped areas. In early days, people also used flails as weapons. The flail usually consisted of a wooden bar or ball studded with metal spikes or barbs. It was joined to a short handle by a length of chain.   A. D. Longhouse

FLAK. See Antiaircraft Defense.

FLAMBEAU RIVER. See Wisconsin (The Land; color picture: Sparkling Water).

FLAME. See FIRE.

FLAME TEST is a way of identifying a chemical element by the color it gives off when held in the flame of a Bunsen burner (see BUNSEN BURNER). The test can be made by dipping a platinum wire or piece of asbestos in a compound of the element, either powdered or in solution. Compounds of barium color the flame yellowish green. Flames of calcium are orange red. Copper gives off an emerald-green color. Lithium's flame is deep red. Sodium's flame is yellow. Strontium gives off a crimson flame. Potassium's flame is violet. An element always gives off flame of the same color.   RALPH G. OWENS

See also MINERAL (Other Identification Tests).

FLAME TETRA is a tropical fish that lives in the rivers of Brazil. The front of its body is yellow and the back is bright red. Flame tetras are about 2 inches (5 centimeters) long and make colorful aquarium fish. The flame tetra is also known as the *red tetra*.

Scientific Classification. The flame tetra belongs to the characin family, *Characidae*. It is in the genus *Hyphessobrycon*, and is species *H. flammeus*.

FLAME THROWER is a weapon of war which shoots a stream of burning fuel in much the way that a fire hose squirts water. The flame belches from the nozzle of a flame gun connected by a flexible tube to two tanks of fuel on the operator's back. A tank of compressed air between the tanks of fuel provides the pressure needed to squirt the fuel through the gun. Portable flame throwers weigh a total of about 70 pounds (32 kilograms) when they are ready to fire.

The Germans introduced flame throwers during World War I, but they were not widely used until United States soldiers used them against the Japanese in World War II. Soldiers used flame throwers against fortifications that could not be captured with rifle fire alone. Flame throwers became a weapon to be feared by the enemy. Soldiers who scoffed at rifle bullets often fled in panic at sight of the long, searing tongue of flame licking toward them. American soldiers called the flame thrower the *GI hotfoot*.

Fuel used in flame throwers during World War I was a mixture of gasoline and oil. During World War II, a jellied gasoline called *napalm* was developed (see NAPALM). By using napalm, soldiers could fire portable flame throwers 200 feet (61 meters). Flame throwers that were mounted on tanks could reach targets 750 feet (230 meters) away. When the jellied fuel hit a target, it scattered into sticky blobs. These blobs bounced through small openings into fortifications. The napalm

stuck to the target and was very difficult to extinguish.

Since the 1940's, flame throwers have served important functions in civilian life. Farmers make much use of flame throwers to burn weeds and destroy such harmful insects as tent caterpillars. Flame throwers can also break rocks and melt snow.   HAROLD C. KINNE, JR.

FLAMENCO, *flah MEHNG koh,* is a kind of dance performed mostly by the Gypsies in Andalusia, a part of southern Spain. Flamenco includes many different kinds of dances. A Gypsy performer makes up steps within the dance according to his or her mood. A guitarist usually accompanies the dancer. People often form a circle around the dancer and encourage him or her by singing, clapping, stamping, and shouting in rhythm with the music. See also SPAIN (picture).   MICHAEL HERMAN

FLAMINGO, *fluh MIHNG goh,* is a bird known for its long, stiltlike legs and curved bill and neck. Flamingos live in many parts of the world and spend their entire life near lakes, marshes, and seas.

Most flamingos stand from 3 to 5 feet (91 to 150 centimeters) tall. The color of a flamingo's feathers—except for some black wing feathers—varies from bright red to pale pink. For example, flamingos of the Caribbean area have coral-red feathers, and South American flamingos have pinkish-white feathers. Most flamingos eat shellfish and small water plants called *algae*. Hairlike "combs" along the edges of the bill strain mud and sand from the food a flamingo finds in the water. Flamingos, like ducks, have webbed feet.

Flamingos live in colonies, some of which have thousands of members. They mate once a year. Flamingos build a nest that consists of a mound of mud. Most of the females lay a single egg in a shallow hole at the top of the nest. The parents take turns sitting on the egg to keep it warm. The egg hatches after about 30 days. Young flamingos leave the nest after about 5 days and form small groups. But they return to the nest to feed on a fluid produced in the digestive system of the parents. The adults dribble this fluid from their mouth into the youngster's bill. After about two weeks, the young form larger herds and start to find their own food. Flamingos live from 15 to 20 years in their natural surroundings. They live even longer in captivity.

Most zoologists classify flamingos into four species. The *greater flamingo* lives in Africa, southern Asia and Europe, southern South America, and the West Indies.

U.S. Army

A Flame Thrower can hurl a tongue of flame 200 feet (61 meters). The operator carries two tanks of fuel and a tank of compressed air to provide the pressure needed to squirt the fuel through the gun. When ready to fire, the portable flame thrower weighs about 70 pounds (32 kilograms).

Jane Burton, Bruce Coleman Inc.

Flamingos live in marshy areas in many parts of the world. These graceful birds feed on small animals and plants that they find in muddy water.

A Young Flamingo, right, lacks the large, bent bill and pinkish color of the adults. The young first leave the nest about five days after hatching.

Jane Burton, Bruce Coleman Ltd.

The *lesser flamingo* lives in the Great Rift Valley of Kenya and Tanganyika in Africa. The other two species, the rare *Andean* and *James'* flamingos, dwell near the highland lakes of the Andes Mountains in South America. Wild flamingos once lived in southern Florida, but people killed them for their beautiful feathers faster than the birds could multiply.

Scientific Classification. Flamingos belong to the flamingo family, *Phoenicopteridae*. The greater flamingo is genus *Phoenicopterus*, species *P. ruber*.   JAMES M. DOLAN, JR.

See also BIRD (pictures: Water Birds, Bird Nests, Types of Beaks).

FLAMINIAN WAY, *fluh MIN ih un*, or VIA FLAMINIA, was an important Roman military road. It led north from Rome to Ariminum (now Rimini) on the Adriatic Sea, a distance of more than 200 miles (320 kilometers). The road was named for Caius Flaminius, a Roman leader. Flaminius started building the road in 220 B.C., as Roman armies moved northward to conquer tribes of Celts living in northern Italy.

The Aemilian Way, an extension of the road, was built in 187 B.C. It crossed the Po River to Mediolanum (now Milan).   WILLIAM P. DONOVAN

FLAMMARION, *FLAH MAH RYAWN*, **CAMILLE** (1842-1925), was one of the most imaginative and colorful writers of science books. He greatly influenced the young people of many countries, and turned their interest to astronomy. He wrote *The Wonders of Heaven* and *Dreams of an Astronomer*. He studied for the priesthood, but poverty forced him to seek work as an engraver. He turned to astronomy and in 1882 took charge of an observatory near Paris, France. There he studied the moon, Mars, and double stars. Later in life, he turned to

more controversial work on psychical research. Flammarion was born in Montigny-le-Roi, France, and lived in or near Paris. His full name was Nicolas Camille Flammarion.   HENRI PEYRE

FLAMSTEED, JOHN. See GREENWICH OBSERVATORY, ROYAL.

FLANAGAN, EDWARD JOSEPH (1886-1948), a Roman Catholic priest, founded Boys Town near Omaha, Nebr., in 1917. He opened the community to boys of all races and religions. His work there was featured in the popular motion picture *Boys Town* (1938). Many institutions similar to Boys Town were founded in the United States and Canada, but they did not all succeed.

Father Flanagan was born in Ballymoe, near Roscommon, Ireland. He came to the United States in 1904, and studied for the priesthood. He completed his studies at the Gregorian University in Rome and at the University of Innsbruck in Austria. Then he became a parish priest in O'Neill, Nebr. His first social service was with a Workingmen's Hostel in Omaha, but he became interested in the treatment of boys who were homeless or had broken the law.   ALAN KEITH-LUCAS

See also BOYS TOWN.

FLANDERS, *FLAN derz*, is a part of northern Europe which was a separate political unit until modern times. Two-thirds of Flanders now forms the provinces of East and West Flanders in northern Belgium and extends slightly into The Netherlands. The rest of Flanders is now part of France. Flanders is an area of rich soils, which are low lying and difficult to drain. The farms near the coast are protected by dikes and drained by canals. Farmers produce hops, fodder, wheat, flax, and sugar beets. Industry in Flanders produces coal and textiles.

The early products of Flanders were wool and flax for use in the manufacture of cloth. A heavy trade in wool grew up, especially with England. As a result, cities developed earlier in Flanders than in most of Europe. Flanders was the market place of the continent in the 1300's and 1400's. The great trading fairs held in Antwerp brought fame and wealth to the city. Ypres, Bruges, and Ghent also grew rich through trade.

The dense population and the wealth of Flanders led to the development of Flemish culture. This culture was marked by a concern for painting, architecture, litera-

WORLD BOOK map

Flanders Is a Historic Region in Europe.

ture, and other refinements of life which gave Flanders a leading place in early European civilization.

For many years, Flanders was ruled by a succession of powerful nobles, each of whom was known as the Count of Flanders. Napoleon made Flanders part of the French Empire. The present division of the Flanders area was made in 1830.   DANIEL H. THOMAS

See also FLEMISH LANGUAGE AND LITERATURE; GHENT; PAINTING (The Renaissance in Flanders).

FLANDERS FIELD is a United States military cemetery near Waregem, Belgium. Buried in this cemetery are the bodies of 368 members of the armed forces who died in World War I (1914-1918). Canadian poet John McCrae wrote the famous poem, "In Flanders Fields" (see McCRAE, JOHN).

FLANNEL is a woven fabric usually made of soft woolen or worsted wool fibers. Flannel may also be made of cotton or rayon. Some flannels, such as baby flannel and fine dress flannel, are delicate. Others, such as the kind that is used for heavy shirts, are thick and coarse.

Textile manufacturers list many types of flannel. Among these are *Canton, French, outing, shaker,* and *suede* flannels. Canton and French flannels have napping on the back of the fabric. Outing, shaker, and suede flannels are napped on both sides.

FLAPS. See AIRPLANE (The Wing).

FLARE. See SUN (Flares; The Sun's Brightness; Terms; The Sun's Stormy Activity).

FLASHBULB is a device that provides artificial light for taking photographs indoors and at night. Flashbulbs are also used to lighten or prevent shadows in pictures taken in bright sunlight. Most flashbulbs are manufactured in the form of *flashcubes* or *flashbars*. Each cube or bar consists of up to 10 flashbulbs. Another type of flash lighting is provided by devices called *electronic flash units*.

How a Flashbulb Works. Flashbulbs, also called *flashlamps*, are made of glass or plastic and are manufactured in many shapes and sizes. Inside the bulb are two stiff zirconium prongs that look like the antennae of an insect. The prongs make up a device called a *primer*, which extends from the base to the center of the bulb. A fine wire filament made of tungsten spans the two prongs and curls around the inside of the bulb.

Cameras contain batteries or small generators that produce electric current. The current travels through the bulb's primer and ignites the filament, creating the flash. The duration and intensity of the flash vary, depending on the amount of filament in the bulb. Flashbulbs are filled with oxygen to make the flash bright. The flash creates heat and a small explosive force. A lacquer coating on the inside and outside of the bulb absorbs the heat and prevents the bulb from shattering.

A device inside the camera triggers the flash at the moment that the shutter is open to its widest point. Most flashbulbs provide a usable light intensity for 15 to 20 thousandths of a second. Small bulbs used with simple cameras can light subjects that are 4 to 10 feet from the camera.

A flashcube is a plastic cube that contains 4 individual bulbs. A reflector stands behind each bulb and directs the light toward the subject. In many cameras, the cube rotates automatically after each exposure.

A flashbar is a flat, rectangular device that contains

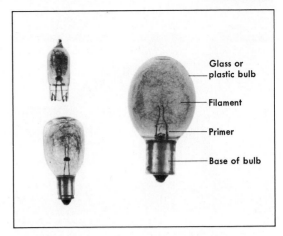

Flashbulbs are made in many shapes and sizes. An electric current from a camera travels through the primer of the bulb and ignites the filament, creating a flash.

Glass or plastic bulb
Filament
Primer
Base of bulb

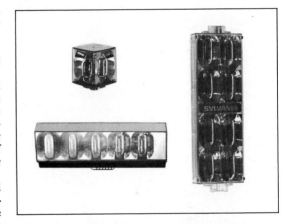

Flashcubes and Flashbars contain several individual bulbs. A flashcube, *upper left,* has 4 bulbs, and flashbars, *right* and *lower left,* have 8 or 10. Each bulb can be used only once.

WORLD BOOK photos by Fred Weituschat

Electronic Flash Units can be attached to a camera or held separately. They contain ionized gas in a glass tube. Electric current makes the gas glow. These units can be used repeatedly.

The Flat-Coated Retriever Has a Thick Coat.

8 or 10 bulbs. Cameras that use an 8-bulb flashbar contain a tiny ceramic cube. The ceramic material is *piezoelectric*—that is, it generates an electric current when struck. The camera's shutter release triggers a tiny hammer that strikes the piezoelectric cube. Electric current from the cube heats a primer in the flashbulb, and this action ignites the filament and sets off the flash.

Electronic Flash Units, also called *speedlights* or *stroboscopic units*, contain ionized gas enclosed in a glass tube. Electric current makes the gas glow in brief bursts of light. The electronic flash is much shorter than the flash of a bulb. In some specialized units, it may last only a millionth of a second. Unlike flashbulbs, electronic flash units can be used repeatedly because the gas is not consumed to produce the flash. Depending on their design, these units use various power sources ranging from small batteries to wall sockets. Some electronic units are small enough to be built into a pocket-size camera, but others are too large and heavy to lift. The large units remain stationary and are used in photographers' studios.

History. The first flash-lighting technique was invented about 1865. It involved the burning of magnesium powder, ribbon, or wire. This technique produced a flash of light, but it also resulted in thick smoke, a strong odor, and sometimes flames. Flashbulbs were introduced in 1929 by the General Electric Company, and such variations as flashcubes and flashbars have been developed since 1963. The electronic flash unit was developed in 1931. KENNETH POLI

See also PHOTOGRAPHY.

FLASHLIGHT is a portable electric light in a metal, fiber, or plastic case. The tiny wire in the bulb of a flashlight is lighted by being brought into contact with the electric current from one or more dry-cell batteries. The beam of light is usually focused by means of a reflector and glass lens. The first dry-cell flashlight was made about 1898 in New York City. Flashlights also can be operated on storage-cell batteries. A flashlight without batteries operates on a generator pumped by hand. See also BATTERY (electric). GENE K. BEARE

FLAT. See MUSIC (The Elements of Music).

FLAT-COATED RETRIEVER is considered a gamekeeper's dog in Great Britain, and is not widely known in the United States. It was bred from two North American dogs, the Labrador retriever and the St. Johns Newfoundland. The dog was first introduced in England, in 1860. It has a thick, fine, flat coat, and is usually solid black or solid *liver* (reddish-brown). The dog weighs from 60 to 70 pounds (27 to 32 kilograms), and stands about 22 inches (56 centimeters) high at the shoulder. MAXWELL RIDDLE

FLATBOAT is a large, raftlike barge used to haul freight and passengers. A flatboat has a flat bottom and square ends. A *keelboat*, sometimes called a flatboat, was a long narrow craft, sharp at one or both ends. It was built on a keel and ribs. These boats carried goods during the westward movement in the United States. Pioneers put their furniture and livestock on flatboats and floated to new settlements. The boats were moved by the current and by long oars which were also used for steering. A vast flatboat freight business grew on the Mississippi in the 1800's. ROBERT H. BURGESS

Flatboats on the Ohio River carried thousands of immigrants to new settlements in the Midwest during the early 1800's.
William A. Croft, *Pioneers in the Settlement of America*

FLATCAR. See RAILROAD (Freight Service).

FLATFISH is a name given to several salt-water fishes. These fishes have a body that appears to be flattened horizontally. The fish actually lies on its side, with both eyes on the same side of the head. When the flatfish is first hatched, it looks like any other kind of fish. But after it has grown from $\frac{1}{2}$ to $\frac{3}{4}$ inch (13 to 19 millimeters) long, one eye begins to move closer to the eye on the opposite side of the head, and the mouth becomes twisted. The eyeless side of the fish stays under and loses its color. The upper side becomes darker. The fish becomes colored to blend with its surroundings. About 130 kinds of flatfishes live in the Atlantic and Pacific oceans, including the flounder and sole. See also FLOUNDER; HALIBUT; SOLE; TURBOT; ANIMAL (color picture: Animal Camouflage). LEONARD P. SCHULTZ

FLATFOOT is a frequently painful condition in which the long arch of the foot flattens out. Flatfoot results when the muscles, ligaments, and connective tissues that normally support the arch weaken, resulting in a *fallen arch*. Poor posture, incorrectly fitted shoes, prolonged standing, and overweight may cause the condition. WILLIAM V. MAYER

FLATHEAD LAKE. See Montana (Rivers and Lakes).

FLATIRON BUILDING is a famous New York City skyscraper. See New York City (Architecture).

FLATTERY, CAPE. See Cape Flattery.

FLATTOP. See Aircraft Carrier.

FLATWORM is a worm with a flattened body. Flatworms live in water or soil, or as parasites on or in the bodies of human beings or animals.

Flatworms are *bilaterally symmetrical*. That is, if the body is divided lengthwise down the middle, the right and left halves are identical. Flatworms are among the lowest forms of animal life to have systems of organs working together. Flatworms have nervous, digestive, reproductive, and *excretory* (waste elimination) systems.

Free-living flatworms include the *planarians*. A planarian can replace lost parts of its body by a process called *regeneration*. If a planarian body is cut into pieces, each piece may grow into a new planarian by replacing the missing parts (see Regeneration).

Parasitic flatworms make up the tapeworm class and the fluke class. Most adult tapeworms infect the intestine of human beings and many kinds of animals. Flukes may be found in the intestine, liver, lungs, blood, and other body parts. Liver flukes are found in cattle, sheep, and dogs. Man becomes infected with flukes by eating uncooked fish, crabs, or vegetables.

People in northern Africa, the Far East, and tropical regions of the Western Hemisphere often have blood flukes called *schistosomes*. Schistosomes usually live in the veins. The eggs work their way out of the body and then hatch into *larvae* (young) in water outside. The larvae infect snails and multiply. Eventually, the free-swimming larvae are released from the snails, and burrow into the skins of animals. If the animal is a suitable *host* (animal in which a parasite lives), the larvae reach the blood vessels and become adults. Most North America schistosomes are parasites of birds. Some burrow into the skins of swimmers and cause swollen, itchy lumps called "swimmer's itch."

Scientific Classification. Flatworms make up the phylum *Platyhelminthes*. The three classes of flatworms are *Turbellaria* (free-living, fresh-water, and salt-water flatworms), *Trematoda* (flukes), and *Cestoidea* (tapeworms).   James A. McLeod

See also Animal (picture: Animals of the Oceans); Fluke; Planarian; Schistosomiasis; Tapeworm.

FLAUBERT, *floh BAIR,* **GUSTAVE** (1821-1880), was a French writer whose novels contain some of the most vivid and lifelike characters and descriptions in literature. Flaubert blends precise observation with a careful attention to language and form. His *Madame Bovary* is considered perhaps the most perfect French novel.

Flaubert was born in Rouen. He lived in solitude, devoting himself to literature. His adoration of artistic beauty was paralleled by his hatred of materialism.

Flaubert tended to be a skeptic and a pessimist. His works are never sentimental or soft, but they are always deeply human. His novels show he was both a realist and a romantic. The realism can be seen in his attention to detail and his objective description of characters and events. The romanticism appears in the exotic subject matter he chose. *Madame Bovary* (1857) is a poetically realistic treatment of a case of adultery in a village in Normandy. *Salammbô* (1862) is a colorful novel about ancient Carthage. *A Sentimental Education* (1869), a kind of autobiography, is an example of strict literary realism. *The Temptation of St. Anthony* (1874) is a marvelous fantasy. *Three Tales* (1880) contains three small masterpieces, each illustrating a different style: "A Simple Heart" (contemporary realism), "Herodias" (Biblical style), and "The Legend of St. Julian the Hospitaller" (medieval style).   Robert J. Niess

See also French Literature (The Great Novelists).

HOW ONE KIND OF FLATWORM GROWS NEW PARTS FOR ITS BODY

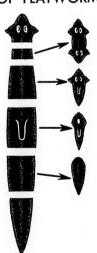

Planarians can reproduce by splitting in two. The tail part may grow a new head; the front part adds a tail.

If you cut a planarian into several pieces, the pieces nearest the head will develop heads at both ends.

If you graft a piece from the head of one worm onto the body of another, a new head will develop and grow.

Split the head of a planarian in half, and two complete heads will form and grow in place of the single head.

Flax Harvesters pull the plants from the ground, *above*, and stack the fiber flax in shocks to dry. Seed pods top the slender flax stalks, *right*. The seeds are used to make linseed oil.

FLAX is a plant raised for its fiber and seed. The fiber can be spun and woven into products that range from coarse rope to delicate linen fabrics and laces. Flaxseeds contain linseed oil, which is used in the manufacture of paints, varnishes, linoleum, and oilcloth. A meal made from the seeds after the oil has been pressed out provides feed for farm animals.

There are about 100 species of flax. They grow chiefly in temperate and subtropical climates. Flax plants are small herbs with green leaves and bright red, yellow, white, or blue flowers. Many people raise them for their beauty. The most important species, however, is the kind raised for seed and fiber. Plants of this species stand 1 to 4 feet (30 to 120 centimeters) high and have small branching stems near the top. They usually have blue flowers, though some varieties have white or pink flowers.

Seed Flax. The world flaxseed output totals about 120 million bushels annually. One bushel equals 56 pounds (25 kilograms). Canada, Russia, India, the United States, and Argentina are the leading flaxseed-producers. But the United States must import flaxseed to fill its needs. North and South Dakota and Minnesota raise most of the U.S. flaxseed. Saskatchewan and Manitoba raise most of Canada's flaxseed.

Seed flax grows well in cool climates with relatively dry soil. It is also grown as a winter crop in subtropical climates. Seed flax can be reaped and threshed with the same machines farmers use to harvest such grain crops as wheat. The seeds are shipped to mills for processing into linseed oil and meal. Much of the flax straw left in the field after harvesting is made into high-strength specialty paper. Such paper is often used for Bibles, certificates, and diplomas. Paper mills make much of the cigarette paper used in the United States from flaxseed plants.

Fiber Flax. Farmers in many parts of the world raise fiber flax. But European farmers produce the most. Russia grows about seven-tenths of the world output. Other important European fiber flax countries include Belgium, Czechoslovakia, France, Hungary, Poland, and Romania. Asiatic fiber flax is raised in China, South Korea, Taiwan, and Turkey. Egypt produces the most flax in Africa. In the Western Hemisphere, Argentina and Chile grow fiber flax. Fiber flax is not grown commercially in the United States. Mills in the United States import fiber flax, chiefly from Europe. The mills make shoes, sewing thread, fish lines, nets, toweling, and other products from it.

Flax usually produces strong, fine fibers with a silky luster. These fibers, called *bast fibers*, lie inside the bark, next to the woody core. The best fibers come from flax plants that have long stems, because these plants have the longest fibers. Fiber cannot be taken from either the roots or small branches of flax plants.

Fiber flax needs a cool, moist climate. It grows best in fertile, well-drained soil that has been cultivated and contains much decayed plant and animal matter. The plants must be harvested at the proper time to obtain the best quality fiber. If they are harvested too early, the fibers will be fine and silky, but weak. If the plants are allowed to become too ripe, the fibers will be stiff and coarse and have poor spinning qualities. In many countries, farmers harvest fiber flax by pulling the plants from the ground by hand. Machines have also been developed to pull flax from the ground.

Processing Fiber Flax. Before flax can be processed for its fiber, the seeds must be removed. This can be done by pulling the plants through coarse combs in a process called *rippling*. Or the plants may be run between rollers that crush the seed bolls and free the seeds

LEADING FIBER FLAX PRODUCING COUNTRIES
Fiber flax produced in 1973

Russia	
	488,300 short tons (443,000 metric tons)
Poland	
	66,690 short tons (60,400 metric tons)
France	
	51,280 short tons (46,500 metric tons)
Romania	
	16,500 short tons (15,000 metric tons)
Czechoslovakia	
	15,400 short tons (14,000 metric tons)

Source: *Production Yearbook, 1973*, FAO.

but do not harm the stems. The seeds are sent to mills to be made into linseed oil.

Next, the flax stems must be soaked in water. This process, called *retting*, frees the fibers by rotting the woody part of the stem. In Russia, farmers spread the flax on the ground and allow the dew to rot the plants. *Dew retting* produces strong, gray linen fibers. The Irish ret in pools of still water. This often causes too much rotting and the linen fibers become weak and brittle. Belgian farmers ret by placing the plants in streams of running water. This method produces strong, pale-yellow fibers. In Belgium and Northern Ireland, farmers also ret by soaking the flax in tanks of warm water. Retting may also be done by treating the plants with certain chemicals. However, chemical retting is not widely used.

After the flax stalks dry, workers put them through a process called *breaking*. They run the stems through grooved rollers. This breaks the woody part of the stems into small pieces called *shives*. The shives are then stripped from the fibers by a process called *scutching*. Scutching machines scrape the shives from the fiber by whirling knives or paddles. Scutching may also be done by hand.

The final step involves combing the fibers. This process, called *hackling*, may be done by machine or by hand. It separates the *line* (long) fibers from the *tow* (short) fibers. For fine linen, hackling must be done repeatedly, using finer and finer combs. The coarse, tow fibers can be made into cord, twines, coarse yarns, and upholstery padding.

History. Flax is one of the oldest known crops. Bits of linen uncovered in Egypt indicate that people there wove flax as early as 5000 B.C. Egyptian mummies more than 4,000 years old have been found wrapped in linen cloth as well as that produced today. The ancient Greeks wore linen clothing, and the Romans made linen paper, as well as cloth.

The use of linen gradually spread throughout Europe. The area that is now Belgium became an important linen producer because the chemicals in the Leie River there were ideal for retting flax. The ruler Charlemagne developed linen-making in what is now France during the A.D. 700's. In the 1600's, skilled Flemish and

USDA

To Prepare Flax for Spinning, workers first comb the fibers with a hackle to separate the short and long fibers.

French workers who left their countries to escape religious persecution helped develop linen spinning and weaving in England, Germany, and The Netherlands.

The American settlers often planted seed flax as their first crop as they moved west. But the invention of the cotton gin by Eli Whitney in 1793 made cotton yarn more economical than linen yarn. For this reason, the United States never produced large amounts of fiber flax. The use of linen in the United States decreased in the mid-1900's with the development of nylon, polyester, and other manufactured fibers. Seed flax acreage also declined as a result of the increasing popularity of latex paints over oil-based paints.

Scientific Classification. Flax plants belong to the flax family, *Linaceae*. They make up the genus *Linum*, which includes about 100 species. Fiber and seed flax are genus *Linum*, species *L. usitatissimum*.   DAVID E. ZIMMER

See also LINEN; LINSEED OIL.

LEADING FLAXSEED-PRODUCING STATES AND PROVINCES

Bushels of flaxseed produced in 1973*

Saskatchewan	8,900,000 bu.
Manitoba	7,600,000 bu.
North Dakota	7,464,000 bu.
South Dakota	5,670,000 bu.
Minnesota	3,119,000 bu.

*One bushel equals 56 pounds (25 kilograms).
Source: U.S. Department of Agriculture; Statistics Canada.

LEADING FLAXSEED-PRODUCING COUNTRIES

Bushels of flaxseed produced in 1973*

Canada	19,409,000 bu.
Russia	18,503,000 bu.
India	17,283,000 bu.
United States	16,437,000 bu.
Argentina	11,889,000 bu.

*One bushel equals 56 pounds (25 kilograms).
Source: *World Agricultural Production and Trade*, February, 1974, U.S. Department of Agriculture.

FLAXMAN, JOHN. See SCULPTURE (European).

FLEA, *flee*, is a small, wingless insect that lives on mammals and birds and sucks blood for food. Fleas are dangerous pests because they can carry the germs that cause plague and typhus. They get the disease germs by biting infected rats and ground squirrels. See BUBONIC PLAGUE; TYPHUS.

A flea has flat sides and a head much smaller than the rest of the body. Strong, spiny legs help fleas move quickly and easily through the hairs or feathers of their host. They puncture the skin with their beaks to get blood.

Fleas live on man, cats, dogs, rats, birds, horses, poultry, rabbits, and many wild animals. A few kinds live only on certain types of animals. But most kinds pass readily from animal to man and from animal to animal. They leave the host as soon as it dies because they must have blood for food.

Fleas are strong and have great leaping ability for their size. Scientists have found that the flea that lives on humans can jump 13 inches (33 centimeters). Fleas can be made to perform tricks such as pulling tiny wagons. *Flea circuses* feature troupes of "trained" fleas.

The Body of a Flea is greatly magnified in this photograph. The flea has a large abdomen where blood is stored.

Hugh Spencer

Kinds of Fleas. The common *European*, or *human, flea* is about $\frac{1}{8}$ inch (3 millimeters) long. It lives in the folds of clothing. It drops its eggs about the house instead of attaching them to clothing. The larvae look like maggots. When they become adults, they seek a host. Some persons attract fleas more than others do, and some become sensitive to the bites. The skin around the bite becomes inflamed in such persons.

The *chigoe*, another kind of flea, is native to South America. But it has spread to Africa and many temperate regions. The female chigoe burrows into the skin to lay eggs. These insects cause ulcers to form on the skin. The flea must be removed before the ulcer will heal. See CHIGOE.

Rat, cat, and dog fleas also may be serious pests. They lay many tiny oval white eggs on the animals or in their sleeping places. When the eggs hatch, the larvae crawl into bedding and into cracks in the floor. They spin their cocoons in dust and appear as adults about two weeks later.

Controlling Fleas. Cleanliness and proper care of pets are the best protection against fleas. Dogs that have fleas should be scrubbed with *derris soaps*, which contain an insecticide. Dusting pets with derris kills the insects. Owners can guard against fleas by changing their pets' bedding frequently. They can destroy the larvae by spraying or dusting the pets' quarters with an insecticide.

Scientific Classification. Fleas make up the order *Siphonaptera*. The common European, or human, flea is a member of the human flea family, *Pulicidae*. It is classified as genus *Pulex*, species *P. irritans*.   ROBERT L. USINGER

FLEABANE, *FLEE bayn*, is a plant often grown in rock gardens. It gets its name because people once thought that the fleabane could drive away or destroy fleas. There are over 130 different kinds of fleabane. *Canada fleabane* is also known as *horseweed*, *colt's-tail*, and *bloodstanch*. It grows as a common weed in Canada and the United States. A fleabane often grown in gardens has violet-colored flowers. These flowers grow in a cluster about $1\frac{1}{2}$ inches (4 centimeters) across. Another garden fleabane has brilliant orange-colored flowers. Much *blue fleabane* grows in dry areas east of the Mississippi.

The Canada fleabane can be gathered while it is flowering and carefully dried. Druggists then sell it as a drug called *erigeron*, or fleabane. Physicians use erigeron to treat diarrhea and dropsy. They also use it to stop the flow of blood. Lotions used to repel mosquitoes often contain oil of fleabane.

Scientific Classification. The fleabanes belong to the composite family, *Compositae*. The Canada fleabane is classified as genus *Conyza*, species *C. canadensis*. The blue fleabane is *Erigeron annuus*. The garden fleabanes are *E. speciosus* and *E. aurantiacus*.   HAROLD NORMAN MOLDENKE

Fleabane in Blossom. This species, the daisy fleabane, is more attractive than many others which are common weeds.

L. W. Brownell

FLEET PRISON, an historic London jail, took its name from its location near Fleet stream. As early as the 1100's, it was the king's prison. In the 1500's and 1600's, it housed Puritans and victims of the Court of the Star Chamber. Later, it was a debtor's prison. In the 1700's, it became noted for cruelty. From the early 1600's until 1753, clergymen performed secret marriages in the prison. These were called "Fleet marriages." The prison was abandoned in 1842, and later torn down.   BASIL D. HENNING

FLEMING. See BELGIUM (The People); FLEMISH LANGUAGE AND LITERATURE.

FLEMING, SIR ALEXANDER (1881-1955), was a British bacteriologist at the University of London. In 1929, he reported the germ-killing power of the green mold, *Penicillium notatum*, from which the life-saving antibiotic, penicillin, was first purified (see ANTIBIOTIC; PENICILLIN). Fleming received the 1945 Nobel prize in medicine, along with Sir Howard Florey and Ernst Chain, for the development of this drug (see FLOREY, LORD; CHAIN, ERNST BORIS).

Fleming's findings opened a new era for medicine, and World War II provided an opportune field trial for penicillin. Fleming discovered penicillin accidentally when he saw that a bit of mold that had fallen from a culture plate in his laboratory had destroyed bacteria around it. Fleming also discovered lysozyme, a substance found in human tears. Even when diluted, this agent can dissolve certain germs.

Fleming was born on a farm in Darvel, Scotland. He attended St. Mary's Hospital Medical School at the University of London. STANLEY E. WEDBERG

FLEMING, IAN LANCASTER (1908-1964), an English novelist, became one of the most popular authors of the mid-1900's. He won fame for his creation of James Bond, a British secret service agent who meets old-fashioned, fantastic adventure in the modern world. Bond, also known by the code name *007*, is the senior of three British agents who used a double-0 code number. The double-0 meant that these agents could kill at their discretion.

Bond appeared first in *Casino Royale* (1953), and then in more than a dozen other books. The books attracted many types of readers. *Diamonds Are Forever* (1956) was a favorite of the more sophisticated readers, while *Doctor No* (1958) had a general appeal like the thrillers of the 1800's. A series of motion pictures based on the novels helped spread Bond's fame.

Fleming was born in London. During World War II, he did espionage work as the personal assistant to the director of British Naval Intelligence. PHILIP DURHAM

FLEMING, JOHN AMBROSE. See VACUUM TUBE; ELECTRONICS (The First Commercial Vacuum Tubes).

FLEMING, SIR SANDFORD (1827-1915), a Canadian civil engineer, built the Intercolonial Railway across Canada and made surveys for the main line of the Canadian Pacific Railway. After 1876, he played a prominent role in establishing standard time zones (see STANDARD TIME). He proposed the use of the 24-hour system of keeping time. He also persuaded the Canadian, Australian, and British governments to cooperate in laying the Pacific cable between Australia and Vancouver in 1902, in an attempt to have a system of communication connecting the entire British Empire.

Fleming was born in Kirkcaldy, Scotland. He moved to Canada when he was 18. He joined the engineering staff of the old Northern Railway, and in 1855 became its chief engineer. He was important in railway development for all Upper Canada. An advocate of transcontinental railroads, he became engineer in chief of the government railroads and a director of the Canadian Pacific Railway. He also paid the expense of locating a railway line in Newfoundland. He retired from active engineering in 1880.

Fleming was also interested in political affairs. He served as chancellor of Queen's University at Kingston, Ont., from 1880 to 1915. ROBERT E. SCHOFIELD

FLEMING VALVE. See VACUUM TUBE.

FLEMISH LANGUAGE AND LITERATURE. The Flemish language is a form of Low German (see GERMAN LANGUAGE). Many people speak Flemish in Belgium, especially in the provinces of East Flanders, West Flanders, Antwerp, Limburg, and Brabant. Some people

also speak Flemish in The Netherlands. Flemish sounds much like the official language of The Netherlands. But many words are not pronounced and spelled the same way in Flemish as they are in Dutch. Flemish also resembles French.

The history of Flemish literature is practically the same as the history of Dutch literature until Belgium was separated from The Netherlands in 1830 (see NETHERLANDS [Arts]). But, during the early 1800's, young Flemish writers began experimenting. Hendrik Conscience wrote the first Flemish novel. Later writers, like poet Jan van Beers and critic Max Rooses, introduced an element of gentle realism. During the 1890's, many writers contributed to a magazine called *Van Nu en Straks*. The works of essayist August Vermeylen and dramatist Herman Teirlinck became widely known.

After World War I, novels by Felix Timmermans and Ernest Claes were translated into many other languages. A group of expressionist poets, led by Paul van Ostaijen, flourished during the same period. In the 1930's, novels by Maurice Roelants explored social and psychological themes. After World War II, popular authors included novelist Daisne, poets Van Wilderode and De Haes, and dramatist Hensen. HELENA M. GAMER

FLESH is the name given to the soft tissues or parts of the body of man and of most animals that have backbones. It is made up chiefly of muscle and connective tissue, but also includes some fat. The flesh is the meaty part of the body which surrounds the skeleton and body cavity. It does not include the organs in the body cavity or the bony and liquid tissues of the body. Animal flesh, or meat, is high in essential nutrients such as fat, protein, and minerals. The word *flesh* also refers to the soft, pulpy parts of fruits and vegetables. W. B. YOUMANS

FLESH-EATING ANIMAL. See CARNIVORE.

FLESH-EATING PLANT. See CARNIVOROUS PLANT.

FLETCHER, JOHN (1579-1625), was an English playwright. For many years, Fletcher's plays were as highly praised as Shakespeare's and Ben Jonson's. Fletcher wrote many kinds of drama, but his fame centers on his skillfully theatrical tragicomedies and such comedies of manners as *The Wild Goose-Chase* (1621). Like similar Restoration plays written later, this play was meant to please a pleasure-loving, sophisticated upper-class audience.

Fletcher was born in Sussex. His success began with his famous collaboration with Francis Beaumont (about 1608-1613). But Fletcher wrote some plays independently before, and many after, this association. Many of the so-called "Beaumont and Fletcher" plays belong solely to Fletcher or to Fletcher working with others (see BEAUMONT, FRANCIS). Shakespeare probably wrote *The Two Noble Kinsmen* and *Henry VIII* with Fletcher. LAWRENCE J. ROSS

FLETCHER V. PECK, an 1810 Supreme Court case, marked the first time the Supreme Court of the United States declared a state law unconstitutional. This decision established the supremacy of the United States Constitution over state laws.

In 1795, members of the Georgia state legislature took bribes to grant land to several companies. The next legislature *revoked* (took back) the grants, but some of the land had already been sold by the companies. The new owners of the land argued that by revoking the grants Georgia had interfered with a lawful contract. The Supreme Court agreed with the landowners and declared the original sale legal. The court ruled that the Constitution prohibited a state from violating a contract.   STANLEY I. KUTLER

FLETTNER, ANTON. See ROTOR SHIP.

FLEUR-DE-LIS, *FLUR duh LEE,* is a French name that literally means *flower of the lily,* but actually refers to the iris. The kings of France used an irislike design in heraldry. Some historians think this design originally represented an iris. Other historians believe the iris was once called a lily, and so the design was called *flower of the lily.* Others claim that the name originally meant *flower of Louis.* According to legend, Clovis I used the fleur-de-lis in the early 500's after an angel gave him an iris for accepting Christianity. *Clovis* is an early form of *Louis.* In 1376, Charles V chose three fleurs-de-lis for his coat of arms.   ARTHUR E. DuBOIS

See also HERALDRY; IRIS (picture); FLAG (color picture: Historical Flags of the World).

FLEURY, ANDRÉ HERCULE DE. See LOUIS (XV).

FLEXNER, ABRAHAM (1866-1959), became an outstanding authority on higher education, especially in the field of medicine. In 1930, he became the first director of the Institute for Advanced Study at Princeton, N.J. (see INSTITUTE FOR ADVANCED STUDY).

Flexner's study of American medical colleges, published in 1910, caused sweeping changes in curriculum and teaching methods. He was associated with the General Education Board, an organization that provided financial aid to U.S. education, from 1913 to 1928. Flexner was born in Louisville, Ky.   GALEN SAYLOR

FLEXOR. See MUSCLE (Skeletal Muscles; diagram).

FLICKER is a large, handsome woodpecker that lives in nearly all the wooded regions in Canada and the United States. It gets its name from its loud call, which sounds like the word "flicker."

Two of the best-known flickers are the *yellow-shafted flicker* and the *red-shafted flicker,* both of which are subspecies of the *common flicker.* The yellow-shafted flicker is a little larger than a robin. It has brownish back feathers, a conspicuous white rump patch, a black collar mark across the breast, and a small red crown patch. People often call this bird the *golden-winged woodpecker,* or *yellowhammer,* because of its golden-yellow underwings. The red-shafted flicker has bright red instead of golden colored underwings.

The flicker builds its nest in holes in trees. Because of this, people sometimes call it the *highhole* or *high-holder.* The bird gathers wood chips with which it builds a bed for its eggs. It lays six or more white eggs.

The flicker gets much of its food on the ground. It eats worms, insects, and berries, and is especially fond of ants. It nests as far north as central Alaska, and migrates in early fall to the southern United States.

Scientific Classification. The flicker belongs to the woodpecker family, *Picidae.* The common flicker is genus *Colaptes,* species *C. auratus.* The yellow-shafted flicker is *C. auratus auratus;* the red-shafted flicker is *C. auratus cafer.*   GEORGE J. WALLACE

See also WOODPECKER; YELLOWHAMMER; BIRD (color picture: Birds That Help Us).

FLICKERTAIL STATE. See NORTH DAKOTA.

FLIGHT. See AIRPLANE (How an Airplane Flies); BIRD (How Birds Fly).

FLIGHT ATTENDANT is a member of the crew on airplane passenger flights. Flight attendants serve as a personal link between the airline and its passengers during the flight. They attend to the individual needs and comforts of the passengers while performing routine flight duties. The flight attendant tries to make the passengers' trip so enjoyable that they will want to fly with the airline again. Attendants receive training that helps them work calmly in an emergency and ensure the safety of the travelers.

The first flight attendants on United States airlines were men. But from the 1930's until the 1970's, the airlines hired only women to serve as attendants. Flight attendants were called stewardesses or hostesses. In 1971, a federal court ruled that a man could not be denied a job as a flight attendant because of his sex. Today, both men and women hold the position, but the majority of flight attendants are women.

Duties. The number of flight attendants assigned to a flight varies according to (1) the airline, (2) the length of the trip, and (3) the type of airplane. Long-distance flights may have as many as 14 flight attendants on the largest jets and 6 on other planes. Most short-run jet flights have at least 3 flight attendants. Flights on twin-engine planes may have only 1 attendant. In the United States, the Federal Aviation Administration (FAA) specifies the minimum number of flight attendants that must be carried on each type of plane.

Before the first passenger boards the plane, flight attendants perform certain duties. For example, they check on flight conditions and the flight schedule. They

Allan Cruickshank

Young Flickers Eagerly Await Feeding Time.

A Flight Attendant serves at least one meal to passengers on most long flights. Attendants must be able to prepare and serve appetizing food in the limited space of the cabin.

Giving Safety Instructions ranks as one of a flight attendant's most important duties. This flight attendant is showing a plane's passengers how to use an emergency oxygen mask.

inspect the plane's cabin and check the food, emergency equipment, and first-aid supplies. As the passengers enter the plane, the flight attendants greet them, show them to seats, and help them put away their coats, hats, and hand luggage.

Before take-off, flight attendants give safety instructions to the passengers over the plane's public address system. They also tell the travelers about the smoking regulations and instruct them on the use of their seat belts. On jet flights, flight attendants demonstrate the use of emergency oxygen masks. If the plane takes the passengers chiefly over water, the attendants show them how to use life jackets.

The attendants make flight announcements before and after take-off. They may report on the weather en route and at the plane's destination, the altitude of the aircraft, and the flight time.

Flight attendants try to make the passengers as comfortable as possible. They provide blankets, pillows, and magazines and keep the cabin neat and clean. They help care for children and infants and give extra attention to elderly or inexperienced travelers. Attendants prepare food attractively and serve meals, snacks, and refreshments. They also answer questions about the aircraft, the route, and travel arrangements at the flight's destination. In case of emergencies, the flight attendants must know how to give first aid. Attendants on international flights must be able to give information on foreign currency, passport regulations, customs, and international travel requirements.

After the passengers leave the plane, the flight attendants submit a flight report if their airline requires it. The attendants always prepare a report in case of an accident, injury, or unusual incident during the flight.

After submitting their reports, the flight attendants are free until their next flight. The average monthly flying time for attendants ranges from 70 to 80 hours, and many hold another job as well. Flight attendants must have their supervisor's approval before taking a second job. Some receive promotional and nonflight assignments. Such assignments include modeling at charity fashion shows and doing other public relations work.

Requirements for flight attendant positions are the same on most U.S. airlines. A candidate must be between 19 and 27 years old and meet normal height and weight standards. Weight must be proportional to height. A candidate's vision, if not 20/20, must be correctable, preferably with contact lenses. A flight attendant candidate must have a pleasant appearance and be able to pass the airline's flight physical examination. Applicants must have at least a high school education, and most airlines require at least two years of college.

Airlines prefer single applicants, but they accept married, widowed, or divorced persons. Most airlines require a candidate to be a citizen of the United States or an immigrant with a permanent residency permit. An applicant for a position with an international airline must be able to speak at least one other language besides English. Flight attendants must accept a base assignment in any city during their first six months of duty.

A person who wishes to become a flight attendant must be confident, enthusiastic, mature, and poised. Flight attendants must enjoy helping people and talking to them.

Training. Flight attendants are trained at special schools, most of which are run by the airlines. The course lasts from three to seven weeks. Most airlines house the trainees in dormitories during the instruction period.

Flight attendant training includes extensive classroom work and practical in-flight experience in a model cabin. Trainees learn to perform their duties skillfully and to handle unusual situations with poise. They study such subjects as child care, first aid, flight theory and procedures, good grooming, meal service, and psychology of passenger service. Candidates for positions on the largest jets receive special training.

Career Opportunities. A career as a flight attendant combines glamour with hard work and provides an opportunity to travel and meet people.

The starting pay for flight attendants varies from airline to airline, but the minimum is about $500 a month. Flight attendants receive regular increases to a maximum of about $900 monthly. Attendants on international flights earn higher salaries. The minimum flying time for flight attendants is about 70 hours a month, and those who fly more than that get paid at an overtime rate. The airline pays flight attendants' expenses while they are away from their base station.

Flight attendants receive excellent employee benefits. For example, they may travel as passengers free or at reduced fares on their own airline and on many other carriers. Most airlines also provide reduced rates for the parents, husband or wife, and children of flight attendants. Paid vacations vary from two to four weeks, depending on length of service. The airlines provide accident, health, and life insurance at reduced rates, sick leave with pay, retirement plans, and educational programs. Most airlines also provide maternity leave.

Many flight attendants with ability and experience have moved up to management positions. For example, a capable flight attendant may become a *purser* and have charge of a plane's cabin-service crew.

Persons interested in information about a specific airline should write the general manager of that company's nearest office. JOHN F. RHODES

FLIGHT DECK. See AIRCRAFT CARRIER.

FLIGHT DIRECTOR. See AIRCRAFT INSTRUMENTS (The Flight Director).

FLIGHT INTO EGYPT. See JESUS CHRIST (The Nativity).

FLIGHT SURGEON. See AVIATION MEDICINE.

FLIGHTLESS BIRD. See BIRD (Kinds of Birds).

FLIN FLON, Manitoba (pop. 8,560), the province's most important mining center, lies on the Saskatchewan border (see MANITOBA [political map]).

The town is sprawled over bare, rocky hills around Ross Lake. Copper and zinc deposits were discovered here in 1915, but were not fully developed until 1930. Water mains and sewers lie on the surface of the ground because digging through the rock terrain is too expensive. Flin Flon was founded in 1914. W. L. MORTON

FLINT is a form of silica, the same material which makes up sand. Most flint is found in the form of fine-grained, dark-gray lumps mixed with chalk and limestone. Pure flint is so hard and even-grained that it chips in smooth curved flakes. Geologists classify flint as a type of *chert* or chalcedony.

In prehistoric times, people valued flint, because they could chip it into sharp tools and weapons. They

made flint spears, knives, and arrowheads. Later, people learned that flint gave a spark when it was struck against some hard metal, and they began using it to start fires. The pioneers fired their flintlock rifles by striking flint against iron (see FLINTLOCK).

Today, flint has little importance as an industrial product. But it is sometimes used to crush hard substances such as ores. ERNEST E. WAHLSTROM

See also ARROWHEAD (picture); FIRE (Methods of Starting Fires).

FLINT (pop. 193,317; met. area pop. 508,664) is Michigan's third largest city. Only Detroit and Grand Rapids are larger. Flint ranks second to the Detroit area as the nation's leading producer of automobiles, automotive parts, and trucks. The city lies on the Flint River, about 60 miles (97 kilometers) northwest of Detroit. For location, see MICHIGAN (political map).

Flint is the largest manufacturing center of the General Motors Corporation, the world's biggest automobile producer. General Motors operates 10 major manufacturing plants in the city, and three of its divisions have their headquarters there. The corporation employs about half of Flint's work force.

Flint is the home of the Flint Institute of Arts and the Flint Symphony Orchestra. The Flint Cultural Center includes an art gallery, concert hall, music center, planetarium, public library, and transportation museum. The cultural center was partly financed by the Mott Foundation, which supports community improvements in Flint (see MOTT FOUNDATION, CHARLES STEWART). Schools in the city include General Motors Institute, Michigan School for the Deaf, and the University of Michigan-Flint.

Chippewa Indians lived in what is now the Flint area when Jacob Smith, the first white settler there, arrived in 1819. Smith, a fur trader from Detroit, built a trading post at a spot where Indians crossed the Flint River. During the 1830's, a community that became known as the Flint River Settlement developed in the area.

Flint was incorporated as a city in 1855. Vast white pine forests near Flint attracted lumbermen to the area during the mid-1800's, and Flint became a center of

The Robert T. Longway Planetarium in Flint, Mich., is part of an educational and cultural center in the city.

lumber milling. By 1900, Flint's factories were making over 100,000 wooden road carts and carriages a year, and Flint became known as the *Vehicle City*.

Flint's automobile industry began to grow rapidly after 1903, when the Buick Motor Company moved from Detroit to Flint. William C. Durant, a Flint road cart manufacturer, took control of Buick in 1904. He founded General Motors in Flint in 1908 and moved the Chevrolet Motor Company's manufacturing operations from Detroit to Flint in 1912. The automobile industry drew thousands of workers to the city, and Flint's population rose from 13,000 in 1900 to 156,000 in 1930.

In 1976, the first buildings opened in a new downtown campus of the Flint branch of the University of Michigan. Other civic plans included construction of Riverfront Center, a convention, entertainment, hotel, and office complex near downtown Flint. Flint is the county seat of Genesee County and has a mayor-council form of government.   LAWRENCE R. GUSTIN

FLINTLOCK firing mechanisms were used on firearms from the 1600's to about 1850. Flintlock weapons had

Metropolitan Museum of Art, New York City
Flintlock Pistols Were Sometimes Used for Dueling.

a piece of flint in the cocking hammer. When the trigger was pulled, the flint struck a piece of steel. This made sparks, which set off the powder charge and fired the bullet. Flintlocks were first used in muskets, then in pistols and rifles. Firearms using percussion caps later replaced flintlock weapons.   JACK O'CONNOR

See also FIREARM; MUSKET.

FLIP. See OCEAN (picture: The *FLIP*).

FLIPPER. See SEAL.

FLOAT CHAMBER. See CARBURETOR.

FLOATING. See SWIMMING; GRAVITY, SPECIFIC (Archimedes' Principle).

FLOATING DOCK. See DRY DOCK.

FLOATPLANE. See AIRPLANE (Seaplanes).

FLOCK. See ANIMAL (Animals That Live Together).

FLODDEN FIELD, BATTLE OF. See SCOTLAND (The House of Stuart).

FLOE. See ICEBERG.

FLOOD is a body of water that covers normally dry land. Most floods are harmful. They may destroy homes and other property and even carry off the topsoil, leaving the land barren. When people are not prepared, sudden and violent floods may bring huge losses. Rivers, lakes, or seas may flood the land. Rivers cause more floods than larger bodies of water do, though river floods may not be more serious. But sometimes floods may be helpful. For example, the yearly floods of the Nile River built up the plains of Egypt and made the Nile Valley one of the most fertile regions in the world. These floods brought fertile soil from lands far to the south and deposited the soil in Egypt.

River Floods. Most rivers overflow their normal channels about once every two years. When a river overflows land where people live, it causes a flood. When a river overflows land where people do not live, it is said to be *in flood*.

The Mississippi-Missouri river system, and the rivers that flow into it, such as the Ohio, are known for their tendency to overflow their banks. So is the Hwang Ho (Yellow River) in China. This river has been called "China's sorrow" because its floods cause such great destruction. The Hwang Ho flows through a channel that has risen from 10 to 20 feet (3 to 6 meters) higher than the plain on either side. The rise of the channel has been caused partly by soil carried in the river. It has also resulted from dikes built by the people. When the Hwang Ho overflows its banks, it sometimes puts an area as large as Great Britain under water.

Common causes of river floods include too much rain at one time and the sudden melting of snow and ice. Under such conditions, rivers may receive more than 10 times as much water as their beds can hold. Heavy rains produce *flash floods* if the rains cause small rivers or streams to rise suddenly and overflow. Flash floods occur chiefly in mountainous areas and do not allow much time for people to be warned of danger. A flash flood at Rapid City, S. Dak., in 1972 killed 238 persons along Rapid Creek. Minor causes of flooding include bridges, piers, filled land, sand bars, and other obstacles to river waters.

In 1927, the Mississippi River overflowed its banks from Cairo, Ill., to the Gulf of Mexico. This flood, the worst in the United States up to that time, destroyed almost $285 million worth of property. The floods of 1936 were serious, but one of the greatest floods in the nation's history occurred in 1937. The Ohio and Mississippi valleys were overrun by the rivers. This flood killed more than 135 persons, left about a million

Wide World
Floodwaters Cause Great Damage when people are not prepared for them. They have often destroyed entire communities. Floods usually occur in the spring, when the water from melting snow and heavy spring rains combine to raise the level of rivers above their banks.

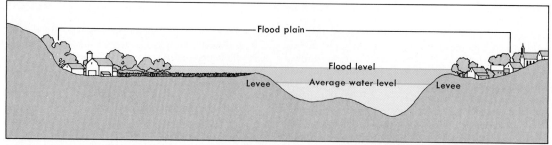

A **Flood Occurs** when a river rises above its normal level and overflows its banks. People have built *levees* (dikes) along some rivers to hold back the high water, but a river may overflow even such barriers. Floodwaters generally cover only a river's *flood plain,* the nearby low-lying land. But sometimes extremely high waters flood a much larger area.

homeless, and destroyed about $400 million worth of property. In 1965, flooding in the upper Mississippi Valley killed about 25 persons and destroyed $140 million worth of property.

The greatest flood damage in U.S. history occurred in 1972. Heavy rain from a tropical storm caused rivers in New York and Pennsylvania to overflow. The resulting floods destroyed or damaged about $3 billion worth of property and left over 15,000 persons homeless.

Seacoast Floods. Most floods from the sea result from hurricanes or other powerful storms that drive water against harbors and push waves far inland. In 1970, a hurricane in the Bay of Bengal, a part of the Indian Ocean, caused the greatest sea flood disaster in history. Huge waves struck the coast of Bangladesh and killed about 300,000 persons. The flood also destroyed the cattle, crops, and homes of millions of other victims.

In The Netherlands, the land lies partly below the level of the sea and faces the constant danger of being flooded. The country is protected by its famous dikes, which wall off the sea. These dikes have seldom failed in modern times.

In other places, there is danger from great tidal waves which come up suddenly and unexpectedly. After the great flood of 1900, Galveston, Tex., built a sea wall. But the storms of 1913 went over the wall. Earthquakes and volcanoes also produce waves. A sea wave caused by an earthquake is called a *tsunami.* During the Good Friday earthquake in Alaska in 1964, tsunamis struck the Kodiak Islands and the southern coast of Alaska. The waves, some as high as 35 feet (11 meters), killed 96 persons and destroyed more than $100 million worth of property. Volcanic waves as high as 50 feet (15 meters) have struck Lisbon, Portugal; Messina, Sicily; and the coast of Japan. In 1883, the volcano Krakatoa in Sunda Strait, west of Java, erupted and raised the surrounding water so high that one ship was carried 1½ miles (2.4 kilometers) inland and was left 39 feet (12 meters) above the sea. Some seacoast floods result from abnormally high tides.

Other Floods. Storms and high winds also cause floods along lakeshores. Some lakeshore floods occur when water moves suddenly from side to side in rhythm. Such a movement of the water of a lake is called a *seiche.*

The failure of man-made structures, such as dams, has caused a number of floods. In 1963, the Vaiont Dam in Italy collapsed, and the resulting flood killed about

1,800 persons. In 1972, a dam on Buffalo Creek in West Virginia burst, and the resulting flood killed 125 persons. The floodwaters destroyed or damaged 1,500 homes and left about 4,000 persons homeless.

Flood Control. Since 1936, the U.S. government has spent about $9 billion to prevent and control floods. Flood control involves building dams to store water and channels to allow it to flow quickly to the sea. It also involves dikes, flood walls, hurricane barriers, and levees that help keep water off the land.

Continuing floods in the Mississippi Valley and other river valleys caused Congress to adopt the Flood Control Act of 1936. In 1938, Congress appropriated $376,700,000 for a five-year program of building and keeping up reservoirs, levees, and flood walls. The engineering work along the Mississippi by the U.S. Army Corps of Engineers stopped the floods of the upper Mississippi from doing damage below Cairo. Before then, the lower Mississippi had been one of the most dangerous flood areas of the world.

In 1943, the rivers that flow into the Mississippi

Control of Floods is made possible by predictions of how much water will be produced by melting snow. People who live along a river can line the river banks with sandbags to keep the river from overflowing when it reaches the predicted height. If the river rises greatly every year, they can build permanent levees.

flooded badly. More than 12 million acres (5 million hectares) of farmland were covered by water, and more than 50,000 persons had to leave their homes. In 1973, the Mississippi-Missouri river system flooded, reaching its highest crest in more than 100 years. Much farmland was flooded, but thousands of people lived safely behind the walls, reservoirs, levees, and dikes between Cairo and New Orleans.

Reducing Flood Losses. Engineers work not only to control floods, but also to reduce flood losses. A program to decrease such losses includes regulations to control permanent construction on the *flood plain* (land that gets flooded) and to make buildings waterproof. Other programs aim to help flood victims by improving methods to warn and evacuate people from flood plains and to provide better insurance and relief aid.

The U.S. Geological Survey and the army engineers identify and map flood hazard areas in the United States. More than 1,300 communities have used this information to set forth regulations for flood plain management. Many of these regulations require that a small strip of land along a waterway be left vacant. Such land is called a *floodway*. Many communities establish a wider area along the floodway for use as farmland or parkland.

Permanent buildings can be located on a flood plain and withstand flood damage. The technique of keeping water out of buildings is called *flood-proofing*. It involves raising buildings off the ground or using waterproof construction materials.

The U.S. government and the Red Cross provide relief for flood victims. They spent about $1 billion to help victims of the severe tropical storm of 1972. Flood insurance is available in about 1,000 communities, and the government pays part of the cost.

The National Weather Service has a network of 12 river forecast centers and 82 district offices that provide flood warnings. Meteorologists measure the height of rivers and the amount of rain and snow to decide whether a flood may occur. They use radar to estimate how much rain or snow will fall in the near future. The National Weather Service can provide enough warning to greatly reduce loss of life and to lower property damage by as much as 15 per cent.   ROBERT W. KATES

Related Articles in WORLD BOOK include:

Conservation	Johnstown	Ohio River
Dam	Levee	Reclamation,
Deluge	Mississippi River	Bureau of
Disaster	Missouri River	Tennessee Valley
Hwang Ho	Basin Project	Authority

FLOOR LEADER. See POLITICAL PARTY (Organizing the Government); HOUSE OF REPRESENTATIVES (Organization).

FLOORING is the general name given to all materials used to cover floors. The most common floorings are wood, concrete, stone, and tile. The main purpose of flooring is to keep rooms clean, dry, and warm.

The first floors were probably only the leveled dirt of the land over which houses were built. For hundreds of years, the houses of poor people continued to have only dirt floors. The log cabins of early American pioneers usually had dirt floors. But ancient peoples used floors of stone and baked clay in large public buildings and temples. The Greeks used marble in their floors. The Romans learned how to make cement. Stone was the most common flooring of public buildings and churches during the Middle Ages. In the 1500's, the Venetians developed *terrazzo*, one of the oldest types of flooring. They made it of granulated marble mixed with gray or white cement.

Wood was first used as flooring in the Middle Ages. *Parquet* floors of different colored woods arranged in designs decorated early palaces. Today, flooring of highly polished hardwoods is the most popular. Other types of flooring include asphalt, cork, linoleum, rubber, plastic, and ceramic tiles (see LINOLEUM; TILE). GEORGE W. WASHA

See also INTERIOR DECORATION (Choosing Patterns).

FLORA is the name given to the plant life of a particular period of time or part of the world. It corresponds to the word *fauna*, which is the term for the animal life of a certain place or time. The term *flora* is taken from the name of the mythological Roman goddess of flowers and spring.

FLORENCE (pop. 460,248) is an Italian city that became famous as the birthplace of the Renaissance. During the Renaissance, from about 1300 to 1600, some of the greatest painters, sculptors, and writers in history lived and worked in Florence.

The city lies on both banks of the Arno River in central Italy, about 60 miles (100 kilometers) east of the Ligurian Sea (see ITALY [political map]). Florence is the capital of both the province of Florence and the region of Tuscany. Its name in Italian is FIRENZE.

Such great artists as Leonardo da Vinci, Fra Angelico, Giotto, and Michelangelo produced many of Florence's magnificent paintings and sculptures. Great writers who lived in the city included Giovanni Boccaccio, Dante, and Petrarch. Florentines also won fame in other fields. For example, the architect Filippo Brunelleschi and the political analyst Niccolò Machiavelli were born in Florence, and the astronomer Galileo did some of his work there.

Today, about a million tourists visit Florence yearly to see its splendid art galleries, churches, and museums. The people of Florence consider Michelangelo's famous statue, *David*, as the symbol of the artistic spirit of their city.

The City covers about 40 square miles (104 square kilometers) in the middle of a rich farming area. The oldest part of Florence lies in a small area divided by the Arno. Most of the city's famous buildings are on the right bank, north of the river. A broad public square called the Piazza della Signoria is a major public gathering spot and tourist attraction on the right bank. Towering over the piazza is the Palazzo Vecchio, or Palazzo della Signoria, a palace that has been the center of local government since the Middle Ages. Many old, impressive churches stand on the right bank of the Arno. The Cathedral of Florence, called the Duomo, is in the Piazza del Duomo. The eight-sided Baptistery, with its beautifully decorated bronze doors by Lorenzo Ghiberti and Andrea Pisano, is part of this piazza. The piazza also features a *campanile* (bell tower) built by Giotto and Pisano.

The tombs of Galileo, Machiavelli, Michelangelo, and other famous Florentines are in the Church of Santa Croce. This church also has frescoes by Giotto. The Church of San Marco and an adjacent museum display a collection of paintings by Fra Angelico and other artists of the 1400's. The chapel of the Church of San Lorenzo has the large stone figures carved by Michelangelo for the tombs of the powerful Medici family.

Many outstanding art galleries and museums are also on the right bank. The famous Uffizi Palace, which once housed government offices, is now an art gallery. It owns one of the world's finest collections of paintings and statues (see UFFIZI PALACE). The National Museum of the Bargello exhibits many masterpieces of Renaissance sculpture. The Galleria dell'Accademia displays medieval and Renaissance sculpture, including Michelangelo's *David*. Two copies of this statue stand elsewhere in Florence.

Florence's most elegant shopping area lies along the Via Tornabuoni, a street in the western part of the old section of the city. Some shops on this street display the kinds of clothing and leather goods that have made Florence famous for fashions.

Six bridges connect the right bank with the Oltrarno, the section of Florence south of the river. Goldsmith and jewelry shops line one of these bridges, the Ponte Vecchio, which was built in 1345. The other bridges replaced bridges destroyed during World War II (1939-1945) by retreating German troops. The present Ponte Santa Trinita is an exact reconstruction of the original bridge, which had stood since 1570.

The Oltrarno includes many antique, silver, and woodcarving shops, but its most famous attraction is the Pitti Palace. This palace—the largest in Florence—was begun in 1458 as a home for Luca Pitti, a wealthy merchant. It now displays an excellent collection of paintings (see PITTI PALACE). The Boboli Gardens, behind the palace, are among the most beautiful gardens in Italy.

Modern apartment buildings stand in Florence's suburbs, which have developed since the 1950's. Industry is concentrated north of the city.

The People. Almost all Florentines are of Italian descent. They speak Italian and belong to the Roman Catholic Church.

Most families in the oldest part of the city live in old stone buildings that lack central heating. Large numbers of families in the suburbs make their homes in modern apartment buildings.

Florentines, like most Italians, eat their largest meal at lunchtime. This meal may include fruit, meat, vegetables, and one of several kinds of noodles called *pasta*, such as spaghetti or ravioli. Other favorites of the people include Chianti wine and beefsteak.

Florence has many public markets. Shoppers meet every morning in the market places and chat as they shop. The Mercato Nuovo, a merchandising square in the heart of Florence, attracts thousands of tourists daily.

Education and Cultural Life. Florence is the home of the University of Florence and several research institutes. The Academy of Fine Arts and the Luigi Cherubini Conservatory of Music are also in the city. Operas are presented at the Teatro Comunale and the Teatro Verdi. Public libraries in Florence include the Laurenziana, the Marucelliana, the Riccardiana, and one of Italy's two national central libraries.

Economy. Florentines have made fine handicrafts since the days of the Renaissance. Many of the people make or sell such handicrafts as leather products, jewelry, mosaics, pottery, and articles made of straw. Tourism is an important economic activity of Florence.

Factories in the city produce clothing, drugs, foods, glass, and plastics. Florence is a major communications and railroad center of Italy.

History. The Etruscans, a tribe that migrated to Italy from Asia, built the first settlement in what is now Florence. They arrived there about 200 B.C., but their settlement was destroyed in 82 B.C. following a Roman civil war. In 59 B.C., the Roman ruler Julius Caesar established a colony on the Arno and named it Floren-

Seymour Linden, De Wys, Inc.

The Ponte Vecchio (Old Bridge) spans the Arno River in Florence. Small shops line both sides of the bridge, a historic landmark built in 1345.

World Film Enterprises, Black Star

Art Treasures of Florence include many statues in the Piazza della Signoria, a square in the heart of the city.

tia. The name later became Florence.

Florence remained a small, unimportant town until about A.D. 1000. It then began to develop into a self-governing area called a *city-state*. Its population grew from perhaps 5,000 in A.D. 900 to about 30,000 in 1200.

The people of Florence developed new processes for refining wool, and the city gained importance for its woolen textiles. Florentine bankers became successful and brought much wealth to the city. The population reached about 100,000 in the early 1300's. Florence fought many wars during the 1300's and early 1400's, gaining and losing territory at various times.

During the 1300's, four Florentines introduced new styles of painting and writing that grew into great achievements of the Renaissance. Giotto painted pictures with realistic figures instead of stiff, formal subjects. In literature, Dante developed Italian as a literary language and Petrarch and Boccaccio renewed interest in the classics. For the next 300 years, Florence was a center of one of the greatest periods of cultural achievement in history.

The wealthy Medici family gained control of Florence in the early 1400's. By that time, Florence had become a strong and almost independent city-state. It controlled part of what is now central Italy. The city achieved its greatest splendor under the most famous Medici, Lorenzo the Magnificent, who ruled from 1469 to 1492. Except for brief periods, members of the Medici family governed until 1737. During their rule, Florentine literature, theater, and opera thrived in Florence and were imitated throughout Europe. See MEDICI.

Florence was the capital of Italy from 1865 to 1870, when the government moved to Rome. Many improvements were carried out in Florence during its period as the capital. For example, the tree-lined boulevards and large piazzas just outside the historical center of Florence were built at that time.

During World War II (1939-1945), several ancient palaces were destroyed during the fighting for Florence. But most of the city's art treasures escaped harm.

In 1966, a flood damaged books, manuscripts, valuable works of art, and museums and other buildings in Florence. Many nations aided in the restoration of the art works. Most of the paintings and manuscripts were saved, though some required years of careful work.

During the 1970's, Florence faced many problems that resulted from a huge increase in the city's population. The number of Florentines grew from about 96,000 in 1861 to 460,248 in 1972. Municipal services, including electricity and water supplies, sometimes fell short of providing enough for everyone. Pedestrians and traffic crowded the narrow streets of the old section. In 1970, private automobiles were banned from the historic center of the city. EMILIANA P. NOETHER

See also ARCHITECTURE (Renaissance; picture: Cathedral of Florence); PAINTING (The Renaissance in Florence; pictures); RENAISSANCE (The Renaissance in Italy); SAVONAROLA, GIROLAMO; SCULPTURE (Italian Renaissance; pictures).

FLORES. See INDONESIA (table: Chief Islands).

FLORES ISLAND, *FLOH rus* (pop. 5,302), famed for its abundant foliage, is the westernmost island of the Portuguese Azores. It covers 55 square miles (142 square kilometers). The main occupations are dairying and cattle raising. Santa Cruz is the chief town. See also AZORES.

FLOREY, LORD (1898-1968), HOWARD WALTER FLOREY, a British bacteriologist, pioneered with Sir Alexander Fleming in developing the antibiotic penicillin (see ANTIBIOTIC; PENICILLIN). He shared the 1945 Nobel prize in medicine with Fleming and Ernst Chain (see FLEMING, SIR ALEXANDER; CHAIN, ERNST BORIS). In 1940 and 1941, his research team at Oxford isolated penicillin in relatively pure form, and tested it.

Florey was born in Adelaide, Australia. He studied at Adelaide University, and, as a Rhodes scholar, at Magdalen College, Oxford. STANLEY E. WEDBERG

FLORICULTURE, *FLOH rih KUL tyur*, is the art, science, and business of growing ornamental plants. Some ornamental plants are grown for outdoor use, others for interior decoration and special occasions.

Raising and marketing cut flowers and decorative plants ranks as a large industry. In mild climates, people grow cut flowers and potted plants outdoors, even in winter. But in cold climates, such plants are grown in greenhouses that can be heated during cold weather. Growers can control the blossoming of flowers. For example, they arrange to have poinsettias for Christmas and lilies for Easter.

Floriculturists control the blooming of flowers by various techniques developed through research. They also control blossoming by planting the flowers on certain dates, by removing the tips of the plants, and by regulating the temperature. Sometimes they artificially lengthen or shorten the amount of light the plant receives each day. Researchers in floriculture have developed long-stemmed carnations, thornless roses, and double snapdragons. Floriculturists work in nurseries, florist shops, and seed companies. HENRY T. NORTHEN

See also CROSS-POLLINATION; FLORIST; GREENHOUSE; HYBRID.

A Sunny Florida Beach

Bathers and Shell Pickers by Eugene Massin from the WORLD BOOK Collection

FLORIDA

THE SUNSHINE STATE

FLORIDA is one of the leading tourist states in the nation. This land of swaying palm trees and warm ocean breezes attracts visitors the year around. Many older persons spend their retirement years in the state. Florida has been nicknamed the *Sunshine State* because of its large number of sunny days. Tallahassee is the capital of Florida and Jacksonville ranks as the state's largest city. Miami Beach, a suburb of Miami, is one of

The contributors of this article are David E. Christensen, coauthor of Florida Reference Atlas; *Malcolm B. Johnson, Editor of the* Tallahassee Democrat; *and Rembert W. Patrick, author of* The Story of Florida.

the most famous resort centers in the world. Other popular seaside resorts in Florida include Daytona Beach, Fort Lauderdale, Palm Beach, and St. Petersburg.

Florida is the southernmost state except for Hawaii. It is sometimes called the *Peninsula State* because it juts southward about 400 miles (640 kilometers) into the sea. The marshy grasslands near the southern tip of the peninsula account for another nickname, the *Everglade State*. Florida faces the Atlantic Ocean on the east, and the Gulf of Mexico on the west. The southern tip of Florida is less than 100 miles (160 kilometers) from Cuba. Florida has a longer coastline than any state except Alaska.

Florida (blue) ranks 22nd in size among all the states, and is the second largest of the Southern States (gray).

Miami Beach News Bureau Photo

Miami Beach, one of North America's most famous resort cities, lies along the Atlantic Ocean just east of Miami. Miami Beach has some of the most luxurious hotels ever built.

Florida's population is growing faster than that of all but a few states. Its industries are expanding, especially in food processing. Florida produces about three-fourths of the nation's oranges and grapefruit. Almost all the frozen orange juice produced in the United States is processed in Florida. Florida also ranks among the leading commercial fishing states.

In 1513, the explorer Juan Ponce de León claimed the Florida region for Spain. In 1958, *Explorer I*, America's first earth satellite, soared into space from Florida's Cape Canaveral. The years between these two famous explorers are rich in Florida history.

Ponce de León named the region for the many flowers he saw there. *Florida* is a Spanish word that means *full of flowers.* In 1565, the Spaniards established St. Augustine, the first permanent white settlement in what became the United States. England gained control of Florida in 1763, but ceded it back to Spain in 1783. After the Revolutionary War, Florida was the only part of southeastern North America that did not belong to the United States.

The United States formally obtained Florida from Spain in 1821, and Congress established the Territory of Florida the next year. Florida became a state in 1845. Shortly before the Civil War began in 1861, Florida left the Union and then joined the Confederacy. Tallahassee was the only Confederate state capital east of the Mississippi River that Union forces did not capture during the war. Florida was readmitted to the Union in 1868. The population of Florida started to swell during the early 1900's, and has been growing ever since that time.

For Florida's relationship to other states in its region, see SOUTHERN STATES.

--- FACTS IN BRIEF ---

Capital: Tallahassee.

Government: *Congress*—U.S. senators, 2; representatives, 15. *Electoral Votes*—17. *State Legislature*—senators, 40; representatives, 120. *Counties*—67.

Area: 58,560 sq. mi. (151,670 km²), including 4,470 sq. mi. (11,577 km²) of inland water but excluding 1,735 sq. mi. (4,494 km²) of Atlantic and Gulf of Mexico coastal water; 22nd in size among the states. *Greatest Distances*—north-south, 447 mi. (719 km); east-west, 361 mi. (581 km). *Coastline*—Atlantic Ocean, 580 mi. (933 km); Gulf of Mexico, 770 mi. (1,239 km).

Elevation: *Highest*—345 ft. (105 m) above sea level in Walton County. *Lowest*—sea level along the Atlantic Ocean.

Population: *Estimated 1975 Population*—8,357,000. *1970 Census*—6,789,443; 9th among the states; distribution, 81 per cent urban, 19 per cent rural; density, 116 persons per sq. mi. (45 persons per km²).

Chief Products: *Agriculture*—oranges, sugar cane, milk, beef cattle, greenhouse and nursery products. *Fishing Industry*—shrimp, lobsters. *Manufacturing*—food products, chemicals, transportation equipment, electric and electronic equipment, printed materials. *Mining*—phosphate rock, petroleum, stone.

Statehood: March 3, 1845, the 27th state.

State Abbreviations: Fla. (traditional); FL (postal).

State Motto: *In God We Trust* (unofficial).

State Song: "Swanee River." Words and music by Stephen Foster.

Constitution of Florida went into effect in 1969. Earlier constitutions went into effect in 1839 (before Florida became a state), in 1861, 1865, 1868, and in 1887.

Constitutional *amendments* (changes) must be approved by a majority of persons voting on them in a general or special election. Amendments may be proposed by the Legislature. Three-fifths of each legislative house must approve the proposed amendment. *Initiative* amendments may be proposed by a petition signed by a specified number of voters. The people may also petition to call a constitutional convention. The petition must then be approved by the voters.

Executive. Florida's governor serves a four-year term and can serve more than one term, but not more than two terms in a row. The governor receives a yearly salary of $50,000. Candidates for governor and lieutenant governor run as a team. Voters cast one vote for the governor and lieutenant governor. For a list of Florida's governors, see the *History* section of this article.

Most state officials are elected. These include cabinet members, Supreme Court justices, circuit court and district court of appeals judges, and public service commissioners. The cabinet consists of the attorney general, commissioner of agriculture, comptroller, secretary of state, commissioner of education, and treasurer. Cabinet members serve four-year terms.

Legislature consists of a 40-member Senate and a 120-member House of Representatives. Senators serve four-year terms, and representatives serve two-year terms. The Legislature meets for a brief organizational session 14 days after November general elections. The regular 60-day session opens on the first Tuesday after the first Monday in April each year. Twenty-day spe-

cial sessions may be called by the governor, by joint agreement of the leaders of each legislative house, or by a three-fifths vote of all members of the Legislature. Most regular or special sessions may be extended by a three-fifths vote of each house.

In 1965, a federal court ordered Florida to *reapportion* (redivide) its Legislature to provide equal representation based on population. The Legislature drew up a reapportionment plan, but the U.S. Supreme Court ruled it unconstitutional. In 1967, a three-judge federal court devised its own reapportionment plan. The Legislature was reapportioned again in 1972.

Courts. The state Supreme Court has a chief justice and six associate justices, all elected to six-year terms. The justices take turns serving two years as chief justice. Florida has four district courts of appeals and 20 circuit courts. Judges of both of these courts are elected for six years. Each county has a county court with one or more judges elected for four years. County courts handle minor civil and criminal cases.

Local Government. Florida's 67 counties can vary their form of government by adopting special county charters approved by the Legislature and the people. Most of the counties are governed by a board of five commissioners and are divided into five districts. County voters elect a resident from each district to serve on the county commission. Other elected county officers include the circuit court clerk, sheriff, supervisor of elections, tax assessor, and tax collector. County officials serve four-year terms.

Chartered counties and municipalities have *home rule* (self-government) to the extent that they may make laws with voter approval. Counties and municipalities also have the power to *consolidate* (combine) and work

The Governor's Mansion in Tallahassee, built in 1957, has stately white columns typical of Southern colonial architecture.
Florida State News Bureau

The Supreme Court Building in Tallahassee is noted for its massive appearance and classical simplicity.
Florida State News Bureau

The State Seal

Symbols of Florida. On the state seal, adopted in 1868, the sun represents glory and splendor, and the authority of the state government. The steamboat is a sign of commerce and growth. The palm tree symbolizes victory, justice, and honor. The flowers stand for hope and joy. The Indian girl strewing flowers shows the influence of various tribes on Florida's history. On the flag, adopted in 1899, the seal lies in a white field crossed by diagonal red bars, which stand for the bars of the Confederate flag.

Bird and flower illustrations, courtesy of Eli Lilly and Company

as a single government. Forms of municipal government in Florida include mayor-council, mayor-commission, and commission-manager.

Taxation. Sales and gross receipts taxes account for almost 60 per cent of the state government's income. Licenses account for an additional 10 per cent. Earnings on investments and deposits and a tax on corporation income provide nearly 10 per cent. The state receives about 20 per cent of its income from federal grants and other U.S. government programs.

Politics. Since the Reconstruction period ended in 1877, all but two of Florida's governors have been Democrats (see RECONSTRUCTION). Only six Republican presidential candidates have won the state's electoral votes since Reconstruction—in 1928, 1952, 1956, 1960, 1968, and 1972. For Florida's voting record in presidential elections, see ELECTORAL COLLEGE (table).

Florida's New State Capitol is 22 stories tall. The Capitol, shown in the sketch below, opened in Tallahassee in 1977.

Office of the Governor

The State Flag

The State Bird
Mockingbird

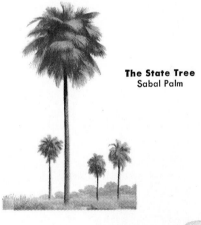

The State Tree
Sabal Palm

The State Flower
Orange Blossom

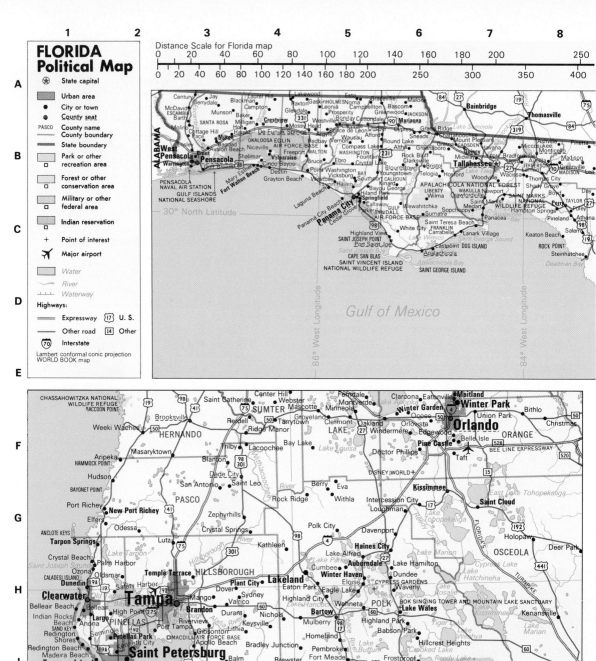
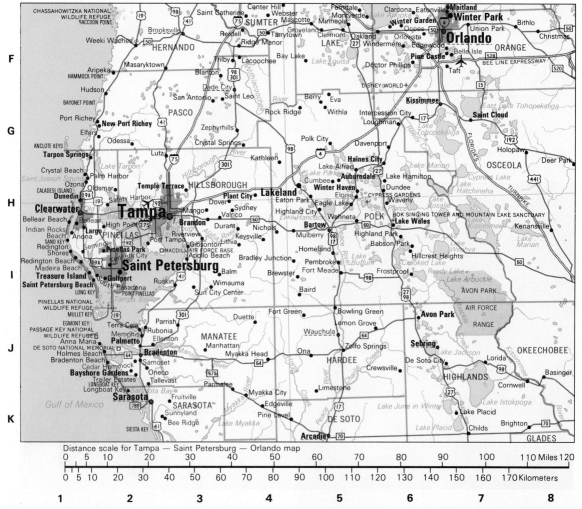

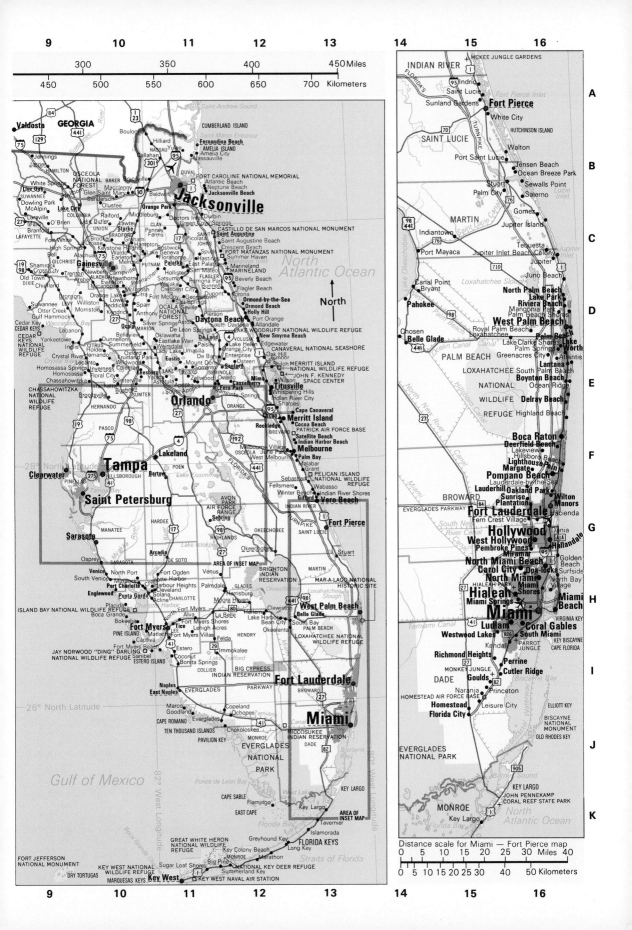

Population

8,357,000 Estimate	1975
6,789,443	Census..1970
4,951,560	" ...1960
2,771,305	" ...1950
1,897,414	" ...1940
1,468,211	" ...1930
968,470	" ...1920
752,619	" ...1910
528,542	" ...1900
391,422	" ...1890
269,493	" ...1880
187,748	" ...1870
140,424	" ...1860
87,445	" ...1850
54,477	" ...1840
34,730	" ...1830

Metropolitan Areas

Bradenton 97,115
Daytona Beach ..169,487
Fort Lauderdale-
Hollywood 620,100
Fort Myers 105,216
Gainesville 104,764
Jacksonville ...621,827
Lakeland-Winter
Haven 228,515
Melbourne-Titus-
ville-Cocoa ...230,006
Miami 1,267,792
Orlando 453,270
Panama City ...75,283
Pensacola 243,075
Sarasota 120,413
Tallahassee ...109,355
Tampa-St.
Petersburg ..1,088,549
West Palm Beach-
Boca Raton ..348,993

Counties

Alachua ..104,764..D 10
Baker .....9,242..B 10
Bay ....75,283..B 5
Bradford ..14,625..C 10
Brevard ..230,006..F 12
Broward ..620,100..I 13
Calhoun ...7,624..B 6
Charlotte ..27,559..H 11
Citrus ....19,196..E 10
Clay ......32,059..C 11
Collier ...38,040..I 11
Columbia ..25,250..C 10
Dade ...1,267,792..J 13
De Soto ..13,060..H 11
Dixie .....5,480..D 9
Duval ...528,865..D 11
Escambia .205,334..A 3
Flagler ...4,454..D 11
Franklin ..7,065..C 6
Gadsden ..39,184..B 7
Gilchrist ..3,551..C 9
Glades .....3,669..H 12
Gulf ......10,096..C 6
Hamilton ...7,787..B 9
Hardee ...14,889..G 11
Hendry ...11,859..I 12
Hernando ..17,004..E 10
Highlands .29,507..G 12
Hillsbor-
ough ...490,265..F 10
Holmes ...10,720..A 5
Indian
River ...35,992..G 13
Jackson ..34,434..A 6
Jefferson ..8,778..B 8
Lafayette ..2,892..C 9
Lake .....69,305..E 11
Lee ......105,216..I 11
Leon .....103,047..B 7
Levy .....12,756..D 9
Liberty ....3,379..C 6
Madison ..13,481..B 8
Manatee ..97,115..G 10
Marion ...69,030..D 10
Martin ...28,035..H 13
Monroe ...52,586..J 12
Nassau ...20,626..B 11
Okaloosa ..88,187..B 4
Okeechobee 11,233..G 12
Orange ..344,311..E 12
Osceola ..25,267..F 12
Palm
Beach ..348,993..F 13
Pasco ...108,865..F 10
Pinellas .522,329..F 9
Polk ....228,515..F 11
Putnam ...36,424..C 11
St. Johns .31,035..C 11
St. Lucie .50,836..G 13
Santa Rosa 37,741..B 3
Sarasota .120,413..H 10
Seminole ..83,692..E 12
Sumter ...14,839..E 10
Suwannee .15,559..B 9
Taylor ...13,641..C 8
Union .....8,112..C 10
Volusia ..169,487..D 12
Wakulla ...8,546..C 7
Walton ...16,087..B 5
Washington 11,453..B 5

Cities, Towns, and Villages

Alachua ...2,252..C 10
Alford ......402..B 6
Altamonte
Springs ..4,391..E 11
Altha ......423..B 6
Anna Maria .1,137..J 2
Anona ....H 1
Apalachicola 3,102.°C 6
Apollo Beach 1,042..I 3
Apopka ...4,045..E 11
Arcadia ...5,658.°G 11
Archer .....898..D 10
Astatula ....388..E 11
Atlantic Beach ...E 11
Atlantis ....425..E 16
Auburndale 5,386..H 5
Avon Park .6,712..J 6
Azalea Park* 7,367..E 11
Babson Park ....I 6
Bagdad ....A 3
Baker ....B 4
Bal
Harbour* .2,038..H 16
Baldwin ....B 11
Bartow ...12,891.°F 11
Bascom .....87..A 6
Bay Harbor
Islands* .4,619..H 16
Bay Lake* ....24..E 12
Bayshore
Gardens .9,255..J 2
Bayview* ....696..C 5
Beacon
Squier* ...2,927..F 10
Bee Ridge ....K 3
Bell ....227..C 9
Belle Glade 15,949..H 13
Belle Isle .2,705..F 7
Belleair ..2,962..H 1
Belleair
Beach ....952..H 1
Belleair
Bluffs* ..1,910..F 9
Belleair
Shores* ...124..H 1
Belleview ..916..D 10
Bellglade
Camp* ..1,892..H 13
Beverly Beach .21..D 12
Biscayne
Park* ...2,717..H 16
Bithlo .....684..F 8
Blountstown 2,384.°B 6
Boca Chica* 2,817..K 11
Boca Grande ....H 10
Boca Raton 28,506..F 16
Bonifay ...2,068.°B 5
Bonita
Springs ..1,932..I 11
Boulogne ...77..B 10
Bowling
Green ...1,357..J 5
Boynton
Beach ..18,115..I 16
Bradenton .21,040.°J 2
Bradenton
Beach ....1,370..J 2
Bradenton South, see
Cedar Hammock
[-Bradenton
South]
Bradley
Junction 1,276..I 4
Brandon ..12,749..H 3
Branford ....820..C 9
Brent ....B 3
Briny Breezes* 481..H 13
Bristol .....626.°B 6
Broadview
Park-Rock
Hill* ....6,049..I 13
Bronson ....698.°D 10
Brooker ....340..C 10
Brooksville 4,060.°E 10
Browardale* 17,444..I 13
Browns
Village* .23,442..J 13
Bryant ....D 14
Buena
Vista* ...3,407..F 10
Bunche
Park* ...5,773..J 13
Bunnell ...1,687.°D 12
Bushnell ...700.°E 10
Callahan ....772..B 11
Callaway ..3,650..C 5
Campbellton ..304..A 6
Canaan, see Midway-
Canaan
Canal Point ....D 14
Cantonment* 3,241..B 3
Cape
Canaveral 4,258..I 13
Cape Coral* 11,470..H 11
Carol City .27,361..H 16
Carrabelle ..1,044..C 7
Carver Ranch
Estates* ..5,515..I 13
Caryville ...724..B 5
Casselberry .9,438..E 12
Cedar Grove .689..C 5
Cedar Hammock
[-Bradenton
South] ..10,820..J 2

Cedar Key ....714..D 9
Center Hill ...371..E 4
Century ...2,679..A 3
Chattahoo-
chee ......7,944..B 6
Chiefland ..1,965..D 9
Chipley ...3,347.°B 5
Chosen ....D 14
Cinco Bayou .362..B 4
Clair Mel, see Palm
River-Clair Mel
Clearwater .52,074.°F 9
Clermont ..3,661..F 5
Clewiston .3,896..H 12
Cloud Lake* .136..D 16
Cocoa ....16,110..F 12
Cocoa
Beach ....9,952..F 13
Cocoa West* 5,779..F 12
Coconut
Creek* ...1,359..I 13
Coleman ....614..E 10
Collier Manor-
Crest-
haven* ...7,202..I 13
Colonial
Hills* ...2,193..F 9
Conway ...8,642..E 12
Cooper City .2,535..G 16
Coral Cove* .1,520..G 10
Coral
Gables ..42,494..H 16
Coral
Springs* .1,489..I 13
Cottondale ..765..B 6
Country
Estates* .1,950..F 9
Crawfordville .°C 7
Crescent
City .....1,734..D 11
Cresthaven, see
Collier Manor-
Cresthaven
Crestview ..7,952.°B 4
Cross City .2,268.°D 9
Crystal Beach ...H 1
Crystal River 1,696..E 10
Crystal Springs ..G 4
Cumbee ...4,963..H 5
Cutler
Ridge ...17,441..I 16
Cypress ....266..B 6
Cypress
Gardens* .3,757..F 11
Cypress
Quarters* .1,310..G 12
Dade City .4,257.°F 4
Dade City
East* ....1,163..E 10
Dade City
North* ...1,837..E 10
Dania .....9,013..G 16
Davenport .1,303..G 6
Davie .....5,859..G 16
Daytona
Beach ..45,327..D 12
Daytona
Beach
Shores* ...768..D 12
De Bary ..3,154..E 11
Deerfield
Beach ..16,662..F 16
De Funiak
Springs ..4,966.°B 5
De Land ..11,641.°D 12
De Leon
Springs ..1,134..D 11
Delray
Beach ..19,915..E 16
Deltona* ..4,868..E 12
Destin ....1,536..B 4
Doctors Inlet ...C 11
Dover .....2,094..H 3
Dundee ...1,660..H 6
Dunedin ..17,639..H 1
Dunnellon .1,146..D 10
Eagle Lake .1,373..H 5
East Auburn-
dale* ....2,621..F 11
East Lake-Orient
Park* ...5,711..H 3
East Naples 6,152.°I 11
East Palatka 1,446..C 11
East Winter
Haven* ..1,148..F 11
Eastpoint ..1,188..C 6
Eaton Park ....H 5
Eatonville .2,024..E 7
Ebro ....125..B 5
Edgewater .3,348..D 12
Edgewood ...392..F 7
Eglin .....7,769..B 4
Egypt Lake* 7,556..F 10
Ellenton ..1,421..J 2
Eloise ....1,504..H 5
El Portal* .2,068..H 16
El Ranchero
Vill-Golf Lake
Estates* .1,859..I 16
Englewood .5,108..H 10
Ensley ....7,181..E 11
Esto ....210..A 5
Eustis ....7,181..E 11
Everglades ..462..J 12
Fellsmere ..813..G 13
Fern Crest
Village ..1,029..I 16
Fern Park .....E 12

Fernandina
Beach ....6,955.°B 11
Five Points* 1,214..B 10
Flagler
Beach ....1,042..D 12
Florahome .....C 11
Floral City ...G 9
Florida City 5,133..J 15
Florida
Ridge* ...1,338..G 13
Forest Hills* 1,215..F 9
Fort Lauder-
dale ...139,590.°I 13
Fort Meade .5,441..I 5
Fort Myers .28,409.°H 11
Fort Myers
Beach ....4,305..I 11
Fort Myers Shores ..H 11
Fort Myers
Southeast* 3,150..H 11
Fort Myers
Southwest* 5,086..H 11
Fort Myers
Villas [-Pine
Manor] ...3,408..I 11
Fort Pierce 29,721.°G 13
Fort Pierce
Northwest* 3,269..G 13
Fort Walton
Beach ...19,994..B 4
Fort White ...365..C 9
Freeport ....518..B 4
Frostproof .2,814..I 6
Fruitland
Park .....1,359..E 11
Fruitville ..1,531..K 3
Gainesville .64,510.°C 10
Gibsonton .....I 3
Gifford ....5,772..G 13
Glen Ridge* ..216..D 16
Glen St. Mary 357..B 10
Golden Beach .849..G 16
Golf* ....50..E 16
Golf Lake Estates,
see El Ranchero
Vill-Golf
Lake Estates
Golfview* ...201..D 16
Goulds ....6,690..I 15
Graceville .2,560..A 5
Grand Ridge .512..B 6
Green Cove
Springs ..3,857.°C 11
Greenacres
City .....1,731..E 16
Greensboro ..716..B 6
Greenville .1,141..B 8
Greenwood ..449..A 6
Gretna .....883..B 7
Grove City* 1,252..H 10
Groveland .1,928..F 5
Gulf Breeze .4,190..B 3
Gulf Gate
Estates* .5,874..G 10
Gulf
Harbors* .1,177..F 9
Gulf Stream* .408..E 16
Gulfport ..9,976..I 2
Hacienda ....15..G 16
Haines City 8,956..H 6
Hallandale .23,849..G 16
Hampton ....386..C 10
Harlem ....2,006..H 12
Hastings ....628..C 11
Havana ....2,022..B 7
Haverhill* .1,034..D 16
Hawthorn ..1,126..D 10
Hernando ...524..E 10
Hialeah ..102,452..H 16
Hialeah
Gardens* ...492..H 16
High Springs 2,787..C 10
Highland Beach 624..F 16
Highland City ..H 5
Highland Park ..H 5
Highland View ..C 6
Hiland Park 3,691..C 5
Hillcrest
Heights ....154..I 6
Hilliard ...1,205..B 11
Hillsboro
Beach ....1,181..F 16
Hobe Sound* 2,029..H 13
Holden
Heights* .6,206..E 11
Holiday
Gardens* .2,132..F 9
Holiday
Hills* ...1,657..F 9
Holly Hill .11,811..D 12
Hollywood 106,873..H 16
Holmes
Beach ....2,699..J 2
Holt ....B 4
Homestead .13,674..J 15
Homestead
Base .....8,257..I 15
Horseshoe
Beach* ....124..C 9
Howey-in-
the-Hills* ..466..E 11
Hudson ...2,278..G 2
Hurlburt* .2,155..B 4
Hypoluxo* ...336..E 16
Immokalee .3,764..I 11
Indialantic 2,685..F 13
Indian Creek* .82..H 16

Indian Harbor
Beach ....5,371..F 13
Indian River
Shores* ....76..G 13
Indian Rocks
Beach ....2,666..I 1
Indian Shores* 791..I 1
Indiantown .2,283..C 15
Indrio ....A 15
Inglis ....449..E 9
Interlachen ..1,338..C 11
Inverness ..2,299.°E 10
Islamorada .1,251..K 13
Islandia* ......8..J 13
Jackson-
ville ...528,865.°B 11
Jacksonville
Beach ....B 11
Jan Phyl
Village* .1,340..F 11
Jasmine
Estates* ..2,967..F 9
Jasper ....2,221.°B 9
Jay ....646..A 3
Jennings ....582..B 9
Jensen Beach .....B 16
June Park .3,090..F 13
Juno Beach .747..D 16
Jupiter ...3,136..C 16
Jupiter Inlet Beach
Colony ....396..C 16
Jupiter Island 295..C 16
Kendall ..35,497..I 16
Kenneth
City ......3,862..I 2
Kensington
Park* ...3,138..K 2
Key Colony
Beach ....371..K 12
Key Largo .2,866..K 13
Key West .29,312.°K 11
Keystone
Heights ...800..C 10
Kissimmee .7,659.°G 7
La Belle ..1,823.°H 11
Lacoochee .1,380..F 4
La Crosse ...365..C 10
Lady Lake ...382..E 11
Lake Alfred .2,847..H 5
Lake Buena
Vista* .....12..F 11
Lake Butler 1,598.°C 10
Lake
Carroll* .5,577..F 10
Lake City .10,575.°C 10
Lake Clarke
Shores ...2,328..E 16
Lake Forest* 5,216..I 13
Lake
Hamilton .1,165..H 6
Lake Helen .1,303..E 12
Lake Hollo-
way* .....6,227..H 4
Lake Magda-
lene* .....9,266..F 10
Lake Mary* .1,924..E 12
Lake Park .6,993..D 16
Lake Placid .656..K 7
Lake Ship
Heights* .1,114..F 11
Lake Wales .8,240..H 6
Lake Worth 23,714..E 16
Lakeland .41,550..F 11
Lantana ...7,126..E 16
Largo ....26,265..H 1
Lauderdale-
by-the-
Sea ......2,879..G 16
Lauderdale Isles,
see Riverland
Village-
Lauderdale Isles
Lauderdale
Lakes* ..10,577..I 13
Lauderhill .8,465..G 16
Laurel Hill ..418..A 4
Lawtey ....636..C 10
Layton, see
Long Key
Lazy Lake* ...48..G 16
Lee ....240..B 9
Leesburg .11,869..E 11
Lehigh Acres 4,394..I 11
Leisure City ..J 15
Leto* .....8,458..F 11
Lighthouse
Point ...10,695..F 16
Live Oak ..6,830.°B 9
Lockhart* .5,809..E 11
Long Key
(Layton) ...100..K 12
Longboat
Key ......2,850..K 2
Longwood .3,203..E 12
Lutz ....G 3
Lynn Haven 4,044..B 5
Macclenny .2,733.°B 10
Madeira
Beach ....4,177..I 1
Madison ...3,737.°B 8
Maitland ..7,157..E 7
Malabar ....634..F 13
Malone .....667..A 6
Manalapan* ..205..E 16
Mango ....H 3
Mangonia
Park ....827..D 16

A Shopping Center in Miami Beach reflects the ability of Florida's cities to keep up with change. This parklike mall, once a busy street, is used mainly by pedestrians. Weary shoppers can ride a bus to their favorite store.

Ewing Galloway

Marathon ...4,397..K 12
Margate ....8,867..F 16
Marianna ..6,741..°B 6
Marineland ....13..C 12
Mary
  Esther ....3,192..B 4
Mascotte ....966..F 5
Mayo ....793.°C 9
McIntosh ....287..D 10
Medley* .....351..J 13
Melbourne .40,236..F 13
Melbourne
  Beach* ...2,262..F 13
Melbourne
  Village ....597..F 12
Melrose
  Park* ....6,111..I 13
Memphis ...3,207..J 2
Merritt
  Island ..29,233..F 12
Mexico Beach* 588..C 6
Miami ..334,859.°J 13
Miami
  Beach ..87,072..H 16
Miami
  Shores ...9,425..H 16
Miami
  Springs .13,279..H 16
Micanopy .....759..D 10
Midway-
  Canaan* ..2,060..E 12
Milligan ....B 4
Milton .....5,360.°B 3
Mims ......8,309..E 12
Minneola ....878..F 5
Miramar ..23,997..G 16
Molino ....B 3
Monticello ..2,473.°B 8
Montverde ....308..E 5
Moore Haven ..974.°H 12
Mount Dora 4,543..E 11
Mulberry ...2,701..H 4
Myrtle
  Grove* ..16,186..B 3
Naples .....12,042..I 11
Naples
  Park* ...1,522..I 11
Naranja ....I 15
Neptune
  Beach ....B 11
New Port
  Richey ...7,137..G 2
New Port Richey
  East-Richey
  Lakes* ...2,758..G 2
New Smyrna
  Beach ..10,580..D 12
Newberry ...1,247..D 10
Niceville ..4,155..B 4
Nokomis
  Laurel* ..3,238..H 10
North Andrews
  Terrace* ..7,082..I 13
North Bay
  Village ..4,831..H 16
North Fort
  Myers ...8,798..H 11
North Lauder-
  dale* ....9,285..I 13
North
  Miami ..34,767..H 16
North Miami
  Beach ..30,544..H 16
North
  Naples* ..3,201..I 11
North Palm
  Beach ...9,035..D 16
North Port ..2,244..H 10
North Reding-
  ton Beach* ..768..I 1
North Winter
  Haven* ...1,659..F 11
Norwood* ..14,973..I 13
Oak Hill .....747..E 12
Oakland .....672..F 6
Oakland
  Park ....16,261..G 16

Ocala ......22,583.°D 10
Ocean City* .5,267..B 4
Ocean Breeze
  Park ....714..B 16
Ocean Ridge .1,074..E 16
Ocoee .....3,937..F 6
Okeechobee .3,715.°G 12
Oldsmar ....1,538..H 2
Olustee ....C 10
Ona ....236..J 5
Oneco ......3,246..J 2
Opa-locka .13,729..H 16
Orange City .1,777..E 12
Orange Lake ......G 9
Orange Park 7,619..C 11
Orchid* ....8..F 13
Orient Park, see
  East Lake-
  Orient Park
Orlando ...99,006.°E 11
Orlovista ....F 6
Ormond
  Beach ..14,768..D 12
Ormond-by-
  the-Sea ..6,002..D 13
Osprey ....1,115..H 10
Otter Creek ...230..D 9
Oviedo .....1,870..E 12
Oxford ....490..E 10
Ozona ....H 1
Pace ....1,776..A 3
Pahokee ...5,663..D 14
Painters Hill* .14..D 12
Palatka ....9,444.°C 11
Palm Bay ...7,176..F 13
Palm Beach .9,086..D 16
Palm Beach
  Gardens* .6,102..D 16
Palm Beach
  Shores ...1,214..D 16
Palm City ....B 16
Palm Harbor .....H 1
Palm River-
  Clair Mel* 8,536..F 10
Palm Shores* .202..F 13
Palm
  Springs ..4,340..E 16
Palma Sola* 1,745..J 2
Palmetto ...7,422..J 2
Panama
  City ....32,096.°C 5
Panama City
  Beach ......67..C 5
Parker ....4,212..C 5
Parkland* ....165..I 13
Parrish ....J 3
Patrick
  North* ...1,652..E 13
Patrick
  South* ...1,583..E 13
Paxton ....243..A 4
Pembroke
  Park* ....3,251..G 16
Pembroke
  Pines ...15,496..G 16
Penney Farms .561..C 11
Pennsuco* .....74..H 16
Pensacola .59,507.°B 3
Perrine ....16,257..I 16
Perry ......7,701.°C 8
Pierson ......654..D 11
Pine Castle ......F 7
Pine Craft* .1,208..G 10
Pine Hills* 13,882..E 11
Pine Manor, see Fort
  Myers Villas [-Pine
  Manor]
Pine Shores* 1,115..G 10
Pinellas
  Park ....22,287..I 2
Plant City .15,451..H 4
Plantation .23,523..G 16
Polk City .....151..G 5
Pomona
  Park ....578..D 11
Pompano
  Beach ...38,587..F 16

Pompano
  Beach
  Highlands* 5,014..I 13
Ponce de Leon 288..B 5
Ponce Inlet* .328..D 12
Port
  Charlotte .10,769..H 10
Port Orange .3,781..D 12
Port Richey .1,487..G 2
Port St. Joe 4,401.°C 6
Port St.
  Lucie ....4,000..B 16
Princeton ....I 15
Progress
  Village* ..2,573..F 10
Punta
  Gorda ....3,879.°H 10
Quincy ....8,334.°B 7
Raiford ......174..C 10
Reddick .....305..D 10
Redington
  Beach ....1,583..I 1
Redington
  Shores ...1,733..I 1
Richey Lakes, see
  New Port
  Richey East-
  Richey Lakes
Richmond
  Heights ..6,663..I 15
Ridge Wood
  Heights* ..2,528..G 10
Riverland Vil-
  lage-Lauder-
  dale Isles* 5,512..I 13
Riverview ...2,225..I 3
Riviera
  Beach ...21,401..D 16
Rock Hill, see
  Broadview Park-
  Rock Hill
Rockledge .10,523..F 12
Royal Palm
  Beach .....475..D 16
Ruskin ....2,414..I 3
Safety
  Harbor ...3,103..H 2
St.
  Augustine 12,352.°C 11
St. Augustine
  Beach .....632..C 12
St. Cloud ..5,041..G 7
St. Leo .....967..G 3
St. Lucie ....428..A 15
St. Marks ....332..C 7
St. Peters-
  burg ...236,413..F 10
St. Petersburg
  Beach ...8,024..I 2
Salerno ....1,161..B 16
Salt Springs .....D 11
Samoset ...4,070..J 2
San Antonio .412..G 3
San Mateo ....D 11
Sanford ...17,393.°E 12
Sanibel ....2,515..I 11
Sarasota ..40,237.°G 10
Sarasota
  North* ...1,737..G 10
Sarasota
  South* ...3,730..G 10
Sarasota
  Southeast* 6,885..G 10
Sarasota
  Springs* ..4,405..G 10
Satellite
  Beach ....6,558..F 13

Scottsmoor ....E 12
Sea Ranch
  Lakes* ....660..F 16
Sebastian ....825..F 13
Sebring ....7,223.°G 11
Seminole ..2,121..I 1
Seville ....D 11
Sewalls
  Point ......298..B 16
Shalimar ....578..B 4
Sharpes ....E 12
Siesta Key* 4,460..G 10
Sneads ....1,550..B 6
Solana ....1,286..H 11
Sopchoppy ...465..C 7
South
  Apopka ...2,293..E 11
South Bay ..2,958..H 13
South
  Daytona ..5,377..D 12
South
  Flomaton* ..329..A 3
South Gate
  Ridge* ...2,043..G 10
South
  Miami ..11,780..I 16
South Miami
  Heights* .10,395..J 13
South Palm
  Beach .....188..E 16
South
  Pasadena ,2,465..I 2
South Patrick
  Shores* .10,313..F 13
South Penin-
  sula* ....3,302..D 12
South
  Venice ...4,680..H 10
Southport ..1,560..B 5
Sparr ....D 10
Springfield ..5,949..C 5
Starke ....4,848.°C 10
Steinhatchee .....C 8
Stuart ....4,820.°G 13
Sun City
  Center ...2,143..I 3
Sunnyland ....K 3
Sunrise ...11,693..I 13
Surfside ...3,614..H 16
Suwannee
  River* ....115..C 9
Sweetwater* 3,357..H 16
Sweetwater
  Creek* ..19,453..F 10
Sydney ....H 4
Taft ......1,183..F 7
Tahitian
  Gardens* .1,286..F 9
Tallahassee 72,624.°B 7
Tamarac* ..22,614..I 13
Tampa ...277,753.°F 10
Tarpon
  Springs .7,118..G 1
Tavares ...3,261.°E 11
Tavernier ....K 13
Temple
  Terrace ..7,347..H 3
Tequesta ..2,642..C 16
Tice ......7,254..H 11
Titusville .30,515.°E 12
Trailer
  Estates ..1,759..J 2
Treasure
  Island ...6,120..I 1
Trenton ...1,074.°D 9
Tri Par
  Estates* .1,080..G 10

Trilby ....F 4
Tyndall ...4,248..C 5
Umatilla ..1,600..E 11
Union Park .2,827..F 7
University* .10,039..H 3
Valparaiso .6,504..B 4
Venice ....6,998..H 10
Vernon .....691..B 5
Vero Beach 11,908.°G 13
Vero Beach
  South* ...7,330..G 13
Virginia
  Gardens* .2,524..J 13
Wahneta ...2,733..H 5
Waldo ....800..C 10
Ward Ridge* ..8..C 6
Warrington 15,848..B 3
Watertown* .3,624..B 10
Wauchula ..3,007.°J 5
Wausau ......288..B 5
Waverly ...1,172..H 6
Webster ....739..E 4
Weeki
  Wachee .....76..F 2
Welaka ......496..D 11
Westbay ....B 5
West Auburn-
  dale* ....2,148..F 11
West Braden-
  ton* .....6,162..J 2
West Eau
  Gallie* ...2,705..F 12
West End* .5,289..D 10
West
  Hollywood ....G 16
West Mel-
  bourne ...3,050..F 13
West Miami* 5,494..H 16
West Palm
  Beach ...57,375.°H 13
West
  Pensacola 20,924..B 3
West Winter
  Haven* ...7,716..F 11
Westville ...266..A 5
Westwood
  Lakes ..12,811..I 15
Wewahitchka 1,733..C 6
White Springs 767..B 9
Whitfield
  Estates* ..1,362..J 2
Whiting
  Field* ....3,439..B 3
Wildwood ..2,082..E 10
Williston ..3,199..D 10
Wilton
  Manors .10,948..G 16
Windermere ..894..F 6
Winston* ..4,505..H 4
Winter Beach .....G 13
Winter
  Garden ...6,238..F 6
Winter
  Haven ..16,136..H 5
Winter
  Park ....21,895..E 7
Winter
  Springs* ..1,161..E 12
Worthington
  Springs* ...214..C 10
Yalaha ....E 11
Yankee-
  town ....490..D 9
Zellwood ....E 11
Zephyrhills .3,600..G 4
Zolfo
  Springs ..1,117..J 5

Sources: Latest census figures (1970 and special censuses). Places without population figures are unincorporated and are not listed in census reports.

FLORIDA /People

The 1970 United States census reported that Florida had a population of 6,789,443. This was an increase of 37 per cent over the 1960 figure, 4,951,560. Only Nevada had a larger percentage of growth during this 10-year period. The U.S. Bureau of the Census estimated that by 1975 the state's population had reached about 8,357,000.

About four-fifths of the people of Florida live in urban areas. That is, they live in or near cities and towns of 2,500 or more. The rest live in rural areas. About 87 per cent of the people live in the state's 16 Standard Metropolitan Statistical Areas (see METROPOLITAN AREA). These areas are Bradenton, Daytona Beach, Fort Lauderdale-Hollywood, Fort Myers, Gainesville, Jacksonville, Lakeland-Winter Haven, Melbourne-Titusville-Cocoa, Miami, Orlando, Panama City, Pensacola, Sarasota, Tallahassee, Tampa-St. Petersburg, and West Palm Beach-Boca Raton. For their populations, see the *Index* to the political map of Florida.

Jacksonville is Florida's largest city. Other large cities, in order of population, are Miami, Tampa, St. Petersburg, Fort Lauderdale, Hollywood, and Hialeah. See the separate articles on Florida cities listed in the *Related Articles* at the end of this article.

About 92 of every 100 Floridians were born in the United States. About 15 per cent are blacks. Many older persons move to Florida from other parts of the United States after they retire. The largest groups of persons from other countries now living in the state came from Britain, Canada, Cuba, Germany, and Russia.

Roman Catholics make up the largest religious group in the state. Other leading religious groups include Baptists, Jews, and Methodists.

Steinmetz, Publix
Diving for Sponges Along Florida's Gulf Coast

Steinmetz, Publix
Seminole Indians Branding a Calf in the Everglades

POPULATION

This map shows the *population density* of Florida, and how it varies in different parts of the state. Population density means the average number of persons who live in a given area.

Steinmetz
Senior Citizens in a retirement village near Bradenton enjoy a game of shuffleboard. Florida's mild, sunny climate lures many persons of retirement age to the state.

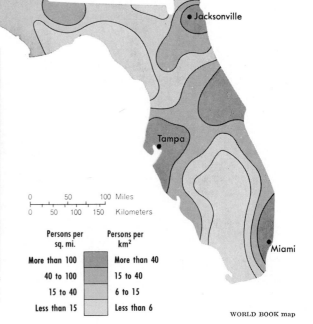

| | 0 | 50 | 100 Miles |
| 0 | 50 | 100 | 150 Kilometers |

Persons per sq. mi.		Persons per km²
More than 100		More than 40
40 to 100		15 to 40
15 to 40		6 to 15
Less than 15		Less than 6

WORLD BOOK map

Annie Pfeiffer Chapel is at Florida Southern College in Lakeland. It is one of nine campus buildings that were designed by architect Frank Lloyd Wright.

University of Miami students study ocean sciences at the Institute of Marine Science on Virginia Key, 7 miles (11 kilometers) from the main campus in Coral Gables.

FLORIDA/*Education*

Schools. Florida's first schools were run by Spanish priests in the 1600's. Spanish and Indian children studied religion and the Spanish language. In the mid-1700's, English colonists provided education for the children of wealthier families. Public education in Florida began in 1868 and was well established by the late 1800's.

The commissioner of education heads the Florida department of education. The commissioner also serves as secretary of the state board of education. Other board members include the governor, secretary of state, attorney general, state treasurer, state comptroller, and commissioner of agriculture. The department of education directs the activities of public schools, community colleges, universities, and vocational education programs. Children between the ages of 7 and 16 must attend school. For the number of students and teachers in Florida, see EDUCATION (table).

Libraries. The St. Augustine Free Public Library is the oldest library in Florida. It opened as a subscription library in 1874. Members of this library contributed money to buy books, which they could use without charge. The state's first free, tax-supported library opened in Jacksonville in 1905.

Today, Florida has about 155 public libraries with about 140 county and city branches. The State Library of Florida in Tallahassee is administered by the Florida Department of State. The P. K. Yonge Memorial Library of Florida History, at the University of Florida, owns the most outstanding collection of books about the state.

Museums. The John and Mabel Ringling Museum of Art in Sarasota has a fine collection of about 1,000 paintings, including many by European masters. A Ringling circus museum is nearby. Other museums in Florida include Cummer Gallery of Art in Jacksonville; Florida State Museum in Gainesville; Society of the Four Arts and Norton Gallery and School of Art, both in West Palm Beach; Lowe Art Museum at the University of Miami; Museum of Fine Arts in St. Petersburg; and Vizcaya-Dade County Art Museum, south of Miami.

—— UNIVERSITIES AND COLLEGES ——

Florida has 27 universities and colleges accredited by the Southern Association of Colleges and Schools. For enrollments and further information, see UNIVERSITIES AND COLLEGES (table).

Name	Location	Founded
Barry College	Miami Shores	1940
Bethune-Cookman College	Daytona Beach	1904
Biscayne College	Miami	1962
Eckerd College	St. Petersburg	1960
Embry-Riddle		
Aeronautical University	Daytona Beach	1962
Flagler College	St. Augustine	1968
Florida, University of	Gainesville	1853
Florida Agricultural and		
Mechanical University	Tallahassee	1887
Florida Atlantic University	Boca Raton	1961
Florida Institute of Technology	Melbourne	1958
Florida International University	Miami	1972
Florida Memorial College	Miami	1892
Florida Southern College	Lakeland	1885
Florida State University	Tallahassee	1857
Florida Technological		
University	Orlando	1963
Jacksonville University	Jacksonville	1934
Miami, University of	Coral Gables	1925
North Florida, University of	Jacksonville	1972
Nova University	Fort Lauderdale	1971
Palm Beach Atlantic College	West Palm Beach	1968
Rollins College	Winter Park	1885
St. Leo College	St. Leo	1963
Seminary of St. Vincent de Paul	Boynton Beach	1960
South Florida, University of	Tampa	1960
Stetson University	De Land	1883
Tampa, University of	Tampa	1931
West Florida, University of	Pensacola	1967

FLORIDA / A Visitor's Guide

Great stretches of sandy beaches and a warm, sunny climate make Florida a year-round vacationland. Southern Florida is one of the world's most beautiful resort areas. Among its many attractions are luxurious oceanfront hotels; Everglades National Park; and the Florida Keys, a group of small islands that extend about 150 miles (241 kilometers) into the sea. People enjoy swimming, fishing, and water skiing in Florida's inland and coastal waters. Visitors may see historic sites that date back to the early Spanish explorers.

© Walt Disney Productions

Steinmetz, Publix

Dolphins in Marineland

Jettie Griffin

Oldest House, in St. Augustine

Walt Disney World, Near Orlando

PLACES TO VISIT

Busch Gardens, in Tampa, cover 300 acres (121 hectares) and contain African animals, rare birds, and tropical plants. Trains and a monorail carry visitors through the area.

Cape Canaveral, near Cocoa Beach, is a major U.S. space and rocket center. The first spacecraft to land men on the moon was launched from the cape.

Circus Winter Quarters, near Venice, is where the Ringling Brothers and Barnum & Bailey Circus rests and rehearses between seasons.

Circus World, near Haines City, offers guests opportunities to walk a high wire, fly a trapeze, or be made up like clowns. The theme park also features a thrill ride and a circus musical show.

Cypress Gardens is about 5 miles (8 kilometers) southeast of Winter Haven. Tropical gardens and water shows make this one of Florida's leading attractions.

Hialeah Park, in Miami, is one of the most beautiful race tracks in the world. The racing season lasts from mid-January to March. But tourists visit the park throughout the year to admire its formal gardens and stately drives and to see its famous flock of flamingos.

John Pennekamp Coral Reef State Park, near Key Largo, is the only underseas park in the continental United States. Visitors can see the living reef formations by diving underwater, or from glass-bottom boats.

Lion Country Safari, near West Palm Beach, is an animal preserve where lions and other wild animals roam free. Visitors may drive through the area in cars.

Marineland, the world's first oceanarium, is between St. Augustine and Daytona Beach on Florida's Atlantic coast. Over 100 kinds of marine life live in their natural surroundings. Marineland was built in 1938.

Oldest House, in St. Augustine, the oldest U.S. city, is now a museum. It was built about 1703.

Ormond-Daytona Beach stretches for about 23 miles (37 kilometers) along the Atlantic coastline. Tides have beaten the beach to the hardness and smoothness of a paved highway. Tourists can drive their cars along the beach.

Parrot Jungle, in South Miami, has brilliantly colored parrots and cockatoos living in a jungle of cypress and live oak trees. Tricks performed by trained parrots and monkeys provide entertainment for visitors.

Sea World, near Orlando, features porpoise and killer whale shows. The marine center also has a colorful water fountain show.

Walt Disney World, near Orlando, features an amusement park and a recreational center. It includes a storybook castle, submarine rides, and facilities for boating, golfing, and horseback riding.

Parklands. Everglades National Park, in southwestern Florida, ranks among the nation's most popular tourist attractions. This park covers 1,400,333 acres (566,695 hectares) and forms the largest subtropical wilderness in the United States. Other Florida parklands managed by the National Park Service include the Fort Jefferson National Monument and the De Soto National Memorial. For more information on these areas and other national parklands in Florida, see the map and tables in the WORLD BOOK article on NATIONAL PARK SYSTEM.

National Forests. Florida has three national forests. The largest, Apalachicola National Forest, spreads across the northwestern part of the state. The other two are Ocala National Forest and Osceola National Forest. For the areas and chief features of these forests, see NATIONAL FOREST (table).

State Parks. Florida has 68 state parks and historic memorials. For information on them, write to Director, Florida Department of Natural Resources, Division of Recreation and Parks, Larson Building, Tallahassee, Fla. 32304.

Steinmetz, Publix   Steinmetz, Publix

The Orange Bowl in Miami   **Circus Quarters Near Venice**

ANNUAL EVENTS

The Orange Bowl football game in Miami on New Year's Day is one of Florida's leading annual events. Many major league baseball teams train in Florida each spring. Horse racing, greyhound racing, and jai alai games are popular. Other annual events include:

January-March: Greek Epiphany Ceremony in Tarpon Springs (January 6); Old Island Days in Key West (January-March); Black Hills Passion Play in Lake Wales (mid-February through Easter); Florida Citrus Festival in Winter Haven (February); Florida State Fair and Gasparilla Carnival in Tampa (February); Desoto Festival in Bradenton (March); Festival of States in St. Petersburg (March).

April-June: Easter Week Festival in St. Augustine (April); Flying High Circus in Tallahassee (May); Fiesta of the Five Flags in Pensacola (June); "Cross and Sword" Official State Play in St. Augustine (June-September).

July-September: Rodeos in Arcadia and Kissimmee (Fourth of July weekend); Firecracker 400 Auto Race in Daytona Beach (Fourth of July); Days in Spain in St. Augustine (August); Labor Day Festival in Daytona Beach (August-September); Florida Folk Festival in White Springs (September).

October-December: Swamp Buggy Days in Naples (October); Beaux Arts Promenade in Fort Lauderdale (November); Gator Bowl Festival and Football Game in Jacksonville (December); Tangerine Bowl Football Game in Orlando (last week in December or first week in January).

Everglades National Park

K. Wagner

Cypress Gardens Near Winter Haven

Ray Atkeson

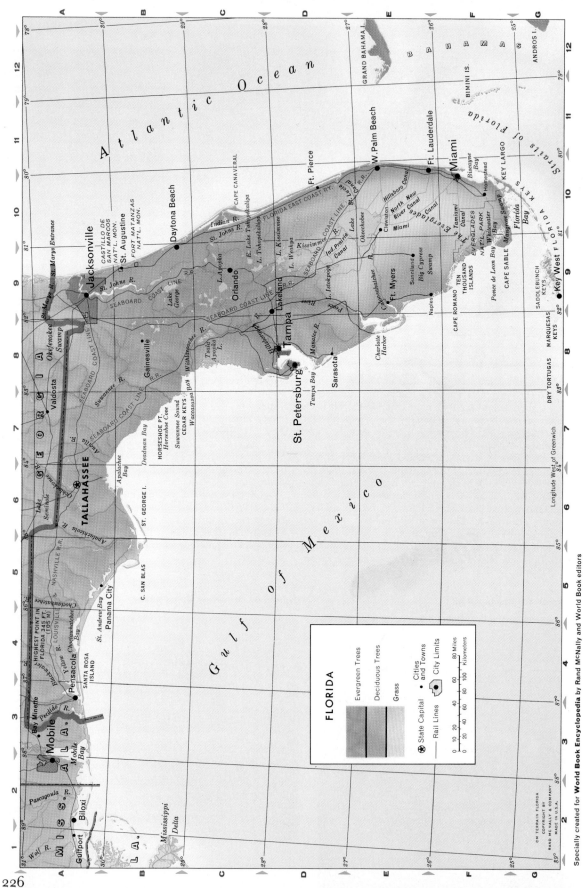

FLORIDA

Evergreen Trees
Deciduous Trees
Grass

⊛ State Capital   • Cities
                        and Towns
— Rail Lines   ⬡ City Limits

0 10 20   40   60   80 Miles
0 20 40 60 80 100 Kilometers

GM TERRAIN FLORIDA
COPYRIGHT BY
RAND McNALLY & COMPANY
MADE IN U.S.A.

Specially created for World Book Encyclopedia by Rand McNally and World Book editors

Alpha Photo Associates

The Everglades are vast swamplands that cover 2,746 square miles (7,112 square kilometers) in southern Florida. Tough sawgrass may grow 12 feet (4 meters) high in the oozing soil, and clusters of trees form "tree islands."

Land Regions of Florida

FLORIDA/The Land

Land Regions. Florida has three main land regions: (1) the Atlantic Coastal Plain, (2) the East Gulf Coastal Plain, and (3) the Florida Uplands.

The Atlantic Coastal Plain is part of an important land region that extends as far north as New Jersey. In Florida, it covers the entire eastern part of the state. The region is a low, level plain ranging in width from 30 to 100 miles (48 to 160 kilometers). A narrow ribbon of sand bars, coral reefs, and islands lies in the Atlantic Ocean, just beyond the mainland. Long shallow lakes, lagoons, rivers, and bays lie between this ribbon and the mainland. Marshes stretch inland from the coast.

Big Cypress Swamp and the Everglades cover most of southern Florida. The Everglades include 2,746 square miles (7,112 square kilometers) of swampy grasslands. Water covers much of this region, especially during the rainy months.

The Florida Keys make up the southernmost part of the state. These small islands curve southwestward for about 150 miles (241 kilometers) off the mainland from Miami. Key Largo is the largest island.

The East Gulf Coastal Plain is also part of a larger land region. It begins at the Gulf of Mexico and extends as far west as western Mississippi and as far north as southern Illinois. In Florida, the East Gulf Coastal Plain has two main sections. One section covers the southwestern part of the peninsula. It joins the Atlantic Coastal Plain in the middle of the Everglades and Big Cypress Swamp. The other section of the East Gulf Coastal Plain curves around the northern edge of the Gulf of Mexico to Florida's western border.

The East Gulf Coastal Plain is similar to the Atlantic Coastal Plain. Long, narrow islands extend along the Gulf of Mexico coastline. Large coastal swamps stretch far inland.

The Florida Uplands is shaped somewhat like a giant arm and hand. A finger of the hand points down the center of the state toward the southern tip of the peninsula. The uplands separate the two sections of the East Gulf Coastal Plain from each other and from the Atlantic Coastal Plain.

The uplands region is higher than Florida's other land regions. But its average elevation is only between 200 and 300 feet (61 and 91 meters) above sea level.

FLORIDA / The Land

Lakes called *sinkholes*, or *lime sinks*, are common in the Florida Uplands. They are formed by cave-ins where a limestone bed near the surface has been dissolved by water action. Pine forests grow in the northern section. Citrus groves thrive in the southern part.

The northern part of the Florida Uplands extends from the northwestern corner of the state along the northern border for about 275 miles (443 kilometers). Its width varies from about 30 to 50 miles (48 to 80 kilometers). This section has fertile valleys and rolling hills of red clay. Many hardwood and softwood forests are found there. The southern part of the Florida Uplands is a region of hills and lakes. It covers an area about 100 miles (160 kilometers) wide and about 160 miles (257 kilometers) long.

Coastline of Florida is 1,350 miles (2,173 kilometers) long. The Atlantic coast has 580 miles (933 kilometers) of shoreline. The Gulf coast is 770 miles (1,240 kilometers) long. When sounds, bays, and offshore islands are included, the Atlantic coastline is 3,331 miles (5,361 kilometers) long and the Gulf coast is 5,095 miles (8,200 kilometers) long. Biscayne Bay, south of Miami, is the one major bay on the Atlantic.

The most important bays along the western coast include Charlotte Harbor, Sarasota, and Tampa. Florida Bay, beyond the southern tip of the peninsula, separates the Florida Keys from the mainland. Apalachee, St. Joseph, St. Andrew, Choctawhatchee, and Pensacola bays stretch along the northern Florida shoreline of the Gulf of Mexico.

Rivers, Lakes, and Springs. The St. Johns River is the largest river in the state. It begins near Melbourne and flows about 275 miles (443 kilometers) northward, almost parallel to the Atlantic coastline. The St. Marys River, along the eastern Florida-Georgia border, flows eastward into the Atlantic. The Perdido River, on Florida's western border, drains into the Gulf of Mexico. The Apalachicola River is northwestern Florida's most important river. It is formed where the Chattahoochee and Flint rivers join at the northern boundary of the state, and flows southward to the Gulf of Mexico. The Suwannee River flows southwestward across northern Florida and also empties into the Gulf. Stephen Foster made this river famous in his song "Old Folks at Home," also known as "Swanee River." Other rivers connect the many lakes of the uplands.

Lake Okeechobee is Florida's largest lake. It covers about 700 square miles (1,800 square kilometers) and is the second largest natural body of fresh water wholly within the United States. Only Lake Michigan covers a larger area. About 30,000 shallow lakes lie throughout central Florida.

Florida has 17 large springs and countless smaller ones. Many of the springs have healthful mineral waters. Wakulla Springs, near Tallahassee, is one of the nation's deepest springs. It has a depth of 185 feet (56 meters). Silver Springs, southeast of Ocala, is the largest spring in the state. Many of the springs are so clear that plant life on the bottom may be seen as deep as 80 feet (24 meters).

Steinmetz, Publix

Big Cypress Swamp, with its towering trees, and the Everglades, with its grassy marshes, make up most of southern Florida.

Winter Haven News Bureau

Winter Haven, in central Florida, is noted for lakes and citrus groves. About a hundred lakes lie within 5 miles (8 kilometers) of the city.

Charles J. Belden

White Sand Dunes stretch along Florida's northern Gulf Coast near Pensacola. They form part of the East Gulf Coastal Plain.

FLORIDA / Climate

Most of Florida has a warm, rainy climate similar to that of the other Southern States. Florida's southern tip has a wet and dry tropical climate like that of Central America and parts of Africa and South America.

Atlantic and Gulf breezes relieve some of the summer heat. Winters are usually mild, even in northern Florida. July temperatures are much the same in the northern and southern parts of the state. Jacksonville, in the north, has an average July temperature of 83° F. (28° C). Miami, in the south, averages 82° F. (28° C) in July. But in January, Miami averages 67° F. (19° C), and Jacksonville's average temperature drops to 56° F. (13° C). The coastal areas have slightly cooler summers and warmer winters than do inland areas. Frosts rarely occur in southern Florida. But occasional cold waves damage crops as far south as the Everglades. The highest and lowest temperatures ever recorded in Florida occurred within 30 miles (48 kilometers) of each other. Tallahassee recorded the lowest temperature, −2° F. (−19° C), on Feb. 13, 1899. Nearby Monticello had the highest temperature, 109° F. (43° C), on June 29, 1931. Nearly all *precipitation* (rain, melted snow, and other forms of moisture) occurs in the form of rain. Florida has an average yearly rainfall of 53 inches (135 centimeters). An average of 32 inches (81 centimeters) falls in the rainy season, from May to October.

Florida lies along the path of many of the hurricanes that sweep across the Atlantic Ocean every summer and fall. Destructive hurricanes hit Florida in 1926, 1928, 1935, 1941, and 1964.

SEASONAL TEMPERATURES

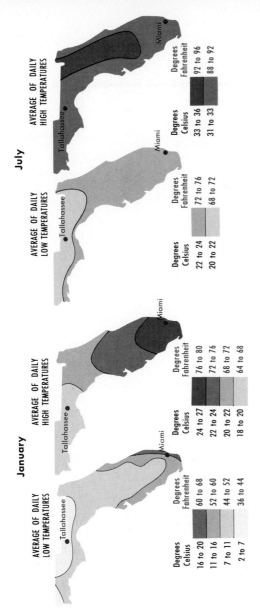

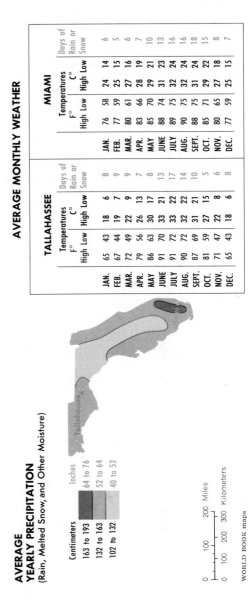

AVERAGE MONTHLY WEATHER

TALLAHASSEE

	Temperatures F° High	Low	C° High	Low	Days of Rain or Snow
JAN.	65	43	18	6	8
FEB.	67	44	19	7	9
MAR.	72	49	22	9	9
APR.	79	56	26	13	7
MAY	86	63	30	17	8
JUNE	91	70	33	21	13
JULY	91	72	33	22	17
AUG.	90	72	32	22	14
SEPT.	87	69	31	21	10
OCT.	81	59	27	15	5
NOV.	71	47	22	8	6
DEC.	65	43	18	6	8

MIAMI

	Temperatures F° High	Low	C° High	Low	Days of Rain or Snow
JAN.	76	58	24	14	6
FEB.	77	59	25	15	5
MAR.	80	61	27	16	6
APR.	83	66	28	19	6
MAY	85	70	29	21	10
JUNE	88	74	31	23	13
JULY	89	75	32	24	16
AUG.	90	75	32	24	16
SEPT.	88	75	31	24	18
OCT.	85	71	29	22	15
NOV.	80	65	27	18	8
DEC.	77	59	25	15	7

WORLD BOOK maps

The main centers of Florida's giant tourist industry lie along the great stretch of coastline. Manufacturing industries are located in many parts of the state. A number of these industries operate near such large cities as Miami, Jacksonville, Tampa, Orlando, and St. Petersburg. Many prosperous farms are in the central and southern parts of the state.

Natural Resources. Florida's natural resources include sandy beaches, a sunny climate, thick forests, rich phosphate and mineral sands deposits, and abundant animal and plant life.

Soil. Most of Florida's soils are sandy, especially in the coastal plains. The most fertile soils are in the southern swamplands. They contain peat and muck. The Florida Uplands are mostly sandy loams and clays of average fertility.

Minerals. Most of Florida lies on top of huge beds of limestone, the state's most plentiful mineral. Florida has the largest phosphate deposits in the United States. Most of the state's phosphate comes from mines in west-central and north-central Florida. Large stores of peat, sand, gravel, and a valuable clay called *fuller's earth* are found throughout the peninsula. The sandy areas of the state have mineral sands including ilmenite, rutile, and zircon. Deposits of brick clays and kaolin, a pottery clay, are found chiefly in Gadsden and Putnam counties. Two oil fields lie east of Fort Myers, and one is in Santa Rosa County.

Forests cover about half the state. Florida has over 360 kinds of trees. Slash pines are the most valuable trees in Florida. The most common hardwood trees are bay, black tupelo, magnolia, oak, and sweet gum. Other common trees include ash, beech, hickory, maple, red cypress, and yellow pines (loblolly and longleaf). Hardwoods and pines are plentiful in the northern half of the state. Mangrove trees flourish in southern Florida's swamplands.

Plant Life. Common wild flowers of Florida include irises, lilies, lupines, orchids, sunflowers, and such climbing vines as Carolina yellow jasmine, Cherokee rose, morning-glory, and trumpet creeper. Other flowers that grow throughout the state include azaleas, camellias, gardenias, hibiscus, oleanders, and poinsettias. The flame vine, or golden bignonia, and the bougainvillea brighten many southern Florida gardens. Dogwood, magnolia, and redbud flourish in the north.

Animal Life. Black bears, deer, Florida panthers, gray foxes, and wildcats live in many parts of the state. Smaller animals such as opossums, otters, raccoons, and squirrels are also common. Florida has the largest colonies of egrets, herons, ibises, pelicans, and water turkeys north of the Caribbean Sea. Alligators live in the swamps.

More kinds of fishes may be found in Florida's waters than in any other part of the world. The fresh-water lakes and rivers are filled with bass, bream, catfish, crappies, and trout. Ocean waters contain bluefish, grouper, menhaden, pompano, red snapper, sailfish, sea trout, mackerel, marlin, and tarpon. Clams, conchs, crabs, crayfish, oysters, scallops, and shrimps live in Florida's coastal waters. Mullet are found in salt and *brackish* (salt marsh) waters.

Production of Goods in Florida

Total value of goods produced in 1975—$11,713,242,000

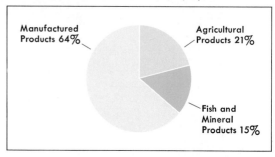

Manufactured Products 64%

Agricultural Products 21%

Fish and Mineral Products 15%

Percentages are based on farm income, value added by manufacture, and value of fish and mineral production. Fish products are less than 1 per cent.

Sources: U.S. government publications, 1976-1977.

Employment in Florida

Total number of persons employed in 1976—2,875,000

	Number of Employees
Wholesale & Retail Trade	727,100
Community, Social, & Personal Services	615,800
Government	552,000
Manufacturing	343,100
Finance, Insurance, & Real Estate	188,000
Transportation & Public Utilities	180,600
Construction	167,000
Agriculture	93,000
Mining	9,200

Sources: *Employment and Earnings*, September 1977, U.S. Bureau of Labor Statistics; *Farm Labor*, February 1977, U.S. Dept. of Agriculture.

Tourist Industry is Florida's leading industry. About 30 million persons visit the state yearly and spend about $9 billion. The main tourist regions lie along the coastlines. The Atlantic Coast serves the greatest number of tourists, but facilities along the Gulf coast and in central Florida are growing rapidly. Florida's tourist trade supports hotels and motels, and facilities for recreation, sports, and transportation.

Manufacturing accounts for 64 per cent of the value of goods produced in Florida. Manufactured goods have a *value added by manufacture* of about $7½ billion yearly. This figure represents the value created in products by Florida's industries, not counting such costs as materials, supplies, and fuels. Florida's chief manufactured products are, in order of importance, food products, chemicals, and electric and electronic equipment.

Food Products have a value added of about $1½ billion yearly. Citrus fruit processing is one of the largest industries in the state. Processing plants, mostly in central Florida, produce fresh citrus fruit juices, canned juices, canned sections of fruit, and citrus by-products. Factories produce about 186 million gallons (704 million liters) of frozen, concentrated orange juice a year. Related industries make wine, jellies, and marmalades. Vegetables are also quick-frozen, canned, and packaged. Other important food-processing industries include the canning of crabmeat, mullet, scallops, shrimps, and turtles.

Chemicals have a value added of about $960 million a year. The chief products are agricultural chemicals, such as fertilizers, and plastics and other synthetic materials. Other products include drugs, paints and varnishes, and soaps and detergents. The major production centers are in Dade and Polk counties.

Other Leading Industries. The manufacture of electric and electronic equipment is the third-ranking industrial activity in Florida, with a value added of about $740 million a year. The production of transportation equipment ranks fourth. Other important industries are printing and publishing and the manufacture of fabricated metal products; paper products; nonelectric machinery; and stone, clay, and glass products.

The assembly and testing of missiles is an important industrial activity in Florida. Many of the missiles are manufactured for the United States space program. Others, including antitank missiles and guided missiles, are produced for the nation's armed services. The tests are held mainly at Eglin Air Force Base near Pensacola.

Agriculture supplies 21 per cent of the value of goods produced in Florida, with a yearly gross income of about $2½ billion. Farmland covers about 15 million acres (6 million hectares), about two-fifths of the state. Florida's 32,000 farms average 407 acres (165 hectares) in size.

Fruits and Nuts account for about $700 million a year, or about a third of the income received for farm products. Oranges are the leading cash crop, accounting for about $500 million a year. Other important citrus fruits include grapefruit, limes, tangerines, and tangelos. The chief citrus grove areas are in central and southern Florida—in De Soto, Hardee, Highlands, Hillsborough, Indian River, Lake, Martin, Orange, Pasco, Polk, and St. Lucie counties. The citrus groves cover about 900,-000 acres (360,000 hectares).

Nuts come from northern and western Florida. Jackson County produces more peanuts than does all the rest of the state. Jackson, Santa Rosa, and Walton rank as Florida's leading pecan-growing centers. Farmers in the southern part of the state raise such tropical and semitropical fruits as avocados, bananas, guavas, mangoes, papayas, and pineapples. Cantaloupes, strawberries, and watermelons thrive throughout Florida.

Field Crops. Soybeans are Florida's most valuable field crop. Farmers grow about 7 million bushels of soybeans yearly. Sugar cane is Florida's second most valuable farm product, with a yearly income of about $310 million. Florida leads the states in sugar cane production. The Everglades region leads in the raising of sugar cane. Other field crops include corn, cotton, peanuts, and tobacco.

Livestock accounts for about $625 million a year—or about a fourth of the total farm income. Farmers raise beef cattle and dairy cattle. Beef cattle and milk are among the state's most valuable farm products. The largest cattle-raising regions are in central and southeastern Florida. Horse farms in Marion County raise thoroughbred race horses. Farmers in the north raise

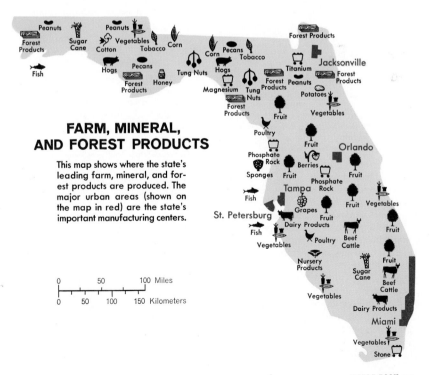

FARM, MINERAL, AND FOREST PRODUCTS

This map shows where the state's leading farm, mineral, and forest products are produced. The major urban areas (shown on the map in red) are the state's important manufacturing centers.

WORLD BOOK map

hogs and cattle. Poultry raising is also important, although Florida imports much of its poultry.

Truck Crops in central and southern Florida have a greater value than those of any other state except California. Tomatoes are the most valuable of Florida's *truck crops* (vegetables grown for market). Tomatoes account for a yearly income of about $150 million. Florida farmers also grow large crops of celery, green peppers, potatoes, snap beans, and sweet corn. The largest vegetable crops come from Broward, Dade, Hendry, Palm Beach, and Seminole counties.

Greenhouse and Nursery Products earn an annual income of about $150 million. These products include flower and vegetable seeds and bulbs.

Mining has an annual value of about $1¾ billion. Mines in Florida account for about 75 per cent of the U.S. production of phosphate rock, or about 37 million short tons (34 million metric tons). Much of the phosphate is used to make fertilizers. Santa Rosa County is

Florida State News Bureau

Dredging Phosphate Rock near Bartow provides raw materials for Florida's chemical industry. Florida has some of the largest deposits of phosphates in the United States.

the chief source of petroleum production in Florida. Pits throughout the state provide limestone for use in road and building construction and in the manufacture of lime and cement. Mines in Gadsden and Marion counties supply fuller's earth, a clay used to filter petroleum. Putnam County produces large amounts of kaolin, a pottery clay. Ilmenite and zircon are taken from the sands near the St. Johns River.

Fishing Industry. Florida is one of the leading commercial fishing states. The state's annual fish catch is valued at about $70 million. It brings in about 168 million pounds (76 million kilograms) of fish each year. Shrimp and lobsters are by far the leading catches, accounting for more than half the total value. Florida accounts for about 10 per cent of the annual U.S. shrimp catch. The most important commercial fishes include catfish, grouper, mackerel, mullet, pompano,

and red snapper. Each year, fishing fleets gather about 4 million pounds (1.8 million kilograms) of clams, oysters, and scallops. They also take in about 65 million pounds (29.5 million kilograms) of blue and stone crabs, lobsters, and shrimp a year. Such fishes as menhaden and shark are also caught in Florida's waters. Factories process these fishes into fertilizer, oil, and feed for poultry and other farm animals.

Florida shrimp boats sometimes travel as far as the coasts of Mexico and Central America. About two-thirds of the supply of red snappers in the United States comes from Florida. Large beds of clams lie in the waters along the northwest coast. The waters off Dade and Monroe counties are major sponge-fishing centers in the United States.

Electric Power. Steam-generating plants produce about 85 per cent of Florida's electric power. Most of these plants are owned by private electric utilities. Nuclear plants supply about 15 per cent of the state's electric power. Hydroelectric power accounts for less than 1 per cent of the electricity produced in Florida.

Transportation. Florida is sometimes called the *aerial crossroads of the Americas* because of its heavy air traffic with Central and South America. The state has about 385 airports. About 30 airlines, including several that belong to other nations, serve the state. Miami International Airport handles much of the air passenger and air freight travel to and from the United States.

Railroads operate on about 4,000 miles (6,400 kilometers) of track in Florida. About 10 rail lines provide freight service, and passenger trains link about 20 Florida cities to other cities. About two-thirds of the state's 98,000 miles (158,000 kilometers) of roads are surfaced. The Sunshine State Parkway connects southern Florida with highways that lead to Georgia and to Florida's west coast. Several interstate highways also cross Florida.

About 15 deepwater ports in Florida serve as ports of entry into the United States. A system of canals in the eastern part of the Everglades helps control and regulate the water supply in southeastern Florida. Florida has a larger section of the Atlantic Intracoastal Waterway than does any other East Coast state. Florida's section of the Gulf Intracoastal Waterway winds along the northwestern part of the state.

Communication. Florida's first newspaper, the *East Florida Gazette*, was established in St. Augustine in 1783. Its publisher was a loyal Englishman named William Charles Wells. In his newspaper, Wells attacked Americans for fighting the Revolutionary War against England. Wells stopped publishing his newspaper and returned to England after the Spanish regained control of Florida in 1783.

Today the state has about 250 newspapers, of which about 60 are dailies. The oldest newspaper still in existence is the *Florida Times-Union*, published daily in Jacksonville. It was established in 1864. Other newspapers include the *Fort Lauderdale News*, *Miami Herald*, *Miami News*, *Palm Beach Post*, *Pensacola Journal*, *St. Petersburg Times*, *Sentinel Star* in Orlando, and *Tampa Tribune*. Florida's first radio station, WQAM in Miami, went on the air in 1921. The first television station in Florida, WTVJ of Miami, began broadcasting in 1949. The state now has about 325 radio stations and 40 television stations.

Indian Days. Burial mounds found along Florida's western coast show that Indians may have lived in the region as long as 10,000 years ago. About 10,000 Indians lived in the Florida region when white men first reached its shores. The Indians belonged to four chief tribes. The Calusa and the Tequesta in the south were hunters and fishermen. The Timucua in the central and northeast regions and the Apalachee in the northwest were farmers and hunters.

Exploration and Spanish Settlement. Legends of a fountain of youth brought the Spanish explorer Juan Ponce de León to the Florida region in 1513. Ponce de León claimed the region for Spain and named it *Florida* because of the many flowers he saw there. The word *florida* in Spanish means *full of flowers*. He returned to Florida in 1521 to start a colony, but was severely wounded in a battle with Indians. He and his followers fled, and Ponce de León soon died.

In 1528, a Spaniard named Pánfilo de Narváez led an expedition of about 400 men to Florida's southwestern coast. He traveled northward searching for gold. But shipwrecks killed Narváez and many of his men. Another Spaniard, Hernando de Soto, landed an expedition in the Tampa Bay area in 1539. He led his men beyond the Florida region and in 1541 became the first European to reach the Mississippi River.

In 1564, a group of *Huguenots* (French Protestants) established a colony on the St. Johns River. They built Fort Caroline near what is now Jacksonville. News of this French colony on Spanish-owned land reached King Philip II of Spain. The king sent a sea captain named Don Pedro Menéndez de Avilés to drive the French from Florida. Menéndez and his men arrived in Florida in 1565. They founded St. Augustine, the first permanent white settlement in what is now the United States. They massacred the French forces and ended French attempts to settle in eastern Florida.

The Spaniards spent much of the next 200 years trying to teach their way of life to the Florida Indians. Meanwhile, England established colonies to the north of Florida, and France built colonies to the west. In the mid-1700's, wars broke out between the English and French colonists. Spain sided with France.

In 1762, English forces captured Cuba. In 1763, Spain gave Florida to England in exchange for Cuba.

The English Period. England divided the Florida region into two separate colonies—East Florida and West Florida. West Florida included the part of the region west of the Apalachicola River. It also included parts of what are now Alabama, Mississippi, and Louisiana. East Florida included the rest of the Florida region. English control of Florida lasted until Spanish forces marched into West Florida in 1779, during the Revolutionary War. The English, already weakened by war, surrendered West Florida to Spain in 1781. Spain regained control of all Florida in 1783.

The Second Spanish Period lasted until 1821. In the early 1800's, Florida was the only part of southeastern North America that did not belong to the United States. Runaway slaves and prisoners and thieving Indians took refuge in the Florida region. Florida settlers fought their Spanish rulers, but Spain refused to sell Florida to

National Park Service

Castillo de San Marcos National Monument, in St. Augustine, has the oldest masonry fort in the United States. The Spaniards began building the fort in 1672. A moat surrounds the structure.

Engraving by an unknown artist from *Pictorial Life of Andrew Jackson* (1847) by John Frost (Newberry Library, Chicago)

The First Seminole War ended in 1818 when Andrew Jackson and his troops drove the Seminole Indians to the Florida peninsula.

the United States. In 1812, a group of eastern Florida settlers rebelled and declared their independence from Spain. But the Spaniards stopped the rebels. During the War of 1812, Spain let England use Pensacola as a naval base. In 1814, American troops led by General Andrew Jackson stormed into Florida and seized Pensacola. During the First Seminole War (1816-1818), Jackson captured Fort St. Marks on the Gulf of Mexico. He then marched as far east as the Suwannee River, and defeated the Seminole Indians. Finally, in 1819, Spain agreed to turn Florida over to the United States. The United States did not actually pay any money to Spain. But it agreed to pay $5 million to American citizens for property damages.

Territorial Days. Florida formally came under U.S. control in 1821. Congress organized the Territory of Florida in 1822. William P. DuVal became the first territorial governor.

Thousands of American settlers poured into Florida. One of the major problems they faced was finding enough land for settlement. Seminole Indians lived in some of the territory's richest farmland. The U.S. gov-

228e

The Acquisition of Florida. Spain gave Florida to the United States in 1819. In return, the United States agreed to pay claims of U.S. citizens against Spain. Andrew Jackson took part in the transfer at Pensacola in 1821.

• Pensacola

★ TALLAHASSEE

The Fountain of Youth. Juan Ponce de León, the Spanish explorer, landed on the Florida coast between St. Augustine and Jacksonville in 1513 during the Easter season. He came in search of a legendary fountain whose waters were supposed to restore youth.

ernment offered land in the Oklahoma region to the Seminole if they would leave Florida territory. Some of the Seminole accepted the offer, but others refused to leave their homes. In 1835, a band of Seminole attacked and massacred Major Francis L. Dade and his troops near what is now Bushnell. This incident started the Second Seminole War. The Seminole were finally defeated in 1842. Most of the Seminole left the territory after the war, but a small band stayed in Florida.

Statehood. In 1839, Florida drew up a constitution in preparation for statehood. But it had to wait for

---
IMPORTANT DATES IN FLORIDA

1513 Juan Ponce de León landed on the Florida coast and claimed the region for Spain.

1528 Pánfilo de Narváez led a Spanish expedition into Florida.

1539 Hernando de Soto led an expedition through Florida.

1564 French Huguenot settlers built Fort Caroline on the St. Johns River.

1565 Pedro Menéndez de Avilés founded St. Augustine.

1763 Spain ceded Florida to England.

1783 Spain regained control of Florida.

1821 Florida came under U.S. control.

1822 Congress established the Territory of Florida.

1835 The Second Seminole War began with the massacre of Major Francis L. Dade and his troops. Most of the Seminole were wiped out during the war.

1845 Florida became the 27th state on March 3.

1861 Florida seceded from the Union and joined the Confederacy.

1868 Florida was readmitted to the Union on June 25.

1906 The project of draining the Everglades started at Fort Lauderdale.

1920-1925 Land speculators poured into the state. The population increased at a tremendous rate.

1938 The Overseas Highway was opened.

1958 The country's first earth satellite, *Explorer I*, was launched on January 31 from Cape Canaveral.

1961 The first U.S. manned space flights were launched from Cape Canaveral.

1969 Florida adopted a new constitution.

1969 *Apollo 11*, the first spacecraft to land men on the moon, was launched from Cape Canaveral (then called Cape Kennedy) on July 16.

1971 The Florida legislature adopted the state's first income tax, a tax on corporation profits.

1977 A new state capitol was completed in Tallahassee.

statehood. Florida would be a slave state, and Congress wanted to maintain a balance between slave and free states. Florida was admitted to the Union as a slave state on March 3, 1845. The following year, Iowa was admitted as a free state. Florida had a population of about 66,500 when it entered the Union. Most of the state's farms were small, and a majority of the farmers did not own slaves.

The Civil War and Reconstruction. In 1860, Abraham Lincoln was elected President. Florida and the other slave states regarded Lincoln as a threat to their way of life. On Jan. 10, 1861, Florida *seceded* (withdrew) from the Union and later joined the Confederacy.

Union forces captured most of Florida's coastal towns early in the Civil War (1861-1865). But Confederate forces won the Battle of Olustee on Feb. 20, 1864. This was the most important battle fought in Florida. In March 1865, a small band of Confederate troops, helped by young boys and old men, successfully defended Tallahassee against Union forces. Tallahassee and Austin, Tex., were the only Confederate state capitals that federal troops did not capture.

During the Reconstruction period after the Civil War, Florida and the other Confederate states came under federal military rule. The defeated states had to meet certain requirements before they could be readmitted to the Union. Florida abolished slavery, but it refused to accept some of the other requirements. For this reason, a strong group of Republicans in Congress blocked Florida and most of the other Confederate states from being readmitted. Republicans gained control of the Florida state government in 1868. Florida was readmitted to the Union on June 25, 1868.

Progress as a State. Florida developed rapidly during the 1880's. Geologists discovered large phosphate deposits. The state government and private investors began to drain the swamplands. New lands were opened for development. Citrus groves were planted in north-central Florida. Resort cities sprang up. People and money from northern states poured into Florida.

A severe freeze during the winter of 1894-1895 damaged much of the state's citrus crops. Citrus growers planted new groves in the south-central part of the state. This move led to the development of southern Florida.

The Early 1900's. In 1906, the state began draining the swampland near Fort Lauderdale. This land soon became one of Florida's richest agricultural regions.

228f

Jacksonville •

St. Augustine •

Oldest City in the U.S. is St. Augustine. Pedro Menéndez de Avilés, a Spanish explorer, founded the settlement in 1565.

• De Land

Citrus Fruit Industry began to develop into big business in Florida in the 1890's. Lue Gim Gong, a Chinese horticulturist in De Land, introduced a new variety of orange, and developed a more hardy type of grapefruit.

Cape
Canaveral

• Tarpon Springs

Sponge Fleet is blessed every year at Tarpon Springs in a colorful religious ceremony. The sponge beds at Tarpon Springs were discovered in 1905.

Franciscan Missions were established in Florida about 1600. The friars raised lemons, oranges, figs, and other fruits never before grown in Florida.

NASA

Apollo 11 Lifts Off from Cape Canaveral (then called Cape Kennedy) on July 16, 1969, to start the trip that featured man's first landing on the moon.

Miami •

• Florida City

HISTORIC
FLORIDA

The Overseas Highway, opened in 1938, links the mainland with Key West. It runs 128 miles (206 kilometers) between Florida City and Key West.

• Key West

FLORIDA

Reports of fantastic profits to be made in Florida real estate swept the country. Hundreds of thousands of land speculators flocked to the state. Florida's population grew at an enormous rate. Seven new counties were formed in 1921. By 1925, Florida's economy had become a swelling bubble of progress and prosperity.

The bubble burst in 1926, when a severe depression hit Florida. Banks closed. Wealthy people suddenly lost their money. Two destructive hurricanes struck Florida's Atlantic coast in 1926 and 1928, killing hundreds of persons. The state had partly recovered from these disasters by the late 1920's. Then, in 1929, the Great Depression struck the United States.

Federal and state welfare measures helped the people of Florida fight the depression. The state created jobs to develop its natural resources. The construction of paper mills by private industries led to forest conservation programs. Cooling plants were built to preserve perishable fruits and vegetables. Farmers established cooperative farm groups and cooperative markets. The state suffered setbacks in 1935 and 1941, when severe hurricanes swept across southern Florida.

The Mid-1900's. Florida's location along the Atlantic Ocean and near the Panama Canal made the state vital to the defense of the Western Hemisphere during World War II (1939-1945). Land, sea, and air bases were established in many parts of the state.

THE GOVERNORS OF FLORIDA

	Party	Term
William D. Moseley	Democratic	1845-1849
Thomas Brown	Whig	1849-1853
James E. Broome	Democratic	1853-1857
Madison S. Perry	Democratic	1857-1861
John Milton	Democratic	1861-1865
Abraham K. Allison	Democratic	1865
William Marvin	None	1865-1866
David S. Walker	Conservative	1866-1868
Harrison Reed	Republican	1868-1873
Ossian B. Hart	Republican	1873-1874
Marcellus L. Stearns	Republican	1874-1877
George F. Drew	Democratic	1877-1881
William D. Bloxham	Democratic	1881-1885
Edward A. Perry	Democratic	1885-1889
Francis P. Fleming	Democratic	1889-1893
Henry L. Mitchell	Democratic	1893-1897
William D. Bloxham	Democratic	1897-1901
W. S. Jennings	Democratic	1901-1905
N. B. Broward	Democratic	1905-1909
Albert W. Gilchrist	Democratic	1909-1913
Park Trammell	Democratic	1913-1917
Sidney J. Catts	Prohibition	1917-1921
Cary A. Hardee	Democratic	1921-1925
John W. Martin	Democratic	1925-1929
Doyle E. Carlton	Democratic	1929-1933
Dave Sholtz	Democratic	1933-1937
Fred P. Cone	Democratic	1937-1941
Spessard L. Holland	Democratic	1941-1945
Millard F. Caldwell	Democratic	1945-1949
Fuller Warren	Democratic	1949-1953
Dan McCarty	Democratic	1953
Charley E. Johns	Democratic	1953-1955
LeRoy Collins	Democratic	1955-1961
Farris Bryant	Democratic	1961-1965
Haydon Burns	Democratic	1965-1967
Claude R. Kirk, Jr.	Republican	1967-1971
Reubin O'D. Askew	Democratic	1971-1979
Robert D. Graham	Democratic	1979-

After the war, Florida's population grew rapidly. Tourism boomed and remained the state's leading source of income. But industrial expansion helped give Florida a balanced economy. Development of industries in such fields as chemicals, electronics, paper and paper products, and ocean and space exploration provided jobs for Florida's swelling labor force.

In the 1950's, Cape Canaveral became a space and rocket center. The nation launched its first satellite from there in 1958, its first manned space flights in 1961, and its first manned spaceship to the moon in 1969. In 1963, after the assassination of President John F. Kennedy, Cape Canaveral was renamed Cape Kennedy.

After Cuba fell under Communist control in the late 1950's, many Cubans fled and came to Florida. In 1962, Russian missiles in Cuba placed Florida and much of the rest of the United States in danger of nuclear attack. President Kennedy forced the Russians to remove the missiles.

Like many Northern and Southern states, Florida faced serious racial problems during the 1950's and 1960's. In 1954, the Supreme Court of the United States ruled that compulsory segregation in public schools was unconstitutional. The Florida Constitution at that time did not permit black children and white children to attend the same schools. Integration of the state's public schools began in Dade County in 1959. By the late 1960's, every county had integrated all or most of its public schools.

In the 1960's, Florida began a stepped-up program to expand its facilities for higher education. This program was partly designed to serve the future demands for personnel in the oceanographic and aerospace industries. During the 1960's, the state opened 4 new universities, several new private colleges, and 13 new public junior colleges. Two other state universities opened in the early 1970's.

A new state constitution went into effect in 1969. The constitution makes it possible for Florida cities and counties to combine and work together as a single government to solve common problems.

Florida Today is continuing its industrial expansion. But the tourist trade remains the top source of income in the 1970's. A poor tourist season could mean financial crisis for Florida. Consumer taxes provide much of the state's income. Tourists thus help support not only the private economy, but also the state government.

Florida's rapid growth has created major problems.

Missile Plant Near Cape Canaveral is built on man-made islands. In this huge plant, workers can assemble and test parts for as many as four Titan III vehicles and their spacecraft at a time.

U.S. Air Force Photo

The increasing population requires more homes, schools, hospitals, and welfare services. Growing numbers of tourists need more highways, hotels, motels, and recreational facilities. In 1971, the legislature adopted a tax on corporation profits to raise money.

Another of Florida's chief problems is how to protect its natural resources. During the early 1970's, protests by conservationists led to the cancellation of work on a large jetport being constructed near the Everglades, and on a canal being built across the state. The conservationists feared that the airport would endanger wildlife in Everglades National Park and that the canal would destroy the natural beauty of the Oklawaha River Valley.

In 1973, Cape Kennedy was renamed Cape Canaveral, the name preferred by Floridians. However, the rocket complex at the cape continued to be known as the John F. Kennedy Space Center.

In 1977, a new state capitol opened in Tallahassee. The building rises 22 stories.　　DAVID E. CHRISTENSEN,

MALCOLM B. JOHNSON, and REMBERT W. PATRICK

FLORIDA/Study Aids

Related Articles in WORLD BOOK include:

BIOGRAPHIES

Bethune, Mary M.	Narváez, Pánfilo de
Cochran, Jacqueline	Osceola
De Soto, Hernando	Ponce de León, Juan
Flagler, Henry M.	Rawlings, Marjorie
Gorrie, John	Kinnan
Johnson, James W.	Smith, Edmund Kirby
Mallory, Stephen R.	

CITIES

Daytona	Miami	Sarasota
Beach	Miami Beach	Tallahassee
Fort Lauderdale	Orlando	Tampa
Hialeah	Pensacola	Tarpon Springs
Jacksonville	Saint Augustine	West Palm Beach
Key West	Saint Petersburg	

HISTORY

Adams-Onís Treaty	Fort Pickens
Confederate States of America	Fountain of Youth
Electoral Commission	Seminole Indians

NATIONAL PARKS AND MONUMENTS

Biscayne National Monument	Fort Jefferson National
Castillo de San Marcos	Monument
National Monument	Fort Matanzas National
De Soto National Memorial	Monument
Everglades National Park	

PHYSICAL FEATURES

Apalachicola River	Florida Keys	Okefenokee
Dry Tortugas	Gulf of Mexico	Swamp
Everglades	Lake	Santa Rosa Island
Florida, Straits of	Okeechobee	Suwannee River

PRODUCTS

For Florida's rank among the states in production, see the following articles:

Grapefruit	Lettuce	Sugar	Tomato
Honey	Orange	Tobacco	Watermelon

OTHER RELATED ARTICLES

Atlantic Intra-	Patrick Air Force Base
coastal Waterway	Pensacola Naval
Cape Canaveral	Air Station
Cypress Gardens	Singing Tower
Eglin Air Force Base	Southern States
Gulf Intracoastal Waterway	Sunshine Skyway

Outline

I. **Government**
   A. Constitution
   B. Executive
   C. Legislature
   D. Courts
II. **People**
   E. Local Government
   F. Taxation
   G. Politics

III. **Education**
   A. Schools　　B. Libraries　　C. Museums
IV. **A Visitor's Guide**
   A. Places to Visit　　B. Annual Events
V. **The Land**
   A. Land Regions
   B. Coastline　　C. Rivers, Lakes, and Springs
VI. **Climate**
VII. **Economy**
   A. Natural Resources　　F. Fishing Industry
   B. Tourist Industry　　G. Electric Power
   C. Manufacturing　　H. Transportation
   D. Agriculture　　I. Communication
   E. Mining
VIII. **History**

Questions

How did Florida get its name?

What are the Florida Keys? The Everglades?

What event of 1894-1895 led to the development of southern Florida?

Where is the U.S. sponge-fishing center?

What is Florida's chief industry?

Why did Spain give Florida to England?

When was the Battle of Olustee fought?

What is Florida's most plentiful mineral?

What major problems does Florida face because of its growing population?

What is Florida's leading cash crop?

Books for Young Readers

CARPENTER, ALLAN. *Florida.* Childrens Press, 1965.

MAY, JULIAN. *These Islands Are Alive.* Hawthorn, 1971.

MELTZER, MILTON. *Hunted Like a Wolf: The Story of the Seminole War.* Farrar, 1972.

SAND, GEORGE X. *The Everglades Today: Endangered Wilderness.* Scholastic Book Services, 1971.

SMITH, MIKE. *Florida.* Coward, 1970.

STOLZ, MARY S. *Lands End.* Harper, 1973. Fiction.

WIER, ESTER. *The Winners.* McKay, 1967. Fiction.

Books for Older Readers

DOUGLAS, MARJORY S. *Florida: The Long Frontier.* Harper, 1967.

JAHODA, GLORIA. *The Other Florida.* Scribner, 1967. *Florida: A Bicentennial History.* Norton, 1976.

LAUBER, PATRICIA. *Everglades Country: A Question of Life or Death.* Viking, 1973.

MORRIS, ALLEN C. *Florida Place Names.* Univ. of Miami Press, 1974.

RAWLINGS, MARJORIE K. *The Yearling.* Scribner, 1938. Fiction.

SHOFNER, JERRELL H. *Nor Is It Over Yet: Florida in the Era of Reconstruction, 1863-1877.* Univ. Presses of Florida, 1974.

SHOUMATOFF, ALEX. *Florida Ramble.* Harper, 1974.

TEBEAU, CHARLTON W. *A History of Florida.* Univ. of Miami Press, 1971.

FLORIDA, STRAITS OF, is a channel at the southern tip of Florida. It connects the Gulf of Mexico with the Atlantic Ocean, and is sometimes called the Gulf of Florida. It was first called the New Bahama Channel. Florida Straits separates southeast Florida and the Florida Keys from the Bahamas on the east and from Cuba on the south. The Gulf Stream passes through the straits, which is 300 miles (480 kilometers) long and from 50 to 150 miles (80 to 240 kilometers) wide. The main channel has depths of 6,000 feet (1,800 meters). The eastern half of the straits includes the shallow waters of the Great Bahama Bank.   KATHRYN ABBEY HANNA

FLORIDA, UNIVERSITY OF, is a combined state university and land-grant college in Gainesville, Fla. Founded in 1853, it is the state's oldest and largest university. It offers programs in accounting, agriculture, architecture, arts and sciences, building construction, business administration, education, engineering, fine arts, forest resources and conservation, journalism and communications, law, and many other fields. The university's Health Center includes colleges of dentistry, health related professions, medicine, nursing, pharmacy, and veterinary medicine. Courses lead to bachelor's, master's, and doctor's degrees. The university also operates the Florida State Museum and several research centers. For enrollment, see UNIVERSITIES AND COLLEGES (table).

Critically reviewed by the
UNIVERSITY OF FLORIDA

FLORIDA AGRICULTURAL AND MECHANICAL UNIVERSITY. See UNIVERSITIES AND COLLEGES (table).

FLORIDA ATLANTIC UNIVERSITY. See UNIVERSITIES AND COLLEGES (table).

FLORIDA INSTITUTE OF TECHNOLOGY. See UNIVERSITIES AND COLLEGES (table).

FLORIDA KEYS are a group of small islands or reefs that stretch in a curved line about 150 miles (241 kilometers) long from Biscayne Bay southwest into the Gulf of Mexico. The word *keys* comes from the Spanish word, *cayo*, which means *small island*. The Keys are remarkable examples of coral formation. They attract a large tourist trade. Industries include sponge, cigar, and canning factories. Key West, farthest from the mainland, has the most important harbor. It is joined with the mainland by an overseas highway 128 miles (206 kilometers) long. Most of the Keys have beautiful beaches. See also FLORIDA (physical map; historic map); KEY WEST.   KATHRYN ABBEY HANNA

FLORIDA MEMORIAL COLLEGE is a coeducational liberal arts school in Miami, Fla. It is affiliated with the Baptist Church. Courses lead to the Bachelor of Science degree. The school was founded in 1892. For enrollment, see UNIVERSITIES AND COLLEGES (table).

FLORIDA SOUTHERN COLLEGE is a coeducational liberal arts school at Lakeland, Fla. It is affiliated with the United Methodist Church, but admits students of all faiths. It has a school of music, a citrus department, and a department of American culture. Many of the buildings on the campus were designed by Frank Lloyd Wright. The college is said to have the world's largest concentration of Wright's architecture. The college was chartered in 1885. For enrollment, see UNIVERSITIES AND COLLEGES (table).   CHARLES T. THRIFT, JR.

See also FLORIDA (picture: Annie Pfeiffer Chapel).

FLORIDA STATE UNIVERSITY is a state-controlled co-educational school at Tallahassee, Fla. It grants degrees in arts and sciences, business, education, engineering science, home economics, law, library science, music, nursing, and social welfare. It also has a full graduate program. Florida State University was founded in 1857. For the school's enrollment, see UNIVERSITIES AND COLLEGES (table).   JOHN E. CHAMPION

FLORIDA TECHNOLOGICAL UNIVERSITY. See UNIVERSITIES AND COLLEGES (table).

FLORIN, *FLAHR in,* is the name of a gold coin first made in Florence in the 1200's. The name comes from the Latin word for flower. The florin bore the imprint of a lily on one side, and the figure of Saint John the Baptist on the other side. Florins, or guilders, are used now in The Netherlands. They have been used in Germany, Austria, Hungary, and Great Britain. The first British florin was issued as a six-shilling gold coin in the reign of Edward III (1327-1377). A silver British florin worth two shillings was first coined in 1849. A British double florin was first coined in 1887. In 1971, the British florin was replaced by a coin of equal value, the 10 new pence piece. See also GUILDER.   FRED REINFELD

FLORISSANT FOSSIL BEDS NATIONAL MONUMENT is near Florissant, Colo. It features fossil insects, leaves, and seeds that date back about 40 million years. Congress authorized the monument in 1969. For the area of the monument, see NATIONAL PARK SYSTEM (table: National Monuments). For location, see COLORADO (political map).   GEORGE B. HARTZOG, JR.

FLORIST is a flower grower or dealer. Retail florists sell cut flowers, potted plants, decorative foliage, corsages, and floral arrangements. They may design flower arrangements for funerals, weddings, parties, displays for businesses, and everyday use in the home. Some florists also sell seeds, bulbs, vases, gifts, ornaments, and equipment for growing and arranging flowers.

Some florists have greenhouses or flower beds in which they grow flowers and plants to sell. But they usually buy most of their flowers from wholesale distributing firms. These firms buy flowers and plants from greenhouses and nurseries that grow them.

The main part of a florist's business comes from customers who visit the shop or order flowers over the telephone. Most florists also deliver flowers by truck.

Some florists belong to flowers-by-wire associations. If florists belonging to such an association receive an order to be delivered to another community, they telephone the order to a member of the association in that community. This florist prepares the order and delivers the flowers ordered. The association handles the finances of these exchanges.

People interested in becoming a florist should love flowers and know how to grow them successfully and to care for them properly. They should be familiar with the varieties of flowers that people in their community like to buy, and be able to advise customers as to which flowers are suitable for particular occasions. The florist must have the artistic ability to design floral arrangements in an interesting and attractive manner, appropriate to their use.

Owners of flower shops should have a thorough knowledge of merchandising, sales, and advertising procedures. Their shop is in many ways a service business, so they must be willing to put in long hours of work

Florists' Telegraph Delivery Assoc.

Florist Shops often have attractively arranged self-service departments. A designer, *inset*, fashions a corsage of orchids.

so that he can fill his customers' orders for flowers.

An education in floriculture is often helpful to a florist, especially if he has a greenhouse or small nursery. Many universities and colleges offer courses in flower production, in retail marketing, and in store management.

Training in other areas of business administration and in art and design are also helpful. An apprenticeship for six months or a year in a retail shop provides one of the best ways for a person to learn how to operate a flower shop.   JOHN H. WALKER

See also FLORICULTURE; FLOWER; GREENHOUSE.

FLOTATION PROCESS is used to separate minerals from each other, or from other materials with which they are mixed. In this process, the material that contains the minerals is first crushed and ground fine. It is then added to a liquid that contains certain chemicals called *flotation reagents*. These chemicals form a film around the particles of one of the ores, and keep the liquid from wetting it. For example, *xanthates* keep water from wetting sulfide ores.

Other chemicals may also be used which will help or hinder the filming of a certain mineral. The liquid is stirred up with air, which rises in bubbles and forms a froth on top. The bubbles stick to the film around the dry particles and carry them to the top. Here they may be skimmed off with the froth. The other minerals or materials remain in the liquid. Special flotation machines have been designed to carry out this process. Flotation is widely used in separating minerals from the ores in which they are found.   A. E. ADAMI

FLOTSAM, *FLAHT sum,* **JETSAM,** *JEHT sum,* and **LAGAN,** *LAG un,* are terms used to describe goods in the sea. Goods found floating in the sea are called *flotsam.* The term includes both goods cast from a vessel in distress and goods that float when a ship sinks.

Jetsam is goods voluntarily cast overboard in an emergency, usually to lighten the vessel. Jetsam sinks and remains under water. *Lagan,* or *ligan,* is cargo which someone has sunk with the definite intention of recovering it later. The person usually ties a buoy to lagan to mark its location.

Flotsam, jetsam, and lagan are not abandoned or derelict property. That is, the owner or master of the ship does not intend to give up the goods permanently. He intends to recover his goods at some later date. Under the maritime law, flotsam, jetsam, and lagan remain the property of their original owner, no matter how long they lie in the sea. The finder may only hold them for salvage, which is a legal reward the owner pays to the finder. Many courts rule that the owner must claim his goods within a year after someone else has recovered them.   WARREN ADAMS JACKMAN

See also SALVAGE.

FLOUNDER is the name of a group of salt-water flatfishes. They live on the sandy and muddy bottoms of bays and along the shores of most seas. There are about 500 different types of flounders. The *winter flounder,* or *blackback,* can be found from Labrador to Cape Hatteras, and makes an important food fish. The *summer flounder,* a popular game fish, ranges from Cape Cod to Florida. It is also known as the *fluke* or the *plaice.*

The flounder has a flattened body with both eyes on the same side of the head. The upper side of the flounder takes on the color of the bottom of the sea where the fish lives. The underside is nearly white. When the flounder first hatches, it looks like a typical fish. After it grows to be about $\frac{1}{2}$ inch (13 millimeters) long, the body becomes flattened, and both eyes appear on one side of the head. The side of the head on which the eyes appear depends on the *species,* or kind, of flounder. Flounders have markings that blend with their surroundings. The fish can lie camouflaged on the bottom of the ocean. This makes it easier for them to catch the shrimp and small fish that form their basic diet. The dab, halibut, and European turbot belong to the flounder group. Flounders are also closely related to soles (see SOLE).

Scientific Classification. Flounders belong to the families *Bothidae* and *Pleuronectidae.* The winter flounder is genus *Pseudopleuronectes,* species *americanus.* The summer flounder is *Paralichthys dentatus.*   LEONARD P. SCHULTZ

See also FLATFISH; HALIBUT; TURBOT; FISH (picture: A Flounder).

A Small Flounder of the Gulf of Mexico. The upper side of this fish imitates remarkably well the appearance of the sand on which the fish rests. As the fish grows, the eye on its lower side moves gradually around to the upper side of its head.

Fish and Wildlife Service

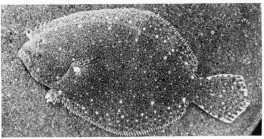

FLOUR

FLOUR is a powdery food made by grinding grain. Most flour is made from wheat and is used to bake bread. Other cereal grains that are ground into flour include barley, corn, millet, oats, rice, and rye. Flour is the basic ingredient of such foods as cakes, cookies, crackers, macaroni, and pancakes.

Bread ranks as the world's most widely eaten food, and people in many countries receive more than half their nourishment from foods made with flour. Each person in the United States eats an average of about 125 pounds (57 kilograms) of flour from wheat and other grains annually. Canadians eat an average of about 135 pounds (61 kilograms) of flour per person each year.

By the 9000's B.C., prehistoric people were grinding crude flour from wild grain by crushing the grain between rocks. Later, the ancient Greeks and Romans used water wheels to power flour mills.

Types of Flour. White flour made from wheat accounts for more than 90 per cent of the flour produced in the United States. There are three main types of white wheat flour: (1) bread flour, (2) cake flour, and (3) all-purpose flour. Bread flour is milled chiefly for commercial bakeries. Cake flour is made for both commercial and home baking. All-purpose flour is used mainly at home.

The three types of flour differ primarily in their protein content. Bread flour contains at least 11 per cent protein, and cake flour contains less than $8\frac{1}{2}$ per cent protein. All-purpose flour, which is a blend of bread flour and cake flour, has a protein content of about $10\frac{1}{2}$ per cent.

When the protein in wheat flour is moistened in dough, it forms a sticky substance called *gluten*. Bread flour dough has strong gluten, cake flour dough has weak gluten, and all-purpose flour dough has a blend of strong and weak glutens. Strong gluten works well with yeast to *leaven* bread, or make it rise. Weak gluten produces tender, crumbly baked goods, but it results in poor yeast-leavened bread. Therefore, bakers use bread flour for breads and use cake flour for pastries. All-purpose flour is used for such foods as cakes, cookies, rolls, and homemade bread, and in sauces.

Bread flour is sometimes called *strong flour* because it forms strong gluten. This kind of flour is also known as *hard-wheat flour* because it comes from varieties of wheat that have hard kernels. Millers call cake flour *weak flour* because it forms weak gluten, or *soft-wheat flour* because it is produced from wheat that has soft kernels.

How Flour Is Milled

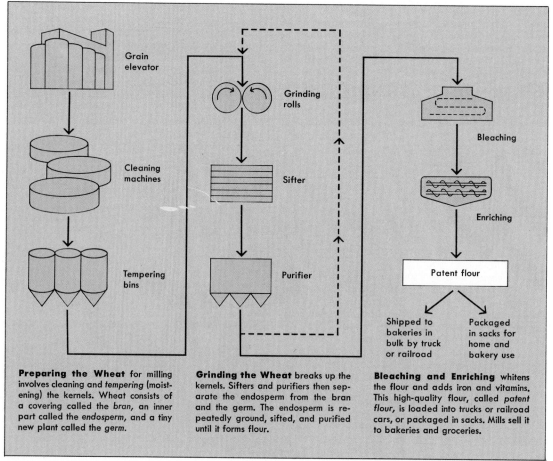

Preparing the Wheat for milling involves cleaning and *tempering* (moistening) the kernels. Wheat consists of a covering called the *bran,* an inner part called the *endosperm,* and a tiny new plant called the *germ.*

Grinding the Wheat breaks up the kernels. Sifters and purifiers then separate the endosperm from the bran and the germ. The endosperm is repeatedly ground, sifted, and purified until it forms flour.

Bleaching and Enriching whitens the flour and adds iron and vitamins. This high-quality flour, called *patent flour,* is loaded into trucks or railroad cars, or packaged in sacks. Mills sell it to bakeries and groceries.

232

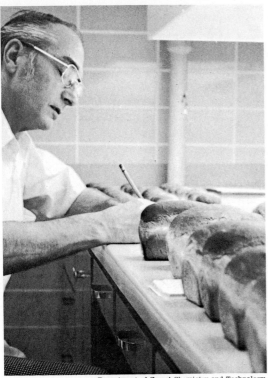

Department of Cereal Chemistry and Technology,
North Dakota State University

A Chemist Tests Samples of Bread made from flour from different *strains* (varieties) of wheat. Seeds from the strains that produce high-quality bread are distributed to farmers for planting.

The term *specialty flours* is used for types of flour other than white wheat flour. They include rye flour, whole-wheat flour, and *mixes*. Mixes consist of flour and other ingredients used to make various foods, such as cakes and pancakes.

How White Flour Is Milled. Wheat kernels form the raw material for flour. They consist of a tough covering called the *bran*, a mellow inner part called the *endosperm*, and a tiny new wheat plant called the *germ*. To make white flour, millers separate the endosperm from the bran and germ and grind the endosperm into flour.

Various cleaning machines first remove dirt, straw, and other impurities from the grain. Next, the wheat is *tempered* (moistened). The moisture makes the endosperm more mellow and the bran tougher.

The tempered wheat passes between a series of rough steel rollers that crush the endosperm into chunks. Pieces of bran and germ cling to the chunks of endosperm or form separate flakes. Then the crushed grain is sifted. The tiniest bits of endosperm, which have become flour, pass through the sifter into a bin. Larger particles collect in the sifter. Next, these larger particles are put into a machine called a *purifier*. There, currents of air blow flakes of bran away from the endosperm particles. The endosperm particles are then repeatedly ground between smooth rollers, sifted, and purified until they form flour. In most mills, about 72 per cent of the wheat eventually becomes flour. The rest is sold chiefly as livestock feed.

Newly milled flour is cream-colored, but some mills bleach it to make it white. They may also add chemicals that strengthen the gluten. Some chemicals both bleach the flour and strengthen the gluten. Such treatments must be carefully controlled because the addition of too much of a chemical ruins the flour.

Wheat is rich in starch, protein, B vitamins, and such minerals as iron and phosphorus. But the vitamins and some of the minerals are chiefly in the bran and germ, which milling removes from white flour. Most millers in the United States and many other countries enrich their product by adding iron and vitamins to white flour made for home use. Most U.S. bakeries use enriched flour, or they add vitamins and minerals to dough made with unenriched white flour.

The enriching of white flour has probably helped millions of people avoid malnutrition. Diseases caused by a lack of B vitamins were common in the United States before 1941. That year, the nation's bakers and millers began enriching white-flour products. Today, few Americans suffer those diseases.

History. People probably began to make crude flour between 15,000 B.C. and 9000 B.C. They used rocks to crush wild grain on other rocks. After farming began about 8000 B.C., people made flour from such cultivated grains as barley, millet, rice, rye, and wheat.

By the 1000's B.C., millers ground grain between two large, flat millstones. Later, domestic animals or groups of slaves rotated the top stone to crush the grain. By the A.D. 600's, windmills were powering flour mills in northern Europe.

Few further advances in milling occurred until 1780. That year, in England, a Scottish engineer named James Watt built the first steam-powered flour mill. In 1802, Oliver Evans, a Philadelphia miller, opened the first such mill in the United States. During the late 1800's, metal rollers replaced millstones in many American and European mills. Edmund La Croix and other millers in Minneapolis, Minn., perfected the purifier in the 1870's. By the early 1900's, automation had made flour mills more productive than ever.

Today, the United States has more than 250 flour mills. They produce about 12 million short tons (10.9 million metric tons) of wheat flour annually. The top flour milling centers in the United States, in order of production, are Buffalo, N.Y.; Minneapolis, Minn.; and Kansas City, Mo. Canada has about 50 flour mills, and they produce about 2 million short tons (1.8 million metric tons) of wheat flour yearly. Montreal is the chief Canadian milling center. The annual world wheat flour production totals about 135 million short tons (122 million metric tons).   Y. POMERANZ

See also BREAD; CORN (Milling); GLUTEN; MACARONI; WHEAT (Wheat Flour).

FLOUR BEETLE is any of several small, reddish, flattened beetles that breed in flour, meal, and other grain products. They often spoil the food. Adult flour beetles are about $\frac{1}{17}$ inch (1.5 millimeters) long. Flour beetles live all over the world, and all year long, in warm buildings.

Scientific Classification. The flour beetle belongs to the family Tenebrionidae. Common species are *Tribolium confusum* and *T. castaneum*.   R. E. BLACKWELDER

FLOW CHART. See COMPUTER (Planning a Program).

Shostal

Bright Yellow Dandelions blossom on meadows and lawns in the U.S. and Canada. The ripened flowers form feathery white parachutes with seeds that the wind carries.

Flowers bloom almost everywhere on earth, from the cold regions of the Far North and South to hot lands near the equator. They dot mountain slopes and brighten steaming jungles. Flowers thrive in fields, woods, deserts, swamps, and along the shores of lakes and oceans.

Night-Blooming Cereus climbs walls and rocky ledges in the West Indies and other warm lands. Gardeners in Hawaii and the Far East also cultivate this type of cactus. Its creamy blossoms open only at night.

Werner Stoy, Camera Hawaii

Base map © Rand McNally & Company

Flower

Cattleya Orchid flourishes in the hot, moist climates of many South-American countries.

Roche

FLOWER. The flowers, or blossoms, of plants and trees bloom almost everywhere on earth. Some flowers grow on high mountains at the edges of snow fields and glaciers. Others live in the shallow parts of oceans. Even hot, dry deserts have many bright blossoms during and after the rainy season. Most flowers need soil in which to grow, but some can grow on tree branches. Others float on lakes and streams. About the only places flowers do not grow are in the ice-covered parts of the Arctic and Antarctic and in the open seas.

The word *flower* may mean either (1) the blossom or (2) the whole plant. *Botanists* (scientists who study plants) use the word flower to mean only the blossom of a plant. They call the whole plant—blossom, stem, leaves, and roots—a *flowering plant*. Any plant that produces some sort of flower, even a tiny, colorless one, is a flowering plant. Grasses, roses, lilies, apple trees, and oaks are all flowering plants.

Flowers are the reproductive parts of flowering plants. The plants could not develop seeds and reproduce without them.

Man depends completely on flowers and flowering plants for his food. Flowering plants include almost all of our grains, fruits, and vegetables. Even the animals that we use for food, such as cattle, hogs, and sheep, live on flowering plants.

There are about 200,000 known kinds of flowers. They range in size from water blossoms so small they can

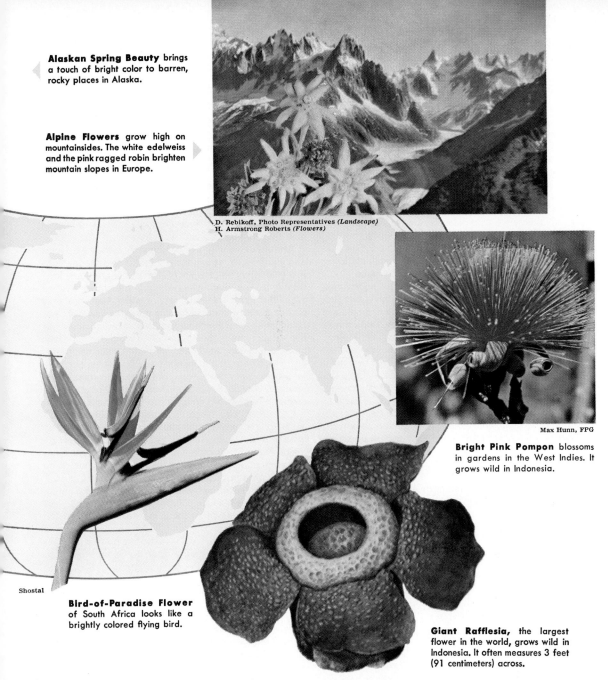

Alaskan Spring Beauty brings a touch of bright color to barren, rocky places in Alaska.

Alpine Flowers grow high on mountainsides. The white edelweiss and the pink ragged robin brighten mountain slopes in Europe.

D. Rebikoff, Photo Representatives (*Landscape*)
H. Armstrong Roberts (*Flowers*)

Max Hunn, FPG

Bright Pink Pompon blossoms in gardens in the West Indies. It grows wild in Indonesia.

Shostal

Bird-of-Paradise Flower of South Africa looks like a brightly colored flying bird.

Giant Rafflesia, the largest flower in the world, grows wild in Indonesia. It often measures 3 feet (91 centimeters) across.

be seen only with a microscope, to tropical flowers that are 3 feet (91 centimeters) wide. Some kinds of flowers, such as those belonging to the grass family, have no petals. Others look like stars, saucers, or balloons. Some even resemble insects, spiders, or birds.

Many flowers have smells that attract the birds or insects which help fertilize them. The smell of flowers ranges from pleasant to unpleasant—from the delightful fragrance of the lily to that of the pelican flower of South America, which smells like rotting meat.

People sometimes use flowers as symbols of certain feelings and emotions. The violet stands for faithfulness, the snowdrop for hope, the daisy for innocence, and the lily for purity. The honeysuckle symbolizes happiness, and the rose and forget-me-not are associated with love. Flowers are also used as symbols of the months of the year. See the articles on the various months in THE WORLD BOOK ENCYCLOPEDIA.

The Importance of Flowers

For Decoration. In every part of the world, people use flowers to decorate their homes. These decorations may range from a single bud in a vase to large, artistic arrangements. Flowers bring a cheerful note to sickrooms. People put wreaths of flowers on statues and monuments, and cover the graves of loved ones with flowers as a sign of respect. Flowers often decorate churches and other places of worship.

235

FLOWER

Young men may present flowers to their sweethearts as tokens of their love. Women wear flowers in their hair or as corsages to add beauty to their appearance. Brides carry bouquets at weddings. Men sometimes pin flowers to their lapels.

As Food. Our common vegetables, fruits, and grains are actually parts of flowering plants. We eat the roots of beets and carrots, the leaves of lettuce, the seeds of beans and peas, the fruits of apples and peaches, and the young stems of asparagus.

Artichokes, broccoli, and cauliflowers are undeveloped groups of flowers. Dandelion and elderberry blossoms are sometimes used to make wine. Cloves, used to flavor many foods, are the pickled flower buds of the tropical clove tree. Pickled flower buds of the caper bush are used as a relish. The petals of the Guatemalan earflower are sometimes used to flavor tea and chocolate.

In Industry. Oils extracted from roses, lilies, jasmines, hyacinths, and other flowers are among the oldest perfumes (see PERFUME). Since ancient times, men have made drugs, such as saffron and opium, from flower blossoms. Dyes, including henna and saffron yellow, are also made from flowers.

The raising and selling of flowers has itself become a large industry. Commercial nurseries and greenhouses grow flowers and small trees and shrubs. They may sell these directly to the public, or sell them wholesale to florists. Florists sell cut flowers, potted flowers, corsages, and flower arrangements. Some grow their own flowers. Others sell the flowers they have bought from nurseries. See FLORICULTURE; FLORIST.

Garden Flowers

Farmers and gardeners in North America raise about 30,000 species, or kinds, of flowering plants. Many kinds of flowering plants are grown for food. But most of the different kinds are garden flowers, grown for decoration. See GARDENING.

Most garden flowers are *herbaceous* plants (plants that do not have woody stems). But others, including golden bells and spiraea, are woody-stemmed. Garden flowers usually need bright sunlight in which to grow. Others grow better in the shade. Some need large amounts of water, while others grow best in well-drained soil. Most

---
INTERESTING FACTS ABOUT FLOWERS

Cherry Blossom Soup, a Japanese delicacy, is made by placing pickled cherry blossoms in hot water. It has a salty flavor.

Flower Clocks that tell the approximate time of day can be made by planting flowers that open and close at certain hours, such as four-o'clocks.

Fossils of flowering plants 165,000,000 years old have been found.

Largest Flower is *Rafflesia arnoldi,* which grows in Indonesia. It may measure 3 feet (91 centimeters) across and weigh 15 pounds (7 kilograms). Its petals may be 1 inch (2.5 centimeters) thick.

Orchids have the longest blooming period. The flowers of certain kinds of orchids may remain open for five weeks or more.

Smallest Flowering Plant is the duckweed, which is about $\frac{1}{50}$ inch (0.5 millimeter) long and $\frac{1}{63}$ inch (0.4 millimeter) wide.

Violets of certain kinds have underground flowers as well as the blossoms that grow above ground.

garden flowers also grow wild, or had ancestors that grew wild. Some are exactly the same as the wild form. Gardeners have bred others to produce huskier or hardier stems, larger or more fragrant flowers, differently colored flowers, or more attractive leaves than in their wild state. Often these man-made changes are temporary. The plants will change back to their wild form in several generations unless a gardener continues to care for the best plants and destroys the others.

Gardeners classify flowers by the length of time the plants live. Annuals live only one year. Biennials live for two years. Perennials live for more than two years.

The length of time a flowering plant normally lives may vary with the climate or the place where it grows. For example, plants that are perennials in warm climates may live only one season in colder areas.

Annuals normally live only one year. But gardeners also use the term *annual* for any plants that bloom within a year after the seeds are planted, no matter how long they live after that. Most annuals are rather easy to grow. But gardeners must *sow,* or plant, large amounts of their seeds, because many may not *germinate,* or sprout. If too many seeds germinate, gardeners usually weed out the weakest ones. Most annuals bloom two or three months after the seeds are planted. When the plants begin to bloom, the gardener usually removes the blossoms before they produce seeds. In this way, most plants produce more flowers over a longer period. Some annuals continue to bloom even after the first frosts of autumn.

Certain annuals, such as cornflowers, cosmos, marigolds, phlox, pinks, and zinnias grow in almost any type of soil. Sweet alyssum, candytuft, and ageratum make attractive borders for flower beds or pathways. Morning-glories, sweet peas, and other annuals climb or twine around sticks, fences, or lattices for support.

Biennials live for two years after the seeds are planted. Most biennials bloom well only during the second year. Gardeners usually plant them in midsummer, and the flowers bloom the next spring. Many biennials are used in formal flower beds. Others make fine borders or backgrounds. Common biennials include Canterbury bells, foxgloves, hollyhocks, and snapdragons.

Perennials. Gardeners usually plant the seeds of perennials in early spring or in midsummer. The flowers bloom the following year. Roses and other perennials with woody stems may live indefinitely. Gardeners may sow perennial seeds in a temporary location where they are protected from the weather. Then, in autumn, they move the seedlings to a permanent place with suitable soil, drainage, and sunlight. Common perennials include asters, bleeding hearts, carnations, columbines, daisies, irises, larkspurs, stonecrops, primroses, and violets. Permanently placed perennials usually form the main spots of interest in a garden.

Wild Flowers

Wild flowers grow almost everywhere—in woods, fields, deserts, jungles, meadows, and swamps; on mountains, prairies, and roadsides; and along streams and seashores. In North America, at least 32,000 kinds of wild flowers grow north of the Rio Grande.

Woodland Flowers thrive on the deep, rich humus formed by decaying leaves and wood (see HUMUS). Most flowers of the woods and forests cannot grow in bright sunlight. Many bloom in early spring, before the sun

Flowers IN FESTIVALS AND CUSTOMS

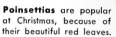

Poinsettias are popular at Christmas, because of their beautiful red leaves.

F.P.G.

H. Armstrong Roberts

White Easter Lilies symbolize purity. As symbols of the season, these flowers are used to decorate churches and homes.

Tulip Festival in Holland, Mich., takes place in May, when the flowers bloom. Many of the people wear Dutch costumes.

Michigan Tourist Council; Fred Bond, Publix

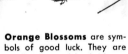

Orange Blossoms are symbols of good luck. They are the flowers used by brides.

Shostal

Three Lions

Brightly Colored Leis, or wreaths, are made from ginger, orchids, plumeria, and other flowers. In Hawaii and other Pacific islands, leis are worn as necklaces.

The Floating Gardens of Xochimilco, in Mexico, are famous for flower vendors who sell their colorful wares from canoes.

Shostal

Shostal

Bunchberry has tiny purple flowers, surrounded by white, petal-like bracts.

Hepaticas peep out from among the fallen leaves and branches on the woodland floor. They are among the first flowers to appear each spring, and may even bloom while snow covers the ground.

Yellow Violet

Purnell, Shostal

Gottscho-Schleisner

Trailing Arbutus, with its spicy odor, is one of the best-loved wild flowers.

John H. Gerard; Shostal

Delicate Violets blossom in shady, sheltered woodland areas. Both the purple violet and the yellow violet grow close to the ground.

Dogtooth Violet is not a violet, but belongs to the same family as the lily.

Trillium blooms in damp, shady woods. Its white petals gradually turn pink.

Frank Cassidy; Gottscho-Schleisner

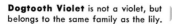

Frank Cassidy

Wild Geraniums dot the woods of eastern North America in spring and early summer.

Spring Beauty opens its delicate flowers in early spring. They live only a few days.

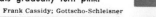

WOODLAND

Rutherford Platt; Booth, Crich, Photo Researchers

Columbine nods its lovely red head in woodlands of the U.S. and Canada.

Shooting Star grows in woods and on prairies from Virginia west to Texas.

Showy Orchis, a kind of orchid, can be pollinated only by female bumblebees.

Rutherford Platt

Ghostly White Indian Pipe gets its food from decaying plants in the soil.

Rutherford Platt

Jack-in-the-Pulpit resembles a minister standing in a pulpit.

Rutherford Platt

Fringed Gentian opens its blue flower only on sunny days.

Roche

May Apple has a cup-shaped flower that hides beneath two large, umbrellalike leaves.

Matteson, Photo Researchers

Gottscho-Schleisner

Pink Lady's-Slipper is as lovely an orchid as its tropical relatives.

Bloodroot has a thick, orange-red root filled with reddish sap which Indians used as warpaint.

239

Bluebonnets in Texas add color to sunlit roadsides, fields, and prairies.

Pasqueflower, or **Easter Flower,** blooms early in the spring.

Scarlet Bugler blooms in sandy places in the Southwest. Hummingbirds get nectar from its bright red flowers.

Bluets are small, delicate flowers common in meadows and sandy woods in the eastern United States and Canada.

Turk's-Cap Lily opens its bright orange and purple-dotted blossoms in wet meadows and low woodlands during the summer.

Goldenrod is a common flower of late summer and autumn.

Oxeye Daisies are sometimes troublesome weeds.

California Poppies cover meadows west of the Rockies with a blanket of gold.

Red Clover is pollinated only by bumblebees. It enriches soil and provides food for livestock.

240

Flowers

OF ROADSIDE, FIELD, AND PRAIRIE

New England Asters brighten open woods, fields, and prairies with their colorful flowers. They bloom in late summer and autumn.

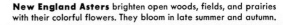

Common Thistle, a troublesome weed, crowds other plants out of fields and wasteland.

Butterfly Weed, a type of milkweed, usually has butterflies flitting around its flowers.

Yellow Lupine has flowers that look like sweetpea blossoms.

Partridge Pea has leaves that fold together when handled.

Bluebells of Scotland grow on ledges and in meadows in northern regions of the world.

Chicory root may be used as a substitute for coffee.

Black-Eyed Susans brighten roadsides and meadows.

Creamcups is named for creamy, cup-shaped blooms.

Toadflax, or **Butter-and-Eggs,** grows as a weed.

Wild Rose ranks as one of the loveliest of wild flowers.

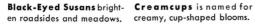

Flowers OF THE DESERT

White Dune Primroses and Yellow Desert Sunflowers brighten the hot, dry, sandy expanses of the southwestern U.S.

Ocotillo

Shostal

Yucca has a cluster of bell-shaped flowers on a tall stem.

Saguaro

Edwards, F.P.G.

Ollis, Black Star

Vrooman, Photo Researchers

Ocotillo and Saguaro bear their flowers high above the desert floor. Saguaro, or giant cactus, may grow up to 50 feet (15 meters) tall.

Prickly Pear is a cactus. Its bright flowers bloom for only one day.

Claret-Cup Cactus was named for its scarlet, cup-shaped blossoms.

Photo Representatives; Shostal

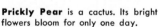

Ollis, Black Star

242

Sand Verbenas thrive in sandy soil in many far western states.

MOUNTAIN *Flowers*

L. Gilpin, Photo Researchers

Bright-Red Snow Plants bloom among low plants and shrubs on top of high mountains.

Calypso, a member of the orchid family, thrives in cool, mossy woods in northern areas.

Emil Muench, Photo Researchers

Shostal

Indian Paintbrush gives a splash of color to the Rockies.

Bob & Ira Spring

Western Anemone has sepals that look like petals.

Bear Grass is not really a grass. It is a kind of lily that grows in mountain meadows.

Mountain Laurel is a blossoming shrub of the eastern U.S.

Gottscho-Schleisner

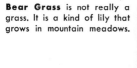

Bob & Ira Spring

Avalanche Lily blooms amid melting snow on high mountains.

Rock Plants force their way between rocks in barren areas high on mountain slopes.

Photo Researchers

Bob & Ira Spring

Swamp Rose Mallow flourishes in salty marshes. The wild plant grows from 4 to 8 feet (1.2 to 2.4 meters) tall and has a pink flower. Cultivated flowers may be white or deep rose.

Western Skunk Cabbage smells like a skunk. A leaflike *spathe* surrounds its small flowers.

Blue Flag, the best-known wild iris, grows in marshes and wet meadows.

Rutherford Platt

Swamp Milkweed lives in sunny swamps and wet places. It ranges from white to purple in color.

Nelson, Brooklyn Botanic Garden; John H. Gerard

Cardinal Flower brightens swamps and marshes with its brilliant red blooms.

Frank Fenner

Mayer, Photo Researchers

Marsh Marigold, or **Cowslip,** is related to the buttercup. It has no petals, but has petal-like *sepals.*

Swamp Buttercups bloom in wet woods and open water in spring.

244

American Lotus flourishes in large colonies on shallow lakes and streams.

Water Lily has sweet-smelling flowers. Its large, flat leaves, called *lily pads*, float lazily on ponds and streams.

Water Hyacinth

Pickerelweed

Yellow Pond Lily

Pickerelweed has its roots buried in the mud. The flower grows above the water. Some leaves are underwater.

Water Hyacinth is a floating plant. Its roots hang freely in the water. The leaves and flowers stick up above the surface.

Yellow Pond Lily has roots anchored in the ground. Its flowers bloom above the water, and the leaves float on top.

ENFOYING *Flowers* INDOORS

Fuchsia

Growing Flowers Indoors can be a rewarding hobby. Many kinds of flowering plants will bloom well in pots, if properly cared for.

Gloxinia

Christmas Begonia

Potted Flowers make fine gifts for holidays, birthdays, anniversaries, and other special occasions. Their beauty lasts for a long time.

African Violet

Flower Boxes, called *planters*, containing geraniums or other colorful flowers, brighten any room.

Cyclamen

Flowering
Crab

SPRING
GARDEN
Flowers

Lilac

Camera Clix   **Scilla**

Frank Cassidy
Creeping Phlox

Frank Cassidy

Sherman, Photo Researchers

Lily of the Valley

**Dwarf
Tulips**

Tulips

Gottscho-Schleisner; Roche

Franklin Photo Agency
Crocus

247

Hyacinth

Forsythia

Daffodil

J. Horace McFarland;
Gottscho-Schleisner

SUMMER GARDEN *Flowers*

Franklin Photo Agency; Bob Taylor, F.P.G.

Lemon Lily and Peony

Morning-Glory

Transvaal Daisy

J. Horace McFarland

Mixed Shades of Delphinium

Gladiolus

Roche

Rose

Iris

Phlox

Fred H. Ragsdale, F.P.G.

Roche

Genereux, F.P.G.

Kwiatkowski

Zinnia

Lincoln, A.P.A.

Snapdragon

Jack Breed, F.P.G.

Rambler Rose

Regal Lily   **Meadow Rue**   **Candlestick Lily**   **Delphinium**   **Sundrops**

The Wayside Gardens Co.

Petunia

J. Horace McFarland

Oriental Poppy

Franklin Photo Agency

Shostal

Hollyhocks

249

FALL GARDEN *Flowers*

Frank Cassidy

Dahlia

Cockscomb

J. Horace McFarland

A Beautiful Fall Garden has chrysanthemums, marigolds, and petunias.

Roche

Salvia

Lincoln, Shostal

Dwarf Marigold

Chrysanthemums

Genereux, F.P.G.

Sherman, Photo Researchers

Cosmos

Camera Clix

Gloriosa Daisy

Roche

250

ARRANGING *Flowers*

Good Housekeeping Magazine

The Japanese have made a fine art of arranging flowers. Their arrangements have graceful lines, pleasing form, and good balance.

Modern Flower Arrangements can be placed in pots, frying pans, or other everyday utensils. The flowers are picked and arranged to harmonize with their surroundings.

Better Homes & Gardens Magazine

A Circle Bouquet can be made of colorful roses, irises, snapdragons, and summer chrysanthemums.

Gottlieb Hampfler, F.P.G.

Lilac and Lily of the Valley form a graceful S curve in this purple and white arrangement.

Black Star

Stately Tulips set in the form of a tall triangle make an attractive formal arrangement.

251

Flowers IN ART

Neue Staatsgalerie, Munich, Germany

National Gallery of Art,
Index of American Design

Tulips decorate a Pennsylvania-Dutch candlebox.

Sunflowers, a still life by Vincent van Gogh, is one of the most famous paintings of flowers.

Painters have used flowers to add realism to an outdoor scene for hundreds of years, as in this detail from *Little Garden of Paradise* by an unknown artist of the Middle Ages.

The Stadelsches Kunstinstitut, Frankfurt am Main, Germany

Nahigian Brothers, Inc.

The Metropolitan Museum of Art,
New York, Roger's Fund, 1930

A Flowering Tree decorates a section of a Javanese sarong.

Persian Rugs have patterns of bright flowers woven with threads of many different colors.

becomes too strong. Others that bloom later thrive on the small amount of sunlight that filters through the leaves of overhanging trees. The length of time that woodland flowers bloom varies. Azaleas, redbuds, and rhododendrons flourish throughout the warm months. Saxifrages and yellow star grass often bloom from spring to fall. Bloodroots, hepaticas, spring beauties, trilliums, and most violets are *tender* plants. They bloom for only a short time in early spring. The part of the plant that grows above the ground withers after the fruit appears. But the roots remain alive year after year.

Trees are also flowering plants. A few, including the cherries, crab apples, mountain ashes, and magnolias, have showy flowers. But most do not. Arrowwoods, spicebushes, witch hazels, and other shrubs grow as underbrush in many wooded areas.

Mountain Flowers. Many attractive flowers flourish near the tops of high mountains where trees cannot grow. Snow fields and glaciers often cover the ground on these peaks. Flowers can grow in these areas only where the sun melts the snow in the warmest months. Plants that grow high on mountains include avalanche lilies, alpine roses, dwarf gentians, edelweiss, moss campions, mountain heaths, and some saxifrages. These plants are called *alpine plants.*

The large, colorful blossoms of many alpine flowers attract the few insects that live on high mountains. These flowers usually produce seeds quickly, because the growing season is short at high altitudes. Many of these small, sturdy plants store food in their fleshy underground parts. Woolly fuzz covers the leaves and stems of many of the plants and cuts down the evaporation of water.

Prairie Flowers. Masses of beardtongues, globe mallows, prairie clovers, prairie rockets, sagebrushes, sunflowers, and many grasses grow on plains and prairies. The roots of most of these plants can withstand the fires that sometimes sweep across the plains. The plants store food in their underground parts. Even though the plant above the ground burns, the roots remain alive and can send up new shoots.

Desert Flowers. Deserts probably have the most unfavorable conditions for plants. Rain usually falls only during a brief season. During the rest of the year, the sun bakes the sandy soil during the day, and the air turns cold at night. Flowering desert plants grow quickly during and after rains. They produce bright flowers that attract insects for pollination. The seeds mature quickly, before the scorching rays of the sun wither the plants.

Many desert annuals survive the long dry season as seeds. Other plants have underground bulbs that send up leaves and flowers only during or immediately after the rainy season (see BULB). Many desert shrubs have no leaves. Others have small, hard leaves that they shed immediately after the rainy season. The stiff, thorny stems and branches of century plants, ocotillos, sagebrushes, and yuccas protect the plants from grazing animals. Thick, fleshy stems filled with spongy, water-holding tissue support most cactus plants. Cacti have sharp spines and mats of stiff bristlelike hairs. Their flowers are usually large and colorful.

Water Flowers. A few flowering plants live in water. Their roots are usually embedded in the mud bottom of a pond or stream. The flowers and leaves of lotuses, pondweeds, water lilies, and many others float on, or project above, the surface of the water. But only the blossoms of eelgrasses and waterweeds reach the surface. Sea grasses and sea wracks are completely submerged, and bloom entirely under water. Duckweeds and water hyacinths float freely on the surface, carried about by water currents and wind. Many kinds of bladderworts float beneath the surface. Their roots do not reach the soil, and only their flowers project above the water. A waxy or slimy water-resistant substance covers the stems of many water plants.

Beach and Shore Flowers. Certain flowering plants prefer sandy seashores, sand dunes, and pine barrens as homes. They often sprawl flat over the sand, with vinelike branches and underground roots and stems. Beach grasses, railroad vines, sandburs, and sea rockets help keep the sand from blowing away. Such plants as glassworts, rose mallows, saltworts, and sea lavenders grow in salt marshes. They can live where the soil, water, and even the air contain salt.

Meadow Flowers. Flowers that grow in open fields and pastures need bright sunshine. They grow best in dry soil. Black-eyed Susans, goldenrods, thistles, and wild roses thrive in sunny places. Thick patches of these plants often form masses of color on the landscape.

Swamp Flowers. Some flowers grow best in wet meadows and along the edges of ponds and streams. These include arrowheads, cardinal flowers, golden clubs, lizard's-tails, purple loosestrifes, and most willows. Other plants, including cattails, cranberries, flags, pitcher plants, and spider lilies, live in marshes, bogs, and swamps. These flowers must have plenty of sunshine, but they cannot grow in dry, or even well-drained, soil.

Tropical Flowers. Thousands of kinds of flowering plants live in tropical forests. They must compete for the sunlight, because there are so many plants. Many are *lianas,* or vines. They climb to the tops of trees and open their flowers and leaves in the sunlight. Other tropical flowering plants are *epiphytes,* or air plants, that live on the trunks and branches of trees. They do not get their food directly from the trees, but from the air and from dirt and decaying leaves that collect around their roots. See also AIR PLANT.

Strange and Unusual Flowers grow in various parts of the world. Some, such as the moonflower and night-blooming cereus, open their flowers only at dusk or at night. Others may blossom both night and day, but have an odor only during certain hours. The leaves of compass plants turn edgewise to the sun during the heat of the day. They resume their normal position in the cool of morning, evening, and night.

Carnivorous plants (plants which trap insects and other small animals) live in many parts of the world. Bladderworts live in water. On their leaves, they have tiny baglike traps in which they catch small water animals. Crawling insects get caught on the broad, sticky leaves of butterworts. Pitcher plants have deep red, globe-shaped flowers. Their hollowed-out leaves resemble pitchers and are partially filled with sweet, sticky fluids. These fluids attract insect visitors, which then drown in them. Little hairs cover the leaves of sundews and dewthreads. A tiny pink droplet of "glue" tips each hair. Insects get stuck to this glue. Then the leaf slowly wraps around them. The Venus's-flytrap has small white

PARTS OF A *Flower*

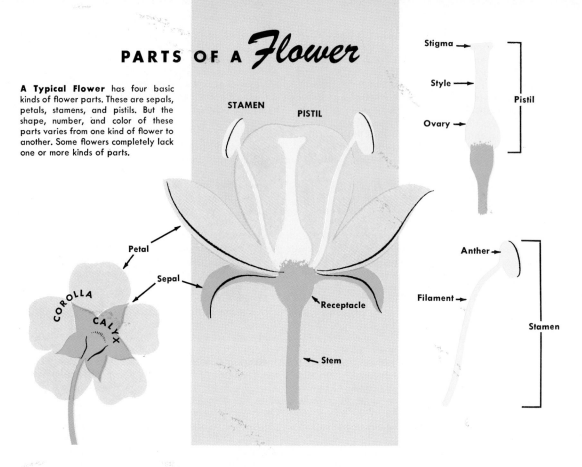

A Typical Flower has four basic kinds of flower parts. These are sepals, petals, stamens, and pistils. But the shape, number, and color of these parts varies from one kind of flower to another. Some flowers completely lack one or more kinds of parts.

STAMEN

PISTIL

Petal

Sepal

COROLLA

CALYX

Receptacle

Stem

Stigma →

Style →

Ovary →

Pistil

Anther →

Filament →

Stamen

---

flowers. It catches insects in a springtrap at the tip of its leaves. Carnivorous plants probably digest the soft parts of the bodies of their victims. See CARNIVOROUS PLANT.

Some flowering plants, including mistletoe and dodder, have become *parasitic*. They attach themselves to other plants and rob them of food. The ghostly white Indian pipes and the blood-red snow plants are *saprophytic*. They live on the dead and decaying vegetable matter in forests. See PARASITE; SAPROPHYTE.

Stranglerfigs, which live in tropical places, begin their lives as ordinary vines. They climb to the tops of neighboring trees. Then they send down *root stems* that grow tightly around the trunks of the trees and choke them. After the trees die and decay, the stranglerfigs remain erect, occupying the position of the trees they killed.

Studying Wild Flowers

The best way to learn about wild flowers is to go to the woods, fields, and mountains to study them where they grow. Botanists usually take notes on the locations and growing habits of interesting plants. Then they may pick some of the plants and preserve them for later study.

To preserve a flowering plant, place it inside a folded sheet of newspaper with large blotters and cardboard outside the newspaper on each side. Tie the package tightly with a strong string, or put a heavy weight on it. If the pressed flowering plant is kept in a warm place, it will dry completely in a few days. You may wish to take plants home before you press them. If so, you can keep them in a long, oval can called a *vasculum*. This can

should be lined with damp newspapers or moss to keep the flowers fresh.

Use glue or gummed tape to mount the dried plant on a large sheet of heavy paper. Label the mounted specimen with its common and scientific names, the date it was picked, its location, and any interesting facts about its growing habits. A collection of mounted, dried flowers is called an *herbarium* (see HERBARIUM). Many books about wild flowers have sections that will help you identify and classify flowers.

When collecting blossoms, remember that in many parks and forests it is against the law to pick flowers. Even in areas not protected by law, do not pick flowers unless they are plentiful. Many wild flowers have shallow roots or take a long time to grow back after the blossoms have been broken off. Picking these flowers may destroy whole plants, or prevent other people from enjoying their beauty for many years.

The Parts of a Flower

A typical flower grows on a *receptacle*, or *torus*, an enlarged part of the flower stalk. The flower consists of four *whorls*, or sets, of parts. These whorls are (1) the calyx, (2) the corolla, (3) the stamens, and (4) the pistils.

The outermost whorl is the *calyx*. Within the calyx is the *corolla*. The calyx and corolla together form the *perianth*. The *stamens*, or male reproductive organs, lie within the corolla. The *pistils*, or female parts of the flower, make up the innermost whorl of parts.

The Calyx is usually made up of small, green, leaf-

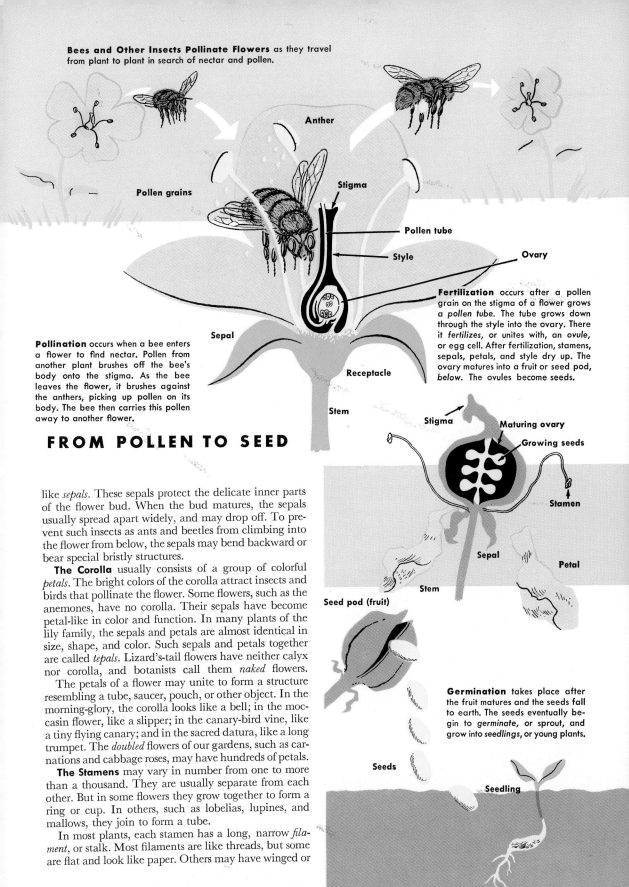

Bees and Other Insects Pollinate Flowers as they travel from plant to plant in search of nectar and pollen.

Anther

Pollen grains

Stigma

Pollen tube

Style

Ovary

Sepal

Fertilization occurs after a pollen grain on the stigma of a flower grows a *pollen tube*. The tube grows down through the style into the ovary. There it *fertilizes*, or unites with, an *ovule*, or egg cell. After fertilization, stamens, sepals, petals, and style dry up. The ovary matures into a fruit or seed pod, *below*. The ovules become seeds.

Pollination occurs when a bee enters a flower to find nectar. Pollen from another plant brushes off the bee's body onto the stigma. As the bee leaves the flower, it brushes against the anthers, picking up pollen on its body. The bee then carries this pollen away to another flower.

Receptacle

Stem

Stigma

Maturing ovary

Growing seeds

Stamen

Sepal

Petal

Stem

Seed pod (fruit)

FROM POLLEN TO SEED

like *sepals*. These sepals protect the delicate inner parts of the flower bud. When the bud matures, the sepals usually spread apart widely, and may drop off. To prevent such insects as ants and beetles from climbing into the flower from below, the sepals may bend backward or bear special bristly structures.

The Corolla usually consists of a group of colorful *petals*. The bright colors of the corolla attract insects and birds that pollinate the flower. Some flowers, such as the anemones, have no corolla. Their sepals have become petal-like in color and function. In many plants of the lily family, the sepals and petals are almost identical in size, shape, and color. Such sepals and petals together are called *tepals*. Lizard's-tail flowers have neither calyx nor corolla, and botanists call them *naked* flowers.

The petals of a flower may unite to form a structure resembling a tube, saucer, pouch, or other object. In the morning-glory, the corolla looks like a bell; in the moccasin flower, like a slipper; in the canary-bird vine, like a tiny flying canary; and in the sacred datura, like a long trumpet. The *doubled* flowers of our gardens, such as carnations and cabbage roses, may have hundreds of petals.

The Stamens may vary in number from one to more than a thousand. They are usually separate from each other. But in some flowers they grow together to form a ring or cup. In others, such as lobelias, lupines, and mallows, they join to form a tube.

In most plants, each stamen has a long, narrow *filament*, or stalk. Most filaments are like threads, but some are flat and look like paper. Others may have winged or

Germination takes place after the fruit matures and the seeds fall to earth. The seeds eventually begin to *germinate*, or sprout, and grow into *seedlings*, or young plants.

Seeds

Seedling

toothlike edges. On top of the filament is an enlargement called the *anther*. The anther usually consists of four baglike structures called *pollen sacs* or *microsporangia*. Dustlike pollen is produced in the sacs. Stamens are called *staminodes* if they lack anthers or if the anthers fail to produce pollen.

The Pistils. The number of pistils in a flower may vary from one to many. In some flowers, several separate pistils may join together to form a single *compound* pistil. Each pistil normally consists of three parts: the *stigma*, the *style*, and the *ovary*.

The *stigma*, at the top, may be large and feathery or small and hard to see. When the stigma is "ripe," its sticky upper surface catches and holds any pollen grains that fall on it. Beneath the stigma, the long, slender *style* leads to a round or long chamber called the *ovary*. Sometimes the pistil has no style, and the stigma rests directly on top of the ovary. The *ovules* (egg cells) that develop into seeds, grow inside the ovary.

Variations in Form. Not all flowers have all four sets of parts. *Incomplete* flowers, such as some buttercups and willows, lack one or more of these sets. Roses, lilies, and other *complete* flowers have them all. *Imperfect* flowers, such as cattails and arrowheads, lack either the stamens or the pistils. But *perfect* flowers have them both. *Staminate* flowers have stamens but no pistils, and *pistillate* flowers have pistils but no stamens.

Dioecious plants, such as poplars or willows, have staminate flowers on one plant, and pistillate flowers on another plant of the same kind. A *monoecious* plant, such as a begonia or castor bean, has both staminate and pistillate flowers on the same plant.

A *polygamous* plant, such as certain kinds of ash, buckwheat, and maple, has both perfect and imperfect flowers on the same plant.

A *radially symmetrical* flower can be cut across through the middle in any of several directions, and both halves will be exactly alike. Buttercups and wild roses are radially symmetrical. Orchids, snapdragons, and sweet peas are *bilaterally symmetrical*, because they produce similar halves only when cut lengthwise.

Flowers may grow singly or together in clusters. All the flowers of a plant together are called an *inflorescence*. Many persons mistakenly refer to an inflorescence as a "flower." For example, a dandelion or a daisy "flower" is actually an inflorescence made up of hundreds of tiny flowers pressed closely together. See INFLORESCENCE.

Bracts are leaflike structures beneath an inflorescence. They may form an *involucre* (circle) beneath the inflorescence. Brightly colored bracts make up the "flowers" of such plants as the poinsettia and flowering dogwood. The true flowers of these plants are found within the circle formed by the bracts.

How Flowers Reproduce

Pollination is the transfer of pollen from the anther to the stigma. It is the first step in the reproduction of flowers. There are two kinds of pollination: (1) cross-pollination and (2) self-pollination.

Cross-Pollination. Wind, water, insects, and other animals may *cross-pollinate* flowers, or transfer the pollen from the anther of one flower to the stigma of another.

VARIATIONS IN FLOWER FORMS

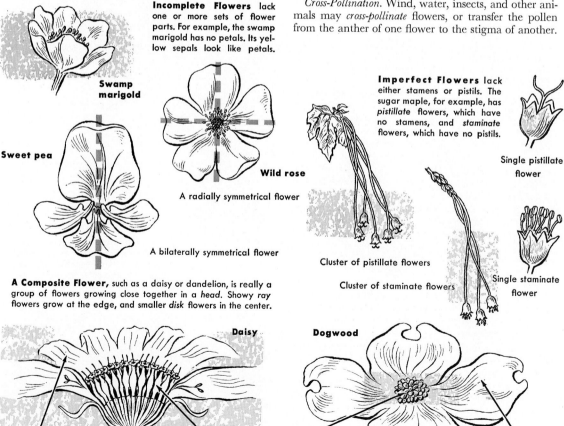

Incomplete Flowers lack one or more sets of flower parts. For example, the swamp marigold has no petals. Its yellow sepals look like petals.

Swamp marigold

Sweet pea

Wild rose

A radially symmetrical flower

A bilaterally symmetrical flower

Imperfect Flowers lack either stamens or pistils. The sugar maple, for example, has *pistillate* flowers, which have no stamens, and *staminate* flowers, which have no pistils.

Single pistillate flower

Cluster of pistillate flowers

Cluster of staminate flowers

Single staminate flower

A Composite Flower, such as a daisy or dandelion, is really a group of flowers growing close together in a *head*. Showy *ray* flowers grow at the edge, and smaller *disk* flowers in the center.

Daisy

Ray flower

Disk flower

Dogwood

Flowers

Bracts

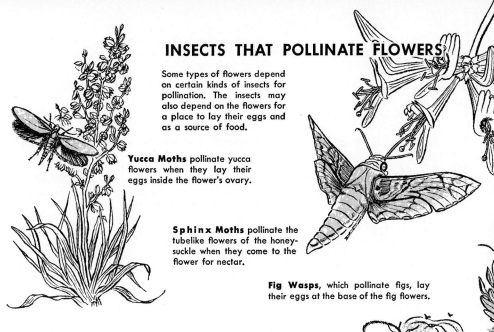

INSECTS THAT POLLINATE FLOWERS

Some types of flowers depend on certain kinds of insects for pollination. The insects may also depend on the flowers for a place to lay their eggs and as a source of food.

Yucca Moths pollinate yucca flowers when they lay their eggs inside the flower's ovary.

Sphinx Moths pollinate the tubelike flowers of the honeysuckle when they come to the flower for nectar.

Fig Wasps, which pollinate figs, lay their eggs at the base of the fig flowers.

Bumblebees pollinate red clover as they visit the flowers in search of pollen for food.

Insects and birds usually cross-pollinate flowers that have colorful corollas or bright calyxes. The colors and odors of the flowers attract insects. But the insects really go to the blossoms for food in the form of pollen and nectar (see NECTAR). Many flowers depend on only a few insects, or even only one kind of insect, for pollination. The red clover depends on the bumblebee, the yucca on the yucca moth, and the fig on the *Blastophaga* wasp. Certain European daisies are pollinated by snails. Even bats pollinate some flowers.

Various parts of the flowers are so constructed that they make sure that visiting insects or birds pollinate the blossoms. The pollen is heavy and sticky, and clings to the visitor's hair or feathers. The lady's-slipper, a kind of orchid, is so shaped that a heavy insect, such as a bumblebee, must force its way into the top of the flower to obtain nectar. To leave, the bee must go through a passage underneath the stamens. The stamens sprinkle their pollen onto the bee's hairy body as it brushes by. This pollen sticks to the pistil of the next flower that the bee visits. Another kind of orchid "shoots" its pollen at insects. When an insect lands on the flower, it sets off a trigger mechanism that throws pollen on the visitor's head. The pipe-vine plant traps insects at the base of a tubular flower where the pistils are ready to receive pollen from another plant. The trap opens only downward, so the insect cannot leave. The trap withers when the stamens, located above it, are ready to shed their pollen. The insects receive this pollen as they crawl out of the withered trap. They carry it to the pistils in the trap of another flower.

Wind pollinates many plants, including birches, corn, grasses, cattails, oaks, and ragweeds. Wind-pollinated plants usually have small, incomplete flowers. They do not need bright colors, fragrance, or nectar to attract insects. They produce much light, dry pollen. The wind carries this pollen to other flowers and deposits it on their large, feathery stigmas. This wind-blown pollen is chiefly responsible for hay fever.

Water pollinates a few kinds of plants. The pollen of eelgrasses and waterweeds floats on the surface until it touches a stigma. Submerged plants are pollinated under water.

Self-Pollination is the transfer of pollen from the stamens of a flower to the stigma of the same flower. Many plants pollinate themselves. These plants include barley, cotton, oats, peas, tobacco, and wheat. When necessary, certain cross-pollinating plants, such as chickweeds and pansies, can also pollinate themselves.

Many flowers grow in such a way that self-pollination cannot take place. In crane's-bills, spiderworts, and others, the stamens develop earlier than the pistils. The stigmas do not become sticky until after the anthers have shed their pollen. The stamens may wither before the pistils are fully grown. Pollen from these stamens cannot possibly fall on the pistil of the same plant at a time when the pistil is ripe. In other flowers, the pistil grows so far out beyond the stamens that self-pollination cannot occur. Such plants must reproduce through cross-pollination. See POLLEN AND POLLINATION.

Fertilization. If a grain of pollen from a flower comes to rest on the stigma of the same kind of flower, it may grow a *pollen tube*. The pollen tube pushes its way down the style to the ovules. There it unites with the *egg cell* within one of the ovules. This union is called *fertilization*. After fertilization, the ovules become seeds, and the ovary grows and develops into a fruit that includes the seeds. For example, we eat the part of the cantaloupe that develops from the ovary and surrounds the seeds.

257

FLOWER

Vegetative reproduction, or reproduction without fertilization and seed formation, takes place in some plants. Fleshy underground parts may divide to grow into new plants. For example, daffodils, hyacinths, and tulips produce underground bulbs. These divide naturally every year, and the daughter bulblets may grow into new plants. Strawberry plants send out stemlike *runners*, or *stolons*, along the ground. A new plant may form at the end of each stolon. A raspberry plant may bend a branch to the ground. A new plant grows where the branch takes root. All these plants also reproduce through fertilization. See REPRODUCTION (Plant Reproduction).

Flower Breeding. Pollen from one kind of plant usually will not fertilize a different kind of plant. But some closely related plants can fertilize each other. Such cross-breeding produces *hybrids* (see HYBRID). These hybrids usually have some characteristics of both parents. Sometimes one plant of a group of seedlings will show a sudden change in flower color or size, leaf-form, or other characteristics. Such a plant is called a *sport*. If its own seeds produce plants that have the same new characteristics, the plant is a *mutant* (see MUTATION).

Gardeners breed hybrids, sports, and mutants by cross-pollinating them with one another, with the parent plants, or with related plants. In this way, they have developed many *cultigens* (garden varieties) of such common flowers as irises, orchids, roses, and tulips.

Sometimes breeders cut off growing parts of a plant and place them in wet sand or peat moss, where they take root. These parts are called *cuttings* or *slips*. This method often saves time, because a plant grown from a cutting matures sooner than one grown from seed. Household plants are often started from slips.

How Flowers Are Named

Common Names. Since earliest times, man has given names to the plants that grow around him. We call these names *vernacular* (common) names. Some flowers are named for the objects they resemble. For example, the Indian pipe looks like a pipe, the pitcher plant resembles a pitcher, and the lady's-slipper is shaped like a shoe. Other flowers are named for animals or insects they resemble. The petals of the tiger lily look somewhat like a tiger's coat, and the butterfly pea looks like a butterfly. Flowers were also named for diseases they were thought to cure, or for the part of the human body they were supposed to affect. People thought the flower of the toothache tree (prickly ash) could cure toothaches, and that liverleaf (hepatica) cured liver diseases.

Common names are confusing, because the same plant often has different names in different parts of the world. Trillium may also be called wake-robin. The same name may be given to totally different plants in different places. For example, the tree with the hardest wood in any region is often called *ironwood*. But the

Text continued on page 261

─── **FAMILIES OF FLOWERING PLANTS** ───

All flowering plants that have separate articles in THE WORLD BOOK ENCYCLOPEDIA are classified below.

Acanthus Family
(Acanthaceae)
Acanthus

Agave Family
(Agavaceae)
Century Plant | Spanish Bayonet
Henequen | Tuberose
Maguey | Yucca

Amaranth Family
(Amaranthaceae)
Amaranth | Pigweed
Cockscomb | Tumbleweed

Amaryllis Family
(Amaryllidaceae)
Amaryllis | Leek
Chive | Narcissus
Daffodil | Onion
Firecracker Flower | Shallot
Garlic | Snowdrop
Jonquil | Star Grass

Arrowroot Family
(Marantaceae)
Arrowroot

Arum Family
(Araceae)
Arum | Philodendron
Caladium | Skunk Cabbage
Calla | Sweet Flag
Elephant's-Ear | Taro
Jack-in-the-Pulpit

Balsam Family
(Balsaminaceae)
Balsam, Garden | Touch-Me-Not

Banana Family
(Musaceae)
Abacá | Bird-of-Paradise
Banana | Flower

Barberry Family
(Berberidaceae)
Barberry | Oregon Grape
May Apple

Beech Family
(Fagaceae)
Beech | Cork
Chestnut | Oak

Begonia Family
(Begoniaceae)
Begonia

Bellflower Family
(Campanulaceae)
Bellflower | Campanula
Bluebell | Canterbury Bell

Bignonia Family
(Bignoniaceae)
Bignonia | Catalpa
Calabash Tree | Jacaranda

Birch Family
(Betulaceae)
Alder | Filbert | Ironwood
Birch | Hazel

Birthwort Family
(Aristolochiaceae)
Ginger | Pelican Flower | Snakeroot

Bladderwort Family
(Lentibulariaceae)
Bladderwort | Butterwort

Bombax Family
(Bombacaceae)
Balsa | Baobab | Kapok

Borage Family
(Boraginaceae)
Cowslip | Lungwort
Forget-Me-Not | Stickseed
Gromwell | Viper's Bugloss
Heliotrope

Box Family
(Buxaceae)
Box

Buckthorn Family
(Rhamnaceae)
Buckthorn | Cascara Sagrada

Buckwheat Family
(Polygonaceae)
Buckwheat | Rhubarb
Dock | Smartweed
Knotgrass | Sorrel

Cactus Family
(Cactaceae)
Cactus | Prickly Pear

Caltrop Family
(Zygophyllaceae)
Creosote Bush | Lignum Vitae

Canna Family
(Cannaceae)
Canna

Caper Family
(Capparidaceae)
Caper

Cashew Family
(Anacardiaceae)
Cashew | Poison Ivy
Mango | Poison Oak
Pepper Tree | Quebracho
Pistachio Nut | Sumac

Casuarina Family
(Casuarinaceae)
Beefwood

Cattail Family
(Typhaceae)
Cattail

———— FAMILIES OF FLOWERING PLANTS (*continued*) ————

All flowering plants that have separate articles in THE WORLD BOOK ENCYCLOPEDIA are classified below.

Coca Family
(Erythroxylaceae)
Coca

Composite Family
(Compositae)

Ageratum	Elecampane
Arnica	Endive
Artichoke	Everlasting
Aster	Feverfew
Bachelor's-Button	Fleabane
Black-Eyed	Gaillardia
Susan	Goldenrod
Blazing Star	Guayule
Boneset	Immortelle
Burdock	Lettuce
Calendula	Marigold
Camomile	Pyrethrum
Canada Thistle	Ragweed
Chicory	Safflower
Chrysanthemum	Sagebrush
Cineraria	Salsify
Cocklebur	Snakeroot
Coltsfoot	Sneezewort
Compass Plant	Sow Thistle
Coreopsis	Strawflower
Cosmos	Sunflower
Dahlia	Tansy
Daisy	Tarragon
Dandelion	Thistle
Devil's	Wormwood
Paintbrush	Zinnia
Edelweiss	

Crowfoot Family
(Ranunculaceae)

Aconite	Hellebore
Adonis	Hepatica
Anemone	Larkspur
Bugbane	Pasqueflower
Buttercup	Peony
Clematis	Snakeroot
Columbine	Wood Anemone
Cowslip	
Goldenseal	

Custard Apple Family
(Annonaceae)

Cherimoya	Pawpaw

Dogbane Family
(Apocynaceae)

Dogbane	Oleander

Dogwood Family
(Cornaceae)

Bunchberry	Dogwood

Duckweed Family
(Lemnaceae)
Duckweed

Ebony Family
(Ebenaceae)

Ebony	Persimmon

Elm Family
(Ulmaceae)

Elm	Hackberry

Evening Primrose Family
(Onagraceae)

Evening Primrose	Fuchsia
Fireweed	Godetia

Figwort Family
(Scrophulariaceae)

Beardtongue	Mullein
Foxglove	Slipperwort
Indian	Snapdragon
Paintbrush	Toadflax
Monkey Flower	Witchweed

Flax Family
(Linaceae)
Flax

Fouquieria Family
(Fouquieriaceae)
Ocotillo

Four-O'Clock Family
(Nyctaginaceae)

Bougainvillea	Sand Verbena
Four-O'Clock	

Frogbit Family
(Hydrocharitaceae)

Eelgrass	Elodea

Fumitory Family
(Fumariaceae)

Bleeding Heart	Dutchman's-
Dicentra	Breeches

Garcinia Family
(Guttiferae)
Mangosteen

Gentian Family
(Gentianaceae)
Gentian

Geranium Family
(Geraniaceae)
Geranium

Gesneria Family
(Gesneriaceae)

African Violet	Gloxinia

Ginger Family
(Zingiberaceae)

Cardamom	Turmeric
Ginger	

Ginseng Family
(Araliaceae)

Ginseng	Spikenard
Ivy	

Goosefoot Family
(Chenopodiaceae)

Beet	Spinach
Glasswort	Sugar Beet
Greasewood	Swiss Chard
Lamb's-Quarters	Tumbleweed

Gourd Family
(Cucurbitaceae)

Calabash	Melon
Casaba	Muskmelon
Chayote	Pumpkin
Cucumber	Squash
Gourd	Watermelon

Grass Family
(Gramineae)

Bamboo	Oats
Barley	Popcorn
Bent	Reed
Bluegrass	Rice
Brome Grass	Rye
Corn	Sandbur
Esparto	Sorghum
Fescue	Sudan Grass
Grain Sorghum	Sugar Cane
Grass	Timothy
Kafir	Wheat
Maize	Wild Barley
Millet	Wild Rice

Heath Family
(Ericaceae)

Arbutus	Labrador Tea
Azalea	Lingonberry
Blueberry	Madroña
Brier	Manzanita
Cranberry	Mountain Laurel
Heath	Rhododendron
Huckleberry	Sorrel Tree
Indian Pipe	Wintergreen

Holly Family
(Aquifoliaceae)

Holly	Winterberry
Maté	

Honeysuckle Family
(Caprifoliaceae)

Black Haw	Snowball
Elder	Twinflower
Honeysuckle	Viburnum

Horse Chestnut Family
(Hippocastanaceae)
Horse Chestnut

Illicium Family
(Illiciaceae)
Illicium

Iris Family
(Iridaceae)

Crocus	Gladiolus
Freesia	Iris

Laurel Family
(Lauraceae)

Avocado	Cinnamon
Bay Tree	Laurel
Camphor	Sassafras

Leadwort Family
(Plumbaginaceae)

Plumbago	Statice

Lecythis Family
(Lecythidaceae)

Anchovy Pear	Cannon-Ball
Brazil Nut	Tree

Lily Family
(Liliaceae)

Aloe	Lily of the Valley
Asparagus	Mariposa Lily
Asphodel	Ramp
Aspidistra	Sego Lily
Colchicum	Smilax
Crocus	Soap Plant
Day Lily	Solomon's-Seal
Dogtooth Violet	Squill
Easter Lily	Star-of-
Fritillary	Bethlehem
Greenbrier	Tiger Lily
Hellebore	Trillium
Hyacinth	Tulip
Lily	

Linden Family
(Tiliaceae)

Basswood	Linden

Lobelia Family
(Lobeliaceae)

Cardinal Flower	Lobelia

Logania Family
(Loganiaceae)
Gelsemium

Loosestrife Family
(Lythraceae)

Crape Myrtle	Henna

Madder Family
(Rubiaceae)

Bedstraw	Coffee
Bluet	Gardenia
Cinchona	Madder

Magnolia Family
(Magnoliaceae)

Bay Tree	Tulip Tree
Magnolia	

Mahogany Family
(Meliaceae)
Mahogany

Mallow Family
(Malvaceae)

Cotton	Hibiscus
Flowering Maple	Hollyhock

259

Indian Mallow
Mallow
Marsh Mallow

Okra
Rose of Sharon

Malpighia Family
(Malpighiaceae)
Acerola

Mangrove Family
(Rhizophoraceae)
Mangrove

Maple Family
(Aceraceae)
Box Elder   Maple

Mignonette Family
(Resedaceae)
Mignonette

Milkweed Family
(Asclepiadaceae)
Milkweed

Milkwort Family
(Polygalaceae)
Snakeroot

Mint Family
(Labiatae)
Balm
Basil
Bergamot
Catnip
Coleus
Horehound
Hyssop
Lavender
Marjoram
Mint

Oswego Tea
Patchouli
Pennyroyal
Peppermint
Rosemary
Sage
Salvia
Spearmint
Thyme

Mistletoe Family
(Loranthaceae)
Mistletoe

Morning-Glory Family
(Convolvulaceae)
Bindweed
Convolvulus
Dodder
Jalap
Moonflower

Morning-Glory
Sweet
Potato

Mulberry Family
(Moraceae)
Banyan
Tree
Bo Tree
Breadfruit
Fig
Hemp

Hop
Mulberry
Osage Orange
Rubber Plant
Upas

Mustard Family
(Cruciferae)
Broccoli
Brussels
Sprouts
Cabbage
Candytuft
Cauliflower
Chinese
Cabbage
Collards
Cress
Horseradish
Kale

Kohlrabi
Mustard
Radish
Rape
Resurrection
Plant
Rutabaga
Stock
Sweet Alyssum
Turnip
Wallflower

Myrtle Family
(Myrtaceae)
Bayberry
Clove
Eucalyptus
Guava

Myrtle
Ohia
Pimento

Nettle Family
(Urticaceae)
Boehmeria   Ramie
Nettle

Nightshade Family
(Solanaceae)
Apple of Sodom
Belladonna
Bittersweet
Capsicum
Cayenne Pepper
Datura
Eggplant
Flowering
Tobacco
Henbane

Jimson Weed
Mandrake
Nightshade
Painted-Tongue
Pepper
Petunia
Potato
Solanum
Tobacco
Tomato

Nutmeg Family
(Myristicaceae)
Nutmeg

Nyssa Family
(Nyssaceae)
Black Tupelo   Tupelo Tree

Olive Family
(Oleaceae)
Ash
Forsythia
Fringe Tree
Jasmine

Lilac
Olive
Privet

Orchid Family
(Orchidaceae)
Lady's-Slipper   Orchid   Vanilla

Orpine Family
(Crassulaceae)
Sedum

Palm Family
(Palmae)
Betel
Cabbage Palm
Coconut Palm
Date Palm
Doum Palm

Ivory Palm
Palm
Palmetto
Palmyra Palm

Parsley Family
(Umbelliferae)
Anise
Caraway
Carrot
Celery
Cicely
Coriander
Cow Parsnip

Dill
Fennel
Hemlock
Parsley
Parsnip
Wild Carrot

Passionflower Family
(Passifloraceae)
Passionflower

Pawpaw Family
(Caricaceae)
Papaya

Pea Family
(Leguminosae)
Acacia
Alfalfa
Bean
Beggarweed
Bird's-Foot
Trefoil
Bluebonnet
Brazilwood
Broom
Carob
Cassia
Clover
Cowpea
Furze
Guar
Honey Locust
Horse Bean
Indigo
Kudzu
Laburnum
Lentil

Lespedeza
Licorice
Lima Bean
Locoweed
Locust
Logwood
Lotus
Lupine
Mesquite
Mimosa
Monkeypod Tree
Paloverde
Partridge Pea
Pea
Peanut
Poinciana
Redbud
Rosewood
Sensitive Plant
Soybean
Sweet Pea

Tamarind
Telegraph Plant
Trefoil

Vetch
Wisteria

Pedalium Family
(Pedaliaceae)
Sesame

Pepper Family
(Piperaceae)
Betel   Cubeb   Kava   Pepper

Phlox Family
(Polemoniaceae)
Phlox

Pickerelweed Family
(Pontederiaceae)
Water Hyacinth

Pineapple Family
(Bromeliaceae)
Pineapple   Spanish Moss

Pink Family
(Caryophyllaceae)
Babies'-Breath   Sweet William
Carnation   Wild Pink
Pink

Plane Tree Family
(Platanaceae)
Sycamore

Plantain Family
(Plantaginaceae)
Plantain   Psyllium

Pokeweed Family
(Phytolaccaceae)
Pokeweed

Pomegranate Family
(Punicaceae)
Pomegranate

Pondweed Family
(Potamogetonaceae)
Eelgrass   Pondweed

Poppy Family
(Papaveraceae)
Bloodroot   Celandine   Poppy

Primrose Family
(Primulaceae)
Cowslip   Loosestrife   Primrose
Cyclamen   Pimpernel

Protea Family
(Proteaceae)
Macadamia Nut

Purslane Family
(Portulacaceae)
Bitterroot   Purslane
Portulaca   Spring Beauty

Quassia Family
(Simaroubaceae)
Ailanthus

Rafflesia Family
(Rafflesiaceae)
Rafflesia

Rose Family
(Rosaceae)
Agrimony
Almond
Apple
Apricot
Beach Plum
Blackberry
Boysenberry
Bramble
Bridal Wreath
Cherry
Cherry Laurel
Cinquefoil
Crab Apple
Dewberry
Eglantine

Hawthorn
Loganberry
Loquat
Mountain Ash
Mountain Avens
Nectarine
Peach
Pear
Plum
Quince
Raspberry
Rose
Sloe
Spiraea
Strawberry

Rue Family
(Rutaceae)

Bergamot	Lemon
Citron	Lime
Citrus	Orange
Grapefruit	Prickly Ash
Kumquat	Tangerine

Rush Family
(Juncaceae)
Rush

Saint John's-Wort Family
(Hypericaceae)
Saint John's-Wort

Sandalwood Family
(Santalaceae)
Sandalwood

Sapodilla Family
(Sapotaceae)
Gum Tree   Sapodilla

Sarracenia Family
(Sarraceniaceae)
Pitcher Plant

Saxifrage Family
(Saxifragaceae)

Currant	Hydrangea
Deutzia	Mock Orange
Gooseberry	Saxifrage

Sedge Family
(Cyperaceae)
Bulrush   Papyrus   Sedge

Soapberry Family
(Sapindaceae)
Litchi   Soapberry

Spiderwort Family
(Commelinaceae)
Spiderwort   Wandering Jew

Spurge Family
(Euphorbiaceae)

Cassava	Poinsettia
Castor Oil	Rubber
Croton	Snow-on-the-
Jumping Bean	Mountain
Kukui	Tallow Tree
Manchineel	Teak

Staff-Tree Family
(Celastraceae)
Bittersweet

Sterculia Family
(Sterculiaceae)
Bottle Tree   Kola Nut
Cacao

Sundew Family
(Droseraceae)
Sundew   Venus's-Flytrap

Sweet Gale Family
(Myricaceae)
Bayberry   Wax Myrtle
Candleberry

Tea Family
(Theaceae)
Camellia   Tea

Teasel Family
(Dipsaceae)
Teasel

Tropaeolum Family
(Tropaeolaceae)
Nasturtium

Valerian Family
(Valerianaceae)
Spikenard   Valerian

Vervain Family
(Verbenaceae)
Teak   Verbena

Vine Family
(Vitaceae)
Grape   Ivy   Virginia Creeper

Violet Family
(Violaceae)
Pansy   Violet

Walnut Family
(Juglandaceae)

Bitternut	Pecan
Butternut	Walnut
Hickory	

Water Lily Family
(Nymphaeaceae)
Lotus   Water Lily

Willow Family
(Salicaceae)

Aspen	Poplar
Cottonwood	Pussy Willow
Osier	Willow

Witch Hazel Family
(Hamamelidaceae)
Sweet Gum   Witch Hazel

Wood Sorrel Family
(Oxalidaceae)
Oxalis

Yam Family
(Dioscoreaceae)
Yam

---

ironwoods of Maine, California, England, and Australia are all different kinds of trees.

Scientific Names are the names botanists give to all plants. These names are in Latin, and are the same in all countries. Scientific names have two parts, the genus and the species. For example, the prairie rose is *Rosa setigera*. This means that it belongs to the genus *Rosa* and is the species *setigera*. The relationship of plants is determined mostly by their reproductive parts. See CLASSIFICATION.

Flower Arranging

Arranging flowers into pleasing and artistic combinations is a popular hobby. People enjoy making a beautiful arrangement. The flowers may come from a backyard garden, a roadside, a forest, or a florist. Flowers add a touch of color to the corner of a room, brighten up a sickroom, or form a pleasing centerpiece for a dining table.

People in many countries enjoy flower arranging. The Japanese are noted for the simplicity and gracefulness they achieve with a few flowers in a vase, or with a single flowering twig. Iranians arrange flowers in tight rows, in which dozens of rosebuds may form one compact bouquet. People on tropical islands in the South Pacific wear flowers in their hair, at their waists, or around their necks, as Hawaiians wear the *lei* (see HAWAII [Clothing]).

Flowers played an important part in religious festivals and celebrations throughout the world long before people used them to decorate homes. In ancient Egypt, each dinner guest received a small garland of flowers. The Aztec Indians of Mexico presented bouquets and wreaths of flowers to honor distinguished guests.

Rules for Flower Arrangements. Flower arrangements vary according to their use—for a sickroom, a party, a formal dinner, a funeral, the breakfast table, or the guest room. Flowers for the sickroom should not have exciting colors or heavy scents. The best arrangement includes only a few flowers, and these should be changed frequently. Arrangements on a dining table should be low, so guests can see over them.

Arrangements also vary according to the setting in which they are placed. The colors of the flowers should harmonize with each other, with the colors in the room, and with the table covering. The size of the arrangement is determined by the size of the room and of the table on which the flowers will stand. Containers should be of suitable color, size, and shape for the flowers being used. For instance, short flowers should be placed in a low container.

To obtain a natural effect, arrange flowers to correspond with their growing habits. For example, leave long stems on tall flowers and place them in a high vase, or so that they will stand tall from a low holder. Use varying stem lengths to avoid an artificial look. Heavy, dark flowers look best near the base of the container, while light colors and delicate shapes look best at the top. Figures of birds and animals, statuettes, and other objects often make arrangements more interesting. Change the water in the container every day to keep the flowers fresh. Each time you change the water, cut off a small portion of the stem of each flower by making a diagonal cut with a sharp knife. Do not use scissors, because they squeeze and crush the stem. If possible, keep flowers out of drafts and away from heat. Withered

FAMOUS *Flowers* OF THE PAST

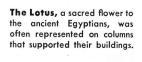

The Fleur-de-Lis, the famous emblem of French kings for hundreds of years, may have been designed after the white Florentine iris.

The Lotus, a sacred flower to the ancient Egyptians, was often represented on columns that supported their buildings.

Camera Clix

The Wars of the Roses were a 30-year struggle for the English throne between two royal houses, York and Lancaster. The York symbol was a white rose, and the house of Lancaster became identified with a red rose.

Florists' Telegraph Delivery, reprinted from *Coronet*, Sept. 1957, © 1957 by Esquire, Inc.

A Biblical Bouquet is a colorful arrangement of some of the plants and flowers mentioned in the Bible. More than 100 plants are named in the Old and New Testaments.

1. Mandrake Flower
2. Hyssop
3. Table of the Ten Commandments
4. Sugar Cane
5. Mandrake Fruit
6. Lily of the Field (Scarlet Lily)
7. Lily of the Field (Anemone)
8. Lotus Seed Pod
9. Spice (Sweet Storax)
10. Lily of the Field (Hyacinth)
11. Date
12. Sugar Cane Leaf
13. Rose of Sharon
14. Apple
15. Lily Flower
16. Grapes
17. Lily of the Field (Crocus)
18. Wheat
19. Ivy
20. Lily Leaf
21. Pomegranate Flower
22. Dill
23. Jug (holding walnuts, almonds, pistachio, and garlic)
24. Castor Leaf
25. Pomegranate Fruit
26. St.-John's-Bread
27. Almonds and Walnuts
28. Rose (now called Narcissus)

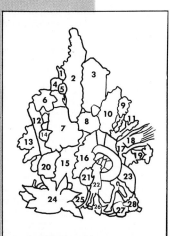

Lifelike Glass Flowers seem to grow on glass models of plants in the Botanical Museum of Harvard University. The models were made by two Bohemian artists, Leopold and Rudolph Blaschka, in their studios in Germany. They based the models on plants in their own gardens and sketches and specimens brought to Germany from the United States. A glass butterfly perches on a glass cornflower, *left*. A bouquet of several kinds of glass flowers, *right*, seems freshly picked from a garden.

flowers can often be freshened by wrapping them in wet newspapers or by putting their stems completely underwater in a cool place, or by dipping the stems in hot water briefly.

Judging Flower Arrangements. Many flower shows include displays of flower arrangements along with other kinds of exhibits. Judges award prizes for these arrangements on the basis of several factors. They consider the color combination, the design and balance of the arrangement, the originality of the display, the suitability of the container and accessories, and the condition of the flowers used. Arrangements may be general, or they may be made for a specific *theme*, or use. If a definite theme is named, the arrangement is also judged for its suitability.

Artificial Flowers

People throughout the world make artificial flowers as decorations and ornaments. The ancient Egyptians made them from stained horn shavings. The Romans made gold and silver flowers. Today, especially in the United States, artificial flowers are made from a kind of plastic called *polyethylene*. Other materials used include silk, linen, cotton, gauze, satin, velvet, ribbon, and metal. The Chinese make flowers from rice paper. The Japanese use the pith of bamboo. In Italy, dyed silkworm cocoons are made into flowers. South American Indians make flowers from feathers.

Artificial flowers are also used for scientific purposes, such as the study of flower structure. Artists make models from such materials as wax and glass. The artists must have painstaking skill and a thorough knowledge of plant structure. Their models can hardly be distinguished from natural blossoms.

The collection of glass flowers in the Botanical Museum of Harvard University is famous throughout the world. Two artist-naturalists, Leopold Blaschka (?-1895) and his son Rudolph (1857-1939), made all the flowers in this collection. They worked together from 1877 until 1895, when Leopold Blaschka died. Rudolph Blaschka continued to work on the flowers until 1936. The collection includes more than 700 kinds of flowers from 164 families of flowering plants, a group of fruits showing the effects of fungus diseases, and thousands of flower parts and magnified details.

Flowers as Emblems

Since earliest times, nations have used flowers as their emblems. The lotus, one of the oldest national flowers, is the emblem of Egypt and India. During the late 1400's, two royal houses of England fought for possession of the English throne. Each side adopted a rose for its emblem. The House of York took a white rose, and the House of Lancaster became identified with a red rose.

——— NATIONAL FLOWERS ———

This table lists the national flowers or symbols of selected countries. These flowers have been officially adopted by the country or traditionally associated with it.

NATION	FLOWER	NATION	FLOWER
Argentina	Ceibo	Indonesia	Jasmine, Rose
Australia	Golden Wattle	Ireland	Shamrock
		Israel	Almond Blossom
Bolivia	Cantua		
Brazil	Cattleya	Japan	Chrysanthemum
Canada	Maple Leaf		
Costa Rica	Cattleya	Laos	Frangipani
Ecuador	Cinchona	Malaysia	Hibiscus
Egypt	Carnation, Rose	Mexico	Dahlia
		Nepal	Rhododendron
England	Rose	Netherlands	Tulip
Finland	Lily of the Valley	New Zealand	Fern
		Norway	Blue Anemone
France	Fleur-de-lis	Philippines	Sampaguita
Germany, West	Blue Cornflower	Rhodesia	Flame Lily
		Scotland	Thistle
Greece	Poppy	South Africa	Protea
Guatemala	White Orchid	Spain	Carnation
		Switzerland	Edelweiss
Honduras	Rose	Venezuela	Orchid
India	Lotus	Wales	Leek

FLOWER

The battles they fought were called the Wars of the Roses (see WARS OF THE ROSES).

The United States has no flower emblem. But each of the states has a flower. In 1891, New York became the first state to select a state flower when its school children voted for the rose. Canada's provinces also have flower emblems. See the accompanying table for state and provincial flowers.

FLOWERS OF THE STATES AND OF THE CANADIAN PROVINCES AND TERRITORIES

Apple (Blossom)
  Arkansas
  Michigan
Arbutus (Mayflower)
  Massachusetts
  Nova Scotia (Trailing)
Bitterroot
  Montana
Black-Eyed Susan
  Maryland
Bluebonnet
  Texas
Camellia
  Alabama
Carnation (Scarlet)
  Ohio
Clover (Red)
  Vermont
Columbine
  Colorado
Dogwood (Flowering)
  British Columbia
  North Carolina
  Virginia
Fireweed
  Yukon
Forget-Me-Not
  Alaska
Goldenrod
  Kentucky
  Nebraska
Hawthorn
  Missouri
Hibiscus
  Hawaii
Indian Paintbrush
  Wyoming
Iris
  Tennessee
Jasmine (Carolina Jessamine)
  South Carolina
Lady's-Slipper
  Minnesota (Pink and White)
  Prince Edward Island
Lilac (Purple)
  New Hampshire
Lily
  Quebec (White Garden Lily)
  Saskatchewan (Prairie Lily)
  Utah (Sego Lily)
Magnolia
  Louisiana
  Mississippi

Mistletoe
  Oklahoma
Mock Orange (Syringa)
  Idaho
Mountain Avens
  Northwest Territories
Mountain Laurel
  Connecticut
  Pennsylvania
Orange (Blossom)
  Florida
Oregon Grape
  Oregon
Pasqueflower (Wild Crocus or Prairie Crocus)
  Manitoba
  South Dakota
Peach (Blossom)
  Delaware
Peony
  Indiana
Pine (Cone and Tassel)
  Maine
Pitcher Plant
  Newfoundland
Poppy (Golden)
  California
Rhododendron
  Washington (Coast Rhododendron)
  West Virginia
Rose
  Alberta (Wild Rose)
  District of Columbia (American Beauty Rose)
  Georgia (Cherokee Rose)
  Iowa (Wild Rose)
  New York
  North Dakota (Wild Prairie Rose)
Sagebrush
  *Nevada
Saguaro (Giant Cactus)
  Arizona
Sunflower
  Kansas
Trillium
  Ontario (White)
Violet
  Illinois
  New Brunswick
  New Jersey
  *Rhode Island
  Wisconsin
Yucca
  New Mexico

All flowers listed above in boldface type have separate articles in THE WORLD BOOK ENCYCLOPEDIA. Color pictures of these flowers are shown with the various state and province articles.

*Unofficial

An Oriental Arrangement shows that a graceful display can be made with only leaves, a figurine, and a flower stalk.

Flower Displays

Planning a Flower Garden. To grow a beautiful garden, careful attention must be given to the arrangement, color scheme, and flowering season of the flowers selected. Tall flowers should form a background for shorter flowers. The flowers should be arranged so that the colors do not clash. Expert gardeners know the flowering season of each plant, and choose the proper types to provide color throughout the various seasons. Perennials usually form the center of interest in a garden, and annuals and biennials fill in corners and odd spaces.

An *old-fashioned garden* has flowers planted in an informal manner. Hollyhocks, snapdragons, roses, spiraea, tulips, and many other blossoms may be used. *Formal gardens* have flowers arranged in definite patterns. The plants used should have a regular form of growth, or be cut into regular forms. *Rock gardens* provide a home for small plants that grow best on or among rocks, and that would attract little attention if planted among more showy flowers. The rocks protect the plants. Water lilies give a formal look to *water gardens*. Swamp plants, such as cardinal flowers, arrowheads, marsh marigolds, and cattails, grow in or around a pool. Flowers planted in *window boxes* brighten up an apartment or a home. A *miniature garden* planted with small or dwarf plants

Cloister Garden at Phipps Conservatories, Pittsburgh, Pa., is an indoor garden. Its flowers blossom in a beautiful greenhouse.

Middleton Gardens, near Charleston, S.C., were landscaped in the mid-1700's. Such formal gardens were popular during that era.

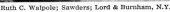

Ruth C. Walpole; Sawders; Lord & Burnham, N.Y.

can make a small yard or an inside room more attractive.

Garden Clubs attract persons who want to talk over their gardening problems and exchange seeds and plants. Some clubs are local groups, and others are state or national organizations. These clubs serve as centers of information for flower growers. Club members often plant seeds and bulbs in parks, vacant lots, and along roadsides. They also try to educate the public to protect wild flowers. Information about garden clubs can be obtained from the National Council of State Garden Clubs, 4401 Magnolia Avenue, St. Louis, Mo. 63110; Garden Club of America, 598 Madison Avenue, New York, N.Y. 10022; and Canadian Horticultural Council, 219 Queen Street, Ottawa, Ont.

Flower Shows are sponsored by amateur garden clubs and professional gardening associations. Gardeners enter their best flowers in various classes of exhibits. Judges select the winners on the basis of such qualities as form, size, color, abundance of blossoms, and quality of leaves. Large botanical gardens, and commercial gardens and nurseries may display their finest flowers to the public in special flower shows or exhibits.

Famous flower shows include the Wilmington Camellia Show, Wilmington, N.C. (March); New England Spring Flower Show, Boston (March); Texas Rose Festival, Tyler, Texas (October); and Chrysanthemum Show,

Chicago (November). Famous flower shows of the various states and provinces may be found in the Annual Events sections of the state and province articles.

Commercial Flower Gardens are maintained by seed firms so they can study and improve the quality of their products. Nurseries that sell cut flowers and ornamental trees and shrubs, and greenhouses that sell retail or to other firms, may also display their blossoms in gardens. Most florists buy their flowers from large greenhouses and nurseries, but some have their own gardens and greenhouses. Seed firms, large greenhouses, and nurseries hold public displays of their gardens to stimulate interest in their products.

Famous Flower Gardens. Probably the most famous gardens in the world are the Royal Botanic Gardens at Kew, England, and at Edinburgh, Scotland. They display a large variety of flowers collected from all parts of the world. The Kew Herbarium is the world center for plant identification and classification.

In the United States, the Middleton Gardens, near Charleston, S.C., are probably the oldest formal gardens. They were established in 1740 by Henry Middleton. The Charleston area also boasts the famous Magnolia and Cypress gardens. The Bellingrath Gardens, near Mobile, Ala., display a fine collection of rare camellias and azaleas. The McKee Jungle Gardens, at Vero

265

Florists Pack Cut Flowers carefully before delivery.

A Florist's Greenhouse may serve as a place to grow flowers and other plants, and also as a display room.

Beach, Fla., exhibit one of America's finest outdoor collections of water lilies. Rare tropical plants, brilliant azaleas, and towering cypress trees flourish in the Florida Cypress Gardens at Winter Haven. California's Municipal Rose Garden at San Jose is world-famous. The International Peace Garden, at the geographical center of North America, honors more than 150 years of peace between Canada and the United States. It lies on top of a large plateau in the Turtle Mountains, on the boundary line between North Dakota and Manitoba.

Famous botanical gardens in the United States include the Arnold Arboretum in Boston; Morton Arboretum at Lisle, Ill.; Boyce Thompson Southwest Arboretum at Superior, Ariz.; Missouri Botanical Garden in St. Louis; New York Botanical Garden in New York City; the Botanical Garden of the University of Michigan; the United States Botanic Garden in Washington, D.C.; the U.S. Plant Introduction Station at Miami, Fla.; and Fairchild Tropical Garden at Coral Gables, Fla.

In Canada, famous gardens include the Butchart Gardens on Vancouver Island near Victoria, B.C.; Stanley Park at Vancouver, B.C.; the rock garden at Banff, Alta.; and Assiniboine and Kildonan parks at Winnipeg, Man. The Maconn Memorial Garden at Ottawa, Ont., has a collection of plants that grow in a temperate climate. The Dale Estate, the largest orchid-producing establishment in Canada, is at Brampton, Ont. Montreal's Mount Royal Park has won fame for its trees, flowers, and botanical garden.

Flowers in Art and Literature

Flowers have been reproduced in paintings, architecture, and designs, and praised in poetry and prose in all civilizations and periods. They have been a favorite subject in still-life paintings from ancient Chinese prints to such recent paintings as Vincent van Gogh's *Sunflowers.* Flower designs often formed the borders of ancient tapestries. Many writers use flowers as symbols in works of fiction and poetry.

Flower patterns add beauty to the decoration of

buildings. The rose window of Gothic architecture is an abstract design inspired by the rose. The ancient Egyptians modeled pillars after the lotus flower. Designers use flower patterns in printed cloth for clothing, draperies, or upholstery. Oriental and Persian rugs are woven with flower designs. China, pottery, and silverware may have floral decorations.

Authors of ancient Greece and Rome, including Sappho, Homer, and Pliny, wrote of the beauty of flowers. Poems about flowers include Wordsworth's "The Daffodils," Tennyson's "Flower in the Crannied Wall," and Bryant's "To a Fringed Gentian." Many authors have written poems and songs that tell of the beauty of gardens.   HAROLD NORMAN MOLDENKE

Related Articles in WORLD BOOK include:

FLOWERING PLANTS

See articles listed in the table, *Families of Flowering Plants,* in this article.

OTHER RELATED ARTICLES

Botany	Garden Club	Pollen and Pollination
Breeding	Gardening	Seed
Bulb	Greenhouse	Shrub
Cross-Pollination	Inflorescence	Spice
Dicotyledon	Leaf	Tree
Floriculture	Monocotyledon	Vegetable
Florist	Perfume	Vine
Fruit	Plant	Weed

Outline

I. **The Importance of Flowers**
   A. For Decoration   B. As Food   C. In Industry
II. **Garden Flowers**
   A. Annuals   B. Biennials   C. Perennials
III. **Wild Flowers**
   A. Woodland Flowers F. Beach and Shore Flowers
   B. Mountain Flowers G. Meadow Flowers
   C. Prairie Flowers   H. Swamp Flowers
   D. Desert Flowers   I. Tropical Flowers
   E. Water Flowers   J. Strange and Unusual
                           Flowers
IV. **Studying Wild Flowers**
V. **The Parts of a Flower**
   A. The Calyx   C. The Stamens   E. Variations
   B. The Corolla D. The Pistils   in Form

Questions

What is your state or province flower?
Why is the blossom important to flowering plants?
What are the four main parts of a flower?
What purpose does the odor of a flower serve?
How do annuals, perennials, and biennials differ?
How do insects help flowers?
What is cross-pollination? How do flowers ensure it?
Why is a dandelion bloom not really a "flower"?
What was the first state to have a state flower?
What is a parasitic flowering plant?
How does pollination differ from fertilization?
Why do seed firms maintain flower gardens?
How do flower clocks tell the approximate time of day?
What is the smallest flowering plant? How large is it?
Why does our existence depend on flowers?

General Flower Books

ARY, SHEILA, and GREGORY, MARY. *The Oxford Book of Wild Flowers.* Oxford, 1970.
ASCHER, AMALIE A. *The Complete Flower Arranger.* Simon & Schuster, 1974.
DEMPSEY, MICHAEL W., and SHEEHAN, ANGELA, eds. *How Flowers Live.* Collins-World, 1970.
FITTER, RICHARD S. R. and ALASTAIR. *The Wild Flowers of Britain and Northern Europe.* Scribner, 1974.
GORDON, ROBERT L. *Professional Flower Arranging for Beginners.* Arco, 1974.
GORER, RICHARD. *The Development of Garden Flowers.* Branford, 1971.
GRIMM, WILLIAM C. *Recognizing Flowering Wild Plants.* Hawthorn, 1974.
GUILCHER, JEAN M., and NOAILLES, R. H. *The Hidden Life of Flowers.* Sterling, 1971.
HOUSE, HOMER D. *Wild Flowers.* Macmillan, 1974.
HUXLEY, ANTHONY J., ed. *Garden Flowers in Color: Vol. 1, Garden Annuals and Bulbs; Vol. 2, Garden Perennials and Water Plants.* Macmillan, 1971.
MILNE, LORUS J. and MARGERY. *Because of a Flower.* Atheneum, 1975.
PERRY, FRANCES. *Flowers of the World.* Crown, 1972.
SCHULER, STANLEY. *The Gardener's Basic Book of Flowers.* Simon & Schuster, 1974.
SPERKA, MARIE S. *Growing Wildflowers: A Gardener's Guide.* Harper, 1973.
STRINGER, MICHAEL. *Wild Flowers.* Arco, 1974.
TENENBAUM, FRANCES. *Gardening with Wild Flowers.* Scribner, 1973.
The Time-Life Encyclopedia of Gardening. 12 vols. Time Inc., 1971-72. Some of the volumes in this series describe flowers.
VANEK, VLASTIMIL. *Garden Flowers.* Transatlantic, 1971.

Regional Flower Books

ARCHIBALD, DAVID, and others. *Quick-key Guide to Wildflowers: Northwestern and Central United States and Adjacent Canada.* Doubleday, 1968.
CRITTENDEN, MABEL, and TELFER, D. W. *Wildflowers of the West.* Celestial Arts (Millbrae, CA 94030), 1975.

DUNCAN, WILBER H., and FOOTE, L. E. *Wildflowers of the Southeastern United States.* Univ. of Georgia Press, 1975.
HITCHCOCK, CHARLES L., and CRONQUIST, ARTHUR. *Flora of the Pacific Northwest.* Univ. of Washington Press, 1973.
KLIMAS, JOHN E., and CUNNINGHAM, J. A. *Wildflowers of Eastern America.* Knopf, 1974.
ORR, ROBERT T. and M. C. *Wildflowers of Western America.* Knopf, 1974.
RICKETT, HAROLD W. *Wild Flowers of the United States: Vol. 1, The Northeastern States; Vol. 2, The Southeastern States; Vol. 3, Texas; Vol. 4, The Southwestern States; Vol. 5, The Northwestern States; Vol. 6, The Central Mountains and Plains.* McGraw, 1966-73.
WELSH, STANLEY L., and RATCLIFFE, WILLIAM. *Flowers of the Mountain Country.* Brigham Young Univ. Press, 1975.

FLOWERING MAPLE is the common name for about 90 kinds of herbs, shrubs, and trees that grow in the temperate parts of all continents except Europe. They usually have heart-shaped leaves and yellow flowers that grow singly or in clusters.

J. Horace McFarland
Flowering Maple

Scientific Classification. Flowering maples are in the mallow family, Malvaceae. The common flowering maple is classified as genus *Abutilon*, species *A. hybridum*.   THEODOR JUST

FLOWERING TOBACCO is the name of several annual and perennial plants in the nightshade family. They are grown for their sweet-scented flowers. They are also called *nicotiana*. Flowering tobaccos grow wild in tropical South America, but are cultivated in the United States.

The leaves of the flowering tobaccos are hairy and sticky. The flowers are yellow, purple, red, or white, and shaped like long tubes. The flowering tobaccos are sensitive to cold, and should be sheltered. They can be grown from seed in rich, light soil. The seeds should be planted in a hotbed or greenhouse in the early spring, and later transplanted outdoors.

J. Horace McFarland
Flowering Tobacco

Scientific Classification. Flowering tobaccos belong to the nightshade family, Solanaceae. They make up the genus *Nicotiana*.   MARCUS MAXON

FLOYD, WILLIAM (1734-1821), was a leader in the American struggle for independence, and a New York signer of the Declaration of Independence. Floyd was born on Dec. 17, 1734, on a farm in Suffolk County, Long Island. He served in the Continental Congress from 1774 to 1777 and from 1778 to 1783. The Continental Congress became the Congress of the Confederation on Mar. 1, 1781. Floyd did important committee work in the New York Congressional delegation. He was an early supporter of the movement to make Thomas Jefferson President.   CLARENCE L. VER STEEG

FLQ. See CANADA, HISTORY OF (The FLQ Crisis).

FLU. See INFLUENZA.

FLÜGELHORN, *FLOO guhl HAWRN,* is a brass wind instrument with three valves that somewhat resembles the cornet. It has a mouthpiece in the form of a deep cone, and a flaring bell. The bore of its tube is wider than that of the cornet. As a result, the flügelhorn has a mellower, less brilliant, and more buglelike tone. Most flügelhorns have a curved tube about $4\frac{1}{2}$ feet (1.4 meters) long. They are pitched in B-flat, and have a range of about $2\frac{1}{2}$ octaves.   KARL GEIRINGER

See also MUSIC (picture: Brass Instruments).

FLUID, *FLOO ihd,* is any substance that flows easily. A slight pressure or force will change the form of a fluid. But fluids are also elastic, so they tend to return to their former size when the pressure is removed. Fluids include all liquids and gases. Water at ordinary temperature is a fluid and a liquid. Air is a fluid and a gas.

A *perfect* fluid is frictionless. That is, it offers no resistance to flow except that of inertia (see INERTIA). A *homogeneous* fluid has the same properties or qualities throughout.

Pressure changes generally do not affect the density of an *incompressible* fluid (see DENSITY). But in practice no liquid is completely incompressible. An *elastic* fluid has greater elastic stresses, or forces resisting changes to size or shape, than viscous stresses, or forces resisting flow. A *viscous* fluid, such as molasses, is thick or slow-flowing because of friction.

See also HYDRAULICS; MECHANICS.

FLUID AMPLIFIER is a small, inflexible device with several connecting *channels* (passages) cut through it. A strong jet of *fluid* (liquid or gas), called the *power jet,* enters through one channel. The power jet is forced toward one or more *output channels* by weaker *control jets* or *flows.* Excess fluid is removed from the fluid amplifier through *vents.*

Fluid amplifiers are connected to make *fluidic circuits.* The circuits are used instead of electrical circuits or mechanical devices for performing certain industrial processes such as timing and counting. They are also used to control parts of airplanes and spacecraft, and for other special purposes.

Several kinds of fluid amplifiers are in use. The *wall-attachment jet amplifier* has channels that are shaped so that the power jet always follows only one of the output channels. Changes in the control flows switch the power jet from one output channel to the other. The *momentum-controlled jet amplifier* has channels that are shaped so that the strength of the control jets determines how much of the power jet enters each output channel.   FORBES T. BROWN

FLUKE, a fish. See FLOUNDER.

FLUKE is any one of a group of parasitic flatworms with only one body segment (see FLATWORM). Flukes live in the intestine, liver, lungs, or blood of human beings and animals. An adult fluke is flat and leaflike and has suckers which hold it to body tissue in the *host* (animal in which it lives). Flukes usually have both male and female organs.

If a person eats improperly cooked fish or crab meat infected by fluke *larvae* (young worms), the larvae may infect the person's body. The larvae of *schistosomes* (blood flukes) burrow into the skin of host animals in water to reach the blood vessels. Human beings suffer from lung, liver, intestinal, and blood flukes. These varieties of flukes are common in the Far East. Blood flukes are also common in some tropical parts of the Western Hemisphere and in Africa.

In the beginning of a fluke's life cycle, eggs escape

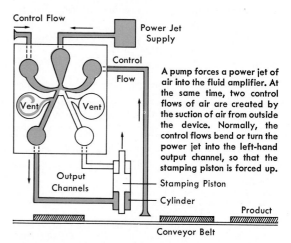

A pump forces a power jet of air into the fluid amplifier. At the same time, two control flows of air are created by the suction of air from outside the device. Normally, the control flows bend or turn the power jet into the left-hand output channel, so that the stamping piston is forced up.

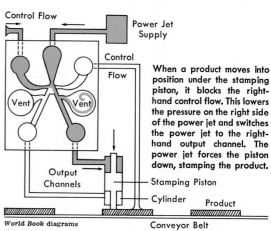

When a product moves into position under the stamping piston, it blocks the right-hand control flow. This lowers the pressure on the right side of the power jet and switches the power jet to the right-hand output channel. The power jet forces the piston down, stamping the product.

World Book diagrams

Bowles Engineering Corp.

A Fluid Amplifier, such as the wall-attachment jet amplifier, *above,* can be used to control machinery. The diagrams, *right,* show how it controls a stamping machine.

from the body of the host and hatch in water. The young worms then develop and multiply in water snails. The fluke larvae escape from the snails into the water and then attach themselves to water plants or enter fish, crabs, insects, or other animals.

Scientific Classification. Flukes compose the class Trematoda of the phylum Platyhelminthes. The liver fluke of human beings is genus *Clonorchis*, species *C. sinensis*. The lung fluke is *Paragonimus westermani*, and a blood fluke is *Schistosoma haematobium*. JAMES A. McLEOD

FLUME is an inclined channel that carries water from a distant source for use in irrigation, logging, placer mining, or water turbines.

FLUORESCENCE, *FLOO uh REHS uhns,* is the light that some substances give off when they absorb energy. Fluorescent substances have many uses. For example, mercury vapor is a fluorescent substance used in highway lights. Fluorescent screens are used in electron microscopes and television picture tubes. Certain harmful compounds in air and water pollution can be detected by their fluorescence. Fluorescence also has many uses in biology, chemistry, and medicine. For example, the drug LSD (lysergic acid diethylamide) fluoresces so strongly that $\frac{1}{10,000,000,000}$ ounce (0.0000000028 gram) can be detected in human tissue.

Different forms of energy produce fluorescence. Electric current causes fluorescence in neon signs. Ultraviolet waves produce light in fluorescent lamps. Beams of electrons striking fluorescent material in a television picture tube produce the picture.

The energy absorbed by a fluorescent substance *excites* (adds energy to) the electrons in the atoms or molecules of the substance. The electrons remain excited for only about $\frac{1}{100,000,000}$ of a second. Then they give off their excess energy as light. The light continues only as long as energy excites the electrons. Materials that are *phosphorescent* discharge a light that disappears more slowly than fluorescent light. Some diamonds, for example, glow for a long time in the dark. See PHOSPHORESCENCE.

Fluorescent light can be of any color, depending on the element or compound affected by the energy. For example, sodium vapor discharges yellow light and neon gives off red light. The arrangement, characteristics, and number of elements in a compound determine the color it gives off. White starch, a compound used in clothes, gives off a blue-white fluorescence.

Fluorescence was described in 1833 by Sir David Brewster, a Scottish physicist. It was named in 1852 by Sir George G. Stokes, a British physicist. RALPH S. BECKER

See also FLUORESCENT LAMP; FLUOROSCOPE; LUMINESCENCE.

FLUORESCENT LAMP is a tube-shaped electric light that has wide use in factories, offices, and schools. In homes, incandescent lamps are more widely used. A fluorescent lamp uses only about a fifth as much electricity as an incandescent lamp to produce the same amount of light. It also produces only a fifth as much heat. For this reason, fluorescent lamps are sometimes called "cool" lights. In addition, they last much longer than incandescent lamps.

A fluorescent lamp consists of a glass tube containing a small amount of mercury and a chemically inactive gas at low pressure. The gas in most fluorescent tubes is argon. The inside surface of the tube has a coating of chemicals called *phosphors* (see PHOSPHOR). At each end of the tube is an electrode, a coil of tungsten wire coated with chemicals called *rare earth oxides*. A fluorescent light fixture includes a device called a *ballast*, which provides voltage to start the lamp and regulates the flow of current in the lamp circuit.

There are three main kinds of fluorescent lamp circuits: (1) preheat, (2) rapid-start, and (3) instant-start. Fixtures using a preheat circuit cost the least and are the type found in most homes. Rapid-start fixtures are more efficient than the preheat type, cheaper to operate and maintain, and widely used commercially.

When a preheat or rapid-start lamp is turned on, electricity flows through the tungsten wire. The wire becomes heated, and the earth oxides on it give off electrons. Some of the electrons strike the argon atoms and *ionize* them—that is, the electrons give the atoms a positive or negative electric charge. When ionized, the argon can conduct electricity. A current flows through the gas from electrode to electrode, forming an *arc* (stream of electrons). Instant-start lamps operate at such high starting voltage that the arc forms immediately. When an electron in the arc strikes a mercury atom, it raises the energy level of another electron in the atom. As this electron returns to its normal state, it gives off invisible ultraviolet rays (see ULTRAVIOLET RAYS). The phosphors that coat the tube absorb these rays and change them into visible light. The color of the light depends on the phosphors used.

HOW A FLUORESCENT LAMP WORKS

A preheat fluorescent lamp needs a *starter* and a *ballast* to operate. The starter switches electricity through the electrodes at each end of the lamp. The current heats the electrodes so they can give off electrons. Then the ballast sends a surge of current between the electrodes to form an *arc* (stream of electrons) in the lamp. The lamp contains mercury vapor. The arc knocks electrons in the mercury atoms out of their normal position. When the electrons return to their position, the atoms give off invisible ultraviolet rays. These rays strike phosphor particles on the walls of the lamp and cause the particles to glow.

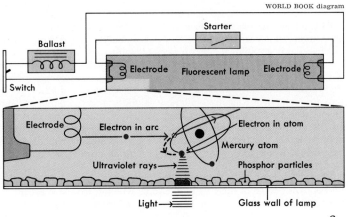

WORLD BOOK diagram

269

FLUORIDATION

The fluorescent lamp was introduced at the New York World's Fair of 1938-1939. Since 1952, fluorescent lamps have ranked ahead of incandescent lamps in sales in the United States.　　　　　　RONALD N. HELMS

See also ELECTRIC LIGHT; FLUORESCENCE.

FLUORIDATION is the addition of chemicals called *fluorides* to water supplies to help teeth resist decay. More than 100 million persons in over 5,000 cities in the United States drink fluoridated water. Some states have laws that require all their cities to fluoridate water.

The study of the effect of fluorides on tooth decay began in the 1930's. Dentists of the U.S. Public Health Service conducted research in communities where the water naturally contained about 1 part of fluoride per 1 million parts of water. The dentists found that children in these communities had up to two-thirds fewer cavities than those living in other areas.

Two cities—Grand Rapids, Mich., and Newburgh, N.Y.—were the first communities in the United States to add fluoride to their water. They both began experimental fluoridation in 1945. By 1950, a small group of dentists and public health officers had persuaded about 75 cities to fluoridate. These experts also helped persuade the Public Health Service, American Dental Association, and other health organizations to support fluoridation.

Many people remained unconvinced of the advantages and safety of fluoridating water. In 1952, a congressional committee recommended that scientists conduct further studies on the effects of fluoride. The subject of fluoridation became extremely controversial. For example, scientists themselves still disagree on whether fluoridation is harmful. Also, many disputes regarding fluoridation result from personal beliefs and cannot be settled by scientific research.

A number of communities in the United States have had their citizens vote on whether their water should be fluoridated. In more than 1,000 elections held from 1945 to 1970, voters opposed fluoridation about 60 per cent of the time. The governments of some European countries have outlawed it.

Arguments for Fluoridation. People who favor fluoridation claim it is the best way to fight tooth decay. They believe it will prevent about two-thirds of all cavities and is completely safe. They argue that fluoridating water is the simplest way to improve everyone's dental health and to reduce dental expenses.

Arguments against Fluoridation. Many people believe fluoridation does not reduce tooth decay nearly so much as has been claimed. They feel that equally effective methods of reducing decay can be used. Opponents of fluoridation maintain that lifelong use of fluoridated water may stain teeth and harm bones. They also argue that not enough is known about how fluorides affect people who consume them over long periods of time. In addition, they say, individuals cannot control their fluoride intake because people drink widely different amounts of water and obtain additional fluoride from food and other sources.

Many opponents believe that adding fluoride to water deprives people of their right to choose whether to have the treatment. They also say that fluoridation is wasteful because most water is used for purposes other than drinking or cooking. They argue that the excess fluoride pollutes the environment.　　EDWARD GROTH III

See also FLUORINE.

FLUORIDE. See FLUORINE; FLUORIDATION.

FLUORINE, *FLOO uh reen*, a chemical element, is a greenish-yellow gas. It combines with other elements more readily than any other chemical element. Fluorine attracts electrons of other elements with a strong force to form compounds called *fluorides*.

Fluorides are found chiefly in the minerals fluorite and cryolite. They have many uses. Crystals of calcium fluoride are used to bend and focus infrared light in analyzing chemical compounds. Compounds of fluorine are also used in the cooling systems of refrigerators and to force the contents out of pressurized "spray" cans. The compound uranium hexafluoride is used to prepare uranium for atomic bombs. Small amounts of fluorides applied to the teeth greatly reduce tooth decay. For this reason, fluorides are added to toothpaste and to the drinking water in many communities.

Fluorine is one of five elements known as halogens. It has the symbol F. Fluorine's atomic number is 9 and its atomic weight is 18.998403. Fluorine melts at $-219.62°$ C ($-363°$ F.) and boils at $-188.14°$ C ($-307°$ F.). Henri Moissan, a French chemist, first isolated fluorine in 1886.　　FRANK C. ANDREWS

See also ELEMENT, CHEMICAL (tables); FLUORIDATION; HALOGEN; URANIUM (Ability to Form Compounds).

FLUORITE, *FLOO uh ryt*, is a soft mineral with a glassy luster. In nature, it is found in blue, violet, yellow, brown, red, green, or colorless deposits. In industry, fluorite is also called *fluorspar* and *fluor*. Great quantities are used to absorb impurities and lower the melting temperature in making steel and aluminum. Hydrofluoric acid, a dangerous industrial chemical, is made from fluorite. Fluorite has been used in making compound lenses and prisms in spectrographs.

Fluorite (CaF_2) deposits are transparent when pure. Some are *fluorescent* or *phosphorescent* and give off visible light when heated, scratched, or exposed to ultraviolet radiation. Fluorite is found throughout the world. Most fluorite mines in the United States are in southern Illinois and western Kentucky. In Canada, it is mined in Newfoundland.　　WILLIAM C. LUTH

See also FLUORESCENCE; FLUORINE; GEM (picture); HARDNESS; MINERAL (picture); SPECTROGRAPH.

FLUOROCARBON, *FLOO uhr uh KAHR buhn*, is any of a group of synthetic organic compounds that contain fluorine and carbon. Many of these chemicals also contain chlorine, and are thus known as *chlorofluorocarbons*. These compounds, often called *Freons*, have many uses.

The two most commonly used fluorocarbons are *trichlorofluoromethane* ($CFCl_3$), also called F-11, and *dichlorodifluoromethane* (CF_2Cl_2), or F-12. Both are nonpoisonous and nonflammable under normal conditions, and they are easily converted from liquid to gas or from gas to liquid form. These properties make the two chemicals useful as propellants in aerosol spray products (see AEROSOL). F-11 and F-12 are also used as refrigerants in air conditioners and refrigerators.

Many scientists believe F-11 and F-12 harm the environment. Studies in the 1970's showed that these chemicals break down molecules of ozone in the earth's upper atmosphere. Ozone, a form of oxygen, protects plants and animals from the harmful ultraviolet rays of the sun. After being used on the earth, F-11 and F-12 slowly rise to the upper atmosphere. There, ultraviolet rays cause them to break up and release chlorine atoms. Each chlorine atom may react with and destroy thousands of ozone molecules. See OZONE.

In 1977, the United States government took steps to restrict the use of F-11 and F-12. It proposed a ban by 1979 of most aerosol spray products containing these fluorocarbons. JAMES P. FRIEND

FLUOROSCOPE, *FLUR uh scohp,* is an instrument that allows a doctor to see a silhouette of the bone structure and internal organs of a living body. The usual type of fluoroscope consists of a large X-ray machine and a fluorescent screen. The patient stands in front of the X-ray machine, and the doctor places the fluorescent screen against the part of the body that he or she wishes to see. X rays are sent through the body and strike the screen. The bones and thick organs partially block the invisible rays, so that partial shadows of X rays are cast upon the fluorescent screen. The fluorescent material radiates light when it receives the invisible X rays. It reproduces the pattern of shadows and light, and the doctor can see an outline of the patient's bones and organs on the screen. It also allows the doctor to see the body organs in operation. When the X-ray machine is turned off, the picture disappears. Doctors fluoroscope their patients only when it is absolutely necessary. An excess of X rays may be harmful to a patient (see RADIATION [Protecting Ourselves from High Energy Radiation]). The American inventor Thomas A. Edison developed the first practical fluoroscope in 1896. Scientists in Italy, Germany, and England had designed earlier but less effective models of the device. See also FLUORESCENCE. JOHN L. LAVAN

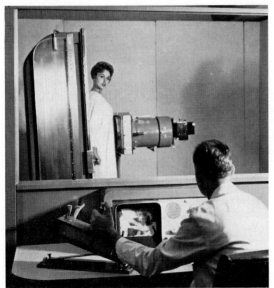

Picker X-Ray Corp.

The Fluoroscope makes it possible to view the bones and internal organs of the body. The patient stands between an X-ray machine and a fluorescent screen. A closed-circuit television camera picks up an image from the screen. The doctor studies the fluoroscope picture on a small television set.

WORLD BOOK photo courtesy Chicago Symphony Orchestra

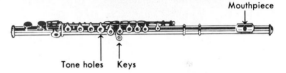

Mouthpiece

Tone holes Keys

The Flute is a woodwind instrument popular in bands and orchestras. A musician plays the flute by blowing across a hole in the mouthpiece and pressing keys that cover the tone holes.

FLUORSPAR. See FLUORITE.

FLUTE is a treble woodwind instrument. A player holds the flute in a horizontal position and produces the tone by blowing across a hole in the mouthpiece. Today, most flutes are made of metal. They have keys, tone holes, and several other holes for finger movements. The *piccolo* is a small flute. This instrument gives off a very high sound (see PICCOLO). The *alto flute,* or *flute d'amour,* is larger and has wider holes than the regular flute. The *bass flute* produces a broad and rich tone because of its lower pitch.

The ancient Egyptians, Greeks, and Chinese used instruments similar to the flute. Some Arab tribes today still use the Egyptian *nay,* or vertical flute. Flute players of the 1600's and 1700's played on cone-shaped instruments made of wood, with few finger holes. In 1846, Theobald Boehm of Munich made the first cylindrical flute of metal. He also arranged the modern system of fingering that makes it possible to place the openings more accurately, and improves the tone. Rudall Carte & Company of London perfected the Boehm flute and brought out variations on it. CHARLES B. RIGHTER

FLUTING. See ARCHITECTURE (Architectural Terms).

FLUX, *fluhks,* in chemistry, is any substance that lowers the melting point of a substance to which it is added. A flux added to ore before melting helps to separate the impurities from the metal. In smelting iron, the flux used is generally limestone. This combines readily with the impurities to form slag, which can then be easily removed. Fluxes made of borax, soda, and potash are used to separate base metal from gold and silver. GEORGE L. BUSH

See also SMELTING.

FLUX VALVE. See GYROSYN COMPASS.

Fran Hall, N.A.S.

A Horsefly's Eyes act as prisms, breaking light into bands of color.

Jane Burton

Grace A. Thompson, N.A.S.

A Housefly Searches for Food on a Crust of Bread. The stiff hairs on the fly's body and legs may carry many disease germs that brush off on anything the insect touches.

The Greenbottle Fly is named for the color of its shiny coat.

FLY is an insect with two wings. The common housefly is one of the best known kinds of flies. Other kinds include blowflies, botflies, crane flies, deer flies, fruit flies, gnats, horseflies, leaf miners, midges, mosquitoes, robber flies, sand flies, tsetse flies, and warble flies.

A number of other insects are often called flies, but they have four wings and are not true flies. These insects include butterflies, caddis flies, damsel flies, dragonflies, May flies, and scorpion flies.

Flies are among the most dangerous pests known to man. They carry germs inside their bodies or in the hair on their bodies. When a fly "bites," or when it touches any object, it leaves some of these germs behind. Flies carry germs that cause such serious diseases as malaria, sleeping sickness, and typhoid fever. These insects also cause diseases in animals and plants.

Scientists have developed many ways to control flies. Some swamps are drained, and others are covered with oil or sprayed with insecticides. These treatments kill newly hatched mosquitoes and other kinds of flies that grow in water. Man also uses chemicals and radioactive materials to prevent the fly eggs from hatching.

Some kinds of flies are helpful. They carry pollen from one plant to another, much as bees do. Scientists use fruit flies in the study of *heredity*. These flies have provided valuable information on how characteristics are passed on from one generation to the next.

Flies live throughout the world. Among the smallest are the midges called *no-see-ums*, which are found in North American forests. They are about $\frac{1}{20}$ inch (1.3 millimeters) long. One of the largest flies is a wood-boring fly of South America. It is 3 inches (7.6 centimeters) long and also measures 3 inches from the tip of one wing to the tip of the other.

Flies are among the fastest of all flying insects. The buzzing of a fly is the sound of its wings beating. A housefly's wings beat about 200 times a second, and some midges move their wings 1,000 times a second. Houseflies fly at an average speed of $4\frac{1}{2}$ miles (7.2 kilometers) per hour. They can fly even faster for short dis-

Dale W. Jenkins, the contributor of this article, is Assistant Director of Bioscience Programs at the National Aeronautics and Space Administration.

--- **FACTS IN BRIEF** ---

Names: *Male,* none; *female,* none; *young,* maggots or wrigglers; *group,* swarm.

Number of Newborn: 1 to 250 at a time, depending on species. As many as 1,000 a year for each female.

Length of Life: Average 30 days in summer for houseflies.

Where Found: Throughout the world.

Scientific Classification: Flies belong to the class *Insecta,* and make up the order *Diptera.*

tances to escape their enemies, which include man and many birds.

There are about 100,000 kinds of flies. They make up an *order* (chief group) of insects. The scientific name of the order is *Diptera*, which comes from Greek words that mean *two wings*. This article provides general information about flies. To learn more about various kinds of flies, see the separate WORLD BOOK articles listed in the *Related Articles* at the end of this article.

The Body of a Fly

A fly's body has three main parts: (1) the head, (2) the thorax, and (3) the abdomen. A thin, elastic shell and fine hair cover the body. Many kinds of flies have dull black, brown, gray, or yellowish bodies. A few kinds, including wasp flies and hover flies, may have bright orange, white, or yellow markings. Some kinds, such as bluebottle flies and greenbottle flies, are shiny blue or green. They seem to sparkle with brassy, coppery, or golden lights.

Head. A fly has two large eyes that cover most of its head. The males of some species have eyes so large that they squeeze against each other. The eyes of most female flies are farther apart.

Like most other kinds of insects, a fly has *compound* eyes made up of thousands of six-sided lenses. A housefly has about 4,000 lenses in each eye. No two lenses point in exactly the same direction, and each lens works independently. Everything a fly sees seems to be broken up into small bits. The insect does not have sharp vision, but it can quickly see any movement.

A fly has two antennae that warn it of danger and help it find food. The antennae grow near the center of the head between the eyes. The size and shape of the antennae vary widely among different species of flies, and even between males and females of the same species. A housefly's antennae are short and thick; a female mosquito's are long and threadlike; and a male mosquito's are long and feathery. The antennae can feel changes in the movement of the air, which may warn of an approaching enemy. Flies also smell with their antennae. The odor of the chemicals in rotting meat and garbage attracts houseflies. The odors of certain chemicals bring vinegar flies to wine cellars.

The mouth of a fly looks somewhat like a funnel. The broadest part is nearest the head, and a tubelike part called the *proboscis* extends downward. A fly uses its proboscis as a straw to sip liquids, its only food.

Flies do not bite or chew because they cannot open their jaws. Mosquitoes, sand flies, stable flies, and other kinds of "biting" flies have needlelike mouth parts hidden in the proboscis. They stab these sharp points into a victim's skin and inject saliva to keep the blood from clotting. Then the flies sip the blood. Blowflies, fruit flies, and houseflies do not have piercing mouth parts. Instead, they have two soft, oval-shaped parts called *labella* at the tip of the proboscis. The flies use these parts somewhat like sponges to lap up liquids, which they then suck into the proboscis. They sip liquids, or turn solid foods such as sugar or starch into liquids by dropping saliva on them.

Thorax. A fly's muscles are attached to the inside shell wall of the thorax. These strong muscles move the insect's legs and wings. A fly has six legs. It uses all its legs when it walks, but often stands on only four legs. The legs of most kinds of flies end in claws which help them cling to such flat surfaces as walls or ceilings. Houseflies and certain other flies also have hairy pads called *pulvilli* on their feet. A sticky substance on the feet helps the insects walk on the smooth, slippery surfaces of windows and mirrors.

A fly's wings are so thin that the veins show through. The veins not only carry blood to the wings, but also help stiffen and support them. Instead of hind wings, a fly has a pair of thick, rodlike parts with knobs at the tips. These parts, called *halteres*, give the fly its sense of balance. They vibrate at the same rate as the wings when the insect is flying.

A fly is airborne as soon as it beats its wings. It does not have to run or jump to take off. In the air, the halteres keep the insect in balance and guide it so it can dart quickly and easily in any direction. A fly does not glide in the air or to a landing as do butterflies, moths, and most other flying insects. A fly beats its wings until its feet touch something to land on. If you pick up a fly, but leave the legs and wings free, the wings begin to beat immediately. Scientists sometimes do this with flies when studying wing movements.

Abdomen. A fly breathes through air holes called *spiracles* along the sides of its body. The abdomen has

BODY OF A HOUSEFLY

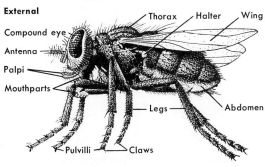

External — Compound eye, Antenna, Palpi, Mouthparts, Thorax, Halter, Wing, Legs, Abdomen, Pulvilli, Claws

Internal — Nerve center, Esophagus, Pharynx, Salivary duct, Stomach, Muscles, Nerve center, Salivary gland, Crop, Intestine, Rectum

KINDS OF MOUTHPARTS

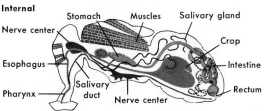

Lapping and Sucking (Housefly) — Compound eye, Antennae, Palpi, Proboscis, Labellum

Biting (Stable fly) — Compound eye, Antenna, Palpus, Proboscis

WORLD BOOK illustration by Tom Dolan

LIFE CYCLE OF THE HOUSEFLY

Eggs   USDA

Larvae   Julian J. Chisholm II

Pupa   Hugh Spencer, NAS

Newly Hatched Adult   USDA

eight pairs of spiracles, and the thorax has two pairs. Air flows through the holes into tubes that carry it to all parts of the fly's body.

The Life of a Fly

A fly's life is divided into four stages: (1) egg, (2) larva, (3) pupa, and (4) adult. At each stage, the fly's appearance changes completely.

Egg. A female fly lays from 1 to about 250 eggs at a time, depending on the species. During her lifetime, one female may produce as many as a thousand eggs. The females of many species simply drop their eggs on water, on the ground, or on other animals. Some species stack the eggs in neat bundles.

At the tip of a female fly's abdomen is an organ called the *ovipositor*, through which the eggs are laid. The housefly usually pushes her ovipositor into soft masses of decaying plant or animal material and lays her eggs there. One kind of mosquito arranges its eggs in groups that look somewhat like rafts. Each egg is held to another by a sticky substance squeezed from the female's body. The eggs float on water until the larvae hatch.

The eggs of many kinds of flies are white or pale yellow, and look like grains of rice. A housefly's eggs hatch in 8 to 30 hours, but the time depends on the

species of fly. Some kinds of mosquitoes lay their eggs during late autumn, but the eggs do not hatch until spring.

Larva of a fly is often called a *maggot* or a *wriggler*. The larvae of most kinds of flies look like worms or small caterpillars. They live in food, garbage, sewage, soil, water, and in living or dead plants and animals.

A fly larva spends all its time eating and growing. It *molts* (sheds its shell and grows a new one) several times as it grows. The larva stage lasts from a few days to two years, depending on the species. The larva then changes into a pupa.

Pupa is the stage of final growth before a fly becomes an adult. The pupae of mosquitoes and some other kinds of flies that develop in water are active swimmers. Most pupae that live on land remain quiet. The larvae build a strong oval-shaped case called a *puparium* around their bodies. Black fly larvae spin a cocoon for protection. Inside the puparium, the larva gradually loses its wormlike look and takes on the shape of the adult fly. After the change is complete, the adult fly bursts one end of the puparium or splits it down the back and crawls out. The pupal stage of a housefly lasts from three to six days in hot weather, and longer in cool weather. The length of time varies among the different species.

Adult. When the adult leaves the puparium, its wings are still moist and soft. The air dries the wings quickly, and blood flows into the wing veins and stiffens them. The thin wing tissue hardens in a few hours or a few days, depending on the species, and the adult flies away to find a mate.

A fly has reached full size when it comes out of the puparium. A small fly grows no larger as it gets older, even though its abdomen may swell with food or eggs.

Adult houseflies live about 30 days in summer. They live longer in cool weather, but are less active. Most adult flies die when the weather gets cold, but many larvae and pupae stay alive during the winter. They develop into adults in spring.   DALE W. JENKINS

Related Articles in WORLD BOOK include:

SOME FLIES THAT SPREAD DISEASE

Fly	Disease	Host
Apple maggots	Bacterial rot	Apples
Black flies	Onchocerciasis (River blindness)	Man
Deer flies	Tularemia (Rabbit fever)	Man, rodents
Fly maggots	Bacterial soft rot	Potato, cabbage, other vegetables
Horseflies	Anthrax	Man, animals
Houseflies	Amebic dysentery	Man, animals
	Typhoid fever	Man
	Bacillary dysentery	Man
	Cholera	Man
Mosquitoes	Filariasis	Man
	Malaria	Man
	Yellow fever	Man, monkeys, rodents
	Dengue	Man
	Encephalitis	Man, horses
Olive fruit fly	Olive knot	Olives
Sand flies	Kala azar	Man
Tsetse flies	African sleeping sickness	Man

FLY CASTING. See FISHING (Reels; Bait).

FLY-UP-THE-CREEK. See HERON.

FLYCATCHER is the name of two families of birds that catch flies and other insects in the air. The flycatcher perches quietly until an insect flies past. Then it darts out quickly and seizes the victim. It closes its bill with a sharp, clicking sound. One of the families of flycatchers lives in America, and the other in Europe. Most of the American flycatchers live in warm climates. Nearly 40 species live in the United States. The more familiar ones include the *Acadian, crested, alder, scissor-tailed, olive-sided, least, yellow-bellied, vermilion, southern crested* or *yellow-hammer,* and *sulfur-bellied* flycatchers. The *kingbird, phoebe,* and *wood pewee* are also flycatchers.

Flycatchers have a wide range of call notes and

S. A. Grimes
A Pair of Acadian Flycatchers Perch by Their Nest.

screams, and some of the notes sound quite musical. The crested flycatcher makes a wild, pleasant sound, somewhat like a whistle. The little alder flycatcher says "RA mee, RA mee." The olive-sided flycatcher calls "pu-pip." This bird also has an amusing call which sounds like "quick, three beers." The least flycatcher calls "chebec" and is sometimes given that name. The sulfur-bellied flycatcher is a noisy bird that calls "kip, kip, kip, kip, squeelya, squeelya." A pair of these birds sometimes sounds like a large group of birds.

As flycatchers move about in search of food, they migrate over a wide area. They may range all the way from Canada to South America in a single year. The scissor-tailed flycatcher lives in the southern Great Plains, New Mexico, and western Texas. The Arkansas kingbird ranges from northern Canada, the Dakotas, western Minnesota, and Kansas to the Pacific Coast. The sulfur-bellied flycatcher ranges from Arizona to Bolivia.

The nesting habits of the flycatchers vary greatly. Some, like the great crested flycatcher, select holes in trees; some, like the phoebe, nest on ledges; and others, like the pewee, make dainty nests.

Scientific Classification. The American flycatchers belong to the New World flycatcher family, *Tyrannidae.* The Acadian flycatcher is genus *Empidonax,* species *E. virescens.* The yellow-bellied is *E. flaviventris;* the least, *E. minimus;* the crested, *Myiarchus crinitus;* the olive-sided, *Nuttallornis borealis;* the scissor-tailed, *Muscivora forficata;* the sulfur-bellied, *Myiodynastes luteiventris.* European flycatchers belong to the Old World flycatcher family, *Muscicapidae.*   ARTHUR A. ALLEN

See also BIRD (color pictures: Other Bird Favorites; Birds' Eggs); KINGBIRD; PHOEBE; WOOD PEWEE; YELLOWHAMMER.

FLYING, in aircraft. See AVIATION.

FLYING BUTTRESS. See ARCHITECTURE (Gothic).

FLYING CLOUD. See MCKAY, DONALD.

FLYING DOCTOR SERVICE, ROYAL. See AUSTRALIA (Transportation and Communication; picture).

FLYING DRAGON is the name commonly given to the so-called flying lizards of southeastern Asia and the East Indies. They grow to be about 8 inches (20 centimeters) long. They do not really fly, but glide by means of folds of skin stretched over extensions of the ribs. Flying dragons glide from branch to branch, or tree to tree, in search of insects and other small animals. In the mating season, the males spread their brightly colored folds of skin to attract the females. These bright folds of skin are usually orange with black markings.

Scientific Classification. Flying dragons are members of the Old World lizard family, *Agamidae.* They are genus *Draco.*   CLIFFORD H. POPE

A Flying Dragon Glides by Spreading Folds of Skin.
American Museum of Natural History

FLYING DUTCHMAN is the name of a legendary ship. The traditional story concerns a sea captain whose punishment for a crime is to sail a ghost ship eternally, without ever coming to port. Richard Wagner wrote an opera called *The Flying Dutchman,* which he based on this famous folklore theme. *Flying Dutchman* was also a nickname for Anthony H. G. Fokker, an airplane designer of World War I.   KNOX WILSON

See also WAGNER, RICHARD (Early Career).

FLYING FARMERS is an international organization of more than 8,000 farmers and ranchers that promotes the use of aviation for agricultural purposes. It has 39 chapters in the United States and Canada.

The association sponsors a program of aviation research and education. It encourages farmers and ranchers to use light aircraft for crop spraying, supervising roundups, locating breaks in fences, and other farm needs. It runs a flight clinic to teach new flying techniques. The association also runs national air tours for members and their families, and cooperates with other groups interested in aviation legislation. The association was founded in 1944. It has national headquarters at Mid Continent Airport, Wichita, Kans. 67209.

Critically reviewed by the INTERNATIONAL FLYING FARMERS, INC.

FLYING FISH

FLYING FISH. The flying fish throws itself from the water with the motion of its strong tail. In the air, it spreads its large fins, which act like wings. Body muscles and the tail fin help the fish to turn in flight. The flight often covers 150 to 1,000 feet (46 to 300 meters). Flying fishes often swim in large groups called *schools*.

Flying fishes live in all warm seas. The California

Harold E. Edgerton

High-Speed Photograph of a Flying Fish, taken off the coast of Southern California, shows the fish in flight. While in flight, the fish looks somewhat like a giant dragonfly.

flying fish grows about 18 inches (46 centimeters) long. The sharp-nosed flying fish lives off both coasts of tropical America. Several species live off the tropical Pacific Islands. Flying fishes make excellent food.

Scientific Classification. Flying fishes make up the flying fish family, *Exocoetidae*. The Atlantic flying fish is genus *Cypselurus*, species *C. heterurus*. The California flying fish is species *C. californicus*. The sharp-nosed flying fish is classified as genus *Fodiator*, species *F. acutus*.   LEONARD P. SCHULTZ

See also GURNARD; FISH (picture: Fish of Coastal Waters and the Open Ocean).

FLYING FORTRESS. See AIR FORCE (color picture); AIR FORCE, UNITED STATES (Between World Wars).

FLYING FOX is a kind of large bat, not a fox. It lives in most tropical regions except South America. It is especially common in Pacific regions. The head and body are about 1 foot (30 centimeters) long, and the wingspread may be over 5 feet (1.5 meters). It gets its name because its face looks like that of a fox.

The flying fox eats mostly fruit, and is more properly known as a *fruit bat*. It also feeds on flower buds, nectar, and pollen. It spends the day hanging in trees, often with other fruit bats. This sometimes makes the tree look as though it is loaded with fruit. Flying foxes can travel long distances for food. Because they can damage

fruit orchards, the U.S. government forbids importation of the animals without a special permit.

Scientific Classification. Flying foxes make up the fruit bat family, *Pteropidae*. The Indian flying fox is genus *Pteropus*, species *P. giganteus*.   CHARLES M. KIRKPATRICK

See also BAT.

FLYING LEMUR, or COLUGO, is a common mammal of Southeast Asia. It is about the size of a cat. A flying lemur looks somewhat like a lemur but is not one (see LEMUR). Flying lemurs can glide as far as 100 yards (91 meters) from tree to tree, but they do not actually fly. Large folds of skin on the animal's sides connect its neck, legs, and tail. When it spreads its legs, this skin forms "wings" used in gliding.

Flying lemurs have a pointed face, large eyes, and brown or gray fur with white spots. They live in rain forests and eat tropical flowers, fruits, and leaves. Most females give birth to one baby every year. Few zoos have flying lemurs, because it is difficult to supply their food.

Scientific Classification: Flying lemurs make up the order *Dermoptera*. The order's single family, *Cynocephalidae*, has one genus, *Cynocephalus*. There are two species, *C. variegatus* and *C. volans*.   PETER CROWCROFT

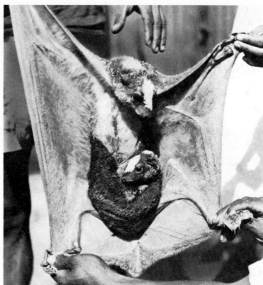

Charles H. Wharton

A Female Flying Lemur Carries Her Baby with Her. The baby fastens its claws tightly to its mother's furry belly. A large membrane, used in gliding, forms a kind of natural cradle when the mother hangs upside down from a branch.

FLYING LIZARD. See FLYING DRAGON.

FLYING SAUCER. See UNIDENTIFIED FLYING OBJECT.

FLYING SQUIRREL is a squirrel that can glide through the air. A fold of skin on each side of its body connects the front and back legs. When a flying squirrel stretches out its legs, the folds of skin form "wings." It glides from tree to tree, using its broad, flat tail to guide its flight. The squirrel's path is downward, then straight, and finally upward. Glides of more than 150 feet (46 meters) have been recorded. Flying squirrels always finish lower than where they started. A high starting point

The Flying Squirrel glides through the air by spreading its legs. Folded skin that grows between the legs stretches out to form "wings." It can glide more than 150 feet (46 meters).

Bernard Hoffman

makes a long glide possible. Flying squirrels live in the forests of Asia, Europe, and North America. American flying squirrels are 8 to 12 inches (20 to 30 centimeters) long, including the tail. Their coat is gray or brownish-red on the upper parts of the body and white or cream-colored on the underparts. Some Asian flying squirrels grow 4 feet (1.2 meters) long.

Flying squirrels nest in the hollows of trees. They hunt for food only at night. Other squirrels hunt by day. Flying squirrels eat berries, birds' eggs, fungi, insects, and nuts. They also eat young birds, and the meat of any *carcasses* (dead animals) they can find.

Scientific Classification. Flying squirrels belong to the subfamily *Petauristinae*, of the squirrel family, *Sciuridae*. The common flying squirrel of the United States is genus *Glaucomys*, species *G. volans*. The larger *G. sabrinus* lives in Canada and the northern United States.   DANIEL BRANT

FLYING TIGERS were a volunteer group of American fliers who fought for Generalissimo Chiang Kai-shek's Chinese government against Japan. Major General Claire Lee Chennault organized the group in 1941. During World War II, they became part of the U.S. Army Air Forces. See also CHENNAULT, CLAIRE LEE.

FLYNN, ELIZABETH GURLEY (1890-1964), was an American labor leader. In 1961, she became the first woman to head the Communist Party in the United States.

Flynn was born in Concord, N.H. Her parents often took her to socialist meetings after the family moved to New York City in 1900. At the age of 15, she began to speak on street corners for workers' rights. In 1906, she joined the Industrial Workers of the World (IWW), an early labor union (see INDUSTRIAL WORKERS OF THE WORLD). She was the leader of several bloody strikes.

In 1920, Flynn helped form the American Civil Liberties Union (ACLU), an organization that works for citizens' rights. She joined the Communist Party in 1937. Flynn spent from January 1955 to May 1957 in prison for violating the Smith Act. This law makes it a crime to urge the violent overthrow of the U.S. govern-

ment. During the 1950's, a period of intense anti-Communist feeling, the Smith Act was used to imprison many Communist leaders. However, the Supreme Court ruled in 1957 that teaching Communism was not, in itself, grounds for conviction.   JUNE SOCHEN

FLYTRAP. See PITCHER PLANT; VENUS'S-FLYTRAP.

FLYWAYS. See BIRD (Bird Migration).

FLYWEIGHT. See BOXING (Weight Classes).

FLYWHEEL is a heavy wheel attached to the shaft of an engine to keep its speed nearly constant. It is used where the forces driving the engine shaft are not constant. The driving forces in a gasoline engine come from a series of explosions in the engine cylinder. The driving forces produce the power needed by the engine's load. Sometimes, the driving forces become momentarily larger than necessary for the engine's load, and the engine speed increases. Then the flywheel absorbs the excess energy and prevents the speed from increasing rapidly. At other times, the driving forces from the cylinder become momentarily smaller than necessary. Then the flywheel's inertia keeps the speed from decreasing quickly. These speed fluctuations are small, usually less than 1 per cent. The fluctuations may occur several times in a single revolution. The flywheel permits an almost steady speed.   E. A. FESSENDEN

Courtesy Chevrolet Motor Div., General Motors

Spoke-Type Flywheels are used for some automatic transmissions on eight-cylinder automobile engines to help keep the speed nearly constant.

See also GASOLINE ENGINE; STARTER; STEAM ENGINE (picture).

FM. See FREQUENCY MODULATION.

FOAL. See HORSE (Life History; table: Terms).

FOAM GLASS. See GLASS (Specialty Glasses).

FOAM RUBBER. See RUBBER (Sponge Rubber).

FOCH, *fawsh,* **FERDINAND** (1851-1929), a French military leader, was acclaimed by many as the greatest Allied general of World War I. He became supreme Allied commander in April, 1918, when a powerful German drive across France seemed on the verge of victory. Foch unified Allied operations and stopped the German drive. Then he launched great counterattacks that drove German forces back into Belgium. Foch's final offensives won the war, and he accepted the German surrender on Nov. 11, 1918.

United Press Int.

Ferdinand Foch

FOCH, FERDINAND

Foch believed that a strong offense was the most effective way to fight a war. But his total reliance on attack early in the war almost ruined his career, because he misjudged the effectiveness of German defensive firepower. He took part in disastrous French offensives in August, 1914, and led offensives that failed in 1915 and 1916. He was finally relieved of his command in December, 1916, seemingly destined for minor duties. One of Foch's great strengths, however, lay in his ability to learn from his earlier failures.

Foch was born in Tarbes, France. He was commissioned in the artillery in 1874. He became a professor at the *École de Guerre*, the French war college, in 1895, and he taught and wrote books on military theory. He became head of the college in 1908.

Foch commanded an army corps at the outbreak of World War I, and helped drive the Germans back from the Marne River in September, 1914. From the fall of 1914 to December, 1916, he commanded the Northern Army Group. In 1917, Foch was made chief of the War Ministry's general staff, and also was intermediary between Henri Pétain, French commander in chief, and other Allied leaders. Foch was promoted to marshal on Aug. 6, 1918, and was elected to the French Academy that same year.

After the war, Foch urged Premier Georges Clemenceau to demand the Rhineland at the Paris Peace Conference in 1919. When the conference denied these demands, Foch bitterly predicted a new war would occur within 20 years.   LARRY H. ADDINGTON

See also WORLD WAR I (The Final Year).

FOCKE, HENRICH. See HELICOPTER (Practical Helicopters).

FOCUS. See EYE (Focusing); LENS.

FODDER is a coarse food fed to farm animals. Farmers make fodder from (1) grasses, including sorghum, cereals, and corn; (2) legumes, such as clover, alfalfa, beans, peas, and peanuts; or (3) roots, such as carrot, potato, turnip, and sugar beet. Fodder may be fed in the green state, or may be dried. Farmers store fodder in *silos* to preserve it for winter use. See also SILO.

FOEHN, *fayn,* is a warm, dry wind that blows down a mountainside. The air loses its moisture as it rises to the mountaintop. It is heated by compression as it comes down the other side of the mountain. Foehns blow frequently in the Alps, and along the eastern slope of the Rocky Mountains, where they are called *chinooks* (see CHINOOK). These winds often bring rapid temperature changes. For example, the temperature at Havre, Mont., rose 33° F. (18° C) in one hour when a chinook arrived on Feb. 15, 1948. Sudden foehns or chinooks frequently cause snow to melt rapidly. These winds often affect the climate where they occur, making it much warmer than at neighboring places.   GEORGE F. TAYLOR

FOETUS, another spelling for *fetus.* See BABY (The Developing Baby).

FOG is a cloud formed so low that it rests near the ground or the surface of a body of water. Fog may be dense or it may be thin. But when the cloud is so thin that it can easily be seen through, it is usually called *mist* or *haze.*

Fog forms in much the same way that a cloud appears about a steaming kettle. The moisture in the warm air coming out of the kettle *condenses* (forms small water

WHAT CAUSES FOG

Fog Forms when moist air near the earth's surface is chilled so that its water vapor condenses. The temperature of the air must be at or below the dew point for the water vapor in the air to condense.

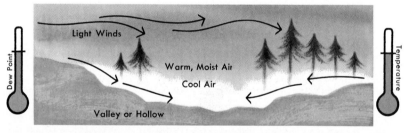

Radiation Fog forms a motionless blanket over the earth. It forms when heat from the ground escapes into the upper air by radiation on a clear night. This chills the air near the ground to its dew point and causes the water vapor in the air to condense.

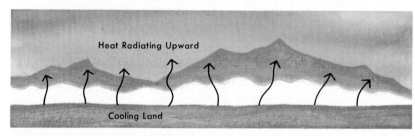

Advection Fog may cover large areas and travel great distances. It forms when warm air blows across cold land or water. The land or water chills the air to its dew point and the water vapor condenses. Advection fogs often occur along seacoasts.

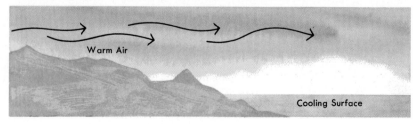

drops) when it strikes the cooler air. In the same way, fog appears when wind blows warm moist air over a cold surface. The sudden chill condenses the moisture.

For any given temperature, there is a definite limit to the amount of water vapor that the air can hold. The warmer the air, the more moisture it can hold before it becomes *saturated* (filled). Fog forms when moist air is cooled below its *saturation temperature*, or *dew point* (see DEW POINT). It also forms when moisture is added to air that is nearly saturated. Both these processes often act at the same time.

The cooling of air which causes the formation of fog most frequently occurs when relatively warm, moist air passes over a colder surface such as a cold ocean current or an area covered by ice or snow. Fogs of this type are called *advection fogs*. They occur frequently along seacoasts and along the shores of rivers and inland lakes. Advection fogs often form in the Newfoundland Banks area, where warm air blows over the cold water of the Labrador Current. Other advection fogs form off the coasts of California and Chile, and along the shores of the Great Lakes. A *radiation fog* may form when air near the ground loses warmth through outward radiation on a clear night. This occurs quite often in valleys during winter. Radiation fogs are common in the San Joaquin Valley of California.

Fog may also form if the amount of moisture in the air increases while the temperature remains constant. This process causes the *frontal fog* that may form at the *front* (boundary) between two air masses of different temperatures. Rain from the warm air mass falls into the cold air mass. Moisture evaporates from the falling rain and saturates the cold air mass, forming fog. A *steam fog* may appear when cold air picks up moisture as it passes over warmer water. Steam fogs are not common. They occur most often in cold climates when the first frigid air of autumn moves over lakes or rivers that have not yet frozen.   GEORGE F. TAYLOR

See also CLOUD; DEW; SMOG; WATER.

FOGHORN. See SIREN.

FOIL. See FENCING.

FOKINE, *faw KEEN,* **MICHEL** (1880-1942), was a great Russian *choreographer* (dance composer). Fokine invented the one-act ballet based on music by a first-rate composer. The dance and scenery in his ballets merge with the mood and drama of the music to create a powerful theater event. Fokine composed more than 60 one-act ballets between 1905 and 1942. The best known include *The Dying Swan, Les Sylphides, Prince Igor, Scheherazade, Le Spectre de la Rose, Petrouchka, L'Epreuve d'Amour,* and *Firebird.*

Fokine was born in St. Petersburg (now Leningrad). There he became soloist with the Maryinsky Ballet (now the Kirov Ballet). He left Russia with Sergei Diaghilev's Ballets Russes in 1909. This marked the beginning of his great career as choreographer. He became a United States citizen in 1932. P. W. MANCHESTER

FOKKER, *FAHK ur,* **ANTHONY HERMAN GERARD** (1890-1939), was a Dutch engineer, pilot, and aircraft manufacturer. He moved to Germany at the age of 20, because of the interest in aviation there. He established his first manufacturing plant near Berlin when he was 22. Fokker designed monoplanes, biplanes, and triplanes. His factories supplied many airplanes for Germany in World War I. After the war, he set up plants

in The Netherlands and the United States. Fokker was born in Kediri, Java.   ROBERT B. HOTZ

FOLGER, CHARLES J. See ARTHUR, CHESTER ALAN (Election of 1884).

FOLGER SHAKESPEARE LIBRARY, in Washington, D.C., houses one of the most important collections of books on British civilization from about 1485 to 1715. It also owns the world's most important collection of books by and about William Shakespeare. The library has more than 145,000 volumes. The most valuable books are protected in fireproof air-conditioned vaults. An exhibition gallery, open free to the public, displays many rare books, pictures, and objects of interest from the Elizabethan period. The small theater in the library is patterned after a typical playhouse of the period.

Henry Clay Folger, a former president of the Standard Oil Company of New York, founded the library in 1930. He left his entire fortune for the trustees of Amherst College to administer toward the development of a great research library. Scholars from all parts of the world come to the library for research in history and literature. The library building was completed in 1932. This magnificent marble structure stands just north of the Library of Congress Annex.   LOUIS B. WRIGHT

FOLIC ACID. See VITAMIN (table).

FOLIO, *FOH lee oh,* is the name used by printers and publishers for a sheet of paper folded once, making four pages, front and back. The word *folio* may also mean the page number of a book. The even-numbered pages, or folios, are always on the left. The odd-numbered folios are on the right side of the bound book or volume.

A *quarto* is a sheet folded twice, making four leaves or eight pages. An *octavo* is a sheet folded into eight leaves or 16 pages. The octavo format, or shape of the book, is the one in most common use. But folio format or octavo format tells nothing about the *size* of a book today, although formerly it did. The size today depends on the dimensions of the sheet of paper before it was folded.

Photo by Emil Otto Hoppé (The Dance Collection, N.Y. Public Library)
Michel Fokine and his wife Vera danced in a 1914 revival of his ballet *Daphnis and Chloë*, based on an ancient Roman story.

A Folk Painting by Edward Hicks shows a scene of Quaker farm life in Pennsylvania during the late 1700's. In several such pictures, Hicks painted his memories of his childhood home, the farm of David Twining. This painting shows Hicks as a boy standing next to Mrs. Twining, *lower right*.

Oil painting on canvas (about 1848)

FOLK ART is a term that refers to the work of painters, sculptors, and craftsmen who have little or no training as artists. Folk artists are ordinary people who create their works for other ordinary people, rather than for museums or wealthy collectors.

Most folk artists know nothing about the basic principles of art. For example, few of them know how to draw the human body accurately or how to use color, light, and perspective properly. Their work shows no awareness of current movements or other developments in the arts. Folk artists solve art problems as best they can. They often create a pleasing picture, carving, or household object without knowing exactly how or why they have succeeded.

Folk art has been produced in many countries for hundreds of years. This article deals with American folk art, especially during its most productive period, from about 1780 to about 1860. Most American folk artists worked in small towns in New England, New York, and Pennsylvania.

American folk artists created a wide variety of works, including paintings, sculptures, and such household objects as dishes, pots, and quilts. They also produced store signs, weather vanes, and other everyday objects. During the 1800's, sailors carved a special kind of folk sculpture called *scrimshaw*.

By 1875, the demand for folk art had declined in America because of the widespread use of machines.

Beatrix T. Rumford, the contributor of this article, is Director of the Abby Aldrich Rockefeller Folk Art Collection in Williamsburg, Va. Unless otherwise credited, the illustrations in this article are from the Abby Aldrich Rockefeller Folk Art Collection.

The machines could manufacture more goods in less time—and with fewer mistakes—than could human hands. But folk art continued in isolated rural areas, and some is still created today.

For many years, scholars and art collectors paid little attention to folk art. The first real interest in American folk art occurred in the late 1920's. At that time, a group of professional artists on vacation in Maine noticed folk art on sale in junk shops. They began to buy it because they admired its fresh, simple quality and its freedom from formal rules.

Today, much folk art is enjoyed simply for its beauty and skillful craftsmanship. In addition, folk art reflects everyday life. Much of it shows the social attitudes, political views, religious feelings, and routine habits of the people of a certain period and place. These elements make folk art a valuable source of information to historians and others interested in ordinary people of the past.

Kinds of Folk Art

Painting. Folk artists painted some subjects from memory and others from life. They often copied or adapted engravings and other kinds of prints that had originally been created by trained artists.

Many American folk painters began by making and decorating business signs. Until about 1870, many Americans could not read, and so shopkeepers used pictorial signs to advertise their products. For example, a sign showing a pig represented a butcher shop. A picture of a boot advertised a shoemaker. Most signs had bright colors and bold designs to catch the eye of passers-by.

The influence of sign painting can be seen in much

early American portrait painting. Portraits were the most common type of folk painting. Artists called *limners* traveled throughout a region, painting likenesses of local residents. These portraits, like store signs, had vivid colors and simple but bold compositions.

In addition to signs and portraits, folk artists painted pictures of houses, landscapes, and ships. Many landscapes showed scenes of life on farms or in small towns. These scenes tell much about now-forgotten activities that once were so common that nobody bothered to write about them.

Sculpture. One of the earliest types of folk sculpture was the *figurehead* of a ship. A figurehead is a statue—of a woman, in most cases—that decorates the bow of a vessel. Early folk carving also included gravestones. A picture of one appears in the WORLD BOOK article on SCULPTURE (1600-1900 [American Sculpture]).

The so-called cigar store Indian was a popular subject for some sculptors. A life-sized wooden figure of an Indian warrior stood outside many shops that sold tobacco products. The Indian figures were first displayed by English merchants of the late 1600's. The merchants used this form of advertisement because Indians had introduced tobacco to the Virginia settlers.

Folk sculptors made animals and other figures for merry-go-rounds. They also carved and decorated toys and *decoys*—wooden figures of ducks and geese used by hunters to attract game birds.

Weather vanes ranked among the most important

The Talcott Family (1832), a water color on paper

Portraits were painted by folk artists called *limners*. While in her early 20's, Deborah Goldsmith traveled throughout northern New York, painting portraits of local residents. This family group ranks among her best-known compositions. The painting provides a valuable record of American clothing and furnishings of the time.

Metal Weather Vanes of the late 1800's were made from wood patterns carved by experienced craftsmen. A folk sculptor designed the weather vane at the right in the form of the Statue of Liberty.

Copper weather vane (after 1886)

Advertisements featured several kinds of folk art. Sculptors skillfully carved wooden Indians, *left*, which stood outside tobacco shops. Painters designed colorful signs, *below*, to advertise a store's products.

Painted wood (1800's);
Virginia Museum of
Fine Arts, Richmond

Oil painting on wood (early 1800's)

Josiah Turner.

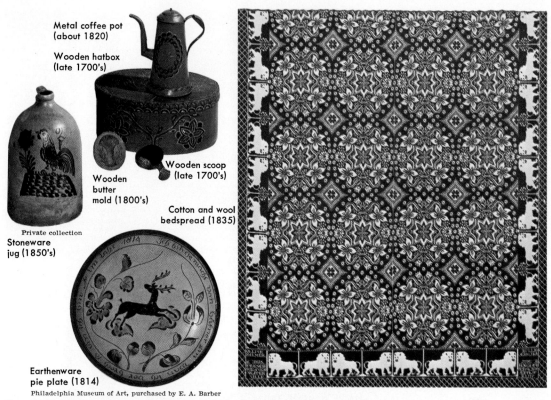

Metal coffee pot
(about 1820)

Wooden hatbox
(late 1700's)

Wooden scoop
(late 1700's)

Wooden
butter
mold (1800's)

Cotton and wool
bedspread (1835)

Private collection
Stoneware
jug (1850's)

Earthenware
pie plate (1814)

Philadelphia Museum of Art, purchased by E. A. Barber

Household Objects were carefully carved and vividly decorated to make them as attractive as possible. Craftsmen used colorful designs in painting the hatbox and kitchen utensils shown above. A weaver chose bold patterns for the bedspread on the right and added an unusual border of lions.

A Dressing Table, built in 1835 by a New England craftsman, was made of cheap wood. The artist painted and decorated the table in imitation of an expensive rosewood piece.

kinds of folk sculpture. Farmers and sailors needed to know about changes in the weather, and so farm buildings and ships had weather vanes to show the direction of the wind.

Household Objects. Folk art included many decorative objects used at home. Some of these objects brightened the inside of a home, and others seemed to make daily chores less boring. A number of folk artists made colorful kitchen utensils of earthenware and tin. Some homemakers specialized in sewing quilts, many of which featured gay colors and lively designs of animals, flowers, and trees.

Many pieces of useful folk art substituted for expensive furniture and utensils that most people could not afford. Some craftsmen used poor-quality wood to make such items as clocks and tables. Folk artists then painted and decorated such pieces to imitate stylish, costly furniture.

Scrimshaw. To help pass the time during long voyages, many sailors made small carvings and engravings of whalebone, ivory, or wood. These objects became known as *scrimshaw.*

Engravings made by American sailors during the 1800's rank as the finest examples of scrimshaw. First, the sailor smoothed and polished the object. Then he scratched a picture or design into the surface with a sharp instrument. Finally, he filled in the engraved lines with colored inks. Some sailors engraved accurate scenes of activities at sea, such as naval battles and whale hunts. Seamen also copied illustrations from books and magazines.

Many pieces of scrimshaw were useful objects, such as knitting needles and corset stays. Sailors sometimes decorated coconut shells, ostrich eggs, and other objects from nature as souvenirs of their travels.

Folk Artists

Most American folk artists probably considered themselves craftsmen rather than artists. They would have used the word *artist* for those who studied and followed traditions of art created through the centuries by Europeans.

The names of most American folk artists have been lost. But a few are known because they wrote their name on their works, developed a recognizable style, or created a large number of items. The best-known of these artists include Erastus Salisbury Field, Edward Hicks, Ammi Phillips, Eunice Pinney, and Wilhelm Schimmel.

Many folk artists were skilled craftsmen who could build houses and ships as well as paint or carve. Edward Hicks, for example, was born in Bucks County, Pennsylvania, and served a seven-year apprenticeship to a local coachmaker as a painter. Then, at the age of 21, Hicks decided to work for himself. He earned his living by lettering signs, but he is best known today for his many versions of a painting he called *The Peaceable Kingdom*.

Some folk artists were amateurs who created folk art for fun, to pass the time, or to impress their neighbors. Still others were students, most of them teen-agers. They painted water colors, made drawings, or embroidered pieces of cloth as classroom assignments. Sometimes such schoolwork produced important pieces of folk art.

A number of folk artists had a regular job and used their artistic talent to increase their income. Schoolteachers, shopkeepers, and even physicians and lawyers earned extra money by selling objects they had created.

Some folk artists traveled throughout a region, trading pieces of their art for food and lodging. During the 1880's, Wilhelm Schimmel wandered through Cumberland County, Pennsylvania, seeking work and begging for food. In exchange for meals, Schimmel gave people animal figures he had carved and then colored with bits of paint. Today, his figures rank among the most prized American folk sculpture.

Folk Art Collections

Several museums in the United States exhibit only folk art or have large folk art collections. Most are in the East, where the majority of folk artists lived.

In New England, folk art can be seen at the Old Sturbridge Village in Sturbridge, Mass.; and at the Shelburne Museum in Shelburne, Vt. The Museum of Fine Arts in Boston also has a large collection.

The Pennsylvania Dutch region of southeastern Pennsylvania was an important center of folk art, and several museums there exhibit such art today. They in-

A Figurehead of a giant eagle decorated the bow of the warship *Lancaster*. The sculptor designed the eagle to symbolize the power and authority of the United States wherever the *Lancaster* sailed.
Painted wood figurehead (about 1875) by John Haley Bellamy; Mariners Museum, Newport News, Va.

Whaling Museum, New Bedford, Mass.
Scrimshaw consisted of carvings and engravings made by sailors during long voyages. The engraving on the sperm whale tooth shown above shows whalers towing a dead whale to their ship.

FOLK ART

Black Folk Art shows the influence of the African heritage of American slaves. A former slave probably carved this wooden figure of a boy with a bucket about 1860. The expressionless face and seated position are features of much African sculpture.

clude the Landis Valley Farm Museum in Lancaster and the Schwenkfelder Museum in Pennsburg. The Museum of Art in Philadelphia and the Bucks County Historical Society in Doylestown, Pa., also have folk art collections.

The New York State Historical Association in Cooperstown exhibits folk art. The Museum of American Folk Art and the Metropolitan Museum of Art, both in New York City, have important collections. Another collection may be seen at the Henry Francis du Pont Winterthur Museum in Winterthur, Del.

The Abby Aldrich Rockefeller Folk Art Collection in Williamsburg, Va., is one of the world's largest museums devoted only to folk art. In Washington, D.C.,

folk art can be seen at the National Gallery of Art and the Smithsonian Institution. In the Midwest, the Henry Ford Museum in Dearborn, Mich., has an outstanding folk art collection. BEATRIX T. RUMFORD

Related Articles in WORLD BOOK include:

Colonial Life in America (Arts and Sciences)	Pennsylvania Dutch (picture)
Feke, Robert	Pickett, Joseph
Hicks, Edward	Sampler
Moses, Grandma	

FOLK COSTUME. See CLOTHING.

FOLK DANCING is the traditional form of social dancing of a nation or ethnic group. Throughout history, almost every culture has developed its own folk dances. These dances have been passed down from generation to generation. People have composed *dance songs*, a type of folk music, to accompany many of the dances.

Most folk dances originated as a form of celebration, religious worship, or a method of controlling mysterious forces. The form and movements of many of these dances were based on superstitious beliefs. For example, a number of early folk dances were performed in a circle because people believed this shape had magical powers. In some early cultures, circular motion was thought to bring good luck or drive away evil.

Early peoples developed dances to celebrate such events as birth, marriage, and even death. In some societies, young people conducted courtship through dances. The *Ländler* of Austria and the *fandango* of Spain are pantomime dances based on gestures of courtship. Other folk dances were originally performed to cure disease, to obtain such favors as plentiful crops, or to celebrate success in battle. The *tarantella* of Italy originated as a method of curing the bite of the tarantula. The Scots once celebrated victories in battle by dancing the *sword dance*.

Through the years, most folk dances lost their original meaning and came to be danced chiefly for recreation. Today, the *square dance* is perhaps the most popular folk dance in the United States. It is usually danced by four couples in a square formation. The dancers swing about, bow, change partners, and perform other lively movements as directed by a caller. Popular European folk dances include the *Irish jig*, the *flamenco* of Spain,

Folk Dancing is an important event at folk festivals throughout the world. The dancers shown at the left in traditional costumes are performing a German folk dance on Bavarian Folk Costume Day. This annual festival is held in Bad Wiessee, West Germany, near Munich.

and the *polka* of Czechoslovakia. Among black African and American Indian groups, traditional dances remain a vital part of religious ceremonies, as well as a form of entertainment.   MELVIN BERGER

See the pictures of dancers in the following articles: CHILE; GREECE; INDONESIA; JEWS; ROMANIA; SPAIN; and YUGOSLAVIA. See also DANCING; LATIN AMERICA (Dancing); SQUARE DANCE.

FOLK LITERATURE. See FOLKLORE; LITERATURE FOR CHILDREN (Folk Literature).

FOLK MUSIC consists of a people's traditional songs. No one knows who created most of the folk songs that have ever been sung or played. Folk songs deal with almost every kind of human activity. Many of these songs express the political or religious beliefs of a people or describe their history. Other folk songs simply provide amusement.

Songs written by professional composers are considered folk music if they become part of a people's traditional music. For example, the American composer Stephen Foster wrote such songs as "Oh! Susanna" and "Swanee River," which are widely accepted as folk music.

Characteristics of Folk Music. The melody and words of a folk song develop over a long period of time. One person makes up a song, and other people hear the song and learn to sing it. These people, in turn, sing the song for others, who also learn the words and melody. In this way, the song passes from person to person, from place to place, and from generation to generation. Through the years, the song is gradually refined and simplified. The melody becomes smoother and more expressive, and the words grow clearer and more direct. Many versions of a song also appear. In addition, the same words may be sung with different tunes, or different words may be used for the same melody.

Most American and European folk songs have a stanza form, which consists of a verse alternating with a chorus. The verses tell the story, and so each verse is different. The words of the chorus remain the same in most folk songs. Many choruses consist of nonsense words or syllables that have no meaning. Sometimes the audience joins in the singing of the chorus.

"Gee, But I Want to Go Home" is an example of a comic verse-chorus folk song. American soldiers sang it during World War I (1914-1918) and World War II (1939-1945). Here are two verses and the chorus:

The coffee that they give you they say is mighty fine:
It's good for cuts and bruises and tastes like iodine.

(chorus) I don't want no more of army life,
    Gee, but I want to go home.

The clothes that they give you they say are mighty fine,
But me and my buddy can both fit into mine.

(chorus) I don't want no more of army life,
    Gee, but I want to go home.

Originally, people sang folk songs with no instrumental accompaniment. Instrumental parts were later added to many tunes. Today, the guitar is the most popular instrument in folk music. Other widely used instruments include the banjo, harmonica, and violin.

Kinds of Folk Music. Most folk songs are ballads that tell simple stories and have simple words and music. Some ballads relate legendary incidents that occurred long ago. For example, "Barbara Allen" is a

tragic love story that dates back at least to the 1600's. There are several versions of the song, some of which originated in England and others in Scotland. Some ballads are based on true events from more recent times. "Peat Bog Soldiers" describes the suffering of prisoners in Nazi concentration camps during the 1930's and 1940's. Many ballads tell about the deeds of heroes. "Casey Jones" praises a brave American railroad engineer, and "John Brown's Body" honors a famous abolitionist.

Certain kinds of folk music deal with a particular activity or occupation. Laborers create *work songs* to help their long days pass more quickly. Popular work songs include "Old Chisholm Trail," sung by cowboys, and "Drunken Sailor," sung by seamen. Some *union songs* call for better conditions for workers. The execution of a famous labor organizer in 1915 inspired the union song "Joe Hill." Prisoners make up *prison songs*. "Midnight Special" tells of the loneliness of prison life. Slaves sang about their suffering in *spirituals*, such as "Go Down, Moses" and "Joshua Fit de Battle ob Jericho." In the mid-1900's, black Americans sang the spirituals "We Shall Overcome" and "Welcome Table" to emphasize their struggle for civil rights.

Some folk songs have no serious purpose and are meant only to entertain. People dance to "Buffalo Gals" and other *dance songs*. A *game song*, such as "Ring-Around-the-Rosy," gives instructions on how to play a certain game. *Nonsense songs*, among them "Arkansas Traveler" and "Frog Went a Courting," are intended to make people laugh.

American Folk Music is noted for its energy, humor, and emotional impact. The major influences on American folk music came from Great Britain and other European countries, and from Africa. However, the songs of American Indians also had a significant part in the heritage of American folk music. In addition, various national and racial groups preserve the folk music of their ancestors. For example, Americans of Spanish ancestry hold folk festivals during which traditional songs are performed.

American Indians consider their songs an extremely important part of their heritage. Traditionally, some tribes believed that gods created all the songs at the beginning of time. These songs can be revealed only in dreams or in other mystical ways. New songs cannot be composed. Indians have judged folk songs by their power, not by their beauty. For example, various tribes have songs to control the weather or to cure illness. They believe the songs must be sung correctly because errors could rob them of their power.

The early American colonists from Great Britain brought their folk music traditions with them, especially the ballad and stanza form. Later settlers from other countries also brought their own folk music, which influenced the colonial songs.

The slaves who were brought to America from Africa had a different musical tradition from that of the Europeans. However, most slaveowners did not allow the blacks to sing or play their native music. As a result, the specific words and melody of the songs were gradually forgotten. But the slaves retained the style of their music and created new songs in the African tradition.

FOLKETING

Most of these songs follow the *call-response* pattern, in which a leader sings a line and the entire group answers. Drums and other percussion instruments play a complex rhythmic accompaniment.

During the mid-1900's, a number of singers gained great popularity performing American folk songs. Some of these singers wrote songs that became part of the American folk tradition. The best known of these songs dealt with social problems, such as poverty and racial prejudice. The leading singer-composers included Bob Dylan, Woody Guthrie, Huddie Ledbetter (known as Leadbelly), and Pete Seeger.   MELVIN BERGER

Related Articles in WORLD BOOK include:

Baez, Joan	Folklore
Ballad	Foster, Stephen Collins
Blues	Guthrie, Woody
Burleigh, Harry Thacker	Jazz
Calypso	Latin America (Music)
Chantey	Seeger, Pete
Country and Western Music	Spiritual
Dylan, Bob	Western Frontier Life
Folk Dancing	(Music)

FOLKETING. See DENMARK (Parliament).

FOLKLORE is any of the beliefs, customs, and traditions that people pass on from generation to generation. Much folklore consists of folk stories, such as ballads, fairy tales, folk tales, legends, and myths. But folklore also includes arts and crafts, dances, games, nursery rhymes, proverbs, riddles, songs, superstitions, and holiday and religious celebrations.

Folklore is as old as humanity. Written records left by the earliest peoples include examples of folklore. As soon as a people develops a writing system, they begin to record folk stories. However, folklore does not have to be written down. Much folklore is passed orally from person to person. Even today, many peoples do not have a written language, but they have folk songs, legends, myths, and other kinds of folklore. Sometimes folklore is handed down by imitation. For centuries, children have learned games, such as jump rope and marbles, by imitating other youngsters.

As people move from one land to another, they take their folklore with them and adapt it to their new surroundings. From the 1500's to the 1800's, for example, thousands of West Africans were transported to the Western Hemisphere as slaves. Many of the slaves enjoyed telling a number of West African folk tales about a sly spider named Anansi. Through the years, the slaves continued to tell tales of Anansi, though the stories about the spider were gradually changed to reflect life in the New World. Today, Anansi remains a popular character in black folklore, both in West Africa and in the Caribbean area.

Origins of Folklore

During the 1800's, scholars believed that folklore in ancient times had been shared by all members of a society. Most ancient peoples lived in rural communities. Through the centuries, large numbers of people moved to cities and gradually lost touch with so-called "authentic" folk traditions. According to the scholars of the 1800's, those traditions were preserved by uneducated peasants called *folk*, whose way of life had changed little for hundreds of years. Two German brothers, Jakob and Wilhelm Grimm, were among the leading folklore scholars. From 1807 to 1814, they collected folk tales from peasants who lived near Kassel, in what is now West Germany. The Grimms believed that by collecting the tales, they were preserving the heritage of all Germans. The stories they collected became famous as *Grimm's Fairy Tales*. But some versions

Erwin E. Smith Collection of Range Life
Photographs, Library of Congress

Telling Folk Tales is a popular pastime. Many legends, songs, and other kinds of folklore are passed orally from person to person. This picture shows American cowboys of the early 1900's listening to stories about Western folk heroes.

Detail of *Children's Games*, an oil painting on oak panel (1560)
by Pieter Bruegel the Elder; Kunsthistorisches Museum, Vienna

Many Children's Games are handed down by imitation. For hundreds of years, youngsters have learned games by watching other children play. This painting of the mid-1500's shows boys and girls playing some games that young people of today enjoy.

Ethnic Folklore preserves the customs of a particular national or racial group. Americans of Swedish ancestry hold an annual festival in Minneapolis that includes Swedish folk dances and songs performed in traditional costumes, *left*.

of these tales are found throughout Europe, the Near East, and Asia.

Today, scholars consider folk to be any group of people who share at least one common linking factor. This factor may be geography, as in folklore of the Ozark Mountains region; religion, as in Jewish folklore; occupation, as in cowboy folklore; or ethnic background, as in Irish-American folklore. Some scholars believe that even a family can be considered folk because many families have their own traditions and stories.

Characteristics of Folklore

Folklore can be short and simple or long and complicated. Brief proverbs, such as "Time flies" and "Money talks," are famous examples of folklore. On the other hand, some Indonesian folk plays begin at sundown and end at dawn.

It is extremely difficult to make up folklore. The songs, stories, and other material that became folklore were, of course, thought up by various people. But those individuals had the rare ability to create a subject and a style that appealed to others through the years. Folklore survives only if it retains that appeal. People would not bother to retell tales or continue to follow customs that had no meaning for them. This is the reason people keep on using the same folklore over and over.

To be considered authentic folklore, an item must have at least two versions. It also must have existed in more than one period and place. For example, scholars have identified more than 1,000 versions of the fairy tale about Cinderella. These versions developed through hundreds of years in many countries, including China, France, Germany, and Turkey.

Changes in folklore often occur as it passes from person to person. These changes, called *variations*, are one of the surest indications that the item is genuine folklore. Variations frequently appear in both the words and music of folk songs. The same lyrics may be used with different tunes, or different words may be set to the same music. The nursery rhymes "Baa, Baa Black Sheep" and "Twinkle, Twinkle Little Star" have the same melody. Some people use the folk saying "As slow as molasses." Others prefer another version, "As slow as molasses in January." Still others say "As slow as molasses in January running uphill."

Kinds of Folklore

Myths are religious stories that explain how the world and humanity developed into their present form. Unlike most types of folk stories, myths are considered true among the people who develop them.

Medieval Folk Musicians traveled throughout France and Germany. They often entertained royalty with long, elaborate songs that celebrated the heroic deeds of legendary kings and knights.

Many Religious Ceremonies include folk traditions. A Navajo medicine man, *right,* and his helpers create a sand painting of a sun god for use in a ritual to treat a sick child. The painting design has been handed down by generations of medicine men.

Many myths describe the creation of the earth. In some, a god creates the earth. In others, the earth emerges from a flood. A number of myths describe the creation of the human race and the origin of death.

Folk Tales are fictional stories about animals or human beings. Most of these tales are not set in any particular time or place, and they begin and end in a certain way. For example, many English folk tales begin with the phrase "Once upon a time" and end with "They lived happily ever after."

Fables are one of the most popular types of folk tales. They are animal stories that try to teach people how to behave. One fable describes a race between a tortoise and a hare. The tortoise, though it is a far slower animal, wins because the hare foolishly stops to sleep. This story teaches the lesson that someone who works steadily can come out ahead of a person who is faster or has a head start.

In many European fairy tales, the hero or heroine leaves home to seek some goal. After various adventures, he or she wins a prize or a marriage partner, in many cases a prince or princess. One popular kind of folk tale has a trickster as the hero. Each culture has its own trickster figure. Most tricksters are animals who act like human beings. In Africa, tricksters include the tortoise; the hare; and Anansi, the spider. The most popular trickster in North American Indian folklore is probably the coyote.

Legends, like myths, are stories told as though they were true. But legends are set in the real world and in relatively recent times.

American folklore includes many legendary heroes. David Crockett was a famous American frontiersman who was elected to the U.S. Congress from Tennessee in 1827. After Crockett died in the battle of the Alamo in 1836, he became a popular figure in American folklore. John Chapman, better known as Johnny Appleseed, planted apple trees from Massachusetts to the Midwest during the early 1800's. He was the hero of a number of legends by the time he died in the 1840's. John Henry was the black hero of many legends in the South. A famous ballad describes how he competed against a steam drill in a race to see whether a man or a machine could dig a tunnel faster. Using only a hammer, John Henry won—but he died when the tunnel caved in.

Many legends tell about human beings who meet supernatural creatures, such as fairies, ghosts, vampires, and witches. A number of legends are associated with famous people who have died. Others tell of holy persons and religious leaders. Some legends describe how saints work miracles.

The action in myths and folk tales ends at the conclusion of the story. But the action in many legends has not been completed by the story's end. For example, a legend about a buried treasure may end by saying that the treasure has not yet been found. A legend about a haunted house may suggest that the house is still haunted.

A number of legends tell about the Loch Ness mon-

Black Folk Dances in America developed from West African religious dances. From the early 1600's to the mid-1800's, thousands of West Africans were transported to the Western Hemisphere as slaves. This water color of the late 1700's shows Southern plantation slaves performing a folk dance. Their musical instruments also originated in West Africa.

ster, a sea serpent in Scotland; and the abominable snowman, a hairy beast in the Himalaya. Some people believe these creatures actually exist. From time to time, various expeditions have tried to find both of them.

Folk Songs have been created for almost every human activity. Some are associated with work. For example, sailors sing songs called *chanteys* while pulling in their lines. Folk songs may deal with birth, childhood, courtship, marriage, and death. Parents sing folk lullabies to babies. Children sing traditional songs as part of some games. Other folk songs are sung at weddings and funerals.

Some folk songs are related to seasonal activities, such as planting and harvesting. Many are sung on certain holidays. The folk song "The Twelve Days of Christmas" is a well-known carol. Some folk songs celebrate the deeds of real or imaginary heroes. But people sing many folk songs simply for enjoyment.

Superstitions and Customs are involved largely in marking a person's advancement from one stage of life to another. For example, many cultures include a custom called *couvade* to protect unborn babies. In couvade, husbands pretend that they are about to give birth. They may avoid eating certain foods considered harmful to the expected baby. They also may avoid working because such activity could injure the unborn child.

A wedding custom called *charivari* is widespread in various European societies. On the wedding night, friends of the bride and groom provide a noisy serenade by banging on pots and pans outside the couple's bedroom. The desire to avoid charivari led to the practice of leaving on a honeymoon immediately after a wedding.

A large number of superstitions and customs supposedly help control or predict the future. The people of fishing communities may hold elaborate ceremonies that are designed to ensure a good catch. Many people try to foretell future events by analyzing the relationships among the planets and stars.

Holidays are special occasions celebrated by a group, and almost all of them include folklore. Christmas is especially rich in folklore. A group may celebrate this holiday with its own special foods and costumes. Many groups have variations of the same folk custom. In a number of countries, for example, children receive presents on Christmas. In the United States, Santa Claus brings the presents. In Italy, an old woman named La Befana distributes the gifts. In some countries of Europe, the gifts come from the Christ Child. In others, the Three Wise Men bring them.

Folklore and the Arts

Folklore has made a major contribution to the world's arts. Many folk stories and folk songs are beautiful works of art themselves. Folklore has also inspired masterpieces of literature, music, painting, and sculpture. The English poet Geoffrey Chaucer used a number of folk tales in his famous *Canterbury Tales*. William Shakespeare based the plots of several of his plays on folk tales. These plays include *King Lear*, *The Merchant of Venice*, and *The Taming of the Shrew*.

Certain legends and myths have attracted artists, composers, and writers for centuries. One legend tells about a medieval German scholar named Faust who sold his soul to the devil. This legend has been the basis of many novels, plays, operas, and orchestral works. *Faust*, a drama by Johann Wolfgang von Goethe, is probably the greatest work in German literature.

Jazz developed largely from folk music of Southern blacks. Classical composers also have incorporated folk melodies into their works. For example, the Czech composer Antonín Dvořák used black spirituals in his famous symphony *From the New World*. The Austrian composer Wolfgang Amadeus Mozart used the melody of "Twinkle, Twinkle Little Star" as the basis of a work he wrote in 1778.

Folklore and Society

Folklore reflects the attitudes and ideals of a society. For example, much folklore reflects how a society regards the roles of males and females in real life. In many

Folk Customs play an important part in most holidays. In many countries, children receive presents on Christmas. Italian boys and girls receive their gifts from a kind witch called La Befana, shown standing on a chair. She gives toys and candy to good youngsters and beats naughty ones with a rod.

examples of Western folklore, women are passive and uncreative. A society that produces such folklore considers men superior to women. This attitude appears in a proverb:

> A whistling maid and a crowing hen
> Are neither fit for gods nor men.

According to the proverb, a girl who whistles like a boy and a hen that crows like a rooster are unnatural. The proverb implies that women should not try to take part in activities traditionally associated with men.

A common wedding custom calls for the groom to carry his bride over the threshold of their home. This custom suggests that the woman is weak and must be carried through the doorway—and presumably through life—by the strong male. In many Western fairy tales, a female is captured by a villain and waits quietly until a heroic male rescues her.   ALAN DUNDES

FOLKWAY is a habit or custom common to the members of a social group. A person who violates the folkways of a group is punished, but in an informal way. The violator may be avoided by other members of the group, or excluded from their activities. But there are no laws against violating folkways.

People see and practice the folkways of their community each day. When a man opens the door for a woman and allows her to go ahead of him, he is observing a folkway. It is also a folkway to walk on the right-hand side of the sidewalk. Anyone who does not do these things may lose the good favor of others.

A folkway arises when many people within a group repeat the same act or courtesy many times. People tend to forget the reasons behind a folkway, and the act becomes automatic. But folkways do not remain unchanged. New folkways appear constantly to meet new conditions. People drop other folkways because they no longer have any meaning.

At times, people come to believe that certain of their folkways are necessary to the welfare of the group. Such folkways are then called *mores* (see MORES). Mores form part of the moral code of a civilization, and often become part of its written laws (see LAW [Systems of Law]). Folkways, mores, moral codes, and written laws all form part of the codes of conduct that each culture sets up.   JOHN F. CUBER

FOLLICLE. See HAIR.

FOLSOM POINT. In 1925, scientists in Folsom, N.M., discovered prehistoric stone spearheads mingled with animal bones. They called the weapons *Folsom points.* Although they found no human bones, scientists used the name *Folsom man* to describe the prehistoric person who must have made and used the pointed weapons. The bones found near the weapons belonged to a species of bison which has long been extinct.

Since 1926, scientists have found similar weapons and animal bones in other parts of New Mexico, and in Colorado and Texas. These discoveries led scientists to question how long human beings have lived in America. At first they thought the weapons might have been washed in among the bones at a later date, so that finding them together was a coincidence.

Amer. Museum of Natural History
This Folsom Point was found near Bison Quarry, New Mexico.

Now most scientists believe that the weapons are the same age as the bones. This suggests that the Folsom man lived in America from about 10,000 to 25,000 years ago.　　　　　WILFRID D. HAMBLY

See also PREHISTORIC PEOPLE; STONE AGE.

FONDA is the family name of three prominent American motion-picture and stage actors, Henry and his two children, Jane and Peter.

Henry Fonda (1905-   ) became noted for his roles as the strong, silent type of hero. He first won fame for his stage performance in *The Farmer Takes a Wife* (1934). He made his film debut in 1935 in the movie version of the play. Fonda's other movies include *The Grapes of Wrath* (1940), *The Ox-Bow Incident* (1943), *My Darling Clementine* (1946), *Twelve Angry Men* (1957), and *Madigan* (1968). He made his most famous stage appearance in *Mr. Roberts* (1948) and in 1955 repeated his starring role in the film version. Henry Jaynes Fonda was born in Grand Island, Nebr. He appeared in more than 60 movies.

Jane Fonda (1937-   ) is known both as a comedienne and a dramatic actress. She won an Academy Award for her acting in *Klute* (1971). Jane Fonda made her Broadway debut in 1960 and her film debut in *Tall Story* (1960). Her later movies include *Sunday in New York* (1964), *Cat Ballou* (1965), *Any Wednesday* (1966), *Barefoot in the Park* (1967), and *They Shoot Horses, Don't They?* (1969). She was born in New York City.

Peter Fonda (1939-   ) is noted for his roles as a rebellious youth. He gained fame for his performance in such movies as *The Wild Angels* (1966) and *Easy Rider* (1969). He was born in New York City and made his stage debut in 1961. He played his first film role in *Tammy and the Doctor* (1963).　　HARVEY R. DENEROFF

FONSECA, MANOEL DEODORO DA. See BRAZIL (The Republic).

FONT. See TYPE (introduction).

FONT, *fahnt,* is a basin used to hold water for baptism. The term *font* comes from the Latin *fons,* meaning *spring.* Fonts are used in most churches that do not practice baptism by *immersion* (submerging a person in water). Most fonts are made of stone. Medieval fonts usually were placed near the main door of the church. They symbolized entrance into the church community. They usually had eight sides, which stood for a new beginning of life.　　ALAN GOWANS

FONTAINEBLEAU, *FAWN TEN BLOH* (pop. 16,778), is a town in northern France about 35 miles (56 kilometers) southeast of Paris (see FRANCE [political map]). It is famous for the magnificent palace which stands just outside the town in a parklike clearing of the Forest of Fontainebleau. The palace was a summer residence for many French kings, and the scene of Napoleon's abdication in 1814. In the 1920's, John D. Rockefeller, Jr., gave France $2,850,000 to restore Fontainebleau, Reims Cathedral, and Versailles.　　ROBERT E. DICKINSON

FONTANA DAM is one of the largest dams in the United States. It is on the Little Tennessee River in western North Carolina. It is part of the Tennessee Valley Authority (see TENNESSEE VALLEY AUTHORITY).

FONTANNE, *fawn TAHN,* **LYNN** (1887?-   ), an English actress, won fame as a costar with her husband, Alfred Lunt (see LUNT, ALFRED). Her beauty and ability helped bring popularity to this famous acting team.

She first acted in America in 1910, and won fame in 1921 as the star of *Dulcy.* She married Lunt in 1922. They acted in plays ranging from such comedies as *Arms and the Man, Reunion in Vienna, Design for Living,* and *The Pirate,* to such serious plays as *Elizabeth the Queen, The Sea Gull, There Shall Be No Night,* and *The Visit.*

Fontanne was born in Essex, England, and studied dramatics with the English actress Ellen Terry. She made her first appearance in London in the Christmas pantomime *Cinderella* in 1905.　　MARY VIRGINIA HEINLEIN

FONTEYN, *fahn TAYN,* **DAME MARGOT** (1919-   ), is generally considered England's leading ballerina and one of the first English dancers to achieve an international reputation. Critics praised her delicate and graceful style and her subtle characterizations.

Dame Margot Fonteyn was born Margaret Hookham in Reigate. Her career has been associated with the Sadler's Wells (later Royal) Ballet since her professional debut in 1934. Royal Ballet director Sir Frederick Ashton created most of his major ballets for her, including *Cinderella, Daphnis and Chloe,* and *Ondine.* Dame Margot is also known for her interpretations of such classics as *Giselle, Sleeping Beauty,* and *Swan Lake.* In 1956, she was made a Dame of the Order of the British Empire. Rudolf Nureyev became her partner in 1962 (see NUREYEV, RUDOLF).　　SELMA JEANNE COHEN

See also BALLET (picture: *Swan Lake*).

Dame Margot Fonteyn and Rudolf Nureyev became dance partners in 1962. They performed in such ballets as *Swan Lake.*

Fred Fehl

FOO-FIGHTER. See UNIDENTIFIED FLYING OBJECT.

FOOCHOW (pop. 900,000), is the capital of Fukien Province in China. The city lies on the Min River, about 30 miles (48 kilometers) from the river's mouth. For location, see CHINA (political map).

Foochow was once a center of tea and camphor trade. In 1842, the city became one of five "treaty ports" in which Great Britain gained special trading rights (see CHINA [The "Unequal Treaties"]). Foochow lost importance as a trading center in the late 1800's. Japanese troops occupied the city several times during World War II (1939-1945). Today, Foochow produces industrial chemicals. Chinese Communist forces use it as a defense center against the nearby Nationalist Chinese island of Matsu.　　RICHARD H. SOLOMON

Food

FOOD is one of our most important daily needs. It gives us energy to work and to play. It makes us grow, and keeps our bodies strong and healthy. Without food, we die. All living things—plants, animals, and man—need food to live and grow. But only plants make their own food. They also provide food for animals and man.

All foods that we eat come from plants and animals. But all people do not eat the same foods. Some people in Central Asia live mostly on milk and milk products. Millions of persons in the Orient eat little else but rice. Eskimos live mostly on meat and fish. But the San Blas Indians of Panama eat mostly fruits and vegetables. Some peoples eat foods that others would not eat. Certain groups in Iran, for example, enjoy sheep's eyes. Some persons in the Far East make a flour of dried, powdered grasshoppers. Other peoples eat such foods as broiled octopus, duck tongues, fish bladders, fried butterfly cocoons, python soup, bird's-nest soup, rooster combs, and shark fins. The kinds of food that people eat depend largely on what plants they can grow and what animals they can raise. It also depends on what foods they can buy from other regions or countries. Customs and religion also influence what people eat.

Food plays an important part in the development of nations. In countries where food is scarce, people have to spend most of their time getting enough to eat. This usually slows down progress, because men have little time to devote to science, industry, government, and art. In nations where food is plentiful and easy to get, men have more time to spend in activities that lead to progress, human betterment, and enjoyment of leisure. The problem of providing good food for everybody has not yet been solved. Many wars have been fought for the control of rich food-producing lands. But it is no longer necessary to go to war for food. Nations are beginning to put scientific knowledge to work for a solution of their food problems. They work together in the Food and Agriculture Organization of the United Nations (FAO) to help hungry nations produce more food (see FOOD AND AGRICULTURE ORGANIZATION).

Kinds of Food

No ancient king had all the kinds of food that a person can buy on a trip to a neighborhood supermarket today. Shoppers can fill their market baskets with enough food to feed a family for a week or more.

At the meat counter, shoppers can find the right size roast for Sunday dinner. They can also buy other cuts of beef, pork, lamb, veal, and poultry, or sea foods for the rest of the week.

At the produce counter, shoppers can choose from a wide variety of fresh fruits and vegetables both in and out of season. These foods may include pineapples from Hawaii, bananas from the West Indies, potatoes from Idaho and Maine, and grapefruit and oranges from California and Florida. If they choose, shoppers can buy canned or frozen fruits and vegetables. The frozen-food counter also provides packaged frozen dinners, soups, fruit juices, and oven-ready baked goods for quick, easy preparation. At the dairy counter, shoppers

Cereals and Bread—2 to 7 pounds (0.9 to 3.2 kilograms)

Milk—5 to 6 quarts (4.7 to 5.7 liters)

Meat—2½ to 4½ pounds (1.1 to 2 kilograms)

Citrus Fruit—2½ to 5 pounds (1.1 to 2.3 kilograms)

Potatoes—2 to 5 pounds (0.9 to 2.3 kilograms)

Leafy Green and Yellow Vegetables— 3½ to 4 pounds (1.6 to 1.8 kilograms)

Other Fruits and Vegetables—3 to 6 pounds (1.4 to 2.7 kilograms)

Eggs—6 to 7 eggs

Dried Beans, Peas, and Nuts—2 to 4 ounces (57 to 110 grams)

Weekly Food Requirements vary according to age, sex, and kind of work a person does. Nutrition experts agree that the average adult should eat the amounts and kinds of food shown above.

may load their market baskets with milk, butter, eggs, margarine, and many kinds of tasty cheeses.

They may also choose from the store's shelves such staple products as flour, spaghetti, bread, coffee, and cocoa. Ready-made cakes, pies, and ice cream make tempting desserts.

The supermarket has hundreds of other items, too. But all the food in the supermarket has one thing in common. It comes from plants or animals.

Food from Plants makes up from 70 to 85 per cent of the people's diets in Brazil, China, Greece, India, Italy, Japan, Mexico, and many African countries. Even in the United States, Canada, Great Britain, and other countries where the people eat much meat, plant foods provide about 60 per cent of the diet.

Grain is the seed of such plants as wheat, rice, rye, and

oats. It is the largest single food item used throughout the world. Almost everyone in the world eats some kind of bread, including English *graham bread*, Scottish *bannocks*, Finnish *tunnbröd*, German *pumpernickel*, Latin-American *arepas*, and Swedish *hardtack*. But all bread—sweet or sour, brown or white, heavy or light—is made from flour, and all flour comes from grain. We often eat cooked rice, oats, corn, and other grain. Food processors make products such as macaroni, spaghetti, and breakfast cereals from grain. Distillers and brewers use grain to make such beverages as whiskey and beer.

Vegetables and Fruits come from several parts of plants. We eat the roots of beets, carrots, and sweet potatoes, and the leaves of cabbage, lettuce, and spinach. Other popular foods include the stems of asparagus, the stalks of celery, the bulbs of onions, and the flowers of cauli-

flower and broccoli. The common white potato comes from the part of the potato plant, called the *tuber*, that grows underground (see TUBER).

Many plants produce fruits that we eat. Some of these fruits, such as cucumbers, peppers, and tomatoes, we call vegetables or vegetable fruits. Others, such as apples, berries, figs, lemons, olives, and oranges, we call simply fruits. Certain trees produce dry fruits that we call nuts. Other foods from plants include spices, sugar, cocoa, coffee, tea, and vegetable oils.

Food from Animals. Between 30 and 40 per cent of the food eaten in Argentina, Australia, Europe, and the United States comes from domestic animals. But in some countries, such as Sri Lanka, India, and South Africa, animal foods may make up less than 20 per cent of the people's diet. The chief foods from animals include butter, cheese, eggs, fish, meat, milk, and poultry.

Most of the meat we eat comes from the flesh of domestic animals, chiefly cattle, hogs, sheep, and poultry. Many persons also eat the hearts, kidneys, livers, tongues, certain glands, and other internal organs of some animals. Fish come from lakes, streams, and oceans. We enjoy other seafoods, including clams, lobsters, crabs, oysters, scallops, and shrimp. Chicken, duck, goose, and turkey are the common poultry meats.

Hogs provide bacon, ham, pork, and sausage. Sheep give us lamb and mutton, and cattle supply beef and veal. In some countries, people may eat meat from other domestic animals. For example, some French people eat horsemeat, and some Greeks and Japanese enjoy goat meat. Hunters in almost all countries seek wild animals for food, as well as for sport. Favorite game meats in the United States include deer, opossum, rabbit, raccoon, squirrel, bear, and such wild fowl as duck, grouse, partridge, pheasant, and quail. In other countries, people may hunt baboons, caribou, elk, elephants, gazelles, monkeys, and snakes for meat. They may also eat ants, grasshoppers, locusts, and other insects.

Animals give us other foods besides meat. We eat animal fats that have been made into lard and other shortenings. Eskimos eat much *blubber*, or fat, from seals, walruses, and whales. Eggs from chickens and ducks are an important food almost everywhere. Some persons eat the eggs of such land and sea birds as emus, gulls, ostriches, plovers, and penguins. In many countries, people enjoy the eggs of alligators, crocodiles, iguanas, turtles, and other reptiles. Caviar, an expensive delicacy, is the *roe* (eggs) of sturgeon and some other large fish.

Milk and milk products are other important foods from animals. In the United States, Canada, and some other countries, cows provide most of the milk. But in southern Europe and the Middle East, the goat is "the poor man's cow." People in India drink buffalo milk and Laplanders enjoy reindeer milk. The yak furnishes milk in Tibet, and Arab herdsmen milk camels. Such dairy foods as butter, buttermilk, cheese, and ice cream come from milk.

How Our Bodies Use Food

Food gives us energy to do work. It provides materials to grow and repair body tissues, and chemicals to regu-late the organs and systems of the body. All foods contain *nutrients*, or chemical building blocks. There are two kinds of nutrients: (1) organic and (2) inorganic. *Organic* nutrients include carbohydrates, fats, proteins, and vitamins. Water and minerals are *inorganic* nutrients.

If we do not eat enough of these necessary nutrients, we become weak, lose weight, and fail to grow properly. We may develop such conditions as anemia, rickets, poor teeth, lack of appetite, and night blindness. If we eat too much, we become fat and the extra weight strains our hearts.

Food restores used-up energy, rebuilds tissue cells that constantly need repair, and develops bones, muscles, and teeth. It keeps the body healthy, strong, and vigorous. It also protects the body against disease. Without food, a strong man can live only seven or eight weeks. Food nutrients must be *digested*, or broken down to a few simple chemicals, before they can be used in the body. For a description of this process, see DIGESTION.

Food as Fuel. When digested food reaches the cells of the body, it is *oxidized*, or slowly burned. This oxidation process releases energy that our bodies use when we eat, dress, run, skate, swim, walk, write, and even breathe and think. Our glands, hearts, muscles, and nerves use energy for their specialized work. Oxidation also produces heat that keeps our body cells at a temperature of about 98.6° F. (37° C). Without this heat, no cell can perform its work or even stay alive. See METABOLISM.

Carbohydrates serve as our chief fuel foods, but *fats* are a more concentrated source. For example, fat furnishes $2\frac{1}{4}$ times as much energy as an equal weight of carbohydrates. We store extra carbohydrates and fats as fatty tissue that serves as a reserve energy source.

We get carbohydrates from such starchy foods as bread, macaroni, potatoes, and rice, as well as from sweet foods such as cake, candy, chocolate, and cookies. Foods high in fats include bacon, butter, cream, margarine, ice cream, and salad dressings. See CARBOHYDRATE; FAT.

Building and Repairing. We need food to build new tissues. Food also repairs worn-out tissues and the damage from infections, wounds, and broken bones. The body uses foods that contain nitrogen for building and repairing. Nitrogen is found only in the amino acids

Don Faulkner, Courtesy Omar Khayyam's

Shish Kebab is an Armenian dish that is made of pieces of lamb, tomatoes, peppers, and onions. The pieces of food are cooked together on a skewer. Shish kebab has become a favorite meal of many people who live in the United States, Canada, and other countries.

Courtesy of *Better Homes and Gardens* Magazine

Pizza Is an International Favorite which originated in Italy. There are many kinds of pizza, but basically, they all consist of a cheese and tomato mix baked on a pie crust. Meat balls, anchovies, onions, sausage, and other ingredients may be added for variety.

Werner Bischof, Magnum

Families in India eat sitting on the floor. Hindus eat only with the right hand and drink only with the left hand.

George Rodger, Magnum

A Coffee Break is enjoyed by Jordanian soldiers. Arabs may boil and cool coffee 7 or 8 times before drinking it.

Constance Stuart, Black Star

In Southeast Africa, women cook meals in kettles which they place over open fires in the courtyard.

Black Star

A Wedding Feast in Lapland, inside the Arctic Circle in Norway, is celebrated by guests in festival costumes.

A Cooked Caterpillar makes a tasty appetizer for a hungry guest at a wedding party in New Guinea.

Photo-Representatives

Werner Bischof, Magnum

The Japanese sit on cushions to eat their meals. They serve their food on low tables and eat with chopsticks.

291

that make up protein nutrients (see AMINO ACID). Protein-rich foods include eggs, fish, legumes, meats, milk, nuts, and poultry. But not all these foods are equally effective for building and repairing tissue. Animal proteins contain more of the amino acids that the body uses for building than plant proteins do. A balanced diet should include at least one-third animal proteins. Our bodies do not store extra proteins. If we eat more proteins than we need for building and repair, we burn them as fuel. See PROTEIN.

Regulation of Body Processes is carried on chiefly by the vitamins and minerals that we get from foods. We need only small amounts of vitamins, but they are just as important for good health as the fuel and repair foods. We get many vitamins and minerals from berries, citrus fruits, eggs, fish, lean meat, liver, milk, salad greens, sea foods, green and yellow vegetables, and whole-grain breads and cereals.

Vitamins serve as "protective regulators." For example, vitamin A helps us to see, especially at night. It builds the body's resistance to infection, and helps keep our skins healthy. The B vitamins increase appetite, build firm muscles, promote growth, and keep the nervous system healthy. Vitamin C keeps our gums and blood vessels healthy, and helps vitamin D build strong teeth and bones. Vitamin K helps our blood to clot.

INTERESTING FACTS ABOUT FOODS

Chinese Egg Rolls and won ton, French crepes suzette, German blintzes, Italian ravioli, Mexican tacos, and Russian piroshki are made of thin dough wrapped around cheese, jam, meat, potatoes, or vegetables.

Headcheese is not really cheese at all, but a jellied meat made from the fleshy parts of a pig's or sheep's head.

Oyster of a Chicken is the dark-meat portion in the bone of the lower back. It is named for its oysterlike shape.

Preserved Eggs, a delicacy in China, take about six months to make and may be stored for about a year. The curing method makes the eggs taste like cheese.

Sandwiches were named for the Earl of Sandwich, an English nobleman of the early 1700's. While playing cards, he ordered a servant to bring him two slices of bread with a piece of roast meat between them.

Tea Leaves are pickled, flavored with garlic and oil, and served as a salad in Burma.

Minerals take part in many body processes. Iron and copper build red blood cells. Calcium and phosphorus help us grow strong bones and healthy teeth. The body needs iodine so that body cells can burn fuel to supply heat and energy. Other minerals that the body uses include compounds of chlorine, cobalt, fluorine, magnesium, manganese, sodium, tin, and zinc.

Food and Diet. Perhaps the easiest way to have a balanced diet is to eat as many different kinds of food as possible. The "Basic Seven" foods recommended by the U.S. Department of Agriculture provide a useful guide for healthy diets. For a description of these foods, see NUTRITION.

Foods of Many Lands

The kinds of foods that people eat vary from country to country. They differ even from region to region within each country. In western Africa, a family's dinner might include cassava or taro root, ants cooked in fat, or small birds roasted in hot coals. In China, the main meal usually consists of rice or millet with soy sauce, soybean cheese, bean sprouts, and a little pork or salted fish. A Latin American might eat baked plantains (a kind of banana), dried peppers, and dried beef. Eskimos dine on raw salmon or seal. African Pygmies get their meats from monkeys, baboons, wild boars, and snakes.

People may cook food over open fires, on heated stones, or in gas or electric ovens. The foods people eat depend on where they live, how much money they have, their religion, their customs, and their beliefs about food.

Geography and Food. The chief foods eaten in any country depend largely on what grows best in its climate and soil. People in tropical areas tend to eat fruits and vegetables, which grow easily in these regions. In temperate areas, people eat more animal foods, because livestock thrives better in cooler regions. However, geography no longer affects what people eat as much as it once did. The development of modern methods of food preservation, and faster transportation have allowed nations to share their food. For example, the people of many lands use sugar from Cuba, coffee from Brazil, and sardines from Norway.

WORLD BOOK photo

Holiday Dinners are served in many U.S. homes on Thanksgiving and other special days. At these meals, families eat traditional foods, such as roast turkey, that are associated with the holidays.

Victor De Palma, Black Star

Spaghetti, an Italian food, is a favorite dish throughout the world. Italians eat it with sauces—or plain as an appetizer.

Many countries and regions specialize in growing certain types of food. The Great Plains of North America and the Ukraine region of Russia produce most of the world's wheat, and are sometimes called the world's "breadbaskets." Many people call China the "rice bowl," and Brazil, the world's "coffeepot." For a description of foods produced in various areas, see AGRICULTURE (Agriculture Around the World), and the Agriculture sections of the continent and country articles.

Economy and Food. The kinds of foods a nation eats depend not only on what it produces, but also on what it can afford to buy from other countries. Buying power depends on a nation's wealth and the kind of economy

it has. For example, people in the underdeveloped countries of Asia eat mostly the foods that grow where they live. They cannot afford to buy foods from other areas. But people in a country such as Canada can buy food from all parts of the world. Great Britain, Sweden, Switzerland, and other industrial countries trade their products for foods produced by agricultural countries. Great Britain grows less than half the food its people need. But it can afford to import about three-fourths of its meat, and any plant food that it lacks. People in highly developed industrial nations generally have the most varied diets, because they have money to buy different kinds of food. They eat the greatest amount of animal foods. These foods are the most expensive kind to produce.

Religion and Food have long been closely connected. The ancient Greeks and Romans worshiped gods and goddesses who ruled over agriculture and hunting. The word *cereal* comes from Ceres, the Roman goddess of fruits and grains. The Bible tells of the early use of food as religious offerings.

Many religions do not permit their followers to eat certain foods. Buddhists are not allowed to eat any meat. Muslims may eat no pork. Hindus consider the cow sacred, and eat no beef. Some Hindus eat no animal foods except milk and dairy products, because their belief forbids them to kill animals. Orthodox Jews avoid certain kinds of foods, including pork, meat from an animal's hindquarters, shellfish such as shrimp and lobsters, and scaleless fish such as catfish. Roman Catholics do not eat meat on certain days during Lent.

Customs influence the ways people eat. Most Americans and Europeans eat from individual plates, using knives, forks, and spoons. Arabs use only their right hands to spoon foods from a central bowl. Chinese and Japanese use chopsticks to pick up food from a small bowl held close to the mouth. Many Orientals sit on the floor and eat from low tables.

Henri Cartier-Bresson, Magnum

Iranian Bread, baked in thin sheets, is a main food in Iran. Other Iranian favorites include cheese, lamb, and rice.

David Seymour, Magnum

A French Chef prepares a flaming specialty in a Paris restaurant. French sauces and recipes are copied throughout the world.

Authenticated News Int.

Suzanne Szasz

Many German Restaurants feature fish on a stick during an Oktoberfest celebration.

American Families enjoy broiling hamburgers and other meat over charcoal at backyard barbecues. Outdoor meals also may include salads and baked potatoes.

Most persons eat at least three meals a day—breakfast, lunch, and dinner. The English and some other Europeans eat a fourth meal, supper, late at night. Meals vary in different countries. Breakfast in the United States, for example, may include fruit or fruit juice, coffee, toast, and a choice of cereal or bacon and eggs. Many persons like pancakes or meat and potatoes for breakfast. In country areas, families usually have their big meal at noon and a lighter meal in the evening. Many families enjoy outdoor meals such as picnics, corn roasts, clambakes, and back-yard barbecues.

Continental Europeans sometimes have an early breakfast of sweet rolls and coffee or hot chocolate, and eat a second breakfast later in the morning. English breakfasts often include *kippers* (salted, smoked herring), or such meat as kidneys or sausage; cooked porridge; toast and marmalade; fresh or stewed fruit; and tea. Another English tradition, tea, or "tiffin," provides an extra meal served in the late afternoon. Its simplest menu usually includes tea and special tea cakes such as crumpets and scones, or biscuits with jam.

Special Foods. Some people restrict their diet to a limited number of foods with high nutritional value. They believe that eating these foods—and avoiding certain others—will result in improved health. For example, they eat whole wheat bread because many nutrients in wheat are lost when it is milled to make flour for white bread. They eat raw vegetables because they believe that cooking vegetables results in the loss of many vitamins and minerals. They sprinkle wheat germ

on many foods for increased vitamins and eat low-fat yogurt as a source of calcium, protein, and riboflavin. They avoid butter, eggs, fatty meats, and other foods that contain much *cholesterol*, a fatty substance that makes up a part of all animal tissue. Many physicians believe that too much cholesterol in the blood can cause certain types of heart disease.

Other special foods include *natural foods* and *organic foods*. Natural foods have no *additives*. Additives are chemicals that manufacturers add to foods to improve their color, flavor, nutritional value, or texture, or to help keep them from spoiling. People who prefer natural foods believe that many additives may have harmful effects on the body. Organic foods include fruits and vegetables grown without the application of pesticides or chemical fertilizers and processed without additives. People who restrict their diet to organic foods believe that many foods from plants treated with pesticides or chemical fertilizers contain traces of these chemicals which may endanger human health. Natural foods and organic foods are sometimes called *health foods*. But the term *health foods* also applies to other foods. For example, vegetarianism is usually considered a health food diet.

Cooking of the same foods varies from country to country. In some countries, for example, people like light, fluffy bread. Compact, heavy loaves are preferred in other lands. Crusts may be hard and crunchy, or thin and delicate. Loaves may be long and thin, big and round, or high and rectangular. Some persons like strong, clear coffee served black or with cream and sugar. But many people in the Middle East prefer thick, sweet Turkish coffee. The British brew strong, dark tea, and usually flavor it with milk and sugar. Orientals prepare clear, light-colored tea and drink it plain.

The foods of most countries have certain special characteristics. Oriental dishes often contain mixtures of many vegetables, nuts, seeds, seasonings, and spices, with small amounts of meat. The Chinese use soy sauce as we use catchup, and people in India season many dishes with curry powder. Cooks in Greece, Italy, and Turkey use much olive oil. French cooks prefer sauces that contain many kinds of herbs, cheeses, and wines. The British use little seasoning except salt and pepper. German cooking favors heavy foods, especially those with a sweet-sour taste. Mexican, Portuguese, and Spanish cooking is often highly seasoned with hot pepper.

Favorite National Foods. Most nations have favorite dishes, many of which have spread to other lands. Many large cities have restaurants that specialize in the favorite dishes of China, France, Italy, Germany, and other countries. Some cooks prepare such dishes as Armenian *shish kebab* (cubed lamb broiled on a skewer); German *wiener schnitzel* (thinly sliced veal fried in a batter of eggs and bread crumbs and served with lemon, anchovies, chopped egg, parsley, and gravy); or Russian *beef Stroganoff* (lean beef cooked in cubes and served with a sauce of mushrooms and sour cream). Grocery stores offer such frozen foods as Italian *pizza pies*, Chinese *egg rolls*, and such canned foods as Mexican *tacos*, Italian *spaghetti* and *ravioli*, and English *plum pudding*.

The Japanese cook *sukiyaki* (strips of meat and vegetables) at the dining table. They also enjoy *tempura* (deep-fried food). Many Russian dishes such as *borscht* (beet or cabbage soup) include *smetana* (sour cream). The English like meat pies, especially *steak and kidney pie*. They usually serve *Yorkshire pudding* (a batter pudding baked in beef drippings) with roast beef. Scottish *haggis* is a boiled pudding made from a sheep's or calf's heart, liver, and lungs, minced with onions, suet, and oatmeal (see HAGGIS). *Huachinango* soup, made from fish, is a favorite in Mexico, and the Danes enjoy *kraasesuppe* (giblet soup with vegetables). A well-known German dish is *hasenpfeffer* (rabbit soaked in vinegar, onions, and spices, and browned in butter). Scandinavians serve appetizers, called *smörgåsbord* in Sweden, and *smørrebrød* in Denmark.

Regional food favorites in the United States include Boston baked beans, New England clam chowder, and Philadelphia scrapple. Kansans enjoy chicken-fried steak and Louisianians serve chicken creole. The *pasty*, a popular food in the Upper Peninsula of Michigan, is dough wrapped around meat and vegetables. Other popular favorites include southern-fried chicken and smoked Virginia ham.

For a description of other national food favorites, see the Food sections of the country articles, such as ARGENTINA (Food).

The Food Industry

The food industry is perhaps the largest and most important in the world. It provides jobs for millions of

Plain and Fancy Cooking can both be an adventure. At a cookout, *left*, campers cook fish they have caught. A fine restaurant, *right*, offers a variety of specially prepared dishes.

persons. In the United States, food growing employs more than 3½ million farm workers, and the processing of food provides jobs for more than 1½ million.

Production. Until the late 1800's, most farmers in the United States produced food chiefly for their own families. They sold or traded any leftover food. A farmer did most of the work by hand, using such animals as horses and oxen to pull plows and other simple farm tools. Modern farm machinery helps farmers raise crops on vast farms that sometimes cover thousands of acres or hectares. In many places, farmers specialize in producing certain kinds of plants, such as fruits, vegetables, or grains. Others operate dairy farms, hog farms, and cattle and sheep ranches, or raise poultry for meat and eggs. See AGRICULTURE (Kinds of Agriculture).

Fish are a vast unplanted food "crop" that grows in the waters of the world. Commercial fishing areas in the United States extend along the entire Atlantic and Pacific coasts, the Gulf of Mexico, and far out to sea. Large quantities of fish are also caught in the Great Lakes. See FISHING INDUSTRY.

Processing. Most foods must undergo some kind of processing before they reach the table. Millers grind wheat, rye, and other grains into flour and cereal foods.

Dairy farmers send milk to creameries and dairy plants for pasteurization and bottling. These plants also produce butter, cream, cheese, buttermilk, canned milk, powdered milk, skimmed milk, and other milk products. Ranchers ship cattle by railroad and truck to stockyards and meat-packing plants in Kansas City, Omaha, Los Angeles, and other cities. Meat-packing plants slaughter animals. Then they process, grade, and pack the meat for shipment to market. Most beef is shipped fresh, but some is salted, dried, or *corned* (pickled or preserved with strong salt water). Bacon and ham are smoked and cured.

Truck farmers and fruit growers pick, clean, and sort their crops. They sell some vegetables and fruits directly to consumers. They sell the rest to companies that process, can, freeze, dry, or chemically preserve fruits and vegetables. See CANNING; FOOD, FROZEN; FOOD PRESERVATION.

Some large fishing vessels carry their own processing equipment. But most fishermen carry their catches into port for processing. Workers wash and clean part of the catch before sending it to market as fresh fish. Sometimes they make "fillets" of the fleshy sides by removing heads, tails, fins, and bones. Most of the catch goes to

25 LEADING FOOD-PROCESSING COMPANIES IN THE UNITED STATES

Company	Sales*	Assets	Employees	Founded	Headquarters
1. Esmark†	$5,300,566,000	$1,757,480,000	47,000	1885	Chicago, Ill.
2. Kraft	4,976,643,000	1,821,854,000	46,790	1923	Glenview, Ill.
3. Beatrice Foods	4,690,569,000	1,844,434,000	67,000	1924	Chicago, Ill.
4. General Foods	3,978,294,000	2,012,932,000	47,000	1929	White Plains, N.Y.
5. Ralston Purina	3,393,800,000	1,556,300,000	59,000	1894	St. Louis, Mo.
6. Borden	3,381,075,000	1,808,479,000	40,400	1899	New York, N.Y.
7. Coca-Cola	3,032,829,000	1,903,065,000	32,952	1886	Atlanta, Ga.
8. PepsiCo	2,727,455,000	1,541,650,000	54,000	1919	Purchase, N.Y.
9. Consolidated Foods	2,726,458,000	1,146,544,000	76,600	1941	Chicago, Ill.
10. CPC International	2,695,800,000	1,459,300,000	42,500	1906	Englewood Cliffs, N.J.
11. Armour	2,653,013,000	739,130,000	17,500	1867	Phoenix, Ariz.
12. General Mills	2,644,952,000	1,328,196,000	51,778	1928	Minneapolis, Minn.
13. United Brands	2,276,559,000	1,085,268,000	48,300	1899	Boston, Mass.
14. Carnation	2,166,957,000	1,079,174,000	22,227	1920	Los Angeles, Calif.
15. Iowa Beef Processors	2,077,158,000	253,437,000	7,400	1960	Dakota City, Neb.
16. Nabisco	2,027,286,000	1,058,530,000	48,000	1898	East Hanover, N.J.
17. Wilson Foods	1,919,433,000	265,741,000	12,000	1853	Oklahoma City, Okla.
18. H. J. Heinz	1,882,359,000	1,168,183,000	32,625	1900	Pittsburgh, Pa.
19. Central Soya	1,836,830,000	431,844,000	9,233	1934	Fort Wayne, Ind.
20. Standard Brands	1,809,964,000	991,868,000	21,200	1929	New York, N.Y.
21. Norton Simon	1,683,793,000	1,418,947,000	26,000	1968	New York, N.Y.
22. Campbell Soup	1,634,762,000	924,328,000	33,445	1869	Camden, N.J.
23. Archer-Daniels-Midland	1,620,777,000	684,060,000	4,739	1902	Decatur, Ill.
24. Quaker Oats	1,473,052,000	854,947,000	23,900	1891	Chicago, Ill.
25. Anheuser-Busch	1,441,146,000	1,268,085,000	13,292	1852	St. Louis, Mo.

*May include sales of nonfood products.   †Formerly Swift & Company.
Sources: "The Fortune Directory," *Fortune*, May 1977, © 1977 Time Inc.; Armour and Company; Wilson Foods Corporation.

10 LEADING FOOD-STORE CHAINS IN THE UNITED STATES

Company	Sales*	Assets	Stores	Founded	Headquarters
1. Safeway Stores	$10,442,531,000	$1,708,946,000	2,451	1902	Oakland, Calif.
2. Great Atlantic & Pacific Tea	6,537,897,000	989,277,000	1,957	1859	Montvale, N.J.
3. Kroger	6,091,109,000	1,233,823,000	1,220	1902	Cincinnati, Ohio
4. Lucky Stores	3,483,174,000	669,862,000	222	1931	Dublin, Calif.
5. Winn-Dixie Stores	3,265,916,000	509,617,000	1,012	1928	Jacksonville, Fla.
6. American Stores	3,207,248,000	513,705,000	787	1917	Wilmington, Del.
7. Jewel Companies	2,981,429,000	811,668,000	604	1899	Chicago, Ill.
8. Food Fair Stores	2,507,040,000	434,342,000	470	1935	Philadelphia, Pa.
9. Southland	2,115,768,000	626,460,000	5,579	1934	Dallas, Tex.
10. Supermarkets General	1,612,692,000	338,405,000	102	1966	Woodbridge, N.J.

*May include nonsupermarket sales.
Sources: "The Fortune Directory," *Fortune*, July 1977, © 1977 Time Inc.; *Moody's Industrial Manual*, 1976.

factories that clean and process fish into frozen, canned, salted, dried, and smoked products. Other seafoods, such as clams and oysters, must have their shells removed before processing. Many fish companies prepare breaded fish and seafoods. Some of these are precooked and quick-frozen.

Transportation of food varies in different parts of the world. In some countries, people simply load food on the backs of animals, haul it in carts, or even carry it themselves. With such slow transportation methods, food can be moved only short distances, usually to local markets.

The commercial transportation of food forms a major part of the food industry. Refrigerated railroad cars and trucks transport fresh and frozen meat, fruits, and vegetables. Foods for export travel in refrigerated ships. Airplanes carry some expensive foods, such as live lobsters. Most food is perishable, and must be handled and transported with great speed.

Marketing. Some farmers sell certain products, such as fresh fruits, vegetables, and eggs, by *direct sale*. They may operate roadside stands at their farms, make regular deliveries to homes, or sell products to a country store. Many farmers take their products to *farmers' markets* in nearby cities. There, individual shoppers and food dealers buy what they need.

Wholesale marketing involves the sale of large quantities of food. Some farmers sell all their food to processing companies. Country shippers, including cooperative marketing associations, may gather foods such as eggs or milk from a group of farmers. They often ship carloads or truckloads of food to wholesalers at *terminal markets* in cities. See COOPERATIVE (Marketing Cooperatives); DISTRIBUTION.

Wholesale meat dealers receive carloads of livestock at the stockyards. Fish wholesalers often buy fish by the ton or boatload at the piers. Wholesalers may auction food to the highest bidder, or sell it to large retailers or independent dealers called *jobbers*. Jobbers sell food to

At a General Store of the 1800's, shoppers bought foods from crates and barrels rather than in small packages as they do today.

small retail stores, hotels, and restaurants, or at smaller public markets.

Retailers sell foods to the consumer. They usually sell small quantities, but keep large stocks of food on hand. A private store owner may sell only a single line of food, such as meats, fruits, or vegetables. Many roadside markets specialize in fresh fruits and vegetables. Bakeries, dairy stores, and delicatessens serve as specialty shops. Some large bakery and dairy companies deliver their products to homes, and also sell some products to food stores.

The neighborhood grocer buys staples from wholesalers; milk, butter, and cream from dairies; and bread from bakeries. He must compete with *supermarkets*, or

Foods Today are plentiful and convenient to buy. A self-service supermarket, *left,* sells fresh and frozen foods, canned and prepared goods, and paper products. Vending machines, *right,* in many public places serve beverages and such foods as sandwiches and soups automatically.

large self-service food stores. Some supermarket chains maintain their own warehouses and processing plants. Some even have farms to grow the food they process. Supermarkets often sell not only food but also such nonfood products as hardware, drugs, cosmetics, phonograph records, books, magazines, and perhaps even some clothing items. See SUPERMARKET.

The consumer can buy meals in many places, including restaurants, diners, cafeterias, and lunch counters. Ships, trains, and planes carry special equipment for serving meals to passengers. Vending machines in many offices and public places supply sandwiches, hot and cold drinks, fruits, desserts, and candy.

Food Controls. Federal, state, and city governments supervise the quality, cleanliness, and purity of foods. Laws protect the public's health, and prevent food companies from making false claims about the products they sell.

State and federal governments have pure-food laws, and set up grading and labeling standards for foods such as fresh fruits and vegetables, eggs, butter, cheese, and canned goods. They require that labels carry accurate information about the quality and weight of food and any substances added to it. They prohibit the use of additives such as food preservatives, seasonings and flavorings, and artificial colorings that may be harmful when eaten. Federal and state governments also have laws concerning weights, measures, and container volumes that protect purchasers from being cheated. Many states, cities, and towns have agencies that check the accuracy of scales and other devices that merchants use to weigh and measure foods. State and federal inspectors examine many foods such as butter, meats, and canned goods. See PURE FOOD AND DRUG LAWS.

The health departments of states and cities set up standards for milk, including minimum fat content and requirements for pasteurization and handling. In addition, they usually require medical examinations of all persons handling food, and inspect sanitary conditions in restaurants and other places that serve meals. Health departments can close places that do not meet the required standards. Some health departments conduct routine examinations of food in wholesale markets and retail stores, and inspect dairy farms, milk-shipping stations, and fishing waters.

Research. Food companies, food growers' associations, meat and canning institutes, fish institutes, and government agencies conduct research connected with the food industry. They experiment with new ways to improve the soil. They breed plants to resist disease, to withstand quick temperature changes, to give greater yields, and to bear better tasting and more nutritious fruits and vegetables. Research on animal feeds and breeding methods shows farmers how to raise cows that give richer milk, hens that lay more eggs, and animals that have more meat.

Chemists, bacteriologists, and other researchers try to increase the storage life and nutritional values of preserved foods. Home economists develop new recipes and such laborsaving foods as pastry mixes. Nutritionists and dietitians seek to improve diets. Engineers design more efficient refrigerators, freezers, stoves, farm machinery, and equipment for processing and transport-

ing foods. Marketing experts study food prices and try to improve buying and selling methods.

Food Through the Ages

Prehistoric People had little choice in what they ate. They did not grow or cook food, but ate only what they could find. Their food probably included mushrooms, nuts, roots, seeds, wild berries, caterpillars, fish, grubs, snakes, worms, and small land animals. When human beings learned to make spears and stone clubs, they began to hunt larger animals for food.

When prehistoric people learned to use fire, they could roast food. When they learned to make pots, they could also boil and stew foods. Next, people probably learned to tame animals and plant seeds. Grain has probably been used for over 20,000 years, and milk from domesticated animals for about 6,000 years. Human beings learned to grind grain into flour, and to feed animals to produce meat. Their way of life changed. People became herders and farmers, and families settled in one place instead of roaming in search of food.

Early Civilizations developed in areas where food was plentiful. The ancient Egyptians could grow three crops a year on the rich soils of the Nile River Basin, because of the warm climate. They raised beans, peas, melons, wheat, barley, grapes, and other crops. The Egyptians used cattle for such farm work as plowing, and threshing and grinding grain. They baked bread and had plenty of wild game and fish. They roasted antelopes, ducks, gazelles, geese, goats, pigeons, sheep, and storks over charcoal fires. They preserved extra food by pickling, smoking, or salting.

The Hebrews lived more simply. They ate rice, vegetables, wheat, barley, bean-flour bread, and a thick lentil soup called *pottage*. They had so much milk from domestic goats and honey from wild bees, that Palestine became known as the *Land of Milk and Honey*.

The early Greeks and Romans had figs, grapes, and olives, as well as domestic animals, seafoods, and wheat and barley for bread and porridge. They "buttered" bread with olive oil, and fermented grapes to make wine. As their populations increased, they reached into other lands for foods. They found cherries in Iran, and apricots, peaches, and spices in the Orient. The Romans took fish from Africa and Spain, grain from Egypt, and plums and dates from Syria. They raised fish in ponds and were the first to set out oyster beds. See the Family Life section in GREECE, ANCIENT; ROMAN EMPIRE.

The Middle Ages. After the Roman Empire fell in the A.D. 400's, Europe no longer traded with distant countries. Feudal lords could import no foods, and had to depend on their own resources. The people grew grain and vegetables, but had little to feed themselves or their domestic animals. Between 1000 and 1300, the Crusades took thousands of Europeans to Eastern lands, where they ate new foods and acquired new tastes. When they returned to Europe, their desire for better food helped renew trade and influenced the exploration of new lands. See FEUDALISM; MIDDLE AGES.

The New World. Christopher Columbus made his famous voyage to America while searching for a short route to India to bring back spices. He did not find spices, but he opened the pantries of Europe to such new vegetables as corn, sweet and white potatoes, squash, and tomatoes. Spanish explorers in South America brought back cassava roots and cacao beans, from which tapioca and chocolate are made. The American colonists enjoyed most of these foods. They had large quantities of fish, game, nuts, and wild fruits. Colonial farmers grew beans, corn, pumpkins, and many other vegetables. They also raised pigs, sheep, and cattle. The Indians showed them where to find salt, and how to cook wild turkeys and lobsters. The colonists also had food in winter, because they smoked hams, cured meats, and salted fish. See COLONIAL LIFE IN AMERICA (Food); PIONEER LIFE IN AMERICA (Food); WESTERN FRONTIER LIFE (Food); INDIAN, AMERICAN (Food).

Foods Today are more plentiful and more varied as a result of advances in science and technology. Farm machinery helps farmers grow more and cheaper food, and up-to-date processing methods increase the variety of foods. Scientific breeding has produced such fruits as tangerines, nectarines, and seedless grapes and grapefruit. Cornish hens and fleshy, small-boned turkeys represent the results of advances in the feeding and breeding of animals. Dehydrated, quick-frozen, and ready-to-serve foods make cooking easier.

In the future, food may be produced in new ways. Experiments with *plankton*, microscopic plants and animals from the ocean, give promise of attractive and nutritious food products. And farmers may be able to grow larger crops by *hydroponic* methods, in which they use water and chemicals rather than soil (see HYDROPONICS). SARAH R. RIEDMAN

Related Articles. See various country articles where local foods are discussed, such as MEXICO (Way of Life). Other related articles in WORLD BOOK include:

KINDS OF FOOD

Bread	Candy	Fruit	Milk	Spice
Breakfast	Cheese	Grain	Nut	Sugar
Cereal	Egg	Meat	Poultry	Vegetable

NUTRITION

Carbohydrate	Digestion	Lipid	Vitamin
Diet	Fat	Nutrition	Weight Control
Dietitian	Health	Protein	

PREPARATION AND PROCESSING

Canning	Dehydration	Food Preservation
Cold	Fishing Industry	Freeze-Drying
Storage	Food, Frozen	Meat Packing
Cooking	Food Additive	Refrigeration

SPECIAL FOOD DISHES

Barbecue	Chili Con Carne	Pemmican
Bird's-Nest Soup	Enchilada	Trepang
Caviar	Haggis	

BEVERAGES

Alcoholic Drink	Cocoa	Maguey	Soft Drink
Chocolate	Coffee	Maté	Tea

OTHER RELATED ARTICLES

Agriculture	Food and	Prehistoric
Aquaculture	Agriculture	People
Cafeteria	Organization	(Food)
Christmas (Christmas	Food and Drug	Rationing
Around the World)	Administration	Restaurant
Climate (Food and	Food Poisoning	Salt
Climate)	Green Revolution	Supermarket
Consumer Protection	Home Economics	Table Setting
Distribution	Knife, Fork,	Thanksgiving
Fast	and Spoon	Day
Flower (As Food)	Kosher	Tree

Outline

I. Kinds of Food
    A. Food from Plants
    B. Food from Animals
II. How Our Bodies Use Food
    A. Food as Fuel
    B. Building and Repairing
    C. Regulation of Body Processes
    D. Food and Diet
III. Foods of Many Lands
    A. Geography and Food
    B. Economy and Food
    C. Religion and Food
    D. Customs
    E. Special Foods
    F. Cooking
    G. Favorite National Foods
IV. The Food Industry
    A. Production
    B. Processing
    C. Transportation
    D. Marketing
    E. Food Controls
    F. Research
V. Food Through the Ages

Questions

What kinds of foods give us energy? What kinds make us grow?

What food makes up the largest item in the world's food supplies?

What different parts of plants do we use as food?

What are five unusual foods eaten in other lands?

All food comes from which two basic sources?

What areas have been called the world's "breadbaskets"?

What animal is often called "the poor man's cow"?

What religious group does not eat meat?

Why did Palestine become known as the *Land of Milk and Honey?*

What country is called the world's "coffeepot"?

Reading and Study Guide

See *Food* in the RESEARCH GUIDE/INDEX, Volume 22, for a *Reading and Study Guide.*

Books for Young Readers

BERRY, ERICK. *Eating and Cooking Around the World: Fingers Before Forks.* Day, 1963.
BUEHR, WALTER. *Food from Farm to Home.* Morrow, 1970.
CARONA, PHILIP B. *Chemistry and Cooking.* Prentice-Hall, 1975.
GRAHAM, ADA. *Great American Shopping Cart: How America Gets Its Food Today.* Simon & Schuster, 1969.
HELFMAN, ELIZABETH S. *This Hungry World.* Lothrop, 1970.
MARR, JOHN S. *The Food You Eat.* Evans, 1973.
SILVERSTEIN, ALVIN and V. B. *The Chemicals We Eat and Drink.* Follett, 1973.
TANNENBAUM, BEULAH, and STILLMAN, MYRA. *Feeding the City.* McGraw, 1971.
WISE, WILLIAM. *Fresh, Canned, and Frozen: Food from Past to Future.* Parents' Magazine Press, 1971.

Books for Older Readers

ARNOLD, PAULINE, and WHITE, PERCIVAL. *Food Facts for Young People.* Holiday, 1968.
BARRONS, KEITH C. *The Food in Your Future: Steps to Abundance.* Van Nostrand, 1975.
HALACY, DANIEL S. *Feast and Famine.* Macrae Smith, 1971.
HYDE, MARGARET O., and FORSYTH, E. H. *What Have You Been Eating? Do You Really Know?* McGraw, 1975.
JOHNSON, ARNOLD H., and PETERSON, M. S., eds. *Encyclopedia of Food Technology.* AVI, 1974.
MARGOLIUS, SIDNEY K. *Health Foods: Facts and Fakes.* Walker, 1973.
SCOTT, JOHN. *Hunger: Man's Struggle to Feed Himself.* Parents' Magazine Press, 1969.
STARE, FREDRICK J., and McWILLIAMS, MARGARET. *Living Nutrition.* Wiley, 1973.

FOOD, FROZEN

FOOD, FROZEN. Freezing is one of the most important methods used to preserve foods. In the United States, food companies freeze over 10 billion pounds (4.5 billion kilograms) of food each year. These foods range from orange juice to ready-to-eat bakery products, vegetables with sauces, and complete precooked meals. In addition, many people freeze foods at home.

Freezing preserves food because it prevents the growth of microorganisms (tiny forms of life), slows down the rate of enzyme action, and lowers the speed at which food-spoiling chemical reactions take place. For a description of how these spoil food, see FOOD PRESERVATION (How Food Spoils).

Almost all frozen foods are *quick-frozen* and stored at temperatures of 0° F. (−18° C) or below. Scientists have no exact definition of quick-freezing as compared to slow-freezing. In slow-freezing, changes take place in the cells of some foods. These changes cause foods to leak fluid during defrosting. This leakage results in undesirable changes in the texture of the food. Also, during slow-freezing the temperature may not be reduced fast enough to prevent spoilage. Thus, quick-freezing might be considered to be any process that freezes food fast enough to prevent spoilage and that causes a minimum change in food cells. However, it is more important to store foods at 0° F. (−18° C) or below than it is to freeze them at extremely fast temperatures.

Commercial freezing of food began in the United States as early as 1865. But early frozen foods were of poor quality, and were frozen too slowly and at too high temperatures. Historians generally credit Clarence Birdseye, a Massachusetts inventor, with developing the modern quick-freezing process. Birdseye used refrigerated moving metal belts to quick-freeze fish in 1925 (see BIRDSEYE, CLARENCE). But large-scale quick-freezing of foods did not begin until 1929 when the Postum Company (now General Foods Corporation) purchased Birdseye's patents.

Commercial Methods of Quick Freezing

There are several methods of quick-freezing foods commercially. The chief methods include (1) air-blast freezing, (2) indirect-contact freezing, (3) nitrogen freezing, and (4) dry-ice freezing.

Frigidaire Div., Gen. Motors Corp.

Freezer Compartments in refrigerators provide a place to preserve most kinds of foods.

Air-Blast Freezing uses a steady flow of cold air to freeze foods moving on a conveyor belt or to freeze packaged foods on trays and racks. The conveyor belt and trays and racks move through an insulated tunnel. Usually the foods are packaged before they are frozen. But some processors expose the food to cold air in a tunnel before placing it in packages.

Indirect-Contact Freezing is done in several ways. One system uses a series of adjustable hollow-walled metal plates. A *refrigerant*, or cooling substance, inside the plate walls, cools the plate surfaces to about −28° F. (−33° C). Workers place packaged foods between the plates, which are then adjusted to make contact with the upper and lower surfaces of the packages. As the cold plates absorb heat, the food freezes solid. Another system uses refrigerated alcohol solutions to freeze foods, chiefly fruit juices, in cans. A screw-type conveyer automatically moves the cans through the freezing solution. This movement shakes the food, and the shaking speeds freezing.

Nitrogen Freezing. In this process, liquid nitrogen under pressure *vaporizes* (turns into a misty gas) and flows through nozzles into the food freezing chamber. The nitrogen vapors, which are extremely cold, take heat from the food, and the food freezes rapidly. The vapors are then collected, recompressed, cooled, and returned to the chamber to be used again. This method costs less and freezes food faster than the air-blast and indirect-contact methods. Its high speed greatly reduces the chance of bacterial growth, cell destruction, and loss of nutrients during freezing.

Dry-Ice Freezing resembles nitrogen freezing, except that it uses *dry ice* (solid carbon dioxide) as the refrigerant. The dry ice vaporizes, and the resulting cold vapors freeze the food quickly. This relatively simple process is used by some commercial food firms that do not have the complex equipment needed for other freezing methods. The process is cheap, and it freezes food as fast as the nitrogen method. However, most companies prefer to use nitrogen for extremely fast freezing because it is easier to handle than carbon dioxide.

Home Freezing

People freeze foods at home by placing them in special cabinet freezers or in refrigerator freezing compartments that operate at 0° F. (−18° C) or below. Freezer capacities vary considerably, however, and it is important not to overload the unit. A 2-cubic-foot (0.06-cubic-meter) freezer will freeze up to about 5 pounds (2.3 kilograms) of food at a time. Some large cabinet units will freeze as much as 40 or 50 pounds (18 or 23 kilograms) at a time. The easiest foods for home freezing include uncooked vegetables, fruits, meats, fish, and poultry. But many people freeze cooked foods such as soups, stews, casseroles, sauces, and baked foods.

In general, most foods make good frozen products and can be stored for a year at 0° F. (−18° C) if properly prepared, packaged, and frozen. Exceptions, for various reasons, include avocados, cabbage, celery, cooked egg whites, custards, fatty fish, grapes, pears, vegetable salads, whole or sliced tomatoes, and some shellfish. These foods should be preserved in some other way.

Preparing Foods for Freezing at home or in the factory involves the same basic steps. But commercial firms use machines to prepare commercial-sized quantities. Also, many commercially frozen foods are the ready-to-eat variety, which need special treatment—precooking, for example—before they are frozen. Basically, foods for freezing are prepared in the same way as those intended for cooking, canning, or immediate table use. They are then packaged and frozen.

Vegetables. Before freezing vegetables, prepare them just as for cooking. Then *blanch* the vegetables, or immerse them in boiling water to destroy enzymes. The time required for blanching vegetables depends on their size. For example, peas as prepared for cooking would require a blanching time of 1 minute, while broccoli needs about $3\frac{1}{2}$ minutes.

After blanching a vegetable, remove it from the boiling water and cool it immediately in running water. Then package the vegetable and freeze it. Vegetables may be packed dry, or in a solution of 1 teaspoon of salt to 1 cup of water (21 milliliters of salt to 1 liter of water). If you use brine, fill the package to within about $\frac{1}{2}$ inch (13 millimeters) of the top. If brine is not used, fill the package to the top.

Fruits should first be prepared as for eating. Do not blanch fruits. Place them directly in the package after preparation. Most fruits should be covered with syrup or mixed with sugar. Blackberries, boysenberries, logan-

berries, and blueberries require no sugar or syrup.

Meat, Poultry, and Fish. Meats need little preparation except trimming of waste parts. They should be cut into cooking-sized portions prior to wrapping, for ease in handling. Poultry requires a thorough washing inside and out after the birds are cleaned and dressed. They may be packaged and frozen without further cutting, or they may be cut into serving portions before packaging. Fish are usually cleaned, cut into fillets, and skinned, or cleaned, scaled, and cut into steaks. Small fish may be frozen whole just as they are caught, or they may be cleaned before freezing. Glazing the frozen fish by dipping them in cold water adds thin coats of ice. The ice helps retain texture and flavor. Cooked shellfish, such as lobsters, shrimps, and crabs, have a limited storage life and should not be frozen at home.

Packaging is an important part of preparing foods for freezing. If frozen foods are not well protected during storage they will lose moisture. This causes changes in appearance called *freezer burn* and speeds up physical and chemical changes in the product. Freezer burn may cause foods to look less glossy, or, in extreme cases, may give them a dried-out appearance.

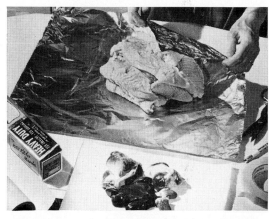

Frozen Foods Must Be Packaged Properly to preserve their flavor, color, and food value. The packages should be sealed tightly so that the foods will not lose their moisture. Cellophane, aluminum foil, and plastic film provide the best wrappings for meat and poultry, *top.* Fruits and vegetables, *bottom,* can be preserved in plastic or aluminum-foil containers, or in waxed cartons.

USDA

Photos courtesy of *Better Homes & Gardens* Magazine

FOOD ADDITIVE

There are many kinds of moisture-vapor-proof wrappings and packages for fruits and vegetables. These include waxed, cylinder-shaped containers; cylindrical cans with snap-on covers; aluminum-foil containers; and waxed, top-opening cartons lined with plastic film.

Preparing Frozen Foods for the Table

Once food is frozen, it should not be thawed until it is ready to be used. Frozen meats, fish, and poultry should be completely thawed before cooking, and then prepared in the usual manner. Meats, fish, and poultry can be defrosted at room temperature, or in the regular food section of a refrigerator. Foods thawed at room temperature should be cooked as soon as they become soft, or else there is danger of spoiling. Thawed frozen foods should never be refrozen because harmful microorganisms can start to grow in the food while it is thawed.

Frozen vegetables need not be thawed before cooking. They should be cooked in as little water as possible, to conserve their food values. Experts suggest about $\frac{1}{4}$ cup (60 milliliters) of water for each pint package (0.47 liter) of frozen vegetables. Bring the water to a boil, add the vegetables, and bring the water to a second boil. Then reduce the heat and allow the food to boil gently until ready to eat. Frozen vegetables require much less cooking than raw ones. Vegetables frozen in a salt solution need no water for cooking.

Fruits may be defrosted at room temperature or in the refrigerator. If defrosted at room temperature, they should be placed in the refrigerator as soon as they thaw. People usually eat frozen fruits without cooking them.　　　　　　　　NORMAN W. DESROSIER

See also FOOD PRESERVATION; REFRIGERATION.

FOOD ADDITIVE is any chemical that food manufacturers intentionally add to one of their products. Some additives increase a food's nutritional value. Others improve the color, flavor, or texture of foods. Still others keep foods from spoiling. Common food additives include iodine, put into salt to prevent goiter, and baking powder, added to dough to make it rise.

Some food additives come from other foods. Scientists also create many synthetic additives in the laboratory. Some people consider food additives dangerous to their health. But many of these chemicals occur naturally in foods that people have eaten for centuries.

Kinds of Additives. Food manufacturers use hundreds of additives in processing various foods. These additives can be classified into six major groups: (1) preservatives; (2) nutritional supplements; (3) flavoring agents; (4) coloring agents; (5) emulsifiers, stabilizers, and thickeners; and (6) acids and alkalis.

Preservatives, such as salt, prevent the growth of bacteria that cause foods to spoil. Preservatives called *antioxidants* keep fats and oils from spoiling and prevent other foods from becoming discolored.

Nutritional Supplements, such as iron, minerals, and vitamins, make foods more nourishing. A number of such supplements, including vitamin B_1 and vitamin B_2, are added to flour. These additives enrich flour and thus improve the nutritional value of bread and other products made from it. Milk with vitamin D added helps prevent rickets, a bone disease.

Flavoring Agents include all spices and natural fruit flavors, as well as such artificial flavors as the vanillin used in ice cream. Some flavoring agents, such as monosodium glutamate (MSG), add no flavor of their own but improve a food's natural flavor.

Coloring Agents make synthetic foods resemble real ones. Margarine manufacturers add yellow coloring to make their product look like butter. Manufacturers also add coloring to many canned foods to replace natural food colors lost in processing. Some coloring agents, such as the orange color added to the skins of oranges, improve the appearance of a food.

Emulsifiers, Stabilizers, and Thickeners help the ingredients in a food to mix and hold together. Algin, an emulsifier, gives ice cream its creamy texture and maintains the mixture of liquids in salad dressings. Carrageen, the most widely used stabilizer, keeps the chocolate particles in chocolate milk from settling. Pectin and gelatin are commonly used to thicken jams and jellies.

Acids and Alkalis help maintain a chemical balance in some foods. For example, alkalis neutralize the high acid content of such canned foods as peas and olives. Some acids add flavor. For example, citric acid added to fruit juice gives it a tart taste. Carbonic acid puts the fizz in soft drinks.

Government Regulations. In the United States, the Federal Food, Drug, and Cosmetic Act of 1938 sets standards for the food industry and requires truthful labeling. This law also requires a manufacturer to prove a new food additive safe before using it. The Food and Drug Administration (FDA) enforces the act. This agency tests many food additives before approving their use.

The Federal Food, Drug, and Cosmetic Act prohibits the use of any food additive if that chemical causes cancer in animals. Such additives have been banned because of concern that they might also cause cancer in humans. In 1970, the FDA prohibited the sale of artificial sweeteners called *cyclamates.* Experiments had shown that cyclamates caused cancer in rats when fed to the animals in large amounts. In 1976, the FDA banned *Red No. 2,* a dye used in foods, drugs, and cosmetics. The agency took steps in 1977 to ban *saccharin,* another artificial sweetener.　　　JEAN MAYER

See also PURE FOOD AND DRUG LAWS.

FOOD AND AGRICULTURE ORGANIZATION (FAO) is a specialized agency of the United Nations (UN). It works to improve the production, distribution, and use of food and other products of farms, forests, and fisheries throughout the world. More than 140 countries belong to the FAO.

The FAO helps developing nations make better use of their agricultural resources and improve their methods of food production. For example, it helps farmers obtain advanced types of seeds and advice on crop rotation and pest control. The organization works for better management of forest and water resources. It also sets up programs to provide information about nutrition. In addition, it supports research on agricultural, fishery, and forestry problems and recommends solutions. The FAO carries out many of its projects for the United Nations Development Program (UNDP) and other organizations.

The Food and Agriculture Organization was established in 1945. It has headquarters in Rome and regional offices throughout the world.

Critically reviewed by the FOOD AND AGRICULTURE ORGANIZATION

See also FOOD SUPPLY (Food Supply Programs); UNITED NATIONS (Fighting Hunger).

FOOD AND DRUG ADMINISTRATION (FDA) is an agency of the United States Department of Health, Education, and Welfare. The FDA administers federal laws designed to ensure the purity of food, the safety and effectiveness of drugs and therapeutic devices, and the safeness of cosmetics. The agency is also concerned with the truthfulness of labels and the safety and honesty of packaging. The principal laws administered by the FDA are the Federal Food, Drug, and Cosmetic Act of 1938 and the Drug Amendments Act of 1962.

The FDA has the responsibility of promoting sanitary conditions in public eating places and interstate travel facilities. It also takes part in joint programs of the federal and state governments to ensure the safety of milk products and shellfish. In 1971, the FDA took over the enforcement of the Radiation Control for Health and Safety Act of 1968. That law was designed to prevent unnecessary exposure to radiation from electronic products, such as television sets and X-ray equipment. The FDA's Bureau of Biologics regulates biological products.

Other activities of the FDA include development of new methods for analyzing products, and research on how various substances affect human beings and animals. The FDA has laboratories and offices in over 100 cities.   Critically reviewed by the FOOD AND DRUG ADMINISTRATION

See also PURE FOOD AND DRUG LAWS.

FOOD AND DRUGS ACT OF 1906. See PURE FOOD AND DRUG LAWS.

FOOD CHAIN. See ECOLOGY; FISH (Fish in the Balance of Nature); SUN (Heat and Light for Life); ENVIRONMENTAL POLLUTION (Other Kinds of Pollution).

FOOD COLORING. See FOOD ADDITIVE (Kinds of Additives).

FOOD FOR PEACE is a United States government program that makes U.S. farm products available to less developed countries and needy people. Under the program, the United States sells or donates farm commodities—chiefly grain and grain products—to many countries in Africa, Asia, and Latin America.

The Food for Peace program was established in 1954. For many years, the program was limited to surplus agricultural products. But in 1966, Congress removed the surplus commodities requirement. Congress authorized the secretary of agriculture to plan U.S. production to help meet the pressing food needs of developing countries. Congress also directed that the program give highest priority to nations that attempt to solve their own problems of food shortages and population growth. The program is administered by the Department of Agriculture, in consultation with the Department of State and other federal agencies.

Critically reviewed by the DEPARTMENT OF AGRICULTURE

FOOD POISONING results from eating food contaminated by bacteria or certain chemicals, such as zinc, lead, and copper. Symptoms of food poisoning usually include nausea, vomiting, cramps, and diarrhea. In some cases, certain muscles may be paralyzed. Food poisoning may be prevented by preparing and storing foods properly with sanitary methods. Contaminated

food may contain living organisms, such as *Salmonella* bacteria, or *toxins* (poisons) produced by such bacteria as *Staphylococcus* (see STAPHYLOCOCCUS). Staphylococcic food poisoning, probably the most common type, is quite mild, and recovery is usually rapid. The bacterium *Clostridium botulinum* causes a more serious poisoning, *botulism* (see BOTULISM). In some cases, botulism may cause respiratory failure and death. Contamination by bacteria is most common in dairy foods, sea foods, and improperly canned foods.   SARAH R. RIEDMAN

See also FOOD PRESERVATION (Using Preserved Foods); BACTERIA (Harmful Bacteria).

FOOD PRESERVATION makes it possible to store food for future use without spoiling. Prehistoric people dried food in the sun or stored it in cool caves. We still use drying (dehydration) and cooling (refrigeration) to preserve food. But science has developed other means of keeping food from spoiling. These include canning, quick-freezing, adding chemicals, freeze-drying, and irradiation.

Because people can preserve food, they can enjoy healthy diets the year around. At the same meal, we may eat refrigerated salmon from Alaska, quick-frozen corn from Iowa, and canned pineapple from Hawaii. Almost everyone eats some preserved foods every day— perhaps frozen orange juice for breakfast, canned soup at lunch, and smoked ham for dinner.

Many people enjoy canning or quick-freezing foods in their homes. But most preserved foods are prepared by the food-processing industry, which employs over 1,500,000 persons in the United States alone.

How Food Spoils

Spoiled foods result from chemical changes and from the growth of tiny forms of life called *microorganisms*.

Chemical Spoilage of foods usually takes place during storage. Stored foods may change color or develop bad odors and flavors as chemical changes occur in their proteins, fats, and carbohydrates. When fats and oils are exposed to air, they *oxidize*, and the foods turn rancid and develop an "old" taste (see OXIDATION). Chemical combinations of sugars and proteins cause *browning*, turning foods to a dark color. Browning often occurs in dried foods.

Chemical substances called *enzymes* cause much food spoilage (see ENZYME). All living things produce enzymes. These substances are important in digestion, and also ripen fruits and vegetables and tenderize meats. Enzymes continuously *split* (break down) starches, proteins, fats, and similar materials into new substances. If their action is not stopped they make foods overripe. They may cause a loss of flavor compounds such as sugars, or of nutrients such as vitamin C.

Microorganisms, such as bacteria, yeasts, and molds, grow in all kinds of food. Some produce substances that make foods decay (see DECAY). Molds that grow in bread and other moist foods often change the flavor of the food. Some bacteria form acids that turn foods sour. Others produce poisons that make people ill (see FOOD POISONING). Yeasts often *ferment* food, or make it alcoholic. Some bacteria produce hydrogen sulfide, a gas that may turn food black if it combines with normal amounts of iron in food. This gas also gives food the

A Cold-Storage Warehouse preserves food by keeping it at low temperatures. Such warehouses are used for dairy products, fruit, vegetables, and meat. The worker shown above is loading cartons of ice cream from a cold-storage warehouse into a refrigerated trailer.

odor of rotten eggs. Bacteria can form so much carbon dioxide or hydrogen gas in canned foods that the pressure may swell or burst the containers.

How Foods Are Preserved

All methods of food preservation are designed to produce healthful, flavorful products. Homemakers and food-processing companies take great care in choosing, preparing, and processing the foods they want to preserve. They must work under clean conditions and use only fresh, high-quality products at the proper stage of ripeness. They must discard any bruised or spoiled food parts and remove parts that are not to be eaten, such as pods, cores, or peels. The chief methods of food preservation include (1) cold storage, (2) canning, (3) freezing, (4) drying, (5) freeze-drying, and (6) curing. In addition, treatment with antibiotic drugs or exposure to ultraviolet rays helps preserve some foods.

Cold Storage keeps food fresh at low temperatures. These temperatures, usually ranging from 30° to 50° F. (−1° to 10° C), do not stop spoilage. But they do slow microorganism growth and enzyme action. The cold-storage life of foods depends on the type of food, the storage temperature, and the amount of moisture present in the air of the storage room. The foods must not dry out or become too moist. Molds often grow on moist foods (see MOLD). Keeping the air in motion around cold-storage food helps maintain a constant temperature. It also removes gases that some foods give off. Some of these gases shorten the storage life of fruit.

Huge *cold-storage warehouses* keep large supplies of apples, apricots, pears, butter, cheese, and eggs for periods of from 6 to 10 months. Most other foods can be stored for only several weeks or a few months. Farmers sometimes harvest fruits and vegetables before they ripen, but after they have reached full size. Some foods ripen during cold storage or shipment in refrigerated railroad cars or trucks. Meat processors use cold storage to *tenderize* meat. They put meat in cold rooms for 7 to 10 days. The cold prevents microorganism spoilage, but allows slow enzyme action that partially breaks down the tougher tissues. This makes the meat more tender. See COLD STORAGE.

Canning has two aims: (1) to *sterilize* food, or make it germ-free, and (2) to keep air away from it. Heating food to high temperatures destroys microorganisms and stops enzyme action. To keep air away from food, canners pack it in airtight metal or glass containers. They remove the air from the containers and seal them with airtight lids. Sealing keeps out microorganisms and helps prevent oxidation of the food. Most canned foods keep well for more than a year.

Food technologists in canning plants test samples of the food at different stages of canning. These experts determine the ripeness and composition of raw foods. They make sure that no foreign matter has entered the cans. They test to see that the canning process has destroyed enzymes and microorganisms that might cause spoilage. Finally, they test to make sure the food meets company and government standards.

The chief canning processes are: (1) the conventional retort method, (2) preheating and hot filling, and (3) fast-canning. Home-canners use about the same methods as commercial canners, but they work with much smaller amounts of food and use less elaborate equipment. See CANNING.

Conventional Retort Method is the most common commercial canning process. It is used to preserve most vegetables, fruits, fish, and meat products. Canners fill and seal the containers, then heat-process the foods. They place the containers in huge *retorts* (cookers) using water or steam to produce germ-killing temperatures of from 212° to 250° F. (100° to 121° C). The sterilizing time depends on the temperature, the container size, and the type of food. The higher the temperature, the faster the food is sterilized. Containers that hold large amounts of food take longer to sterilize than containers holding smaller amounts.

Home-canners use a similar method called *raw packing* to can fruits and tomatoes. They place raw or partially heated foods in sterile jars and cook them in a pressure cooker, or a hot-water bath if the food is very acid. Another home-canning method called *hot packing* is used for vegetables, meats, and fruit preserves. In hot packing, canners heat food to the boiling point, but do not cook it before putting it in containers. The sealed containers are then sterilized by pressure cooking.

Preheating and Hot Filling. In this method, canners first heat the food thoroughly in open kettles or in devices called *heat exchangers*. Then they put the hot food into sterilized containers and seal the containers. Heat from the hot food kills any microorganisms that may enter the containers during the filling process. Commercial canners use this method only to preserve very acid foods such as orange juice, tomato paste, and jams or

Harshe-Rotman & Druck Inc.

TV Dinners are precooked and frozen by food processors and reheated by people at home. The equipment shown above squirts butter on the vegetables included in a TV dinner.

jellies. Temperatures used in preheating and hot filling do not exceed 200° F. (93° C). Nonacid foods, such as meat or fish, require higher temperatures for sterilization. Home-canners use preheating and hot filling mainly to can fruits and to make jellies, preserves, and pickles. They call it the *open-kettle* method.

Fast-Canning methods use high temperatures, from 250° to 280° F. (121° to 138° C), for short periods of time. Fast canning prevents certain changes in foods that occur during longer heating periods. Processors use this method with only a few kinds of foods, because chemical changes occur during storage after processing. Commercial foods processed by fast canning include baby foods, cream-style corn, potted meats, and sauces.

In one fast-canning method, called *flame sterilization*, a direct flame heats filled and sealed cans while they rotate at 40 to 50 revolutions per minute. The rotation mixes the contents of the cans and so helps the heat penetrate quickly. Commercial canners in the United States use flame sterilization to preserve only tomatoes and acid fruits. However, this method is used in canning a wide variety of foods in Australia, Europe, and South America.

Freezing ranks after canning as one of the most widely used methods of food preservation. Homemakers and commercial food processors freeze most kinds of fruits and vegetables, and some kinds of meat, fish, poultry, and dairy products. Food companies also freeze a variety of precooked foods ranging from French-fried potatoes to complete meat dinners. For a description of the methods that are used to freeze foods, see FOOD, FROZEN.

Drying, or dehydration, removes most of the moisture from food. Microorganisms cannot grow on dry food. Drying also reduces the size and weight of foods, making them easier to transport and store. Dried foods play an important part in feeding troops in wartime. Soldiers can easily carry small packages of dried foods such as milk, eggs, and powdered coffee. See DEHYDRATION.

Food processors blanch vegetables and some fruits before drying to prevent changes caused by enzymes. In *blanching*, the foods are exposed to steam or boiling water. Processors often treat apples, apricots, pears, and peaches with sulfur-dioxide gas to prevent enzyme and

Castle & Cooke, Inc.

Canning packs food in airtight containers and sterilizes it to prevent spoilage. This worker is operating a machine that seals cans of sliced pineapple. The contents of the cans are then sterilized by heat in huge containers called *retorts*.

other chemical changes, especially browning. Food can be dried in the sun, in kilns, in special machines called *dehydrators*, and in spray chambers.

Sun-Drying is the oldest method of drying food. Processors spread the food on trays and expose it to the sun. After several days, enough moisture has evaporated to make the food safe for storage. Processors sun-dry many fruits, some vegetables, and some fish. People sometimes use this method to dry apples at home.

Kiln-Drying uses heat from a furnace or stove to evaporate moisture from food. The furnace or stove stands on the lower floor of a building called a *kiln*. The food is put on the slatted floors of the upper stories, and heat rises through the openings between the slats. Kiln-drying may take several days. During this period, processors turn and move the food several times to make sure it becomes thoroughly dry.

Dehydrators take less time than the other means of drying to process the same amount of food. Some dehydrators use a partial vacuum to make water evaporate at a low temperature. Due to the lower temperature, fewer chemical changes caused by heat take place.

Processors dehydrate eggs, milk, fruit and vegetable juices, and other liquid or partly liquid foods by *spray-drying*. In this method, liquid food is sprayed through nozzles into specially designed drying chambers. Food particles collect at the bottoms of the chambers as powder. *Hot-blast* drying is used chiefly for vegetables. Dehydrators force hot air over food put on trays in special chambers. As the heated air flows over the food, it absorbs and carries off moisture.

Freeze-Drying removes water from food while the food is still frozen. The frozen food is cooled to about −20° F. (−29° C). Then it is placed on trays in a vacuum chamber, and heat is carefully applied. In this method, the frozen water in the food is evaporated without melting. The food does not undergo high temperatures until most of the moisture has been removed. Drying takes from 4 to 12 hours, depending on the type of food, particle size, and the drying system used. Freeze-dried foods are usually packed in an inert gas such as nitrogen. They must be packaged in moisture-proof containers. Freeze-drying usually produces higher quality dried foods, but it costs more than other drying methods. See FREEZE-DRYING.

Curing slows the growth of microorganisms inside food, and often destroys many of those on the food surfaces. Curing consists of salting, smoking, cooking, and drying, or some combination of these treatments. In some kinds of curing, certain chemical compounds other than salt may be used, but the amounts and kinds of chemicals are regulated. Federal and state laws prevent the use of chemicals that might make people ill. The most widely used chemicals include salt, sugar, vinegar, and wood smoke. Some of the other chemicals permitted with certain foods include potassium and sodium nitrite, sulfur dioxide, and benzoic acid. The U.S. Department of Agriculture limits the amount of sodium nitrite used in curing. Under certain conditions, sodium nitrite can combine with other chemicals to form compounds that may cause cancer.

Salt must be used in large amounts to control microorganism growth. Because salt has a strong taste, proc-

Grant Heilman

A Smokehouse is used by meat-packing companies to cure ham, bacon, and other meats, such as this bologna. Smoking also gives meat a special flavor that many people enjoy.

essors can use large amounts only in foods where it adds flavor, such as beef, pork, and fish. They usually put such foods in salt-water solutions to soak up salt, or rub dry salt into the food. Pickled foods are preserved with salt (see PICKLE).

Sugar in large amounts slows the growth of microorganisms. Cooks and food processors add sugar or syrup to jams and jellies, and usually to canned or frozen fruits, to help preserve them. Sugar also improves the flavor of these foods. Condensed milk contains sugar as a preserving agent.

Vinegar is used to pickle green tomatoes, cucumbers, cauliflower, onions, beets, herring, sardines, and other foods that taste good sour. Acetic acid in vinegar slows microorganism growth.

Wood Smoke contains chemicals that slow the growth of microorganisms. But smoking changes the odor and flavor of food. Food processors use it only to preserve meats or fish, because smoking does not ruin the flavors of these products. Smoking preserves meat and fish well if combined with salting and drying. Meat to be smoked, such as ham, bacon, and other salt-cured products, is hung in a *smokehouse*. A slow-burning fire provides the smoke.

Antibiotics are chemical compounds produced by living microorganisms (see ANTIBIOTIC). Doctors use antibiotics to destroy microorganisms that make people ill. Scientists found that they can also be used to hamper microorganisms that spoil food. In Canada, food processors dip fish into a weak solution of the antibiotics Aureomycin and Terramycin. This slows the growth of microorganisms and extends the time fish can be kept in refrigerated storage. Antibiotics are also added to refrigerated sea water, which preserves fish while they are being transported by ship.

Ultraviolet Rays can destroy most microorganisms, but their use in preserving food is not widespread. They are used to kill spores in the air in bakeries, control mold in packaged cheese, and reduce bacterial damage in meat. Meat packers expose meat to ultraviolet rays while tenderizing it. The rays sterilize the surface of the meat, where most microorganisms live. Packers can keep such meat at temperatures up to 60° F. (16° C) for several days without microorganism spoilage. Meats that are not *irradiated*, or treated with ultraviolet rays, must be kept at lower temperatures. The relatively high temperature allows tenderizing enzymes to work faster. See IRRADIATION; ULTRAVIOLET RAYS.

Using Preserved Foods

When consumers buy preserved foods, they must take care to select good quality products. They should never buy cans with swelled ends, called *swells* or *springers*. Such cans may contain foods spoiled by gas-producing microorganisms. They should also avoid frozen foods that do not feel solid to the touch. Such foods may be spoiled.

Canners use brand names that correspond to their best, or *fancy*, products; their medium, or *extra-standard*, grades; and their lowest, or *standard*, products. Consumers should learn to identify these brands. The size of cans is important for economical buying. Food preserved in large cans costs less per cup than food preserved in smaller cans. But buying large cans may be wasteful, if they contain more food than the family can use before some spoils. The labels of all cans show the weight of their contents.

The federal government sets minimum standards for the quality of food and the amount per can for many canned foods sold in interstate commerce. Government regulations also require that many of the materials used in preserving foods be listed on the container label. See PURE FOOD AND DRUG LAWS.

Storage. Unopened canned foods should be kept in a cool, dry place. After opening a can, you can refrigerate the remaining food in the can or in another container. The can or container should be covered.

Cured, smoked, and fresh meats and fish should be kept in the refrigerator, near the freezing compartment. They should be wrapped or covered with waxed paper, plastic, or aluminum foil.

Dried foods must be stored in moistureproof containers, or in a very dry place. Many dried foods keep best under refrigeration. It is not necessary to refrigerate such dried foods as rice and beans.

Preparation. Cooks should prepare preserved foods carefully to keep as much of the food value as possible.

Home-Canned Foods, when improperly prepared, sometimes contain the poison that causes botulism (see BOTULISM). A wise precaution is to boil nonacid home-canned foods for several minutes. This destroys any poison that may be present in the food.

Commercially Canned Foods are considered to be free from the danger of botulism. Canners cook their products at temperatures high enough to kill the organism that produces the poison. Canners often pack vegetables in a weak brine solution. This liquid should be eaten, because it is rich in vitamins. Before heating commercially canned foods that contain little or no fluid, a little water or a small piece of butter should be added. Melting of the butter indicates that the food has been heated sufficiently. It also adds to its flavor.

Salt-Cured Meats should be washed thoroughly in clear water before cooking. This removes excess salt from the meat. Cooks can also get rid of excess salt by *parboiling* (boiling for a short time), then pouring off the water and boiling the meat again in fresh water.

Dried Foods must be *rehydrated* (have water restored) before eating. Some foods require presoaking in warm water for several hours before cooking. The amount of water needed to rehydrate varies with the type of food and the quantity. The cooking time varies with the method of preparation and the type of food.

History

Early Methods. Prehistoric people probably dried grains, nuts, fruits, roots, and other plant products in

The Ancient Egyptians preserved food. This 3,000-year-old wallpainting shows Egyptians making wine from grapes, *top*, and drying fowl and storing it in salt-filled jars, *bottom*.

FOOD PRESERVATION

the sun. They may have stored certain foods such as acorns in cool, dry caves. After fire was discovered, cave dwellers probably dried foods faster and learned to smoke meat. The ancient Romans imported ice and snow to use in cooling and preserving foods. The early peoples of Asia preserved food with spices and sugar. They dried such fruits as apricots, prunes, and figs. The pioneers of the American Colonies preserved foods by smoking them or by pickling them in vinegar, spices, and brine.

Many people helped in developing modern food preservation. In the late 1600's, the Dutch scientist Anton van Leeuwenhoek became the first to observe, draw, and describe bacteria and other microorganisms. Lazzaro Spallanzani, an Italian naturalist, showed in 1765 that bacteria are not the product of spontaneous generation (see SPONTANEOUS GENERATION). In the 1850's, the great French chemist Louis Pasteur proved that, although some microorganisms help produce beer and wines, the growth of the wrong types of microorganisms might spoil these beverages.

Modern Food Preservation began in France in 1795 when Nicolas Appert (1749?-1841), a candymaker, worked out the first canning method. He put precooked foods in sealed glass bottles and heated them in boiling water. This method spread to other countries after Appert published his reports in 1810.

William Underwood (1787-1864), who came to the United States from England, established the canning industry in America. He opened a canning plant in Boston in 1820. Underwood's company is still a well-known canning firm. Metal containers came into use during the 1820's. In 1825, Thomas Kensett, who was a canner in New York City, obtained the first United States patent for tin-plated cans. The canning industry in the United States grew rapidly until it became one of the largest food-preserving industries. Each year canners process more than 20 billion pounds (9 billion kilograms) of food having a retail value of about $4½ billion.

The development of refrigeration took place mainly in the United States. In the early 1800's, people used ice to keep food fresh. Ice-refrigerator cars came into use during the mid-1800's for shipping fresh meats, fruits, and vegetables. Mechanical refrigeration was developed during the late 1800's. Mechanical refrigerators for homes began to replace iceboxes by 1920, and became standard equipment in United States households by 1940.

Foods had been preserved by freezing long before Clarence Birdseye developed the quick-freezing process in the 1920's. Until then, however, freezing was not an important method for preserving food. Earlier, foods selected to be frozen were often of poor quality, and processors used slow-freezing methods with generally poor results. Today, with improved methods, processors freeze more than 10 billion pounds (4.5 billion kilograms) of food a year, with a retail value of more than $2 billion.

Food was not dried in great volume in the United States until World War I, when dried food became important for feeding soldiers. The need for such food during World War II led to the development of standard dried items, including "instant" coffee, dried milk, and dried eggs.   GEORGE K. YORK

Related Articles in WORLD BOOK include:

METHODS OF PRESERVING FOOD

Canning	Food, Frozen	Jelly and Jam
Cold Storage	Freeze-Drying	Meat Packing
Dehydration	Irradiation	Refrigeration

PRESERVATIVES

Antibiotic	Spice	Sulfur Dioxide
Dry Ice	Sugar	Vinegar
Salt		

OTHER RELATED ARTICLES

Bacteria	Fermentation	Pure Food and
Birdseye,	Leeuwenhoek,	Drug Laws
Clarence	Anton van	Spallanzani, Lazzaro
Botulism	Mold	Sterilization
Enzyme	Pasteur, Louis	Yeast

Outline

I. **How Foods Spoil**
  A. Chemical Spoilage
  B. Microorganisms
II. **How Foods Are Preserved**
  A. Cold Storage   E. Freeze-Drying
  B. Canning   F. Curing
  C. Freezing   G. Antibiotics
  D. Drying   H. Ultraviolet Rays
III. **Using Preserved Foods**
  A. Storage
  B. Preparation
IV. **History**

Questions

What two factors cause food to spoil?
What chemical preservatives can be used in food safely?
Why should the liquid in canned foods be eaten?
In what country did modern food preservation begin?
Who developed the quick-freezing process?
On what factors does the time required to sterilize foods depend?
How do ultraviolet rays preserve food?
Should you buy cans with swelled ends? Explain.
Should you store an opened can of food in the refrigerator?
Why are dried foods important in wartime?

FOOD SERVICE INDUSTRY. See RESTAURANT.

FOOD STAMP PROGRAM is a U.S. government plan to help low-income households buy more and better food than they normally could afford. It serves people receiving welfare aid and others with low incomes.

Persons apply to join the program at area welfare or public assistance offices. For a household to be eligible, it must have an income below a specified level. Its members must live together and buy food together. With certain exceptions, each adult member who is unemployed and able to work must register with the state employment service and try to find a job.

Each participating household gets a certain number of food stamps, depending on its income and size. The stamps cannot be used to buy such nonfood items as alcoholic beverages and tobacco. Grocers redeem the stamps through banks or wholesale food dealers. Local banks send the stamps to federal reserve banks.

The program was established by the Food Stamp Act of 1964. It is administered by the Food and Nutrition Service of the U.S. Department of Agriculture through state and local welfare and public assistance agencies.

See also WELFARE.

The Food Supply in Poor and Rich Countries differs greatly, in many cases because of differences in farm output. At the left, farmers in Nepal receive a ration of rice seed, which will produce barely enough food for their needs. At the right, a U.S. farmer harvests a huge crop of soybeans.

FOOD SUPPLY

FOOD SUPPLY is the total amount of food available to all the people in the world. No one can live without food, and so the supply of food has always been one of the human race's chief concerns. The food supply depends mainly on the world's farmers. They raise the crops and livestock that provide most of our food. The world's food supply varies from year to year because the production of crops and livestock varies. Some years, terrible losses result from droughts, floods, or other natural disasters. Yet the world's population grows every year, and so the worldwide demand for food also constantly increases. Food shortages and famines occur when the food supply falls short of the amount needed.

The food supply varies not only from year to year but also from country to country. Most of the poor, *developing* nations of Africa, Asia, and Latin America seldom have enough food for most of their people. Millions of people in these countries go hungry. During years of famine, millions may die of starvation. In almost all *developed* nations, on the other hand, the majority of people have an adequate diet. But in few countries is the food supply equally distributed. In nearly every nation, some people have more than enough to eat while others live in constant hunger.

Most people in the developed countries have an adequate diet for several reasons. Almost all the developed nations lie in the world's *temperate* regions—that is, be-

tween the tropics and the polar areas. The soil and climate in temperate regions are generally well suited for farming. In addition, the developed nations have money for agricultural research and so have been able to solve various problems associated with agriculture in temperate regions. Most farmers in the developed countries can afford the fertilizers and other materials needed to produce large amounts of food. Finally, the developed countries have enough food because their population grows more slowly than their food supply.

Unlike the developed countries, most developing nations lie in or near the tropics. The soil and climate in these regions are generally not so well suited to large-scale food production as they are in temperate regions. Nor do the developing nations have much money for agricultural research. As a result, they have made relatively little progress in solving the problems of tropical agriculture. In addition, many farmers in the developing countries cannot afford to buy the fertilizers and other materials they need to produce more food. All these conditions limit food production. But the developing nations have too little food chiefly because their population grows nearly as fast as—or faster than—their food supply.

The world's population passed 4 billion in the mid-1970's and is increasing about 2 per cent a year. At this rate of growth, the number of people in the world will double in 35 years. Food production must also double during this time to feed the added people.

Many experts believe that food production will be unable to keep up with population growth unless the birth rate falls sharply. This theory was first developed in detail by the British economist Thomas Robert Malthus in the late 1700's (see MALTHUS, THOMAS ROBERT). In the past, population growth was controlled mainly by a high death rate. But during the 1900's, improved

Lester R. Brown, the contributor of this article, is President of Worldwatch Institute, a private, nonprofit organization that researches problems of worldwide concern, including food supply problems. He is also the author of By Bread Alone *and other books on the food supply.*

FOOD SUPPLY

living standards and medical advances have reduced the death rate in the majority of countries. Today, most people who agree with Malthus consider family planning to be the only practical method of reducing population growth. This article discusses these and other food supply problems. It also discusses human food needs, food sources, and food supply programs.

Basic Human Food Needs

Experts usually determine the adequacy of a person's diet by the amount of *calories* and *protein* it provides. Protein is one of the chief *nutrients* (nourishing substances) found in food. It is needed to build and maintain body cells. Other nutrients are *carbohydrates* (starches and sugars), fats, minerals, and vitamins. Calories are units of energy supplied by food. Carbohydrates and fats normally provide most of the calories in the human diet. Protein supplies the rest. People who lack sufficient calories in their diet are said to be *undernourished*. A person whose diet seriously lacks any nutrient is said to be *malnourished*. Protein malnutrition is by far the most common type of malnutrition.

The majority of people who do not get enough protein in their diet also lack sufficient calories. To make up for a continuing lack of calories, the human body changes more and more protein into energy. As a result, less protein is available to build and maintain body cells. Most malnutrition is therefore protein-calorie malnutrition—an inadequate supply of both protein and

calories in the diet. As many as 500 million persons throughout the world—about an eighth of the world's population—suffer from protein-calorie malnutrition. The great majority of these people live in developing countries, and most are young children. Many victims die before they are 5 years old. Many others grow up with severe mental and physical handicaps. See NUTRITION (Protein-Calorie Malnutrition).

Calories. The amount of calories a person needs each day depends on the person's sex, age, body build, and degree of physical activity. A husky house painter, for example, requires far more calories than does a slightly built office worker. The United Nations (UN) estimates that a moderately active man of average weight—that is, 143 pounds (65 kilograms)—needs at least 3,000 calories a day. A moderately active woman of average weight—that is, 121 pounds (55 kilograms)—needs about 2,200. Children and young people up to 19 years of age require an average of 820 to 3,070 calories, depending on sex, weight, and age.

Daily calorie *consumption* (intake) by all people in the poorest developing countries averages under 2,000—far less than most people require. In many developed countries, daily calorie consumption averages over 3,200 —far more than most people require.

Protein in the human diet consists of *animal protein* and *plant protein*. Dairy products, eggs, fish, and meat are the chief sources of animal protein. The best sources of plant protein are members of the pea family. These plants, which are called *legumes* or *pulses*, include beans, peas, and peanuts. *Cereal grains* also supply plant pro-

Per Capita Distribution of the World's Calorie Supply

This graph shows the number of food calories that would be available daily *per capita* (for each person) in the world's major regions if the calories were divided equally among all the people in the region. The dotted red line indicates the daily calorie requirement for a moderately active woman of average weight—that is, 121 pounds (55 kilograms). The dotted blue line shows the requirement for a moderately active man of average weight—that is, 143 pounds (65 kilograms).

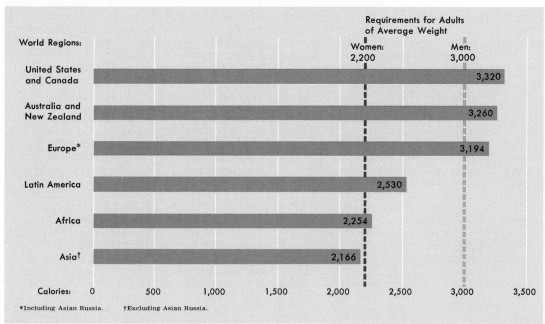

Requirements for Adults of Average Weight

World Regions:		Women: 2,200	Men: 3,000
United States and Canada			3,320
Australia and New Zealand			3,260
Europe*			3,194
Latin America		2,530	
Africa	2,254		
Asia†	2,166		

Calories: 0   500   1,000   1,500   2,000   2,500   3,000   3,500

*Including Asian Russia.   †Excluding Asian Russia.

Sources: *Population, Food Supply, and Agricultural Development*, FAO, 1975. *Handbook on Human Nutritional Requirements*, FAO, 1974. Supply figures are 1969-1971 averages.

tein. The main cereal grains are barley, corn, millet, oats, rice, rye, sorghum, and wheat.

Protein is made up of molecules called *amino acids*. The human body must have certain amino acids to build and maintain body cells. Most sources of animal protein provide all the essential amino acids—and in the proportions the body requires. These food sources can thus supply all of a person's daily protein needs. On the other hand, many sources of plant protein do not supply the complete combination of amino acids. One or more of the essential amino acids are missing or insufficient. For example, cereal grains by themselves do not provide a full combination of amino acids. But if grain is eaten together with certain legumes, especially protein-rich soybeans, it can meet a person's protein needs. See PROTEIN.

People differ in their protein requirements, just as they do in their calorie requirements. But a person's protein needs also depend on the quality of the protein consumed. People require less protein if their diet includes some animal protein than if it includes only plant protein. The UN estimates that a man of average weight needs at least 37 grams of protein daily, if the protein is entirely animal protein. A woman of average weight needs about 29 grams. Children and young people up to 19 years of age require an average of 14 to 38 grams. In every case, a person's requirement increases if the protein is mainly plant protein.

Daily protein consumption by all people in the poorest developing countries averages about 40 grams. But most of the protein is plant protein. Average protein consumption in these countries therefore falls short of the minimum requirement. In addition, most people in these countries have too few calories in their diet. As a result, much of the protein they consume is used to meet their energy needs rather than to build and maintain body cells. Protein consumption by all people in many developed countries averages as high as 80 to 100 grams daily. Most of the protein is animal protein and therefore far exceeds the minimum need. The extra protein provides added calories. If the calories exceed the amount required, the body stores the excess as fat.

Major Sources of Food

Cereal Grains are the world's most important food source. Worldwide, they supply more than half the calories and much of the protein that people consume. Grain is also a chief ingredient in most livestock feed and so is involved in the production of meat, eggs, and dairy products. Cereal grains are of such great importance that food experts often use the size of the grain supply as a measure of the total food supply.

Almost all the grain grown in developing countries is *food grain*—that is, people consume it directly as food. They may simply cook the grain as a main dish. Or they may use it to make bread, noodles, or some other food. People in developed countries also consume grain directly. But in addition, they use much of the grain as *feed grain*, which is fed to livestock. People consume this grain indirectly in the form of livestock products.

Grains used chiefly as feed in some countries are used chiefly as food in other countries. For example, most of the corn grown in the United States is used for livestock feed. But in some African and Latin-American countries, corn is an important food grain.

Per Capita Protein Supply in the United States and India

In the United States, a developed country, the daily per capita protein supply is twice as large as in India, a developing country. In addition, the supply of high-quality, animal protein in the United States is five times as large as in India.

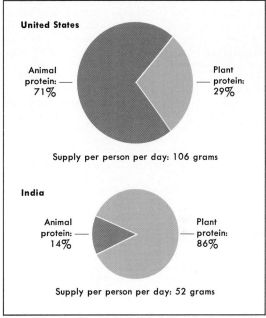

United States

Animal protein: — 71%

Plant protein: — 29%

Supply per person per day: 106 grams

India

Animal protein: — 14%

Plant protein: — 86%

Supply per person per day: 52 grams

Source: *Population, Food Supply, and Agricultural Development*, FAO, 1975. Figures are 1969-1971 averages.

Livestock and Fish are the main sources of animal protein. On a worldwide basis, meat, eggs, and dairy products supply about 85 to 90 per cent of the animal protein in the human diet. Fish provide a large percentage of the animal protein in certain countries, such as Japan, Norway, and the Philippines. But worldwide, fish supply only about 10 to 15 per cent of the animal protein people consume.

Other Major Food Sources. In certain areas of the world, people depend heavily on food sources other than grain, livestock, or fish. Soybeans and other legumes rank second only to rice as a source of food in many Asian countries. Potatoes are a major food in parts of Europe and South America. People in some tropical areas rely largely on such native foods as bananas, *cassava* (a starchy root), and sweet potatoes or yams. Of all these foods, only legumes provide an adequate supply of essential amino acids.

Conditions That Affect the Food Supply

The world's food supply consists mainly of food produced during the current year. But it also includes *reserves*, or *stocks*, left over from previous years. Food reserves are necessary to help prevent shortages after bad farming years. To build up reserves, the countries of the world overall must produce more food in a year than they consume. But few countries produce a surplus. The United States produces by far the largest surplus. Argentina, Australia, Canada, and New Zealand

FOOD SUPPLY

also regularly produce a food surplus, though far less than that produced by the United States.

Most countries produce either just enough food to meet their needs or not enough. If a country fails to produce enough food for all its people, it must import additional supplies or face a shortage. Most developed countries that do not produce sufficient food can afford to import the extra supplies they need. Great Britain and Japan are examples of such countries. But most developing countries cannot afford to import all the additional food their people require. Since the early 1950's, world food production has doubled, but so has the worldwide demand. As a result, many countries rely on food imports, chiefly from the United States.

The amount of food a country produces depends partly on its agricultural resources, such as land and water. No country has an unlimited supply of these resources. The worldwide food supply is thus affected by (1) limited agricultural resources and (2) the ever-increasing demand for food. The food supply within countries is also affected by problems of distribution.

Limited Agricultural Resources. Farming requires various resources—especially land, water, energy, and fertilizer. Land is the chief agricultural resource. Land

The Relation Between Food Production and Population

This graph shows the percentage contributions to world food production and world population of each of the major world regions. Asia, Africa, and Latin America have 75 per cent of the world's people but produce less than 45 per cent of its food.

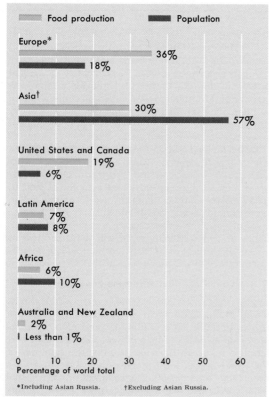

Food production   Population

Europe*
36%
18%

Asia†
30%
57%

United States and Canada
19%
6%

Latin America
7%
8%

Africa
6%
10%

Australia and New Zealand
2%
Less than 1%

0   10   20   30   40   50   60
Percentage of world total

*Including Asian Russia.   †Excluding Asian Russia.

Source: FAO. Figures are for 1975.

used for growing crops must be fairly level and fertile. But most of the world's good cropland is already in use, and most of the unused land lies in remote areas, far from markets and transportation.

All crops require water to grow, but rainfall is distributed unevenly over the earth's surface. Some farmers can depend on rainfall for all the water they need. Other farmers must use irrigation water—if it is available—because the rainfall is too light or uncertain. But the supply of irrigation water is limited, and farmers in some countries use nearly all the available supply.

Many farmers depend heavily on energy resources—particularly petroleum fuels—to operate tractors, irrigation pumps, and other farm equipment. They use fertilizers—especially nitrogen fertilizers—to enrich the soil. At present, most nitrogen fertilizers are made from natural gas. But the world's supplies of petroleum and natural gas are strictly limited. In fact, the supplies may become extremely short or nearly exhausted by the early 2000's. Farmers will therefore need other sources for energy and nitrogen fertilizers.

Meanwhile, the cost of petroleum fuels and fertilizer has soared. Most farmers in developed countries can afford the higher costs. But many farmers in developing countries cannot and so are unable to increase their food production. In every country, higher prices for energy and fertilizer add to the cost of food.

Increased use of agricultural resources can help farmers produce more food. But it can also cause environmental problems. For example, increased use of nitrogen fertilizers sometimes creates a build-up of nitrogen compounds in the soil. Rain water eventually washes these compounds into rivers and streams, where they contribute to water pollution.

Increased Demand for Food chiefly reflects the growth in the population of the world. To a lesser extent, it also reflects higher living standards, which allow people to eat both bigger and better meals.

The Effect of Population Growth. Experts measure a country's food supply by the amount that would be available *per capita* (for each person) if the food were distributed equally among all the people. The food supply thus depends not only on the total amount of food but also on the number of people who must be fed.

The developed and developing countries both increased food production more than 25 per cent during the 1960's. During this period, the population of the developed nations grew about 10 per cent. The amount of food available per capita in these countries therefore increased greatly. But the population of the developing countries grew nearly 25 per cent during the 1960's. The population growth therefore almost equaled the gain in food production, and so little food was left over to help improve people's diets. In some developing nations, the population increases faster than food production. The per capita food supply in these countries thus continually declines.

In an attempt to avoid disastrous food shortages in the future, many developing countries have promoted birth control programs (see BIRTH CONTROL). But lack of education and various other social and economic obstacles have prevented the programs from reaching or influencing most of the people.

The Effect of Higher Living Standards. As people improve their living standards, especially through in-

The Growth in Food Production and Population

The developing countries have difficulty improving their food supply because their population grows nearly as fast as—or faster than—their food production. The reverse is true of most developed countries. The three graphs below illustrate this difference.

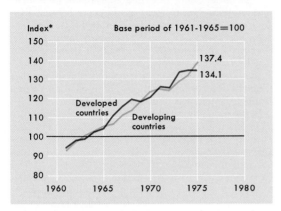

The Growth of Food Production in the developing countries equaled that in the developed countries from 1961 through 1975.

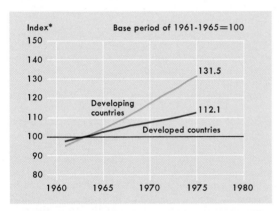

Population Growth was much less in the developed nations from 1961 through 1975 than it was in the developing nations.

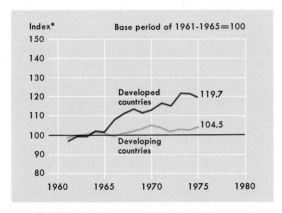

The Per Capita Increase in Food Production was therefore much greater in the developed countries. The developing nations had little food left over to help improve people's diets.

*Shows changes in relation to the base period of 1961-1965.
Source: FAO.

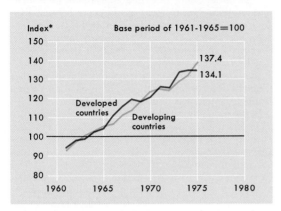

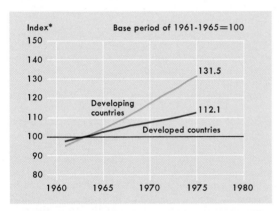

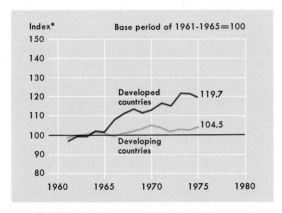

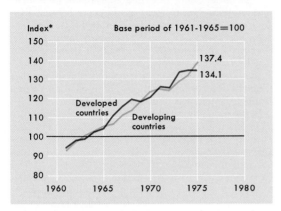

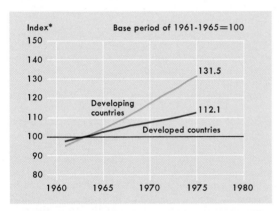

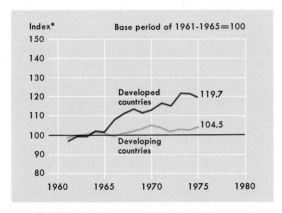

creased personal income, they usually eat more food. In time, they also generally begin to eat more expensive foods, particularly more meat. Greater meat consumption usually calls for an increase in the amount of grain used for livestock feed. For this reason, many countries with a high standard of living also have a high per capita consumption of grain.

The people of the United States directly consume an average of about 150 pounds (68 kilograms) of grain per person annually. But about 1,500 pounds (680 kilograms) of grain per person is fed to U.S. livestock each year. Americans consume this grain indirectly in the form of meat, eggs, and dairy products. Total per capita grain consumption in the United States thus averages about 1,650 pounds (748 kilograms) annually.

Total per capita grain consumption in the developing countries averages about 400 pounds (180 kilograms) a year. Almost all this grain is consumed directly. On the average, people in the United States therefore consume more than four times as much grain as do people in the developing countries.

Distribution Problems. In many developing countries, the majority of people are too poor to buy all the food they need. Much of the available supply therefore goes to the small minority of people who can afford it. The developing countries also lack modern facilities for the transportation and storage of food. In many cases, supplies cannot be delivered immediately to every area where they are needed, and they cannot be safely stored to await shipment. As a result, large quantities of food spoil or are eaten by mice, rats, and insects.

Methods to Increase the Food Supply

Most increases in the food supply result from greater farm output. Farm output can be increased in two main ways: (1) by developing new farmland and (2) by making existing farmland more productive. Two other methods to increase the food supply involve (1) reducing the demand for feed grain and (2) developing new sources of food.

Developing New Farmland is difficult and costly. The largest areas of land that could be developed for farming lie in Africa south of the Sahara and in the Amazon River Basin of South America. Much of this land is covered with dense forests, and the tropical soil and climate are not ideal for farming. As a result, the countries that control the two regions often have difficulty getting farmers to settle and develop the land.

Making Farmland More Productive. Farmers have two main methods of making their land more productive. (1) They may increase their use of irrigation, energy, and fertilizer. (2) They may use improved varieties of grains and livestock, which produce higher crop yields and larger amounts of livestock products. Farmers in developed countries have used both methods during much of the 1900's. In the 1950's and 1960's, farmers in some developing countries also adopted both methods to increase their production of wheat and rice. Their effort proved so successful that it has been called the *Green Revolution.*

The development of high-yield varieties of rice and wheat made the Green Revolution possible. But the revolution also required greater use of irrigation water, energy, and fertilizer. Many farmers got the water from wells and installed electric or diesel-powered pumps to bring the water to the surface. To get the highest yields, farmers had to enrich their soil with fertilizers. During the 1960's, these methods helped such countries as India and Mexico double their wheat production.

The Green Revolution can continue to make farmland more productive. For example, if farmers in the tropics have enough water, fertilizer, and other essential resources, they can grow two or three crops a year on the same land, instead of one crop. But the Green Revolution's ability to increase the food supply is limited. As we have seen, many farmers in developing countries cannot afford the additional resources that the Green Revolution requires. But in any case, greater use of these resources makes land more productive only up to a point. Most farmers in the United States, for example, use 7 to 10 times as much fertilizer on each unit of land as do most farmers in developing countries. But U.S. grain yields are only about twice as large as those in developing countries.

Although farmland can be made more productive, the ever-rising costs of energy and fertilizer drive food prices higher and higher. And millions of people throughout the world cannot afford to buy all the food they need even at lower prices. Ways must therefore be found to expand food production at a cost that most people can afford.

The best hope for making farmland more productive lies with agricultural research. For example, research scientists are working to develop varieties of grain that not only produce higher yields but also have other improved characteristics. Such a grain might supply a more complete combination of amino acids, make more efficient use of water and fertilizer, and provide better resistance to insects and disease. But it is extremely dif-

Marc & Evelyne Bernheim, Woodfin Camp, Inc.

Research in Tropical Agriculture seeks to increase food production in developing countries, most of which lie in the tropics. This researcher in India is studying tropical plant diseases.

ficult to develop a plant variety that has so many different characteristics. The necessary research therefore takes much time and money.

Reducing the Demand for Feed Grain would increase the amount of calories and protein available for human consumption. This increase would occur because livestock consume more calories and protein than they produce. Beef cattle are especially inefficient in this respect. For every 8 to 10 pounds (3.6 to 4.5 kilograms) of grain that beef cattle consume, they produce only 1 pound (0.45 kilogram) of meat. But 8 pounds of grain supplies about 10 times as many calories and more than 4 times as much protein as a pound of beef supplies.

In the past, almost all beef cattle grazed on grass and other *forage* up to the time they were slaughtered. But since the mid-1900's, many cattle-fattening establishments called *feed lots* have opened in the United States, Canada, and certain other developed countries. A feed lot fattens cattle on grain. Today, most U.S. beef cattle are fattened on feed lots and so consume enormous quantities of grain. The demand for feed grain would lessen greatly if the cattle industry returned to its earlier practice of raising cattle chiefly on forage. Some cattle raisers have already made the change. As a result, the percentage of cattle fattened on U.S. feed lots declined in the mid-1970's.

The demand for feed grain would also decline if people in the developed countries ate less meat. Most people in the United States, for example, could probably reduce their meat consumption as much as 30 per cent without ill effects.

Developing New Sources of Food. Such oilseed crops as coconuts, cottonseed, peanuts, and soybeans are all valuable sources of protein. Soybeans have an especially high protein content and have long been an important food in Asia, where they originated. But with this exception, none of these oilseed crops is a major source of food anywhere in the world. Instead, the crops are grown mainly for their oil, which is used to make such products as margarine and salad dressing. The protein, however, remains in the meal, the part of the seed that is left after the oil has been removed. Most of the meal is used for livestock feed.

Since the mid-1900's, food processors have been working to make the protein in oilseed meal available for human consumption. They have developed a variety of inexpensive, specially flavored foods from soybean meal. Some of these products, especially those in beverage form, have been successfully marketed in developing countries in various parts of the world. Food processors are now working to convert coconut, cottonseed, and peanut meal into foods that will have a broad appeal. All three crops are widely grown in the tropics and so could provide millions of people in developing countries with inexpensive protein.

Scientists and food processors have also developed methods of enriching food. For example, scientists have produced artificial amino acids, which can be added to bread and other grain products to improve the quality of their protein.

Food Supply Programs

Various organizations sponsor programs to increase and improve the world's food supply. The chief international organizations include two United Nations

Alain Nogues, Sygma

Emergency Food Supplies are provided for thousands of disaster victims annually. These Red Cross workers are distributing emergency rations to victims of a flood in Bangladesh.

(UN) agencies—the Food and Agriculture Organization (FAO) and the World Bank. Another major agency, the Organization for Economic Cooperation and Development (OECD), is made up of developed non-Communist countries. The World Food Council, a group of food experts appointed by the UN, helps coordinate the work of the various international organizations. Many developed nations have set up their own agencies to help increase the world's food supply.

A number of important food supply programs are sponsored by religious and other private groups. For example, the Rockefeller Foundation, an organization founded in the United States by the Rockefeller family, has long been one of the biggest contributors to agricultural research in developing countries.

Technical and Financial Programs work to expand farm output in developing countries. The FAO sponsors the chief technical assistance programs. These programs are designed mainly to train farmers in modern agricultural methods. The United Nations Development Program also sponsors technical aid programs (see UNITED NATIONS [Economic and Technical Aid]). Most financial help for agriculture in the developing countries is in the form of low-interest loans. The OECD, the World Bank, and various regional banks associated with the World Bank provide most of the loans. In 1976, the UN established the International Fund for Agricultural Development to obtain additional loan funds from prosperous UN members. The United States offers technical aid and loans chiefly through its Agency for International Development.

Food Aid Programs provide shipments of food to countries that need emergency aid. Members of the OECD contribute most of this aid. The United States is the largest contributor. Most U.S. assistance is administered through the federal government's Food for Peace program. The World Food Program, sponsored by the

UN and the FAO, channels donations from individual countries to nations in need of aid. Many private charitable organizations also supply food aid.

Research Programs. Various scientific research programs seek to increase both the quality and the quantity of the food supply. For example, a variety of corn with an improved amino acid content was developed in the 1960's. But the new variety gives relatively low yields. Scientists are now working to develop a high-yield variety with the improved amino acid content.

Research scientists are also seeking ways to conserve agricultural resources. As we have seen, some of this research is aimed at developing varieties of grain that make more efficient use of water and fertilizer. Animal scientists are conducting similar experiments to develop varieties of cattle that produce more meat from the same amount of feed.

Many research projects are carried out at about 10 agricultural research institutes jointly sponsored by the FAO, the World Bank, the Ford and Rockefeller foundations, and several other organizations. The institutes have been established in developing countries, and each specializes in a particular type of research. In Mexico, for example, the International Center for the Improvement of Maize and Wheat is trying to produce improved varieties of corn, wheat, and certain other grains. Some of the institutes, such as the International Rice Research Institute in the Philippines, are working to develop varieties of plants and livestock that are specially suited to tropical climates. For more information on agricultural research, see AGRICULTURAL RESEARCH SERVICE; RESEARCH (Agriculture).

A World Food Reserve. In 1974, representatives from 130 countries attended a UN-sponsored World Food Conference in Rome. The representatives adopted a plan to set up a unified world food reserve. The world's reserves now consist of the individual reserves of the major exporting countries. Each country administers its own reserve. Under the new plan, each country will continue to hold its own reserve, but it will work with participating countries in the use of the reserve. Reserve supplies can thus be directed to parts of the world where they are needed most.   LESTER R. BROWN

Related Articles. See AGRICULTURE, FOOD, and NUTRITION with their lists of *Related Articles*. See also the following articles:

Agency for International   Food for Peace
  Development   Foreign Aid
Birth Control   Green Revolution
Famine   Population
Fishing Industry   Standard of Living
Food and Agriculture   Technical Assistance
  Organization   World Bank

Outline

I. **Basic Human Food Needs**
    A. Calories
    B. Protein
II. **Major Sources of Food**
    A. Cereal Grains
    B. Livestock and Fish
    C. Other Major Food Sources
III. **Conditions That Affect the Food Supply**
    A. Limited Agricultural Resources
    B. Increased Demand for Food
    C. Distribution Problems

FOOD VALUES

Questions

Why do most developing countries seldom have enough food?

What are four methods to increase the food supply?

What plants are the world's most important source of food? Why?

Why did a great increase in food production during the 1960's do little to help improve people's diets in the developing countries?

What is protein-calorie malnutrition? Why is it harmful?

What are two United Nations agencies that sponsor food supply programs?

Which country produces the most surplus food?

How do higher living standards affect the food supply?

What is the Green Revolution?

How would a reduction in the demand for feed grain increase the food supply? Why?

FOOD VALUES. See NUTRITION.

FOOD WEB. See ECOLOGY (The Activities); FISH (Fish in the Balance of Nature).

FOOL HEN. See GROUSE.

FOOLISH FIRE. See WILL-O'-THE-WISP.

FOOLS, FEAST OF. See FEAST OF FOOLS.

FOOL'S GOLD. See PYRITE; MINERAL (color picture).

FOOLSCAP is paper that has been cut to about 13 inches (33 centimeters) wide and about 17 inches (43 centimeters) long. A jester, or *fool*, in medieval courts often wore a conical cap, sometimes trimmed with bells, which was called a *fool's cap*. Early papermakers used a fool's cap watermark for paper of this size.

FOOT, in poetry. See POETRY (Metrical Patterns).

FOOT is a unit of length in the customary system of measurement used in the United States. It is equal to one-third of a yard, and contains 12 inches. One foot equals 0.3048 meter.

The foot measurement was originally based on the length of the human foot. But the human foot varied in size too much to be used in measuring. When the English fixed the yard at 36 inches, they set the foot as one-third of a yard. One story says the yard was set by measuring the length of the arm of King Henry I. Historians do not believe this, because only a giant would have arms 36 inches (91 centimeters) long.

A *square foot* is a unit of area. It is equal to the area of a square whose sides are 1 foot long. It contains 12 x 12, or 144, square inches (929 square centimeters). A *cubic foot* is a unit of volume. It is equal to the volume of a cube 1 foot high, 1 foot wide, and 1 foot deep. It contains 12 x 12 x 12, or 1,728, cubic inches (28,327 cubic centimeters). The *board foot* is a unit measure for logs and lumber. It is 1 foot long, 1 foot wide, and 1 inch (2.54 centimeters) thick. The symbol for foot is '.

E. G. STRAUS

See also WEIGHTS AND MEASURES.

FOOT is the structure at the end of the leg, on which humans and some animals stand. In animals that walk on all four legs, the ends of the front and hind limbs, or feet, are much the same. In humans, birds, and animals such as the kangaroo that walk on their hind limbs, the foot is heavier and stronger than its counterpart on the forelimb, the hand.

The Bones. The human foot has 26 bones. They are (1) the seven *tarsals*, or ankle bones; (2) the five *metatarsals*, or instep bones; and (3) the 14 *phalanges*, or toe bones. The tarsal bones are the *talus, calcaneus, navicular, cuboid*, and the three *cuneiform* bones. They form the heel and back part of the instep. The metatarsal bones connect the cuneiforms and the cuboid with the phalanges, and form the front part of the instep. The big toe has two phalanges. Each of the other toes has three. The ends of the phalanges meet the underside of the metatarsals to form the *ball of the foot*.

The Arches. The bones of the foot form three arches, two running lengthwise and one running across the instep. The arches provide the natural elastic spring of the foot in walking or jumping. The main arch reaches from the heel bone to the ball of the foot. It is called the *long medial* or *plantar* arch. This arch presses down on the ground only at the heel and ball of the foot, and thus prevents jars which might shock the spinal column. A thick layer of flexible cartilage covers the end of the bones of the arch (see CARTILAGE). The cartilage helps make the arch shock-absorbent. The *lateral* arch runs along the outside of the foot, and the *transverse* or *metatarsal* arch lies across the ball of the foot. The condition known as *flatfoot* may be caused by the breakdown of the arches of the foot (see FLATFOOT).

Ligaments and Muscles support the arches of the foot. The *long plantar* ligament is very strong. It keeps the bones of the foot in place and protects the nerves, muscles, and blood vessels in the hollow of the foot. The foot has as many muscles as the hand. But its structure permits less flexibility and freedom of movement than does that of the hand.

Tough, thick skin covers the *sole*, or bottom, of the foot. A thick pad of fatty tissue lies between the skin and the bones and the plantar ligament. This layer of fat acts like an air cushion to protect the inner parts

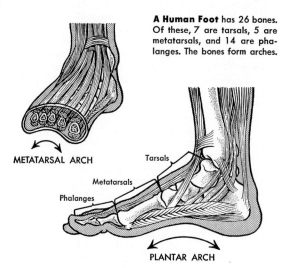

A Human Foot has 26 bones. Of these, 7 are tarsals, 5 are metatarsals, and 14 are phalanges. The bones form arches.

METATARSAL ARCH

Tarsals

Metatarsals

Phalanges

PLANTAR ARCH

of the foot from pressure on the foot and from jarring.

Disorders of the foot, such as corns, often result from wearing badly fitted shoes.　　　WILLIAM V. MAYER

Related Articles in WORLD BOOK include:

Achilles' Tendon	Bunion	Footprinting
Animal (picture:	Callus	Immersion Foot
Kinds of Feet)	Chilblain	Podiatry
Ankle	Clubfoot	Transverse Arch
Athlete's Foot	Corn	

FOOT, MICHAEL (1913-   ), is a British political leader. In 1976, he became deputy prime minister, leader of the House of Commons, and lord president of the Council—a largely honorary Cabinet post. Foot was named to these offices following James Callaghan's election as Labour Party leader by the party's members of Parliament. Callaghan became prime minister as a result of the elections. Foot had received the second largest number of votes.

Foot is a leader of the left wing of the Labour Party. The left wing calls for increased spending on social welfare programs and for government ownership of business.

Foot was born in Plymouth, England, and attended Oxford University. He became a newspaper

Pictorial Parade
Michael Foot

columnist and editor and a forceful left wing critic of British government policies. From 1945 to 1955, Foot represented a district of Plymouth in the House of Commons. He has represented the Ebbw Vale district of Wales since 1960. He was secretary of state for employment from 1974 to 1976.　　　RICHARD ROSE

FOOT-AND-MOUTH DISEASE is a highly contagious disease of animals. It is also called *hoof-and-mouth disease*. It attacks cattle, sheep, hogs, and other animals with *cleft* (divided) hoofs. The disease rarely attacks human beings. However, a person may get it by drinking milk from infected cows or by handling diseased animals. Blisters are the main symptom of the disease. They break out first in the animal's mouth and later on its feet. The disease has been known in Europe since 1809. The first outbreak in the United States was in 1870. Since then there have been at least nine outbreaks. Although the disease spreads rapidly, the U.S. government has organized effective control methods.

Cause and Symptoms. In 1957, scientists isolated and photographed the virus that causes foot-and-mouth disease. It is one of the smallest viruses that cause animal diseases. After the virus enters the animal, it takes from two to four days for signs of the disease to appear. Early symptoms include fever, smacking of the lips, and drooling. The animal does not want to move around and shows considerable stiffness when it tries to walk. In about two days, the mouth, tongue, and inner side of the lips show blisters, and saliva drops from the mouth.

The blisters break in two or three days and leave ulcers. These may heal quickly or very slowly. Soon the animal becomes lame. To ease the pain, it draws up first one foot and then the other. The blisters then appear on the skin above the hoof. Later the hoof may separate in

places. The teats of cows often break out in blisters. In the more dangerous form of the disease, death may occur suddenly. As high as 70 per cent of these cases are fatal. In ordinary cases, the death rate is from 1 to 5 per cent. Although the disease does not kill many animals, it causes inflamed udders and losses in milk and flesh.

Measures of Control. As soon as an outbreak is reported in the United States, federal and state authorities quarantine the farm, the locality, or even the whole state. The authorities kill the infected and exposed animals, and bury them in quicklime. Their sheds and pens are disinfected, and all infected feed and litter is burned. Persons who come in contact with infected animals are required to wear rubber clothing that can be disinfected.　　　D. W. BRUNER

FOOT-CANDLE is a unit of measurement of *illumination*, the amount of light that falls on an object. The foot-candle is part of the customary, or English, system of measurement.

Two factors determine the amount of light that an object receives: (1) the *luminous intensity* (brightness) of the light source and (2) the distance between the light source and the object. As the luminous intensity of the light source increases, illumination also increases. As the distance increases, illumination decreases.

To calculate foot-candles (*fc*), scientists use the formula $fc = \dfrac{cd}{d^2}$. Cd is the luminous intensity of the light, measured in *candelas* (see CANDELA). *D* is the distance between the light source and the object, measured in feet.

In the metric system, units of measurement for illumination include the *lux* and the *phot*. Distance is measured in meters to calculate luxes, and in centimeters to calculate phots.　　　RONALD N. HELMS

See also LIGHT (The Brightness of Light; diagram: Basic Units); LIGHTING (Quantity of Light).

FOOT-POUND is a unit in the customary, or English, system of measurement. It is used to measure *work* and *energy*.

Physicists define work as the product of force and distance when a force moves an object through a distance. One foot-pound is the amount of work done when a force of 1 pound moves an object a distance of 1 foot. If a force of 2 pounds moves an object 3 feet, the work done therefore equals 6 foot-pounds.

Energy is the ability to do work. The foot-pound is used to measure all forms of energy. One foot-pound equals the quantity of energy needed to lift a 1-pound object to a height of 1 foot. Thus, for example, 6 foot-pounds of mechanical energy are needed to lift a 2-pound object 3 feet high.

The rate at which work is done is called *power*. To measure power, the amount of time required to do the work is considered along with force and distance. Power may be measured either in foot-pounds per second or in horsepower. One horsepower equals 550 foot-pounds per second (see HORSEPOWER).

In the metric system of measurement, work and energy are measured in *joules*. One foot-pound equals 1.356 joules.　　　HUGH D. YOUNG

See also ENERGY (Measuring Energy); JOULE; WORK.

FOOT RACE. See RUNNING.

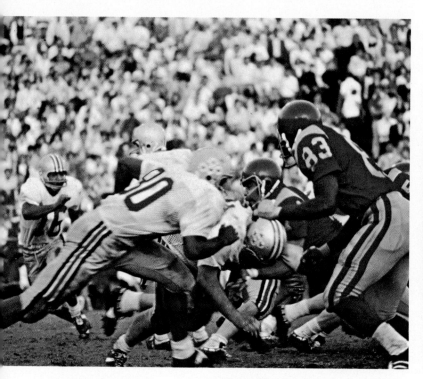

Football Games Are Colorful Spectacles. Fans enjoy the rugged action, and peppy cheerleaders help them root for their favorite team.

FOOTBALL

FOOTBALL is an exciting sport played by elementary school, high school, college, and professional teams. Every football season, millions of fans crowd into huge stadiums to watch two teams try to move the ball across each other's goal line. Millions more watch college games on television, as well as televised competition in the two major professional leagues—the National Football League (NFL) and the Canadian Football League (CFL).

Football developed from soccer, a kicking game played with a round ball. Soccer is called *football* in most countries. In American football, the players carry or throw the ball much more than they kick it, and the ball itself is shaped like an egg.

Football players once needed little more than strength and speed. Today, a good football team combines strength, speed, skillful planning, and split-second teamwork—and the ability to fool the other team.

FOOTBALL / How to Play Football

The Football is a pointed, oval-shaped ball. It is about 11 inches (28 centimeters) long and more than 7 inches (18 centimeters) in diameter at the center. The ball is sometimes called a *pigskin* because it once was made of pig's hide. For many years, the best footballs have been made of cowhide, but rubber and plastic are also used. A football is made of four pieces of material sewn together with tight, inside seams. It has a rubber lining that is blown up to an air pressure of $12\frac{1}{2}$ to $13\frac{1}{2}$ pounds per square inch (0.88 to 0.95 kilogram per square centimeter). The ball weighs from 14 to 15 ounces (397 to 425 grams).

Ara Parseghian, the contributor of this article, was formerly Head Football Coach at the University of Notre Dame. The photographs for the article were taken for WORLD BOOK by Lee Balterman and Phil Bath, unless otherwise noted.

Leather laces along one seam provide a good grip for passing the ball. The laces once closed an opening that was used to insert the lining after the ball had been stitched. Today, the lining is molded inside the ball before stitching.

The Field is a level area 360 feet (110 meters) long and 160 feet (49 meters) wide. White lines called *yard lines* run across the field every 5 yards (4.6 meters), and lines called *sidelines* run down each side. A football field is sometimes called a *gridiron* because it looks somewhat like a cooking utensil called a gridiron. The *goal lines* are 100 yards (91 meters) apart, and the *end zones* extend 10 yards (9 meters) beyond each goal line. The white lines are numbered from the goal lines to the 50-yard line or *midfield*. Two broken lines called *inbounds lines* or *hash marks* run parallel to the sidelines. For college games, the hash marks are 53 feet 4 inches (16.3 meters) from each sideline, dividing the field into thirds. For professional games, they are 70 feet 9 inches (21.6 meters) from each sideline. All plays start with the ball between the hash marks or on a hash mark. If a play ends out of bounds, or between a hash mark and a sideline, the ball is placed on the hash mark for the next play.

In high school and college football, two *goal posts*,

--- **FOOTBALL PLAYS** ---

Buck is a power play in which the runner tries to gain a few yards by driving between two of his linemen.

Counter is any play in which the action goes one way and the ball carrier goes another way.

Dive is a split-T power play in which the quarterback runs parallel to the line of scrimmage and gives the ball to a back. The runner then usually follows a tackle who is blocking straight ahead.

Dropback is a play in which the quarterback retreats into a protective "pocket" of blockers to throw a pass.

Off-Tackle is a running play in which the defensive end is blocked toward the sideline, and the defensive tackle is blocked inward, opening a hole for the runner.

Option is a variation of the dive play. As the quarterback runs parallel to the line, another back runs next to him. If the quarterback sees he is about to be tackled, he tosses the ball to the other man. Otherwise, he continues to run with the ball.

Rollout is a passing play in which the quarterback retreats a bit from the line of scrimmage and runs toward the sideline before throwing the ball.

Screen is a pass play in which the receiver is behind a screen of blockers at or near the line of scrimmage.

Sneak is usually called when a team needs only a few yards. The quarterback keeps the ball and drives straight ahead behind the blocking of the center and guards.

Sweep is a running play around either end.

Trap is a play in which a defensive lineman is allowed into the backfield, and then is blocked from the side. The ball carrier runs into the hole left by the trapped lineman.

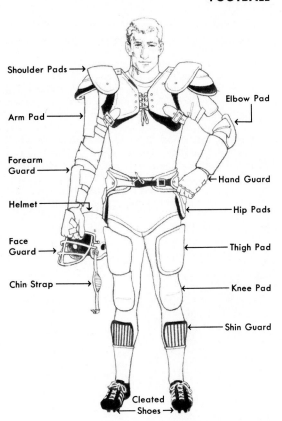

Shoulder Pads • Arm Pad • Forearm Guard • Helmet • Face Guard • Chin Strap • Elbow Pad • Hand Guard • Hip Pads • Thigh Pad • Knee Pad • Shin Guard • Cleated Shoes

Protective Equipment helps prevent football injuries. The amount of padding varies. Tackles, guards, and centers wear the most because they do the most blocking and tackling. Ends and backfield men wear less because they must run at top speed.

DIAGRAM OF A FOOTBALL FIELD

The gridiron is marked with white lines. Yard lines run across the field every five yards. Hash marks run down the field crossing the yard lines. College hash marks (shown in red) divide the field into thirds. Professional hash marks (shown in blue) are close to the center of the field. Goal posts stand on the end lines.

WORLD BOOK Diagram

100 yards from Goal Line to Goal Line

Goal Line • Goal Line

53 feet 4 inches • 70 feet 9 inches

Hash Marks (College) • Hash Marks (Professional)

53 feet 4 inches • 18 feet 6 inches

End Line, 160 feet • Goal Post • Goal Post • End Line

53 feet 4 inches • 70 feet 9 inches

End Zone 10 yards • End Zone 10 yards

Side Line, 120 yards from End Line to End Line

each 20 feet (6 meters) high, stand 10 yards (9 meters) behind each goal line. A crossbar connects them 10 feet (3 meters) above the ground. The posts are 18 feet 6 inches (5.6 meters) apart in high school games, and 23 feet 4 inches (7 meters) apart for college games. In professional football, the goal posts, 18 feet 6 inches (5.6 meters) apart, rise 20 feet (6 meters) from the crossbar. A single post 6 feet (1.8 meters) behind the end line curves forward to support the crossbar over the line.

Playing Time. College and professional football games are 60 minutes long. A game is divided into two 30-minute *halves*, each consisting of two 15-minute *quarters*. The teams change goals at the end of each quarter. A 15- to 20-minute intermission between halves is called *half-time*. There is a rest period of 1 or 2 minutes at the end of the first and third quarters. High school games are 48 minutes long, with 12-minute quarters.

The clock is stopped (1) after each incomplete pass, (2) after a team scores, (3) if a player is injured, or (4) if

Kickoff starts a football game and puts the ball in play. The kicker places the ball on a tee, *left,* and the kicking team lines up behind him. It cannot advance until the ball has been kicked, *below.* Two or three men on the receiving team stand downfield. One of them catches the ball and runs with it, and the others block for him.

the ball carrier crosses a sideline and goes out of bounds. In college games, the clock is also stopped after a first down. High school, college, and professional teams are allowed three time outs in each half.

The Kickoff starts each half of a game. The team that kicks off to begin the game is decided by a toss of a coin. The team that wins the coin toss can (1) choose to kick off or receive, or (2) choose the goal it will defend. For the start of the second half, the team that had lost the coin toss has its choice of kicking off or receiving, or choosing the goal it will defend.

A team also kicks off after it scores a touchdown or a field goal. Most kickers *place-kick* a kickoff. Before kicking the ball, they stand it at an angle on a tee. In high school and college games, kickoffs come from the 40-yard line. Kickoffs in the National Football League come from the 35-yard line.

The receiving team usually places two or three players near the goal line to catch the ball. After the receiver catches the ball, he runs it back as far as he can toward the kicking team's goal line. His teammates provide interference by blocking members of the kicking team, who try to down the runner. A *touchback* occurs if the kickoff carries out of the end zone or if the receiver downs the ball in the end zone. The ball is then put in play on the receiving team's 20-yard line.

A ball carrier is downed when any part of his body other than his feet and one hand touches the ground, or if he goes out of bounds. In professional football, the ball carrier must be downed by an opponent. If the ball carrier slips and falls, he can get up and keep running.

After the receiver has been downed, his team has four *downs* (plays) in which to advance the ball at least 10

yards and gain a *first down*. After each first down, the team with the ball gets another four downs to gain 10 more yards.

The Players. The team with the ball is called the *offensive* team, and the other team is the *defensive* team. Before each play, the two teams line up facing each other along the *line of scrimmage*. This imaginary line runs parallel to the yard lines, and passes through the tip of the ball nearest the defensive team's goal.

The offensive team must have at least seven players within a yard of the line of scrimmage. The most common lineup has three linemen on each side of the *center*. The two linemen next to the center are called *guards*, and the next two are the *tackles*. The two outside linemen are called *ends*. The backfield men are the *quarterback*, two *halfbacks*, and the *fullback*. One halfback may be placed near the line as a pass receiver called a *flanker*.

The defensive team lines up in any way it thinks will provide the greatest protection against the runs and passes of its opponent. There are usually four to seven linemen, one to four *linebackers* just behind them, and four backs.

Plays. The offensive team tries to advance the ball by running with it, or by passing or kicking it. Most plays start with the quarterback standing directly behind the center and calling a series of numbers or code words. These *signals* indicate what the play will be and when it will start. They are decided when the offensive team meets in a *huddle* before lining up to start the play. On most plays, the center quickly hands the ball through his legs to the quarterback. The quarterback either gives the ball to one of the other backs, or keeps it and runs or passes.

On a running play, there are three basic ways that the ball carrier may get past the line of scrimmage. He can use (1) speed, (2) power, or (3) deception—or a combination of all three. Using speed, the runner tries to get through a defensive area before the defense can tackle him. In power football, the offensive team attempts to outman its opponent by blocking the defenders out of the way. Teams usually try to deceive their opponents with plays in which the action seems to go in one direction, but the ball carrier goes another way.

Running plays go through five basic areas: (1) outside the right end; (2) off-tackle right, or inside the right end; (3) up the middle, or through the center and guard areas; (4) off-tackle left, or inside the left end; or (5) outside the left end.

On a passing play, the passer throws the ball to a player who then runs with it. A *forward pass* is thrown toward the opposing team's goal, and must be thrown from behind the line of scrimmage. Forward passes may be thrown to and by the four backs and two of the linemen, almost always the ends. The other five linemen must stay behind the line of scrimmage until the pass has been thrown. A *lateral pass* is thrown toward the sidelines or to the rear. It may be thrown by any player to any other player anywhere on the field.

A player in the backfield can *punt* (kick) the ball at any time. The punter drops the ball and kicks it before it touches the ground. Punting gives the ball to the other team. But even if the opposing team gets the ball, the punting team may gain an advantage by moving the ball farther from its own goal line. A team rarely punts except on fourth down, after it has failed to advance the ball at least 10 yards. But sometimes a team

Selection of Plays involves careful planning by the coaches and the quarterback. A coach in the press box, *left above,* watches the game and telephones suggestions to a coach on the sidelines, *left below.* The coaches and the quarterback then choose plays they think will gain the greatest yardage. Using code words and numbers, the quarterback gives the team its instructions in a huddle, *below.*

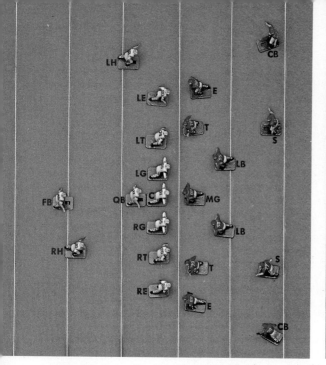

WORLD BOOK photos, courtesy Tudor Metal Products

DIAGRAM OF A RUNNING PLAY

Offensive Players

Center (C)
Left Guard (LG)
Right Guard (RG)
Left Tackle (LT)
Right Tackle (RT)
Left End (LE)
Right End (RE)
Quarterback (QB)
Fullback (FB)
Left Halfback (LH)
Right Halfback (RH)

Defensive Players

Middle Guard (MG)
Tackles (T)
Ends (E)
Linebackers (LB)
Safeties (S)
Cornerbacks (CB)

For a running play, the offensive team (shown in white) might line up in a type of winged T-formation, *left*. From this formation, the quarterback drops back and gives the ball to the fullback, who runs toward the right side of the line, *right*. The right tackle and right end clear a path for the fullback by blocking the defensive tackle. The other offensive players block various defensive men to keep them away from the fullback.

Linemen Get Set at the line of scrimmage before each play. No man on either team is allowed to move across the line until the center hands the ball to the quarterback, who stands directly behind him.

316

The Quarterback Hands Off to the fullback, but pretends to keep the ball so he can draw tacklers away from the fullback.

Running with the Ball requires speed and balance. The runner must avoid tacklers and keep a tight grip on the ball.

Blockers Run Ahead of the Ball Carrier and try to keep tacklers away from him. A blocker uses either a shoulder block, *left,* driving a shoulder into an opponent, or a body block, *right,* throwing his body across the opponent's thighs.

A Tackler Hits the Ball Carrier from any angle. The tackler usually hits with his shoulders and body, and then wraps his arms around the ball carrier's legs. He must keep a tight hold so the runner cannot squirm away and gain extra yardage.

317

The Officials Use a Yardage Chain to check whether the offense has advanced the ball 10 yards for a first down. The chain is normally kept on the sidelines. For close measurements, it is brought to the spot where the ball has been downed.

The Referee Signals a Foul. If an offensive player commits a foul, his team is penalized by a loss of yards or the loss of a down. If a defensive man commits a foul, the offense gains yardage or a down, or both. Penalties differ for various fouls.

unexpectedly punts on one of the first three downs. Such a punt is called a *quick kick* and is intended to catch the defensive team by surprise and thus reduce its chances for a runback.

Teams try not only to advance the ball, but also to gain the best possible *field position*. A team is in good field position when it has the ball in its opponent's half of the field. Good field position allows a team to use more daring strategy, because the ball is far from its own goal.

The offensive team loses possession of the ball if (1) it fails to make a first down; (2) it punts; (3) the ball carrier *fumbles*, or drops the ball, and a defensive player recovers it; or (4) a defensive player *intercepts*, or catches, a pass.

Scoring. There are four ways to score points in a football game. A team gets points by scoring (1) a touchdown, (2) a conversion, (3) a field goal, or (4) a safety.

A *touchdown* counts six points. A touchdown is scored when a team moves the ball across the opponent's goal line. The offensive team scores nearly all the touchdowns. The offensive team scores a touchdown by running the ball over the goal line or by catching a pass in the end zone. Occasionally, the defensive team scores a touchdown. For example, a defensive player may intercept a pass and run the ball for a touchdown. The defense may also recover a blocked punt or a fumble in the opponent's end zone for a touchdown.

Immediately after scoring a touchdown, a team tries for a *conversion*, or *point after touchdown*. The ball is put in play from the 3-yard line in college games and the 2-yard line in National Football League and most high school games. Most conversions are made by place-kicking the ball over the crossbar of the goal posts. A team scores one point by successfully place-kicking the conversion. In college ball, successfully running or passing the conversion counts two points. In high school and National Football League games, a successful conversion counts one point whether it is place-kicked, run, or passed.

A *field goal*, worth three points, is made by place-kicking the ball over the crossbar between the goal posts from anywhere on the field. A *safety*, worth two points, is scored by the defensive team when the ball carrier is downed in his own end zone, or if the ball carrier steps out of his end zone.

Formations. In the early days of football, strategy was fairly simple. One team usually tried to run over or around the other. Through the years, coaches came up with different strategies to fool the opposition. These strategies consisted either of special plays or of various series of plays. Entire systems of play gradually developed. Today, there are three major systems, each named after its basic player formation. These formations are the (1) *T-formation*, (2) *single wing*, and (3) *double wing*.

In the T-formation, the quarterback lines up directly behind the center. The three other backs line up in a row about four yards behind and parallel to the line of scrimmage. When viewed from above, this formation looks like the letter T. But a T-formation can be any system in which the quarterback takes a direct snap from the center. In the split-T, for example, the quarter-

back takes the ball and runs parallel to the line of scrimmage. He can run with the ball, toss it to another back, or throw a pass.

In the single wing formation, three backs line up in a row about four yards behind and parallel to the line of scrimmage. One back is *winged* outside one of the ends. In the double wing formation, two backs are behind the line and one *wingback* is outside each end. In both these formations, the center snaps the ball to any of the backs who are behind the line.

Many formations combine parts of the three major formations. The winged-T formation, for example, is a T-formation with a wingback. To confuse the defense, a team may use an I-formation. In this formation, the backs line up behind one another and behind the center. They usually shift into other positions just before the ball is snapped.

The Officials. Four to seven officials supervise a football game. If a player breaks any of the rules, the officials call a penalty on his team. All the officials have equal rights to call penalties.

The *referee* is the chief official, and has general control of the game. He stands behind the offensive team, and blows a whistle to declare the ball in play or *dead* (out of play). The *umpire* stands behind the defensive line and watches for fouls in the line. The *head linesman* stands at one end of the line of scrimmage. He marks the forward progress of the ball and supervises the marking crew, which moves up and down one sideline keeping track of the downs and the distance gained. The *field judge* stands on the opposite side of the field from the head linesman and is responsible for timing the game.

The Offense Usually Punts on Fourth Down. The center snaps the ball directly to the punter, *left*, who must get his kick away before a defensive man can rush in and block it, *right*.

DIAGRAM OF A PASS PLAY

A pass play can begin, *left*, with the offense (shown in white) in the same type of T-formation as for a running play. The quarterback drops back with the ball, *right*, and waits for the right halfback, right end, and left end to run certain patterns downfield. The other backs and some linemen form around the quarterback to protect him from the defensive men who try to rush in. Other defensive players guard the pass receivers. The quarterback passes when he spots an open receiver.

A Successful Pass Play requires speed and accuracy. After the quarterback has dropped back to pass, he must find a receiver in the clear. Then he must throw the ball, *left*, within the receiver's reach. The amount of time he has depends on how well his blockers protect him from the defense. A perfect pass may result in a catch in the end zone for a touchdown, *right*.

Touchdown! The ball carrier dives over a mass of linemen piled up on the goal line, *left*. The official's signal for a touchdown, *above*, indicates that at least a part of the ball was carried over the goal line for the score.

A Place Kick can be used to score a point after touchdown or a field goal. The ball must be kicked over the crossbar and between the uprights of the opposing team's goal post.

Defensive Players Leap to Block a Kick and prevent a score. Blockers on the kicking team try to keep the defensive men from rushing in toward the ball and the kicker.

FOUL SIGNALS

Offside

Interference

Illegal Procedure

Delay of Game

Holding

Roughing the Kicker

Ineligible Receiver Downfield

Illegal Motion

Personal Foul

Clipping   WORLD BOOK photos

College and professional games both have a *back judge*. In college games, he stands beyond the line of scrimmage, and assists the other officials when play moves downfield. In professional games, he stands about 15 yards behind the offensive team, and watches for fouls in the backfield. Professional games also have a *line judge*. He stands opposite the head linesman, and helps watch for fouls in the line.

———————————— FOULS AND PENALTIES ————————————

Clipping is committed when one player blocks another from behind. **Penalty**—15 yards.

Delay of Game occurs when the offensive team does not put the ball in play in 25 seconds or less after the last play, or after the referee has started play. In professional football, 30 seconds are allowed. This foul can also be called on the defensive team for slowing play. **Penalty**—5 yards.

Illegal Motion or **Illegal Procedure** is called if the offensive team does not have seven men on the line, or if an offensive player moves forward before the center snaps the ball. **Penalty**—5 yards.

Interference is called if either the pass receiver or the pass defender is tackled or blocked after the ball has been thrown, and before either has a chance to catch the ball. **Penalty**—If the defender interferes, the offensive team receives a first down at the point of the foul. If the receiver interferes, the offensive team is penalized 15 yards plus the loss of a down.

Holding is called on an offensive player who blocks with his hands away from his body, or stops a player by some method other than a legal block. Defensive holding is called if a defender grabs a blocker. **Penalty**—10 or 15 yards for offensive holding, or 5 yards for defensive holding. In professional football, the offensive team also gets a first down if a defensive player is caught holding.

Offside is called if a player crosses the line of scrimmage before the ball has been snapped. **Penalty**—5 yards.

Officials Use Hand Signals to show what is happening on the field. The signals for various fouls, *left,* are usually given by the referee. Other signals, including the one indicating a first down, *above,* can be given by any of the officials.

318d

First Football Game, 1869; Collection of William Boyd (WORLD BOOK Photo by Tom Morton)

The First College Football Game was played between Rutgers and Princeton in 1869. Details recalled by some of the players helped William Boyd paint a picture of the game many years later.

Beginnings. Football began in the mid-1800's, when a game similar to soccer was played in the East. The object of the game was simply to kick a round ball across the other team's goal line. The teams sometimes consisted of as many as 30 or even more players.

As the soccerlike game became popular, stricter rules were adopted and schools began to organize teams. The first college football game was played on Nov. 6, 1869, in New Brunswick, N.J. Rutgers defeated the College of New Jersey (now Princeton University), 6 to 4.

In 1874, the first of several changes brought football closer to today's game. That year, Harvard played McGill University of Montreal. The visiting Canadians, instead of playing the soccerlike kicking game, picked up the ball and ran with it. They scored by either carrying or kicking the ball over the goal line. The McGill players also tackled the Harvard ball carrier. McGill's game, played between 15-man teams, was a variation of rugby football, a game that developed from soccer in England (see RUGBY FOOTBALL). The Harvard team liked the new version of football, and introduced it to other college teams in the United States. Running, blocking, and tackling soon became as important as kicking.

Shortly after Eastern colleges began to play the rugby-type football game, they began changing and improving it. About 1880, they adopted rules allowing a team to keep possession of the ball while trying to make a first down. Also, the number of men on each team was reduced to 11. The rules concerning possession and first down improved the game by giving teams time to plan strategy for advancing the ball. At first, a team had to advance the ball only five yards in three plays for a first down. Many of the early rules varied from game to game, and depended on agreement between the teams beforehand.

During the 1880's, football spread quickly from Eastern colleges to high schools and community playgrounds throughout the East and Midwest. Many towns organized football teams and developed rivalries with one another.

By 1900, football consisted mostly of running, blocking, and tackling. Teams ran with the ball to advance it, but kicking was still the most frequent way of scoring. Soon, merely kicking the ball over the goal line became too easy. To make scoring more difficult, a narrow goal area in the middle of the goal line was added. The ball had to be kicked into this area for a score. Later, goal posts marked the goal area, and finally a crossbar was placed between the posts.

Violence and the Forward Pass. As running, blocking, and tackling became more and more important in football, so did strength and wrestling ability. Football games became violent, and many players were injured.

318e

Early Football Stars William (Pudge) Heffelfinger, *left,* and T. Lee (Bum) McClung played for Yale from 1888 to 1891.

The Four Horsemen of Notre Dame formed an outstanding backfield from 1922 to 1924. These famous players were, *left to right,* right halfback Don Miller, fullback Elmer Layden, left halfback Jim Crowley, and quarterback Harry Stuhldreher.

Many games seemed more like organized fights than athletic events. Some players wore uniforms with straps on the shoulders and hips so teammates could pull them forward and advance the ball. Members of the other team tried to pull them backward.

In 1905, President Theodore Roosevelt saw a photograph of an injured football player and threatened to ban the game if such violence continued. Some college presidents prohibited football at their schools because of the frequent injuries.

In 1906, college coaches and faculty members changed the rules of football to take some of the stress away from running and blocking. A back was now allowed to throw the ball forward to another back or to an end.

The first forward pass was thrown for an 18-yard gain by Wesleyan University against Yale in 1906. But passing did not become popular until 1913, in a game between Notre Dame and Army. The Army team was favored to win because it was stronger and heavier than Notre Dame. But Gus Dorais, the Notre Dame quarterback, threw the ball several times to Knute Rockne, a star end, and Notre Dame won, 35 to 13.

Forward passing quickly became an established part of football and helped make the game more popular

---

MAJOR COLLEGE FOOTBALL CONFERENCES

Most major college football teams belong to an athletic conference. Those that do not belong to a conference are called *independents.* Leading independent teams include Air Force, Army, Miami (Fla.), Navy, Notre Dame, Penn State, Pittsburgh, South Carolina, Syracuse, and Tulane.

Atlantic Coast Conference	Ivy League	Big Eight Conference	Western Athletic Conference
Clemson	Brown	Colorado	
Duke	Columbia	Iowa State	Brigham Young
Georgia Tech	Cornell	Kansas	Colorado State
Maryland	Dartmouth	Kansas State	New Mexico
North Carolina	Harvard	Missouri	San Diego State
North Carolina State	Pennsylvania	Nebraska	Texas (at El Paso)
Virginia	Princeton	Oklahoma	Utah
Wake Forest	Yale	Oklahoma State	Wyoming

Pacific Ten Conference	Southeastern Conference	Big Ten Conference	Southwest Athletic Conference
Arizona	Alabama	Illinois	
Arizona State	Auburn	Indiana	Arkansas
California (at Berkeley)	Florida	Iowa	Baylor
Oregon	Georgia	Michigan	Houston
Oregon State	Kentucky	Michigan State	Rice
Stanford	Louisiana State	Minnesota	Southern Methodist
Southern California	Mississippi	Northwestern	Texas
UCLA (University of California at Los Angeles)	Mississippi State	Ohio State	Texas A&M
Washington	Tennessee	Purdue	Texas Christian
Washington State	Vanderbilt	Wisconsin	Texas Tech

MAJOR COLLEGIATE BOWL GAMES

Game	Location	Year Started
Bluebonnet Bowl	Houston, Tex.	1959
Cotton Bowl	Dallas, Tex.	1937
Fiesta Bowl	Tempe, Ariz.	1971
Gator Bowl	Jacksonville, Fla.	1946
Hall of Fame Classic	Birmingham, Ala.	1977
Liberty Bowl	Memphis, Tenn.	1959
Orange Bowl	Miami, Fla.	1933
Peach Bowl	Atlanta, Ga.	1968
Rose Bowl	Pasadena, Calif.	1902
Sugar Bowl	New Orleans, La.	1935
Sun Bowl	El Paso, Tex.	1936
Tangerine Bowl	Orlando, Fla.	1947

MAJOR COLLEGIATE ALL-STAR GAMES

Game	Location	Year Started
All-America Bowl	Tampa, Fla.	1969
Blue-Gray	Montgomery, Ala.	1938
East-West	Palo Alto, Calif.	1925
Hula Bowl	Honolulu, Hawaii	1951
Senior Bowl	Mobile, Ala.	1950

HEISMAN TROPHY WINNERS

Year	Player	School	Position
1935	Jay Berwanger	Chicago	Back
1936	Larry Kelley	Yale	End
1937	Clint Frank	Yale	Back
1938	Davey O'Brien	Texas Christian	Back
1939	Nile Kinnick	Iowa	Back
1940	Tom Harmon	Michigan	Back
1941	Bruce Smith	Minnesota	Back
1942	Frank Sinkwich	Georgia	Back
1943	Angelo Bertelli	Notre Dame	Back
1944	Les Horvath	Ohio State	Back
1945	Doc Blanchard	Army	Back
1946	Glenn Davis	Army	Back
1947	Johnny Lujack	Notre Dame	Back
1948	Doak Walker	Southern Methodist	Back
1949	Leon Hart	Notre Dame	End
1950	Vic Janowicz	Ohio State	Back
1951	Dick Kazmaier	Princeton	Back
1952	Billy Vessels	Oklahoma	Back
1953	Johnny Lattner	Notre Dame	Back
1954	Alan Ameche	Wisconsin	Back
1955	Howard Cassady	Ohio State	Back
1956	Paul Hornung	Notre Dame	Back
1957	John Crow	Texas A&M	Back
1958	Pete Dawkins	Army	Back
1959	Billy Cannon	Louisiana State	Back
1960	Joe Bellino	Navy	Back
1961	Ernie Davis	Syracuse	Back
1962	Terry Baker	Oregon State	Back
1963	Roger Staubach	Navy	Back
1964	John Huarte	Notre Dame	Back
1965	Mike Garrett	Southern California	Back
1966	Steve Spurrier	Florida	Back
1967	Gary Beban	UCLA	Back
1968	O. J. Simpson	Southern California	Back
1969	Steve Owens	Oklahoma	Back
1970	Jim Plunkett	Stanford	Back
1971	Pat Sullivan	Auburn	Back
1972	Johnny Rodgers	Nebraska	Back
1973	John Cappelletti	Penn State	Back
1974	Archie Griffin	Ohio State	Back
1975	Archie Griffin	Ohio State	Back
1976	Tony Dorsett	Pittsburgh	Back
1977	Earl Campbell	Texas	Back
1978	Billy Sims	Oklahoma	Back

University of Illinois Athletic Association

The Galloping Ghost, Red Grange of Illinois, scored on each of his first five carries against Michigan in 1924.

than ever. Passing let smaller, faster players compete successfully, and required careful planning and the use of many different plays.

College Football became organized in 1876. That year, Harvard, Yale, Princeton, and Columbia formed the American Intercollegiate Football Association, the first college football conference. Today, most of the more than 600 college and university football teams belong to one of about 60 college conferences. These conferences set standards for competition and are made up of teams of about the same strength.

Conference members and independent teams belong to one of two intercollegiate athletic organizations—the National Collegiate Athletic Association (NCAA) or the National Association of Intercollegiate Athletics (NAIA). These organizations establish standard rules and supervise competition among member teams.

Every week during the football season, the Associated Press and United Press International choose the 10 best college football teams in the United States. The two news services pick the top teams from the members of the 11 major conferences and from leading independent teams. Not all the major teams represent the largest colleges and universities. The Football Writers' Association of America considers a team major if it belongs to one of the 11 main conferences or if it plays at least half its games against other major teams. The Associated Press ranking is prepared by about 50 sports writers and broadcasters. The United Press International selections are made by 35 college coaches. At the end of the season, each news service awards a trophy to the team it chooses as national champion.

After each season, a number of high-ranking teams play in various bowl games. The first bowl game was played in 1902, when Michigan defeated Stanford, 49 to 0, in the Rose Bowl. Most bowl games are played in late December and on New Year's Day. Other post-season games are all-star contests. The teams that play in all-star games are made up of outstanding players who are seniors at colleges and universities.

Outstanding college players are also honored by being named to various all-America teams. All-America selections started in 1889 when Walter Camp, a former

FOOTBALL

Yale star, and Caspar Whitney, a sportswriter, named 11 players as the best in the nation at their positions. Today, many newspapers, magazines, news services, and athletic foundations pick all-America teams.

Many clubs and organizations present awards to college players each year. The Downtown Athletic Club of New York City awards the John W. Heisman Memorial Trophy to the player voted best in the country by a group of sportswriters. The Maxwell Club of Philadelphia gives the Robert Maxwell Memorial Trophy to a top player. The National Football Hall of Fame on the Rutgers campus in New Jersey honors both players and coaches.

Professional Football. The town teams of the late 1800's became the first professional football teams when they began paying college players to play for them. The first game between two professional teams took place one Sunday in 1895, when a team from Latrobe, Pa., played the team from nearby Jeannette. Latrobe beat Jeannette, 12 to 0. Each player in that game received $10. Soon, with increased competition between town teams, especially in the Midwest, college football players were being paid as much as $600 a game. Ever since, many leading college players have

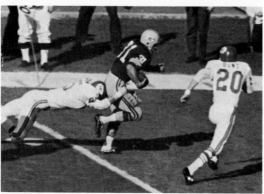

Vic Stein

The First Super Bowl was won by the Green Bay Packers in 1967. The Packers defeated the Kansas City Chiefs, 35-10. This picture shows Packer fullback Jim Taylor scoring a touchdown.

National Football League

American Conference

Eastern Division	Central Division	Western Division
Baltimore Colts	Cincinnati	Denver Broncos
New England	Bengals	Kansas City Chiefs
Patriots	Cleveland	Oakland
Buffalo Bills	Browns	Raiders
Miami	Houston Oilers	San Diego
Dolphins	Pittsburgh	Chargers
New York Jets	Steelers	Seattle
		Seahawks

National Conference

Eastern Division	Central Division	Western Division
Dallas Cowboys	Chicago Bears	Atlanta Falcons
New York Giants	Detroit Lions	Los Angeles Rams
Philadelphia	Green Bay	New Orleans
Eagles	Packers	Saints
St. Louis Cardinals	Minnesota	San Francisco
Washington	Vikings	49'ers
Redskins	Tampa Bay	
	Buccaneers	

Professional Football Champions

National Conference*

Season	Champion	Season	Champion
1933	Chicago Bears	1952	Detroit Lions
1934	New York Giants	1953	Detroit Lions
1935	Detroit Lions	1954	Cleveland Browns
1936	Green Bay Packers	1955	Cleveland Browns
1937	Washington Redskins	1956	New York Giants
1938	New York Giants	1957	Detroit Lions
1939	Green Bay Packers	1958	Baltimore Colts
1940	Chicago Bears	1959	Baltimore Colts
1941	Chicago Bears	1960	Philadelphia Eagles
1942	Washington Redskins	1961	Green Bay Packers
1943	Chicago Bears	1962	Green Bay Packers
1944	Green Bay Packers	1963	Chicago Bears
1945	Cleveland Rams	1964	Cleveland Browns
1946	Chicago Bears	1965	Green Bay Packers
1947	Chicago Cardinals	1966-1967	†Green Bay Packers
1948	Philadelphia Eagles	1967-1968	†Green Bay Packers
1949	Philadelphia Eagles	1968-1969	Baltimore Colts
1950	Cleveland Browns	1969-1970	Minnesota Vikings
1951	Los Angeles Rams	1970-1971	Dallas Cowboys

Season	Champion	Season	Champion
1971-1972	†Dallas Cowboys	1975-1976	Dallas Cowboys
1972-1973	Washington Redskins	1976-1977	Minnesota Vikings
		1977-1978	†Dallas Cowboys
1973-1974	Minnesota Vikings	1978-1979	Dallas Cowboys
1974-1975	Minnesota Vikings		

American Conference**

Season	Champion	Season	Champion
1960	Houston Oilers	1969-1970	†Kansas City Chiefs
1961	Houston Oilers	1970-1971	†Baltimore Colts
1962	Dallas Texans	1971-1972	Miami Dolphins
1963	San Diego Chargers	1972-1973	†Miami Dolphins
1964	Buffalo Bills	1973-1974	†Miami Dolphins
1965	Buffalo Bills	1974-1975	†Pittsburgh Steelers
1966-1967	Kansas City Chiefs	1975-1976	†Pittsburgh Steelers
1967-1968	Oakland Raiders	1976-1977	†Oakland Raiders
		1977-1978	Denver Broncos
1968-1969	†New York Jets	1978-1979	†Pittsburgh Steelers

*National Football League until 1970.
†Won Super Bowl.
**American Football League until 1970.

Fran Tarkenton, quarterback of the Minnesota Vikings, holds several National Football League passing records. He also became noted for his ability to elude tacklers.

continued their football careers on professional teams.

In the early days of professional football, college players often played for their schools on Saturdays and for professional teams on Sundays. Today, a man is not allowed to play professional football or to sign a contract with a professional football team while playing on a college team.

Professional football was disorganized until 1920, when the American Professional Football Association was founded. The 11 teams in the association included what later became the Chicago Bears and the St. Louis Cardinals. In 1922, the organization was renamed the National Football League (NFL). No one paid much attention to the NFL until 1925. That year, Red Grange, the star Illinois halfback, joined the Bears after the college season for a series of exhibition games. Grange's fame as a runner attracted about 200,000 fans during a 10-game tour and greatly increased interest in professional football.

In 1933, the National Football League divided into

two conferences. The Chicago Bears, champions of the Western Conference, beat the New York Giants of the Eastern Conference that fall for the first world championship.

The All-America Football Conference was formed in 1944, and began competition in 1946. The new 8-team league took many players from the NFL, but never became so successful as the older league. In 1950, the two leagues merged into a 13-team league rather than continue competing with each other. The league was reduced to 12 teams in 1951.

During the 1950's, professional football gained great nationwide popularity. Television networks began paying millions of dollars for the rights to televise games. As money from television increased, so did players' salaries—and more college stars aimed for careers in professional football.

In 1960, the popularity of professional football led to the founding of the American Football League (AFL). This eight-team league competed with the NFL both for college stars and for older NFL players. Teams of both professional leagues offered some college stars as much as $500,000 in salary and bonus over a period of several years. In 1966, the two leagues agreed to end their competition by merging into one league in 1970.

Following the merger agreement, the NFL expanded to 16 teams, and the AFL to 10 teams. In 1970, the merger led to a new National Football League consisting of an American Conference and a National Conference. Three teams from the former National League

Star Running Backs of the 1970's included O. J. Simpson, *left,* and Walter Payton, *right.* In 1973, Simpson, then with the Buffalo Bills, became the first professional player to gain 2,000 yards in a season. Payton, of the Chicago Bears, set a pro record of 275 yards in one game in 1977.

FOOTBALL

—Baltimore, Cleveland, and Pittsburgh—joined the teams from the former American League, so that the National Conference and the American Conference each would have 13 teams. The addition of Tampa Bay and Seattle in 1976 gave each conference 14 teams. Each conference has three divisions. The division winners and the next two teams with the best record in each conference play to determine the conference champions. These champions then play for the NFL championship in a game called the *Super Bowl*.

The teams in both conferences obtain college players through a draft. Each team chooses men who have completed their college playing careers. First choice goes to the team that ended the previous season with the poorest record in the two conferences. The winner of the Super Bowl chooses last. No team can sign a player who has been drafted by another team. The practice of drafting college football players was started in 1936 by the NFL.

A new professional football league, the World Football League (WFL), began play in 1974 with 12 teams. Several of the teams experienced financial difficulties and the league was reorganized in 1975. Despite the addition of several former NFL stars, most of the teams still had financial problems. The league collapsed and ceased operations during the 1975 season.

Players, coaches, and others who have made outstanding contributions to professional football are honored in the National Professional Football Hall of Fame, established in 1962 in Canton, Ohio.

FOOTBALL / *Other Kinds of Football*

Canadian Football is played by 12-man teams on a field 110 yards (100 meters) long and 65 yards (59 meters) wide. The 12th man usually lines up in the backfield, but he may be used as an end. The offensive team has three downs to advance the ball 10 yards.

Scoring in Canadian football is the same as in U.S. football, with one exception. The Canadian field has a *dead-ball line* 25 yards (23 meters) behind each goal line. On a kick, the receiving team must advance the ball out of the area between the dead-ball line and the goal line. If it does not do so, the kicking team scores one point, called a *single*. A punt over the dead-ball line scores one point for the kicker's team.

Although hockey is Canada's major college sport, more than 30 Canadian colleges and universities compete in four regional football conferences. The conference champions meet in post-season playoffs, with the two finalists playing in the Canadian College Bowl. The national champion is awarded the Vanier Cup.

Teams of the Canadian Football League play professional football in Canada. The league is divided into an Eastern Conference and a Western Conference. The conference champions play for the Grey Cup championship each November or December (see GREY CUP).

Six- and Eight-Man Football are played on a field 80 yards (73 meters) long and 40 yards (37 meters) wide. The player who receives the ball from the center must pass it to a teammate. Players must not leave their feet to block an opponent. An eight-man team consists of five linemen and three backs. A six-man team has three linemen and three backs.

Touch Football differs from regular football in that the ball carrier is downed when merely touched by an opponent. The players usually stand upright when blocking. Touch football can be played by almost any number of players on a field of any size. *Pass ball* and *flag ball* are similar to touch football.   ARA PARSEGHIAN

——— CANADIAN FOOTBALL LEAGUE ———	
EASTERN CONFERENCE	**WESTERN CONFERENCE**
Hamilton Tiger-Cats	British Columbia Lions
Montreal Alouettes	Calgary Stampeders
Ottawa Rough Riders	Edmonton Eskimos
Toronto Argonauts	Saskatchewan Roughriders
	Winnipeg Blue Bombers

FOOTBALL / *Study Aids*

Related Articles in WORLD BOOK include:

Brown, Jim	Namath, Joe	Thorpe, Jim
Camp, Walter C.	Rockne, Knute K.	Unitas, John
Grange, Red	Rozelle, Pete	United States
Halas, George S.	Rugby Football	(picture)
Heisman Memorial	Simpson, O. J.	Warner, Pop
Trophy	Soccer	White, Byron R.
Lombardi, Vince	Stagg, Amos A.	

Outline

I. How to Play Football
  A. The Football
  B. The Field
  C. Playing Time
  D. Kickoff
  E. The Players
  F. Plays
  G. Scoring
  H. Formations
  I. The Officials

II. History
  A. Beginnings
  B. Violence and the Forward Pass
  C. College Football
  D. Professional Football

III. Other Kinds of Football
  A. Canadian Football
  B. Six- and Eight-Man Football
  C. Touch Football

Questions

When is the ball carrier downed in college football? In professional football?

What is the line of scrimmage? A lateral pass?

When and where was the first college football game?

How do professional football teams choose college players?

What are four ways by which the offensive team can lose possession of the ball?

Why did President Theodore Roosevelt threaten to ban football?

What is the difference between the T-formation and the single-wing formation?

How did the 1874 game between Harvard and McGill affect football in the United States?

How does the field in Canadian football differ from that in U.S. football?

When was the forward pass first widely used?

FOOTE, ANDREW HULL (1806-1863), was a Union Navy officer during the Civil War. He became the first American naval officer to command a flotilla of iron-clad gunboats in battle. His fleet joined the army in attacks on Fort Henry on the Tennessee River and on Fort Donelson on the Cumberland River in February, 1862. He helped break the Confederate line of defense in the surrounding area. He became a rear admiral in July, 1862.

A temperance society he founded on board the U.S.S. *Cumberland* in 1843 led to the abolishment in 1862 of the serving of liquor on U.S. warships. Foote commanded the U.S.S. *Perry* along the coast of Africa in operations against the slave trade from 1849 to 1851.

Foote was born on Sept. 12, 1806, in New Haven, Conn., and studied briefly at the U.S. Military Academy. He joined the navy at the age of 16.   RICHARD S. WEST, JR.

FOOTHILL. See HILL.

FOOTNOTE is a note printed in small type at the bottom of a page. It is used to give information that is too long or too detailed to be included in the original statement. Footnotes sometimes explain a word or idea that might easily be misunderstood, but more often they merely cite the source or authority for what the author says. Footnotes help to keep sentences short and free of excess facts. For example, a student writing a composition about the aardvark might want to tell some fact about this animal that he had learned from THE WORLD BOOK ENCYCLOPEDIA. The following sentence would be awkward:

In an article entitled AARDVARK on page 2 of Volume A of THE WORLD BOOK ENCYCLOPEDIA, it is stated that in the 1600's Dutch settlers in Africa gave the aardvark its name.

When a footnote is used, however, the sentence can be quickly and easily read:

The aardvark received its name from Dutch settlers in Africa in the 1600's.[1]

---

[1]"Aardvark," WORLD BOOK ENCYCLOPEDIA, Vol. A, p. 2.

A number in small type is commonly used to draw attention to a footnote. An asterisk (*), or a dagger (†), or a double dagger (‡) may be used instead of a number.

Footnotes referring to a book should list the name of the author first, the book title second, and the page number third. Those referring to magazine articles list the author first, the title of the article second, the name of the magazine third, the volume fourth, the date of issue fifth, and the page number sixth.   R. B. DOWNS

FOOTPRINTING provides a system of identification similar to fingerprinting (see FINGERPRINTING). It can be important in both criminal and civil cases, particularly in those instances where fingerprints cannot be obtained because of mutilation or complete dismemberment. For example, the United States Federal Bureau of Investigation devotes a part of its identification files to maintaining footprint records.

Newborn infants are often footprinted for identification. Such prints are obtained in maternity wards and hospitals by applying printer's ink to the sole and then pressing the foot lightly against white paper. In general, such footprints are kept in the individual hospital for future reference.   J. EDGAR HOOVER

FORAKER, MOUNT. See MOUNT FORAKER.

FORAMINIFER. See PROTOZOAN (The Sarcodina).

FORBES, ESTHER (1891-1967), was an American author. She won the 1943 Pulitzer prize in American history for her brilliant historical biography, *Paul Revere and the World He Lived In*. While writing this book, she became interested in the apprentice boys of Boston, and the part they played in the Revolutionary War. After finishing the adult biography, Miss Forbes wrote for young people the novel, *Johnny Tremain*, about an apprentice in the exciting days of the Boston Tea Party. This book won the Newbery medal in 1944. She also wrote such American historical novels as *A Mirror for Witches* (1928), *Paradise* (1937), *The General's Lady* (1938), *The Running of the Tide* (1948), and *Rainbow on the Road* (1954).

Eric Schaal

Esther Forbes

Esther Forbes was born in Westboro, Mass. She studied at the University of Wisconsin.   EVELYN RAY SICKELS

FORBES' ROAD. See PENNSYLVANIA STATE ROAD.

FORBES-ROBERTSON, SIR JOHNSTON (1853-1937), was one of the most distinguished English actor-managers. His best-known roles included the leading parts in *Hamlet*, *Macbeth*, *Caesar and Cleopatra*, and *The Passing of the Third Floor Back*. He made five tours of the United States, the first in 1885 and the last in 1915. Forbes-Robertson was born in London. He studied to be a painter at the Royal Academy, but in 1874 he went on the stage. He was knighted in 1913, and retired from the theater in 1916.   RICHARD MOODY

FORBIDDEN CITY. See LHASA; PEKING.

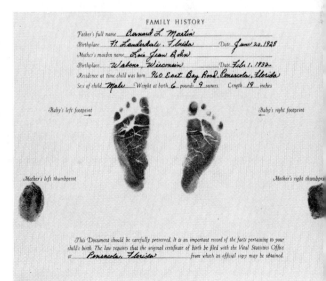

Franklin C. Hollister Co.

Footprints of a Newborn Baby are made in many hospitals. They appear on the hospital certificate along with the mother's thumbprints and a record of the facts about the child's birth.

FORCE

FORCE, in physics, is any cause that starts, stops, or changes motion. A force can be described as a push or a pull on an object. When you throw a ball into the air, it falls to the ground. We say that its *weight*, or the pull of the earth's gravity, causes it to fall. We call the attraction of the ball toward the earth the *force of gravity*. When a magnet attracts small pieces of iron, we say that *magnetic force* moves the iron. When a baseball player catches a ball in his glove, he produces a force that stops the ball from moving. There are many kinds of force, but physicists have discovered that they all act in a similar way.

Measuring Force. Physicists measure a force by the change in *velocity* (speed in one fixed direction) that it produces on a known mass in a given time. For example, in units of the metric system, 1 newton of force acting on 1 kilogram of mass can change its velocity by 1 meter per second. This change in velocity is called the *acceleration* of that mass. In units of customary measurement, 1 *poundal* of force acting on 1 pound of mass can change its velocity by 1 foot per second. A poundal equals 0.031 pounds of force. See ACCELERATION; MASS; VELOCITY; WEIGHTS AND MEASURES.

The branch of physics that studies the motion of bodies, and the action of forces in changing or producing motion, is called *dynamics*. The principles of dynamics were summed up by the English scientist Sir Isaac Newton in his three *Laws of Motion* (see MOTION [Newton's Laws of Motion]). Newton's second law of motion gives the relationship between force, mass, and acceleration. This law states that every change of motion, or acceleration, is proportional to the force that caused it, and in the same direction as the force. Physicists express this relationship in the formula $F=ma$, where F is force, m is mass, and a is acceleration. This formula can be rewritten $a=\dfrac{F}{m}$. So, the greater the force, the greater the acceleration will be for the same mass.

Newton's first and third laws of motion are also important to an understanding of force and its effects. The first law of motion says that a body at rest remains at rest, and a body in motion remains in motion with a constant speed along a straight line, unless some outside force changes that motion. Newton's third law of motion states that the action of every force is accompanied by an equal reaction in the opposite direction. The laws of motion rank among the great cornerstones of physics and play an important part in understanding the principles behind all moving objects.

Composition of Forces. If two forces act on the same body or at the same point at the same time, they give the effect of a third force. This third force can be represented in a diagram called the *parallelogram of forces*. An example of a parallelogram of forces is shown in Figure 1. Lines *AB* and *AC* stand for ropes attached to the front of a wagon at point *A*. A child pulls on each rope. A girl pulls on rope *AB* in the direction shown by the arrow, and a boy pulls on *AC* in the direction shown by its arrow. Ignoring friction, the result of these two forces is that the wagon moves in the direction shown by line *AD*. The two different forces working together have produced a resultant force. Suppose that one of the children is bigger and stronger. The

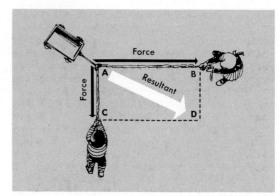

Figure 1

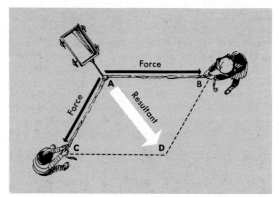

Figure 2

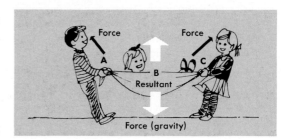

Figure 3

stronger will pull with greater force than his playmate and contribute more to the resultant force. Thus, the wagon will move nearer to the direction in which the stronger child is pulling.

We can also show this effect on the parallelogram. *AB* and *AC* can represent not only the direction of the forces, but also their *magnitude* (strength).

If the child pulling on rope *AB* is twice as strong as the child pulling on rope *AC*, then we can make the line *AB* twice as long as line *AC*. If you measure the lines in Figure 1, you will see that this is true. Thus, the diagonal line *AD* represents the direction of the resultant and its magnitude. It is the same as if the stronger child had pulled the wagon from *A* to *B*, and the weaker child had then pulled it from *B* to *D*. Another way to state this is that the resultant *AD* is the single force which, acting alone, can produce the same effect as the forces of *AB* and *AC* acting together.

When *AB* and *AC* represent motions, the parallelogram shows the composition of motions. *AD*, the direction in which the body moves, is called the *resultant motion*. If *AB* and *AC* represent forces, then the combination is known as the composition of forces, and *AD* is the *resultant force*.

Calculating Resultants. You can use a parallelogram of forces to calculate the resultant from any combination of forces by using the rules of geometry. For example, in Figure 1, suppose that the force of the pull along *AB* is just strong enough to lift a 40-pound rock, while the pull along *AC* is just enough to lift a 30-pound rock. We must then draw *AC* three-fourths as long as *AB*. When we complete the diagram, we can measure the length of *AD*. This will give the resultant force. Geometry has a rule for finding the length of the side *AD* of the triangle *ABD* when we know the length of the other sides. Note that the side *BD* is the same as the side *AC*. The rule is that $AD =$ the square root of $(AB)^2 + (AC)^2$, or $AD = \sqrt{(AB)^2 + (AC)^2}$. This is the same as $\sqrt{40^2 + 30^2}$, which equals $\sqrt{2,500}$, or 50. Thus, the magnitude of the resultant is 50 pounds. This rule works only when the forces are at right angles and the parallelogram is a rectangle, as in Figure 1. The parallelogram can still be used, however, if the forces act at a sharper or wider angle. A diagram for such forces is shown in Figure 2. The rules of trigonometry must be used to calculate this diagonal. See TRIGONOMETRY (Solving Triangles).

Other diagrams can be drawn to show what happens when more than two forces act on a single point. First, find the resultant for any two forces. Then, using the first resultant, find the resultant for it and a third force, and so on.

Figure 3, showing a child sitting in a blanket held by two other children, is an example of the resultant of three forces. The three forces acting on the girl in the blanket are the force of gravity, or the girl's weight, and the pull of each child holding the blanket. Gravity pulls downward on the girl in the blanket. The force from each child holding the blanket combine to produce an upward resultant acting on the girl in the blanket. When this resultant and the weight of the girl balance exactly, the girl and the blanket will move neither up nor down.

The resolution of forces plays an important part in such engineering problems as designing bridges and cranes. Engineers have to know the forces involved in order to design structures to carry specific loads.

Fields of Force. You can easily see how the force of a man pushing against a door moves it open, or how the force of a rope pulls a wagon attached to it. However, other kinds of forces seem to work without any contact between objects. *Gravitation*, or the force that pulls objects toward one another, works right through space. Weight and falling are the familiar results of this sort of attraction by the earth when it pulls on objects near its surface. *Magnetism* is another force that seems to work on objects at a distance. Forces of this kind are said to act through *fields of force*. A field of force extends out into space around the body, or magnet. See GRAVITATION; MAGNET AND MAGNETISM (Science Project).

Fundamental Forces. Physicists consider four forces to be the fundamental forces in the universe. These basic forces, from weakest to strongest, are (1) gravitation, (2) electromagnetic, (3) weak nuclear, and (4) strong nuclear. Other forces in nature are simply forms of these four forces.

Gravitation acts chiefly between large quantities of matter separated by great distances, such as the earth and the sun. Electromagnetic force is millions of times as strong as gravitation, but it acts over shorter distances. Electromagnetic force produces both electrical and magnetic forces. It is also the force that binds atoms together to form molecules. Scientists do not completely understand the weak and strong nuclear forces. These forces are millions of times as strong as electromagnetic force. Weak and strong nuclear forces act only within atoms themselves.

S. Y. LEE

Related Articles in WORLD BOOK include:

Adhesion	Moment (in physics)
Centrifugal Force	Motion (Newton's
Centripetal Force	Laws)
Cohesion	Newton, Sir Isaac
Dynamics	Parallel Forces
Dyne	Physics
Electromotive Force	Pound
Energy	Power
Friction	Pressure
Gravitation	Statics
Gyroscope	Strength of
Inertia	Materials
Jet Propulsion (Thrust)	Torque
Magnet and Magnetism	Weight

FORCE BILL. Several measures passed or considered by the United States Congress, which authorized the use of military power to enforce federal law, were known as Force Bills. The first force bill was sometimes called the "Bloody Bill." It became a law on March 2, 1833, after South Carolina had declared the protective tariff laws of 1828 and 1832 "null, void, and no law" within the borders of the state (see NULLIFICATION). The bill authorized the President to use the armed forces of the United States to collect the duties. A compromise tariff was passed, and bloodshed was averted.

During the period of Reconstruction three other force bills were passed. Two of them (one signed May 31, 1870, and another February 28, 1871) were designed to enforce the Fifteenth Amendment (Negro suffrage). An act of April 20, 1871, otherwise known as the Ku Klux Klan Act, was intended to enforce the Fourteenth Amendment (civil rights).

The Lodge Election Bill of 1890, which passed the House of Representatives but not the Senate, was also called a force bill. Its purpose was to prevent discrimination against Negro voters in the Southern States. It was denounced in the South as an attempt to bring back the horrors of Reconstruction.

JOHN DONALD HICKS

FORD is a place where a stream or river can be crossed. During early times, men had to cross a waterway by wading through or swimming across its shallow part. During wartime, soldiers must often *ford* (cross) water where bridges have been blown up. They sometimes do this by placing *pontoons* (portable floats) in a straight line across the water. These floating pontoon bridges can support troops and vehicles.

See also PONTOON BRIDGE.

323

FORD

Henry Ford

Henry Ford II

FORD is the name of the family that built the Ford Motor Company into one of the largest industrial companies in the world.

Henry Ford (1863-1947) developed the mass-produced "Model T" automobile and sold it at a price the average person could afford. He pioneered in the use of assembly-line methods. Because of the savings in time and money made by mass production, Ford could offer more cars to the American public at a lower price than anyone before him. He sold more than 15 million "Model T's" over the 19-year period from 1908 to 1927. More than half the automobiles sold in the United States during that period were Fords.

Early Years. Ford was born on a farm which has since become part of the city of Dearborn, Mich. He attended grammar school near his home. Later he became a machinist in Detroit. He began to experiment with engines about 1890, and completed his first gasoline engine in 1893.

His first automobile, completed in 1896, is on exhibition at Dearborn, Mich. It is not at all like any present-day automobile. The body looks like a small, crude, wooden box. It has a single seat, a steering tiller, bicycle wheels, and an electric bell on the front. Ford made the cylinder of the engine from the exhaust pipe of a steam engine, and made the flywheel out of wood. But this queer-looking car still runs.

The Industrialist. Ford organized the Ford Motor Company in 1903. At first, like his competitors, he made automobiles that only well-to-do people could afford. But later he came to believe that every man, no matter what his income, should own an automobile. The result was the inexpensive "Model T." It brought great financial success for him and his company. Ford drew national attention to this success early in 1914. He announced that from then on, the company would share its profits with its employees. At the same time, Ford cut the working day from 9 to 8 hours, and set the minimum wage for every employee over 21 years of age at $5 a day. Up to that time, unskilled workers had been receiving $1 a day and skilled workers, $2.50 a day.

Ford believed that most of the profits should be used to increase the size of the company's factories. This was an unusual idea at that time. The other stockholders of the Ford Motor Company wanted to split the profits among themselves, in the form of dividends. Ford did not like this opposition, so he bought out all the other stockholders in 1919. From that time until January, 1956, the Ford family had sole control of the giant company.

The Pacifist and Philanthropist. In December, 1915, Ford paid the expenses of a "peace trip" to Europe for about 150 men and women. The group, though well-intentioned, did not have the approval of the U.S. government, and broke up after a few weeks. Ford was at first opposed to the United States' taking part in either World War I or II. After the country was at war, however, he used his plants to capacity in manufacturing war materials.

Ford developed the V-8 engine in 1932, a feature that many other automobile makers adopted later. He took a less active part in company affairs after that time, devoting himself to hobbies. He established Greenfield Village, a group of American historical buildings and landmarks, in Dearborn, Mich. (see GREENFIELD VILLAGE). He also established the Henry Ford Museum in Dearborn. The museum exhibits man's progress in such fields as science, invention, handicraft, transportation,

Henry Ford, foreground, stands with his first Ford automobile in front of the Detroit workshop where the car was built.

324

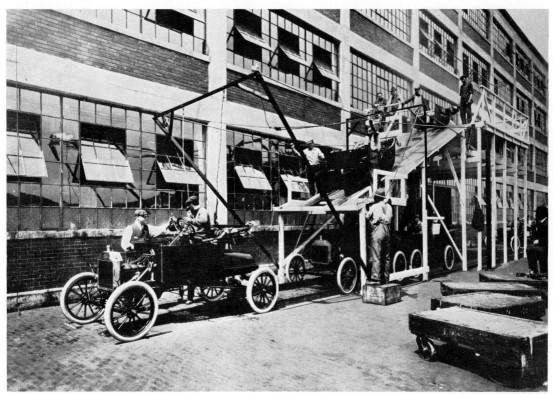

In 1914, an Early Assembly Line Was Used to Build Model T Automobiles in the Ford Plant at Highland Park, Mich.

manufacturing, and agriculture. With his son, Edsel, he donated large amounts of money and Ford Motor Company stock to the philanthropic Ford Foundation (see Ford Foundation).

When the United States entered World War II, Ford announced that he would build a plant that could produce one bomber an hour. His Willow Run, Mich., plant was the largest aircraft assembly plant in the world, and made B-24 Liberator bombers until the end of the war.

With author Samuel Crowther, Ford wrote *My Life and Work*, *Today and Tomorrow*, and *Moving Forward*.

Edsel Bryant Ford (1893-1943), Ford's son, succeeded him as president of the Ford Motor Company in 1919. Henry Ford resumed the presidency when Edsel died in 1943.

Henry Ford II (1917-   ) reorganized the Ford Motor Company in the middle and late 1940's and brought it back from the verge of bankruptcy to a paying basis.

Ford was born in Detroit, the eldest son of Edsel Bryant Ford. When his father died in 1943, Ford was released from the Navy to return to the family business at Dearborn. He became a vice-president that year, executive vice-president in 1944, and took over the presidency from his grandfather in September, 1945.

Ford reorganized his company in 1944. In July, 1945, he became the first manufacturer to exhibit a 1946 model car. When he became president in 1945, he reorganized the company more drastically. It had not been doing well financially. Its net loss in 1946 was $8 million. Ford's reorganization and business ability turned the tide in the opposite direction. The company made a net profit of about $430 million in 1955. More than $1,300,000,000 had been spent on expansion.

Henry Ford II became chairman of the board of Ford Motor Company in 1960. In 1967, he helped found the National Urban Coalition, an organization that works to solve urban problems. The next year, Ford organized the National Alliance of Businessmen to provide jobs for the "hard-core" unemployed. In 1970, he became chairman of the National Center for Voluntary Action, an organization that promotes volunteer service programs.   Smith Hempstone Oliver

See also Automobile (How the Auto Industry Grew); Ford Motor Company; Michigan (color picture).

FORD, FORD MADOX (1873-1939), was an English author of complex and symbolic novels which show the influence of the psychological novels of Henry James. Ford's best-known work is a series of novels called *Parade's End*. The series consists of *Some Do Not* (1924), *No More Parades* (1925), *A Man Could Stand Up* (1926), and *The Last Post* (1928). The series traces changes in English society during and after World War I. In *The Good Soldier* (1915), Ford symbolically revealed the declining influence of the upper class in English life. Ford and Joseph Conrad wrote two novels together, *The Inheritors* (1901) and *Romance* (1903).

Ford was born Ford Madox Hueffer in Merton, England. He edited two famous literary magazines, the *English Review* and the *Transatlantic Review*, and was writer-in-residence at Olivet (Mich.) College from 1937 until his death.   John Espey

GERALD R. FORD

FORD, GERALD RUDOLPH (1913-   ), was the only Vice-President of the United States to become President upon the resignation of a chief executive. Richard M. Nixon resigned as President on Aug. 9, 1974, and Ford took office that same day. When Nixon left the presidency, he faced almost certain impeachment because of his role in the Watergate political scandal.

Ford had been Vice-President for only eight months when he took office as President. Nixon had appointed him to succeed Vice-President Spiro T. Agnew, who resigned while under criminal investigation for graft. Ford was the first person to be appointed to fill a vacancy in the vice-presidency. He also was the only person to serve as both Vice-President and President who did not win election to either office. In 1976, Ford was defeated in his bid for a full term as President by former Governor James E. Carter, Jr., of Georgia, his Democratic opponent.

Ford, a Michigan Republican, had been elected to the U.S. House of Representatives 13 straight times before he replaced Agnew. He also had served as House minority leader.

The American people warmly welcomed Ford to the presidency. He had a calm, friendly manner and an unquestioned reputation for honesty. But Ford's popularity dropped sharply about a month later after he pardoned Nixon for all federal crimes that Nixon might have committed as President. Many Americans felt that Nixon should have been brought to trial in the Watergate scandal. Others believed that Nixon should not have been pardoned until he admitted his role in the scandal. Ford was challenged by major economic problems, including a recession, rapid inflation, and high unemployment. The economy began to recover in 1975, though the unemployment rate remained high. U.S. foreign policy suffered a major defeat in 1975, when the Vietnam War ended with a Communist victory.

Ford was a big, athletic man who loved sports. He often turned to the sports section of his newspaper before reading any other news. Ford starred as a football player in high school and college, and football had a major influence on his life. "Thanks to my football experience," he once said, "I know the value of team play. It is, I believe, one of the most important lessons to be learned and practiced in our lives." Ford swam regularly and also enjoyed golf and skiing.

Early Life

Family Background. Ford was born on July 14, 1913, in Omaha, Nebr. He was named for his father, Leslie Lynch King, who operated a family wool business there. Leslie's parents were divorced about two years after his

J. F. terHorst, the contributor of this article, is a Columnist for The Detroit News-Universal Press Syndicate *and the author of* Gerald Ford and the Future of the Presidency.

birth. His mother, Dorothy Gardner King, then took him to Grand Rapids, Mich., where she had friends. In 1916, she married Gerald Rudolph Ford, the owner of a small paint company in the city. Ford adopted the child and gave him his name. The stocky, blond youth, who became known as "Jerry," grew up with three younger half brothers, James, Richard, and Thomas.

Jerry's real father also remarried. Jerry had a half brother, Leslie H. King; and two half sisters, Marjorie King Werner and Patricia King.

Boyhood. Jerry's parents encouraged him to develop pride in civic responsibility. His stepfather participated in programs to aid needy youths in Grand Rapids and took an active interest in local politics. His mother devoted much of her time to charity projects and other activities of the Grace Episcopal Church, where the Fords worshiped. Jerry joined the Boy Scouts and achieved the rank of Eagle Scout, the highest level in Scouting. He later proudly referred to himself as the nation's "first Eagle Scout Vice-President."

Jerry was a strong, husky boy and excelled in sports. He first gained public attention as the star center of the South High School football team. He was selected to the all-city high school football team three times and was named to the all-state team in his senior year.

At school, Jerry usually wore a suit and tie, though most boys in those days wore a sport shirt, slacks, and sweater. He studied hard and received good grades. He also won a contest sponsored by a local motion-picture theater to choose the most popular high school senior in Grand Rapids.

As a teen-ager, Jerry waited on tables and washed dishes at a small restaurant across the street from South High School. One day, his real father came in and introduced himself to the startled youth. Jerry knew about his natural father but had not seen him since his parents' divorce. King asked Jerry if he would like to live with the King family. Jerry said he considered the Fords his family. Later, in 1936, King helped Ford get a summer job as a ranger in Yellowstone National Park.

College Student. Ford entered the University of Michigan in 1931. He earned good grades and played center on the undefeated Michigan football teams of 1932 and 1933. In 1934, his teammates named him the team's most valuable player. He played center on the college team that lost to the Chicago Bears, 5 to 0, in the 1935 All-Star Football Game.

The White House

38TH PRESIDENT
OF THE
UNITED STATES
1974-1977

The United States flag had
50 stars when Gerald R.
Ford became President.

Ford graduated from Michigan in 1935. The Detroit Lions and the Green Bay Packers offered him a contract to play professional football, but Ford had decided to study law. He accepted a job as assistant football coach and boxing coach at Yale University, hoping he could also study law there. Ford coached full time at Yale from 1935 until 1938, when he was accepted for admission by the Yale Law School.

While at Yale, Ford became a partner in a modeling agency in New York City. His partner, Harry Conover, a model, operated the agency. In March, 1940, Ford modeled sports clothes for an article in *Look* magazine.

IMPORTANT DATES IN FORD'S LIFE

1913 (July 14) Born in Omaha, Nebr.

1935 Graduated from the University of Michigan.

1942-1946 Served in the U.S. Navy during World War II.

1948 (Oct. 15) Married Elizabeth (Betty) Bloomer.

1948 Elected to the first of 13 successive terms in the U.S. House of Representatives.

1965 Became House minority leader.

1973 (Dec. 6) Became Vice-President of the United States.

1974 (Aug. 9) Succeeded to the presidency.

1976 Lost presidential election to James E. Carter, Jr.

The agency succeeded, but Ford became dissatisfied with his share of the profits and soon sold his interest.

Ford received his law degree from Yale in 1941. He ranked in the top third of his graduating class.

Grand Rapids Lawyer

In June, 1941, Ford was admitted to the Michigan bar. Shortly afterward, he and Philip W. Buchen, a former roommate at the University of Michigan, opened a law office in Grand Rapids. The United States entered World War II in December, 1941, and Ford soon volunteered for the United States Navy.

Naval Officer. Ford entered the Navy in April, 1942, and became an ensign. He taught physical training at a base in Chapel Hill, N.C., for a year. Then he became the physical-training director and assistant navigation officer of the U.S.S. *Monterey*, an aircraft carrier. In 1943 and 1944, the *Monterey* took part in every big naval battle in the Pacific Ocean. Ford was discharged in January, 1946, as a lieutenant commander.

Entry into Politics. Ford resumed his law career in Grand Rapids and also became active in a local Republican reform group. Leaders of the organization, called the Home Front, included U.S. Senator Arthur H. Vandenberg of Michigan, who had helped establish the United Nations, and Ford's stepfather. The two

326a

FORD, GERALD RUDOLPH

Young Jerry, shown at the age of 2½, liked to play with his dog, Spot. The youth later became active in the Boy Scouts and rose to Eagle Scout, the highest level in Scouting.

One of Ford's Boyhood Homes was this frame house on Union Street in Grand Rapids, Mich. His family lived in the house from 1923 until 1929, when they moved to East Grand Rapids.

men urged Ford to challenge U.S. Representative Bartel J. Jonkman in the Republican primary election of 1948.

Jonkman believed that the United States should stay out of foreign affairs as much as possible. Vandenberg and Ford had supported that policy before World War II, but the war changed their views. Ford defeated Jonkman in the primary and then beat Fred Barr, his Democratic opponent in the November election. The voters of Michigan's Fifth Congressional District re-elected Ford 12 straight times.

Marriage. In 1947, Ford met Elizabeth (Betty) Bloomer (April 8, 1918-   ). She was born in Chicago and moved to Grand Rapids with her family when she was 3 years old. Her father, William S. Bloomer, was a machinery salesman. Her mother, Hortense, took an active interest in Grand Rapids community affairs.

As a child, Betty became interested in dancing. She continued to study the dance and, during the 1930's, joined a New York City group directed by the noted dancer Martha Graham. Betty also worked as a fashion model. In 1942, she returned to Grand Rapids and married William Warren, a local furniture salesman. They were divorced in 1947.

When Ford met Betty, she was working as a fashion coordinator for a Grand Rapids department store. They were married on Oct. 15, 1948, just before Ford first won election to the U.S. House of Representatives. Ford campaigned on the day of his wedding and arrived late for the ceremony. The Fords had four children, Michael Gerald (1950-   ), John Gardner (1952-   ), Steven Meigs (1956-   ), and Susan Elizabeth (1957-   ).

Career in Congress

Rise to Power. Ford gained a reputation as a loyal Republican and a hard worker during his early terms in Congress. He was named to the defense subcommittee of the House Appropriations Committee in 1953 and became known as a military affairs expert. Some Republican leaders mentioned Ford as a possible candidate for the vice-presidential nomination in 1960. But the nomination went to Henry Cabot Lodge, Jr., the U.S. ambassador to the United Nations.

During the early 1960's, Ford became increasingly popular among young Republican congressmen. In 1963, they helped elect him chairman of the Republican Conference of the House. In this position, his first leadership role in the House, Ford presided at meetings of the Republican representatives.

In November, 1963, President Lyndon B. Johnson established the Warren Commission to investigate the assassination of President John F. Kennedy. Johnson appointed Ford as one of the seven members. Ford and a member of his staff, John R. Stiles, later wrote a book about Lee Harvey Oswald, *Portrait of the Assassin* (1965).

House Minority Leader. In 1965, Ford was chosen House minority leader. As minority leader, he urged Republican congressmen to do more than just criticize the proposals of Democrats, who held a majority in the House. Ford worked for Republican alternatives to Democratic programs.

Ford attracted national attention when he appeared with Senate Minority Leader Everett M. Dirksen on a series of televised Republican press conferences. The series, which reporters called the "Ev and Jerry Show," drew increased attention to Republican views.

Ford supported President Johnson's early policies in the Vietnam War. But by 1967, with no end of the war in sight, Ford began to strongly attack U.S. military strategy in Vietnam. That year, he gave a speech entitled "Why Are We Pulling Our Punches in Vietnam?" The speech encouraged Republicans to oppose

Ford Starred at Center on the University of Michigan football team, which named him its most valuable player in 1934. He later coached football and boxing at Yale University.

The Ford Family in 1948. Seated are, *left to right,* Gerald's half brother James, Mrs. Dorothy Ford, and Gerald. Standing are half brother Thomas, Gerald R. Ford, Sr., and half brother Richard.

Johnson's war policies. In addition, Republicans and Southern Democrats joined under Ford's leadership in opposing many of Johnson's social programs. Ford considered these programs either too costly or unnecessary.

In 1968, Richard M. Nixon was elected President. The Democrats kept control of both houses of Congress, but Ford helped win approval of a number of Nixon's policies concerning the Vietnam War and inflation.

In 1970, Ford led an effort to impeach William O. Douglas, a liberal associate justice of the Supreme Court of the United States. Ford strongly criticized Douglas' vote in a case involving Ralph Ginzburg, the editor of a magazine that had paid the justice $350 for an article. Ford also objected to Douglas' encouragement of political dissent in various writings. The matter ended after a House investigating committee reported a lack of evidence to support Douglas' impeachment.

The Resignation of Agnew. In 1972, Nixon and Vice-President Spiro T. Agnew won re-election in a landslide. That same year, Ford won election to his 13th successive term in the House.

Early in 1973, federal investigators uncovered evidence that Agnew had accepted bribes. The charges covered the period that Agnew had served as Baltimore County Executive and then as governor of Maryland, and later as Vice-President. As a result of the investigation, Agnew resigned from the vice-presidency on Oct. 10, 1973. Nixon nominated Ford to replace Agnew. The nomination required the approval of both houses of Congress under procedures established in 1967 by the 25th Amendment to the United States Constitution. Previously, vacancies in the vice-presidency had remained unfilled until the next presidential election.

The Senate approved Ford's nomination by a 92 to 3 vote on November 27. The House approved it, 387 to 35, on December 6, and Ford was sworn in as the 40th

Vice-President later that day. He became the first appointed Vice-President in the nation's history.

Vice-President (1973-1974)

Shortly before Ford became Vice-President, the House of Representatives started impeachment proceedings against Nixon. Some members of congress believed that Nixon was hiding evidence related to the Watergate scandal, which had begun in June 1972. The scandal arose after Nixon's re-election committee became involved in a burglary at Democratic national headquarters in the Watergate building complex in Washington, D.C. Later, evidence linked several top

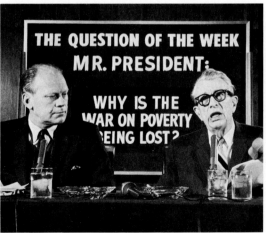

House Minority Leader Ford appeared with Senate Minority Leader Everett M. Dirksen in a series of televised press conferences. Reporters nicknamed the series "The Ev and Jerry Show."

White House aides with the burglary or with an effort to conceal information about it.

Speaking Tour. The Watergate scandal shook public confidence in Nixon, even though he insisted he had no part in it. As Vice-President, Ford went on a nationwide speaking tour and expressed his faith in Nixon. He addressed business, civic, and youth groups in cities throughout the country. Ford also took part in many Republican fund-raising activities and campaigned for Republican candidates. By mid-1974, the Vice-President had visited about 40 states and made several hundred public appearances.

The Resignation of Nixon. In July 1974, the House Judiciary Committee recommended that Nixon be impeached. It voted to adopt three articles of impeachment for consideration by the full House of Representatives. The first article accused the President of interfering with justice by acting to hide evidence about the Watergate burglary from federal law-enforcement officials. The other articles charged that Nixon had abused presidential powers and illegally withheld evidence from the judiciary committee.

Ford continued to defend Nixon, arguing that the President had committed no impeachable offense. Ford also predicted that the House of Representatives would not impeach Nixon.

Then, on August 5, Nixon released transcripts of taped White House conversations that clearly supported the first proposed article of impeachment. Almost all of Nixon's remaining support in Congress collapsed immediately. The Republican leaders of both the House and the Senate warned Nixon that he faced certain impeachment and removal from office.

Nixon resigned as President on the morning of August 9. At noon that day, Ford took the oath of office as the 38th President of the United States. Warren E.

VICE-PRESIDENT AND CABINET

Vice-President.............	*Nelson A. Rockefeller
Secretary of State..........	*Henry A. Kissinger
Secretary of the Treasury....	*William E. Simon
Secretary of Defense........	*James R. Schlesinger
	*Donald H. Rumsfeld (1975)
Attorney General..........	William B. Saxbe
	*Edward H. Levi (1975)
Secretary of the Interior.....	*Rogers C. B. Morton
	Stanley K. Hathaway (1975)
	Thomas S. Kleppe (1975)
Secretary of Agriculture.....	*Earl L. Butz
	John A. Knebel (1976)
Secretary of Commerce......	Frederick B. Dent
	*Rogers C. B. Morton (1975)
	*Elliot L. Richardson (1975)
Secretary of Labor..........	Peter J. Brennan
	John T. Dunlop (1975)
	W. J. Usery, Jr. (1976)
Secretary of Health, Education, and Welfare....	*Caspar Weinberger
	*F. David Mathews (1975)
Secretary of Housing and Urban Development.......	*James T. Lynn
	*Carla A. Hills (1975)
Secretary of Transportation..	Claude S. Brinegar
	*William T. Coleman, Jr. (1975)

*Has a biography in WORLD BOOK.

THE WORLD OF

WORLD EVENTS

1975 Civil wars broke out in Angola and Lebanon.

1975 The Vietnam War ended.

1975 Manned U.S. Apollo and Soviet Soyuz space vehicles linked up in space in the Apollo Soyuz Test Project.

1975 Francisco Franco, ruler of Spain since 1936, died.

1976 Mao Tse-tung, leader of the Chinese Communist Revolution and ruler of China since 1949, died.

UNITED STATES EVENTS

The United States flag had 50 stars when Ford became President.

1974 (Aug. 9) Ford succeeded to the presidency after Richard M. Nixon became the first President to resign from office.

1974 Ford pardoned Nixon for all federal crimes that Nixon may have committed during his Administration.

1974 A recession struck the nation.

1975 The unmanned *Viking I* became the first U.S. spacecraft to land on Mars.

1975 Ford escaped two attempted assassinations in California.

1976 Americans celebrated the *bicentennial* (200th anniversary) of their nation's founding.

Burger, chief justice of the United States, administered the presidential oath of office to Ford in the East Room of the White House. Ford became the only President in the nation's history who had not been elected to either the presidency or the vice-presidency.

Ford's Administration (1974-1977)

Ford kept all of Nixon's Cabinet officers at the start of his Administration. He nominated Nelson A. Rockefeller, former governor of New York, as Vice-President. Rockefeller took office in December 1974, after both the Senate and the House of Representatives confirmed his nomination.

Early Problems. When Ford became President, he was challenged at home by soaring inflation and a loss of public confidence in the government. Inflation was causing hardship among many Americans, especially the poor and the elderly. Sharp rises in prices also threatened to cause a severe business slump.

Public faith in government had plunged to its lowest level in years, largely because of the Watergate scandal. In addition, the Nixon impeachment crisis had slowed

PRESIDENT FORD

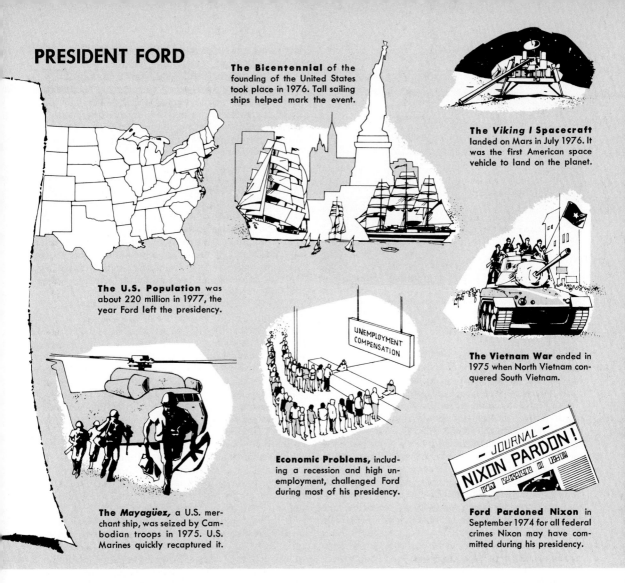

The Bicentennial of the founding of the United States took place in 1976. Tall sailing ships helped mark the event.

The Viking I Spacecraft landed on Mars in July 1976. It was the first American space vehicle to land on the planet.

The U.S. Population was about 220 million in 1977, the year Ford left the presidency.

The Vietnam War ended in 1975 when North Vietnam conquered South Vietnam.

Economic Problems, including a recession and high unemployment, challenged Ford during most of his presidency.

The Mayagüez, a U.S. merchant ship, was seized by Cambodian troops in 1975. U.S. Marines quickly recaptured it.

Ford Pardoned Nixon in September 1974 for all federal crimes Nixon may have committed during his presidency.

the work of many federal agencies and created confusion about various government policies.

Fighting on the Mediterranean island of Cyprus provided the first foreign crisis for the new President. In August 1974, Turkish troops invaded Cyprus and took control of a large part of the island. The take-over occurred after Turkish Cypriots strongly protested the formation of a new government by Greek Cypriots. Angry Greeks, Greek Cypriots, and Americans of Greek ancestry charged that the United States should have used its influence to stop the Turks.

The National Scene. Relations between Ford and the Democratic-controlled Congress were strained. Congress passed few of his major proposals. Ford vetoed over 50 bills. He believed most of these bills would have increased the rate of inflation.

The Nixon Pardon severely hurt Ford's early popularity. On Sept. 8, 1974, he pardoned Nixon for all federal crimes the former President might have committed as chief executive. Ford said he took the action to end divisions within the nation and to "heal the wounds that had festered too long." But the pardon angered millions of Americans. Many of them believed that the government should have brought Nixon to trial if it had enough evidence to do so. Many others felt that Ford should not have granted the pardon until Nixon had admitted his involvement in the Watergate scandal.

The Amnesty Program was announced by Ford eight days after he pardoned Nixon. The new President offered amnesty to draft dodgers and deserters of the Vietnam War period. The program required most of these men to work in a public service job for up to two years. About 22,000 of the approximately 106,000 eligible men applied for amnesty under the program. Most of the rest objected to the work requirement and refused to apply.

The Economy. At the beginning of his Administration, Ford called inflation the nation's "public enemy Number 1." With quick congressional approval, he established the Council on Wage and Price Stability to expose any inflationary wage and price increases.

Ford also proposed tax increases for corporations, families, and individuals. But he dropped these plans

Sygma

Ford Took the Oath of Office As President on Aug. 9, 1974. Mrs. Betty Ford watched Warren E. Burger, chief justice of the United States, administer the oath in the East Room of the White House.

later in 1974 after a recession struck the nation. Ford then introduced legislation to create public service jobs for the unemployed and to lower federal income taxes. Congress passed both measures.

Early in 1975, inflation slowed and the economy began to recover. But in May that year, more than 9 per cent of the nation's labor force had no jobs—the highest level of unemployment since 1941. The unemployment rate dropped slowly during the recovery. In October 1976, it stood at about 8 per cent.

Two Attempted Assassinations of Ford occurred in California during September 1975. The first attempt, by Lynette Alice Fromme, a follower of a convicted murderer named Charles Manson, took place on September 5 in Sacramento. A Secret Service agent saw Fromme pointing a pistol at Ford and grabbed the gun before it was fired. On September 22, Sara Jane Moore, who had been associated with groups protesting U.S. government policies, shot at Ford in San Francisco but missed.

Both women were convicted of attempted assassination of a President and sentenced to life imprisonment.

Foreign Affairs. Ford relied heavily on the guidance of Secretary of State Henry A. Kissinger, who had also been Nixon's chief adviser on foreign policy. In 1975, Ford and Kissinger helped Egypt and Israel settle a territorial dispute that had resulted from a war between the two nations in 1973. Ford also worked to continue Nixon's program to improve U.S. relations with China and Russia.

The Vietnam War ended in April 1975, after Communist North Vietnam conquered South Vietnam. That same month, Communist troops also took over Cambodia, which borders Vietnam on the west. Shortly before South Vietnam fell, Ford asked Congress to give that nation more than $700 million in emergency military aid. But Congress felt the aid could not save South Vietnam and rejected the request. Ford arranged for the evacuation of refugees from South Vietnam. About 100,000 of them came to the United States.

The Mayagüez Seizure. In May 1975, Cambodian Communist troops seized the *Mayagüez*, a U.S. merchant ship, in the Gulf of Siam. Ford sent 200 U.S. Marines to the area, and they quickly recaptured the ship and rescued its 39 crew members.

Life in the White House was relaxed and informal during Ford's presidency. The Fords impressed visitors with their personal warmth and friendly hospitality. They liked to entertain and invited over 900 guests to a White House Christmas Party for members of Congress in 1974. The Fords especially enjoyed dancing.

Susan Ford was the only one of the four Ford children who lived in the White House during most of Ford's presidency. She entered Mount Vernon College in Washington in 1975. Susan's Siamese cat, Shan, was one of the family pets. Another was the President's dog, a golden retriever named Liberty.

Betty Ford underwent surgery for breast cancer about a month after Ford became President. She won the admiration of millions when she resumed her busy schedule of activities after recovering from the operation. Mrs. Ford also became noted for her support of women's rights. She campaigned for adoption of the Equal

The White House

The President's Family in the White House. From left to right are sons John and Steven, Mrs. Ford, Ford, daughter Susan, and daughter-in-law Gayle and her husband, Michael.

Rights Amendment to the U.S. Constitution. This amendment was designed to give women the same rights men had in business and other fields.

The 1976 Election. Former Governor Ronald Reagan of California challenged Ford for the 1976 Republican presidential nomination. The two fought a close, bitter contest in the state primary elections. Ford narrowly won nomination on the first ballot at the Republican National Convention in Kansas City. At his request, the convention nominated Senator Robert J. Dole of Kansas for Vice-President. Their Democratic opponents were former Governor James E. Carter, Jr., of Georgia and Senator Walter F. Mondale of Minnesota.

During his campaign against Carter, Ford pledged to continue policies that he believed had brought about the economic recovery and the slowdown in the inflation rate. Carter charged that Ford had mismanaged the economy. He argued that Ford's policies had contributed to the continuing high rate of unemployment. The campaign included the second series of nationally televised debates between presidential candidates in U.S. history. The first series took place in 1960 between John F. Kennedy, the Democratic candidate, and Nixon, then the Republican nominee. In the 1976 election, Carter defeated Ford by 1,678,069 popular votes out of over 81½ million. Ford carried 27 states, while Carter carried 23 states and the District of Columbia. But Carter received 297 electoral votes compared to Ford's 240. Reagan received one electoral vote. See ELECTORAL COLLEGE (table).   J. F. terHORST

Questions

Who first encouraged Ford to seek public office?
What national problems did Ford face when he became President?
What new approach did Ford develop for the Republicans in the House after he became minority leader?
What high honor did Ford earn as a Boy Scout?
What influence did football have on Ford's life?
Under what provision of the United States Constitution did Ford become Vice-President?
Why was Ford's succession to the presidency unique?
What action severely hurt Ford's early popularity?
What recreational activities did Ford enjoy?
What was the "Ev and Jerry Show"?

FORD, HANNIBAL CHOATE (1877-1955), an American inventor and engineer, developed equipment to control the range and accuracy of gunfire. He perfected the method that allowed guns to aim accurately from the rolling decks of a ship at sea. Ford helped Elmer A. Sperry develop the gyroscope in 1909 and was Sperry's chief engineer from 1910 to 1915 (see GYROSCOPE; SPERRY, ELMER A.).

Ford formed the Ford Instrument Company in 1915 and became its first president. Later it became a division of the Sperry-Rand Corporation. He helped make many improvements on typewriters and also invented an automatic bombsight. Ford was born in Dryden, N.Y.   ROBERT P. MULTHAUF

FORD, HENRY. See FORD (family).

FORD, JOHN (1586-1639?), was an English dramatist. Many critics of the 1900's, particularly T. S. Eliot, ranked several of Ford's tragedies as second only to those of Shakespeare. Two of Ford's tragedies, *The Broken Heart* (1629) and *'Tis Pity She's a Whore* (about 1633), appeal to today's audiences because of the modern psychology of the characters' motivations. Both plays concern the power of love and the tragedy resulting from its frustrations. *'Tis Pity She's a Whore*, because its subject is incest, verges on sensationalism, yet it is only a plot like *Romeo and Juliet* developed with more highly individualized psychology.

Little is known of Ford's life. He was connected with the legal profession and may have turned to writing plays to increase his income. His dramas apparently were not popular in his own time.   ALAN S. DOWNER

FORD, JOHN (1895-1973), became the first motion-picture director to win Academy Awards for four movies. He won the awards for *The Informer* (1935), *The Grapes of Wrath* (1940), *How Green Was My Valley* (1941), and *The Quiet Man* (1952). Ford became famous for staging outdoor motion pictures with a keen sense of background and deep feeling for people. His major outdoor and western movies include *The Iron Horse* (1924), *The Hurricane* (1937), *Stagecoach* (1939), *Fort Apache* (1948), *She Wore a Yellow Ribbon* (1949), *Wagonmaster* (1951), *Mogambo* (1952), *The Horse Soldiers* (1959), and *Cheyenne Autumn* (1964).

Ford was born in Portland, Me. His real name was Sean Aloysius O'Feeney. Ford began his directing career in 1914 and directed more than 200 movies. In 1973, President Richard M. Nixon awarded Ford the Presidential Medal of Freedom.   HOWARD THOMPSON

FORD FOUNDATION is the world's largest philanthropic organization. It seeks to advance human welfare, mainly through grants for educational purposes. The foundation assists individuals, institutions, and communities in working to improve education, promote the arts, and solve social problems.

The Ford Foundation has given or pledged about $4.8 billion since it was established in 1936. This money has gone to more than 7,100 institutions and organizations in the United States and about 95 other countries. The foundation makes most of its U.S. grants to schools, private research institutes, and voluntary organizations.

Programs. The Ford Foundation supports programs in six fields: (1) education and research, (2) the arts, (3)

national affairs, (4) international affairs, (5) communications, and (6) resources and the environment.

In education and research, the foundation grants funds to aid universities, colleges, and other schools. Since the early 1960's, it has increased its assistance to provide higher education for larger numbers of black students and other minority-group students. It also supports research in primary and secondary education.

In the arts, the foundation assists individual artists in music, theater, and the dance. The foundation also helps finance symphony orchestras, ballet and opera companies, and other artistic organizations.

In national affairs, the Ford Foundation has helped blacks and other minorities through community action, housing, job training, and other programs. It has also supported efforts to improve the quality of working life, the effectiveness of government, and the performance of courts and law enforcement agencies.

In international affairs, the foundation grants funds to developing countries to help them build institutions needed for long-range growth. The foundation has supported university research programs and courses of study in the problems of developing countries. It also supports research, training, and educational programs in family planning.

In communications, the Ford Foundation has given more than $250 million since 1952 to aid noncommercial broadcasting. The foundation helped establish the Public Broadcasting Service and has helped finance local news and community affairs programs. It also supports activities concerning communications policy, journalism education, and the responsibility of the news media.

In resources and the environment, the foundation supports research on energy, land use, and resource scarcity. It also supports environmental public interest law activities and the training of environmental managers.

History. The automobile manufacturer Henry Ford and his son, Edsel, established the Ford Foundation in 1936. Until 1950, most of its grants went to charitable and educational institutions in Michigan. That year, the foundation became a national organization.

The foundation has headquarters at 320 E. 43rd Street, New York, N.Y. 10017. For assets, see FOUNDATIONS (table). Critically reviewed by the FORD FOUNDATION

FORD MOTOR COMPANY ranks as one of the giants of American industry. The company manufactures various models of Ford, Lincoln, and Mercury automobiles. It also makes Ford trucks and tractors, farm machinery, and industrial engines and accessories. The company also manufactures advanced products for space and military use. Ford Motor Company wholly owns the Philco-Ford Corporation, Ford Motor Credit Company, The American Road Insurance Company, and the Ford Leasing Development Company.

Ford has 65 assembly and manufacturing plants in the United States. The largest of these plants is the Rouge complex near Detroit, Mich. It covers 1,200 acres (486 hectares) and employs 35,000 persons. The Rouge plant has its own dock for lake freighters.

Ford also has manufacturing subsidiaries in Great Britain, Canada, Belgium, Germany, Australia, Argentina, Brazil, and Mexico, and maintains other sales and assembly facilities in Europe, the Middle East, South America, Malaysia, Singapore, South Africa, New Zealand, and the Philippines. For the sales and assets of the Ford Motor Company, see MANUFACTURING (table: 100 Leading U.S. Manufacturers).

Henry Ford organized the company in 1903. The success of the "Model N," brought out in 1906, led to the introduction of the famous "Model T" in 1908. Affectionately known as the "Tin Lizzie," this simple and inexpensive car became very popular. All but the body could be assembled in 93 minutes on an assembly line established at the Ford factory in Highland Park, Mich., in 1913. The "Model T" finally gave way to the "Model A" in 1927.

In 1932, Ford brought out the "V-8" engine. The company acquired control of the Lincoln Motor Car Company in 1922, and has grown steadily over the years. Henry Ford II, grandson of the founder, took over the presidency in 1945 and became chairman of the board in 1960.

Ford family interests controlled the company until 1956. In January 1956, the Ford Foundation sold 10,200,000 shares of its Ford company stock to the public. This was the largest single stock issue ever offered to the public up to that date. Ford Motor Company became a publicly owned company. It has more than 372,000 stockholders.

Critically reviewed by FORD MOTOR COMPANY

See also FORD (family); FORD FOUNDATION.

FORDHAM UNIVERSITY is a coeducational school in New York City. It is governed by a board of trustees consisting of 15 laypersons and 11 members of the Society of Jesus. Fordham College of Arts and Sciences accepts men only. The university has schools of business, law, education, general studies, and social services; and a college of philosophy and letters for Jesuits. In 1964, the university added Thomas More College, a college of arts and sciences for women. Fordham was founded in 1841. For enrollment, see UNIVERSITIES AND COLLEGES (table). CHARLES J. DEANE

FORDNEY-McCUMBER TARIFF ACT. See TARIFF (United States Tariffs).

FORD'S THEATRE. See LINCOLN, ABRAHAM (Assassination); NATIONAL PARK SYSTEM (National Historic Sites).

FOREARM. See ARM.

FORECASTING, WEATHER. See WEATHER with pictures; METEOROLOGY; WEATHER SERVICE, NATIONAL.

FORECASTLE. See SHIP (table: Nautical Terms).

FORECLOSURE. See MORTGAGE.

FOREFATHERS' DAY. See DECEMBER (Special Days).

FOREIGN AGRICULTURAL SERVICE is an agency of the United States Department of Agriculture. Its main purpose is to develop markets in other countries for farm products from the United States. It also acts as an information agency to tell American farmers and trade groups what is happening in agriculture throughout the world. The service performs these duties through a staff in Washington, D.C. It also has agricultural experts stationed at diplomatic posts in other countries.

The Foreign Agricultural Service tries to reduce or eliminate unreasonable foreign tariffs or other trade barriers erected against United States agricultural products. Much of this work is done through the

General Agreement on Tariffs and Trade (GATT), of which the United States is a member. The service also works with private trade groups to increase the foreign demand for United States farm products.

Critically reviewed by FOREIGN AGRICULTURAL SERVICE

FOREIGN AID refers to the money, goods, or services that governments and private organizations give to help other nations and their people. Both private groups and governments give aid to help less developed nations fight poverty, disease, and ignorance. But since the start of the Cold War in the 1940's, foreign aid has also become an important part of foreign policy for many nations.

The governments of many countries give aid to support three foreign policy goals: (1) to promote national security; (2) to increase international trade; and (3) to achieve political objectives. The nations giving aid try to strengthen their own national defenses by strengthening friendly or neutral governments. They also give aid to create or maintain trade and investment ties with other nations. And when they give foreign aid, they expect the receiving nations to support, or at least not oppose, their political policies.

Aid in Solving Food Shortages includes technical assistance. United States farm experts teach modern farming methods to increase production. Experts from the Agency for International Development, *above*, advise Venezuelan sugar cane farmers.

Kinds of Foreign Aid

Foreign aid takes many forms. It may be CARE packages of food or clothing for needy people, or Peace Corps volunteers working in villages. It could be technicians who teach others such things as modern farming methods or how to operate heavy construction machinery. It could also be long-term loans to help developing countries build roads and power plants.

Foreign aid includes money, supplies, and technical assistance to help another country build up its economic and military power. But it does not include military forces sent to help another country. Nor does it include international trade, private international investment, or diplomatic efforts to help other countries.

Private aid is offered by voluntary nongovernment organizations, such as CARE and the Red Cross. Governments give *official*, or *public*, aid. Official aid given by one country to another is called *bilateral* aid. Aid given by a group of countries through the United Nations or other institutions is called *multilateral* aid.

About three-fourths of all official aid is bilateral. In the mid-1970's, such aid amounted to about $13½ billion a year. In the mid-1970's, the United States gave the largest amount of economic aid. Other leading contributors included Canada, France, Great Britain, Japan, Saudi Arabia, and West Germany.

United States Aid Programs

Large-scale foreign aid began during World War II (1939-1945). From the early 1940's to the mid-1960's, the United States gave or lent about $140 billion in foreign aid. At one time or another, almost every country in the world has received U.S. aid. Since World War II, about a third of all U.S. aid has gone to help other nations build up their armed forces. The rest has gone to teach people new skills, to provide emergency aid for people who lacked food or homes, and to build up national wealth and income in poor countries. Changes in types of aid and in the countries receiving aid reflect changes in U.S. interests since 1940.

World War II Aid. From 1940 through 1945, the United States gave about $46 billion worth of supplies and equipment to its allies, especially Great Britain and Russia. It gave much of this aid through the Lend-Lease Program. During this period, the U.S. also started a technical and development assistance program for Latin America, and gave funds to war relief programs.

Relief and Reconstruction. One of the most pressing needs at the end of World War II was to provide food and shelter for millions of people in Europe and Asia. Another was to help the people rebuild their war-torn

Photos courtesy of Agency for International Development

Aid to Education provides funds and teachers for schools and universities in many countries. The Agency for International Development helped finance the Indian Institute of Technology at Kanpur, India, *left*.

FOREIGN AID

countries. The United Nations Relief and Rehabilitation Administration (UNRRA), an organization financed largely by U.S. grants, helped meet these needs. So did U.S. loans to Great Britain and other nations. But these were only temporary measures. In 1948, the United States began the first broad reconstruction program, the Marshall Plan (European Recovery Program). The plan gave the countries of Western Europe about $13 billion for rebuilding over a period of four years.

Economic Development and Mutual Security. After the Marshall Plan, U.S. interests turned to promoting the economic development and military security of developing countries in Africa, Asia, and Latin America. In 1949, the U.S. Congress approved President Harry S. Truman's proposed Point Four Program to give technical assistance to these countries.

The threat of Communism changed the emphasis in foreign aid. Americans were concerned about the Communist takeover in China in 1949, the Korean War in the 1950's, and increasing Cold War tensions between the United States and Russia. To stop the spread of Communism, the U.S. helped found the North Atlantic Treaty Organization (NATO), and pledged military aid to NATO members. It gave military and economic aid to developing countries facing Soviet or Chinese pressure. These countries included Greece, Laos, South Korea, South Vietnam, Taiwan, and Turkey. The U.S. has also given mutual security aid to India, Pakistan, Yugoslavia, and other developing countries it considered to be of major political importance.

In 1957, the United States set up a Development Loan Fund. It lent money on easy terms to developing countries so that they could build up their economies. Countries could also get bilateral help from the Export-Import Bank, another agency of the U.S. government.

In the 1960's, Presidents John F. Kennedy and Lyndon B. Johnson strongly supported technical assistance and economic development programs. In 1961, Congress established the Agency for International Development (AID) to administer all U.S. bilateral aid programs, and Kennedy established the Peace Corps. Thousands of American Peace Corps volunteers have lived and worked with people in developing countries to help them improve their living conditions. In 1961, the U.S. and 19 Latin American countries formed the Alliance for Progress to promote economic development and social reform in Latin America. Under the Food for Peace Program, which was set up in 1954, food shipments to needy nations averaged about $1½ billion a year during the 1960's.

But in the early 1970's, the United States reduced its foreign aid program. Public support for foreign aid weakened. The United States felt it needed the money more for military and domestic programs. It also had to end a balance of payments deficit caused by the nation spending more money abroad than foreigners spent in the United States. Many Americans were disappointed in the results foreign aid had achieved.

Other Countries' Aid Programs

Other nations besides the United States give economic aid to developing countries. France gives much aid to its overseas territories and to its former colonies

Leading Contributors of Foreign Aid
Economic aid given in 1975

Contributor	Aid (in millions)	Aid as Per Cent of GNP*
United States	$4,007.0	0.26%
France	2,090.9	0.69%
West Germany	1,688.8	0.44%
Japan	1,147.7	0.24%
Saudi Arabia	917.2	2.96%
Canada	879.7	0.61%
Great Britain	863.4	0.43%
The Netherlands	604.0	0.89%
Sweden	566.0	0.93%
Australia	506.8	0.69%
Iran	485.4	0.97%
United Arab Emirates	403.7	5.53%
Belgium	377.7	0.71%
China	375.0	0.16%
Russia	350.0	0.04%

Leading Recipients of Foreign Aid
Economic aid received in 1975

Recipient	Aid (in millions)	Aid as Per Cent of GNP*
India	$1,389.2	1.47%
Bangladesh	921.9	9.00%
Indonesia	677.3	2.42%
Israel	467.1	3.94%
Pakistan	426.4	4.12%
Egypt	324.0	2.84%
Papua New Guinea	304.3	24.94%
Vietnam	296.5	6.59%
Tanzania	276.5	12.23%
South Korea	240.2	1.28%

*Gross National Product (GNP). The GNP is the total value of goods and services produced by a country in a year.
Sources: Organization for Economic Cooperation and Development; U.S. Department of State.

in Africa. Belgium, Great Britain, and other former colonial powers also give aid to their former colonies.

Russia has given large amounts of military and economic aid to several countries, including Afghanistan, Cuba, Egypt, India, North Korea, and Vietnam. Other countries have been less concerned than Russia and the U.S. with aid for security purposes. They are more interested in promoting trade, cultural, or diplomatic ties. In addition to aid, these countries arrange commercial loans to finance purchases of their exports. France, Italy, and Japan rely heavily on such lending.

France gives the most technical assistance because most of its aid goes to Africa, which lacks trained people. Belgium, Great Britain, Italy, and West Germany also supply much technical assistance.

The non-Communist countries coordinate their bilateral aid through the Organization for Economic Cooperation and Development (OECD). The countries providing aid often negotiate as a group with aid-receiving countries to determine the size and use of aid programs.

Multilateral Aid Programs

About a fourth of all official foreign aid is multilateral. A large part of this aid is channeled through the United Nations and United Nations agencies. Most multilateral aid goes for development and technical assistance, and disaster relief. Multilateral agencies generally do not offer military aid.

Technical Assistance and Relief. United Nations technical assistance, refugee, and relief programs are financed mostly by contributions from member governments. A large share of these contributions goes to the United Nations Development Program (UNDP). The UNDP selects aid projects and distributes funds to various agencies to carry out the projects. Each agency also receives funds directly from member countries.

Five agencies carry out much of the UN's technical assistance work in developing countries. (1) The Food and Agriculture Organization of the United Nations (FAO) promotes agricultural development. (2) United Nations Educational, Scientific and Cultural Organization (UNESCO) gives educational and scientific assistance. (3) The World Health Organization (WHO) helps countries improve their health services. (4) United Nations Children's Fund (UNICEF) helps fight children's diseases, and aids needy children and mothers. (5) The International Labor Organization (ILO) conducts labor training programs. Other agencies also give technical assistance. The United Nations Industrial Development Organization (UNIDO) was formed in 1966 to give advice on industrial development. Special agencies aid refugees.

The United Nations Conference on Trade and Development (UNCTAD) does not give aid. But it serves as a forum for its members to frame aid and trade policies to benefit developing countries. For more information on most of the UN's specialized agencies, see UNITED NATIONS (Specialized Agencies).

Worldwide Lending Programs help developing countries finance development projects. The International Bank for Reconstruction and Development (World Bank), an independent UN agency, makes long-term loans to member governments at reasonable interest rates. The International Development Association (IDA), a World Bank affiliate, makes loans to less developed member countries, allowing 50 years to repay at very low interest. Another World Bank affiliate, the International Finance Corporation (IFC), invests in private enterprises in developing countries.

Regional Development Programs aid poor countries in particular areas. The Inter-American Development Bank (IDB), an instrument of the Alliance for Progress, makes long-term development loans to Latin American countries. Founded in 1959, the IDB is financed mainly by the U.S. government. Headquarters are in Washington, D.C. The Asian Development Bank, established in 1965, lends money to governments and private enterprises in Asia. The bank's original financing came mainly from the United States, Japan, India, and Australia. Headquarters are in Manila, the Philippines. The African Development Bank, financed by over 25 African countries, makes loans to promote economic and social development in Africa. Founded in 1964, the bank has headquarters in Abidjan, Ivory Coast.

Two agencies of the European Economic Community (EEC) aid developing countries. The Overseas Development Fund provides grants to associate members of the EEC in Africa. The EEC-sponsored European Investment Bank makes development loans to the African associates, and to Greece and Turkey.   JOHN PINCUS

Related Articles in WORLD BOOK include:

Agency for International   Alliance for Progress
  Development   Asian Development Bank

Developing Country
European Community
Export-Import Bank of
  the United States
Food and Agriculture
  Organization
Food for Peace
Foreign Policy
International Development
  Association
International Finance
  Corporation
International Labor
  Organization
International Trade

Lend-Lease
Marshall Plan
Peace Corps
Point Four Program
Technical Assistance
UNESCO
United Nations
United Nations Relief and
  Rehabilitation Administration
World (The Interdependence of Nations)
World Bank
World Health Organization

FOREIGN BILL OF EXCHANGE. See ECONOMICS (World Finance).

FOREIGN CORRESPONDENT reports the news from important places in other countries. Such reporters may work for a newspaper, magazine, press association, or radio or television network in their own country.

Increasing interest in international affairs has assured foreign correspondents a permanent place in American journalism. Their stories provide the most reliable public report of affairs in other nations. The press associations, Associated Press and United Press International, employ many of the foreign correspondents who report to American readers. Others are heard through major radio and television networks.

Foreign correspondents who have become best known are those who served during wars. Richard Harding Davis covered the Spanish-American War, the Boer War, the Russo-Japanese War, and the early part of World War I (see DAVIS, RICHARD HARDING). In World War II, Ernie Pyle's columns from Great Britain, Africa, and Europe appeared in many papers. His columns were written in a simple, folksy style, and became highly popular (see PYLE, ERNIE).

In early American newspapers, foreign news was copied from papers brought from other countries, mostly England. Merchant ships brought these papers. But there was little opportunity for really effective foreign correspondence until ocean cables became available after 1858. The invention of the wireless and the development of radio increased the demand for fast reporting of events abroad.   JOHN ELDRIDGE DREWRY

See also WAR CORRESPONDENT.

FOREIGN EXCHANGE. See MONEY (table); INTERNATIONAL TRADE (Financing International Trade); ECONOMICS (World Finance).

FOREIGN LANGUAGE STUDY. See LANGUAGE (Learning a Foreign Language).

FOREIGN LEGION, or LÉGION ÉTRANGÈRE, is one of the world's most colorful and gallant fighting forces. The Legion is a unit of the French government, but consists of volunteers. Most Legionnaires come from countries other than France. Frenchmen are forbidden to join the Legion, but some enlist by giving false nationalities.

Men who apply for duty in the Legion must be between 18 and 40 years old. They must pass a strict physical examination. Legionnaires enlist for five years.

The Legion does not make its records public, and an atmosphere of mystery, exaggeration, and glamour surrounds it. Some men join the Legion to escape political punishment, and others to seek adventure. Still others join to avoid punishment for crime. However, the Legion accepts no known criminals, and the number of criminals in the unit has been exaggerated in many fictional accounts. Doctors, lawyers, merchants, and priests have served as Legionnaires. Whatever their reasons for joining, the Legionnaires rank among the world's best soldiers.

Discipline in the Legion is harsh. But the unit never lacks recruits. About 350,000 men have served in the Legion. Today, it has about 8,000 members. The Legion's headquarters are in Aubagne, France, just outside Marseille.

Louis Philippe created the Legion in 1831, for service outside France. Its original purposes were to offer a haven for foreign mercenaries serving in the Swiss Guard, and to assist in the conquest of Algeria. A total of 4,000 men, most of them Poles, Spaniards, Germans, and Italians, were organized into nationalistic battalions. Each group spoke its own language. The Legion's flag then, as now, was the tricolor, on which appears a globe marked *France* and the words: "The King of the French to the Foreign Legion." The Legion's most famous uniform consisted of baggy red trousers and a high-collar blue coat. During World War I, the Legion wore the blue of the French army. Shortly after the war, it adopted the present khaki uniform. The Legion's insignia is a small red grenade that spouts seven flames.

The Legion has served most frequently in colonial wars. But it has also participated in France's major wars. After its work in Algeria, it fought for Spain in the Carlist War of 1835. Only 500 men survived the three years in Spain and returned to Algeria. For the next 50 years, the Legion was involved in subduing and making peace with the people of Algeria and Morocco. When it was not fighting, it was erecting buildings. Legionnaires constructed the first European-style buildings in almost every city in North Africa. During these 50 years, the Legion also fought elsewhere, and underwent organizational changes.

In 1854, two regiments fought in the Crimean War. About 450 Legionnaires were killed in the war. In 1859, two regiments fought the Austrians in Italy, in an attempt to revive France's empire. Nearly 150 Legionnaires died in the campaign. In 1863, Napoleon III involved the Legion in another desperate and hopeless cause. The Legion formed part of the French army sent to Mexico to support Maximilian's attempt to seize authority in that country. In that campaign, which lasted until 1867, the Legion lost about 470 men.

A handful of Legionnaires bravely fought the Battle of Camerone in Mexico on April 30, 1863. The date of that battle is considered the sacred date of the corps, and Legionnaires throughout the world observe it each year. They conduct memorial services, and retell the story of the men who withstood the assaults of 2,000 enemy soldiers and refused to surrender. Of the last six Legionnaires who made a final bayonet charge, three survived and were captured. The officer in charge lost his wooden hand. It now rests in a place of honor in the Legion's Hall of Fame in Aubagne, France.

When Germany invaded France in 1870, the Legion sent help to the mother country. Their capture of Or-

léans was the only bright spot in the tale of French resistance. In 1885, four battalions went to Indochina to protect that colony against local uprisings. After successfully accomplishing this mission, the units were organized into the Fifth Regiment, and stationed permanently in Indochina.

During World War I (1914-1918), the first two regiments of the Legion supplied four other regiments for service in France. About 45,000 Legionnaires fought Germany. Of these, nearly 31,000 were killed, wounded, or missing in action. As a result of its gallant actions, the Legion became one of the most decorated French military units of World War I.

In World War II (1939-1945), Legionnaires served in many parts of the world. At first, they fought the Japanese in Indochina, and against Nazi Germany in France and Norway. Later, some units fought for Vichy France. But most units joined General Charles de Gaulle and served in North Africa, France, and Germany.

After World War II, the Legion again became a haven for political refugees and ex-soldiers, particularly Germans. With up-to-date equipment, it was again called upon to fight in Indochina from 1946 to 1954, this time against Communist rebels. The Legion sparked the final heroic resistance at Dien Bien Phu. When Algeria became independent in 1962, Legion headquarters moved from Sidi Bel Abbès, Algeria, to Aubagne, France. Through the years, most of the Legion's units moved out of Africa. Today, the majority of the units are stationed in France and the Pacific Islands controlled by France.　　　　　　　CHARLES MERCER

FOREIGN OFFICE. See DIPLOMACY.

FOREIGN POLICY is the whole set of objectives which a government seeks in its relations with other governments. It ordinarily seeks to gain them by *diplomacy* (official negotiations between states). But it may also try to secure them through war. The announced aims of a nation are usually peace, security, and justice. But each country judges what these objectives mean in its own case.

A nation usually has several broad aims which remain the same even though its political parties or its form of government may change. French foreign policy has traditionally been concerned with the security of the country's northeast frontiers, often endangered by German attack. Great Britain tried to maintain a balance of power in Europe. A cornerstone of United States foreign policy was the Monroe Doctrine, a policy designed to prevent European interference in the affairs of North and South America (see MONROE DOCTRINE). After World War II ended in 1945, the containment policy of the United States tried to prevent Communist expansion (see COLD WAR). Major changes in warfare and in world politics since the war have caused these traditional policies to be altered and new policies to be added.

Influences on Foreign Policy

Broad national objectives have to be supported by specific actions. Shaping foreign policy involves a series of choices among a variety of alternative possible courses. Foreign policy is a continuous process, because each new step depends on former action and the changes it causes in the behavior of other nations.

Alliances. All countries need the cooperation of other nations. They continually modify their own policies in order to obtain and preserve allies. For example, after World War II, the United States needed the cooperation of European nations in trying to "contain" Russia. It tried to strengthen countries which shared the American interest in halting the spread of Russian Communism. The United States offered economic aid to war-devastated Western Europe through the Marshall Plan and other programs of foreign aid. It also entered an alliance of western democracies, the North Atlantic Treaty Organization (NATO). Russia in turn reacted to the joint activities of the Western nations, and Russian moves then required shifts in American policies.

The foreign policies of allies may conflict with each other when put into practice. For instance, the traditional American attitude against colonialism sometimes created tensions when the United States had to work with other powers that had colonies.

Domestic Policies sometimes interfere with foreign policy. For example, United States farm programs have unintentionally produced great surpluses of some commodities. The United States has disposed of some surpluses abroad at far below the world market price. This action has caused friction between the United States and some of its allies whose economies depend on the export of the same commodities.

Historical and Social Traditions in a country play a large part in its foreign policy. For example, Canadian foreign policy differs from that of the United States, even though both are English-speaking democracies with a long record as good neighbors. Until 1931, Canada was a part of the British Empire. Therefore, Canadians have been more concerned about European affairs, and less interested in the Far East than have Americans. Social relations in a country also make a difference in its foreign policy. Canada has two peoples, English- and French-speaking. Its government must act so as not to antagonize the large French minority, which is traditionally more "isolationist."

Economic Factors also enter into foreign policy. Canada's economy depends greatly on the export of products from its fields, forests, and mines. Canadians are still in the expensive process of industrializing. Trade questions are therefore more important in Canadian foreign policy than in that of the United States.

Shaping Foreign Policy

The Executive takes the initiative in shaping a nation's foreign policy because the state must speak with one voice. The chief executive receives advice from his foreign minister and the foreign office. The Department of State aids the President of the United States. The Ministry of External Affairs serves this function in Canada. The foreign service of the executive branch provides information and carries out the policy. Other executive departments, such as defense and treasury, participate in foreign policy to some extent.

The Legislature can usually approve or disapprove of actions already taken by the administration. The American governmental system is based on a separation of powers. For this reason, policy making is more difficult in the United States than in many other democracies. The United States Senate must agree by a two-thirds vote to treaties concluded by the President. The House of Representatives, as well as the Senate, must approve of expenditures made to carry out foreign policy.

Public Opinion. In a democracy, the executive cannot move too far in any direction contrary to public sentiment. In dictatorships, the person or persons heading the government can make rapid decisions without immediate need to secure popular consent. Americans historically favored a policy of isolationism. Such a policy worked during the 1800's because European nations were too occupied with conflicts among themselves to be able to threaten North America. But after the United States was drawn into two world wars, American leaders were able to convince the American people that the United States should abandon isolationism and act as a great power. Since World War II, American public opinion has generally supported worldwide foreign commitments.

Many nations try to reach beyond foreign governments directly to the people. A country's information services carry out such programs. For example, the United States Voice of America broadcasts to many countries, including Russia. Economic aid and technical assistance programs, student and teacher exchanges, and the Peace Corps program are other means used by the U.S. government to build good will overseas.

Other Factors directly or indirectly shape foreign policy. No government can long uphold a foreign policy that does not balance with the nation's capabilities. Its power to carry out a policy depends on resources and geographical location, and on the education, skills, and loyalty of the people. Policy-makers must also consider a country's military strength, its experience in diplomacy, and its ability to win support from the governments of other nations.   WILLIAM T. R. FOX

Related Articles. See the History section of the country articles, such as FRANCE (History). See also CANADA, HISTORY OF; UNITED STATES, HISTORY OF. See also:

Council on Foreign	Foreign Service
Relations	International Law
Diplomacy	International Relations
Foreign Aid	International Trade
Foreign Policy Association	

FOREIGN POLICY ASSOCIATION (FPA) is a national organization whose purpose is to increase the interest and understanding of Americans in world affairs. The FPA works independently of the government and of political parties. It sponsors the annual *Great Decisions* program, in which participants study and discuss eight major foreign policy issues.

The FPA publishes *Headline Series* five times a year. Each of these booklets contains analyses of major foreign policy problems and world areas written by experts. The association also publishes a kit of "Foreign Policy Briefs" for candidates and voters during presidential election years. The briefs discuss the foreign policy issues of special concern to the nation.

The Foreign Policy Association was founded in 1918. It is financed by individuals, corporations, and foundations, and by the sale of its publications and services. It has national headquarters at 345 E. 46th Street, New York, N.Y. 10017.

Critically reviewed by the FOREIGN POLICY ASSOCIATION

FOREIGN RELATIONS. See FOREIGN POLICY; INTERNATIONAL RELATIONS.

FOREIGN SERVICE

FOREIGN SERVICE is the principal operational force through which the international affairs of the United States government are conducted. The Foreign Service is administered by the U.S. Department of State. The service provides trained personnel for U.S. embassies and consulates in other countries. Members of the Foreign Service also fill many positions in the Department of State in Washington, D.C. They are often assigned to work in other government agencies that have a direct interest in foreign affairs.

Service

Foreign Service posts abroad fall into two categories, diplomatic and consular. Chiefs of *diplomatic* missions, or embassies, are appointed by the President and accredited to the chief of state of the host country. An ambassador heads an embassy. He or she is a personal representative of the President of the United States. *Consular* officers assist American citizens abroad and handle U.S. business and commercial affairs overseas. Consular officers are not accredited to the host government and cannot represent the President.

Members of the Foreign Service perform administrative work in U.S. embassies, missions, and consulates; negotiate with government officials of other countries; report to the U.S. Department of State on economic, political, and social conditions; issue passports and visas; protect the interests and welfare of U.S. citizens abroad; and interpret U.S. policies to governments and citizens of other countries. Some members of the Foreign Service perform specialized tasks in economics, international commercial and labor affairs, and administration.

Most newly appointed Foreign Service officers receive orientation at the Foreign Service Institute (FSI) in Washington, D.C., before they are sent abroad. The institute teaches the languages and customs of other countries, gives advanced instruction in foreign affairs, and provides training in specialized activities of the Foreign Service. Senior Foreign Service officers often go back to the institute for special training before starting new assignments. The institute also offers courses for the spouses and dependents of Foreign Service officers and other government officials who work overseas.

Foreign Service personnel serving overseas may receive allowances for living expenses if government-owned quarters are not available. They may also receive allowances for travel and official entertainment. The government may provide additional living expenses for personnel in cities where the cost-of-living index is higher than in Washington, D.C. Foreign Service employees usually serve at overseas posts for periods of five to seven years out of ten years. On assignments of this length, the government provides home leave at its own expense after two to three years.

Personnel

There are approximately 9,000 persons in the Foreign Service. About 3,400 work in the United States, most of them at the Department of State in Washington. The rest serve in other countries. Foreign Service personnel receive their appointments on a merit basis. Considera-

tion is also given to geographic distribution and to the recruitment of women and members of minority groups so that the work force of the Foreign Service is broadly representative of the American people.

Members of the Foreign Service fall into three basic classifications: Foreign Service officers, Foreign Service Reserve officers, and Foreign Service Staff officers and employees.

Foreign Service Officers are appointed by the President with the advice and consent of the Senate. They fill most of the officer positions in the diplomatic and consular corps. Foreign Service officers are assigned to positions both in the United States and abroad. These positions are in administrative, consular, economic and commercial, and political fields, and do not require a high degree of continuity or specialization. They are graded from Class 8, the lowest class, up to Class 1. The positions of career minister and career ambassador rank above Class 1. Salaries range from about $11,000 to about $57,500 for the highest paid officers, who are ambassadors.

All Foreign Service officer appointments are made on a competitive basis. Applicants must be at least 21 years old—or 20, if they have already completed their junior year of college. They must also be U.S. citizens. There is no upper age limit. But applicants must be able to serve at least one complete tour of duty abroad before the mandatory retirement age of 60. A tour of duty is about two or three years long.

Candidates must first take a written examination. The test is given once each year in December in about 150 cities in the United States and at all U.S. embassies and consulates. Candidates who pass the written examination then undergo a one-hour oral examination before a panel of three Foreign Service officers. The panel tries to judge the candidate's ability to analyze ideas and problems, ability to work with others, creativity, intellectual curiosity, and other qualities. Candidates who are recommended for further consideration undergo a background investigation and a medical examination. All dependents who would accompany the candidate abroad also receive medical examinations.

After completing these steps, the candidates receive a final review in which all relevant information is evaluated. The names of the candidates who pass are placed on a rank-order register. The candidates on the register receive appointments at the Class 8 or 7 levels in relation to their standing on the register and as vacancies occur.

Foreign Service Reserve Officers are appointed by the secretary of state. There are two categories of reserve officers—limited and unlimited. Limited Foreign Service Reserve officers are recruited from federal agencies and private organizations to meet a need for skills not available in the regular officer staff. Their appointments are limited to not more than five years. But some may be extended up to five more years.

Foreign Service Reserve Unlimited officers receive unlimited status only after three years of continuous and satisfactory service as Limited Foreign Service Reserve officers. They must successfully undergo an oral interview and receive a certificate verifying the continuing need for the officer's services. They are assigned primarily to highly specialized positions. These include positions in such fields as communications, engineering, finance security, geography, medicine, and physical sciences.

Reserve officers receive salaries based on the same pay scale structure as that of Foreign Service officers.

Foreign Service Staff Officers and Employees are also appointed by the secretary of state. They are assigned to clerical, secretarial, and technical positions. Staff members in grades 7 to 1 make up the officer corps of the Foreign Service Staff. Staff salaries range from about $8,000 to about $27,000.

History

Beginnings. In the early years of the United States, many people took literally the injunction of President George Washington to avoid foreign entanglements, and opposed having any representation abroad. This opposition was so great that even the highest-ranking American diplomats sent abroad held only the rank of minister, instead of ambassador. Such a diplomat often carried only the title of *chargé d'affaires.*

Early U.S. diplomats included Benjamin Franklin, Thomas Jefferson, John Adams, John Jay, and James Monroe. In those early years, the top yearly salary for ministers was $9,000. They had to pay their own travel expenses, provide their own living quarters, and hire their own secretaries. In spite of the low respect diplomats received, four of the first six United States presidents had a diplomatic background.

The *spoils system,* or appointment and promotion on a political basis, dominated the Foreign Service throughout the 1800's and early 1900's. U.S. representation abroad consisted mainly of untrained personnel. Diplomatic posts served as rewards for service, and often went to political hacks and wealthy campaign contributors.

The Rogers Act. World War I imposed new responsibilities on the Foreign Service, and brought about substantial reforms. In 1924, John Jacob Rogers, a Massachusetts congressman, succeeded in legislating improvements in the Foreign Service through the Rogers Act, the basis of the present U.S. Foreign Service. This act combined the consular and diplomatic branches of the Foreign Service. The act also established difficult competitive examinations for Foreign Service career officers, and put promotion on a merit, rather than a political, basis. The act established the first retirement and disability pay system. It also installed the system of extra allowances so that competent people without private fortunes could accept overseas appointments.

After World War II, greater changes occurred in the Foreign Service. Many stemmed from the Foreign Service Act of 1946. This legislation gave ambassadors and ministers their first pay raises in nearly 100 years. It raised pay levels generally, and set up a new class system for the Foreign Service.

Many top-ranking ambassadors still receive appointments on political grounds, but at least two-thirds of the chiefs of overseas posts have advanced through the Foreign Service ranks.

In addition to the Foreign Service, overseas personnel of other government agencies, such as the International Communication Agency, also conduct U.S. business abroad.   Critically reviewed by the DEPARTMENT OF STATE

See also CONSUL; DIPLOMACY; DIPLOMATIC CORPS; STATE, DEPARTMENT OF.

FOREIGN SERVICE, SCHOOL OF. See GEORGETOWN UNIVERSITY.

FOREIGN TRADE. See INTERNATIONAL TRADE.

FOREIGN TRADE ZONE is an area in the United States where importers may store, exhibit, and process foreign goods without paying *customs duties* (import taxes). The zones are policed by the U.S. Customs Service. Customs officials collect duty only if the goods entering the United States are to be used or sold. If the goods are exported directly from the zones, no duty is paid. In other countries, foreign trade zones are sometimes called *free trade zones* or *free ports* (see FREE PORT).

The United States has foreign trade zones in about 30 of its almost 300 *ports of entry.* Ports of entry are cities with customs facilities where goods may enter the country legally. The Foreign-Trade Zones Board—made up of the secretaries of commerce, the treasury, and the army—administers the zones. The board was established in 1934. An executive secretary in the Department of Commerce directs the program for the Foreign-Trade Zones Board.   HAROLD J. HECK

FOREMAN, GEORGE (1949-   ), an American boxer, was the world heavyweight champion from January 1973, to October 1974. He won the title with an upset victory over Joe Frazier, the previous champion. Foreman lost the title when he was knocked out by Muhammad Ali. The defeat was Foreman's first after 40 straight victories, 37 of them by knockout, since he turned professional in 1969.

George Edward Foreman was born in Marshall, Tex. He dropped out of high school in Houston and, in 1965, joined the Job Corps, a government program for training unemployed youths. He learned how to box in the Job Corps. Foreman first became famous for winning the heavyweight championship at the 1968 Olympic Games. In 1977, Foreman announced his retirement from boxing. At that time he had won 46 professional fights and lost 2.   HERMAN WEISKOPF

Wide World

George Foreman

FORENSIC BALLISTICS. See BALLISTICS.

FOREORDINATION, *FAWR awr duh NAY shuhn,* is the belief that every event is *foreordained,* or decreed beforehand, by God. Supporters of this doctrine argue that if God does not ordain every event, He cannot be said to be all-powerful. Foreordination in its extreme form teaches that, by God's mysterious choice, some people are destined for hell and others are destined for heaven.

Many religious traditions have taught some form of foreordination. But it is most often associated with John Calvin, whose ideas influenced the Congregationalists, Baptists, Presbyterians, and Episcopalians (see CALVIN, JOHN). In recent years, most churches have moderated or ceased to emphasize the doctrine of foreordination.   HOWARD R. BURKLE

See also PREDESTINATION.

FORESHORTENING. See PERSPECTIVE.

Jerry Frank, DPI

Robert Frerck, Dimensions

Jacques Jangoux

Tropical Rain Forest

Tropical Seasonal Forest

Savanna

Different Kinds of Forests grow in different parts of the world. Many scientists divide the world's forests into the six main *formations* (types) shown in the photographs above and on the next page. The forests that make up each formation have similar plant and animal life.

FOREST

FOREST is a large area of land covered with trees. But a forest is much more than just trees. It also includes smaller plants, such as mosses, shrubs, and wild flowers. In addition, many kinds of birds, insects, and other animals make their home in the forest. Millions upon millions of living things that can only be seen under a microscope also live in the forest.

Climate, soil, and water determine the kinds of plants and animals that can live in a forest. The living things and their environment together make up the forest *ecosystem*. An ecosystem consists of all the living and nonliving things in a particular area and the relationships among them.

The forest ecosystem is highly complicated. The trees and other green plants use sunlight to make their own food from the air and from water and minerals in the soil. The plants themselves serve as food for certain animals. These animals, in turn, are eaten by other animals. After plants and animals die, their remains are broken down by bacteria; tiny soil-dwelling animals; and plants called *fungi*. This process returns minerals to the soil, where they can again be used by green plants to make food.

Paul F. Maycock, the contributor of this article, is Professor of Botany at Erindale College, University of Toronto.

Although individual members of the ecosystem die, the forest itself lives on. If the forest is wisely managed, it provides us with a continuous source of wood and many other products.

Before people began to clear the forests for farms and cities, great stretches of forestland covered about 60 per cent of the earth's land area. Today, forests occupy about 30 per cent of the world's land. The forests differ greatly from one part of the world to another. For example, the steamy, vine-choked rain forests of central Africa are far different from the cool, towering spruce and fir woods of northern Canada.

This article provides general information on the importance of forests and describes the structure of forests. It also discusses the major kinds of forests in the world and in the United States and Canada. Finally, the article describes how forests work as an ecosystem and how they have changed and developed through the ages. For detailed information on forest products and forest management, see the articles FOREST PRODUCTS and FORESTRY.

The Importance of Forests

Forests have always had great importance to human beings. Prehistoric people got their food mainly by hunting and gathering wild plants. Many of these people lived in the forest and were a natural part of it. With the development of civilization, people settled in towns and cities. But they still returned to the forest to get timber and to hunt.

Temperate Deciduous Forest

Temperate Evergreen Forest

Boreal Forest

Today, people depend on forests as much as ever, especially for their (1) economic value, (2) environmental value, and (3) enjoyment value. The science of forestry is concerned with increasing and preserving these values by careful management of forestland.

Economic Value. Forests supply many products. Wood from forest trees provides lumber, plywood, railroad ties, and shingles. It also is used in making furniture, tool handles, and thousands of other products. In many parts of the world, wood serves as the chief fuel for cooking and heating.

Various manufacturing processes change wood into a great number of different products. Paper is one of the most valuable products made from wood. Other processed wood products include cellophane, plastics, and such fibers as rayon and acetate.

Forests provide many important products besides wood. Latex, which is used in making rubber, and turpentine come from forest trees. Various fats, gums, oils, and waxes used in manufacturing also come from trees. In some primitive societies, forest plants and animals make up a large part of the people's diet.

Unlike most other natural resources, such as coal, oil, and mineral deposits, forest resources are renewable. As long as there are forests, people can count on a steady supply of forest products.

Environmental Value. Forests help conserve and enrich the environment in several ways. For example, forest soil soaks up large amounts of rainfall. It thus prevents the rapid runoff of water that can cause erosion and flooding. In addition, the rain water is filtered as it passes through the forest soil and becomes *ground water*. This ground water flows through the ground and provides a clean, fresh source of water for streams, lakes, and wells.

Forests also help renew the oxygen in the air we breathe. As the trees and other green plants make food, they release oxygen into the air. People and nearly all other living things need oxygen to live. If green plants did not continuously supply new oxygen, almost all life would soon stop.

Forests also provide a home for many plants and animals that can live nowhere else. Without the forest, many kinds of wildlife could not exist.

Enjoyment Value. The natural beauty and peace of the forest offer a special source of enjoyment. In the United States, Canada, and many other countries, huge forestlands have been set aside for the enjoyment of the people. Many people use these forests for such recreational activities as camping, hiking, and hunting. Others visit the forest simply to enjoy the scenery and to relax in the quiet beauty.

The Structure of Forests

Every forest has various *strata* (layers) of plants. The five basic forest strata, from highest to lowest, are (1) the canopy, (2) the understory, (3) the shrub layer, (4) the herb layer, and (5) the forest floor.

The Canopy consists mainly of the *crowns* (branches and leaves) of the tallest trees. The most common trees in the canopy are called the *dominant* trees of the forest. Certain plants, especially climbing vines and epiphytes, may grow in the canopy. *Epiphytes* are plants that grow on other plants for support but absorb from the air the water and other materials they need to make food.

The canopy receives full sunlight. As a result, it pro-

336a

The Structure of the Forest

Every forest has various *strata* (layers) of plants. The five basic strata, from highest to lowest, are (1) the canopy, (2) the understory, (3) the shrub layer, (4) the herb layer, and (5) the forest floor. This illustration shows the strata as they might appear in a temperate deciduous forest.

The Canopy

The tops of the tallest trees in the forest make up the canopy. This layer receives full sunlight. As a result, it produces more food than does any other layer. In some forests, the canopy is dense, almost forming a roof over the forest. But in other forests, such as this one, the canopy is more open, permitting much more sunlight to reach the lower layers. Many climbing and flying animals live in the canopy, where they can find plentiful food.

The Understory

Shorter trees that grow beneath the canopy form the understory. The understory trees receive less sunlight than do the trees of the canopy. They therefore produce less food. However, the understory provides sufficient food, as well as shelter, for many kinds of forest animals.

The Shrub Layer

The shrub layer consists mainly of shrubs—that is, woody plants which have more than one stem and do not grow as tall as trees. Forests with a more open canopy and understory, such as this one, have a much heavier shrub layer than do those with dense tree growth. Many birds and insects live in the shrub layer.

The Herb Layer

Small, soft-stemmed plants, such as ferns, grasses, and wild flowers, make up the herb layer. This layer receives limited sunlight. Yet even in forests with dense tree layers, enough sunlight reaches the ground to support some herb growth. The animal life of the herb layer includes such small animals as insects, mice, and snakes and such large animals as bears, deer, and wolves.

The Forest Floor

The forest floor serves as the wastebasket for the upper strata. It is covered with animal droppings, leaves, and dead animals and plants. These wastes are broken down by earthworms, fungi, and insects and by countless bacteria and other microscopic life. This process, called *decomposition*, returns basic chemical elements to the soil, where they can be used for new plant growth.

Canopy

Understory

Shrub Layer

Herb Layer

Forest Floor

WORLD BOOK illustration by Jean Helmer

duces more food than does any other layer. Fruit-eating birds, and insects and mammals that eat leaves or fruit, live in the canopy.

The Understory is made up of trees shorter than those of the canopy. Some of these trees are smaller species that grow well in the shade of the canopy. Others are young trees that may in time join the canopy layer. Because the understory grows in shade, it is not as productive as the canopy. However, the understory provides food and shelter for many forest animals.

The Shrub Layer consists mainly of shrubs. Shrubs, like trees, have woody stems. But unlike trees, they have more than one stem, and none of the stems grows as tall as a tree. Forests with a dense canopy and understory may have only a spotty shrub layer. The trees in such forests filter out so much light that few shrubs can grow beneath them. Most forests with a more open canopy and understory have heavy shrub growth. Many birds and insects live in the shrub layer.

The Herb Layer consists of ferns, grasses, wild flowers, and other soft-stemmed plants. Tree seedlings also make up part of this layer. Like the shrub layer, the herb layer grows thickest in forests with a more open canopy and understory. The herb layer is the home of forest animals that live on the ground. They include such animals as insects, mice, snakes, turtles, and ground-nesting birds.

The Forest Floor is covered with clumps of moss and with the wastes from the upper layers. Leaves, twigs, and animal droppings—as well as dead animals and plants—build up on the forest floor. Among these wastes, an incredible number of small *organisms* (living things) can be found. They include earthworms, fungi, insects, and spiders, plus countless bacteria and other microscopic life. All these organisms break down the waste materials into the basic chemical elements necessary for new plant growth.

Kinds of Forests

Many systems are used to classify the world's forests. Some systems classify a forest according to the characteristics of its dominant trees. A *needleleaf forest*, for example, consists of a forest in which the dominant trees have long, narrow, needlelike leaves. Such forests are also called *coniferous* (cone-bearing) because the trees bear cones. The seeds grow in these cones. A *broadleaf forest* is made up mainly of trees with broad, flat leaves. Forests in which the dominant trees shed all their leaves during certain seasons of the year, and then grow new ones, are classed as *deciduous forests*. In an *evergreen forest*, the dominant trees shed old leaves and grow new ones continuously and so remain green throughout the year.

In some other systems, forests are classified according to the usable qualities of the trees. A forest of broad-leaf trees may be classed as a *hardwood forest* because most broadleaf trees have hard wood, which makes fine furniture. A forest of needleleaf trees may be classed as a *softwood forest* because most needleleaf trees have softer wood than broadleaf trees have.

Many scientists classify forests according to various *ecological systems*. Under such systems, forests with similar climate, soil, and amounts of moisture are grouped into *formations*. Climate, soil, and moisture determine the kinds of trees found in a forest formation. One common ecological system groups the world's forests into six major formations. They are (1) tropical rain forests, (2) tropical seasonal forests, (3) temperate deciduous forests, (4) temperate evergreen forests, (5) boreal forests, and (6) savannas.

Tropical Rain Forests grow near the equator, where the climate is warm and wet the year around. The largest of these forests grow in the Amazon River Basin of South America, the Congo River Basin of Africa, and throughout much of Southeast Asia.

Of the six forest formations, tropical rain forests have the greatest variety of trees. As many as 100 species—none of which is dominant—may grow in 1 square mile (2.6 square kilometers) of land. Nearly all the trees of tropical rain forests are broadleaf evergreens, though some palm trees and tree ferns can also be found. In most of the forests, the trees form three canopies. The upper canopy reaches about 150 feet (46 meters) high. A few exceptionally tall trees, called *emergents*, tower above the upper canopy. The understory trees form the two lower canopies.

The shrub and herb layers are thin because little sunlight penetrates the dense canopies. However, many climbing plants and epiphytes crowd the branches of the canopies, where the sunlight is fullest.

Most of the animals of the tropical rain forests also live in the canopies, where they can find plentiful food. These animals include such flying or climbing creatures as bats, birds, insects, lizards, mice, monkeys, opossums, sloths, and snakes.

Tropical Seasonal Forests grow in certain regions of the tropics and subtropics. These regions have a definite wet and dry season each year or a somewhat cooler climate than that of the tropical rain forest. Such climatic conditions occur in Central America, central South America, southern Africa, India, eastern China, and northern Australia and on many islands in the Pacific Ocean.

Tropical seasonal forests have a great variety of tree species, though not nearly as many as the rain forests have. They also have fewer climbing plants and epiphytes. Unlike the trees of the rain forest, many tropical seasonal species are deciduous. The deciduous trees are found especially in regions with distinct wet and dry seasons. The trees shed their leaves during the dry season.

Tropical seasonal forests have a canopy about 100 feet (30 meters) high. One understory grows beneath the canopy. Bamboos and palms form a dense shrub layer, and a thick herb layer blankets the ground. The animal life resembles that of the rain forest.

Temperate Deciduous Forests grow in eastern North America, western Europe, and eastern Asia. These re-

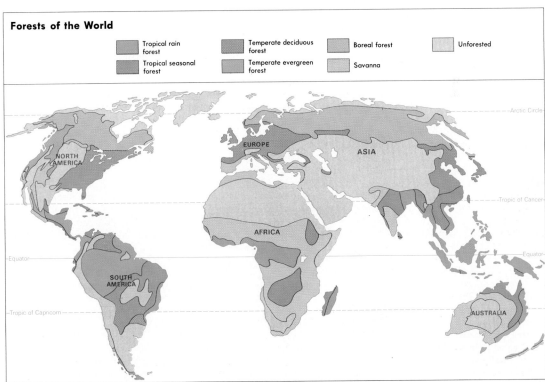

Forests of the World

Tropical rain forest Temperate deciduous forest Boreal forest Unforested

Tropical seasonal forest Temperate evergreen forest Savanna

WORLD BOOK map; adapted from *Physical Elements of Geography* by Trewartha, Robinson, and Hammond.
Copyright © 1967 by McGraw-Hill, Inc. Used with permission of McGraw-Hill Book Company.

gions have a *temperate* climate, with warm summers and cold winters.

The canopy of temperate deciduous forests is about 100 feet (30 meters) high. Two or more kinds of trees dominate the canopy. Most of the trees in these forests are broadleaf and deciduous. They shed their leaves in fall. The understory, shrub, and herb layers may be dense. The herb layer has two growing periods each year. Plants of the first growth appear in early spring, before the trees have developed new leaves. These plants die by summer and are replaced by plants that have grown in the shade of the leafy canopy.

Large animals of the temperate deciduous forests include bears, deer, and, rarely, wolves. These forests are also the home of hundreds of smaller mammals and birds. Many of the birds migrate south in fall, and some of the mammals hibernate during the winter.

Some temperate areas support mixed deciduous and evergreen forests. In the Great Lakes region of North America, for example, the cold winters promote the growth of heavily mixed forests of deciduous and evergreen trees. Forests of evergreen pine and deciduous oak and hickory grow on the dry coastal plains of the Southeastern United States.

Temperate Evergreen Forests. In some temperate regions, the environment favors the growth of evergreen forests. Such forests grow along coastal areas that have mild winters with heavy rainfall. These areas include the northwest coast of North America, the south coast of Chile, the west coast of New Zealand, and the southeast coast of Australia. Temperate evergreen forests also cover the lower mountain slopes in Asia, Europe, and western North America. In these mountain regions, the cool climate favors the growth of evergreen trees.

The strata and the plant and animal life vary greatly from one temperate evergreen forest to another. For example, the mountainous evergreen forests of Asia, Europe, and North America are made up of conifers. The coastal forests of Australia and New Zealand, on the other hand, consist of broadleaf evergreen trees.

Boreal Forests are found in regions that have an extremely cold winter and a short growing season. The word *boreal* means *northern*. Vast boreal forests stretch across northern Europe, Asia, and North America. Similar forests also cover the higher mountain slopes on these continents.

Boreal forests, which are also called *taiga*, have the simplest structure of all forest formations. They have only one uneven layer of trees, which reaches up to about 75 feet (23 meters) high. In most of the boreal forests, the dominant trees are needleleaf evergreens—either spruce and fir or spruce and pine. The shrub layer is spotty. However, mosses and lichens form a thick layer on the forest floor and also grow on the tree trunks and branches. There are few herbs.

Many small mammals, such as beavers, mice, porcupines, and snowshoe hares, live in the boreal forests. Larger mammals include bears, deer, foxes, moose, and wolves. Birds of the boreal forests include ducks, loons, owls, warblers, and woodpeckers.

Savannas are areas of widely spaced trees. In some savannas, the trees grow in clumps. In others, individual trees grow throughout the area, forming an uneven,

widely open canopy. In either case, most of the ground is covered by shrubs and herbs, especially grasses. Savannas are found in regions where low rainfall, poor soil, frequent fires, or other environmental features limit tree growth.

The largest savannas lie in the tropics, between heavy forests and grasslands. Tropical savannas grow throughout much of Central America, Brazil, Africa, India, Southeast Asia, and Australia. Most temperate savannas, which are called *woodlands*, grow between forests and grasslands and between forests and deserts.

Animals of the tropical savannas include giraffes, lions, tigers, and zebras. Temperate savannas have such animals as bears, deer, elk, and pumas.

Forests of the United States and Canada

The United States and Canada are rich in forests. Before the first white settlers arrived in the 1600's, forests covered most of the land from the Atlantic Ocean to the Mississippi River. Altogether, nearly 40 per cent of the land north of Mexico was forested at that time. More than half this forestland was in Canada and Alaska, where only a small portion has been cleared. Even in the lower United States, forests still grow on much of the original forestland. Today, the United States, excluding Hawaii, has about 753 million acres (305 million hectares) of forests. Canada has about 796 million acres (322 million hectares). In both countries, forests cover about a third of the land area.

The forests of the United States and Canada include all the major formations discussed in the previous section, except for tropical rain forests. The U.S.-Canadian forests can be divided into many smaller formations. One common system recognizes nine U.S.-Canadian formations. They are (1) subtropical forests, (2) southern deciduous-evergreen forests, (3) deciduous forests, (4) northern deciduous-evergreen forests, (5) temperate savannas, (6) mountain evergreen forests, (7) Pacific coastal forests, (8) boreal forests, and (9) subarctic woodlands.

Subtropical Forests thrive along the coasts of the Atlantic Ocean and the Gulf of Mexico in the Southeastern United States. In these regions, the climate stays hot and humid throughout the year.

In southern Florida, raised areas of the swampy Everglades support forests of live oak, mahogany, and sabal palm. These forests have a dense undergrowth of ferns, shrubs, and small trees. Epiphytes and vines crowd the branches of the taller trees. Broadleaf-evergreen forests grow farther north, along the edges of the Atlantic and Gulf coasts. The dominant trees in these forests are bay, holly, live oak, and magnolia. Thick growths of Spanish moss, an epiphyte that looks like long gray hair, hang from the branches.

Southern Deciduous-Evergreen Forests grow on the flat, sandy coastal plains of the Southeastern United States. The forests extend along the Atlantic Coastal Plain from New Jersey to Florida and along the Gulf Coastal Plain from Florida to Texas. These regions have long, hot summers and short winters.

Most of the forests consist of evergreen pine and deciduous oak. Pitch pine is the most common evergreen in the northern part of these forests. Going southward, pitch pine is replaced, in order, by loblolly, longleaf, and slash pine.

Forests of the United States and Canada

- Tropical rain forest
- Subtropical forest
- Southern deciduous-evergreen forest
- Deciduous forest
- Northern deciduous-evergreen forest
- Temperate savanna
- Mountain evergreen forest
- Pacific coastal forest
- Boreal forest
- Subarctic woodland
- Unforested

CANADA

UNITED STATES

MEXICO

Arctic Circle

Tropic of Cancer

WORLD BOOK map

Deciduous Forests occupy a region bounded by the coastal plains on the south and east, the Great Lakes on the north, and the Great Plains on the west. This region has dependable rainfall and distinct seasons. Severe frosts and heavy snows occur during winter in the northern parts of this formation.

The northern part of the deciduous forest region was once covered by glaciers. But the glaciers did not reach the southern portion, which has the oldest and richest deciduous forest in North America. This forest lies in the central Appalachian Mountains region. The dominant trees of the forest include ash, basswood, beech, buckeye, cucumber magnolia, hickory, sugar maple, tulip tree, and several kinds of oaks.

In most deciduous forests outside the central Appalachians, fewer species of trees dominate. For example, various kinds of oaks dominate the forests from southern New England to northwestern Georgia. Hickory and tulip trees—and in drier areas several species of pine—grow among the oak trees. Beech and sugar maple trees dominate the northeastern and north-central deciduous forests. However, these forests also have many other kinds of trees, such as black cherry, red maple, red oak, and white elm. The northwestern deciduous

forests are dominated by basswood and maple. Some oak trees also grow in these forests.

Northern Deciduous-Evergreen Forests stretch from the Great Lakes across southeastern Canada and northern New York and New England. In this region of cold winters and warm summers, deciduous trees of the south are mixed with conifers of the north.

The dominant evergreens throughout much of this region include white cedar, hemlock, and jack, red, and white pine. The chief broadleaf species include basswood, beech, sugar maple, white ash, and yellow birch. In moist areas, hemlock and white cedar grow in mixed stands with black ash and white elm. Drier areas have forests of red and white pine, which is mixed with some ironwood and red oak. Areas that are neither especially dry nor moist support maple or beech forests. The region's swamps are covered with black spruce and larch.

Temperate Savannas are found in areas of Canada and the United States that have fairly light annual rainfall and a long season of dryness. Most of these areas lie between heavily wooded forests and grasslands and between forests and deserts.

Temperate savannas dominated by aspen grow in

337

FOREST

North Dakota, Manitoba, Saskatchewan, and Alberta. Outside this region, oak, pine, or both oak and pine dominate the temperate savannas of North America. Savannas of bur oak, mixed in some areas with other oaks or hickory, extend in a belt from Manitoba through Texas. Coniferous savannas of juniper and piñon pine cover the dry foothills of the Rocky Mountains from Idaho to northern Mexico. In California, the foothills of the Sierra Nevada have similar savannas of blue oak and digger pine. Along the coast of southern California, the climate supports a broadleaf savanna of various species of oaks.

Mountain Evergreen Forests grow above the foothill savannas of the mountains of the western United States and Canada. In general, the climate in the mountains becomes colder, wetter, and windier with increasing altitude. The forests of the lower and middle slopes are called *montane forests*. Those of the upper slopes are known as *subalpine forests*.

In the Rockies, the lower montane forests consist of unmixed stands of ponderosa pine. At higher elevations, Douglas fir becomes dominant. Douglas fir is mixed with grand fir in the northern Rockies and with blue spruce and white fir in the southern Rockies. Above this zone lie the cold, snowy subalpine forests, which are dominated by Engelmann spruce and subalpine fir. Lodgepole pine is also common in both the montane and subalpine zones, especially in areas that have been affected by fire. The highest elevation at which trees can grow is called the *timber line*. Beyond this point, the climate is too severe for tree growth. In the timber-line regions, the trees grow in a scattered, savannalike way. The timber-line regions are dominated by bristlecone pine in the southern Rockies, by limber pine in the central Rockies, and by Lyall's larch and whitebark pine in the northern Rockies.

In the Sierra Nevada, incense cedar grows in moist areas of the lower montane forests. Douglas fir, Jeffrey pine, ponderosa pine, and sugar pine thrive on drier slopes. In central California, magnificent stands of giant sequoia trees grow on the western slopes of the Sierra Nevada. The sequoias are the bulkiest, though not the tallest, of all the world's trees. The largest sequoias measure about 100 feet (30 meters) around at the base. White fir dominates the upper montane forests of the Sierra Nevada. At subalpine elevations, the mountains support forests of red fir mixed with lodgepole pine and mountain hemlock. These subalpine forests thin out into savannas of bristlecone and whitebark pine at elevations near the timber line.

Pacific Coastal Forests extend along the Pacific Ocean from west-central California to Alaska. The warm currents of the Pacific help give this region a mild climate the year around. Warm, moisture-filled winds from the ocean bring heavy annual precipitation.

Huge conifers dominate the Pacific coastal forests. Forests of redwood, one of the world's tallest trees, grow along a narrow coastal strip from central California to southern Oregon. Many of these giants tower more than 300 feet (91 meters). Inland from the redwoods and to the north, grow magnificent forests of Douglas fir, Sitka spruce, western hemlock, and western red cedar. Along the coast of northern Washington

and southern British Columbia, the high annual precipitation supports thick temperate rain forests. These forests, with their moss-covered Douglas fir, Sitka spruce, and Pacific red cedar, make up a damp, green wilderness found nowhere else in North America.

Boreal Forests sweep across northern North America from northwestern Alaska to Newfoundland. In this region of severe cold and heavy snowfall, winter lasts seven to eight months. However, the short growing season has dependable rainfall and many hours of daylight each day. The boreal forests are dominated by coniferous evergreens, chiefly balsam fir, black spruce, jack pine, and white spruce. Some areas support stands of larch, which is a deciduous conifer. Such deciduous broadleaf trees as balsam poplar, trembling aspen, and white birch grow in areas that have been burned over by forest fires. The boreal forests have many *bogs* (areas of wet, spongy ground). Some of the bogs are treeless. Other bogs, called *muskegs*, are covered by a deep mat of moss on which dwarfed conifers grow.

Subarctic Woodlands lie along the northern edge of the boreal forests. The climate in this region is bitterly cold, with low precipitation and an extremely brief growing season. These conditions force the trees to grow in a widely spaced, savannalike fashion. Black spruce dominates most of the region. Other boreal trees, such as aspen, larch, white birch, and white spruce, grow in some places. North of the woodlands lies the Arctic tundra, where trees cannot survive.

The Life of the Forest

Forests are filled with an incredible variety of plant and animal life. For example, scientists recorded nearly 10,500 kinds of organisms in a deciduous forest in Switzerland. The number of individual plants and animals in a forest is enormous.

All life in the forest is part of a complex ecosystem, which also includes the physical environment. Ecologists study forest life by examining the ways in which the organisms interact with one another and their environment. Such interactions involve (1) the flow of energy through the ecosystem, (2) the cycling of essential chemicals within the ecosystem, and (3) competition and cooperation among the organisms.

The Flow of Energy. All organisms need energy to stay alive. In forests, as in all other ecosystems, life depends on energy from the sun. However, only the green plants in the forest can use the sun's energy directly. Through a process called *photosynthesis*, they use sunlight to produce food.

All other forest organisms rely on green plants to capture the energy of sunlight. Green plants are thus the *primary producers* in the forest. Animals that eat plants are known as *primary consumers* or *herbivores*. Animals that eat herbivores are called *secondary consumers* or *predators*. Secondary consumers themselves may fall prey to other predators, called *tertiary* (third) *consumers*. This series of primary producers and various levels of consumers is known as a *food chain*.

In a typical forest food chain, tree leaves (primary producers) are eaten by caterpillars (primary consumers). The caterpillars, in turn, are eaten by shrews (secondary consumers), which are eaten by owls (tertiary consumers). Energy, in the form of food, passes from one level of the chain to the next. But much energy

Decomposers, such as bacteria, fungi, and insects, play a vital role in recycling chemical elements through the forest ecosystem. They break down dead plant and animal matter into basic substances that green plants need to grow. The bracket fungi shown here are growing on fallen trees in a tropical rain forest and speeding their decay.

Jacques Jangoux

is lost at each level. Therefore, a forest ecosystem can support, in terms of weight, far more green plants than herbivores and far more herbivores than predators.

The Cycling of Chemicals. All living things are made up of certain basic chemical elements. The supply of these chemicals is limited, and so they must be recycled for life to continue.

The *decomposers* of the forest floor play a vital role in chemical recycling. The decomposers include bacteria, earthworms, fungi, some insects, and certain single-celled animals. These organisms obtain food by breaking down dead plants and the wastes and dead bodies of animals into their basic chemicals. The elements pass into the soil, where they are absorbed by the roots of growing plants. Without decomposition, the supply of such essential elements as nitrogen, phosphorus, and potassium would soon be exhausted.

Some chemical recycling does not involve decomposers. Green plants, for example, release oxygen during photosynthesis. Animals—and plants as well—need this chemical to *oxidize* (burn) food and so release energy. In the oxidation process, animals and plants give off carbon dioxide, which the green plants need for photosynthesis. Thus the cycling of oxygen and carbon dioxide works together and maintains a steady supply of the two chemicals.

Competition and Cooperation. Every forest animal and plant must compete with individuals of its own and similar species for such necessities as nutrients, space, and water. For example, red squirrels in a boreal forest must compete with one another—and with certain other herbivores—for conifer seeds, their chief food. Similarly, the conifers compete with one another and

with other plants for water and sunlight. This competition helps ensure that the forest organisms best adapted to the environment will survive and reproduce.

Cooperation among the organisms of the forest is common. For many species, it is necessary for survival. For example, birds and mammals that eat fruit rely on plants for food. But the plants, in turn, may depend on these animals to help spread their seeds. Similarly, certain fungi grow on the roots of living trees. The fungi obtain food from the tree, but they also help the tree absorb needed water and nutrients.

For a diagram of a forest ecosystem, see ECOLOGY.

Forest Succession

In forests and other natural areas, a series of orderly changes may occur in the kinds of plants and animals that live in the area. This series of changes is called *ecological succession.* Areas undergoing succession pass through one or more *intermediate* stages until a final *climax* stage is reached. Forests exist in intermediate or climax stages of ecological succession in many places.

To illustrate how a forest develops and succession occurs, let us imagine an area of abandoned farmland in the Southeastern United States. The abandoned land will first support communities of low-growing weeds, insects, and mice. The land then gradually becomes a meadow as grasses and larger herbs and shrubs begin to appear. At the same time, rabbits, snakes, and ground-nesting birds begin to move into the area.

In a few years, young pine trees stand throughout the meadow. As the trees mature, the meadow becomes an intermediate forest of pines. The meadow herbs and shrubs die and are replaced by plants that grow better

A forest develops through a series of changes in the kinds of plants and animals that live in an area. This process is called *ecological succession*. The pictures below show how a forest might develop and succession occur on abandoned farmland in the Southeastern United States.

WORLD BOOK illustrations by Jean Helmer

A Grassy Meadow develops during the first few years. Pine seedlings appear throughout the meadow.

An Evergreen Forest gradually develops. But young pines need full sun, and so deciduous trees form the understory.

A Deciduous-Evergreen Forest is established as the old pines die. Deciduous trees fill in the gaps in the canopy.

A Wholly Deciduous Forest finally develops. This forest is the *climax* (final) stage in the succession.

in the shade of the pine canopy. As the meadow plants disappear, so do the food chains based on them. New herbivores and predators enter the area, forming food chains based on the plant life of the pine forest.

Years pass, and the pines grow old and large. But few young pines grow beneath them because pine seedlings need direct sunlight. Instead, broadleaf trees—particularly oaks—form the understory. As the old pines die, oaks fill the openings in the canopy. Gradually, a mixed deciduous-evergreen forest typical of the Southeastern United States develops.

But the succession is still not complete. Young oaks grow well in the shade of the canopy, but pines do not. Therefore, a climax oak forest may eventually replace the mixed forest. However, pine wood is much more valuable than oak wood. For this reason, foresters in the Southeast use controlled fires to check the growth of oaks and so prevent the climax forest from developing.

Different successional series occur in different areas. In southern boreal regions, for instance, balsam fir and white spruce dominate the climax forests. If fire, disease, or windstorms destroy some of these coniferous forests, an intermediate forest of trembling aspen and white birch may develop in its place. These deciduous trees grow better in direct sunlight and on unprotected, bare ground than do fir and spruce.

The aspen-birch forest provides the protection young boreal conifers need, and soon spruce and fir seedlings make up most of the understory. In time, these conifers grow taller than the aspen and birch trees. The deciduous species cannot reproduce in the shade of the new

canopy, and gradually the climax forest of fir and spruce trees is reestablished.

The History of Forests

The First Forests developed in marshlands about 365 million years ago, during the Devonian Period. They consisted of tree-sized club mosses and ferns, some of which had trunks nearly 40 feet (12 meters) tall and about 3 feet (1 meter) thick. These forests became the home of the first amphibians and insects.

By the beginning of the Carboniferous Period—about 345 million years ago—vast swamps covered much of North America. Forests of giant club mosses and horsetails up to 125 feet (38 meters) tall grew in these warm swamps. Ferns about 10 feet (3 meters) tall formed a thick undergrowth that sheltered huge cockroaches, dragonflies, scorpions, and spiders. In time, seed ferns and primitive conifers developed in the swamp forests. When plants of the swamp forests died, they fell into the mud and water that covered the forest floor. The mud and water did not contain enough oxygen to support decomposers. As a result, the plants did not decay but became buried under layer after layer of mud. Over millions of years, the weight and pressure on the plants turned them into great coal deposits.

Later Forests. As the Mesozoic Era began, about 225 million years ago, severe changes in climate and in the earth's surface wiped out the swamp forests. In the new, drier environment, gymnosperm trees became dominant. *Gymnosperms* are plants whose seeds are not enclosed in a fruit or seedcase. The gymnosperm trees included seed ferns and primitive conifers like those that grew in the swamp forests. They also included cycad and ginkgo trees, which became widespread. Gymnosperm trees formed forests that covered much of the earth. Amphibians, insects, and large reptiles lived in these forests.

The first flowering plants appeared about 130 million years ago, during the Cretaceous Period. Flowering plants, which are called *angiosperms*, produce seeds enclosed in a fruit or seedcase. Many angiosperm trees became prominent in the forests. They included magnolias, maples, poplars, and willows. Flowering shrubs and herbs became common undergrowth plants.

At the start of the Cenozoic Era, about 65 million years ago, the earth's climate turned cooler. Magnificent temperate forests then spread across North America, Europe, and Asia. The forests included a wealth of flowering broadleaf trees and needleleaf conifers. Many birds and mammals lived in these forests.

Modern Forests. The earth's climate continued to turn colder, and about 1½ million years ago the Pleistocene Ice Age began. Several great waves of glaciers advanced over much of North America and Europe and then retreated. By the time the last glacier retreated—about 10,000 years ago—the ice sheets had destroyed large areas of the temperate forests in North America and Europe. Only the temperate forests of southeastern Asia remained largely untouched.

The forests of the world took on their modern distribution after the Ice Age. For example, the great boreal forests developed across northern Europe and North

The Earth's Early Forests

Paleozoic Era (600 million to 225 million years ago)

The first forests developed about 365 million years ago during the Devonian Period. By the beginning of the Carboniferous Period—about 345 million years ago—swampy forests covered much of North America. These forests consisted of giant club mosses and horsetails up to 125 feet (38 meters) tall. The plants of the Carboniferous forests were later formed into great coal deposits.

Carboniferous Forest

Mesozoic Era (225 million to 65 million years ago)

During the Mesozoic Era, severe changes in climate and in the earth's surface wiped out the swamp forests. By the start of the Jurassic Period—about 180 million years ago—forests of *gymnosperm* trees covered much of the earth. Gymnosperm trees produce seeds that are not enclosed in a fruit or a seedcase. The gymnosperm trees included conifers, cycads, ginkgoes, and seed ferns.

Jurassic Forest

Cenozoic Era (65 million years ago to the present)

Magnificent temperate forests covered much of North America, Europe, and Asia during the Tertiary Period, which lasted from 65 million to 1¾ million years ago. These forests included a variety of flowering broadleaf trees and needleleaf conifers. The Pleistocene Ice Age, which began about 1½ million years ago, destroyed most of the temperate forests in North America and Europe.

Tertiary Forest

America. But the world's forest regions are not permanent. Today, for instance, temperate forests are invading the southern edge of the boreal region. Another ice age or other dramatic environmental changes could greatly alter the world's forests.

Human activities have had tremendous impact on modern forests. Since agriculture began about 10,000 years ago, large forest areas have been cleared for farms and cities. Modern forestry practices and concern for the environment have helped check forest destruction in many temperate regions. But population growth and increased agriculture and industrialization continue to result in much forest destruction, especially in tropical areas. PAUL F. MAYCOCK

Related Articles. See TREE with its list of *Related Articles*. See also NATIONAL FOREST (table) and the *Natural Resources* section of the various country, state, and province articles. Other related articles include:

Conservation
Ecology
Forest Products
Forest Service

Forestry
Jungle
Petrified Forest
Tropical Rain Forest

Outline
I. The Importance of Forests
  A. Economic Value
  B. Environmental Value
  C. Enjoyment Value
II. The Structure of Forests
  A. The Canopy
  B. The Understory
  C. The Shrub Layer
  D. The Herb Layer
  E. The Forest Floor
III. Kinds of Forests
  A. Tropical Rain Forests
  B. Tropical Seasonal Forests
  C. Temperate Deciduous Forests
  D. Temperate Evergreen Forests
  E. Boreal Forests
  F. Savannas
IV. Forests of the United States and Canada
  A. Subtropical Forests
  B. Southern Deciduous-Evergreen Forests
  C. Deciduous Forests
  D. Northern Deciduous-Evergreen Forests
  E. Temperate Savannas
  F. Mountain Evergreen Forests
  G. Pacific Coastal Forests
  H. Boreal Forests
  I. Subarctic Woodlands
V. The Life of the Forest
  A. The Flow of Energy
  B. The Cycling of Chemicals
  C. Competition and Cooperation
VI. Forest Succession
VII. The History of Forests

Questions
How do forests help conserve and enrich the environment?

Where is the oldest deciduous forest in North America?

How does an *intermediate* forest differ from a *climax* forest?

Which layer of the forest produces the most food? Why?

Where do forests of the world's bulkiest trees grow? What are these trees?

When did the first forests develop? What did they consist of?

How do deciduous and evergreen forests differ?

How does the forest food chain work?

What is the *timber line?*

Which kind of forest has the greatest variety of trees?

FOREST, NATIONAL. See NATIONAL FOREST.

FOREST, PETRIFIED. See PETRIFIED FOREST.

FOREST CONSERVATION. See CONSERVATION (Forest Conservation); FORESTRY.

FOREST FIRE. See AIRPLANE (Special-Purpose Planes); FORESTRY.

FOREST PRODUCTS

FOREST PRODUCTS have provided people with food, shelter, clothing, and fuel since the beginning of civilization. Prehistoric people ate berries and nuts that grew in forests. They built shelters from the branches of trees and wore clothing made of plant materials. By about 500,000 B.C., they used wood as a fuel to make fire.

Today, people throughout the world use more wood for fuel than for any other purpose. In the developing nations, about 90 per cent of the people rely on firewood for cooking and heating. In the United States and other industrialized countries, wood is used chiefly as a building material and as a source of pulp for making paper. The construction of a typical American house requires about 18,000 *board feet* of wood. A board foot is 1 foot (30 centimeters) long, 1 foot wide, and 1 inch (2.5 centimeters) thick. The amount of paper and paperboard used annually in the United States averages 575 pounds (261 kilograms) per person.

There are thousands of forest products, but most can be classified into one of two main groups, *wood products* or *chemical products*. Wood products are made directly from wood. They include lumber, plywood, and other construction materials. Chemical products are manufactured by breaking down wood cells through chemical processes. Such products may be entirely different from wood. For example, cellophane, lacquer, paper, and

Harry E. Troxell, the contributor of this article, is Professor of Wood Science and Technology at Colorado State University.

rayon do not look or feel like wood—but all are made from it. Other forest products come from the bark, fruit, gum, leaves, and sap of trees. Each person in the United States uses enough forest products yearly to make up a tree 100 feet (30 meters) tall and 16 inches (41 centimeters) in diameter.

Wood Products

Wood has many characteristics that make it an important construction material. It can be easily shaped with tools and fastened with nails, screws, staples, and adhesives. It is light but strong. Wood provides insulation against electricity, heat, cold, and sound. It can hold paint and other finishes, and it does not rust. Unlike metal construction materials, wood is a *renewable resource*—that is, a new supply grows after the timber has been harvested. Some of the chief wood structural materials are *round timbers, lumber, plywood and veneers,* and *composition board.*

Round Timbers include *pilings, poles,* and *posts.* Pilings are driven into the ground as foundations for buildings, wharves, and other heavy structures. Poles link overhead telephone wires and power lines. Posts are used chiefly to build fences and corrals.

Round timbers are simply trees that have been stripped of their branches and bark, and cut into logs of a desired length. The logs are dried and treated with various chemical preservatives, such as creosote and pentachlorophenol. The chemicals help the wood resist decay for about 40 years.

Lumber includes boards and larger pieces of wood that have been sawed from logs. The construction in-

Some Kinds of Forest Products   Trees from forests provide thousands of wood, chemical, and other products that people use every day. Wood products include lumber and plywood. Chemical products, such as charcoal and paper, are made from wood by various chemical processes. Other forest products include nuts and turpentine.

WORLD BOOK illustrations by David Cunningham

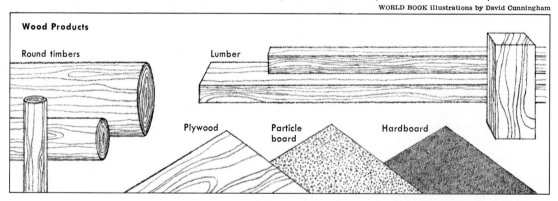

Wood Products

Round timbers   Lumber

Plywood   Particle board   Hardboard

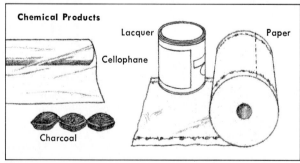

Chemical Products

Cellophane   Lacquer   Paper

Charcoal

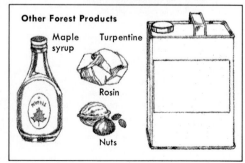

Other Forest Products

Maple syrup   Turpentine

Rosin

Nuts

dustry uses about 75 per cent of the lumber manufactured in the United States. The rest goes to factories that make baseball bats, crates, furniture, railroad ties, shingles, toys, and thousands of other products.

Wood scientists classify lumber as *softwood* or *hardwood*, depending on the kind of tree. Softwood trees stay green the year around, and hardwood trees lose their leaves every autumn. However, this classification system does not indicate the hardness of lumber because various softwoods are harder than some hardwoods. Most softwoods can be easily sawed, planed, chiseled, or bored, and so they are used chiefly for structural work. Such woods include cedar, Douglas fir, hemlock, and pine. Hardwoods have beautiful grain patterns and are widely used for floors, furniture, and paneling. Popular hardwoods include birch, maple, oak, sweet gum, walnut, and mahogany.

Plywood and Veneers. Plywood consists of an odd number of thin layers of wood glued together. The layers, called *veneers*, are arranged so that the grain pattern of each layer is at a right angle to the grain of the next layer. This arrangement gives plywood several advantages over lumber. Plywood shrinks, swells, and warps less than lumber, and it can be easily nailed near the edges without splitting. In addition, less expensive woods can be used for the inside layers of plywood than for the outer surfaces. Thus, plywood can look like expensive wood but cost less. Manufacturers may also glue hardwood veneers to softwood lumber, combining the advantages of each type of wood. Plywood and veneers are widely used in the construction and furniture industries.

Composition Board includes *particle board, insulation board*, and *hardboard*. These materials are made from small pieces of wood left over in sawmills and paper mills. Particle board consists of flakes of wood that have been mixed with an adhesive and pressed into a board. Much particle board is covered with veneers and used in making cabinets, doors, and furniture. Insulation board is made by exploding chips of wood into fibers by means of high-pressure steam. The wet fibers are then matted into a board. Insulation board may be cut into tiles and used in soundproof ceilings. Hardboard is made in much the same way as insulation board, but the fibers are dried before being compressed. Hardboard is harder than solid wood and is used in furniture and television and radio cabinets.

Chemical Products

Wood cells consist of three chief substances, *cellulose, lignin*, and *hemicelluloses*. Cellulose is the main ingredient of the fibers that give wood its strength and structure. Lignin holds the fibers together. Hemicelluloses combine with cellulose and lignin to form the walls of wood cells. Manufacturers make thousands of products from cellulose. Lignin has far fewer uses, but it is used in such products as artificial vanilla, cosmetics, and soil conditioners. Hemicelluloses have little importance as a source of forest products.

Some of the most valuable products made from cellulose include paper, fibers, films, and plastics. Charcoal is also a widely used chemical product of wood. It does

Some Uses of Forest Products

Wood Products

Hardboard

Cabinets	Paneling
Containers	Signs
Furniture	

Insulation Board

Ceiling tile	Sheathing

Lumber

Baseball bats	Furniture
Boats	Mine timbers
Bowling pins	Musical
Boxes	instruments
Building	Pencils
materials	Railroad ties
Cabinets	Shingles
Caskets	Toys
Crates	Window frames
Flooring	

Particle Board

Cabinets	Furniture
Doors	Paneling

Plywood

Airplanes	Concrete forms
Boats	Containers
Boxes	Doors
Building	Furniture
materials	Paneling
Cabinets	

Round Timbers

Bridges	Telephone poles
Fence posts	Utility poles
Foundations	

Sawmill Wastes

Bedding for	Insulation board
animals	Packing
Floor-sweeping	material
compounds	Particle board
Fuel	Pulp chips
Hardboard	

Veneer

Barrels	Matches
Baskets	Paneling
Boxes	Tabletops
Cabinets	Tongue depressors
Crates	Toothpicks
Furniture	

Chemical Products

Charcoal

Explosives	Fuel
Filters	

Lignin

Animal feeds	Plastics
Artificial	Road-building
vanilla	materials
Drilling muds	Soil conditioners
Pharmaceuticals	

Wood Pulp

Acetate	Photographic
Cardboard	film
Cellophane	Plastics
Explosives	Rayon
Lacquer	Triacetate
Paper	

Other Forest Products

Bark

Adhesives	Fuel
Cork	Soil mulch
Dyes	Tannic acid

Fruit

Beechnuts	Hickory nuts
Black walnuts	Pecans
Blueberries	Pine nuts
Cranberries	

Gum

Pine oil	Tall oil
Rosin	Turpentine

Leaves

Cedar-needle	Ornamental
oil	wreaths
Holly	Pine-needle oil

Sap

Maple sugar	Maple syrup

FOREST PRODUCTS

not come from cellulose alone, but from the entire wood substance. Charcoal is made by heating wood until it is *charred* (scorched).

Paper. In the United States, about 98 per cent of the cellulose obtained from trees is made into paper. To make most kinds of paper, manufacturers cut the wood into chips and "cook" them in various chemical solutions to form a pulp. The pulp is washed and passed through a series of screens that remove unwanted substances, leaving cellulose fibers and water. After being drained, bleached, and washed again, the pulp is matted into a sheet. A machine squeezes the sheet between rollers and dries it to form paper or paperboard. Heavy paperboard for cartons and other industrial products accounts for about half the output of U.S. paper mills.

Fibers and Films made from wood are manufactured by treating sheets of cellulose with a variety of chemical solutions. These solutions turn the cellulose into a thick liquid. The liquid is forced through tiny holes or narrow slits and treated with chemicals to make specific fibers and films.

Cellulose fibers, such as acetate and rayon, are widely used in making clothing, draperies, and upholstery.

Cellulose films include cellophane and photographic film.

Plastics manufactured from wood are among the toughest produced. They are made by combining cellulose with chemicals to obtain such compounds as cellulose acetate, cellulose acetate butyrate, and ethyl cellulose. Manufacturers mold these compounds into simple shapes, such as sheets and tubes. The molded plastics are then sent to companies that use them in making various products, including combs, tool handles, and toys.

Charcoal is made by heating wood in an oven that contains little or no air. During this process, called *destructive distillation*, the wood gives off various gases and turns into charcoal. Charcoal is an important fuel in many developing countries, but in the United States it is used mainly in barbecue cooking. Charcoal may also be purified to form *activated charcoal*, which can be used to remove odors and impurities from air and many substances.

Other Forest Products

Although most forest products are made from wood, many come from the bark, fruit, gum, leaves, and sap of trees.

Bark from the cork oak tree provides cork for such

10 LARGEST FOREST PRODUCTS COMPANIES IN THE UNITED STATES

Company	Forest Products Sales	Total Sales*	Total Employees	Year Founded	Headquarters
1. Georgia-Pacific Corporation	$3,038,000,000	$3,038,000,000	34,200	1927	Portland, Ore.
2. International Paper Company	2,933,098,000	3,540,600,000	52,290	1898	New York, N.Y.
3. Weyerhaeuser Company	2,868,376,000	2,868,376,000	47,210	1900	Tacoma, Wash.
4. Champion International Corporation	2,560,200,000	2,910,520,000	46,930	1937	Stamford, Conn.
5. Boise Cascade Corporation	1,904,251,000	1,931,530,000	35,230	1931	Boise, Ida.
6. Crown Zellerbach Corporation	1,659,155,000	2,135,624,000	32,000	1870	San Francisco, Calif.
7. St. Regis Paper Company	1,604,956,000	1,642,132,000	28,000	1899	New York, N.Y.
8. Kimberly-Clark Corporation	1,574,302,000	1,585,302,000	27,630	1872	Neenah, Wis.
9. Scott Paper Company	1,291,300,000	1,373,770,000	20,600	1879	Philadelphia, Pa.
10. Mead Corporation	985,700,000	1,599,342,000	26,200	1846	Dayton, O.

*Includes all sales and services.
Source: Investors Management Sciences, Inc., 1976 figures.

STATES AND PROVINCES LEADING IN FOREST PRODUCTS

Wood cut each year

British Columbia
78,589,000 cu. yds. (60,085,600 m³)

Oregon
56,631,000 cu. yds. (43,297,500 m³)

Washington
51,756,000 cu. yds. (39,570,300 m³)

Quebec
42,785,000 cu. yds. (32,711,500 m³)

California
31,249,000 cu. yds. (23,891,600 m³)

Georgia
29,223,000 cu. yds. (22,342,600 m³)

Alabama
27,586,000 cu. yds. (21,091,000 m³)

Ontario
24,678,000 cu. yds. (18,867,700 m³)

Mississippi
24,107,000 cu. yds. (18,431,100 m³)

Louisiana
22,309,000 cu. yds. (17,056,500 m³)

Sources: U.S. Department of Agriculture; Statistics Canada. Latest available figures—1974 for provinces, 1970 for states.

COUNTRIES LEADING IN FOREST PRODUCTS

Wood cut each year

Russia
500,927,800 cu. yds. (383,000,000 m³)

United States
440,588,900 cu. yds. (336,866,000 m³)

China
246,291,200 cu. yds. (188,310,000 m³)

Brazil
214,234,900 cu. yds. (163,800,000 m³)

Canada
180,262,100 cu. yds. (137,825,000 m³)

Indonesia
175,692,300 cu. yds. (134,331,000 m³)

India
164,000,900 cu. yds. (125,392,000 m³)

Nigeria
82,590,300 cu. yds. (63,147,000 m³)

Sweden
74,306,000 cu. yds. (56,813,000 m³)

Japan
56,318,400 cu. yds. (43,060,000 m³)

Source: FAO. 1974 figures.

products as bottle stoppers, bulletin boards, and insulation. The bark of the hemlock and other trees furnishes tannic acid for processing animal hides into leather.

Fruit harvested from forest trees includes pecans and pine nuts. Blueberry bushes and cranberry vines also grow in many forests. In addition, forest trees provide seeds for nurseries that grow seedlings.

Gum from certain pine trees is made into rosin and turpentine. Rosin is used in manufacturing such products as paint, paper, and varnish. Turpentine serves as a thinner in paints and varnishes and as a source of many industrial chemicals.

Leaves of forest trees furnish ornamental greenery for Christmas and other occasions. Forests also provide Christmas trees, but most Christmas trees sold in the United States are grown commercially.

Sap from certain maple trees can be made into maple syrup. Most maple syrup comes from the northeastern United States and from Ontario and Quebec in Canada.

The Forest Products Industry

The manufacture of forest products is a major industry in the United States and Canada. The U.S. forest products industry employs more than 1,300,000 men and women and produces about $23 billion worth of goods annually. The industry has about 40,000 manufacturing plants. Forest products companies own about 67 million acres (27 million hectares) of commercially valuable forestland in the United States. They also harvest timber in state and national forests under government leases. In addition, they buy logs from the owners of small wooded areas.

Canada's forest products industry ranks as the nation's leading manufacturer. More than 250,000 persons work for Canadian companies that make forest products. These firms produce about $3½ billion worth of goods yearly. Canada is the world's largest producer of *newsprint*, the paper on which newspapers are printed. It makes about 9 million short tons (8.2 million metric tons) of newsprint annually, nearly 40 per cent of the world total. About two-thirds of the newsprint used in the United States comes from Canada. HARRY E. TROXELL

Related Articles. See WOOD with its list of *Related Articles*. See also the following articles:

Acetate	Fiberboard	Paper	Sap
Bark	Gum	Rayon	Tannic Acid
Charcoal	Lacquer	Resin	Tar
Cork	Lumber	Rosin	Turpentine
Creosote	Naval Stores	Rubber	Veneer

FOREST RANGER. See FORESTRY; FOREST SERVICE.

FOREST RESERVE. See NATIONAL FOREST (History).

FOREST SERVICE is an agency of the United States Department of Agriculture. The agency has the task of promoting the best possible use of forest land. It manages about 188 million acres (76.1 million hectares) of national forests and other lands. Forest Service rangers try to protect these forests against insects, disease, and fire. The rangers preserve wildlife and supervise grazing. They see that no more timber is cut in any one year than a single year's growth can replace. They keep a cover of plants on sloping land to guard against rapid soil erosion and floods. The rangers also supervise camping and picnic areas, and keep up a system of lookout stations, telephone lines, two-way radio communication, and roads and trails. They often help rescue lost or injured people.

The agency cooperates in various ways with state and local governments and private landowners. For example, it advises and assists them in protecting and planting forests.

The Forest Service carries on research programs at eight experimental stations; the Forest Products Laboratory, Madison, Wis.; and the Institute of Tropical Forestry in Puerto Rico. It also conducts research projects at sites throughout the United States. Founded as the Bureau of Forestry, the agency became the Forest Service in 1905. Critically reviewed by the FOREST SERVICE

See also NATIONAL FOREST.

FORESTER. See FORESTRY; FOREST SERVICE.

FORESTER, CECIL SCOTT (1899-1966), was an English novelist who won fame for his fictional creation of Horatio Hornblower, a British naval hero of the 1800's. Hornblower's exciting adventures, his coolness and inventiveness under stress, and his weakness for women endeared him to a large reading public. He rises from midshipman to admiral in a series of novels which includes *Beat to Quarters* (1937), *Flying Colours* (1938), *A Ship of the Line* (1939), and *Lord Hornblower* (1946).

Forester believed his other novels, especially *The General* (1936), were equal to the Hornblower books. But his readers overwhelmingly favored the naval hero. Forester was born in Cairo, Egypt, and was educated in England. He lived in the United States from 1945 until his death. JOHN ESPEY

FORESTERS, ANCIENT ORDER OF, is a fraternal benefit society which was founded in England in 1745. The American branch was introduced in Philadelphia in 1832 and now is organized into three high courts and about 450 subcourts. Headquarters are located at 248 Boylston St., Boston, Mass. 02116. The order was introduced into Canada in 1898. Insurance benefits are paid to families of members. There are about 1,700,000 members. See also FORESTERS OF AMERICA.

FORESTERS, INDEPENDENT ORDER OF, is a fraternal benefit society founded in Newark, N.J., in 1874. The society operates in Canada, the United States, and the British Isles. Organized into 26 High Courts, it has 540,000 life insurance certificates in force. The order extends to eligible members certain fraternal benefits, including a home for aged members, grants for the care of Forester orphans, and financial assistance for the treatment of cancer, poliomyelitis, tuberculosis, and certain infectious diseases. Headquarters are at 789 Don Mills Road, Don Mills, Ont.
Critically reviewed by the INDEPENDENT ORDER OF FORESTERS

FORESTERS OF AMERICA is a fraternal benefit society which was once part of the Ancient Order of Foresters. It provides insurance for its members and has paid out over $100 million for members' illnesses, benevolent purposes, and for death benefits. The branches of the Foresters are organized in the form of 12 Grand Courts and about 400 Subordinate Courts.

The Ancient Order of Foresters was founded in Leeds, England, in 1745 and became active in the United States in 1832. In 1889, the American branch seceded from the English order and became a separate organization. It has headquarters at 161 Massachusetts Ave., Boston, Mass. 02115. JEAN B. GODDU

See also FORESTERS, ANCIENT ORDER OF.

Weyerhaeuser Co.

Georgia-Pacific Corp.

Harvesting and Planting Trees Mechanically contributes to efficient management of timber resources. The powerful jaws of tree shears, *left*, fell trees in a fraction of the time of a saw. A planting gun, *right*, digs a hole, inserts a seedling, and pats down the soil in one operation.

FORESTRY is the science of managing forest resources for human benefit. The practice of forestry helps maintain an adequate supply of timber for the manufacture of lumber, plywood, paper, and other wood products. It also includes the management of such valuable forest resources as water, wildlife, grazing areas, and recreation areas.

In general, forests provide the greatest benefits when they are managed with the goal of providing several benefits at once. This concept, called *multiple use forest management*, is applied in the national forests of the United States and in most state forests. These forests furnish about a third of the timber harvested annually in the United States. They also provide water for communities; shelter for wildlife; grazing land for livestock; and recreation areas for campers, hikers, and picnickers.

In some forests, however, the importance of one resource may outweigh that of others. For example, companies that manufacture paper or other wood products manage their forests primarily for maximum timber production. The U.S. forest products industry owns about 67 million acres (27 million hectares) of forestland. This acreage equals about half that of the forest-

David M. Smith, the contributor of this article, is Morris K. Jesup Professor of Silviculture at Yale University and the author of The Practice of Silviculture.

land owned and managed for timber production by the federal, state, and local governments. However, industrial forests produce about as much commercial timber yearly as do government forests. Private individuals own about 300 million acres (120 million hectares) of small woodland areas, but few of these forests are well managed.

This article discusses the scientific management of forest resources. For information on the various products made from trees, see FOREST PRODUCTS. For a discussion of forest ecology, see FOREST.

Managing Timber Resources

The goal of managing timber resources is to achieve an approximate balance between the annual harvest and growth of wood. This balance, called a *sustained yield*, ensures a continuous supply of timber. It is achieved by managing forests so they have about equal areas of trees of each age group, from seedlings to mature trees. The science of harvesting and growing crops of trees for sustained yield is called *silviculture*. The practice of silviculture requires that foresters know how various species of trees grow in different climates and soils, and how much sunlight and water the trees need. Foresters also use the science of genetics to breed trees that have improved growth rates and greater resistance to diseases and pests.

Harvesting. There are four chief methods of harvesting timber: (1) clearcutting, (2) seed tree cutting,

(3) shelterwood cutting, and (4) selection cutting. Each cutting method is also a way of replacing the crop. New trees grow from seeds produced by the remaining or surrounding trees, from sprouting stumps, or from seeds or seedlings that foresters plant.

Clearcutting is the removal of all the trees in a certain area of a forest. The area may range in size from 1 to 600 acres (0.4 to 243 hectares) or more. Clearcutting is the best harvesting method for trees that need maximum sunlight to develop, such as jack pine and lodgepole pine. It is also the method generally used when a forest is to be replaced by planting.

Seed Tree Cutting resembles clearcutting, but foresters leave a few trees widely scattered in the harvested area to provide a natural source of seeds. These seed trees are removed after the new *stand* (large group of trees) is established. Seed tree cutting can be used with loblolly pine, longleaf pine, and other southern pines.

Shelterwood Cutting involves harvesting timber in several stages over a period of 10 to 20 years. Foresters establish a new stand as the old one is removed. Shelterwood cutting can be used with such trees as ponderosa pine, red pine, and white pine, which require shade during their first few years of growth. It also allows the growth of some trees in a stand to continue after the majority of the trees have ceased growing well.

Selection Cutting is the harvesting of small patches of mature trees to make room for younger trees and new growth. The trees are removed on the basis of age and size and their nearness to other trees. However, foresters leave many older trees standing to produce seeds. Selection cutting leaves only small openings in a forest, and so it works best with trees that grow well in shade. Such trees include American beech, hemlock, and sugar maple. Forests may be harvested by selection cutting every 5 to 30 years.

Planting. Foresters plant new timber crops by a process called *artificial reforestation*. They either plant seeds directly in the harvested land, or they raise seedlings in a nursery and transplant these young trees in the forest. The process is called *afforestation* when these methods are used to plant trees on land that was never covered by a forest.

Direct seeding works best on cultivated land or on land where a timber crop has been destroyed by fire. The seeds are treated with a chemical repellent, which prevents animals from eating them, and are sown sometime between late autumn and early spring. Airplanes or helicopters are generally used to scatter the seeds, but seeds may also be placed in the ground with hand tools. About 30,000 seeds per acre (74,000 seeds per hectare) are usually sown to assure an adequate crop.

Forests are planted with seedlings in late winter or early spring, before the buds of the seedlings have opened for the growing season. Seedlings grow in a nursery for one to four years before being transplanted in the forest. Foresters generally plant about 800 trees per acre (1,976 trees per hectare), using hand tools or various kinds of planting machines. A person can plant approximately 1 acre (0.4 hectare) a day by hand—about as much land as a machine can plant in an hour.

Tree Improvement involves breeding trees for superior growth rates and increased resistance to diseases and pests. Foresters begin this process by searching forests for trees that are straighter and faster growing than most of their species. Such trees, sometimes called *supertrees*, must also have high-quality wood and be healthy and free of harmful insects and other pests. Tree improvement programs breed chiefly *conifers* (evergreens) because these trees supply most of the wood used by the forest products industry.

After foresters find a superior tree, they take cuttings, called *cions*, from its branches. The cions are brought to a nursery and *grafted* (joined) to the roots of 2-year-old trees (see GRAFTING). The cions receive nutrients through the roots of the young trees but keep the characteristics of the tree from which they were cut. Foresters then take pollen from the male cones of the cions and pollinate the female cones of cions from other superior trees. The foresters keep careful records of the cions used for each pollination.

How Timber Is Harvested

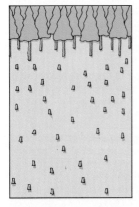 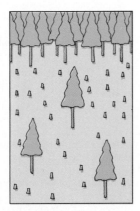  

WORLD BOOK diagrams by David Cunningham

Clearcutting removes all the trees in a large area. It provides full sunlight in which new seedlings can develop.

Seed Tree Cutting leaves a few scattered trees in the harvested area to provide a good source of seeds for a new crop.

Shelterwood Cutting, which is used for trees that require shade to develop, removes trees in several stages.

Selection Cutting involves harvesting small patches of mature trees to make room for younger trees and new ones.

FORESTRY

After pollination, the female cones produce seeds that are planted in the nursery and grow into seedlings. Foresters transplant the seedlings on special plantations and closely watch the growth of the trees. If the trees from a particular set of parents appear to be developing into supertrees, the seeds from those parents may be produced commercially.

Managing Other Forest Resources

Water. Nearly all forests serve as *watersheds*—that is, sources of water for rivers and streams. The soil of forests collects water by soaking up rain and melted snow. Watershed management largely involves keeping the forest soil porous so it can absorb a maximum amount of water.

The soil of a forest is covered by a spongy layer of leaves and twigs, called *litter*. The action of earthworms, insects, rodents, and decaying roots creates spaces within the soil. When rain or snow falls, the water is absorbed by the litter and these spaces in the soil. Much of the water is used by plants, and some flows underground and then into rivers, streams, and wells. If forest soil becomes too hard and nonporous, water flows over the surface of the ground, carrying mud and other materials into nearby streams. This runoff damages other soil, pollutes the water of the streams, and may even cause flooding.

Foresters help keep soil porous in several ways. They plant trees or shrubs in open areas in the forest to assure a continuous supply of litter. They regulate livestock grazing to maintain a good cover of grass and to prevent the animals from packing down the

Georgia-Pacific Corp.

A Forest Campground may provide cooking facilities, electrical outlets, and plumbing. Foresters plan recreation areas to meet the needs of campers without harming the environment.

earth. Foresters also make sure that truck roads built for logging operations are carefully built to prevent damage to the soil.

Wildlife. Forests provide homes for a wide variety of wildlife, including bears, birds, deer, fish, foxes, and rodents. Wildlife management involves maintaining a balance between the number of animals in a forest and the supply of food, water, and shelter.

Forests that consist of a mixture of young and old trees generally support the greatest variety of wildlife. Dense forests of old, tall trees provide good homes for birds, insects, and such climbing mammals as raccoons and squirrels. But the shade in such forests prevents the growth of enough herbs, shrubs, and small trees to feed deer and other large animals that live on the ground. Therefore, foresters cut down patches of trees to let in sunlight. Hollow trees are left to serve as dens and nesting places. New plants soon begin to sprout in the clearings, providing food for wildlife. The animals tend to feed along the edges of the clearings, near the protective cover of the trees.

Wildlife management also involves controlling animal populations by regulating hunting. During food shortages caused by overpopulation of wildlife, the animals may damage trees by feeding on bark, buds, and twigs.

Grazing Land. Many forests in dry areas have widely spaced trees with heavy growths of grass and shrubs in-between. Farmers who own small woodlands in such areas often let their livestock graze there. In the Western United States, thousands of ranchers use the wide grasslands of the national forests as a source of feed for cattle and sheep. However, the use of rangeland must be carefully regulated to prevent overgrazing, which can damage watersheds.

Foresters preserve grasslands—and protect watersheds—chiefly by making sure that livestock roam over the entire range. In this way, the animals do not use up the grass or pack down the soil too much in any one area. Foresters sometimes fence off rangeland into many pastures and rotate the grazing among them. To keep

U.S. Forest Service

Foresters Prevent Soil Erosion by planting trees on barren areas, above. The tree roots help hold the soil in place and soak up great amounts of rain and melted snow.

livestock moving on open ranges, watering holes may be developed at scattered locations. Placing salt licks away from the water also contributes to better use of the range.

In addition to controlling overgrazing, foresters maintain grasslands through cultivation. For example, they kill brush, weeds, and poisonous plants with chemicals and then sow the area with seeds. Foresters also may restrict grazing on some land for a year or more to allow new grass to grow there.

Recreation Areas. The scenic beauty and natural resources of forests provide opportunities for many recreational activities, including camping, hiking, fishing, and hunting. In the United States, millions of people visit the state and national forests annually. In addition, many forest products companies open areas of their woodlands to the public, chiefly for hunting and fishing. Small, privately owned wooded areas also provide recreational benefits.

Many areas of state and national forests are managed primarily for recreation. Government foresters carefully plan these areas to provide maximum benefits to visitors with minimum harm to the forests. Before developing a campground, for example, foresters study such factors as the terrain, the amount of shade, and the availability of water in the area. They can then install picnic tables, cooking equipment, electrical outlets, plumbing, roads and trails, and parking areas without seriously upsetting the ecological balance of the forest.

Protecting Forest Resources

The full benefits of forest resources can be obtained only if timber is protected from fires, diseases, and insect pests. Fire is a great threat to forests because it can

U.S. Forest Service

Fighting a Forest Fire involves removing the fuel from the path of the flames. Fire fighters may clear leaves, wood, and other material from the forest floor with axes and shovels, *above*.

cause tremendous damage in a short time. In the United States, fires destroy about 3 million acres (1.2 million hectares) of timber annually. But the destruction caused by diseases and pests is even greater—nearly seven times that of fire.

Fire. About 90 per cent of the forest fires in the United States are caused by human beings. Most of the rest start when lightning strikes trees. Little can be done to avoid fires caused by lightning, but fires caused by people can be prevented. Smokers start many fires by carelessly dropping lighted matches and cigarettes in forests. Other forest fires are set deliberately. Forest fires can best be prevented by educating people to understand the value of forests and the importance of protecting them. During dry seasons, when fires can easily start, foresters may close a forest to the public to reduce the danger of fire.

Foresters watch for fires from lookout towers in a forest. These towers have binoculars, direction finders, and other equipment to locate fires, and a telephone or short-wave radio to call fire fighters to the burning area. Fires may also be spotted by airplane patrols.

Forest fires feed on fallen leaves, twigs, and other decaying material on the forest floor. The task of extinguishing a forest fire largely involves removing this blanket of fuel. Fire-fighting crews spray water or chemicals on the burning area to cool the fire and slow its progress. They then can get close enough to the flames to dig a *fire line*. The fire fighters start a fire line by clearing all brush, logs, and trees from a wide strip around the fire. Then they scrape away the litter and some of the soil with axes, shovels, or bulldozers. Fire fighters called *smoke jumpers* may parachute from airplanes or helicopters to dig a fire line in an area that is difficult to reach by land.

After creating a fire line, the fire fighters may set *backfires* to burn the area between the line and the forest fire itself. Backfires remove additional fuel and widen the fire line to help stop the spread of the flames. After a fire dies, the fire fighters clear any flammable material from the edge of the burned area. This action prevents the material from smoldering and starting new fires.

Under certain conditions, fire can be used as a tool to benefit a forest. In a process called *prescribed burning*, foresters may set small fires in the litter on the forest floor to reduce the potential fuel for a fire. Prescribed burning also kills insect pests and the seedlings of unwanted trees. This technique must be used with extreme caution.

Diseases and Pests. Most tree diseases are caused by fungus infections. Diseases attack trees chiefly by clogging the flow of sap, killing the leaves, or rotting the roots or wood. Some of the most destructive tree diseases in the United States include beech bark disease, chestnut blight, Dutch elm disease, oak wilt, and stem blister rusts that affect pines.

Insects that damage trees include bark beetles, sucking insects, and *defoliators*. Bark beetles feed on a tree's inner bark. Sucking insects suck the fluid from trees. Defoliators eat leaves. Various kinds of bark beetles destroy thousands of evergreens yearly in the Southern and Western United States. Defoliators, which include spruce budworms and tussock moths, also attack ever-

349

greens. One defoliator, the gypsy moth, is especially harmful to oak trees. Sucking insects, such as aphids and scales, feed on all types of trees.

Foresters control diseases and pests by three chief methods: (1) biological controls, (2) silvicultural controls, and (3) direct controls. Biological controls fight diseases and pests with natural enemies. For example, foresters might increase the number of birds in a forest to reduce the insect population. Silvicultural controls use methods of timber management to make a forest undesirable for diseases and pests. Foresters follow such silvicultural practices as removing old, weak trees that are easy prey for fungi and insects. Direct controls include the use of chemical pesticides to kill fungi and insects. The chemicals can upset the ecological balance of a forest, and so pesticides are generally used only if biological or silvicultural controls fail.

History

People have used forest resources since prehistoric times. Throughout history, the use of forests has been regulated when shortages of timber have occurred. During the Middle Ages, forest wildlife was protected to ensure a sufficient supply of game for the nobility to hunt. Forest management developed as a science during the 1800's in Europe, chiefly in France, Germany, and the Scandinavian countries.

In the United States, the early settlers treated the nation's vast timberland as though it would last forever. They cleared much more land than they needed for their homes and crops. Lumbermen destroyed large areas of forestland by wasteful logging methods, and few people worried about abandoned, cutover forests. Some of this land still lies barren.

By 1891, a conservation movement had started, and Congress authorized the President that year to set aside wooded areas called *forest reserves*. The U.S. Forest Service was established in 1905, with Gifford Pinchot as its first chief (see PINCHOT, GIFFORD). The Forest Service was given control of the forest reserves, which in 1907 became known as national forests. Today, national forests cover about 187 million acres (75.7 million hectares).

In 1911, Congress passed the Weeks Law, which authorized the government to purchase forests that serve as watersheds for important rivers and streams. The Clarke-McNary Act of 1924 expanded the Weeks Law to cover the purchase of land necessary for timber production. The act also provided that the government make funds available to the states to protect all forests from fire. In 1947, Congress passed the Forest Pest Control Act. This law provided for federal cooperation with states and owners of private forests to control insect pests and diseases.

The Multiple Use-Sustained Yield Act was passed in 1960. It directed that the national forests be managed to produce a sustained yield of timber and an adequate supply of other forest resources. In 1964, Congress passed the Wilderness Act, which provided for the preservation of *wilderness areas* in national forests and on other federal lands. No roads or buildings may be built in wilderness areas, and hunting and timber harvesting are forbidden there. In the late 1970's, wilderness areas

covered about 13 million acres (5.3 million hectares), mostly in national forests.

During the 1970's, a long-standing controversy deepened over the emphasis on timber production in the national forests compared with the management of other resources. The use of clearcutting came under especially severe criticism by some conservationists, who charged that the practice leaves ugly patches of barren land. The Forest and Rangeland Renewable Resources Planning Act was passed in 1974 to establish procedures for continually reviewing the management of American forests. DAVID M. SMITH

Related Articles. See FOREST and FOREST PRODUCTS with their lists of Related Articles. See also the following articles:

Aphid	Nursery
Conservation	Scale Insect
Dutch Elm Disease	Tree Farming
Forest Service	Tussock Moth
Gypsy Moth	Wildlife Conservation
National Forest	

FORFEITURE is a legal punishment or penalty by which a person guilty of wrongdoing or breach of contract has some right or possession taken from him. A person who drives too fast may have his driver's license taken from him and thus *forfeit* his right to drive. A corporation may forfeit its charter if it abuses its privileges. Ordinarily, in the United States, forfeitures of this type can be made only by court action or by administrative action which is later subject to review by a court. *Civil*, or *contractual*, forfeiture occurs when a person fails to perform his duties under a contract. For example, when a person fails to pay a premium on an insurance policy, he may forfeit his right to coverage under the policy. JOHN ALAN APPLEMAN

FORGAILL, DALLÁN. See IRISH LITERATURE (Early Irish Literature).

FORGE. See FORGING (Forging by Hand; picture); BLACKSMITH.

FORGERY, *FAWR jur ih*, is deliberately tampering with a written paper for the purpose of deceit or fraud. Common kinds of forgery include fraudulently signing another person's name to a check or document, changing the figures on a check to alter its amount ("kiting" a check), and making changes in a will or contract. The punishment for forgery is usually imprisonment. Intent to defraud must be proved before a person can be convicted of forgery. Skilled forgers can imitate a person's handwriting almost exactly, but handwriting experts are usually able to detect forgery. Literary forgers have tried to pass off their forged documents as rare manuscripts. FRED E. INBAU

FORGERY BOND. See INSURANCE (Fidelity, Forgery, and Surety Bonds).

FORGET-ME-NOT is a little flower which belongs to the borage family. It grows in both wild and cultivated forms in temperate regions. Many forget-me-nots are European kinds that have been brought to the United States. The forget-me-not plant has a hairy stem and light green leaves. The flowers are usually a sky-blue color with yellow centers. They are tiny and grow in clusters. Several other kinds of forget-me-not flowers are white or pink. The buds of the flowers are pink.

A few forget-me-nots grow in cool, damp places, but others thrive in dry soil. Several perennial kinds are

A. W. Ambler, NAS

The Forget-Me-Not, according to a legend dating back to the 1400's, has a magic quality. People who wear this flower are supposedly never forgotten by those who love them.

grown in gardens and are well suited to flower beds or borders. *Victoria, Blue Bird,* and *Royal Blue* are annual varieties.

The forget-me-not is the symbol of friendship and of true love. The flower appears in many legends. In German legend, *forget me not* were the last words a lover spoke before he drowned trying to get the flower for his sweetheart. According to another legend, all the plants and animals shrank away from Adam and Eve when they were expelled from the Garden of Eden, except for one tiny blue flower that said, "Forget me not!" The British poet Alfred, Lord Tennyson spoke of the "sweet forget-me-nots that grow for happy lovers."

Scientific Classification. The common forget-me-not belongs to the borage family, *Boraginaceae.* It is genus *Myosotis,* species *M. scorpioides. Myosotis* means *mouse ear,* and refers to the leaves.   MARCUS MAXON

FORGING is a method of shaping metal by heating it, then hammering or pressing it into a desired form. Almost any metal or combination of metals can be forged. Some of the forgeable materials are iron, steel, nickel, titanium, aluminum, and bronze.

When metal is forged, its internal make-up changes. It loses its grainy structure and becomes more fiberlike. This fiberlike structure gives the forged article more strength. Forgings are particularly useful for objects that take heavy wear, such as turbine blades for jet-aircraft engines, propeller shafts for ships, and locomotive parts.

Forging by Hand is one of the oldest shaping operations known to man. The simplest kind of forging is that done by a workman called a *blacksmith.* The blacksmith heats the metal until it is red hot in a furnace, or *forge.* The furnace is an open fireplace with a blower, or set of bellows, to force air into the fire and make it hotter. The blacksmith lifts the hot metal from the furnace with a pair of tongs. Then he holds it against an anvil and beats it into shape with a hand hammer.

Forging with Hammers. Most forged articles are made by big forging hammers. A single forging hammer may be as tall as a four-story building and weigh more than 1,000,000 pounds (450,000 kilograms). Five men operating this machine can turn out more forgings in an hour than five blacksmiths could make in a year. A single forged piece, or *forging,* can weigh more than 200,000 pounds (91,000 kilograms).

In forging with hammers, tools called *dies* shape the desired article. One die fits on the top of the article and another die fits on the bottom. When the dies are pressed, or hammered, together, they squeeze hot metal into the desired shape. See DIE AND DIEMAKING.

Smith, or *flat-die, forgings* are made on machines called *open-frame,* or *double-frame, hammers.* The lower die is held stationary while the upper die moves up and down in a series of blows by steam power.

Drop-hammer, or *impact-die, forgings* are produced when the heated metal is forced into impressions cut into the upper and lower dies. In the same manner as in flat-die forging, the upper die moves up and down repeatedly

Bethlehem Steel Corp.

A Hydraulic Press Forge squeezes a mass of heated metal between two dies. The shape of the dies determines the final shape of the metal. The operator wears protective clothing from head to foot to guard against heat and glare.

with steam or electric power. A drop hammer can turn out articles many times faster than flat-die forging, and produce shapes that are impossible by flat-die methods.

Press forging uses a squeezing action, rather than a series of blows. The dies are similar to those used for impact-die forging. The operators squeeze the dies together using either mechanical or hydraulic pressure.

Upset forging covers such operations as the forming of heads on nails or bolts. The forging is held firmly for part of its length. The free end is forced into the impression of a die. The work in upset forging is done horizontally, rather than vertically.   ROY A. KROPP

See also HYDRAULICS; STEAM HAMMER.

FORK. See KNIFE, FORK, AND SPOON.

FORLANINI, ENRICO. See HELICOPTER (Early Experiments); HYDROFOIL (Development).

FORMALDEHYDE, *fawr MAL duh hyd*, is probably most familiar as the solution used to preserve insects and other biological specimens. August Wilhelm von Hofmann, a German chemist, discovered it in 1867.

Formaldehyde is also used for disinfecting, embalming, and for making compounds such as urea resins and organic dyes. The plastics industry uses formaldehyde with carbolic acid to make Bakelite (see BAKELITE). *Formacone,* or *paraformaldehyde,* a solid polymer of formaldehyde, is used to make fumigating candles.

Chemists prepare formaldehyde by oxidizing methanol (methyl alcohol), or simple petroleum gases such as methane, in the presence of catalysts. Most formaldehyde is used in the form of *formalin,* a water solution containing 35 to 40 per cent formaldehyde.

Formaldehyde is the simplest member of the aldehyde class of organic compounds. It is a colorless gas, easily soluble in water. It has a stifling odor, and can irritate the eyes and nose. Its chemical formula is $HCHO$, and it boils at $-21°$ C $(-6°$ F.).   E. CAMPAIGNE

See also ALDEHYDE.

FORMALIN. See FORMALDEHYDE.

FORMIC ACID is an important industrial chemical. Its name comes from the Latin word *formica,* which means *ant.* It was first obtained from the distillation of ants in 1670. Formic acid causes the irritating sting that results from the bite of a red ant. It is also found in pine needles and stinging nettles.

Formic acid is prepared commercially from carbon monoxide and sodium hydroxide. The textile industry uses it in dyeing wool-fast colors, and the rubber industry uses it for coagulating rubber latex.

Pure formic acid is a clear, fuming liquid that has a penetrating odor. It is highly corrosive and causes skin blisters on contact. Formic acid has the chemical formula $HCOOH$. It mixes readily with water, and boils at about $101°$ C $(214°$ F.).   JOHN E. LEFFLER

FORMOSA. See TAIWAN.

FORMULA. See BABY (Feeding); in science, see ALGEBRA (Writing Formulas); CHEMISTRY.

FORREST, EDWIN (1806-1872), became one of the first great American actors. His most successful Shakespearean role was Othello. He first appeared on the American stage in 1820, and dominated it for nearly 30 years. He was born in Philadelphia. WILLIAM VAN LENNEP

FORREST, NATHAN BEDFORD (1821-1877), was a Confederate general in the Civil War. He was a brilliant cavalry leader. He enlisted as a private in the Confederate Army in June, 1861, and became a lieutenant colonel in command of a troop of cavalry by October. Forrest had no military education, but he enjoyed amazing success as a strategist and tactician.

Forrest escaped with his men from the Battle of Fort Donelson and fought at Shiloh in 1862 (see CIVIL WAR [War in the West]). General Forrest then developed raiding tactics that turned his cavalry into a fearsome striking force. At Brice's Cross Roads, Miss., in June, 1864, he won a battle that was a model for cavalry warfare. When asked the secret of his victory, he is said to have replied, "To git thar fustest with the mostest men."

Forrest became a lieutenant general in February, 1865. He was beaten by the Union Army at Selma, Ala., in April, 1865. Forrest was born in Bedford County, Tennessee.   FRANK E. VANDIVER

FORRESTAL, JAMES VINCENT (1892-1949), was the first United States secretary of defense. He served from September, 1947, until March, 1949. Forrestal also served as secretary of the Navy from 1944 to 1947. During this period, he helped build the U.S. fleet into the largest in the world. In 1954, the Navy named a class of aircraft carriers the *Forrestal* in honor of him.

When Congress passed the National Security Act in 1947 to unify the armed forces, it created a civilian secretary of national defense. President Harry S. Truman appointed Forrestal to the post. Forrestal resigned in 1949 because of mental and physical exhaustion. The strain of his job was blamed by many for his suicide two months later.

United Press Int.
James V. Forrestal

Forrestal was born in Beacon, N.Y. In World War I, he served as a naval aviator and then turned to a financial career in New York City.   HARVEY WISH

FORSSMANN, *FORCE mahn,* **WERNER** (1904-   ), a German surgeon and urologist, shared the 1956 Nobel prize for medicine for his work on cardiac catheterization. This involves the insertion of a small tube into a vein through which it reaches the heart. The procedure is used to measure blood pressure inside the heart, to draw off blood samples, and to decide what part of the heart is defective and whether or not to operate. Forssmann was born in Berlin, Germany.   NOAH D. FABRICANT

FORSTER, E. M. (1879-1970), was an English novelist, essayist, and literary critic. His novels show his interest in personal relationships and in the social, psychological, and racial obstacles to such relationships. His fiction stresses the value of following generous impulses.

Forster's most highly praised novels are *Howards End* (1910) and *A Passage to India* (1924). *Howards End* is a social comedy about several English middle-class characters. It reflects Forster's ideal of an "aristocracy of the sensitive, the considerate, and the plucky." *A Passage to India* describes the clash between English and traditional Indian cultures in India.

Forster's four other novels are *Where Angels Fear to Tread* (1905), *The Longest Journey* (1907), *A Room with* a *View* (1908), and *Maurice* (completed in 1914, published in 1971, after the author's death). His nonfiction includes *Aspects of the Novel* (1927), a book of literary criticism; *Abinger Harvest* (1936), a collection of essays; and *Two Cheers for Democracy* (1951), another book of essays. Edward Morgan Forster was born in London.   DARCY O'BRIEN

See also BLOOMSBURY GROUP.

FORSYTHIA, *fawr SIHTH ee uh,* is a shrub which belongs to the olive family. It grows as high as 9

J. C. Allen

The Forsythia's Yellow Blossoms Grow in Clusters.

feet (2.7 meters), and has spreading, arched branches. People sometimes call the forsythia the *golden bell,* because its yellow flowers look like tiny, golden bells. One to six flowers grow in clusters. They bloom in early spring before the leaves appear. The leaves grow 3 to 5 inches (8 to 13 centimeters) long, and are egg-shaped. They usually have jagged edges. Gardeners can grow the forsythia in any garden soil. The forsythia is named for the British botanist William Forsyth.

Scientific Classification. Forsythias belong to the olive family, *Oleaceae.* Different forsythias are genus *Forsythia,* species *F. suspensa* and *F. viridissima.*   J. J. LEVISON

See also FLOWER (picture: Spring Garden Flowers).

FORT originally was a fortified building or place that provided defense against attack. On the American frontier, forts also served as trading posts. Many cities that grew up around forts bear their names, including Fort Wayne, Ind. The term *fort* now applies to permanent army posts. For information on various forts, see the articles and cross references on forts following this article. See also BLOCKHOUSE; CASTLE.   HUGH M. COLE

FORT AMADOR, Panama Canal Zone, is the headquarters of the U.S. Navy Forces, Southern Command. The fort lies on the Bay of Panama at the Pacific end of the Panama Canal. It was built in 1917, and named after Manuel Amador Guerrero, first president of the Republic of Panama. Located nearby is Quarry Heights, headquarters of the U.S. Southern Command, which directs all Army, Navy, and Air Force units in the Caribbean area.   SAMUEL J. ZISKIND

FORT AMHERST. See CANADA (National Historic Parks and Sites).

FORT ANCIENT. See OHIO (Places to Visit [Indian Mounds]).

FORT ANNE. See CANADA (National Historic Parks and Sites).

FORT BATTLEFORD. See CANADA (National Historic Parks and Sites).

FORT BEAUSÉJOUR. See CANADA (National Historic Parks and Sites).

FORT BELVOIR, Va., houses the United States Army Engineer Center. The fort covers 9,288 acres (3,759 hectares) along the Potomac River. It lies 18 miles (29 kilometers) south of Washington, D.C. Chief activities there include the Army engineer school and engineer research and development laboratories. The Army founded Camp Belvoir in 1912, and named it after the ruins of Belvoir Manor. The site was once part of an estate owned by Lord Thomas Fairfax, a neighbor of George Washington.   SAMUEL J. ZISKIND

FORT BENJAMIN HARRISON, Ind., is the headquarters of the U.S. Army Finance Center and School. It is also the home of The Adjutant General's School and Army reserve units. The post lies 12 miles (19 kilometers) northeast of Indianapolis, and covers 2,680 acres (1,085 hectares). It was founded in 1903, and named for President Benjamin Harrison.   SAMUEL J. ZISKIND

FORT BENNING, Ga., is the site of the U.S. Army Infantry Center. This command includes the infantry school and the infantry board. The school also conducts airborne and ranger training courses. The post covers 182,000 acres (73,650 hectares). It lies 9 miles (14 kilometers) south of Columbus on the Chattahoochee River. The Army established Camp Benning in 1918, and named it after Brigadier General Henry L. Benning, a native of Columbus, who served in the Confederate Army during the Civil War.   SAMUEL J. ZISKIND

U.S. Army

A Paratroop Trainee practices parachute jumping at Fort Benning, the chief training center for U.S. airborne troops.

FORT BLISS

FORT BLISS, Tex., houses the United States Army Air Defense Center, which trains troops to operate anti-aircraft artillery and guided missiles. Fort Bliss is located near El Paso. Its firing ranges in Texas and New Mexico cover about 1,177,000 acres (476,310 hectares). It is named for Lieutenant Colonel William Bliss, a son-in-law of President Zachary Taylor.   SAMUEL J. ZISKIND

FORT BRAGG, N.C., is the home of airborne combat units of the United States Army. It also houses the Special Warfare Center, which trains troops in psychological and guerrilla warfare. The post lies 10 miles (16 kilometers) northwest of Fayetteville, and covers 132,000 acres (53,420 hectares). It was founded in 1918, and named for Braxton Bragg, a Confederate Army general in the Civil War.

The Army trained its first two airborne divisions, the 82nd and the 101st, at Fort Bragg during World War II. After the war, the post became the headquarters of the 82nd Airborne Division and the XVIII Airborne Corps.   SAMUEL J. ZISKIND

FORT BROWN. See BROWNSVILLE.

FORT CHAMBLY. See CANADA (Historic Parks).

FORT CHRISTINA. See DELAWARE (picture).

FORT CONDÉ. See ALABAMA (Exploration).

FORT CREVECOEUR. See HENNEPIN, LOUIS.

FORT DEARBORN was built near the mouth of the Chicago River, close to the site of Chicago's present Michigan Avenue Bridge. Soldiers under the command of Captain John Whistler built the fort in 1803. It was named after General Henry Dearborn. The double stockade had blockhouses on two corners, enclosed log barracks, stables, and an Indian agency.

A garrison of soldiers at the fort protected the few Americans on the frontier from Indian attack. Soon after the War of 1812 began, the troops and settlers were ordered to move to Fort Wayne for greater safety. The soldiers feared Indian attacks on the way, and urged Captain Nathan Heald to stay within the stockade. He insisted on obeying orders, destroyed all ammunition

that could not be carried, and left the post with about 100 troops and settlers on Aug. 15, 1812.

A band of 500 Potawatomi and allied Indians attacked the Americans near the fort (at the eastern end of Chicago's present Eighteenth Street). They killed more than half of the Americans, captured the rest, and burned the fort the next day.

Fort Dearborn was rebuilt about 1816, and torn down in 1836. By then the danger of Indian attack in the area had passed.   WALKER D. WYMAN

See also DEARBORN, HENRY.

FORT-DE-FRANCE, *FAWR duh FRAHNS* (pop. 85,-219), is the capital city of the island of Martinique. Three forts guard its large harbor. The city provides the island with a natural naval base on the Caribbean Sea. Fort-de-France has palm-lined streets, bright-colored

Air France

Fort-de-France is the capital of Martinique. The city lies on a deep natural harbor on the west coast of the island.

Chicago Park District

A Replica of Fort Dearborn was built in 1933 for Chicago's Century of Progress Exposition, and later dismantled. It contained articles used by settlers at the time the original fort was built.

houses, a waterfront park, and a modern airport. It serves as an outlet for the sugar, rum, and fruit which are Martinique's main products. Educational institutions include a school of arts and crafts, and a law school. See also MARTINIQUE.   H. F. RAUP

FORT DES MOINES. See DES MOINES (Government).

FORT DIX, N.J., is a center of U.S. Army infantry training. It covers 33,122 acres (13,404 hectares) and lies 17 miles (27 kilometers) southeast of Trenton. An Army Personnel Center processes troops for overseas duty. It also discharges or releases soldiers from the Army. The fort, founded in 1917, was named after John A. Dix, a Civil War major general. In World War II, it trained and shipped overseas parts of five corps, ten divisions, and an air force. After the war, it discharged more than 1¼ million soldiers.   SAMUEL J. ZISKIND

FORT DONELSON. See CIVIL WAR (Fort Henry and Fort Donelson); NATIONAL PARK SYSTEM (table: National Military Parks).

FORT DUQUESNE, *doo KAYN,* was built by the French in 1754 at the fork of the Monongahela and Allegheny rivers. French forces had driven Virginian frontiersmen from this site. The French named the fort after the Marquis Michel-Ange Duquesne, governor general of Canada. The Battle of the Great Meadows took place near the fort in 1754. The French defeated a band of militiamen led by George Washington. This battle marked the beginning of the French and Indian War.

In 1755, the French defeated General Braddock in another battle near Fort Duquesne. Three years later, the French burned the fort and fled northward when they learned that a British force was approaching. The British built Fort Pitt nearby on the Monongahela. Pittsburgh later rose on this site.   WALKER D. WYMAN

See also FRENCH AND INDIAN WARS.

FORT EDMONTON. See EDMONTON (History).

FORT EUSTIS, Va., houses the U.S. Army Transportation Center. It covers 8,000 acres (3,200 hectares), and lies 11 miles (18 kilometers) south of Williamsburg. Other activities include the Army transportation school, aviation matériel laboratories, and transportation engineering agency. Fort Eustis has the nation's only all-military-operated railway system. The post was set up as a Coast Artillery training area in 1918, and named for Brigadier General Abraham Eustis, an artillery officer of the early 1800's.   SAMUEL J. ZISKIND

FORT FREDERICA NATIONAL MONUMENT is on Saint Simons Island in Georgia. It contains the ruins of a fort built in the 1700's. Governor James Edward Oglethorpe had the fort built as a defense against the Spaniards. For its area, see NATIONAL PARK SYSTEM (table: National Monuments).

FORT FRONTENAC stood near the present site of Kingston, Ont., overlooking the St. Lawrence and Cataraqui rivers. At first, it was a log fort named Cataraqui. Comte de Frontenac, governor of French possessions in North America, built it in 1673. In 1675, the fort was renamed in his honor. It was later enlarged and rebuilt in stone. British forces captured Fort Frontenac in 1758, and held it until it was torn down in 1819.   JEAN BRUCHÉSI

FORT GARRY. See WINNIPEG (History).

FORT GEORGE G. MEADE, Md., houses headquarters of the First United States Army. This command controls units and posts in 15 eastern states.

Other commands located at the fort include the National Security Agency and the Army Air Defense Engineering Agency. The fort covers about 14,000 acres (5,670 hectares) and lies 18 miles (29 kilometers) southwest of Baltimore. The Army set up the post in 1917. It is named for Maj. Gen. George Gordon Meade, who commanded the Army of the Potomac in the Civil War.   SAMUEL J. ZISKIND

FORT GORDON, Ga., is the home of the U.S. Army Signal School, the Dwight D. Eisenhower Medical Center, and the First Basic Training Brigade. It lies 15 miles (24 kilometers) southwest of Augusta, and covers about 56,000 acres (22,700 hectares). It was founded in 1941 as an infantry training center, and named for Lt. Gen. John B. Gordon, a Confederate Army officer and former governor of Georgia.   SAMUEL J. ZISKIND

FORT HENRY, BATTLE OF. See CIVIL WAR (Fort Henry).

FORT HOOD, Tex., houses some of the armored units of the United States Army. It lies 2 miles (3 kilometers) west of Killeen, and covers 216,000 acres (87,410 hectares). The post was founded in 1942 as Camp Hood, and named for John B. Hood, Civil War commander of the Texas Brigade. It became a permanent fort in 1950. North Fort Hood lies 17 miles (27 kilometers) to the north.   SAMUEL J. ZISKIND

FORT JEFFERSON NATIONAL MONUMENT is located on the Dry Tortugas Islands, 68 miles (109 kilometers) west of Key West, Fla. The fort was established in 1846. It was a federal prison from 1863 to 1873. Scientists find unusual bird and marine life in the area. Fort Jefferson National Monument was established in 1935. For its area, see NATIONAL PARK SYSTEM (table: National Monuments).   C. LANGDON WHITE

FORT JOHNSON. See SOUTH CAROLINA (Places to Visit [Forts]).

FORT KNOX, Ky., houses the United States Army Armor Center. This command includes the armor school, armor board, bullion depository, and armor training center. The post covers 110,000 acres (44,500 hectares), and lies 35 miles (56 kilometers) south of Louisville. The government took over part of the present post for army maneuvers in 1918. Camp Knox was established in 1918, and named for Major General Henry Knox, the first secretary of war. Its name became Fort Knox in 1933. The post has been called "the Home of Armor," because the Army created its first armored force here in 1940. Four combat armored divisions were trained at Fort Knox during World War II.

The U.S. Treasury Department completed its gold depository there in 1936. The depository contains about $5 billion worth of gold. During World War II, the Constitution, Declaration of Independence, Gutenberg Bible, Lincoln's Gettysburg Address, and Magna Carta were placed in the depository at Fort Knox for safekeeping.   SAMUEL J. ZISKIND

See also MONEY (picture: Vaults at Fort Knox).

FORT-LAMY. See N'DJAMENA.

FORT LANGLEY. See CANADA (Historic Parks).

FORT LAUDERDALE, Fla. (pop. 139,590), is a major resort city and a leading vacation and retirement center. It lies on the Atlantic Ocean, about 25 miles (40 kilometers) north of Miami. For location, see FLORIDA (political map). Fort Lauderdale's location and warm climate have made it one of the fastest growing cities of the United States. The city's population increased from about 18,000 in 1940 to about 140,000 during the mid-1970's. Fort Lauderdale and Hollywood, to the south, form a metropolitan area with a population of about 620,100.

During the 1800's, Seminole Indians lived in what is now Fort Lauderdale. White settlers, most of whom farmed and fished for a living, first arrived in the area in the 1890's. They named their settlement after a fort that Major William Lauderdale had built there in 1838, during the Second Seminole War.

Description. Fort Lauderdale, the county seat of Broward County, covers about 30 square miles (80 square kilometers). This area includes 3 square miles (8 square kilometers) of inland water. The city has about 85 miles (137 kilometers) of navigable canals and waterways. Fort Lauderdale is sometimes called the *Venice of America*, though it does not have canals instead of streets, as does the city of Venice, Italy. Fort Lauderdale also has about 6 miles (10 kilometers) of ocean beaches, where people can go boating, fishing, and swimming.

Cultural attractions in the city include the Museum of the Arts and the Parker Playhouse. The Fort Lauderdale Opera Guild and the Symphony Society present various types of musical performances. Fort Lauderdale is the home of Nova University.

Construction and tourism rank as Fort Lauderdale's leading sources of income. The Fort Lauderdale metropolitan area has about 680 manufacturing plants. Their chief products, in order of value, include printed materials, electrical equipment, machinery, and transportation equipment.

Port Everglades, at the south end of Fort Lauderdale, serves as a major port for cargo ships and passenger cruisers. Airlines use Fort Lauderdale-Hollywood International Airport.

Government and History. Fort Lauderdale has a council-manager form of government. The voters elect the five members of the city council to a two-year term. The candidate who receives the most votes becomes mayor. The council hires a city manager to serve as the chief administrator of the local government.

The city had a population of only about 150 when it was incorporated in 1911. After World War II ended in 1945, a tourist boom resulted in a rapid population growth. Fort Lauderdale received national attention during the 1960's, when thousands of college students began to spend their spring vacation there. By the early 1970's, more than 800,000 tourists visited the city yearly.   MIKE MORGAN

FORT LEAVENWORTH, Kans., is the home of the Army Command and General Staff College, the senior tactical school of the United States Army. The fort covers about 6,000 acres (2,400 hectares) on the west bluff of the Missouri River, 25 miles (40 kilometers) northwest of Kansas City. The Army and Air Force operate a military prison, the U.S. Disciplinary Barracks. The fort was named for Colonel Henry Leavenworth, who founded it in 1827.   SAMUEL J. ZISKIND

See also KANSAS (Places to Visit).

FORT LEE, Va., is the home of the United States Army Quartermaster Center and School. It lies 3 miles (5 kilometers) east of Petersburg, and covers 6,583 acres (2,664 hectares). The post was founded in 1917, and named for Gen. Robert E. Lee of the Confederate Army. It became a permanent fort in 1950. Between World War I and World War II, the post served as a wildlife sanctuary. During World War II, Fort Lee gave basic training to about 300,000 persons, and its Quartermaster School graduated more than 53,000 officers and other military personnel.   SAMUEL J. ZISKIND

FORT LENNOX NATIONAL HISTORIC PARK. See CANADA (National Historic Parks and Sites).

FORT LEONARD WOOD, Mo., is a center for U.S. Army engineer training. It covers 90,000 acres (36,000 hectares) and lies in the Clark National Forest, 120 miles (193 kilometers) southwest of St. Louis (see MISSOURI [map]). The post was built in 1941 and named for Maj. Gen. Leonard E. Wood, who was Army chief of staff from 1910 to 1914. During World War II, it trained about 320,000 soldiers. Fort Leonard Wood provides basic infantry training for thousands of Army recruits from a 13-state area in the Midwestern United States.   SAMUEL J. ZISKIND

FORT LEWIS. See TACOMA.

FORT LOUDOUN DAM. See TENNESSEE VALLEY AUTHORITY (The Dams).

FORT LOUIS. See ALABAMA (Exploration).

FORT MALDEN NATIONAL HISTORIC PARK. See CANADA (Historic Parks).

FORT MARION NATIONAL MONUMENT. See CASTILLO DE SAN MARCOS NATIONAL MONUMENT.

FORT MASSACHUSETTS. See MISSISSIPPI (Places to Visit).

FORT MATANZAS NATIONAL MONUMENT is near Saint Augustine, Fla. The Spanish built the fort in the early 1740's. It served as a defense for Saint Augustine against French colonizers. Saint Augustine is the oldest city in the United States. The monument was established in 1924. For area, see NATIONAL PARK SYSTEM (table: National Monuments).

FORT McCLELLAN, Ala., is the home of the United States Army Training Center. The center is a training site for enlisted women and women officers. The fort covers 45,746 acres (18,513 hectares) about 6 miles (10 kilometers) northeast of Anniston. Chemical warfare training and testing is done at the chemical center and school there.

Fort McClellan was established in 1917. It was named for Maj. Gen. George B. McClellan, who served as commander of Union forces during the early years of the Civil War.   SAMUEL J. ZISKIND

FORT McHENRY NATIONAL MONUMENT AND HISTORIC SHRINE is in Baltimore, Md. Francis Scott Key composed "The Star-Spangled Banner" as he watched a battle at the fort during the War of 1812. The monument was established in 1939. For area, see NATIONAL PARK SYSTEM (table: National Monuments).

See also MARYLAND (picture: The Star-Spangled Banner Flies Day and Night over Historic Fort McHenry).

FORT McPHERSON, Ga., serves as the headquarters of the United States Army Forces Command. This command supervises the training and combat readiness of the Army's active and reserve forces. The fort covers 504 acres (204 hectares) and lies within the city limits of Atlanta. The Army made it a permanent post in 1889, and named it after Maj. Gen. James B. McPherson, a Union Army commander killed in the Battle of Atlanta during the Civil War. SAMUEL J. ZISKIND

FORT MIMS. See ALABAMA (Territorial Days).

FORT MONMOUTH, N.J., is the chief training and development center for U.S. Army communications-electronics activities. It covers 2,042 acres (826 hectares), and lies about 30 miles (48 kilometers) south of New York City. Major commands at the fort include the headquarters of the U.S. Army Electronics Command, the signal school, and the electronics research and development laboratories. The post was established in 1917. It received its present name in 1925. SAMUEL J. ZISKIND

FORT MONROE, Va., houses the headquarters of the United States Army Training and Doctrine Command. This command controls all Army individual schooling and training and manages the Army ROTC program. The post lies on Old Point Comfort at the mouth of the James River, about 11 miles (18 kilometers) north of Norfolk. It overlooks the entrance to Hampton Roads and covers 1,190 acres (482 hectares).

Engineers began building a fort there in 1819, although the site had been fortified as early as 1609. In 1832 the post was named Fort Monroe, after President James Monroe. Poet Edgar Allan Poe served at Fort Monroe before he entered West Point. Robert E. Lee supervised construction activities at the fort in the early 1830's. Jefferson Davis, President of the Confederacy, was imprisoned at Fort Monroe for two years after the Civil War. SAMUEL J. ZISKIND

FORT MOULTRIE, *MOO trih,* or *MOOL trih,* is a fort on Sullivan's Island at the main entrance to Charleston Harbor, S.C. Settlers first called it Fort Sullivan. In 1776, the fort withstood a British attack designed to capture Charleston and make it a base of British operations in the South. The attack included 10 British ships under Sir Peter Parker, carrying a strong force of British troops under Sir Henry Clinton. They withdrew after 10 hours. The American forces at Charleston numbered 6,500 men, of whom 435 were stationed at Fort Sullivan. They were commanded by Colonel William Moultrie, for whom the fort was renamed. This defense saved the South temporarily from invasion. Clinton again tried to conquer South Carolina later in the war, and Fort Moultrie fell on May 7, 1780.

Just before the Civil War, a United States garrison occupied Fort Moultrie. It was abandoned by its commander, Major Anderson, who moved his troops to Fort Sumter on December 26, 1860. During the bombardment of Sumter the following April, Fort Moultrie served as Confederate headquarters.

Edgar Allan Poe was once a sergeant major at Fort Moultrie, and wrote "Israfel" there. WALKER D. WYMAN

See also FLAG (color picture: Flags in American History); FORT SUMTER; MOULTRIE, WILLIAM.

FORT NECESSITY was a fortification built by George Washington in 1754. It was located in southwestern Pennsylvania. Washington surrendered it to the French in 1754. The French allowed his army to march out of the fort and return home. The site became a national battlefield site in 1931 and a national battlefield in 1961. It covers 912 acres (369 hectares).

See also WASHINGTON, GEORGE (Surrender of Fort Necessity).

FORT NIAGARA was built by the French in 1726 on land bought from the Seneca Indians. It stood on the eastern shore of the Niagara River and guarded a narrow passage which led to the rich fur lands west of the river. British forces captured the fort during the French and Indian War. They used it during the Revolutionary War as a starting point for raids against western settlers. Fort Niagara remained in British hands until 1796, when the Jay Treaty finally gave it to the United States. The British captured the fort again during the War of 1812. It remained in British hands until 1815.

Fort Little Niagara was the name of another fort in the same region. The French built this fort in 1751, and destroyed it during the French and Indian War to prevent the British from taking it. WALKER D. WYMAN

FORT PECK DAM, on the Missouri River in northeastern Montana, is the largest earth-fill dam in the United States. It contains 125,600,000 cubic yards (96,028,000 cubic meters) of earth. Fort Peck Dam was completed in 1940. It stretches for nearly 4 miles (6 kilometers) across the Missouri. The main section is 10,578 feet (3,224 meters) long, and a dike section on the west riverbank is 10,448 feet (3,185 meters) long. The dam is 250 feet (76 meters) high. The reservoir holds 19.1 million acre-feet (23.6 billion cubic meters) of water. See also DAM (picture). T. W. MERMEL

FORT PICKENS was a U.S. military post on Santa Rosa Island near Pensacola, Fla. It remained under federal control throughout the Civil War. When Florida *seceded* (withdrew) from the Union in January, 1861, Lieutenant Adam J. Slemmer moved a small body of federal soldiers into Fort Pickens. Union and Confederate authorities agreed that the Union would not reinforce the fort, and the Confederate States would not attack it. But after Confederate forces fired on Fort Sumter, S.C., on April 12, 1861, and the war began, the Union rushed reinforcements to Fort Pickens. The defenders withstood a surprise attack on Oct. 9, 1861. See also SANTA ROSA ISLAND. FRANK L. KLEMENT

FORT PITT. See PITTSBURGH (History).

FORT PONTCHARTRAIN. See DETROIT (History).

FORT PRINCE OF WALES. See CANADA (National Historic Parks and Sites); MANITOBA (Places to Visit).

FORT PULASKI NATIONAL MONUMENT is on the coast of Georgia. It includes a massive brick fort which Union forces captured in 1862. The old-style brick defenses could not withstand the rifled cannon attack of the Union artillery. The 5,616-acre (2,273-hectare) monument was established in 1924. C. LANGDON WHITE

FORT RANDALL DAM is part of the upper Missouri River Basin development program. The dam lies in south-central South Dakota near Lake Andes above old Fort Randall. United States Army engineers began building this electric-power and navigation project in 1946. They completed it in 1956. The dam is one of the largest in the world. It is 165 feet (50 meters) high and 10,700 feet (3,261 meters) long. The earth-fill dam contains 53 million cubic yards (41 million cubic meters) of earth. Its reservoir can store 6.1 million acre-feet (7.5 billion cubic meters) of water. The power plant has a capacity of 320,000 kilowatts, and began operating in 1954. T. W. MERMEL

FORT RECOVERY. See OHIO (Places to Visit).

FORT RILEY, Kans., is the home of combat units of the Fifth United States Army. The fort covers 56,000 acres (22,700 hectares). It lies about 2 miles (3 kilometers) northeast of Junction City. The army set up the post in 1853, and later named it for Maj. Gen. Bennett Riley, who fought in the Mexican War. Many cavalry regiments were organized at the post, including Maj. Gen. George A. Custer's Seventh Cavalry. Fort Riley became known as "the cradle of the cavalry." See also KANSAS (Places to Visit). SAMUEL J. ZISKIND

FORT RODD HILL NATIONAL HISTORIC PARK. See CANADA (National Historic Parks and Sites).

FORT RUCKER, Ala., houses the U.S. Army Aviation Center. This command trains pilots and maintenance workers for the Army's own air force of small fixed-wing airplanes and helicopters. The center's major activities include the Army Aviation School and Aviation Test Board. The post lies 25 miles (40 kilometers) northwest of Dothan. It was founded in 1942, and named for Edmund Rucker, a Confederate Army general. Four divisions trained there for combat in World War II, and one for service in the Korean War. SAMUEL J. ZISKIND

FORT SAINTE MARIE. See ONTARIO (Early Settlement).

FORT SAM HOUSTON, Tex., houses the headquarters of the Fifth United States Army. This command directs units and posts in 14 states. The fort covers 3,365 acres (1,362 hectares) and lies within the city limits of San Antonio. Brooke Army Medical Center, on the post, is the world's largest medical training center. The post dates from 1850, when the Army rebuilt the Alamo. In 1890, the post was named in honor of the first president of the Republic of Texas. The Army organized its first aviation unit there. SAMUEL J. ZISKIND

FORT SHAFTER, Hawaii, is a U.S. Army post that covers 1,344 acres (544 hectares) northwest of Honolulu's chief urban area. The Army set up the post as Kahauiki Military Reservation in 1899. Later, it was named for Major General William R. Shafter, who fought in the Spanish-American War. It was once a cavalry post, and became a permanent fort in 1956. SAMUEL J. ZISKIND

FORT SILL, Okla., is the site of the United States Army Field Artillery and Missile Center. This center controls the Army artillery and missile school and Army field artillery missile training activities. The post covers about 94,315 acres (38,168 hectares) near Lawton. The Army established Fort Sill in 1869 to keep watch over the Comanche and Kiowa tribes. It named the post after Brigadier General Joshua W. Sill, who was killed in the Civil War. The grave of the famous Apache chief Geronimo is at Fort Sill. SAMUEL J. ZISKIND

FORT SMITH, Ark. (pop. 68,006; met. area pop. 160,-421), is the state's most important manufacturing center. People often call it the *Industrial Capital* of the state. It is a railroad center on the western border of Arkansas, and the second largest city in the state. Fort Smith stands on a high point of land where the Poteau River flows into the Arkansas River (see ARKANSAS [political map]). Part of its metropolitan area lies in Oklahoma. Large coal and natural gas fields and soybean farms surround the city. Fort Smith factories produce about 100 different products, including furniture.

In 1817, Army Major Stephen H. Long (1784-1864)

established Fort Smith to keep peace between the Osage and Cherokee Indians. Major Long called the site Belle Point. The fort was called Fort Smith in honor of General Thomas A. Smith, Long's superior officer and commander of the military district. Fort Smith was incorporated as a town in 1842. During the California gold rush in 1849, Fort Smith became the meeting point for thousands of prospectors journeying to the West. The discovery of natural gas near the city about 1900 gave the growing Fort Smith industries a cheap source of power. In 1969, a federal navigation project on the Arkansas River made it possible for barges to reach Fort Smith. The city became an important port on the Arkansas River Navigation System. Fort Smith has a council-manager form of government, and is the seat of Sebastian County. WALTER L. BROWN

See also ARKANSAS (Climate).

FORT SNELLING. See MINNEAPOLIS (History).

FORT STANWIX was a military fortification during the Revolutionary War. It stood in the east-central part of New York just east of Lake Oneida. The city of Rome, N.Y., now stands on the fort site.

FORT STANWIX NATIONAL MONUMENT, in Rome, N.Y., was authorized in 1935 as a memorial to the Revolutionary War and U.S. colonial history. For area, see NATIONAL PARK SYSTEM (table: National Monuments). GEORGE B. HARTZOG, JR.

FORT SUMTER. In 1860, South Carolina seceded from the Union and prepared to seize the United States forts in the harbor at Charleston, S.C. Major Robert Anderson (1805-1871) directed the harbor defenses. He made his headquarters in Fort Moultrie. He realized that South Carolina troops would soon attack Fort Moultrie and that it would be difficult to defend his position. He moved his headquarters to Fort Sumter.

In April, 1861, Pierre Beauregard, the Confederate general, demanded the surrender of the fort. Anderson refused. The vigorous bombardment which followed began the Civil War. On April 14, Union troops evacuated the fort. The Confederates permitted Anderson and his command to leave with their weapons and their flag. The Confederates held Fort Sumter until February, 1865. In April of that year, troops again raised the United States flag over the fort. JOHN DONALD HICKS

See also BEAUREGARD, PIERRE G. T.; CIVIL WAR (Secession); FORT MOULTRIE; SOUTH CAROLINA (color picture: Fort Sumter); RUFFIN, EDMUND.

FORT SUMTER NATIONAL MONUMENT lies in Charleston Harbor, South Carolina. It was authorized in 1848 as a Civil War memorial. For area, see NATIONAL PARK SYSTEM (table: National Monuments). See also FORT SUMTER; NATIONAL PARK SYSTEM (picture).

FORT SUPPLY DAM is a federal flood-control project located in northwestern Oklahoma. It is on Wolfe Creek near its junction with the North Canadian River. The dam is an earth-fill structure 11,865 feet (3,616 meters) long and 85 feet (26 meters) high. The reservoir has a storage capacity of 106,100 acre-feet (131 million cubic meters) of water. The dam was completed in 1942.

FORT TICONDEROGA, on Lake Champlain in New York State, was an important stronghold during the Revolutionary War. It commanded the invasion route by water from Canada. When hostilities began, a group of Americans organized an expedition to seize the fort. The group included Ethan Allen, a Vermont colonial

Fort Ticonderoga, a military stronghold on Lake Champlain during the Revolutionary War, has been rebuilt as a museum.

Robert H. Glaze, Artstreet

leader. On May 10, 1775, Allen and Benedict Arnold led the *Green Mountain Boys* (Vermont soldiers) in a surprise attack and captured the fort without loss of life. The British recaptured the fort in 1777, but abandoned it in 1780 when they gave up hope of using the invasion route.

In 1908, the fort was rebuilt, and a museum was opened there. The museum contains articles used by soldiers of the Revolution.   WALKER D. WYMAN

FORT UNION NATIONAL MONUMENT is near Watrous, N.Mex. The army built the fort in 1851 to protect travelers on the nearby Santa Fe Trail from unfriendly Indians. It became a national monument in 1954. For area, see NATIONAL PARK SYSTEM (table: National Monuments).

FORT VANCOUVER NATIONAL HISTORIC SITE is in Vancouver, Wash. It preserves the site of a stockaded fur-trading post. From 1825 to 1849, the post served as the western headquarters and depot for the Hudson's Bay Company. It became a national historic site in 1961. For area, see NATIONAL PARK SYSTEM (table: National Historic Sites).

FORT WAYNE (pop. 184,989; met. area pop. 361,-984) is a commercial and industrial center in northeastern Indiana. Among Indiana's cities, only Indianapolis and Gary are larger. Fort Wayne lies about 130 miles (209 kilometers) northeast of Indianapolis. For location, see INDIANA (political map).

Description. Fort Wayne, the county seat of Allen County, covers about 50 square miles (130 square kilometers). The St. Marys and St. Joseph rivers join within the city to form the Maumee River.

Cultural attractions in Fort Wayne include the Fort Wayne Philharmonic Orchestra and the Philharmonic Opera Guild. The Community Center for the Performing Arts is the home of the Fort Wayne Ballet, the Civic Theater, and other fine-arts groups. The city's mu-

seums include the Lincoln Library and Museum of the Lincoln National Life Foundation and the Allen County-Fort Wayne Historical Museum. A campus of Indiana University-Purdue University is in Fort Wayne. Other institutions of higher education include the Indiana Institute of Technology and St. Francis College. Fort Wayne's biggest tourist attraction, the Three Rivers Festival, is a spectacle of parades and historical displays held in July.

The Fort Wayne area has about 375 manufacturing plants. Their chief products include automotive parts, electrical machinery, electronic parts and equipment, and transportation equipment. Two major airlines and freight and passenger trains serve the city.

History. The Miami Indians lived in what is now the Fort Wayne area before white settlers arrived. A United States Army officer, Major General "Mad Anthony" Wayne, built a fort there in 1794. The fort and the town that grew up around it were named in his honor. Fort Wayne was incorporated as a city in 1840.

Fort Wayne was a fur-trading center until the 1830's. In 1832, construction began at Fort Wayne on the Wabash and Erie Canal, which linked Lake Erie with the Wabash River. Fort Wayne's population grew as Irish and German immigrants came to work on the canal and in related industries. A railroad was built through the city in 1854 and helped attract industry.

Dale Stedman, Stedman Studio

Downtown Fort Wayne is one of Indiana's chief commercial centers. The domed Allen County Courthouse, *center*, and other nearby buildings overlook Freiman Park, *foreground*.

By 1900, the population had grown to over 45,000.

In the late 1970's, Fort Wayne planned major construction projects for the downtown area. They included a community-convention center and an office building complex. Fort Wayne has a mayor-council form of government.   JOHN ANKENBRUCK

FORT WELLINGTON. See CANADA (Historic Parks).
FORT WILLIAM, Ontario. See THUNDER BAY.
FORT WOOD. See LIBERTY ISLAND.

FORT WORTH

FORT WORTH, Tex. (pop. 393,476; met. area 2,378,-353), is a major industrial city and one of the nation's chief aircraft producers. It ranks as a leader among Southwestern cities as a market for grain and oil. Fort Worth lies about 30 miles (48 kilometers) west of Dallas in north-central Texas (see TEXAS [political map]).

Major Ripley A. Arnold founded Fort Worth in 1849 as an army post to protect settlers from Indian attacks. The post was named for Major General William J. Worth, a hero of the Mexican War. Fort Worth is still occasionally called "Cowtown." The city got this early nickname because of its history as a cattle-marketing center. Business expansion has made Fort Worth one of the fastest-growing urban centers in Texas.

The City. Fort Worth occupies about 236 square miles (611 square kilometers) in the center of Tarrant County. The city's metropolitan area covers 11 counties, a total of 8,567 square miles (22,188 square kilometers). The Dallas-Fort Worth metropolitan area is one of the most highly populated regions in the United States.

Fort Worth's main business district lies on the south bank of the Trinity River, which runs through the center of the city. The 37-story Fort Worth National Bank on Throckmorton Street is Fort Worth's tallest building. At the southeast end of the downtown area, the Tarrant County Convention Center covers 14 city blocks between Houston and Commerce streets.

More than 98 per cent of Fort Worth's people were born in the United States, and almost 75 per cent were born in Texas. Fewer than 20 per cent of the people are Negroes. Persons of Mexican ancestry make up about 6 per cent of the population. Baptists form the largest religious group in Fort Worth, followed by members of the Churches of Christ and the Disciples of Christ.

Economy of Fort Worth is based on manufacturing, which employs about half the workers in the area. The city has about 780 factories. Fort Worth's largest industries make airplanes, helicopters, and other military products. Its aircraft plants are among the largest in the nation. Other Fort Worth products include food products, mobile homes, oil-well equipment, and shipping containers. Fort Worth is also one of the Southwest's leading grain-milling and storage centers.

Fort Worth lies in the center of a rich oil-producing region, and about 35 oil companies have offices in the city. About 40 insurance firms have their headquarters in Fort Worth. The city ranks as a major wholesale outlet for the Southwest. It is served by railroad passenger trains, 9 rail freight lines, 5 bus lines, and about 40 truck lines. Two interstate highways intersect in the downtown area. The Greater Southwest International Airport lies about 16 miles (26 kilometers) northeast of the city. The Dallas-Fort Worth Airport lies about midway between the two cities.

Education and Cultural Life. Fort Worth is the home of the Southwestern Baptist Theological Seminary, Texas Christian University, and Texas Wesleyan College. A branch of the University of Texas is in nearby Arlington. Tarrant County Junior College has two campuses in Fort Worth. The city's public school system consists of 115 elementary and high schools. Fort Worth also has about 40 private schools and about 20 church-supported schools.

The *Star-Telegram* is the only daily newspaper in Fort Worth. Seven television stations and about 20 radio stations serve the city.

Fort Worth has a ballet company, an opera company, and a symphony orchestra. Many people enjoy summer musicals at the Casa Mañana theater-in-the-round. The William Edrington Scott Theatre features plays and motion pictures. Fort Worth's annual Southwestern Exposition and Fat Stock Show is one of the nation's largest livestock shows. The Texas Rangers of the American Baseball League play their home games at Turnpike Stadium in nearby Arlington.

The Fort Worth Museum of Science and History, one of the largest children's museums in the United States, has live animals in some exhibits. The Amon Carter Museum of Western Art displays paintings and sculpture of the West by the American artists Frederic Remington and Charles M. Russell. The Fort Worth Art Center also exhibits works by American artists. The Kimbell Art Museum includes a large collection of English paintings.

In Forest Park, 3 miles (5 kilometers) west of downtown, the Fort Worth Zoological Park has more than 600 kinds of animals. The park also has the actual homes of early Fort Worth settlers in a log cabin village. The nearby Botanic Gardens feature about 150,000 plants.

Government. Fort Worth has a mayor-council form of government. Voters elect the mayor and eight councilmen to two-year terms. The mayor and councilmen all serve without salary. The council employs a city manager as the administrative head of the government. The city manager carries out policies established by the council, prepares the budget, and appoints and dismisses department heads. Fort Worth gets most of its income from property and sales taxes.

History. On June 6, 1849, Major Ripley A. Arnold established an Army post called Fort Worth to protect settlers from attacks by Indians. The soldiers left in 1853, and many settlers moved into the Army buildings. Fort Worth became the county seat of Tarrant County in 1860. During the 1860's and 1870's, the people traded with cowboys driving cattle to markets in Kansas. Fort Worth was incorporated as a city in 1873.

In 1876, the Texas and Pacific Railroad reached Fort Worth. Cattle could now be shipped directly from the city. Fort Worth's first flour mill opened in 1882. As the cattle and grain industries developed, the city's population grew from 500 persons in 1870 to 26,688 in 1900.

In 1902, the Swift and Armour companies built large meat-packing plants in Fort Worth. The meat industry helped Fort Worth's population reach 73,312 by 1910. The discovery of several oil fields in West Texas about 1915 brought more people to Fort Worth. By 1930, the city's population had climbed to 163,447. The Great Depression almost stopped Fort Worth's growth during the 1930's. Only 14,000 new residents settled there between 1930 and 1940.

During World War II (1939-1945), Fort Worth became a center for the manufacture of airplanes, helicopters, and other military products. Jobs created by defense industries caused a sharp population rise during

Fort Worth is one of the largest industrial cities in Texas. The Tarrant County Convention Center, *center*, and Fort Worth Water Gardens, *foreground*, are at the edge of the main business district.

and after the war. The city had 356,268 persons by 1960.

Unemployment in the defense and oil industries again slowed Fort Worth's growth during the 1960's and early 1970's. Almost half of Fort Worth's workers are employed in manufacturing, and so the city needs industrial jobs for steady growth and a strong economy. Fort Worth depends heavily on jobs in defense plants, especially in the General Dynamics factory.

A movement of people and trade away from the city into the suburbs also affected Fort Worth's growth during the 1960's. To slow this trend, city leaders began an urban renewal program. Private investors planned new office buildings and remodeling projects in the central business district. In October, 1965, the voters approved a $33.9-million bond issue—the largest in Fort Worth's history—to pay for new park and recreation facilities, street repairs, a new city hall and police building, and other improvements.

Fort Worth's development has been affected by a traditional rivalry with Dallas, which has a larger population and a stronger economy. Efforts toward greater cooperation led to construction of the Dallas-Fort Worth Airport, which opened in 1974.   WALTER B. MOORE

FORT WRIGHT COLLEGE. See UNIVERSITIES AND COLLEGES (table).

FORTALEZA, *FAWR tuh LAY zuh* (pop. 529,933; met. area pop. 973,452), is the capital of the state of Ceará in Brazil. For location, see BRAZIL (political map). This part of Brazil has little rain and the land is not fertile. Fortaleza is a busy commercial and cultural center. It exports metal ores, cotton, and hides. It was settled in 1611 and became a *vila* (town) in 1726.   MANOEL CARDOZO

FORTAS, ABE (1910-   ), was appointed an associate justice of the Supreme Court of the United States by President Lyndon B. Johnson in 1965. In 1968, Johnson nominated Fortas for the position of chief justice. Johnson withdrew the nomination at Fortas' request after a Senate filibuster prevented a vote on the nomination. Fortas resigned from the court in 1969 fol-

lowing widespread criticism of his association with the Wolfson Family Foundation. Financier Louis E. Wolfson had been convicted of stock manipulation in 1967. After joining the court, and at a time when Wolfson was under federal investigation, Fortas had agreed to perform services for the Wolfson Foundation. He was to receive $20,000 a year for life from the foundation, but he later canceled the agreement.

Fortas was born in Memphis, Tenn. He graduated from Southwestern College and Yale Law School. From 1933 to 1937, he was an assistant professor of law at Yale. Fortas held many government posts. He became undersecretary of the interior in 1942. He entered private law practice in Washington, D.C., in 1947. He became known as an outstanding appeals lawyer and a defender of civil liberties.   CARL T. ROWAN

FORTEN, JAMES (1766-1842), was an American Negro businessman who won fame as an abolitionist during the early 1800's. He believed that most American Negroes wanted to live as free men in the United States. He opposed efforts being made at the time to help blacks move to Africa.

Forten was born in Philadelphia, the son of free parents. He served as a powder boy on an American ship during the Revolutionary War in America (1775-1783). Forten was captured in the war—at the age of 15 —and spent seven months on a British prison ship. In 1786, he got a job in a Philadelphia sailmaking shop. Forten rose to foreman two years later and became owner of the business in 1798. About that time, he invented a device that helped crewmen handle heavy sails. The invention greatly aided his business, and Forten became wealthy.

During the War of 1812, Forten helped recruit about 2,500 Negroes as part of a force to defend Philadelphia against a British invasion. In 1817, he presided over a meeting of Philadelphia blacks who protested the American Colonization Society's attempts to resettle free Negroes in Africa. During the 1830's, he contributed much money to the noted abolitionist William Lloyd

361

Garrison and to Garrison's antislavery newspaper, *The Liberator*. Forten also helped runaway slaves seeking freedom in the North.　　　　OTEY M. SCRUGGS

FORTRAN. See COMPUTER (Writing a Program).

FORTRESS OF LOUISBOURG. See CANADA (National Historic Parks and Sites).

FORTUNA, *fawr TYOO nuh*, was the goddess of chance in Roman mythology. Her name was Tyche in Greece. Fortuna brought good or bad luck to men whether or not they deserved it. Temples were built to her at Antium. Fortuna appears in art with a rudder to show her power to guide lives. She is also shown holding a horn of plenty as a symbol of riches. The word *fortune* comes from her name.　　　　H. L. STOW

FORTUNETELLING is the practice of predicting future events by methods generally considered illogical and unscientific. Persons who claim to foretell the future are called *fortunetellers*.

Some fortunetellers say they have powers of *clairvoyance*—that is, they claim to have knowledge of future events without using any known senses. Scientists do not know whether clairvoyance actually exists. Most fortunetellers, however, do not claim to have clairvoyant powers. Instead, they use special systems of prediction. Some of these systems are complicated, and fortunetellers often say they are scientific. But most scientists consider such systems to be *pseudosciences* (false sciences).

Fortunetelling has been especially popular during certain periods of history. For example, the ancient Greeks and Romans believed the gods spoke to them through prophets called *oracles*. Many persons went to oracles for advice about the future. In later times, the Christian church discouraged fortunetelling. However, an ancient type of fortunetelling called *astrology* became extremely popular in Europe during the Renaissance, the period from about 1300 to about 1600. Some forms of fortunetelling remain popular today, especially in primitive societies and underdeveloped countries. Most Americans regard fortunetelling as a form of amusement, but many believe in it sincerely.

Methods of Fortunetelling. Throughout history, hundreds of different fortunetelling methods have been used. One of the most famous methods involves gazing into a crystal ball. Many methods of fortunetelling seem to depend entirely on chance. For example, fortunetellers have made predictions based on the order in which a rooster ate grains of wheat placed on letters drawn on the ground. Predictions also have been based on the shape taken by oil poured on water, or on segments of writing chosen from a book at random.

However, fortunetellers claim that mysterious causes and relationships, not chance, make their predictions possible. For example, astrology is based on the belief that the sun, moon, planets, and stars control the lives of human beings. Therefore, the positions and movements of these celestial bodies supposedly can be used to predict the future.

Other fortunetelling systems include *numerology* and *palmistry*. In numerology, a fortuneteller makes predictions through numbers based on a person's name and birth date. In palmistry, a fortuneteller tries to foresee an individual's future by studying the lines,

markings, shape, and the size of the person's hand.

Some fortunetellers only pretend to rely on special systems. For example, a fortuneteller may investigate a client's background and then impress him by relating many things about the client. A fortuneteller also may rely on a broad knowledge of human nature. He knows what most people want to hear, and so he makes statements about the future that could apply to almost anyone. He then observes his client's reactions to these statements and develops a more detailed prediction on the basis of these reactions.

Dangers of Fortunetelling. Most fortunetelling is based on the idea that mysterious forces control human life. Therefore, a belief in fortunetelling may rob a person of trust in his own ability to control his future. Also, some individuals have lost large sums of money to dishonest fortunetellers.

Some people argue that honest fortunetellers may give harmless—and even sensible—advice to troubled persons who cannot afford psychiatric help. However, businesses and marriages have been wrecked because a person acted on bad advice given by a fortuneteller. Some states and cities have laws against fortunetelling. In general, however, these laws are poorly enforced, and Americans spend millions of dollars annually on fortunetelling.　　　　MARCELLO TRUZZI

Related Articles in WORLD BOOK include:

Astrology	Magic	Omen
Augur	Necromancy	Oracles
Clairvoyance	Nostradamus	Palmistry
Divination	Numerology	Superstition
Graphology	Occult	

FORTY IMMORTALS. See FRENCH ACADEMY.

FORTY-NINER was a gold-seeker who rushed to California after gold was discovered there in 1848. The first forty-niners reached San Francisco on the steamer *California* on Feb. 28, 1849. Ships from all parts of the world carried other men there. But the greatest number arrived in covered wagons by way of the Oregon Trail. By the end of the year, the forty-niners had increased California's population from 20,000 to over 107,000. The forty-niners were the first of still heavier migrations to California during the following years. See also CALIFORNIA (The Gold Rush); GOLD RUSH (picture); GOLDEN GATE.　　　　OSCAR O. WINTHER

FORTY-TWO-LINE BIBLE. See GUTENBERG, JOHANNES.

FORUM is an assembly for discussing questions of public interest. See PANEL DISCUSSION; SYMPOSIUM.

FORUM, ROMAN, was the section of ancient Rome that served as the center of government. It was the administrative, legislative, and legal center of the Republic and of the Roman Empire. Many important and beautiful buildings and monuments stood in the Forum. These included the *Curia* (Senate House), the temples of Concord and Saturn, the Basilica Julia and Basilica Aemilia, the Arch of Septimius Severus, and the *Tabularium* (Hall of Records).

Events in the Forum often affected the rest of the known world. Marcus Tullius Cicero's stirring speeches on the floor of the Curia in the 60's B.C. saved the Republic from a rebellion led by Catiline. There, too, in 27 B.C., the senate gave Augustus the powers that made him the first emperor of Rome. Romans went to the Forum to hear famous orators speak and to see the valuables seized after distant battles.

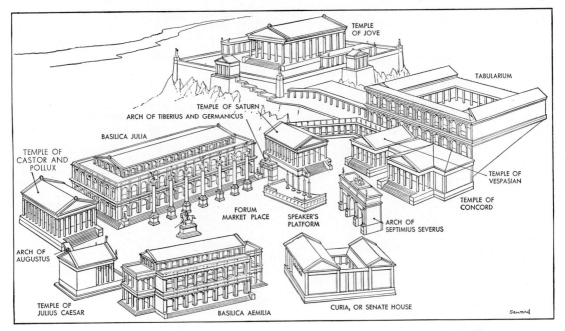

The Early Roman Forum Had This Arrangement During the Period of Its Greatest Magnificence.

In Rome's earliest days, the Forum area was a swamp used as a cemetery by the people of surrounding villages. The Etruscans turned these villages into the city of Rome and drained the marshes, probably in the 500's B.C. Residents built shops and temples around the edges of the Forum area. The Forum became the civic and legal center of Rome by the mid-100's B.C., and the merchants moved their shops to other parts of the city.

The barbarians who invaded Rome in the A.D. 400's did not destroy the Forum. But the Forum's buildings gradually crumbled after the fall of Rome, and people came to call the Forum *Cow Plain* because it had become so desolate. Excavations have since uncovered many of the ancient columns and arches. Rome had other forums, some with architecture as outstanding as that of the Roman Forum. Several emperors named forums in their own honor. But only the first forum was called *Forum Romanum* (Roman Forum). FRANK C. BOURNE

See also ROME (Forums; picture: Roman Forum); ROMAN EMPIRE (picture: The Roman Forum).

FOSBURY FLOP. See HIGH JUMP.

FOSCOLO, UGO (1778-1827), was an Italian author. His *Le ultime lettere di Jacopo Ortis* (1802, revised in 1817), is sometimes considered the first modern Italian novel. It is the tragic story of a young student's love for Teresa, a woman whose hand has been promised to another man, Odardo. The story is told in the form of letters, and shows the influence of Johann von Goethe's *The Sorrows of Young Werther*. Many of Foscolo's odes and sonnets tell in a lyrical yet classical style about his personal sufferings and disappointments. His best-known poem, *The Sepulchers* (1806-1807), is an ode that stresses the importance of graves as living reminders of one's forefathers.

Foscolo was born on the island of Zákinthos in the Ionian Sea. His early poetry is filled with his desire to see Italy unified. In 1815, Foscolo left Italy for England, where he taught Italian and wrote essays for magazines and newspapers. SERGIO PACIFICI

FOSDICK, HARRY EMERSON (1878-1969), became one of the best-known Protestant preachers in the United States. He devoted his entire career as a preacher, professor, and author to the conflict between science and religion. He preached the right of science to its place in the world. Fosdick opposed the views held by the Fundamentalists (see FUNDAMENTALISM).

Fosdick served as pastor of the First Baptist Church in Montclair, N.J.; and the First Presbyterian Church, Park Avenue Baptist Church, and the nondenominational Riverside Church, all located in New York City. Fosdick was professor of preaching at Union Theological Seminary in New York City from 1915 to 1946. He served with the Y.M.C.A. in England, Scotland, and France during World War I.

Fosdick's many books include *The Meaning of Prayer, The Manhood of the Master, The Modern Use of the Bible, On Being a Real Person*, and an autobiography, *The Living of These Days*.

Born in Buffalo, N.Y., Fosdick was graduated from Colgate University. He also studied at Union Theological Seminary and Columbia University. L. J. TRINTERUD

FOSS, JOSEPH JACOB (1915-   ), was a leading United States fighter pilot in the South Pacific during World War II. He also served as Republican governor of South Dakota from 1955 to 1959. During the war, Foss led a United States Marine Air Force unit known as *Joe's Flying Circus*. The unit shot down 72 Japanese planes. Foss destroyed 26 of them. He received the Congressional Medal of Honor, Bronze Star, Silver Star, and the Purple Heart. He was the director of operations for the Central Air Defense Force in the Korean War. Foss was commissioner of the American Football League from 1959 to 1966. He was born near Sioux Falls, S. Dak. See also WAR ACES. EVERETT W. STERLING

363

Fossils of such prehistoric animals as the Gorgosaurus, *left,* are displayed in many museums. Scientists have reconstructed the skeletons of many creatures by using disconnected bones found in the ground. Fossil hunters must dig carefully to remove such bones without damaging them.

FOSSIL is the record or remains of a plant or animal that lived in the past. A fossil may be a whole animal preserved in ice, a bone or tooth hardened by minerals, an insect encased in amber, a footprint, or the outline of a leaf. Fossils tell scientists what life was like millions of years before human beings existed. The earliest forms of life were simple, one-celled creatures. The oldest fossils known to scientists are *algae* and *bacteria* (one-celled plants) that were alive over 3,100,000,000 years ago. The next oldest are many-celled plants and animals. Finally, about 600 million years ago, plants and animals developed hard skeletons and shells that have left good records of their remains in rocks.

Many gaps exist in the record. For example, scientists have found deposits of carbon more than 2,700,000,000 years old. They believe plants formed this carbon, but they cannot identify the plants. Plants and animals that live in dry areas leave fewer fossils than those that live in damp places or in water. Dissolved minerals in the water help form fossils. Creatures without hard parts leave few fossils. Some animals, including flying reptiles and birds, were so delicate that few left remains.

But in spite of the gaps, scientists have pieced together a record of plants, animals, and people that lived in past ages. For a description of animals of the past, see PREHISTORIC ANIMAL; for a description of early human beings, see PREHISTORIC PEOPLE.

Scientists determine when fossils were formed by finding out the age of the rocks in which they lie (see GEOLOGY). They also measure the amount of certain chemicals in the fossils to tell how long the fossils have been in the earth (see PREHISTORIC ANIMAL [Determining When Prehistoric Animals Lived]).

Kinds of Fossils

Most dead plants and animals are eaten by animals or decayed by bacteria or fungi. Only those buried quickly and protected from decay can become fossils. Hard parts, such as wood, shells, bones, and teeth, decay less easily than soft parts, such as skin and muscles. So hard parts are more likely to be preserved. Most of our knowledge of past life comes from studying the preserved hard parts of plants and animals.

Fossils may be preserved in several different ways. The chief kinds of fossils are (1) petrified fossils, (2) molds and casts, (3) prints, and (4) whole animals and plants.

Petrified Fossils are the remains of plants and animals that have turned to stone. The remains may be petrified in three main ways. Many fossils are formed by *replacement.* Water dissolves away the original substance of the plant or animal. As the substance dissolves, minerals replace it. In *permineralization,* minerals fill in the small air spaces in bones or shells without changing the original shape of the object. The actual bone or shell remains, strengthened by the minerals. In *carbonization,* leaves or the soft parts of animals turn to carbon. Other chemicals escape, leaving a record of the shape of the plant or animal as a thin film of carbon.

Molds and Casts. Living things sometimes become buried in mud, clay, or other material that hardens around them. Later, the bodies dissolve away, leaving openings within the hard material that are natural *molds* of the original. Scientists can fill these molds with wax, plastic, or plaster to make *artificial casts,* or duplicates of the outer surface of the original. They let the filler harden and then crack away the outer shell. Sometimes, minerals slowly fill a mold while it lies in the ground. This forms a *natural cast.*

Resin, or sap, from trees sometimes trapped insects and other small animals. The resin hardened into clear amber, and the animals dried to a film of carbon lining the amber mold. The insects are preserved so well that scientists can count the tiny hairs and wing scales on

Samuel Paul Welles, the contributor of this article, is Research Associate at the University of California's Museum of Paleontology in Berkeley and coauthor of From Bones to Bodies.

their bodies. But if the scientists dissolve away the amber, the specimen inside crumbles to bits.

About 20 million years ago, an ancient lava flow buried a rhinoceros. The animal's body formed a mold in the lava, and some charred bones and teeth were preserved. When the Columbia River wore its way down through the lava, it cut through the rear of the mold. Scientists crawled inside the mold and made a plaster cast of the animal. From this cast and the bone and teeth fragments, they identified the rhinoceros.

Prints may be molds of thin objects, such as leaves or feathers, or they may be tracks or footprints left by extinct animals. Prints are preserved when the soft mud in which they are made hardens into stone. Some prints show veins and pores in leaves. Others show the bodies and fins of extinct reptiles and fishes, and even the thin, skinlike wings of flying reptiles. Prints also preserve details of the skin of some dinosaurs.

Footprints and tracks may provide a *paleontologist* (scientist who studies prehistoric life) with valuable information. The depth, size, and distance between footprints may tell a paleontologist the length and weight of the animal that left them. Scientists have found footprints left by birds, mammals, amphibians, and dinosaurs and other reptiles, including flying reptiles. Even animals without skeletons left tracks.

Whole Animals and Plants are rarely preserved. Most fossils consist only of shells, teeth, bones, and other hard parts. Flesh and other soft parts almost always decay too quickly to be preserved.

The earliest fossil egg known came from rocks in Texas that are probably 270 million years old. It is of an early mammal-like reptile. The famous dinosaur eggs found by the explorer Roy Chapman Andrews in 1923 came from 135 million-year-old rocks in Mongolia. Fossil birds' eggs are found in rocks formed during the last 60 million years. These eggs are usually of waterfowl that made their nests in lowlands. In the damp lowland areas, mud and other fine sediment covered the eggs and fossilized them.

In a few rare cases, whole animals are preserved in ice or tar. A woolly rhinoceros found preserved in tar had parts of the flesh and skin attached to its skeleton. Woolly mammoths and woolly rhinoceroses have been preserved where they fell into crevasses in deep ice. The flesh of these animals is frozen, as meat is frozen in a freezer. It may be eaten if it is thawed quickly.

Entire plants are almost never preserved as fossils. But, in some places, trunks of trees were preserved when they were buried under sand and mud containing volcanic ash. Groups of these trunks, some still standing, later became petrified forests. See PETRIFIED FOREST.

Studying Fossils

Hunting for Fossils. Almost all fossils are found in *sedimentary* rocks, or rocks that have been built up in layers from small particles. These rocks lie beneath about three-fourths of the land surface of the earth. Most of them contain fossils. Fossils of different animals and from different times in the earth's history are found in different places. To find a certain kind of fossil, a scientist must go where the rocks that contain this kind of fossil lie near the earth's surface. A scientist studying dinosaurs might go to Colorado, Wyoming, or Alberta in Canada. A scientist interested in horses might search

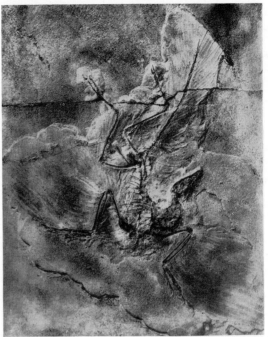

From *The Vertebrate Story* by A. S. Romer;
© 1958, The University of Chicago Press

One of the Earliest Birds, *Archaeornis,* left this fossil in limestone rocks in southern Germany. The bird was about the same size as a crow. The fossil shows clear prints of feathers.

Hal Roth

The Head of a 30-Million-Year-Old Stingless Bee was perfectly preserved in amber. Sap from a tree trapped the insect and later hardened into a glasslike amber shell.

Fish Skeleton was preserved by *permineralization*. In this process, air spaces in the fish's body became filled with minerals.

Dinosaur Egg, *center,* was laid about 135 million years ago. It is compared here with a hen's egg, *left,* and an alligator egg, *right.* Because their shells broke easily, prehistoric eggs were seldom preserved as fossils.

Fossil of *Ichthyosaurus,* a fishlike reptile, is so well preserved that outlines of the soft parts of the body can be seen.

Fossils of Trilobites, relatives of modern crabs and lobsters, show the horizontal sections of the animals' shells.

the Great Plains and the Rocky Mountain basins. Fossils may be found anywhere that sedimentary rocks lie exposed. They might be in your own back yard. But the best collecting areas are places where wind and water have cut deep into rocks and exposed large areas. Fossils lie nearer to the surface in these places.

When the scientist reaches an area he thinks may contain fossils, he begins searching places where the soil has worn away from the rocks. If he wants to study plants or *invertebrates* (animals without backbones), he splits open rocks to find fossils inside them. To study larger animals, he searches for fragments of bones or teeth that stick out of the ground.

When the fossil hunter finds a few fragments of bone or a tooth, he must locate the place where the rest of the animal lies buried. This may be near the fragments, or a distance away. Sometimes fossils lie in hard-to-reach places. The scientist digs away the rock from above the skeleton. First he uses large tools, or even explosives, to remove the rock. But as he works nearer to the skeleton, he uses smaller tools. He may do the final cleaning with small awls and paintbrushes.

As he uncovers the fossil, the paleontologist protects it with shellac or plastic. Then he covers it with strips of wet paper. Next he adds a series of burlap strips dipped in plaster of Paris to form a *jacket* that protects and supports the fossil. He may strengthen a large specimen by putting sticks or timbers inside the jacket. When the exposed surface is completely covered with hardened plaster, the whole fossil is rolled over. The scientist places another jacket on the other side. The skeleton encased in its plaster jacket resembles a waffle in a waffle iron. It is ready to be packed and shipped

to a museum. At the museum, scientists carefully uncover the fossil. They clean away remaining rock and rebuild broken or missing parts with plaster. The skeleton is then ready for study or display.

Mounting Fossils. Once a fossil is cleaned, it is ready for mounting. The simplest mount for skeletons is *bas-relief.* Workers clean off the best side of the skeleton. They strengthen the other side and fasten the slab to the wall. This kind of mounting displays the fossil as it was buried.

The *free mount* is the most spectacular kind of mounting. Scientists remove each bone from the rock, clean it, and strengthen it. Then they make a small model to show the position of the final mount. Next they weld a steel framework together to support the skeleton. Then they fasten the bones to the outside of the framework to hide the steel. In the finished mount, the skeleton seems to stand by itself.

Fossils of small animals and of plants may be merely cleaned, and placed on a shelf or on the wall. Often scientists *reconstruct* an animal or plant to show what it looked like in life. An artist may make a scale model out of plaster, or paint or sketch a picture. Labels tell the story of the fossil, and explain what scientists think the animal or plant was like when it was alive. See DINOSAUR (picture: Reconstructing a Skeleton).

What Scientists Learn from Fossils. Fossils tell about the past history of life on earth, and of the past changes in geography. Since fossils show a continuous array of living things for the last 600 million years, we know that the climate for that time has been uniform enough to support life. Fossil shellfish indicate that the rocks that contain them formed under the ocean. Paleontolo-

American Museum of Natural History

Bony Armor of a Dinosaur, rather than the animal's skeleton, has been preserved in this fossil. The armor grew beneath the animal's skin and served as a protective covering.

Peabody Museum of Natural History, Yale Univ.

Salamander Fossil was found in Switzerland in the early 1700's. Some scientists of that time mistook it for the skeleton of a man drowned in the great flood described in the Bible.

Field Museum of Natural History

A Split Rock reveals a fossil of part of a leaf from a fern plant that lived about 250 million years ago.

gists find such rocks high in the Alps, Andes, Himalayas, and Rockies. They know that these areas, once under water, were lifted up to form mountain ranges.

Fossils, especially of plants, tell what past climates were like. Fossil palms and magnolias about 80 million years old found in Greenland indicate a warm, moist climate at that time. Fossils also tell when certain continents were connected. For example, Bering Strait, part of the North Pacific Ocean, was a land bridge at several different times. Camels and rhinoceroses crossed this land from America to Asia. Bison, elephants, and mastodons crossed it going in the other direction.

Paleontologists study fossils by comparing them in detail with other fossils and with living animals and plants. They measure, draw, photograph, and describe the fossils to determine their closest relatives. Paleontologists have found that fossils most like living forms occur in rocks nearest the surface. In lower and lower layers, fossils become less and less like living plants and animals. Thus, certain *strata* (layers) have particular kinds of fossils. Paleontologists use these fossils to identify the strata wherever they occur.

The long series of fossil animals and plants found in succeeding layers of the earth's crust builds up the story of past life. It presents evidence to support the theory of evolution of life (see EVOLUTION). Many fossils are missing from the record. But in a few cases, including the horse, the history of change through the ages is almost complete.　　　　SAMUEL PAUL WELLES

Related Articles in WORLD BOOK include:

Andrews, Roy Chapman	Paleontology
Archaeology	Prehistoric Animal
Cuvier, Baron	Prehistoric People
Earth (History; picture)	Rock (Organic Sediments)
Geology	Smith, William
Insect (picture)	Teilhard de Chardin, Pierre
Osborn (Henry F.)	Tree (Fossil Trees)

FOSSIL BUTTE NATIONAL MONUMENT, an area of rare fish fossils, is in southwestern Wyoming near Kemmerer. The fossils date from the Paleocene and Eocene epochs, two periods in the earth's history from 40 to 65 million years ago. The site became a national monument in 1972. For its area, see NATIONAL PARK SYSTEM (table: National Monuments).　　　CHARLES C. KEELY, JR.

FOSTER, SIR GEORGE EULAS (1847-1931), served as acting prime minister of Canada in 1920 while Sir Robert Borden was ill. Foster was a member of the Canadian House of Commons from 1882 to 1900, and from 1904 to 1921. He was Canadian minister of finance from 1888 to 1896 and minister of trade and commerce from 1911 to 1921. In 1921, Foster accepted an appointment to the Canadian Senate, where he served until his death. He was also elected a vice-president of the League of Nations Assembly of 1921. He was born in Carleton County, New Brunswick, and was educated at the University of New Brunswick.　　　J. K. CHAPMAN

FOSTER, STEPHEN COLLINS (1826-1864), was one of America's best-loved songwriters. He composed sentimental Negro songs that were called "plantation melodies." These songs are deeply moving in their sincerity and their simplicity. Foster's most popular works include "Old Folks at Home" (also known as "Swanee River," see SUWANNEE RIVER); "My Old Kentucky Home, Good Night," "Old Black Joe," and "Massa's in de Cold, Cold Ground." He also wrote such rollicking songs as "Oh! Susanna" and "Camptown Races," and such romantic songs as "Beautiful Dreamer" and "Jeanie with the Light Brown Hair." He wrote more than 200 songs, and wrote the words as well as the music for most of them.

Foster was born on July 4, 1826, near Lawrenceville, Pa. (now part of Pittsburgh). He had little musical training, but he had a great gift of melody. At the age of 6, he taught himself to play the clarinet, and he could pick up any tune by ear. He composed "The Tioga Waltz" for piano at 14. Two years later his first song, "Open Thy Lattice, Love," was published.

He wrote his first minstrel melodies, which he called "Ethiopian songs," in 1845. These were "Lou'siana Belle" and "Old Uncle Ned." Blackface minstrel shows, in which white entertainers blackened their faces, were becoming popular in the United States (see MINSTREL SHOW). Foster decided to write songs for the

University of Pittsburgh

Stephen Foster

minstrels and to improve the quality of their music.

He went to Cincinnati in 1846 to work as a bookkeeper for his brother. He wrote "Oh! Susanna" in 1846. Soon it became the favorite song of the "forty-niners" in the California gold rush. He married Jane McDowell in 1850, and settled in Pittsburgh to work as a composer. He arranged with the minstrel leader, E. P. Christy, to have his new songs performed on the minstrel stage. Foster was a poor businessman, and he sold many of his most famous songs for very little money. He lived in New York City from 1860 until his death, struggling against illness, poverty, and alcoholism.

Courtesy of Stephen Foster Memorial, White Springs, Florida

Foster's "Jeanie with the Light Brown Hair" may have been inspired by the composer's wife. It was published in 1854.

Some of Foster's songs became so popular during his lifetime that they were adapted (with suitable words) for Sunday school use. The American composer Charles Ives often quoted Foster's tunes in his own music when he wanted a real American flavor. Because Foster's songs are deeply rooted in American folk traditions, the best of them have become part of the American cultural heritage.   GILBERT CHASE

FOSTER PARENT is a person who provides a home for one or more children who are not legally members of his family. About 170,000 married couples in the United States serve as foster parents. Most foster parents have children of their own.

Most foster parents care for children under the supervision of a public or private social agency that has the basic responsibility for the youngsters. Such agencies find foster parents for children whose natural parents cannot provide adequate care. In some cases, the natural parents abused, deserted, or neglected the children. In others, the parents suffer from long-term mental or physical illness. The separation from his natural family and the adjustment to a foster family can be unpleasant experiences for a child. Foster parents try to provide a family environment that will encourage the child to grow up normally.

Foster parents, natural parents, and social agencies work together in planning the care of each child. Some children remain in foster homes until they reach adulthood. But for many foster children, the arrangement is temporary. Some are returned to their natural homes after their natural parents become capable of caring for them. Social agencies find adoptive homes for others.

In the United States, a foster parent must be licensed by his state government. License requirements for foster parents include good health, adequate housing, and certain qualities of personality and family life. Social agencies generally pay for part of the clothing, food, and medical care required by foster children under their supervision.   HELEN D. STONE

See also ADOPTION.

FOUCAULT, FOO KOH, **JEAN BERNARD LÉON** (1819-1868), a French physicist, used a revolving mirror to measure the speed of light. Some types of measuring apparatus still use adaptations of his method. Foucault proved in 1850 that light travels more slowly in water than in air, and that the speed varies inversely with the index of refraction. He also made various improvements in the mirrors of reflecting telescopes. Foucault demonstrated the rotation of the earth on its axis with a pendulum experiment, and also by using a gyroscope that maintained its axis in a fixed direction while the earth turned relative to that direction (see GYROSCOPE; PENDULUM [picture: Foucault Pendulum]). He also discovered the existence of eddy currents, which are produced in a conductor moving in a magnetic field. Foucault was born in Paris.   R. T. ELLICKSON

FOUL BROOD. See BEE (Enemies).

FOULARD, foo LAHRD, is a cloth woven in twill (raised diagonal lines). It is a soft, light fabric of silk, cotton, or rayon, and is always printed. Clothing makers use foulard for neckties, bathrobes, dresses, and suit and coat linings. It comes in 27- to 40-inch (69- to 102-centimeter) widths.

FOUNDATION. See BUILDING CONSTRUCTION; HOUSE.

FOUNDATIONS are organizations that aid research, cultural progress, and human welfare. Gifts of money from wealthy persons and groups help establish and finance most foundations. Three of the best-known foundations in the United States are the Ford Foundation, the Rockefeller Foundation and the Lilly Endowment. Their grants total about $290 million a year.

The government does not tax most foundations because foundations do not make profits. However, some kinds of foundations pay a tax on the income received from their investments. Many foundations are called *corporations, endowments, funds,* or *trusts.* There are about 26,000 foundations in the United States, not including privately endowed colleges, hospitals, and scientific societies. These foundations have assets of about $29 billion. Americans give about $29,400,000,000 to charity every year. The foundations give about $2,100,000,000, or about 7 per cent of this amount. Canada, Great Britain, and Western Europe have a much smaller number of foundations than the United States has.

How Foundations Are Organized

A foundation can be organized as a *trust* or as a *nonprofit corporation* (see CORPORATION; TRUST). It is easier to set up a trust than a nonprofit corporation, because there are fewer legal formalities. A nonprofit corporation can operate with greater freedom, however, because the law does not restrict its powers so narrowly. Both types of foundations are governed by a *trustee* or *trustees,* or legally appointed administrators. The trustees may administer the foundation themselves, or may hire executives to manage the foundation's work.

Foundations are also organized according to the way they spend their funds. A *perpetuity* can spend only the income from its assets. For example, its assets may consist of stocks that pay regular dividends. A *liquidating foundation* must spend all its money within a specified period of time. An *optional foundation* can spend either its income or both the income and the assets. The Carnegie Corporation of New York is a perpetuity. The Julius Rosenwald Fund was self-liquidating. The Rockefeller Foundation is an optional foundation.

Kinds of Foundations

Private Foundations often bear their founders' names and are usually the best known to the public. They include the Carnegie Corporation of New York, the Ford Foundation, and the Rockefeller Foundation. Some private foundations have charters that allow them to operate freely in fields such as education, health, and public welfare. However, many persons organize foundations for specific purposes. If foundations of this kind are organized as perpetuities, they often outlive their original aim. For example, the Bryan Mullanphy Fund, established in St. Louis in 1851, furnished "relief to all poor emigrants and travelers coming to St. Louis on their way . . . to settle in the West." By 1900, it became impossible to find enough persons who could qualify.

Business Foundations are established by business firms. They seldom have large assets, and usually depend on the firms for funds. They often concentrate their work in areas of interest to the founding firms. Business foundations include the United States Steel Foundation, the Westinghouse Educational Foundation, and the General Foods Fund.

Union Foundations, established by labor unions, usually operate in the field of education. Many of them provide scholarships for needy children. For example, the Sidney Hillman Foundation, established by garment workers' unions in 1947, gives college and university scholarships to promising students.

Community Foundations or TRUSTS differ from other foundations, because the people of various communities control them. They depend on private gifts, however. Community foundations usually give money to local welfare programs, rather than to more general projects. Frederick H. Goff, a Cleveland banker, helped establish the Cleveland Foundation, the first community foundation, in 1914.

The Work of Foundations

Foundations carry out their work in two ways. *Grant-making foundations* give money to organizations or persons working in a certain field. Most of the larger foundations do this. *Operating foundations* employ their own staffs to do their work. Some foundations use both methods.

Education has always been one of the chief areas of foundation interest. For example, the General Education Board, a Rockefeller charity, worked to raise the level of secondary and higher education in the Southern States. The Carnegie Foundation for the Advancement of Teaching provides pensions for retired college teachers and their widows (see CARNEGIE FOUNDATION FOR THE ADVANCEMENT OF TEACHING). The Ford Foundation gave money to raise the salaries of teachers in private colleges and universities in the United States. The Ford Foundation has the largest assets of any foundation (see FORD FOUNDATION). The Ford Foundation and the Carnegie Corporation of New York together established the National Merit Scholarship Corporation in 1955. The scholarship corporation provides college and university scholarships. The National Merit scholarships are awarded to outstanding high school students (see SCHOLARSHIP).

Social Welfare. For many years, various foundations have given money to help needy persons. But in the 1950's, research programs designed to solve specific social problems began to replace gifts to charity. For example, the Field Foundation, Inc., and the Russell Sage Foundation have sponsored important programs dealing with the psychological, health, and social problems of youth and the aged (see FIELD FOUNDATION, INC.; SAGE FOUNDATION, RUSSELL).

Health and Medicine attract much foundation aid. For example, the Carnegie Corporation sponsored a study of medical education by Abraham Flexner that resulted in a vast improvement in medical schools in the United States (see FLEXNER, ABRAHAM). The Rockefeller Foundation aids medical research, and has sponsored valuable campaigns against hookworm, malaria, and yellow fever (see ROCKEFELLER FOUNDATION). The Robert Wood Johnson Foundation sponsors programs to improve the quality of health care in the United States and the public's access to it. The John and Mary R. Markle Foundation offers scholarships and fellowships for medical study and research. The Albert and Mary Lasker Foundation gives several grants in medical

FOUNDATIONS

research each year. Several community and private foundations aid the handicapped, such as victims of defective hearing, sight, and speech. The Foundation for Child Development supports this work.

Science. Foundations often support scientific projects that the federal government will not finance. Before World War II, the Rockefeller Foundation provided funds for the construction of a cyclotron at the University of California. Research resulting from this project helped in the development of the atomic bomb. The Carnegie Corporation of New York provides funds for the National Research Council, an agency devoted to science research. The National Science Foundation, a federal government agency, also encourages science

LEADING UNITED STATES FOUNDATIONS

Name	Assets	Founded	Address
1. Ford Foundation*	$2,070,728,000	1936	320 E. 43rd St., New York, N.Y. 10017
2. Lilly Endowment*	1,142,605,000	1937	2801 N. Meridian St., Indianapolis, Ind. 46208
3. Johnson Foundation, Robert Wood*	970,653,746	1936	Forrestal Center, P.O. Box 2316, Princeton, N.J. 08540
4. Rockefeller Foundation*	747,252,258	1913	1133 Avenue of the Americas, New York, N.Y. 10036
5. Kellogg Foundation, W. K.*	747,012,414	1930	400 North Ave., Battle Creek, Mich. 49016
6. Kresge Foundation*	623,624,842	1924	2401 W. Big Beaver Rd., Troy, Mich. 48084
7. Mellon Foundation, Andrew W.*	623,417,000	1969	140 E. 62nd St., New York, N.Y. 10021
8. Pew Memorial Trust*	512,074,000	1948	1529 Walnut St., Philadelphia, Pa. 19102
9. Duke Endowment*	380,071,263	1924	30 Rockefeller Plaza, New York, N.Y. 10020
10. Sloan Foundation, Alfred P.*	256,662,156	1934	630 Fifth Ave., New York, N.Y. 10020
11. Mott Foundation, Charles Stewart*	255,843,124	1926	510 Mott Foundation Building, Flint, Mich. 48502
12. Carnegie Corporation of New York*	246,844,732	1911	437 Madison Ave., New York, N.Y. 10022
13. Mellon Foundation, Richard King	231,365,000	1947	525 William Penn Place, Pittsburgh, Pa. 15230
14. Houston Endowment	201,713,218	1937	P.O. Box 52338, Houston, Tex. 77052
15. Bush Foundation	198,967,000	1953	W-962 First National Bank Building, St. Paul, Minn. 55101
16. Hartford Foundation, John A.	179,828,166	1929	405 Lexington Ave., New York, N.Y. 10017
17. Rockefeller Brothers Fund	152,611,018	1940	30 Rockefeller Plaza, New York, N.Y. 10020
18. Gannett Newspaper Foundation, Frank E.	148,871,883	1935	49 S. Fitzhugh St., Rochester, N.Y. 14614
19. Brown Foundation	142,115,000	1951	P.O. Box 13646, Houston, Tex. 77019
20. Cleveland Foundation	139,953,000	1914	700 National City Bank Building, Cleveland, Ohio 44114
21. New York Community Trust	137,684,347	1923	415 Madison Ave., New York, N.Y. 10017
22. Penn Foundation, William	125,669,000	1945	920 Suburban Station Building, 1617 John F. Kennedy Blvd., Philadelphia, Pa. 19103
23. Commonwealth Fund*	123,522,162	1918	1 E. 75th St., New York, N.Y. 10021
24. Moody Foundation	116,609,000	1942	704 Moody National Bank Building, Galveston, Tex. 77550
25. Dow Foundation, Herbert H. and Grace A.	111,014,000	1936	P.O. Box 632, Midland, Mich. 48640
26. Welch Foundation, Robert A.	110,830,000	1954	2010 Bank of the Southwest Building, Houston, Tex. 77002
27. Fleischmann Foundation, Max C.	109,024,512	1951	P.O. Box 1871, Reno, Nev. 89505
28. Kenan Charitable Trust, William R., Jr.	107,320,000	1965	120 Broadway, Room 3046, New York, N.Y. 10005
29. Board of Directors of City Trusts, City of Philadelphia	106,000,000	1869	21 S. 12th St., Philadelphia, Pa. 19107
30. De Rance	104,568,520	1946	7700 W. Blue Mound Road, Milwaukee, Wis. 53213
31. Longwood Foundation	102,245,852	1937	2024 DuPont Building, Wilmington, Del. 19898
32. Alcoa Foundation	101,654,148	1952	1501 Alcoa Building, Pittsburgh, Pa. 15219
33. Northwest Area Foundation	100,528,883	1950	West 975, First National Bank Building, St. Paul, Minn. 55101
34. Danforth Foundation*	98,948,826	1927	222 S. Central Ave., St. Louis, Mo. 63105
35. Surdna Foundation	96,177,826	1917	200 Park Ave., New York, N.Y. 10017
36. Guggenheim Memorial Foundation, John Simon*	90,014,000	1925	90 Park Ave., New York, N.Y. 10016
37. Atlantic Foundation	86,000,000	1964	P.O. Box 6337, Lawrenceville, N.J. 08648

IMPORTANT CANADIAN FOUNDATIONS

Name	Assets	Founded	Address
Atkinson Charitable Foundation	$16,950,951	1942	One Younge St., Toronto, Ont. M5E 1E5
Bickell Foundation, J. P.	34,312,497	1951	National Trust Co., 21 King St. E., Toronto 210, Ont.
Donner Canadian Foundation	†20,000,000	1950	P.O. Box 122, Toronto-Dominion Centre, Toronto 111, Ont.
Lévesque Foundation, J. Louis	† 7,000,000	1961	360 Rue St. Jacques, Montreal, Que.
McConnell Foundation, J. W.	†65,000,000	1937	630 Dorchester Blvd. W., Montreal 101, Que.
McLaughlin Foundation, R. Samuel	†18,000,000	1951	National Trust Co., 21 King St. E., Toronto, Ont. M5C 1B3
Vancouver Foundation	40,421,327	1943	1177 W. Hastings St., Vancouver 1, B.C.
Winnipeg Foundation	10,471,200	1921	701 Montreal Trust Bldg., Winnipeg, Man. R3B 1N3

*Has separate article in WORLD BOOK.   †Estimates from various sources.

Sources: Questionnaires to foundations in 1972, 1973, and 1976.

research. But this foundation depends on Congress for funds (see NATIONAL SCIENCE FOUNDATION).

Literature and the Fine Arts are helped by the foundations that award scholarships and fellowships to talented persons. The John Simon Guggenheim Memorial Foundation has been one of the leaders in giving this kind of aid. The Ford Foundation has helped the American Council of Learned Societies, which uses part of these funds for scholarships and fellowships. The Ford Foundation also has given money to universities and colleges for the publication of scholarly books. The Carnegie Corporation of New York helps strengthen liberal arts programs in universities and colleges. It also has contributed to art and music appreciation by providing universities and colleges with reproductions of art works and recordings of music. The A. W. Mellon Educational and Charitable Trust gave about $20 million to build and maintain the National Gallery of Art in Washington, D.C. (see NATIONAL GALLERY OF ART).

Religion. Few large foundations aid specific religious groups, but many small foundations make such gifts. Several foundations have given large sums to interdenominational programs and religious education. The Edward W. Hazen Foundation has contributed to religious education in colleges. The Sealantic Fund, a Rockefeller charity, aids theological schools and the American Association of Theological Schools.

Citizenship has interested many foundations. The Maurice and Laura Falk Foundation has helped a number of universities and colleges train students for participation in politics. The Ford Foundation and one of the independent foundations it created, The Fund for the Republic, have made many large grants to support education in citizenship and democracy.

International Understanding. Many foundations support programs in the United States and in other countries to improve international relations. In 1910, Andrew Carnegie established the Carnegie Endowment for International Peace. The Carnegie Endowment helps encourage mutual knowledge and understanding among nations. The Carnegie Endowment, W. K. Kellogg Foundation, Rockefeller Foundation, and others support *exchange programs*. These programs help Americans study and teach in other countries, and bring persons from other countries to study and teach in the United States.

Other Interests. Foundations have many special interests. For example, the Ford Foundation established Resources for the Future, Inc., an organization interested in the conservation of natural resources. The Twentieth Century Fund, Inc., aids and conducts programs in city and regional planning. The Buhl Foundation is also interested in regional planning. It operates Chatham Village, a model community in Pittsburgh.

Canadian Foundations

Canadian foundations do not have the same freedom as U.S. foundations. The government carefully regulates their growth. Canada does not have as many foundations as the United States, nor are they so large. Outstanding Canadian foundations include the Atkinson Charitable Foundation and the J. P. Bickell Foundation. Both have headquarters in Toronto, and limit most of their activities to the province of Ontario. The Atkinson Charitable Foundation gives university and college fellowships to needy students, and supports missionary work among Indians and Eskimos. The J. P. Bickell Foundation aids students and medical research, and makes other gifts to charity. Several large Canadian cities have community foundations, including Vancouver and Winnipeg. Their programs resemble those of community foundations in the United States.

History

The earliest foundations appeared in ancient Egypt and the city-states of ancient Greece. The Greek philosopher Plato established a fund to support his academy. Many Roman emperors set up municipal foundations for the relief of the poor. During the Middle Ages, the Roman Catholic Church administered many private funds for hospitals, schools, and other charitable causes.

The United States had few foundations before the Civil War. In 1790, Benjamin Franklin's will established funds for the poor in Boston and Philadelphia. In 1846, the Smithsonian Institution was founded with funds left by the scientist James Smithson, "for the increase and diffusion of knowledge among men."

The Peabody and Slater funds became the first modern foundations in the United States. George Peabody, an American banker, founded the Peabody Fund in London in 1867. John Fox Slater, a manufacturer, founded the Slater Fund in New York in 1882. They created the funds to aid education in the South following the Civil War. Andrew Carnegie, one of the greatest steel manufacturers in the United States, spread the idea in the early 1900's that people with large fortunes should devote part of their wealth to the betterment of humanity. Carnegie established many foundations, including the Carnegie Endowment for International Peace and the Carnegie Corporation of New York. Many other wealthy people, such as Edward S. Harkness and Andrew W. Mellon, followed Carnegie's example. The number of foundations in the United States has increased steadily in recent years. Extremely high income and inheritance taxes have been a significant factor in promoting this growth.   JOSEPH C. KIGER

Related Articles in WORLD BOOK include:

BIOGRAPHIES

For a list of biographies relating to Foundations, see the Related Articles at the end of PHILANTHROPY.

FOUNDATIONS

See the separate articles on the foundations in the *table* with this article. See also the following WORLD BOOK articles:

Carnegie Endowment for International Peace	Juilliard Musical Foundation
Carnegie Foundation for the Advancement of Teaching	Mayo Foundation
	New York Foundation
	Peabody Education Fund
Carnegie Hero Fund Commission	Sage Foundation, Russell
	Southern Education Foundation
Fels Fund, Samuel S.	United States Steel Foundation
Field Foundation	

OTHER RELATED ARTICLES

Brookings Institution	Rhodes Scholarship
Endowment	Rosenwald Fund, Julius
Fellowship	Scholarship
Research	

FOUNDING FATHERS

FOUNDING FATHERS were statesmen of the Revolutionary War period, particularly those men who wrote the Constitution of the United States. The founding fathers included Benjamin Franklin, Alexander Hamilton, James Madison, George Washington, and other delegates to the Constitutional Convention of 1787. See also CONSTITUTION OF THE UNITED STATES.

FOUNDRY is a shop where workers make one-piece metal *castings*, or molded metal products. Products made in foundries range from engine blocks to toy soldiers. The process of pouring melted metals into molds is called *founding*. The metals commonly used include iron, steel, brass, bronze, aluminum, lead, zinc, and magnesium (see CAST AND CASTING). Dies can also be made in foundries (see DIE AND DIEMAKING).

Foundries that turn out heavy castings often do their founding in large pits in the floor. Overhead cranes ease the work of lifting and carrying the heavy molds and castings from place to place. Sometimes foundries have narrow-gauge tracks and small cars to move finished work.

See also AUTOMATION (Making Railroad Wheels); FORGING; HEAT (picture: Man Uses Heat).

FOUNTAIN is a jet or stream of water that springs from the ground or from a man-made structure, as the result of pressure. In a natural fountain, this pressure comes from the weight of a great amount of water collected in a *reservoir* (container) some distance away.

The water follows an underground passage from the reservoir to the fountain outlet. Pumps supply the pressure in man-made fountains.

Many famous fountains occur in nature. In Vaucluse, in southern France, a tremendous volume of water shoots into the air every minute from a circular pool surrounded by lofty cliffs. The waters of this natural fountain flow off through a ravine to form a number of brooks.

Fountains in America. Most American fountains are man-made, and are powered by electric motors. Some people consider the *Tyler-Davidson Fountain* in Cincinnati, Ohio, one of the finest in the world. It was cast in Munich, Germany, at a cost of $200,000. Lorado Taft designed a fountain called *The Spirit of the Great Lakes* in Chicago. Five female figures represent the five Great Lakes of North America (see TAFT, LORADO [picture]). The *Buckingham Memorial Fountain* in Chicago is the largest lighted fountain in the world (see CHICAGO [Places to Visit]).

European Fountains. In ancient Greece and Rome, most people were too poor to have water brought to their homes. So they drew their household water from one of the many well-designed fountains scattered throughout the countryside. The Greeks told a legend about a wood nymph, Arethusa, who bathed in a river one day. The river god pursued Arethusa, but the goddess Diana changed her into a lovely fountain to save her (see ARETHUSA).

In Italy, people especially like the *Fontana Maggiore* in Perugia, and the *Trevi Fountain* and *The Fountain of*

Designed by Niccolo Salvi and Giuseppe Pannini and completed (1762) with statues by Gian Battista Maini and Pietro Bracci; Holmes, Ewing Galloway

Fountain of Trevi, Rome's most magnificent public fountain, *left*, features the sea-god Neptune in a chariot of shells, being pulled by sea horses and tritons. Streams of water pour from the mouths of dolphins on the stone fountain of La Fama in Madrid, *above.*

Jets of Water Form an Unusual Fountain at the south end of an artificial lake at the General Motors Technical Center in Warren, Mich. Pressure causes the water to become a cloudy mist at the top of the 115-foot (35-meter) water curtain.

the Rivers in Rome. Germans admire the *Schöne Brunnen* at Nuremberg. The French take pride in the beautiful *Fontaine des Innocents* in Paris and the fountains at Versailles.   WILLIAM T. ARNETT

See also ARTESIAN WELL; GEYSER; GREECE, ANCIENT (color picture, At the Fountain House).

FOUNTAIN OF CASTALIA. See PARNASSUS.

FOUNTAIN OF YOUTH was an imaginary spring. Many legends were told about it in both Europe and America. Its waters were supposed to make old persons young, and to heal all kinds of sickness. Tribes of Indians in Central America and the West Indies thought the spring was in the Bahama Islands. Spanish explorers searched for it throughout the area. Ponce de León searched for the fountain in Florida, but he never found it. A spring in St. Augustine, Fla., is shown today as one that he discovered.   WALTER C. LANGSAM

FOUNTAIN PEN. See PEN.

FOUR CORNERS is the only place in the United States where four states meet. Arizona, Colorado, New Mexico, and Utah come together at this point (see ROCKY MOUNTAIN STATES [map]). A monument marks the site. It is surrounded by a concrete platform which bears the seals of the four states.

FOUR-CYCLE ENGINE. See GASOLINE ENGINE.

FOUR-EYED FISH. See ANABLEPS.

FOUR FREEDOMS. President Franklin D. Roosevelt, in a message to Congress on Jan. 6, 1941, said that any settlements made after World War II should be based on "four freedoms." He defined these four freedoms as freedom of speech, freedom of worship, freedom from want, and freedom from fear.

He asked Congress for laws allowing him to lend or lease war materials to countries fighting the Axis, or to any country whose defense was important to the United States (see LEND-LEASE). President Roosevelt's words were as follows:

"In the future days, which we seek to make secure, we look forward to a world founded upon four essential human freedoms.

"The first is freedom of speech and expression—everywhere in the world.

"The second is freedom of every person to worship God in his own way—everywhere in the world.

"The third is freedom from want—which, translated into world terms, means economic understandings which will secure to every nation a healthy peaceful life for its inhabitants—everywhere in the world.

"The fourth is freedom from fear—which, translated into world terms, means a worldwide reduction of armaments to such a point and in such a thorough fashion that no nation will be in a position to commit an act of physical aggression against any neighbor—anywhere in the world."

373

The 4-H Emblem is a four-leaf clover with an H on each leaf. The four H's stand for *head, heart, hands,* and *health.*

National 4-H Council

Many 4-H'ers work on clothing projects. These members are learning to sew and will display their project in a fashion show.

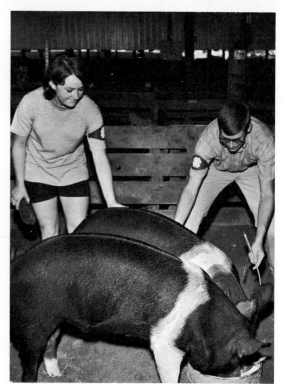

National 4-H Council

Exhibiting Hogs at the County Fair is part of a 4-H livestock project. Members may also raise cattle, poultry, or sheep.

4-H is an organization that helps young people learn useful skills, serve their communities, and have fun together. The 4-H slogan is "Learn by Doing." Members learn skills through working on a variety of projects either by themselves or together with other members of a community 4-H club. These projects deal with clothing, food, health, raising animals, safety, and many other subjects.

The four H's stand for *head, heart, hands,* and *health.* Members show their high ideals with their motto, *Make the Best Better,* and with this pledge:

I pledge
My *Head* to clearer thinking,
My *Heart* to greater loyalty,
My *Hands* to larger service, and
My *Health* to better living,
for my club, my community, my country, and my world.

More than 80 countries have 4-H or similar organizations. Over 5½ million young people in the United States, Puerto Rico, Guam, and the Virgin Islands belong to 4-H. Almost 1¼ million more young people receive assistance from 4-H, even though they are not members. Canadian 4-H clubs have almost 75,000 members.

In the United States, anyone 9 through 19 years old may join 4-H. In Canada, the ages for membership vary depending on the province. Most members belong to neighborhood 4-H clubs, which have at least one adult volunteer leader. But teen-agers may also start a 4-H special interest group, such as a workshop on managing money. Unlike 4-H clubs, special interest groups are only temporary. After a group completes one workshop, it may start another or the members may join other special interest groups. Young people may also belong to 4-H through a 4-H television series, which guides them in doing projects at home.

Most 4-H clubs serve their communities with one or more special projects a year. For example, a club might plant trees or conduct a bicycle safety program. Many 4-H clubs prepare educational exhibits for community fairs.

There is no official 4-H uniform. But many members sew 4-H emblems on their clothing. The emblem is a green four-leaf clover with a white H printed on each leaf.

The 4-H movement began in the United States during the early 1900's. At first, only farm children belonged to the organization. They worked on such projects as canning, and raising livestock, poultry, and crops. City youngsters joined 4-H in greater numbers after clubs added projects of greater interest to them, such as automobile care and safety and career studies. Today, about a fourth of the 4-H members in the United States live on farms. The rest live in other rural areas and in cities, towns, and suburbs.

The Cooperative Extension Service, a joint project of the federal, state, and county governments, guides 4-H work in the United States. The extension service works in cooperation with state land-grant universities (see LAND-GRANT COLLEGE OR UNIVERSITY). An extension office in nearly every county in the United States employs one or more agents. The agents recruit and as-

374

sist local 4-H leaders and help members with their projects.

Projects and Activities

Individual Projects. Each 4-H member carries out at least one project a year. In most states, he or she may select the project from a list of 50 to 100 choices. A member may also design his own project. A 4-H project may involve almost any subject that encourages the young person to learn and to use his imagination.

Some subjects have several project levels, and so members may continue working in these subject areas over a number of years. Other projects are for certain age groups. For example, projects for older members include career studies and money management.

Many 4-H members who live in rural areas choose projects that deal with crops and livestock, farm machinery, forestry, and marketing. Both city and rural members enjoy projects involving clothing, conservation, food, home improvement, photography, and woodworking.

Various 4-H projects that were once limited to farm youngsters have been developed to serve members in cities as well. A rural youngster, for example, may choose a project in raising and caring for his horse. A city youth who does not own a horse may select a project in horsemanship. Projects that once helped rural youths learn how to raise crops have also been made more flexible for city members. For example, suburban youths may learn how to plant large gardens. Inner city members, who have limited space, may learn how to tend backyard plots, window boxes, or indoor plants.

Each 4-H member receives a booklet that explains the requirements of his project. The booklet also contains information and questions to make the member think and learn about his subject. A booklet for a gardening project, for example, might include facts on soils and fertilization, planting and cultivation, plant diseases, and insect control.

The county extension office provides visual aids and other teaching materials. County agents and volunteer leaders visit members at home to review their projects.

Many 4-H members finish a year's project by preparing an educational exhibit about their subject for a local or county fair. Other members finish their project work by taking part in fashion shows, tractor-operator contests, or other special activities related to their projects. Some members prepare talks and demonstrations to share what they have learned. Members may earn medals, certificates, ribbons, trophies, and scholarships for their work.

Group Activities. Each 4-H club meets at least once a month in a member's home or a public building. Most meetings allow time for club business, an educational program, and games or other recreation. Adult volunteer leaders take part in the activities.

During the educational part of the meeting, a club member may present a talk or demonstration or lead a group discussion. A business or civic leader might speak to the club about his work. Clubs with several members involved in the same project may hold separate educational meetings about that topic. An adult with an interest in the subject may serve as a project leader.

Teen-agers interested in a particular subject, such as conservation or health, may organize a joint project or workshop dealing with that subject. Members of such 4-H special interest groups need not belong to a local club. After completing a project or workshop, the group may start another one. Or the members may join other special interest groups.

Most 4-H clubs carry on community service activities. For example, they may assist when bloodmobiles visit their neighborhood, or they may lead community beautification programs. Many 4-H clubs fight such problems as drug abuse and pollution. Club members may help the aged, the blind, the mentally retarded, and the poor.

Members of 4-H get together for all kinds of recreation. They hold picnics and sporting events and go on hikes. Some clubs organize music and drama programs.

Conservation and Environmental Pollution are topics of interest to 4-H members in both urban and rural areas. These 4-H'ers are using screens and sieves to test for pollution in a stream.

Camping is a favorite 4-H activity, and more than 430,-000 members attend 4-H camps each summer.

Older 4-H members may join county senior clubs and councils or county junior leader groups. Members of these organizations are especially active in community service programs. They also develop leadership abilities as they help younger 4-H members with their projects.

Organization

In the United States, the federal, state, and county governments contribute funds to 4-H work through the Cooperative Extension Service. They also cooperate in employing the county extension agents. The state land-grant universities and the U.S. Department of Agriculture supply educational materials for 4-H members. They also help organize national and state 4-H events.

The 4-H program in Canada receives support from the federal and provincial governments. The Provincial Extension Service, an agency similar to the U.S. Cooperative Extension Service, has offices in each province. Business and nonprofit organizations also support 4-H in both the United States and Canada.

Young people may join a 4-H club already in their community, or they may organize a new club. In the United States, members join through their county extension office. In Canada, they enroll through the provincial 4-H agencies. The United States has about 134,-000 local clubs, and Canada has about 6,000.

Most 4-H clubs choose their own adult volunteer leaders. Many select a parent or other relative of a club member. Teen-agers may become junior or teen leaders after several years of 4-H work. They assist adult leaders and help younger members with their work and their project records.

Each 4-H club elects its own officers, decides whether to collect dues, and makes other local rules. The officers may receive special training from older 4-H youths and from adults. Members and leaders together plan their club's program for the year.

County extension agents help organize 4-H programs within the county. They also help train leaders.

Each state has a 4-H leader at the state land-grant university. State leaders and their staffs choose the 4-H projects their state will offer and organize statewide 4-H events. They also help prepare aids and materials for members and volunteer leaders. At the national level, 4-H is directed by an assistant administrator and a staff for 4-H and youth programs in the U.S. Department of Agriculture.

4-H Sponsors. In the United States, the National 4-H Council, a nonprofit corporation, supports 4-H work on a nationwide basis. The council helps arrange and conduct 4-H activities and events, operates public information services, and develops educational materials.

The council publishes project handbooks, leaders' guides, and the *National 4-H News*, a magazine for adult and junior 4-H leaders. It organizes sponsored programs in which outstanding 4-H members receive awards for their work. These awards include medals of honor, scholarships, and free trips to national 4-H events. The council also operates the National 4-H Supply Service, a mail-order house that offers more than 1,500 items bearing the 4-H emblem.

The National 4-H Center in Washington, D.C., is managed by the council. Club members may attend summer courses on leadership and citizenship at the center. The council also holds leader-training and professional improvement sessions at the center and at other locations throughout the United States.

The council sponsors the International 4-H Youth Exchange and other international programs. About 2,000 adults and young people annually participate in the council's international 4-H programs.

The National 4-H Council was established in 1976. It resulted from the merger of two previous 4-H sponsors—the National 4-H Service Committee and the National 4-H Foundation. A 20-member board of trustees administers the National 4-H Council. Its work is supported by contributions from corporations, foundations,

Food Projects teach 4-H members cooking skills. They learn the principles of nutrition and how to prepare balanced meals.

Projects for Older Members may help them choose a career. The 4-H group shown above is discussing management planning.

and individuals. The council has offices at 150 N. Wacker Drive, Chicago, Ill. 60606, and at 7100 Connecticut Avenue NW, Washington, D.C. 20015.

In Canada, the provincial departments of education administer the 4-H programs in each province. Two national groups—the Canadian Council on 4-H Clubs and the Canadian 4-H Foundation—provide educational support. The council coordinates 4-H programs and events in Canada, and the foundation raises funds for 4-H. Members of both groups represent business and nonprofit organizations and the national and provincial governments. The council and foundation have their headquarters at 185 Somerset Street W., Ottawa, Ont. K2P 0J2.

National, State, and County Events. Soon after Thanksgiving each year, about 1,600 American 4-H members meet in Chicago for the National 4-H Congress. Most delegates receive free trips to the congress as winners of state, district, or national 4-H contests in such areas as 4-H projects or citizenship. The congress also honors individuals and business firms for their services to 4-H. Delegates discuss problems that affect young people in the United States and hear speeches by leaders in agriculture, government, industry, and science.

Each spring, about 250 delegates from the United States and Canada attend the weeklong National 4-H Conference in Washington, D.C. The conference delegates tour the city, hear speakers, and help plan 4-H programs.

The United States observes National 4-H Week each year during the first full week of October. Newspaper and magazine articles and radio and television programs stress the educational values of 4-H. During the week, clubs review their work and plan new programs.

Many states sponsor meetings similar to the national conferences. Other state as well as county events include fairs, workshops, camps, and exhibitions.

Each November, the Canadian Council on 4-H Clubs sponsors a weeklong National 4-H Conference in Toronto. About 80 Canadian and 10 American 4-H members participate in the conference. They tour Toronto,

meet government and business officials, discuss social and economic issues, and exchange ideas about 4-H work.

History

The 4-H movement started in the United States in many places at about the same time. During the 1890's and early 1900's, educators in several states began programs to teach farm children useful skills. In 1896, Liberty Hyde Bailey, a naturalist at Cornell University, began to publish nature study leaflets for country schools and to organize nature study clubs.

Corn, canning, and poultry clubs that stressed learning by doing started in several Southern and Midwestern states in the early 1900's. Schoolteachers and school superintendents organized most of these clubs. In 1902, A. B. Graham, a township school superintendent in Ohio, began one of the first clubs similar to today's local 4-H clubs. Graham's club held regular meetings with planned programs. Members worked on projects dealing with corn and other vegetables, flowers, and soil testing.

In 1902, the University of Illinois helped O. J. Kern, a county school superintendent, organize local agricultural clubs in Winnebago County, Illinois. In 1904, Will B. Otwell, an Illinois agricultural leader, encouraged 8,000 Illinois farm boys to exhibit their corn projects at the Louisiana Purchase Centennial Exposition in St. Louis. W. H. Smith, a county school superintendent, began to organize local corn clubs in Holmes County, Mississippi, in 1907. Girls' canning clubs started in South Carolina in 1910.

The U.S. Department of Agriculture encouraged the formation of the clubs. It appointed Seaman A. Knapp, who had established a cotton demonstration farm in Texas in 1903, to direct club work. Southern land-grant colleges joined with the Agriculture Department in sponsoring the clubs. In 1914, the Smith-Lever Act established the Cooperative Extension Service. The act also granted states federal funds to organize boys' and girls' agricultural clubs, and each state soon set up a club department. Gradually, boys and girls began joining the same clubs, as they do today.

During the early 1920's, agricultural clubs throughout the United States adopted the 4-H emblem and the name 4-H Club. Clubs in Iowa had begun to use a clover emblem with white H's about 1910.

Agricultural clubs grew more slowly in Canada. The first clubs began in 1913. But they were not organized nationally until 1931, when the government formed the Canadian Council on Boys' and Girls' Clubs. In 1952, the council changed its name to the Canadian Council on 4-H Clubs. Most Canadian clubs have both boys and girls.

Today, more than 80 nations have 4-H or similar organizations. In several countries, the groups have not adopted all parts of the 4-H program. But all the groups work to help young people develop useful skills and become productive citizens.   Critically reviewed by the

NATIONAL 4-H COUNCIL, INCORPORATED

See also AGRICULTURAL EDUCATION; COUNTY AGRICULTURAL EXTENSION AGENT; COUNTY EXTENSION HOME ECONOMIST.

National 4-H Council

Horsemanship Projects may involve raising horses. Many rural and suburban 4-H'ers exhibit their horses at shows.

FOUR HORSEMEN OF NOTRE DAME

FOUR HORSEMEN OF NOTRE DAME. See FOOTBALL (picture).

FOUR HORSEMEN OF THE APOCALYPSE, *uh PAHK uh lips*, are beings mentioned in the sixth chapter of the last book of the New Testament of the Bible, The Revelation of St. John the Divine. The chapter tells of a scroll in God's right hand that is sealed with seven seals. When the first four of these seals are opened, four horsemen appear. Their horses are white, red, black, and pale (literally, greenish-yellow). The horsemen represent Conquest, War, Famine, and Death.

The four horsemen are often featured in art and literature. The German engraver Albrecht Dürer drew a series about them. The Spanish writer Vicente Blasco Ibáñez wrote a World War I novel titled *The Four Horsemen of the Apocalypse.* MERRILL C. TENNEY

See also APOCALYPSE.

FOUR-O'CLOCK, also called the MARVEL-OF-PERU, is an attractive perennial from tropical America. It is easy to grow, and is cultivated as an annual in North America. The four-o'clock grows from 2 to 4 feet (61 to 120 centimeters) high. Its fragrant flowers may be white, pink, red, yellow, or a mixture of several of these colors. What seem to be flowers are actually colorful *involucres* (modified bracts) surrounding the tiny true flowers. The four-o'clock gets its name because its flowers open late in the afternoon and close in the morning.

The plant grows well in almost any kind of soil. It can be started from seeds, or from its roots, saved for planting in the spring. The four-o'clock makes an attractive, bushy border plant.

J. Horace McFarland
Four-O'Clock

Scientific Classification. Four-o'clocks are in the four-o'clock family, *Nyctaginaceae.* The marvel-of-Peru is genus *Mirabilis*, species *M. jalapa.* ROBERT W. SCHERY

FOURDRINIER MACHINE. See PAPER (How Paper Is Made).

FOURIER, *FOO ree ay*, **CHARLES** (1772-1837), was an important French socialist. He criticized the social conditions of his times, and held that society could be improved if private property were eliminated.

Fourier thought society could be improved through an economic and social regrouping of people. He wanted to create small, self-sufficient farm communities of about 1,600 persons each. Each person would own a share of the property in these communities. All persons would be required to work, but they could choose their own type of work. Fourier's ideas attracted many

Bettmann Archive
Charles Fourier

followers. But he could not get enough money to start such a venture. He was born François Marie Charles Fourier in Besançon, France. BRISON D. GOOCH

FOURNEYRON, BENOÎT. See TURBINE (History).

FOURRAGÈRE. See INSIGNIA.

FOURTEEN POINTS were a set of principles proposed by President Woodrow Wilson as the basis for ending World War I and for keeping the peace. On Jan. 8, 1918, in an address before both houses of Congress, Wilson stated these proposals, which became famous as the *Fourteen Points.* They included "open covenants openly arrived at," removal of economic barriers, and "adjustment of all colonial claims." They also proposed arms reductions, territorial readjustments, and the formation of a "general association of nations."

Wilson never offered any detailed explanation of how the Fourteen Points might be made to work. In spite of this vagueness, millions of persons hailed the principles as the basis for a free world, united in peace. But at the Paris Peace Conference in 1919, Wilson encountered much opposition to the Fourteen Points. His principles were almost lost in the compromises he was forced to make in the peace treaties. NORMAN D. PALMER

For a summary of the text of the Fourteen Points, see WILSON, WOODROW (The Fourteen Points).

FOURTEENTH AMENDMENT to the United States Constitution forbids the states to deny any citizen the rights granted by federal law. It also declares that all citizens are entitled to equal protection of the law. The original purpose of the amendment was to provide citizenship for former slaves and give them full civil rights. Amendment 14 went into effect on July 9, 1868.

Through the years, the Supreme Court of the United States has interpreted the 14th Amendment in different ways. In 1905, in the case of *Lochner v. New York*, the court ruled that state laws regulating wages and hours violated the 14th Amendment. The court held that such laws hampered the right of employers and employees to bargain without government interference. The court reversed this decision in 1937. It ruled that a state had the right to regulate wages, hours, and working conditions in the best interests of the people.

The court applied the equal-protection clause of the 14th Amendment in 1954, in the case of *Brown v. Board of Education of Topeka.* In that case, the court held that separate schools for blacks and whites did not meet the constitutional requirement for equal protection of the law. The Supreme Court has also applied the equal-protection principle to sex discrimination and other civil rights cases. JUNE SOCHEN

See also CONSTITUTION OF THE U.S. (Amendment 14); GOVERNMENT (The Fourteenth Amendment).

FOURTH DIMENSION. We usually think of space as having three dimensions, length, width, and height, as in a cube. Solid geometry is based on three-dimensional space. But many problems cannot be solved by considering only three dimensions. For example, a problem in making an airplane may involve temperature changes at certain heights above sea level at a certain place. Temperature is the fourth dimension in this problem.

Complicated relationships in geometry are usually solved by algebra. Algebra can be applied to four quantities as easily as to three. Four-dimensional geometry is in the same relation to solid geometry as solid geometry is to plane geometry. The language of geometry is used even though a fourth dimension cannot be visualized.

Two mathematicians, Hermann Grassmann (1809-1877) and Georg Friedrich Riemann (1826-1866), applied mathematics to geometry of four and more dimensions. Hermann Minkowski (1864-1909) studied a special case for a point moving in space. The four quantities were three distances used to fix the point of intersection, and the time. This space-time was used by the scientist Albert Einstein in the theory of relativity that he developed in the early 1900's.

Four-dimensional problems are used in the study of all spheres in space. The four "dimensions," or quantities, are three distances used to fix the position of the center of the object, and the radius of the sphere.

Time is often the fourth dimension. Matter, distance, and time are too closely related to be separated. In order to know exactly where a star is, an astronomer must know the direction it is traveling, its position relative to other stars at different points along its path, and also the star's rate of speed. Time is a necessary dimension in astronomical measurement. An airplane pilot uses time to tell the plane's location on a map. A pilot who leaves New York City and flies straight southwest can trace the plane's line of flight on a map. But to tell its exact position on the line, the plane's speed per hour must be multiplied by the number of hours in flight. For example, if the plane has had an average speed of 200 miles an hour for two hours, it is 400 miles along the line. PHILIP FRANKLIN

See also RELATIVITY (Special Theory of Relativity; General Relativity Theory).

FOURTH ESTATE is a name often given to the newspaper profession. Among the members of the fourth estate are those who gather, write, and edit the news for the press. The phrase *Fourth Estate* is believed to have first been used in writing by Thomas Babington Macaulay. In 1828, he wrote in an essay that "The gallery in which the reporters sit has become a fourth estate of the realm." He was adding a term to those already used for the three estates, or classes, of the English realm. These were lords spiritual, lords temporal, and commons. The three estates later came to stand for government, while reference to a Fourth Estate described any other influential body in English political life, such as the army or the press. EARL F. ENGLISH

FOURTH OF JULY. See INDEPENDENCE DAY.

FOURTH REPUBLIC. See FRANCE (History; Government).

FOVEA CENTRALIS. See EYE (The Image on the Retina).

FOWL. See POULTRY; CHICKEN.

FOWLER, HENRY HAMILL (1908-   ), served as secretary of the treasury from 1965 to 1968 under President Lyndon B. Johnson. He had served as undersecretary of the treasury from 1961 to 1964.

Fowler served as legal counsel to the Tennessee Valley Authority (TVA) from 1934 to 1939. During World War II, he served as counsel to the War Production Board. From 1946 to 1951, Fowler practiced law in Washington, D.C. In 1952, he was named to head the Defense Production Administration. Later that year, he was appointed director of the Office of Defense Mobilization. Fowler was born in Roanoke, Va., and was graduated from Yale University. CARL T. ROWAN

G. Ronald Austing, Bruce Coleman, Inc.

The Gray Fox is the only member of the dog family that frequently climbs trees. It may scamper into the branches to escape an enemy or, apparently, for no reason at all.

FOX is a bushy-tailed, sharp-snouted member of the dog family. True foxes include the arctic fox, the gray fox, and the red fox. Several foxlike animals are also called foxes. Foxes and foxlike animals live throughout the world, except in Antarctica and Southeast Asia and on some islands. They may be found in farmlands and forests, on deserts, and even in wooded areas of some cities and suburbs.

Foxes are quick, skillful hunters. The red fox can easily catch a dodging rabbit. This fox can also creep silently toward a bird, then rush up and pounce on it.

Some kinds of foxes, especially the arctic fox and the red fox, have long, soft fur that is valued highly. People trap foxes for their fur and also raise the animals on fur farms (see FUR).

Some people hunt the red fox because of its skill in trying to avoid capture. Many hunters seek only the excitement of the chase and do not kill the fox. The hunters use hounds to follow the scent of the fox. But the fox may double back on its trail or run into water, making its scent difficult to follow.

Most foxes are about the same size. Gray foxes and red foxes, the commonest kinds in the United States and Canada, grow from 23 to 27 inches (58 to 69 centimeters) long. The tail measures an additional 14 to 16 inches (36 to 41 centimeters). Most of these animals weigh from 8 to 11 pounds (3.6 to 5 kilograms).

The Body of a Fox

Most species of foxes resemble small, slender dogs. But unlike most dogs, foxes have a bushy tail. These animals also have large, pointed ears and a long, sharp snout.

A fox has keen hearing and an excellent sense of smell. It depends especially on these two senses in

Joseph A. Davis, the contributor of this article, is General Curator of the North Carolina Zoological Park in Asheboro, N.C.

© Kojo Tanaka, Animals Animals

Jane Burton, Bruce Coleman Ltd.

Red Foxes live in family groups. An adult male and female, *above*, stay together after mating until their pups mature. The same pair may mate year after year. The eyes of all fox pups, *right*, do not open until about nine days after the animals are born.

locating prey. A red fox can hear a mouse squeak over 100 feet (30 meters) away. Foxes quickly see moving objects, but they sometimes do not notice objects that are motionless.

A fox has five toes on each front foot, but the first toe is not completely developed. This toe, called a *dewclaw*, does not reach the ground. Each hind foot has only four toes. When the animal walks or trots, its hind paws step into the tracks of the front paws.

Most foxes carry their tails straight backward when running. The tail droops when the animal walks. A fox may sleep with its tail over its nose and front paws. Many foxes have a scent gland on the tail. Scent from this gland gives foxes a distinctive odor.

The Life of a Fox

Most knowledge about foxes comes from studies of the red fox. The information in this section refers mostly to the red fox, but other species do not differ greatly.

Foxes live in family groups while the young are growing up. At other times, they live alone or in pairs. They do not form packs as wolves do. A male and a female mate in early winter. They play together and cooperate in hunting. If one of a pair of foxes is chased by an enemy, its mate may dash out of a hiding place and lead the pursuers astray.

Foxes communicate with one another with growls, yelps, and short yapping barks. A fox also makes *scent stations* by urinating at various spots. The scent stations tell foxes in the area that another fox is present.

─────────── **FACTS IN BRIEF** ───────────

Names: *Male,* dog; *female,* vixen; *young,* pup or cub.

Gestation Period: 49 to 79 days, depending on species.

Length of Life: Up to 14 years.

Where Found: Throughout the world except Antarctica, Southeast Asia, and some islands.

Scientific Classification: Foxes belong to the dog family Canidae. The bat-eared fox is *Otocyon megalotis.* The gray fox is *Urocyon cinereoargenteus.* The kit fox is *Vulpes velox.* The red fox is *Vulpes fulva.* The maned wolf is *Chrysocyon brachyurus.* The raccoon dog is *Nyctereutes procyonoides.*

J. Simon, Bruce Coleman Inc.

Dens of various kinds of foxes may be underground, in a hollow log or tree, in a cave, or among rocks. Most red foxes enlarge burrows of badgers or woodchucks, but some dig their own dens.

Young. A female fox gives birth to her young in late winter or early spring. A young fox is usually called a *pup,* but may also be called a *cub.* Red foxes have from four to nine pups at a time, and gray foxes have from three to five. Both the *vixen* (female) and the *dog* (male) bring their pups food and lead enemies away from them.

A newborn fox weighs about 4 ounces (110 grams) and has a short muzzle and closed eyes. Its eyes open about nine days after birth. Pups drink the mother's milk for about five weeks. Then they begin to eat some solid food and leave their den for short periods. Later, the pups wrestle with one another and pounce on insects, leaves, sticks, and their parents' tails. The adults also bring live mice for the young to pounce on. Later, the adults show the pups how to stalk prey. The pups start to live on their own in late summer and may wander far from their place of birth. The parents may separate then or in early fall and rejoin during the winter.

Dens. Foxes settle in dens after mating. A fox den may be underground, in a cave, among rocks, or in a hollow log or tree. Some red foxes dig their own dens, but most use burrows abandoned by such animals as woodchucks. The foxes may enlarge a burrow if necessary. An underground den may be as long as 75 feet (23 meters) and have several entrances. A main tunnel leads to several chambers that the animals use for nests and for storing food. Two pairs of red foxes may share one burrow. Gray foxes dig less than red foxes. Most gray foxes live in caves, rock piles, logs, or tree holes.

Many kinds of foxes live in dens only while raising pups. After the pups have grown old enough to hunt for themselves, the adults and the pups both sleep in the open most of the time.

Food. Foxes eat almost any animal they can catch easily, especially mice and other kinds of rodents. They also hunt birds, frogs, insects, lizards, and rabbits. Foxes also eat many kinds of fruit and the remains of dead animals. Most species hide the uneaten parts of their prey. They dig a shallow hole, drop the meat in, and spread dirt over it. A fox returns to the stored food, both to feed and, apparently, to check on it.

Some foxes may prey on farmers' chickens if the birds roam freely or if the chicken coops are not closed tightly. But foxes help farmers by eating mice and rats. In some areas where foxes had been killed off, rodents increased so much that farmers brought in other foxes.

Hunting. Foxes hunt mostly at night and remain active the year around. They often roam grassy meadows and listen for the squeaks of mice. The grass conceals the mice, but if a fox sees a slight movement of blades of grass, it jumps onto the spot. Foxes sometimes stand on their hind legs to get a better view in tall grass. A fox also may lie in wait and pounce on a ground squirrel or a woodchuck as the victim leaves its burrow.

Kinds of Foxes

Red Foxes live throughout most of Asia, Europe, and northern North America. They are the most common foxes of Canada and the northern United States.

The majority of red foxes have bright rusty-red or red-orange fur, with whitish fur on the belly. They have blackish legs and a white tip on the tail. But not all red foxes have red coats. Some, called *silver foxes*, have coats of black fur tipped with white. Silver foxes may appear blackish, gray, or frosty silver, depending on the length of the white tips. Silver foxes with black fur are called *black foxes*. Other red foxes, called *cross foxes*, have

THE SKELETON OF A FOX

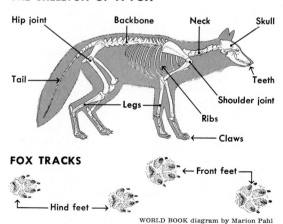

Hip joint · Backbone · Neck · Skull · Teeth · Shoulder joint · Ribs · Claws · Tail · Legs

FOX TRACKS

← Front feet → · Hind feet →

WORLD BOOK diagram by Marion Pahl

Mark Boulton, National Audubon Society

The Bat-Eared Fox received its name because its large rounded ears resemble those of some bats. This fox, which lives in the dry grasslands of Africa, often suns itself near its burrow.

rusty-red coats with a large black cross at the shoulders. The cross extends down the middle of the back. Silver foxes, cross foxes, and typical red foxes may be born at the same time to the same parents.

Kit Foxes, also called *swift foxes*, roam the grasslands and deserts of western North America. The kit fox has sandy yellow-gray fur with a black tip on the tail. This fox, a close relative of the red fox, measures from 15 to 20 inches (38 to 51 centimeters) long, not including a tail 11 inches (28 centimeters) long. It weighs from 4 to 6 pounds (1.8 to 2.7 kilograms). This animal got its name because its small size is like that of a kitten. See ANIMAL (Animals of the Desert [picture]).

Gray Foxes live throughout most of the United States, Mexico, and Central America, and in part of northern South America. Some live in the far southern parts of Canada. They are the most common foxes of the southern United States. The back of a gray fox has the color of salt and pepper mixed together. The animal's underparts are whitish. The sides of the neck, shoulders, and legs, and the underside of the tail are rust-colored. The tail of the gray fox has a black tip. This fox is also called the *tree fox* because it often climbs trees.

Arctic Foxes live in the far northern regions of Asia, Europe, and North America. The long fur of the arctic fox's coat protects the animal from the extreme cold. The arctic fox has shorter, more rounded ears than most other foxes. These small ears let less body heat escape than larger ears would. Arctic foxes are about the same size as red foxes. See ARCTIC FOX.

Fennecs, the smallest kind of foxes, live in the deserts of North Africa and Arabia. A fennec grows only about 16 inches (41 centimeters) long and weighs 2 to 3 pounds (0.9 kilogram to 1.4 kilograms). It has pale sandy fur with whitish underparts. Its ears are 4 to 6 inches (10 to 15 centimeters) long. They have a large surface area through which the animal can lose body heat to keep from becoming overheated. See FENNEC.

Bat-Eared Foxes, also called *big-eared foxes*, live in dry areas of eastern and southern Africa. A bat-eared fox has large ears that resemble those of a fennec. It has a gray-brown back and sandy underparts. This animal is about the size of a red fox. Bat-eared foxes feed mostly on insects, especially termites. They also eat fruits and such rodents as mice and rats. Bat-eared foxes can change direction sharply while running at full speed, and this ability helps them catch rodents.

South American "Foxes" are not true foxes, but they resemble foxes. They include several grayish or brownish animals of various sizes. The largest one, the *maned wolf*, grows as long as 4 feet (1.2 meters) and may weigh 50 pounds (23 kilograms). It is called a wolf because of its large size, but it looks like a long-legged red fox. It has long, yellowish-orange fur that grows especially long and manelike along the middle of its back. The maned wolf has such long legs in proportion to its body that it is often called the "fox that walks on stilts." It feeds on insects, small animals, and fruits. See ANIMAL (Bodies [picture: Stiltlike Legs]).

Raccoon Dogs, which live in eastern Asia, have chunky, grayish bodies and masked faces that make them look like raccoons. But these animals are closely related to foxes. They are no more closely related to raccoons than are any other members of the dog family. A raccoon dog measures about 22 inches (56 centimeters) long, not including a tail 6 inches (15 centimeters) long. It weighs up to 18 pounds (8 kilograms). Raccoon dogs that live in places with bitter cold winters sleep during much of the winter. JOSEPH A. DAVIS

FOX, CHARLES JAMES (1749-1806), a brilliant English statesman and speaker, became a friend of the American colonies in their fight for freedom. He also defended the French Revolution when most British statesmen, including Edmund Burke, opposed it. He was sympathetic, had a warm personality, and was an eloquent speaker.

Fox was born in Westminster. In 1768, he entered Parliament as a Tory, but later joined the Whig Party. Because of his support in Parliament of the American colonies during the Revolutionary War, King George III became his enemy. His career was also disturbed by the opposition of William Pitt. Fox had a major role in the preliminaries of the impeachment of Warren Hastings (see HASTINGS, WARREN). Fox became England's secretary for foreign affairs in 1806. ANDRÉ MAUROIS

Lithograph by Leopold Grozelier;
Chicago Historical Society

George Fox

FOX, GEORGE (1624-1691), an English religious leader, founded the Society of Friends, or Quakers, about 1647. He taught that the presence of the "Inner Light" in the individual should aid that person's conscience in guiding his faith and actions. His followers were first called *Quakers* because Fox once told a British judge "to tremble at the word of the Lord." See QUAKERS.

As a young man, Fox believed that he had received a divine call, and began going from place to place preaching his ideas of religion. He advised people to give up their worldly pleasures. He made missionary trips through Ireland, Scotland, the West Indies, North America, and The Netherlands, and had many followers. He was imprisoned and publicly punished many times because of his religious beliefs. Fox was born in Leicestershire, England. GEORGE L. MOSSE

FOX, PAULA (1923-   ), an American author, won the 1974 Newbery medal for her children's novel *The Slave Dancer*. This story describes the experiences of a white boy and a black slave aboard an American ship carrying slaves from Africa in 1840.

Paula Fox was born in New York City. Her other children's books include *How Many Miles to Babylon?* (1967), *The Stone-Faced Boy* (1968), *Portrait of Ivan* (1969), and *Blowfish Live in the Sea* (1970). She also has written several books for adults. ZENA SUTHERLAND

FOX HUNT, or RIDING TO HOUNDS, is a sport that originated in England in about the middle 1700's. The

H. Armstrong Roberts

Foxhounds are used in packs for hunting foxes. This kind of fox hunting is popular in England, and it is occasionally enjoyed in certain parts of the United States.

sport consists of finding a wild fox, and hunting it by scent with a pack of hounds especially trained for the purpose. The fox hunters, mounted on horses bred and trained for the sport, follow the hounds across the countryside, over fences, ditches, and streams. This group of mounted followers is called the *field*. It is led by the *master of foxhounds*. The pack of hounds is managed in the hunting field by the *huntsman*.

The first packs of hounds used only for fox hunting were established in England. Colonial settlers in Virginia, Maryland, and Pennsylvania brought the sport to America. GILBERT MATHER

See also AMERICAN FOXHOUND; ENGLISH FOXHOUND; VIRGINIA (color picture).

FOX INDIANS. See SAUK INDIANS.

FOX TERRIER is a small, lively, black-and-white dog. There are two kinds of fox terriers, the *smooth-coated* and the *wire-haired*. The only difference between them is that the wire-haired type has longer and harsher hair. The fox terrier weighs about 15 to 19 pounds (7 to 9 kilograms). It has a white coat, with black or tan patches, or both. Owners usually cut the tail short a few days after the dog is born. The quick action of the short upright tail gives the dog a gay look. The fox terrier's ears fold over into a V-shaped end. The head is somewhat long and squarely built. A good fox terrier should have legs well suited for running. Its front legs should be straight. The English first bred fox terriers. They used them to hunt foxes. After the hounds had driven a fox into its burrow, the terrier went in and drove it out. To do this, the dog had to have hard muscles, quickness, and courage. Fox terriers make delightful companions and are popular as pets. See also DOG (color picture: Terriers). JOSEPHINE Z. RINE

FOX TROT is a ballroom dance that combines short, rapid steps with occasional slides and glides. The name *fox trot* is used to include all ballroom dancing done in walking time. The fox trot began in the United States, about 1912. In its first form, the dance consisted mainly of alternating short and long steps in a somewhat trotting fashion. Later, slow steps and quick fox trots appeared. The *blues* music of the late 1920's was popular for the slow fox trot. *Swing* music is usually played for the fast fox trot.

FOXFIRE. See WILL-O'-THE WISP.

W. Atlee Burpee
The Foxglove is a valuable source of the powerful heart stimulant, digitalis.

FOXGLOVE is the name for a group of plants belonging to the figwort family. The foxglove gets its name from its flowers, which are shaped somewhat like fingers. The leaves of the purple foxglove contain a powerful poison called *digitalis*. In rare cases, children and animals have died from eating foxgloves. Physicians use small amounts of digitalis to treat certain heart diseases (see DIGITALIS).

The foxglove grows from 2 to 4 feet (61 to 120 centimeters) tall. The long oval leaves grow along the stem. The flowers are purple, lilac, yellow, or white —the deeper-colored ones more or less spotted. They are bell-shaped, and grow along one side of a wandlike cluster. The plants are biennials or short-lived perennials, usually dying after the second season. New seed should be planted yearly to keep foxglove in continual bloom.

Scientific Classification. Foxgloves belong to the figwort family, *Scrophulariaceae*. Purple foxglove is genus *Digitalis*, species *D. purpurea*. H. D. HARRINGTON

See also SUPERSTITION (The Role of Superstitions).

FOXHOUND is a medium-sized hound. Packs of hounds hunt foxes by following their scent on the ground. The American Kennel Club recognizes two distinct breeds, American and English. See AMERICAN FOXHOUND; ENGLISH FOXHOUND. OLGA DAKAN

FOXX, JIMMY (1907-1967), became one of the leading home run hitters in baseball history. A big, strong right-handed batter, Foxx hit 534 home runs during 21 seasons in the major leagues.

A first baseman, Foxx played for the Philadelphia

Athletics under manager Connie Mack from 1925 to 1935. He also played for the Boston Red Sox (1936-1942), the Chicago Cubs (1942-1944), and the Philadelphia Phillies (1945). He had a .325 lifetime batting average in the major leagues. He was elected to the National Baseball Hall of Fame in 1951. James Emory Foxx was born in Sudlersville, Md. JOSEPH P. SPOHN

FRA ANGELICO, *frah ahn JEH lee koh* (1400?-1455), was an Italian painter. He helped pioneer Renaissance methods of art in the city of Florence. His strong, plain figures in measured space reflected the newer ideas of his time, but he continued to use the bright, unshadowed colors that were traditional. He had many imitators who added sentimental flavor to his style. Such work has been credited to him.

Fra Angelico was a Dominican monk. When the great new monastery of San Marco in Florence was established about 1435, he became a member and remained one until his death. He covered the walls of the monastery with religious images. Many of his other paintings are now collected there as a museum of his work. One of his paintings, *The Annunciation*, appears in the PAINTING article. Fra Angelico's other works include *The Coronation of the Virgin* and *The Nativity*.

Fra Angelico was born in Vecchio, Italy. He became a monk in Fiesole when he was 19, and was known as Fra Giovanni da Fiesole. Later, his admirers called him Fra Angelico (angelic brother). CREIGHTON GILBERT

See also CHRISTMAS (color picture: *The Nativity*); AQUINAS, SAINT THOMAS (picture).

The *Madonna of Humility* by Fra Angelico shows the artist's skill in combining delicate colors with simple, graceful figures.

Oil painting on wood panel; National Gallery of Art, Washington, D.C., Andrew W. Mellon Collection

WORLD BOOK photo

Students Learn That Fractions with a Common Denominator Can Be Added.

FRACTION. The word *fraction* means a part of something. The part is usually small. For example, an accident may happen "in a fraction of a second." You may read in a history book that "only a fraction of the settlers survived the Indian attack."

But, in arithmetic, a fraction is a *number*, such as $\frac{1}{2}$ or $\frac{1}{4}$. It tells what part of something is taken. The part can be small or large. For example, a fraction can stand for a slice of an apple or a quarter of the moon. When you count the number of things in a group, you use *whole numbers*, such as 1, 2, and 3. You can add, subtract, multiply, and divide fractions to solve problems just as you can whole numbers.

Fractions are used everywhere. You may tell a friend, "I will meet you in three quarters ($\frac{3}{4}$) of an hour." You may buy half ($\frac{1}{2}$) a pint of ice cream. Or you may share a candy bar by giving one third ($\frac{1}{3}$) to each of two friends. Learning to use fractions is an important part of arithmetic.

The Language of Fractions

Fraction Names. Suppose you break a stick into two pieces of the same length. If you lay the two pieces side by side, you can see that they are of equal length. You can say that each piece is *one half* of the whole stick.

In the same way, you can break a candy bar into two pieces of the same size. You can tear a piece of paper into two pieces that have the same size. You can divide a pie into two equal pieces by cutting along a line down its center. In each of these cases, you split a whole into two parts that are *equal*, or alike, in some way. In each case, you can say that either one of the two parts is *one half* of the whole.

─────── **FRACTION TERMS** ───────

Bar is the short line that separates the numerator from the denominator in a fraction.

Cancel means to strike out a number by putting a line through it.

Common, in arithmetic, means *shared* or *the same*. Two fractions with the same denominator, such as $\frac{1}{5}$ and $\frac{2}{5}$, have a *common denominator*.

Convert a fraction means to change a fraction's form, but not its value. For example, $\frac{4}{6}$ can be converted to $\frac{8}{12}$.

Denominator is the number written below the bar in a fraction. The denominator of $\frac{2}{3}$ is 3. The denominator tells into how many parts a whole has been divided.

Equal Fractions are fractions that have the same value, but may have different forms. For example, $\frac{1}{2}$ and $\frac{2}{4}$ are equal fractions.

Improper Fraction is a fraction whose numerator equals, or is greater than, its denominator. For example, $\frac{3}{3}$ and $\frac{7}{4}$ are improper fractions.

Mixed Number is an abbreviated way of writing the sum of a whole number and a proper fraction. For example, the mixed number $2\frac{1}{4}$ really means $2+\frac{1}{4}$.

Numerator is the number written above the bar in a fraction. The numerator of $\frac{2}{3}$ is 2. The numerator tells how many parts are taken.

Proper Fraction is a fraction whose numerator is smaller than its denominator. For example, $\frac{3}{4}$ is a proper fraction, because 3 is smaller than 4.

Reduce a fraction means to convert a fraction to an equal fraction with a smaller numerator and denominator. But the new fraction has the same value.

Term refers to either the numerator or the denominator of a fraction. *Lower terms* means a smaller numerator and denominator. *In lowest terms* means that the numerator and denominator of a fraction cannot be made smaller.

Value of a fraction is the number that the fraction stands for. Equal fractions, such as $\frac{2}{3}$ and $\frac{6}{9}$, have the same value and stand for the same number.

382

If you cut something into *three* equal parts, you call each part *one third* of the whole. If you cut something into four equal parts, you call each part *one quarter* or *one fourth* of the whole. If you cut something into five equal parts, you call each part *one fifth*.

If you and a group of your friends stand in a line, you can use an *ordinal number name* to describe your position in the line. The ordinal number names are *first, second, third, fourth, fifth, sixth*, and so on. For example, you can say "I am the *third* person in the line." Or, you can say, "I live on the *fourteenth* floor of that apartment building." or, "My father celebrates his *forty-third* birthday tomorrow."

Except in the case of *half* or *quarter*, you use the names of the ordinal numbers to name fractions. For example, each day has 24 hours. That is, each day has 24 parts. So you can say that one hour is *one twenty-fourth* of a day. Five hours are *five twenty-fourths* of a day.

Writing Fractions with Numbers. A pound contains 16 ounces. Suppose a piece of meat weighs 9 ounces. You can say that the meat weighs *nine sixteenths* of a pound. Suppose you want to use numbers, instead of words, to write nine sixteenths. Something like "9 16ths" might be awkward or confusing. In arithmetic, you put the 9 above the 16, with a *bar*, or short line, between the two numbers:

$$\frac{9}{16}$$

When you see this expression you still read it *nine sixteenths*. But when you tell a friend how to write nine sixteenths, you might find it easier to say *nine over sixteen*. Sometimes you may see the bar slanted: 9/16. But one number usually appears over the other, with a bar between them.

In arithmetic, we call an expression such as $\frac{9}{16}$ a *fraction*. Each of the two numbers, 9 and 16, has a name of its own. The number above the bar, 9, is the *numerator* of the fraction. *Numerator* means *numberer*. It tells the number of parts. For example, in the fraction $\frac{9}{16}$ there are nine parts. The number below the bar, 16, is the *denominator* of the fraction. *Denominator* means *namer*. It tells the name, or size, of the parts that make up the whole. For example, the parts in $\frac{9}{16}$ are *sixteenths*.

Every fraction has this form:

$$\frac{\text{Numerator}}{\text{Denominator}}$$

We call both the numerator and the denominator *terms* of the fraction. For example, in $\frac{9}{16}$ the numerator 9 is one term and the denominator 16 is the other term.

Equal Fractions. Mary sees 12 cookies on a plate. Suppose she takes four of them.

$$\frac{4}{12} \text{ of } 12$$

She has taken 4 of the 12 cookies, so she has taken *four twelfths*, or $\frac{4}{12}$, of the cookies.

Suppose someone has arranged the same 12 cookies in pairs. Now there are six piles of two cookies each. Suppose Mary takes two of these piles.

$$\frac{2}{6} \text{ of } 12$$

She still has four cookies, just as before. But she has taken two of the six piles. So you can say that she has taken *two sixths*, or $\frac{2}{6}$, of the cookies.

Suppose someone has arranged the 12 cookies in three piles of four cookies each. Suppose Mary takes one of these piles.

$$\frac{1}{3} \text{ of } 12$$

Again, she has four cookies. But she has taken one of the three piles. So you can say that she has taken *one third*, or $\frac{1}{3}$, of the cookies.

Now look at this sentence, which has a blank to be filled in:

Mary took_____of the dozen cookies.

You can write $\frac{1}{3}$ in the blank space. Or you can write $\frac{2}{6}$. Or you can write $\frac{4}{12}$. In each case, the sentence will be correct. It will mean that Mary took 4 cookies from the 12 on the table.

We say that the fractions $\frac{1}{3}$, $\frac{2}{6}$, and $\frac{4}{12}$ are *equal*. Using an *equality sign* (=), we can write this out. The equality sign means that what is on one side of the sign has the same value as what is on the other side.

$$\frac{1}{3} = \frac{2}{6} \quad \text{or} \quad \frac{1}{3} = \frac{4}{12} \quad \text{or} \quad \frac{2}{6} = \frac{4}{12}$$

This means that any one of the three fractions is equal to any other one of the three.

Converting and Reducing Fractions. Suppose Mary sees 60 cookies on a plate. To take $\frac{1}{3}$ of them, she will have to pick up 20 cookies, leaving 40. You can see that three 20's are 60.

$$\frac{1}{3} = \frac{20}{60}$$

You can see that there are many fractions equal to $\frac{1}{3}$. For example, $\frac{2}{6}$, $\frac{4}{12}$, and $\frac{20}{60}$ all equal $\frac{1}{3}$. *You can form a new equal fraction by multiplying the original fraction "above and below" by some whole number.* Multiplying "above and below" means multiplying both the numerator and the denominator by the same whole number. For example, suppose you multiply $\frac{1}{3}$ "above and below" by 10:

$$\frac{1 \times 10}{3 \times 10} = \frac{10}{30}$$

And $\frac{10}{30}$ is equal to $\frac{1}{3}$.

If you multiply "above and below" by 1, then by 2, then by 3, and so on, you will eventually get every fraction equal to $\frac{1}{3}$.

$$\frac{1}{3} = \frac{2}{6} = \frac{3}{9} = \frac{4}{12} = \frac{5}{15} = \frac{6}{18}, \text{ and so on.}$$

FRACTION

You can divide "above and below," too. For example, you can divide the fraction $\frac{6}{18}$ above and below by 6:

$$\frac{6 \div 6}{18 \div 6} = \frac{1}{3}$$

To convert, or change, a fraction to an equal fraction, you may have to both multiply and divide above and below. It is usually easier to divide first, then multiply. For example, suppose you want to convert $\frac{6}{18}$ to twenty-fourths. First, divide $\frac{6}{18}$ above and below by 3:

$$\frac{6 \div 3}{18 \div 3} = \frac{2}{6}$$

Multiply this result above and below by 4:

$$\frac{2 \times 4}{6 \times 4} = \frac{8}{24}$$

When you divide above and below, the new fraction has *lower terms* than the original fraction. That is, the new fraction has a smaller numerator and denominator than the original fraction. For example, $\frac{2}{6}$ has a smaller numerator and denominator than $\frac{6}{18}$. Conversion of a fraction to one that has a smaller numerator and denominator is called *reduction to lower terms.*

You can convert a fraction such as $\frac{8}{24}$ to $\frac{4}{12}$, $\frac{2}{6}$, and $\frac{1}{3}$ by dividing each fraction above and below by the same number. When you cannot divide above and below any further, the fraction is *in lowest terms.* Here are some fractions in lowest terms:

$$\frac{1}{3} \qquad \frac{2}{3} \qquad \frac{7}{12} \qquad \frac{8}{15}$$

Look at $\frac{8}{15}$. Aside from 1, the only whole numbers you can use to divide evenly into 8 are 2, 4, and 8 itself. You cannot divide 15 evenly by 2, 4, or 8. So $\frac{8}{15}$ is in lowest terms.

Here is an example of reduction. Suppose you want to reduce $\frac{36}{60}$ to lowest terms. You can begin by dividing $\frac{36}{60}$ above and below by 2 and then go on:

$$\frac{36 \div 2}{60 \div 2} = \frac{18}{30} \qquad \frac{18 \div 2}{30 \div 2} = \frac{9}{15} \qquad \frac{9 \div 3}{15 \div 3} = \frac{3}{5}$$

So $\frac{36}{60}$ reduced to lowest terms is $\frac{3}{5}$. Of course, you can do the problem more quickly if you see at once that 36 and 60 can both be divided by 12:

$$\frac{36 \div 12}{60 \div 12} = \frac{3}{5}$$

Cancellation. You can usually shorten the work of reducing a fraction to lowest terms by *cancellation. Cancel* means *strike out.* Here is the longer way of reducing the fraction $\frac{4}{6}$ to lowest terms:

$$\frac{4 \div 2}{6 \div 2} = \frac{2}{3}$$

In cancellation, you divide above and below by the same whole number. But you strike out the old numerator and denominator and write new ones:

$$\frac{\cancel{4}^{\,2}}{\cancel{6}_{\,3}} = \frac{2}{3}$$

Here are two more examples of cancellation:

$$\frac{\cancel{\cancel{\cancel{36}}}}{\cancel{\cancel{\cancel{60}}}} = \frac{3}{5} \qquad \frac{\cancel{\cancel{12}}}{\cancel{\cancel{36}}} = \frac{1}{3}$$

You should always remember that cancellation is just a way of shortening written work. It is not a mathematical method. The *method* consists of dividing both the numerator and denominator. See CANCELLATION.

Comparing Fractions

To find $\frac{2}{3}$ of a certain group, you can separate the group into three equal parts, or *thirds.* Then you take *two* of these thirds. So $\frac{2}{3}$ is *twice* as large as $\frac{1}{3}$.

The fraction $\frac{8}{37}$ is larger than the fraction $\frac{5}{37}$. To find $\frac{5}{37}$ of a group, you separate the group into *thirty-sevenths.* To get $\frac{5}{37}$, you take *five* of the *thirty-sevenths.* To get $\frac{8}{37}$, you take *eight* of these same *thirty-sevenths.* And eight is larger than five.

Whenever two fractions have the same denominator, the one with the larger numerator is the larger fraction. For example, $\frac{4}{5}$ is larger than $\frac{2}{5}$, and $\frac{9}{26}$ is larger than $\frac{5}{26}$.

To find which of two fractions is larger, convert them to forms with the same denominator. Then compare the numerators.

You can always find a suitable denominator *by multiplying together the denominators of the two fractions.* But a smaller denominator can often be used instead. The denominator you use for both fractions is called the *common denominator.* If this denominator is the smallest that can be used, it is called the *least common denominator.*

Which is larger, $\frac{3}{5}$ or $\frac{7}{12}$? First, you must convert these fractions to forms that have the same denominator. You can find a suitable denominator by multiplying the denominators of $\frac{3}{5}$ and $\frac{7}{12}$: $5 \times 12 = 60$. So 60 will be the new denominator. Now you must convert $\frac{3}{5}$ to a form that has the denominator 60. To do this, you can multiply $\frac{3}{5}$ above and below by 12, because $5 \times 12 = 60$.

$$\frac{3 \times 12}{5 \times 12} = \frac{36}{60}$$

Next, you must convert $\frac{7}{12}$ to a form that has the denominator 60. You can multiply $\frac{7}{12}$ above and below by 5, because $12 \times 5 = 60$.

$$\frac{7 \times 5}{12 \times 5} = \frac{35}{60}$$

Now you can compare $\frac{36}{60}$ and $\frac{35}{60}$. You can see that $\frac{36}{60}$ is larger than $\frac{35}{60}$. So $\frac{3}{5}$ is larger than $\frac{7}{12}$.

Here is another example. Which is larger, $\frac{7}{10}$ or $\frac{11}{15}$? To find a suitable denominator, multiply 15 by 10: $15 \times 10 = 150$. But perhaps you will see that the smaller denominator of 30 will also work, because both 15 and 10 divide evenly into 30. Now you must convert the fractions:

$$\frac{7 \times 3}{10 \times 3} = \frac{21}{30} \qquad \frac{11 \times 2}{15 \times 2} = \frac{22}{30}$$

So $\frac{11}{15}$ is larger than $\frac{7}{10}$. In this example, 30 is the least common denominator.

Operations with Fractions

Adding Fractions. Suppose you see 12 blocks in a row. The first four blocks make a third of the group.

$$\frac{1}{3}$$

The next four make another third. So do the last four. If you put the first third and the second third together, you will have two thirds of the group of blocks.

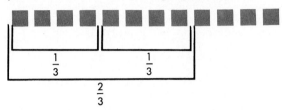

$$\frac{1}{3} \qquad \frac{1}{3}$$
$$\frac{2}{3}$$

When you put groups together, you *add* the numbers of the groups. For example, if you put together a group of three and a group of two, you get a group of five. You write this $3+2=5$. We think of adding fractions in much the same way. If you add a third of a group to another third of the group, you get two thirds of the group. You write this $\frac{1}{3}+\frac{1}{3}=\frac{2}{3}$.

Suppose you want to find the sum of $\frac{4}{12}$ and $\frac{3}{12}$. Look at the 12 blocks again. Four blocks make $\frac{4}{12}$ of the whole group of 12 blocks. Three blocks make $\frac{3}{12}$. The fraction $\frac{3}{12}$ represents three blocks. If you put together the group of four blocks and the group of three blocks, you have a group of seven blocks. The group of seven blocks is $\frac{7}{12}$ of the whole group.

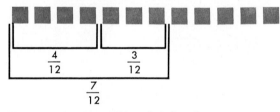

$$\frac{4}{12} \qquad \frac{3}{12}$$
$$\frac{7}{12}$$

You can write this addition $\frac{4}{12}+\frac{3}{12}=\frac{7}{12}$.

To add fractions with the same denominator, add their numerators. Write this sum above the denominator of the original fractions. The new fraction is called the *sum* of the two original fractions. Here are three examples:

$$\frac{1}{4}+\frac{2}{4}=\frac{3}{4}$$

$$\frac{36}{293}+\frac{20}{293}=\frac{56}{293}$$

$$\frac{1}{12}+\frac{2}{12}+\frac{5}{12}=\frac{8}{12} \text{ or } \frac{2}{3}$$

How can you add $\frac{1}{4}$ and $\frac{1}{3}$? These fractions do not have the same denominator. But you can easily convert them to fractions that do have the same denominator. You can find the common denominator of the two fractions by multiplying their present denominators: $4 \times 3 =$

12. Next, you must convert them to forms with the denominator 12:

$$\frac{1 \times 3}{4 \times 3}=\frac{3}{12} \qquad \frac{1 \times 4}{3 \times 4}=\frac{4}{12}$$

Now $\frac{3}{12}$ and $\frac{4}{12}$ have the same denominator. You can add them by adding the numerators together:

$$\frac{3}{12}+\frac{4}{12} = \frac{3+4}{12} = \frac{7}{12}$$

So $\frac{1}{4}+\frac{1}{3}=\frac{7}{12}$.

Subtracting Fractions. When you take away one group from another group, you *subtract* one number from another. For example, if you take away a group of two from a group of five, you get a group of three. You write this $5-2=3$. We think of subtracting fractions in the same way.

To subtract one fraction from another with the same denominator, subtract one numerator from the other. The denominator remains the same. Look at the dozen blocks again. Suppose you have a group of four blocks.

$$\frac{4}{12}$$

This is $\frac{4}{12}$ of the whole group. Suppose you take away three blocks from the group of four.

You have one block, or $\frac{1}{12}$, of the group remaining. Here is the way you write the subtraction:

$$\frac{4}{12}-\frac{3}{12} = \frac{4-3}{12} = \frac{1}{12}$$

Suppose you want to subtract fractions with denominators that are not alike. You must convert the fractions to forms that have the same denominator. Then you can subtract one numerator from the other. For example, subtract $\frac{1}{6}$ from $\frac{3}{4}$. First, you must convert the fractions, using the common denominator 12:

$$\frac{3 \times 3}{4 \times 3}=\frac{9}{12} \qquad \frac{1 \times 2}{6 \times 2}=\frac{2}{12}$$

Now you can subtract the numerators:

$$\frac{9}{12}-\frac{2}{12}=\frac{9-2}{12}=\frac{7}{12}$$

So $\frac{3}{4}-\frac{1}{6}=\frac{7}{12}$.

Suppose you want to combine several fractions, some by addition and some by subtraction. Here is an example:

$$\frac{5}{8}+\frac{1}{6}-\frac{2}{3}=?$$

The first two fractions have 8×6, or 48, for a common denominator. But you can see that 8 and 6 both divide evenly into 24. The denominator 3 of the third fraction also divides evenly into 24. So 24 is the least common denominator for all three fractions. Converting, you find that $\frac{5}{8}=\frac{15}{24}$, $\frac{1}{6}=\frac{4}{24}$, and $\frac{2}{3}=\frac{16}{24}$. Now you can combine the numerators:

$$\frac{15}{24}+\frac{4}{24}-\frac{16}{24}=\frac{15+4-16}{24}$$

$$\frac{19-16}{24}=\frac{3}{24}$$

$$\frac{3}{24}=\frac{1}{8}$$

$$\frac{5}{8}+\frac{1}{6}-\frac{2}{3}=\frac{1}{8}$$

Multiplying by a Fraction. Suppose you have a group of 12 blocks. To find a third of this group, you can divide 12 by 3: $12\div3=4$. So one third of the group of 12 blocks is four blocks. And $\frac{1}{3}$ of 12 is $12\div3=4$.

To find two thirds of a group of 12, you can divide by 3 and multiply by 2.

$$\frac{2}{3}\text{ of }12=2\times(12\div3)=2\times4=8$$

Or, you can multiply by 2 first, and then divide by 3:

$$\frac{2}{3}\text{ of }12=(2\times12)\div3=24\div3=8$$

In each case above, you may say that you are multiplying 12 by the fraction $\frac{2}{3}$. Instead of writing $\frac{2}{3}$ of 12, you can write $\frac{2}{3}\times12$. Then you find $\frac{2}{3}\times12$ by multiplying by 2 and dividing the result by 3, as above: $2\times12=24$ and $24\div3=8$ (or: $12\div3=4$ and $4\times2=8$). *To multiply a number by a fraction, you can divide the number by the denominator, then multiply the result by the numerator. Or, you can multiply the number by the numerator, then divide the result by the denominator.*

Here is an example of multiplying by a fraction. John is paid 50¢ an hour to cut grass. He works 48 minutes. How much should he be paid? First, an hour consists of 60 minutes. So John has worked $\frac{48}{60}$ of an hour. You can reduce the fraction $\frac{48}{60}$:

$$\frac{48\div12}{60\div12}=\frac{4}{5}$$

So John has worked $\frac{4}{5}$ of an hour. Because he receives 50¢ an hour, he should receive $\frac{4}{5}$ of 50¢ for his work.

$$\frac{4}{5}\times50=4\times(50\div5)=4\times10=40$$

So John should receive 40¢ for his work. Many practical problems call for multiplication by a fraction.

Multiplying Two Fractions. John earned $\frac{4}{5}$ of 50¢ and saved $\frac{3}{8}$ of this amount. How much did he save?

That is, what is $\frac{3}{8}$ of $\frac{4}{5}$ of 50? Here is the way you can write this problem:

$$\frac{3}{8}\times\left(\frac{4}{5}\times50\right)$$

You can see how this problem may be solved in four steps. First, multiply 50 by 4: $50\times4=200$. Second, divide 200 by 5: $200\div5=40$. So $\frac{4}{5}$ of 50 is 40. Third, multiply 40 by 3: $40\times3=120$. Fourth, divide 120 by 8: $120\div8=15$. So $\frac{3}{8}$ of $\frac{4}{5}$ of 50 is 15. John saved 15¢. Multiplication of two fractions helps to solve many arithmetic problems in everyday life.

But you can do the two multiplications first, then the two divisions. If you multiply by 4 and then by 3, it is the same as multiplying by 12, the product of 4 and 3. Similarly, if you divide by 5 and then by 8, it is the same as dividing by 40, the product of 5 and 8.

$$\frac{3}{8}\times\left(\frac{4}{5}\times50\right)=\left(\frac{3\times4}{8\times5}\right)\times50=\frac{12}{40}\times50$$

The fraction $\frac{12}{40}$ is the *product* of $\frac{3}{8}$ and $\frac{4}{5}$. You can reduce this fraction: $\frac{12}{40}=\frac{3}{10}$. Now you can find $\frac{3}{10}$ of 50:

$$\frac{3}{10}\times50=3\times(50\div10)=3\times5=15$$

To multiply two fractions, multiply their numerators together and multiply their denominators together. Write these two products as the numerator and denominator, respectively, of a new fraction.

Here is another example of multiplying two fractions. Mary buys $\frac{2}{3}$ of a dozen rolls. She keeps $\frac{3}{4}$ of her purchase for herself and gives the rest to a friend. How

many does she keep? Or, what is $\frac{3}{4}$ of $\frac{2}{3}$?

$$\frac{3}{4}\times\frac{2}{3}=\frac{3\times2}{4\times3}=\frac{6}{12}=\frac{1}{2}$$

So Mary keeps $\frac{1}{2}$ of a dozen rolls, or 6 rolls.

This example illustrates an important point. A product, such as 3×2, consists of two *factors*, 3 and 2. Similarly, 4×3 consists of two factors, 4 and 3. *If you can divide one factor by a number, this has the same effect as dividing the product by the number.* For example, suppose you want to divide 3×2 by 2:

$$\frac{3\times2}{2}=\frac{3\times\overset{1}{2}}{\underset{1}{2}}=\frac{3\times1}{1}=\frac{3}{1}=3$$

The product 3×2 contains the factor 2. So you can divide this factor by 2, as shown above, rather than divide the whole product, 6. The result is the same as dividing 6 by 2. *You show the division by cancellation.* You must show that $2 \div 2 = 1$ in two places, above and below. For example, you must *not* leave a factor of zero, because $3 \times 0 = 0$. So you must write 1 in two places.

You can use the same method in the example of Mary and the rolls.

$$\frac{3}{4} \times \frac{2}{3} = \frac{\overset{1}{\cancel{3}} \times \overset{1}{\cancel{2}}}{\underset{2}{\cancel{4}} \times \underset{1}{\cancel{3}}} = \frac{1 \times 1}{2 \times 1} = \frac{1}{2}$$

In this case, there is a factor of 3 in the numerator and a factor of 3 in the denominator. You can divide above and below by 3. This replaces the factors of 3 in the numerator and denominator with factors of 1. There is a factor of 2 in the numerator and a factor of 4 in the denominator. You can divide above and below by 2. This replaces the factor of 2 in the numerator with a factor of 1, and the factor of 4 in the denominator with a factor of 2. You indicate these results by cancellation.

Dividing by a Fraction. How many dimes make two dollars? Two dollars are 200 cents, and a dime is 10 cents. To find the answer, you can divide the value in cents of two dollars (200) by the value in cents of a dime (10): $200 \div 10 = 20$. So there are 20 dimes in two dollars. Or, there are 20 tenths in two.

How many half dollars make three dollars? As in the example above, you might divide the value of three dollars (3) by the value in dollars of a half dollar ($\frac{1}{2}$):

$$3 \div \frac{1}{2} = ?$$

You probably know the answer already. There are two half dollars in a dollar. So there are 3×2 half dollars in three dollars.

$$3 \times 2 = 6$$

There are six half dollars in three dollars. So you can see that to divide by $\frac{1}{2}$, you must multiply by 2. To divide by $\frac{1}{3}$, you multiply by 3. To divide by $\frac{1}{4}$, you multiply by 4.

Four children have three candy bars. Suppose each candy bar is cut into four pieces. This makes 3×4, or 12 pieces altogether. How many pieces can each child have?

Divide the number of pieces by the number of children: $12 \div 4 = 3$. So each child gets three pieces, or $\frac{3}{4}$ of a candy bar.

Using the same example, look at a different question: How many $\frac{3}{4}$ candy bars are there in 3 candy bars? You can write the question this way:

$$3 \div \frac{3}{4} = ?$$

You know the answer, 4, from the previous example: each of the four children gets $\frac{3}{4}$ of a candy bar. But how can you find the answer using fractions?

First, multiply 3, the number of bars, by 4, the number of pieces into which each bar is cut: $3 \times 4 = 12$. This is the same as finding how many fourths there are in 3. The number 1 is the same as $\frac{4}{4}$, or $\frac{4}{4} \times 1$, so the number 3 is $\frac{4}{4} \times 3$, or $\frac{12}{4}$. When you multiply the number of bars by the number of pieces, you find that three bars consist of 12 fourths, or pieces.

Second, divide 12, the number of pieces, by 3, the number of pieces each child receives: $12 \div 3 = 4$. In other words, how many groups of 3 fourths, or pieces, are there in 12 fourths, or pieces?

Here is the way you write this process:

$$3 \div \frac{3}{4} = 3 \times \frac{4}{3} = \frac{3 \times 4}{3} = \frac{12}{3} = 4$$

You "turn over," or *invert*, the fraction $\frac{3}{4}$ so you can multiply 3×4 to find the number of fourths in 3.

You can see that the way to divide by $\frac{3}{4}$ is to multiply by $\frac{4}{3}$. The fraction $\frac{4}{3}$ is the fraction $\frac{3}{4}$ "turned over," or inverted. You invert a fraction when you replace it with another fraction in which the old numerator and denominator have been switched. *To divide by a fraction, invert the fraction and multiply.*

Here is another example. A recipe calls for $\frac{2}{3}$ of a cup of flour. If you have 8 cups of flour, how many times can you make the recipe?

$$8 \div \frac{2}{3} = 8 \times \frac{3}{2} = \frac{8 \times 3}{2} = \frac{24}{2} = 12$$

So you can make the recipe 12 times.

Finding the Least Common Denominator

You must often find the least common denominator for two or more fractions. To learn how to do this, you must first learn about *divisors* and *multiples*.

Divisors. A *divisor* of a number is any number that divides into the original number evenly. For example, 2 is a divisor of 6: $6 \div 2 = 3$. But 4 is not a divisor of 6 because you cannot divide 6 by 4 evenly.

To find all the divisors of a number, try to divide it by each whole number in succession—first by 1, then by 2, then by 3, and so on. Whenever the division comes out even, write down both the divisor you used and the *quotient* (the result of division) you found. *Both* divisor and quotient will be divisors of the number. For example, divide 6 by 1: $6 \div 1 = 6$. Write down 1 and the quotient 6. Both 6 and 1 are divisors of 6. Next, divide 6 by 2: $6 \div 2 = 3$. Write down 2 and 3, because they are also divisors of 6. Keep on trying whole numbers as divisors only up to the point where the quotient still comes out larger than the whole number you are trying. For example, because $6 \div 3 = 2$ and 2 is smaller than 3, you will not have to try 3 or any larger whole number. So the divisors of 6 are 1, 2, 3, and 6.

For another example, find the divisors of 36. By trying each whole number in succession, you will find that you will only need 1, 2, 3, 4, and 6. You will not have to try any whole numbers larger than 6. You will have found the quotient 36 with the divisor 1, the quotient 18 with the divisor 2, the quotient 12 with the divisor 3,

FRACTION

and the quotient 9 with the divisor 4. So the divisors of 36 are 1, 2, 3, 4, 6, 9, 12, 18, and 36.

Multiples. When you multiply a number by a whole number, the resulting product is called a *multiple* of the original number. Suppose the original number is 8. Multiplying 8 by 1 gives 8. Multiplying 8 by 2 gives 16. Multiplying 8 by 3 gives 24. So 8, 16, and 24 are some of the multiples of 8.

When you try to find a common denominator for two fractions, you are really trying to find a *common multiple* of the fractions' denominators. Look at the numbers 6 and 8. You can see that $6 \times 8 = 48$, and that $8 \times 6 = 48$. So the product 48 is a multiple of both 6 and of 8. But 48 is not the *least* common multiple of 6 and 8.

To find the least common multiple of two numbers, multiply one of the two numbers by each divisor of the other number. Test each result to see if you can divide it by the number whose divisors you have been using. That is, divide each result by the second number. For example, find the least common multiple of 8 and 6. The divisors of 6 are 1, 2, 3, and 6. Multiply 8 by each divisor of 6. Divide each result by 6. Here is what you will find:

$1 \times 8 = 8$	No. You cannot divide 8 by 6.
$2 \times 8 = 16$	No. You cannot divide 16 by 6.
$3 \times 8 = 24$	Yes. You can divide 24 by 6.

So 24 is the least common multiple of 6 and 8. *The least common multiple is the least common denominator.* The least common denominator for fractions with denominators of 6 and 8 will be 24.

Here is a subtraction example:

$$\frac{25}{36} - \frac{3}{20} = ?$$

To find the least common denominator for these fractions, you must find the least common multiple for 36 and 20. First, you must find the divisors of 20. Divide 20 by each whole number in succession. You will have to try only 1, 2, 3, and 4. The divisors of 20 are 1, 2, 4, 5, 10, and 20. Now you must multiply 36 by each divisor of 20, and test to see if you can divide the result by 20. (Perhaps you will see at once that any multiple of 20 will end in zero.)

$1 \times 36 = 36$	No. You cannot divide 36 by 20.
$2 \times 36 = 72$	No. You cannot divide 72 by 20.
$4 \times 36 = 144$	No. You cannot divide 144 by 20.
$5 \times 36 = 180$	Yes. You can divide 180 by 20.

So 180 is the least common denominator for fractions with denominators of 36 and 20. Now you can convert the fractions:

$$\frac{25 \times 5}{36 \times 5} = \frac{125}{180} \qquad \frac{3 \times 9}{20 \times 9} = \frac{27}{180}$$

And complete the subtraction:

$$\frac{125}{180} - \frac{27}{180} = \frac{98}{180}$$

$$\frac{98}{180} = \frac{49}{90}$$

Improper Fractions and Mixed Numbers

Improper Fractions. The fraction $\frac{4}{3}$ might puzzle a beginner, because you cannot split a group into three equal parts and take away four of them. To see what $\frac{4}{3}$ means, think of two trays in a bakery. Each tray holds a dozen cupcakes.

Each tray has three even rows of cupcakes. So each row consists of $\frac{1}{3}$ of a dozen cupcakes. If you buy four rows, you get $\frac{4}{3}$ of a dozen cupcakes. The fraction $\frac{4}{3}$ means one dozen and $\frac{1}{3}$ of another dozen. To find the number of cupcakes, multiply 12, a dozen, by $\frac{4}{3}$:

$$\frac{4}{3} \times 12 = 4 \times (12 \div 3) = 4 \times 4 = 16$$

So you get 16 cupcakes if you buy four rows.

If the numerator of a fraction is smaller than the denominator, the fraction is called a *proper fraction*. For example, $\frac{3}{4}$ is a proper fraction, because the numerator, 3, is smaller than the denominator, 4. If the numerator equals or is larger than the denominator, the fraction is an *improper fraction*. For example, $\frac{4}{4}$ is an improper fraction, because the numerator 4 equals the denominator 4. And $\frac{15}{4}$ is an improper fraction, because 15 is larger than 4.

Fractions such as $\frac{2}{2}$, $\frac{3}{3}$, or $\frac{4}{4}$ of a dozen are the same as the dozen itself. You can see this by finding $\frac{3}{3}$ of 12:

$$\frac{3}{3} \times 12 = 3 \times (12 \div 3) = 3 \times 4 = 12$$

Multiplying by $\frac{3}{3}$ is the same as multiplying by 1. So $\frac{1}{1} = 1$, $\frac{2}{2} = 1$, $\frac{3}{3} = 1$, and so on.

Whole numbers appear as fractions in another way. What is $\frac{2}{1}$ of a dozen?

$$\frac{2}{1} \times 12 = 2 \times (12 \div 1) = 2 \times 12 = 24$$

Multiplying by $\frac{2}{1}$ is the same as multiplying by 2. So $\frac{2}{1} = 2$, $\frac{3}{1} = 3$, $\frac{4}{1} = 4$, and so on.

Look at the fraction $\frac{36}{3}$. You can divide 3 evenly into 36:

$$\frac{36}{3} = 36 \div 3 = 12$$

The quotient, or result, of this division is the number value of the fraction $\frac{36}{3}$. *You can always change an improper fraction into a quotient. If the denominator divides evenly into the numerator, the quotient is the number value of the fraction.*

Mixed Numbers. Look at the fraction $\frac{11}{4}$. You can rewrite this fraction as a sum:

$$\frac{11}{4} = \frac{8}{4} + \frac{3}{4}$$

Because $\frac{8}{4}=2$, you can write $\frac{11}{4}$ this way:

$$\frac{11}{4}=2+\frac{3}{4}$$

You usually write $2+\frac{3}{4}$ as $2\frac{3}{4}$. The expression $2\frac{3}{4}$ is an abbreviated form of the sum. It does *not* mean $2\times\frac{3}{4}$. Expressions such as $2\frac{3}{4}$ that consist of a whole number and a fraction are called *mixed numbers*.

Here is an example of changing an improper fraction to a mixed number. Suppose you want to change $\frac{389}{12}$. First, divide 389 by 12: $389\div12=32$ with a remainder of 5. This division shows that $389=32\times12+5$. Here is the mixed number:

$$\frac{389}{12}=32+\frac{5}{12}=32\frac{5}{12}$$

If the denominator does not divide evenly into the numerator, you can write an improper fraction as a mixed number.

Suppose you want to change a mixed number into an improper fraction. For example, change $8\frac{2}{3}$ into an improper fraction. First, change the 8 to thirds:

$$8=\frac{8}{1}=\frac{8\times3}{1\times3}=\frac{24}{3}$$

Now you can add the 8 and the $\frac{2}{3}$:

$$8\frac{2}{3}=8+\frac{2}{3}=\frac{24}{3}+\frac{2}{3}=\frac{26}{3}$$

This is not hard to do mentally, with a little practice.

Decimal Fractions

Fractions such as $\frac{4}{10}$, $\frac{7}{100}$, or $\frac{5}{1,000}$ are *decimal fractions*. They have denominators of 10, or 10 multiplied by itself a certain number of times. But decimal fractions are written *without a denominator* as part of the decimal number system. For example, $\frac{4}{10}$ is written 0.4, and $\frac{5}{1,000}$ is written 0.005. Decimal fractions have great importance in everyday arithmetic, especially in the metric system of measurement. Learning to use them is an important part of understanding fractions. See Decimal Numeral System (Decimal Fractions).

Fractions and the Number Scale

Look at a foot ruler. It is marked off in inches. Its left end represents 0 or zero. It extends to 12 at its right end. Now look at the first inch:

Within the first inch, you will find a mark midway between 0 and 1 that shows the fraction $\frac{1}{2}$. There are two lengths, one from 0 to $\frac{1}{2}$ and the other from $\frac{1}{2}$ to 1. We speak of each length as *one half inch*.

You will also find marks that divide the inch into four equal lengths. We speak of each of these four lengths as *one fourth inch*. If each inch on the ruler has been divided into fourths, we say that the ruler has been *graduated* in one fourth or quarter inches.

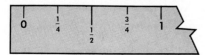

Rulers are usually graduated in eighths or sixteenths of an inch, as well as in halves and quarters.

The important idea you should understand is that *every fraction has a place of its own on the ruler*. It does not matter if the place is marked or not.

Now try to forget the ruler and think of its edge as a line. The marks along the edge are points on the line:

The arrow suggests that the line extends on and on to the right. It can extend as far as we want—a thousand, million, billion, or even endlessly. *Each fraction has its place on this line of numbers that stretches from 0 into the distance.* We call the line of numbers a *number scale*.

Suppose you want to locate the fraction $\frac{5}{4}$ on the scale. Starting from 0, you count off five fourths to the right. You can mark the place of $\frac{5}{4}$ on the scale. You can locate other fractions on the scale in the same way.

If you locate other fractions on the scale, you will discover two interesting things. First, *equal fractions have the same place on the line*. If you locate $\frac{1}{2}$, $\frac{2}{4}$, and $\frac{4}{8}$ on the scale, you will see that they all fall at the same point—the point midway between 0 and 1. Second, *if one fraction is greater than another, its place lies to the right of the place of the smaller fraction*. For example, you will find that $\frac{4}{12}$ lies to the right of $\frac{3}{12}$. If you reduce these fractions, $\frac{4}{12}=\frac{1}{3}$ and $\frac{3}{12}=\frac{1}{4}$. And $\frac{1}{3}$ lies to the right of $\frac{1}{4}$.

Look at the part of the scale from 0 to $\frac{5}{4}$. The fraction $\frac{5}{4}$ marks off a definite part of the line. *We use fractions to measure the lengths of parts of a line.*

If you study fractions on the number scale, you will realize that *fractions are numbers*. You can add, subtract, multiply, and divide fractions. You can use fractions for sizes and lengths, and for dozens of other measurements. You can even think of whole numbers as fractions. For example, you can think of 2 as $\frac{2}{1}$.

When you think about fractions, you must be careful to understand the difference between *form* and *value*. The fractions $\frac{2}{3}$ and $\frac{4}{6}$ are two different forms. But they have the same value. That is, they have the same place on the number scale, and they stand for the same number. When you write $\frac{2}{3}=\frac{4}{6}$, you say that the number or value is the same, even though the forms are different.

Handling Fractions

After some practice, you will begin to think of fractions as numbers. Then you no longer will need so many special rules for handling fractions. You will be able to use the same rules, no matter what combination of whole numbers, mixed numbers, and common fractions you have.

For example, the *order* in which you multiply whole numbers does not matter. The same rule applies to fractions. You do not need to think of $4\times\frac{1}{2}$—"the sum of four halves" as any different from $\frac{1}{2}\times4$—"half of

FRACTION

four." Both fractions are the product of $\frac{4}{1}$ and $\frac{1}{2}$. Their order does not matter:

$$4\times\frac{1}{2}\ \text{or}\ \frac{1}{2}\times4=\frac{4}{1}\times\frac{1}{2}=\frac{4\times1}{1\times2}=\frac{4}{2}=2$$

You will find different ways of working with fractions. Suppose you want to divide $23\frac{7}{8}$ by $5\frac{3}{4}$. Here is one way:

$$23\frac{7}{8}\div5\frac{3}{4}=\frac{191}{8}\div\frac{23}{4}$$

$$=\frac{191}{\underset{2}{8}}\times\frac{\overset{1}{4}}{23}$$

$$=\frac{191}{46}=4\frac{7}{46}$$

Here is another way of working the same problem:

$$23\frac{7}{8}\div5\frac{3}{4}\ =\ \frac{23\frac{7}{8}}{5\frac{3}{4}}\ =\ \frac{23+\frac{7}{8}}{5+\frac{3}{4}}$$

Now multiply above and below by 8, the least common multiple of the denominators 4 and 8:

$$\frac{\left(23+\frac{7}{8}\right)\times8}{\left(5+\frac{3}{4}\right)\times8}=\frac{184+7}{40+6}$$

$$=\frac{191}{46}\ \text{or}\ 4\frac{7}{46}$$

Suppose you want to multiply $3\frac{7}{8}$ by 4. You must multiply each part of the sum $3+\frac{7}{8}$ by 4:

$$4\times3\frac{7}{8}=4\times\left(3+\frac{7}{8}\right)$$

$$=4\times3+4\times\frac{7}{8}$$

$$=12+\frac{7}{2}$$

$$=15\frac{1}{2}$$

Fun with Fractions

A Mind-Reading Trick. Think of the fraction $\frac{2}{3}$. Multiply by 2. Add 18. Divide by 2. Subtract the fraction you started with. That is, subtract $\frac{2}{3}$. Your answer will be 9. Here are the steps:

$$\frac{2}{3}\times2=1\frac{1}{3}$$

$$1\frac{1}{3}+18=19\frac{1}{3}$$

$$19\frac{1}{3}\div2=\frac{58}{3}\div2=\frac{29}{3}=9\frac{2}{3}$$

$$9\frac{2}{3}-\frac{2}{3}=9$$

Try this with any fraction you please in place of $\frac{2}{3}$. The answer will always be 9. Now you can say to a friend, "Think of a fraction. Multiply by 2. Add 18. Divide by 2. Subtract the number you started with. Do not tell me your answer. I know what it is. It is 9."

A Fraction Slide Rule. Here is a way to make a "slide rule" for adding and subtracting fractions and mixed numbers. First, take two rulers graduated in sixteenths. On one ruler, extend the graduation marks across the whole width of the ruler. For example, at the $\frac{1}{2}$ mark draw a line across the ruler so you can read $\frac{1}{2}$ on the bottom edge of the ruler. Instead of rulers, you can mark two scales on cardboard like the ones in the picture below. These scales are graduated in quarters or fourths instead of sixteenths.

Now, put the two rulers together, so that the zeros, 1's, 2's, 3's, and so on, match up. Suppose you want to find $2\frac{3}{4}+1\frac{7}{8}$. Slide the upper scale to the right so that its zero point is over $2\frac{3}{4}$ on the lower scale.

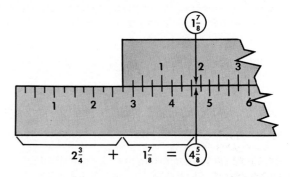

$$2\frac{3}{4}\ +\ 1\frac{7}{8}\ =\ 4\frac{5}{8}$$

Find the $1\frac{7}{8}$ mark on the upper scale. Now read the answer, $4\frac{5}{8}$, on the lower scale below the upper $1\frac{7}{8}$. You will find it interesting to discover how to subtract with your "slide rule." ROBERT L. SWAIN

Related Articles in WORLD BOOK include:

Outline

Practice Fraction Examples

1. Bill is $62\frac{1}{2}$ inches tall. Mary is $56\frac{1}{4}$ inches tall. How much taller is Bill than Mary?

2. Dave's house stands on a quarter-acre plot. His father bought the three-eighths acre plot next to it. What is the size of the combined plots of land of both Dave and his father?

3. Mr. Barry uses $\frac{3}{4}$ of a teaspoon of instant coffee to make one cup. How many teaspoons of instant coffee should he use to make six cups?

4. John wants to saw a board into four equal pieces. He finds that the board is 7 feet $3\frac{5}{8}$ inches long. How long should he make each piece?

5. If there are 52 weeks in a year, how many weeks would there be in an average month?

6. If Mr. Baker earns $120 a week and Mr. Katz earns $500 a month, who is the better paid? How much more a month does he earn? Use the average number of weeks from the preceding example.

7. Mrs. Dugan is having a rug cleaned. The rug measures 7 feet by 11 feet. Cleaning costs 80¢ for each square yard. What will be the cost of cleaning the rug?

8. Jerry can "step off" distances. The average length of his step is $2\frac{1}{2}$ feet. The length of his room measures 7 steps, and the width measures 6 steps. How long is Jerry's room? How wide?

9. The boys ask Bill to "step off" 50 yards so they can run the 50-yard dash. Bill's step measures $2\frac{1}{3}$ feet. How many steps should he take to measure 50 yards?

10. A breakfast cereal comes in two sizes. The standard 1 pound 4 ounce box costs two for 27¢. The large 3 pound 8 ounce box costs 36¢. How much money do you save by buying the large size?

Answers to the Practice Examples

1. $6\frac{1}{4}$ inches	6. Mr. Baker; $20
2. $\frac{5}{8}$ acre	7. $6.85
3. $4\frac{1}{2}$ teaspoons	8. $17\frac{1}{2}$ feet; 15 feet
4. 1 ft. $9\frac{29}{32}$ in.	9. 64+ steps
5. $4\frac{1}{3}$ weeks	10. $1\frac{4}{5}$¢ for $3\frac{1}{2}$ pounds

FRACTIONAL DISTILLATION. See DISTILLATION; PETROLEUM (Distillation; picture: Refining Petroleum).

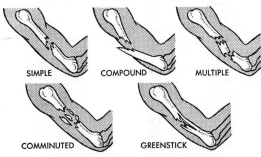

SIMPLE   COMPOUND   MULTIPLE

COMMINUTED   GREENSTICK

FIVE TYPES OF FRACTURES

FRACTURE, *FRACK chur*, means the breaking of a bone. There are several kinds of fractures. In a *simple* or *closed fracture*, a bone breaks, but the skin over it does not. Thus, there is no danger of infection from outside germs. In a *compound*, or *open fracture*, both the bone and skin break, and there is danger of infection. *Multiple fracture* means there is more than one break in a bone. *Comminuted fracture* means the bone has splintered, or shattered. In a *greenstick fracture*, the break cuts only part way through the bone.

Persons of all ages break bones. But the bones of aged persons are more fragile than the bones of young persons. They break more easily and heal more slowly.

A physician can detect a fracture in several ways. Usually, there is pain, soreness, or tenderness in a fracture area. Swelling and discoloration also occur.

Sometimes, there is movement of the bone under the skin and obvious deformity. *Crepitus* often signals a broken bone. Crepitus is a harsh grating sound caused when the broken ends of the bone rub together. In some cases, only an X ray will reveal a fracture. Fractures should be treated only by physicians. The injured part of the body should be kept motionless until a physician arrives.   MARSHALL R. URIST

FRAGMENTATION is the breaking of any material into small pieces. The fragmentation bomb or shell is used against troops, trucks, and grounded aircraft. Such a bomb or shell has a heavy case that breaks into thousands of small *fragments* (pieces) when it explodes.

Bombs of this type are usually about 18 inches (46 centimeters) long and about 3 inches (8 centimeters) in diameter. They are made of a can of TNT with a heavy iron rod coiled around the can. The bombs have sensitive fuzes that explode the instant they touch something. Instead of digging a deep hole, or crater, in the ground as other bombs do, fragmentation bombs spray small pieces of their casings over the surface. Fragmentation shells fired from artillery guns operate the same way. Their fuzes usually are set so the shells burst in the air.   JOHN D. BILLINGSLEY

See also BOMB (Explosive Bombs).

FRAGONARD, *FRAH GAW NAHR*, **JEAN HONORÉ** (1732-1806), was a French artist who painted in the highly ornamental style of the Rococo period (see PAINTING [Rococo]). Perhaps his best works were the panels called *The Progress of Love*, which he painted for Madame du Barry. His painting, *The Swing*, appears in color in the PAINTING article.

Fragonard was born in Grasse, France. He won the Prix de Rome in 1752. The award enabled him to study in Italy. He became a member of the French Academy in 1765, and turned to painting decorative scenes of the witty, sentimental type then popular. Fragonard ranks as a superior colorist and as one of the great French masters in painting, although his subjects are no longer particularly admired.   JOSEPH C. SLOANE

FRAME CONSTRUCTION. See BUILDING CONSTRUCTION; HOUSE.

FRAMINGHAM STATE COLLEGE. See UNIVERSITIES AND COLLEGES (table).

FRANC, *frank*, is the standard coin of France. The franc is also used in Belgium, Luxembourg, Switzerland, and many other countries. For the franc's value in each country, see MONEY (table: Values).

Chase Manhattan Bank Money Museum

The French Franc. On one side are the words "République Française" ("French Republic"), *left*. The other has the motto "Liberté, Égalité, Fraternité" ("Liberty, Equality, Fraternity").

The Arc de Triomphe in Paris is a symbol of French patriotism. Under the stone arch and the French flag lies the tomb of France's Unknown Soldier of World War I.

◀

▶

The French Countryside has long been a favorite subject of painters. France has produced great artists for hundreds of years. They have developed many styles that spread to other countries.

FRANCE

FRANCE is the largest country of Western Europe. It ranks second to Russia in area among all the European nations. France has about a fourth as many people as the entire United States, even though it is only about twice as large as the state of Colorado.

Paris, the capital and largest city of France, is one of the world's great cities. For hundreds of years, Paris has been a world capital of art and learning. Many great artists have produced their finest masterpieces there. Every year, millions of tourists visit such famous landmarks as the Cathedral of Notre Dame and the Louvre, one of the world's largest art museums.

There is much more to France than just Paris, however. The snow-capped Alps form the border between France and Italy. Sunny beaches and steep cliffs stretch along the French coast on the Mediterranean Sea. Fishing villages dot the Atlantic coast of northwestern France. The peaceful, wooded Loire Valley has many historic *châteaux* (castles). Colorful apple orchards, dairy farms, and vineyards lie throughout much of the countryside. Many regions have fields of golden wheat.

The French are famous for their enjoyment of life. Good food and good wine are an important part of everyday living for most French people. The wines of France are considered the best in the world. Almost every restaurant and area has at least one special recipe of its own. The delicious salads, sauces, and soups of France are copied by cooks in most parts of the world.

France has a long and colorful history. Julius Caesar and his Roman soldiers conquered the region before the time of Christ. Then, after Rome fell, the Franks and other Germanic tribes invaded the region. France was named for the Franks. By the A.D. 800's, the mighty Charlemagne, king of the Franks, had built a huge kingdom. In 1792, during the French Revolution, France became one of the first nations to overthrow its king and set up a republic. A few years later, Napoleon Bonaparte seized power. He conquered much of Europe before he finally was defeated. During World Wars I and II, France was a bloody battleground for Allied armies and the invading German forces.

France is not only a beautiful and historic country, it is also rich and powerful. France has great automobile, chemical, and steel industries. It is a leader in growing wheat, vegetables, and many other crops. France stands fifth among the countries of the world in its trade with other nations, as measured by exports.

The contributors of this article are John W. Hackett, Deputy Director for Financial Affairs at the Organization for Economic Cooperation and Development; J. A. Laponce, Professor of Political Science at the University of British Columbia; Lawrence M. Sommers, Chairman of the Department of Geography at Michigan State University; and Gordon Wright, William H. Bonsall Professor of History Emeritus at Stanford University.

Village of Breux, Normandie by Constantin Kluge from the WORLD BOOK Collection

France also plays an important part in world politics. Its foreign policies affect millions of persons in other countries.

The political importance of France today resulted partly from the leadership of Charles de Gaulle, who served as president from 1958 to 1969. De Gaulle established a strong French republic. He looked on France as a world power and followed a policy independent of both the United States and the Communist nations. He ended close military ties with the United States, refused to allow Great Britain to join the European Common Market, and tried to improve relations with Communist countries. De Gaulle's actions angered many other nations, but to the proud people of France he was a symbol of their nation's greatness. Many of his policies were continued after he left office.

── FACTS IN BRIEF ──

Capital: Paris.

Official Language: French.

Form of Government: Republic; 96 Metropolitan Departments; 5 Overseas Departments; 4 Overseas Territories; 1 Territorial Collectivity; 1 Condominium. *Head of State*—President (7-year term). *Head of Government*—Prime Minister (appointed by the President). *Parliament*—National Assembly (491 Deputies, 5-year terms); Senate (280 Senators, 9-year terms).

Area: Metropolitan France (mainland and Corsica), 211,208 sq. mi. (547,026 km²). *Greatest Distances*—east-west, 605 mi. (974 km); north-south, 590 mi. (950 km). *Coastline*—2,300 mi. (3,701 km).

Elevation: *Highest*—Mont Blanc, 15,771 ft. (4,807 m) above sea level. *Lowest*—below sea level along the delta of the Rhône River.

Population: Metropolitan France, *Estimated 1979 Population*—54,040,000; distribution, 76 per cent urban, 24 per cent rural; density, 256 persons per sq. mi. (99 persons per km²). *1975 Census*—52,544,400. *Estimated 1984 Population*—56,000,000.

Chief Products: *Agriculture*—barley, corn, flowers, flax, fruits, livestock (mainly beef and dairy cattle, hogs, and sheep), oats, potatoes, rice, rye, sugar beets, wheat. *Fishing*—cod, crabs, herring, lobsters, mackerel, oysters, sardines, shrimps, tuna. *Manufacturing*—aircraft, aluminum, automobiles, chemicals, clothing, dairy products (mainly butter and cheese), electrical and nonelectrical machinery, furniture, iron and steel, jewelry, paper, perfume, textiles, wine. *Mining*—bauxite, coal, gypsum, iron ore, potash, uranium.

National Anthem: "La Marseillaise."

National Holiday: Bastille Day, July 14.

National Motto: *Liberté, Égalité, Fraternité* (Liberty, Equality, Fraternity).

Money: *Basic Unit*—franc. One hundred centimes equal one franc. See MONEY (table: Values). See also FRANC.

393

FRANCE / Government

France is a democratic republic with a president, a prime minister (also called premier), and a Parliament. Its present government, called the *Fifth Republic*, has been in effect since 1958. The First Republic was established in 1792 during the French Revolution. Between 1792 and 1958, the structure of the French government changed many times.

The Fifth Republic was created to end serious weaknesses in the Fourth Republic, which had been established in 1946. Almost all the powers of the Fourth Republic were in the main house of Parliament, the *National Assembly*. The president had little power, and the Assembly could easily vote the prime minister and the cabinet out of office. In fact, the Assembly did so an average of twice a year.

Many political parties were represented in the Assembly. No party ever had more than 30 per cent of the seats in the Assembly during the Fourth Republic. The parties formed alliances to establish a majority group, but these alliances did not last long. When a majority group broke up, the prime minister and the cabinet lost the support they needed to stay in office.

In 1958, France faced the threat of civil war over the question of Algerian independence. The Fourth Republic was too weak to handle the problem. General Charles de Gaulle, France's hero of World War II, formed a new government. It wrote a new constitution that increased the executive powers, and made it more difficult for the Assembly to force the cabinet to resign. The constitution gave the president the power to submit treaties and constitutional amendments to the voters for approval. The president also was given the power to dissolve the Assembly before its term ended, and to call new elections. In a national emergency, the president was allowed to take all executive and legislative powers. The voters' approval of this constitution established the Fifth Republic.

President and Prime Minister. The president of France is elected to a seven-year term by voters aged 18 or older. The president can serve an unlimited number of terms. The president appoints the prime minister and the *Council of Ministers* (cabinet), which is headed by the prime minister. The prime minister directs the day-to-day operations of the government.

Parliament. The National Assembly consists of 491 *deputies*, elected by the voters to five-year terms. The less powerful house of Parliament is the Senate. It has 280 members. Senators are elected to nine-year terms by regional and city electoral colleges. If the houses of Parliament disagree on a proposed law, the prime minister may ask the Assembly to cast the deciding vote.

Local Government. The basic unit of local government in France is the *commune*. France has about 38,000 communes, which vary in size from small villages to large cities. Except for Paris, each commune is governed by an elected council whose members select one of their number as mayor. For a discussion of the government of Paris, see PARIS (Government).

Mainland France and the island of Corsica are divided into 96 *metropolitan departments*. Each department is administered by a *prefect*, appointed by the national government. The prefects are assisted by elected coun-

Publix Pictorial

Bourbon Palace is the meeting place of the National Assembly, the main house of France's Parliament. It was completed in 1728.

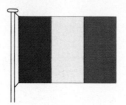

H. E. Harris & Co.

The French Flag is called the *tricolor*. In 1789, King Louis XVI first used its three colors to represent France.

An Unofficial Symbol of France, adopted in 1953, has emblems used by ancient Rome to represent a republic.

cils. France has many overseas possessions. See the separate articles listed under Overseas Possessions in the *Related Articles* at the end of this article.

Courts are in the major cities of each department. Appeals from civil and criminal courts may be taken to *Courts of Appeal*. The *Courts of Assizes* hear cases involving murder and other very serious crimes. The decisions of the Courts of Appeal and of Assizes are generally final. But the *Court of Cassation*, the highest court of France, may review these decisions. It can return cases to the lower courts for new trials.

Armed Forces. Men between the ages of 18 and 35 must serve 16 months of active duty in the French armed forces. About 565,000 persons serve in the army, navy, and air force.

France, the largest Western European country, is about 7 per cent the size of the United States, not counting Alaska and Hawaii.

WORLD BOOK map

France Map Index

395

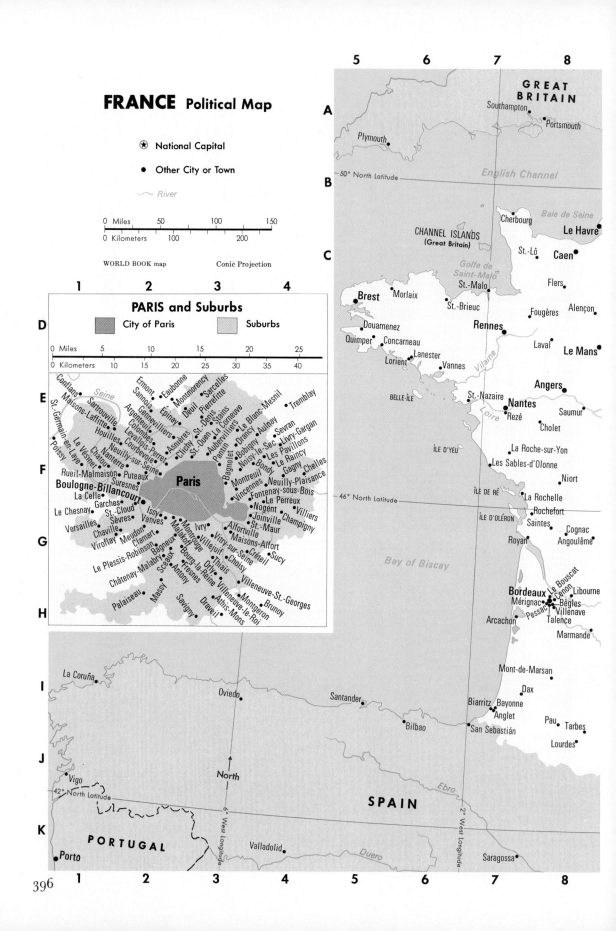

FRANCE Political Map

⊛ National Capital

● Other City or Town

〜 River

0 Miles 50 100 150
0 Kilometers 100 200

WORLD BOOK map   Conic Projection

PARIS and Suburbs

▨ City of Paris   ▨ Suburbs

0 Miles 5 10 15 20 25
0 Kilometers 10 15 20 25 30 35 40

GREAT BRITAIN

Southampton
Portsmouth
Plymouth

English Channel

50° North Latitude

Cherbourg
Baie de Seine
Le Havre
St.-Lô
Caen

CHANNEL ISLANDS
(Great Britain)

Golfe de Saint-Malo
St.-Malo
Flers
Brest
Morlaix
St.-Brieuc
Fougères
Alençon
Douarnenez
Rennes
Quimper
Concarneau
Laval
Le Mans
Lorient
Lanester
Vannes

BELLE-ÎLE
St.-Nazaire
Angers
Nantes
Saumur
Rezé
Cholet

ÎLE D'YEU
La Roche-sur-Yon
Les Sables-d'Olonne

ÎLE DE RÉ
Niort
46° North Latitude
La Rochelle
ÎLE D'OLÉRON
Rochefort
Royan
Saintes
Cognac
Angoulême

Bay of Biscay

Le Bouscat
Bordeaux Cenon Libourne
Mérignac Bègles
Pessac Villenave
Arcachon Talence
Marmande

Mont-de-Marsan
Dax
Biarritz Bayonne
La Coruña
Oviedo
Santander
Anglet
Pau Tarbes
San Sebastián
Lourdes
Bilbao

Vigo
Ebro
SPAIN

42° North Latitude

PORTUGAL
Porto
Valladolid
Duero
Saragossa

Paris and Suburbs labels

Conflans
Ermont
Eaubonne
Seine
Sannois
Montmorency
Sarcelles
Maisons-Laffitte
Gennevilliers
Déuil
Pierrefitte
Sartrouville
Epinay
St.-Denis
Stains
St.-Germain-en-Laye
Argenteuil
Asnières
Houilles
Colombes
St.-Ouen La Coneuve
Le Blanc-Mesnil
Tremblay
Le Vésinet
Levallois-Perret
Clichy
Aubervilliers
Drancy
Aulnay
Poissy
Chatou
Courbevoie
Pantin
Noisy-le-Sec
Sevran
Nanterre
Neuilly-sur-Seine
Bobigny
Les Pavillons
Livry-Gargan
Puteaux
Bagnolet
Bondy
Le Raincy
Rueil-Malmaison
Montreuil
Gagny
Chelles
Suresnes
Vincennes
Neuilly-Plaisance
Boulogne-Billancourt
Paris
Fontenay-sous-Bois
La Celle
Le Perreux
Villiers
Garches
Nogent
Le Chesnay
St.-Cloud
Issy
Joinville
Champigny
Sèvres
Vanves
Ivry
St.-Maur
Versailles
Chaville
Montrouge
Alfortville
Sucy
Viroflay
Meudon
Malakoff
Vitry-sur-Seine
Créteil
Clamart
Bagneux
Villejuif
Maisons-Alfort
Le Plessis-Robinson
Bourg-la-Reine
Choisy
Châtenay-Malabry
Sceaux
Orly
Thiais
Villeneuve-St.-Georges
Fresnes
Antony
Villeneuve-le-Roi
Montgeron
Palaiseau
Massy
Savigny
Draveil
Athis-Mons
Brunoy

396

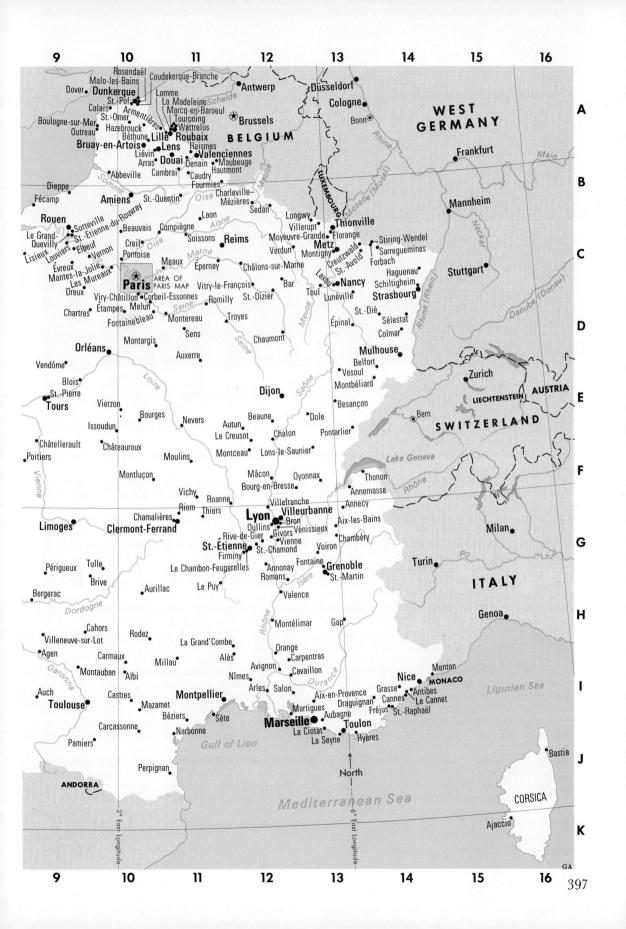

Village Festivals are yearly events throughout France. This dance is part of a festival in the Provence region.

FRANCE/People

Among the people of France, there are some small regional differences in language and traditions. The major regional difference is between the people of Paris and those of the rest of France. No other French city equals Paris as a center of cultural, economic, and political activity. Every year, thousands of persons move to Paris to enjoy its varied advantages.

Population. Since World War II ended in 1945, France's population has increased by about 1 per cent a year. In 1979, France had more than 54 million persons.

About three-fourths of the French people live in cities and towns of at least 2,000 persons. About a sixth live in the Paris metropolitan area, one of the largest in the world. France has 39 cities with populations of over 100,000. Five of them have more than 300,000 persons. In order of size, they are Paris, Marseille, Lyon, Toulouse, and Nice. See the articles on French cities listed in the *Related Articles* at the end of this article.

In ancient times, peoples called *Gauls* lived in what is now France (see GAUL). Roman, Germanic, and then Norse invaders came from the south, east, and north. The Romans brought peace to the warring Gallic tribes, and Roman law became the basis of modern French law. The name of France came from Germanic conquerors called *Franks.* Many persons of northeastern France have Germanic ancestors. The people of Normandy trace their ancestry back to the Norse people who settled there. Many other groups came from various parts of Europe and Africa and settled in France. They included Belgians, Italians, Poles, and Spaniards.

Language. The French language began to develop with the invasions of the ancient Romans. The Gauls

adopted the Latin tongue of the Roman soldiers, and gradually changed it through the years. Later invaders added new words to the language, and the changes continued. For a discussion of the French language, including its development, see FRENCH LANGUAGE.

Some persons of Provence, where the Roman influence was particularly strong, speak Provençal. This language also developed from Latin. Breton, a Celtic language similar to Welsh, is spoken in Brittany. Along the Pyrenees Mountains, separate groups speak Basque and Catalan. Flemish is used in Flanders, and forms of German are heard throughout Alsace and in parts of Lorraine. But wherever any of these languages are spoken, most of the people also speak French.

Education. French children between the ages of 6 and 16 must go to school. About 85 per cent of the children in elementary schools attend public schools. About 75 per cent of the high school students go to public schools. The others attend private schools, most of which are operated by the Roman Catholic Church.

The French educational system is highly centralized. The Ministry of National Education decides what courses should be taught and what teaching methods should be used in elementary and high schools throughout the country. The ministry grants all graduation certificates in public schools. All students graduating from public schools must take the same state examinations.

Children between the ages of 2 and 6 may attend free nursery schools. Reading is taught during the last year of these schools. Children from 6 to 13 attend elementary schools, most of which are separate schools for boys or girls. Students in elementary schools study language and mathematics in the morning and arts, physi-

Boulevards of Paris are famous for their sidewalk cafes where Parisians enjoy sipping coffee or wine under the trees. Fashionable shops along the boulevards sell such items as women's clothing, perfume, gloves, and handbags.

cal education, and social studies in the afternoon. At the age of 11, many children begin a four-year period of observation by their teachers. After this period, the teachers tell the parents whether the children may enter a general high school or a trade school. A student recommended for a vocational school can enter a general high school by passing an examination.

The general high schools, called *collèges* and *lycées*, prepare students to enter universities. The last year of these schools is a period of specialized study in one of five areas. These areas are philosophy, experimental sciences, mathematics, mathematics and technology, and economics and social sciences. This year compares in difficulty with the second year of university work in the United States or Canada. About 40 per cent of the students study philosophy, the most popular specialized course. A *baccalauréat* examination completes this program. The examination is so hard that from 30 to 50 per cent of the students fail it. The baccalauréat degree is granted by the Ministry of National Education. Most French universities admit students who have this degree.

Vocational schools offer study programs that last from three to five years. These programs include job training in such fields as business, crafts, farming, industry, and teaching.

A law reforming French state universities was passed in 1968 and gradually went into effect in 1969 and 1970. Before the reform, France had 23 state universities, each made up of separate schools of law, literature, sciences, medicine, and pharmacy.

Under the reform law, the state universities were replaced by 61 smaller state universities, each with many departments rather than separate schools. Each of these

POPULATION

This map shows the population distribution of France. Each dot represents 25,000 persons. The five cities on the map have the largest metropolitan populations.

WORLD BOOK map

new universities selects its courses and teaching methods. Students have a voice in university administration. Tuition is free. The government provides financial support and grants all state university degrees.

France also has schools of higher education called *Grandes Écoles* (Great Schools). They prepare students for high-ranking careers in the civil and military services, commerce, education, industry, and other fields. Only about a tenth of the students pass the entrance examinations for these state-operated schools.

Museums and Libraries. France has about 30 government-owned museums. The best known, the Louvre in Paris, is one of the largest art museums in the world (see LOUVRE). Many old castles and palaces, once the homes of kings and emperors, are national historical museums. They include the palace at Versailles, built by King Louis XIV (see VERSAILLES). Other French museums have important scientific exhibits.

Public libraries are in all large French cities. France's national library, the Bibliothèque Nationale in Paris, is similar to the U.S. Library of Congress. It has more than six million books, and is one of the largest libraries in Western Europe (see BIBLIOTHÈQUE NATIONALE). Other important libraries include the Mazarine Library of the Institute of France, the country's major learned society. The University of Paris also has fine libraries.

Religion. More than 80 per cent of the French people are Roman Catholics. Less than 2 per cent are Protestants. France also has some Jews and Muslims. From 1801 to 1905, the French government recognized Roman Catholicism as the religion of the majority of the people. Bishops and priests were state officials, and were paid by the government. This church-state connection, established by Napoleon and Pope Pius VII, was broken by French law in 1905.

The Louvre in Paris is one of the largest art museums in the world. It has nearly 250,000 drawings, paintings, statues, and other works of art. The Louvre attracts more than 2 million visitors a year, and is especially popular with tourists.

Doumic, Pix

Rene Burri, Magnum

French Students on each elementary grade level are taught the same courses, no matter where in France they go to school.

Holidays. Most French holidays and festivals are closely connected with the Roman Catholic Church. Many cities celebrate Shrove Tuesday, the last day before Lent, with a merry carnival called *Mardi Gras*. The Mardi Gras celebration in Nice includes a colorful parade, and attracts many tourists. Most villages honor their local patron saints with a festival in July.

On *Noël* (Christmas), French families hold reunions and the children receive gifts (see CHRISTMAS [In France]). The people also exchange gifts on *Le Jour de l'An* (New Year's Day). On *Pâques* (Easter), the children receive colored candy eggs and chocolate chickens. Church bells do not ring from Good Friday to Easter. Some parents tell their children that the bells fly to Rome and drop the candy eggs when they return.

The French national holiday is Bastille Day, July 14. It marks the capture of the Bastille, a fortified prison, by the people of Paris in 1789, during the French Revolution. A large military parade is held in Paris on Bastille Day. At night, the people watch fireworks and dance in the streets until dawn.

Cooking is considered an art by the French. They are world famous for their salads, sauces, and soups. Almost every region, city, and restaurant of France has its own food specialty. These specialties include *truffles* (mushroomlike plants) in the Guyenne region, snails in Burgundy, sausages in Arles and Lyon, omelets in Mont St. Michel, and pressed duck in Paris.

Sports. The greatest national sporting event in France is the *Tour de France*, a bicycle race. Every summer, more than a hundred professional cyclists race around almost the entire country. They ride daily for nearly a month, and finish in Paris. Thousands of spectators line the route and cheer them along. France's most popular team sport is *soccer*, a form of football. Almost every area and region has its own team. The French also enjoy *boules* (a form of bowling), fishing, ice skating, rugby, skiing, swimming, and tennis.

French Family Life is much like that in the United States or Canada. This family is visiting the father's parents in Le Havre. The roof of the grandparents' apartment house provides a view of the harbor, where the father works as a shipping agent.

On Market Day, many French farmers bring their fruits, vegetables, and other products into the cities and towns. Housewives buy the foods in busy public squares such as this one in Carcassonne.

Bastille Day, July 14, is France's national holiday. An annual parade in Paris celebrates the capture of the Bastille, a prison, during the French Revolution.

Outdoor Camping is a popular vacation activity in France. Millions of Frenchmen, including entire families, go camping every year. The government operates thousands of campsites throughout the country.

Basque Fishermen unload a basket of fish caught in the Bay of Biscay. The Basques of France live in the Pyrenees region along the Spanish border.

Ewing Krainin

Castles, called *châteaux*, stand in the Loire Valley of France. The château at Villandry is famous for its beautiful gardens.

French Sculpture of the Late 1800's is represented by the masterpieces of Auguste Rodin.

Monument to Balzac by Auguste Rodin, The Museum of Modern Art, New York

FRANCE / *Arts*

Architecture. During the 1100's and 1200's, French architects developed the towering style of the Gothic cathedral. Famous examples include Notre Dame in Paris and the cathedrals of Amiens, Chartres, and Reims. During the Renaissance, French kings and nobles built many magnificent *châteaux* (castles), especially in the Loire Valley. The palace of Versailles, designed in the baroque style, is one of the finest palaces in the world. During the 1900's, the architect Le Corbusier developed many new styles. See ARCHITECTURE (with pictures); GOTHIC ART; LE CORBUSIER.

Literature of France became highly developed during the Middle Ages. François Villon was France's greatest poet of the period. The books of François Rabelais and the essays of Michel de Montaigne gave expression to the reforming spirit of the Renaissance. French writers of the 1600's and 1700's set examples of quality for all Europe, especially in drama. The greatest dramatists were Pierre Corneille, Molière, and Jean Racine.

The novel became the most important form of writing during the 1800's. Major novelists included Honoré de Balzac, Gustave Flaubert, Victor Hugo, and Émile Zola. Charles Baudelaire and Arthur Rimbaud led new movements in poetry. Important novelists of the 1900's include Albert Camus, André Gide, Marcel Proust, and Jean-Paul Sartre. See FRENCH LITERATURE.

Painting. During the 1800's, French artists led new movements in painting. Paris became the art capital of the world, and held this position until World War II. Impressionism, the best-known movement, included such painters as Edouard Manet, Claude Monet, Camille Pissarro, and Pierre Auguste Renoir. Great French painters in other movements included Jacques Louis David (neoclassicism); Eugène Delacroix and Théodore Géricault (romanticism); Paul Cézanne and Paul Gauguin (post-impressionism); Georges Braque (cubism); and Yves Tanguy (surrealism). Many great artists born in other countries have lived in France. They include Marc Chagall, Pablo Picasso, and Vincent van Gogh. See PAINTING (The 1800's; The 1900's).

Sculpture. French sculptors decorated the Gothic cathedrals with many religious, royal, and imaginary figures. During the Renaissance, Jean Goujon and others adopted the graceful Italian style. Since that period, France has had many fine sculptors, including Jean Antoine Houdon, Auguste Rodin, and Aristide Maillol. See SCULPTURE.

Music. France's composers have been less outstanding than its artists and writers. But many have won fame, including Louis Hector Berlioz, Georges Bizet, Claude Debussy, Charles Gounod, Darius Milhaud, and Maurice Ravel. See MUSIC (History).

Modern French Architecture is represented by this apartment building, completed in 1952 and designed by Le Corbusier.

Historic French Furniture was richly decorated. This furniture of the Louis XV period is in the palace of Versailles.

French Impressionist Painting developed during the late 1800's. This important style took its name from *Impression: Sunrise* by Claude Monet.

A Modern French Artist, Jean Dubuffet, created *The Gardener* from leaves of plants.

The Comedies of Molière, including *The Miser*, poked fun at the weaknesses, foolish behavior, and false values of the French people during the 1600's.

Tapestry Makers in the town of Aubusson weave wallhangings from colorful yarn.

FRANCE / *The Land*

The Îles Chausey and other islands lie north of the rugged coast of Brittany. Lobster fishing is an important industry on these small islands, which are in the Golfe de St. Malo.

France has wide differences in geography. The northern and western regions consist mainly of flat or rolling plains. Hills and mountains rise in the eastern, central, and southern parts of France. France has 10 main land regions. They are (1) the Brittany-Normandy Hills, (2) the Northern France Plains, (3) the Northeastern Plateaus, (4) the Rhine Valley, (5) the Aquitanian Lowlands, (6) the Central Highlands, (7) the French Alps and Jura Mountains, (8) the Pyrenees Mountains, (9) the Mediterranean Lowlands and Rhône-Saône Valley, and (10) the island of Corsica.

The Brittany-Normandy Hills region has low, rounded hills and rolling plains. This region consists of ancient rock covered by poor soils, with some fertile areas along the coast. Apple orchards, dairy farms, and grasslands crisscross the land, and thick hedges separate the fields. Many bays indent the rugged coast and have important fishing harbors.

The Northern France Plains have highly fertile soils and productive industries. The plains are flat or rolling, and are broken up by forest-covered hills and plateaus. This heavily populated region includes Paris, where about a sixth of the French people live. The Paris Basin is a large, circular area drained by the Seine and other major rivers. East of Paris, a series of rocky ridges resembles the upturned edge of a huge saucer. Coal is mined near the Belgian border.

The Northeastern Plateaus share the Ardennes Mountains with Belgium. This wooded region becomes a little more rugged to the southeast in the Vosges Mountains. It has great deposits of iron ore, and produces much iron and steel. Farmers raise livestock and a variety of crops

on the lower slopes and in the valleys. Lumbermen operate in the large forests.

The Rhine Valley has steep slopes and flat bottom lands. Trees and vines cover the slopes, and rich farmlands lie along the Rhine River. This river, which forms part of France's boundary with Germany, is the main inland waterway in Europe. Important roads and railways follow its course.

Land Regions of France

404

FRANCE Physical Map

Physical Features

Aisne River .... B 6
Allier River .... D 5
Alpes Cottiennes .. D 7
Alpes Grées .... D 7
Alps .... D 7
Ardennes (Plateau) B 6
Argonne (Plateau) . B 6
Baie de Seine ...... B 3
Belfort Gap .... C 7
Belle-Île .... C 2
Bretagne,
 Collines de ...... B 2
Cap de la Hague ... B 3
Carlit (Mtn.) ...... E 5
Causses (Plateau) . D 4
Cévennes (Mts.) ... D 5
Chambon Dam ...... D 7
Doubs River .... C 6
English Channel ... B 2
Étang de Carcans .. D 3
Garonne River ..... D 4
Gavarnie Falls ..... E 3
Gave d'Oloron ..... E 3
Génissiat Dam ..... C 6
Gironde (Estuary) . D 3
Golfe de St. Malo .. B 2
Groix, Île de ...... C 2
Gulf of Lion ...... E 5

Hyères, Îles d' ..... E 6
Isère River .... D 6
Jura Mts. .... C 7
Lac de Grand-Lieu .C 3
Lannemezan,
 Plateau de ...... E 3
Les Écrins
 (Mountain) ...... D 7
Little St. Bernard
 Pass .... D 7
Loir River .... C 4
Loire River .... C 4
Lorraine, Plateau . B 7
Maritime Alps ..... D 7
Marne River .... B 5
Massif Central .... D 5
Mediterranean Sea .E 6
Meuse River .... B 6
Meuse, Côtes de .. B 6
Mont Blanc .... D 7
Mont Cenis Pass ... D 7
Mont Pelat .... D 7
Mont St. Michel
 (Island) .... B 3
Monts du Forez ... D 5
Monts du Morvan .C 6
Moselle (Mosel)
 River .... B 7

Nivernais, Côtes du C 5
Noirmoutier, Île de C 2
Normandie,
 Collines de ...... B 3
Oise River .... B 5
Oleron, Île d' ..... D 3
Or, Côte d' .... C 6
Perche, Collines du C 4
Pertuis Breton .... C 3
Pic de Montcalm ..E 4
Pointe de Barfleur . B 3
Pyrenees (Mts.) ... E 3
Quiberon,
 Presqu'île de .... C 2
Rance River .... B 3
Ré, Île de .... C 3
Rhine River .... B 7
Rhône River .... D 6
Riviera .... E 7
Saône River .... C 6
Sarthe River ...... C 4
Seine River .... B 4
Somme River ...... B 4
Vienne River ...... C 4
Vire River .... B 3
Visoulet (Mtn.) .... D 7
Vosges Mountains . B 7
Yonne River .... C 5

Historic Provinces

ALSACE .... B 7
ANGOUMOIS ..... D 3
ANJOU .... C 3
ARTOIS .... A 5
AUNIS .... D 3
AUVERGNE .... E 3
BÉARN .... E 3
BERRY .... C 4
BOURBONNAIS .. C 5
BRITTANY .... B 2
BURGUNDY .... C 6
CHAMPAGNE .... B 5
COMTAT
 VENAISSIN ..... D 6
DAUPHINÉ .... D 6
FLANDERS .... A 5
FOIX .... E 4
FRANCHE-COMTÉ C 6
GASCONY .... D 3
GUYENNE .... D 3
ÎLE-DE-FRANCE .. B 5
LANGUEDOC ..... E 5
LIMOUSIN .... D 4
LORRAINE .... B 6
LYONNAIS .... D 6
MAINE .... C 3
MARCHE .... C 4
NICE .... E 7
NIVERNAIS .... C 5
NORMANDY ...... B 3
ORLÉANAIS ...... C 4
PICARDY .... B 5
POITOU .... C 3
PROVENCE .... E 6
ROUSSILLON .... E 5
SAINTONGE ...... D 3
SAVOY .... D 7
TOURAINE .... C 4

French Geographic Terms

Alpes .... mountains
Baie .... bay
Cap .... cape
Colline(s) ..... hill(s)
Côte(s) .... hill(s)
Étang .... lagoon
Fôret .... forest
Gave .... stream
Golfe .... gulf
Hauteur(s) .... hill(s)
Île(s) .... island(s)
Lac .... lake
Massif .... upland
Mont(s) .. mountain(s)
Pic .... peak
Pointe .... point
Presqu'île .. peninsula

The Loire River, about 650 miles (1,050 kilometers) long, is the longest river entirely within France. Much of the Loire flows through the fertile Northern France Plains. The Loire Valley is famous for its *châteaux* (castles) built hundreds of years ago.

In Alsace, on the Northeastern Plateaus, vineyards spread over the rolling valleys and lower slopes of the Vosges Mountains. The region also has large forests and many potash deposits.

The Central Highlands include peaks as high as 6,000 feet (1,800 meters). The tallest mountains rise in the Auvergne section. Soils are rich in some valleys, but are poor in most of the region.

In the French Alps, the country's highest mountains, cattle graze in pastures above the thickly forested slopes.

The Aquitanian Lowlands are drained by the Garonne River and the streams that flow into it. Sandy beaches lie along the coast. Inland, the region has pine forests, rolling plains, and sand dunes. Its many vineyards supply grapes for France's important wine industry. Oil and natural gas fields are in the Landes area, a forested section south of the major seaport of Bordeaux.

The Central Highlands, or *Massif Central,* is thinly populated. The soils are poor, except in some valleys where rye and other crops are grown. Cattle and sheep graze on the lower grasslands, and forests cover the higher slopes. Coal is mined near St.-Étienne. The Loire River, about 650 miles (1,050 kilometers) long, rises in the Cévennes Mountains. It is the longest river entirely within France. See LOIRE RIVER.

The French Alps and Jura Mountains border on Italy and Switzerland. Snow-capped Mont Blanc, the highest point in France, rises 15,771 feet (4,807 meters). Many tourists visit nearby Chamonix and other ski resorts in the mountains. Mountain streams provide much hydroelectric power. See ALPS; JURA; MONT BLANC.

The Pyrenees Mountains extend along France's border with Spain. Many peaks in this range rise more than 10,000 feet (3,000 meters). The rugged mountains have poor soils and are thinly populated. See PYRENEES.

The Mediterranean Lowlands and Rhône-Saône Valley region has productive farming areas, and irrigation is used widely. Fruits, vegetables, and wine grapes are important products. Marseille, on the Mediterranean Sea, is the leading seaport of France. The coast also includes the Riviera, a famous resort area. See RHÔNE RIVER; RIVIERA.

Corsica is a Mediterranean island about 100 miles (160 kilometers) southeast of mainland France. It has hills and mountains similar to those of the Central Highlands. The island has generally poor soils and a steep, rocky coastline. Crops are grown in the valleys, and sheep graze in the mountains. See CORSICA.

FRANCE / Climate

The climate varies widely among the various regions of France. The differences in climate are closely related to the distance of the land from the Atlantic Ocean or the Mediterranean Sea. Westerly winds that blow in from the Atlantic strongly influence the climate of western France. The coastal regions there have a rainy climate with mild winters and cool summers.

To the east, away from the Atlantic, the climate changes sharply between seasons. These inland regions have hot summers and cold winters, with medium rainfall throughout the year. The mountainous regions receive the most *precipitation* (rain, melted snow, and other forms of moisture), most of it in summer. Heavy winter snows fall in the Alps and Jura Mountains, and huge glaciers are found in the Alps.

Along the Mediterranean Sea, the lowlands have hot, dry summers and mild winters with some rainfall. Swift, cold north winds called *mistrals* sometimes blow over southern France and cause crop damage (see MISTRAL). The Alps shield the sunny Riviera from the cold north winds during much of the year.

A. L. Goldman, Rapho Guillumette

The Sunny French Riviera, a world-famous vacation area, is warmed by breezes from the Mediterranean Sea.

AVERAGE JANUARY TEMPERATURES

Degrees Fahrenheit	Degrees Celsius
above 39	above 4
36 to 39	2 to 4
32 to 36	0 to 2
below 32	below 0

AVERAGE JULY TEMPERATURES

Degrees Fahrenheit	Degrees Celsius
above 72	above 22
64 to 72	18 to 22
50 to 64	10 to 18
below 50	below 10

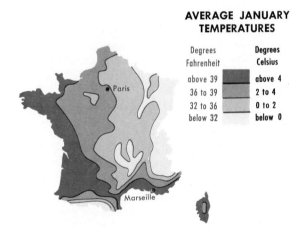

AVERAGE YEARLY PRECIPITATION
(Rain, Melted Snow, and Other Moisture)

Inches	Centimeters
more than 39	more than 100
31 to 39	80 to 100
24 to 31	60 to 80
less than 24	less than 60

```
0    100   200   300   400  Miles
0  100 200 300 400 500 600  Kilometers
```

WORLD BOOK maps

AVERAGE MONTHLY WEATHER

	PARIS					MARSEILLE				
	Temperatures F.°		Temperatures C°		Days of Rain or Snow		Temperatures F.°		Temperatures C°		Days of Rain or Snow
	High	Low	High	Low			High	Low	High	Low	
JAN.	42	32	6	0	15	JAN.	53	38	12	3	10
FEB.	45	33	7	1	13	FEB.	52	37	11	3	9
MAR.	52	36	11	2	15	MAR.	55	38	13	3	8
APR.	60	41	16	5	14	APR.	59	41	15	5	10
MAY	67	47	19	8	13	MAY	65	46	18	8	10
JUNE	73	52	23	11	11	JUNE	72	52	22	11	9
JULY	76	55	24	13	12	JULY	78	58	26	14	6
AUG.	75	55	24	13	12	AUG.	83	61	28	16	4
SEPT.	69	50	21	10	11	SEPT.	82	61	28	16	5
OCT.	59	44	15	7	14	OCT.	76	57	24	14	7
NOV.	49	38	9	3	15	NOV.	67	50	19	10	10
DEC.	43	33	6	1	17	DEC.	59	43	15	6	11

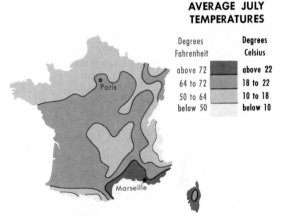

Sources: Comité National de Géographie, Paris; Air Ministry, Meteorological Office, London.

France is one of the rich nations of the world, and its people have a high standard of living. The prosperity resulted largely from sweeping economic changes made since the 1940's. Before World War II, the French economy was based chiefly on small, old-fashioned farms and business firms. After the war ended in 1945, the government worked to modernize the economy. New methods of production and trade were developed through a series of national plans. These improvements, which are still going on, have brought ever-increasing production. For France's rank in the output of various products, see the articles listed under Products and Industry in the *Related Articles* at the end of this article.

France's Gross National Product

Total gross national product in 1975—$304,600,000,000

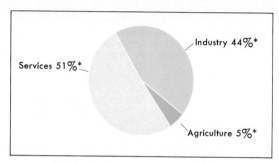

Services 51%*

Industry 44%*

Agriculture 5%*

The Gross National Product (GNP) is the total value of goods and services produced by a country in a year. The GNP measures a nation's total economic performance. It can also be used to compare the economic output and growth of countries.

Production and Workers by Economic Activities

Economic Activities	Per Cent of GDP* Produced	Employed Workers†	
		Number of Persons	Per Cent of Total
Manufacturing	35	5,961,000	28
Community, Social, & Personal Services	19	4,559,000	21
Hotels, Restaurants, & Trade	16	3,502,000	17
Government	10	**	**
Construction	9	1,981,000	9
Agriculture, Forestry, & Fishing	5	2,452,000	12
Transportation & Communication	5	1,162,000	5
Finance, Insurance, Real Estate, & Business Services	**	1,189,000	6
Housing	‡	—	—
Mining	§	185,000	1
Utilities	§	174,000	1
Other Services	1	**	**
Total	100	21,165,000	100

*Based on gross domestic product (GDP) in 1974. GDP is gross national product adjusted for net income sent or received from abroad.
†Figures are for 1974.
**Included in Community, Social, & Personal Services.
‡Included in Finance, Insurance, Real Estate, & Business Services.
§Included in Manufacturing.
Sources: Yearbook of Labor Statistics 1975, ILO; Yearbook of National Accounts Statistics 1975, UN; World Bank.

Natural Resources play an important part in France's prosperity. Rich soils are the country's most important natural resource. France also has plentiful water and large deposits of some minerals.

Soils. More than 90 per cent of France's total land area is fertile. The richest farmlands lie in the north and northeast, where wheat and sugar beets are the chief crops. The rainier northwest consists mainly of grasslands, used for grazing cattle and sheep, and orchards. Many of the drier areas of southern France have good soils for growing grapes. Soils are generally poor in the Central Highlands and on Corsica.

Minerals. Iron ore is France's most important mineral deposit. Most of it comes from Lorraine, and helps make that region a major steel producer. Great deposits of bauxite, from which aluminum is made, are found in southeastern France. Alsace has much potash, used in making fertilizers. France has small deposits of *nonferrous* (without iron) metals such as copper, lead, and zinc. The country also has several important coal deposits and some natural gas, petroleum, and salt.

Forests cover about a fifth of France. Heavily forested sections include the Northeastern Plateaus, the Central Highlands, the southwestern coastal areas, and the slopes of the Alps, Juras, Pyrenees, and Vosges. Many forests are being planted in the Landes area of southwestern France for use by the pulp and paper industry. Pine trees and cork oaks grow along the dry Mediterranean coast and on Corsica. Forest fires are common in these regions. Other trees of France include ashes, beeches, cypresses, and olives.

Manufacturing. France has many more manufacturing industries than it had before World War II. Large corporations control the new industries. But even the largest French corporations are small compared with the industrial giants of the United States. The Paris area is France's manufacturing center, and it produces a wide variety of products. To spread industry more evenly, the government helps companies establish plants in the less industrialized western areas. These areas have many new electronics factories that produce computers, radios, and television sets.

The great French automobile industry is chiefly in Paris, and a large plant operates near Rennes. About 300,000 workers produce about $3\frac{1}{3}$ million cars and trucks a year. The government-owned Renault automobile company is the largest in France. The aircraft industry has expanded rapidly at Toulouse since the war. The chemical industry is also growing rapidly. Petrochemicals, made from petroleum, are produced mainly in Berre and Lacq in southern France, and in Rouen.

The French iron and steel industry is based largely on iron ore mined in France. The aluminum industry uses about 90 per cent of the bauxite taken from French mines. Its production has increased about 600 per cent since World War II. Local and imported wood goes into the production of furniture, lumber, and pulp and paper. The famous French perfume industry, based in Paris, uses flowers grown in southeastern France.

Cotton and silk textiles have traditionally been important French products. But this industry is growing at a slower rate than the production of nylon and other

FARM, MINERAL, AND FOREST PRODUCTS

This map shows where the leading farm, mineral, and forest products are produced. The map also shows the major industrial areas and the areas that have little or no agricultural or industrial importance.

Mainly Cropland
Mainly Pastureland
Major Industrial Area
Nonproductive Area

0   50   100   150 Miles
0 50 100 150 200 Kilometers

WORLD BOOK map – FGA

Grapes of Alsace are used in making wine, one of France's chief products. More wine is produced in France than in any other country. Much of the high-quality wine is exported.

Automobile Production in France is one of the highest in the world. The government owns this Renault factory west of Paris.

Robert Doisneau, Rapho Guillumette

Doumic, Pix

artificial fibers. The Lyon area, long a silk center, has new artificial-fiber factories. Paris, the fashion capital of the world, produces much of the nation's clothing.

In the big cities, the preparation of fancy home-cooked meals is decreasing, and the use of precooked and frozen foods is increasing. As a result, food processing has grown in importance. France has long been famous for processing wine and cheese. The wine is aged, sometimes for many years, in deep cellars or caves. France produces much butter, and about 300 kinds of cheese, including Brie, Camembert, and Roquefort.

About 10 million clocks and watches are made yearly in France, chiefly in communities in the Alps and the Jura Mountains. Several plants produce nuclear materials for peacetime and military uses.

Agriculture. Since World War II, French farming methods have been modernized rapidly. Production has increased, in spite of a heavy movement of farmers to the cities. French farmers have about a million tractors, compared with 30,000 before the war, and almost all the farms have electricity. Many small, scattered plots of land belonging to the same farm have been regrouped with government help into larger units. Over 1 million acres (400,000 hectares) a year have been reorganized, making modern equipment more useful. French farms average $37\frac{1}{2}$ acres (15.2 hectares), compared with about 385 acres (156 hectares) in the United States.

The farmers of France earn about two-thirds of their income by raising meat and dairy animals. About a fourth of the nation's land consists of grassland, used for grazing. Beef cattle are the chief meat animals, and lambs and sheep are also important. French peasants have always raised some chickens and hogs, and specialized, large-scale production of these animals is expanding rapidly. Much of the milk produced on the dairy farms is used in making butter and cheese.

Crops grow on more than a third of France's land. Livestock feeds, including barley, corn, oats, and potatoes, are grown on most of the cropland. Large farms in the Paris Basin and the north grow most of the wheat, France's leading single crop. The farmers produce more wheat than the nation can use. As a result, the government encourages farmers to grow less wheat and more of other crops. The big wheat farms rotate wheat with sugar beets and potatoes. Other important crops include chicory, colza, flax, flowers, forage beets, fruits, hops, rice, rye, tobacco, and vegetables.

Most grapes used in making wine are grown in southern France. The Mediterranean region produces grapes used in making the cheaper kinds of wine. Grapes for high-quality wine come from several regions, including Alsace, Bordeaux, Burgundy, Champagne, and the Loire Valley. Each region produces grapes that have their own special flavor. Grapes from southwestern France are used in making brandy.

Mining. About 96 per cent of France's iron ore comes from Lorraine. Coal is also mined there and near Lille. Among Western European nations, only Greece produces more bauxite than France. Discoveries of natural gas at Lacq, in southwestern France, have attracted many industries since 1949. Most petroleum mined in France comes from the Landes area. French mines also produce gypsum, potash, uranium, and other minerals.

Fishing. French commercial fishing brings in a yearly catch of about 878,000 short tons (797,000 metric tons). Fishing crews work off the French coasts, or sail the Atlantic Ocean to the waters of Iceland and Newfoundland. Many fishing fleets operate from Brittany and Normandy. Seafood taken by French crews includes cod, crabs, herring, lobsters, mackerel, oysters, sardines, shrimps, and tuna.

Tourism. More than six million persons a year visit France. Paris, one of the most beautiful cities in the world, attracts many visitors. Some tourists go to famous vacation resorts in the Alps or on the Riviera. Others enjoy motoring or bicycling through the colorful countryside, and viewing historical sights such as the *châteaux* (castles) of the Loire Valley.

Electric Power. French homes and industries need four times as much power as they required before World War II. Coal-burning plants, which supplied 80 per cent of the power before the war, now provide less than half. Hydroelectric plants have been expanded, especially in the Alps and the Jura Mountains. In 1961, the French government started to build the world's first tidal power plant. This plant started operations in 1966. It uses the tides of the English Channel in the mouth of the Rance River. These tides are among the highest in the world, and may reach a height of 44 feet (13 meters). The government also operates some nuclear plants, which produce about 8 per cent of France's electricity.

Foreign Trade of France, as measured by exports, is the fourth largest in the world. It ranks after the United States, West Germany, and Japan. France belongs to the European Economic Community, usually called the *Common Market* (see EUROPEAN COMMUNITY). About 40 per cent of France's trade is with Common Market countries, chiefly West Germany. About 15 per cent of the total trade is with other countries in the French Community. This organization includes most of France's former colonies in Africa.

Transportation. Since the 1700's, France has had more road mileage in relation to its size than any other European country. Today, it has about 50,500 miles (81,270 kilometers) of national highways, 173,600 miles (279,380 kilometers) of local highways, and 263,500 miles (424,060 kilometers) of local roads. About one of every two families owns an automobile. In 1965, the world's longest highway tunnel was built through Mont Blanc. The Mont Blanc Tunnel is $7\frac{1}{4}$ miles (11.7 kilometers) long, and connects France with Italy.

The French railway system, owned and operated by the government, has about 22,000 miles (35,000 kilometers) of track. The railroad network forms a cobweb pattern. Its lines extend from Paris to various parts of France. A railroad tunnel, $8\frac{1}{2}$ miles (13.7 kilometers) long, through Mont Cenis links France with Italy.

Orly Airport, near Paris, is the busiest airport in France. Its terminal handles about $12\frac{3}{4}$ million passengers a year. The Charles de Gaulle Airport, also near Paris, opened in 1974. Air France, a government-owned airline, serves about 60 countries throughout the world. Another government-owned airline, Air Inter, provides service among all the large cities of France.

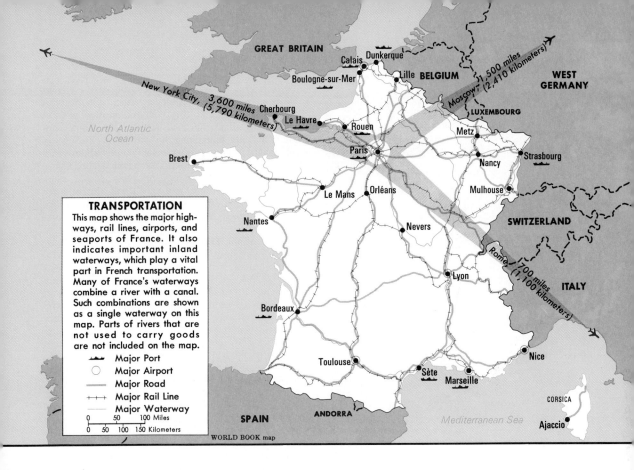

TRANSPORTATION

This map shows the major highways, rail lines, airports, and seaports of France. It also indicates important inland waterways, which play a vital part in French transportation. Many of France's waterways combine a river with a canal. Such combinations are shown as a single waterway on this map. Parts of rivers that are not used to carry goods are not included on the map.

- Major Port
- Major Airport
- Major Road
- Major Rail Line
- Major Waterway

0   50   100 Miles
0   50   100   150 Kilometers

French Merchant Ships dock at Le Havre on the English Channel to pick up cargo for export. The cargo is brought to the seaport from Paris and other cities by railroad and inland waterway.

More than 10,000 ships and barges operate on France's 4,780 miles (7,693 kilometers) of navigable rivers and canals. These rivers include the Rhine, Rhône, and Seine. Northern and eastern France have well-developed canal systems. Ocean-going ships dock at the many fine French seaports.

Communication. France has about 120 daily newspapers, with a total sale of more than 10 million copies. Paris newspapers account for about a third of this total. One Paris paper, *France-Soir*, sells more than 800,000 copies a day. Eight other French dailies have sales of over 300,000 copies. The largest newspaper outside Paris, *Ouest-France* of Rennes, sells about 575,000 copies a day. It prints 50 regional editions, each with some local news about one of the 50 communities.

A government-controlled broadcasting system operates one radio network and three television networks. Color television broadcasting began in 1967. The broadcasting system's income is provided by annual taxes on all radios and television sets. France also has a few privately owned radio stations.

A government agency supervises France's motion-picture industry. The agency's activities include giving financial aid to producers and scheduling new films. France has almost 5,800 motion-picture theaters. They must show films made in France during at least 5 of every 13 weeks.

Telephone and telegraph lines connect all parts of France. The country has over 5,700,000 telephones.

The Amphitheater of Nimes was built nearly 2,000 years ago after Rome conquered Gaul (present-day France). Public games were held there. During the Middle Ages, the amphitheater was made into a fort by filling the doors and windows with bricks. About 200 homes were built inside, and remained there until the 1800's. Today, the amphitheater is used for bullfights.

Early Days. In ancient times, tribes of Celts and other peoples lived in what is now France. The Romans called the region *Gallia* (Gaul). Roman armies began to invade Gaul about 200 B.C. By 121 B.C., Rome controlled the Gallic land along the Mediterranean Sea and in the Rhône Valley. Julius Caesar conquered the entire region between 58 and 51 B.C. The people, called *Gauls*, soon adopted Roman customs and ways of life. They dressed like the Romans, and used the Latin language of the invaders. Gaul prospered under Roman rule for hundreds of years, in spite of barbarian invasions during the A.D. 200's and 300's. See CELT; GAUL.

Victory of the Franks. The border defenses of the West Roman Empire began to crumble in the A.D. 400's. Germanic tribes from the east, including Burgundians, Franks, and Visigoths, crossed the Rhine River and entered Gaul. They killed many Gauls and drove others west into what is now Brittany. Clovis, the king of the Salian Franks, defeated the Roman governor of Gaul in 486 at Soissons. Clovis then defeated other Germanic tribes in Gaul, and extended his kingdom. He founded the Merovingian *dynasty* (a series of rulers from the same family), and adopted Christianity. See CLOVIS; FRANK; MEROVINGIAN.

The Carolingian Dynasty. By the mid-600's, the Merovingian kings had become weak rulers, interested chiefly in personal pleasures. Pepin of Herstal, the chief royal adviser, gradually took over most of the royal powers. His son, Charles Martel, extended the family's power. Charles received the title of *Martel* (the Hammer) after defeating an invading Arab army near Tours in 732. He became king of the Franks in all but title. See CHARLES MARTEL.

Charles Martel's son, Pepin the Short, overthrew the last Merovingian ruler and became king of the

The Royal Court of France at the time of King Charles V is shown in this miniature painting of the 1300's.

Bibliothèque Nationale, Paris (Giraudon)

———— KINGS AND EMPERORS OF FRANCE ————

Ruler	Reign	Ruler	Reign
*Hugh Capet	987-996	*Louis XI	1461-1483
Robert II	996-1031	*Charles VIII	1483-1498
*Henry I	1031-1060	*Louis XII	1498-1515
Philip I	1060-1108	*Francis I	1515-1547
Louis VI	1108-1137	*Henry II	1547-1559
Louis VII	1137-1180	*Francis II	1559-1560
*Philip II	1180-1223	*Charles IX	1560-1574
Louis VIII	1223-1226	*Henry III	1574-1589
*Louis IX	1226-1270	*Henry IV	1589-1610
Philip III	1270-1285	*Louis XIII	1610-1643
*Philip IV	1285-1314	*Louis XIV	1643-1715
Louis X	1314-1316	*Louis XV	1715-1774
John I	1316	*Louis XVI	1774-1792
Philip V	1316-1322	*Napoleon I	1804-1814
*Charles IV	1322-1328	*Louis XVIII	1814-1815
*Philip VI	1328-1350	*Napoleon I	1815
John II	1350-1364	*Louis XVIII	1815-1824
*Charles V	1364-1380	*Charles X	1824-1830
*Charles VI	1380-1422	*Louis Philippe	1830-1848
*Charles VII	1422-1461	*Napoleon III	1852-1870

*Has a separate biography in WORLD BOOK.

Franks in 751. He founded the Carolingian dynasty, and enlarged the Frankish kingdom. He also helped develop the political power of the pope by giving Pope Stephen II a large gift of land north of Rome. See PAPAL STATES; PEPIN THE SHORT.

Pepin's son, Charlemagne, was one of the mightiest conquerors of all time. After Charlemagne became king of the Franks, he went on more than 50 military campaigns and expanded his kingdom far beyond the borders of what is now France. He also extended the pope's lands. In 800, Pope Leo III crowned Charlemagne Emperor of the Romans. For the story of Charlemagne and a map of his empire, see CHARLEMAGNE.

Charlemagne died in 814, and his three grandsons later fought among themselves for control of his huge empire. They divided it into three kingdoms in 843. In the Treaty of Verdun, one grandson, Charles the Bald, received most of what is now France. The second kingdom consisted of much that is now Germany. The third kingdom lay between the other two. It consisted of a strip of land extending from the North Sea to central Italy. The middle kingdom north of Italy was divided between the other two in 870. See VERDUN, TREATY OF.

The Capetian Dynasty. By the late 900's, the Carolingian kings had lost much power, and the strength of the nobles had increased. The kings became little more than great feudal lords chosen by the other feudal nobles to lead them in war (see FEUDALISM). But in peacetime, most of their authority extended only over their personal estates. In 987, the nobles ended the Carolingian line of kings and chose Hugh Capet as their king. He started the Capetian dynasty. Many historians mark the beginning of the French nation from the coronation of Hugh Capet. See CAPETIAN DYNASTY; HUGH CAPET.

For many years, the Capetian kings controlled only their royal *domain* (land), between Paris and Orléans. The great feudal nobles ruled their own domains almost independently. The dukes of Normandy were the most powerful of these nobles. Normandy became the most unified and best administered feudal state in Europe. In 1066, the Norman Duke William, later called William the Conqueror, invaded England and became king. See NORMAN CONQUEST; WILLIAM (I, the Conqueror).

Growth of Royal Power. The Capetian kings gradu-

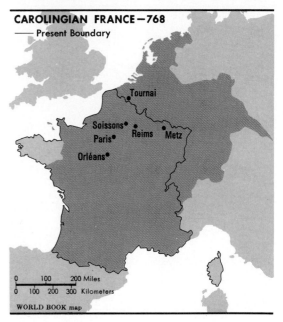

CAROLINGIAN FRANCE—768
—— Present Boundary

Tournai
Soissons• Reims• •Metz
Paris•
Orléans•

0   100   200 Miles
0 100 200 300 Kilometers
WORLD BOOK map

IMPORTANT DATES IN FRANCE

58-51 B.C. Julius Caesar conquered Gaul.

A.D. 486 Clovis, a king of the Franks, defeated the Roman governor of Gaul.

800 Charlemagne became emperor of the Romans.

987 Hugh Capet was crowned king of France.

1302 Philip IV called together the first States-General, the ancestor of the French Parliament.

1309-1377 The popes lived in Avignon.

1337-1453 France defeated England in the Hundred Years' War.

1598 Henry IV issued the Edict of Nantes, which gave limited religious freedom to Protestants.

1789-1799 The French Revolution took place. It ended absolute rule by French kings.

1792 The First Republic was established.

1799 Napoleon seized control of France.

1804 Napoleon founded the First Empire.

1814 Napoleon was exiled; Louis XVIII came to power.

1815 Napoleon returned to power, but was defeated at Waterloo. Louis XVIII regained the throne.

1848 Revolutionists established the Second Republic.

1852 Napoleon III founded the Second Empire.

1870-1871 Prussia defeated France in the Franco-Prussian War. The Third Republic was begun.

1914-1918 France fought on the Allied side in World War I.

1939-1940 France fought on the Allied side in World War II until defeated by Germany.

1940-1942 Germany occupied northern France.

1942-1944 The Germans occupied all France.

1946 France adopted a new constitution, establishing the Fourth Republic.

1946-1954 A revolution in French Indochina resulted in France's giving up the colony.

1949 France joined the North Atlantic Treaty Organization.

1954 Revolution broke out in the French territory of Algeria.

1957 France joined the European Common Market.

1958 A new constitution was adopted, marking the beginning of the Fifth Republic. Charles de Gaulle was elected president.

1960 France exploded its first atomic bomb.

1962 France granted independence to Algeria.

1963 The French air force was armed with atomic bombs.

1966 De Gaulle withdrew French troops from NATO.

1969 De Gaulle resigned as president.

ally added more territory to their personal lands, and became stronger than any of their rivals. In addition, every Capetian king for over 300 years had a son to succeed him on the throne. As a result, the nobles' power to select kings died out. The nobles were further weakened because many of them left France between 1100 and 1300 on crusades to capture the Holy Land from the Muslims. See CRUSADES.

Philip II, called Philip Augustus, was the first great Capetian king. After he came to the throne in 1180, he

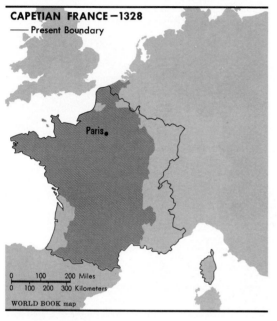

CAPETIAN FRANCE—1328
—— Present Boundary

Paris

0   100   200 Miles
0 100 200 300 Kilometers

WORLD BOOK map

more than doubled the royal domain, and tightened his control over the great nobles. Philip built up a large body of government officials, many of them from the middle class. He also developed Paris as a permanent, expanding capital. See PHILIP (II) of France.

The handsome Philip IV, called Philip the Fair, rebelled against the pope's authority. He taxed church officials, and arrested a bishop and even Pope Boniface VIII. Philip won public approval for his actions in the first States-General, a body of Frenchmen that he called together in 1302. This group was the ancestor of the French Parliament. In 1305, through Philip's influence, a French archbishop was elected pope and became Pope Clement V. In 1309, Clement moved the pope's court from Rome to Avignon, where it remained until 1377. See PHILIP (IV); POPE (The Troubles of the Papacy).

A Period of Wars. The last Capetian king, Charles IV, died in 1328 without a male heir. A cousin succeeded him as Philip VI and started the Valois dynasty. King Edward III of England, a nephew of the last Capetian king, also claimed the French throne. In 1337, Edward landed an army in Normandy. This invasion started a series of wars between France and England known as the Hundred Years' War (1337-1453). The English won most of the battles. But the French, after

Bibliothèque Nationale, Paris (Larousse)

Traveling Musicians called *jongleurs* entertained the people of France during the Middle Ages. These two performers decorate the manuscript of a Latin song of the 1000's.

their victory at Orléans under Joan of Arc, drove the English out of most of France. See HUNDRED YEARS' WAR; JOAN OF ARC, SAINT; VALOIS.

Louis XI laid the foundations for absolute rule by French kings. During the Hundred Years' War, the kings had lost much of their power to the French nobles. Louis regained this power. His greatest rival was Charles the Bold, Duke of Burgundy. Charles died in battle in 1477 while trying to conquer the city of Nancy, and Louis seized most of his vast lands. See LOUIS (XI).

Francis I invaded northern Italy, and captured Milan in 1515. In a later Italian campaign, Francis was defeated by Charles V of the Holy Roman Empire. French wars against the Holy Roman Empire continued into the reign of Henry II. The Empire and England were allies. In 1558, this alliance gave Henry an excuse to seize the port city of Calais, England's last possession in France. See FRANCIS (I) of France; HENRY (II) of France.

Religious Wars. During the early 1500's, a religious movement called the Reformation developed Protestantism in Europe. Many French people became Protestants. They followed the teachings of John Calvin, and were called *Huguenots*. After 1540, the government persecuted the Huguenots severely, but they grew in number and political strength. During the late 1500's, French Roman Catholics and the Huguenots fought a series of civil wars that lasted more than 30 years. In 1572, thousands of Huguenots were killed in France during the Massacre of Saint Bartholomew's Day. See CALVIN, JOHN; HUGUENOTS.

Henry III died in 1589 without a male heir. He was followed by Henry of Navarre, who became Henry IV and started the Bourbon dynasty. But Roman Catholic forces prevented him from entering Paris because he was the leader of the Huguenots. In 1593, Henry became a Roman Catholic to achieve peace. He entered the capital the next year. In 1598, Henry signed the Edict of Nantes, which granted limited freedom of worship to the Huguenots. See BOURBON; HENRY (III and IV) of France.

The Age of Absolutism. The great power of the French kings and their *ministers* (high government officials) grew steadily from the 1500's to the 1700's. France became a strong nation, largely through the efforts of these ministers. The first important minister was Maximilien de Béthune, Duke of Sully, who served Henry IV. Sully promoted agriculture and such public works as highways and canals. He also reduced the *taille*, the chief tax on the common people. The actual ruler behind Louis XIII was his prime minister, Armand Jean du Plessis, Cardinal Richelieu. Richelieu increased French royal power more than any other man. See RICHELIEU, CARDINAL.

Louis XIV was the outstanding example of the absolute French king. He is said to have boasted: "I am the State." After his prime minister died in 1661, Louis declared that he would be his own prime minister. In 1685, Louis canceled the Edict of Nantes and began to persecute the Huguenots savagely. About 200,000 Huguenots fled France, which weakened the country's economy. Louis' minister of finance, Jean Baptiste Colbert, promoted a strong economy. But the construction of Louis' magnificent palace at Versailles and a series of major wars drained France's finances. Louis tried to rule supreme in Europe. He was stopped by military alliances that included England, Spain, the Holy Roman Empire, and other nations. See GRAND ALLIANCE; LOUIS XIV; SUCCESSION WARS (The War of the Spanish Succession).

The French Revolution. By the late 1700's, great discontent had swept through France. The common people, members of the middle class, and nobles were all dissatisfied, but for different reasons. The government was bankrupt, and Louis XVI was too weak to handle the situation. In 1789, the people's discontent finally led to the French Revolution, which lasted for 10 years. In 1792, the First French Republic was formed. For an account of the causes, violence, and reforms of the French Revolution, see FRENCH REVOLUTION.

Napoleon. During the French Revolution, Napoleon Bonaparte rose through the ranks of the army. He became a general in 1794, and his power grew rapidly. In 1799, Napoleon overthrew the revolutionary French government and seized control of France. He ruled until 1814, and again for about three months in 1815 before his final defeat at Waterloo. For the story of Na-

poleon's life, military campaigns, and rule, and a map of his empire, see NAPOLEON I.

The Revolutions of 1830 and 1848. The Bourbon dynasty returned to power when Louis XVIII came to the throne in 1814. Napoleon again seized power in 1815, but lost it to Louis later that year. Charles X followed Louis and tried to re-establish the total power of the earlier French kings. He was overthrown in the July Revolution of 1830. See CHARLES (X) of France; JULY REVOLUTION; LOUIS (XVIII).

REVOLUTIONARY FRANCE—1799
—— Present Boundary

Rhine River

Paris

CORSICA

0   100   200 Miles
0   100   200   300 Kilometers

WORLD BOOK map

The Directory, a five-man board, governed France from 1795 to 1799, during the last half of the French Revolution.

Engraving, *Audience du Directoire en Costume* (Bulloz, Paris)

The revolutionists placed Louis Philippe on the throne. He belonged to the Orléans branch of the Bourbon family. France was peaceful and prosperous during Louis Philippe's reign. But the poorer classes became dissatisfied because only the wealthy could vote or hold public office. The February Revolution of 1848 overthrew the government and established the Second Republic. All Frenchmen received the right to vote. See LOUIS PHILIPPE; REVOLUTION OF 1848.

The voters elected Louis Napoleon Bonaparte, a nephew of Napoleon, to a four-year term as president in 1848. He seized greater power illegally in 1851, and declared himself president for 10 years. In 1852, he established the Second Empire and declared himself Emperor Napoleon III. See NAPOLEON III.

The Franco-Prussian War. During the 1860's, France became alarmed over the growing strength of Prussia. France feared that a united Germany under Prussian leadership would upset Europe's balance of power. After a series of disputes, France declared war on Prussia in 1870. Prussia defeated France the next year. In the peace treaty following the Franco-Prussian War, France gave Alsace and part of Lorraine to the new German Empire. See BALANCE OF POWER; FRANCO-PRUSSIAN WAR.

The Third Republic. After disastrous Prussian victories in 1870, the French revolted against Napoleon III. They established the Third Republic, and in 1871 elected a National Assembly. In 1875, the Assembly voted to continue the republic, and wrote a new constitution for France.

French strength and prosperity grew until World War I began in 1914. French explorers and soldiers won a vast colonial empire in Africa and Asia. Only Great Britain had a larger overseas empire. France strengthened its army, and formed a military alliance with Russia in 1894 and the *Entente Cordiale* (cordial understanding) with Great Britain in 1904. French industries expanded steadily, especially after 1895.

Most Frenchmen were satisfied with the Third Republic, but many thought the government needed stronger leadership. The president had little power or influence. A cabinet, headed by the prime minister, held political leadership. Parliament could vote the cabinet out of office at any time, and often did so.

World War I. During the early 1900's, France and Germany had disagreements over colonial territories, and each country feared an attack by the other. In 1907, France established a diplomatic agreement called the Triple Entente with Great Britain and Russia. The French strengthened their army and prepared for war. Soon after the start of World War I (1914-1918), Germany invaded France. During the four years of fighting, millions of French servicemen were killed or wounded. For the story of France in the war, see WORLD WAR I.

Between World Wars. In the Treaty of Versailles, signed in 1919, France recovered Alsace and the German part of Lorraine from Germany. France and other Allied nations also were awarded *reparations* (payments for war damages) from Germany. Germany fell behind in making these payments. As a result, French and

Belgian troops occupied the Ruhr Valley of Germany in 1923. After Germany agreed to keep up the payments, the troops were withdrawn in 1925. See ALSACE-LORRAINE; RUHR (History); VERSAILLES, TREATY OF.

The French did much to re-establish good relations with Germany. France joined other Allied nations and Germany in the Rhineland Security Pact of 1925. This agreement in part guaranteed the security of the French-German border. France reduced Germany's reparations, and dropped various controls over Germany set up by the Treaty of Versailles. Suggestions by Aristide Briand, the French foreign minister, led to the Kellogg Peace Pact of 1928 (see KELLOGG PEACE PACT). It was signed by France, Germany, and 13 other nations. But in 1929, France began building the Maginot Line, a fortified line of defense against Germany.

During the 1930's, the worldwide economic depression and the rise of Adolf Hitler in Germany caused serious political unrest in France. In 1933, for example, the French Parliament overthrew five cabinets. The French Communist party grew, and several new Fascist groups were organized (see FASCISM). In 1938, the government began to give in to the demands of Nazi Germany. As part of this policy of *appeasement*, France signed the Munich Agreement, under which Czechoslovakia was forced to give territory to Germany (see MUNICH AGREEMENT).

World War II began when Germany invaded Poland on Sept. 1, 1939. Two days later, France and Great Britain declared war on Germany. On May 10, 1940, the Germans attacked Belgium, Luxembourg, and The Netherlands. They invaded France through Belgium on May 12, passing northwest of the Maginot Line. The Germans launched a major attack to the south on June 5, and entered Paris on June 14. On June 22, France signed an armistice with Germany. The Germans occupied the northern two-thirds of France, and southern France remained under French control. Southern France was governed at Vichy by Henri Philippe Pétain, who largely cooperated with the Germans. See PÉTAIN, HENRI PHILIPPE.

After France fell, General Charles de Gaulle fled to London. He invited all French patriots to join a movement called *Free France*, and continue fighting the Germans. This *resistance* movement also spread throughout France. Some groups of Frenchmen called *Maquis* hid in hilly areas and fought the Germans. After Allied troops landed in French North Africa in November, 1942, German troops also occupied southern France. The Germans tried to seize the French fleet at Toulon, but the French sank most of the ships. See DE GAULLE, CHARLES; MAQUIS.

On June 6, 1944, the Allies landed in France in Normandy. They landed in southern France on August 15. After fierce fighting and heavy loss of lives, the Allied troops entered Paris on August 25. De Gaulle soon formed a *provisional* (temporary) government and became its president. In 1945, France became a charter member of the United Nations. For the story of France in the war, see WORLD WAR II.

The Fourth Republic. In October, 1945, the French people voted to have the National Assembly write a new constitution creating the Fourth Republic. In this election, French women voted for the first time. De Gaulle resigned as president in January, 1946, over

later. But France refused to give up Algeria, the home of almost a million French settlers. France gradually built up its army in Algeria to about 500,000 men, and the war continued through the 1950's. See ALGERIA (The Algerian Revolt).

In spite of the costly colonial wars, France's economy grew rapidly. By the late 1950's, it had broken all French production records. The boom developed with U.S. aid and a series of national economic plans begun

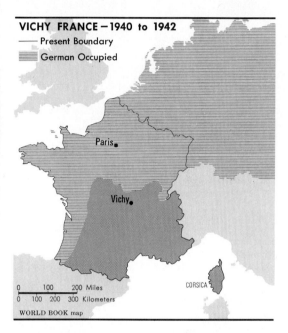

VICHY FRANCE – 1940 to 1942
—— Present Boundary
▨ German Occupied

Paris

Vichy

CORSICA

0   100   200 Miles
0 100 200 300 Kilometers

WORLD BOOK map

Wide World

Henri Philippe Pétain, *second from right,* became French head of state during World War II. He arranged an armistice with Germany in 1940, and largely cooperated with the Germans. In 1941, he met with German Reich Marshal Hermann Goering, *right.* Pétain was imprisoned for treason after the war.

disagreements with the Assembly. The new constitution, much like that of the Third Republic, went into effect in October, 1946. De Gaulle opposed it because it did not provide strong executive powers.

France received much aid from the United States, and rebuilt its cities and industries which had been badly damaged during the war. But political troubles at home and colonial revolts overseas slowed the nation's economic recovery. France became a major battlefield in the Cold War between Communist Russia and the Western nations (see COLD WAR). The Communist party was one of the largest in France after the war, and it controlled the chief labor unions. Communist-led strikes in 1947 and 1948 crippled production across the country. In 1949, France became a charter member of the anti-Communist North Atlantic Treaty Organization (NATO).

The first colonial revolt began in French Indochina in 1946. Indochina was eventually divided into Cambodia, Laos, and North and South Vietnam. The French withdrew from Indochina in 1954 after suffering heavy losses. See INDOCHINA (French Indochina).

Later in 1954, revolution broke out in the French territory of Algeria. To prevent revolutions in Morocco and Tunisia, France made them independent in 1956. Other French colonies in Africa received independence

in 1946. French businessmen and government officials were determined to prove that France's greatness had not disappeared. Between 1947 and 1958, France helped form several economic organizations that were important steps toward a European confederation. For discussions of them, see EUROPE, COUNCIL OF; EUROPEAN COMMUNITY; EUROPEAN MONETARY AGREEMENT.

The Fifth Republic. By 1958, many Frenchmen thought it was useless to continue fighting in Algeria. But the idea of giving up Algeria angered many army leaders and French settlers there. They rebelled in May, 1958, and threatened to overthrow the government by force unless it called De Gaulle back to power. De Gaulle became prime minister with emergency powers for six months. His government prepared a new constitution, which the voters approved on Sept. 28, 1958. This constitution established the Fifth Republic. It gave the president greater power than ever before, and sharply reduced the power of Parliament. In December, the Electoral College elected De Gaulle to a seven-year term as president.

De Gaulle's government continued the war in Algeria, but still without success. De Gaulle hoped the Algerians would agree to a peace with some French control. By 1961, however, it was clear that only independence would end the rebellion. Peace talks began

404m

Charles de Gaulle made France a nuclear military power. In 1963, wearing a protective robe, the French president inspected the Pierrelatte nuclear laboratory in southern France.

in April, 1961, and ended in March, 1962, with a cease-fire. At De Gaulle's urging, French voters approved Algerian independence in April. Algeria became independent on July 3, 1962, and about three-fourths of the French settlers there returned to France.

Algerian independence set off a wave of bombings and murders in France and Algeria by the Secret Army Organization (OAS). This group, which included many army officers, opposed independence for Algeria. The OAS tried several times to kill De Gaulle. In 1962, the OAS founder and leader, General Raoul Salan, was captured in Algeria and sentenced to life imprisonment.

After the Algerian crisis, some French politicians tried to weaken De Gaulle's strong rule. They wanted to re-establish the former power of Parliament and reduce that of the president. But De Gaulle made the presidency even stronger. He declared that the president should have nationwide support and be elected by all the voters, not just by the Electoral College. In October, 1962, a huge majority of the voters approved a constitutional amendment that provided such elections.

France Today. The high level of prosperity and economic growth of the 1950's continued into the 1960's. New methods of production and ways of life are changing France rapidly. Most of France's farms and factories use modern production methods. New houses and apartment buildings have risen throughout the country.

In spite of this prosperity, many French workers still vote for Communist candidates in elections. These voters believe they are not getting a fair share of the economic gains. Many poor farmers are discontented because they cannot afford to modernize their farms.

De Gaulle's main interest lay in France's foreign policy. He believed that the French are "a race created for brilliant deeds," but cannot achieve greatness with

their "destiny in the hands of foreigners." Because of this belief, De Gaulle was generally uncooperative with the United States. He feared the loss of French independence to the United States in NATO and the United Nations. He dreamed of France's leading the nations of Western Europe in an alliance free of either American or Russian influence. But the other Western European nations, especially Great Britain, preferred to maintain close ties with the United States.

After De Gaulle returned to power in 1958, he acted with great firmness to put his ideas into action. In 1959, he forced the United States to remove the nuclear warheads it had stored in France. He did this because the United States refused to let France share control of the warheads. In 1960, France tested its first atomic bomb. In 1965, the French launched a space satellite. France exploded its first hydrogen bomb in 1968.

In 1963, De Gaulle prevented Great Britain from joining the European Economic Community, also called the European Common Market. Among other reasons, he believed Britain's ties with the United States would give America too much influence in Europe's economy. In 1964, in spite of U.S. disapproval, France recognized Communist China. De Gaulle also gradually withdrew most of the French armed forces assigned to NATO. He believed the United States had too much power over the French forces in the organization.

In 1965, De Gaulle withdrew France's representative from European Economic Community headquarters in Brussels, Belgium. De Gaulle acted in protest against a move to give the organization greater political control over member nations. The French walkout ended in January, 1966, but the disagreement did not end.

De Gaulle's foreign policy angered many Europeans and Americans. But it was popular with the French. In 1965, De Gaulle was re-elected to a seven-year term.

In 1966 and 1967, De Gaulle withdrew all French troops from NATO. He also declared that NATO military bases, headquarters, and troops had to be removed from France by April, 1967. His deadline was met. France withdrew from the NATO alliance militarily, but it remained a member politically.

Massive strikes and demonstrations by workers and students in May, 1968, paralyzed France and weakened its economy. De Gaulle called a general election in June, and his supporters won more than 70 per cent of the seats in the Assembly. In 1969, De Gaulle asked for minor constitutional reforms and said he would resign if the voters did not pass them. The people voted against the reforms in April, and De Gaulle resigned.

Georges Pompidou, a former member of De Gaulle's Cabinet, was elected president in June, 1969. In August, the government devalued the franc to help stabilize the economy (see DEVALUATION). Pompidou also worked to improve France's relations with Great Britain. In 1971, he met with British Prime Minister Edward Heath. The two leaders reached general agreement on terms for Britain's entry into the European Common Market.

Pompidou died in April, 1974. In May, Valéry Giscard d'Estaing, head of the Independent Republican Party, was elected president. Giscard d'Estaing had been Pompidou's finance minister.   JOHN W. HACKETT,

J. A. LAPONCE, LAWRENCE M. SOMMERS, and GORDON WRIGHT

Related Articles in WORLD BOOK include:

POLITICAL AND MILITARY LEADERS

See the table *Kings and Emperors of France* with this article. Other biographies in WORLD BOOK include:

Barras, Vicomte de	Lamartine, Alphonse
Bonaparte (Lucien)	Laval, Pierre
Briand, Aristide	Marat, Jean P.
Catherine de Médicis	Mazarin, Jules Cardinal
Charles Martel	Mirabeau, Comte de
Chateaubriand, François R. de	Montcalm, Marquis de
Claudel, Paul	Murat, Joachim
Clemenceau, Georges	Necker, Jacques
Colbert, Jean B.	Ney, Michel
Condorcet, Marquis de	Pétain, Henri P.
Corday, Charlotte	Poincaré, Raymond
Daladier, Édouard	Pompidou, Georges J. R.
Danton, Georges J.	Richelieu, Cardinal
De Gaulle, Charles A. J. M.	Robespierre
Eugénie Marie de Montijo	Rochambeau, Comte de
Foch, Ferdinand	Roland de la Platière,
Gambetta, Léon Michel	Marie Jeanne
Genêt, Edmond C. É.	Saxe, Comte de
Giraud, Henri H.	Sieyès, Emmanuel J.
Giscard d'Estaing, Valéry	Talleyrand
Godfrey of Bouillon	Talon, Jean B.
Guizot, François P. G.	Thiers, Louis A.
Herriot, Édouard	Tocqueville, Alexis de
Joffre, Joseph J. C.	Vauban, Sebastien Le P.
Lafayette, Marquis de	Weygand, Maxime

CITIES AND TOWNS

Amiens	Dijon	Lyon	Rennes
Avignon	Dunkerque	Marseille	Rouen
Bordeaux	Fontainebleau	Metz	Saint-
Brest	Grenoble	Nancy	Étienne
Calais	La Rochelle	Nantes	Strasbourg
Carcassonne	Le Havre	Nice	Toulon
Cherbourg	Le Mans	Nîmes	Toulouse
Clermont-	Lille	Orléans	Tours
Ferrand	Limoges	Paris	Versailles
Dieppe	Lourdes	Reims	Vichy

HISTORY

Agincourt,	Dauphin	Louisbourg
Battle of	Directory	Mississippi
Austerlitz,	Feudalism	Scheme
Battle of	Franco-Prussian War	Poitiers, Battle of
Bastille	Frank	Reformation
Bonaparte	French and	Renaissance
Bourbon	Indian Wars	Revolution of 1848
Continental	French Revolution	States-General
System	French Union	Succession Wars
Crécy,	Fronde	Waldenses
Battle of	Huguenots	World War I
Crimean War	Hundred Years' War	World War II
Crusades	July Revolution	Zouaves

OVERSEAS POSSESSIONS

French Guiana	New Caledonia
French Polynesia	New Hebrides Islands
French Southern and	Reunion
Antarctic Territories	Saint Pierre and Miquelon
Guadeloupe	Wallis and Futuna Islands
Martinique	

PHYSICAL FEATURES

Aisne River	Cape Gris-Nez	Isère River
Alps	Corsica	Jura
Ardennes Mountains	Dover, Strait of	Loire River
and Forest	English Channel	Lusse Tunnel
Bay of Biscay	Garonne River	Marne River
Belfort Gap	Gavarnie Falls	Mont Blanc

Pyrenees	Saône River	Somme River
Rhône River	Seine River	Vosges Mountains

PRODUCTS AND INDUSTRY

For France's rank among other countries, see:

Aluminum	Iron and Steel	Salt
Automobile	Leather	Ship
Barley	Lumber	Sugar
Cheese	Manufacturing	Sugar Beet
Chemical Industry	Nuclear Energy	Textile
Clothing	Oats	Tuna
Corn	Potato	Uranium
Electric Power	Publishing	Wheat
Flax	Rubber	Wine

REGIONS

Alsace-Lorraine	Burgundy	Gascony	Provence
Brittany	Flanders	Normandy	Riviera

OTHER RELATED ARTICLES

Architecture	École des	Motion Picture
Army (Major	Beaux-Arts	(Postwar
Armies)	Eiffel Tower	European)
Basques	Fleur-de-Lis	Music
Bastille Day	Foreign Legion	Navy (The
Bibliothèque	French Academy	World's Ma-
Nationale	French Language	jor Navies)
Bicycle Racing	French Literature	Norman
(Road Racing)	Furniture	Painting
Christmas (In France)	Gendarme	Premier
Code Napoléon	Institute of	Salic Law
Court (Other Court	France	Sculpture
Systems)	Louvre	Sorbonne
Democracy (French	Maginot Line	Statue of
Contributions	Marseillaise	Liberty
to Democracy)	Martinmas	Theater
Doll (History;		(France)
picture)		Tuileries

Outline

I. Government
    A. The Fifth Republic   D. Local Government
    B. President and   E. Courts
        Prime Minister   F. Armed Forces
    C. Parliament

II. People
    A. Population   D. Museums and   F. Holidays
    B. Language   Libraries   G. Cooking
    C. Education   E. Religion   H. Sports

III. Arts
    A. Architecture   C. Painting   E. Music
    B. Literature   D. Sculpture

IV. The Land
V. Climate
VI. Economy
    A. Natural Resources   F. Tourism
    B. Manufacturing   G. Electric Power
    C. Agriculture   H. Foreign Trade
    D. Mining   I. Transportation
    E. Fishing   J. Communication

VII. History

Questions

What major changes in French government were made by Charles de Gaulle?

How did France get its name?

What is the principal religion of France?

How did the Romans influence French ways of life?

What is France's chief crop? Chief mineral deposit?

Who seized control after the French Revolution?

Where is the world's longest highway tunnel?

What led to De Gaulle's return to power in 1958?

What is France's cultural and economic center?

How does France rank in foreign trade?

Reading and Study Guide

See *France* in the RESEARCH GUIDE/INDEX, Volume 22, for a *Reading and Study Guide*.

FRANCE, ANATOLE (1844-1924), was the pen name of Jacques Anatole François Thibault, a French novelist and critic. He won the 1921 Nobel prize for literature.

France was born in Paris, the son of a well-to-do bookseller. His childhood was filled with the magic of literature. In his autobiography, *My Friend's Book* (1885), France recalled the pleasures of those years and the mental stimulation he received from Paris, especially its libraries and bookshops.

France's first successful novel was *The Crime of Sylvester Bonnard* (1881). Beginning in 1886, he wrote a literary column for the newspaper *Le Temps*. His clear and elegant style, the subtlety of his observation, and his disinterested rejection of extreme causes gained him the reputation of being a friendly, easy-going man. France's novel *Thaïs* (1890) seemed to symbolize his ideals of pleasure and wisdom.

The famous Dreyfus affair, which shook the nation, led France to write about political and social issues (see DREYFUS, ALFRED). His novels of the 1900's reflect his part in the struggle for social justice that took place in the country. He began to ridicule society and its institutions in *Penguin Island* (1908), his most famous novel, and in *The Gods are Athirst* (1912) and *The Revolt of the Angels* (1914). The irony of these novels has been compared to that of the works of Voltaire.   EDITH KERN

FRANCESCA, PIERO DELLA. See PIERO DELLA FRANCESCA.

FRANCESCATTI, *frahn ches KAHT tih,* **ZINO** (1905-   ), a French violinist, became noted for his concert performances in Europe and America. He has won acclaim for his full rich tone. Francescatti made his first public appearance at the age of 5. He made his formal debut at the Paris Opera in 1927. Francescatti was born in Marseille, France.   DOROTHY DeLAY

FRANCHISE, *FRAN chyz,* is a privilege that a government or a company grants to a corporation or an individual. A franchise involves certain rights, such as business rights, that most corporations and persons do not have. Cities and states grant most franchises approved by a government.

Most public utility companies, which furnish such necessities as electricity, gas, or water, operate under a franchise. They have the right—an exclusive right in most cases—to use whatever public property they need to provide their services. For example, a telephone company may erect its poles along a city street. A government may also give a franchise company the right of eminent domain (see EMINENT DOMAIN).

In return for the right to use public property, a government may require a franchise firm to provide equal service to all persons. Such companies may also have to pay a franchise tax. In addition, the government may specify the prices a franchise company can charge. A firm that holds a franchise may not refuse to perform any required duty on the grounds that it would be unprofitable. However, public authorities try to assure a profit for the company by considering the firm's investment and operating costs when they fix its price rates. In most cases, a government grants a franchise for a specific number of years.

Private businesses also use franchise arrangements. In this type of franchise, a company grants a person or corporation the privilege of selling the firm's product in a particular area. Such franchises make up a large part of the economy of the United States and Canada. Firms that operate on a franchise basis include automobile dealers, auto-parts suppliers, beer and soft-drink distributors, chain stores of various kinds, hotels, restaurants, and service stations.

The term *franchise* may also refer to a citizen's right to vote.   JOHN ALAN APPLEMAN

See also PUBLIC UTILITY.

FRANCIA, JOSÉ GASPAR RODRÍGUEZ DE. See PARAGUAY (Independence).

FRANCIS was the name of two Holy Roman Emperors.

Francis I (1708-1765) became Holy Roman Emperor in 1745, nine years after he married Maria Theresa of Austria, the oldest child of Emperor Charles VI. Maria Theresa made Francis co-regent, but she was the actual ruler. Their son, Joseph II, became emperor in 1765. See MARIA THERESA.

Francis II (1768-1835) was the last monarch to hold the title of Holy Roman Emperor. He became ruler of Austria in 1792, and was elected Holy Roman Emperor in the same year. He joined Russia and England in wars against the French Republic and Napoleon. Napoleon decisively defeated the combined armies of Austria and Russia at Austerlitz, in 1805. A year later, Napoleon formed the Confederation of the Rhine, and the Holy Roman Empire ended. Earlier, Francis had taken the title of Emperor Francis I of Austria. Francis joined Russia, Prussia, and England against Napoleon in 1813, and helped to form the Holy Alliance after Napoleon's defeat (see HOLY ALLIANCE).

Francis adopted an extremely reactionary policy. Liberal and national movements frightened him, and he refused to let his conservative minister, Prince Metternich, change Austria's constitution (see METTERNICH, PRINCE VON). His last testament warned his successor to "Rule and change nothing." ROBERT G. L. WAITE

FRANCIS was the name of two kings who ruled France in the 1500's.

Francis I (1494-1547) became king in 1515, succeeding Louis XII, who was both his cousin and his father-in-law. He was intelligent, fond of pleasure, and devoted to the arts. He was also ambitious, inconstant, and somewhat dishonest. He began his reign brilliantly with the great victory of Marignano in 1515. This gave him a foothold in northern Italy.

It soon became clear, however, that the interests and ambitions of France clashed with the Holy Roman Empire, which included Spain and Germany. Francis and the Holy Roman Emperor Charles V carried on a bitter struggle for years (see CHARLES [V] Holy Roman Emperor). Francis was captured and imprisoned in 1525, in another Italian campaign. He won his freedom in 1526 by making false promises. The last war between Francis I and Charles V ended in 1544 without having made great changes. Francis had shown himself greedy for power and indifferent about how he obtained it.

Francis persecuted the Protestants, but not so severely as some of his successors. Possibly the king would have been more savage against them if he had not given most of his attention to other affairs. He enjoyed beautiful surroundings, took an interest in new art and literature, and spent money lavishly. Such activities gave him a reputation as a patron of the Renaissance in France.

Francis II (1544-1560), grandson of Francis I, became king in 1559, but died the next year. Mary, Queen of Scots, was his wife. In his reign began the long, bitter rivalry between the noble houses of Guise and Bourbon, which cost France so much during the religious wars between Catholics and Huguenots.   William C. Bark

See also Catherine de Médicis; France (A Period of Wars); Huguenots; Mary, Queen of Scots.

FRANCIS DE SALES, SAINT (1567-1622), was born at Thorens in Savoy. He was educated at the College of Clermont in Paris, France. There he became so devoted to the Blessed Virgin Mary that he took a vow of chastity and dedicated himself to her service. After becoming a doctor of law in Padua, he entered the priesthood and was ordained in 1593. In 1602, he became bishop of Geneva. He and Saint Jane de Chantal established the Visitation Order, the purposes of which were teaching and the care of the sick. His most popular work is *An Introduction to the Devout Life*. He was canonized in 1665, and his feast day is January 29.   Fulton J. Sheen

FRANCIS FERDINAND, Archduke of Austria. See World War I (Death of an Archduke).

FRANCIS JOSEPH (1830-1916) was the aged ruler of the dual monarchy of Austria-Hungary at the beginning of World War I. He ruled as emperor of Austria for 68 years. His popularity, as well as military force, held the widely different elements of the dual monarchy together. When his heir and nephew, Archduke Francis Ferdinand, was assassinated in 1914, Francis Joseph declared war on Serbia. This led to World War I (see Serbia; World War I).

Francis Joseph became Emperor of Austria in 1848, a year of national revolutions. He was a member of the

Francis Joseph

ancient ruling family of Hapsburg (see Hapsburg). During his long reign Austria prospered, although it suffered several military defeats. In the war against Sardinia and France in 1859, Austria lost the province of Lombardy (see Sardinia, Kingdom of). Prussia defeated Austria and three smaller German states in the Seven Weeks' War of 1866. As a result, Austria lost much of its influence in Germany (see Seven Weeks' War). Francis Joseph then adopted more liberal internal policies, allowing the Hungarians equal rights. This brought about the Austro-Hungarian empire, and Francis Joseph took the additional title of King of Hungary in 1867 (see Austria-Hungary).

Francis Joseph's only son, Rudolph, killed himself in 1889. An Italian anarchist killed Francis Joseph's wife, Elizabeth. A nephew, Charles I, succeeded him as emperor (see Charles I).   Gabriel A. Almond

FRANCIS OF ASSISI, *uh SEE zee,* **SAINT** (1181?-1226), founded the Franciscan religious order of the Roman Catholic Church. His simple life of poverty inspired many men during the Middle Ages. Today, many people admire Francis because of his love of peace and his respect for all living creatures.

St. Francis in Ecstasy (about 1480), a tempera and oil painting on a wood panel; © The Frick Collection, New York City

Saint Francis of Assisi was one of the most popular saints of the Middle Ages. This painting by the Italian artist Giovanni Bellini shows Francis about to receive the *stigmata*—wounds resembling those that Jesus received at the Crucifixion. The gentle animals and peaceful landscape symbolize the saint's love of nature and all living things.

FRANCIS XAVIER

Francis, the son of a prosperous textile merchant, was born in Assisi, Italy. As a young man, he took an active part in the city's commercial, political, and social life. Francis was captured while fighting in a war between Assisi and the nearby city of Perugia. He spent most of 1202 and 1203 in an enemy prison. The suffering he saw during the war caused him to think about the meaning and purpose of his life.

In 1205, after seeing a vision of Christ, Francis changed his way of life. He disowned his father, rejected his inheritance, and began to devote his life to rebuilding churches and serving the poor. Francis adopted absolute poverty as his ideal. He tried to pattern his life after Christ's by preaching the Gospel and healing the sick. Soon, Francis started to attract followers.

In 1209 or 1210, Pope Innocent III approved the formation of the Franciscan order by Francis. Although many of his followers became priests, Francis remained a layman. See FRANCISCANS.

In 1212, while traveling to Syria to convert the Muslims, Francis was shipwrecked on the coast of Yugoslavia. He tried to go to Morocco as a missionary but became ill in Spain and could not continue. In 1219, Francis accompanied the crusaders to Egypt. There, he tried to convert the sultan but failed.

Francis returned to Italy in 1220. He continued to preach but let others administer the Franciscans. In 1224, while Francis prayed on Mount Alvernia near Florence, the *stigmata* appeared on his body. The stigmata are five wounds resembling those suffered by Jesus on His hands, feet, and side during the Crucifixion. Two years later, Francis died near Assisi in the Portiuncula chapel, his favorite church and the first headquarters of the Franciscans. Francis was *canonized* (declared a saint) in 1228. His feast day is October 4.

Francis expressed his religious ideals in poems as well as through his ministry. In "Canticle of the Sun," he showed his love for all living things. His poems also contributed to the development of Italian literature. About 100 years after Francis' death, a Franciscan collected stories about the saint and his companions in *The Little Flowers of Saint Francis*.   WILLIAM J. COURTENAY

FRANCIS XAVIER. See XAVIER, SAINT FRANCIS.

FRANCISCANS, *fran SIHS kuhnz,* are members of one of the three great Roman Catholic religious orders founded by Saint Francis of Assisi. The first is that of the *Friars Minor.* They were first called the *gray friars,* because they wore gray robes. The second is the order of Franciscan nuns, the *Poor Clares,* and the third is the *Brothers and Sisters of Penance,* or the *Tertiaries.*

The Friars Minor received the approval of Pope Innocent III in 1209. They took vows of poverty, chastity, and obedience. This order now has three branches, the Friars Minor, the Friars Minor Conventuals, and the Friars Minor Capuchins (see CAPUCHINS).

The *Poor Clares* were founded by Saint Clare, a follower of Saint Francis, in 1212. At first, they followed the rules of the Friars Minor, but their rules were later modified by Saint Colette, and approved by Pope Urban IV in 1283. The *Tertiaries* include lay people, monks, and nuns. This order was founded about 1221.

The early Franciscans devoted themselves to a spiritual care of the people, but soon turned to educational

work as well. They established many missions in the United States and Canada, especially among the Indians living along the Pacific Coast.   FULTON J. SHEEN

See also FRANCIS OF ASSISI, SAINT; FRIAR; EL CAMINO REAL; CALIFORNIA (History); WILLIAM OF OCKHAM.

FRANCIUM, *FRAN sih um* (chemical symbol, Fr), is an unstable element whose chemical properties resemble those of cesium. It is formed by the radioactive decay of actinium. It may also be made by bombarding thorium in an atom smasher. Francium's atomic number is 87. The mass number of its most stable isotope is 223. All of the known isotopes of francium are radioactive, and the element decays to form radium or astatine. Two Americans, Fred Allison and Edgar J. Murphy, were once believed to have discovered francium in 1930. Scientists now credit Marguerite Perey of France with the discovery. She reported it in 1939, and named the element *actinium K.* She changed its name to *francium* in 1947 to honor France.   K. L. KAUFMAN

FRANCK, *frank,* **CÉSAR AUGUSTE** (1822-1890), was a leading composer of instrumental music during the late 1800's. He combined strictness of form with profound and often somewhat mystical thought.

One of his best-known works is the *Symphony in D minor* (1888). It firmly established Franck's reputation as a symphony composer. His other contributions include symphonic poems and the *Symphonic Variations* (1885) for piano and orchestra, which are popular works in the piano concerto form. Franck composed music for the organ and for the piano. His piano compositions include the famed *Prelude, Chorale, and Fugue* (1884).

Franck also wrote chamber music. His better-known works of this type include four *Trios Concertants* for piano, violin, and cello (1841-1842), the *Quintet in F minor* (1879) for piano and strings, the *Sonata in A major* (1886) for violin and piano, and the *String Quartet in D major* (1889).

Franck was born in Liège, Belgium. He showed considerable talent for the piano and settled in Paris, where he served as a teacher and an organist in 1844. Franck was appointed professor of organ at the Paris Conservatory in 1872.   HANS ROSENWALD

FRANCK, JAMES (1882-1964), a German scientist, collaborated with Gustav Hertz in 1914 to prove the Niels Bohr theory of atomic structure. Franck and Hertz received the 1925 Nobel prize in physics for research proving that electrons occupy certain energy levels in atoms. This research confirmed Bohr's theory (see BOHR [Niels]). Franck also won recognition for his research in photochemistry and photosynthesis. He was awarded the Max Planck medal in 1953.

Franck was born in Hamburg, Germany, and studied at Heidelberg and the University of Berlin. He taught physics and chemistry in Berlin and in Göttingen. He became professor of physics at the University of Chicago in 1938.   RALPH E. LAPP

FRANCO, FRANCISCO (1892-1975), was dictator of Spain from 1936 until his death in 1975. He came to power shortly after the start of the Spanish Civil War. In that war, he led the rebel Nationalist Army to victory over the *Loyalist* (Republican) forces. After the war ended in 1939, Franco held complete control of Spain. His regime was similar to a Fascist dictatorship. He carried out the functions of chief of state, prime minister, commander in chief, and leader of the Falange, the only political party permitted (see FALANGE ESPAÑOLA). He adopted the title of *El Caudillo* (The Leader). In the early years of his regime, he tried to eliminate all opposition. He later eased some restrictions.

His Early Life. Franco was born Francisco Franco Bahamonde in El Ferrol del Caudillo, in the province of La Coruña. His father was a naval officer. Young Franco was trained as an army officer at the Infantry Academy of Toledo. Between 1912 and 1927, he held important command posts in Spanish Morocco. His troops there helped put down a long rebellion against Spanish rule. He was made a general at the age of 34.

Black Star
Francisco Franco

In 1931, Spain became a republic. During the next five years, disputes involving Spanish political groups became increasingly severe. At first, Franco avoided becoming involved. But when the moderate conservatives won the election of 1933, Franco became identified with them. In 1934, Franco helped put down a revolt by *leftists*, who wanted sweeping changes in Spain's way of life. In 1935, he became army chief of staff. The following year, the leftists won the election and sent Franco to a post in the Canary Islands.

Military leaders plotted to overthrow the leftist government in 1936. Franco delayed taking part in the plot, but he was promised command of the most important part of the army. The revolt began in July 1936 and it started a total civil war. Two and a half months later, the rebel generals named Franco commander in chief and dictator. Franco's forces, called Nationalists, received strong support from Italy and Germany. On April 1, 1939, after 32 months of bitter fighting, the Nationalists gained complete victory.

As Dictator, Franco kept Spain officially neutral during World War II. But he sent "volunteers" to help Germany fight Russia. After the war, the victorious Allies would have little to do with Spain because of Franco's pro-Fascist policies. The Western powers became more friendly toward Franco during the Cold War with Russia, because he was against Communism. In 1953, Franco signed an agreement with the United States. He permitted the United States to build air and naval bases in Spain in exchange for economic and military aid. This aid helped bring about industrial expansion. Spain's living standard rose, although it remained one of the lowest in Western Europe.

In the early 1960's, opposition to Franco became more outspoken. Miners and other workers went on strike, though strikes were illegal. Opposition groups organized in secret. Franco relaxed police controls and economic restriction somewhat. In 1966, strict press censorship was relaxed.

Franco declared, in 1947, that Spain would be ruled by a king after he left office. In 1969, Franco named Prince Juan Carlos to be king and head of state after Franco's death or retirement. Juan Carlos is the grand-

son of King Alfonso XIII, who left Spain in 1931. Franco died in November 1975, and Juan Carlos became king (see JUAN CARLOS I).   STANLEY G. PAYNE

See also SPAIN (Government; History).

FRANCO-PRUSSIAN WAR began as a struggle between France and Prussia in 1870. Then the other German states joined, and the conflict became one between France and Germany.

Events Leading up to the War. Prussia had overthrown Austria in the Seven Weeks' War and placed itself at the head of the German states. Emperor Napoleon III of France allowed himself to be influenced by patriots who wanted to humiliate Prussia. Otto von Bismarck, Prussia's chancellor, was equally anxious for a struggle. Bismarck hoped to strengthen the unity of the German states by having them fight France.

An excuse for war was easily found. Prince Leopold of Hohenzollern, a Roman Catholic relative of the Prussian king, had been offered the Spanish crown. The French felt that if Leopold ruled Spain, the Hohenzollern family would become too powerful. Leopold refused the crown, but France insisted that no Hohenzollern should ever accept the Spanish throne.

Count Benedetti, the French ambassador, presented this demand to Wilhelm I of Prussia at Ems, in Prussia. Wilhelm received Benedetti politely, but refused the French demand. He then sent a telegram to Bismarck telling what had happened. Bismarck condensed this "Ems dispatch" in such a way that it aroused great fury when it was published in France on July 14, 1870. The French declared war on July 19.

Progress of the War. Both countries entered the struggle with enthusiasm. General Helmuth Karl von Moltke, head of the Prussian Army, had made careful preparations for war with France. The French were largely unprepared.

The Germans defeated the French at Weissenburg, Wörth, and Spichern, and inflicted severe losses. The French armies under Marshal MacMahon and Marshal Bazaine were separated and kept apart by the Germans. Bazaine was defeated and surrounded at Metz. MacMahon, who had been ordered to march to the relief of Bazaine, met the Germans in a great battle near Sedan. The French were overwhelmed, MacMahon's army surrendered, and the Emperor Napoleon III was taken prisoner. Bazaine later surrendered at Metz.

The End of the War. When the news of the defeat at Sedan reached Paris, the French deposed Napoleon and prepared to defend the city. The army and the citizens of Paris fought bravely, but they had to yield the city to the Germans early in 1871. The war ended with the Treaty of Frankfurt, which was signed on May 10, 1871. The treaty provided that France would give Alsace and part of Lorraine to Germany, pay Germany one billion dollars, and support a German army of occupation until the sum was paid.

Neutral powers considered the Treaty of Frankfurt very harsh. The indemnity was the largest in the history of modern Europe up to that time. France resolutely set itself to pay the money, and, to the astonishment of the world, did so in less than three years. French industry was stimulated by the need to produce enough to pay the debt.

Results. The Franco-Prussian War abolished the North German Confederation and created a new German Empire. It helped set the stage for World War I by increasing French and German hostility. ROBERT G. L. WAITE

Related Articles in WORLD BOOK include:

Alsace-Lorraine	Napoleon III
Balloon (Balloons in War)	Prussia
Bismarck	Seven Weeks' War
Germany (History)	Thiers, Louis Adolphe
Hohenzollern	Wilhelm (I) of Germany
Moltke (Count Helmuth Karl von)	World War I (Causes)

FRANCOLIN, *FRANG koh lin,* is a kind of partridge. It grows about a foot long, and may be richly barred or spotted. The male generally is black and white, with a handsome black head and white ear patch. The female is brownish. The *common francolin* lives in parts of southern Asia and southern Europe. Other francolins may be much more plainly colored. They live throughout the whole of Africa, and in southern Asia and Europe.

Scientific Classification. Francolins belong to the partridge, pheasant, and quail family, *Phasianidae.* The common francolin is a member of genus *Francolinus,* and is species *F. francolinus.* JOSEPH J. HICKEY

See also PARTRIDGE; QUAIL.

FRANK was a member of a confederation of Germanic peoples that attacked the Roman Empire beginning in the A.D. 200's. Franks were divided into two branches, the Salians and the Ripuarians. The Salians settled in the Low Countries on the lower Rhine, near the North Sea. The Ripuarians moved into the region around what are now the cities of Trier and Cologne, Germany, on the middle Rhine.

Clovis, a king of the Salian Franks, began a massive invasion of Roman Gaul (now France) in 486. He defeated Gauls, Romans, Visigoths, and others to create a kingdom stretching from east of the Rhine River to the Pyrenees Mountains. Clovis was the first great Germanic ruler to adopt orthodox Christianity, in place of the heresy called *Arianism* practiced by the East Germanic peoples (see ARIANISM). When Clovis died in 511, the Franks, though outnumbered by their Gallo-Roman neighbors 20 to 1, had such a firm hold on Gaul that the region was called France after them.

Frankish history is divided into two periods, the

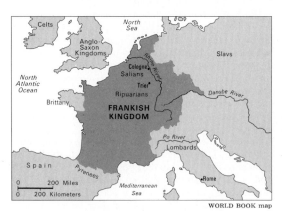

The Frankish Kingdom in A.D. 768

WORLD BOOK map

Merovingian, from about 481 to 751, and the *Carolingian,* 751 to 987. Charlemagne, who was king of the Franks from 768 to 814, created a vast empire. In 800, Pope Leo III crowned him emperor of the Romans. After the time of Charlemagne, the Frankish empire began to break up into what later became the kingdoms of France, Germany, and Italy. WILLIAM G. SINNIGEN

See also CHARLEMAGNE; CHARLES MARTEL; CLOVIS I; FEUDALISM; MEROVINGIAN.

FRANK, ANNE (1929-1945), a German-Jewish girl, wrote a vivid, tender diary while hiding from the Nazis during World War II. Anne was born in Frankfurt, Germany. She and her family moved to The Netherlands in 1933 after the Nazis began to persecute Jews. In 1942, during the Nazi occupation of The Netherlands, the family hid in a secret attic in an Amsterdam office building. Anne recorded her experiences in a diary. Two years later, the family was betrayed and discovered. Anne died in the Nazi concentration camp at Belsen. Her diary was published in 1947, and later was made into a play and a film, both called *The Diary of Anne Frank.*

Wide World

Anne Frank

FRANK, ILYA M. See NOBEL PRIZES (table: Nobel Prizes for Physics—1958).

FRANKENSTEIN is a famous horror novel written by Mary Wollstonecraft Shelley. The book tells the story of a monster that has been created from parts of dead bodies by a young medical student named Victor Frankenstein. The monster has no name in the book, but it has mistakenly been called "Frankenstein." In the beginning, the monster is gentle. But when people scorn it because of its ugliness, it becomes hateful, and turns to murder. Eventually, Frankenstein dies and the monster disappears.

The book was published in 1818 under the title *Frankenstein, or The Modern Prometheus.* Many motion pictures have been based on the character of the monster. Most of the motion pictures have little relationship to Shelley's book. JAMES DOUGLAS MERRITT

See also SHELLEY, MARY WOLLSTONECRAFT.

FRANKENTHALER, HELEN (1928-), an American artist, is a leading abstract expressionist painter. Her works illustrate the physical process involved in creating a painting, rather than communicating an idea through the subject. Colors run into one another in her paintings, and forms overlap visibly. Some areas remain unpainted, so that the canvas itself is part of the painting.

Frankenthaler developed a painting technique called *soak-stain,* which involves pouring thin layers of paint on raw canvas. After the paint soaks into the canvas, the color becomes an actual part of the painting surface. In this way, Frankenthaler rejected brushwork texture and allowed the color and texture of the paint itself to become major elements of the painting. Her painting *Pre-Dawn* is reproduced in the PAINTING article. Frankenthaler was born in New York City. GREGORY BATTCOCK

FRANKFORT, Ky. (pop. 21,902), is the capital of Kentucky and the county seat of Franklin County. People sometimes call Frankfort the *Bluegrass Capital* because of its central location in the Bluegrass Region. The city lies within S-loops of the Kentucky River on a plain surrounded by hills, about 45 miles (72 kilometers) east of Louisville (see KENTUCKY [political map]).

The Kentucky River divides Frankfort into north and south sections, connected by three bridges. The north side includes the older residential section, the Old Capitol, and the main business district. The New Capitol and the Executive Mansion stand in the southern section. The New Capitol, completed in 1910, is three stories high and resembles the United States Capitol in design. Kentucky State University is in Frankfort. Whiskey distilling is the city's chief industry.

Frankfort has many points of historical interest. The Old Capitol is now the home of the Kentucky Historical Society. Beautiful old homes of famous Kentucky statesmen, judges, and military men line the "Corner of Celebrities," a three-block area in north Frankfort.

The Virginia Legislature founded Frankfort in 1786 on land owned by General James Wilkinson (1757-1825), later Commander of the American Armies of the West. Frankfort has a council-manager form of government.   THOMAS D. CLARK

See also KENTUCKY (color picture: The State Capitol; pictures: The Kentucky Governor's Mansion, Floral Clock).

FRANKFURT, *FRAHNK furt* (pop. 660,400), is the transportation hub of West Germany. It stands on the banks of the Main River, about 100 miles (160 kilometers) southeast of Cologne. For location, see GERMANY (political map). A network of railroads and highways links the city with all parts of Western Europe. The Frankfurt airport covers a larger area than any other airport in Europe. A river and canal system links the city with the North Sea. Frankfurt has three harbor areas, and ranks third among Germany's inland ports. The city's full name is Frankfurt am Main.

The city is a world center of commerce and banking. The Rothschild family opened its first bank there in 1798 (see ROTHSCHILD). Frankfurt holds two great trade fairs a year. The fair held in September opened first in 1240 and the February fair started in 1330. The city also holds many specialized fairs. Factories in Frankfurt produce chemicals, machinery, electrical equipment, and precision instruments.

Allied bombers leveled nearly half of Frankfurt during World War II, including the birthplace of Johann Wolfgang Goethe. But the city was rebuilt after the war, and American aid helped restore Goethe's home as a museum. The city changed Frankfurt University's name to Johann Wolfgang Goethe University in 1932.

Frankfurt's geographical position made it important from the time of the Roman Empire. The shallow ford in the Main River provided the easiest north-south river crossing in all Germany. The Franks forded the river in early times, and the city's name means *ford of the Franks* (see FRANK). Merchants traveling between Mediterranean countries and northern Europe naturally passed through Frankfurt. In about A.D. 500, the Franks seized a Roman fort at the crossing and founded a settlement. After 1356, Holy Roman Emperors were elected in Frankfurt. The city served as headquarters

for the U.S. occupation forces in Germany from 1945 to 1955. The U.S. Air Force still maintains the Rhein-Main air base, which is located just outside Frankfurt.   JAMES K. POLLOCK

FRANKFURT, TREATY OF. See FRANCO-PRUSSIAN WAR.

FRANKFURTER. See SAUSAGE.

FRANKFURTER, FELIX (1882-1965), served as an associate justice of the Supreme Court of the United States from 1939 until he retired in 1962. Before that time, Frankfurter spent 25 years as professor of law at Harvard University, and was an influential adviser to Presidents Woodrow Wilson and Franklin D. Roosevelt.

As a Supreme Court justice, Frankfurter was independent, forward-looking, and judicial-minded. His writings include *The Case of Sacco and Vanzetti; The Public and Its Government; The Commerce Clause Under Marshall, Taney and Waite;* and *Mr. Justice Holmes and the Supreme Court.*

Frankfurter was born in Vienna, Austria, and came to the United States in 1894. He was graduated from the College of the City of New York and Harvard Law School. He held several posts in Washington, D.C., during World War I, and went to the Versailles Peace Conference in 1919, where he served as a legal aide to President Wilson.   MERLO J. PUSEY

FRANKINCENSE, or OLIBANUM, is a fragrant gum resin obtained from certain trees that grow in Africa and Asia. Since ancient times, it has been burned as an incense during religious services. The Bible says that one of the wise men brought Jesus a gift of frankincense (Matt. 2).

Frankincense is the hardened resin from the bark of trees of the genus *Boswellia*. The resin hardens into pale-colored drops called *tears*. These tears are used as incense in religious services. Perfumers dissolve the natural resin in alcohol to get a product called *olibanum absolute*. When steam is passed through olibanum absolute, it yields an oil perfumers call *essential oil*. This essential oil is added to perfumes to give a long-lasting, spicy fragrance.   PAUL Z. BEDOUKIAN

FRANKING AND PENALTY PRIVILEGES are ways of sending official matter through the United States mails without prepayment of postage. The Vice-President, members of and delegates to Congress, and certain other officials of the Congress use the *franking privilege*. They use it to mail official correspondence, public documents, the Congressional Record, seeds, and agricultural reports. The mailer puts his signature or its facsimile on each piece of mail instead of a postage stamp. Widows of former presidents may frank all their domestic mail. Congress appropriates money to pay the U.S. Postal Service for the postage involved in these franking privileges.

Departments, offices, and agencies of the executive branch of the government use the *penalty privilege* without prepayment of postage for mailing official matter. Each item bears a printed clause citing the penalty for private use of this privilege. Each division pays the Postal Service the amount of postage chargeable on its penalty mail at regular postal rates.

Critically reviewed by the U.S. POSTAL SERVICE

Detail of a pastel portrait (1783) by Joseph-Sifrède Duplessis; New York Public Library (Bettmann Archive)

Franklin Served His Nation as a Statesman, Scientist, and Public Leader.

BENJAMIN FRANKLIN

FRANKLIN, BENJAMIN (1706-1790), was a jack-of-all-trades and master of many. No other American, except possibly Thomas Jefferson, has done so many things so well. During his long and useful life, Franklin concerned himself with such different matters as statesmanship and soapmaking, book-printing and cabbage-growing, and the rise of tides and the fall of empires. He also invented an efficient heating stove and proved that lightning is electricity.

As a statesman, Franklin stood in the front rank of the men who built the United States. He was the only man who signed all four of these key documents in American history: the Declaration of Independence, the Treaty of Alliance with France, the Treaty of Peace with Great Britain, and the Constitution of the United States.

Franklin's services as minister to France helped greatly in winning the Revolutionary War. Many historians consider him the ablest and most successful diplomat that America has ever sent abroad.

Franklin led all men of his day in the study of electricity. As an inventor, he was unequaled in the United States until the time of Thomas A. Edison. People still quote from Franklin's *Sayings of Poor Richard* and read his *Autobiography*. Franklin helped establish Pennsylvania's first university and its first public hospital.

Franklin's fame extended to Europe as well as America. Thomas Jefferson hailed him as "the greatest man and ornament of the age and country in which he lived." A French statesman, Count Honoré de Mirabeau, called him "the sage whom two worlds claimed as their own."

Early Life

Benjamin Franklin was born in Boston, Mass., on Jan. 17, 1706. He was the 15th child and youngest son in a family of 17 children. His parents, Josiah and Abiah Franklin, were hard-working, God-fearing folk. His father made soap and candles in his shop "at the sign of the Blue Ball" on Milk Street.

Student and Apprentice. Benjamin attended school in Boston for only two years. He proved himself excellent in reading, fair in writing, and poor in arithmetic. Josiah Franklin decided that he could not afford further education for his youngest son. He kept Benjamin home after the age of 10 to help cut wicks and melt tallow in the candle and soap shop.

Franklin's schooling ended, but his education did not. He believed that "the doors of wisdom are never shut," and continued to read every book that he could get. He worked on his own writing style, using a volume of the British journal *The Spectator* as a model. His prose became clear, simple, and effective. The boy also taught himself the basic principles of algebra and geometry, navigation, grammar, logic, and the natural and physical sciences. He studied and partially mastered French, German, Italian, Spanish, and Latin. He eagerly read such books as *Pilgrim's Progress*, Plutarch's *Lives*, Cotton Mather's *Essays to Do Good*, and Daniel Defoe's *Robinson Crusoe*. Franklin made himself one of the best-educated men of his time.

Franklin did not care much for the trade of candle-making. When the boy was 12, his father persuaded him to become an apprentice to his older brother James, a printer. James proved to be a good teacher, and Benjamin a good pupil. He soon became a skilled printer. He wrote several newspaper articles, signed them "Mrs. Silence Dogood," and slipped them under the printshop door. James admired the articles, and printed several of them. But he refused to print any more when he discovered that Benjamin had written them. The brothers quarreled frequently, and Benjamin longed to become his own master. At 17, Franklin ran away to Philadelphia, which was then the largest city in the British colonies. The story of his arrival there has become a classic of American folklore. Many tales describe the runaway apprentice trudging manfully up Market Street with a Dutch dollar in his pocket, carrying one loaf of bread under each arm and eating a third.

Printer. From 1723 to 1730, Franklin worked for various printers in Philadelphia and in London, England, where he was sent to buy printing presses. He became the owner of his own print shop in 1730, when he was 24. He began publishing *The Pennsylvania Gazette*, writing much of the material for this newspaper himself. His name gradually became known throughout the colonies. Franklin had a simple formula for business success. He believed that a successful man had to work just a little harder than any of his competitors. As one of his neighbors said: "The industry of that Franklin is superior to anything I ever saw . . . I see him still at work when I go home from the club; and he is at work again before his neighbors are out of bed."

Later in 1730, Franklin married Deborah Read, the daughter of his first Philadelphia landlady. Deborah was not nearly so well educated as her husband. Her letters to him have many misspelled words. The Franklins were a devoted couple. He addressed his letters to "my dear Debby," and she signed her replies, "your afeckshonet wife."

Franklin had three children, two boys and a girl. One of the boys, William, became governor of New Jersey.

The First Citizen of Philadelphia

Publisher. Franklin's printing business prospered from the start. He developed *The Pennsylvania Gazette* into one of the most successful newspapers in the colonies. He always watched carefully for new ideas. Historians credit him as the first editor in America to publish a newspaper cartoon, and to illustrate a news story with a map. He laid many of his projects for civic reform before the public in the columns of his newspaper. Franklin published *The Pennsylvania Gazette* from 1729 until 1766.

But Franklin achieved even greater success with *Poor Richard's Almanac* than with his newspaper. He wrote and published the almanac for every year from 1733 to 1758. The fame of the almanac rests mainly on the wise and witty sayings that Franklin scattered through each issue. Many of these sayings preach the virtues of industry, frugality, and thrift. "Early to bed and early to rise, makes a man healthy, wealthy, and wise." "God helps them that help themselves." "Little strokes fell great oaks." Other sayings reflect a shrewd understanding of human nature. "He's a fool that makes his doctor his heir." "He that falls in love with himself will have no rivals." See POOR RICHARD'S ALMANAC.

Civic Leader. Franklin never actively sought public office, although he was interested in public affairs. In 1736, he became clerk of the Pennsylvania Assembly. The poor service of the colonial postal service disturbed him greatly. Hoping to improve matters, he agreed to become Philadelphia's postmaster in 1737. He impressed the British government with his efficiency in this position, and in 1753 he became deputy postmaster general for all the colonies. Franklin worked hard at this job, and introduced many needed reforms. He set up the first city delivery system and the first Dead-Mail Office (see DEAD-MAIL OFFICE). He speeded foreign mail deliveries by using the fastest packet ships available across the Atlantic Ocean. To speed domestic mail service, he hired more post riders, and required his couriers to ride both night and day. Franklin also helped Canada establish its first regular postal service. He opened post offices at Quebec, Montreal, and Trois Rivières in 1763.

Printer and Publisher

Bettmann Archive

As an Author, Franklin signed the pen name Richard Saunders to his famous *Poor Richard's Almanac.*

He also established messenger service between Montreal and New York.

Franklin was public-spirited, and worked constantly to make Philadelphia a better city. He established the world's first subscription library. The members of this library contributed money to buy books, and then used them free of charge. The original collection still exists. Fire losses in Philadelphia were alarmingly high, and Franklin organized a fire department. He reformed the city police when he saw that criminals were getting away without punishment. The city streets were unpaved, dirty, and dark, so he started a program to pave, clean, and light them. The people of Philadelphia shamefully neglected the sick and insane during Franklin's time. He raised money to help build a city hospital, the Pennsylvania Hospital, for these unfortunates. Scientists in the city were not organized, so Franklin set up the American Philosophical Society to bring them together. The city had no school for higher education, so Franklin also helped to found the academy that grew into the University of Pennsylvania. As a result of these and other projects, Philadelphia became the most advanced city in the 13 colonies.

The Scientist

Experiments with Electricity. Franklin was one of the first persons in the world to experiment with electricity. He conducted his most famous electrical experiment at Philadelphia in 1752. He flew a homemade kite during a thunderstorm, and proved that lightning is electricity. A bolt of lightning struck the kite wire and traveled down to a key fastened at the end, where it caused a spark. Then he tamed lightning by inventing the lightning rod (see LIGHTNING ROD). He urged his fellow citizens to use this device as a sure "means of securing the habitations and other buildings from mischief from thunder and lightning." When lightning struck Franklin's own home, the soundness of his invention became apparent. The lightning rod saved the building from damage. Franklin's lightning rod demonstrated his saying that "An ounce of prevention is worth a pound of cure." Authorities generally agree that Franklin created such electrical terms as *armature, condenser,* and *battery.*

Franklin's experiments with electricity involved some personal risk. He knocked himself unconscious at least once. He had been trying to kill a turkey with an electric shock, but something went wrong and Franklin, not the bird, was stunned. When he regained consciousness, he said: "I meant to kill a turkey, and instead, I nearly killed a goose."

Other Studies. Franklin's scientific interests ranged far beyond electricity. He became the first scientist to

Bettmann Archive

As a Printer, Franklin bought a press with Hugh Meredith in 1729. He became sole owner the next year.

As an Apprentice, Franklin began his lifelong career in printing and publishing at the age of 12.

study the movement of the Gulf Stream in the Atlantic Ocean. He spent much time charting its course and recording its temperature, speed, and depth. Franklin was the first to show scientists and naval officers that sailors could calm a rough sea by pouring oil on it. He favored daylight-saving time in summer. It struck him as silly and wasteful that people should "live much by candle-light and sleep by sunshine."

Franklin gave the world several other valuable inventions in addition to the lightning rod. The Franklin stove proved most useful to the people of his day. By arranging the flues in his own stove in an efficient way, he could make his sitting room twice as warm with one fourth as much fuel as he had been using. People everywhere appreciate his invention of bifocal eyeglasses most of all. This invention allowed both reading and distant lenses to be set in a single frame. Franklin discovered that disease flourishes in poorly ventilated rooms. Franklin also showed Americans how to improve acid soil by using lime. He refused to patent any of his inventions, or to use them for profit. He preferred to have them used freely as his contribution to the comfort and convenience of everyone.

Franklin quickly appreciated the inventive efforts of other people. He once said that he would like to return to earth a hundred years later to see what progress humanity had made. The first successful balloon flight took place in 1783, during Franklin's stay in Paris. Many bystanders scoffed at the new device and asked, "What good is it?" Franklin retorted, "What good is a newborn baby?"

Franklin's scientific work won him many high honors. The Royal Society of London elected him to membership, a rare honor for a person living in the colonies. Publishers translated his writings on electricity into French, German, and Italian. The great English statesman William Pitt told the House of Lords that Franklin ranked with Isaac Newton as a scientist. He called Franklin "an honor not to the English nation only but to human nature."

The Public Servant

The Plan of Union. In the spring of 1754, war broke out between the British and French in America (see FRENCH AND INDIAN WARS). Franklin felt that the colonies had to unite for self-defense against the French and Indians. He printed the famous "Join or Die" cartoon in his newspaper. This cartoon showed a snake cut up into pieces that represented the colonies.

Franklin presented his Plan of Union at a conference of seven colonies at Albany, N.Y. This plan tried to bring the 13 colonies together in "one general government." It contained some ideas that were later included in the Constitution of the United States. The delegates at the Albany Congress approved Franklin's plan, but the colonies failed to ratify it. Said Franklin: "Everyone cries a union is absolutely necessary, but when it comes to the manner and form of the union, their weak noddles are perfectly distracted." See ALBANY CONGRESS.

The war forced Franklin to turn his attention to the unfamiliar field of military matters. Early in 1755, General Edward Braddock and two British regiments arrived in America with orders to capture the French stronghold of Fort Duquesne, at the point where the Allegheny and Monongahela rivers met. The British had trouble finding horses and wagons for the expedition, and Franklin helped provide the necessary equipment. He was one of many who tried to give Braddock a timely warning. He remarked that, above all, the British must avoid a surprise attack by the French and Indians. But Braddock ignored Franklin's warning. As a result, the French and Indians ambushed the British on the banks of the Monongahela River. Braddock was killed, and the British army was almost destroyed. In

Public-minded Citizen

Bettmann Archive

The Subscription Library Franklin set up at Philadelphia in 1731 was the first of its kind in the world.

The City Hospital he organized was the first in America.

Postal Service improved when Franklin became deputy postmaster general in 1753.

The Academy he helped found later became the University of Pennsylvania.

the meantime, Franklin raised volunteer colonial armies to defend frontier towns, and supervised construction of a fort at Weissport in Carbon County, Pennsylvania.

A Delegate in London. In 1757, the Pennsylvania legislature sent Franklin to London to speak for the colony in a tax dispute with the *proprietors* (descendants of William Penn living in Great Britain). The proprietors controlled the governor of the colony, and would not allow it to pass any tax bill for defense unless their own estates were left tax-free. In 1760, Franklin finally succeeded in getting a bill through parliament that taxed both the colonists and the proprietors. Franklin remained in Britain for most of the next 18 years (1757-1775) as a sort of unofficial ambassador and spokesman for the American point of view.

A serious debate developed in Great Britain in the early 1760's at the end of the French and Indian War. The French, who lost the war, agreed to give the British either the French province of Canada or the French island of Guadeloupe in the West Indies. At the height

the Boston Tea Party if the British government would agree to repeal its unjust tax on tea (see BOSTON TEA PARTY). The British ignored his proposal. Franklin realized that his usefulness in Britain had ended, and sadly sailed for home on March 21, 1775. He had done everything possible to keep the American colonies in the empire on the basis of mutual respect and good will.

The Statesman

Organizing the New Nation. Franklin arrived in Philadelphia on May 5, 1775, about two weeks after the Revolutionary War began. The next day, the people of Philadelphia chose him to serve in the Second Continental Congress. Franklin seldom spoke at the Congress, but became one of its most active and influential members. He submitted a proposed Plan of Union that contained ideas from his earlier Albany Plan of Union. This plan laid the groundwork for the Articles of Confederation. Franklin served on a commission that went to Canada in an unsuccessful attempt to persuade the French Canadians to join the Revolutionary War. He worked on committees dealing with such varied

Scientist and Inventor

Franklin and His Kite showed the world that lightning is actually electricity.

Franklin's Glasses. He invented bifocal lenses, for both distance and reading use.

Barton, Franklin Institute

His Lightning Rod saved many buildings from fires caused by lightning.

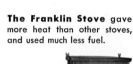

The Franklin Stove gave more heat than other stoves, and used much less fuel.

Foster, Franklin Institute

of the argument, Franklin published a pamphlet that shrewdly compared the boundless future of Canada with the relative unimportance of Guadeloupe. Europeans and Americans read it carefully. Some historians believe that it influenced the British to choose Canada.

Franklin also took part in the fight over the Stamp Act (see STAMP ACT). He seems to have been rather slow to recognize that the proposed measure threatened the American colonies. But once he realized its dangers, he joined the struggle for repeal of the act. This fight led to one of the high points of his career. On Feb. 13, 1766, Franklin appeared before the House of Commons to answer a series of 174 questions dealing with "taxation without representation." Members of the House threw questions at him for nearly two hours. He answered as briefly and clearly as he could. His knowledge of taxation problems impressed everyone, and his reputation grew throughout Europe. The Stamp Act was repealed a short time later, and Franklin received much of the credit.

Political relations between Great Britain and the colonies grew steadily worse. Franklin wanted America to remain in the British Empire, but only if the rights of the colonists could be recognized and protected. He pledged his entire fortune to pay for the tea destroyed in

matters as printing paper money, reorganizing the Continental Army, and finding supplies of powder and lead.

The Continental Congress chose Franklin as Postmaster General in 1775 because of his experience as a colonial postmaster. The government directed him to organize a postal system quickly. He soon had mail service from Portland, Me., to Savannah, Ga. He gave his salary to the relief of wounded soldiers.

Franklin helped draft the Declaration of Independence, and was one of its signers. During the signing ceremonies, John Hancock warned his fellow delegates, "We must be unanimous; there must be no pulling different ways; we must all hang together." "Yes," Franklin replied, "we must indeed all hang together, or assuredly we shall all hang separately."

Minister to France. Shortly after the Declaration of Independence was adopted, Congress appointed Franklin as minister to France. The war was not going well at the time, and Congress realized that an alliance with France might mean the difference between victory and defeat. Late in 1776, at the age of 70, Franklin set forth on the most important task of his life.

Franklin received a tremendous welcome in Paris. The French people were charmed by his kindness, his simple dress and manner, his wise and witty sayings,

Statesman and Diplomat

Bettmann Archive

Title Guarantee & Trust Co., N.Y.

Franklin Traveled to Europe many times representing the colonies, *above*. He was elected to the Second Continental Congress in 1775, and served on a committee inspecting the army, *above right*. Later, he discussed peace terms with Lord Howe, *right*. But the talks failed, and the war went on.

and his tact and courtesy in greeting the nobility and common people alike. Crowds ran after him in the streets. Poets wrote glowing verses in his honor. Portraits and busts of him appeared everywhere.

In spite of Franklin's popularity, the French government hesitated to make a treaty of alliance with the American colonies. Such a treaty would surely mean war with Great Britain. So with tact, patience, and courtesy, Franklin set out to win the French government. His chance came after General John Burgoyne's army surrendered at Saratoga. The French were impressed by this American victory, and agreed to a treaty of alliance. The pact was signed on Feb. 6, 1778. Franklin then arranged transportation to America for French officers, soldiers, and guns. He managed to keep loans and gifts of money flowing to the United States. Many historians believe that without this aid the Americans could not have won their independence.

Franklin next helped draft the Treaty of Paris, which ended the Revolutionary War. France, Great Britain, and Spain all had interests in the American colonies, and Franklin found it difficult to arrange a treaty that satisfied them all. The treaty gave the new nation everything it could reasonably expect. Franklin was one of the signers of the Treaty of Paris in 1783.

The Twilight Years

Franklin returned to Philadelphia in 1785. For the next two years, he served as president of the executive council of Pennsylvania. This office resembled that of a governor today. In 1787, Pennsylvania sent the 81-year-old Franklin as one of its delegates to the Constitutional Convention. It met in Independence Hall to draft the Constitution of the United States. Age and illness kept him from taking an active part. But his wisdom and common sense helped keep the convention from breaking up in failure. Franklin was the oldest delegate at the convention.

Franklin also helped the convention settle the bitter dispute between large and small states over representation in Congress. He was one of the principal authors of the so-called Great Compromise. The compromise sought to satisfy both groups by setting up a two-house Congress. In his last formal speech to the convention, Franklin appealed to his fellow delegates for unanimous support of the Constitution.

Franklin's attendance at the Constitutional Convention was his last major public service. However, his interest in public affairs continued to the end of his life. He rejoiced in Washington's inauguration as the first President of the United States. He hoped that the example of the new nation would lead to a United States of Europe. In 1788, he was elected president of the first antislavery society in America. Franklin's last public act was to sign an appeal to Congress calling for the speedy abolition of slavery.

Franklin died on the night of April 17, 1790, at the age of 84. About 20,000 persons honored him at his funeral. He was buried in the cemetery of Christ Church in Philadelphia beside his wife, who had died in 1774. Franklin accomplished much in many fields, but he began his will with the simple words: "I, Benjamin Franklin, printer . . ." Franklin left $5,000 each to Boston and Philadelphia, part to be used for public works after 100 years, and the rest after 200 years. Part of this money has been used to establish the Franklin Technical Institute, a trade school in Boston, and the Franklin Institute, a scientific museum in Philadelphia.

His Place in History

Franklin led all the people of his time in his lifelong concern for the happiness, well-being, and dignity of humanity. George Washington spoke for a whole generation of Americans in a letter to Franklin in 1789: "If to be venerated for benevolence, if to be admired for talents, if to be esteemed for patriotism, if to be beloved for philanthropy, can gratify the human mind, you must have the pleasing consolation to know that you have not lived in vain."

Franklin's name would almost certainly be on any list of the half-dozen greatest Americans. His face has appeared on postage stamps, and on the coins and paper money of the United States. Two Presidents of the United States proudly bore his name: Franklin Pierce and Franklin D. Roosevelt. Critics hailed Carl Van Doren's *Benjamin Franklin* as one of the best biographies published in the United States in the 1900's.

Philadelphia has also revered the memory of its most famous citizen. The University of Pennsylvania named its athletic field in his honor. One of the show places of the city is the spacious Benjamin Franklin Parkway. Midway along the Parkway stands the Franklin Institute, dedicated to popularizing the sciences that Franklin loved so well. This building contains the Benjamin Franklin National Memorial, with its great statue of the seated philosopher by James Earle Fraser. The Franklin Institute has also set up a reconstruction of Franklin's printing shop, with his own printing presses (see FRANKLIN INSTITUTE).　　　MALCOLM R. EISELEN

Related Articles in WORLD BOOK include:

American Literature (Politics)	Harmonica	Poor Richard's
Cartoon (Early	Kite	Almanac
Cartoons; picture)	Lightning	Rebus
Glasses (picture)	Philadelphia	Stamp Collecting (picture)

Outline

I. Early Life
  A. Student and Apprentice　　　B. Printer
II. The First Citizen of Philadelphia
  A. Publisher　　　B. Civic Leader
III. The Scientist
  A. Experiments with Electricity　B. Other Studies
IV. The Public Servant
  A. The Plan of Union　B. A Delegate in London
V. The Statesman
  A. Organizing the New Nation
  B. Minister to France
VI. The Twilight Years
VII. His Place in History

Questions

How did Franklin happen to become a printer?
What famous newspaper did Franklin establish?
In what ways did Franklin help Philadelphia become the most advanced city in the 13 colonies?
How did Franklin become one of the best-educated men of his time?
Why did Franklin run away to Philadelphia?
What was Franklin's formula for business success?
What is considered to be Franklin's greatest contribution as a colonial statesman?
What did Franklin do with his salary as postmaster general?
How many years did Franklin attend school?
What was Franklin's last major public service?

Reading and Study Guide

See *Franklin, Benjamin,* in the RESEARCH GUIDE/INDEX, Volume 22, for a *Reading and Study Guide.*

Books to Read

ASIMOV, ISAAC. *The Kite That Won the Revolution.* Houghton, 1963.
COHEN, I. BERNARD. *Benjamin Franklin: Scientist and Statesman.* Scribner, 1975.
DAUGHERTY, JAMES. *Poor Richard.* Viking, 1941.
DONOVAN, FRANK R. *The Many Worlds of Benjamin Franklin.* Harper, 1964.
FLEMING, THOMAS J. *The Man Who Dared the Lightning: A New Look at Benjamin Franklin.* Morrow, 1971. *Benjamin Franklin, A Biography in His Own Words.* Harper, 1972.

FRANKLIN, BENJAMIN. *Autobiography.* Many editions are available.
SANDERLIN, GEORGE W. *Benjamin Franklin As Others Saw Him.* Coward, 1972.
VAN DOREN, CARL C. *Benjamin Franklin: A Biography.* Viking, 1956. Written from Franklin's own notes, this long, scholarly study won a Pulitzer prize.

FRANKLIN, DISTRICT OF, is made up of the islands in the Canadian Arctic Archipelago, and the Boothia and Melville peninsulas of the Canadian mainland. It was named for Sir John Franklin, an explorer of the Canadian northwest. The district is a part of the Northwest Territories of Canada. Canada established it in 1895. It is believed to have rich oil and mineral resources. Its area is 549,253 square miles (1,422,559 square kilometers), including 7,500 square miles (19,425 square kilometers) of inland water. The district has a population of about 9,300. See also FRANKLIN, SIR JOHN; NORTHWEST TERRITORIES.　　　R. A. J. PHILLIPS

FRANKLIN, SIR JOHN (1786-1847), pioneered English exploration in the Arctic area. He lost his life looking for the Northwest Passage.

Franklin was born in Lincolnshire, England, and joined the British Navy at the age of 15. He was a midshipman on Matthew Flinders' voyage around Australia in 1803. In 1819, Franklin explored the mouth of the Coppermine River while leading his first Arctic expedition. He led his second Arctic expedition in 1825 and 1826. In 1845, he led the best-equipped expedition to enter the Arctic up to that time. No one returned from it. Lady Franklin's courage inspired many expeditions to search for her husband. A full exploration of the North American Arctic regions resulted. Finally, Roald Amundsen navigated the Northwest Passage between 1903 and 1906. Other explorers found two of Franklin's campsites in 1930.　　　JAMES G. ALLEN

See also NORTHWEST PASSAGE.

FRANKLIN, JOHN HOPE (1915-　　), an American historian, has written many books about black Americans. His book *From Slavery to Freedom* (1947) is a widely praised account of blacks in America.

Franklin was born in Rentiesville, Okla. He earned a bachelor's degree at Fisk University, and master's and doctor's degrees at Harvard University. He taught at colleges in North Carolina from 1939 to 1947, and then at Howard University until 1956. Franklin was a professor at Brooklyn College from 1956 to 1964. Since that time, Franklin has taught at the University of Chicago, where he became head of the history department in 1967.

His books include *The Free Negro in North Carolina* (1943), *The Militant South* (1956), *Reconstruction after the Civil War* (1961), and *The Emancipation Proclamation* (1963). He is coauthor of a junior high school textbook, *Land of the Free* (1966).　　　EDGAR ALLAN TOPPIN

FRANKLIN, ROSALIND ELSIE (1920-1958), was a British chemist and molecular biologist. She made important X-ray studies of *deoxyribonucleic acid,* commonly called *DNA,* which transmits genetic information from one generation to the next (see CELL). Franklin's work contributed greatly to the construction in 1953 of a model of the structure of DNA. This model was built by the biologists James D. Watson of the United States and Francis H. C. Crick of Great Britain. Franklin's research also helped verify the accuracy of the model.

Franklin made other important contributions to chemistry and molecular biology through her use of X-ray diffraction techniques (see X RAYS [In Scientific Research]). Her structural analysis of coals and chars promoted a better understanding of their properties. She also determined the complex structure of the tobacco mosaic virus, which attacks tobacco plants.

Franklin was born in London and graduated from Cambridge University in 1941. She died of cancer at the age of 37.   MARJORIE C. CASERIO

FRANKLIN, STATE OF, was never admitted to the Union. It was organized as a state between 1784 and 1788, and had its own constitution and governor. In 1784, North Carolina ceded part of its western lands to the federal government. Before Congress could vote to accept the region, North Carolina withdrew the offer. The people of the region set up a separate state because they were left without state or federal protection. They

State of Franklin

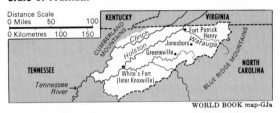

WORLD BOOK map-GJa

named it for Benjamin Franklin, probably in hopes of gaining his support. John Sevier was elected governor. Representatives of North Carolina and other congressmen opposed admitting Franklin to the Union.

Franklin, however, governed itself as a state for 4 years. Because money was scarce, people received furs, whiskey, and tobacco as salaries. North Carolina gained control of the area in 1788, and pardoned its leaders. The voters elected Sevier to the North Carolina Senate. In 1789, North Carolina once again ceded its western lands to the United States. Franklin became part of eastern Tennessee in 1796, and Sevier became the first governor of Tennessee.   MARSHALL SMELSER

See also SEVIER, JOHN; TENNESSEE (Territorial Years; map: Historic Tennessee).

FRANKLIN INSTITUTE, located in Philadelphia, Pa., is a nonprofit scientific and educational institution. It includes the Science Teaching Museum, the Fels Planetarium, the Franklin Institute Research Laboratories, the Bartol Research Foundation, and a library. The institute's rotunda is the Benjamin Franklin National Memorial.

The Science Teaching Museum has exhibits that demonstrate the fundamentals and applications of the sciences. The Fels Planetarium projects a replica of the stars and the planets. The laboratories conduct research and development for private firms and for government agencies. They specialize in engineering, chemistry, physics, and systems sciences. The Bartol Research Foundation performs basic research in astronomy, astrophysics, cosmic radiation, and nuclear physics.

The institute, founded in 1824, was named for Benjamin Franklin. In 1826, it first published its *Journal of the Franklin Institute*, a leading scientific publication in the United States. The institute grants certificates and awards, including the Franklin Medal, to persons

or organizations for their work in the sciences. It is located at 20th and Benjamin Franklin Parkway, Philadelphia.   Critically reviewed by the FRANKLIN INSTITUTE

See also FRANKLIN, BENJAMIN (The Twilight Years).

FRANKLINITE. See ZINC.

FRANKLIN'S GULL is not a sea bird like most gulls. It lives on the prairies during the summer. Franklin's gull is also called the *prairie pigeon*. It breeds from southern Canada to Oregon and east to Iowa. It spends the winter from Louisiana to South America. Franklin's gull is about 14 inches (36 centimeters) long. It is white, with a bluish-gray back. Its head and neck are dark gray in the summer, but turn white in winter. It has a red bill tipped with black.

Flocks of these birds fly over the prairies, giving flutelike cries. Franklin's gull makes its nest of rushes among the reeds of marshy lakes. Thousands of the birds build colonies of many nests fairly close together. By the end of May, the female has laid 2 or 3 eggs, dull white to olive, with brown blotches. Franklin's gull helps the farmer by eating many harmful insects.

Scientific Classification. Franklin's gull belongs to the gull and tern family, *Laridae*. It is genus *Larus*, species *L. pipixcan*.   ALFRED M. BAILEY

See also GULL.

FRANZ JOSEF. See FRANCIS JOSEPH.

FRANZ JOSEF LAND is a group of about 85 islands in the Arctic Ocean, north of Novaya Zemlya. The islands cover about 8,000 square miles (21,000 square kilometers) and are part of Russia. No one lives on most of the islands. They are the most northerly land of the Eastern Hemisphere. The largest islands in the group include Alexandra Land, George Land, Wilczek Land, and Graham Bell Island. In July, the mean temperature of this ice-covered land ranges from 8.2° to 10° F. ($-13.2°$ to $-12°$ C). In winter, the mean temperature is $-22°$ F. ($-30°$ C). But gales may force the temperature as low as $-50°$ F. ($-46°$ C). An Austro-Hungarian expedition discovered the islands in 1873. Russia claimed them in 1926.   THEODORE SHABAD

FRASER, DOUGLAS ANDREW (1916-   ), became president of the United Automobile Workers (UAW), one of the largest labor unions in the United States, in 1977. He succeeded Leonard Woodcock, who retired.

Fraser was born in Glasgow, Scotland, and moved to Detroit with his family when he was 6 years old. In 1934, he went to work as a metal finisher for the De Soto division of the Chrysler Corporation. He joined the UAW shortly after the union was founded in 1935. In 1943, at the age of 27, Fraser became president of one of the UAW's local unions in Detroit.

During the 1950's, Fraser served eight years as an administrative assistant to Walter P. Reuther, who was then president of the United Automobile Workers. From 1970 to 1977, Fraser served as a vice-president of the union and as director of several UAW departments.   JAMES G. SCOVILLE

FRASER, JAMES EARLE (1876-1953), was a well-known American sculptor. He completed his most famous work, the Indian statue *The End of the Trail*, when he was only 20. He designed the buffalo nickel issued by the United States Treasury in 1913. He also produced the bust of Theodore Roosevelt that stands in the

FRASER, JOHN MALCOLM

U.S. Senate Chamber. Fraser was born in Winona, Minn. JEAN LIPMAN

FRASER, JOHN MALCOLM (1930-   ), became prime minister of Australia in 1975. Fraser, the leader of Australia's Liberal Party, succeeded Gough Whitlam, the leader of the Labor Party, as prime minister.

Whitlam's government was dismissed in November 1975 by Australia's governor general, Sir John Kerr, after the Senate rejected the national budget. Kerr appointed Fraser prime minister and instructed him to form a temporary government until an election could be held. The Liberal and Country parties combined forces to win the election in December, and Fraser continued as prime minister. Fraser again led the combined Liberal and Country parties to victory in the election held in 1977. As prime minister, Fraser worked to limit government spending, to reduce unemployment, and to strengthen Australia's ties with the United States and Britain.

Australian Information Service
John Malcolm Fraser

Fraser was born near Melbourne, Victoria, and received a master's degree from Oxford University in England. In 1955, he was elected to the Australian House of Representatives. From 1966 to 1971, Fraser served successively as minister for the army, minister for education and science, and minister for defence. Fraser became head of Australia's Liberal Party in March 1975. C. M. H. CLARK

FRASER, SIMON (1776-1862), was a fur trader and explorer in what is now the Canadian province of British Columbia. He worked for the North West Company, a Montreal fur-trading firm. In 1805, he was put in charge of the company's operations west of the Rocky Mountains. He built that area's first trading posts and explored many of its rivers. In 1808, Fraser explored what is now called the Fraser River.

Fraser was born in Bennington, Vt. He moved with his family to Canada when he was a young child. P. B. WAITE

FRASER RIVER, famous for its salmon fisheries, lies within the Canadian province of British Columbia. It follows a course from its source in the Rocky Mountains, and empties into the Strait of Georgia near Vancouver, B.C. For location, see BRITISH COLUMBIA (map).

The Fraser River drains almost the entire southern half of British Columbia, an area of about 142,000 square miles (367,800 square kilometers). The river is about 850 miles (1,370 kilometers) long. The Chilcotin, Nechako, and Thompson rivers are its chief tributaries. Highways and railroads follow the Fraser through the southern interior of British Columbia. Sir Alexander Mackenzie, a Canadian trader, reached the river in 1793. It was named for Simon Fraser, a Canadian fur trader who followed it to the sea in 1808. The river was the scene of a gold rush in 1858. D. F. PUTNAM

FRATERNAL INSURANCE. See INSURANCE (How Life Insurance Is Sold).

FRATERNAL SOCIETY is an association of persons drawn together by common interests. The society may be organized chiefly to provide companionship and pleasure for its members, or it may be set up to furnish its members with certain benefits such as life, accident, and health insurance. Fraternal societies sometimes take part in civic programs or social work.

Many fraternal societies are secret lodges, with passwords, ceremonies, and initiation rites. Each society adopts its own constitution and bylaws, and sets up its own rules of procedure. Most societies restrict their membership. Some fraternal societies admit only men as members, while a few limit their membership to women. Many fraternal societies for men have auxiliary chapters or organizations to which mothers, wives, daughters, and sisters of members can belong. A few fraternal societies are limited to a single state, but almost all have national or even international membership.

Governing Methods. Fraternal societies elect representatives from local chapters to serve on a governing board within the limit of a district usually covering a state. Each society elects delegates to its national convention from the memberships of the various lodges or from the governing boards of the various states or districts. The delegates in turn elect the officers who make up the supreme governing body. These officers serve until the next national convention is held.

History. Early fraternal societies were somewhat like the English *friendly societies* which first appeared in the 1500's. Working people organized these clubs to provide sickness and death benefits for members. Several fraternal societies founded branches in the United States and Canada during the early 1800's.

The Ancient Order of United Workmen, founded by John Upchurch in 1868, was the first fraternal society in the United States to pay substantial death benefits in the form of insurance to a deceased member's family. Other groups organized fraternal societies on the model of the Ancient Order of United Workmen. Many of these societies in later years merged with other groups to form the present fraternal societies. Early fraternal societies performed a genuine service by furnishing life insurance to members whose incomes were so low they could not otherwise have enjoyed insurance benefits.

The National Fraternal Congress was formed in 1886 to provide state regulation and uniform legislation for fraternal benefit societies. In 1901, certain fraternal societies formed the Associated Fraternities of America. The two associations united in 1913 to form the National Fraternal Congress of America. FOSTER F. FARRELL

Related Articles in WORLD BOOK include:

B'nai B'rith	Knights of Pythias
De Molay, Order of	Maccabees
Eagles, Fraternal Order of	Masonry
Eastern Star, Order of the	Moose, Loyal Order of
Elks, B.P.O. of	Odd Fellows, Inde-
Foresters, Ancient Order of	pendent Order of
Foresters, Independent	Rainbow for Girls
Order of	Red Men, Improved
Foresters of America	Order of
Good Templars, International	Rosicrucian Order
Organization of	Royal Arcanum, Su-
Hibernians in America,	preme Council of the
Ancient Order of	Tammany, Society of
Job's Daughters,	Woodmen of America,
International Order of	Modern
Knights of Columbus	

FRATERNITY is a society of college or university students and alumni. Fraternities are often called *Greek-letter societies*, because most fraternities form their names by combining two or three letters of the Greek alphabet. The word *fraternity* comes from the Latin word *frater*, meaning *brother*. Members of a fraternity pledge to keep the group's ceremonies and mottoes secret. Most fraternities are for men, but some admit both men and women. Women's organizations for college students and alumnae are discussed in the *Sorority* article (see SORORITY).

The best-known kind of fraternity is the *general* or *social fraternity*. *Professional fraternities* are made up of persons preparing for, or working in, such professions as education, law, medicine, and science. Fraternities called *honor* and *recognition societies* select their members for exceptional achievement in a general or specific area. A student may join only one general fraternity. But a general fraternity member may also join a professional fraternity, an honor society, or both.

Most fraternities have *chapters* (local units) in several schools in the United States and Canada. Intercollegiate, national, and international fraternities of all kinds include about 22,000 chapters and about 8,600,000 members. Local fraternities serve only a single school.

Fraternities began in the United States. Phi Beta Kappa was the first fraternity. It was founded in 1776 at William and Mary College as a general fraternity. It later became an honor society. The Kappa Alpha Society was founded in 1825 at Union College in Schenectady, N.Y. It is the oldest continuing general fraternity. Theta Xi, the first professional fraternity, was founded in 1864 at Rensselaer Polytechnic Institute. It became a general fraternity in 1926. Phi Delta Phi was founded in 1869 at the University of Michigan for law students. It ranks as the oldest continuing professional fraternity.

General Fraternities

Membership. To join a social fraternity, a student must be invited by its members. The invitation to join, called a *bid*, must be approved by the chapter members. Bids are made following a period called *rushing*. During rushing, students who are interested in joining a fraternity attend parties to learn about various fraternities and meet their members. Students who accept bids are called *pledges*. A pledge must prove his ability to live, study, and work with fraternity brothers before he is finally accepted for membership. A pledge who fills all requirements is initiated and receives a *fraternity pin* (badge).

Activities. Fraternities are well known for social activities, such as dances and parties. But they also play an important role in other aspects of college life. They encourage members to work for good grades, and they stress participation in athletic, cultural, political, social, and other activities. Most fraternities maintain a fraternity house, where members live. Fraternity life provides experience in self-government and develops skills in cooperation, leadership, and relations with other persons. Fraternities aid charity programs, extend hospitality to students from other countries, and provide funds for scholarships to fellow students and for summer camps for children. Most fraternities have alumni chapters and associations that advise chapters in financial affairs.

Organization. Each general fraternity chapter is a self-governing unit. But they are regulated by college officials and their own interfraternity council.

Most colleges have an interfraternity council. The council consists of representatives from all fraternities on campus. It regulates rushing, settles interfraternity disputes, and enforces conduct codes.

Representatives from each chapter of a national fraternity meet every year or two years in a national convention to decide fraternity policy. National officers, usually alumni, are elected at the conventions. Most national fraternities have a permanent staff and publish a magazine.

The National Interfraternity Conference, Inc., established in 1909, provides a forum for its 52 member fraternities. It sponsors an annual meeting. The National Interfraternity Conference has headquarters at 8770 Purdue Road, Indianapolis, Ind. 46240.

Professional Fraternities

Professional fraternities are similar to general fraternities in many ways. But professional fraternities are made up of persons with a common academic or occupational interest. Some professional groups require higher academic standing than do general fraternities. Members may not pledge other fraternities in the same profession, but they may pledge a general fraternity. There are over 75 intercollegiate professional fraternities for men. Most of them belong to the Professional Inter-

—— LARGEST PROFESSIONAL FRATERNITIES, HONOR SOCIETIES, AND RECOGNITION SOCIETIES IN THE U.S.* ——

Name	College Chapters	Alumni Chapters	Year Founded	Where Founded	National Headquarters
Kappa Delta Pi (Education)†	330	35	1911	University of Illinois	West Lafayette, Ind.
Phi Beta Kappa (Scholarship)†	214	53	1776	College of William and Mary	Washington, D.C.
Phi Kappa Phi (Scholarship)†	188	2	1897	University of Maine	Ann Arbor, Mich.
Sigma Xi (Scientific)†**	§244	None	1886	Cornell University	New Haven, Conn.
Phi Delta Kappa (Education)††	§462	None	1906	Indiana University	Bloomington, Ind.
Tau Beta Pi (Engineering)†	172	48	1885	Lehigh University	Knoxville, Tenn.
Phi Eta Sigma (Freshmen)†	171	None	1923	University of Illinois	Auburn, Ala.
Alpha Phi Omega (Service)**	575	50	1925	Lafayette College	Kansas City, Mo.
Scabbard and Blade (Military)†	143	None	1905	University of Wisconsin	Stillwater, Okla.
Pi Gamma Mu (Social Science)†	153	None	1924	Southwestern College	Winfield, Kans.

*Ranked by total membership since fraternity was founded.
†Honor Society.
**Recognition Society.
††Professional Fraternity.
§Includes noncollege chapters.
Source: WORLD BOOK questionnaires sent to fraternities in 1975 and 1976.

Name	College Chapters	Alumni Chapters	Year Founded	Where Founded	National Headquarters
Acacia	50	10	1904	University of Michigan	Boulder, Colo.
Alpha Chi Rho	26	33	1895	Trinity College (Conn.)	North Brunswick, N.J.
Alpha Delta Phi	23	None	1832	Hamilton College	Baltimore, Md.
Alpha Epsilon Pi	50	34	1913	New York University	St. Louis
Alpha Gamma Rho	52	85	1904	Ohio State University	Des Plaines, Ill.
Alpha Kappa Lambda	30	5	1914	University of California	Fort Collins, Colo.
Alpha Phi Alpha	236	249	1906	Cornell University	Chicago
Alpha Phi Delta	17	17	1914	Syracuse University	Pittsburgh
Alpha Sigma Phi	52	29	1845	Yale University	Delaware, Ohio
Alpha Tau Omega	146	100	1865	Virginia Military Institute	Champaign, Ill.
Beta Sigma Psi	13	15	1925	University of Illinois	St. Louis, Mo.
Beta Theta Pi	105	110	1839	Miami University	Oxford, Ohio
Chi Phi	45	35	1824	Princeton University	Atlanta
Chi Psi	28	28	1841	Union College (N.Y.)	Ann Arbor, Mich.
Delta Chi	67	16	1890	Cornell University	Iowa City
Delta Kappa Epsilon	41	55	1844	Yale University	New York City
Delta Phi	15	18	1827	Union College (N.Y.)	Lancaster, Pa.
Delta Psi	8	9	1847	Columbia University	New York City
Delta Sigma Phi	102	27	1899	City University of New York	Denver
Delta Tau Delta	114	90	1858	Bethany College (W. Va.)	Indianapolis
Delta Upsilon	88	68	1834	Williams College	Indianapolis
FarmHouse	23	25	1905	University of Missouri	St. Joseph, Mo.
Kappa Alpha Order	101	48	1865	Washington and Lee University	Atlanta
Kappa Alpha Psi	201	204	1911	Indiana State University	Philadelphia
Kappa Delta Rho	23	41	1905	Middlebury College	Indianapolis
Kappa Sigma	180	100	1869	University of Virginia	Charlottesville, Va.
Kappa Sigma Kappa	5	None	1867	Virginia Military Institute	Fairmont, W. Va.
Lambda Chi Alpha	200	208	1909	Boston University	Indianapolis
Omega Psi Phi	226	258	1911	Howard University	Washington, D.C.
Phi Beta Sigma	160	170	1914	Howard University	New York City
Phi Delta Theta	141	110	1848	Miami University	Oxford, Ohio
Phi Gamma Delta	110	125	1848	Washington and Jefferson College	Lexington, Ky.
Phi Kappa Psi	76	90	1852	Washington and Jefferson College	Cleveland
Phi Kappa Sigma	47	15	1850	University of Pennsylvania	Philadelphia
Phi Kappa Tau	111	111	1906	Miami University	Oxford, Ohio
Phi Kappa Theta	60	6	1889	Brown and Lehigh universities	Worcester, Mass.
Phi Lambda Chi	5	1	1939	State College of Arkansas	North Little Rock, Ark.
Phi Mu Delta	17	19	1918	University of Massachusetts	Lancaster, Pa.
Phi Sigma Epsilon	60	30	1910	Kansas State Teachers College	Indianapolis
Phi Sigma Kappa	85	47	1873	University of Massachusetts	Drexel Hill, Pa.
Pi Kappa Alpha	170	60	1868	University of Virginia	Memphis, Tenn.
Pi Kappa Phi	91	40	1904	College of Charleston	Charlotte, N.C.
Pi Lambda Phi	41	45	1895	Yale University	Norwalk, Conn.
Psi Upsilon	26	32	1833	Union College (N.Y.)	Paoli, Pa.
Sigma Alpha Epsilon	187	165	1856	University of Alabama	Evanston, Ill.
Sigma Alpha Mu	36	40	1909	City University of New York	Indianapolis
Sigma Chi	167	210	1855	Miami University	Evanston, Ill.
Sigma Nu	168	130	1869	Virginia Military Institute	Lexington, Va.
Sigma Phi	10	11	1827	Union College (N.Y.)	New York City
Sigma Phi Epsilon	210	25	1901	University of Richmond	Richmond, Va.
Sigma Pi	86	36	1897	Vincennes University	Vincennes, Ind.
Sigma Tau Gamma	68	15	1920	Central Missouri State University	Warrensburg, Mo.
Tau Delta Phi	30	20	1910	City University of New York	New York City
Tau Epsilon Phi	52	30	1910	Columbia University	Atlanta
Tau Kappa Epsilon	310	40	1899	Illinois Wesleyan University	Indianapolis
Theta Chi	150	56	1856	Norwich University	Trenton, N.J.
Theta Delta Chi	34	None	1849	Union College (N.Y.)	Boston
Theta Xi	70	30	1864	Rensselaer Polytechnic Institute	St. Louis
Triangle	31	32	1907	University of Illinois	Evanston, Ill.
Zeta Beta Tau	100	50	1898	City University of New York	Manhasset, N.Y.
Zeta Psi	40	41	1847	New York University	New York City

Source: WORLD BOOK questionnaires sent to fraternities in 1975 and 1976.

fraternity Conference. Professional fraternities include more than 2,100 chapters and a million members.

Honor and Recognition Societies

Honor societies are either *departmental* or *general*. A departmental honor society selects men and women who have excellent academic records in a specific area of study. A general honor society selects members from all fields of study. A *recognition* society selects those who have done outstanding work in an area such as retailing or community service.

Critically reviewed by the NATIONAL INTERFRATERNITY CONFERENCE

See also PHI BETA KAPPA; SIGMA XI.

FRAUD is an intentional untruth or a dishonest scheme used to take deliberate and unfair advantage of another person or group of persons. *Actual fraud* includes cases of misrepresentation designed specifically to cheat others, as when a company sells lots in a subdivision that does not exist. Actual fraud includes something said, done, or omitted by a person with the design of continuing what he knows to be a cheat or a deception. *Constructive fraud* includes acts or words that tend to mislead others, as when a man sells his automobile without telling the purchaser that the car stalls often.

Ordinarily, the person wronged by another's fraud may sue the wrongdoer and recover the amount of damages caused by the fraud or deceit. But the person wronged must be able to prove damages.

Statute of Frauds, enacted in England in 1677, required certain common types of contracts, such as those dealing with real estate or employment for over a year, to be in writing. The states of the United States and the provinces of Canada have laws based on this statute.   FRED E. INBAU

FRAUNCES TAVERN, *FRAWN sez*, is famous as the place where George Washington said farewell to his officers on Dec. 4, 1783. The tavern stands at the corner of Broad and Pearl streets in New York City. It is one of the oldest houses in the city. Long Room, where this event took place, contains Revolutionary War flags and many relics. Étienne de Lancey, a wealthy Huguenot, built it as a residence in 1719. In 1762, Samuel Fraunces, a West Indian, bought the house and opened it as the Queen's Head Tavern. The Sons of the Revolution bought the building and restored it between 1904 and 1907.   MARSHALL SMELSER

FRAZER, SIR JAMES GEORGE (1854-1941), Scottish anthropologist, wrote the famous *Golden Bough*. This book traces the development of the world's religions from their earliest forms. He also wrote *Totemism and Exogamy; Description of Greece; Superstition in the Growth of Institutions;* and *Anthologia Anthropologica*. Frazer was born in Glasgow and was educated at Glasgow and Cambridge universities. He taught social anthropology at the University of Liverpool.   DAVID B. STOUT

FRAZIER, EDWARD FRANKLIN (1894-1962), a sociologist, was a leading authority on Negro life in the United States. His writings prompted studies of how such forces as slavery and the prejudices of whites affected the Negro family. Frazier's best-known book is *The Negro Family in the United States* (1939).

Frazier was born in Baltimore. He attended Howard and Clark universities before earning a doctor's degree from the University of Chicago in 1931. He taught at several schools from 1916 to 1934. He headed the sociology department at Howard University from 1934

to 1959. He was president of the American Sociological Society in 1948. His books include *The Free Negro Family* (1932), *The Negro in the United States* (1949), *Black Bourgeoisie* (1957), and *The Negro Church in America* (published in 1964, after his death).   EDGAR ALLAN TOPPIN

FRÉCHETTE, LOUIS HONORÉ. See CANADIAN LITERATURE (Literary Expansion).

FRECKLES are small, brown marks which most frequently appear on the skin of the face and hands. When pigment, or coloring matter, accumulates in small spots in the outer skin, or *epidermis*, freckles appear. Freckles usually occur in large numbers. Exposure to sunlight can increase the size and number of freckles. Freckles are often hereditary. Cold freckles are freckles on parts of the skin not exposed to the sun.   W. B. YOUMANS

FREDERIC, HAROLD (1856-1898), played an important part in the rise of realism in American fiction. He believed that writers should describe realistically the life they had experienced. His best novels portray the narrow, grim small-town life of his native upstate New York in the late 1800's. Frederic also was interested in the impact of new ideas and in the developing political and industrial forces of the day.

Frederic's best novel, *The Damnation of Theron Ware* (1896), describes the influence of new social and religious ideas on a rigid small-town congregation and its minister. In *Seth's Brother's Wife* (1887), Frederic portrayed the mingling of politics and journalism in a small town. *The Lawton Girl* (1890) concerns the greed and social neglect arising from industrial expansion.

Frederic was born in Utica, N.Y. He lived in England as a correspondent for the *New York Times* from 1884 until his death.   DEAN DONER

FREDERICK was the name of three Prussian kings. Frederick III was also German emperor.

Frederick I (1657-1713), the first king of Prussia, was the son of Frederick William, the great elector of Brandenburg (see FREDERICK WILLIAM). He succeeded to his father's title in 1688. He crowned himself king of Prussia in 1701, with the permission of Emperor Leopold I. He founded the University of Halle and the Academy of Sciences. He was born at Königsberg, East Prussia (now Kaliningrad, Russia).

Frederick II (1712-1786) became known as Frederick the Great. He started his reign in 1740 by invading Silesia, one of the finest provinces of Maria Theresa of Austria. This caused the War of the Austrian Succession and the Seven Years' War, in which Frederick brilliantly held off the combined armies of Austria, France, and Russia (see MARIA THERESA; SEVEN YEARS' WAR; SUCCESSION WARS). He kept Silesia and expanded Prussia further when he joined with Austria and Russia in the first partition of Poland. Frederick built a strong government and an efficient army. He encouraged industry and agriculture. He also made Prussia a

Frederick the Great
Oil portrait by Johann George Ziesenis, Kurpfälzisches Museum, Heidelberg

Frederick Barbarossa was a leader of the Third Crusade, which began in 1189. He drowned in 1190 on his way to the Holy Land. This miniature of the late 1100's shows Barbarossa leading his troops during the crusade.

rival to Austria for control of other German states.

Frederick has been called an "enlightened despot." He wanted efficient government, but he did not believe his subjects could rule themselves. He liked philosophy, and included Voltaire, the French writer, among his friends. Voltaire hailed him as "the Philosopher King." Thirty volumes of Frederick's writings, including his correspondence with philosophers, scientists, and artists, were published in 1857. The German people remember Frederick as a strong king and a great military hero. Frederick was born in Berlin, the son of Frederick William I of Prussia and Princess Sophia of Hanover, the sister of George II of England.

Frederick III (1831-1888), the only son of Wilhelm I, became king of Prussia and emperor of united Germany in 1888. He died of cancer just three months after he succeeded his father. He believed in parliamentary government and took an important part in political affairs during his father's reign. Bismarck, the chancellor of Imperial Germany, opposed Frederick's liberal views (see BISMARCK). Frederick was born in Potsdam. He married the Princess Royal Victoria, daughter of Queen Victoria of England. Their oldest son was Wilhelm II (see WILHELM [II]).   ROBERT G. L. WAITE

See also PRUSSIA.

FREDERICK, Danish kings. See FREDERIK.

FREDERICK was the name of three Holy Roman emperors.

Frederick I (1121?-1190), called *Barbarossa* or *Red Beard*, succeeded his uncle Conrad III as king of Germany in 1152. He became Holy Roman emperor in 1155. The German people admired and respected him as a great national hero. In 1180, he defeated his great rival for power in Germany, Henry the Lion, Duke of Saxony and Bavaria. He enforced his authority in Germany and the Slavic borderlands to the east.

He was less successful in a bitter struggle against Pope Alexander III and the Lombard League of North Italian cities. The league defeated Frederick at the Battle of Legnano in 1176. It was in this battle that foot soldiers recorded their first great victory over feudal cavalry. The Lombard cities forced Frederick to grant them self-government in the Peace of Constance in 1183. The emperor started on the Third Crusade to the Holy Land in 1189, but drowned the next year while crossing a river. A German legend, however, says that Barbarossa never really died but is sleeping beside a huge table in the Kyffhäuser Mountains. When his beard grows completely around the table, the legend says, he will arise and conquer Germany's enemies.

Frederick II (1194-1250), called *Stupor Mundi* (The Amazement of the World), was one of the most brilliant rulers of the Middle Ages. He was an excellent administrator, an able soldier, and one of the leading scientists of his time. He understood several languages and encouraged the development of poetry and sculpture. His book on falcons is still consulted by experts.

Frederick belonged to the royal Hohenstaufen family (see HOHENSTAUFEN). He was the son of the Holy Roman Emperor Henry VI and grandson of Frederick I. Frederick II was crowned king of the Romans (king of Germany) when he was 2 years old, and king of Italy when he was 4. He became Holy Roman emperor in 1215, and made himself king of Jerusalem in 1229.

Frederick governed his Sicilian kingdom well. He established the University of Naples in 1224 and made the University of Salerno the best school of medicine in Europe. Throughout his life, he was in conflict with the popes and the rising towns of Germany and Italy.

Frederick III (1415-1493), crowned in 1440, was a poor ruler, and lost much of his empire.   ROBERT G. L. WAITE

See also CRUSADES (Other Crusades).

FREDERICK THE GREAT. See FREDERICK (II) of Prussia.

FREDERICK WILLIAM (1620-1688), often called the *Great Elector*, ruled Brandenburg from 1640 to 1688. Brandenburg later became the heart of the powerful Prussian kingdom.

During his rule, Frederick William laid the foundations for the future military greatness of Prussia. He was only 20 years old when he succeeded his father as *elector* (ruler). He ruled Brandenburg during the last eight years of the Thirty Years' War (see THIRTY YEARS' WAR). The war had brought ruin to Brandenburg. Frederick William began as quickly as possible to regulate the finances, to send new people to the deserted towns, and to build a standing army.

Frederick William fought against both King Louis XIV of France and King Charles XI of Sweden. He defeated Swedish troops in an important battle at Fehrbellin, Germany, in 1675.

After making peace, he devoted his time to improving his territory. He encouraged industries, opened canals, and established a postal system. He reorganized the universities of Frankfurt and Königsberg, and also founded the Royal Library in Berlin. At his death,

Frederick William left to his son Frederick I a prosperous country. ROBERT G. L. WAITE

FREDERICK WILLIAM was the name of four kings of Prussia.

Frederick William I (1688-1740) was one of the great builders of Prussian power. He became king in 1713. He was a stern and absolute monarch who once remarked, "Salvation is God's affair; everything else belongs to me." He expected absolute obedience from his subjects and once imprisoned his own son, Frederick the Great, for disobedience.

Frederick William I dominated an efficient government, strengthened the economy, and trained an army of 80,000 men. His one expensive hobby was collecting tall soldiers. He purchased or kidnaped them from all parts of Europe. During his reign, he took a large area of Pomerania from Sweden. Frederick William I was the son of Frederick I of Prussia.

Frederick William II (1744-1797) became king after the death of his uncle, Frederick the Great, in 1786. He was born in Berlin, the grandson of Frederick William I. He was a weak king, and conditions in Prussia became worse during his reign.

Frederick William III (1770-1840) became king when his father, Frederick William II, died in 1797. Napoleon defeated his armies at the battles of Jena and Auerstädt in 1806. He signed the Peace of Tilsit in 1807, which gave half his land to France. This disastrous treaty brought on a great reform movement in Prussia, led by Baron vom und zum Stein.

The king joined in the War of Liberation against Napoleon, and in the Holy Alliance of 1815. He also supported Prince Metternich in putting down liberal movements. See LOUISE OF MECKLENBURG-STRELITZ; METTERNICH, PRINCE VON; NAPOLEON I.

Frederick William IV (1795-1861) became king after the death of his father, Frederick William III, in 1840. Ten years later, he granted his subjects a limited constitution. He became insane in 1858. His brother Wilhelm became king in 1861. ROBERT G. L. WAITE

See also GERMANY (History).

FREDERICKSBURG, Va. (pop. 14,450), one of the nation's most historic cities, is the marketing center of a fertile farming area. It lies on the Rappahannock River about halfway between Richmond, Va., and Washington, D.C. (see VIRGINIA [political map]). The homes of George Washington's mother and sister are in Fredericksburg, as are James Monroe's law offices. Across the river is Ferry Farm, where Washington spent part of his boyhood. FRANCIS B. SIMKINS

FREDERICKSBURG, BATTLE OF. See CIVIL WAR (Fredericksburg).

FREDERICKSBURG AND SPOTSYLVANIA COUNTY BATTLEFIELDS MEMORIAL NATIONAL MILITARY PARK. See NATIONAL PARK SYSTEM (table).

FREDERICTON (pop. 45,248) is the capital of the Canadian province of New Brunswick. The city lies on the Saint John River, in southwestern New Brunswick. For location, see NEW BRUNSWICK (political map).

Fredericton's leading industries include food processing, woodworking, and the manufacture of leather goods and small boats. The provincial government employs about a fifth of the city's work force. Fredericton is the home of the Beaverbrook Art Gallery and Christ Church Cathedral, one of the finest examples of Gothic architecture in North America. The city is also the home of Mary Washington College, the University of New Brunswick, and St. Thomas University.

Maliseet and Micmac Indians once lived in what is now the Fredericton area. The British founded Fredericton in 1762 on the site of an abandoned French settlement. They named the settlement in honor of Prince Frederick, the second son of King George III. After the Revolutionary War in America ended in 1783, about 6,000 persons from the United States moved to Fredericton because they wanted to remain British subjects. The city became the capital of New Brunswick in 1785. The provincial legislative building was built in downtown Fredericton in 1880 (see NEW BRUNSWICK [picture: The Legislative Building]).

In 1973, several surrounding communities united with Fredericton, and the city's population rose from 24,254 to more than 44,000. The area of the city increased from 23 to 51 square miles (60 to 132 square kilometers). A $7½-million urban renewal project called Kings Place opened in Fredericton in 1974. It includes business offices and a shopping center. Fredericton has a mayor-council form of government. STERLING KNEEBONE

FREDERIK, or FREDERICK, is the name of two kings of Denmark who were members of the House of Schleswig-Holstein-Sonderburg-Glücksburg.

Frederik VIII (1843-1912) ruled Denmark for six years after the death of his father, Christian IX, in 1906. His kindly and democratic manner won him the affection and respect of his people. Frederik was born in Copenhagen. He was a scholarly man, and served as chancellor of the University of Copenhagen for a time. He was the brother of Queen Alexandra of England and of King George I of Greece. His second son, Charles, became King Haakon VII of Norway, and his oldest son, Christian X, succeeded him.

Frederik IX (1899-1972) the oldest son of Christian X, was king from 1947 until his death in 1972. He had served as crown prince for 35 years and as regent during World War II when his father was injured. He married Princess Ingrid of Sweden in 1935. His oldest daughter, Margrethe, succeeded him. RAYMOND E. LINDGREN

FREDERIKSTED, *FREHD rihk stehd* (pop. 1,531), is the chief commercial center of St. Croix, one of the Virgin Islands. The city lies on the western tip of the island. It handles about 80 per cent of the imports of the island, and exports sugar. Victorian houses with lacy galleries line the streets of the town. Nearby ruins of sugar plantations remind visitors of earlier days.

FREE ASSOCIATION. See PSYCHOANALYSIS.

FREE CITY is an independent city-state with its own government. Such city-states developed in Italy and Germany during the Middle Ages. The German free cities received their independence in the 1100's as a reward for helping the German emperor against the nobles. They were not counted among the cities of the Holy Roman Empire. The free cities included Hamburg, Lübeck, and Bremen. They became states in the German Empire in 1871, but kept special tariff privileges until 1888. Danzig (now Gdańsk, Poland) and Fiume (now Rijeka, Yugoslavia) were free cities for a time under the League of Nations. J. SALWYN SCHAPIRO

See also CITY-STATE; GDAŃSK; RIJEKA.

FREE ENTERPRISE SYSTEM

FREE ENTERPRISE SYSTEM is the economic system of the United States, Canada, and some other countries. This system is based on individual economic freedom. It stresses private economic decisions, both by individuals and by companies. A free enterprise system is also called a *private enterprise economy*, a *market economy*, or *capitalism*.

Free enterprise systems operate without an overall central economic plan. No one person, group, or government agency decides what or how much should be produced, or what prices should be charged for goods and services. Business people are generally free to make these decisions themselves. Individuals are also free, for the most part, to decide how they will earn and spend their incomes.

Most economies have some elements of free enterprise and some elements of government control. The United States and Canada allow as much economic freedom as any country today. Government plays an important part in their economies, but free enterprise lies at the heart of their economic systems.

All people, in all times and places, have struggled with the same basic economic problem—making choices. No nation has ever had enough productive resources to satisfy all the wants of its people. Therefore, people must decide which of the many things they want are most important. They must also decide who, among all those who want the available goods and services, shall have them. Some societies are organized so that decisions are made in agreement with long-standing traditions. For example, a tribe may hunt today just as its ancestors did hundreds of years ago. The food obtained from the hunt may also be divided in an age-old way. Other societies may be organized so that some central authority makes the decisions of what to produce and for whom. In such planned societies as China or Russia, planners in the central government make the major economic decisions.

Judged by the test of wealth produced, free enterprise has been the most successful way of making economic choices. It has produced the highest standards of living in history. At the same time, it has given people the freedom of making many of their own economic decisions.

The basic idea of free enterprise can be summed up this way: Put people on their own to make economic decisions, and let them reap the rewards or lack of rewards from those decisions.

This article presents a brief overview of the free enterprise system—what it is, how it developed, and how it works. For a more complete understanding of this and other economic systems, read the articles on ECONOMICS; MARKET; MONOPOLY AND COMPETITION; PRICE; PRODUCTION; DISTRIBUTION; COMMUNISM; and SOCIALISM.

Development of Free Enterprise

Throughout most of history, most people have had their basic economic decisions made for them. Small groups of people in each society have decided what

John R. Coleman, the contributor of this article, is Chairman of the Edna McConnell Clark Foundation, and the author of Comparative Economic Systems.

goods and services should be produced, and who should get what share of them. The idea that people might do better if left on their own came late in history. No one country or age can claim all the credit for this idea. But free enterprise took its first firm hold in England, during the 1700's.

Free enterprise developed in England as a reaction against government control of economic life. From the 1500's to the 1700's, England's economic system, called *mercantilism*, aimed at making the country the most powerful European nation. *Mercantilists* (followers of mercantilism) believed the import of gold, together with a favorable balance of trade, would help the country grow rich and powerful. Their policies required strict government regulation of the entire economy. For example, the government encouraged the export of goods, but placed high taxes on the import of goods. It favored manufacturing at the expense of agriculture. It denied workers the right to organize because this might have raised production costs. See MERCANTILISM.

Many English industrialists who came into power during the mid-1700's found government controls increasingly hard to live with. The American colonists also became more and more discontented with the restrictions England placed on their economic life. For a more detailed discussion of the Americans' dislike for these policies, see REVOLUTIONARY WAR IN AMERICA (Events Leading to the Revolution).

No one person invented the idea of free enterprise. However, Adam Smith, a Scottish philosopher and one of the world's first great economists, was the first to describe and analyze it. In his book *The Wealth of Nations* (1776), he criticized mercantilism, and defended free enterprise on moral grounds. Smith argued that all people benefited most when each individual followed his or her own self-interest. If a person wanted a good income, he or she could get it best by selling some product or service that society most wanted. If the person judged the market correctly, he or she would succeed. If the person misjudged the market, he or she would suffer. The person's misfortune would be a signal to others not to enter that particular field.

In Smith's time, government still represented a small group of people making decisions for others. Smith concluded that, to the greatest extent possible, government should keep its hands off the economy.

Smith's central idea has undergone many changes. But it still lies at the heart of the economic systems of the United States and Canada. Other countries with a large degree of free enterprise include France, Great Britain, Japan, and West Germany.

How Free Enterprise Works

Free enterprise rests firmly on the belief that each person knows what is best for himself or herself. It assumes that a person can make wise decisions concerning what career to prepare for and what brands to buy. The right of a person to own property is also basic to a free enterprise economy. Under such a system, individuals or private firms own most raw materials, factories, and other means of production. The owners are free, within certain important limitations, to use their property as they see fit and to profit from it.

In turn, under a free enterprise system people are expected to live with the results of their decisions. A young man may decide to get a job after high school, rather than pay for further education. He will begin earning money immediately. But he will probably earn less during his lifetime because of his limited education.

Economic decisions are made in what economists call the *market*. In the market, economic forces operate to determine prices. Producers try to get the highest possible prices for their goods or services. Consumers, on the other hand, try to buy at the lowest price. The supply of and demand for a good or service act upon each other to determine the *market price*.

The Role of Profits. Profits and losses play an important part in a free enterprise economy. In such an economy, private businessmen bring various resources together to produce goods and services. First, the businessmen decide what to produce. Then they organize production by combining money, manpower, machinery, materials, and know-how. The main reason men take the risk of entering and staying in business is that they expect to earn profits. Economists define *profit* as earnings over and above all costs. Businessmen do not always earn profits. Sometimes their costs are higher or their sales are lower than they expected—and they lose money.

In a sense, profits and losses play the same role that tradition or a ruler's commands play in other societies. They signal what should or should not be produced. The chief difference is in who gives the signals. In economies based on tradition or command, the signals come from what someone else says people should want to pay for. In a free enterprise economy, the signals result from what people show they are willing to pay for. A business can make a profit only by providing something that people are willing and able to buy. The desire for profits tends to assure that businessmen will produce the goods and services that are most wanted.

The Role of Competition. A free enterprise system permits men to follow their own self-interest. But what can the system do about those who charge prices that are too high or sell products of poor quality? Adam Smith realized that men would abuse power if they had a chance to do so. He found the answer to this problem in the workings of competition. Dissatisfied customers would simply turn to other sources of supply. This was ample protection against goods that were too high in price or too low in quality.

The term *free enterprise system* seems to stress the freedom to start and operate a business. But it also refers to the freedom of workers to choose and change jobs. Competition helps regulate the labor market. Suppose an employer offers a worker less than his effort and skills entitle him to receive. In a completely free economy, another employer would probably be happy to hire the worker away and pay him more for his services. Or suppose an employee or a group of employees demands wages that the employer thinks are too high. The employer might find other workers who are willing to do the job for what he thinks it is worth.

Competition acts as a sort of "policeman" in a free enterprise system. But people's attitudes toward this policeman are not always the same. People are happy with competition among sellers when they themselves are buying. They are less happy when they are the sellers and other sellers try to outdo them in price, service, or quality.

If there are few enough sellers, and they are free to do as they wish, they may join together to raise prices and limit quality and quantity. For this reason, someone must police the policeman. In the United States, the federal and state governments have passed many laws and regulations that attempt to keep competition free and fair. Maintaining and enforcing competition is a necessary government task in all free enterprise systems.

Free Enterprise in the United States

No country has ever had a pure free enterprise system. Each nation has modified the decisions of the market in some ways to achieve various goals. These changes have been made through government, and have generally been in agreement with the public opinion of the time. Most changes have been made in an attempt to improve the welfare of large numbers of people. Many economists use the terms *mixed free enterprise* and *modified free enterprise* to describe economies that rely mainly, but not entirely, on free enterprise. These terms are often applied to the economies of the United States and Canada.

In the United States, the government has always had some influence on the economic system. For instance, the government has always regulated foreign trade and provided for the defense of its citizens. The United States still has basically a free enterprise economy, but the economic role of government has greatly expanded through the years.

During the 1900's, government expenditures have risen sharply. Heavy defense spending since 1940 has made the U.S. government the single biggest buyer of goods and services. Today, more than a fifth of the nation's goods and services are bought by federal, state, and local governments.

The government has also entered some fields of economic activity that involve projects too big for private industry to handle. Examples include the Tennessee Valley Authority (TVA) in the 1930's and the space program in the 1960's.

Since the 1930's, the government has set up many social welfare programs. These programs have been designed to give special aid to groups handicapped by illness, unemployment, poverty, or discrimination. Leading welfare measures include Social Security, minimum wage laws, and parts of the civil rights laws. Such programs have produced bitter dispute over the government's entrance into free markets. Opponents of these welfare laws think that markets should be left alone to distribute goods and services among the people. Supporters of the laws want a fairer distribution than they believe would result from free markets alone.

The Great Depression of the 1930's caused millions of workers to lose their jobs. To prevent such a situation from happening again, the government strives to maintain employment at as high a level as possible. It uses its strong taxing, spending, and credit powers in an attempt to achieve maximum employment, production, and incomes without large increases in prices.

The rise of strong labor unions has also affected the free enterprise system. Wages for many industrial jobs are set by collective bargaining between companies and unions. This process does not look much like the free enterprise system that Adam Smith praised. Yet market forces still make themselves felt at the bargaining table. For instance, the balance between the supply of labor and the demand for that labor increases the bargaining power of either the company or the union. See LABOR MOVEMENT (Arranging Contracts).

Since the nation was founded, Americans have debated the proper role of government in the economy. Most Americans express overwhelming support for some form of free enterprise economy. But they differ on the ways in which the economy can be made to work best to achieve progress, stability, justice, and freedom.

Free Enterprise and the Planned Economies

Just as no country has a pure free enterprise system, neither does any nation have pure socialism or pure communism. All the world's economies might be compared to points along an unbroken line. At one end would be the nations that rely most completely on free enterprise. At the other end would be those that depend most heavily on central planning. The United States and Canada would be closest to the free enterprise end, and China would be nearest the completely planned end. However, all the world's economies have some elements of free enterprise and some elements of planning. See COMMUNISM; SOCIALISM.

Mixtures of free enterprise and central planning do not erase basic differences among economies. Since the 1930's, the U.S. government has taken a larger and larger part in the nation's economic affairs. On the other hand, Russia is relying more and more on prices in market places to distribute goods and services. These facts do not hide the wide gaps between the two countries. Americans still make far more economic choices for themselves than Russians do. Both nations face the same problem of making economic choices in their daily affairs. Each is constantly undertaking changes in its system to make those choices.   JOHN R. COLEMAN

See also ECONOMICS with its list of Related Articles.

For a *Reading and Study Guide*, see *Free Enterprise System* in the RESEARCH GUIDE/INDEX, Volume 22.

FREE METHODIST CHURCH is a religious denomination. It follows the Methodist teachings of John Wesley and the free will doctrine of the Arminians. The church was founded in 1860 by ministers and members of the laity who had been excluded from the Genesee Conference of the Methodist Episcopal Church because they tried to restore historic Wesleyan principles to the church. They believed in simplicity of life and worship; rent-free seats in churches; abolition of slavery; and freedom from secret societies. See METHODISTS.

The church maintains a strong missionary program. Headquarters are in Winona Lake, Ind. The church's full name is the Free Methodist Church of North America.   Critically reviewed by the FREE METHODIST CHURCH

FREE-PISTON ENGINE, sometimes called a *gasifier*, generates hot gases usually used to run a turbine. It can burn nearly any liquid fuel, from kerosene to peanut oil. Most free-piston engines have one or more pairs of pistons mounted facing each other in a cylinder. These pistons work much like the pistons in a diesel engine, except that they are not connected to a crankshaft.

Burning fuel makes the pistons bounce back and forth against cushions of air trapped in the ends of a compressor cylinder. As the pistons move toward each other, they compress air, raising it to a high temperature. When fuel is injected, it explodes, drives the pistons apart, and produces hot gases. The pistons also compress

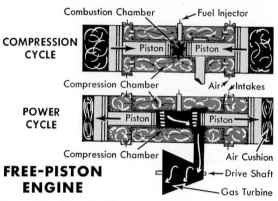

FREE-PISTON ENGINE

Free Pistons bounce off cushions of air. As the pistons move inward, *top*, they compress air. Fuel explodes, creating hot gases that drive the pistons apart, *bottom*. Compressed air sweeps the gases to a turbine before the pistons bounce in again.

air in a chamber around the cylinder. After the explosion, this air forces the gases through the turbine. Some of these engines have only one piston used as an air compressor or a pile driver.

Pateras Pescara, a Spanish engineer, is credited with inventing the engine in the 1920's.   E. W. KETTERING

See also DIESEL ENGINE; PISTON; TURBINE (Gas).

FREE PORT is an area where traders may bring in goods from foreign countries without paying import duties. The goods are free from most customs laws as long as they remain within the limits of the port.

Several free ports were established during the 1800's to help shippers engaged in foreign trade. They included Penang (now Georgetown, Malaysia) and Singapore, which were opened in 1824, and Hong Kong, which has been a free port since 1842. About 10 nations maintain free ports today.

Although relatively few free ports exist today, many countries have special trade areas located near seaports or airports that serve much the same purpose as free ports. In most countries, the official name for such areas is *free trade zone*. The United States calls them *foreign trade zones*. See FOREIGN TRADE ZONE.

Free ports and foreign trade zones encourage foreign trade by making it easier for buyers and sellers to carry on such trade. These special areas usually allow traders to store, exhibit, sort, repack, and reship their goods without paying import duties.   HAROLD J. HECK

FREE SILVER was a plan to put more money in circulation in the United States by coining silver dollars. It was backed chiefly by farmers and silver miners in the late 1800's, when the U.S. government usually used gold coins to redeem paper money.

Supporters of the free-silver plan wanted all silver that was brought to the mint made into coins on a standard that made 16 ounces of silver equal to 1 ounce of gold. The 16-to-1 standard had existed before the U.S. Treasury stopped making silver dollars in 1873.

Farmers believed the plan would help them get higher prices for crops. Miners and silver producers also favored it. The Populist Party supported the free-silver plan in the 1892 elections, and Democrat William Jennings Bryan urged the adoption of the free-silver plan when he ran for President in 1896. The issue died after Alaskan gold discoveries in 1896 increased the supply of money. CHARLES B. FORCEY and LINDA R. FORCEY

See also POPULISM; BRYAN (William Jennings).

FREE SOIL PARTY was a political group organized in Buffalo, N.Y., in 1848. The party opposed the extension of slavery into the territories and the admission of new slave states to the Union. Many members of the party had once belonged to the Liberty Party (see LIBERTY PARTY). The Free Soil Party was joined and strengthened by a discontented faction of the Democratic Party in New York known as the Barnburners.

Martin Van Buren became the Free Soilers' candidate for President in 1848. Their campaign slogan was "Free Soil, Free Speech, Free Labor, and Free Men." The party did not carry any state, but it polled over 291,000 votes. Thirteen Free Soil candidates were elected to the House of Representatives. A coalition of Free Soilers and Democrats elected Salmon P. Chase to the Senate in 1848, and Charles Sumner in 1851.

The Free Soil Party lost the support of the Barnburners before the presidential election of 1852 (see BARNBURNERS). This loss cut the party strength far below what it had been in the preceding election, but the Free Soil candidate for the presidency, John P. Hale, still polled 156,000 votes. Before the election of 1856, the remnants of the Free Soil Party had joined forces with the newly formed Republican Party. DONALD R. MCCOY

FREE STATE. See MARYLAND (The Early 1900's).

FREE TRADE is the policy of permitting the people of a country to buy and sell where they please without restrictions. The term is generally used to describe the conditions of trade between countries, but it may also apply to the conditions of trade within a country. A nation that follows the policy of free trade does not prevent its citizens from buying goods produced in other countries, or encourage them to buy at home.

The opposite of free trade is *protection*, the policy of protecting home industries from outside competition. This protection may be provided by placing *tariffs*, or special taxes, on foreign goods; by restricting the amounts of goods that people may bring into the country; or in many other ways.

The Theory of Free Trade is based on the same reasoning as the idea that there should be free trade among the sections of a country. Consumers in Indiana gain by buying oranges from California, where the fruit can be grown less expensively. They would also gain by buying woolen goods from England if the goods could be produced there at less cost than in America.

Free-trade thinking is based on the principle of *comparative advantage* (see INTERNATIONAL TRADE). According to this principle, market forces lead producers in each area to specialize in the production of goods on which their costs are lower. Each area imports goods that are costlier for it to produce. Such a policy leads to the greatest total worldwide production, so that consumers receive the largest possible supply of goods.

Objections to Free Trade. Despite superior efficiency under free trade, most countries favor some protection.

One reason is the unsettled state of world affairs. Many persons believe that, so long as there is risk of war, a nation should not be too dependent on foreign supplies. Another reason is the protectionist economic policy followed by some other nations. Today, as the United States shifts away from protection, except in agriculture, many of these nations are increasingly emphasizing protection for themselves. These countries are mainly the less-developed nations of the world that seek to protect their "infant" industries, more or less as the United States did in the 1800's.

Those who favor free trade argue that protection leads to national isolation, national jealousies, and threats of war, which in turn necessitate even greater protection. They believe that free trade leads to understanding and world peace. HAROLD J. HECK

Related Articles in WORLD BOOK include:

Customs Union	Free Port
European Community	Latin America (Latin-
European Free	American Trade Relations)
Trade Association	Smith, Adam
Exports and Imports	Tariff

FREE VERSE is a kind of poetry without meter, and often without rhyme (see METER). It replaces the regular beat of poetic meter with a kind of stress called *strophic rhythm*. The stresses rise and fall with the thought or emotion of the words. Free verse retains other poetic devices, such as alliteration, assonance, and balance. For an example of free verse, see Walt Whitman's poem under Enjoying Poetry in the POETRY article. See also the section Verse and Melody of the same article.

FREE WILL is the theory that human beings have the power to make their own choices about what they will do. It implies that people are able to decide for themselves which of several courses of action they will follow. The theory opposite to free will is *determinism*. Many kinds of determinism exist, but determinists believe that people do not really make choices.

There are two ways of looking at free will. One view is that all human actions are free because they come spontaneously from within. Midway between this theory and determinism is the position that in some actions people are determined, and in some they are free. People have free will when they can deliberate and choose between alternate plans. JAMES COLLINS

FREEDMEN'S BUREAU. The close of the Civil War found the blacks of the South free, but homeless and penniless. In 1865, Congress created the Freedmen's Bureau to help the blacks. The Bureau furnished supplies to destitute blacks, supervised contracts between freedmen and their employers, and protected their rights. The Bureau also sought to help them in many other ways. General Oliver O. Howard became commissioner in charge of the Bureau. An assistant commissioner was located in each of the former Confederate States.

In 1866, Congress greatly extended the Bureau's powers. The Freedmen's Bureau continued its work until 1872, spending over $17 million. The Democrats in the South strongly criticized it. They charged that agents of the Freedmen's Bureau worked in the interests of the Republican Party and set the blacks up against their former masters. JOHN DONALD HICKS

FREEDOM

FREEDOM is the ability of a person to make his own choices and to carry them out. The words *freedom* and *liberty* mean much the same thing. For a person to have complete freedom, there must be no restrictions on how he thinks, speaks, or acts. He must know what his choices are, and he must have the power to decide among those choices. He also must have the means and the opportunity to think, speak, and act without being controlled by anyone else.

From a legal point of view, a person is free if society imposes no unjust, unnecessary, or unreasonable limits on him. Society must also protect his rights—that is, his basic liberties, powers, and privileges. A free society tries to distribute freedom equally among all its people.

Today, many societies put a high value on legal freedom. But people have not always considered it so desirable. Through the centuries, for example, many men and women—and even whole societies—have set goals of self-fulfillment or self-perfection. They have believed that achieving those goals would do more to make a person "free" than would the legal protection of his rights in society. Many societies have thought it natural and desirable for a few persons to restrict the liberty of all others. This article discusses the ways that governments and laws both protect and restrict freedom.

Kinds of Freedom

Most legal freedoms can be divided into three main groups: (1) political freedom, (2) social freedom, and (3) economic freedom.

Political Freedom gives people a voice in government and an opportunity to take part in its decisions. This freedom includes the right to vote, to choose between rival candidates for public office, and to run for office oneself. Political freedom also includes the right to criticize government policies, which is part of free speech. People who are politically free can also form and join political parties and organizations. This right is part of the freedom of assembly.

In the past, many people considered political freedom the most important freedom. They believed that men and women who were politically free could vote all other freedoms for themselves. But most people now realize that political liberty means little unless economic and social freedom support it. For example, a person's right to vote does not have much value if he lacks the information to vote in his own best interests.

Social Freedom includes freedom of speech, of the press, and of religion; freedom of assembly; academic freedom; and the right to due process of law.

Freedom of Speech is the right of a person to say publicly or privately what he believes. Political liberty depends on this right. People need to hold free discussions and to exchange ideas so they can decide wisely on political issues. Free speech also contributes to political freedom by making government officials aware of public opinion. See FREEDOM OF SPEECH.

Freedom of the Press is the right to publish facts, ideas, and opinions without interference from the government or from private groups. This right extends to radio, television, and motion pictures as well as to printed material. Freedom of the press may be considered a special type of freedom of speech, and it is important

for the same reasons. See FREEDOM OF THE PRESS.

Freedom of Religion means the right to believe in and to practice the faith of one's choice. It also includes the right to have no religion at all. See FREEDOM OF RELIGION.

Freedom of Assembly is the right to meet together and to form groups with others of similar interests. It also means that a person may associate with anyone he wishes. On the other hand, no one may be forced to join an association against his will.

Academic Freedom is a group of freedoms claimed by teachers and students. It includes the right to teach, discuss, research, write, and publish without interference. Academic freedom promotes the exchange of ideas and the spread of knowledge. See ACADEMIC FREEDOM.

Due Process of Law is a group of legal requirements that must be met before a person accused of crime can be punished. By protecting an individual against unjust imprisonment, due process serves as a safeguard of personal freedom. Due process includes a person's right to know the charges against him. The law also guarantees the right to obtain a legal order called a *writ of habeas corpus*. This writ orders the police to free a prisoner if no legal charge can be placed against him. It protects people from being imprisoned unjustly. See DUE PROCESS OF LAW; HABEAS CORPUS.

Economic Freedom enables a person to make his own economic decisions. This freedom includes the right to own property, to use it, and to profit from it. Workers are free to choose and change jobs. Any person has the freedom to save money and invest it as he wishes. Such freedoms form the basis of an economic system called *free enterprise* (see FREE ENTERPRISE SYSTEM).

The basic principle of free enterprise is the policy of *laissez faire*, which states that government should not interfere in economic affairs. According to laissez faire, everyone would be best off if allowed to pursue his own economic interests without restriction or special treatment from government.

Since the 1930's, economic freedom has come to mean that everyone has the right to a satisfactory standard of living. This concept of economic freedom, sometimes called "freedom from want," often conflicts with the principle of laissez faire. For example, government has imposed minimum-wage laws that limit the smallest amount of money per hour an employer can pay. Laws also protect workers' rights to reasonable hours, holidays with pay, and safe working conditions. And if a person cannot earn a living because of disability, old age, or unemployment, he receives special aid.

Limits on Freedom

The laws of every organized society form a complicated pattern of balanced freedoms and restrictions. Some persons think of laws as the natural enemies of freedom. In fact, people called *anarchists* believe that all systems of government and laws destroy liberty (see ANARCHISM). Actually, the law both limits and protects the freedom of an individual. For example, it forbids a person to hit his neighbor. But it also guarantees that the person will be free from being hit.

Reasons for Limits on Freedom. The major reason for restricting freedom is to prevent harm to others. To achieve the goal of equal freedom for everyone, a government may have to restrict the liberty of certain individuals or groups to act in certain ways. In the United States, for example, restaurant owners no longer have the freedom to refuse to serve persons because of race.

Society also limits personal freedom in order to maintain order and keep things running smoothly. When two cars cannot cross an intersection at the same time without colliding, traffic regulations specify which should go first.

Also, every person must accept certain duties and responsibilities to maintain and protect society. Many of these duties limit freedom. For example, a citizen has the duty to vote, and he must pay taxes and serve on a jury. The idea of personal freedom has nearly always carried with it some amount of duty to society.

Limits on Political Freedom. Democracies divide political power among the branches of government, between government and the citizens, and between the majority and minority parties. These divisions of power restrict various liberties. For example, citizens have the right to vote. As a result, elected officials must respect voter opinion. They are not free to govern as they please. A system called the *separation of powers* divides authority among the three branches of government— executive, legislative, and judicial. Each branch is limited by the others' power. Majority rule does not give the majority party the liberty to do whatever it wants. No matter how large the majority, it can never take away certain rights and freedoms of the minority.

Limits on Social Freedom prevent people from using their liberty in ways that would harm the health, safety, or welfare of others. For example, free speech does not include the right to shout "Fire!" in a crowded theater if there is no fire. Freedom of speech and of the press do not allow a person to tell lies that damage another's reputation. Such statements are called *slander* if spoken and *libel* if written.

The law also prohibits speeches or publications that would endanger the nation's peace or security. Under certain conditions, it forbids speeches that call on people to riot. It also outlaws *sedition* (calling for rebellion).

In addition, many governments limit freedom of speech and of the press to protect public morals. For example, many states of the United States have laws against *pornography* (indecent pictures and writings). See OBSCENITY AND PORNOGRAPHY.

The government limits freedom of religion by forbidding certain religious practices. For example, it prohibits human sacrifice. It also bans *polygamy* (marriage to more than one person at a time), though Islam and other religions permit the practice.

Most other social freedoms can be restricted or set aside to protect other people or to safeguard the nation. For example, people may not use freedom of assembly to disturb the peace or to block public streets or sidewalks. The writ of habeas corpus may be suspended during a rebellion or an invasion.

Limits on Economic Freedom. In the past, most governments put few limits on economic freedom. They followed a policy of not interfering in economic affairs.

But since the 1800's, the development of large-scale capitalism has concentrated wealth in the hands of relatively few people. This development has convinced many persons that government must intervene to protect underprivileged groups and promote equality of economic opportunity. Such beliefs have led to in-

creased restrictions on big business and other powerful economic groups. For example, the Supreme Court of the United States once ruled that minimum-wage laws violated the "freedom of contract" between employer and employee. But today, laws regulate wages, hours, and working conditions; forbid child labor; and even guarantee unemployment insurance. Most people believe these laws protect economic freedom rather than violate it.

Economic freedom is also limited when it conflicts with other people's rights or welfare. For example, no one is free to cheat others. A hotelkeeper's right to do what he chooses with his property does not allow him to refuse a room to persons of a certain race or religion. A manufacturer's freedom to run his factory as he wishes does not allow him to dump its wastes into other people's drinking water.

History

In Ancient Greece and Rome, only the highest classes had much freedom. By about 500 B.C., Athens and several other Greek city-states had democratic governments. Citizens could vote and hold office, but they made up a minority of the population. Women, slaves, and non-Greeks did not have these rights.

During Rome's years as a republic, from 509 to 27 B.C., the highest classes had many liberties. But the lower classes could not hold public office or marry into upper-class families. Lowest of all were the slaves, who, as a form of property, had no legal rights.

The Middle Ages produced a political and economic system called *feudalism*. Under feudalism, the peasants known as *serfs* had little freedom, but nobles had much. Lower-ranking noblemen furnished troops and paid taxes to a higher-ranking nobleman called their *lord*. The lower-ranking noblemen were known as the lord's *vassals*. Vassals had many important rights. For example, a lord had to call his vassals together and get their permission before he could collect extra taxes. Another custom called for disputes between a vassal and his lord to be settled by a court of the vassal's *peers*— men of the same rank as he.

In 1215, King John of England approved a document called Magna Carta. This document made laws of many customary feudal liberties. For example, it confirmed the tradition that the king could raise no special tax without the consent of his nobles. This provision brought about the development of Parliament. In addition, the document stated that no free man could be imprisoned, exiled, or deprived of property, except as provided by law. The ideas of due process of law and trial by jury developed from this concept. Most important of all, Magna Carta established the principle that even the king had to obey the law. See MAGNA CARTA.

In the Middle Ages, the Christian church restricted freedom of thought in Europe. The church persecuted Jews, Moslems, and others who disagreed with its beliefs. It restricted writings it considered contrary to church teachings. But church teachings also acted as a check on the unreasonable use of political power.

The Renaissance and the Reformation emphasized the importance of the individual. As a result, people began to demand greater personal freedom. Anabaptists and other Protestant groups elected their own ministers and held free and open discussions. These practices carried over into politics and contributed to the growth of democracy and political freedom. In 1620, for example, the Puritans who settled in Massachusetts signed an agreement called the Mayflower Compact. In this document, they agreed to obey "just and equal laws."

During the Age of Reason, many people began to regard freedom as a natural right. Parliament passed the English Bill of Rights in 1689. This bill eliminated many powers of the king and guaranteed the basic rights and liberties of the English people.

At the same time, the English philosopher John Locke declared that every person is born with natural rights that cannot be taken away. These rights include the right to life and to own property; and freedom of opinion, religion, and speech. Locke's book *Two Treatises of Government* (1689) argued that the chief purpose of government was to protect these rights. If a government did not adequately protect the citizens' liberty, they had the right to revolt.

In 1776, the American colonists used many of Locke's ideas in the Declaration of Independence. For example, the declaration stated that people had God-given rights to "Life, Liberty and the pursuit of Happiness."

As the Industrial Revolution spread during the 1700's, the free enterprise system became firmly established. The Scottish economist Adam Smith argued for the laissez faire policy in his book *The Wealth of Nations* (1776).

During the 1700's, three important French philosophers—Montesquieu, Jean Jacques Rousseau, and Voltaire—spoke out for individual rights and freedoms. Montesquieu's book *The Spirit of the Laws* (1748) called for representative government with separation of powers into executive, legislative, and judicial branches. Rousseau declared in his book *The Social Contract* (1762) that government was based on a voluntary contract between the ruler and the people. Voltaire's many writings opposed government interference with individual rights.

The writings of these three men helped cause the French Revolution, which began in 1789. The revolution was devoted to liberty and equality. It did not succeed in making France a democracy. But it did wipe out many abuses and limit the king's powers.

The Revolutionary War in America (1775-1783) brought the colonies independence from Great Britain. In 1789, the Constitution of the United States established a democratic government with powers divided among the President, Congress, and the federal courts. The first 10 amendments to the Constitution took effect in 1791. These amendments, known as the Bill of Rights, guaranteed such basic liberties as freedom of speech, press, and religion; and the right to trial by jury.

The 1800's brought into practice many beliefs about freedom that had developed during the Age of Reason. In 1830, and again in 1848, revolutionary movements swept over much of Europe. Many European monarchs lost most of their powers. By 1848, the citizens of many nations had won basic civil liberties and at least the beginnings of democratic government. These nations included Belgium, Denmark, and Holland. Most European nations also ended slavery during the 1800's. In 1865, the 13th Amendment to the Constitution abolished slavery in the United States. The 15th Amendment, adopted in 1870, gave former slaves the right to vote.

Workers also gained many important rights during the 1800's. Many nations, including Great Britain and the United States, passed laws that regulated working conditions in factories. Workers in several countries won the right to form labor unions.

The 1900's. After World War I ended in 1918, many European nations established representative democracies. A number of them also gave women the right to vote. The United States did so in 1920 with the 19th Amendment. By 1932, 16 European nations had become republics governed by elected representatives.

By the 1930's, many people no longer believed that the simple absence of restrictions could make them free. Instead, the idea of freedom expanded to include employment, health, and adequate food and housing. In 1941, President Franklin D. Roosevelt reflected this broad view in his "four freedoms" message. He called for four freedoms—freedom of speech, freedom of religion, freedom from want, and freedom from fear—to be spread throughout the world. For the text of Roosevelt's message, see FOUR FREEDOMS.

In 1948, the United Nations General Assembly adopted the Universal Declaration of Human Rights. This declaration listed rights and freedoms that the UN thought should be the goals of all nations.

In the 1960's, the civil rights struggle by blacks resulted in much important legislation in the United States. The 24th Amendment to the Constitution, adopted in 1964, banned poll taxes in federal elections. The Civil Rights Act of 1964 forbade employers and unions to discriminate on the basis of race, religion, or national origin. It also prohibited hotels and restaurants from such discrimination in serving customers.

In 1972, Congress passed the so-called Equal Rights Amendment to the Constitution and sent it to the states for ratification. This amendment would guarantee equality of rights under the law to all persons regardless of sex.   Critically reviewed by WILLIAM C. HAVARD

Related Articles in WORLD BOOK include:

Academic Freedom	Democracy
Bill of Rights	Freedom of Religion
Censorship	Freedom of Speech
Civil Rights	Freedom of the Press
Communism (Personal	Privacy, Right of
Freedom)	Voting

FREEDOM, ACADEMIC. See ACADEMIC FREEDOM.

FREEDOM DAY, NATIONAL, falls on February 1. It commemorates the day a resolution was signed proposing an amendment to the Constitution to outlaw slavery. Congress adopted the resolution, and President Abraham Lincoln signed it on Feb. 1, 1865. Amendment 13 was ratified by the states and was proclaimed on Dec. 18, 1865 (see CONSTITUTION OF THE UNITED STATES). It freed all slaves in the North. Lincoln's Emancipation Proclamation of Jan. 1, 1863, had freed only the slaves in territories that were in rebellion against the United States (see EMANCIPATION PROCLAMATION).

In 1948, Congress authorized the President to proclaim the first day of February in each year as National Freedom Day. President Harry S. Truman made Feb. 1, 1949, the first such day.   ELIZABETH HOUGH SECHRIST

FREEDOM OF RELIGION is the right of a person to believe in and practice whatever faith he chooses. It also includes the right of an individual to have no religious beliefs at all.

Like most rights, freedom of religion is not absolute. Most countries prohibit religious practices that injure people or that are thought to threaten to destroy society. For example, most governments forbid human sacrifice and *polygamy*, the practice of having more than one wife or husband at the same time.

Throughout most of history, people have been persecuted for their religious beliefs. The denial of religious liberty probably stems from two major sources —personal and political. Religion touches the deepest feelings of countless people. Strong religious views have led to intolerance among various faiths. Some governments have close ties to one religion and consider people of other faiths to be a threat to political authority. A government also may regard all religion as politically dangerous because religion places allegiance to God above allegiance to the state.

The question of morality has caused many conflicts between church and state. Both religion and government are concerned with morality. They work together if the moral goals desired by the state are the same as those sought by the church. But discord may result if they have different views about morality.

In the United States. The desire for religious freedom was a major reason for the settlement of America by Europeans. The Puritans and many other groups came to the New World to escape religious persecution.

The First Amendment of the United States Constitution guarantees that "Congress shall make no law respecting an establishment of religion, or prohibiting the free exercise thereof. . . ." This provision originally protected religious groups from unfair treatment by the federal government only. Until the mid-1800's, New Hampshire and some other states had laws that prohibited non-Protestants from holding public office. Several states, including Connecticut and Massachusetts, even had official state churches. Since the 1920's, however, the Supreme Court of the United States has ruled that the states must uphold the First Amendment.

Today, freedom of religion remains an issue in the United States. Various court rulings have interpreted the First Amendment to mean that the government may not promote or give special treatment to any religion. Judges have struck down plans that called for the government to give financial aid to religious schools. The courts have also ruled unconstitutional a number of programs to teach the Bible or recite prayers in public schools. See RELIGIOUS EDUCATION.

But church and state are not completely separated in the United States. The nation's motto is *In God We Trust*. Sessions of Congress open with prayers, and court witnesses swear oaths on the Bible.

Christian moral views have had a predominant influence on U.S. laws because most of the nation's people are Christians. In 1878, for example, the Supreme Court upheld a federal law against polygamy, even though this law restricted the religious freedom of one Christian group, the Mormons. At that time, the Mormon faith included belief in polygamy. But the laws and the courts agreed with the view of most Americans that polygamy is immoral.

In Other Countries. Religion has been discouraged or even forbidden in countries ruled by dictators. For example, the governments of China, Russia, and other Communist nations have persecuted religion on a large scale. A person's highest allegiance, they believe, belongs to Communism, not to a Supreme Being. Communist dictators consider religion a competitor for such allegiance. Although they do not forbid religion entirely, they make it difficult for people to practice any faith. Communist authorities have imprisoned religious leaders and have closed churches. Russia has conducted intensive propaganda campaigns to persuade people not to attend church. China has imprisoned or expelled foreign missionaries.

In some countries that have an official state church, or where most of the people belong to one church, other faiths do not have religious freedom. Spain, almost all of whose people are Roman Catholics, did not permit Jews or Protestants to hold public services for much of its history. This ban was dropped in 1967. Many Muslim nations persecute Christians and Jews. Even in countries whose governments do not officially deny religious liberty, members of minority religions may have economic or social disadvantages. Catholics in Northern Ireland, which is mostly Protestant, complain of such unfair treatment.

Other countries, including England, Scotland, and Sweden, have state churches. But the governments of these nations grant freedom of worship to other religious groups. In some countries, the government provides equal support for all religions. The Netherlands, for example, gives funds to three school systems—Catholic, Protestant, and nonreligious.

History. Many ancient peoples permitted broad religious freedom. These peoples worshiped many gods and readily accepted groups with new gods. Jews and, later, Christians could not do so because they worshiped only one God. They also believed that allegiance to God was higher than allegiance to any ruler or state. Some ancient peoples did not accept these beliefs, and they persecuted Christians and Jews.

During the Middle Ages, from the A.D. 400's to the 1500's, the Roman Catholic Church dominated Europe and permitted little religious freedom. The church persecuted Jews and Muslims. It punished people for any serious disagreement with its teachings. In 1415, the Bohemian religious reformer John Huss was burned at the stake because he challenged the pope's authority.

The Reformation, a religious movement of the 1500's, gave birth to Protestantism. The Catholic Church and Catholic rulers persecuted various Protestant groups. Many Protestant denominations persecuted Catholics and other Protestant groups as well. But by the 1700's and 1800's, the variety of religions that resulted from the Reformation had led to increased tolerance in many countries. These countries included England, The Netherlands, and the United States. On the other hand, intolerance remained strong in some countries. Poland and Russia, for example, severely persecuted Jews. One of the most savage religious persecutions in history occurred during the 1930's and 1940's, when Nazi Germany slaughtered about 6 million Jews. LOREN P. BETH

See also CHURCH AND STATE.

FREEDOM OF SPEECH

FREEDOM OF SPEECH is the right to say publicly or privately what one believes. The term covers all forms of expression, including books, newspapers, magazines, radio, television, and motion pictures. Many scholars consider freedom of speech a natural right.

In a democracy, freedom of speech is a necessity. Democratic governments give people the right to express their opinions freely because democracy is government of, by, and for the people. The people need information to decide what they believe are the best possible political and social policies. And government officials need to know what the majority of people believe and want.

Most nondemocratic nations deny freedom of speech to their people. The governments of these countries operate under the theory that the ruler or governing party "knows best" what is good for the people. Such governments believe that free discussion would interfere with the conduct of public affairs and would create disorder.

Limitations. All societies, including democratic ones, put various limitations on what people may say. They prohibit certain types of speech that they believe might harm the government or the people. But drawing a line between dangerous and harmless speech can be extremely difficult.

Most democratic nations have four major restrictions on free expression. (1) Laws covering *libel* and *slander* prohibit speech that endangers the privacy or reputation of individuals (see LIBEL; SLANDER). (2) Some laws forbid speech that offends public decency by using obscenities or by encouraging people to commit acts considered immoral. (3) Laws against spying, treason, and urging violence prohibit speech that endangers life, property, or national security. (4) Other laws forbid speech that invades the right of people not to listen to it. For example, a Republican would not have the right to address a meeting of Democrats unless they invited him.

In the United States. Freedom of speech was one of the goals of the American colonists that led to the Revolutionary War (1775-1783). Since 1791, the First Amendment to the United States Constitution has protected freedom of speech from interference by the federal government. Since 1925, the Supreme Court of the United States has protected free speech against interference by state or local governments. The court has done this by using the *due process* clause of the 14th Amendment (see DUE PROCESS OF LAW).

On the other hand, the government restricts some speech considered dangerous or immoral. The first major federal law that limited speech was the Sedition Act of 1798 (see ALIEN AND SEDITION ACTS). This law provided fines and imprisonment for speaking or writing against the government.

In the late 1800's, Congress passed several laws against obscenity. But during the 1900's, court decisions generally have eased such restrictions. For example, judges lifted the bans on such famous books as *Ulysses* by James Joyce, in 1933, and *Lady Chatterley's Lover* by D. H. Lawrence, in 1960. See OBSCENITY AND PORNOGRAPHY.

The Espionage Act of 1917 and the Sedition Act of 1918, passed during World War I, forbade speeches and publications that interfered with the war effort. Since 1919, the courts have ruled on a speech on the basis of whether it presents "a clear and present danger" to the nation. In 1940, Congress passed the Smith Act, which made it a crime to publish or distribute material that urges the overthrow of the United States government.

Most periods of increased restrictions on speech occur when threats to individuals, national security, or social morality seem grave. During such times of stress, the courts have provided little protection for individual freedom. In the early 1950's, for example, fear of Communism was strong in the United States because of the Korean War and the conviction of several Americans as Russian spies. In 1951, the Supreme Court upheld the Smith Act in the case of 11 leaders of the Communist Party convicted for advocating the overthrow of the government. Since the mid-1950's, however, the courts have become more concerned about personal rights and have provided greater protection for freedom of speech.

In Other Countries. The development of freedom of speech in most Western European countries and English-speaking nations has resembled that in the United States. In various other countries, this freedom has grown more slowly or not at all.

Some major powers, including Great Britain and France, have severe restrictions on free expression in the interests of national security. Such smaller countries as Denmark and Switzerland have less concern about security and, consequently, fewer restrictions. Ireland perhaps has stricter controls over freedom of expression than does any other Western nation. These controls are based on the moral teachings of the Roman Catholic Church, to which about 95 per cent of the Irish people belong.

The rulers of some countries have simply ignored or have taken away constitutional guarantees of freedom of speech. In 1967, for example, a military dictatorship took power in Greece and suspended many freedoms. The rulers of China, Russia, and Spain severely limit freedom of speech. These dictators believe they alone hold the truth. Therefore, they say, any opposition to them must be based on falsehood and regarded as dangerous.

History. Throughout history, men have fought for freedom of speech. During the 400's B.C., the city-state of Athens in ancient Greece gave its citizens considerable freedom of expression. Later, freedom of speech became closely linked with many struggles for political and religious freedom. These struggles took place during the Middle Ages, from about the A.D. 400's to the 1500's. They also played an important part in the Reformation, a religious movement of the 1500's that gave rise to Protestantism.

In the 1600's and 1700's, a period called the Age of Reason, many people began to regard freedom of speech as a natural right. Such philosophers as John Locke of England and Voltaire of France based this idea on their belief in the importance of the individual. Every man, they declared, has a right to speak freely and to have a voice in his government. Thomas Jefferson also expressed this idea when he wrote the Declaration of Independence.

During the 1800's, democratic ideas grew and increasing numbers of people gained freedom of speech. At the same time, however, the growth of cities and industry required more and more people to live and work in large groups. To some people, such as the German philosopher Karl Marx, the interests of society became more important than those of the individual. They thought nations could operate best under an intelligent central authority, rather than with democracy and individual freedom.

In the 1900's, a number of nations have come under such totalitarian forms of government as Communism and fascism. All these nations have abolished or put heavy curbs on freedom of speech.

Technological advances have helped create a centralization of both power and communications in many industrial nations. A government can use such power to restrict speech, so that the "little man" with an idea to express finds it difficult to reach an audience. On the other hand, the same technological advances have produced new means of communication that could lead to increased freedom of speech.   LOREN P. BETH

See also CENSORSHIP; FREEDOM; FREEDOM OF THE PRESS; PUBLIC OPINION.

FREEDOM OF THE PRESS is the right to publish facts, ideas, and opinions without interference from the government or from private groups. This right applies to the printed media, including books and newspapers, and to the electronic media, including radio and television.

Freedom of the press has been disputed since modern printing began in the 1400's, because words have great power to influence people. Today, this power is greater than ever because of the many modern methods of communication. A number of governments place limits on the press because they believe the power of words would be used to oppose them. Some governments have taken control of the press and use it in their own interests.

Most publishers and writers, on the other hand, fight for as much freedom as possible.

Democratic governments grant freedom of the press as part of their effort to encourage the exchange of ideas. Citizens of democracies need information to help them decide whether to support the policies of their national and local governments. In a democracy, freedom of the press applies not only to political and social issues but also to cultural, religious, and scientific matters.

Most democratic governments limit freedom of the press in three major types of cases. In such cases, these governments believe that press freedom could endanger individuals, national security, or social morality. (1) Laws against *libel* protect individuals from writings that could threaten their reputation or privacy (see LIBEL). (2) Laws against *sedition* (urging revolution) and treason work to prevent the publication of material that could harm a nation's security. (3) Laws against obscenity aim at protecting the morals of the people.

Dictatorships do not allow freedom of the press. The rulers of these governments believe they alone hold the truth—and that opposition to them endangers the nation.

In the United States, freedom of the press is guaranteed by the First Amendment to the Constitution. All state constitutions also include protection for press freedom. Court decisions help make clear the extent and the limits of this freedom. In general, censorship before publication is forbidden (see CENSORSHIP).

The U.S. press regulates itself to a great extent. For example, most publishers do not print material that they know is false or that could lead to crime, riot, or revolution. They also avoid publishing libelous material, obscenities, and other matter that might offend a large number of readers. In addition, because the press in the United States depends heavily on advertising income, it sometimes does not publish material that would displease its advertisers.

Freedom of the press was one goal of the American

Wide World

Colonial Officials burned copies of John Peter Zenger's *New York Weekly Journal* to try to stop criticism of the British government. This diorama, part of an exhibit on Zenger's fight for freedom of the press, is in the Federal Hall National Memorial in New York City.

FREEDOM OF THE PRESS

Colonies in their struggle for independence from Great Britain. The libel trial of John Peter Zenger in 1735 became a major step in the fight for this freedom. Zenger was the editor of the *New York Weekly Journal*, which criticized the British government. A jury found Zenger innocent after his attorney argued that Zenger had printed the truth and that truth is not libelous. See ZENGER, JOHN PETER.

The severest restrictions on the press in the United States—and in all other countries—are imposed during times of stress, especially wartime. During World War II (1939-1945), for example, Congress passed laws banning the publication of any material that could interfere with the war effort or harm national security.

During the late 1960's and early 1970's, criticism by the U.S. press of the nation's involvement in Vietnam became increasingly widespread. This criticism helped broaden public opposition to the Vietnam War and probably influenced the government's change in policy toward the war. In 1971, the government tried to stop *The New York Times* and *The Washington Post* from publishing parts of a secret study of the war. The government claimed that publication of the so-called *Pentagon Papers* could harm national security. But the Supreme Court blocked the government's action.

Also in the 1960's and 1970's, many judges issued rulings frequently referred to as *gag orders*. The orders forbade the press to publish information that judges thought might violate a defendant's right to a fair trial. Such information might include confessions made by defendants or facts about their past. The press argued that gag orders violated the First Amendment. In 1976, the Nebraska Press Association challenged a Nebraska gag order before the Supreme Court. The court ruled that such orders are unconstitutional, except in extraordinary circumstances.

In Other Countries. Freedom of the press exists largely in the Western European countries, the English-speaking nations, and Japan. It is present to a limited extent in some Latin-American countries.

Press restrictions vary greatly from country to country. In Great Britain, for example, the press restricts itself on what it prints about certain aspects of the private lives of members of the royal family. In Italy, the press restricts itself on what it prints about the pope. Such nations as Australia and Ireland have strict obscenity laws. But the obscenity laws in such countries as Norway and Sweden are not strict. Denmark dropped all its obscenity laws during the 1960's. Nations with strict racial segregation—such as South Africa and Rhodesia—may have freedom of the press in general. But the governments restrict press discussion of racial issues.

The governments of many countries have strict overall controls on the press. In Spain, censorship boards check all publications to make sure they follow government guidelines and agree with official policy. A number of nations in Asia, Latin America, and the Middle East have similar restrictions. The governments of China, Russia, and other Communist nations own and operate the press themselves. The Communist Party in each of these countries makes sure that the press follows party policies. Communist governments use the press largely to spread propaganda.

History. Rulers and church leaders restricted the writing and distribution of certain material even before there was a press. In those days, when everything was written by hand, books considered offensive were banned or burned. Since the A.D. 400's, the Roman Catholic Church has restricted material that it considers contrary to church teachings.

Early printers had to obtain a license from the government or from some religious group for any material they wanted to publish. In 1644, the English poet and political writer John Milton criticized such licensing in his pamphlet *Areopagitica*. This essay was one of the earliest arguments for freedom of the press. In time, Great Britain and other nations ended the licensing system. By the 1800's, the press of many countries had considerable freedom.

Freedom of the press led to some abuses. In the late 1800's, for example, some U.S. newspapers published false and sensational material to attract readers. Some people favored government regulation to stop such abuses by the so-called "yellow press." But in most cases, the press accepted its responsibility to the public. Self-regulation made government action unnecessary.

During the 1900's, the press in many countries has lost its freedom. For example, the Fascists in Italy and the Nazis in Germany destroyed press freedom and used the press for their own purposes. Civilian or military dictatorships rule many of the countries created since the end of World War II. All these governments censor the press heavily. LOREN P. BETH

See also FREEDOM; FREEDOM OF SPEECH.

FREEDOM RIDER. See BLACK AMERICANS (The "Black Revolution"); KENNEDY, JOHN F. (Civil Rights).

FREEDOM TRAIL. See BOSTON (Downtown Boston).

FREEHOLD. See ESTATE.

FREEHOLDER. See COLONIAL LIFE IN AMERICA (Land Ownership).

FREEMAN, DOUGLAS SOUTHALL (1886-1953), a United States historian and editor, became a leading authority on the history of the Confederacy. He won a Pulitzer prize in 1935 for *R. E. Lee*, a biography he worked on for 19 years. He also shared a Pulitzer prize with John A. Carroll and Mary W. Ashworth for *George Washington*. Many historians consider this work the most authoritative Washington biography. He also wrote *Lee's Lieutenants* (three volumes), *The South to Posterity*, and *Virginia—A Gentle Dominion*. Freeman wrote vividly about military history and problems.

He served as editor of the *Richmond* (Va.) *News Leader* from 1915 to 1949. He also worked as radio commentator from 1925 until his death. Freeman was born in Lynchburg, Va., the son of a Confederate veteran. He graduated from Richmond College and received a Ph.D. from Johns Hopkins University. MERLE CURTI

FREEMAN, MARY ELEANOR WILKINS (1852-1930), wrote short stories and novels about New England women and village life. She ranks second only to Sarah Orne Jewett in this type of writing. Her ghost stories, such as *The Wind in the Rose Bush*, also are distinguished. She wrote more than 230 short stories, 12 novels, a play, and two volumes of verse. Her works include *A New England Nun and Other Stories*. She was less successful with her novels, which include *Pembroke* and *Adventures of Ann Bost*. Born in Randolph, Mass., she later lived in Vermont and in New Jersey. EDWARD WAGENKNECHT

FREEMAN, ORVILLE LOTHROP (1918-   ), served as secretary of agriculture from 1961 to 1969, under Presidents John F. Kennedy and Lyndon B. Johnson. He was governor of Minnesota from 1955 to 1961.

Freeman graduated from the University of Minnesota in 1940. During World War II, he served with the U.S. Marine Corps. He was wounded in action and received the Purple Heart. After the war, he earned his law degree and was a member of a Minneapolis law firm from 1947 to 1955.

Harris & Ewing
Orville L. Freeman

He was chairman of the Minnesota Democratic-Farm-Labor Party from 1948 to 1950. He was born in Minneapolis.   ERIC SEVAREID

FREEMAN'S FARM, BATTLES OF. See REVOLUTIONARY WAR IN AMERICA (Defeat at Saratoga; table).

FREEMASONRY. See MASONRY.

FREEPORT DOCTRINE. See LINCOLN, ABRAHAM (The Debates with Douglas).

FREER GALLERY OF ART, in Washington, D.C., is a government museum famous for its collections of Oriental art. These include paintings, sculpture, bronzes, glass, jade, lacquer, pottery, and metalwork from the Near and Far East. The gallery has important Biblical manuscripts in Greek, Aramaic, and Armenian. It also has many works by James Whistler and other American painters of the late 1800's. The museum library contains 40,000 volumes. The museum staff carries on research in the arts and cultures represented in the collections. The Smithsonian Institution administers the building and endowment fund. Charles Lang Freer, a Detroit industrialist, gave his collections and an endowment to the Smithsonian by deed of gift executed in 1906.

Critically reviewed by the SMITHSONIAN INSTITUTION

FREESIA, *FREE zhah*, is a fragrant, attractive plant belonging to the iris family. It is a native of South Africa, but gardeners throughout the world cultivate it in greenhouses. It has a *corm* (bulblike stem) and long, narrow leaves shaped like swords. The white, rose, salmon, or yellow flowers have yellow blotches at the center and grow in clusters that look like spikes. Many people plant the freesia because the flowers bloom in winter. They plant the corm indoors about mid-August. It grows better in a cool greenhouse where the night temperature is not above 50° F. (10° C). When the flowers appear, the plant should be watered freely.

J. Horace McFarland
Freesia

Scientific Classification. The freesia belongs to the iris family, *Iridaceae*. The freesia is genus *Freesia*, species *F. refracta*.   ALFRED C. HOTTES

FREESTONE. See LIMESTONE.

FREETHINKER is a person who refuses to accept the authority of a church or the Bible. A freethinker insists on his freedom to form his religious opinions on the basis of his own reasoning powers.

The name *freethinker* goes back to the 1600's, when Anthony Collins used it in his *Discourse of Freethinking*. He and his friend, John Toland, argued against the authority of the Christian Church. Later, Lord Bolingbroke and David Hume were among the leading English Freethinkers. In France, Voltaire was the leader of a group which argued for "natural" religion, as against revealed religion. Freethinking became fashionable in Germany during the reign of Frederick the Great. At the present time, few freethinkers belong to organized groups. Modern freedom of religion has made such organized bodies unnecessary.   LOUIS O. KATTSOFF

FREETOWN (pop. 178,600) is the seaport capital of Sierra Leone. It stands on the estuary of the Sierra Leone River, and has an excellent harbor. The city has a tropical climate. Temperatures average 80° F. (27° C), and rainfall totals about 150 inches (381 centimeters) a year. For location, see SIERRA LEONE (map).

Industries in Freetown include fish processing and soap factories and ship repair yards. Exports include chromite, diamonds, ginger, gold, kola nuts, palm oil and kernels, and platinum. British philanthropists founded the city in 1787 as a home for freed slaves. The city served as an important naval base during World Wars I and II.   HIBBERD V. B. KLINE, JR.

FREEWAY is a highway designed to carry heavy traffic with little interference from roads or highways entering it. Other roads and highways cross over or under a freeway. Most freeways are divided with a strip of land between opposing traffic lanes. Two or more lanes run in each direction. Some people mistakenly call any toll-free divided highway a freeway.

FREEZE-DRYING, or LYOPHILIZATION, is a process that removes water from a substance to preserve the substance for future use. Drug companies use freeze-drying in the preparation of many medicines. Biologists use it in preparing animal specimens for display in museums, or parts of organisms for microscopic study. The process is used to preserve some foods and beverages and to restore valuable papers damaged by water.

Freeze-drying differs from other drying methods because the substance is frozen before being dried. The item is then placed in a refrigerated vacuum chamber. There, any water in the product changes from ice to water vapor. Unlike other drying processes, freeze-drying does not shrink the substance or lessen its ability to dissolve in a liquid. For this reason, freeze-drying is useful for certain drugs and for coffee and tea, all of which must dissolve rapidly. The low temperature at which the process takes place allows serums and other drug solutions to retain their original characteristics.

Hikers and military personnel often carry freeze-dried foods because these products are light and compact. But freeze-drying is not widely used for food preservation because the difficulties of freeze-drying animal and plant cells make it uneconomical.   HAROLD T. MERYMAN

See also COFFEE (Instant Coffee); DEHYDRATION; FOOD PRESERVATION (Freeze-Drying).

FREEZING POINTS OF DIFFERENT LIQUIDS

Mercury freezes at —38° F. (—39° C). It is used for thermometers because most regions do not have temperatures below —38° F.

◀

▶

Water freezes at 32° F. (0° C). The freezing point of water is the basis for measuring temperatures.

Alcohol freezes at —202° F. (—130° C). It is mixed with the water in automobile radiators to keep it from freezing.

found its way into the cracks of rock will freeze during the winter and expand. This creates great cracks and breaks off pieces here and there. An iceberg floats because water expands in freezing. The ice is less dense than water, and so the ice floats.

Another interesting fact is that the freezing point is lowered by pressure. Ice melts when pressure is applied to it although it freezes again when the pressure is removed. This quality of ice enables us to enjoy the pleasures of skating. The weight of the skater melts for an instant a thin strip of ice beneath the skate blade, and the skater literally glides along on a film of water. You can make a snowball because the pressure of your hands momentarily melts the snow.　　　RALPH G. OWENS

See also ICE; REGELATION; THERMOMETER; FOOD, FROZEN.

FREIGHT is manufactured goods or raw materials transported from one place to another. In the United States, railroads carry the greatest amount of freight. But truck freight has increased steadily since the 1940's. Shipping by water is usually the cheapest way to send freight. Pipelines are used to ship liquids and gases. Shipping by air has increased since the 1950's. But its high cost makes it practical only for covering a long distance in a short time. Freight rates vary with the type of freight and with competition.

Freight rates are usually expressed in dollars and cents per specific weight for shipping and handling between specific destinations. The Interstate Commerce Commission sets rates for all interstate carriers except airplanes. The Civil Aeronautics Board regulates air transportation. A state commerce commission sets rates for freight carried within the state.　　　JOHN H. FREDERICK

FREEZING is the process that turns a liquid into a solid when its temperature is lowered to a certain point. Each substance has its own *freezing point*, which is always the same under ordinary conditions. The freezing point of pure water is 32° Fahrenheit or 0° Celsius—a fact that is depended upon in making a thermometer. Except in mixtures and solutions, the freezing point of the liquid is also the *melting point* of the solid. Ice melts to water again at the temperature of 32° F. (0° C). This is sometimes called the *point of fusion*.

Different fluids have different freezing points. Mercury, for example, freezes at —38° F. (—39° C). A mercury thermometer will not work below this temperature. But alcohol does not freeze until it reaches a temperature of —202° F. (—130° C). For this reason, thermometers for exceedingly cold regions are made with alcohol. For the same reason, people put alcohol in automobile radiators in cold weather. Salt water freezes at a lower temperature than fresh water. Seawater freezes at about 28.5° F. (—1.9° C). The more salt there is in solution, the lower the freezing point drops.

Most substances contract when they freeze, but water expands when it freezes. This explains why water pipes sometimes burst on "freezing cold" nights. This also accounts for one form of erosion. The moisture that has

Related Articles in WORLD BOOK include:

Airline (Carrying Cargo)	Pipeline
Barge	Railroad (What Makes
Bill of Lading	Up a Railroad)
Civil Aeronautics Board	Ship
Interstate Commerce	Transportation
Manifest	Truck and Trucking

FREISCHÜTZ, DER. See OPERA; WEBER, CARL MARIA.

FRÉMONT, *FREE mahnt,* **JOHN CHARLES** (1813-1890), sometimes called "The Pathfinder," explored much of the area between the Rocky Mountains and the Pacific Ocean. In 1856, he was the first Republican candidate for President of the United States, but he lost to James Buchanan. He served in the Army and Navy, and as a United States Senator from California.

As a second lieutenant in the Army Topographical Corps, Frémont worked as a surveyor in the Carolina mountains. He made his first important independent survey to the Wind River chain of the Rockies in 1842. During this trip, he met Kit Carson, who served as the guide for his expeditions. Frémont's *Report of the Exploring Expedition to the Rocky Mountains* described this trip, and established his reputation.

Frémont explored part of the Oregon country in 1843. He visited Fort Vancouver, and then moved to the Carson River in Nevada early in 1844. From there he went to California, which was then a Mexican province. He returned to St. Louis in August 1844.

The third expedition, in 1845, was organized with the Mexican War in prospect. Frémont aroused the suspicions of the Mexican authorities in California, and they ordered him to leave. However, by the summer of 1846 he was inspiring discontented Americans in the Sacramento Valley to organize the "Bear Flag" revolt (see CALIFORNIA [Mexico Surrenders]).

Commodore Robert Stockton of the Navy and General S. W. Kearny of the Army became involved in a dispute over conflicting orders, and Frémont sided with Stockton. When Kearny won, he had Frémont court-martialed for insubordination (see KEARNY, STEPHEN W.). The Army dismissed Frémont from the service. President James K. Polk overruled the dismissal, but Frémont then resigned from the Army. He made a

fourth expedition in 1848, but it failed. He then settled in California, and served as a U.S. Senator from September, 1850, until March, 1851.

Early in the Civil War, President Abraham Lincoln gave him command of the Union Army's Western Department. But Frémont issued a proclamation taking over the property of rebelling Missouri slaveowners, and freeing their slaves. His act aroused the public and angered Lincoln, who transferred him to West Virginia. Later, he served from 1878 to 1883 as territorial governor of Arizona.

Frémont was born in Savannah, Ga., on Jan. 21, 1813, and studied at Charleston (S.C.) College. He married Jessie Benton, the daughter of the powerful Senator Thomas Hart Benton of Missouri, in 1841. Mrs. Frémont became a regular writer for magazines after her husband lost his wealth in the 1870's. She helped him write his memoirs, and wrote several books describing her own experiences.   WILLIAM P. BRANDON

See also LINCOLN, ABRAHAM (Election of 1864).

FRENCH, DANIEL CHESTER (1850-1931), an American sculptor, made the statue of Abraham Lincoln for the Lincoln Memorial in Washington, D.C. *Death Staying the Hand of the Sculptor*, a memorial relief in Forest Hills Cemetery, Boston, is considered his most important work. Probably his best work is of the human figure, in a simple realistic style. Born in Exeter, N.H., French taught himself and studied for a year in Italy. His first important work, *The Minute Man*, was completed when he was 23, for the 100th anniversary of the Battle of Concord. See also LINCOLN MEMORIAL (picture); MINUTEMAN (picture).   JEAN LIPMAN

FRENCH, JOHN DENTON PINKSTONE (1852-1925), EARL OF YPRES, commanded the first units of British soldiers sent to France in World War I. French returned to Great Britain in December, 1915, to lead the home forces. He served as chief of Great Britain's General Staff from 1912 to 1914. After World War I, he was lord lieutenant, or British governor, of Ireland from 1918 to 1921. French became a navy midshipman when he was 14 years old, but joined the army four years later.   ALFRED F. HAVIGHURST

FRENCH ACADEMY, or ACADÉMIE FRANÇAISE, is an organization of French scholars and men of letters. It was founded in 1635. The 40 members of the Academy are called *The Immortals.* Many French people consider election to the Academy the highest honor a French writer can achieve. But the Academy, located in Paris, France, has repeatedly refused to elect writers who had original or revolutionary ideas. Many great French writers, including Denis Diderot, Jean Jacques Rousseau, Honoré de Balzac, Gustave Flaubert, and Émile Zola, were never members of the Academy. Some persons believe that the Academy has been a fine influence on French literature. Others believe that it has been far too conservative and traditional.

One of the Academy's aims has been to purify the French language and set standards of good usage. It set out to publish a comprehensive dictionary of the French language, and the first edition appeared in 1694. The Academy supervises revision, and seven later editions have been published, the most recent in the 1930's.   R. FREEMAN BUTTS

Engraving by J. C. Fry; Chicago Historical Society

John Charles Frémont became famous as an American explorer, soldier, and political leader. He became the first candidate of the Republican party for President in 1856.

FRENCH AND INDIAN WARS

FRENCH AND INDIAN WARS broke out between the French and the British in North America from 1689 to 1763. These four wars grew out of European conflicts, but also resulted from local problems.

Both Great Britain and France wanted to extend their possessions in North America, mainly because of the fur trade. British colonies in North America spread along the Atlantic Coast in a narrow strip east of the Appalachian Mountains. French settlements lay north of the British colonies, along the Saint Lawrence River and the Great Lakes, and eventually spread southward along the Mississippi River. The British claimed all the territory that stretched inland from their colonies along the coast. The French claimed all the land drained by the rivers they had explored.

Other causes underlying the wars included disputed claims to fishing grounds off the coast of Newfoundland, and religious differences between French Roman Catholics and British Protestants. Both French and British colonists had the support of Indian allies and regular troops from their home countries. The French and Indian Wars resulted in Great Britain's final victory over France, and in the loss of most of France's possessions in North America.

King William's War (1689-1697) took its name from King William III of England. It formed part of a European struggle called the *War of the League of Augsburg*. King William's War began when French and Indian forces attacked the English colonies just south of Canada, in New York and the New England states. Raiders attacked Schenectady, N.Y., Haverhill, Mass., and Dover, N.H. The British organized their colonial forces and Indian allies, and counterattacked.

This war ended in 1697, not because anything had been decided, but because European powers had signed the Treaty of Ryswick. By this treaty, both sides surrendered all the American territory that they had gained during the war. The colonial possessions of both sides remained almost unchanged.

Queen Anne's War (1702-1713), named for Queen Anne of England, grew out of the European struggle known as the *War of the Spanish Succession*. Spain also took part in this war, which centered in New England and in Florida and South Carolina. As in King William's War, the French and their Algonkian Indian allies raided settlements near the Canadian border. They also destroyed Deerfield, Mass., in an important battle. The British in turn seized Port Royal, the principal town of Acadia. In the South, the English took, but soon abandoned, the town of Saint Augustine in Spanish Florida. Spanish forces unsuccessfully attacked Charleston, S.C.

Queen Anne's War ended with the signing of the Peace of Utrecht in 1713. By the terms of the treaty, France surrendered to Great Britain the Hudson Bay region, Newfoundland, and Acadia, which was also called Nova Scotia. France kept only Cape Breton Island and the islands of the Saint Lawrence. The boundaries of what Britain had won were so vaguely defined that they invited renewed fighting.

King George's War (1744-1748), named for the British King George II, was the North American counterpart of the *War of the Austrian Succession*. Fighting again broke out between British and French colonists in the north. New England colonial troops under William Pepperell took the French fortress of Louisbourg, on Cape Breton Island, in 1745. But the Treaty of Aix-la-Chapelle, which ended the war, returned the fortress to the French. The treaty provided for each side to give back what it had won in the war.

The French and Indian War (1754-1763) was the last and most important conflict over French and British possessions in North America. Unlike the three earlier wars, which began in Europe and then spread to America, this struggle broke out first in America. Its European counterpart, the *Seven Years' War*, began two years later, in 1756.

Territorial rivalries had become more intense as British and French settlements expanded over the years. The two countries could not agree on the boundaries of Acadia (see ACADIA). Disputes also arose over the Great Lakes region and the land around lakes George and Champlain. Most important, both countries claimed the vast area between the Allegheny Mountains and the

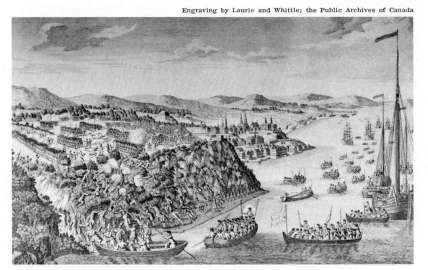

The Battle of Quebec in 1759 ended in victory for Great Britain. This engraving shows British troops led by General James Wolfe storming the Plains of Abraham, above the city.

The French and Indian War

The French and Indian War led to the end of France's colonial empire in North America. The war also established British dominance over most of the French possessions there. This map shows where the major battles of the war took place.

▢	British possession
▨	French possession
——	Colonial boundary
✳	Major battle
▪	Fort
•	City

0   200 Miles
0   200 Kilometers

WORLD BOOK map

Mississippi River. The French called their North American possessions *New France*. In 1749, the French explorer Céloron de Bienville traveled through the Ohio River Valley to reinforce France's claim there. The first Ohio Company sent Christopher Gist to survey the same area in 1750. In 1753 the French built a chain of forts along the Allegheny River in Pennsylvania. Lieutenant Governor Robert Dinwiddie of Virginia sent George Washington to the commander of the new forts, protesting against French occupation of the area. But the French refused to leave. In 1754, Washington led a small force of colonial troops to force the French to withdraw. They were attacked and defeated near Fort Duquesne (now Pittsburgh), in the war's first battle.

Meanwhile, representatives of seven colonies met in Albany, N.Y., to plan military action. Benjamin Franklin also proposed a plan for political union, but the delegates did not adopt it. See ALBANY CONGRESS.

French Successes. In 1755, General Edward Braddock led a band of British soldiers against Fort Duquesne. Braddock was unfamiliar with North American methods of warfare, which often involved surprise attacks from behind trees and concealed spots. He refused to take advice from his experienced American officers, who included Washington. Braddock and his soldiers marched into an ambush. Many were killed, but Washington succeeded in leading some of them to safety.

The British also failed to take Crown Point and Fort Niagara. They succeeded in capturing Fort Beauséjour in what is now New Brunswick. But much bad feeling was aroused when New England colonial troops exiled a large group of French Acadians for disloyalty.

The Marquis de Montcalm took over the leadership of the French forces in 1756, and led attacks against Fort Oswego and Fort William Henry. The French troops outfought the English and seized both these forts.

British Victories. William Pitt became the political leader of Great Britain in 1756. His leadership gave new life to the British cause in North America. British forces in 1758 captured Louisbourg, Fort Frontenac, and Fort Duquesne. In July, 1759, they took Fort Niagara, Fort Ticonderoga, and Crown Point. Meanwhile, General James Wolfe began to besiege the city of Quebec, which was held by 15,000 French troops under General Montcalm. In September, after a siege of almost three months, Wolfe's army stormed the Plains of Abraham, above the city. A short but decisive battle ended in British victory (see QUEBEC, BATTLE OF). The fall of Quebec marked the real end of the French and Indian War, although the struggle continued until General Jeffery Amherst took Montreal in 1760.

By the terms of the Treaty of Paris, signed in 1763, Great Britain received Canada and most French possessions east of the Mississippi River. The Spanish territory of Florida also went to Great Britain. Spain received all French land west of the Mississippi, and the Isle of Orleans, which included the city of New Orleans and controlled the mouth of the Mississippi. France's great colonial empire in North America was reduced to only two tiny islands south of Newfoundland, Saint Pierre and Miquelon. The Caribbean islands of Martinique and Guadeloupe were returned to France as part of the bargain. Spain remained Great Britain's only rival in North America.   RICHARD HOFSTADTER

Related Articles in WORLD BOOK include:

Acadia
Aix-la-Chapelle, Treaties of
Amherst, Lord Jeffery
Braddock, Edward
Coureurs de Bois
Fort Duquesne
Fort Niagara
Franklin, Benjamin (The Plan of Union)
Grand Alliance

Montcalm, Marquis de
Paris, Treaties of
Rogers' Rangers
Ryswick, Treaty of
Seven Years' War
Succession Wars
Utrecht, Peace of
Washington, George
Wolfe, James

FRENCH BULLDOG is a strong, heavy little dog. It weighs from 18 to 28 pounds (8 to 13 kilograms). This bulldog has a more pleasant face than the English one. It has a large, square head, rounded ears, and a short nose. Its chunky body is broader in front than in back. It has soft, loose skin that usually is wrinkled on its face and shoulders. Its coat is usually brindle, but may be white with brindle patches. See also Dog (picture: Non-sporting Dogs).   JOSEPHINE Z. RINE

FRENCH CANADA. See QUEBEC; CANADA; CANADA, HISTORY OF.

FRENCH CANADIANS. See CANADA (People); CANADIAN LITERATURE.

FRENCH CHALK. See SOAPSTONE.

FRENCH EQUATORIAL AFRICA, a region in central Africa, was once a French colony. It included what are now four independent nations: Central African Empire, Chad, Congo, and Gabon. Each nation has a separate article in WORLD BOOK.

The region formerly called French Equatorial Africa covers 969,114 square miles (2,509,994 square kilometers). Nearly all the people in the region are black Africans. Bantu-speaking peoples live in the south. Fulah, Sara, and Tibbu groups live in the north.

The region has vast forest and mineral resources. The richest known mineral deposits lie in Gabon. Chief products include cotton, rice, meat, peanuts, cacao, coffee, timber, manganese, and oil.

The first French colonists arrived in Equatorial Africa in 1839, and settled on the Gabon River. In 1849, they founded Libreville as the capital of the colony. The capital was later moved to Brazzaville.

The four territories of French Equatorial Africa were offered the chance to become independent republics in November, 1958. All of them chose to become self-governing states. They became independent nations in August, 1960.   JAMES W. FERNANDEZ

FRENCH FOREIGN LEGION. See FOREIGN LEGION.

French Equatorial Africa, shown in black, was once a French colony. Four independent countries now occupy this area.

WORLD BOOK map

French Guiana

⊛ Capital

• Other City or Town

— Road

▲ Highest Known Elevation

〜 River

WORLD BOOK maps

FRENCH GUIANA, *gee AH nuh,* is an overseas *department* (state) of France on the northeastern coast of South America. It is bordered on the west by Surinam, on the east and south by Brazil, and on the north by the Atlantic Ocean. It covers about 35,135 square miles (91,000 square kilometers) and has a population of about 67,000. Cayenne is the capital and largest city.

Almost all the people of French Guiana are blacks or *Creoles* (people of mixed black and white ancestry). Most of the people live along the coast. The interior of French Guiana is largely wilderness. The interior has important mineral and forest resources, but they have not been developed. French Guiana depends heavily on France for financial support.

Historically, French Guiana has been known for its penal colonies. For about 150 years, France sent convicts to French Guiana. Political prisoners were kept on Devils Island, an offshore isle. Other convicts were

Anthony P. Maingot, the contributor of this article, is Associate Professor of Sociology at Florida International University.

kept in prison camps at Kourou and Saint-Laurent. The prison camps were widely known for their cruelty. The French finally closed them in 1945 and sent the prisoners back to France. In the 1960's, France turned the camp at Kourou into a space research center.

Government. French Guiana was made an overseas department of France in 1946. It is governed much like the departments in France (see DEPARTMENT). A *prefect* (governor), appointed by the French government, administers French Guiana. He is assisted by a general secretary and an elected council of 16 members. French Guiana has one representative in each house of the French Parliament. The court system in French Guiana is much like that of France (see FRANCE [Courts]).

People. About 90 per cent of the people of French Guiana are Negroes or Creoles. They are descendants of slaves who were brought to French Guiana during the 1600's and 1700's. The rest of the people are American Indians, Chinese, Europeans, Indochinese, Lebanese, and Syrians. The Indians were the first people to live in French Guiana. Today, they live in the interior. Most of the rest of the people live along the coast.

Most French Guianans speak French, the department's official language. Many Creoles also speak a dialect that is a mixture of French and English. Most of the people are Roman Catholics.

Children are required by law to attend school. French Guiana has both public and private elementary schools, a high school, and two vocational schools. About 75 per cent of the people can read and write.

After French Guiana became an overseas department of France in 1946, the French government built hospitals and clinics there. It has also waged campaigns to wipe out leprosy, malaria, and tuberculosis in the department.

The Land and Climate. French Guiana has three land regions—a coastal plain in the north, a hilly plateau in the center, and the Tumuc-Humac Mountains in the south. Rain forests cover most of the country. More than 20 rivers flow north through French Guiana to the Atlantic Ocean. The most important rivers are the Maroni and the Oyapock. The Maroni forms part of the border between French Guiana and Surinam. The Oyapock flows along French Guiana's border with Brazil.

French Guiana has a tropical climate. Temperatures average about 80° F. (27° C) throughout the year. About 130 inches (330 centimeters) of rain falls annually, most of it from December to June.

Economy. French Guiana has an underdeveloped economy. The department depends on France for money to operate its government, to help support its industries, and to pay for health care and other services. Most of the workers are employed by the government.

French Guiana's chief industries include gold mining and the processing of agricultural and forest products. A shrimp industry is being developed. The leading farm products include bananas, cattle, corn, pineapples, rice, sugar cane, and yams. The farmers do not raise enough food to feed the people, and so much food must be imported.

The interior of French Guiana has rich, well-watered soil; valuable timberland; and large deposits of bauxite, an ore used in making aluminum. But these resources have not been developed.

History. The French were the first Europeans to settle in what is now French Guiana. They came in the early 1600's, when many European nations were building colonial empires in the Americas. French Guiana became a French colony in 1667. Since then, the region has been under French control, except for a short period in the early 1800's when it was ruled by British and Portuguese military forces.

France began to send political prisoners to French Guiana during the French Revolution in the 1790's. In

Cayenne, the Capital of French Guiana, lies on an island at the mouth of the Cayenne River. About half the French Guianan people live in the city.

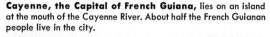
Guy Delabergerie

Devils Island, a small isle off the French Guianan coast, was for many years a brutal prison camp for political prisoners of France. The camp was closed in 1945.

Hassoldt Davis, Rapho Guillumette

FRENCH GUINEA

1854, a formal prison system was established in the colony. About 70,000 persons were held in the prisons from 1852 to 1945, when France closed them.

French Guiana became an overseas department of France in 1946. Since then, French Guiana has worked, with the help of France, to develop its economy and improve the life of its people. A few French Guianans have demanded independence for French Guiana. But most of the people want French Guiana to remain an overseas department of France.　　ANTHONY P. MAINGOT

See also CAYENNE; PENAL COLONY.

FRENCH GUINEA. See GUINEA (country); FRENCH WEST AFRICA.

WORLD BOOK photo, courtesy
Chicago Symphony Orchestra

The French Horn is an important brass instrument in an orchestra or a band. A musician uses one hand to press the key-levers in various combinations to produce notes. He places his other hand inside the bell to control the horn's tone.

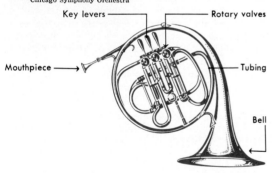

Key levers — Rotary valves

Mouthpiece → — Tubing

— Bell

FRENCH HORN is a brass instrument made from a thin metal tube about 16 feet (5 meters) long, twisted into coils which flare out into a wide bell. It has a funnel-shaped mouthpiece, but no reed. The player's lips serve as the reed. Originally, *crooks* (extensions of the tube) were used to change the horn's pitch by changing its length. In 1754, Anton Joseph Hampel, of Dresden, Germany, invented a method called *stopping* the horn. A player would change the instrument's tone and pitch by inserting the fingers of his right hand into the bell. This technique is still used for special effects. But since the 1800's, most French horns have been equipped with three or four pistons, or rotary valves, respectively, for smooth and quick changes of pitch. The French horn's warm and mellow tone blends well with wood-wind instruments. Most orchestras today use four French horns. See also MELLOPHONE.　　KARL GEIRINGER

FRENCH INDOCHINA. See INDOCHINA.

FRENCH LANGUAGE is the official language of France, its overseas territories, and associated states. It is also an official language of Belgium, Canada, Haiti, Luxembourg, Switzerland, and the United Nations. More people speak such languages as Chinese, English, Russian, or Spanish than speak French. But French is so widely spoken that it ranks with English as an international language. More than 80 million persons speak French as their mother tongue, and millions of others use it as a second language.

The beautiful and harmonious French language has served for hundreds of years as the language of diplomats. Its clear style and regular *syntax* (arrangement of words) make it ideal for diplomatic, legal, and business use, and for prose.

About half the words in the English language come from French. English began to absorb French words after the Norman conquest of England in 1066. The king's court and courts of justice used French, but the ordinary people continued to speak English. French words gradually became part of English. For example, the words *mouton*, *boeuf*, and *porc*, which the nobility used instead of *sheep*, *ox*, and *swine*, became *mutton*, *beef*, and *pork* in English. Thousands of French terms have been adopted, in whole or in part, into English. They include such words as *art*, *army*, *bouillon*, *dinner*, *dress*, *faith*, *fashion*, *fraud*, *garage*, *government*, *hors d'oeuvre*, *pardon*, *preach*, *prison*, *sermon*, and *theater*. The motto of the British royal arms is in French, *Dieu et mon droit* (God and my right), and the motto of Minnesota is *L'Etoile du Nord* (The Star of the North).

French Grammar

Nouns and Adjectives. Few French nouns have *inflections*, or changes of form (see INFLECTION). All nouns are either masculine or feminine. For example, *the book* (*le livre*) is masculine, and *the chair* (*la chaise*) is feminine. Descriptive adjectives are usually made feminine by adding *e*. For example, the feminine of *petit* (small) is *petite*. Plurals are most commonly formed by adding *s* to the singular. The plural of *le petit livre* is *les petits livres*. The plural of *la petite chaise* is *les petites chaises*. *Le* and *la* are the masculine and feminine singular forms of the definite article *the*. *Les* is the masculine and feminine plural form.

Verbs. French has 14 tenses, 7 simple and 7 compound (see TENSE). The *simple* tenses are formed by adding endings to the infinitive or to the stem of the verb. The *compound* tenses are made up of the past participle of the verb and an appropriate form of one of the auxiliary verbs *avoir* (to have) or *être* (to be).

French verbs are classified according to the endings of their infinitives. They fall into three groups: *-er* verbs, such as *donner* (to give); *-ir* verbs, such as *finir* (to finish); and *-re* verbs, such as *vendre* (to sell). French has many irregular verbs.

Word Order in French is similar to that of English. A sentence is made negative by placing *ne* before the verb and *pas* after it. A question is formed by inverting the order of the sentence or by placing the phrase *est-ce que* (is it that) before it. The following are the affirmative, negative, and interrogative forms of the sentence *John gives the books to my friends:*

Affirmative: *Jean donne les livres à mes amis.*
Negative: *Jean ne donne pas les livres à mes amis.*

Interrogative: *Jean donne-t-il les livres à mes amis?* or *Est-ce que Jean donne les livres à mes amis?*

In the perfect tense, a past tense, the forms are:

Affirmative: *Jean a donné les livres à mes amis.*
Negative: *Jean n'a pas donné les livres à mes amis.*
Interrogative: *Jean a-t-il donné les livres à mes amis?* or *Est-ce que Jean a donné les livres à mes amis?*

Pronunciation of French is often difficult for English-speaking people. The French rarely pronounce final consonants except for the letters *c, f, l,* and *r.* For example, *lits* (beds) is pronounced *lee,* and *et* (and) is pronounced *ay.* French vowels are sharp, clear, single sounds. A few do not occur in English. For example, there is no exact equivalent for the *u* of *lune* (moon). It is a "whistled" sound between *ee* and *oo.* Nasal sounds occur in syllables ending in *n* or *m,* as in *bon* (good). The French *r,* pronounced with the uvula at the back of the soft palate, sounds throatier than the English *r.* The French often link words together when speaking, so that a phrase such as *les hommes* (the men) is pronounced *layz OM.*

Development

Beginnings. French, one of the Romance languages, developed from Latin (see ROMANCE LANGUAGE). When Julius Caesar conquered Gaul (France) in the 50's B.C., he found the people speaking a language called Gaulish. The Gauls gradually adopted the language of the Roman soldiers. This language, called *vulgar* or *popular* Latin, differed from the Latin used by educated persons. The Gauls did not learn to speak popular Latin as the soldiers spoke it. They tended to change the vocabulary on the basis of the way the words sounded. For example, a Gaul hearing the stressed syllables *bon* and *ta* of the word *bonitatem* (kindness) shortened the word to *bonta.* This became *bonté* in modern French.

The new language kept few old Gaulish words. Only about 360 Gaulish words became part of modern French. The Franks, who invaded Gaul during the A.D. 400's and gave their name to the country, contributed about a thousand words to French. Norsemen, who occupied northern France in the 800's, added about 90 words. Many French words also came from Greek. As the language developed, the grammar changed. For example, the six Latin cases merged into two, and the number of tenses decreased.

Old French. By the 700's, popular Latin had evolved so completely into *la langue romane,* or Romance, that few persons could read Latin without the aid of a dictionary. The new language first appeared in written form in the "Oaths of Strasbourg," a treaty signed by two of Charlemagne's descendants in 842.

Beginning in the 900's, Romance developed in France into two distinct dialects of *Old French,* each with many minor dialects. The *langue d'oc* flourished in the south, and the *langue d'oïl* prevailed in the north. These terms grew out of the word for *yes,* which was *oc* in the south and *oïl* in the north. The most famous dialect of the langue d'oc was *Provençal,* the language of the troubadours (see TROUBADOUR). But the dialect of the langue d'oïl spoken in the area around Paris became the accepted tongue throughout France.

Modern French. The Renaissance added learned Greek and Latin words to the French vocabulary. Contacts with Spaniards and Italians in the 1500's brought other new words. During the 1600's, writers and scholars standardized the structure of the language. By the 1700's, a French author could say with justification, *Ce qui n'est pas clair n'est pas français* ("What is not clear is not French"). Today, French is considered one of the clearest and most precise of all languages. BOYD G. CARTER

See also FRENCH LITERATURE; FRENCH ACADEMY.

FRENCH WORDS AND PHRASES

NUMBERS

un, *uhng,* one	**trente,** *trawngt,* thirty
deux, *duhr,* two	**quarante,** *kah RAWNGT,* forty
trois, *trwah,* three	**cinquante,** *sang KAWNGT,* fifty
quatre, *kah truh,* four	**soixante,** *swah SAWNGT,* sixty
cinq, *sangk,* five	**soixante-dix,** *swah sawngt DEES,* seventy
six, *sees,* six	**quatre-vingts,** *kah truh VANG,* eighty
sept, *set,* seven	**quatre-vingt-dix,** *kah truh vang DEES,* ninety
huit, *weet,* eight	
neuf, *nuhf,* nine	
dix, *dees,* ten	**cent,** *sawng,* one hundred
vingt, *vang,* twenty	

DAYS OF THE WEEK

lundi, *luhng DEE,* Monday	**vendredi,** *vawng druh DEE,* Friday
mardi, *mahr DEE,* Tuesday	**samedi,** *sahm DEE,* Saturday
mercredi, *mair cruh DEE,* Wednesday	**dimanche,** *dee MAWNG shuh,* Sunday
jeudi, *jhuhr DEE,* Thursday	

MONTHS OF THE YEAR

janvier, *jhawng VEEAY,* January	**août,** *oo,* August
février, *fay VREEAY,* February	**septembre,** *sep TAWNG bruh,* September
mars, *mahrs,* March	**octobre,** *ohk TOH bruh,* October
avril, *ah VREEL,* April	**novembre,** *noh VAWNG bruh,* November
mai, *may,* May	**décembre,** *day SAWNG bruh,* December
juin, *jhwang,* June	
juillet, *jhwee YEH,* July	

Pronunciation of nasal sounds, as in *blanc,* is indicated by a final *ng.*

COMMON WORDS

après, *ah PREH,* after	**jaune,** *JOHN uh,* yellow
aujourd'hui, *oh jhoor DWEE,* today	**joli,** *johl EE,* pretty
blanc, *blawng,* white	**madame,** *mah DAHM,* madam
bleu, *bluhr,* blue	**mademoiselle,** *mahd mwah ZEHL,* miss
chose, *shohz,* thing	**maison,** *may ZOHNG,* house
court, *koor,* short	**mauvais,** *moh VAY,* bad
dans, *dawng,* in, into	**mère,** *mair,* mother
de, *duh,* of, from	**monsieur,** *muh SEEYUH,* Mr., sir
enfant, *awng FAWNG,* child	**où,** *oo,* where
être, *EH truh,* to be	**père,** *pair,* father
femme, *fahm,* woman	**pour,** *poor,* for
fermer, *fehr MAY,* to close	**rouge,** *roozh,* red
frère, *frair,* brother	**sans,** *sawng,* without
garçon, *gahr SOHNG,* boy, waiter	**soeur,** *suhr,* sister
gris, *gree,* gray	**vert,** *vair,* green

COMMON EXPRESSIONS

au revoir, *oh ruh VWAHR,* good-by
bonjour, *bohng JHOOR,* hello
comment allez-vous? *koh mawng tah lay VOO,* how are you?
merci beaucoup, *MAIR see boh KOO,* thank you very much
parlez-vous français? *par lay voo frawng SAY,* do you speak French?
quelle heure est-il? *kel ur eh TEEL,* what time is it?
qu'est-ce que c'est? *kehs kuh SEH,* what is it?
s'il vous plaît, *seel voo PLEH,* please
très bien, *treh BYANG,* very well

FRENCH LITERATURE

FRENCH LITERATURE. French authors have contributed to every literary form—drama, poetry, the essay, the novel, and the short story. No one genius towers over French literature as Shakespeare stands out in English literature. But, during the last thousand years, many great writers have made the literature of France one of the most creative in the world.

The French have great love for their language and their literature. They, more than many other peoples, turn to their writers for inspiration. They give authors greater fame and honor than other peoples do. French authors often speak intimately and personally of themselves. But they have always been concerned with broader problems in politics, morals, theology, and philosophy. For example, Montaigne expounded the philosophic ideas of the 1500's. Bossuet preached on the religious controversies that raged during the 1600's. Montesquieu set forth principles that inspired reforms in the government of France during the 1700's. A French poet of the 1900's, Paul Valéry, drew on the scientific developments and political events of his age to express his ideas on the nature of man and the future of western civilization.

Since its earliest days, French literature has made significant contributions to the writings of other nations. For example, Shakespeare borrowed from the work of Montaigne. Montesquieu's *The Spirit of the Laws* became an American classic in the 1700's. The names of French writers have become universal symbols of certain attitudes and styles. Voltaire represents brilliance and wit; Blaise Pascal, spiritual force; Jean

Racine, an understanding of passion; and Montaigne, a devotion to truth. Masterpieces of French literature have been translated into almost every major language. They are read in all parts of the world.

Characteristics of French Literature

Two strong contradictory voices run through most of French literature, forming a sort of dialogue. At no period has one major view of man been allowed to stand unchallenged. Every theory has called forth an opposing theory. But no theory ever really dominates the other. For example, two kinds of humanism opposed one another during the Renaissance in the 1500's. The humorist François Rabelais proclaimed the natural goodness of man. But the religious reformer John Calvin preached on the corruption of human nature. In the first half of the 1600's, René Descartes formulated a philosophic method that emphasized the powers of human reason. During the same years, Pascal asked human reason to humble itself.

A preoccupation with religious problems has been a major characteristic of French literature since its beginnings. This interest in religion recurs with greater persistence and vitality than does any other subject. It appears in all forms of writing from Pierre Corneille's tragedy on sainthood, *Polyeucte*, to Molière's comedy on religious hypocrisy, *Tartuffe*. Most French writers can be classified according to their acceptance or rejection of religion. During the Renaissance, Calvin held strict religious views, and protested against Rabelais' pagan naturalism. In the 1600's, Pascal defended religion and accused Montaigne of dangerous skepticism. Voltaire attacked organized religion in the 1700's

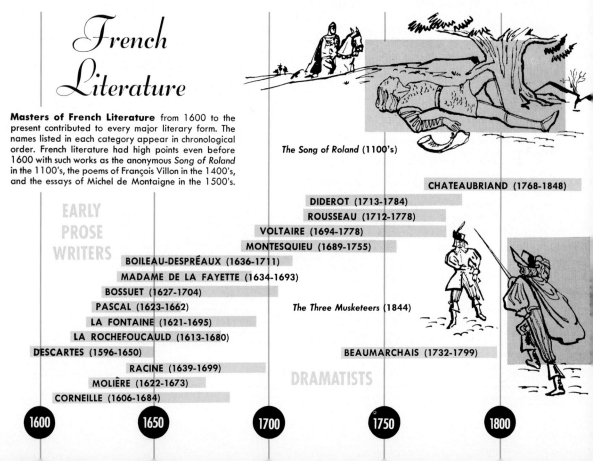

French Literature

Masters of French Literature from 1600 to the present contributed to every major literary form. The names listed in each category appear in chronological order. French literature had high points even before 1600 with such works as the anonymous *Song of Roland* in the 1100's, the poems of François Villon in the 1400's, and the essays of Michel de Montaigne in the 1500's.

The Song of Roland (1100's)

CHATEAUBRIAND (1768-1848)

EARLY PROSE WRITERS

DIDEROT (1713-1784)
ROUSSEAU (1712-1778)
VOLTAIRE (1694-1778)
MONTESQUIEU (1689-1755)
BOILEAU-DESPRÉAUX (1636-1711)
MADAME DE LA FAYETTE (1634-1693)
BOSSUET (1627-1704)
PASCAL (1623-1662)
LA FONTAINE (1621-1695)
LA ROCHEFOUCAULD (1613-1680)
DESCARTES (1596-1650)

The Three Musketeers (1844)

BEAUMARCHAIS (1732-1799)

RACINE (1639-1699)
MOLIÈRE (1622-1673)
CORNEILLE (1606-1684)

DRAMATISTS

1600   **1650**   **1700**   **1750**   **1800**

and sought to destroy the influence of Bossuet and Pascal. During the 1800's, François de Chateaubriand attempted to reinstate Bossuet and Pascal and to undermine Voltaire. Some scholars interpret all French literature as a battle between those who have faith and those who do not.

Early French Literature

Narrative Poetry was the first important form of French literature. Long epic poems called *chansons de geste* (songs of deeds) appeared in the 1000's and 1100's. These poems celebrated the deeds of Charlemagne and other heroes (see CHARLEMAGNE). Many scholars believe that monks wrote most of the chansons de geste to glorify the founders and protectors of their monasteries. The chansons de geste formed a cycle of poems, of which *The Song of Roland* is the most famous.

A second group of poems called *romans courtois*, or courtly romances, grew up with the chansons de geste. They dealt with themes of love, magic, and chivalry. Chrétien de Troyes, who wrote from about 1160 to 1190, became the most popular author of courtly romances. He tried to combine the warlike ideals of the chansons de geste with a new romantic attitude toward women. He often drew on the legends of King Arthur.

The outstanding French narrative poem of the Middle Ages was *The Romance of the Rose*, an allegory in two parts. Guillaume de Lorris, who lived in the early 1200's, wrote the first part before 1250, and Jean de Meung (1250?-1305?) wrote the second part nearly 50 years later. The first part is a manual of courtly love. The second part attacks social evils of the period. It begins a type of moral philosophy that appears later in the works of Rabelais, Molière, and Voltaire.

Lyric Poetry flourished in the Provençal region of southern France during the 1100's. Wandering minstrels called *troubadours* composed songs of love and adventure to entertain the noblemen and ladies. They wrote short poems called *chansons de toile* (sewing songs) to accompany needlework, weaving, or dancing. *Trouvères* in northern France followed the troubadours in the 1200's, and adopted many of their forms.

Wars, famine, and poverty ravaged France in the 1400's. Poets wrote about death, fortune, exile, the vanity of the world, the flight of time, and the cruelty of love. These themes found their purest expression in the art of Charles d'Orléans (1391-1465) and of François Villon (1431- ?), the first great French poet. In his two *Testaments*, Villon described himself as a poverty-stricken culprit.

Early Prose lagged far behind poetry in its development. The only important form to appear early was the *chronicle* (history of the day). Geoffroi de Villehardouin (1160?-1213?) described the Fourth Crusade in his *Conquest of Constantinople*. Jean de Joinville (1224?-1317) included many anecdotes from the life of Louis IX in his *History of Saint Louis*. In his *Chronicles*, Jean Froissart (1337?-1410?) described the Hundred Years' War. Froissart was a careful researcher, and based much of his history on eyewitness accounts.

The Renaissance

The Renaissance came to France in the early 1500's and brought sweeping spiritual and intellectual

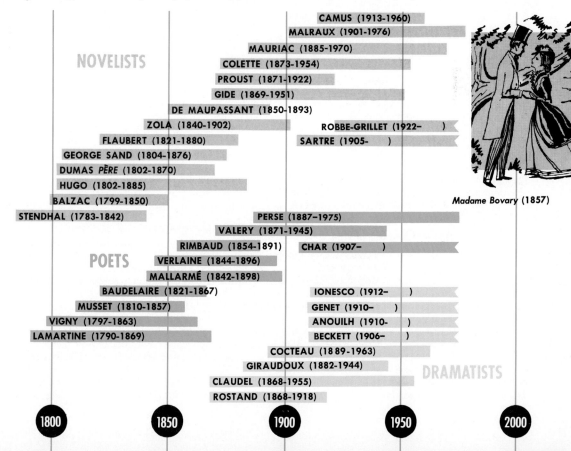

NOVELISTS

CAMUS (1913-1960)
MALRAUX (1901-1976)
MAURIAC (1885-1970)
COLETTE (1873-1954)
PROUST (1871-1922)
GIDE (1869-1951)
DE MAUPASSANT (1850-1893)
ZOLA (1840-1902)
ROBBE-GRILLET (1922–   )
FLAUBERT (1821-1880)
SARTRE (1905-   )
GEORGE SAND (1804-1876)
DUMAS *PÈRE* (1802-1870)
HUGO (1802-1885)
BALZAC (1799-1850)
STENDHAL (1783-1842)

Madame Bovary (1857)

PERSE (1887–1975)
VALERY (1871-1945)
RIMBAUD (1854-1891)
CHAR (1907–   )
VERLAINE (1844-1896)
POETS
MALLARMÉ (1842-1898)
BAUDELAIRE (1821-1867)
IONESCO (1912–   )
MUSSET (1810-1857)
GENET (1910–   )
VIGNY (1797-1863)
ANOUILH (1910-   )
LAMARTINE (1790-1869)
BECKETT (1906–   )
COCTEAU (1889-1963)
GIRAUDOUX (1882-1944)
DRAMATISTS
CLAUDEL (1868-1955)
ROSTAND (1868-1918)

1800   1850   1900   1950   2000

changes. Scholars and thinkers rediscovered the literature of the ancient world. Writers adopted new attitudes toward art and philosophy. Humanists made man, rather than God, the center of their study.

The Humanists. The prose of François Rabelais (1494?-1553?) proved that literature could be a mighty instrument of thought. The vitality, scholarship, and optimism of the Renaissance appear in the pages of Rabelais' *Gargantua*. This book is a story about giants. But it also sets forth the creed of the new humanism. It rejects the otherworldliness of the Middle Ages and proclaims the new ideals of science and humanity.

The spirit of the Renaissance appears in a quieter and more controlled form in the *Essays* of Michel de Montaigne (1533-1592). Montaigne did not have the coarseness, comic effects, or exaggerated optimism of Rabelais. The personal essay form, which he invented, suited his own habits and thinking. Montaigne's *Essays* present his philosophy of life. He appears to be a skeptic, because he contradicts accepted beliefs. His motto is *Que sais-je?* ("What do I know?"). But Montaigne is concerned more with pointing out incoherences and errors in man's thought than with founding a philosophy of skepticism.

The Pléiade, a group of seven poets, represents the most spectacular triumph of French poetry during the Renaissance. The term *Pléiade* comes from the *Pleiades,* a cluster of seven stars. The Pléiade poets broke with the traditions of the Middle Ages. They turned to ancient Greek and Latin sources for themes, studied their poetic meter and versification, and adapted new forms from Italian Renaissance poetry. They first established the *alexandrine* (12-syllable line) as the principal meter in French poetry (see METER). Pléiade poets united mythology and nature, and combined learned ideas with popular poetry. Some of their poems show great tenderness and hopefulness. Pierre de Ronsard (1524-1585), the greatest of the Pléiade, became the most celebrated poet of Europe in his time.

Joachim Du Bellay (1522-1560), a member of the Pléiade, wrote the first important book of criticism in France. This book, *Defense and Glorification of the French Language*, appeared in 1549. Du Bellay treated the ancient writers with almost fanatical respect, and advised French authors to imitate their forms deliberately. He sought to prove that French equaled Greek and Latin in dignity. Although Du Bellay's book was wordy and contradictory, it served as a guidebook for French poets for over 100 years.

The 1600's—The Classical Age

The magnificent palace at Versailles where Louis XIV held his court was the visible expression of the ideals of the 1600's. "The Grand Monarch" ruled with an iron hand. To add to the glory of his reign, Louis encouraged the growth of the arts. Under his patronage, France enjoyed a golden age of literature.

The influence of François de Malherbe (1555-1628) dominated literature during the first half of the 1600's. His work as grammarian, poet, and critic helped define the rules of French *classical art*, a style that occupies a central place in the history of French culture. Classical literature reflected the absolute submission to authority characteristic of the period. Writers adopted what they believed had been the standards of ancient times, and followed strict stylistic rules. Reason and restraint became the criteria of good writing.

The *Discourse on the Method of Rightly Conducting the Reason and Seeking for Truth in the Sciences* by René Descartes (1596-1650), published in 1637, was the first important philosophical work written in French. Descartes' method of reasoning, known as *Cartesian rationalism*, influenced most forms of literature in the 1600's, and continued for a long time to mold the spirit of French logic.

Classical Prose. The aristocrats who gathered at Versailles cultivated all forms of writing. They held regular *salons* (intellectual meetings) where writers tried to outdo one another in wit and originality. Madame de Sévigné (1626-1696) set the standards for taste and fashion in her newsy letters to her daughter. Jacques Bénigne Bossuet (1627-1704) wrote solemn sermons on life and death and the majesty of God. In his sermons, he used a language of great lyrical style that often resembled poetry. The Duc de la Rochefoucauld (1613-1680) created pithy maxims that expressed his belief in the egotism and self-love of man. Jean de la Bruyère (1645-1696) recorded his impressions of people around him in satirical character sketches.

Blaise Pascal (1623-1662), a physicist, mathematician, and philosopher, perhaps created the true French prose style—sensitive and indirect in its complexity, spirited and alive in its movement, and always animated by the light of intuition. In his *Provincial Letters*, he used straightforward, clear sentences, constructed according to the logical development of the thought. His 18 letters range in tone from irony to protest and indignation. They criticize the Jesuits for what Pascal considered their lax and indulgent view of morality. The genius of Pascal reveals itself best in his *Pensées* (*Thoughts on Religion and Other Subjects*).

Jean de la Fontaine (1621-1695) created the first literary fables in verse form. He called his Fables "the one hundred act comedy whose stage set is the universe." Each fable is like a dramatization. Its scenes, characters, and dialogues are remarkably clear.

Nicolas Boileau-Despréaux (1636-1711) became the leading literary critic of the period. He was a craftsman and painstaking theorist. His defense of reason established a bond of agreement between himself and other thinkers of his day.

Drama was the supreme expression of French classical literature. The three masters of classical drama were Pierre Corneille (1606-1684), Jean Racine (1639-1699), and Molière (1622-1673).

Corneille was the first dramatist to apply "the three unities" successfully in French tragedy. The principles of unity of space, time, and action supposedly came from the Greek philosopher Aristotle. Corneille mastered the alexandrine couplet, which became the classic French verse form. His best tragedies include *The Cid, Horace,* and *Cinna.* The poetry of these works is a poetry of action. It is an intellectual language that describes the feelings and dilemmas of the characters.

Racine's fame as a dramatist results partly from his emphasis on a single tragic action and his psychological acuteness in portraying character. But Racine's greatness also rests on his poetic gifts, the elegance of his expression, and the magic of his style. In his theatrical verse, Racine found a mode of expression that most essentially approaches the grace and mystery of poetry. He particularly triumphed in making the pure sound of his alexandrine line express perfectly the tragic sentiment of his dramas.

Molière wrote some of the greatest comedies in the history of the theater. Much of the humor of Molière's plays comes from his sharp, biting dialogue. He knew the language of the common people; of the *bourgeoisie* (middle class); and of the *précieux* (members of the upper class), who used ornate, affected speech. Molière wrote several comedies in verse form, including *The School for Wives*, *Tartuffe*, and *The Misanthrope*.

The 1700's—The Age of Philosophers

Respect for traditions began to crumble during the first half of the 1700's. Writers and others expressed increasing dissatisfaction with existing institutions. Their new theories about government, religion, and society helped bring about the French Revolution.

The Philosophes, or philosophers and liberal writers of the 1700's, insisted on the rights of free opinion. They helped establish a scientific spirit in France that has had a deep effect on all civilization.

Pierre Bayle (1647-1706) was one of the first religious freethinkers of the 1700's. He maintained that it was impossible to reconcile reason with faith. Bayle became a forceful advocate of religious toleration. He and the philosophers who came after him made factual truth the goal of their investigations.

In 1721, six years after the death of Louis XIV, Montesquieu (1689-1755) published *The Persian Letters*, a volume that testified to the new spirit of the age. This work is a detailed attack on the system of government, disguised as correspondence between two Persians.

About the same time, the reputation of Voltaire (1694-1778) as a poet and dramatist began to spread. He became the defender of all just causes. Voltaire mastered a brilliant prose style with which he attacked political and religious institutions. He was at his best when he heaped scorn and ridicule on persons and doctrines he loathed. Voltaire's philosophical tales, such as *Candide* and *Micromégas*, have such a fine sense of order and design that they almost resemble problems in mathematics.

Jean Jacques Rousseau (1712-1778) was a kind of prophet, advocating a return to nature. He claimed that the evils of humanity come from civilization, and he regarded primitive man as "the noble savage." His emphasis on individual rights and dignity helped inspire leaders of the French Revolution. His *Confessions*, a frank, detailed description of his own development, started a literary style still popular today.

The Encyclopédie, or *Encyclopedia*, was one of the most important literary productions of the 1700's. This monumental work covered all branches of human activity. Denis Diderot (1713-1784), a philosopher, poet, and playwright, spent 20 years editing it. Diderot and his associates started the *Encyclopédie* as a translation of Ephraim Chambers' *Cyclopaedia*. But they soon expanded it into a vast work that included contributions from almost every important writer of the period. The *Encyclopédie* was published between 1751 and 1780. This work helped bring the prestige of French literature and French taste to all parts of Europe.

Experiments in Form. Literary styles in the 1700's represented a transition from the classicism of the 1600's to the freer forms of the 1800's. Writers experimented with new forms and tried to modify old ones. One of the most important new forms was the *picaresque*, a long, rambling account of the adventures of a roguish, often comic, hero. The picaresque was a forerunner of the modern novel. The best-known picaresque of the period was *Gil Blas* by Alain René Lesage (1668-1747).

Drama declined during the 1700's. Under Diderot's influence, dramatists gave up heroic themes and began to write about the life of the times. Few of the new *bourgeois dramas* had literary merit. But they paved the way for the social-problem plays that became important in the 1800's and 1900's. The one outstanding playwright of the time was Pierre de Beaumarchais (1732-1799). The wit and fearless mockery of his comedies, *The Marriage of Figaro* and *The Barber of Seville*, brought him wide acclaim as a social reformer. The playwright presented the nobility in an atmosphere of frivolity, intrigue, and love-making. But he gave significance to only one figure, the valet Figaro. Some of Figaro's speeches predict the revolution that exploded at the end of the 1700's.

The 1800's—Romanticism and Realism

Rousseau's last book, *Reveries of the Solitary Stroller*, written from 1776 to 1778, was the earliest expression of a new romantic temperament that dominated much of French literature during the next 100 years. The romantic movement broke the conventions and restrictions of classicism. Romantic writers glorified emotion, sentiment, and passion, and spoke of "liberty in art." The writings of François de Chateaubriand (1768-1848) laid the basis for romanticism. But Victor Hugo (1802-1885) first stated the principles of the movement in 1827 in the preface to his play *Cromwell*.

Even during the height of romanticism, a number of writers began to revolt against its exaggerated emotionalism and flowery forms. These *realists* spoke of "sincerity in art." Their goal was to describe their observations with scientific accuracy and without comment. The *naturalists* who followed the realists wrote about the ugly and the abnormal. They concentrated on crime, slum conditions, and the lowest aspects of human nature. Realism and naturalism gained their greatest popularity in the second half of the 1800's.

Poetry Reborn. After almost two hundred years of decline, poetry flowered again during the 1800's. The young romantics turned to nature for inspiration. They saw their own moods and feelings reflected in the wildness and unpredictability of nature. In his *Poetic Meditations*, Alphonse de Lamartine (1790-1869) wrote of love, death, nature, and religious faith. Alfred de Vigny (1797-1863) attacked the infidelity of nature in his poems. But Victor Hugo was the glory and dominating power of the whole movement. He raised nature to a level of religious significance, and exercised a lasting influence upon French literature.

A group of poets called the *Parnassians* reacted against romanticism, and concentrated on perfection of form and expression. Led by Leconte de Lisle (1818-1894), these poets followed the "art for art's sake" theories of Théophile Gautier (1811-1872).

The most creative period of post-romantic poetry came after the short reign of the *Parnassus School*, in the second half of the 1800's. Many critics consider Charles Baudelaire (1821-1867) the greatest French poet of the period. His book *The Flowers of Evil* (1857) was both a great achievement as poetry and a major criticism of prevailing ideas of art. During the first 40 years of the 1900's, Arthur Rimbaud (1854-1891) was considered the greatest French poet by several critics. The images he used from 1870 to 1873 continued to influence later European and American poets. Rimbaud, Paul Verlaine (1844-1896), and Stéphane Mallarmé (1842-1898) led the *symbolist movement* in poetry. They believed that the poetry should convey feelings and impressions by means of images and symbols. Mallarmé maintained that a work of art has no other value than its value as art. He believed that the subject of all poems is poetry. A poet's duty, according to Mallarmé, is to gain an increasing degree of self-awareness in order to understand and explain the unknown in himself. Mallarmé's theories made him the literary model for some of the outstanding writers of the 1900's.

The Great Novelists. The earliest example of a modern novel in France was *The Princess of Clèves* by Madame de La Fayette (1634-1693), published in 1678. In the 1700's, *Manon Lescaut* by l'Abbé Prévost (1697-1763) continued the tradition of a psychological story with few characters. The novel gradually became the most important literary form of the 1800's.

George Sand (1804-1876) symbolized the romantic revolt in such novels as *Indiana* and *Lélia*. Later, both she and Victor Hugo wrote novels about social problems. Hugo's powerful novels *The Hunchback of Notre Dame* and *Les Misérables* won great fame.

Stendhal (1783-1842) learned that writing gave him the happiness he could not find in life. His two masterpieces, *The Red and the Black* and *The Charterhouse of Parma*, are partly autobiographical novels. They became noted for their detailed psychological description of proud, strong characters in love and war.

Honoré de Balzac (1799-1850) called his long series of novels *The Human Comedy*. He considered the work a history of social customs. About 100 novels, short novels, and short stories, written between 1829 and 1848, make up the series. Balzac's repertory of more than 2,000 characters places him in company with Molière and Shakespeare as a great "creator of souls."

Gustave Flaubert (1821-1880) followed Balzac in his love of detail and his careful observation of facts. Flaubert spent five years writing his most famous book, *Madame Bovary*. It portrays French provincial life in the mid-1800's. Flaubert believed that an author must remain completely detached from his subject.

Émile Zola (1840-1902) led the naturalist movement in literature. His series about the Rougon Macquart family traces the history of a Parisian family through several generations. Zola treated his characters as the products of their heredity and environment. His novels provided much ammunition for social reformers.

Guy de Maupassant (1850-1893) specialized in realistic short stories. Many of his brutal, vivid tales portray the lives of Norman peasants.

French Literature Today

The Four Masters. During the early 1900's, four men ranked as the leading French writers. They were Paul Claudel (1868-1955), André Gide (1869-1951), Marcel Proust (1871-1922), and Paul Valéry (1871-1945).

Claudel has an important place in modern Roman Catholic thought both as a poet and as a dramatist. The seriousness of Claudel's religious feelings dominates his work. His verse plays, such as *The Satin Slipper*, express his belief in the eternal relationship between man and woman and between mankind and God.

Gide contributed to almost all forms of literature. His critical writings had as much influence as his fiction. Gide's untiring curiosity and critical spirit place him in the tradition of Montaigne. In his criticism, Gide emphasized the theme that man must remain detached and dissatisfied so he can always change and grow. Gide's best-known fiction includes the short novels *The Immoralist* and *Strait Is the Gate* and the novel *The Counterfeiters*.

Proust's seven-part *Remembrance of Things Past* is one of the greatest novels ever written. It describes every level of French society, especially the aristocracy and the rich middle class. The novel also explores the development of a writer's career.

Valéry continued the poetic tradition established by Mallarmé. The hero of Valéry's *Fragments du Narcisse* (*Fragments of Narcissus*) is a kind of philosopher searching for self-knowledge. In *The Marine Cemetery*, Valéry visits his boyhood home on the Mediterranean coast and meditates on death while visiting the graves of his ancestors.

Surrealism, one of the most significant modern French artistic and literary movements, flourished especially from about 1924 to 1935. Surrealist writers and painters relied on such mental forces as dreams and the subconscious in creating their works. The leader of the movement was the poet André Breton (1896-1966). Surrealism also attracted many leading young French poets of the early 1900's, including Louis Aragon (1897-   ), Robert Desnos (1900-1945), Paul Éluard (1895-1952), and Pierre Reverdy (1889-1960).

Poetry After Surrealism. The leading French poets of the mid-1900's were René Char (1907-   ) and Saint-John Perse (1887-1975). Char joined the surrealists about 1930 but soon left the movement. He set most of his poems in the French countryside near the Mediterranean Sea. These works show Char's love of nature and his hostility toward industrial society.

Perse wrote in a more traditional style than the surrealists. He composed three great epics—*Anabasis*, *Exile*, and *Seamarks*. They deal with such universal themes as man's urge to explore and conquer unknown lands. His poem *Winds* uses the winds that blow over the earth to symbolize man's spirit and the forces of history.

Existentialism is a philosophical movement that dominated French literary and philosophic thought during the 1940's and 1950's. Existentialism deals with man's major philosophical and psychological problems, including the nature of liberty and responsibility. The movement's leader, Jean-Paul Sartre (1905-   ), expressed his ideas in philosophical writings and in the novel *Nausea* and the plays *No Exit* and *The Flies*. Another leading existentialist writer was Albert Camus (1913-1960). In Camus' novel *The Stranger*, the hero feels he is a stranger in the world. He does not believe in God or in the ability of people to progress.

Theater of the Absurd refers to the works of several playwrights who first gained recognition in the early 1950's. They used unrealistic dramatic techniques to show what they believed was the meaningless nature of human existence. In *Waiting for Godot*, Samuel Beckett (1906-   ) presented two tramps trying to convince themselves that they exist. In *The Balcony*, Jean Genet (1910-   ) explored the nature of reality and the difficulty of defining good and evil. Eugène Ionesco (1912-   ) dramatized his belief in the absurdity of human speech and the inadequacy of language. One of Ionesco's best-known plays is *The Chairs*.

The New Novel is a term for an experimental form of fiction that first appeared in the 1950's. Leaders of the New Novel movement included Michel Butor (1926-   ), Alain Robbe-Grillet (1922-   ), and Nathalie Sarraute (1902-   ). These writers abandoned such traditional storytelling elements as realistic characters and plots. Their novels concentrate on precise descriptions of events and objects as experienced or seen by the characters.   WALLACE FOWLIE

Related Articles in WORLD BOOK include:

EARLY FRENCH LITERATURE

Chrétien de Troyes	Roland	Trouvère
Froissart, Jean	Troubadour	Villon, François

THE RENAISSANCE

Du Bellay, Joachim	Montaigne, Michel de
Gargantua and Pantagruel	Rabelais, François
Marot, Clément	Ronsard, Pierre de

THE 1600'S—THE CLASSICAL AGE

Boileau-Despréaux, Nicolas	La Fayette, Madame de
Bossuet, Jacques	La Fontaine, Jean de
Classicism	La Rochefoucauld, Duc de
Corneille, Pierre	Malherbe, François de
Cyrano de Bergerac,	Molière
Savinien de	Pascal, Blaise
Descartes, René	Perrault, Charles
Fénelon, François de S.	Racine, Jean
La Bruyère, Jean de	

THE 1700'S—THE AGE OF PHILOSOPHERS

Age of Reason	Lesage, Alain René
Bayle, Pierre	Marivaux, Pierre
Beaumarchais, Pierre de	Montesquieu
Chénier, André	Rousseau, Jean Jacques
Diderot, Denis	Sade, Marquis de
Figaro	Voltaire

THE 1800'S—ROMANTICISM AND REALISM

Balzac, Honoré de	Mérimée, Prosper
Baudelaire, Charles	Mistral, Frédéric
Brieux, Eugène	Musset, Alfred de
Chateaubriand, François de	Naturalism
Daudet, Alphonse	Nerval, Gérard de
De Maupassant, Guy	Rimbaud, Arthur
Dumas, Alexandre	Romanticism
Flaubert, Gustave	Rostand, Edmond
France, Anatole	Sainte-Beuve, Charles
Gautier, Théophile	Sand, George
Goncourt (family)	Sardou, Victorien
Hugo, Victor	Scribe, Augustine Eugène
Lamartine, Alphonse de	Staël, Madame de
Mallarmé, Stéphane	Stendhal

Sully-Prudhomme, René	Verne, Jules
Symbolism	Vigny, Alfred de
Taine, Hippolyte	Zola, Émile
Verlaine, Paul	

FRENCH LITERATURE TODAY

Anouilh, Jean	Existentialism	Perse, Saint-John
Apollinaire,	Genet, Jean	Prévert, Jacques
Guillaume	Gide, André	Proust, Marcel
Beauvoir,	Giraudoux, Jean	Rolland, Romain
Simone de	Ionesco, Eugène	Romains, Jules
Beckett, Samuel	Malraux, André	Saint-Exupéry,
Breton, André	Martin du Gard,	Antoine de
Camus, Albert	Roger	Sartre, Jean-Paul
Claudel, Paul	Mauriac, François	Surrealism
Cocteau, Jean	Maurois, André	Valéry, Paul
Colette		

OTHER RELATED ARTICLES

Drama	French Language	Poetry
French Academy	Novel	

Outline

I. Characteristics of French Literature
II. Early French Literature
  A. Narrative Poetry   C. Early Prose
  B. Lyric Poetry
III. The Renaissance
  A. The Humanists   B. The Pléiade
IV. The 1600's—The Classical Age
  A. Classical Prose   B. Drama
V. The 1700's—The Age of Philosophers
  A. The Philosophes   C. Experiments in Form
  B. The Encyclopédie
VI. The 1800's—Romanticism and Realism
  A. Poetry Reborn   B. The Great Novelists
VII. French Literature Today
  A. The Four Masters   D. Existentialism
  B. Surrealism   E. Theater of the Absurd
  C. Poetry After   F. The New Novel
    Surrealism

Questions

How have French authors shown an interest in religion?

Why has literature been so significant in France?

What did the *Pléiade* achieve? The *Philosophes*?

Who were the *troubadours*? The *trouvères*?

What was the *Encyclopédie*? Why was it important?

How did the realists differ from the romantics?

What were the *chansons de geste*? The *chansons de toile*?

Who were the leaders of the symbolist movement?

How did the theories of Jean Jacques Rousseau inspire the French Revolution?

What were the major contributions of (1) Montaigne? (2) Guy de Maupassant? (3) Jean-Paul Sartre?

Reading and Study Guide

See *French Literature* in the RESEARCH GUIDE/INDEX, Volume 22, for a *Reading and Study Guide*.

FRENCH MOROCCO. See MOROCCO (History).

FRENCH POLYNESIA is an overseas territory of France. It covers 1,544 square miles (4,000 square kilometers) of land in the Pacific Ocean, about 2,500 miles (4,020 kilometers) southeast of Hawaii. About 142,000 people live in the territory. French Polynesia includes Clipperton Island, and the Austral, Gambier, Marquesas, Society, and Tuamotu island groups.

See also AUSTRAL ISLANDS; GAMBIER ISLANDS; MARQUESAS ISLANDS; SOCIETY ISLANDS; TUAMOTU ISLANDS; PACIFIC ISLANDS (picture: Village Life).

FRENCH QUARTER. See NEW ORLEANS (Downtown New Orleans).

FRENCH REVOLUTION

FRENCH REVOLUTION. The ten years between 1789 and 1799 were a time of struggle and violence in France. The French Revolution began when Louis XVI called the States-General to provide money for his bankrupt government. It ended when Napoleon Bonaparte became first consul of France. During these ten years thousands of aristocrats, including the king and queen, lost their lives on the guillotine. Revolutionary leaders rose, then lost popularity, and died on the guillotine.

At the beginning of the Revolution, the king, in theory, held supreme power in France. By the time it ended, power had passed to the hands of the great and growing middle class. The Bourbon kings came back to the throne in 1814 and 1815, after each defeat of Napoleon. But absolute government was gone for good. The Revolution did not make France a democracy, but it did make France a limited monarchy.

Causes of the Revolution. French commerce and industry grew rapidly in the 1700's, and a new class of merchants and manufacturers began to gain great wealth. But France's government and social organization, which had grown up during the Middle Ages, made no changes to make room for the new class. The king claimed to rule the country by divine right (see DIVINE RIGHT OF KINGS). Noblemen lived in great luxury, but many peasants did not have enough to eat. The unfair system of taxation caused great hardships, particularly for the lower classes. Noblemen and clergymen did not have to pay the tax on land. The middle and lower classes carried the greater part of the tax burden.

At the same time, the people began taking interest in new ideas about freedom. Many men of learning had come to think that perhaps government was not a thing kings exercised by divine right. They suggested that it was an agreement shared by the ruler and the people. The middle class felt hampered by ancient legal, political, and religious institutions. This class began to organize the people and to prepare for revolution.

The first Treaty of Paris further discredited the old regime. The treaty, signed in 1763, gave the French empire in India and North America to the British. This was a national humiliation and a severe economic blow to the French middle class.

When Louis XVI followed his grandfather, Louis XV, on the throne, the government was almost bankrupt. Louis XV had been a selfish, wasteful, inefficient ruler. Louis XVI refused to follow the advice of his ministers that he make sorely needed reforms. By his refusal, he brought the country to the verge of revolution.

The Revolution Begins. The American Revolution had been expensive for the French. France had given money to aid the Americans, and the king's treasury was empty in 1787. The *Parlement* (high court) had rebelled against the king's wishes. The king could raise more money only by calling a meeting of the States-General, the French national assembly. The last meeting of this body had been held in 1614. The first meeting of the new States-General took place at Versailles on May 5, 1789.

Before it could consider any other problems, the assembly had to decide how it was going to count its vote. It was divided into three *estates* (classes) according to a system that had developed in the Middle Ages.

Clergymen made up the first estate, noblemen the second, and the rest of the people the third. Under the old voting system, each estate had one vote. Members of the third estate realized that they could not hope to make any reforms unless they could persuade either the first or the second estate to agree with them.

The third estate wanted each member of the whole assembly to have a vote, but the nobles and clergy refused. Representatives from the third estate then withdrew from the assembly. They met on a nearby tennis court and declared themselves the legal National Assembly of France. They also took the famous Oath of the Tennis Court, pledging that they would not disband until they had given France a constitution. Many nobles and members of the lower clergy joined this new group, which was known as the Constituent Assembly. The king was finally forced to recognize them. But Louis was not satisfied with the course of events. He dismissed his chief minister, Jacques Necker, and planned to dismiss the Assembly.

The people of Paris rose on July 14 and stormed the Bastille, a fortress-prison, in an effort to secure arms and to free many political prisoners. In the fighting, they murdered the governor of the prison. The king was forced to recall Necker as his chief minister. But the mob in Paris, aroused by revolutionary leaders, began to play a more and more important part in the Revolution. In October, a mob from Paris, made up largely of women, invaded the royal palace at Versailles. The royal family had to turn for protection to the National Guard, an armed force organized by the Assembly to keep order. At the same time, peasants in various parts of France began uprisings against their feudal lords. French noblemen, including the king's brother, began fleeing the country.

Acts of the Assembly. During the next two years, the National Assembly passed laws which wiped out many abuses of the old feudal system. The nobles gave up most of their rights, privileges, and titles. At first it was intended that the government should pay them for their losses, but later even this provision was abolished.

The Assembly accepted a famous document, the Declaration of the Rights of Man, on Aug. 26, 1789. The National Assembly then drew up a constitution, which made France a constitutional monarchy with a one-house legislature. According to the constitution, the king could declare war and make peace only with the consent of the legislature. France was divided into departments, and the departments were divided into districts and cantons. Voters had to be taxpayers, or "active citizens." The property of the church and of the nobles who had fled the country was seized by the government, and notes called *assignats* were issued against the property to provide public funds. The clergy had to take an oath of loyalty to the new constitution. Some of them did, but many refused to do so. The National Assembly voted that none of its members could be elected to the new chamber, the Legislative Assembly. It dissolved itself on Sept. 30, 1791, to make way for the new government.

The king did not really accept the acts of the Assembly, although he appeared to do so. In June, 1791, he tried to escape from France with his family. He was recognized at Varennes and was brought back to Paris. Leaders used this attempt to arouse the suspicion of the people, who believed that Louis was plotting against

France with noblemen who had fled the country and with the governments of other countries. Many countries still had kings who ruled by the doctrine of divine right. They distrusted the French revolutionary movement, fearing it might spread to their own countries.

The Legislative Assembly. The new assembly met on October 1, 1791. It had 745 members, elected by "active citizens," and it represented mainly the middle class. Radical revolutionary clubs, most of them formed in 1789, quickly became an important force in the new government. Robespierre led the *Jacobin* clubs, and Georges Jacques Danton, Jean Paul Marat, and Camille Desmoulins were members of the *Cordeliers*. These men dominated one group in the assembly, called *the Mountain,* because their seats were in the highest part of the hall, on the speaker's left. Near them sat another important group, called *the Gironde* because their leaders came from a district of the same name. Members of *the Plain* sat in the low central section of the hall. More conservative members sat on the speaker's right. Many historians believe that the terms *left* and *right* for political parties may have originated in the Legislative Assembly. Gradually, as the Revolution continued, the Jacobins gained more power.

France was plunged into war against Prussia and Austria in April, 1792. The principal task of the Assembly became the management of the war. A national army was formed. At first the enemies of France were successful, and news of defeats in battle drove the Paris mob to frenzy. They believed that the king was plotting

Engraving by Pierre-Philippe Choffard after a drawing by Jean Duplessi-Bertaux; Bibliothèque Nationale, Paris

Rebellions Against the Revolution developed in many French cities. Supporters of the king led an uprising in Lyon in 1793. After the revolutionists put down the revolt, many royalists were massacred, *above*, by forces led by Jean Marie Collot d'Herbois.

Engraving by A. L. d'Argent; Bibliothèque Nationale, Paris

The Royal Family of France Faced an Angry Mob at Versailles in 1789. Revolutionary leaders later tried King Louis XVI and Queen Marie Antoinette for treason. Both were executed in 1793.

with foreign rulers to betray France. In August, 1792, a band of rioters broke into the royal palace (the Tuileries), killed the king's famous Swiss Guards, who had been ordered not to fire, and forced the king to turn to the Legislative Assembly for protection. The Assembly imprisoned him and his family and took all his powers.

More defeats led to the September massacre, during which organized mobs broke into the prisons and killed over 1,000 persons. Order was restored after the French army won a battle at Valmy. The radical party won control of the Assembly. It called for the election of a National Convention to frame a new constitution because the constitutional monarchy of 1791 ended with the removal of the king.

The Convention met on September 20, 1792. It was elected by vote of all male citizens, and had 749 members. Almost its first act was to declare France a republic. The danger of invasion was met by strengthening the army, which continued to win victories. The two groups which had been strongest in the Legislative Assembly, the Gironde and the Mountain, now formed the conservative and radical parties in the Convention. At first the Girondists were in the majority. The two groups began to struggle for power. The radicals, backed by the Paris government, wished to carry the revolution farther than the upper middle class desired.

Louis XVI was placed on trial for betraying his country. Many Girondists wished to spare his life, but he was declared guilty and executed. In April, 1793, the Convention appointed a Committee of Public Safety to watch over France's internal security. The radicals gained power step by step until, in June, 1793, they drove out the Girondist leaders and arrested them.

The Reign of Terror. With the rise to power of the Committee of Safety, the Revolution entered its most terrible stage. The Committee took over actual rule of France. Its leaders included Danton, Robespierre, Lazare Nicolas Marguerite Carnot, and Jean Marie Collot d'Herbois. Hundreds and hundreds of people were sent to the guillotine because they aroused the suspicion of some member of the Committee (see GUILLOTINE). Paris became accustomed to the rattle of two-wheeled carts called *tumbrels* as they carried persons through the streets to the guillotine. Scenes from these terrible times have appeared in many novels and stories. A famous scene from the Reign of Terror climaxes Charles Dickens' *A Tale of Two Cities.*

Commissioners were sent to the provinces, where they worked with the local Jacobin clubs and carried on reigns of terror there. The aristocrats, including Marie Antoinette, Queen of France, were executed first. Then came the moderates, including the Girondists. Finally the radicals began to struggle for power among themselves. Robespierre succeeded in having Danton and other former leaders condemned and executed. Later the people turned on Robespierre, and he, too, met his death by the guillotine. The revolutionists did not carry on the Terror for its own sake, but as a method of political control. France was seriously threatened by enemies both inside and outside the country. Robespierre and the other leaders believed that neither France nor the Revolution was safe as long as these enemies lived. Even Robespierre's death was the result of a political

The Death of Marat spurred on the Reign of Terror. A girl from the provinces, Charlotte Corday, stabbed him while he took a bath. Jacques Louis David painted *The Death of Marat.*

struggle. The men who condemned him wanted to end his power, not to end the Terror.

The End of the Revolution. France was meanwhile winning victories on the battlefield. French armies had not only pushed back the invaders, but were carrying the Revolution to foreign soil. An army officer, Napoleon Bonaparte, was attracting notice as a military genius. A group of moderates gained control of the Convention, and the Revolution ended. The power of the Paris Commune and of the Jacobin clubs was broken. The people of Paris rioted, but the riots were suppressed.

The Convention framed a constitution (1795) which provided for a new government. The legislature was to consist of two chambers, and executive power was given to a board of five directors. The people rebelled against the Convention's provision that two-thirds of the new representatives were to be chosen from among the members of the Convention. But Napoleon fired "a whiff of grape-shot" into the mob, the Convention was dissolved, and the new government took office.

From 1795 to 1799, the revolutionary fervor abated. France's financial affairs were in a bad state, and the country continued to be threatened by enemies abroad and dissatisfied people at home. Some people believed that a stronger central government was needed. Napoleon, who was in Egypt, returned unexpectedly, and made himself dictator of France. WILLIAM F. MCDONALD

Related Articles in WORLD BOOK include:

BIOGRAPHIES

Barras, Vicomte de
Corday, Charlotte

Danton, Georges Jacques
Du Barry, Madame

Lafayette, Marquis de	Necker, Jacques
Louis (XVI)	Orléans (Louis P. J.)
Marat, Jean Paul	Robespierre
Marie Antoinette	Roland de la Platière, M. J.
Mirabeau, Comte de	Sieyès, Emmanuel Joseph
Napoleon I	Talleyrand

Background and Causes

Bastille	Rousseau, Jean J.
Divine Right of Kings	States-General
Rights of Man, Declaration of the	Versailles

The Revolution

Directory	Girondists	Jacobins	Reign of Terror
Émigré	Guillotine	Marseillaise	Sans-Culotte

Other Related Articles

Clothing	Liberty, Equality,	Swiss Guards
(The 1700's)	Fraternity	Tricolor
Liberty Cap	Parlement	Tuileries

See also *French Revolution* in the Research Guide/Index, Volume 22, for a *Reading and Study Guide*.

FRENCH SOMALILAND. See Djibouti (country).

FRENCH SOUTHERN AND ANTARCTIC TERRITORIES are overseas possessions of France. They include the Kerguelen and Crozet *archipelagos* (groups of islands) and Amsterdam and Saint Paul islands, all in the south Indian Ocean. The islands cover about 2,920 square miles (7,563 square kilometers). The territories also include Adélie Coast, an area in Antarctica claimed by France. A High Administrator and Consultative Council, both appointed by the French government, govern the territories.

Kerguelen Island, the largest island, covers about 2,700 square miles (6,993 square kilometers). It is about 2,100 miles (3,380 kilometers) southeast of Madagascar. The Crozet Archipelago lies about 850 miles (1,370 kilometers) west of the Kerguelen group. Both groups are cold, damp, and windy. Penguins, whales, and elephant seals live there. Amsterdam and Saint Paul lie about 800 miles (1,300 kilometers) northeast of the Kerguelen group. They have a milder climate, and lobster and cod are caught in the surrounding waters.

Only scientists live in the territories. They study physical forces within and above the earth, including the weather and animal and plant life. Germaine Caron

FRENCH SUDAN. See Mali.

FRENCH UNION was the organization that linked France with its overseas territories from 1946 to 1958. It consisted of *Metropolitan France*, made up of France, Algeria, and Corsica; *Overseas Departments* such as French Guiana; *Overseas Territories* such as Madagascar; and *Associated Territories*, including Cameroon and the New Hebrides Islands. The president of France governed the union with a council and an assembly. In 1958, under the Fifth Republic, France replaced the union with a new system called the *French Community*. The French Community is a loose economic association, rather than a political organization.

FRENCH WEST AFRICA was a federation of eight territories in western Africa. France administered the territories from 1895 to 1958. Dakar, now the capital of Senegal, was the capital. French West Africa included eight territories that are now independent countries: Dahomey (now Benin), French Guinea (now Guinea), French Sudan (now Mali), Ivory Coast, Mauritania, Niger, Senegal, and Upper Volta. For details on the economy, government, history, land, and people, see the articles on each of these countries in World Book.

The Land. French West Africa spread over 1,789,186 square miles (4,633,970 square kilometers). It covered most of the great African bulge that juts into the Atlantic Ocean. It occupied about one-seventh of the African continent. An area of rolling plains, it has tropical rain forests along the southern coasts, a belt of *savanna* (thick grasslands) across the center, and the barren Sahara in the North.

History. Before Europeans took control of what became French West Africa, the people of the region were divided into many groups. Some of the groups were loose associations of families living in small areas without centralized authority. Others were more elaborate states, with central governments that controlled large populations.

Several great empires bordered the Sahara. The Ghana Empire was strongest during the A.D. 1000's. The Mali Empire reached its height in the 1300's. The Songhai Empire flourished in the 1500's.

The Portuguese were the first Europeans to explore the west African coast. They arrived in the late 1400's. Then came the French, the Dutch, and the English. The English were mainly interested in buying slaves they could sell in the West Indies and America. In 1624, King Louis XIII of France granted a French company a charter to trade in Senegal. The French established St. Louis, now a city in Senegal, as a fortified trading post at the mouth of the Sénégal River in 1658.

Throughout the 1700's, Britain and France fought for control of this area. In 1815, Britain finally recognized French control of St. Louis and Gorée at the tip of Cape Verde peninsula. But France did not seriously extend its control throughout French West Africa until the late 1800's. In 1895, France grouped its colonies in western Africa under the authority of a gov-

WORLD BOOK map

French West Africa, *shown in black, was a federation of eight territories in western Africa until 1958. But now eight separate and independent countries cover this region.*

ernor general. Dakar became the governor general's headquarters in 1902.

France proclaimed a constitution for the Federation of West Africa in 1904. But many areas were far from being completely controlled. Some remained under military authority until after 1945.

French West Africa became a federation of eight overseas territories within the French Union in 1946. France extended citizenship rights to the Africans, but gave only some of them the right to vote. In 1947, France started an economic development program for the federation. In 1956, France gave all Africans in the federation the right to vote.

When France adopted a new constitution in 1958, French Guinea voted to leave the French Union and became an independent country. The other seven territories voted to remain associated with France within the new French Community. But by the end of December 1958, these territories had voted to become autonomous republics.

In 1960, French Sudan and Senegal united to form the Mali Federation. They negotiated with France for full independence, but agreed to remain in the French Community. The Mali Federation broke up in August, 1960, and French Sudan became the Republic of Mali. The other five republics then asked for complete independence. All of them had received their freedom by the end of 1960. The republics all became members of the United Nations.   IMMANUEL WALLERSTEIN

Related Articles in WORLD BOOK include:

Arab	Cape Verde	Mali	Niger River
Benin	Guinea	Mauritania	Senegal
Berbers	Ivory Coast	Niger	Upper Volta

FRENCH WEST INDIES consists of several small islands at the eastern end of the Caribbean Sea (see WEST INDIES [map]). They are part of the island chain, the Lesser Antilles. The islands cover about 1,112 square miles (2,880 square kilometers) and have a population of about 754,000. The French West Indies makes up two overseas departments of the French Republic. These two departments are named Guadeloupe and Martinique, after the two major islands of the French West Indies (see GUADELOUPE; MARTINIQUE).

FRENCHTOWN. See WAR OF 1812 (Raisin River).

FRENEAU, *free NO*, **PHILIP** (1752-1832), was an early American poet and journalist. His admirers called him the "Poet of the American Revolution." Freneau wrote articles in favor of Jeffersonian democracy. He opposed first the British monarchy and later American conservative statesmen. In poems like "The Indian Burying Ground," he helped people discover the beauties of America's wilderness and the pathos of the vanishing Indian. He was born in New York City. See also AMERICAN LITERATURE (Patriotism and Wit).   PETER VIERECK

FRENULUM. See MOTH (Thorax; picture).

FREON. See FLUOROCARBON.

FREQUENCY. See ELECTRIC GENERATOR (A Simple Generator); SOUND (Characteristics); WAVE BAND.

FREQUENCY MODULATION, usually called simply FM, is a method of sending sound signals on radio waves. Frequency modulation and *amplitude modulation* (AM) are the two chief means of transmitting music and speech.

A radio wave has a fixed *frequency*, the number of times the wave vibrates per second. It also has a definite *amplitude* (size). In frequency modulation, the frequency of the transmitting radio wave is made higher or lower to correspond with the vibrations of the sound to be sent. But the amplitude of the wave is not varied. In contrast, amplitude modulation keeps the frequency of the transmitting wave constant. But it changes the wave's amplitude in accordance with the vibrations of the sound signal being transmitted.

FM has some advantages over AM. It is relatively free of static from thunderstorms and of other types of interference that affect AM broadcasts. FM also provides a more faithful reproduction of music and speech.

One of the main uses of frequency modulation is FM radio broadcasting. The transmission of stereophonic programs ranks as an important development in this area. In FM stereo broadcasting, sound signals from two microphones or from both *channels* (transmission paths) of a stereo record are sent on the same radio wave. Transmitting a program by this method is called *multiplexing*. For the best results, a listener needs a special receiver that can "decode" the sounds from the two channels and send them through two separate speakers.

A commercial FM station can transmit special programs of uninterrupted music in addition to its regular or stereo broadcasts. Such programs provide pleasant background music for offices, restaurants, and stores.

Frequency modulation also has other uses. For example, television stations transmit the audio portion of their programs by this method. Telephone companies also use frequency modulation in *microwave radio relaying*, a system designed to send long-distance phone calls.

Edwin H. Armstrong, an American electrical engineer, invented frequency modulation in 1933. FM became widely used in the 1940's.   RICHARD W. HENRY

See also RADIO (How Radio Works); HIGH FIDELITY.

FRESCO, *FRES koh*, is a painting made with water colors on fresh plaster. *Fresco* is the Italian word for *fresh*. To make a fresco, the artist usually first makes a drawing, called a *cartoon*, in the exact size of the proposed picture. A smaller sketch in colors is also made. Then fresh plaster—as much as can be painted in a day—is laid on the surface to be decorated. On this, the artist places the cartoon and traces the outlines. The artist is then ready to paint. The work must proceed rapidly because the plaster cannot be painted over once it is dry. Any unpainted plaster left at the end of the day is cut away. The lime of the plaster penetrates the paint and acts as a binder. Fresco colors are clear and pure, but lack depth.

Fresco painting reached its height in Italy during the Renaissance. Among the most celebrated frescoes of that period are the decorations of the Sistine Chapel in the Vatican, by Michelangelo. *The Creation of Adam*, a fresco on a ceiling panel in the Sistine Chapel, appears in color in the PAINTING article. Raphael painted other Vatican frescoes. The frescoes in the Church of San Marco in Florence, by Fra Angelico, and those of Luini (1475?-1532?) in Saronno and Milan are also famous. A German artist, Peter von Cornelius, revived interest in fresco painting during the 1800's. Two Mexican artists, Diego Rivera and José Clemente Orozco, inspired a revival of frescoes in the United States. Rivera's *Agrarian Leader Zapata* and a detail of one of

This Spanish Fresco was painted about 1220 on a wall of the chapter house of the monastery of San Pedro de Arlanza in northwestern Spain.

Orozco's frescoes, *An Epic of American Civilization*, appear in color in the PAINTING article.   THOMAS MUNRO

Related Articles in WORLD BOOK include:

Cartoon	Mural
Fra Angelico	Orozco, José Clemente
Ghirlandajo, Domenico	Painting (Fresco Painting)
Giotto	Raphael
Martini, Simone	Rivera, Diego
Michelangelo	

FRESNO (pop. 165,972; met. area pop. 413,329) is the main marketing and distribution center of central California. The city is often called the raisin-growing capital of the world. It lies in Fresno County, in the middle of the fertile San Joaquin Valley. For the location of Fresno, see CALIFORNIA (political map).

Irrigation from the nearby Kings and San Joaquin rivers helped make Fresno County the nation's leading farm county. Farmers there grow more than 200 crops. The largest fig orchards in the United States flourish near Fresno, and 60 per cent of the nation's raisins are grown there.

Fresno's chief industry is the packing, processing, canning, and shipping of fruit. Factories in the city manufacture such products as chemicals, farm machinery, plastics, and soap. Fresno is the home of the Fresno Opera Association and the Fresno Philharmonic Orchestra. Universities in the city include California State University, Fresno; Fresno Pacific College; and Mennonite Brethren Biblical Seminary.

Yokut Indians lived in what is now the Fresno area when investors began buying land there in the 1860's. No one really knows how the area got the name *Fresno*, which is the Spanish word for *ash tree*. Mexican ranchers may have named Fresno after the white ash trees that grew there.

Leland Stanford, a builder of the Central Pacific Railroad, realized that the area had ideal farmland. In 1872, the railroad built the town of Fresno Station. Several irrigation canals were built during the 1870's and 1880's, and the town became a farming center. Fresno was incorporated as a city in 1885. In 1889, George Roeding, a botanist, demonstrated that Smyrna fig trees in the Fresno area would bear fruit. His discovery led to the founding of a great industry.

In the mid-1900's, the growth of industry related to farming helped create a population boom in Fresno. The city's population jumped from 60,685 in 1940 to 165,972 in 1970. Urban renewal in downtown Fresno led to the opening of a shopping mall in 1965 and the Fresno Community and Convention Center in 1966. Fresno is the county seat of Fresno County and has a council-manager form of government.   SCOTT E. TOMPKINS

FRET. See GUITAR.

FREUD, *froyd,* **ANNA** (1895-   ), is an Austrian-born leader in the field of child psychoanalysis, the treatment of children's mental illnesses. Her work has been influenced by the psychoanalytic theories of her father, the famous Austrian physician Sigmund Freud (see FREUD, SIGMUND).

Anna Freud believes children go through various normal stages of psychological development. She maintains that psychoanalysts must have knowledge of these stages to diagnose and treat mental illness in children. According to her, such knowledge can be obtained only through research involving the direct observation of children.

FREUD, SIGMUND

Freud was born in Vienna. She has conducted most of her research at the Hampstead Child Therapy Course and Clinic, which she established in London in 1938. The clinic's activities include the treatment of mentally ill children, helping handicapped youngsters, and training workers in child therapy.   GEORGE H. POLLOCK

FREUD, *froyd,* **SIGMUND** (1856-1939), was an Austrian physician who revolutionized ideas on how the human mind works. Freud established the theory that unconscious motives control much behavior. He thus greatly advanced the field of psychiatry. His work has helped millions of mentally ill patients. His theories have brought new approaches in child rearing, education, and sociology and have provided new themes for many authors and artists. Most people in Western society view human behavior at least partially in Freudian terms.

His Life

Freud was born on May 6, 1856, in Freiberg, Moravia, a region that is now part of Czechoslovakia. He was the oldest of eight children, and his father was a wool merchant. When Freud was 4 years old, his family moved to Vienna, the capital of Austria. He graduated from the medical school of the University of Vienna in 1881. Freud later decided to specialize in *neurology,* the treatment of disorders of the nervous system.

In 1885, Freud went to Paris to study under Jean-Martin Charcot, a famous neurologist. Charcot was working with patients who suffered from a mental illness now called *hysteria.* Some of these people appeared to be blind or paralyzed, but they actually had no physical defects. Charcot demonstrated that their real problem was mental, and that the physical symptoms could be relieved through hypnosis.

Freud returned to Vienna in 1886 and began to work extensively with hysterical patients. He gradually formed ideas about the origin and treatment of mental illness. Freud used the term *psychoanalysis* for both his theories and his method of treatment. When he first presented his ideas in the 1890's, other physicians reacted with hostility. But Freud eventually attracted a group of followers, and by 1910, he had gained international recognition.

During the following decade, Freud's reputation continued to grow. But two of his early followers, Alfred Adler and Carl Jung, split with Freud and developed their own theories of psychology (see ADLER, ALFRED; JUNG, CARL). Freud was constantly modifying his own ideas, and in 1923, he published a revised version of many of his earlier theories. That same year, he learned he had cancer of the mouth. He continued his work, though the cancer made working increasingly difficult. In 1938, the Nazis gained control of Austria. Under their rule, Jews were persecuted. Freud, who was

Dr. W. Hoffer
Sigmund Freud

Jewish, went to England with his wife and children to escape persecution. He died there of cancer in 1939.

Freud wrote many works. However, his most important writings include *The Interpretation of Dreams* (1900), *Three Essays on the Theory of Sexuality* (1905), *Totem and Taboo* (1913), *General Introduction to Psychoanalysis* (1920), *The Ego and the Id* (1923), and *Civilization and Its Discontents* (1930).

His Theories

On Behavior. Freud observed that many patients behaved according to drives and experiences of which they were not consciously aware. He thus concluded that the unconscious plays a major role in shaping behavior. He also concluded that the unconscious is full of memories of events from early childhood—sometimes as far back as infancy. Freud noted that if these memories were especially painful, people kept them out of conscious awareness. He used the term *defense mechanisms* for the methods by which individuals did this. Freud believed that patients used vast amounts of energy in forming defense mechanisms. Tying up energy in defense mechanisms could affect a person's ability to lead a productive life, causing an illness that Freud called *neurosis.*

Freud also concluded that many childhood memories dealt with sex. He theorized that sexual functioning begins at birth, and that a person passes through several psychological stages of sexual development. During this passage from infant sexuality to adult sexuality, an individual makes many self-discoveries and learns to control his or her sexual impulses. Freud believed that the normal pattern of sexual development is interrupted in some individuals. These people become *fixated* at an earlier, immature stage. He felt that such fixation could contribute to mental illness in adulthood.

On the Mind. Freud divided the mind into three parts: (1) the *id,* (2) the *ego,* and (3) the *superego.* He recognized that each person is born with various instincts, such as the drive to satisfy hunger and the drive to satisfy sexual needs. The id is the mental representation of these biological instincts. It does not distinguish between the internal mind and the outside environment. For example, the id stimulates the eating drives, but it makes no distinction between a mental image of food and the food itself.

The ego distinguishes between the internal mind and external reality. It controls behavior that bridges the gap between mental images and the outside world. For example, the ego directs a hungry person to look for and to eat real food.

The superego governs moral behavior. It is the mental representation of society's moral code. The superego seeks to limit behavior based on the drives of the id.

In mentally healthy individuals, the three parts of the mind work in harmony. But in others, the parts may conflict. For example, the superego might oppose all sexual behavior, thus preventing fulfillment of the id's sexual drives. If the parts of the mind oppose one another, psychological disturbance can result.

On Treatment. At first, Freud treated neurotic patients by using the hypnotic techniques he had learned from Charcot. But he modified this approach several years later and simply had patients talk about whatever was on their minds. He called this technique *free*

association. By free associating—that is, by speaking freely—the patient sometimes came upon earlier experiences that contributed to the neurosis.

Often, however, the painful memories that caused the neurosis were held in the unconscious through defense mechanisms. Freud then analyzed the random thoughts that had been expressed during free association. He did this in an effort to penetrate the patient's defense mechanisms. He also interpreted the patient's dreams, which he believed were symbolic clues to unconscious memories. After he felt he understood the root of the problem, Freud talked with the patient about the person's earlier experiences. He paid particular attention to the painful feelings—hostility or love, for example—that the patient directed at Freud himself. Through this *transference* of past feelings to the present, the patient could be relieved of the painful memories. The symptoms of the neurosis might then disappear.

His Influence

Freud ranks as one of the most influential thinkers in history. His research and writings changed the way many people thought about human nature. The strongest impact of Freud's theories occurred in psychiatry and psychology. Some psychiatrists and psychologists disagree with certain of his ideas. However, Freud's work on the origin and treatment of mental illness helped form the basis of modern psychiatry. In psychology, Freud especially influenced the field of abnormal psychology and the study of the personality.

Freud's theories on sexual development led to open discussion and treatment of sexual matters and problems. His stress on the importance of childhood helped teach the value of giving children an emotionally nourishing environment. Freud's insights also influenced the fields of anthropology and sociology. Most social scientists accept his concept that an adult's social relationships are patterned after the individual's early family relationships.

Attitudes toward antisocial behavior have also been influenced by Freud. Many parents and teachers believe that behavior problems can be caused by a child's emotional conflicts. Similarly, many criminologists are convinced that large numbers of people commit crimes because of unconscious drives. Many such people can be helped more effectively by psychiatric care than by a prison sentence.

In art and literature, Freud's theories encouraged understanding of *surrealism* (see SURREALISM). Like psychoanalysis, surrealistic painting and writing explores the inner depths of the unconscious mind. Freudian concepts have provided subject matter for many authors and artists, and critics frequently analyze art and literature in Freudian terms.   GEORGE H. POLLOCK

See also DREAM; LIBIDO; OEDIPUS COMPLEX; PSYCHOANALYSIS; SUBCONSCIOUS.

FREUDIAN THEORY. See PSYCHOANALYSIS.

FREY, *fray,* or FREYR, *frayr,* was the Norse god who promoted fertility in crops and animals. Like his father Njord and his sister Freyja (see FREYJA), he was one of the Vanir, all of whom were associated with fertility. Frey had power over rain and sunshine. The Norse people prayed to him for good crops and peace.

Frey was said to possess many fine gifts made for him by the dwarfs. One was a magic sword that fought by itself. Another was a ship that could sail on land and sea, and was large enough to carry all the gods, but could also be folded up to fit in his pocket. Frey rode on a boar with golden bristles, high above the earth. Once he fell in love with Gerd, a giant's daughter. A poem in the *Edda* tells the story of his courtship. He gave away his sword to win her.   EINAR HAUGEN

See also EDDA; MYTHOLOGY (Teutonic).

FREYJA, *FRAY ah,* was the goddess of love and beauty in Norse mythology. She was the sister of Frey (see FREY). Men were advised to call upon her for help in affairs of the heart, and they were told that songs of love were pleasing to her. She rode to battle with Odin, and claimed half the men who were killed. A pair of cats pulled her chariot.

Freyja married a god named Oder. He deserted her and went to other lands. She often wept over the loss of him, and her tears were drops of gold. The worship of Freyja was common in Scandinavia, but it was not known elsewhere. She partially replaced Frigg, who was the love goddess in England and Germany.   EINAR HAUGEN

See also FRIGG; MYTHOLOGY (Teutonic).

FRIANT DAM is an irrigation dam on the upper San Joaquin River east of Fresno, Calif. The dam is part of the Central Valley Project, which provides irrigation, flood control, and electric power. Friant Dam is a concrete, gravity-type structure, 319 feet (97 meters) high and 3,488 feet (1,063 meters) long. Its reservoir holds 520,500 acre-feet (642,030,000 cubic meters) of water. It was completed in 1942 by the United States Bureau of Reclamation. See also CENTRAL VALLEY PROJECT; DAM (Masonry Dams).   T. W. MERMEL

FRIAR is a general name applied to members of religious orders of men who originally lived only as *mendicants* (beggars). They had no possessions or fixed place to live. The older term *monk* differs from *friar,* in that monks live permanently with one local group or monastery, and aim at withdrawal from the world. The friar strives to be free of worldly goods so that he may engage more efficiently in preaching, missionary work, or other charitable undertakings.

The four chief mendicant orders are the Dominicans, the Franciscans, the Carmelites, and the Augustinians, or Austins. The term *friar* comes from the Latin word for *brother.* The founders were men of humble spirit, who called their followers by the simple title of *brother.* Saint Francis, the founder of the Franciscans, called his followers *friars minor* (lesser brothers). The founder of the Dominicans, Saint Dominic, termed his order the *preaching friars.* In England, the friars were popularly named after the colors of their *habits* (robes). Thus the Franciscans were called the *gray friars,* the Dominicans, *black friars,* and the Carmelites, *white friars.* These terms are still used in the names of English streets and localities.   FULTON J. SHEEN

See also CAPUCHINS; CARMELITES; DOMINICANS; FRANCISCANS; MONK.

FRIARS MINOR. See FRANCISCANS.

FRICK, FORD (1894-1978), was national commissioner of baseball from 1951 to 1965. While he was commissioner, four teams were added to the major leagues. Ford Christopher Frick was born in Wawaka, Ind., and was graduated from DePauw University. He worked on newspapers in Colorado Springs and Denver, Colo., and in New York City. He made radio sports broadcasts from 1930 until 1934, when he became president of the National Baseball League. Frick helped popularize night baseball. He was named to the National Baseball Hall of Fame in 1970. ED FITZGERALD

FRICK, HENRY CLAY (1849-1919), was an American industrialist. He controlled much of the coke production in the Pittsburgh area, and arranged a very favorable union with the Carnegie Steel Company. He served as chairman of the company from 1889 to 1900. He was influential in the merger in 1901 that formed the United States Steel Corporation, of which he later became a director. Frick was born in West Overton, Pa. He left his home and a fine art collection to New York City as a museum. Frick also gave generously to Princeton University, and left a park of 150 acres (61 hectares) to the city of Pittsburgh. JOHN B. McFERRIN

FRICTION, *FRICK shun,* is the property that objects have which makes them resist being moved across one another. If two objects with flat surfaces are placed one on top of the other, the top object can be lifted without any resistance except that of gravity. But if one object is pushed or pulled along the surface of the other, there is a resistance caused by friction.

Friction has many important uses. It makes the wheels of a locomotive grip the rails of the track. It allows a conveyor belt to turn on pulleys without slipping. You could not walk without friction to keep your shoes from sliding on the sidewalk. This is why it is hard to walk on ice. The smooth surface of the ice produces less friction than a sidewalk, and allows shoes to slip.

Friction also has disadvantages. It produces heat that may cause objects to wear. This is why oil and other lubricating liquids are used to fill spaces between moving machinery parts. The liquid reduces friction and makes the parts move more easily and produce less heat.

Kinds of Friction. There are three chief kinds of friction. *Sliding* or *kinetic* friction is produced when two surfaces slide across each other, as when a book moves across a table. *Rolling friction* is the resistance produced when a rolling body moves over a surface. The friction between an automobile tire and a street is rolling friction. *Fluid friction* or *viscosity* is the friction between moving fluids or between fluids and a solid. Thinner fluids have less viscosity than thicker fluids, and usually flow faster. See VISCOSITY.

Laws of Friction. The basic law of friction says that the force needed to overcome friction is proportional to the total *normal,* or perpendicular, force pressing one surface against the other. That is, when the weight of a box being pulled across a floor is doubled, the force necessary to pull it must be doubled. When the box weighs four times as much, four times as much force must be used to pull it. The ratio between the weight being moved and the force pressing the surfaces together is called the *coefficient of friction (C.F.).* The value of *C.F.* depends on the type of surfaces moving against each other. The coefficient of friction equals the force needed to move an object divided by the force pressing the surfaces together. This can be written $C.F. = \dfrac{F}{P}.$

For example, suppose a force of 30 pounds (*F*) is needed to pull a block weighing 80 pounds (*P*) across a flat surface. The coefficient of friction (*C.F.*) equals 30 divided by 80, or 0.375. In a similar example using the metric system, the force would be measured in units called *newtons.* Suppose a force of 45 newtons is needed to slide a block weighing 12.2 kilograms. The block presses down with a force of 120 newtons. This is because gravity at the earth's surface pulls with a force of 9.8 newtons for every kilogram an object weighs, and 9.8 times 12.2 equals 120. The coefficient of friction equals 45 divided by 120, or 0.375.

The coefficient of friction varies with the different materials used. The *C.F.* of wood sliding on wood is between 0.25 and 0.50. Metal sliding on metal has a *C.F.* between 0.15 and 0.20. The frictional force due to rolling friction is about $\frac{1}{100}$ as much as that due to sliding friction. But various conditions, including hardness, smoothness, and diameter of the materials, affect rolling friction. To design machines, engineers must know the various coefficients of friction.

Oil reduces friction. The *C.F.* for iron rolled on oiled wood, for example, would be much less than .018. The kind of surface has almost no effect when it is covered with oil or other liquids. The friction then depends on the viscosity of the liquid and the relative speed between the moving surfaces. S. Y. LEE

See also BEARING; FIRE (How Fire Is Produced); HEAT (Friction).

FRIDAY is the sixth day of the week. The name comes from the Anglo-Saxon word *Frigedaeg,* which means *Frigg's day.* Frigg was a goddess of love in Norse mythology (see FRIGG). The Scandinavians considered Friday their luckiest day. But people today associate Friday the 13th with bad luck. One of the many explanations for this belief is that Christ was crucified on Friday, and 13 men were present at the Last Supper. People have called Friday *hangman's day* because it once was the day for the execution of criminals. In memory of the crucifixion, some Christians fast on Fridays, except on a feast day, such as Christmas. Christians observe *Good Friday* two days before Easter in memory of Christ's suffering. The Jewish Sabbath begins at sunset on Friday. Friday is also a holy day among Muslims. Muslims also celebrate the creation of Adam on Friday. GRACE HUMPHREY

See also BLACK FRIDAY; GOOD FRIDAY; WEEK.

Lars Hedman   Exxon Corporation

Kinds of Friction include sliding friction, *above left,* and rolling friction, *above right.*

FRIEDAN, BETTY (1921-   ), is considered the founder of the women's liberation movement in the United States. She first gained fame from her book *The Feminine Mystique* (1963). In this book, she protested that society puts pressure on women to be housewives only and not to seek a career.

In 1966, Friedan helped found the National Organization for Women (NOW) to fight for equal rights for women. She led a nationwide protest called the Women's Strike for Equality on Aug. 26, 1970. That date marked the 50th anniversary of the granting of the vote to U.S. women. In 1971, Friedan helped form the National Women's Political Caucus, which encourages women to seek political office. Betty Naomi Goldstein Friedan was born in Peoria, Ill., and graduated from Smith College in 1942.   CYNTHIA FUCHS EPSTEIN

Jack Lenahan, *Chicago Sun-Times*
Betty Friedan

See also NATIONAL ORGANIZATION FOR WOMEN.

FRIEDLAND, BATTLE OF. See NAPOLEON I.

FRIEDMAN, MILTON (1912-   ), is an American economist whose controversial theories sparked widespread debate. He was awarded the 1976 Nobel prize in economics.

Friedman argued against government intervention in the economy, claiming that the forces of a free market will efficiently solve most economic problems. He rejected the theories of John Maynard Keynes and his followers. Keynesian economists call for short-term changes in government spending to control the economy. Instead, Friedman urged a gradual, continuous increase in the money supply to promote economic growth. He set forth these theories in his book *A Monetary History of the United States, 1867-1960* (1963). In *Capitalism and Freedom* (1962), Friedman proposed a *negative income tax*. Under this plan, families with incomes below a certain level would get cash payments from the government.

Friedman was born in New York City and received a Ph.D. degree from Columbia University. He taught economics at the University of Chicago from 1946 to 1977. He then moved to Stanford University's Hoover Institution on War, Revolution, and Peace.   LEONARD S. SILK

FRIENDLY ISLANDS. See TONGA.

FRIENDS, SOCIETY OF, or RELIGIOUS SOCIETY OF FRIENDS, is another name for the Quakers, a Christian religious denomination. For information about the Quakers' history and worship, see QUAKERS.

FRIENDS UNIVERSITY is a private, coeducational, liberal arts school in Wichita, Kans. It is affiliated with the Society of Friends (Quakers). Friends University grants A.B., B.Sc., and B.Mus. degrees. It was founded in 1898. For enrollment, see UNIVERSITIES AND COLLEGES (table).   ROY F. RAY

FRIENDSHIP 7. See GLENN, JOHN HERSCHEL, JR.; SPACE TRAVEL (table: Manned Space Flights).

FRIETCHIE, *FREECH ee*, **BARBARA,** is the heroine of John Greenleaf Whittier's poem "Barbara Frietchie" (1864). The poem describes a supposed incident during the Civil War when the Confederate general "Stonewall" Jackson and his troops marched through Frederick, Md. Ninety-year-old Barbara Frietchie was the only resident of the town who risked the anger of the Confederate troops by flying a Union flag. Jackson saw the flag and ordered it shot down. But she grasped the flag as it fell, and waving it defiantly:

> "Shoot, if you must, this old gray head,
> But spare your country's flag," she said.

Jackson was moved by the old woman's bravery and permitted her to fly the flag as the troops marched through town. No one knows for sure whether the incident actually occurred, but a woman named Barbara Fritchie (1766-1862), also spelled Frietchie, actually lived in Frederick. A reproduction of her home stands on the supposed site of the incident (see MARYLAND [Places to Visit; picture]).   B. A. BOTKIN

FRIEZE. See ARCHITECTURE (Architectural Terms [Entablature]).

FRIGATE is a warship used chiefly to escort amphibious and merchant ships. Frigates are used for patrol duty as well. These ships can launch rockets and torpedoes against submarines. Frigates have radar and sonar to detect enemy aircraft, surface ships, and submarines.

Most frigates of the United States Navy belong to the *Knox* class. These ships are used mostly for antisubmarine warfare. They measure 438 feet (131 meters) long, and steam turbines propel them at speeds of more than 27 knots (nautical miles per hour). In addition to their antisubmarine weapons, these frigates have a

WORLD BOOK illustration by George Suyeoka

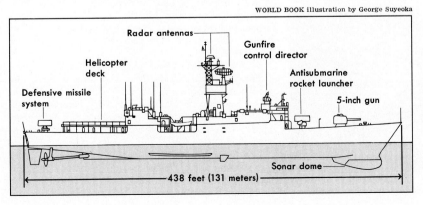

Radar antennas

Helicopter deck

Gunfire control director

Antisubmarine rocket launcher

Defensive missile system

5-inch gun

Sonar dome

438 feet (131 meters)

Frigates serve as patrol ships and as escorts for amphibious and merchant ships. Those of the *Knox* class, such as the frigate shown at the left, are used largely for antisubmarine warfare.

FRIGATE BIRD

5-inch (127-millimeter) gun and short range missiles for use against enemy planes. Each *Knox* class frigate also carries a helicopter.

Frigates of the *Oliver Hazard Perry* class, launched in 1976, can fire missiles against ships and aircraft. They also carry a 3-inch (76-millimeter) gun, torpedoes, and a helicopter. These frigates measure 445 feet (133½ meters) long, and gas turbines propel them at about 28 knots.

In 1794, frigates became the first warships authorized by the United States Congress. The frigate *Constitution*, nicknamed *Old Ironsides*, ranks as one of the nation's most famous ships. It is docked on the Charles River near Boston (see CONSTITUTION [ship]).

During World War II (1939-1945), the U.S. Navy had a class of escort ships called frigates. After the war, the Navy used the term *frigate* for large destroyer-type ships. In 1975, the Navy reclassified most of these ships as cruisers. NORMAN POLMAR

See also CRUISER; NAVY, UNITED STATES (picture: Combat Ships of the Navy).

FRIGATE BIRD is a sea bird with a large wingspread and unusually great powers of flight. People sometimes speak of it as the most graceful bird of the seas. It is a relative of the pelican, and is also called *man-of-war bird*.

Frigate birds live in the tropics throughout the world. They are about 40 inches (100 centimeters) long, but their wings spread to about 8 feet (2.4 meters). Black feathers with a metallic sheen cover the upper part of their bodies. The females, or both sexes of some species, have white feathers on the underside. The young birds have white heads. In nesting season, the male grows a bright scarlet pouch under its bill. It can blow up this pouch like a balloon.

Frigate birds breed in colonies and build their nests on rocks, high cliffs, or trees on uninhabited islands. They eat fish, which they catch from the surface of the sea or steal from other birds.

Scientific Classification. Frigate birds form the frigate bird family, *Fregatidae*. The frigate bird of the coast of southeastern United States is genus *Fregata*, species *F. magnificens*. Those of the Pacific and Indian oceans are *F. minor* and *F. ariel*. ALEXANDER WETMORE

FRIGG, or FRIGGA, was a goddess in Norse mythology. She was the wife of Odin (see ODIN) and the mother of Balder. She knew all things and was originally a divinity of love and fertility, like the younger Freyja (see

The Long-billed Frigate Bird Lives in the Tropics.

FREYJA). People worshiped her in Germany and England as well as in Scandinavia. It is her name we have in Friday, corresponding to the Latin words *veneris dies*, "Venus' day." EINAR HAUGEN

FRIGID ZONE. See ZONE.

FRIJOLES. See MEXICO (Food).

FRIML, *FRIM'l,* **RUDOLF** (1879-1972), composed such highly successful operettas as *The Firefly, Rose Marie*, and *The Vagabond King*. He wrote much light, pleasing music. His popular "Donkey Serenade" was included in the motion-picture version of *The Firefly* in 1937. Friml was born in Prague, then a part of Austria. He studied piano and composition at the Prague Conservatory, and came to the United States in 1901 as accompanist for violinist Jan Kubelik. He remained in this country after a second tour in 1906, appearing as a concert pianist. GILBERT CHASE

FRINGE BENEFITS. See LABOR MOVEMENT (Arranging Labor Contracts).

FRINGE TREE is a small tree or large shrub named for its threadlike or fringelike white flower petals. It is also called *old man's beard*. The fringe tree grows up to 35 feet (11 meters) high. Its delicate flowers bloom in early spring. Fringe trees grow wild in the United States from New Jersey and southern Pennsylvania,

N.Y. Botanical Gardens
The Fragrant Fringe Tree Flowers Have Four Petals.

south to Florida and west to southern Missouri. They thrive on rich, well-drained soil along the banks of rivers and streams. Gardeners plant fringe trees as ornamentals as far north as southern New England. Fringe trees have hard, heavy, pale-brown wood. The bark contains substances that can be used as medicines. A smaller kind of fringe tree grows wild in China.

Scientific Classification. The fringe tree belongs to the olive family, *Oleaceae*. The common fringe tree is genus *Chionanthus*, species *C. virginica*. T. EWALD MAKI

FRINGING REEF. See CORAL (Coral Reefs).

FRISCH, KARL VON (1886-), an Austrian zoologist, was a pioneer in the field of animal behavior. Frisch and two naturalists—Konrad Lorenz of Austria and Nikolaas Tinbergen, who was born in The Netherlands—won the 1973 Nobel prize for physiology or medicine.

Frisch's best-known work dealt with the communication system of bees. He discovered that bees "dance" in certain patterns to tell members of their hive where to find food. These patterns can indicate the distance and

J. Horace McFarland

Fritillary Flowers Have Six Sword-Shaped Petals.

direction of food from the hive (see BEE [The Workers; diagram: A Field Worker]). Frisch also showed that fish can see colors. Scientists had previously thought fish were color-blind.

Frisch was born in Vienna. He studied at the Universities of Munich and Vienna and received a Ph.D. degree from the latter institution in 1910. From 1910 to 1958, he taught at several European universities. Frisch wrote many books, including *Bees: Their Vision, Chemical Senses, and Language* (1971) and *A Biologist Remembers* (1967), an autobiography.   JOHN A. WIENS

FRISCH, MAX (1911-   ), a Swiss author, became one of the leading writers in the German-speaking world after World War II. His novels and plays concern the problem of identity and the question of how man can find his true self. According to Frisch, the images imposed on us by others, and the images we in turn impose on others, falsify and destroy the authenticity of human personality and individual existence. In his novels *I Am Not Stiller* (1954), *Homo Faber* (1957), and *Wilderness of Mirrors* (1964), Frisch shows the shallowness of man's view of others and his inability to understand his own identity. Frisch's plays, notably *Don Juan and the Love for Geometry* (1953), *The Firebugs* (1957-1958), and *Andorra* (1961), deal with the same themes. Frisch was born in Zurich.   PETER GONTRUM

FRISCH, RAGNAR (1895-1973), a Norwegian economist, shared the 1969 Nobel prize in economics with Jan Tinbergen of The Netherlands. The two men received the award for their work on the development of mathematical models used in *econometrics* (mathematical analysis of economic activity). The Nobel prize in economics was awarded for the first time in 1969.

Frisch was born in Oslo and graduated from Oslo University. He served as a professor in social economy and statistics at the university from 1931 until his retirement in 1965. Frisch led a number of theoretical investigations concerning production, economic planning, and national accounting. He helped establish the Econometric Society in 1930 and was chief editor of its journal, *Econometrica*, until 1955. Frisch also served as an adviser to various underdeveloped countries, including Egypt and India.   LEONARD S. SILK

FRISIAN ISLANDS, *FRIZH un*, are a group of islands near the coasts of Denmark, The Netherlands, and West Germany. For location, see GERMANY (map); NETHER-

LANDS (map). The islands are protected by embankments because of the danger of sea floods. The sea wears away land from some islands and deposits it on others. The islanders live by fishing, growing potatoes, and tending sheep and cattle.   BENJAMIN HUNNINGHER

FRITILLARY, *FRIT uh LER ih,* is the common name for a *genus* (group) of herbs that belong to the lily family. This group is made up of nearly a hundred different species of plants that grow throughout the North Temperate Zone. Fritillaries have nodding, bell-shaped flowers. All fritillaries bloom in the spring. Most fritillaries are hardy plants, and grow well in good garden soil. Popular kinds of fritillaries include the *crown imperial* and the *checkered lily,* or *snakes-head.* The crown imperial has brick or yellow-red flowers. The checkered lily has checkered or veined purple-colored flowers.

Scientific Classification. The fritillary belongs to the lily family, *Liliaceae.* The crown imperial fritillary is genus *Fritillaria,* species *F. imperialis.* The checkered lily is *F. meleagris.*   THEODOR JUST

FRITZ, JOHN. See IRON AND STEEL (Famous Men).

FROBISHER, *FRO bish er,* **SIR MARTIN** (1535?-1594), was one of the first English navigators to search for a Northwest Passage to India and the East. He became known as one of the greatest seamen of the reign of Queen Elizabeth I. He fought against the Spanish Armada, and was knighted for his services.

His three attempts to reach Asia by sailing west extended geographic knowledge. On the first voyage in 1576, he rounded the southern end of Greenland, visited Labrador, and became the first European to sail into the bay on Baffin Island. This bay now bears his name. Frobisher took back to England rock that some persons thought was gold ore. This touched off a scramble to join in his second voyage in 1577. Frobisher annexed the country to England on this trip, and returned with 200 short tons (180 metric tons) of rock. On his third voyage, in 1578, he sailed with 15 ships and 41 miners. He entered what later became Hudson Strait, but made no further attempts at discovery. This time he brought back some 1,300 short tons (1,180 metric tons) of the rock. But it proved valueless, and interest in the Northwest Passage declined. Frobisher was born in Altofts, Yorkshire.   JAMES G. ALLEN

FROEBEL, *FRU bul,* or **FRÖBEL, FRIEDRICH** (1782-1852), a German educator, founded the kindergarten system of educating very young children (see KINDERGARTEN). He started a *kindergarten,* or *children's garden,* in 1837. Others had established such schools earlier, but he was the first to name it a kindergarten.

He believed that a child should develop impulses that come from within. He felt that a teacher or parent should cooperate with nature, and guide the functions of the child as these impulses develop. Children learn by doing things, he reasoned, and their play could be organized to teach as well as to amuse. His ideas influenced teachers to favor tasks (selected by the pupils) that help them learn how to live and work with each other. He wrote *The Education of Man, Education by Development,* and *Mother Play and Nursery Songs.*

Froebel was born in Oberweissbach in Thuringia. He founded the Universal German Educational Institute in Griesheim in 1816.   CLAUDE A. EGGERTSEN

E. R. Degginger

Harold Hungerford

Frogs vary greatly in color and size. The spotted, brownish-green leopard frog, *above*, measures from 2 to 3½ inches (5 to 9 centimeters) long. The colorful arrow poison frog, *top right*, grows from 1 to 2 inches (2.5 to 5 centimeters) long. The green tree frog, *bottom right*, is less than 2 inches long.

Alvin E. Staffan

FROG

FROG is a small, tailless animal with bulging eyes. Almost all frogs also have long back legs. The strong hind legs enable a frog to leap distances far greater than the length of its body. Frogs live on every continent except Antarctica. But tropical regions have the greatest number of species. Frogs belong to a class of animals called *amphibians*. Most amphibians, including most frogs, spend part of their life as a water animal and part as a land animal.

Frogs are related to toads but differ from them in several ways. The section *Kinds of Frogs* describes the basic differences between frogs and toads.

The first frogs appeared on earth about 180 million years ago. More than 2,000 species of frogs and toads have developed from these early ancestors. Some species spend their entire life in or near water. Others live mainly on land and come to the water only to mate. Still other species never enter the water, not even to mate. Many kinds are climbers that dwell in trees. Others are burrowers that live underground.

Throughout history, frogs have been the source of superstitions. One old myth says that frogs fall from the sky during a rain. Actually, many species that live underground leave their burrows during or after a rain at the start of the mating season. Because people seldom see these frogs the rest of the year, they imagine the animals fell from the sky with the rain.

The Body of a Frog

The giant, or Goliath, frog of west-central Africa ranks as the largest frog. It measures nearly a foot (30

W. Frank Blair, the contributor of this article, is Professor of Zoology at the University of Texas.

centimeters) long. The smallest species grow only ½ inch (1.3 centimeters) long. Frogs also differ in color. Most kinds are green or brown, but some have bright, colorful markings.

Although different species may vary in size or color, almost all frogs have the same basic body structure. They have large hind legs, short front legs, and a flat head and body with no neck. Adult frogs have no tail, though one North American species has a short, tail-like structure. Most frogs have a sticky tongue attached to the front part of the mouth. They can rapidly flip out the tongue to capture prey (see TONGUE [picture]).

Like higher animals, frogs have such internal organs as a heart, liver, lungs, and kidneys. However, some of the internal organs differ from those of higher animals. For example, a frog's heart has three chambers instead of four. And although adult frogs breathe by means of lungs, they also breathe through their skin.

Legs. A few burrowing species have short hind legs and cannot hop. But all other frogs have long, powerful hind legs, which they use for jumping. Many frogs can leap 20 times their body length on a level surface. Frogs also use their large hind legs for swimming. Most water-dwelling species have webbed toes on their hind feet. The smaller front legs, or arms, prop a frog up when it sits. The front legs also help break the animal's fall when it jumps. Frogs that live in trees have tiny pads on the ends of their fingers and toes. The pads help the animal cling to the tree trunk as it climbs.

Skin. Most frogs have thin, moist skin. Many species have poison glands in their skin. The poison oozes onto the skin and helps protect the frog. If an enemy grabs a frog, the poison irritates the enemy's mouth and causes the animal to release the frog. Frogs have no hair, though the males of one African species, the so-called hairy frog, look hairy during the mating season. At that time, tiny, blood-rich growths called *papillae*, which resemble hair, grow from the sides of the frog's body.

Skeleton of a Grass Frog

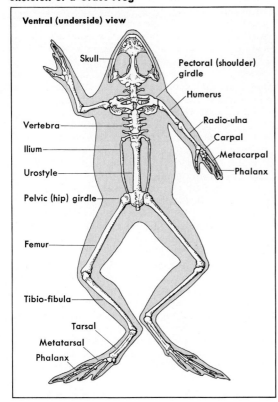

Ventral (underside) view

Skull
Pectoral (shoulder) girdle
Humerus
Radio-ulna
Carpal
Metacarpal
Phalanx
Vertebra
Ilium
Urostyle
Pelvic (hip) girdle
Femur
Tibio-fibula
Tarsal
Metatarsal
Phalanx

Some species of frogs change their skin color with changes in the humidity, light, and temperature. Frogs shed the outer layer of their skin many times a year. Using their forelegs, they pull the old skin off over their head. They then usually eat the old skin.

Senses. Frogs have fairly good eyesight, which helps them in capturing food and avoiding enemies. A frog's eyes bulge out, enabling the animal to see in almost all directions. Frogs can close their eyes by pulling the eyeballs deeper into their sockets. This action closes the upper and lower eyelids. Most species also have a thin, partly clear inner eyelid attached to the bottom lid. This inner eyelid, called the *nictitating membrane*, can be moved upward when a frog's eyes are open. It allows the frog to protect its eyes without completely cutting off its vision.

Many frogs have a large disk behind each eye. These disks are eardrums. Sound waves cause the eardrums to vibrate. The vibrations travel to the inner ear, which is connected by nerves to the hearing centers of the brain.

Most frogs have a delicate sense of touch. It is particularly well developed in species that live in water. A frog's tongue and mouth have many taste buds, and frogs often spit out bad-tasting food. The frog's sense of smell varies from species to species. Frogs that hunt mostly at night or that live underground have the best sense of smell.

Voice. Male frogs of most species have a voice, which they use mainly to call females during the mating season. In some species, the females also have a voice. But the female's voice is not nearly so loud as the male's.

Internal Organs of a Male Grass Frog

A frog's internal anatomy resembles that of higher animals in many ways. In addition, frogs are small and easily available. For these reasons, frogs have long been used for dissection in basic biology classes. The drawing at the left shows the organs that are visible when the frog's belly is cut open. The drawing at the right shows the structures behind the first layer of organs.

WORLD BOOK illustrations by Marion Pahl

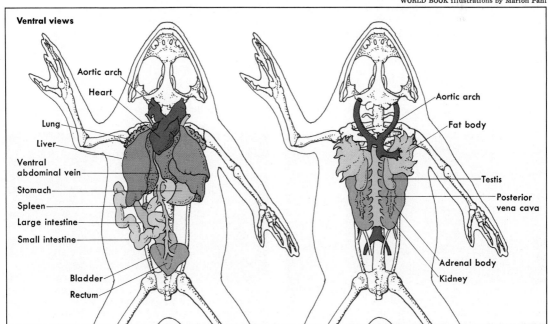

Ventral views

Aortic arch
Heart
Lung
Liver
Ventral abdominal vein
Stomach
Spleen
Large intestine
Small intestine
Bladder
Rectum

Aortic arch
Fat body
Testis
Posterior vena cava
Adrenal body
Kidney

Grant Heilman

Anthony Bannister, NHPA

A Male Frog, above, sounds a mating call by puffing out its throat and forcing air over its vocal cords. It uses this call to attract a female.

A Frog's Sticky Tongue is used to capture prey. The green frog shown at the left is about to eat a fly. The disk behind its eye is an eardrum.

A frog produces sound by means of its *vocal cords.* The vocal cords consist of thin bands of tissue in the *larynx* (voice box), which lies between the mouth and lungs. When a frog forces air from its lungs, the vocal cords vibrate and give off sound.

Among many species, the males have a *vocal sac,* which swells to great size while a call is being made. Species that have a vocal sac produce a much louder call than do similar species that have no sac. Some species have a vocal sac on each side of the head. Others have a single sac in the throat region.

The Life of a Frog

Frogs, like all other amphibians, are *cold-blooded*— that is, their body temperature tends to be the same as the temperature of the surrounding air or water. Frogs that live in regions with cold winters hibernate. Some species hibernate in burrows. Others spend the winter buried in mud at the bottom of a pond or stream, breathing through their skin. During hibernation, a frog lives off materials stored in its body tissues.

Mating. Most frogs of tropical and semitropical regions breed during the rainy season. In other regions, most species breed in spring or in early summer.

The majority of frogs, including most species that live on land, mate in water. The male frogs usually enter the water first. They then call to attract mates. Their call also helps direct other males to a pool suitable for mating. Each species has its own mating call. Naturalists can identify many kinds of frogs more easily by their call than by their appearance. Female frogs respond only to the call made by males of their own species. Males of some species also have a territorial call. This call warns other males of the same species that a certain area is occupied and that intruders are not welcome.

After a female frog enters the water, a male grasps her and clings to her back. In this position, the male fertilizes the eggs as they leave the female's body. The eggs hatch within 3 to 25 days, depending on the species and the water temperature. Higher water temperatures speed up development, and lower temperatures slow it down. Among most species, a tiny, tailed animal known as a *tadpole* or *polliwog* hatches from the egg.

Eggs. The eggs of different species vary in size, color, and shape. A jellylike substance covers frog eggs, providing a protective coating. This jelly also differs from species to species.

Many frogs lay eggs that have a dark and a light side. For example, green frogs, leopard frogs, wood frogs, and bullfrogs lay black-and-white eggs. The eggs of the pickerel frog are brown and bright yellow. The light-colored side of the egg contains the yolk, the heaviest part of the egg. Because it weighs more, the light-colored side is always on the bottom. If the eggs are disturbed and the light-colored side is turned up, the eggs soon turn over again.

Some species of frogs lay several thousand eggs at a time. But only a few of these eggs develop into adult frogs. Ducks, fish, insects, and other water creatures eat many of the eggs. Even if the eggs hatch, the tad-

Treat Davidson, NAS

In Water, a frog uses its strong hind legs for swimming. Many water-dwelling species, such as the North American bullfrog, above, have webbed toes on their hind feet as well.

Stephen Dalton, NHPA

On Land, the frog's muscular hind legs are used for jumping. The legs of the large edible frog, above, have still another use. People throughout Europe eat them.

The Life of a Frog   A frog's life has three stages: (1) egg, (2) tadpole, and (3) adult frog. Most female frogs lay a clump of several hundred eggs in water. A male frog clings to the female's back and fertilizes the eggs as she lays them. Tiny fishlike tadpoles hatch from the eggs. As the tadpoles grow, they develop legs and a froglike body. In time, they become adult frogs and can live out of water.

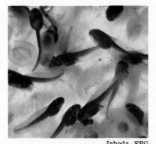

Jahoda, FPG

Newly hatched tadpoles

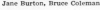

E. S. Ross

Jane Burton, Bruce Coleman Inc.

Frog eggs and egg laying   **Older tadpole, with legs**   Giuseppe Mazza   **Frog near completion of metamorphosis**

poles also face the danger of being eaten by larger water animals. In addition, the pond or stream in which the eggs were laid sometimes dries up. As a result, the tadpoles die.

Certain tropical frogs lay their eggs in rain water that collects among the leaves of plants or in holes in trees. Other tropical species attach their eggs to the underside of leaves that grow over water. When the eggs hatch, the tadpoles fall into the water.

Among some species, one of the parents carries the eggs until they hatch. For example, the female of certain South American tree frogs carries the eggs on her back. Among another species of frog, the midwife toad, the male carries the eggs wound around his hind legs. Males of another species, Darwin's frog, carry the eggs in their vocal pouch.

Some tropical frogs lay their eggs on land. They lay them under logs or dead leaves. These frogs have no tadpole stage. A young frog hatches from the egg and begins life as a land animal.

Tadpoles are not completely developed when they hatch. At first, the tadpole clings to some support in the water, using its mouth or a tiny sucker. A tadpole has no neck, and so its head and body look like one round form. The animal has a long tail and resembles a little fish. It breathes by means of gills.

A tadpole's form changes as the animal grows. Its tail becomes larger and enables the animal to swim about to obtain food. Tadpoles eat plants and decaying animal matter. In time, the tadpole begins to grow legs. The hind legs appear first. Then the lungs begin to develop and the front legs appear. The digestive system changes, enabling the frog that develops to eat live animals. Just before its *metamorphosis* (change) into a frog, the tadpole loses its gills. Finally, a tiny frog, still bearing a stump of a tail, emerges from the water. Eventually, the animal absorbs its tail and assumes its adult form.

Some tadpoles are so small they can hardly be seen. But a fully developed bullfrog tadpole may measure 6 to 7 inches (15 to 18 centimeters) long. It may take two or even three years for a bullfrog tadpole to develop into a frog. But among some species, the tadpoles change into adults within a few weeks.

Adult Frogs. After a frog becomes an adult, it may take a few months to a few years before the animal is mature enough to breed. The green frog and the pickerel frog mature in about three years. Scientists do not know how long frogs live in the wild. In captivity, a bullfrog may live more than 15 years. But frogs probably do not live nearly this long in nature. They may be eaten by such enemies as hawks, herons, raccoons, snakes, turtles, and fish.

Adult frogs eat mainly insects and other small animals, including earthworms, minnows, and spiders. Most frogs use their sticky tongue to capture prey. But they flip out their tongue only at moving prey. Furthermore, they tend to flip it at any small moving object. As a result, large adult frogs sometimes eat small frogs of their own or other species.

Kinds of Frogs

Frogs and toads make up the order *Salientia*, or *Anura*, one of the three main groups of amphibians. Most zoologists divide this order into at least 13 families of living frogs and toads.

One family of salientians consists of *true frogs*. *True toads* make up another family. Most true toads have a broader, flatter body and darker, drier skin than do most true frogs. True toads are commonly covered with warts, but true frogs have smooth skin. Unlike most true frogs, the majority of true toads live on land. The adults go to water only to breed. For more information on true toads, see TOAD.

Of the other families in the order Salientia, some closely resemble true frogs, and others closely resemble

465

true toads. Still others have features of both true frogs and true toads. Certain salientian families other than the true toads also have the word *toad* as part of their common name.

The most common frogs in the United States and Canada belong to the true frog and tree frog families.

True Frogs live on every continent except Antarctica. They are most common in Africa. The majority of true frogs live in or near water. They have long hind legs, smooth skin, a narrow waist, and webbed hind feet.

About 20 kinds of true frogs live in the United States. Many of these frogs also live in Canada. The leopard frog, or grass frog, is the most widespread. Leopard frogs range from the Atlantic coast to eastern California and from northern Canada to the Mexican border. The bullfrog, which may grow up to 8 inches (20 centimeters) long, ranks as the largest American and Canadian frog. Other common true frogs of the United States and Canada include the green frog, the pickerel frog, and the wood frog. Unlike most other true frogs, the wood frog spends much of its time away from water. It lives in damp wooded areas of Alaska, Canada, and the Midwestern and Eastern United States.

Tree Frogs, like true frogs, live on all continents except Antarctica. Most tree frogs measure less than 2 inches (5 centimeters) long and dwell in trees.

About 25 species of tree frogs live in the United States. Some of these species are also found in Canada. Common species in the Eastern United States include the green tree frog, the gray tree frog, and the spring peeper. Western tree frogs include the California tree frog, the canyon tree frog, and the Pacific tree frog. Some North American tree frogs, called chorus frogs and cricket frogs, live mainly on the ground.

Other Frogs of the United States include leptodactylid frogs, narrow-mouthed toads, spadefoot toads, and tailed frogs.

Leptodactylid Frogs make up a large family of frogs that live mainly in Australia and South America. Those found in the United States include the barking frog, the cliff frog, and the white-lipped frog. The barking frog and the cliff frog live on rocky cliffs in Texas. These frogs lay their eggs under rocks. Tiny frogs hatch from the eggs, without going through the tadpole stage. The white-lipped frog lives in the southern Rio Grande Valley area of Texas. The female white-lipped frog lays her eggs in a hole near water. She then beats the egg jelly into a foam. The tadpoles live in the foam nest until rain washes them into the nearby water.

Narrow-Mouthed Toads live throughout most tropical and subtropical regions. As their name suggests, these frogs have an extremely narrow mouth. The eastern narrow-mouthed toad, the Great Plains narrow-mouthed toad, and the sheep frog are the only members of this family that live in the United States. All three species live in burrows and eat ants and termites.

Spadefoot Toads live in Asia, Europe, North America, and northwestern Africa. These frogs are called spadefoots because most of them have a sharp-edged spadelike growth on each hind foot. They use this growth as a digging tool.

Spadefoot toads live throughout much of the United States. They dwell underground and are usually seen only after a rain. Several species live in dry regions of the Great Plains and the Southwest. These spadefoots may remain in their burrows for weeks at a time to stay moist. They breed following heavy rains, often laying their eggs in temporary ponds. The tadpoles develop rapidly. If enough food is available, tiny adults may emerge in only 12 days.

Tailed Frogs live in swift mountain streams of the northwestern United States and southwestern Canada. The males have a taillike structure. It is not a true tail but an organ used to fertilize the eggs while they are inside the female. The tailed frog is the only frog that fertilizes the eggs this way.

Frogs and Human Beings

Frogs benefit us in many ways. They eat large numbers of insects, which might otherwise become serious pests. Frogs also provide us with food. The meaty hind legs of larger frogs are considered a delicacy in many countries. In the United States, people mainly eat the legs of bullfrogs, green frogs, and leopard frogs. Frogs also are used widely in the laboratory. Medical researchers use frogs to test new drugs, and students dissect frogs to learn about anatomy.

Human beings are, in fact, the frog's worst enemy. People obtain most of the frogs used for food and in the laboratory from the wild. Furthermore, people destroy the homes and breeding places of frogs by replacing natural areas with cities and farms. They also pollute and so poison the waters in which frogs dwell.

Scientific Classification. True frogs make up the family Ranidae. All North American true frogs are in the genus *Rana*. Tree frogs make up the family Hylidae. Leptodactylid frogs make up the family Leptodactylidae; narrow-mouthed toads, the family Microhylidae; and spadefoot toads, the family Pelobatidae. The tailed frog belongs to the family Leiopelmatidae.   W. FRANK BLAIR

Outline

I. **The Body of a Frog**
    A. Legs   C. Senses
    B. Skin   D. Voice
II. **The Life of a Frog**
    A. Mating   C. Tadpoles
    B. Eggs   D. Adult Frogs
III. **Kinds of Frogs**
    A. True Frogs
    B. Tree Frogs
    C. Other Frogs
IV. **Frogs and Human Beings**

Questions

How many species of frogs are there?

Which is the most widespread frog in the United States and Canada?

How do tadpoles breathe? How do adult frogs?

In what ways do frogs benefit us?

What do tadpoles eat? What do adult frogs eat?

How did spadefoot toads get their name?

Why are some frogs able to climb trees?

What is the function of a male frog's territorial call?

What are some of the changes a tadpole undergoes during its metamorphosis into a frog?

What is the function of the *nictitating membrane*?

FROHMAN, *FROH muhn,* was the name of two brothers who were famous theatrical managers. Their theatrical group practically controlled the American theater from 1895 to 1910. Both brothers were born in Sandusky, Ohio.

Daniel Frohman (1851-1940) was known for many years as the dean of American theatrical producers. He began his career as business manager of the Madison Square Theatre in New York City, and soon managed his own companies and theaters.

Charles Frohman (1860-1915) has been called the "theatrical Napoleon of America." At one time, he owned and operated theaters in London as well as in New York City. In a typical season, he presented 25 plays and employed 795 actors. Maude Adams, Ethel Barrymore, and John Drew were among the actors who became stars under his management. Frohman died in the *Lusitania* disaster in 1915.   BARNARD HEWITT

FROISSART, *frwah SAHR,* **JEAN** (1337?-1410?), a French poet and historian, wrote *The Chronicles of France, England, Scotland, and Spain.* This four-volume work describes events from 1325 to 1400, especially the Hundred Years' War (see HUNDRED YEARS' WAR). *The Chronicles* are based partly on what Froissart actually witnessed and partly on research. His history is not always accurate, but he described vividly the manners and personalities of the times. One critic said, "Froissart's whole business was to live in the fourteenth century, and tell us what he saw there." William Morris and other writers of the 1800's drew materials for some of their narrative poems from *The Chronicles.* Froissart also wrote of his school days and early love affairs in "L'Espinette Amoureuse."

During the 1360's, he served five years as secretary to Queen Philippa of England. He studied to be a priest, but preferred writing of chivalry and adventure. He was born in Valenciennes, France.   FRANCIS J. BOWMAN

FROMM, *frahm,* **ERICH** (1900-   ), is a German-born social psychoanalyst. He became a leading supporter of the idea that most human behavior is a learned response to social conditions. In adopting this concept, Fromm rejected much of the theory of the noted Austrian psychiatrist Sigmund Freud. Freud maintained that instincts determine most human behavior.

Fromm applies the ideas of sociology to psychoanalysis. He studies the social and cultural processes by which people come to learn and act out the behavior expected of them by their society.

Fromm has written numerous books that reflect his many fields of interest, such as philosophy, psychology, religion, and sociology. His major works include *The Art of Loving* (1956) and *The Heart of Man* (1964).

Fromm was born in Frankfurt. He earned his Ph.D. degree from the University of Heidelberg in 1922. In 1933, Fromm came to the United States to lecture at the Institute for Psychoanalysis in Chicago. A year later, he settled in the United States. He became a U.S. citizen in 1940. Since 1934, Fromm has held various positions in psychoanalytical institutions in the United States and has taught at universities in the United States and Mexico.   GEORGE H. POLLOCK

FROND. See FERN.

FRONDE, *frawnd,* was a revolt of nobles against the French monarchy. The word means *sling,* a popular game among French boys. Historians do not know how the revolt got its name. In 1648, the Parlement of Paris rebelled against French tax policies. The Prince of Condé led armies that crushed the rebellion in 1649. Condé himself then led a new revolt in 1650. It failed in 1652, and the monarchy became stronger than it had been before the revolt.

FRONDIZI, ARTURO. See ARGENTINA (New Political Crises).

FRONT. See WEATHER (illustrations; Fronts).

FRONT ORGANIZATION is one that serves as a cover for illegal or subversive activities.

FRONT RANGE. See COLORADO (Land Regions).

FRONTAL BONE. See HEAD.

FRONTENAC, *FRAHN tuh nak* or *frawnt NAHK,* **COMTE DE** (1620-1698), LOUIS DE BUADE, was governor of New France, the French colonies in Canada, in the late 1600's. He helped establish France's power in America so firmly that it lasted for more than 50 years after his death.

He was appointed governor in 1672. His stern, military ways and his hot temper often got him into trouble with the civil authorities in the province. But he knew when to be tactful and when to be masterful with the Indians. The colony prospered under his rule.

Frontenac encouraged exploration of the west, and aided the expeditions of Robert Cavelier, Sieur de la Salle; Louis Joliet; and Father Marquette. But he quarreled constantly with Bishop Laval and the priests, mainly about using brandy in the Indian trade. The

Detail of a water color by de Rinzy; the Public Archives of Canada

The Comte de Frontenac served two terms as governor of the French colonies in Canada during the late 1600's. This watercolor shows Frontenac, seated in a canoe, on his way to Fort Cataraqui, which he built on Lake Ontario in 1673.

church objected to this. He was recalled to France in 1682.

Seven years later, however, he was again appointed governor, as New France needed his stern rule. The French planned to drive the English out of North America, or hold them in a narrow strip of land along the Atlantic. Frontenac began campaigns against the Iroquois Indians, whom the English encouraged in their attacks on New France. Warfare followed on the New York and New England frontiers. Frontenac's bands of French fighters and Algonkian Indians were not able to make permanent conquests. In 1690, Frontenac defended Quebec against an English fleet. Six years later, his forces laid waste the villages and lands of the Iroquois. The Treaty of Ryswick, in 1697, stopped the war for a time. Frontenac died less than a year later.

Frontenac became a soldier as a boy, and was made a brigadier general at the age of 26. He served in Flanders, Germany, Italy, Hungary, and Crete before he became governor of New France. IAN C. C. GRAHAM

See also CANADA, HISTORY OF (French Rule).

FRONTIER. See PIONEER LIFE IN AMERICA; WESTERN FRONTIER LIFE; WESTWARD MOVEMENT.

FRONTISPIECE. See BOOK (Printed Books).

FROST. The lacy ice crystals which may form on trees and windowpanes on a winter morning are frost.

Frost is formed when air containing moisture in the form of water vapor is cooled to below freezing temperature. The moisture then condenses and collects as frost on solid objects.

Frost is usually formed at night, and in much the same way as dew. During the daytime the earth soaks up a great deal of heat from the sun's rays. As soon as the sun sets, the earth starts to cool. The surface of the ground cools rapidly, and the moisture which hangs in the air in gas, or vapor form, begins to condense, or change to liquid. This causes it to change to drops of water, or dew, which collect on objects. If the temperature goes below the freezing point of 32° F. (0° C), moisture passes directly from the gaseous to the solid state. This process is called *sublimation*, and results in the formation of ice crystals called *frost* or *hoarfrost*.

More frost is formed on a clear night than on a cloudy one, because the ground cools faster on clear nights when there are no clouds to reflect heat back to earth. During the growing season, farmers watch the sky closely on chilly nights, for a cloudless sky sometimes means a killing frost. Plants die because low temperatures cause the plant juices to freeze and swell up, bursting delicate plant cells. Modern means of weather forecasting usually make it possible for farmers to know when a heavy frost is coming. They can then work to save their crops by using devices such as smudge-pot fires.

See also DEW; HOARFROST; JACK FROST; SMUDGE POT.

Upper left photo by Ewing Galloway. All other photos courtesy of the National Weather Service.

Frost forms when water vapor in the air condenses at a temperature below freezing. On cold nights, frost may coat plants and blades of grass, as shown in the photograph at the upper left. Frost also occurs in delicate patterns of ice crystals on solid surfaces, as shown in the other photographs.

FROST, ROBERT LEE (1874-1963), became the most popular American poet of his time. He won the Pulitzer prize for poetry in 1924, 1931, 1937, and 1943. In 1960, Congress voted him a gold medal "in recognition of his poetry, which has enriched the culture of the United States and the philosophy of the world." Frost's public career reached a climax in January, 1961, when he read his poem "The Gift Outright" at the inauguration of President John F. Kennedy.

His Life. Frost was born in San Francisco on March 26, 1874. After the death of his father in 1885, his family moved back to New England, the original family home. Frost attended schools in Lawrence, Mass., and later briefly attended Dartmouth and Harvard colleges. In the early 1890's, he worked in New England as a farmer, an editor, and a schoolteacher, absorbing the materials that were to form the themes of many of his most famous poems. His first volume of poetry, *A Boy's Will*, appeared in 1913. His final collection, *In the Clearing*, appeared in 1962. Frost died on Jan. 29, 1963.

His Poems. Frost's poetry is identified with New England, particularly Vermont and New Hampshire. Frost found inspiration for many of his finest poems in the landscapes, folkways, and speech mannerisms of this region. Frost's poetry is noted for its plain language, conventional poetic forms, and graceful style. He was so expert a poet that many of his earliest poems are as richly developed as his later poems.

Frost is sometimes praised for being a direct and straightforward writer. While he is never obscure, he cannot always be read easily. His effects, even at their simplest, depend upon a certain slyness for which the reader must be prepared. In "Precaution," he wrote:

> I never dared be radical when young
> For fear it would make me conservative
> When old.

In his longer, more elaborate poems, Frost writes about complex subjects in a complex style.

Frost tends to restrict himself to New England scenes, but the range of moods in his poetry is rich and varied. He assumes the role of a puckish, homespun philosopher in "Mending Wall." In such poems as "Design" and "Bereft," he responds to the terror and tragedy of life. He writes soberly of vaguely threatening aspects of nature in "Come In" and "Stopping by Woods on a Snowy Evening." In the latter poem, he wrote:

> My little horse must think it queer
> To stop without a farmhouse near
> Between the woods and frozen lake
> The darkest evening of the year.

A similar varied pattern can be found in Frost's character studies. "The Witch of Coos" is a comic account of the superstitions of rural New England. In "Home Burial," this same setting is the background of tragedy centering around a child's death. In "The Hill Wife," Frost shows the loneliness and emotional poverty of a rural existence driving a person insane.

By placing man and nature side by side, Frost often appears to write the kind of romantic poetry associated with England and the United States in the 1800's. There

Wide World

Robert Frost became famous for his poems about rural life in New England.

is, however, a crucial difference between his themes and those of the older tradition. The romantic poets of the 1800's believed man could live in harmony with nature. To Frost, the purposes of man and nature are never the same, and so nature's meanings can never be known by man. Probing for nature's secrets is futile and foolish. Man's best chance for serenity does not come from understanding his natural environment. Serenity comes from working usefully and productively amid the external forces of nature. Frost often used the theme of "significant toil"—toil by which man is nourished and sustained. This theme appears in such famous lyrics as "Birches," "After Apple-Picking," and "Two Tramps in Mud Time." CLARK GRIFFITH

FROSTBITE is the effect of extreme cold on the body. Frostbite usually affects the ears, nose, hands, and feet. A frostbitten area is numb and unnaturally white. Early symptoms of frostbite include tingling, numbness, and pain. Severe freezing of deeper tissues is dangerous, and often results in gangrene (see GANGRENE).

Doctors treat frostbite by restoring circulation and warmth to the affected part. Rubbing frostbite with snow or ice is dangerous because it might remove skin and damage the tissue. The safest treatment is to warm the part gradually under blankets or in warm, but not hot, water. The patient should be kept in a warm room, with the affected part slightly raised. In the early stage of treatment, only dry sterile dressings should be used. Wet antiseptic dressings may be used on the affected area if gangrene sets in. No pressure should be applied. Frostbitten areas may remain sensitive to cold. BENJAMIN F. MILLER

See also CHILBLAIN; FIRST AID (Frostbite); IMMERSION FOOT.

FROUDE, *frood,* was the family name of two famous English brothers. They were born in Dartington, England, and graduated from Oxford University.

William Froude (1810-1879) was an engineer and naval architect. He developed the first scientific methods for testing ship models. Froude designed the deep *bilge keel* (thin vanes along a ship's bottom) used to help stabilize British warships. He also designed a dynamometer that was large enough to measure the power of marine engines. ROBERT E. SCHOFIELD

James Anthony Froude (1818-1894) was a historian. His 12-volume *History of England* (1856-1870) has a pleasing, vigorous style. Froude edited Thomas Carlyle's *Reminiscences* (1881) and *Letters and Memorials of Jane Welsh Carlyle* (1883). He taught modern history at Oxford from 1892 until his death. FRANCIS J. BOWMAN

FROZEN FOOD. See FOOD, FROZEN.

FRUCTOSE. See SUGAR (Sources); CARBOHYDRATE (Simple Carbohydrates).

FRUIT

FRUIT is the part of a flowering plant that contains the plant's seeds. Fruits include acorns, cucumbers, tomatoes, and wheat grains. However, the word *fruit* commonly refers to the juicy, sweet or tart kinds that people enjoy as desserts or snacks. The word comes from the Latin word *frui*, meaning *enjoy*. Popular fruits include apples, bananas, grapes, oranges, peaches, pears, and strawberries.

Many fruits are nutritious as well as appetizing. For example, oranges and strawberries contain large amounts of Vitamin C. Most fruits have a high sugar content, and so they provide quick energy. Fruits alone cannot provide a balanced diet, however, because the majority of them supply little protein.

The world's fruit growers raise millions of tons of fruit annually. Fruit growing is a branch of *horticulture*, a field of agriculture that also includes the raising of nuts, vegetables, flowers, and landscape crops. Most nuts are actually fruits, as are such vegetables as cucumbers, green peppers, and tomatoes. To prevent confusion, horticultural scientists define a fruit as an edible seed-bearing structure that (1) consists of fleshy tissue and (2) is produced by a *perennial*. A perennial is a plant that lives for more than two years without being replanted. The horticultural definition of a fruit excludes nuts and vegetables. Nuts are firm rather than fleshy. Most vegetables are *annuals*—that is, the plants live for only one season.

In some cases, the horticultural definition of a fruit conflicts with the definition used by botanists and with common usage. For example, watermelons and muskmelons are fruits, and most people regard them as such. But they grow on vines that must be replanted annually, and so horticulturists regard melons as vegetables. Rhubarb is sometimes considered a fruit. But people eat the leafstalk of the rhubarb plant, not the seed-bearing structure. Therefore, horticulturists classify rhubarb as a vegetable.

This article discusses fruits chiefly from a horticultural point of view. The last section tells about fruits from a botanical viewpoint.

How Horticulturists Classify Fruits

Most of the fruits that are widely raised in North America today were originally brought from other regions. For example, apples, cherries, and pears originated in Europe and western Asia. Apricots and peaches first came from China, and lemons and oranges from China and Southeast Asia. All these fruits are now grown in any part of the world that has a favorable climate.

All fruits need at least some moisture, and most require considerable amounts. Dates and olives are among the few fruits that can be grown in dry regions without irrigation.

Horticulturists classify fruits into three groups, based on temperature requirements for growth: (1) temperate fruits, (2) subtropical fruits, and (3) tropical fruits.

How Horticulturists Classify Fruits

Any seed-bearing structure produced by a flowering plant is a fruit. But the word *fruit* has a more limited meaning in common usage and in horticulture, the branch of agriculture that includes fruit growing. Thus, the word usually refers to the edible sweet or tart fruits that are popular foods and widely grown farm crops. Horticulturists classify these fruits into three groups, based on temperature requirements for growth: (1) temperate fruits, (2) subtropical fruits, and (3) tropical fruits. Some examples of each of these types are shown below.

WORLD BOOK illustrations by James Teason

Cranberries
Apricot
Apple
Blueberries
Gooseberries
Plums

Dates
Pear
Avocado
Grapefruit
Lemon
Olives

Mango
Litchis
Papaya
Banana

Temperate Fruits must have an annual cold season to grow well. They are raised mainly in the Temperate Zones, the regions between the tropics and the polar areas.

Subtropical Fruits need warm or mild temperatures throughout the year but can survive occasional light frosts. They are grown chiefly in subtropical regions.

Tropical Fruits cannot stand frost. They are raised mainly in the tropics. Large quantities of some species, especially bananas and pineapples, are exported.

Temperate Fruits must have an annual cold season to grow properly. They are raised chiefly in the Temperate Zones, the regions between the tropics and the polar areas. Most temperate fruits come from Europe and North America, but Asia and Australia also have major producing areas.

The principal temperate fruits are apples, apricots, cherries, peaches, pears, and plums. In addition, most *small fruits*, which grow on plants smaller than trees, are raised mainly in the Temperate Zones. They include blueberries, cranberries, grapes, raspberries, and strawberries.

Subtropical Fruits require warm or mild temperatures throughout the year but can survive an occasional light frost. They are grown chiefly in subtropical regions.

The most widely grown subtropical fruits are the citrus group, which includes grapefruit, lemons, limes, and oranges. Oranges, the leading citrus crop, are grown throughout the subtropics, from southern Japan to southern Europe. In the United States, Florida produces by far the most oranges. Citrus crops are also raised on some farms in the tropics, but the somewhat cooler climate of the subtropics produces better-tasting and more attractive fruit. Other subtropical fruits include dates, figs, olives, pomegranates, and certain types of avocados.

Tropical Fruits are raised mainly in the tropics and cannot stand even a light frost. Bananas and pineapples, the best-known tropical fruits, are grown throughout the tropics, and much of each crop is exported. The majority of other tropical fruits are consumed locally for the most part. They include acerolas, cherimoyas, litchis, mangoes, mangosteens, and papayas.

Growing Fruit

Almost all species of fruits grow on plants that have a woody stem. Such plants are trees, bushes, or woody vines. Fruits that grow on trees include apples, cherries, lemons, limes, oranges, and peaches. Most small fruits grow on bushes, but grapes come from woody vines. Bananas and strawberries grow on plants that have a soft, rather than a woody, stem.

Fruit crops, unlike most other crops, are not grown from seeds. Plants grown from seeds may vary in many ways from generation to generation. But growers strive to produce plants that will bear fruits of uniform type, appearance, and quality. Such fruits bring the highest prices when marketed. Fruit plants produce fruits of uniform quality if grown *vegetatively*—that is, from certain parts of desirable plants, such as stems, buds, and roots. The part that is grown develops new tissues and new parts identical to those of the parent plant.

Fruit plants are produced vegetatively in three main ways: (1) by grafting, (2) from cuttings, and (3) from specialized plant structures. Most fruit trees are reproduced by grafting. In this process, a bud or piece of stem from one tree is joined to a *rootstock* from another. A rootstock is a root or a root plus its stem. The resulting tree will have most of the same characteristics as the tree from which the bud or stem was taken. However, the rootstock may determine such characteristics as the size and productivity of the new tree.

Some fruit plants are produced from *cuttings* or from specialized structures. Most cuttings are pieces of stem that grow roots when placed in water or moist soil. Specialized structures called *runners* are used to grow strawberry plants. Runners are long, slender shoots that mature strawberry plants send out along the ground. A runner placed in soil develops into a new plant.

Some fruit growers produce their own plants from grafts, cuttings, or specialized structures. But most growers buy plants from nurseries that specialize in producing them.

The branch of horticulture that deals with fruit growing is called *pomology*. Pomologists have developed highly efficient methods of planting and caring for fruit crops, and most fruit farms use these techniques.

There are three main steps in growing fruit: (1) planting, (2) caring for the crop, and (3) harvesting.

Planting. Fruit crops are perennials, and so they do not have to be replanted annually as do most other crops. After the original planting, a fruit farmer need only replace plants that become unproductive. Many fruit plants remain productive for 30 to 50 years or even longer. In mild climates, farmers generally plant trees, bushes, and vines in fall. In cold climates, planting usually takes place in spring.

Most bushes are planted from 3 to 5 feet (0.9 to 1.5 meters) apart in rows that are 6 to 10 feet (1.8 to 3 meters) apart. Rows of grapevines are spaced about 10 feet (3 meters) apart. In the past, farmers almost always grew full-sized fruit trees. In most cases, the trees were planted from 20 to 40 feet (6 to 12 meters) apart to allow room for growth. Today, many farmers prefer to grow dwarf trees, which are planted close together. The branches of each tree may grow up a supporting framework called a *trellis*. The trellis enables all the fruit to receive the maximum amount of sunlight, and so the crop ripens better and faster than it otherwise would. Fruit is also easier to harvest from dwarf trees than from full-sized trees.

Caring for the Crop. Most fruit growers use special machinery to fertilize, cultivate, and otherwise care for their crops. Fruit crops must be fertilized at least once a year. Some fertilizers are applied to the soil, and others are sprayed on the plants. Many fruit growers cultivate the soil around young fruit plants periodically. This practice helps control weeds and thus encourages the growth of the crop. Most fruit crops grown in extremely dry regions must be irrigated. Farmers use various methods, such as ditches and sprinklers, to distribute irrigation water.

In many cases, the branches of a young fruit tree must be *trained* so that the tree develops a uniform shape and a sturdy structure. Training may involve propping the trunk or tying the branches, or it may consist entirely of pruning. Pruning strengthens a plant by ridding it of unproductive branches. Nearly all fruit plants have to be pruned at least once annually. In addition, most fruit farmers remove some of the crop from the trees during the early stages of the fruit's growth. This practice, called *thinning*, helps increase the size of the remaining fruit.

The majority of fruit growers use chemical pesticides to protect their crops against diseases and insect pests. Most pesticides are sprayed or dusted on crops by tractor-driven machinery or specially equipped light

A Mechanical Cherry Picker shakes a cherry tree to loosen the fruit. The cherries drop onto outstretched cloths, roll onto a conveyor, and are deposited in a tank of salt water. The fruit floats in the water and thus is protected from being bruised.

airplanes or helicopters. Plant breeders have also developed varieties of fruit plants that resist certain diseases and harmful insects.

Sudden spring frosts can endanger fruit crops in temperate or subtropical regions. Farmers use water distributed by sprinklers to protect small-fruit crops from frosts. Water releases heat as it freezes. If it is sprinkled onto the crops continuously, it keeps the tender flowers and young fruits from freezing. Farmers use heaters to protect tree crops from spring frosts.

Harvesting. Fruits are bruised more easily than most other crops, and so they must be harvested with greater care. Most are picked by hand. However, the increasing cost of hand labor has encouraged the use of fruit-harvesting machines. Some of these machines have arms that shake the fruit loose from the plants. The loosened fruit drops onto outstretched cloths. Other mechanical fruit pickers have fingers that "comb" the fruit from the plants.

Marketing Fruit

The United States is the world's leading fruit-producing country. It raises more than 10 per cent of all the apples, lemons, pineapples, and plums; about 20 per cent of the peaches and strawberries; more than 25 per cent of the oranges; and nearly 65 per cent of the grapefruit. California is the nation's chief fruit-growing state. Other leaders include Florida, Michigan, New York, Oregon, and Washington.

Most fruit scheduled to be sold fresh is taken from the orchard or field by truck and delivered to a packing house. Many large fruit farms have their own packing facilities. Commercial packing houses are centrally located in fruit-growing regions. Most large packing houses are fully mechanized. Machines wash the fruit, sort it according to size and quality, and pack each batch into containers. The fruit is then shipped to market or stored for future delivery. Railroads and trucks carry most overland shipments of fruit. Most overseas shipments travel by ocean freighter.

Fruits can be stored for varying lengths of time under controlled conditions. Temperate tree fruits must be stored at temperatures near freezing. Some kinds of apples can be kept fresh for about a year under such conditions. On the other hand, most small fruits remain fresh only a few days or weeks in cold storage. Tropical and subtropical fruits can be stored for a few weeks or months under temperature-controlled conditions. The temperatures, though cool, must be well above freezing. The amount of oxygen ordinarily present in the air promotes spoilage of fruit. The storage time for all fruits can be lengthened by reducing the oxygen supply.

Much fruit is shipped directly from farms to food processors. Processing plants preserve fruit by such methods as canning, drying, and freezing. See FOOD, FROZEN; FOOD PRESERVATION.

Developing New Varieties of Fruit

Occasionally, an individual plant develops an unexpected characteristic. For example, a fruit tree may suddenly start to bear fruit of a different color. Such a plant is called a *sport*. Growers have used sports to develop many new cultivated varieties of fruit. Cultivated varieties are also known as *cultivars*. The trees of Delicious apples originally produced only pale-colored, striped fruit. Then, some of the branches on individual trees began to bear solid-red apples. By grafting these branches onto appropriate rootstocks, growers produced the attractively colored varieties of Delicious apples available today.

Sports often play an important role in the development of new varieties of fruit. But the majority of new varieties are produced by a process called *selection*. In selection, plants grown from seed are examined for various desirable qualities. An individual plant may thus be singled out for high productivity or for the superior color, texture, or flavor of its fruit. By reproducing this plant vegetatively, the desirable characteristic is preserved from one generation to the next. If the desirable quality persists, the fruit may be classed as a new variety.

In addition to selection, modern fruit growers also use a technique called *crossing* or *hybridization*. In this process, pollen is taken from a plant that has been selected for a particular desirable trait. The pollen is placed in the flower of a plant selected for another desirable quality. Some of the plants grown from the resulting seed may have the desirable characteristics of both parents. Occasionally, one of these plants may prove worthy of being classed as a new variety. In most cases, however, the entire process of selection and hybridization must be repeated many times to produce a new variety. Hybridization is a highly useful technique because it enables growers to produce varieties with more and more desirable qualities.

How Botanists Classify Fruits

Fruit, the seed-bearing structure of a flowering plant, develops from the *ovaries* of the flowers. An ovary is a hollow structure near the base of a flower. It may hold one seed or more than one, depending on the species of the plant. See TREE (diagram: How Most Trees Reproduce [Fruit-Bearing Trees]).

The wall of an ovary of mature fruit, in which the seed is fully developed, has three layers. The outer layer is called the *exocarp*, the middle layer is known as

Simple Fruits   Simple fruits are classified into two main groups, depending on whether their tissue is fleshy or dry. Fleshy simple fruits include most of the seed-bearing structures that are commonly called fruits. They are divided into three main types: (1) berries, (2) drupes, and (3) pomes. The drawings below show some examples of each of these types and of several dry simple fruits.

Berries consist entirely of fleshy tissue, and most species have many seeds. The seeds are embedded in the flesh. This group includes only a few of the fruits that are commonly known as berries.

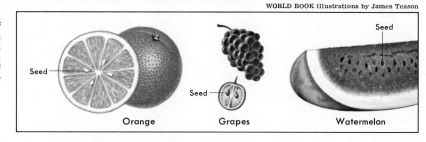

Orange   Grapes   Watermelon

Drupes are fleshy fruits that have a hard inner stone or pit and a single seed. The pit encloses the seed.

Peach   Cherries   Plum

Pomes have a fleshy outer layer, a paperlike core, and more than one seed. The seeds are enclosed in the core.

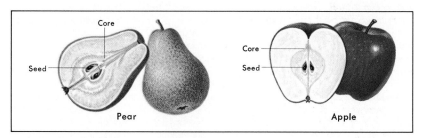

Pear   Apple

Dry Simple Fruits are produced by many kinds of trees, shrubs, garden plants, and weeds. The seed-bearing structures of nearly all members of the grass family, including corn and wheat, belong to this group.

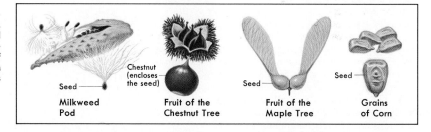

Milkweed Pod   Fruit of the Chestnut Tree   Fruit of the Maple Tree   Grains of Corn

Compound Fruits   A compound fruit consists of a cluster of seed-bearing structures, each of which is a complete fruit. Compound fruits are divided into two groups, (1) aggregate fruits and (2) multiple fruits.

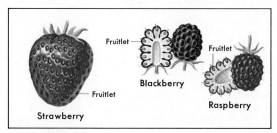

Blackberry   Raspberry

Strawberry

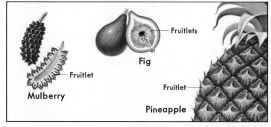

Fig

Mulberry   Pineapple

Aggregate Fruits include most of the fruits that are commonly called berries. Each fruitlet of a blackberry or raspberry is a small drupe. Each "seed" of a strawberry is a dry fruitlet.

Multiple Fruits include mulberries, figs, and pineapples. Mulberry fruitlets are small drupes. Each "seed" in a fig and each segment of a pineapple is a fruitlet.

473

Leading Fruits in the United States
Value and quantity of production in 1977

Fruit	Value	Short Tons	Metric Tons	Leading States in Quantity of Production
Grapes*	$652,357,000	4,226,000	3,833,800	California, New York, Washington, Pennsylvania, Michigan
Oranges	648,552,000	10,595,000	9,611,600	Florida, California, Texas, Arizona
Apples	620,979,000	3,351,000	3,040,000	Washington, New York, Michigan, California, Pennsylvania
Peaches*	268,195,000	1,363,000	1,236,500	California, South Carolina, Pennsylvania, Georgia, New Jersey
Strawberries	214,947,000	325,000	294,800	California, Oregon, Florida, Washington, Michigan
Grapefruit	167,528,000	3,029,000	2,747,000	Florida, Texas, California, Arizona
Plums and Prunes	135,318,000	717,000	650,500	California, Oregon, Michigan, Washington, Idaho
Cherries	126,915,000	254,000	230,400	Michigan, Washington, Oregon, California, Utah
Pears*	111,130,000	775,000	703,100	California, Washington, Oregon, New York, Michigan
Lemons	87,538,000	973,000	882,700	California, Arizona
Avocados	79,451,000	141,000	127,900	California, Florida
Pineapples	62,500,000	690,000	626,000	Hawaii
Apricots	31,973,000	142,000	128,800	California, Washington, Utah
Nectarines	30,450,000	150,000	136,100	California
Tangerines	29,850,000	249,000	225,900	Florida, California, Arizona
Cranberries	28,682,000	106,000	96,200	Massachusetts, Wisconsin, New Jersey, Washington, Oregon
Olives*	22,467,000	62,000	56,200	California
Raspberries	13,904,000	14,000	12,700	Washington, Oregon
Limes	11,610,000	40,000	36,300	Florida
Figs	10,511,000	39,000	35,400	California
Tangelos	9,696,000	216,000	196,000	Florida
Blackberries	8,842,000	10,000	9,100	Oregon, Washington
Temples	8,740,000	171,000	155,100	Florida
Papayas	8,388,000	31,000	28,100	Hawaii

*4-year average, 1974 through 1977. Source: U.S. Department of Agriculture.

the *mesocarp*, and the inner layer is the *endocarp*. The three layers together are called the *pericarp*.

Botanists classify fruits into two main groups: (1) simple fruits and (2) compound fruits. A simple fruit develops from a single ovary, and a compound fruit develops from two or more ovaries.

Simple Fruits are by far the largest group of fruits. They are divided into two types, depending on whether their pericarp is fleshy or dry.

Fleshy Simple Fruits include most of the seed-bearing structures that are commonly called fruits. There are three main kinds of these fruits: (1) berries, (2) drupes, and (3) pomes.

Berries have an entirely fleshy pericarp. Botanists classify bananas, blueberries, grapes, green peppers, muskmelons, oranges, tomatoes, and watermelons as berries. Some berries, including watermelons and muskmelons, have a hard rind. Such fruits are called *pepos*. Other berries, including the citrus fruits, have a leathery rind. They are called *hesperidiums*. Raspberries, strawberries, and most of the other fruits commonly known as berries are actually compound fruits.

Drupes have an exocarp that forms a thin skin. The endocarp develops into a stone or pit, and only the mesocarp is fleshy. Such fruits include apricots, cherries, peaches, and plums.

Pomes are fleshy fruits with a paperlike core. Apples and pears are pomes.

Dry Simple Fruits include the pods of the bean plant, the milkweed, the pea plant, and the locust tree; the grains of the corn, rice, and wheat plants; and nuts. Botanists regard nuts as single-seed fruits with a hard pericarp called a shell. The seed is the edible part. Acorns, chestnuts, and hazelnuts are true nuts. But many so-called nuts are classed otherwise by botanists. For example, almonds and walnuts are the seeds of drupes.

Compound Fruits consist of a cluster of ripened ovaries. There are two main types of compound fruits,

aggregate fruits and *multiple fruits*. Aggregate fruits develop from single flowers, each of which has many ovaries. Blackberries and raspberries are aggregate fruits. The strawberry is a special type of aggregate fruit. Each "seed" in a strawberry is actually a complete fruit. The flesh surrounding the seeds develops from the base of the flower rather than from the ovaries. Multiple fruits develop from a cluster of flowers on a single stem. Figs, mulberries, and pineapples are multiple fruits. JULES JANICK

Related Articles in WORLD BOOK include:

TEMPERATE FRUITS

Apple	Cranberry	Nectarine
Apricot	Currant	Oregon Grape
Beach Plum	Dewberry	Peach
Blackberry	Gooseberry	Pear
Blueberry	Grape	Plum
Boysenberry	Huckleberry	Quince
Casaba	Loganberry	Raspberry
Cherry	Melon	Strawberry
Crab Apple	Muskmelon	

SUBTROPICAL FRUITS

Avocado	Grapefruit	Olive
Citron	Kumquat	Orange
Citrus	Lemon	Persimmon
Date and Date Palm	Lime	Pomegranate
Fig	Loquat	Tangerine

TROPICAL FRUITS

Acerola	Banana	Litchi	Papaya
Anchovy	Cherimoya	Mango	Pineapple
Pear	Guava	Mangosteen	Tamarind

OTHER RELATED ARTICLES

Berry	Grafting	Pruning
Bramble	Horticulture	Raisin
Burbank, Luther	Hybrid	Rose (The Rose
Canning	Jelly and Jam	Family)
Drupe	Nut	Smudge Pot
Espalier	Pectin	Spraying
Food, Frozen	Pome	Vitamin
Food Preservation	Prune	Wine

474

FRUIT BAT. See FLYING Fox.

FRUIT FLY. There are several kinds of flies whose larvae eat their way through different fruits. Fruit flies include some of the most harmful agricultural pests.

Croy, Black Star
A Fruit Fly

Members of one family of these insects are called *peacock flies* because of their habit of strutting on fruit. They are small insects with many colors and beautiful wings. They lay their eggs in fruits, berries, nuts, and other parts of plants. The larvae which hatch from the eggs are the small white maggots that tunnel their way through the fruit. This family of fruit flies includes the important *Mediterranean fruit fly*, *Oriental fruit fly*, *Mexican fruit fly*, the various cherry fruit flies, and the apple maggot. Quarantine laws prevent bringing infested fruit into the United States. Control methods include chemical sprays and bringing in parasites to eat the flies.

The *pomace*, or *vinegar*, *flies* also are called fruit flies. Their maggots breed chiefly in decaying fruit and in crushed grapes in wineries. Scientists often use one species of pomace fly, *Drosophila melanogaster*, in heredity studies, partly because this fly reproduces rapidly.

Scientific Classification. Peacock flies belong to the family *Tephritidae*, or *Trypetidae*. The pomace flies form the family *Drosophilidae*. The most important pomace fly is genus *Drosophila*, species *D. melanogaster*.   ROBERT L. USINGER

See also APPLE MAGGOT; HEREDITY (Science Project); MEDITERRANEAN FRUIT FLY.

FRUIT PRESERVATION. See FOOD PRESERVATION.

FRUSTUM. See CONE; PYRAMID.

FRY. See FISH (How Fish Live; picture).

FRY, CHRISTOPHER (1907-   ), is an English dramatist. Fry wrote in verse at a time when most other playwrights were writing in prose. His plays were praised at first, but most critics no longer rank them highly. The verse is often witty, but it often seems pompous. Unlike the verse of Shakespeare and other Elizabethan dramatists, it does little to reveal character.

Fry's first play, *The Boy with a Cart* (1939), is a religious work. He wrote other religious plays, but gained his greatest success with the nonreligious comedies *A Phoenix Too Frequent* (1946), *The Lady's Not for Burning* (1949), and *Venus Observed* (1950). His other plays include *A Sleep of Prisoners* (1951) and *Curtmantle* (1961).

Fry was born CHRISTOPHER HARRIS in Bristol. He also wrote for films and provided well-received translations of several modern French plays.   MALCOLM GOLDSTEIN

FRY, ELIZABETH GURNEY (1780-1845), a British reformer, was among the first to insist that prisoners need help rather than punishment in becoming good citizens. Her work aroused the conscience of officials, and led to many reforms. She was horrified by conditions in Newgate Prison in London, particularly among the women. Many women had their children with them in prison. Although it was considered dangerous to go among the prisoners, she visited them, found work for them, started schools for their children, and insisted on better living conditions. She also began a simple form of nurses' training and a free school at her home. Elizabeth Fry was born in Norfolk, England. ALAN KEITH-LUCAS

FRY, FRANKLIN CLARK (1900-1968), was one of America's most prominent Lutheran clergymen. He became president of the United Lutheran Church of America in 1945 and of the Lutheran World Federation in 1957. After 1954, he served as chairman of the central committee of the World Council of Churches. Fry was born in Bethlehem, Pa.   L. J. TRINTERUD

FRYING. See COOKING (Methods).

FU-CHOU. See FOOCHOW.

FUCHS, KLAUS. See ROSENBERG.

FUCHS, *fyooks,* **SIR VIVIAN ERNEST** (1908-   ), is a British geologist and Antarctic expert. He headed the British Commonwealth Trans-Antarctic Expedition in 1957 and 1958. Sir Edmund Hillary led the New Zealand party. The expedition, the first known party to cross Antarctica, covered 2,158 miles (3,473 kilometers) in 99 days, and made geophysical observations. Fuchs became director of the British Antarctic Survey in 1958. See also ANTARCTICA (International Cooperation; picture: The First Antarctic Crossing). JOHN EDWARDS CASWELL

FUCHSIA, *FYU shuh,* a house and garden plant, is cultivated in America and Europe. There are about 70 kinds of fuchsias. Most grow wild in tropical America. Some are shrubs, and others are trees or climbers.

Fuchsias grown indoors are often called *lady's eardrops*. They are small and green, and not woody. The flowers droop from long, dangling pollen stalks.

Gardeners grow fuchsias easily from cuttings. The cut-

J. Horace McFarland
Fuchsia Flowers are funnel-shaped and colored purple, red, white, or pink. Many fuchsias are used for indoor winter plants.

tings should be planted in the spring in light, porous soil, with plenty of water and protection from strong sunlight. Indoors, fuchsias should be kept watered and out of direct sunshine. The fuchsia is named after the German botanist and physician, Leonhard Fuchs.

Scientific Classification. Fuchsias belong to the evening primrose family, *Onagraceae*. The fuchsias most commonly planted in greenhouses and gardens are genus *Fuchsia*, species *F. coccinea; F. fulgens;* and *F. hybrida.* MARCUS MAXON

See also FLOWER (color picture: Enjoying Flowers).

FUEGIAN. See TIERRA DEL FUEGO.

FUEL

FUEL is any substance that produces useful heat or power when burned. We use fuels to heat our homes in winter and to cook our food. Without fuels, our airplanes, trains, and automobiles could not run, and most of our factories would be idle.

Nature produces the common fuels such as coal, oil, and natural gas. These fuels, called *fossil fuels*, come from beneath the earth's surface, where they were formed millions of years ago from plants and animals. Chemical plants make gasoline, kerosene, and other fuels from these common fuels. Man also uses nuclear fuels that provide heat and power from atomic energy. In addition, electricity can be classed as a fuel when it is used to produce heat, as in an electric stove.

Early man discovered fire and burned wood as a fuel as long as 200,000 years ago. The Chinese used coal, oil, and natural gas as fuels as early as 1100 B.C. Today, fuel production is one of the world's leading industries. In the early 1970's, shortages of some fuels in the United States led to concern that the nation might be facing an energy crisis (see PETROLEUM [Energy Crisis]; GAS [History of the Gas Industry]).

Kinds of Fuel

The fuels man uses can be divided into five main groups. These are: (1) solid fuels, (2) liquid fuels, (3) gas fuels, (4) atomic fuels, and (5) chemical fuels. The common solid, liquid, and gas fuels consist chiefly of carbon and hydrogen, or combinations of these two elements called *hydrocarbons* (see HYDROCARBON). Most of these fuels also contain small amounts of nitrogen, oxygen, sulfur, and ash. When a common fuel burns, the hydrogen and carbon react with oxygen in the air to form new products. In the process, they give off heat (see COMBUSTION; OXIDATION). Atomic fuels give off heat through the *fission* (splitting) or *fusion* (joining together) of atoms (see FISSION; FUSION). Chemical fuels burn by reacting with oxygen, but contain elements such as boron and magnesium instead of carbon.

Solid Fuels. The chief solid fuels are coal, wood, peat, charcoal, and coke.

Coal ranks as one of the world's most important fuels. The three main kinds of coal are: (1) bituminous, (2) anthracite, and (3) lignite. *Bituminous coal*, or *soft coal*, is the most important coal used by industry. It not only supplies heat and power, but factories also change it into coke, gas fuels, and valuable chemical products such as drugs, and plastics. *Anthracite*, also called *hard coal*, has value as a fuel, because it burns without smoke. *Lignite*, or *brown coal*, contains much moisture and produces less heat than anthracite or bituminous coal.

Wood was once man's chief fuel. But coal, coke, petroleum, and other fuels have largely replaced it.

Peat, like lignite, contains much moisture and therefore is a poor fuel. It represents the in-between step in nature's process of changing plant remains into coal.

Charcoal and *Coke* are manufactured fuels. Plants make charcoal by heating wood in kilns or retorts that resemble large ovens. Charcoal is used in chemical processes and as a fuel for picnic grills and fireplaces. Fuel plants make coke by heating certain kinds of bituminous coal in ovens until most of the gases have been driven out. The coke that remains after heating

SOLID FUELS	B.T.U. A POUND
Anthracite Coal	12,700
Bituminous Coal	9,400-14,900
Carbon, Graphite	14,093
Charcoal	13,000
Coke	12,600
Lignite	7,000
Peat (Air Dried)	7,000
Wood (Air Dried)	6,900

LIQUID FUELS	B.T.U. A POUND
Alcohol, Denatured	11,600
Alcohol, Ethyl	13,161
Alcohol, Methyl	10,259
Crude Oil	19,460
Diesel Oil	19,550
Fuel Oils	18,320-19,650
Gasoline	21,400
Kerosene	19,810
Liquid Hydrocarbons (Pure)	
Benzene	19,068
Decane	20,483
Hexane	20,771
Octane	20,591
Toluene	19,537
Xylene	18,650

Heat Values of Fuels are often measured in British thermal units. A British thermal unit (B.T.U.) is the amount of heat needed to raise the temperature of one pound of water one degree Fahrenheit. The metric system measures heat in *calories*. One B.T.U. equals

is used principally as a fuel for making iron and steel.

Liquid Fuels. Refineries make the main liquid fuels from crude oil, or petroleum. When crude oil comes from the ground, it is a complex mixture of many different liquid hydrocarbons. Refineries *refine*, or separate, the mixture into fuels such as gasoline, kerosene, and light and heavy fuel oils. Liquid fuels have several advantages over solid fuels. They are easier to handle, store, and transport. Except for the heavy fuel oils, liquid fuels contain almost no ash or other impurities.

Gasoline provides the main fuel for the engines of automobiles, airplanes, and other vehicles. *Kerosene* has become the basic fuel for commercial jet aircraft. Jet fuel used by the military is a mixture of gasoline, kerosene, and oils with low freezing points. People once used kerosene mainly as a fuel for lamps and stoves. Refineries refine *fuel oils* into several grades. Diesel engines and furnaces in homes and industry burn the lightest fuel oils. The heaviest grades, known as *residual fuel oils*, are thick, heavy oils. They are burned as a fuel chiefly by large ships and power plants such as those that produce electricity. Other liquids such as

476

HEAT VALUES OF FUELS

CHEMICAL FUELS	B.T.U. A POUND
Aluminum	13,310
Beryllium	29,160
Boron	25,120
Diborane	31,390
Hydrogen	51,605
Lithium	18,460
Lithium Hydride	17,770
Magnesium	10,640
Pentaborane	29,150
Silane	17,160
Silicon	13,160
Titanium	8,190

GAS FUELS	B.T.U. A CUBIC FOOT
Acetylene	1,488
Butane	3,392
Butylene	3,190
Carbon Monoxide	322
Ethane	1,789
Ethylene	1,614
Manufactured Gases	
Blue or Water Gas	290
Carbureted Water Gas	540
Coke Oven or Coal Gas	550-575
Oil Gas	550-960
Producer Gas	135-175
Methane	1,015
Natural Gas	970-1,200
Pentane	4,200
Propane	2,573
Propylene	2,383

252 calories. Heating engineers measure chemical, liquid, and solid fuels by weight. They measure gas fuels by volume. The heat values of fuels depend on their composition and on their weight and ash content.

alcohol may be used to power rockets, or burned in small stoves. Some oils made from plants and animal fat serve as fuels for candles and lamps.

Gas Fuels include natural and manufactured gases.

Natural Gas ranks as the most important gas fuel in the United States and Canada. It comes from wells drilled deep underground. Vast networks of pipelines carry the gas from the wells to cities and towns in almost all parts of the United States. Natural gas makes an ideal fuel. When burned, it gives off almost twice as much heat as the common manufactured gases, and leaves no ashes or other waste.

Natural gas is a mixture of hydrocarbon gases that consist chiefly of *methane*. Gas companies remove some of the heavier hydrocarbons in natural gas as it leaves the wells. These hydrocarbons are called *natural gasoline* and are blended with refinery-made gasoline. The gas companies may also remove lighter hydrocarbons, such as *propane* and *butane*, from natural gas. These gas fuels are sometimes called *liquefied petroleum*, or *LP*, *gas*. Dealers distribute LP gas in small pressure containers to farm and suburban homes for use as a fuel for cooking

and heating. Methane, which is the lightest hydrocarbon, is a widely used fuel in homes and industry.

Manufactured Gases are made from coal, coke, or petroleum by a number of processes. A fuel gas called *coke oven gas* or *coal gas* is recovered as a byproduct when coal is heated in ovens or retorts to make coke. Gas companies break petroleum down into a fuel gas known as *oil gas* by heating it. A fuel gas called *blue gas* or *water gas* can also be made through a chemical reaction between hot coke and steam.

Atomic Fuels must have atoms that can either split or fuse in a *chain* (continuous) reaction to produce heat and power. Only a few materials have atoms that can split in this way. Uranium-235 is the most important of these materials. Hydrogen is the only material that has been fused, but not in a controlled reaction. Atomic fuels have the advantage of compactness. One pound (0.5 kilogram) of uranium-235 is about the size of a walnut, but this amount produces as much heat as 1,500 short tons (1,360 metric tons) of coal. See NUCLEAR ENERGY.

Chemical Fuels are man-made substances, sometimes called *exotic fuels*. They provide the great power needed to drive jet aircraft and rockets. There are two kinds of these fuels. One is for jet engines that operate where oxygen from the air is available to burn the fuel. The other is for rockets that fly outside the earth's atmosphere and must carry both fuel and oxygen. Examples of the first kind of chemical fuels include compounds made of hydrogen and boron. Some of these compounds produce half again as much heat as kerosene jet fuels.

Common liquid chemical fuels for rockets include alcohol and kerosene. These fuels are burned with oxygen or other *oxidizers*, such as nitric acid, that easily give up oxygen. Scientists have also developed solid chemical fuels for rockets and missiles. These fuels consist of particles of an oxidizer bound together by a material such as rubber or plastic. The binding material serves as the fuel.　　　　HARLAN W. NELSON

Related Articles in WORLD BOOK include:

ATOMIC FUELS

Plutonium	Thorium	Uranium

CHEMICAL FUELS

Aluminum	Boron	Lithium	Silicon
Beryllium	Hydrogen	Magnesium	Titanium

GAS FUELS

Acetylene	Carbon	Ethane	Gas
Butane and	Monoxide	Ethylene	Methane
Propane	Coke Oven Gas		

LIQUID FUELS

Alcohol	Gas Oil	Kerosene	Oil	Toluene
Benzene	Gasoline	Octane	Petroleum	

SOLID FUELS

Bark	Coal	Lignite	Wood
Charcoal	Coke	Peat	

OTHER RELATED ARTICLES

Combustion	Heating (Sources	Rocket (Kinds
Electricity	of Heat)	of Rocket
Energy Supply	Nuclear Energy	Engines)
Fire	Power	Solar Energy
Heat		

FUEL CELL

FUEL CELL is a device that produces electricity from a fuel and an *oxidizer*, a substance that combines with the fuel. The fuel and oxidizer react chemically at two separate *electrodes* (electrical terminals), which produces the direct electric current. This description also applies to an ordinary battery. But in a battery, the electrodes themselves are the fuel and oxidizer and are used up in the reaction. In a fuel cell, the fuel and oxidizer are added from outside the cell and the electrodes remain largely unchanged.

Today, fuel cells are used only to supply electricity for special uses. For example, fuel cells provided the electricity for the Apollo spacecraft. These cells used hydrogen as the fuel and oxygen as the oxidizer. They produced about $1\frac{1}{2}$ kilowatts of power.

Scientists and engineers hope to lower the cost and increase the reliability of fuel cells. They are working to produce cells that can be run directly on low-cost fuels, such as diesel fuel, gasoline, or natural gas. Oxygen in the air would be the oxidizer in these cells. Future uses for fuel cells may include furnishing electricity and heat for homes and powering military vehicles or civilian electric cars.

The main advantage of fuel cells over other methods of generating electricity is their high efficiency. Most electric power today is generated by machines that use heat. The efficiency of these machines is limited. In theory, fuel cells can change chemical energy into electricity without any change in temperature. However, today's fuel cells do produce some waste heat.

In a fuel cell, the fuel is oxidized at the fuel electrode and gives up electrons (see OXIDATION). These electrons make up the electricity produced by the cell. The electrons flow through an outside circuit and then back to the oxidizer electrode. There, another reaction with the oxidizer occurs, and *ions* (electrically charged atoms) are formed. These ions flow through the *electrolyte* (current-carrying solution) between the electrodes and complete the electric circuit.

There are two kinds of fuel cells. In *primary* cells, the fuel and oxidizer are used only once. In *secondary* cells, the products of the reactions are regenerated so that the fuel and oxidizer can be reused. There are three types of primary cells. One type uses a water solution electrolyte. Other kinds of primary cells use *molten* (melted) salt or solid electrolytes. C. GORDON PEATTIE

FUEL INJECTION is a system for squirting fuel into the cylinders of diesel and gasoline engines. It replaces the carburetor when used on gasoline engines (see CARBURETOR). With fuel injection, a pump forces fuel under high pressure to a nozzle at each cylinder. On most diesel engines, these nozzles inject the fuel directly into the cylinders. On most gasoline engines that use fuel injection, and on some diesels, the nozzles spray the fuel into an *intake port*, or chamber, near each cylinder. There the fuel mixes with air before a valve opens to admit the mixture into the cylinder. The fuel may be injected into the intake port in a continuous stream or only when the intake valve opens.

Fuel injection overcomes several disadvantages of carburetors. A carburetor mixes air and fuel. Heat from the engine vaporizes this mixture to make it burn properly. The expansion of the heated air reduces the

FUEL INJECTION

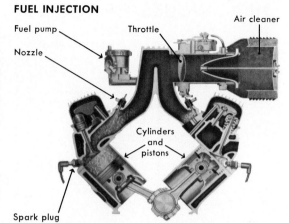

Fuel-Injection Systems feed fuel to diesel engines and some gasoline engines. A pump forces fuel to a nozzle at each cylinder. The nozzles inject the fuel. Controls link the pump to the throttle, which regulates the air flow to the cylinders.

amount of air going to the cylinders. The cylinders get differing amounts of the vapor, depending on their distance from the carburetor. Some of the gasoline often fails to burn, because of improper vaporization. The engine may *flood* (get too much gasoline), or ice up in winter and vapor lock in summer (see VAPOR LOCK).

Fuel injection includes an air-flow system and a fuel system. Electronic or mechanical controls link the two systems so that each cylinder gets the same amount of fuel. The cylinders also get only the amount of fuel that will burn in the amount of air that enters them. The nozzles break the fuel into a fine spray so that it all burns. The cylinders get more air, because the air does not have to be heated. This increases power and does not waste unburned fuel. Cold engines start quickly and run smoothly. The throttle controls only the air flow. Therefore, the engine cannot be flooded.

Fuel injection has always been used on diesel engines. Its use on some airplane and racing-car engines began after World War II. It came into use for American passenger automobiles in 1957. E. W. KETTERING

See also DIESEL ENGINE; GASOLINE ENGINE.

FUEL PUMP. See FUEL INJECTION.

FUEL VALUE OF FOODS. See NUTRITION.

FUGITIVE SLAVE LAW was a law which provided for the return of runaway slaves who escaped from one state to another. A clause in the Ordinance of 1787 provided for the return of slaves who had escaped to the free Northwest Territory. In 1793, Congress passed a fugitive slave law which allowed owners to recover their slaves merely by presenting proof of ownership before a magistrate. An order was then issued for the arrest and return of an escaped slave, who was allowed neither a jury trial nor the right to give evidence in his own behalf. Under this law, free Negroes living in the North were sometimes kidnaped and taken South as slaves. For this reason, some of the Northern states gave orders not to help in the recovery of fugitive slaves.

By the middle of the 1800's, the law of 1793 was no longer in force, but one item in the Compromise of 1850 revived it in an aggravated form. The new law imposed heavy penalties upon persons who aided a slave's escape or interfered with a slave's recovery. Some Northern states passed *personal liberty laws*, which sometimes prohibited state and local officers from obeying the national fugitive slave laws. JOHN DONALD HICKS

FUGUE. See AMNESIA.

FUGUE is a musical composition in which the different parts are introduced in succession and follow one another in the manner of a flight or chase. The term comes from *fuga*, the Latin word for *flight*. Johann Sebastian Bach was one of the greatest composers of fugues of all time. The strict fugue form is made up of an *exposition*, a *discussion*, and a concluding section, or *climax*, which often contains *stretto*. In stretto, the subjects and answers overlap, much as in "rounds."

The exposition begins with the *subject* (theme) by the first voice in the principal key. Then the second voice gives the *answer*, which is merely the subject transposed a fifth upward or a fourth downward. The first voice meanwhile gives a *countersubject*. The third voice then introduces the original subject an octave below or above the principal key, and a fourth voice paralleling the second voice answers. The discussion is made up of less formal repetitions of the subject and answer.

In the *double fugue*, two subjects in different parts are introduced at the start. There are also *free fugues*, or *fughettas*, which introduce the subjects in succession, without discussion or stretto. RAYMOND KENDALL

FUJI, MOUNT. See MOUNT FUJI.

FUKUOKA, *FOO koo OH kuh* (pop. 853,270), is the commercial center of the island of Kyushu in Japan (see JAPAN [political map]). Factories in Fukuoka produce dolls, machinery, paper, pottery, and textiles.

FULANI, *foo LAH nee*, are a people of the grassy regions of western Africa. The more than 5 million Fulani live as far west as Senegal and as far east as Cameroon. For hundreds of years, most Fulani have been cattle herders and have lived as minority groups among various agricultural peoples.

The Fulani originated in what are now Senegal and Guinea. A group of Fulani called the Tucolor built a powerful empire there during the A.D. 600's. The Fulani gradually spread eastward and reached Nigeria and Cameroon in the early 1800's.

Many Fulani became Muslims in the early 1700's and conquered a number of their neighbors in holy

Marilyn Silverstone, Magnum

Fulani Girls often wear earrings and necklaces. The Fulani are one of the largest ethnic groups in Nigeria.

wars. Between 1804 and 1809, Uthman Dan Fodio, a Muslim religious leader, conquered most of the Hausa states of Northern Nigeria. He then established an empire consisting of several Fulani states. Uthman's empire remained powerful until the British conquered Northern Nigeria in 1903. Many Fulani still live in the northern part of Nigeria. JOHN MIDDLETON

FULBRIGHT, J. WILLIAM (1905-   ), an Arkansas Democrat, served in the United States Senate from 1945 to 1974. He was chairman of the Senate Foreign Relations Committee from 1959 to 1974. Fulbright became a leading critic of U.S. involvement in the Vietnam War (1957-1975). During the 1960's and early 1970's, Fulbright was a spokesman for those who wanted Congress to have more control over presidential warmaking powers. He sponsored the Fulbright Act of 1946, which provides funds for the exchange of students between the United States and other countries (see FULBRIGHT SCHOLARSHIP).

James William Fulbright was born in Sumner, Mo., and entered the University of Arkansas at the age of 16. He graduated from Arkansas in 1925 and from the George Washington University Law School in 1934. From 1925 to 1928, he studied at Oxford University in England as a Rhodes scholar. Fulbright served as president of the University of Arkansas from 1939 to 1941 and was elected to the United States House of Representatives in 1942. He criticized U.S. foreign policy in his books, including *Old Myths and New Realities* (1964) and *The Arrogance of Power* (1967). WILLIAM J. EATON

FULBRIGHT SCHOLARSHIP is an award by the United States government for research, teaching, or graduate study. The scholarship program was begun under the Fulbright Act of 1946, named for its sponsor, Senator J. William Fulbright of Arkansas. It seeks to promote better understanding between the peoples of the United States and other countries.

The annual awards allow U.S. citizens to study or work in other lands and permit persons of other countries to study or work in the United States. About 110 countries have participated in the program, and over 120,000 scholarships have been awarded, about 42,000 of them to U.S. citizens.

Money for the awards came at first from the sale of surplus World War II equipment to other countries. The U.S. government and participating countries and universities now fund the program. The U.S. International Communication Agency (ICA) administers it. The Board of Foreign Scholarships selects the award winners. Interested persons may contact one of the following agencies.

For graduate study: The Institute of International Education, 809 United Nations Plaza, New York, N.Y. 10017.

For secondary-school teaching: The U.S. Office of Education, Division of International Education, Department of Health, Education, and Welfare, Washington, D.C. 20201.

For university lecturing and post-doctoral research: The Council for International Exchange of Scholars, 11 Dupont Circle NW, Suite 300, Washington, D.C. 20036. J. WILLIAM FULBRIGHT

FULCRUM. See LEVER.

FULGURITE. See GLASS (History of Glass).

FULLBACK. See FOOTBALL; RUGBY FOOTBALL.

FULLER, ALFRED CARL (1885-1973), founded the Fuller Brush Company. He started making brushes in Somerville, Mass., in 1906. Fuller developed his company by using the door-to-door selling method. Fuller salesmen called at about 9 of every 10 American homes and sold more than $800 million worth of Fuller brushes and other products in the firm's first 50 years. He was born in Nova Scotia, Canada. DONALD L. KEMMERER

FULLER, BUCKMINSTER (1895-   ), is an American designer who has sought to express the technology and needs of modern life in buildings and enclosures of space. He has an intense interest in expanding man's ability to control larger areas of his environment and still have a close relationship with nature. His designs show the influence of such natural molecular structures as the tetrahedron. Fuller has solved many design problems in such diversified fields as automobiles, buildings, and cities. His influence has been spread through his lectures, teaching, and writings. A collection of essays he wrote discussing his theories and designs was published as *Ideas and Integrities* (1963).

Richard Buckminster Fuller was born in Milton, Mass. He gained international attention in 1927 by designing an all-metal prefabricated home called a *Dymaxion house.* Between 1932 and 1935, he designed a revolutionary bullet-shaped three-wheeled auto. Since World War II, he has concentrated on designing large, lightweight prefabricated enclosures that he calls *geodesic domes.* DAVID GEBHARD

FULLER, MARGARET (1810-1850), was an American journalist and reformer. She became a leader of a philosophical movement called *transcendentalism* (see TRANSCENDENTALISM).

Architectural model (1927) by Buckminster Fuller;
Museum of Modern Art, New York City

Fuller's *Dymaxion House* was built around a mast so it could be lifted and easily moved from one site to another.

Sarah Margaret Fuller was born in Cambridgeport, Mass., near Boston. She began her journalistic career by serving from 1840 to 1842 as editor in chief of the transcendentalist magazine *The Dial.* Under her guidance, *The Dial* became one of the most important periodicals in American literary history. From 1844 to 1846, she wrote literary criticism for the *New York Tribune.* Her book *Papers on Literature and Art* (1846) grew out of her contributions to the *Tribune.*

As a reformer, Fuller campaigned for women's rights. Her most important book, *Woman in the Nineteenth Century* (1845), explores the political, economic, social, and intellectual status of women. She was far ahead of her time in her criticism of discrimination against women because of their sex.

Fuller went to Europe in 1846. The next year, she married the Marchese Angelo Ossoli, a follower of the Italian patriot Giuseppe Mazzini. The couple participated in the Italian revolution of 1848 and 1849. During a voyage to the United States, they and their son drowned when their ship sank. JOHN CLENDENNING

FULLER, MELVILLE WESTON (1833-1910), served as Chief Justice of the United States from 1888 to 1910. He was a capable Court administrator. But he clung to the doctrine of states' rights in a time of problems that required increasing federal regulation. Fuller's two best-known decisions declared the national income tax unconstitutional, and, by interpretation, greatly weakened the 1890 Sherman Antitrust Act (see TRUST [Trust Legislation]).

Fuller was born in Augusta, Me. He graduated from Bowdoin College and studied law at Harvard University. He was a Chicago corporation lawyer from 1856 to 1888. He served as a member of the Illinois constitutional convention in 1862, and later was a member of the Illinois legislature. Fuller was an arbitrator of the Anglo-Venezuelan dispute and a member of the Permanent Court of Arbitration at The Hague, from 1900 to 1910. JERRE S. WILLIAMS

FULLER THEOLOGICAL SEMINARY. See UNIVERSITIES AND COLLEGES (table).

FULLER'S EARTH is a claylike material that bleaches and purifies fats and oils. It consists of 50 to 80 per cent silica. Bleaching and purifying occur when particles of fuller's earth remove asphalt and resin from fatty or oily substances. The particles do this by *adsorbing* (collecting and holding) the asphalt and resin (see ABSORPTION AND ADSORPTION).

Petroleum companies use fuller's earth to purify crude oil and to lighten its color. Fuller's earth is also used to purify animal and vegetable oils. People once used a powdered form of it to remove grease from cloth and wool. Fuller's earth gets its name from this process, called *fulling.* WALTER E. REED and BARRIE WALL

FULMAR, *FOOL mer,* an ocean bird, is one of the petrels. The northern fulmar is the size of a duck. Its yellow bill is nearly as long as its head. The feet of the fulmar are webbed. The bird's hind toe is reduced to a claw.

This bird breeds on rocky shores and makes a shallow nest in high, rocky places. It lays only one egg in the nest. The fulmar feeds on any animal matter, but prefers fatty substances like whale blubber. Great numbers of fulmars follow whaling boats. The fulmar is valuable for its feathers, down, and oil. The people of Saint Kilda,

Eric Hosking

The Northern Fulmar Builds Its Nest on Rocky Cliffs.

Detail of an oil portrait (about 1806 to 1810) by Rembrandt Peale; Detroit Institute of Arts, gift of the Ford Foundation

Robert Fulton

an island near Scotland, eat the bird's flesh and eggs.

The fulmar lives in far northern seas from Melville Island to Greenland and Svalbard. In winter, it goes south to the Massachusetts coast and the southern coasts of Great Britain. It is common around Saint Kilda Island, the Outer Hebrides, and Scotland.

Scientific Classification. The fulmar belongs to the family *Procellariidae*. The northern fulmar is genus *Fulmarus*, species *F. glacialis*.   ALEXANDER WETMORE

See also PETREL.

FULTON, ROBERT (1765-1815), was an American inventor, civil engineer, and artist. He is best known for designing and building the *Clermont*, the first commercially successful steamboat. This boat ushered in a new era in the history of transportation. Fulton also made important contributions to the development of the submarine and to canal transportation. In addition, he showed talent as an artist.

Early Years. Fulton was born Nov. 14, 1765, on a farm near Little Britain in Lancaster County, Pennsylvania. He spent his boyhood in Lancaster, and showed inventive talent at an early age. He turned out lead pencils, household utensils for his mother, and skyrockets for a town celebration. Fulton developed a hand-operated paddle wheel for use on a rowboat, and constructed a rifle with sight and bore of original design.

Fulton went to Philadelphia at the age of 17, and was apprenticed to a jeweler. He soon began to make a name for himself as a painter of miniatures and portraits. He saved enough money to buy a farm for his mother. At the age of 21, he went to England to study with the fashionable American artist Benjamin West. In London, Fulton was able to make a moderate living as an artist. But he became increasingly interested in scientific and engineering developments. After 1793, he gave his full attention to this field, and painted only for amusement. Fulton began to travel. He studied science and higher mathematics, and learned French, Italian, and German.

The Inventor. Fulton had been interested for many years in the idea of steam propulsion for a boat. But his first enthusiasm was for canal development. He designed new types of canal boats, and a system of inclined planes to replace canal locks. Other mechanical problems challenged him. He invented a machine for making rope and one for spinning flax. He made a labor-saving device for cutting marble, and invented a dredging machine for cutting canal channels.

About 1797, Fulton turned his attention to the submarine. This project claimed most of his energies until 1806. He realized the dangers which submarines would bring to naval warfare, but thought that they might serve to limit sea war and piracy, for that very reason. Fulton's experimental submarines were able to dive and surface, and he succeeded in blowing up anchored test

Courtesy of The New-York Historical Society, New York

The *Clermont*. Inventor Robert Fulton painted this water color sketch of his famous steamboat in 1808. The boat made its first successful trip up the Hudson River.

craft. But the problem of propulsion under water was never satisfactorily solved. Fulton's submarine ideas interested both Napoleon Bonaparte and the British Admiralty, but neither ever adopted them wholeheartedly.

In 1802, Robert R. Livingston, the United States minister to France, interested Fulton in turning his attention to the steamboat. An experimental boat, launched on the Seine River in Paris in 1803, sank because the engine was too heavy. But a second boat, which was built in the same year, operated successfully. Fulton ordered an engine from the British firm of Boulton & Watt, and returned to the United States in 1806.

Builds the *Clermont*. Fulton directed the building of a steamboat in New York in 1807. This boat, which he called *The North River Steamboat*, became famous as the *Clermont*. On Aug. 17, 1807, this vessel began its first successful trip up the Hudson River from New York City to Albany. After some alterations, the boat sailed in regular passenger service on the Hudson.

The *Clermont* was not the first steamboat to be built, but it was the first to become a practical and financial success. Part of Fulton's success was due to his concern for passenger comfort. His handbills announced: "Dinner will be served at exactly 2 o'clock . . . Tea with meats . . . Supper at 8 in the evening" and "A shelf has been added to each berth, on which gentlemen will please put their boots, shoes, and clothes, that the cabin will not be encumbered."

After the financial and mechanical success of his first boat, Fulton became occupied with building and operating others, and with expanding his activities to other parts of the country. He built two steamboats similar to the *Clermont*, and two ferries, for New York harbor. He defended the monopolies that a number of state legislatures had granted to him and Robert Livingston. He also experimented with the firing of guns under water. His findings became the basis of later developments in this field.

Fulton designed and built a steam warship, *Fulton the First*, for the defense of New York harbor in the War of 1812, but died before the completion of this remarkable craft. Congress authorized the construction of this vessel in 1814, after an investigation by naval experts. The statue of Fulton in Statuary Hall, Washington, D.C., honors his achievements. JOHN H. KEMBLE

See also CLERMONT; FITCH, JOHN; LIVINGSTON, ROBERT R.; STEAMBOAT; SHIP (The *Clermont*).

FUMAROLE, *FYOO muh rohl*, is a hole or vent in the ground that gives off volcanic gases. Most fumaroles occur in volcanic regions, such as Yellowstone National Park. The gases given off usually are steam mixed with carbon dioxide, hydrogen, hydrogen sulfide, hydrogen chloride, and nitrogen. Some of the gases are poisonous. Others cause choking. Fumaroles that give off sulfurous gases are called *solfataras*. G. A. MACDONALD

FUMIGATION, *FYOO muh GAY shuhn*, is the use of smoke or gases to drive away and kill insects, mice, and other rodents or vermin. Exterminators seal the house or apartment which is to be fumigated. They pipe the gas or smoke in, and, in a short time, it kills the insects or rodents. The most common poisons used for fumigation include cyanide, formaldehyde, and chlorine gases. Sulfur gases were once used, but they harmed the walls and

furniture. All fumigating gases are poisonous, and should be used only by persons who have been trained. Most large communities now have professional exterminators.

Fumigation was once used to disinfect houses in which someone had had a communicable disease such as smallpox. Health officials no longer follow this practice because cleanliness and hygiene have been found to be more effective in killing the germs. W. V. MILLER

See also CHLORINE; FORMALDEHYDE; INSECTICIDE.

FUNCHAL, *fun SHAHL* (pop. 43,768), is the capital, largest city, and chief port of the Madeira Islands. The Madeiras belong to Portugal and lie in the Atlantic Ocean off the northwest coast of Africa. Funchal is on the southern coast of the island of Madeira. The city's pleasant climate makes it a popular resort.

Portuguese settlers founded Funchal in 1421. The city has many beautiful gardens and a cathedral that dates from the 1400's. Funchal's economy is based on the tourist trade and the export of sugar and the famous Madeira wines. The city also produces ceramics and linen embroidery. Funchal has a modern airport, and airlines connect the city with western Europe and northern Africa. DOUGLAS L. WHEELER

See also MADEIRA ISLANDS (picture).

FUNCTION, in mathematics. See ALGEBRA (Functions); CALCULUS.

FUNCTIONAL ILLITERACY. See ILLITERACY.

FUNDAMENTAL ORDERS. See CONNECTICUT (English Settlement).

FUNDAMENTALISM is a broad movement within Protestantism in the United States. The movement tries to preserve what it considers the basic ideas of Christianity against criticism by liberal theologians.

At the end of the 1800's, many liberal religious scholars challenged the accuracy of the Bible. They also used historical research to question previously accepted Christian beliefs. The liberals attempted to adjust Christian theology to then new discoveries in the sciences, particularly in biology and geology. Many Christians believed the work of the liberals threatened the authenticity and even the survival of Christianity.

Between 1910 and 1912, anonymous authors published 12 small volumes entitled *The Fundamentals*. The fundamentalist movement got its name from these booklets. The authors tried to explain what they felt were basic Christian doctrines that should be accepted without question. These doctrines included the absolute accuracy of the Bible, including the story of creation and accounts of miracles. Other doctrines included the Virgin Birth of Jesus, Christ's atonement for the sins of humanity through His Crucifixion, and Christ's Second Coming.

Fundamentalists had an impact on many Protestant denominations, especially among Baptists and Presbyterians. Many fundamentalists broke away and formed new churches. ROBERT L. FERM

See also BOB JONES UNIVERSITY.

FUNDY, BAY OF. See BAY OF FUNDY.

FUNDY NATIONAL PARK. See CANADA (National Parks).

FUNERAL CUSTOMS are special ceremonies performed after a person dies. Throughout history, humankind has developed such customs to express grief, comfort the living, and honor the dead.

Nearly all religions include the belief that human

beings survive death in some form. For many people, a funeral symbolizes a passage from one life to another, rather than the end of a person's existence. Such a ceremony, which is associated with the completion of one phase of life and the beginning of another, is called a *rite of passage*. Other rites of passage include baptism, initiation of young people into adulthood, and marriage.

Funeral customs vary from society to society, but many of the same practices are found throughout the world. These practices include public announcement of the death; preparation of the body; religious ceremonies or other services; a procession; a burial or other form of disposal; and mourning.

Preparation of the Body varies among different peoples. Typically, however, the corpse is laid out and washed. Sometimes it is painted or anointed with oils. It is then dressed in new or special garments or wrapped in a cloth called a *shroud*. In most societies, the body is placed in a coffin, also called a casket, or other container.

Many peoples hold an all-night watch called a *wake* beside the corpse. They may do so in the belief that the wake comforts the spirit of the dead or protects the body from evil spirits. In the past, another reason for a wake was to watch for signs of life. Before modern tests were developed, an unconscious person might be mistaken for dead.

In the United States and Canada, funeral directors preserve most bodies by a process called *embalming*. An embalmer removes the blood and injects a chemical solution into the veins to retard decay. The embalmer also uses cosmetics to restore a more natural appearance to the dead person, who may have been disfigured by a long illness or an accident. Such treatment is common in North America because most bodies are kept several days or more before the funeral. During this period, relatives and friends come to view the body. Embalming is not required by law except in special circumstances, such as if a body is to be transported or stored. In other countries, embalming is rare because most people are buried within a day or two after death.

The Funeral may include prayers, hymns and other music, and speeches called *eulogies* that recall and praise the dead person. In the United States, many funeral services take place at a funeral home with the embalmed body on display. After the service, a special vehicle called a *hearse* carries it in a procession to the cemetery or crematory. A final brief ceremony is held before the body is buried, or cremated in a special furnace. After many funerals, the mourners return with the bereaved family to their house and share food. Later, a tombstone or other monument is erected to record the dead person's life and mark the place of burial.

Burial is the most common method of disposal in Christian, Jewish, and Muslim countries. Human burial developed from the belief that the dead rise again. Like a seed, according to this belief, a body is planted in the earth to await rebirth.

Cremation is customary in Buddhist and Hindu nations and is increasing in the United States and Can-

Robert Fulton, the contributor of this article, is Professor of Sociology and Director of the Center for Death Education and Research at the University of Minnesota.

ada. However, Orthodox Jews, Roman Catholics, and some Protestant groups oppose this practice. They believe the body is the temple of the soul or of the Holy Spirit and should not be destroyed. Other religions do not object to cremation.

Some societies dispose of their dead in other ways. For example, the Sioux Indians of North America place their dead on high platforms. Some groups of Aborigines, the original inhabitants of Australia, leave dead bodies in trees. In Tibet, bodies are sunk in water. The Parsis, a religious group who live mainly in India, take their dead to special enclosures called *towers of silence*. There, birds pick the bones clean. The Parsis believe the earth and fire are sacred and must not be violated by burying or burning a corpse.

Mourning is the expression of grief after a death. People in mourning may deny themselves amusement, avoid certain foods, or wear special clothing. Until the 1940's, Americans and Europeans wore black armbands and hung funeral wreaths on their doors while in mourning. Some societies regard a period of mourning as a time of uncleanliness. They believe death contaminates the survivors and makes them *taboo* (set apart as cursed or sacred). See TABOO.

History. As early as 60,000 years ago, prehistoric people observed special ceremonies when burying their dead. Neanderthal graves, for example, contain tools, weapons, and evidence of flowers. The ancient Egyptians and other early peoples placed food, jewels, and other goods in tombs. Such provisions showed the belief that a person continued to exist after death and had the same needs as in life. The Egyptians also developed embalming into an advanced technique called *mummification*. They believed the spirit would someday return to inhabit the body. Therefore, it had to be preserved to prevent the soul from perishing.

During the 1900's, traditional funeral and mourning practices have declined in the United States. Ideas concerning death and the treatment of the dead are in a state of change. Criticism of North American funeral practices as needlessly elaborate and expensive has led many people to seek alternatives. For example, some families prefer to hold a memorial service at their home or church.

However, the funeral fills important emotional needs for the living. It focuses attention upon the grief of the survivors and provides a public ceremony that helps them acknowledge and accept their loss. A funeral also helps the survivors express their feelings and discharge their grief.   ROBERT FULTON

Related Articles in WORLD BOOK include:

Catacombs	Funeral Director	Potter's Field
Cemetery	Mask (Burial Masks	Pyramids
Crypt	and Death Masks;	Sarcophagus
Death	picture)	Suttee
Embalming	Mummy	Tomb
Epitaph	Necropolis	Wake

FUNERAL DIRECTOR is a person who prepares the dead for burial or other form of disposition. The funeral director also performs other services at the time of death. A funeral director is also called a *mortician* or an *undertaker*. In some states, a person who is licensed to provide funeral services is called an *embalmer*.

FUNGI

Responsibilities. An important service of a funeral director is to supervise the embalming of the body for temporary preservation. Embalming is done by removing the blood and body fluids and injecting a preserving fluid into the arteries. Embalming may also include restoring facial features that were disfigured by an accident or prolonged illness.

A funeral director organizes the kind of funeral or other arrangement desired by the family or friends of the dead person. The director obtains a burial permit, notifies relatives and the press, and plans with the clergy for services. Services may be held in the home, a church, or the funeral home, and at the grave or crematory. Services may also be nonreligious.

Most funeral homes have a chapel, a casket-selection room, and a preparation room. A funeral director's equipment may include a hearse, also called a casket coach; a flower car; limousines; and an ambulance.

Funeral directors are in a position to offer experienced and sympathetic advice to the mourners. In some cases, they assist families for several months following the funeral. They may help relatives collect insurance and death benefits from social security, from unions, or from fraternal and veterans' organizations.

History. Throughout history, people in all societies have regarded the disposal of the dead as a solemn act requiring group concern and accompanied by certain ceremonies. Patterns of conduct have developed out of a sense of loss, grief, and mystery caused by death. Religious beliefs and practices have been the most important of these patterns. The funeral director helps people perform ceremonies that follow their beliefs and customs.

By the mid-1800's, the functions performed by a funeral director had become a service occupation in the United States. By 1900, funeral directors were required by law to have certain training and to meet other qualifications.

As a Career. In the United States, about 22,000 funeral homes employ about 65,000 persons. Most funeral directors have both a funeral director's and an embalmer's license or a combination license.

Each state establishes its own licensing requirements, but nearly all the states require a high school diploma. About 25 states require up to two years of college. Every state also requires at least a year of study in funeral-service education, plus an apprenticeship from six months to three years. The most common apprenticeship is for one year. All applicants for a license must pass a state board examination. The American Board of Funeral Service Education has approved more than 30 funeral-service education schools.

Information about a career in funeral direction may be obtained from the National Funeral Directors Association, 135 W. Wells Street, Milwaukee, Wis. 53203.

Critically reviewed by the NATIONAL FUNERAL DIRECTORS ASSOCIATION

See also EMBALMING; FUNERAL CUSTOMS; MUMMY.

FUNGI, *FUHN jy,* are simple nongreen plants. They lack chlorophyll, the green coloring matter that higher plants use to make food. Fungi have no leaves, roots, or stems. This article discusses only the plants that scientists call *true fungi.* For information about other organisms sometimes grouped among the fungi, see the WORLD BOOK articles on BACTERIA and SLIME MOLD.

According to *mycologists,* scientists who study fungi, there are more than 100,000 species of these plants. The most common include mildews, molds, and mushrooms.

Parts of a Fungus. Except for yeasts and other one-celled fungi, the main part of a fungus consists of thousands of threadlike cells called *hyphae.* These tiny, branching cells form a tangled mass called a *mycelium.* In many kinds of fungi, the mycelium grows beneath the surface of the material on which the plant is feeding. For example, the mycelium of a mushroom grows underground. The umbrella-shaped growth known as a mushroom is actually the *fruiting body* of the mushroom plant. The fruiting body produces cells called *spores,* which develop into new plants. Spores are smaller and simpler than the seeds of green plants, but they have the same function.

Yeasts and other one-celled fungi are too small to be seen without a microscope. However, the fruiting bodies of many fungi can be seen with the unaided eye, and the largest of these structures measure more than 3 feet (91 centimeters) in diameter.

How a Fungus Lives. Fungi live almost everywhere in the soil, water, and air. Some fungi are parasites that feed on living plants and animals. Others, called *saprophytes,* live on decaying matter. Still other fungi live together with other plants in ways that benefit both organisms. Such a relationship is called *symbiosis.* For example, a fungus and a simple plant called an *alga* may live together symbiotically. They form a plant called a *lichen* (see LICHEN). Some fungi also live on the roots of higher plants in a symbiotic relationship known as a *mycorrhiza.* The fungus gets moisture and carbohydrates from the green plant. In return, the fungus helps supply the green plant with nitrogen and such essential minerals as phosphorus and zinc. Many species of trees, shrubs, and herbs have mycorrhizas.

Fungi cannot produce their own food because they do not contain chlorophyll. They must take carbohydrates, proteins, and other nutrients from the animals, plants, or decaying matter on which they live. Fungi discharge chemicals called *enzymes* into the material on which they feed. The enzymes break down complex carbohydrates and proteins into simple compounds that the hyphae can absorb.

Department of Plant Pathology, University
of Wisconsin-Madison (S. A. Vicen)

Some Kinds of Fungi live on the roots of green plants in relationships called *mycorrhizas,* which benefit both species. In the example shown above, the white threadlike hyphae of a mushroom grow together with the roots of Norway spruce trees.

Black Bread Mold

Black bread mold is one of the most common fungi. A 10-day growth of this mold covers the slice of bread shown at the left. The hyphae and fruiting bodies of the mold are visible in the microscopic photograph in the center. The diagram at the right shows these and other parts of the mold.

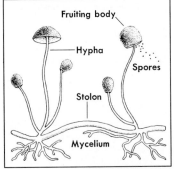

Fruiting body

Hypha

Spores

Stolon

Mycelium

Runk/Schoenberger from
Grant Heilman

WORLD BOOK illustration
by Margaret Ann Moran

Most kinds of fungi reproduce by forming spores. Some spores are produced by the union of *gametes* (sex cells). Others, called *asexual* or *imperfect* spores, are produced without the union of sex cells. Many fungi produce spores both sexually and asexually. Most spores are scattered by the wind and by water. Mushrooms and some other fungi discharge their spores. A spore that lands in a spot favorable for growth soon begins to produce a new fungus plant.

Yeasts can produce spores, but they almost always reproduce by *budding*. When a yeast buds, a bulge forms on the cell. A cell wall grows and separates the bud from the original cell, and the bud then develops into a new yeast.

The Importance of Fungi. Fungi break down complex animal and plant matter into simple compounds. This process of *decomposition* enriches the soil and makes essential substances available to plants in a form they can use. Through decomposition, fungi also return carbon dioxide to the atmosphere, where green plants reuse it to make food.

Fungi play a major role in a number of foods. For example, mushrooms and truffles are considered delicacies by many people (see TRUFFLE). Cheese manufacturers add molds to Camembert and Roquefort cheeses to ripen them and provide their distinctive flavors.

Yeasts cause the *fermentation* that produces alcoholic beverages. In the fermentation process, yeasts break down sugar into carbon dioxide and alcohol. Baker's yeast causes bread to rise by producing carbon dioxide from the carbohydrates in the dough. The carbon dioxide gas bubbles up through the dough and causes it to rise. Someday, yeasts may become an important new source of food. Some people already eat yeasts as a rich source of protein and B vitamins.

Some molds produce important drugs called *antibiotics*. Antibiotics weaken or destroy bacteria and other organisms that cause disease. Penicillin, the first and most important antibiotic, was discovered in 1929 by Sir Alexander Fleming, a British bacteriologist. *Penicillium notatum* is one of several green molds that produce penicillin, which physicians use in treating many diseases caused by bacteria.

Some fungi cause great damage. Parasitic fungi destroy many crops and other plants. Important parasitic fungi that attack plants include mildews, rusts, and smuts. Others produce diseases in animals and people. Some mushrooms are poisonous and can cause serious illness or death if eaten. Molds spoil many kinds of food. In damp climates, mildews and other fungi can ruin clothing, bookbindings, and other materials.

Scientific Classification. Botanists traditionally consider fungi as part of the plant kingdom. Under this system, the true fungi make up the phylum Eumycophyta in the subkingdom Thallophyta (see PLANT [A Classification of the Plant Kingdom]). However, many biologists consider fungi to be a separate kingdom. They classify the true fungi as phylum Eumycota within this fungi kingdom.   ORSON K. MILLER, JR.

Related Articles. See FUNGUS DISEASE with its list of *Related Articles.* See also the following articles:

Mold	Plant (Fungi)	Saprophyte
Mushroom	Puffball	Yeast
Parasite		

FUNGICIDE is a chemical substance that is used to kill growths called *fungi* that are harmful to human beings and plants. Diseases caused by fungi can destroy or seriously damage food crops. A fungus disease destroyed the potato crop in Ireland and caused the Irish potato famine in which about 750,000 persons died in the 1840's. Fungus also caused the chestnut blight that killed thousands of American chestnut trees in the United States during the early 1900's.

Grant Heilman

Some Penicillium Molds, such as the one shown above, cause citrus fruits to spoil. Others ripen certain cheeses.

Corn Smut has infected this corn plant. Smuts and other parasitic fungi cause great damage to grain crops.

FUNGUS DISEASE

Great quantities of fungicides are sold each year to protect plants and human beings from fungus diseases. Fungicides are sprayed or dusted on plants to kill fungus diseases called *rusts, mildews, smuts,* and *molds.* They are used to protect potatoes, apples, and other crops from fungus diseases called *blight* and *scab.* Many kinds of seeds are dipped in a fungicide to prevent *damping-off,* a disease that prevents seeds from *germinating* (starting to grow).

Human beings use preparations containing a fungicide to prevent such diseases as *athlete's foot.* Fabrics are treated with fungicides to prevent rotting.

Inorganic Fungicides are made from metal compounds. Copper compounds have been widely used to protect against mildew on fruit trees, grapevines, and vegetables, and to treat seeds. Among the copper compounds is Bordeaux mixture, which contains copper sulfate and lime. Other compounds contain carbonate, chloride, hydroxide, and sulfate. Sulfur and lime-sulfur are used to control scab and another fungus disease called *brown rot,* which attack fruit. Mercury compounds are used on seeds and lawns.

Organic Fungicides are poisonous chemical compounds that contain carbon, hydrogen, and oxygen atoms. Most organic fungicides are *synthetic* (man-made). Formaldehyde and chloranil are used to treat seeds and potatoes. Maneb, nabam, and zineb are sprayed on the leaves of fruit trees and on vegetables and cereal grasses to kill rusts and fungi that cause blight. Organic fungicides containing mercury compounds are used to treat seeds and soils. Others are used to prevent rot in wood, rope, tents, and some paints.

Fungicides must be poisonous to fungi. But they must not be harmful to the plants they are supposed to protect. Fungicides should be used with care, because many will be harmful to plants if they are applied too heavily. Many fungicides are poisonous to humans. They should be stored where small children, livestock, and pets cannot get them. Some fungicides also leave poisonous deposits on food crops. The deposits must be cleaned off before these crops are used.   W. V. MILLER

Related Articles in WORLD BOOK include:

Bordeaux Mixture	Fungus Disease	Mildew	Rust
Fungi	Insecticide	Mold	

FUNGUS DISEASE. Many kinds of fungi live and feed on the tissues of living plants and animals (see FUNGI). These *parasites* often cause diseases in the plants and animals they infect.

Diseases of Plants. The most important fungi that live on plants include smuts, rusts, and mildews. They affect many kinds of plants. One kind of fungus disease, chestnut blight, has destroyed American chestnut trees. Dutch elm disease, caused by a fungus, threatens to eliminate the elm trees of the United States. Fungus diseases in plants sometimes spread rapidly. To avoid crop losses, farmers may use *fungicides,* chemicals that kill fungi (see FUNGICIDE). Breeders try to develop plants that will resist fungus attacks.

Diseases of Human Beings and Animals. Fungi that infect people and animals may cause skin disorders or serious illness. *Actinomycosis,* or lumpy jaw, is a fungus disease of cattle and other animals. But it may also affect people. Other fungus diseases of human beings include *blastomycosis, coccidioidomycosis,* and *moniliasis.* These diseases often attack the lungs. *Thrush,* a fungus disease of the throat, is found mainly in infants. *Tinea* (ringworm) affects parts of the skin. An increased use of antibiotics has aided the spread of fungus infections in people. Antibiotics often kill bacteria in the body that destroy fungi.   WILLIAM F. HANNA

Related Articles in WORLD BOOK include:

Athlete's Foot	Ergot	Mildew	Smut
Blight	Fungi	Ringworm	Thrush
Damping-Off	Fungicide	Rot	(disease)
Dutch Elm	Histoplasmosis	Rust	Wilt
Disease	Lumpy Jaw		

FUNJ SULTANATE was a Muslim empire in what is now Sudan in northeastern Africa. The empire began in the early 1500's and fell in 1821. It reached its height between 1600 and 1650 when Funj armies conquered neighboring peoples. The Funj became greatly feared in the region between the Red Sea and the Nile River.

The origin of the black-skinned Funj people is uncertain. They may have descended from Shilluk raiders from the White Nile region. In the early 1500's, the Funj adopted Islam, the Muslim religion. In 1504, they founded their capital, Sennar, south of the present-day city of Wad Madani. The sultanate went on to conquer the northern region of Sudan and nearly all the area between the Blue Nile and White Nile, south of the present-day city of Khartoum. From 1600 to 1650, the Funj used a slave army built by the sultan Badi II Abu Daqn to further extend their empire.

Between 1650 and 1750, the Funj nobles became jealous of the sultans' power and revolted frequently. Finally, in 1761, a group of officers deposed the ruling sultan. A period of decline followed, and the empire fell in 1821 after Egypt invaded it.   LEO SPITZER

FUNK, CASIMIR. See VITAMIN (History).

FUNNY BONE is not a bone, but a sensitive place at the bend of the elbow. In this area, the *ulnar nerve* lies between the skin and bone. The nerve is relatively unprotected because it lies near the surface. Even a slight blow on this area stimulates the nerve. This produces pain and a tingling sensation that travels into the ring finger and little finger. Sometimes the funny bone is referred to as "the crazy bone."   MARSHALL R. URIST

Humerus

ULNAR NERVE

Radius

Ulna

FUNSTON, *FUN stun,* **FREDERICK** (1865-1917), was a major general in the United States Army. He won the name "Fighting Bantam of the Army" because he was only 5 feet 5 inches (165 centimeters) tall.

Funston joined the rebel forces in Cuba against the Spaniards in 1896. During the Spanish-American War, he commanded troops in the Philippine Islands. In 1901, he helped capture Emilio Aguinaldo, the Philippine guerrilla leader. After the San Francisco earthquake in 1906, he was placed in charge of the city to restore order. He commanded U.S. forces at Veracruz, Mexico, in 1914. Funston was born in New Carlisle, Ohio.   H. A. DEWEERD

FUR is the thick growth of hair that covers the skin of many kinds of animals. People make coats and other warm clothing from fur. They value fur for its beauty as well as for the warmth that it provides.

Fur consists of a combination of stiff, oily *guard hair* on top and thick *underfur* beneath. The guard hair sheds moisture, and the underfur acts as an insulating blanket that keeps the animal warm.

Because fur comes from wild animals, it cannot be flawless like cloth, which is manufactured from fibers. The work involved in repairing imperfect pelts and then sewing them together into clothing contributes to the high cost of fur garments. In some years, the scarcity of fur-bearing animals makes prices rise even higher.

Fur that comes from animals is called *natural fur*. Natural furs account for about 99 per cent of the dollar value of fur garment sales in North America. Manufacturers also produce *artificial fur*, which looks like many kinds of fashionable natural furs but costs far less and is not as warm.

Prehistoric people wore animal skins for warmth and protection. They also used fur skins for blankets, rugs, and wallhangings. During the 400's B.C., an active fur market operated in Athens, Greece. Fur became a luxury during medieval times, when only kings and princes wore such extremely expensive furs as ermine and sable.

The desire for furs stimulated much of the early exploration of North America. In the 1600's, fur trading became the most important industry in Canada. See FUR TRADE.

Today, the fur industry plays an important role in the economies of many nations. More than half of the world's fur supply comes from fur ranches, where fur-bearing animals are raised in pens. The rest of the fur comes from trapping wild animals. During the 1960's and 1970's, some wildlife protection groups began to protest the trapping of animals for fur.

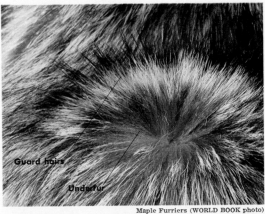

Maple Furriers (WORLD BOOK photo)

Fur consists of long *guard hairs* and thick *underfur*. The guard hairs shed moisture, and the underfur keeps the animal warm.

Russia produces more fur than any other nation. The United States ranks as the second largest producer, followed by Canada. The fur garments produced annually in the United States have a total wholesale value of about $400 million. The wholesale value of Canadian fur garment production exceeds $150 million annually. Both the United States and Canada export millions of dollars worth of fur pelts yearly. Major importers of fur include France, Great Britain, Greece, Italy, Japan, Switzerland, the United States, and West Germany.

Kinds of Fur

Natural Fur. The most popular natural furs used for clothing include beaver, fox, mink, muskrat, and raccoon. Chinchilla, mink, Persian lamb, and sable are

Some Important Furs

Fur	Fur Family	Animal's Main Habitat	Description
*Beaver	Rodent	North America	Dark brown; short, thick fur.
*Chinchilla	Rodent	Fur ranches	Blue-gray; long, branched, fine fur.
*Ermine	Weasel	Russia	White; short, thick fur.
Fisher	Weasel	Canada	Dark brown; short, soft fur.
Fitch	Weasel	Europe, Russia	Yellow; long, silky fur.
*Fox	Dog	Asia, Europe, North America	Red, blue, silver, white; long, soft fur.
*Lynx	Cat	North America, Russia	Beige; long, silky fur.
*Marten	Weasel	Asia, North America	Blue-brown; soft, thick fur.
*Mink	Weasel	North America, Russia	Brown, gray, white; long, silky fur.
*Mole	Mole	The Netherlands, Scotland	Blue, gray; soft, thick fur.
*Muskrat	Rodent	North America, Russia	Brown; long, silky fur.
Nutria	Rodent	South America	Dark brown; short, soft fur.
*Opossum	Opossum	South America, United States	Creamy; short, rough fur.
*Otter	Weasel	North America, South America	Brown; short, thick fur.
Persian Lamb	Sheep	Afghanistan, Russia, South West Africa	Black, brown, gray; woolly, tightly curled fur.
*Rabbit	Rodent	Australia, Europe, Japan, North America	White, brown, gray; short, fluffy fur.
*Raccoon	Raccoon	China, North America	Beige, brown, yellow; long, coarse fur.
*Sable	Weasel	Canada, Russia	Dark brown; long, silky fur.
*Seal	Seal	Alaska, Canada, Russia, South West Africa, Uruguay	Gray, salmon, silver, white; short, silky or stiff fur.
*Skunk	Weasel	North America	Black; long, silky fur.
*Squirrel	Rodent	Asia, Europe, North America	Gray; short, soft fur.

*Has a separate article in WORLD BOOK.

Some Kinds of Fur

Mink ranges in color from white to many shades of gray and brown.

Fox fur is long and soft. The most popular shades include red, white, and silver.

Muskrat fur is light brown. Some is dyed to resemble other kinds of fur.

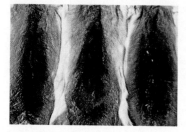

Chinchilla is highly prized for its luxurious softness and unusual coloration.

Sable, one of the most beautiful and expensive furs, has a brown color.

Maple Furriers (WORLD BOOK photos)

Beaver may be sheared to reveal the soft underfur, *left,* or left natural, *right.*

among the most fashionable and most expensive furs.

Furs vary greatly in color, texture, and value. Colors range from jet-black to snow-white, with many shades of brown, blue, gray, red-orange, and tan. Fur texture varies from the velvety softness of beaver to the coarseness of raccoon. Some furs, including beaver, mink, and nutria, are warmer and more durable than others. In the late 1970's, the price of a fur pelt in the United States ranged from 25 cents for a squirrel skin to $800 for a top quality lynx skin.

Rodents provide more skins for furs than any other group of animals. Beavers, muskrats, and other rodents make up more than three-fourths of the total wild fur catch in the United States and Canada. The weasel family supplies the greatest number of pelts from fur ranches. Weasels include such valuable fur-bearing animals as ermines, minks, and sables.

Artificial Fur consists of synthetic fibers that have been processed to look like real fur. Artificial furs be-

Natural and Artificial Persian Lamb image placeholder

Maple Furriers (WORLD BOOK photo)

Natural and Artificial Persian Lamb differ in appearance, as a close-up photograph shows. The natural fur is on the left.

come increasingly popular when the prices of genuine fur rise. The most popular "fake furs" are imitation lamb, mink, muskrat, and seal. Manufacturers make artificial furs by weaving and knitting synthetic fibers into *pile fabrics.* Pile consists of soft, clipped fiber ends. Manufacturers treat the pile to make it look like real fur. Natural fur fibers are sometimes woven into the pile to make it feel more like genuine fur.

How Fur Is Obtained

Fur Ranching. Millions of foxes and minks are raised yearly on ranches in the United States, Canada, and many European countries. Ranches in Afghanistan, Russia, and South West Africa raise Karakul sheep, whose fur is called *Persian lamb* (see KARAKUL). Ranchers raise chinchillas in Europe, North America, South Africa, South America, and Rhodesia. More than 50 per cent of the furs produced in the United States, and about 40 per cent of those produced in Canada, come from ranches.

The first fur ranches were established in the 1880's in Prince Edward Island, Canada. Today, fur ranchers conduct breeding programs based on the principles of genetics. Skilled ranchers breed their animals to produce offspring of particular colors and sizes or with other special characteristics.

Trapping. Most fur trapping takes place during the winter, when furs are thickest, longest, and shiniest. Each trapper sets a series of traps called a *trap line* along riverbanks and at other spots that the animals visit frequently. In most cases, the traps kill the animals almost immediately.

After collecting their catches, the trappers skin the animals. They use two main methods of skinning, *cased* and *open.* Ermines, minks, and other small animals are skinned by the cased method. The trapper slits

488

a line across the rump from leg to leg and peels the pelt off inside out. Beavers and other larger animals are skinned by the open method. The trapper slits a line up the belly and peels the pelt off from side to side. Trappers scrape the skins clean of all fat and tissue, dry the skins, and ship them to market.

Some wildlife protection groups oppose the trapping of animals for fur. These groups especially object to the use of *leg-hold traps*. The jaws of such traps snap shut on an animal's leg and hold the animal until the trapper arrives to kill it. Many trappers now use the more humane *Conibear trap*, which snaps the animal's spine and usually causes almost instant death.

Government conservation programs regulate fur trapping in every state of the United States except Hawaii, which has no fur-bearing animals, and in every Canadian province. Each state and province issues trapping licenses and determines when and where trapping may take place. Regulations also set limits on the number of animals that may be trapped at one time. The United States and many other nations prohibit the import of furs of animals that are in danger of becoming extinct. These animals include cheetahs, leopards, tigers, and wolves. See WILDLIFE CONSERVATION.

Marketing Fur

Most ranchers and trappers ship their furs to one of the great auction houses in the major fur-trading centers of the world. In the United States, the chief auction houses operate in Greenville, S.C.; Minneapolis, Minn.; New York City; and Seattle. Major Canadian auction houses are in Montreal; North Bay, Ont.; Regina, Sask.; Vancouver, B.C.; and Winnipeg, Man. Leading European fur auction centers include Leningrad, Russia; London; and Oslo, Norway. The Hudson's Bay Company in Canada is the world's largest fur-trading firm.

Representatives of auction houses visit trappers and ranchers to arrange the shipment of pelts to market. The largest cargoes of furs come to market from November through February. Fur dealers, manufacturers,

J. C. Allen & Son

Fur Ranches, such as the one shown above, raise large numbers of foxes, minks, and other fur-bearing animals.

and retailers attend the auctions. Buyers may examine several hundred thousand pelts in the warehouses on *examining days*. The furs are auctioned off on *sales days*. Buyers must pay for their purchases on or before the *prompt day*, which is usually about a month after the sales day. On the prompt day, the furs are shipped according to the buyers' instructions.

Processing Fur

Dressing. Pelts bought at fur auctions must be cleaned and made flexible by a process called *dressing*. First, the pelts are softened in a salt solution that removes all excess tissue and grease. Next, the processors apply a special grease to the leather and put the skins into a machine called a *kicker*. The kicker has wooden feet that pound the grease into every pore of a skin. The pelts are then placed in revolving drums, where they are cleaned and dried with special sawdust and compressed air. Later, the processors may pluck out the long guard hairs, leaving only the thick fur fibers. The

Fur Buyers inspect pelts at a fur merchant's storeroom and decide which ones to purchase. The storeroom contains pelts of various fur-bearing animals from many parts of the world.

American Fur Industry

Pelts Are Matched according to color, luster, thickness, and other features. Matched pelts enable a manufacturer to produce a garment that has the same color and texture throughout.

How a Fur Coat Is Made

Making a fur coat requires the labor of many highly skilled workers. The illustrations below show some of the important steps involved in converting raw pelts into a finished garment.

The photographs for this page were taken for WORLD BOOK at Maple Furriers unless otherwise credited.

WORLD BOOK photo by Fred Weituschat

Dressing begins with the removal, by hand or by machine, of any bits of flesh that are still attached to the pelts.

Trimming. Workers trim off the heads, paws, bellies, rumps, and tails. These parts are used to make cheaper garments.

Slicing is one of many techniques used by fur cutters. This step involves cutting the pelts into long diagonal strips.

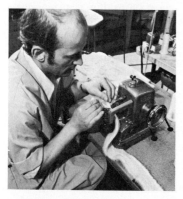

Sewing. An operator sews the strips together to form lengthened, narrow pelts. Then the pelts are sewn into a sheet of fur.

Maple Furriers (Milt & Joan Mann)

Blocking consists of shaping the sheet of fur by stapling it to a large board on which the pattern of the coat has been drawn.

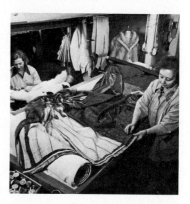

Finishing. The sheet of fur is made into a coat, which is then cleaned. Finally, workers sew in the lining of the coat.

fur may also be sheared shorter to give it a plush effect.

Dyeing. Many furs are dyed to improve their appearance or to make them look like other types of fur. Processors may put furs into a vat of dye, or they may dye entire coats by hand. Sometimes dark fur is bleached and then dyed a pale shade. In a special dyeing process called *tipping*, only the tips of the fur fibers are dyed. This process makes furs resemble darker pelts of the same variety. Tipping helps the manufacturer match several pelts to be used in the same coat.

Cutting and Sewing. Furs differ in quality and appearance, and so manufacturers must carefully grade and match processed skins. A manufacturer makes the pattern for a garment and then selects the skins to be used. Workers stretch the skins and trim off the heads, paws, bellies, rumps, and tails. These parts are used to make cheaper garments.

A worker called a *cutter* trims and shapes the skins to make the best use of the material. An *operator* then sews the skins together to form a sheet of fur that approximately matches the shape of the pattern. Next, a worker called a *blocker* applies small amounts of water to the skin to make it stretch just enough to cover the edges of the pattern. Then the fur is *blocked*,

or *nailed*, to a large pine board and left to dry. Later, any surplus material is trimmed away, and the fur is sewn into a garment. Finally, the garment is cleaned and the lining is sewn in.

In the United States, a law called the *Fur Products Labeling Act* requires manufacturers to place a label in a conspicuous place on all fur garments. This label must provide certain information, including: (1) the name in English of the animal that produced the fur; (2) the country of origin, if the fur is imported; and (3) whether the fur has been dyed or bleached. If the fur contains paws, bellies, or other scrap parts, that fact must also appear on the label. In addition, the label on a used garment must clearly indicate that the article is second-hand.   SIDNEY S. SCHIPPER

Related Articles. See the articles on the animals marked by an asterisk in the table *Some Important Furs* in this article. See also the following articles:

Animal (pictures)   Pribilof Islands
Astor (John Jacob)   Siberia (picture)
Canada (Fur Industry)   Trapping

FUR TRADE was one of the earliest and most important industries in North America. The fur trading industry played a major role in the development of the

United States and Canada for more than 300 years.

The fur trade began in the 1500's as an exchange between Indians and Europeans. The Indians traded furs for such goods as tools and weapons. Beaver fur, which was used in Europe to make felt hats, became the most valuable of these furs (see BEAVER). The fur trade prospered until the mid-1800's, when fur-bearing animals became scarce and silk hats became more popular than felt hats made with beaver. Today, almost all trappers sell their pelts. But some Eskimo and Indian trappers in Canada still trade their furs to fur companies for various goods.

The Early Fur Trade. The earliest fur traders in North America were French explorers and fishermen who arrived in what is now Eastern Canada during the early 1500's. Trade started after the French offered the Indians kettles, knives, and other gifts as a means to establish friendly relations. The Indians, in turn, gave pelts to the French. By the late 1500's, a great demand for fur had developed in Europe. This demand encouraged further exploration of North America. The demand for beaver increased rapidly in the early 1600's, when fashionable European men began to wear felt hats made from beaver fur. Such furs as fox, marten, mink, and otter also were traded.

In 1608, the French explorer Samuel de Champlain established a trading post on the site of the present-day city of Quebec. The city became a fur-trading center. The French expanded their trading activities along the St. Lawrence River and around the Great Lakes. They eventually controlled most of the early fur trade in what became Canada. The French traders obtained furs from the Huron Indians and, later, from the Ottawa. These tribes were not trappers, but they acquired the furs from other Indians. The French also developed the fur trade along the Mississippi River.

During the early 1600's, English settlers developed a fur trade in what are now New England and Virginia. English traders later formed an alliance with the Iroquois Indians and extended their trading area from Maine down the Atlantic Coast to Georgia.

European business companies handled a large number of the furs shipped from North America during the 1600's and 1700's. The most famous of these firms, the Hudson's Bay Company, was established in 1670. It was founded by a group of English merchants, with the help of two French fur traders, Sieur des Groseilliers and Pierre E. Radisson. The English government gave the company sole trading rights in what is now the Hudson Bay region. See HUDSON'S BAY COMPANY; GROSEILLIERS, SIEUR DES; RADISSON, PIERRE E.

During the 1700's, French and British fur traders competed bitterly over trading rights in the region between the Allegheny Mountains and the Mississippi River. This competition, plus other conflicts between the two nations, led to the French and Indian War in 1754. Great Britain won the war in 1763 and took over France's colonial empire in North America.

In 1783, British merchants in Montreal founded the North West Company to compete with the Hudson's Bay Company. The traders of the new firm were called "Nor Westers." They led many daring expeditions in

The Fur Trade in North America

The fur trade played a key role in the development of Canada and the United States from the 1500's to the mid-1800's. This map shows the chief areas of the fur trade in North America. The groups that controlled these areas and the periods in which the trade flourished under each group are shown below.

French
1500's to 1763

Colonial American
1600's to late 1700's

Hudson's Bay Company
1670 to 1850's

North West Company
1783 to 1821

Russian
1790's to 1850's

American
1820's to 1850's

→ Fur export route

• Trading post

· City

0   1,000 Miles

0   1,000 Kilometers

WORLD BOOK map

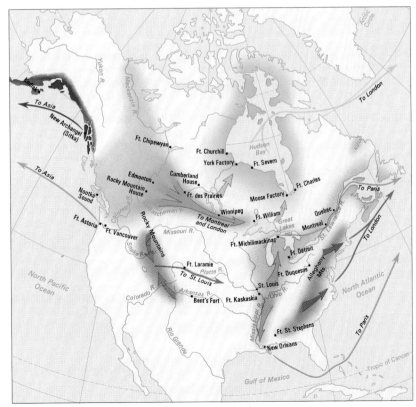

The Annual Rendezvous, *above,* was a center of Western fur trading in the 1800's. Trappers assembled at these gatherings in the Rocky Mountains to trade or sell their pelts to fur companies.

search of fur in far western Canada. However, the company failed financially and, in 1821, merged with the Hudson's Bay Company. See NORTH WEST COMPANY.

During the late 1700's, Russia began to develop the fur trade in the area that is now Alaska. The Russian-American Company was established there in 1799.

The 1800's. The Lewis and Clark expedition to the Pacific Ocean in 1805 and 1806 led to the development of fur trading in the West. Several companies competed heavily for this western trade. They included firms headed by John Jacob Astor, William H. Ashley, Pierre Chouteau, and Manuel Lisa. See ASTOR (John Jacob); ASHLEY, WILLIAM H.; CHOUTEAU (family).

Many Indians of the West had little interest in trapping, and so the fur-trading companies hired white frontiersmen to obtain pelts. These trappers became known as "mountain men" because they roamed through wild areas of the Rocky Mountains in search of fur. Such mountain men as Kit Carson, John Colter, and Jedediah Smith became famous for their roles in the settlement of the West.

Ashley, the head of the Rocky Mountain Fur Company, began to hold an annual trappers' gathering in the Rocky Mountains in 1825. At each gathering, called a *rendezvous,* trappers sold their furs and bought supplies for the next year. The rendezvous saved the men the time and trouble of traveling long distances to various trading posts.

The fur trade started to decline in the Eastern United States by the late 1700's. The decline resulted chiefly from the clearing of large areas for settlement. As more and more land was cleared, fur-bearing animals became increasingly scarce. Overtrapping of fur-bearing animals

hurt the fur trade in the Western United States and Western Canada. In addition, the value of beaver fur dropped sharply in the 1830's, when European hat manufacturers began to use silk instead of felt. By 1870, most fur-trading activity had ended.

Effects of the Fur Trade. The fur trade contributed to the development of British and French empires in North America. During the 1600's, the prospect of wealth from the fur trade attracted many Europeans to the New World. Traders and trappers explored much of North America in search of fur. They built trading posts in the wilderness, and settlements grew up around many of the posts. Some of these settlements later became such major cities as Detroit, New Orleans, and St. Louis in the United States; and Edmonton, Montreal, Quebec, and Winnipeg in Canada.

The fur trade led to conflict between France and Great Britain in America. Rivalries over trading alliances also arose among Indian tribes that wanted to obtain European goods. The fur trade promoted friendly relations between the Indians and white traders. However, it also brought Indian hostility toward white settlers because the clearing of land threatened the supply of fur-bearing animals.

The claims of fur traders played a part in establishing the border between the United States and Canada. For example, the areas of trade controlled by U.S. and British traders helped determine the border in the region of the Great Lakes.   JOHN ELGIN FOSTER

Related Articles in WORLD BOOK include:

Fraser, Simon	Henry, Alexander	Simpson, Sir
Fur	McKay, Alexander	George
Hearne, Samuel	Robidoux (family)	Trading Post

FURFURAL, *FUR fuh ral,* is a liquid chemical that is used in many industries. Manufacturers use it in making nylon, plastics, and other products. Furfural changes from colorless to yellow and finally dark brown when it is exposed to the air. Its vapor irritates the eyes, nose, and throat.

In the manufacture of nylon, furfural is changed into tetrahydrofuran (THF). When THF is treated with certain acids, it changes into a compound used to make nylon. Butadiene, a material used in *synthetic* (artificial) rubber, can be made from THF. THF is also used as a solvent to dissolve other substances in industry.

Furfuryl alcohol, another compound made from furfural, is used in making resins which protect metals from *corroding* (being eaten away). Many synthetic resins are made with furfural. Manufacturers use these synthetic resins to make plastic products. Because furfural kills various fungi, germs, and insects, it is used in fungicides, germicides, and insecticides. Rubber manufacturers use furfural to speed up the vulcanization process used to make rubber harder and more durable.

Chemists call furfural a selective solvent because it will dissolve some materials in a mixture and not others. Petroleum refineries use furfural to dissolve the harmful carbon and sulfur compounds found in impure lubricating oils. Furfural is also used to refine other petroleum products such as diesel fuel.

Chemical manufacturers prepare furfural by mixing acid with waste plant materials such as corn cobs or the hulls of cottonseeds, oats, or rice. Furfural is also found in some natural oils. Johann Döbereiner, a German chemist, reported his discovery of furfural in 1832. He accidentally obtained the chemical by treating sugar with sulfuric acid and manganese dioxide. American chemists discovered the methods now used to manufacture furfural in the early 1920's.

Furfural is an organic chemical with the formula C_4H_3OCHO. It belongs to the aldehyde chemical family and is sometimes called *furfuraldehyde* (see ALDE-HYDE). Furfural freezes at $-37.6°$ F. ($-38.7°$ C) and

boils at $323°$ F. ($161.7°$ C). It is about 1.16 times as dense as water.   OTTO THEODOR BENFEY

FURIES, *FYOO reez,* were the terrible goddesses of vengeance in Greek and Roman mythology. The Greeks called them *Erinyes.* At first there were many furies. But later there were only three—Alecto, Tisiphone, and Megaera. They had snakes in their hair and about their bodies, and had wings made of scales of brass.

The Furies punished people for every kind of crime. It did not matter if people had done wrong without knowing it. They still were punished. The Furies pursued the guilty ones even into the Lower World, and drove them mad. Aeschylus in his *The Furies* and Virgil in the *Aeneid* wrote about them.   PADRAIC COLUM

See also ORESTES.

FURLONG is an English unit of measurement of length equal to 40 rods, or $\frac{1}{8}$ mile (0.2 kilometer). Furlong originally meant the length of one furrow in a plowed field. This was indefinite because farmers plowed many different lengths of furrows. Gradually the furlong became a standard length. Among the old English writers, the furlong was one-eighth of a mile in each of the world's different standards for a mile. In the 800's, the word meant the same as the Latin *stadium*, which was one-eighth of the Roman mile. The furlong is seldom used today except on horse-race tracks. See also WEIGHTS AND MEASURES.   E. G. STRAUS

FURMAN UNIVERSITY is a coeducational liberal arts school located 5 miles (8 kilometers) north of Greenville, S.C. It offers instruction in fine arts, humanities, mathematics and natural sciences, and social sciences. Courses lead to bachelor's and master's degrees. The college for men was authorized by the South Carolina Baptist State Convention in 1825, and classes began in 1827. It is the oldest Baptist college in the South. In 1933, Furman combined with the Greenville Woman's College. For enrollment, see UNIVERSITIES AND COLLEGES (table).   GORDON W. BLACKWELL

Detail from Greek vase painting of the late 300's B.C.; The British Museum, London

Furies were avenging goddesses in Greek mythology. This vase pictures them in an event from the play *The Furies* by Aeschylus. The goddesses were usually shown with snakes on their bodies and with wings made of brass.

493

FURNACE

FURNACE is an enclosed structure in which fuel is burned to produce heat. Most furnaces are built of metal, brick, or a combination of these fireproof materials. A furnace may be used to produce heat for comfort, to boil water to make steam, or to heat materials for manufacturing purposes. Furnaces are built to obtain the greatest amount of heat from the fuel used and to focus the heat where it is most needed.

Furnaces for Home Heating. *Warm-air* furnaces burn coal, coke, gas, or oil. They heat air, causing it to rise through *ducts* (tubes) to house openings called *registers*. When cool, the air returns through a cold-air register to the furnace. A *forced-air* furnace has a blower that directs and increases the flow of warm air. Because the blower directs the air, a forced-air furnace can be located on the same floor as the rooms being heated.

A furnace connected to a *steam boiler* heats water until it forms steam that passes through pipes to various rooms. A furnace connected to a *hot-water boiler* does not heat water to the boiling point, but circulates hot water through the pipes and radiators. A *forced hot-water* system uses a pump to force the water through the pipes to give faster circulation. Most gas and oil furnaces operate automatically by use of a thermostatic control (see THERMOSTAT). Coal and coke furnaces can be made semi-automatic by installing a *stoker* to feed the fuel to the furnace. They are not entirely automatic, because ashes must be removed.

Care of home furnaces is important. The ash pits in coal and coke furnaces should be emptied regularly. Oil and gas burners should be serviced at least once every two years. All furnaces, chimneys, and air ducts should be vacuumed every year or so. The sealing of furnace joints should be checked every few years.

Industrial Furnaces are used to heat-treat metals and to generate steam. They are also used to manufacture bricks, cement, glass, iron, steel, and other materials. They produce extremely high temperatures. Most of them burn coal or coke. Others use electricity, gas, oil, or powdered coal to produce heat. One industrial furnace, the *blast furnace*, is used to make iron from iron ore. Fans blow air under pressure into the furnace and make the fire extremely hot.

Electric furnaces have certain advantages over other industrial types. Metalworkers often need temperatures that range from 3500° to 5000° F. (1830° to 2800° C). Only electric furnaces can produce these temperatures. Also, electric furnaces do not produce gases that may harm metals being melted. Furnaces that burn coal, coke, gas, and oil can produce temperatures of 2800° F. (1540° C) and higher. These temperatures are high enough for the manufacture of bricks, iron, and steel, and for other industrial uses.

The three main types of electric furnaces are the arc, resistance, and induction furnaces. Heat from an *arc* furnace comes from an electric arc formed between carbon electrodes. A *resistance* furnace works much like a home toaster. It produces heat by passing an electric current through a material. The material becomes very hot by resisting the passage of current.

An *induction* furnace sends an alternating current through a conductor coiled around an insulated container that holds the material to be melted. The alternating current has a magnetic field that *induces* a current in the material. This induced current heats the material. If a material such as glass, that does not allow induced currents to be set up within it, is to be melted, the container is made of carbon. The furnace generates heat within the container. The container then melts the material. See INDUCTION, ELECTRIC.

Atomic furnaces or *nuclear reactors* have been developed for use in producing power. Their fuel is uranium or plutonium. Heat is provided by *nuclear fission* (the splitting of atoms) instead of by combustion. Careful shielding is necessary because of radiation. See NUCLEAR REACTOR.

Solar furnaces are used to produce temperatures of 8000° F. (4400° C) and higher. In a solar furnace, a series of flat and curved mirrors reflects the sun's rays to a single spot in an oven. See SOLAR ENERGY (Capturing Solar Energy; pictures).   JAMES B. JONES

See also BLAST FURNACE; HEATING; IRON AND STEEL (How Iron Is Made; Methods of Making Steel); ELECTRIC FURNACE; KILN.

TYPES OF FURNACES FOR HOME HEATING

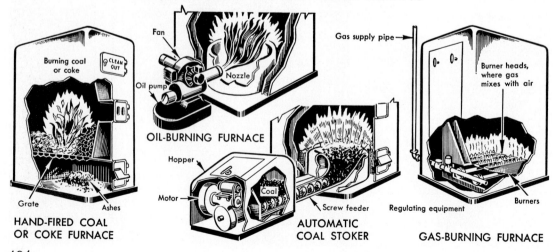

HAND-FIRED COAL OR COKE FURNACE

OIL-BURNING FURNACE

AUTOMATIC COAL STOKER

GAS-BURNING FURNACE

Well-Designed Furniture contributes beauty and comfort to daily life. The chairs, sofas, and tables in this living room reflect the clean, simple lines of modern furniture styles.

FURNITURE

FURNITURE consists of chairs, tables, beds, and other movable pieces that provide comfort and convenience in our daily lives. Many kinds of furniture are used in homes, schools, and offices. We relax on comfortable couches, and we store various belongings in chests, dressers, and bookcases. Desks provide a place for study and paperwork. Numerous television sets and phonographs have handsome cabinets, and so they also serve as pieces of furniture. In many homes, a piano is an impressive piece of furniture.

In addition to being useful, furniture is attractively designed to make our surroundings more pleasant. Furniture works with other decorative and useful objects to beautify a room. Such items, including rugs and carpets, curtains, draperies, lamps, and pictures, are called *furnishings*.

Most furniture is made of wood or wood products. But furniture makers also use glass, metal, plastics, and a variety of other materials.

Certain pieces of the finest furniture rank among the world's greatest works of art. Over the years, expert designers and *artisans* (skilled craftworkers) have created richly decorated furniture in various styles. Many of these artisans were regarded as artists equal to the most famous painters and sculptors of their day. Today, museums display examples of their furniture as masterpieces of art.

People who study the history of furniture have given names to the different styles. Some styles are named for important people. For example, Louis XIV furniture is named for King Louis XIV of France. Other styles are named for historical periods. Thus, the Federal style of American furniture recalls the beginning of the federal system of government in the United States. Still other styles, such as art nouveau, take their name from an art movement.

The history of furniture can be seen as a series of styles that become popular for a time and then fall from fashion. Designers then revive earlier styles, adapting them to fit the taste of the time.

The history of furniture is closely related to the history of human culture. For thousands of years, all fine furniture was designed to accommodate the tastes of royalty and the nobility and other wealthy people. These people considered furniture a symbol of their power and rank rather than a practical necessity. Beginning in the A.D. 1500's, a middle class of people gradually developed in Western countries. People of this class wanted furniture that was comfortable and suited to their homes. By the 1800's, the tastes of middle-class buyers set the standard for furniture styles. Most furniture made today is still designed to be practical, comfortable, and easy to maintain.

This article describes the history of furniture from its earliest period to the present time. For a discussion of the importance of furniture in interior decoration, see the WORLD BOOK article INTERIOR DECORATION.

John W. Keefe, the contributor of this article, is the Curator of European Decorative Arts at the Art Institute of Chicago.

The ancient Egyptians created the first known fine furniture about 3000 B.C. Later, the Greeks and then the Romans developed outstanding furniture in their own characteristic styles. The age of Greek and Roman culture was followed by the Middle Ages, a period that in general produced little important furniture.

Ancient Egypt (3100 B.C.-1090 B.C.). The ancient Egyptians considered the ownership of furniture a mark of social rank. The best-made and most beautiful furniture decorated the palace of the Egyptian king. Members of the nobility, wealthy officials, and landowners also possessed fine furniture. The common people had only one piece of furniture—a three-legged stool—in their simple homes.

Egyptian furniture makers did some of their best work in designing beds. Most beds had legs shaped like the legs of an animal, usually a lion. These beds led to the development of couches in the shape of an animal, such as a lion or a leopard.

Egyptian artisans also made fine chairs. The finest chairs had a seat of woven cord covered with a removable cushion. The development of the armchair was probably the most lasting Egyptian contribution to furniture design. Other Egyptian furniture included boxes, cabinets, and small tables.

Ancient Greece (about 1100 B.C.-A.D. 400). In ancient Greece, as in ancient Egypt, only persons of the highest social rank possessed much furniture. Most Greek citizens owned only a three-legged stool and perhaps a crudely made table.

The Greeks borrowed many furniture forms, including the bed and the couch, from the Egyptians. Beds became major pieces of household decoration in Greece because they were used for dining as well as for sleeping. During a meal, a person would lie on his or her side, leaning on one elbow for support.

Greek artisans produced a variety of seating furniture. The most important were the thrones made for people of high rank. Some thrones had a low back decorated with one or more carvings of animal heads. Others had a high back with flowerlike carvings. The arm supports were in the form of rams' heads. The most common type of Greek chair, called the *klismos*, had curved legs. The front legs curved forward, and the rear legs curved to the back.

The Greeks used tables more than the Egyptians did. Most Greek tables had three legs that ended in feet shaped like hoofs or paws. Greek artisans decorated the finest furniture with inlaid patterns of fine wood, silver, gold, and gems. They either carved ivory to form the feet or cast them in silver or bronze.

Ancient Rome (700's B.C.-A.D. 400's). The Romans borrowed many furniture forms from the Greeks but gave them a distinctly Roman character. For example, the Romans used more bronze and silver in their furniture than did the Greeks. Romans used the Greek klismos but made it heavier and larger. They also covered it with upholstery. Roman furniture makers adopted a Greek stool design and developed it into a

Egyptian Museum, Cairo, Egypt
(Metropolitan Museum of Art/Lee Boltin)

An Ancient Egyptian Throne, *above,* which belonged to King Tutankhamon, is decorated with carvings of lion heads and paws.

Relief from a gravestone
(about 400 B.C.); Archaeological
Museum, Athens, Greece
(Raymond V. Schoder, S.J.)

A Simply Built Chest, *right,* is typical of the furniture of the Middle Ages. Carvings were a common form of furniture decoration during this period.

Church of St. Mary, Stoke D'Abernon,
England (Hanford Photography)

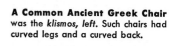

A Common Ancient Greek Chair was the *klismos, left.* Such chairs had curved legs and a curved back.

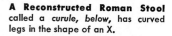

A Reconstructed Roman Stool called a *curule, below,* has curved legs in the shape of an X.

Rijksmuseum, Nijmegen,
The Netherlands

stool called a *curule*. The curule had two pairs of legs. The delicate, curved legs in each pair were crossed in the form of an X.

Tables were very popular among the Romans. Many tables had three or four legs connected by crossbars. The *slab table* was a major Roman contribution to table design. The tabletop consisted of a large slab of marble or wood, which rested on carved upright marble slabs. Artisans sculptured various designs into the upright slabs, including animals, flowers, fruits, and vines.

The Middle Ages (400's-1300). During the period of European history called the Middle Ages, skillful furniture making generally became a lost art. Most furniture of the Middle Ages was coarse and unrefined by the standards of ancient Greece and Rome. Furniture makers painted or *gilded* (coated with gold) most pieces to disguise their crude construction. As in earlier times, people of high rank owned the best furniture.

Landowners and church officials of the Middle Ages traveled frequently. They usually took their furniture and other possessions with them on their journeys. Much furniture thus was designed to be portable. Large pieces were put together in such a way that they could be taken apart and carried easily. Chests were used for storage as well as for seats.

During the 1200's, a new Western European art style called *Gothic* influenced the design of furniture. Artisans decorated their furniture, especially chests and cupboards, with arches, columns, and other features of Gothic architecture.

FURNITURE/*Oriental Furniture*

In the Oriental countries, as in Egypt and Europe, only high-ranking officials and wealthy people owned finely crafted furniture. The artisans of China, Japan, and India produced the most noteworthy Oriental furniture. The earliest high-quality Oriental furniture was produced in China during the 200's B.C.

China. By the time of the Han dynasty (202 B.C.-A.D. 220), the Chinese had developed several furniture forms. The most characteristic was the *k'ang*, a platform on which a person could lie to sleep or rest. The Chinese of this period grouped a variety of small stools and tables around the k'ang.

Later Chinese furniture falls into two categories: household furniture and the furniture used in royal palaces. Chinese household furniture was simple and practical. Palace furniture was larger, heavier, and more richly decorated than household furniture.

A notable characteristic of all Chinese furniture was the skillful manner in which artisans joined the parts. They used no pegs or nails and seldom used glue. Instead, they carved the edges of parts so expertly that the parts fitted together tightly.

By the early 1400's, the Chinese were using low dining tables supported by gracefully curved legs now known as *cabriole* legs. A cabriole leg has S-shaped curves, and it ends with a decorative foot. Beginning in the 1700's, this design became an important feature of Western furniture and was given the French name *cabriole*. The best-known Chinese chair design had a single vertical *splat*—a piece of wood that formed the center of the chair's back.

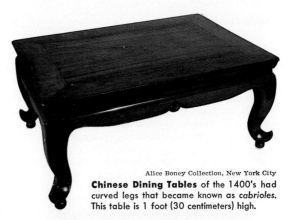

Chinese Dining Tables of the 1400's had curved legs that became known as *cabrioles*. This table is 1 foot (30 centimeters) high.

A Typical Chinese Chair of the 1500's had a single vertical *splat* that formed the center of the chair's back.

A Japanese Cabinet of the early 1600's is made of lacquered wood. The doors and shelves are decorated with grapevine designs.

497

Japan. Japanese architectural styles largely determined that country's furniture styles. Earthquakes occurred frequently in Japan, which resulted in the building of light, one-story buildings. In both home and palaces, the Japanese used small, lightweight cabinets, chests, and writing tables rather than large, heavy pieces. The Japanese customarily sat and slept on floor mats, and so they used no chairs or beds. Their furniture was simple in shape, but it was beautifully decorated with colorful designs of flowers, animals, and scenes from Japanese literature. Japanese artisans lacquered the furniture to give it a glossy finish. This use of lacquer gave the furniture a distinctive quality. Japanese furniture makers also beautified their work with shell inlays and rich fabrics.

India. The earliest important pieces of Indian furniture were chairs designed to be used by members of the nobility. Such thrones later developed into four-legged platforms on which a person sat with legs folded. Many of these thrones had the shape of a flower blossom. A person sat on cushions and used pillows for a backrest. Indian beds were covered with luxuriously upholstered cushions and mattresses.

FURNITURE/*The Renaissance*

The Renaissance was a period of European history that lasted from about 1300 to 1600. A major characteristic of the period was a revival of interest in *classical* cultures—that is, the cultures of ancient Greece and Rome. Classical art thus had a strong influence on furniture designed during the Renaissance. Italian artisans created the first important Renaissance furniture. Their work attracted much attention in other European countries, especially France, England, and Spain.

Italy. During the Renaissance, the palaces of Italian nobles became famous for their luxurious interiors, which included fine furniture and magnificent paintings. Actually, these palaces contained few pieces of furniture by today's standards. The best-furnished room in a palace was the *studio*, a library in which the owner kept books, manuscripts, gems, medals, and small sculptures. These items rested on shelves in beautifully ornamented cupboards.

Chests continued to be important articles of furniture, as they were in the Middle Ages. During the early 1500's, a large type of chest called a *cassone* was carved, gilded, and painted with scenes from classical history and mythology. A new form of chest called the *cassapanca* developed from the cassone. The cassapanca had a backrest and arms, and it was used as a sofa as well as a chest. Large cupboards called *sideboards* or *credenzas* became popular pieces of Italian furniture. Artisans decorated them with columns and other features of classical architecture.

France. French Renaissance furniture can be divided into two important styles, called Francis I and Henry II. Each of these styles was named after a French king. Francis I ruled from 1515 to 1547. Henry II ruled from 1547 to 1559.

Before the reign of Francis I, French furniture re-

© The Frick Collection, New York City

An Italian Renaissance Chest called a *cassone, above,* is made of fine wood and beautifully carved. Such chests were the most popular type of furniture in Italy during the Renaissance.

Château de Beauregard, Blois, France (P. Hinous, Agence TOP)

A French Renaissance Cabinet, *above,* was designed in the Henry II style, which became popular during the mid-1500's. Such cabinets had a small upper section that rested on a larger base. Furniture makers decorated these pieces with carvings of human figures and scenes from Greek and Roman mythology.

English Furniture of the Renaissance was solid and sturdy, as this picture indicates. The picture shows the drawing room of Hardwick Hall, an English estate, as it looked in the 1590's. The room has a new and distinctly English furniture form, a dining table called a *draw-table*, foreground. The length of the table could be increased by drawing its halves apart and adding leaves. Carvings of mythical winged beasts support the tabletop.

flected the Gothic style of the late Middle Ages. A new style developed after Francis brought leading Italian artists to France to remodel the royal *château* (castle) at Fontainebleau. In redesigning the château, the Italian artisans introduced decorative *motifs* (designs) that revolutionized French art of the period. These motifs included the use of columns; carved human heads surrounded by scrolls; carved bands, called *strapwork*, which imitated tooled leather bookbindings; and *niches* (hollowed-out areas in walls).

The Italian-inspired Francis I style of furniture lasted until the mid-1500's. The Henry II style, which was more varied and more identifiably French, then replaced it. Carved human figures still played an important decorative role, as did carved animals. Columns and arches served as supports for tables. But the new style gave furniture a lighter appearance. For example, French artisans refined the traditional cabinet form by placing a small upper section on a larger base.

England. The Italian Renaissance influenced England largely because of the encouragement of King Henry VIII, who ruled England from 1509 to 1547. Henry invited Italian artists and artisans to work in England. English furniture makers then blended the Italian ornamental style with traditional English designs to create an English Renaissance style.

A number of distinctly English furniture forms appeared during the reign of Queen Elizabeth I, who ruled from 1558 to 1603. One of these forms was the *draw-table*, a large oak dining table made in halves that could be drawn apart. The length of this table could be increased by adding one or two top sections called *leaves* after drawing the halves apart. Another fashionable English design was the *court cupboard*, which had open shelves for displaying valuable plates and silverware. The cupboard had legs that were decorated with classical and Italian Renaissance motifs. Perhaps the most impressive pieces of English Renaissance furniture were beds, which featured handsome carvings and expensive fabrics.

Spain developed a Renaissance style that combined Spanish, Italian, and Moorish influences. The Moors were North African Muslims who had invaded Spain in the A.D. 700's. The Moorish impact on Spanish furniture appeared in an emphasis on gilding and the use of geometric designs made with ivory and wood inlays.

A major contribution of Spanish artisans was the design of a portable cabinet called a *vargueno*. The vargueno's door was hinged at the lower edge. When opened, the door served as a writing desk. The vargueno had many small drawers and a central cupboard.

A Portable Cabinet called a *vargueno* was a contribution of Spanish artisans. Varguenos had a door that could serve as a desk. This vargueno, made about 1600, rests on another cabinet.

499

An Italian Tabletop of the 1600's is decorated with semiprecious stones in a technique called *pietre dure*. Other popular tabletops of the period were made of marble or inlaid wood.

The Early 1600's were years during which most of Europe was engaged in political and religious wars. This warfare hindered the development of the arts in many European countries. Only Italy and The Netherlands enjoyed peace, and Italian artisans especially became an important source of new furniture design. Dutch furniture makers achieved excellence in creating beautiful floral designs with inlays of tropical woods and *mother-of-pearl* (the lining of certain sea shells).

In France, King Henry IV established royal furniture workshops in the Louvre in Paris. He financed the workshops and brought leading artisans from other countries to work in them.

Italy led in furniture development largely because many rich Italian merchants were building great palaces during the period. These merchants wanted the finest furniture for their palaces, and Italian artisans supplied it.

Many Italian tables had a base modeled on the slab tables of ancient Rome. Other tables had a top made of marble or inlaid wood on a base sculptured in the form of mythical creatures, shells, floral designs, and human figures. Sculptured human figures also supported cabinets, candlestands, and some chairs.

Italian artisans created fashions for chests, cabinets, and cupboards that spread throughout Europe. The cassone of the 1500's developed into a long credenza with a number of doors. The credenza, in turn, gradu-

The Louis XIV Style was known for its luxury. Louis Le Vau, the French architect who designed this room, combined beautiful furniture with works of art and architectural decorations to achieve an elegant effect. The sofa and high-backed chairs are typical of the Louis XIV style.

State Beds, which featured a carved canopy and luxurious drapings, were important pieces of furniture among the nobility and the wealthy during the late 1600's. Daniel Marot, an influential French furniture maker, designed this state bed for the royal bedroom in Hampton Court Palace, near London.

ally developed into two new forms. One form was a tall two-door cabinet. The other was a tall chest of drawers that rested on a stand.

Many people of the early 1600's considered the quality of upholstery to be a measure of a householder's social rank. As a result, beds—which were richly decorated with silk, velvet, and other luxurious fabrics—became major pieces of furniture. Such large *state beds* were placed in the main room of a palace or large house as well as in the bedrooms.

Louis XIV Furniture was the most notable furniture of the late 1600's. Louis XIV had become king of France in 1643, when he was only 4 years old. He took control of the French government in 1661, after the death of France's chief minister, Jules Cardinal Mazarin. Louis, who was then 23 years old, devoted himself to making France the cultural and political center of the Western world. He considered furniture making and the decorative arts to be politically important because he could use them to glorify his position as king. Louis bought a building on the outskirts of Paris, turned it into workshops, and staffed the shops with expert artisans. He commissioned them to create furnishings for his residences. These furnishings created a new national style of art.

Actually, the artisans worked almost entirely on a single project in Versailles, where they converted a royal hunting lodge into a luxurious royal palace. The noted French architect Charles Le Brun supervised the huge Versailles project and hired artisans from other countries. The decorating and furnishing of the Versailles palace became such a large undertaking that many foreign artisans took up permanent residence in France. Many of them married French women and had children who became furniture makers, creating a native French group of artisans.

The remarkable style of the furnishings made for the Versailles palace became known as the *Louis XIV* style.

This luxurious style was particularly notable for two important characteristics. One was a *veneer* technique invented by a French cabinetmaker, André Charles Boulle. In this technique, artisans "sandwiched" a *veneer* (thin layer of material) between two veneers of a contrasting material. Artisans used such materials as brass, ebony, and a dull silvery metal called pewter. They then cut through the layers to create contrasting scrolled patterns. These veneers were applied to Louis XIV cabinets, writing tables, and other furniture. Le Brun and Louis himself were responsible for the second characteristic—furniture of solid silver made for the main rooms at Versailles.

The French Influence Spreads. The furnishings of the Versailles palace set the standard for other royal palaces, and soon French furniture styles were imitated in palaces throughout Europe. But there were also political and religious reasons for the spread of French influence.

The national religion of France was Roman Catholicism, but most French artisans were Protestants. The French Protestants, called *Huguenots*, enjoyed religious freedom under the Edict of Nantes, which was issued by King Henry IV in 1598. In 1685, Louis XIV took away the Huguenots' freedom by canceling the edict. Most of the artisans then fled to The Netherlands or to England. There, they worked among the nobles and wealthy merchants and so established a taste for French design in the two countries.

Daniel Marot became one of the most influential Huguenot artisans both in The Netherlands and in England. Marot worked for William III, who was a Dutch prince before he became king of England in 1689. Marot also designed the interiors and furniture for Hampton Court Palace, near London. His designs created a demand in the late 1600's for high-backed chairs with French-style upholstered seats and backs. Marot's work also led to a fashion for state beds with drapery even more luxurious than that used in France.

501

Stavros S. Niarchos Collection (Josse)

A Low Chest of Drawers called a *commode* became a popular furniture form of the 1700's. The commode above has curves of bronze. Curved decorations were basic to the *rococo* style of the early 1700's.

The French Neoclassical Style of the late 1700's, *right*, featured light, graceful furniture with straight lines. The influence of ancient Roman art can be seen in the decorations on the furniture and walls.

Queen's Salon (1781), Versailles, France (Lauros, Giraudon)

Artisans in France and England dominated furniture design during the 1700's. Furniture makers in other countries interpreted the French and English designs and developed them into individual national styles.

French Styles

The Régence Style of the early 1700's received its name because a *regent* (temporary ruler) governed France during the period. After Louis XIV died in 1715, his 5-year-old grandson became King Louis XV. Because of the king's youth, his uncle, the Duke of Orléans, was appointed regent. The duke disliked the formality of Versailles and moved the royal court to Paris. There, a less ceremonial life style developed among the people of the court. They lived in residences called *town houses*, which were smaller and more intimate than the palace at Versailles. The style of furniture created for these town houses became known as the Régence style.

Régence furniture had a lighter, more graceful quality than Louis XIV furniture, emphasizing curves and delicate floral designs. Perhaps its most important characteristic was the use of the cabriole leg, which was inspired by Chinese furniture.

During the Régence period, the French cabinet-makers André Charles Boulle and Charles Cressent developed a low chest of drawers called a *commode*. This form became one of the most popular of the 1700's and was made with regional variations throughout Europe.

The Rococo Style. During the 1730's, the Régence style took on the features of a new style called *rococo*. The leading designer of rococo furniture was Juste-Aurèle Meissonnier. His motifs stressed swirling curves, *asymmetrical* (irregular) designs, and carvings in the form of rocks and shells. The name *rococo* came from the word *rocaille*, which was used to describe the rock-and-shell

European Room by Mrs. James Ward Thorne, Art Institute of Chicago

French Provincial Furniture was a comfortable style favored by middle-class people in the French provinces. This bedroom of the 1700's includes a tall cupboard and a bed set into the wall.

designs. The rococo style was also called the *Louis XV* style.

Rococo furniture was designed to blend with the overall architectural plan of a room. For example, artisans designed tables, mirrors, benches, and beds so that they could be set into wall niches provided by the architect. Oriental furniture styles also influenced rococo design. A style called *chinoiserie*, loosely based on Chinese motifs, became especially popular. Oriental lacquer also became fashionable.

The Neoclassical Style, called the *Louis XVI* style in France, replaced the rococo style by the late 1750's. The word *neoclassical* is a combination of the prefix *neo*, which means *new*, and the word *classical*. Neoclassical design thus reflected a renewed interest in the furniture motifs of ancient Greece and Rome. Neoclassical designers gradually eliminated the numerous curves of the rococo style in favor of the straight outlines of classical furniture. In place of elaborate rococo decorations, neoclassical artisans used thin pieces of plain wood arranged in geometric designs.

Much neoclassical furniture was inspired by classical motifs that were discovered in the mid-1700's by archeologists in two ancient Roman cities, Pompeii and Herculaneum. The cities had been buried by an eruption of Mount Vesuvius in A.D. 79.

The Queen Anne Style of the early 1700's featured splat-backed upholstered chairs and large desks called *secretaries*. The style introduced the cabriole leg into English furniture design.

The Chippendale Style dominated English and American furniture of the mid-1700's. The three chairs in the room shown above have carved mahogany legs, which are characteristic of the style. The influence of Chinese furniture design appears in the splat-backed chair on the left.

Dining room at Osterley Park House (about 1770); the National Trust, London

The English Neoclassical Style was begun by Robert Adam, a Scottish architect, in the 1760's. His light, harmonious designs can be seen in this dining room. A mirror in a richly carved frame hangs above a table called a *sideboard*. Carved plaster ornaments decorate the walls and ceiling.

English Styles

The Palladian Style was popular in England during the early 1700's. It was named after Andrea Palladio, an Italian architect of the 1500's. English artisans adopted elements of Palladio's style, which was based on the style of Roman architecture. For example, they decorated chests and cupboards with such architectural features as columns, ornamental moldings called *cornices*, and triangular top sections called *pediments*.

The Queen Anne Style. The Palladian style was so expensive to produce that only wealthy people could

Henry Francis DuPont Winterthur Museum, Wilmington, Del.

Early American Furniture was simple and sturdy. Most of the designs were based on English styles. The room at the left dates from about 1670. The cupboard, with its open shelves and a closed cabinet, reflects the influence of a type of English furniture called a *court cupboard.*

afford it. The English middle class used a less expensive—and more comfortable—style. It was called the Queen Anne style after the queen who ruled England from 1702 to 1714. The Queen Anne style introduced the cabriole leg into English furniture design.

Chippendale Furniture. In 1754, the English cabinetmaker Thomas Chippendale published a book of furniture designs. It was the first book dealing entirely with furniture to be published in England, and it had a tremendous influence. In the book, Chippendale did not introduce any new styles. But he portrayed existing styles, especially the rococo, with such freedom and vigor that his designs were widely copied. His influence became so widespread that the name Chippendale has come to mean almost any English and American rococo furniture of the mid-1700's.

English Neoclassical Furniture. Robert Adam, a Scottish architect and furniture designer, introduced the neoclassical style into England in the 1760's. Adam borrowed some of his ideas from the French neoclassical style, but he also contributed many original elements. For decoration, he used delicate floral motifs, ram and ox heads, and other features inspired by ornaments on Roman buildings and tombs. Adam introduced the sideboard, or credenza, into English furniture. He also became known for skillfully blending furniture into the architectural plan of a room.

A number of English furniture makers adopted Adam's neoclassical style during the late 1700's. Two of the best known, George Hepplewhite and Thomas Sheraton, prepared design books that popularized the style. The furniture made according to Adam's original designs was very expensive. Hepplewhite, Sheraton, and other furniture makers simplified the designs to reduce the cost of the furniture and make it appealing to middle-class buyers.

Early American Furniture

In the English colonies of North America, furniture design generally reflected the styles that were popular in England at the time. However, colonial artisans developed variations of the English styles. Starting about 1790, the most common early American style was a neoclassical variation called the *Federal* style. This style took its name from the young nation's new federal form of government. Duncan Phyfe, the leading American furniture designer of the period, worked in New York City and helped make it the manufacturing center for the Federal style. High-quality furniture was also produced by artisans in Boston; Philadelphia; and Newport, R.I.

The Federal Style of American furniture began about 1790. It was influenced by the straight lines of English neoclassical furniture. The pieces in the Federal bedroom shown above were largely based on designs created by such English furniture makers as George Hepplewhite and Thomas Sheraton.

Until the early 1800's, furniture fashions were set largely by the tastes of nobles and other wealthy people. But beginning in the early 1800's, the tastes of the middle class set the standard for furniture fashions. People of the middle class wanted variety and novelty in furniture design. As a result, a great number of styles became popular for a short time and were then replaced by new styles.

During the 1800's, many furniture expositions were held in major cities in the United States and Europe. At these expositions, furniture makers from many countries displayed their own designs and viewed the designs of others. These designs greatly influenced public taste. The expositions thus had the effect of establishing international furniture styles. The United States and European countries adopted the same major styles, with some regional differences.

The furniture of the 1800's falls into two categories: (1) furniture based on historical styles and (2) furniture intended to be truly original. Some furniture makers simply copied earlier styles. Others used earlier styles as models but changed them to give them freshness and new vigor. The invention of new furniture-making machines during the 1800's helped designers develop new styles. With these machines, designers could use materials in new ways. For example, they could use such materials as cast iron and wire in ways that had been impossible.

The Empire Style, the first major style of the 1800's, originated while Emperor Napoleon I ruled the French empire. Like Louis XIV, Napoleon wanted to use furniture as a symbol of political greatness. As a result, Empire furniture was impressive—large and heavy.

Empire artisans borrowed designs from Egyptian, Greek, and Roman furniture. They made chairs with curved rear legs shaped like those on the Greek klismos. They decorated furniture with such classical subjects as lions, sphinxes, and sculptured female figures called *caryatids*. Empire commodes, writing tables, and desks called *secretaries* were designed to fit into the overall plan of a room.

The Regency Style, a neoclassical style, was fashionable in England and the United States along with the Empire style. The Regency style was named after the period from 1811 to 1820, when the Prince of Wales served as regent for King George III of England. Most Regency furniture combined Egyptian, Chinese, and Gothic motifs with neoclassical elements. The style featured couches with ends shaped like scrolls, and chairs loosely modeled on the klismos. Stools based on the Roman curule also were popular.

Regency artisans used little carved ornamentation. They often used a decorative technique called *penwork*, in which artists inked designs on light-colored wood or a painted white surface. Regency artisans also decorated furniture with brass inlays.

The Biedermeier, or Restoration, Style. After the fall of Napoleon I in 1815, the majestic Empire style went out of fashion. A more informal style favored by middle-class people replaced it. This new style was called either by its German name, *Biedermeier,* or by its French name, *Restoration.* The name Biedermeier came from a comic

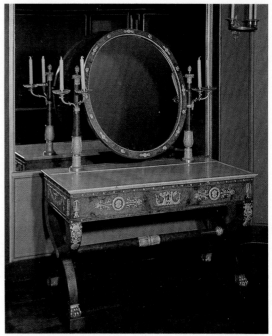

Fratelli Fabbri Editori, Milan, Italy

An Empire-Style Dressing Table, *above,* features a round mirror and built-in candleholders. The table also has a marble top and curved, crossed legs like the legs of the Roman curule.

Art Institute of Chicago

Biedermeier Furniture of the early 1800's had an informal, practical style. The chair and drop-front desk shown above illustrate the appealing simplicity of the style.

character in German popular literature (see BIEDER-MEIER). The term Restoration refers to the restoration of the French monarchy after the fall of Napoleon's empire. The style produced comfortable, practical furniture that had simple lines and simple decoration. The most important forms were desks, display cabinets, small work tables, and pianos.

Historical Revivals. From the 1830's to the late 1800's, a number of earlier styles were revived. The most important styles, in the order in which they appeared, were the Gothic, rococo, and Renaissance revivals. People used each style in a particular room. They placed Gothic furniture in the library, rococo in the *drawing room* (parlor) and bedroom, and Renaissance in the dining room.

Most Gothic revival furniture consisted of neoclassical forms with Gothic ornaments. These ornaments included pointed arches and decorative patterns called *tracery*. The style was particularly popular in England, where a variation called the *Elizabethan revival* became fashionable. In France, Gothic revival was known as the *cathedral* or *troubadour* style.

The rococo revival replaced the Gothic revival in the 1840's. Chairs and sofas in this style had cabriole legs and oval backs based upon the Louis XV style of the 1700's. Artisans decorated pieces with rocaille carving and introduced large pieces, such as mirrored wardrobes, sideboards, and display cabinets. Such pieces remained popular throughout the 1800's.

The Renaissance revival began in the court of the French emperor Napoleon III, who ruled from 1852 to 1870. It achieved the greatest popularity in the late 1870's and the 1880's. Artisans of this period tried to reproduce the furniture designs of the 1400's and 1500's. Designers emphasized angular forms and richly upholstered chairs, sofas, and stools.

Art Nouveau was an art movement that developed as a revolt against the historical revival styles. It began

Parlor of Lansdowne, Natchez, Miss.
(Mrs. George M. Marshall)

Parlor Furniture in the Rococo Revival Style, *above,* has cabriole legs and oval backs edged with fine wood carvings.

in the 1800's and lasted until the early 1900's. Art nouveau furniture featured design elements based on natural forms, such as blossoms, roots, stalks, and vines. Artisans combined these forms with a graceful motif called a *whiplash* curve. Art nouveau decorations also included female heads surrounded by flowing hair.

Middle-class buyers could not afford the handmade and expensive art nouveau furniture. After wealthy buyers tired of the style's specialized designs, it fell from fashion. But the popularity of art nouveau and its rejection of traditional styles greatly contributed to design developments in furniture of the 1900's.

Musée de l'Ecole de Nancy, Nancy, France (Gilbert Mangin)

Art Nouveau was a decorative style characterized by a graceful curve known as a *whiplash* curve. This feature appears in both the furniture and the wall and ceiling decorations in the dining room shown at the left.

During the 1900's, many designers have rejected traditional furniture styles. The designers of this period have made use of new manufacturing methods and new materials to revolutionize both the appearance and the function of furniture.

A variety of modern furniture styles has appeared during the 1900's, but most of the styles share a number of characteristics. The chief characteristic of modern furniture is its *abstract* form—that is, its appearance is not based on recognizable forms, such as animals or human figures. Most modern furniture has little decoration. Designers have used as few materials as possible and have selected materials that are lightweight, hard, and smooth. They have reduced the number of parts in a piece of furniture. For example, modern tables and chairs may have only one support instead of the traditional four legs. Such reductions in materials and parts have made manufacturing simpler and less costly.

Modern designers have also reduced the number of furniture forms used in a room. For example, some designers have eliminated traditional cabinets and cupboards and replaced them with sets of drawers and shelves called *storage units*. Some storage units are built into walls and become part of a room's architecture. Others are *modular units*, which can be moved and combined in various ways to fit a particular setting or to rearrange space in an area.

Early Styles

De Stijl (The Style) was an art movement that began in The Netherlands about 1917. Led by the Dutch architect and furniture designer Gerrit Rietveld, the De Stijl movement produced furniture that emphasized abstract, rectangular forms. Rietveld used only the three primary colors—blue, red, and yellow. The pure geometric forms of De Stijl furniture and the lightness and clarity of the new design influenced most later styles of the 1900's.

The Bauhaus was a school of design founded by the German architect and educator Walter Gropius in 1919. Perhaps the most important Bauhaus contribution to furniture design was the development of the use of *tubular steel*. Tubular steel is steel tubing that can be bent and shaped to form furniture frames and supports. This use of tubular steel reduced the number of expensive joints in a piece of furniture and the amount of upholstery needed to cover the piece.

Marcel Breuer, a Bauhaus instructor, introduced tubular steel in his *Wassily* chair in 1925. Breuer made this light, elegant, and comfortable chair of chrome-plated tubular steel and leather. In 1929, Ludwig Mies Van der Rohe, a director of the Bauhaus, created his famous *Barcelona* chair of curved steel bars and leather cushions. The chair's curved, X-form legs recalled the style of the curule stools of ancient Rome.

Organic Design is the name often given to the work of the American architect Frank Lloyd Wright. Wright believed that furniture should fit naturally into its surroundings. Like other pioneers of modern furniture design, Wright reduced his forms to basic geometric outlines. But, unlike De Stijl and Bauhaus furniture, which could be used interchangeably in most homes or offices, each piece of Wright furniture was an original design intended to blend into a specific setting.

Art Deco was a popular art movement during the 1920's and 1930's. It showed the influence of art nouveau but eliminated the curves and naturalistic carvings common in that earlier style. Art deco designers created streamlined shapes that stressed geometric proportions

Organic Design—a creative technique promoted by the American architect Frank Lloyd Wright—results in furniture that closely matches its architectural setting. The photograph at the left shows the dining room in Wright's Robie House, which was built in Chicago in 1909.

Classics of Modern Furniture Design

The chairs shown below rank among the furniture masterpieces of the 1900's. Their designs, as in Mies Van der Rohe's Barcelona chair and Eero Saarinen's tulip chair, have a light, airy appearance that is typical of most modern furniture. The caption beneath each picture gives the name of the designer, the date the chair was created, and the chair's most important materials.

Atelier International

Gerrit Rietveld (1917)
Painted Wood

Knoll International

Marcel Breuer (1928)
Cane and Steel Tubing

Knoll International

Mies Van der Rohe (1929)
Steel and Leather

I C F, Inc.

Alvar Aalto (1934)
Molded Plywood

Herman Miller, Inc.

Charles Eames (1946)
Plywood and Metal

Knoll International

Hans Wegner (1949)
Wood and Cane

Knoll International

Harry Bertoia (1952)
Metal Rods and Wire

Knoll International

Eero Saarinen (1957)
Plastics and Aluminum

and emphasized the fine quality of the materials. Unlike most other modern styles, which were undecorated, art deco used various decorative motifs, notably lightning bolts, wheels and circles, pyramids, and waterfalls.

Modern Scandinavian Design originated in the 1920's in the Scandinavian countries—Denmark, Sweden, and Norway—and in Finland. Kaare Klint, a Danish architect, is considered the first of several leaders of the modern Scandinavian style. Most Scandinavian furniture was made with native hardwoods, notably birch. The use of wood gave the style a warmer, more natural quality than modern furniture that relied on steel.

Recent Developments

The United States became a major furniture design center during the 1940's, largely through the activities of the Museum of Modern Art in New York City. In 1940, the museum established a department of industrial art, which held furniture exhibitions and sponsored competitions in furniture design. Several of the designs entered in these competitions had great international impact. The museum brought worldwide attention to many American designers, notably Charles Eames and Eero Saarinen. Many experts consider Eames the first internationally important American furniture designer.

In 1940, Eames and Saarinen won a museum competition for their design for an armchair. The arms, back, and seat of the chair were joined in one molded plywood form. In 1946, Eames designed a chair in which the plywood seat was attached to a thin frame of chrome-plated rods by rubber disks. The disks allowed the parts of the chair to shift with the weight of the sitter, thus providing extra comfort. In 1957, Saarinen created the *tulip suite*, a cluster of curved chairs and a table, all made of fiberglass and mounted on single, slender aluminum supports. The suite consisted only of chairs and a table because Saarinen wanted to eliminate other forms of furniture.

During the 1900's, large companies have been formed that design and manufacture furniture. One of the most famous is Knoll International, founded in New York City in 1938 by Hans Knoll. This company produces furniture created by many leading modern designers. Milan, Italy, became notable among several design centers that have also appeared since the mid-1900's.

Although designers of the 1900's have revolutionized furniture, most buyers still purchase furniture made in traditional styles. The French and English styles of the 1700's and 1800's are especially fashionable and are manufactured by modern furniture makers.

FURNITURE/The Furniture Industry

During the 1700's and early 1800's, furniture making in America was a craft rather than an industry. All the furniture made during this period was produced in small woodworking shops.

The manufacture of furniture became an important industry in the United States in the mid-1800's. Large factories were built to serve the demands of middle-class people, who wanted a wide variety of furniture. The Midwest became the chief furniture-producing region because it had an abundant supply of hardwoods and was close to water transportation routes. Chicago, Cincinnati, and St. Louis became important furniture-manufacturing cities.

During the 1800's, Grand Rapids, Mich., was the most famous furniture center in the United States. William Haldane, a cabinetmaker, built the first furniture factory in Grand Rapids in 1848. Later, other furniture factories opened in that city. Artisans and designers from England, The Netherlands, Sweden, and Switzerland settled in Grand Rapids. Their skill and ideas added to the quality of furniture produced there.

Since the end of World War II (1939-1945), the South has replaced the Midwest as the leading U.S. furniture-making region. Today, factories in the South manufacture furniture worth more than half the value of all the furniture made in the United States. The Midwest now produces about a fifth of the value of all furniture made in the United States.

More than 5,000 manufacturers make furniture in the United States. They employ over 300,000 persons. During the mid-1970's, Americans spent more than $8.3 billion annually on commercially produced furniture, making it one of the leading consumer industries in the country.   JOHN W. KEEFE

Baker Furniture

Furniture Making often requires much handwork in addition to work done by machines. This worker applies a coloring substance to get a matching finish on all parts of a chest.

FURNITURE/Study Aids

Related Articles in WORLD BOOK include:

BIOGRAPHIES

STYLES

OTHER RELATED ARTICLES

Outline

I. Early Furniture
  A. Ancient Egypt   C. Ancient Rome
  B. Ancient Greece   D. The Middle Ages
II. Oriental Furniture
  A. China
  B. Japan
  C. India
III. The Renaissance
  A. Italy   C. England
  B. France   D. Spain
IV. The 1600's
  A. The Early 1600's
  B. Louis XIV Furniture
  C. The French Influence Spreads
V. The 1700's
  A. French Styles
  B. English Styles
  C. Early American Furniture
VI. The 1800's
  A. The Empire Style
  B. The Regency Style
  C. The Biedermeier, or Restoration, Style
  D. Historical Revivals
  E. Art Nouveau
VII. The 1900's
  A. Early Styles
  B. Recent Developments
VIII. The Furniture Industry

Questions

Who was the leading designer of the Federal style in American furniture?

What was a *klismos?* A *curule?*

How did the Bauhaus influence furniture design in the 1900's?

What is a *cabriole* leg?

How did classical art influence Italian Renaissance furniture?

What were the two most important characteristics of the Louis XIV style?

How did Japanese architecture influence Japanese furniture design?

What were some characteristics of the Regency style? The Régence style?

Who was Kaare Klint? Eero Saarinen?

How did the rococo style differ from the neoclassical style?

FURTSEVA, *FOOR tseh vah,* **EKATERINA,** *yeh kah teh REE nah* (1910-1974), was the first woman to serve on the Presidium of the Russian Communist party Central Committee. She joined the Central Committee in 1952, and served on its Presidium from 1956 to 1961. She served as minister of culture from 1960 to 1974. She was born in Tver (now Kalinin) province. She joined a Communist youth group at 14, and became a Communist party official at 20.   ALBERT PARRY

FURTWÄNGLER, *FOORT veng lur,* **WILHELM** (1886-1954), was a noted German musical conductor. He conducted orchestras in Lübeck, Mannheim, Vienna, Berlin, and other European cities from 1911 to 1922. He succeeded Arthur Nikisch as permanent conductor of both the Berlin Philharmonic Orchestra and the Leipzig Gewandhaus Orchestra in 1922. Furtwängler made his debut in the United States with the New York Philharmonic Symphony in 1925. He was born in Berlin, Germany.   DAVID EWEN

FURZE, a spiny shrub of the pea family, grows wild in Europe and is sometimes called *gorse,* or *whin.* The furze has many dark-green branches which are covered with spines. It grows to a height of 4 feet (1.2 meters) or more and has fragrant yellow flowers. The furze can be grown from cuttings or from seeds in a sand-and-gravel soil. See also LEGUME.

Scientific Classification. The furze is in the pea family, *Leguminosae.* It is genus *Ulex,* species *U. europaeus.* J. J. LEVISON

FUSE is a device used to cause an explosion. There are two general types, *safety fuse* and *detonating fuse.* The safety fuse allows the person setting off the explosion to reach safety before the blast occurs. A safety fuse is made of black powder enclosed in jute, cotton yarns, and waterproofing materials. When lit, the black powder burns slowly until the flame reaches the explosive. The flame sets off the charge. A blasting cap must be attached to the fuse if dynamite is to be exploded. A detonating fuse has a core of high explosive. It explodes with great violence and is used principally to set off dynamite in quarry blasting. Either a combination of safety fuse and blasting cap, or an electric blasting cap explodes this fuse. In military use, the word is usually spelled *fuze.*   JULIUS ROTH

See also AMMUNITION; BLASTING; DYNAMITE; EXPLOSIVE.

FUSE, ELECTRIC. Because of electrical resistance, the passage of electric current through wire produces heat. When the current is large enough the wire gets hotter. All circuits are in constant danger of suddenly being obliged to carry such heavy currents that they will set fire to materials around them. A short circuit in a home may be caused quite easily by accident, and could start a fire that might destroy the home. An electric fuse prevents this. The current passes through the fuse from the main power line to the house wiring. The wires in the fuse are of an alloy which melts at low temperature, and are made to carry a certain amount of current. This amount is called the fuse's *rating.* When the current reaches a dangerous amount, the wire melts, or fuses, and the circuit is broken. A fuse may be considered a kind of circuit breaker (see CIRCUIT BREAKER).

There are two kinds of house fuses, *plug fuses* and *cartridge fuses.* Cartridge fuses are long and narrow. They carry heavy currents. A plug fuse screws into a socket and carries smaller currents. Fuses are generally rated at between 15 and 25 amperes.

FUTURE BUSINESS LEADERS OF AMERICA

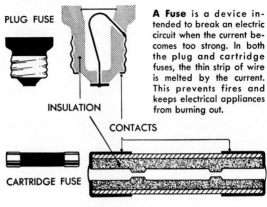

PLUG FUSE

INSULATION

CONTACTS

CARTRIDGE FUSE

A Fuse is a device intended to break an electric circuit when the current becomes too strong. In both the plug and cartridge fuses, the thin strip of wire is melted by the current. This prevents fires and keeps electrical appliances from burning out.

TWO TYPES OF HOME FUSES

It is dangerous to replace a burned-out fuse with a penny, as some people do. The coin closes the circuit again, but does nothing to remove the overload on the line. The house is still in danger if too strong a current is passed, because the penny will not melt and stop the flow of current, as the fuse did.   PALMER H. CRAIG

See also ELECTRIC CIRCUIT.

FUSEE. See FIREWORKS (Other Uses).

FUSEL OIL is an unpleasant-smelling, colorless liquid. It is found in alcohols made from fermented potatoes, rye, barley, and other vegetable matter. The oil is made up mainly of a mixture of amyl alcohols. Chemists remove the oil from the alcohols by a distilling process. Fusel oil is used to make essential oils and varnishes.

FUSELAGE. See AIRPLANE (Fuselage).

FUSIBLE METAL. See ALLOY (Characteristics of Alloys).

FUSING POINT. See MELTING POINT; FREEZING.

FUSION, in physics, takes place when lightweight atoms *fuse* (join together) to form a heavier atom and release energy. Fusion reactions are often called *thermonuclear* reactions because they take place at temperatures higher than 180,000,000° F. (100,000,000° C).

The sun's energy comes from the fusion of light hydrogen atoms to form a helium atom. The energy of the hydrogen bomb comes from the fusion of *deuterium* and *tritium,* two heavy isotopes of hydrogen (see HYDROGEN BOMB; ISOTOPE). These isotopes fuse to form helium. Scientists are experimenting with ways to control fusion reactions for peaceful purposes.

See also NUCLEAR ENERGY (Nuclear Fusion); STAR (Why Stars Shine).

FUTURE BUSINESS LEADERS OF AMERICA-PHI BETA LAMBDA is a national vocational education organization for students interested in business, office, or business education careers. Future Business Leaders of America (FBLA) is the organization's division for high school students, and Phi Beta Lambda (PBL) is the division for students at the college level. There are more than 8,000 FBLA and PBL chapters with over 180,000 members in the United States, Guam, Puerto Rico, and the Virgin Islands. The organization was founded in 1942 and its headquarters are at 1908 Association Drive, Reston, Va. 22091.   Critically reviewed by

FUTURE BUSINESS LEADERS OF AMERICA-PHI BETA LAMBDA

Future Farmers study for careers in agriculture. On a field trip, *right,* a guide tells members of the FFA about the various kinds of trees that grow in an area. The organization's emblem is shown above.

FUTURE FARMERS OF AMERICA (FFA) is an organization for high school students who study vocational agriculture. It helps them prepare for careers in agriculture and *agribusiness* (business involving agriculture). It also trains them to become responsible citizens and leaders in their communities. FFA forms part of the agricultural education program in many public schools. Members gain practical experience through FFA activities while they study school courses in agriculture. They also develop leadership and learn to cooperate with others. Both boys and girls may join the FFA. The United States Department of Health, Education, and Welfare sponsors the FFA nationally.

The official motto of the Future Farmers of America expresses its entire program:

> Learning to do,
> Doing to learn;
> Earning to live,
> Living to serve.

In *learning to do*, FFA members study practical and scientific agriculture to become good farmers or prepare themselves for other careers in agriculture.

In *doing to learn*, members work on projects from which they gain practical experience.

In *earning to live*, FFA members manage farms or agribusiness enterprises that produce income.

In *living to serve*, members develop qualities of competent leadership and responsible citizenship, and work to improve their school and community.

The FFA slogan is "The Successful Farmer of Tomorrow is the Future Farmer of Today." The FFA emblem has an owl, a plow, and a rising sun within the cross section of an ear of corn. An American eagle appears above this design. The owl represents wisdom and

Horticulture is one of the most popular areas of vocational study in the FFA program. These young people are taking care of a new crop of hothouse tomatoes.

An Annual Corn Drive conducted by Future Farmers in Minnesota raises funds for a camp for the handicapped. FFA members collect and sell corn that local farmers donate to the drive.

Local, County, and State Fairs enable FFA members to exhibit animals and crops they have raised. The livestock judging contest shown above took place at the Florida State Fair.

knowledge, and the plow stands for labor and tilling the soil. The rising sun symbolizes the new day that will dawn when all farmers learn to work together. The corn stands for the agricultural interest that is common to all FFA members, and the eagle stands for the national scope of the FFA.

More than 485,000 students belong to the Future Farmers of America in about 7,800 high school chapters in the United States and Puerto Rico. A school must have a full-time vocational agriculture teacher before it can form an FFA chapter. Only boys and girls who are studying vocational agriculture may join. They may continue their membership for three years after they leave high school, or until they reach the age of 21, whichever is longer. Members wear distinctive blue corduroy jackets. The emblems and names on the jackets are embroidered in gold and blue, the FFA colors.

What Future Farmers Do

Training. Each FFA member carries out a supervised project. The project is designed to put into practice the knowledge gained in vocational agriculture classes. Members usually start with small projects when they are freshmen in high school. They may raise a pig or calf, or cultivate crops on a small patch of land. But the goal is to broaden the scope of the enterprise and become established after four to six years. Agriculture teachers visit each student to supervise and help with the project.

FFA chapters often help beginners by organizing a "pig chain" or a "calf chain." The chapter gives a student a pig or calf with the agreement that he or she will give the chapter its first female offspring. This female is passed on to another student to start a project.

513

FUTURE FARMERS OF AMERICA

The FFA occasionally lends money to beginning students whose families cannot give them the money for a good start in farming, or helps them obtain needed credit. In some areas, an FFA chapter or a school may own a farm or greenhouse where members who do not have land at home can work on their projects. The organization encourages members to expand their farming programs or agribusiness experiences so that, by the time they complete high school, they will be prepared to farm on a full-time basis, or to be employed in an agribusiness.

FFA members study career opportunities in agriculture. With their teachers, they go on field trips to nearby farms to observe good farming practices and farm management. They also visit agricultural experiment stations and agribusinesses to see the development and results of new agricultural methods. They study farm economics, marketing, and soil conservation and improvement, and learn how to keep accurate, complete financial records. The FFA also trains members in farm mechanics. It teaches them how to select, use, care for, and repair farm machinery. Members also study horticulture.

By participating in chapter meetings, FFA members learn to follow parliamentary procedure, to speak in public, and to cooperate with their fellow students in programs to improve themselves and their communities. The organization recommends that chapters meet regularly at least once a month and that they hold special meetings as needed.

Activities. FFA members exhibit the animals and crops they have raised in local, county, and state fairs. Chapters participate in contests at the local, state, and national levels. Contests are held in livestock, dairy, and poultry judging; agricultural mechanics skills; dairy products and meats evaluation; horticulture; and farm management. The contests teach students judging and technical skills, and instill a spirit of competition among FFA members. The members also participate in dairy herd improvement associations, livestock breeders' groups, business associations, and other organizations that work to improve agriculture.

Local chapters sponsor recreational activities and organize educational tours. They conduct safety campaigns and home-improvement projects, and hold annual parent-student banquets. FFA chapters sometimes organize and manage community fairs. Through the FFA *Building Our American Communities* program, FFA chapters across the nation have participated in community improvement activities.

FFA members enjoy camping during the summer months. Many states have FFA leadership centers that provide summer fun and offer leadership training courses for members.

Degrees. FFA members are awarded various degrees for their achievements in agricultural projects, community service, cooperation, leadership, and scholarship. When a student joins the FFA, he or she becomes a *Greenhand*, and may buy and wear a small bronze pin bearing the FFA emblem.

After one year, Greenhands receive the *Chapter Farmer* degree if their participation in the organization has been satisfactory. They may now wear a silver FFA

Future Farmers of America

The FFA's International Program encourages cooperation and understanding among nations. This Future Farmer team is competing in a dairy judging contest in Wales.

pin. Most FFA members receive the Chapter Farmer degree.

A third degree, the *State Farmer*, is much harder to attain. State associations of the FFA award this degree for outstanding achievement in agricultural career development, leadership, and scholarship. They present it at annual state conventions. Among other things, a State Farmer must have worked at least 600 hours, or earned at least $500 and deposited it in a bank or invested it productively. Each state association awards the degree to no more than 3 of every 100 members a year. A State Farmer wears a gold emblem pin.

The *American Farmer* degree is the highest FFA rank. The national organization presents it each year to members nominated by the state associations. Each

─────── **PURPOSES OF THE FFA** ───────

1. To develop competent, aggressive, rural, and agricultural leadership.
2. To create and nurture a love of country life.
3. To strengthen the confidence of members in themselves and their work.
4. To create more interest in the intelligent choice of agricultural occupations.
5. To encourage members to develop individual farming programs and to become established in agricultural careers.
6. To encourage members to improve the farm home and its surroundings.
7. To participate in worthy undertakings for the improvement of agriculture.
8. To develop character, train for useful citizenship, and foster patriotism.
9. To participate in cooperative effort.
10. To encourage and practice thrift.
11. To encourage improvement in scholarship.
12. To provide and encourage the development of organized rural recreational activities.

state may nominate one candidate for each 667 members. In order to encourage students to maintain their interest in agriculture, only FFA members who have been out of high school for at least one year may be nominated. Each American Farmer receives a gold key and partially paid travel expenses to the national convention.

The FFA also presents honorary degrees to men and women who perform exceptional service to the organization. These individuals receive *Honorary Chapter*, *State*, or *American Farmer* degrees and pins.

Awards are designed to encourage FFA members to do better work in vocational agriculture. The Future Farmers of America Foundation, Inc., sponsors 19 proficiency awards for FFA members, including awards for agricultural mechanics, agricultural processing, agricultural sales and service, horticulture, natural resources, and production agriculture. This foundation, organized in 1944, is supported by donations from more than 1,500 businesses. It presents four Star Farmer and four Star Agribusinessman awards each year at the national FFA convention to winners chosen from among the American Farmer candidates. Other national awards are made for group achievements in chapter activities and to winners of the national FFA public speaking contest.

Individual states present awards at state FFA conventions. Local chapters award medals to outstanding members during their annual parent-member banquets or at special school assemblies. They offer the awards in various fields, including farm mechanics, electrification, horticulture, soil and water management, and farm safety. The chapters present awards to more than 80,-000 students each year.

Organization

Local Chapters of the FFA are sponsored by the vocational agriculture departments of local high schools. The chapters elect their own officers, choose committees, and hold regular business meetings. Chapter officers usually serve as delegates to state conventions. The vocational agriculture teacher in each high school is the advisor for the local chapter.

State Associations in the individual states aid the local chapters. A state board for vocational education sponsors each state association, and the state supervisor of vocational agriculture is its advisor. State associations elect officers at an annual state convention. The state president and other state officers usually serve as delegates to the annual national convention in Kansas City, Mo.

National Organization. Delegates to the national convention each year elect a Board of National Officers made up of a president, a secretary, and four vice-presidents. Each vice-president represents one of the FFA's four administrative regions. The regions are Central, Eastern, Southern, and Western. The FFA also has an adult board of directors made up of five members of the Agricultural Education Service of the Department of Health, Education, and Welfare, and four state supervisors of agricultural education. State supervisors hold regional conferences and choose their four board members.

The Board of National Officers meets three times a year with the Board of Directors to conduct the business

of the national organization. The Board of Directors has final authority, but in most cases it accepts the recommendations of the Board of National Officers. The two boards may refer questions of policy to the national convention.

The head of the Agricultural Education Service of the Office of Education in the Department of Health, Education, and Welfare is the national FFA adviser. A member of the adviser's staff serves as national FFA executive secretary. The state boards for vocational education and the local high school departments of vocational agriculture help carry out FFA programs. Part of the funds to operate the FFA come from annual dues that are paid by each member. Members pay $1.50 a year in national dues. The organization's headquarters are at the National FFA Center, P.O. Box 15160, Alexandria, Va. 22309.

History

In 1917, Congress passed the Smith-Hughes Act, which gave the government the power to establish a national program of vocational education. It also permitted the government to pay half the cost of a vocational agriculture program in each state. The government now pays only about a sixth of the cost. The states and local communities pay the rest. A Federal Board for Vocational Education administered the Smith-Hughes Act at first. Later, the Department of Health, Education, and Welfare took over the management of the program.

In the early 1920's, vocational-agriculture students formed clubs in many communities throughout the country. In some states the local clubs joined in statewide associations. One of these state associations, the Future Farmers of Virginia, formed in 1926, became the model for the Future Farmers of America. In November, 1928, representatives from the state associations met in Kansas City, Mo., to establish a national farm organization for high school boys. They adopted a constitution and founded the Future Farmers of America. Congress granted it a charter in 1950.

In 1955, the FFA began a program to improve international understanding. The FFA has helped set up Future Farmers organizations in Colombia, Costa Rica, Japan, Mexico, Peru, and the Philippines. The FFA also operates an international exchange program. Members can gain work experience on farms in Australia and New Zealand, Europe, and South America.

FFA maintains a supply service that sells FFA jackets, jewelry, and other items bearing its emblem. The organization publishes a *National FFA Calendar* and *The National FUTURE FARMER* magazine. The magazine is sent every other month to all FFA members as part of their membership dues.

Critically reviewed by the FUTURE FARMERS OF AMERICA

Related Articles in WORLD BOOK include:
Agricultural Education
Agricultural Experiment Station
Agriculture
Fairs and Expositions
Farm and Farming
4-H
Future Homemakers of America
Smith-Hughes Act

The Future Homemakers of America includes HERO chapters, which prepare students for employment in home economics related occupations. The students shown above are learning how to plan and operate a restaurant.

FUTURE HOMEMAKERS OF AMERICA is a national organization for junior high and high school students of home economics or related subjects. Its members participate in various activities designed to build character and increase the understanding of classroom subjects. More than 450,000 boys and girls belong to the organization. About 12,000 local chapters operate in the United States and its territories.

The Future Homemakers of America is a private, non-profit organization supported entirely by the dues of its members. Sponsors of the group include the United States Office of Education and the American Home Economics Association.

The organization consists of two types of chapters—Future Homemakers of America (FHA) chapters and Home Economics Related Occupations (HERO) chapters. FHA chapters study such homemaking skills as child care, cooking, and household management. HERO chapters prepare members for employment in such fields as the clothing business, the food industry, and interior decoration. A student may belong to both FHA and HERO.

Activities. Most of the organization's activities are conducted by local FHA and HERO chapters. Chapter members participate in group activities and in individual projects. Local chapters conduct activities in three main areas: (1) the community, (2) the home, and (3) the school.

Community Activities enable members to learn job skills and help solve local problems. For example, many HERO chapter members gain practical experience by

An FHA Member can get practical experience by doing volunteer work in the community. This girl is learning about child development by working with youngsters at a day-care center.

FHA/HERO Chapters

A Clean-Up Campaign improves the environment and helps FHA members learn how various discarded items can be recycled.

working for a local business, such as a factory or restaurant. Members also may volunteer as aides at hospitals or nursing homes. Some FHA and HERO chapters conduct clean-up campaigns in their community and learn how various discarded items can be *recycled* (used again). Other chapters help with fund drives that collect money for many community projects.

Home Activities prepare members to manage a household. Some FHA and HERO chapters learn how to plan a family budget and spend money wisely. Other chapters refinish old furniture and learn about decorating a home. Many chapters discuss family life and ways that members of a family can work together to solve problems. Still other chapters study home safety and learn how to use small appliances and electric tools.

School Activities enable chapter members to help other students and practice home economics skills. Many

FUTURE SCIENTISTS OF AMERICA

FHA and HERO chapters conduct campaigns to encourage students to continue their education at least through high school. Other chapters operate food stands at their school's athletic events. They also may display posters that explain what foods make up a balanced diet. Many FHA members practice their cooking skills by preparing special meals for students and teachers.

Organization. The Future Homemakers of America was founded in 1945. It is organized on three levels—national, state, and local.

National Headquarters sets general policies for the Future Homemakers of America. The group consists of a national executive council and a national board of directors. Young people make up the executive council. The board of directors consists of both adults and students. A headquarters staff, located at 2010 Massachusetts Avenue NW, Washington, D.C. 20036, assists in developing and administering the organization's programs. *Teen Times*, the official publication of the Future Homemakers of America, is published by the national headquarters.

State Associations assist the local chapters in each state. For example, representatives of the state associations visit local chapters and explain how chapter activities can be conducted. An adult adviser directs each state association, and students serve as officers.

Local Chapters design and conduct activities based on community needs and the interests of individual members. Local FHA and HERO chapters are organized through the schools. Home economics teachers serve as chapter advisers. All officers of local chapters are young people. Critically reviewed by the FUTURE HOMEMAKERS OF AMERICA

See also HOME ECONOMICS.

FUTURE NURSES. See NURSING (Career Information).

FUTURE SCIENTISTS OF AMERICA is a national program for high school science students. It encourages industry, professional societies, science teachers, and students to develop a greater interest in science. The program, sponsored by the National Science Teachers Association, was established in 1952.

The program provides student congresses, youth

FHA/HERO Chapters

Students Help Set Policy at meetings of the National Board of Directors of the Future Homemakers of America. The board consists of both young people and adults.

Red Cross Train (1914), an oil painting by Gino Severini;
The Solomon R. Guggenheim Museum, New York City

Futurist Paintings express the energy, speed, and excitement that the movement saw in the machine age. Most of these paintings feature multiple images and overlapping fragments of color.

tours, science club activities, and awards for student science projects. It publishes the Vistas of Science paperback book series and such booklets as *Careers in Science Teaching*. Industrial and technical organizations help support the program. Future Scientists of America has about 2,000 clubs with about 60,000 members. Its headquarters are at 1201 Sixteenth Street NW, Washington, D.C. 20036.

FUTURES. See COMMODITY EXCHANGE.

FUTURISM was an Italian art movement that flourished from 1909 to about 1916. It was the first of many art movements that tried to break with the past in all areas of life. Futurism glorified the power, speed, and excitement of the machine age. From the French cubist painters and multiple-exposure photography, the Futurists learned to break up realistic forms into multiple images and overlapping fragments of color. By such

means, they tried to show the energy and speed of life. In literature, Futurism demanded the abolition of traditional sentence structures and verse forms.

Futurism was created by the poet Filippo Marinetti. In 1909, Marinetti issued the first of many defiant proclamations published by the Futurists. He was soon joined by the painters Giacomo Balla, Carlo Carrà, Luigi Russolo, and Gino Severini, and the painter and sculptor Umberto Boccioni. Boccioni's Futurist sculpture *Unique Forms of Continuity in Space* is reproduced in the SCULPTURE article.

By 1916, Futurism had lost most of its vigor. Despite its short life, Futurism influenced the theories and works of such modern art movements as Dadaism, Expressionism, and Surrealism. MARCEL FRANCISCONO

See also BOCCIONI, UMBERTO; PAINTING (Futurism); SCULPTURE (Modern International).

FUZE. See FUSE.